Modern Chinese Stories and Novellas

MODERN ASIAN LITERATURE SERIES

MODERN CHINESE STORIES AND NOVELLAS
1919–1949

EDITED BY
JOSEPH S. M. LAU, C. T. HSIA,
AND LEO OU-FAN LEE

COLUMBIA UNIVERSITY PRESS
New York   1981

Library of Congress Cataloging in Publication Data
Main entry under title:

Modern Chinese stories and novellas, 1919–1949.

(Modern Asian literature series)
Bibliography: p.
Includes index.
1. Chinese fiction—20th century—Translations into
English.   2. English fiction—Translations for Chinese.
I. Lau, Joseph S. M., 1934–   . II. Hsia, Chih-tsing,
1921–   . III. Lee, Leo Ou-fan. IV. Title.
V. Series.
PL2658.E8M6   895.1′301   80–27572
ISBN 0–231–04202–7
ISBN 0–231–04203–5 (pbk.)

Columbia University Press
New York   Guildford, Surrey

Modern Asian Literature Series

Contents

Preface

In preparing this anthology, we have adopted one of the editorial principles embraced by C. T. Hsia in *Twentieth-Century Chinese Stories* (New York, 1971): "to impress upon the Western reader the strength and vitality of modern Chinese fiction" through stories chosen for their "literary interest and their representative importance." The present work is a larger one because it is by design a comprehensive anthology of stories and novellas representing the best that has been produced since the Literary Revolution in 1917. We have included, therefore, a number of important works already available in English translations, our rationale being that, as a textbook, this anthology should contain all the stories essential to our understanding of the development of modern Chinese fiction.

The period of 1919 to 1949, in which these stories were first published, represents one of the most significant periods in modern Chinese literary history. This anthology reflects, therefore, the accumulated legacies of the May Fourth Movement and its aftermath. This crop of "new literature" differs notably not only from its late Ch'ing predecessors but also from what has been produced since 1949. Literary developments in the People's Republic of China have since taken a course very different from these three decades. Moreover, there has emerged another vital stream of modern Chinese literature in the Republic of China in Taiwan. Each has its own concept of defining reality, its own set of moral assumptions and literary sensibilities. Since anthologies covering these two contemporary strains already exist or are in preparation, there seems no need for us to duplicate these efforts.[1]

Except for those cases mentioned later in this preface, all translations were especially commissioned for this anthology. In matters related to the technique of translation, the Editors' main emphases have been readability and fidelity to the original. No passage in the Chinese text has been regarded as too vulgar to

---

[1] Notably Chi Pang-yuan, et al., eds., *An Anthology of Contemporary Chinese Literature,* 2 vols. (Taipei: National Institute for Compilation and Translation, 1975). Joseph S. M. Lau, ed., *Chinese Stories from Taiwan: 1960–1970* (New York: Columbia University Press, 1976). Kai-yu Hsu and Ting Wang, eds., *The Literature of the People's Republic of China* (Bloomington: Indiana University Press, 1980). Under contract for Indiana University Press, C. H. Wang and Joseph S. M. Lau are now preparing a comprehensive anthology of Taiwan literature since 1895 to the present time.

For a checklist of modern Chinese literature in translation, consult: Donald A. Gibbs and Yun-chen Li, *A Bibliography of Studies and Translations of Modern Chinese Literature: 1918–1942* (East Asian Center: Harvard University, 1975), and Winston L. Y. Yang and Nathan K. Mao, eds., *Modern Chinese Fiction: A Guide to Its Study and Appreciation: Essays and Bibliographies* (Boston: G. K. Hall, 1980).

merit expurgation. However, no rules have been set pertaining to the translation of personal names or epithets. We believe that each story has a mood and a convention of its own. Thus, while the hero in Chao Shu-li's story can formally be transliterated as "Fu-kuei," we feel that "Lucky" fits the immediate context better. Except in the cases of "The Merchant's Wife," "Horse-bell Melons," and those stories previously published, all the footnotes supplied by the translators have either been amended or supplemented by the Editors. The romanization used in this anthology is the Wade-Giles system.

As principal editor, I wish to acknowledge the unstinting collaboration of my co-editors, C. T. Hsia and Leo Ou-fan Lee, whose counsel and assistance have been invaluable. I further wish to thank the Graduate School of the University of Wisconsin, Madison, for the award of summer grants and Project Assistantships, without which this project would never have been accomplished. I am especially grateful to all the translators who have generously given of their time and labor for this undertaking.

More than perfunctory thanks are also due to the following individuals at Wisconsin: Pi-twan H. Wang and Jane Parish Yang, Project Assistants and doctoral candidates in the Department of East Asian Languages and Literature, for reading the manuscripts and making valuable suggestions for correction. To Susan MacKerer, Admissions Assistant in the Department of East Asian Languages and Literature, for typing some of the manuscripts.

Thanks are also due to Teresa Mei of the Cornell University Libraries for her patience in answering all sorts of queries related to the question of text and original dates of publication. To Y. W. Ma and Anthony C. Yu, whose interest and encouragement have sustained my faith in the necessity of anthologizing, I offer my warm gratitude. To Karen Mitchell, editor of Columbia University Press, I want to indicate my indebtedness for her most conscientious editorial work and valuable suggestions for rearranging the format of this anthology. To Howard Goldblatt and George Cheng of San Francisco State University, I would like to express my sincere appreciation for their contribution of a bibliography of modern Chinese fiction.

Finally, a most special note of thanks is due my wife, Yu-shan Lau, who encouraged me to spend most of my waking hours working in the office. Without her patience and understanding, this anthology could not have been completed.

All the stories by Lu Hsün are translated by Yang Hsien-yi and Gladys Yang and are reprinted from *Selected Stories of Lu Hsün* (Peking, 1960), with minor revisions by Leo Lee and Lawrence Herzberg of Indiana University, Bloomington. Mao Tun's "Spring Silkworms," translated by Sidney Shapiro, is reprinted from *Spring Silkworms and Other Stories* (Peking, 1956), with minor editorial changes. Hsiao Chün's "Goats" originally appeared in *Renditions* (4, Spring

1975), a Chinese-English translation magazine published by the Comparative Literature and Translation Center, the Chinese University of Hong Kong. For inclusion in this anthology, the translator Howard Goldblatt has made a few stylistic changes in the original translation. Grateful acknowledgment is due to George Kao and Stephen Soong, editors of *Renditions,* for permission to reprint.

C. T. Hsia, our co-editor, has kindly allowed us to reprint in this book four translations from his *Twentieth-Century Chinese Stories:* Yü Ta-fu's "Sinking," Shen Ts'ung-wen's "Quiet," Wu Tsu-hsiang's "Fan Village," and Eileen Chang's "The Golden Cangue," all with minor revisions in the translations. Aside from these four, we are generally indebted to Hsia for his monumental *History of Modern Chinese Fiction* (New Haven, 1961; 2d ed., 1971, hereafter cited as *History*), which was the first book to discuss from a humanistic and moral perspective so many of the stories and novellas included in the present volume. Hsia is also responsible for assembling the pictures of the authors appearing at the end of the Introduction. In this connection we are especially grateful to Eileen Chang, Ch'ien Chung-shu, and Ling Shu-hua for sending us their individual portraits, to Hsu Kai-yu and Ms. Hsü Ta-ch'un, respectively, for pictures of Shen Ts'ung-wen and Lu Ling, and to K'ung Lo-sun, Secretary of the Chinese Writers' Association and editor of the *Literary Gazette (Wen-i pao),* Peking, China, for photographs of several authors, deceased and living, taken in the thirties and forties.

We have made extensive use of Hsia's *History* both in compiling the anthology and in preparing the biographical sketches of authors that appear before each group of stories. Other reference works consulted include: Howard Boorman, ed., *Biographical Dictionary of Republican China,* 4 vols. (New York, 1970); *Biographical Dictionary of Chinese Writers: A Draft Version (Chung-kuo wen-hsüeh-chia tz'u-tien: cheng-ch'iu i-chien-kao,* Peking, 1978); Li Li-ming, *Brief Biographies of Six Hundred Modern Chinese Authors (Chung-kuo hsien-tai liu-pai tso-chia shiao-chuan,* Hong Kong, 1977).

In cooperation with Wai-leung Wong of the Chinese University of Hong Kong, I am preparing a Chinese edition of this anthology to be published in Hong Kong; technical details that will be of interest to the specialist are being reserved for that edition.

JOSEPH S. M. LAU

Introduction

C. T. Hsia

In this companion volume to *Traditional Chinese Stories: Themes and Variations* (ed. Y. W. Ma and Joseph S. M. Lau), my co-editors and I have chosen forty-four works by twenty authors to represent the achievement in fiction during the three decades, 1919–1949. Forty-one of these are short stories of various lengths while three can be safely called novellas: Hsü Ti-shan's "Yü-kuan," Lao She's "An Old Tragedy in a New Age," and Eileen Chang's "The Golden Cangue." Even in an anthology of this size, of course, we cannot include a full-length novel without sacrificing diversity of representation; fortunately, many novels of our authors dating from the same period, such as Mao Tun's *Midnight,* Lao She's *Cat Country* and *Rickshaw,* Pa Chin's *The Family* and *Cold Nights,* Hsiao Hung's *The Field of Life and Death* and *Tales of Hulan River,* and Ch'ien Chung-shu's *Fortress Besieged,* are readily available in translation to meet the needs of the serious reader. Our volume covers practically all fiction writers of the first rank who rose to fame in the twenties and thirties, but of the new writers of the forties we have included only four—Chao Shu-li, Ch'ien Chung-shu, Lu Ling, and Eileen Chang—though Ting Ling, a famous writer since the late twenties, is represented solely by her stories of the forties. Scholars agree that for that decade Yenan fiction is best represented by Chao Shu-li and Ting Ling and Shanghai fiction by Eileen Chang and Ch'ien Chung-shu. But since there is yet no critical consensus regarding the relative merits of several important novelists to emerge from the Nationalist interior during the war years, we can only exercise our best judgment in preferring Lu Ling above the others, both for his unmistakable talent and for his copious productivity.

The reader of the last volume, if previously unacquainted with modern Chinese fiction, will find a different type of fare awaiting him in this one. While he might miss the wide range of themes, along with the knights-errant, ghost-wives, alchemists, and other such characters that contribute so much to the exotic flavor of the previous anthology, at the same time he will find our selections little encumbered with notes on historical or literary allusions, and on the whole both easier and more engrossing to read because of their conformity to a Western mode of realistic narrative. The "Questing Man" retains his thematic importance in modern Chinese fiction, but he is altogether of a different breed from the archetype defined in *Traditional Chinese Stories* as "a selfless seeker of supernatural power through an exceedingly difficult journey for the salvation of someone else." The questing hero in the modern fiction seeks nothing less than the salvation of his suffering compatriots, or of the nation as a whole. Of course, he expects no supernatural aid in this task—unless he is the type of stupid and gullible patriot satirized in Chang T'ien-i's *The Strange Knight of Shanghai.* For all modern writers seeking the salvation of Mother China, her shame appears especially visible through the gross superstitions of her religious populace. Thus these writers have nothing but contempt for Buddhist and Tao-ist priests, shamans, and witch doctors who, in addition to their cupidity and quackery, reconcile the believers to a miserable existence on earth. Quite unlike the other volume, supernaturalism plays no part in *Modern Chinese Stories and Novellas* unless it is the playful kind of satiric machinery that we find in Ch'ien Chung-shu's "The Inspiration."

Confucianism, insofar as it is identifiable with the gentry and the official establishment, does not fare much better: the hypocritical gentleman forever mouthing proverbs and getting angry with the wicked modern ways is an object of derision in some of our selections from Lu Hsün, Lao She, and Chang T'ien-i. All of our twenty authors were of course brought up on the Confucian classics and may be called Confucian if we regard kindness, sympathy, and charity as Confucian virtues. But the inoperancy of these virtues in the society around them makes our writers angry and harsh: their humanitarianism, while reconcilable with Confucian teaching, is nevertheless something more deeply rooted in the Western tradition. Even with the only two of our writers whose religious sense remains intact—Hsü Ti-shan as a Christian convert and Shen Ts'ung-wen as a philosophical Taoist nostalgic for a premoral condition of humanity—their humanitarian anger against the oppressors of the people remains quite apparent.

In view of the abundance of love stories in the other anthology, one would expect an even larger supply of such stories in this one, since it is during the twentieth century that Chinese youth finally gained the right to court and marry whomever they will without parental approval. A large quantity of love stories and novels were indeed produced in the twenties and thirties by identifiably modern writers, but they all appear quite dated by reason of their excessive sentimentality. The most poignant love story in our volume remains the thwarted courtship of a timid student home from abroad for an old-fashioned girl in "The Golden Cangue"; their silent communion contrasts sharply with the verbosity of the gushy lovers in the fiction of the twenties. Ch'ien Chung-shu, responsible for the sole satiric fantasy in our volume, also provides in "Souvenir" the only adult example of a tale of seduction and adultery that compares well with some famous European models in its classical restraint and psychological precision. From the many untranslated stories of Eileen Chang we could have chosen another of comparable maturity, but few modern writers of an earlier period have written a love story of equal irony and detachment. Typically, the would-be lover in Yü Ta-fu's "Sinking," a Chinese student in Japan, is thwarted from his search for an Eve by his perpetual awareness of his alienation, and the young lovers in both Tuan-mu

Hung-liang's "The Rapid Current of the Muddy River" and Wu Tsu-hsiang's "Fan Village" must stand united against their enemies. Though their potential for idyllic happiness is stressed, in neither story is their love relationship the central concern.

The modern Chinese writer discards the baggage of traditional beliefs and even finds romantic love an expendable luxury because, as I have said elsewhere, of his "obsessive concern with China as a nation afflicted with a spiritual disease and therefore unable to strengthen itself or change its set ways of inhumanity" (*History*, pp. 533–34). Because of this obsession with China, modern Chinese literature far surpasses the bulk of traditional Chinese literature in moral seriousness and human understanding. It is a rare traditional poet who is seriously concerned with the sufferings of common man, and it is a rarer playwright or novelist who writes of women as vibrant human beings in their own right. During the three decades of our coverage, all writers shared a larger vision of humanity where the common man and woman, and the common child as well, are as much entitled to respect as the officials and scholars of the past. This is a revolutionary change of the most fundamental nature. The modern writer not only writes with greater candor than the scholar-official of the old days, but sees himself or herself as an observer and recorder of the truth about Chinese society. Every story in our volume, though some may provide pat answers in accordance with socialist or Communist teaching, is fundamentally true; most were disconcerting to their contemporary readers, and should remain disconcerting for their disclosure of some ugly aspects of Chinese society, though in time we may be more concerned about the generic and aesthetic features of this type of realistic fiction than its truth-telling power. Not since the age of philosophers in pre-Ch'in times has there been a period in China when its writers were primarily engaged in truth speaking. Though truth speaking has met with official disapproval and punishment on the China mainland since 1949, the intellectual revolution of the previous decades cannot be easily overturned. Whenever circumstances permit, mainland writers will still speak out for freedom and for the common man.

After the Opium War the Chinese began to perceive themselves as an endangered nation, but the further perception that China was inhumane did not dawn on them until they began to read Western thought and literature. By the late Ch'ing period novelists were habitually contrasting the barbarity (*yeh-man*) of their country to the civilization (*wen-ming*) of Western nations. Among the intellectual leaders of the May Fourth era, the American-educated Hu Shih no less than the Japanese-educated Lu Hsün and Chou Tso-jen openly acknowledged the vast inferiority of Chinese civilization after their exposure to Western thought and literature, particularly of the nineteenth and early twentieth centuries. When Chou Tso-jen spoke out in 1918–1919 for a "humane literature" and a "literature of the common man," he was expressing for a whole generation of Western-influenced writers and readers their radically altered understanding of the function and profession of literature. In late 1920 several young writers, including Mao Tun, Yeh Shao-chün, and Hsü Ti-shan of our volume, responded to Chou's call by forming the Literary Association (Wen-hsüeh yen-chiu hui), whose principal organ, *The Short Story Magazine* (*Hsiao-shuo yüeh-pao*), became the first major journal of humane literature realistically concerned with the problems and sufferings of the common man.

The subsequent ideological split of the May Fourth writers and intellectuals into a left wing and a liberal wing was unfortunate but inevitable, but the succeeding good writers, whatever their political persuasion, never lost sight of the humane importance and enhanced dignity of their profession. Their fundamental repudiation of the old literary culture remained intact, along with their fundamental disgust with the old society. If we continue to honor Lu Hsün on the centennial of his birth in 1981, it is not because he is the greatest of modern Chinese writers, as the Communist critics would have us believe. It is rather because his stories and early essays have effected a permanent revolution in attitude toward their national past for the succeeding generations of writers and readers. Since Lu Hsün, it has not been possible to reinculcate upon the minds of the young an unqualified respect for the Chinese tradition without inviting disbelief and ridicule. Again with the exception of Ch'ien Chung-shu, a satirist engrossed in the follies and foibles of modern intellectuals, all our writers in this volume share an attitude of disgust toward the old society, even though a trio of less angry writers—Hsü Ti-shan, Shen Ts'ung-wen, and Eileen Chang—accept its pervasive influence as a necessary condition under which their characters have to live. It is their defeat or triumph under the most absurd circumstances that engages these writers' creative interest, and not the circumstances themselves.

However disagreeable their circumstances, the heroes and heroines of traditional Chinese stories inhabit a moral universe and act in full expectation that virtue will be rewarded and vice punished. Hence the numerous instances in our companion anthology of divine intervention in behalf of the good to demonstrate the visibility and efficacy of the moral principle in human affairs. Modern Chinese writers find this moral principle much less in evidence, and even Hsü Ti-shan is too good a Christian to stress the material rewards accruing to good conduct: on the contrary, his good characters find their spiritual improvement sufficient reward for being mistreated by the world. Alienated from traditional beliefs by intellectual choice, the authors of our volume are thus no different from modern Western writers in seeing man as a much smaller creature, and his fate more pathetic or ironic. Only the objects of satire—the Confucian gentlemen, the landlords, and the big merchants—are as self-assured and as much mired in greed and lust as the villains in traditional fiction. Barring the resolute heroes of romantic-revolutionary novels, the good characters are much less sure of themselves and very often reconcile themselves to their smallness and transience by developing an ironic attitude of self-mockery. Thus even the earliest writers in this volume, Lu Hsün and Yeh Shao-chün, quite often strike a Chekhovian note, which makes them so very different from the authors of traditional fiction.

This Chekhovian quality is also quite conspicuous in our selections from Pa

Chin, Hsiao Chün, Ting Ling, and Hsiao Hung. Pa Chin, whose early novels in the romantic-revolutionary mode are quite bad, is at his Chekhovian best in "The General" and "Piglet and Chickens." The former story is about a Russian exile in a Chinese city, presumably Shanghai, who pretends to be an ex-general so as to forget the humiliation of being supported by his prostitute-wife, also a White Russian. The Chinese widow in the latter story, who tries to augment her income by raising a piglet and some chickens, is no less pathetic because her only weapon is her abusive language, which does nothing to prevent defeat in her contention with her landlady and some of her fellow tenants. Our two selections from the Manchurian writer Tuan-mu Hung-liang, written under the stimulus of the Japanese invasion, are sustained on a heroic note, though some of his best tales are equally noted for their irony and pathos. His "Nocturne in March" (*San-yüeh yeh-ch'ü*), also about Russian exiles in Shanghai, is, I believe, an even finer story than "The General." A Chekhovian quality also distinguishes some of Eileen Chang's best stories, though "The Golden Cangue" is in the tragic mode because its heroine, however unhappy, remains a fanatic unreconciled to her fate.

Beginning with Lu Hsün, Chinese story writers frequently write of modern intellectuals like themselves, who, while wishing to accomplish something big for their country, soon become aware of their individual smallness and the magnitude of the reactionary forces with which they have to contend. In *The Romantic Generation of Modern Chinese Writers*, Leo Lee has rightly noted the persistence of a Promethean strain in modern Chinese literature which is conspicuously romantic. During the three decades of our anthology, veneration for Romain Rolland and his masterpiece *Jean-Christophe* (rarely mentioned by American intellectuals today, but once popular enough to become a Modern Library Giant) was a fact attested to by a great many writers, and the creation of a modern Chinese hero in the image of Jean-Christophe was consciously striven for, but without success. The dedicated hero of invincible will looms large in the type of romantic-revolutionary fiction once highly popular; he eventually hardens into the Party "cadre" who works day and night on behalf of the people in Communist novels. This figure is barely visible in our anthology, however, because we prefer stories of greater realism in which modern intellectuals are viewed more ironically. Lü Wei-fu of Lu Hsün's "In the Wine Shop" is a self-confessed failure whose earlier zest for modern enlightenment has been crushed by economic necessity and by his continual regard for maternal wishes. But the first-person narrator, sipping wine alone as a total stranger in his home town (as the author was during his return to Shaohsing in the winter of 1919–1920) is even more an object of ironic contemplation: he is much more famous and successful than his former classmate, but is he any nearer his goal of awakening the Chinese people? Lu Hsün's helpless sympathy for a childhood companion in "My Old Home" and for a dismissed servant in "The New Year's Sacrifice" is also in subtle counterpoint with an awareness of his own impotence and estrangement despite—or rather because of—his own success as a modern intellectual.

The intellectual heroes of Yü Ta-fu's "Sinking" and Hsiao Chün's "Goats" fare even worse, one a suicidal student in Japan and the other a political prisoner in his own country. But if the sea tempts the former to drown himself partly in protest against his country's weakness, it provides for the latter the only gleam of hope in his otherwise viewless confinement. Like so many writers of the thirties, Hsiao Chün has espoused socialism, if not Communism, as the only hope for China's future, and in "Goats," his finest story, he presents his case for hope without ever raising his voice to denounce his captors or the whole rotten system that has made possible the inhumane treatment of petty thieves. In contrast to his own prolonged confinement, however, two Russian boys named Kolya and Alyosha are about to be released after a brief stay in the prison, and they intend forthwith to go to Russia rather than stay with their exiled parents in Shanghai. If there is a land of hope for Chinese intellectuals in the thirties, it is the Soviet Union. Thus Hsiao Chün's hero is quite envious of the boys willing to return even though they have only seen Soviet Russia in picture magazines and movies. What they know by heart is what their parents have taught them: the poems of Pushkin, Lermontov, and Tolstoy.

They recited the poems and songs they could recall, especially the younger one, and when he began to chant Pushkin's "My Nurse," I was moved to the point that I could no longer hold back my tears.
"Children, listen to me . . ."
Softly I too recited for them all the poems that I knew and could remember. But the children couldn't understand their meaning. I explained them and at the same time said:
"In your homeland all these are very popular poems."
The children—the younger one, that is—draped himself around my neck.
"We are friends!"

Since Alyosha and Kolya are common familiar names for Russian boys, I cannot be certain if Hsiao Chün had read Dostoevsky's *The Brothers Karamazov* and has alluded to it in his choice of these names. In the subplot of that novel Alyosha Karamazov moves among a group of boys whose leader is Kolya Krassotkin. Athough Alyosha can do nothing to prevent the tragic contentions in his own home, his gentle persuasion of these nihilist boys asserts a note of hope at the end of the novel. In "Goats," however, the roles of mentor and students have been reversed: our Chinese Alyosha, who is a young man of experience and suffering, now plays the part of a wonder-struck boy who listens to the children's poetry recitation and shares their dream of eventual freedom and happiness in a Soviet paradise. He is so wrapped up in their impending liberation that he doesn't even think of his wife and friends in other prisons. The boys, on their part, are ready to forsake their parents even though they are much more ignorant of the conditions in Soviet Russia than even the Chinese hero, who could at least recite some of the revolutionary poems popular in their homeland. The short story ends with the hero receiving a letter from his Russian friends:

Once I received a letter from the two Russian kids. They said they had already reached Harbin, had received entry from their country, and were about to strike out across Siberia and return to their homeland. In the letter they wrote:

"Mr. ——, haven't you had your fill of the ocean yet? Wishing you good health."

Yes, my dear little friends, I'm still watching the ocean, watching the same slice of ocean . . . I'm healthy . . .

I shook my head, and some strands of hair fluttered down onto the letter; this time I was truly smiling.

One is almost tempted to spoil his happiness by saying, "Wait until you get their next letter from Moscow!" But perhaps once there, they are not even allowed to write to their Chinese friend anymore.

"Goats" is a truly moving story, especially in its graphic account of the torture and death suffered alike by the goat thief and his three stolen goats. The reader almost allows the hero the sentimental dream of a better homeland, in his captive role as a numb spectator of all the senseless brutality around him. Disgusted with political repression in China, writers like Hsiao Chün are not really much better informed about conditions in Stalinist Russia than the two eager immigrants; judging by "Goats" and other stories in the hopeful vein, it is quite evident that the leftist authors of the thirties are confusing the noble humanism and humanitarianism of Pushkin, Lermontov, and Tolstoy with the new cynicism and brutality of a Soviet state.

Pa Chin, an anarchist, does not share the delusions of the more orthodox writers on the left. He believes in the teachings of Kropotkin and is much more drawn to the pre-Bolshevik revolutionaries of Czarist Russia, such as Vera Figner and Sophia Perovskaya. As we have seen, he even extends his sympathy to the Russian "general" and his wife. But Pa Chin is one with the orthodox leftists in his scornful attitude toward the liberal intellectuals of the thirties. There can be no doubt whatever that the protagonist of "Sinking Low" is a caricature of several prominent intellectuals of that period—Hu Shih for his insistence on historical research, his management of the Boxer Indemnity Fund for advanced students, and his pacific stand on Japanese aggression; and Chou Tso-jen and Lin Yutang for their espousal of the familiar essayists of the late Ming period and their cultivation of their own garden in deliberate retreat from national affairs. The protagonist's unhappy relationship with his giddy and flirtatious wife suggests the poet Hsü Chih-mo, whose notorious courtship of Lu Hsiao-man ended in marital disillusionment. Throughout the forties, Communist writers would continue to attack Hu Shih, Chou Tso-jen, and Lin Yutang in a grossly unfair fashion for their supposed crimes. But in his story Pa Chin takes these three to task not so much for their obstruction of leftist enlightenment as for their betrayal of the causes they had earlier espoused. The suffering of the Chinese people as individuals and as a nation should have remained their primary concern (as has been Pa Chin's throughout his writing career, with a brief interlude as a compliant Communist propagandist in the fifties). In the context of the primacy of this unfinished task—to strengthen China against foreign aggression and to alleviate the sufferings of its people—we can see why he should regard historical research for its own sake, the young scholars' quest for fame, and the remapping of literary tradition for the greater glory of individualist authors as idle pursuits.

If Pa Chin is properly indignant against the "lost leaders" of the new culture movement in 1934, he himself might be included in the blanket attack on all fashionable authors of the thirties in Ch'ien Chung-shu's grotesque caricature of The Writer in "The Inspiration" (1946). Edward Gunn has grouped the most brilliant Shanghai writers of the forties under the broad label of Antiromanticism.[1] But Ch'ien Chung-shu is not so much antiromantic as temperamentally Augustan and classic. With the exception of a few critics and scholars under the influence of Irving Babbitt, one can say that the portion of Western literature that seized the Chinese imagination begins with Rousseau, Blake, and Goethe. In China as in other Asian nations, it is the Romantic Movement with its enhanced respect for the individual and its discrediting of all institutional authorities that made possible the exposure of the glaring ills of a traditional Oriental society. Ch'ien Chung-shu is almost unique in modern Chinese literature for his affiliations with Pope and the Augustans as well as for his satiric preoccupation with his fellow writers and scholars. If he pokes fun at the romantic, revolutionary, and leftist writers in "The Inspiration," in another story, "The Cat" (*Mao*), he ridicules with equal composure what the leftist camp would have called the reactionary writers: Chou Tso-jen, Lin Yutang, and Shen Ts'ung-wen. These writers too are patently under the Romantic influence. Ch'ien Chung-shu is salutary in providing a refreshing way of looking at the modern tradition without seriously challenging our estimate of the writers affected. As a short-story writer and novelist, he is at his best (as in "Souvenir") for his Augustan discernment of the human heart and all its wiles and pretenses. His is a different kind of satire from the dominant type exposing inhumanity and injustice.

For the three decades of literature represented in our anthology, the abiding question is not why people are so ridiculous or stupid (as in "The Inspiration"), but why people are so unkind and cruel. The pat answer that the feudal system or society is entirely to blame, subscribed to by Pa Chin in the thirties, is certainly not adequate, since we find in the stories of Chang T'ien-i, Wu Tsu-hsiang, and Lu Ling so many sadistic characters whose delight in torturing others cannot be explained solely in terms of their class background. In "The Golden Cangue," Eileen Chang surpasses even these writers in exposing the worsening madness of its heroine, who destroys the chances of happiness for her own children to compensate for her own unhappiness. While implicitly condemning the moral turpitude of a social system which makes it possible for an elder brother to sell his sister to the paralytic son of a wealthy family, the author stresses nevertheless the volitional aspect of the unhappy victim's moral decline. In at least this one story, then, the human will is even more of a corrupting agent than the environment.

In our stories, if male members of the gentry are mostly seen in unflattering roles, as hypocrites and oppressors, representatives of the underprivileged classes are usually depicted as persons of moral integrity even by the strictest Confucian

[1] See Edward M. Gunn, Jr., *Unwelcome Muse: Chinese Literature in Shanghai and Peking, 1937–1945* (New York, 1980).

standards. This is so because the poor cannot gain our sympathy unless they are seen as honorable and upright, thrifty and diligent. Old T'ung Pao, the peasant hero of Mao Tun's "Spring Silkworms," for instance, still lives by the traditional maxim that personal honesty and hard work ensure economic self-sufficiency even though he is now living in a harsher world of rural bankruptcy. While Mao Tun has to depict T'ung Pao and his family in their habitual piety and diligence to earn our sympathy, as a Marxist writer, he shows at the same time how wrong-headed they are to place their trust in their betters and in Heaven when they should have followed the lead of the old man's youngest son, Ah To, whose lack of traditional piety actually marks the beginning of his modern enlightenment. There is a sequel to the story, "Autumn Harvest," in which the deliberate contrast between father and son is exploited even further to prove that, for all his immoral behavior, Ah To is right after all, as T'ung Pao himself, now increasingly ridiculed, acknowledges on his deathbed.

The hero of Chao Shu-li's "Lucky," another peasant cut in the traditional mold, suffers worse tribulations than Old T'ung Pao but is eventually saved from pauperdom and ignominy with the aid of the Communist cadres. Of the twenty authors in this volume, Chao Shu-li was the only one unschooled in Western literature; he had become Communist without ever being modern, and his story can be read as a simple Communist fable. Yet because of the naïveté of his vision, he has drawn in Lucky an archetypal orphan whose exemplary virtue would have moved the gods to assist him if he had inhabited the world of traditional fiction. He is the modern Tung Yung—one of the twenty-four exemplary sons and daughters in traditional folklore, who sells himself as a slave so as to have enough money to give his father a decent funeral. After Tung has observed his mourning period, he goes to serve his master and meets on the road a young woman who offers to be his wife and whose miraculous skills as a weaver soon restore him to freedom. She says in parting, "I am the Weaving Maid from Heaven. Because you are a filial son, the Heavenly Emperor ordered me to repay your debt."[2] The modern Tung Yung has no such luck; at fifteen or so, he is betrothed to an orphan of eight, who lives in his home as a child bride. At twenty-two, he has to marry her to please his dying mother, and has to buy a coffin and provide a funeral upon the latter's death. On account of these expenses, he borrows thirty dollars from his uncle Myriad Wang, who is also the clan leader of his village. Lucky becomes virtually his uncle's slave, trying to pay off the debt and its accumulated interest in the next few years. In the process, he is dispossessed of land and house, earns a bad reputation as a gambler, turns fugitive, and doesn't dare to confront Myriad Wang until many years later, following the liberation of his village by the Communists. Though loving and faithful even when her husband is away for years as a fugitive, Silver Flower is of course no heavenly maiden who can ransom her husband with only ten days' work. "Lucky" retains the framework of a fairy

---

[2] Yang Hsien-yi and Gladys Yang, trs., *The Man Who Sold A Ghost: Chinese Tales of the 3rd–6th Centuries* (Peking, 1958), p. 11.

tale, but its main interest lies in recounting the tribulations of the hero and indicting Myriad Wang as a representative of the landlord class for his impossible usury and callous exploitation of poor peasants.

Discounting the possible exaggeration of Myriad Wang's villainy, I am inclined to believe that he represents a perennial figure in Chinese villages who has oppressed the peasants for centuries. It is true that from the late Ch'ing to the war with Japan, China had fallen on hard times, and people tended to be even more cruel when there was not enough food for everybody. The satiric fiction of the late Ch'ing and the fiction of our three decades are in that sense especially reflective of their times. But we must also remember that it is the Chinese scholars' traditional preoccupation with Confucian learning and polite letters that has made possible a literary image of traditional China little plagued by large-scale suffering and injustice, except for reminders to the contrary from some of its popular poetry, fiction, and drama. It is also good to remember that Western reports on conditions in China by earlier missionaries as well as more recent historians and journalists have largely confirmed what modern Chinese writers have to say about their country. Thus Theodore White's capsule description of Chinese villages in the forties in no way deviates from what we have learned from Lu Hsün or Hsiao Hung:

> If Chungking was noisy, as all Chinese towns were noisy, the village, as most villages, was silent— the somber, brooding silence of countryside which I later came to recognize as the sound of emotionless vacuum. Nothing happened in villages; people grew up, lived and died in their villages, lashed to the seasons, to the fields, to the crops, their lives empty of any information but gossip, any excitement except fear.[3]

Among academic historians as well, an increasing interest in Chinese social and local history has meant that they are beginning to see a traditional China which is in every way as cruel and callous as the China depicted by modern novelists. Further research along the lines of Jonathan Spence's *The Death of Woman Wang* (New York, 1978), which is about some humble residents of a poor county in seventeenth-century China, will continue to corroborate the massive evidence of inhumanity supplied by modern Chinese fiction.

Tung Yung of the Han dynasty is a legendary figure, but in Han times, because of the government's promotion of filial piety, many an orphan of Tung Yung's poverty did sell himself out as a slave in order to provide his deceased parent with a proper burial. And in modern times, a landlord like Myriad Wang could not charge such exorbitant rates of interest on his loans were it not for the fact that a desperate orphan has to turn to him in order to maintain his self-respect in the eyes of his clan. Chao Shu-li blames Lucky's tribulations on an evil landlord and usurer, but surely his need to observe a financially ruinous ritual dictates his contraction of an impossible debt in the first place. For Tung Yung and Lucky

---

[3] Theodore H. White, *In Search of History: A Personal Adventure* (New York, 1978), p. 86.

alike, it is their obligatory fulfillment of a familial duty rather than their filial piety per se that changes their status from free men to enslaved.

Our anthology supplies other incidents illustrating a truism about the traditional Chinese family, namely, that junior and female members must subordinate themselves to the elders lest they violate a set of arbitrary regulations ensuring the family's honor and continuation. While most rich men buy concubines as a matter of course, even the most shrewish of wives cannot stop her husband from buying one if she herself is without a son. The middle-aged scholar in Jou Shih's "A Slave-Mother" is quite henpecked, but even his wife encourages him to rent a poor man's wife so that the family line may be continued. The title heroine of Shen Ts'ung-wen's "Hsiao-hsiao," a child bride like Silver Flower, is made pregnant by a farm hand. Though a peasant girl in the primitive region of West Hunan, she has nevertheless violated the honor of her husband's family and must be either drowned or sold as a concubine. In the pastoral scheme of Shen's story, she is spared either fate and lives on to see her bastard marrying in time a child bride. Shen Ts'ung-wen is entitled to his idyllic vision of a child of nature surviving unscathed, but of course he is the last person to be oblivious of the fate of many a Hunanese maiden who embraced death after a brief affair with a sailor or soldier.

It is because the family comes first that Myriad Wang can flog Lucky with the clan's support and even rally it to the idea of punishing him with death. He exhorts the clan thus: "This—this Lucky has lived long enough! The latest is that he's working in the town as hired musician at funerals. If people outside the clan hear of this, how will we ever be able to face them again? A common ancestral line, a common burial ground—if we of the Wang clan get this muck smeared on us, none of us will ever be clean again!" The same thought runs through the mind of a T'ang nobleman over a thousand years ago when he hears of his son's degradation as a professional singer at funerals. The reader of "The Courtesan Li Wa" (in *Traditional Chinese Stories*) will surely remember the scene where the nobleman, after scolding the wastrel for disgracing the family, forthwith "stripped his son and used a horse whip to flog him several hundred times. The young man, overcome by pain, fell unconscious. The father left him for dead."[4] It is true that the pride of the nobleman is genuinely hurt, whereas Myriad Wang is merely simulating anger to get rid of Lucky for good. But the same moral prejudice prevails in both scenes: a wastrel should be dead rather than disgrace the family by entering a mean profession. Little wonder that the point of so many modern Chinese novels is the ultimate decision of the young hero or heroine to leave the family and exercise an independence in the outside world of revolutionary action. Despite its artistic flatness, the overwhelming response of the young readers of the thirties and forties to Pa Chin's *The Family,* which features such a hero, was mainly due to their recognition of its truthfulness as a chronicle of a large-size family of Confucian gentility in any province, any city.

[4] Y. W. Ma and Joseph S. M. Lau, eds., *Traditional Chinese Stories: Themes and Variations* (New York, 1978), p. 168.

As is amply demonstrated in *The Family*, women have been the main victims of traditional Chinese society. By Han times the existence of such bibles for women as the lady scholar Pan Chao's *Nü-chieh* (Precepts for Women) indicated already the rigid codification of female subservience and chastity in a society run by men for their convenience and pleasure. From Han to the late Ch'ing, except for a tiny minority who made some mark in literature and the arts, ordinary women who aspired to posthumous fame in local or national history have been invariably those whose heroic acts of wifely constancy or filial piety, resulting nearly always in death, compelled male admiration. Since at least Sung times the crippling of nearly all urban women by deforming their feet at a tender age had added further injury to insult, and the rise of Neo-Confucianism in the same period with its even harsher insistence on female chastity could not be coincidental.

By the Ming–Ch'ing period the misery of women and the depravity of some of them in contriving for pleasure and power despite their subjection to male domination have been spectacularly displayed in such novels as *Chin P'ing Mei* and the *Dream of the Red Chamber* (or *The Story of the Stone; Hung-lou meng*) as well as the much less read verse narratives, written by women themselves, known as *t'an-tz'u*. This literary record notwithstanding, a systematic examination of the biographies of notable women in all the local gazetteers dating from that period and earlier will add immeasurably to the heart-rending record of appalling inhumanity, which amply justifies Lu Hsün's indictment of China as a cannibalistic society.

The women's lot has considerably improved during the three decades covered by our anthology. But precisely because of their changed attitude toward Chinese society and toward women in general, our authors have left us an astounding gallery of memorable female characters, young, middle-aged, and old, from the twice-widowed Hsiang-lin's wife of Lu Hsün's "The New Year's Sacrifice" to the mad woman Ch'i-ch'iao and her captive daughter Ch'ang-an in Eileen Chang's "The Golden Cangue." There can be no doubt that these women leave on the whole a far stronger impression on the reader than the male characters in this volume. While both Lu Hsün and Yeh Shao-chün are as noted for their sympathetic portrayal of lonely and pitiful men—K'ung I-chi, the teacher in "Rice," and the old man in "Solitude"—as of women, quite a number of their male characters are objects of satire, such as Ssu-ming and his Confucian friends in Lu Hsün's "Soap." Given the nature of Chinese society in the pre-Communist decades, it was quite inevitable that story writers of satiric disposition should treat many of their central male characters as embodiments of its hypocritical and wicked ways, as is the case with Lao She's "An Old Tragedy in a New Age," Chang T'ien-i's "The Bulwark" and "Midautumn Festival," and Lu Ling's "The Coffins." The protagonists of these stories are certainly sharply visualized, but as satiric vignettes, they do not assume an independent existence outside their tales and do not haunt us the way some of the women characters do for their wrongs.

It is altogether fitting that, given the brutalization and enslavement of Chinese women over the millennia, far more female characters than male should stand for outraged humanity in modern Chinese fiction, while nearly all the women writers of our period, including Ling Shu-hua, Ting Ling, Hsiao Hung, and Eileen Chang of this volume, should be particularly drawn to the fate of Chinese women and include in their portrayals some heroines who represent their own frustrated idealism in a still male-chauvinist society. Of our three stories with a Communist setting, if Chao Shu-li's "Lucky" gives an unqualified endorsement of Communist benevolence in a liberated village, it is appropriate that Ting Ling, whose early stories are famous for their nihilist idealism, should display so much sympathy for the young heroines of "When I Was in Hsia Village" and "In the Hospital": Chen-chen, afflicted with venereal disease for her Party-approved work among the Japanese and now an outcast in her village; and Lu P'ing, an obstetrician shocked by the callousness of a Yenan hospital and censured for reformist ardor. Ting Ling too was censured by the Communist authorities in Yenan for the latter story and for an editorial pleading the women's cause in the following year (1942). Mao Tse-tung gave his *Talks at the Yenan Forum on Literature and Art* that May in direct response to the grievances expressed by Ting Ling, Hsiao Chün, and other like-minded authors.

The heroines of Lu Hsün's "The New Year's Sacrifice" and Jou Shih's "A Slave-Mother" are unfortunate women of an earlier age long before Communism had penetrated into Chinese villages. Hsiang-lin's wife of the former story, upon being widowed, is forcibly sold by her mother-in-law for a sum of money, and the slave-mother is given on loan to the scholar by her destitute husband for a hundred dollars. Though Chen-chen and Ch'i-ch'iao come close, no other women in our volume suffer greater ignominy than these two. Yet if they cannot have much affection for their husbands, what stands out is their instinctive, unfeigned maternal love, which defines their humanity without mitigating their suffering. Hsiang-lin's wife becomes in the eyes of others a crazed person because she constantly tells of the death of her son, and the slave-mother suffers as much mental anguish when torn from her firstborn son to serve a stranger as when torn from her second son to return to her long estranged husband. Though he is initially a brute who has no compunction in boiling her newborn daughter alive, and though she cannot expect to see her second son ever again, toward the end the slave-mother's fate is somewhat kinder than that of Hsiang-lin's wife, since there is every indication that her first son will return her love.

The heroines of Ling Shu-hua's two stories, though urban women of higher social status, lead lives as unfree and predetermined as those of Hsiang-lin's wife and the slave-mother. Like so many daughters of genteel families, the Eldest Young Mistress of "Embroidered Pillows" regards her skill in needlework as her best recommendation on the marriage market. Lately she has devoted half a year embroidering a pair of back cushions. Though in the admiring eyes of a woman servant she still looks "as fresh and delicate as a scallion," she is actually a drudge doing close work in the summer heat and impairing her eyesight into the bargain. The servant predicts that upon the delivery of the finished cushions to a cabinet secretary's house, "the matchmakers will be coming to see you; the gate will be trampled down by the crowd." Actually, these same cushions will be trampled and actually vomited upon the day they arrive at the secretary's house, thus foreshadowing Eldest Young Mistress's future if she ever becomes a daughter-in-law in an official family. The wife of the shopkeeper Ching-jen in "The Night of Midautumn Festival" is not particularly sympathetic for her cold indifference toward her husband's dying foster sister. However, the story of the foster sister, which tells us much about Ching-jen, is not essential to our understanding of his wife's fate; quarrel over any other issue could easily have caused a rift between the recently married couple once the euphoria of the first months wore off. And once Ching-jen decides to find fault with his wife, he immediately notices that she has ugly features. It is also very easy—and traditional—for his mother to blame her for not keeping him at home when he has turned into a libertine and spendthrift. The heroine herself is also in character when she blames the ruin of her life on that unfortunate quarrel over the foster sister, and so is her mother in counseling her to accept her fate and "wait for your next life." Though Ching-jen's wife is almost as much abused by her husband as is the slave-mother by hers, all the readily proffered explanations for her failure in life comment powerfully on feudal mentality and lend her story its special pathos.

In Hsiao Hung's "Hands" the schoolgirl Wang Ya-ming is as much a symbol of unwanted humanity as is Hsiang-lin's wife in Lu Hsün's story. But whereas the latter lives and dies a victim of feudal cruelty and superstition, Wang Ya-ming's maltreatment in a modern girls' school is all the more accusatory of the supposed modern enlightenment that has failed to instill kindness and remove class barriers. She is a poor dyer's daughter whose blackened hands serve effectively to isolate her from everyone in the school, with the exception of the sympathetic first-person narrator. Wang Ya-ming is ostensibly expelled for her poor academic performance, and yet this unkind deed will dash all her father's hopes for betterment and probably hasten her to a grave.

Not all authors in this volume are content to view this feminine suffering with mere sympathy and indignation. Despite their tribulations, the heroines of Hsü Ti-shan's "The Merchant's Wife" and "Yü-kuan" reach out for a deeper understanding of life's meaning in which sufferings have their appropriate place. Yü-kuan's quest for self-knowledge, especially, makes her tale a triumphant testament of human spirituality. Whereas Shen Ts'ung-wen's Hsiao-hsiao remains inviolable by feudal morality by virtue of her animal grace and whereas Eileen Chang's Ch'i-ch'iao, married against her will into a decadent upper-class family, steadily deteriorates until she becomes the most corrupt and cruel representative of her adopted class, the humble missionary woman Yü-kuan makes a conscious choice to lead a good life and eventually succeeds after she has seen through her self-deception during the long years of her widowhood.

Though Hsü Ti-shan, Shen Ts'ung-wen, and Eileen Chang transcend humanitarian realism to reach for a larger or more complex view of life, their stories do not gainsay the evilness of feudal society or the victimization of women in that society. The young heroine of Shen's "Three Men and One Woman" dies by swallowing gold, surely in protest against her parents' arbitrary arrangement of her marital future. The author's casual comment that such deaths occur too often to bother the survivors does not lessen the cruelty of such tragedies. It is only because Shen Ts'ung-wen is mainly concerned with the strange fulfillment such a death brings to a smitten youth that it is passed over lightly. The girl's fate is worth exploring in itself, though Shen has not done so in the story.

Since it is not possible to discuss all of our forty-four selections in a short Introduction, I have passed over many in silence because they have already been discussed in my *History of Modern Chinese Fiction*. For the same reason I have paid particular attention to those stories not mentioned in that book, such as Pa Chin's "The General" and "Sinking Low," Jou Shih's "A Slave-Mother," Hsiao Chün's "Goats," Hsiao Hung's "Hands," and Chao Shu-li's "Lucky." With the four exceptions already noted, all our twenty writers are humanitarian and satiric realists primarily concerned with the old society with all its victims and its perpetrators of cruelty and injustice. Many of these writers, of course, also wrote political or revolutionary fiction concerned with the making of a new China in accordance with some socialist or utopian dream. And insofar as the new China that came into being in 1949 has not lived up to the aspirations of the May Fourth era, the literary record of our three decades shows by and large a strain of political naïveté for its failure to forewarn against any possible resurgence of the forces of reaction and tyranny. The best fiction of our period, however, is little tainted with political naïveté or political didacticism in its obsession with the ugly realities of contemporary China. In culling some of the best short fiction from these decades, therefore, our collection stands as a proud and moving record of an old nation's attempt to regain its humanity and redefine its identity through fearless self-criticism.

Lu Hsün, 1930

Hsü Ti-shan, 1939

Yeh Shao-chün, early 1950s

Yü Ta-fu, 1930s

Mao Tun, 1930

Lao She, 1956

Ling Shu-hua, 1955

Jou Shih, early 1930s

Shen Ts'ung-wen, 1973

Ting Ling, early 1950s

Pa Chin, 1978

Chao Shu-li, 1950s

Chang T'ien-i, early 1950s

Hsiao Hung and Hsiao Chün, 1930

Wu Tsu-hsiang, 1946–1947

Ch'ien Chung-shu and his wife Yang Chiang, 1961

Tuan-mu Hung-liang, 1942

Lu Ling with wife (left) and friend, 1980

Eileen Chang, early 1940s

Modern Chinese Stories and Novellas

LU HSÜN
(1881–1936)

Lu Hsün (pen name of Chou Shu-jen), was born to a gentry family in Shao-hsing, Chekiang. He had received a traditional education before he enrolled in a new-style mining school and a naval academy in Nanking. Graduated at the top of his class, he was sent to Japan in 1902 on a government scholarship. He eventually decided to study Western medicine partly because, so he later claimed, his father had died a victim of traditional Chinese quacks. His studies at the Sendai Medical School were not distinguished, and he soon realized that his inclination was toward the humanities. In 1905, he left Sendai to devote his full energies to literary endeavors.

His proposed new magazine did not materialize, and the two-volume set of European translations, *Stories from Abroad* (*Yü-wai hsiao-shuo chi,* 1909), which he published in collaboration with his younger brother, Chou Tso-jen, sold very poorly. In 1909, Lu Hsün returned to China in frustration and taught biology at schools in Hangchow and his home town, Shaohsing. Later, he was invited to Peking to serve as a section head in charge of libraries and museums at the Ministry of Education of the newly founded Republic. After almost a decade of mental depression, an invitation from a friend to write for *New Youth* (*Hsin ch'ing-nien*), the leading intellectual magazine of its time, suddenly released his creative energies. His first story for that monthly, "The Diary of a Madman" (*K'uang-jen jih-chi,* 1918) was truly revolutionary in impact for its radical critique of Chinese society. In the next eight years he wrote two dozen stories, including the six indubitable classics chosen for our volume. Collected in *Outcry* (*Na-han,* 1923) and *Wandering* (*P'ang-huang,* 1926), these stories established Lu Hsün's reputation as the finest short-story writer of that period.

Before Lu Hsün left Peking in 1926, he had taught Chinese literature at National Peking University, Peking Women's College, and the National Normal University. After brief sojourns in Amoy and Canton, he finally moved to Shanghai and settled down with his common-law wife, Hsü Kuang-p'ing, a former student, until his death in 1936. As a result of his experiences in Canton and Shanghai, where he became increasingly disillusioned with the high-handed measures of the Nationalist Government, Lu Hsün turned toward the left. The last decade of his life, in which he gradually gave up fictional writing in favor of the pithy, satiric *tsa-wen*, was by no means uneventful. He became bitterly embroiled in several debates on literature and politics with various literary groups on both the left and the right. Though he was the titular head of the League of the Leftwing Writers (a Communist organization dominating the literary scene from 1930 to 1936), and the acknowledged leading writer in Shanghai, he did not enjoy a harmonious relationship with those members of the Chinese Communist Party working behind the scenes at the League. Nevertheless, his commitment to his new Marxist conviction was unswerving. In 1936, he and his disciples clashed with Chou Yang, then known as Chou Ch'i-ying, the Party's literary commissar in Shanghai, in the famous "Battle of Slogans" because of what Lu Hsün believed to be Chou's compromising policy toward non-leftist forces. Sick at heart at the time of his death, he has bequeathed to posterity a voluminous legacy of stories, essays, translations, letters, diaries, studies of classical Chinese literature, and collections of European woodcut art which he had promoted.

Enjoying a wide following in his lifetime and exerting a tremendous impact on modern Chinese literature, Lu Hsün was lionized and later deified by the Chinese Communists under Mao Tse-tung. He still remains the most renowned writer-intellectual of modern China.

L.O.F.L.

K'ung I-chi

by Lu Hsün

Translated by Yang Hsien-yi and Gladys Yang

The wine shops in Luchen are not like those in other parts of China. They all have a right-angled counter facing the street, where hot water is kept ready for warming wine. When men come off work at midday and in the evening they buy a bowl of wine; it cost four coppers twenty years ago, but the price has risen to ten coppers. Standing beside the counter, they drink it warm, and relax. Another copper will buy a plate of salted bamboo shoots or peas flavored with aniseed to go with the wine, while for a dozen coppers you can buy a meat dish. But most of these customers belong to the short-coated class, few of whom can afford this. Only those in long gowns enter the adjacent room to order wine and dishes, and sit and drink at leisure.

At the age of twelve I started work as a waiter in Prosperity Tavern, at the entrance to the town. The tavern keeper said I looked too foolish to serve the long-gowned customers, so I was given work in the outer room. Although the short-coated customers there were easy to talk to, there were quite a few who would make a fuss. They would insist on watching with their own eyes as the yellow wine was ladled from the keg, looking to see if there were any water at the bottom of the wine pot, and inspecting for themselves the immersion of the pot in hot water. Under such keen scrutiny, it was very difficult for me to dilute the wine. So after a few days the manager decided I was not suited for this work. Fortunately I had been recommended by someone influential, so he could not dismiss me, and I was transferred to the dull work of warming wine.

From that time on I stood all day behind the counter, fully engaged with my duties. Although I did nothing wrong at this job, I found it rather monotonous and uninteresting. Our manager was a fierce-looking individual, and the customers were a morose lot, so that it was impossible to be gay. Only when K'ung I-chi came to the tavern could I laugh a little. That is why I still remember him.

K'ung was the only long-gowned customer to drink his wine standing. He was a big man, with a pale complexion and scars that often showed among the wrinkles of his face. He had a large, unkempt beard, streaked with white. Although he wore a long gown, it was dirty and tattered, and looked as if it had not been washed or mended for over ten years. He used so many archaisms in his speech, it was impossible to understand half of what he said. As his surname was K'ung, he was nicknamed "K'ung I-chi," the first three characters in a children's copybook. Whenever he came into the shop, everyone would look at him and chuckle. And someone would call out:

"K'ung I-chi! There are some fresh scars on your face!"

Ignoring this remark, K'ung would come to the counter to order two bowls of heated wine and a dish of peas flavored with aniseed. For this he produced nine coppers. Someone else would call out, in deliberately loud tones:

"You must have been stealing again!"

"How can you ruin a man's good name so groundlessly?" he would ask, opening his eyes wide.

"What good name! The day before yesterday I saw you with my own eyes being hung up and beaten for stealing books from the Ho family!"

Then K'ung would flush, the veins on his forehead standing out as he remonstrated: "Taking a book can't be considered stealing . . . Taking a book! . . . Can the business of a scholar be considered stealing?!" Then followed sayings that were hard to understand, like "A gentleman keeps his integrity even in poverty,"[1] and a jumble of archaic expressions until everybody was roaring with laughter and the whole tavern was filled with merriment.

From gossip I heard behind his back, K'ung I-chi had studied the classics but had never passed the official examination. With no way of making a living, he grew poorer and poorer, until he was practically reduced to begging. Luckily, he was a good calligrapher, and could do copy work in exchange for a bowl of rice to eat. Unfortunately he had a bad disposition: he liked drinking and was lazy. So after a few days he would invariably disappear, taking books, paper, brushes, and inkstone with him. After this had happened several times, nobody wanted to employ him as a copyist again. Then there was no alternative for him but occasional pilfering. In our tavern his behavior outshone everyone else's. He never failed to pay up, although sometimes, when he had no ready money, his name would appear on the chalk board where we listed debtors. However, in less than a month he would always settle his account, and his name would be wiped off the board again.

After he had drank half a bowl of wine, K'ung's flushed face would return to normal. But then someone would ask:

"K'ung I-chi, do you really know how to read?"

When K'ung looked as if such a question were beneath contempt, they would continue: "How is it you never got through even the lowest official examination?"

At that K'ung would look disconsolate and ill at ease. His face would turn pale and his lips move, but only to utter those unintelligible classical expressions. Then everybody would laugh heartily

again, and the whole tavern was filled with merriment.

At such times, I could join in the laughter without being scolded by my master. In fact he often put such questions to K'ung himself, to evoke laughter. Knowing it was no use talking to them, K'ung would chat with us children. Once he asked me:

"Have you had any schooling?"

When I nodded, he said, "Well then, I'll test you. How do you write the character *hui* in *hui-hsiang* peas?"[2]

I thought, "I'm not going to be tested by a beggar!" So I turned away and ignored him. After waiting for some time, he said very earnestly:

"You can't write it? I'll show you how. Mind you remember! You ought to remember such characters, because later when you have a shop of your own, you'll need them to make up your accounts."

It seemed to me I was still very far from owning a shop; besides, our employer never entered *hui-hsiang* peas in the account book. Amused but irritated, I answered listlessly: "Who wants you as a teacher? Isn't it the *hui* character with the grass radical?"

K'ung was delighted, and tapped two long fingernails on the counter. "Right, right!" he said, nodding. "Only there are four different ways of writing *hui*. Do you know them?" My patience exhausted, I scowled and made off. K'ung I-chi had dipped his finger in wine, in order to trace the characters on the counter. But when he saw how indifferent I was, he sighed and looked most disappointed.

Sometimes children in the neighborhood, hearing laughter, came to join in the fun, and surrounded K'ung I-chi. Then he would give them peas flavored with aniseed, one to each of them. After eating the peas, the children would still hang round, their eyes on the dish. Flustered, he would spread his fingers to cover the dish and, bending forward from the waist, would say: "There isn't much left. I haven't much as it is." Then straightening up to look at the peas again, he would shake his head. "Not much! Verily, not

---

[1] From the *Analects* of Confucius.   [2] Aniseed.

much, forsooth!" Then the children would scamper off, with shouts of laughter.

K'ung I-chi could make everyone happy like this, but we got along all right without him too.

One day, a few days or so before the Midautumn Festival, the tavern keeper was laboriously making out his accounts. Taking down the board from the wall, he suddenly said: "K'ung I-chi hasn't been in for a long time. He still owes nineteen coppers!" That made me realize how long it was since we had seen him.

"How could he come?" one of the customers said. "His legs were broken in that last beating."

"Ah!"

"He was stealing again. This time he was fool enough to steal from Mr. Ting, the provincial scholar! As if anybody could get away with that!"

"What then?"

"What then? First he had to write a confession, then he was beaten. The beating lasted nearly all night, until his legs were broken."

"And then?"

"Well, his legs were broken."

"Yes, but after that?"

"After? . . . Who knows? He may be dead."

The tavern keeper asked no more questions, but went on slowly making up his accounts.

After the Midautumn Festival the wind grew colder every day, as winter came on. Even though I spent all my time by the stove, I had to wear my padded jacket. One afternoon, when the shop was empty, I was sitting with my eyes closed when I heard a voice:

"Warm a bowl of wine."

The voice was very low, yet familiar. But when I looked up, there was no one in sight. I stood up and looked toward the door, and there, facing the threshold, beneath the counter, sat K'ung I-chi. His face was haggard and lean, and he looked in a terrible condition. He had on a ragged lined jacket, and was sitting cross-legged on a mat

which was attached to his shoulders by a straw rope. When he saw me, he repeated:

"Warm a bowl of wine."

At this point my employer stuck his head out over the counter and asked:

"Is that K'ung I-chi? You still owe nineteen coppers!"

"That . . . I'll settle next time," replied K'ung, looking up disconsolately. "Here's ready money; the wine must be good."

The tavern keeper, just as in the past, chuckled and said:

"K'ung I-chi, you've been stealing again!"

But instead of protesting vigorously, the other simply said:

"It's nothing to joke about."

"Joke? If you didn't steal, why did they break your legs?"

"I fell," said K'ung in a low voice. "I broke them in a fall." His eyes pleaded with the tavern keeper to let the matter drop. But now several people had gathered round, and they all laughed. I warmed the wine, carried it over, and set it on the threshold. He produced four coppers from his ragged coat pocket, and placed them in my hand. As he did so I saw that his hands were covered with mud—he must have crawled there on them. Presently he finished the wine and, amid the laughter and comments of the others, slowly dragged himself off by his hands.

A long time went by after that without our seeing K'ung again. At the end of the year, when the tavern keeper took down the board, he said, "K'ung I-chi still owes nineteen coppers!" At the Dragon Boat Festival the next year, he said the same thing again. But when the Midautumn Festival came, he did not mention it. And another New Year came round without our seeing any more of him.

Nor have I ever seen him since—probably K'ung I-chi is really dead.

Medicine

by Lu Hsün

Translated by Yang Hsien-yi and Gladys Yang

I

It was autumn, in the early hours of the morning. The moon had gone down, but the sun had not yet risen, and all that remained was a dark blue layer of sky. Apart from night prowlers, everything was asleep. Old Shuan suddenly sat up in bed. He struck a match and lit the grease-covered oil lamp, which shed a ghostly light over the two rooms of the teahouse.

"Are you going now, dad?" queried an old woman's voice. And from the small inner room a fit of coughing was heard.

"Hmm."

Old Shuan listened as he fastened his clothes, then stretching out his hand said, "Give it to me."

After some fumbling under the pillow his wife produced a packet of silver dollars which she handed over. Old Shuan pocketed it nervously, patted his pocket twice, then lighting a paper lantern and blowing out the lamp went into the inner room. A rustling was heard, and then more coughing. When all was quiet again, Old Shuan called softly: "Son! . . . Don't you get up! . . . Your mother will see to the shop."

Receiving no answer, Old Shuan assumed his son must be sound asleep again; so he went out into the street. The street was pitch black and empty. All that could be seen clearly was the gray road. The light from the lantern fell on his pacing feet. Here and there he came across a few dogs, but none of them barked. It was much colder than indoors, yet Old Shuan's spirits rose, as if he

had grown suddenly younger and possessed some miraculous life-giving power. He lengthened his stride. And the more he walked, the clearer the road became, the brighter the sky.

Absorbed in his walking, Old Shuan was startled when he saw distinctly the crossroad ahead of him. He walked back a few steps and found a shop with its doors shut. He hobbled under the eaves and stood still, leaning against the door. After some time he began to feel chilly.

"Uh, an old chap."

"Seems rather cheerful . . ."

Old Shuan was startled again and, opening his eyes, saw several men passing in front of him. One of them even turned back to look at him, and although he could not see him clearly, the man's eyes shone with the glare of a predator, like a famished person at the sight of food. Looking at his lantern, Old Shuan saw it had gone out. He patted his pocket—the hard packet was still there. Then he looked around and saw many strange people, in twos and threes, wandering about like lost souls. However, when he gazed steadily at them, he could not see anything else strange about them.

Presently he saw some soldiers strolling around. The large white circle on their uniforms, both in front and behind, was clear even at a distance; and as they drew nearer, he saw the dark red border too. The next second, with a trampling of feet, a crowd rushed past. Thereupon the small groups which had arrived earlier suddenly formed a solid mass and rushed forward like a tidal wave. Just before the crossroad, they came to a sudden stop and grouped themselves in a semi-circle.

Old Shuan looked in that direction too, but could only see a mass of people's backs. Craning their necks as far as they would go, they looked like so many ducks held and lifted by some invisible hand. For a moment all was still; then a sound was heard, and a stir swept through the on-lookers. There was a rumble as they pushed back, sweeping past Old Shuan and nearly knocking him down.

"Hey! Give me the cash, and I'll give you the goods!" A man clad entirely in black stood before him, his eyes like daggers, making Old Shuan shrink to half his normal size. This man thrust one huge extended hand toward him, while in the other he held a roll of steamed bread, from which crimson drops were still dripping to the ground.

Hurriedly Old Shuan fumbled for his dollars, and trembling he was about to hand them over, but he dared not take the object. The other grew impatient and shouted: "What are your afraid of? Why not take it?" When Old Shuan still hesitated, the man in black snatched his lantern and tore off its paper shade to wrap up the roll. This package he thrust into Old Shuan's hand, at the same time seizing the silver and giving it a cursory feel. Then he turned away, muttering, "Old fool . . ."

"Whose sickness is this for?" Old Shuan seemed to hear someone ask, but he made no reply. His whole mind was on the package, which he carried as carefully as if it were the sole heir to an ancient house. Nothing else mattered now. He was about to transplant this new life to his own home, and reap much happiness. The sun had risen, lighting up the broad highway before him that led straight home and the worn tablet behind him at the crossroad with its faded gold inscription: "Ancient Pavilion."

II

When Old Shuan reached home, the shop had been cleaned, and the rows of tea tables shone brightly; but no customers had arrived. Only his son sat eating at a table by the wall. Big beads of sweat rolled off his forehead and his lined jacket clung to his spine. His shoulder blades stuck out so sharply that an inverted V seemed stamped there. At this sight, Old Shuan's brow, which had been relaxed, contracted again. His wife hurried in from the kitchen, with expectant eyes and a tremor on her lips:

"Get it?"

"Yes."

They went together into the kitchen, and discussed things for a while. Then the old woman went out, to return shortly with a dried lotus leaf which she spread on the table. Old Shuan unwrapped the crimson-stained roll from the lantern paper and transferred it to the lotus leaf. Little Shuan had finished his meal, but his mother exclaimed nervously:

"Sit still, Little Shuan! Don't come over here."

Adjusting the fire in the stove, Old Shuan put the green package and the red and white lantern paper into the stove together. A red-black flame flared up, and a strange odor permeated the shop.

"Smells good! What kind of snack are you having?" The hunchback had arrived. He was one of those who spend all their time in teashops, the first to come in the morning and the last to leave. Now he had just stumbled to a corner table facing the street, and sat down. But no one answered his question.

"Puffed rice gruel?"

Still no reply. Old Shuan hurried out to brew tea for him.

"Come here, Little Shuan!" His mother called him into the inner room, set a stool in the middle, and sat the child down. Then, bringing him a round black object on a plate, she said gently:

"Eat it up . . . then you'll get better."

Little Shuan picked up the black object and looked at it. He had the oddest feeling, as if he were holding his own life in his hands. He split it open very carefully. From within the charred crust a jet of white vapor escaped, then disappeared, leaving only two halves of a steamed white flour roll. Soon it was all eaten, the flavor completely forgotten. Only the empty plate was left in front of him. His father and mother were standing one on each side of him, their eyes apparently pouring something into him and at the same time extracting something. His small heart began to beat faster, and, putting his hands to his chest, he began to cough again.

"Sleep for a while; then you'll be all right," said his mother.

Obediently, Little Shuan coughed himself to sleep. The woman waited until his breathing was regular, then covered him lightly with a much patched quilt.

III

The shop was crowded, and Old Shuan was busy, carrying a big copper kettle to pour tea for one customer after another. There were dark circles under his eyes.

"Aren't you well, Old Shuan? . . . What's wrong with you?" asked one graybeard.

"Nothing."

"Nothing? . . . No, I suppose from your smile, there couldn't be," the old man corrected himself.

"It's just that Old Shuan's busy," said the hunchback. "If his son—" But before he could finish, a heavy-jowled man burst in. He wore a dark brown shirt, unbuttoned and fastened carelessly with a broad dark-brown sash at his waist. As soon as he entered, he shouted to Old Shuan:

"Has he eaten it? Any better? Fate's with you, Old Shuan. What luck! If I didn't hear of things so quickly—"

Holding the kettle in one hand, the other straight by his side in an attitude of respect, Old Shuan listened with a smile. In fact, all present were listening respectfully. The old woman, dark circles under her eyes too, came out smiling with a bowl containing tea leaves and an added olive, over which Old Shuan poured boiling water for the newcomer.

"This is a guaranteed cure! Not like other things!" declared the heavy-jowled man. "Just think, brought back warm, and eaten warm!"

"Yes, indeed, we couldn't have managed it without Uncle K'ang's help." The old woman thanked him warmly.

"A guaranteed cure! Eaten warm like this. A

roll dipped in human blood like this can cure any consumption!"

The old woman seemed a little disconcerted by the word "consumption," and turned a bit pale. However, she forced a smile again at once and found some pretext to leave. Meanwhile the man in brown was indiscreet enough to go on talking at the top of his voice until the child in the inner room was wakened and started coughing.

"So you've had a great stroke of luck for your Little Shuan! Of course his sickness will be cured completely. No wonder Old Shuan keeps smiling." As he spoke, the graybeard walked up to the man in brown, and lowered his voice to ask:

"Mr. K'ang, I heard the criminal executed today came from the Hsia family. Who was it? And why was he executed?"

"Who? Son of Widow Hsia, of course! Young scoundrel!"

Seeing how they all hung on his words, Mr. K'ang's spirits rose even higher. His jowls quivered, and he made his voice as loud as he could.

"The worthless rogue didn't want to live, simply didn't want to! I didn't get anything out of it this time. Even the clothes stripped from him were taken by Red-eye, the jailer. Our Old Shuan was luckiest, and after him Third Uncle Hsia, who pocketed the whole reward—twenty-five taels of bright silver—and didn't have to spend a cent!"

Little Shuan walked slowly out of the inner room with his hands pressed against his chest, coughing repeatedly. He went to the kitchen, filled a bowl with cold rice, added hot water to it, and sitting down started to eat. His mother, hovering over him, asked softly:

"Do you feel better, son? Still as hungry as ever?"

"A guaranteed cure!" K'ang glanced at the child, then turned back to address the company. "Third Uncle Hsia is really crafty. If he hadn't informed, even *his* family would have been executed, and their property confiscated. But instead? Silver! That worthless young rogue was a real scoundrel! Even locked up in prison he still tried to incite the jailer to revolt!"

"No! The idea of it!" A man in his twenties, sitting in the back, expressed his indignation.

"You know, Red-eye went to sound him out, but he started chatting with him. He said the great Ch'ing empire belongs to all of us. Just think: is that the way people should talk? Red-eye knew he had only an old mother at home, but had never imagined he was so poor. He couldn't squeeze anything out of him. He was already bursting with anger, and then the young fool tried to 'pacify the tiger by scratching its head,' so he gave him a couple of slaps."

"Red-eye packs quite a wallop. Those slaps must have been hard to take."

"The lowly scamp was not afraid of being beaten. He even said how sorry he was."

"Nothing to be sorry about in beating a wretch like that," said Graybeard.

K'ang looked at him superciliously and said with a sarcastic grin, "You misunderstood. The way he said it, he was sorry for Red-eye."

His listeners' eyes took on a glazed look, and no one spoke. Little Shuan had finished his rice and was perspiring profusely all over, his head steaming.

"Sorry for Red-eye—that's crazy! He must have gone crazy!" said Graybeard, as if he had suddenly seen the light.

"He must have been crazy!" echoed the man in his twenties.

The customers came to life once more, and started talking and laughing. Under cover of the noise, the child was seized by a fit of coughing. K'ang went up to him, clapped him on the shoulder, and said:

"A guaranteed cure! Don't cough like that, Little Shuan! A guaranteed cure!"

"Crazy!" agreed the hunchback, nodding his head.

IV

The land alongside the West Gate was actually public land. The zigzag path running across it, made by the shoe soles of passersby seeking a short cut, had become a natural boundary line. To the left of the path were buried executed criminals or those who had died of neglect in prison. To the right of the path were the clustered graves of the poor. The piled-up layers of grave mounds on both sides looked like the rolls laid out for a rich man's birthday.

The Ch'ing-ming Festival[1] that year was unusually cold. Willows were only just beginning to put forth new shoots no larger than grains of rice. Shortly after daybreak, Old Shuan's wife brought four dishes and a bowl of rice to set before a new grave in the right section, and cried for a while before it. When she had burned paper money she sat on the ground in a stupor as if waiting for something; but for what, she herself did not know. A breeze sprang up and rippled her short hair, which was certainly whiter than the previous year.

Another woman came down the path, also mostly white-haired and in tattered clothes. Carrying an old, round, red-lacquered basket with a string of paper money hanging from it, she walked haltingly, pausing after every few steps. When she saw Old Shuan's wife sitting on the ground watching her, she hesitated, and a flush of shame spread over her pale face. However, she finally summoned up her courage and crossed over to a grave in the left section, where she set down her basket.

That grave was directly opposite Little Shuan's, separated only by the small path. As Old Shuan's wife watched the other woman set out four dishes of food and a bowl of rice, then stand up to wail and burn paper money, she thought: "It must be her son in that grave too." The older woman wandered around and gazed aimlessly for a while, then suddenly she began to tremble and stagger backwards, her staring eyes completely dazed.

Fearing she might go crazy from grief, Old Shuan's wife couldn't help getting up and stepping across the path, to say quietly: "An old woman like you shouldn't grieve so . . . Let's go back now."

The other nodded, with her eyes still gazing out into space, and she muttered softly: "Look! What's that?"

[1] A spring festival roughly equivalent to Easter time, around April 5, at which the Chinese worship at the graves of their ancestors. It is also known as "Tomb-sweeping Day."

Looking where she pointed, Old Shuan's wife saw that the grave in front had not yet been overgrown with grass, so that ugly patches of brown earth still showed through. But when she looked up carefully, she was rather startled—in plain view at the top of the small round grave was a wreath of red and white flowers.

Both of them suffered from failing eyesight, yet they could see these red and white flowers clearly. There were not many, but they were placed in a circle; and although not very fresh, they were neatly set out. Little Shuan's mother looked around at her own son's grave and those of other people, dotted only with a few small pale flowers that had managed to withstand the cold. Suddenly she felt a certain discontent and emptiness, and didn't want to investigate things any further.

In the meantime the old woman had gone a few steps closer to the grave, to look more carefully. "They have no roots," she said to herself. "They can't have grown here by themselves. Who could have been here? Children don't come here to play, and none of our relatives ever come. What is this all about?" She puzzled over it, until suddenly her tears began to fall, and she cried aloud:

"Son, they all wronged you, and you do not forget. Is your grief still so great that today you worked this wonder to let me know?"

She looked all around, but could see only a crow perched on a leafless bough. "I know," she continued. "They murdered you. But a day of reckoning will come, Heaven will see to it. Just close your eyes in peace . . . If you are really here, and can hear me, make that crow fly onto your grave as a sign."

The breeze had long since died down, and the dry grass stood stiff and straight as copper wires. A faint, tremulous sound vibrated in the air, then faded and died away. All around was deathly still. They stood in the dry grass, looking up at the crow; and the crow, on the rigid bough of the tree, its head drawn in, perched immobile as iron.

Time passed. More people, young and old, came to visit the graves.

Old Shuan's wife felt somehow as if a load had been lifted from her mind and, wanting to leave, she urged the other:

"Let's go back now."

The old woman sighed, and listlessly picked up the rice and dishes. After a moment's hesitation she started off slowly, still muttering to herself:

"What is this all about?"

They had not gone thirty paces when they heard a loud caw behind them. Startled, they looked round and saw the crow stretch out its wings, brace itself to take off, then fly like an arrow toward the far horizon.

My Old Home

by Lu Hsün

Translated by Yang Hsien-yi and Gladys Yang

Braving the bitter cold, I traveled more than seven hundred miles back to the old home I had left over twenty years before.

It was late winter. As we drew near my former home the day became overcast and a cold wind blew into the cabin of our boat, while all one could see through the chinks in our bamboo awning were a few desolate villages, void of any sign of life, scattered far and near under the somber yellow sky. I could not help feeling depressed.

Ah! Surely this was not the old home I had remembered for the past twenty years?

The old home I remembered was not in the least like this. My old home was much better. But if you asked me to recall its peculiar charm or describe its beauties, I had no clear impression, no words to describe it. And now it seemed this was all there was to it. Then I rationalized the matter to myself, saying: Home was always like this, and although it has not improved, still it is not so depressing as I imagine; it is only my mood that has changed, because I am coming back to the country this time without any illusions.

This time I had come with the sole object of saying goodbye. The old house our clan had lived in for so many years had already been sold to another family, and was to change hands before the end of the year. I had to hurry there before New Year's Day to say goodbye forever to the familiar old compound, and to move my family far from the old home town they knew to the other place where I was making a living.

At dawn on the second day I reached the gateway of my home. Broken stems of withered grass on the roof, trembling in the wind, made it very clear why this old house would inevitably change hands. Several branches of our clan had probably already moved away, so it was unusually quiet. By the time I reached our own house my mother was already at the door to welcome me, and my eight-year-old nephew, Hung-erh, rushed out after her.

Though Mother was delighted, she was also trying to hide a certain feeling of sadness. She told me to sit down, rest, have some tea, and not discuss the business of moving just yet. Hung-erh, who had never seen me before, stood watching me at a distance.

But finally we had to talk about moving. I said that I had already rented a place elsewhere, and I had bought a little furniture; in addition it would be necessary to sell all the furniture in the house in order to buy more things. Mother agreed, saying that the luggage was nearly all packed, and about half the furniture that could not easily be moved had already been sold. Only it was difficult to collect the money for it.

"You must rest for a day or two, and call on our relatives to pay your respects. Then we can go," said Mother.

"That's fine."

"Then there is Jun-t'u. Each time he comes here he asks about you, and wants very much to see you again. I told him the probable date of your return home, and he may be coming any time."

At this point a strange picture suddenly flashed into my mind: a golden moon suspended in a deep blue sky and beneath it the seashore, planted as far as the eye could see with jade-green watermelons. In their midst a boy of eleven or twelve, wearing a silver necklet and grasping a steel pitchfork in his hand, was thrusting with all his might at a *zha*[1] which dodged the blow and escaped between his legs.

This boy was Jun-t'u. When I first met him he was just over ten—that was thirty years ago. At that time my father was still alive and the family well off, so I was really a "young master." That year it was our family's turn to take charge of a big ancestral sacrifice, which came around only once in thirty years or more, and so was an important one. In the first month the ancestral images were presented and offerings made, and since the sacrificial vessels were very fine and there was such a crowd of worshippers, it was necessary to guard against theft. Our family had only one part-time laborer. (In our district we divide laborers into three classes. Those who are hired by the day are called dailies; and those who farm their own land and only work for one family at New Year, during festivals, or when rents are being collected are called part-timers.) And since there was so much to be done, he told my father that he would send for his son Jun-t'u to look after the sacrificial vessels.

When my father gave his consent I was overjoyed, because I had long since heard of Jun-t'u and knew that he was about my own age, born in the intercalary month.[2] When his horoscope was told it was found that of the five elements, the earth element was lacking, so his father called him Jun-t'u, "Intercalary Earth." He could set traps and catch small birds.

I looked forward every day to New Year, for New Year would bring Jun-t'u. At last, one day when the end of the year came, Mother told me that Jun-t'u had come, and I flew to see him. He was standing in the kitchen. He had a round, ruddy face and wore a small felt cap on his head and a gleaming silver necklet around his neck. From this it was obvious that his father doted on him and, fearing he might die, had made a pledge with the gods and Buddhas, using the necklet as a talisman. He was very shy, and I was the only person he was not afraid of. When there was no one else there, he would talk with me, so in a few hours we were close friends.

I don't know what we talked of then, but I remember that Jun-t'u was in high spirits, saying that since he had come to town he had seen many new things.

The next day I wanted him to catch birds.

"I can't do it," he said. "It's only possible after a heavy snowfall. On our sands, after it snows, I sweep clear a patch of ground, prop up a big threshing basket with a short stick, and scatter husks of grain beneath. When the birds come there to eat, I tug on a long, long string tied to the stick, and the birds are caught in the basket. There are all kinds: wild pheasants, woodcocks, wood-pigeons, 'blue-backs' . . ."

Accordingly I really hoped it would snow.

"Just now it's too cold," said Jun-t'u another time, "but you must come to our place in summer. In the daytime we'll go to the seashore to look for shells and 'Buddha hands.' In the evening when dad and I go to see the watermelons, you'll come along too."

"Is it to look out for thieves?"

"No. If passersby are thirsty and pick a watermelon, folk down our way don't consider it stealing. What we have to look out for are badgers, hedgehogs, and *zha*. When under the moonlight you hear the crunching sound made by the *zha* when it bites the melons, then you take your pitchfork and creep stealthily over . . ."

I had no idea then what this thing called *zha* was—and I am not much clearer now for that matter—but somehow I felt it was something like a small dog, and very fierce.

"Don't they bite people?"

"You have a pitchfork. You go across, and when you see it you strike. It's a very cunning creature and will rush toward you and get away between your legs. Its fur is as slippery as oil . . ."

[1] *Zha* is a word invented by Lu Hsün for a kind of animal which most commentators have taken to mean "badger."

[2] The Chinese lunar calendar reckons three hundred and sixty days to a year, and each month comprises twenty-nine or thirty days, never thirty-one. Hence every few years a thirteenth, or intercalary, month is inserted in the calendar.

I had never known that all these fresh and exciting things existed: at the seashore there were shells all colors of the rainbow; watermelons were exposed to such danger, yet all I had known of them before was that they were sold in the fruit and vegetable shop.

"On our shore, when the tide comes in, there are lots of jumping fish, each with two legs like a frog . . ."

Jun-t'u's mind was a treasure house of such strange lore, all of it unknown to my other friends. They were ignorant of all these things and, while Jun-t'u lived by the sea, they like me could see only the four corners of the sky above the high courtyard wall.

Unfortunately, a month after New Year Jun-t'u had to go home. I was so upset I burst into tears and he hid in the kitchen, crying and refusing to come out, until finally his father carried him off. Later he had his father bring me a packet of shells and a few very beautiful feathers, and I sent him presents once or twice, but we never saw each other again.

Now that my mother mentioned him, this childhood memory sprang into life like a flash of lightning, and I seemed to see my beautiful old home. So I answered:

"Fine! And he—how is he?"

"He? Things aren't going very well for him," said Mother. And then, looking out of the door: "Here come those people again. They say they want to buy our furniture; but actually they'll casually walk off with something. I must go and watch them."

Mother stood up and went out. The voices of several women could be heard outside. I called Hung-erh to me and started talking to him, asking him whether he could write, and whether he would be glad to leave.

"Are we going to take the train?"

"Yes, we're going to take the train."

"And a boat?"

"First we'll take a boat."

A strange shrill voice suddenly rang out:

"Looking like this! With such a long moustache!"

I looked up with a start, and saw a woman of about fifty with prominent cheekbones and thin lips standing in front of me. With her hands on her hips, not wearing a skirt but with her trousered legs apart, she seemed just like a thin, spindly-legged compass in a box of geometrical instruments.

I was really startled.

"Don't you know me? Why, I have held you in my arms!"

I was even more taken aback. Fortunately my mother came in just then and broke in:

"He's been away so long, you must excuse his forgetting. You should remember," she said to me, "this is Mrs. Yang from across the road. She has a beancurd shop."

Then, of course, I remembered. When I was a child there was a Mrs. Yang who used to sit nearly all day long in the beancurd shop across the road, and everybody used to call her Beancurd Beauty. She used to powder herself, and her cheekbones were not so prominent then nor her lips so thin; besides, she sat there the whole day, so that I had never noticed this resemblance to a compass. In those days people said that, thanks to her, that beancurd shop did a very good business. But, probably on account of my age, she had made no impression on me, so that later I forgot her entirely. However, the Compass was extremely indignant and looked at me contemptuously, just as one might look at a Frenchman who had never heard of Napoleon or an American who had never heard of Washington. Smiling sarcastically she said:

"You had forgotten? Naturally I am beneath your notice."

"Certainly not . . . I . . ." I answered nervously, getting to my feet.

"Then you listen to me, Master Hsün. You have grown rich, and they are too heavy to move, so you can't possibly want these worn-out pieces of furniture anymore. You had better let me take them away. Poor people like us can make use of them."

"I haven't grown rich. I must sell these in order to buy—"

"Oh, come now, you have been made the intendant of a circuit; how can you still say you're not rich? Hah! You can't hide anything from me."

I knew there was nothing I could say, so I kept quiet and just stood still there.

"Come now, really, the more money people have the more miserly they get, and the more miserly they are the more money they get," jabbered the Compass, as she turned away indignantly and walked slowly off, casually picking up a pair of my mother's gloves and stuffing them into her pocket as she left.

After this a number of relatives in the neighborhood came to call. In the intervals between entertaining them I did some packing, and so three or four days passed.

One very cold afternoon, I sat drinking tea after lunch when I was aware of someone coming in, and turned my head to see who it was. At the first glance I gave an involuntary start, hastily stood up, and went over to welcome him.

The newcomer was Jun-t'u. But although I knew at a glance that this was Jun-t'u, it was not the Jun-t'u I remembered. He had grown to twice his former size. His round face, once ruddy, had become sallow and now had deep lines and wrinkles; his eyes too were like his father's, the rims swollen and red. I knew that most peasants who work by the sea and are exposed all day to the wind from the ocean were like this. He wore a shabby felt cap and just a very thin padded jacket, and was shivering from head to foot. He carried a package wrapped in paper and a long pipe. His hands were not the plump red hands I remembered, but coarse and clumsy and chapped, like the bark of a pine tree.

I was delighted, but I didn't know what words to use, so I only said:

"Oh! Jun-t'u—so it's you? . . ."

There were so many things then to talk about that I wanted to spew them out like a string of beads: woodcocks, jumping fish, shells, *zha* . . . But something seemed to hold me back. Everything just swirled around in my head and I couldn't get the words out.

He stood there, joy and sadness both showing on his face. His lips moved, but not a sound did

he utter. Finally, assuming a respectful attitude, he said clearly:

"Master!"

I felt a shiver run through me, for I knew then what a lamentably thick wall had grown up between us. Yet I could not say anything.

He turned his head to call:

"Shui-sheng, bow to the master." Then he pulled forward a boy who had been hiding behind his back, and this was just the Jun-t'u of twenty years before, only a little paler and thinner, and he had no silver necklet.

"This is my fifth," he said. "He hasn't had any experience with social occasions, so he's shy and awkward."

Mother came downstairs with Hung-erh, probably after hearing our voices.

"I got your letter some time ago, madam," said Jun'-t'u. "I was really so pleased to know the master was coming back."

"Now, why are you so polite? Didn't you consider yourselves brothers in the past?" said Mother gaily. "Why don't you still call him Brother Hsün as you used to?"

"Oh, you are really too . . . What bad manners that would be. I was a child then and didn't understand." As he was speaking Jun-t'u motioned Shui-sheng to come and bow, but the child was shy, and stood stock still behind his father.

"So he is Shui-Sheng? Your fifth?" asked Mother. "We are all strangers, you can't blame him for feeling shy. Hung-erh had better take him out to play."

When Hung-erh heard this he went over to Shui-sheng, and Shui-sheng went out with him, entirely at his ease. Mother asked Jun-t'u to sit down, and after a little hesitation he did so; then, leaning his long pipe against the table, he handed over the paper package, saying:

"In winter there is nothing worth bringing; but these few green beans we dried ourselves, if you will excuse the liberty, sir."

When I asked him how things were with him, he just shook his head.

"In a very bad way. Even my sixth can do a little work, but still we haven't enough to eat . . . and then there is no security . . . all sorts of people want money, there is no fixed rule . . . and the harvests are bad. You grow things, and when you take them to sell you always have to pay several taxes and lose money, while if you don't try to sell, the things will only spoil . . ."

He kept shaking his head; yet, although his face was lined with wrinkles, not one of them moved, just as if he were a stone statue. No doubt he felt intensely bitter, but could not openly express himself. After a pause he took up his pipe and began to smoke in silence.

From her chat with him, Mother learned that he was busy at home and had to go back the next day; and since he had had no lunch, she told him to go to the kitchen and fry some rice for himself.

After he had gone out, Mother and I both shook our heads over his hard life: many children, famines, taxes, soldiers, bandits, officials, and landed gentry, all had been so hard on him that he seemed a wooden image of a man. Mother said that we should offer him all the things we didn't need to take with us, letting him choose for himself.

That afternoon he picked out a number of things: two long tables, four chairs, an incense burner and candlesticks, and a balance. He also asked for all the ashes from the stove (in our region we cook over straw, and the ashes can be used to fertilize sandy soil), saying that when we left he would come to take them away by boat.

That night we talked again, but not of anything serious; and the next morning he went away with Shui-sheng.

After another nine days it was time for us to leave. Jun-t'u came in the morning. Shui-sheng did not come with him—he had just brought a little girl of five to watch the boat. We were very busy all day, and had no time to talk. We also had quite a number of visitors, some to see us off, some to fetch things, and some to do both. It was nearly evening when we left by boat, and by that time everything in the house, however old or shabby, large or small, fine or coarse, had been cleared out.

As we set off, in the dusk, the green mountains on either side of the river became deep blue, receding toward the stern of the boat.

Hung-erh and I, leaning against the cabin window, were both watching the indistinct scene outside, when suddenly he asked:

"Uncle, when shall we go back?"

"Go back? Do you mean that before you've left you want to go back?"

"Well, Shui-sheng has invited me to his home . . ." He opened wide his black eyes, engrossed in thought.

Mother and I both felt rather sad, and so Jun-t'u's name came up again. Mother said that ever since our family started packing up, Mrs. Yang from the beancurd shop had come over every day, and the day before in the ash-heap she had unearthed a dozen bowls and plates, which after some discussion she insisted must have been buried there by Jun-t'u, so that when he came to remove the ashes he could take them home at the same time. After making this discovery Mrs. Yang was very pleased with herself, and flew off taking the dog-teaser with her. (The dog-teaser is used by poultry keepers in our parts. It is a wooden cage inside which food is put, so that hens can stretch their necks in to eat but dogs can only look on furiously.) And it was a marvel, considering the thick-soled shoes on her bound feet, how fast she could run.

I was leaving the old house farther and farther behind, while the hills and rivers of my old home were also receding gradually ever farther in the distance. But I felt no regret. I only felt that all around me was an invisible high wall, cutting me off from others, and this depressed me thoroughly. The vision of that small hero with the silver necklet among the watermelons had formerly been as clear as day, but now it suddenly blurred, adding to my depression.

Mother and Hung-erh fell asleep.

I lay down, listening to the water rippling beneath the boat, and knew that I was going my own way. I thought: although there is such a barrier between Jun-t'u and myself, the children still have much in common, for wasn't Hung-erh thinking of Shui-sheng just now? I hope they will not be like us, that they will not allow a barrier to grow up between them. Then again, I wouldn't want them, because they want to be alike, to have a treadmill existence like mine nor to suffer like Jun-t'u until they become stupefied, nor yet, like others, to lead a cruel life of dissipation. They should have a new life, a life we never experienced.

The thought of hope made me suddenly afraid. When Jun-t'u asked for the incense burner and candlesticks I had laughed at him to myself, to think that he still worshipped idols and could not put them out of his mind. Yet what I now called hope, wasn't it nothing more than an idol I had created myself? The only difference was that what he desired was close at hand, while what I desired was less easily realized.

As I dozed, a stretch of jade-green seashore spread itself before my eyes, and above a round golden moon hung in a deep blue sky. I thought: hope cannot be said to exist, nor can it be said not to exist. It is just like pathways over the land. For actually there were no paths originally, but when many people traveled one way, a road was made.

The New Year's Sacrifice

by Lu Hsün

Translated by Yang Hsien-yi and Gladys Yang

New Year's Eve according to the lunar calendar seems after all more like the real New Year's Eve; for, to say nothing of the villages and towns, even in the air there is a feeling that the New Year is coming. From the pale, lowering evening clouds issue frequent flashes of lightning, followed by a rumbling sound of firecrackers celebrating the departure of the Hearth God; while, nearer by, the firecrackers explode even more violently, and before the deafening report dies away the air is filled with a faint smell of powder. It was on such a night that I returned to Luchen, my native place. Although I call it my native place, I had had no home there for some time, so I had to put up temporarily with a certain Mr. Lu, the fourth son of his family. He is a member of our clan, and belongs to the generation before mine, so I ought to call him "Fourth Uncle." An old student of the imperial college who took to Neo-Confucianism, he was very little changed in any way; I found him slightly older but without any moustache as yet. When we met, after exchanging a few polite remarks he said I was fatter, and after saying that I was fatter he immediately started a violent attack on the reformers. I knew this was not meant personally, because the object of the attack was still K'ang Yu-wei.[1] Nevertheless, conversation proved difficult, so that in a short time I found myself alone in the study.

The next day I got up very late, and after lunch went out to see some relatives and friends. The day after I did the same. None of them was greatly changed, simply slightly older; but every family was busy preparing for "the sacrifice." This is the great end-of-year ceremony in Luchen, when people reverently welcome the God of Fortune and solicit good fortune for the coming year. They kill chickens and geese and buy pork, scouring and scrubbing until all the women's arms turn red in the water. Some of them had twisted silver bracelets on their wrists. After the meat is cooked some chopsticks are thrust into it at random, and it is called the "offering." It is set out at dawn, when incense and candles are lit, and they reverently invite the God of Fortune to come and partake of the offering. Only men can be worshippers, and after the sacrifice they naturally continue to let off firecrackers as before. This happens every year, in every family, provided they can afford to buy the offering and firecrackers; and this year they naturally followed the old custom.

The day grew overcast. In the afternoon it actually started to snow; the biggest snowflakes, as large as plum blossom petals, fluttered about the sky; and this, combined with the smoke and air of activity, made Luchen appear in a ferment. When I returned to my uncle's study the roof of the house was already white with snow. The room also appeared brighter, the great red temple-rubbing hanging on the wall showing up very clearly the character for Longevity written by the

[1] A famous reformer (1858–1927) who advocated constitutional monarchy.

Taoist saint Ch'en Tuan.[2] One of a pair of scrolls had fallen down and was lying loosely rolled up on the long table, but the other was still hanging there, bearing the words: "By understanding reason we achieve tranquillity of mind." Aimlessly, I went to leaf through the books on the table beneath the window, but all I could find was a pile of what looked like an incomplete set of *K'ang-hsi's Dictionary,* a variorum edition of *Reflections on Things at Hand,* and a volume of *Commentaries on the Four Books.*[3] At all events, I made up my mind to leave the next day.

Besides, the very thought of my meeting with Hsiang Lin's wife the day before made me uncomfortable. It happened in the afternoon. I had been visiting a friend in the eastern part of the town. As I came out I met her by the river, and seeing the way she fastened her eyes on me I knew very well she meant to speak to me. Of all the people I had seen this time at Luchen none had changed as much as she: her hair, which had been streaked with white five years before, was now completely white, quite unlike someone in her forties. Her face was fearfully thin and dark in its sallowness, and had moreover lost its former expression of sadness, looking as if carved out of wood. Only an occasional flicker of her eyes showed she was still a living creature. In one hand she carried a wicker basket, in which was a broken bowl, completely empty; in the other hand she held a bamboo pole longer than herself, split at the bottom: it was clear she had become a beggar.

I stood still, waiting for her to come and ask for money.

"You have come back?" she asked me first.

"Yes."

"That is very good. You are a scholar, and have traveled too and seen a lot. I just want to ask you something." Her lusterless eyes suddenly gleamed.

I never would have guessed she would say something like this. I stood there in amazement.

"It is this." She drew two paces nearer, and lowered her voice, and said very confidentially: "After a person dies, is there really a soul that lives on?"

As she fixed her eyes on me I was seized with foreboding. A shiver ran down my spine and I felt more nervous than during an unexpected examination at school, when unfortunately the teacher stands by one's side. Personally, I had never given the least thought to the existence of spirits. In this instance how should I answer her? Hesitating for a moment, I reflected: "It is the tradition here to believe in spirits, yet she seems to be skeptical—perhaps it would be better to say she hopes: hopes that there is immortality and yet hopes that there is not. Why increase the worries of people nearing the end of their lives? To give her something to look forward to, it would be better to say there is."

"There may be, I think," I told her hesitantly.

"Then, there must also be a Hell?"

"What, Hell?" Greatly startled, I could only try to evade the question. "Hell? According to reason there should be one too—but not necessarily. Who cares about it anyway?"

"Then will all the people of one family who have died see each other again?"

"Well, as to whether they will see each other again or not—" I realized now that I was a complete fool; for all my hesitation and reflection I had been unable to answer her three questions. Immediately I lost confidence and wanted to say the exact opposite of what I had previously said. "In this case . . . as a matter of fact, I am not sure. Actually, regarding the question of ghosts, I am not sure either."

Taking advantage of the pause in her questioning, I walked off, and beat a hasty retreat to my

---

[2] A hermit at the beginning of the tenth century.

[3] *K'ang-hsi's Dictionary (K'ang-hsi tzu-tien)* was compiled under the auspices of Emperor K'ang-hsi (r. 1662–1722). *Reflections on Things at Hand (Chin-ssu lu)* is a collection of Neo-Confucianist writings in the Sung Dynasty (960–1279), comprising the works of Chou Tun-i, Ch'eng Hao, Ch'eng I, and Chang Tsai, and compiled by their contemporaries Chu Hsi and Lü Tsu-ch'ien. A variorum edition of this work was published in the early Ch'ing (1644–1911), edited by Mao Hsing-lai and Chiang Yung. *Commentaries on the Four Books* is a work especially prepared for the candidates for the imperial civil service examinations in the Ch'ing Dynasty. The four books are the Confucian *Analects (Lun-yü)*, *The Great Learning (Ta-hsüeh)*, *The Doctrine of the Mean (Chung-yung)*, and *Mencius (Meng-tzu)*.

uncle's house, feeling exceedingly uncomfortable. I thought to myself: "I'm afraid my answer will prove dangerous to her. Probably it's just that when other people are celebrating she feels lonely all by herself, but could there be another reason? Could she have had some premonition? If there is another reason, I shall be held responsible to a certain extent." Finally, however, I ended by laughing at myself, thinking that such a chance meeting could have no great significance, and yet here I was pondering it so carefully; no wonder certain educators called me a neurotic. Moreover I had distinctly said, "I am not sure," contradicting my previous answer; so that even if anything did happen, it would have nothing at all to do with me.

"I am not sure" is a most useful phrase.

Inexperienced and rash young men often take it upon themselves to solve people's problems for them or choose doctors for them, and if by any chance things turn out badly, they are probably held to blame; but by simply concluding with this phrase "I am not sure," one can free oneself of all responsibility. At this time I felt even more strongly the necessity for such a phrase, since even in speaking with a beggar woman there was no getting along without it.

However, I continued to feel uncomfortable on this, as if I had had a premonition of some misfortune to come. In that oppressive snowy weather, in the gloomy study, this discomfort increased. It would be better to leave: I should go back to town the next day. The boiled shark's fins in the Fu-hsing Restaurant used to cost a dollar for a large portion, and I wondered if this cheap and delicious dish had increased in price or not. Although the friends who had accompanied me in the old days had scattered, the shark's fins still had to be tasted even if it was by me alone. In any event, I made up my mind to leave the next day.

After experiencing many times that things which I hoped would not happen and felt should not happen invariably did happen, I was desperately afraid this would prove another such case. And, indeed, strange things did begin to happen.

Toward evening I heard several people conversing in the inner room, as if they were discussing something; but soon the conversation ended, and all I heard was my uncle saying loudly as he walked out: "Not earlier nor later, but just at this time—sure sign of a bad character!"

At first I felt astonished, then very uncomfortable, thinking these words must refer to me. I looked outside the door, but no one was there. I contained myself with difficulty until their servant came in before dinner to brew a pot of tea, when at last I had a chance to make some inquiries.

"With whom was Mr. Lu angry just now?" I asked.

"It's Hsiang Lin's wife again," he replied briefly.

"Hsiang Lin's wife? How was that?" I asked again.

"She's passed away."

"Dead?" My heart suddenly missed a beat. I almost jumped up out of my seat, and my face probably turned pale. But since he did not raise his head, he was probably quite unaware of how I felt. Then I controlled myself, and asked:

"When did she die?"

"When? Last night, or else today . . . I can't say for sure."

"How did she die?"

"How did she die? Why, from poverty, of course." He answered placidly and, still without having raised his head to look at me, went out.

However, my agitation was short-lived, for now that something I had felt imminent had already taken place, I no longer had to take refuge in saying "I'm not sure," or find comfort in the servant's expression "dying of poverty." My heart felt lighter. Only from time to time something still seemed to weigh on it. Dinner was served, and my uncle solemnly kept me company. I wanted to ask about Hsiang Lin's wife but knew that although he had read, "Ghosts and spirits demonstrate the inherent balance in nature,"[4] he had retained many superstitions, and on the eve of this New Year's sacrifice it was out of the question to mention anything like death or illness. In case of necessity one could use veiled allusions, but unfortunately I did not know how to, so although

---

[4] An observation by the Neo-Confucianist Chang Tsai, in *Reflections on Things at Hand.*

questions kept rising to the tip of my tongue, I had to hold them back. From his solemn expression I suddenly suspected that he saw me as choosing not earlier nor later but just this time to come and trouble him, and that I was also a bad character; therefore to set his mind at rest I told him at once that I intended to leave Luchen the next day and go back to the city. He did not press me greatly to stay. So we quietly finished the meal.

In winter the days are short and, now that it was snowing, darkness already enveloped the whole town. Everybody was busy beneath the lamplight in their homes, but outside the windows it was very quiet. Snowflakes fell on the thickly piled snow, making a whispering sound, which made me feel even more lonely. I sat by myself under the yellow gleam of the vegetable-oil lamp and thought, "That poor woman, whom people abandoned in the dust as a tiresome and worn-out plaything, once left her own imprint in the dust. Those who enjoy life must have wondered at her for wishing to prolong her existence; but now at least she has been swept clear by eternity. Whether spirits exist or not I do not know; but in the present world when a meaningless existence ends, so that someone whom others are tired of seeing is no longer seen, it is just as well, both for the individual concerned and for others." I listened quietly to the whispering sound of the snowflakes falling outside the window, still pursuing this train of thought, until gradually I felt less ill at ease.

Fragments of her life, seen or heard before, now combined to form one whole.

She did not belong to Luchen. One year at the beginning of winter, when my uncle's family wanted to find a new maidservant, Old Mrs. Wei brought her in and introduced her. Her hair was tied with white bands, and she wore a black skirt, blue jacket, and pale green bodice. She was about twenty-six, and the skin of her face was pale, but her cheeks still had a rosy color. Old Mrs. Wei called her Hsiang Lin's wife. She said that she was a neighbor of her mother's family, and because

her husband was dead she wanted to go out to work. My uncle knit his brows and my aunt immediately understood that he disapproved of her because she was a widow. She looked very suitable, though, with big strong feet and hands, and a meek expression in her eyes. She had said nothing but showed every sign of being tractable and hard-working. So my aunt paid no attention to my uncle's frown, but kept her. During the period of probation she worked from morning to night, as if she found resting dull, and she was so strong that she could do a man's work. Accordingly, on the third day it was settled, and each month she was to be paid five hundred cash.

Everybody called her Hsiang Lin's wife. They did not ask her own name; but since she was introduced by someone from Wei Village who said she was a neighbor, presumably her name was also Wei. She was not very talkative, only answering when other people spoke to her, and her answers were brief. It was not until a dozen days or so had passed that they learned little by little that she still had a very strict mother-in-law at home and a younger brother-in-law more than ten years old, who could cut wood. Her husband, who had been a woodcutter too, had died in the spring. He had been ten years younger than she.[5] This little was all that people learned from her.

The days passed quickly. She worked as hard as ever; she would eat anything, and did not spare herself. Everybody agreed that the Lu family had found a very good maidservant, who really got through more work than a hard-working man. At the end of the year she swept, mopped, killed chickens and geese, and sat up to boil the sacrificial meat, all singlehandedly, so the family did not have to hire extra help. Nevertheless she, on her side, was satisfied; gradually the trace of a smile appeared at the corner of her mouth. She became plumper and her skin whiter.

New Year was scarcely over when she came back from washing rice by the river looking pale, and said that in the distance she had just seen a man wandering on the opposite bank who looked

---

[5] In old China, it used to be common in country districts for young women to be married to boys of ten or eleven. The bride's labor could then be exploited by her husband's family.

very like her husband's cousin, and probably he had come to look for her. My aunt, much alarmed, made detailed inquiries, but failed to get any further information. As soon as my uncle learned of it he frowned and said, "This is bad. She must have run away from her husband's family."

Before long this inference that she had run away was confirmed.

About a fortnight later, just as everybody was beginning to forget what had happened, Old Mrs. Wei suddenly called, bringing with her a woman in her thirties who, she said, was the maidservant's mother-in-law. Although the woman looked like a villager, she behaved with great self-possession and had a ready tongue in her head. After the usual polite remarks she apologized for coming to take her daughter-in-law home, saying there was a great deal to be done at the beginning of spring, and since there were only old people and children at home they were short-handed.

"Since it is her mother-in-law who wants her to go back, what is there to be said?" was my uncle's comment.

Thereupon her wages were reckoned up. They amounted to one thousand seven hundred and fifty cash, all of which she had left with her mistress without spending a single coin. My aunt gave the entire amount to her mother-in-law. The latter also took her clothes, thanked Mr. and Mrs. Lu, and went out. By this time it was noon.

"Oh, the rice! Didn't Hsiang Lin's wife go to wash the rice?" my aunt exclaimed some time later. Probably she was rather hungry, so that she remembered lunch.

Thereupon everybody set about looking for the rice basket. My aunt went first to the kitchen, then to the hall, then to the bedroom; but not a trace of it was to be seen anywhere. My uncle went outside, but could not find it either; only when he went right down to the riverside did he see it, set down squarely on the bank, with a bundle of vegetables beside it.

Some people there told him that a boat with a white awning had moored there in the morning, but since the awning covered the boat completely they did not know who was inside, and before this

incident no one had paid any attention to it. But when Hsiang Lin's wife came to wash rice, two men looking like people from the mountains jumped off the boat just as she was kneeling down, and seizing hold of her, carried her on board. After a few shouts and cries, Hsiang Lin's wife became silent: they had probably stopped up her mouth. Then two women walked up, one of them a stranger and the other Old Mrs. Wei. When the people who told this story had tried to peer into the boat they could not see very clearly, but Hsiang Lin's wife seemed to be lying there tied up on the floor of the boat.

"Disgraceful! However . . ." said my uncle.

That day my aunt cooked the midday meal herself, and my cousin Ah Niu lit the fire.

After lunch Old Mrs. Wei came again.

"Disgraceful!" said my uncle.

"What is the meaning of this? How dare you come here again!" My aunt, who was washing dishes, started scolding as soon as she saw her. "You recommended her yourself, and then plotted to have her carried off, causing all this stir. What will people think? Are you trying to make a laughingstock of our family?"

"*Ai-ya,* I was really taken in! Now I have come especially to clear up this business. When she asked me to find her work, how was I to know that she had left home without her mother-in-law's consent? I'm very sorry, Mr. Lu, Mrs. Lu. Because I'm so old and foolish and careless, I have offended my patrons. However, it's lucky for me that your family is always so generous and kind, and unwilling to be hard on your inferiors. This time I promise to find you someone good to make up for my mistake."

"However . . ." said my uncle.

Thereupon the business of Hsiang Lin's wife was concluded, and before long it was also forgotten.

Because the maidservants hired later were all lazy or fond of stealing food, or else both lazy and fond of stealing food, with not a good one in the lot, only my aunt still spoke of Hsiang Lin's wife. On such occasions she would always say to herself, "I wonder what has become of her now?" meaning that she would like to have her back. But by the following New Year she too gave up hope.

The New Year's holiday was nearly over when Old Mrs. Wei, already half tipsy, came to pay her respects, and said it was because she had been back to Wei Village to visit her mother's family and stayed a few days that she had come late. During the course of conversation they naturally came to speak of Hsiang Lin's wife.

"She?" said Mrs. Wei cheerfully. "She's in luck now. When her mother-in-law dragged her home, she had already promised her to the sixth son of the Ho family in Ho Village. Not long after she reached home they put her in the bridal chair and sent her off."

"*Ai-ya!* What a mother-in-law!" exclaimed my aunt in amazement.

"Ah, madam, you really talk like a great lady! We country folk, poor women, think nothing of that. She still had a younger brother-in-law who had to be married. And if they hadn't found her a husband, where would they have found the money for his wedding? [6] But her mother-in-law is a clever and capable woman, who knows how to drive a good bargain, so she married her off into the mountains. If she had married her to someone in the same village, she wouldn't have got so much money; but since very few women are willing to marry someone living deep in the mountains, she got eighty thousand cash. Now the second son is married, the presents only cost her fifty thousand, and after paying the wedding expenses she still has over ten thousand left. Just think, doesn't this show she knows how to drive a good bargain?"

"But was Hsiang Lin's wife willing?"

"It wasn't a question of being willing or not. Of course anyone would have protested. They just tied her up with a rope, stuffed her into the bridal chair, carried her to the man's house, put on the bridal headdress, performed the ceremony in the hall, and locked them in their room; and that was that. But Hsiang Lin's wife is quite a character. I heard she really put up a big struggle, and everybody said she was different from other people

because she had worked in a scholar's family. We go-betweens, madam, see a great deal. When widows remarry, some cry and shout, some threaten to commit suicide, some when they have been carried to the man's house won't go through with the ceremony, and some even smash the wedding candlesticks. But Hsiang Lin's wife was different from the rest. They said she shouted and cursed all the way, so that by the time they had carried her to Ho Village she was completely hoarse. When they dragged her out of the chair, although the two chair-bearers and her young brother-in-law used all their strength, they couldn't force her to go through the ceremony. The moment they were careless enough to loosen their grip— gracious Buddha!—she threw herself against a corner of the table and knocked a big hole in her head. The blood poured out; and although they used two handfuls of incense ashes and bandaged her with two pieces of red cloth, they still couldn't stop the bleeding. Finally it took all of them together to get her shut up with her husband in the bridal chamber, where she went on cursing. Oh, it was really dreadful!" She shook her head, cast down her eyes and said no more.

"And after that what happened?" asked my aunt.

"They said the next day she still didn't get up," said Old Mrs. Wei, raising her eyes.

"And after that?"

"After that? She got up. At the end of the year she had a baby, a boy, who was two this New Year's. [7] These few days when I was at home some people went to Ho Village, and when they came back they said they had seen her and her son, and that both mother and baby are fat. There is no mother-in-law over her, the man is a strong fellow who can earn a living, and the house is their own. Well, well, she is really in luck."

After this even my aunt gave up talking of Hsiang Lin's wife.

But one autumn, two New Years' after they heard how lucky Hsiang Lin's wife had been, she actually reappeared on the threshold of my un-

---

[6] In old China, because of the labor value of the peasant woman, the man's family virtually bought the wife.

[7] It was the custom to reckon a child as one year old at birth, and to add another year to his age at New Year.

cle's house. On the table she placed a round bulb-shaped basket, and under the eaves a small roll of bedding. Her hair was still wrapped in white bands, and she wore a black skirt, blue jacket, and pale green bodice. But her skin was sallow and her cheeks had lost their color; she had a docile look, and her eyes, with their tear-stained rims, were no longer bright. Just as before, it was Old Mrs. Wei, looking very benevolent, who brought her in, and who explained at length to my aunt:

"It was really a bolt out of the blue. Her husband was so strong, nobody could have guessed that a young fellow like that would die of typhoid fever. First he seemed better, but then he ate a bowl of cold rice and the sickness came back. Luckily she had the boy, and she can work, whether it is chopping wood, picking tea leaves, or raising silkworms; so at first she was able to carry on. Then who could believe that the child too would be carried off by a wolf? Although it was nearly the end of spring, wolves still came to the village—how could anyone have guessed that? Now she's all on her own. Her brother-in-law came to take the house, and turned her out; so she has really no way open to her but to come and ask help from her former mistress. Luckily this time there is nobody to stop her, and you happen to be wanting a new servant, so I have brought her here. I think someone who is used to your ways is much better than a new hand . . ."

"I was really stupid, really . . ." Hsiang Lin's wife raised her listless eyes to say. "I only knew that when it snows the wild beasts in the glen have nothing to eat and may come to the villages; I didn't know that in spring they came too. I got up at dawn and opened the door, filled a small basket with beans, and called our Ah Mao to go and sit on the threshold and shell the beans. He was very obedient and always did as I told him: he went out. Then I chopped wood at the back of the house and washed the rice, and when the rice was in the pan and I wanted to boil the beans I called Ah Mao, but there was no answer; and when I went out to look, all I could see was beans scattered on the ground, but no Ah Mao. He never went to other families to play; and in fact at each place where I went to ask, there was no sign of

him. I became desperate, and begged people to go to look for him. Only in the afternoon, after looking everywhere else, did they go to look in the glen and see one of his little shoes caught on a bramble. 'That's bad,' they said, 'he must have met a wolf.' And sure enough when they went further in there he was, lying in the wolf's lair, with all his entrails eaten away, his hand still tightly clutching that little basket—" At this point she started crying, and was unable to complete the sentence.

My aunt had been undecided at first, but by the end of this story the rims of her eyes were rather red. After thinking for a moment she told her to take the round basket and bedding into the servants' quarters. Old Mrs. Wei heaved a long sigh as if relieved of a great burden. Hsiang Lin's wife looked a little more at ease than when she first came and, without having to be told the way, quietly took away her bedding. From this time on she worked again as a maidservant in Luchen.

Everybody still called her Hsiang Lin's wife.

However, she had changed a great deal. She had not been there more than three days before her master and mistress realized that she was not as lively or active as before. Since her memory was much worse, and her impassive face never showed the least trace of a smile, my aunt already expressed herself very far from satisfied. When the woman first arrived, although my uncle frowned as before, he still did not object very strongly because they invariably had such difficulty in finding servants. But secretly he warned my aunt that while such people may seem very pitiful, they exert a bad moral influence. Thus although it would be all right for her to do ordinary work she must not join in the preparations for sacrifice; they would have to prepare all the dishes themselves, for otherwise they would be unclean and the ancestors would not accept them.

The most important event in my uncle's household was the ancestral sacrifice, and formerly this had been the busiest time for Hsiang Lin's wife; but now she had very little to do. When the table was placed in the center of the hall and the curtain fastened, she still remembered how to set out the wine cups and chopsticks in the old way.

"Hsiang Lin's wife, put those down!" said my aunt hastily. "I'll do it!"

She sheepishly withdrew her hand and went to get the candlesticks.

"Hsiang Lin's wife, put those down!" cried my aunt hastily again. "I'll fetch them."

After walking around several times without finding anything to do, Hsiang Lin's wife could only go reluctantly away. All she did that day was to sit by the stove and feed the fire.

The people in the town still called her Hsiang Lin's wife, but in a different tone than before; and although they still talked to her, their manner was colder. She did not mind this in the least, only, looking straight in front of her, she would tell everybody her story, which was never out of her mind day or night.

"I was really stupid, really," she would say. "I only knew that when it snows the wild beasts in the glen have nothing to eat and may come to the villages; I didn't know that in spring they came too. I got up at dawn and opened the door, filled a small basket with beans, and called our Ah Mao to go and sit on the threshold and shell them. He was very obedient and always did as I told him: he went out. Then I chopped wood at the back of the house and washed the rice, and when the rice was in the pan and I wanted to boil the beans I called Ah Mao, but there was no answer; and when I went out to look, all I could see was beans scattered on the ground, but no Ah Mao. He never went to other families to play; and in fact at each place where I went to ask, there was no sign of him. I became desperate, and begged people to go to look for him. Only in the afternoon, after looking everywhere else, did they go to look in the glen and see one of his little shoes caught on a bramble. 'That's bad,' they said, 'he must have met a wolf.' And sure enough when they went further in there he was, lying in the wolf's lair, with all his entrails eaten away, his hand still tightly clutching that small basket—" At this point she would start crying and her voice would trail away.

This story was rather effective, and when men heard it they often stopped smiling and walked away disconcerted. The women not only seemed to forgive her, but their faces immediately lost their contemptuous look and they added their tears to hers. There were some old women who had not heard her speaking in the street, who went especially to look for her in order to hear her sad tale. When her voice trailed away and she started to cry, they joined in, shedding the tears which had gathered in their eyes. Then they sighed, and went away satisfied, exchanging comments.

She asked nothing better than to tell her sad story over and over again, often attracting three or four listeners. But before long everybody knew it by heart, until even in the eyes of the most kindly, Buddha-fearing old ladies not a trace of tears could be seen. In the end, almost everyone in the town could repeat her tale by heart and it bored and exasperated them to hear it.

"I was really stupid, really . . ." she would begin.

"Yes, you only knew that in snowy weather the wild beasts in the mountains had nothing to eat and might come down to the villages." Promptly cutting short her recital, they walked away.

She would stand there open-mouthed, looking at them with a dazed expression, and then go away too, as if she also felt disconcerted. But she still brooded over it, hoping from other topics such as small baskets, beans, or other people's children, to lead up to the story of her Ah Mao. If she saw a child of two or three, she would say, "Oh dear, if my Ah Mao were still alive, he would be just as big . . ."

Children seeing the look in her eyes would take fright and, clutching the hems of their mothers' clothes, try to tug them away. Thereupon she would be left by herself again, and finally walk away disconcerted. Later everybody knew what she was like, and it only needed a child present for them to ask her with an artificial smile, "Hsiang Lin's wife, if your Ah Mao were alive, wouldn't he be just as big as that?"

She probably did not realize that her story, after having been tasted and appraised by people for so many days, had long since become stale, only exciting disgust and contempt; but from the way people smiled she seemed to know that they were cold and sarcastic, and that there was no need for her to say any more. She would simply look at them, not answering a word.

In Luchen people celebrate the New Year in a big way: they busy themselves from the twentieth day of the twelfth month on with preparations. That year my uncle's household found it necessary to hire a temporary manservant, but since there was still a great deal to do they also called in another maidservant, Liu Ma, to help. Chickens and geese had to be killed; but Liu Ma was a devout woman who abstained from meat, did not kill living things, and would only wash the sacrificial dishes. Hsiang Lin's wife had nothing to do but feed the fire. She sat there, resting, watching Liu Ma as she washed the sacrificial dishes. A light snow began to fall.

"Dear me, I was really stupid," began Hsiang Lin's wife, as if to herself, looking at the sky and sighing.

"Hsiang Lin's wife, there you go again," said Liu Ma, looking at her impatiently. "I ask you: that wound on your forehead, wasn't it then you got it?"

"Uh-huh," she answered vaguely.

"Let me ask you: what made you willing after all?"

"Me?"

"Yes. What I think is, you must have been willing; otherwise—"

"Oh dear, you don't know how strong he was."

"I don't believe it. I don't believe he was so strong that you really couldn't keep him off. You must have been willing, only you put the blame on his being so strong."

"Oh dear, you . . . you try for yourself and see." She smiled.

Liu Ma's lined face broke into a smile too, making it wrinkled like a walnut; her small beady eyes swept Hsiang Lin's wife's forehead and fastened on her eyes. As if rather embarrassed, Hsiang Lin's wife immediately stopped smiling, averted her eyes, and looked at the snowflakes.

"Hsiang Lin's wife, that was really a bad bargain," continued Liu Ma mysteriously. "If you had held out longer or knocked yourself to death, it would have been better. As it is, after living with your second husband for less than two years, you are guilty of a great crime. Just think: when you go down to the lower world in the future, these two men's ghosts will fight over you. To whom will they give you? The King of Hell will have no choice but to cut you in two and divide you between them. I think, really . . ."

Then terror showed in her face. This was something she had never heard in the mountains.

"I think you had better take precautions beforehand. Go to the temple of the earth gods and buy a threshold to be your substitute, so that thousands of people can walk over it and trample on it, in order to atone for your sins in this life and avoid torment after death."

At the time Hsiang Lin's wife said nothing, but she must have taken this to heart, for the next morning when she got up there were dark circles under her eyes. After breakfast she went to the temple of the earth gods at the west end of the village, and asked to buy a threshold. The temple priests would not agree at first, and only when she shed tears did they give a grudging consent. The price was twelve thousand cash.

She had long since given up talking to people, because Ah Mao's story was received with such contempt; but news of her conversation with Liu Ma that day spread, and many people took a fresh interest in her and came again to tease her into talking. As for the subject, that had naturally changed to the scar on her forehead.

"Hsiang Lin's wife, I ask you: what made you willing after all that time?" one would cry.

"Oh, what a pity, to have had that knock for nothing," another looking at her scar would agree.

Probably she knew from their smiles and tone of voice that they were making fun of her, for she always looked steadily at them without saying a word, and finally did not even turn her head. All day long she kept her lips tightly closed, bearing on her head the scar which everyone considered a mark of shame, silently shopping, sweeping the floor, washing vegetables, preparing rice. Only after nearly a year did she take from my aunt her accumulated wages. She changed them for twelve silver dollars, and asking for leave, went to the west end of town. In less time than it takes for a meal she was back again, looking much comforted, and with an unaccustomed light in her eyes. She told my aunt happily that she had bought a threshold in the temple of the earth gods.

When the time came for the ancestral sacrifice at the winter equinox, she worked harder than ever, and seeing my aunt take out the sacrificial utensils and with Ah Niu carry the table into the middle of the hall, she went confidently to fetch the wine cups and chopsticks.

"Put those down, Hsiang Lin's wife!" my aunt called out hastily.

She withdrew her hand as if it had been burned, her face turned ashen-gray, and instead of fetching the candlesticks she just stood there dazed. Only when my uncle came to light the incense and told her to go did she walk away. This time the change in her was very great, for the next day not only were her eyes sunken but even her spirit seemed broken. Moreover, she became very timid, not only afraid of the dark and shadows but also at the sight of anyone. Even her own master or mistress made her look as frightened as a little mouse that has come out of its hole in the daytime. For the rest, she would sit stupidly, like a wooden statue. In less than half a year her hair began to turn gray, and her memory became much worse, reaching the point where she was constantly forgetting to go and prepare the rice.

"What has come over Hsiang Lin's wife? It would really have been better not to have kept her that time." My aunt would sometimes speak like this in front of her, as if to warn her.

However, she remained this way, so that it was impossible to see any hope of her improving. They finally decided to get rid of her and tell her to go back to Old Mrs. Wei. While I was at Luchen they were still only talking of this; but judging by what happened later, it is evident that this was what they must have done. Whether after leaving my uncle's household she became a beggar, or whether she went first to Old Mrs. Wei's house and later became a beggar, I do not know.

I was awakened by firecrackers exploding noisily nearby, saw the yellow oil lamp's glowing light, the size of a bean, and heard the splutter of fireworks as my uncle's household celebrated the sacrifice. I knew that it was nearly dawn. I felt bewildered, hearing as in a dream the confused continuous sound of distant firecrackers which seemed to form one dense cloud of noise in the sky, joining the whirling snowflakes to envelop the whole town. Wrapped in this medley of sound, relaxed and at ease, the doubt which had preyed on me from dawn to early night was swept clean away by the atmosphere of celebration. I felt only that the saints of heaven and earth had accepted the sacrifice and incense and were all reeling with intoxication in the sky, preparing to give the people of Luchen boundless good fortune.

In the Wine Shop

by Lu Hsün

Translated by Yang Hsien-yi and Gladys Yang

During my travels from the North to the Southeast I made a detour to my home, then to S——. This town is only about ten miles from my native place, and by small boat can be reached in a few hours. I had taught in a school there for a year. In the depth of winter, after a snowfall, the landscape was bleak. Indolence and nostalgia combined finally made me put up for a short time in the Lo Szu Inn, one which had not been there before. The town was small. I looked for some old colleagues I thought I might find, but not one was there: they had long since gone their separate ways. When I passed the gate of the school, I found that too had changed its name and appearance, which made me feel quite a stranger. In less than two hours my enthusiasm had waned, and I rather reproached myself for coming.

The inn in which I stayed rented rooms but did not supply meals; food could be ordered from the outside, but it was quite unpalatable, tasting like mud. Outside the window was only a stained and spotted wall, covered with withered moss. Above was the lead-colored sky, dead white without a trace of brilliance; moreover a light flurry of snow had begun to fall. I had had a meager lunch to begin with, and had nothing to do to while away the time, so quite naturally I thought of a small wine shop I had known very well in the old days, called the One Barrel House, which, I reckoned, could not be far from the hotel. I immediately locked the door of my room and set out for this tavern. Actually, all I wanted was to escape the boredom of my visit, rather than to really drink. The One Barrel House was still there, its narrow, moldering front and dilapidated signboard unchanged. But from the landlord down to the waiter there was not a single person I knew—in the One Barrel House too I had become a complete stranger. Still I walked up the familiar flight of stairs in the corner of the room to the little upper storey. Up here were the same five small wooden tables, unchanged. Only the back window, which originally had a wooden lattice, was now fitted with panes of glass.

"A catty of yellow wine. Dishes? Ten slices of fried beancurd, with plenty of pepper sauce!"

As I gave the order to the waiter who had come up with me, I walked to the back and sat down at the table by the window. This upstairs room was absolutely empty, which enabled me to take possession of the best seat, from which I could look out on to the deserted courtyard beneath. The courtyard probably did not belong to the wine shop. I had looked out at it many times before in the past, sometimes in snowy weather too. Now, to eyes accustomed to the North, the sight was sufficiently striking: several old plum trees, rivals of the snow, were actually in full blossom as if entirely oblivious of winter; while beside the crumbling pavilion there was still a camellia with a dozen crimson blossoms standing out against its thick, dark green foliage, blazing in the snow as bright as fire, indignant and arrogant, as if despising the traveler's wanderlust. I suddenly remembered the moistness of the heaped snow here, clinging, glistening and shining, quite unlike the dry northern snow which, when a high wind blows, will fly up and fill the sky like mist . . .

"Your wine, sir," said the waiter listlessly, and put down the cup, chopsticks, wine pot, and dish. The wine had come. I turned to the table, set everything straight, and filled my cup. I felt that the North was certainly not my home, yet when I came south I could only be considered a stranger. The dry snow up there, which flew like powder, and the soft snow here, which clung lingeringly, seemed equally alien to me. The wine tasted quite pure, and the fried beancurd was excellently cooked. The only pity was that the pepper sauce was too thin, but then the people of S— had never understood pungent flavors.

Probably because it was only afternoon, the place had none of the atmosphere of a tavern. I had already drunk three cups, but apart from myself there were still only four bare wooden tables in the place. Looking at the deserted courtyard I began to feel lonely, yet I did not want any other customers to come up. I could not help being irritated by the sound of footsteps on the stairs, and was relieved to find it was only the waiter. And so I drank another two cups of wine.

"This time it must be a customer," I thought, for the footsteps sounded much slower than those of the waiter. When I judged that he must be at the top of the stairs, I raised my head rather apprehensively to look at this unwelcome company. I gave a start and stood up. I never guessed that here of all places I should unexpectedly meet a friend—if such he would still let me call him. The newcomer was an old classmate who had been my colleague when I was a teacher, and although he had changed a great deal I knew him as soon as I saw him. Only he had become much slower in his movements, very unlike the nimble and active Lü Wei-fu of the old days.

"Ah, Wei-fu, is it you? I never expected to meet you here."

"Oh, it's you? Neither did I ever . . ."

I urged him to join me, but only after some hesitation did he seem willing to sit down. At first I thought this very strange, and felt rather hurt and displeased. When I looked closely at him he had still the same disorderly hair and beard and pale oblong face, but he was thinner and weaker. He looked very quiet, or perhaps dispirited, and his

eyes beneath their thick black brows had lost their alertness; but when he looked slowly around in the direction of the deserted courtyard, from his eyes suddenly flashed one of those piercing looks which I had seen so often at school.

"Well," I said cheerfully but somewhat awkwardly, "it's been about ten years now since we've seen each other. I heard long ago that you were at Tsinan, but I was so terribly lazy I never wrote."

"I was just the same. I've been at T'ai-yüan for more than two years now, with my mother. When I came back to fetch her I learned that you had already left, left once and for all."

"What are you doing in T'ai-yüan?" I asked.

"Teaching in the family of someone from the same province."

"And before that?"

"Before that?" He took a cigarette from his pocket, lit it, and put it in his mouth, then, watching the smoke as he puffed, said reflectively, "Simply futile work, equivalent to doing nothing at all."

He also asked what had happened to me since we separated. I gave him a rough idea, at the same time calling the waiter to bring a cup and chopsticks, so that he could share my wine while we had another two catties heated. We also ordered dishes of food. In the past we had never stood on ceremony, but now we began to be so formal that neither would choose a dish, and finally we decided on four suggested by the waiter: peas spiced with aniseed, cold meat, fried beancurd, and salted fish.

"As soon as I came back I knew I was a fool." Holding his cigarette in one hand and the wine cup in the other, he spoke with a bitter smile. "When I was young, I saw the way bees or flies stopped in one place. If they were frightened they would fly off, but after flying in a small circle they would come back again to land in the same place; and I thought this really very foolish, as well as pathetic. But I didn't think that I would fly back myself, after only flying in a small circle. And I didn't think you would come back either. Couldn't you have flown a little farther?"

"That's difficult to say. Probably I too have simply flown in a small circle." I also spoke with a rather bitter smile. "But why did you fly back?"

"For something quite futile." In one gulp he emptied his cup, then took several pulls at his cigarette and opened his eyes a little wider. "Futile— but you may as well hear about it."

The waiter brought up the freshly heated wine and dishes, and set them on the table. The smoke and the hot steam of the fried beancurd seemed to make the upstairs room more cheerful, while outside the snow fell still more thickly.

"Perhaps you knew," he went on, "that I had a little brother who died when he was three, and was buried here in the country. I can't even remember clearly what he looked like, but I have heard my mother say he was a very lovable child, and very fond of me. Even now it brings tears to her eyes to speak of him. This spring an elder cousin wrote to tell us that the ground beside his grave was gradually being invaded by water, and he was afraid before long it would slip into the river: we should go at once and do something about it. As soon as my mother discovered this, she became very upset, and couldn't sleep for several nights—she can read letters by herself, you know. But what could I do? I had no money, no time: there was nothing that could be done.

"Only now, taking advantage of my New Year's holiday, I have been able to come south to move his grave." He drained off another cup of wine, looked out of the window, and exclaimed: "Could you find anything like this up North? Flowers in thick snow, and beneath the snow unfrozen ground. So the day before yesterday I bought a small coffin, because I figured that the one under the ground must have rotted long ago—I took cotton and bedding, hired four workmen, and went into the country to move his grave. At the time I suddenly felt very happy, eager to dig up the grave, eager to see the body of the little brother who had been so fond of me: this was a new sensation for me. When we reached the grave, sure enough, the river water was encroaching on it and was already less than two feet away. The pitiful grave had not had any earth added to it for two years, and had sunk in. I stood in the snow, firmly pointed it out to the workmen, and said: 'Dig it up!'

"I'm really a commonplace fellow. I felt that my voice at that point was rather unnatural, and that this order was the greatest I had given in all my life. But the workmen didn't find it at all strange, and simply set to work to dig. When they reached the enclosure I had a look, and indeed the wood of the coffin had rotted almost completely away, leaving only a heap of splinters and small fragments of wood. My heart beat faster and I set these aside myself very carefully, wanting to see my little brother. However, I was taken by surprise. Bedding, clothes, skeleton, all were gone! I thought: 'These have all rotted away, but I always heard that the most difficult substance to rot is hair; perhaps there's still some hair.' So I bent down and looked carefully in the mud where the pillow should have been, but there was none. Not a trace remained."

I suddenly noticed that the rims of his eyes had become rather red, but realized at once that this was the effect of the wine. He had scarcely touched the dishes, but had been drinking incessantly, so that he had already drunk more than a catty, and his looks and gestures had all become more vigorous, so that he gradually resembled the Lü Wei-fu I had known. I called to the waiter to heat two more measures of wine, then turned back and, taking my winecup and facing him, listened in silence to what he had to tell.

"Actually it need not really have been moved again; I had only to level the ground, sell the coffin, and that would have been the end of it. Although there would have been something rather singular in my going to sell the coffin, still, if the price were low enough the shop from which I bought it would have taken it, and at least I could have saved a little money for wine. But I didn't do so. I still spread out the bedding, wrapped up in cotton some of the clay where his body had been, covered it up, put it in the new coffin, moved it to the grave where my father was buried, and buried it beside him. Because I used bricks to enclose the coffin I was busy again most of yesterday, supervising the work. In this way I can consider the affair ended, at least enough to deceive my mother and set her mind at rest. Well, well, you look at me like that! Do you blame me for being so different from before? Yes, I still remember the time when we went together to the city temple to pull off the gods' beards, how all day long we used to discuss methods of revolutionizing China until we even came to blows. But now I'm like this, willing to let things slide and to compromise. Sometimes I think: 'If my old friends were to see me now, probably they would no longer acknowledge me as a friend.' But that's what I'm like now."

He took out another cigarette, put it in his mouth, and lit it.

"Judging from your expression, you still seem to have hope for me. Naturally I'm much more passive then before, but there are still some things I realize. This makes me grateful to you, though at the same time rather uneasy. I'm afraid I'm just letting down the old friends who even now still have some hope for me . . ." He stopped and took a few drags at his cigarette before going on slowly: "Only today, just before coming to the One Barrel House, I did something futile, and yet it was something I was glad to do. My former neighbor on the east side was called Chang Fu. He was a boatman and had a daughter called Ah Shun. When you came to my house in those days you might have seen her, but you certainly wouldn't have paid any attention to her, because she was so small then. Nor did she grow up to be pretty, having just an ordinary thin oval face and pale skin. Only her eyes were unusually large, with very long lashes, and the whites were as clear as a cloudless night sky—I mean the cloudless sky of the North when there's no wind; the moon here is not so bright. She was very capable. She lost her mother when she was in her teens, and it was her job to look after a small brother and sister; she also had to wait on her father, and all this she did very competently. She was economical too, so that the family's livelihood gradually became secure. There was scarcely a neighbor who did not praise her, and even Chang Fu often expressed his appreciation. When I set off on my journey home this time, my mother remembered her—old people's memories are so long. She recalled that in the past Ah Shun once saw someone wearing red velvet flowers in her hair, and wanted a spray for herself. When she couldn't get one she cried nearly all night, so that she was beaten by her father, and her eyes remained red and swollen for two or three days. These red flowers came from another province, and couldn't be bought even in S——, so how could she ever hope to have any? Since I was coming south this time, my mother told me to buy two sprays to give her.

"Far from feeling vexed at this commission, I was actually delighted. I was really glad to do something for Ah Shun. The year before last, I came back to fetch my mother, and one day when Chang Fu was at home I happened to start chatting with him. He wanted to invite me to take a bowl of buckwheat gruel, telling me that they added white sugar to it. You see, a boatman who could have white sugar in his house was obviously not poor, and must eat very well. I let myself be persuaded and accepted, but begged that they only give me a small bowl. He quite understood, and said to Ah Shun: 'These scholars have no appetite. You can use a small bowl, but add more sugar!' However, when she had prepared the concoction and brought it in, it still gave me a start, for it was a large bowl, as much as I would eat in a whole day. Compared with Chang Fu's bowl, it's true, it did look small. In all my life I had never eaten this buckwheat gruel, and now that I tasted it, it was really unpalatable, though extremely sweet. I carelessly swallowed a few mouthfuls, and decided not to eat any more when I happened to catch a glimpse of Ah Shun standing far off in one corner of the room. Then I hadn't the heart to put down my chopsticks. I saw in her face both hope and fear—fear, no doubt, that she had prepared it badly, and hope that we would find it to our liking. I knew that if I left most of the food in my bowl she would feel very disappointed and apologetic. So I screwed up my courage, opened my mouth wide, and shoveled it down, eating almost as fast as Chang Fu. It was then that I learned the agony of forcing oneself to eat; I remember when I was a child and had to finish a bowl of brown sugar mixed with medicine for worms that I experienced the same difficulty. I felt no resentment, though, because her half-suppressed smile of satisfaction, when she came to take away our empty bowls, repaid me amply for all my discomfort. That night, although indigestion kept me from sleeping well and I had a series of nightmares, I still wished her a lifetime of happiness, and hoped the world would change for the better for her sake. Such thoughts were only the traces of my dreams of the old days. The next instant I laughed at myself, and promptly forgot them.

"I didn't know before that she had been beaten on account of a spray of artificial flowers, but when my mother spoke of it I remembered the buckwheat gruel incident, and became unaccountably diligent. First I made a search in T'ai-yüan, but none of the shops had them. It was only when I went to Tsinan—"

There was a rustle outside the window, as a pile of snow slipped down from the camellia tree which it had bent beaneath its weight; then the branches of the tree straightened themselves, showing even more clearly their dark thick foliage and blood-red flowers. The leaden color of the sky deepened. Small sparrows chirped, probably because evening was near, and since the ground was covered with snow they could find nothing to eat and would go early to their nests to sleep.

"It was only when I went to Tsinan"—he looked out of the window for a moment, turned back and drained a cup of wine, took several puffs at his cigarette, and went on—"only then did I buy the artificial flowers. I didn't know whether those she had been beaten for were this kind or not; but at least these were also made of velvet. I didn't know either whether she liked a deep or a light color, so I bought one spray of red, one spray of pink, and brought them both here.

"That same afternoon, as soon as I had finished lunch, I went to see Chang Fu, having stayed an extra day just for this. His house was there all right, only looking rather gloomy; or perhaps that was simply my imagination. His son and second daughter—Ah Chao—were standing at the gate. Both of them had grown. Ah Chao was completely different from her sister, and simply looked like a ghost; but when she saw me come up to their house, she quickly ran inside. When I asked the little boy, I found that Chang Fu was not at home. 'And your elder sister?' At once he

stared at me wide-eyed, and asked me what I wanted her for; moreover he seemed very fierce, as if he wanted to leap on me and bite me. Hesitantly I walked away. Nowadays I just let things slide . . .

"You have no idea how much more afraid I am of calling on people than I used to be. Because I know very well how unwelcome I am, I have even come to dislike myself. Knowing this, why should I deliberately inflict myself on others? But this time I felt my errand had to be carried out, so after some reflection I went back to the firewood shop almost opposite their house. The shopkeeper's mother, Old Mrs. Fa, was there at least, and still recognized me. She actually asked me into the shop to sit down. After an exchange of polite remarks I told her why I had come back to S—— and why I was looking for Chang Fu. I was taken aback when she heaved a sigh and said:

"'What a pity Ah Shun didn't have the good fortune to wear these flowers.'

"Then she told me the whole story, saying, 'It was probably last spring that Ah Shun began to look pale and thin. Later she would often start crying suddenly, and if you asked her why, she wouldn't say. Sometimes she even cried all night, until Chang Fu lost his temper and scolded her, saying she had waited too long to marry and had gone mad. When autumn came, first she had a slight cold and then she took to her bed, and after that she never got up again. Only a few days before she died, she told Chang Fu that she had long ago become like her mother, often spitting blood and perspiring at night. She had hidden it, afraid that he would worry about her. One evening her uncle Chang Keng came to demand money—he was always doing that—and when she didn't give him any he smiled coldly and said, "Don't act so proud; your man isn't any better than I am!" After that she fell into a state of depression, but she was too shy to ask her father about it and could only cry. As soon as Chang Fu learned about this, he told her what a decent fellow her future husband was; but it was too late. Besides, she didn't believe him. "It's a good thing I'm already like this," she said. "Now nothing matters any more." '

"The old woman also said, 'If her man was really not as good as Chang Keng, that would be truly frightful! He'd have been worse than a chicken thief, and what sort of scoundrel would that be! But when he came to the funeral I saw him with my own eyes: his clothes were clean and he looked very respectable. He said with tears in his eyes that he had worked hard all those years on the boat to save up money to marry, but now the girl was dead. It was obvious that he was actually a good man, and everything Chang Keng said was false. It was a pity Ah Shun believed such a rascally liar, and died for nothing. But we can't blame anyone else: it was Ah Shun's fate.'

"Since that was the case, my business was finished too. But what about the two sprays of artificial flowers I had brought with me? Well, I asked her to give them to Ah Chao. This Ah Chao no sooner saw me than she fled as if I were a wolf or some monster; I really didn't want to give them to her. However, I did give them to her, and I have only to tell my mother that Ah Shun was delighted with them, and that will be that. Who cares about such futile affairs anyway? One only wants to muddle through them somehow. When I've gotten through New Year I'll go back to teaching the Confucian classics as before."

"Are you teaching that?" I asked in astonishment.

"Of course. Did you think I was teaching English? First I had two pupils, one studying the *Book of Songs,* the other *Mencius.* Recently I have got another, a girl, who is studying the *Canon for Girls.*[1] I don't even teach mathematics; not that I wouldn't teach it, but they don't want it taught."

"I would really never have guessed that you would be teaching such books."

"Their father wants them to study these. I'm an outsider, so it's all the same to me. Who cares about such futile affairs anyway? There's no need to take them seriously."

His whole face was scarlet as if he were quite drunk, but the gleam in his eyes had died down. I gave a slight sigh, and for a time found nothing to say. There was a clatter on the stairs as some customers came up. The first was short, with a round bloated face; the second was tall with a conspicuous red nose. Behind them were others, and as they walked up, the small upper floor shook. I turned to Lü Wei-fu, who was trying to catch my eyes; then I called the waiter to bring the bill.

"Is your salary enough to live on?" I asked as I prepared to leave.

"I have twenty dollars a month, not quite enough to manage on."

"Then what do you mean to do in the future?"

"In the future? I don't know. Just think: has any of our many plans turned out as we hoped in the past? I'm not sure of anything now, not even of what I will do tomorrow, or the next minute . . ."

The waiter brought up the bill and gave it to me. Wei-fu did not behave as formally as before. He just glanced at me, then went on smoking and allowed me to pay.

We went out of the wine shop together. His hotel lay in the opposite direction from mine, so we said goodbye at the door. As I walked alone toward my hotel, the cold wind and snow beat against my face, but I felt refreshed. I saw that the sky was already dark, woven together with houses and streets into the white, shifting web of thick snow.

---

[1] A book giving the feudal standard of behavior for girls, and the virtues they should cultivate.

Soap

by Lu Hsün

Translated by Yang Hsien-yi and Gladys Yang

With her back to the north window in the slanting sunlight, Ssu-ming's wife with her eight-year-old daughter, Hsiu-erh, was pasting paper money for the dead when she heard the slow, heavy footsteps of someone in cloth shoes and knew her husband was back. Paying no attention, she simply went on pasting paper money. But the tread of cloth shoes drew nearer and nearer, until it finally stopped beside her. Then she could not help looking up to see Ssu-ming before her, hunching his shoulders and stooping forward to fumble desperately under his cloth jacket in the inner pocket of his long gown.

By dint of twisting and turning at last he extracted his hand with a small oblong package in it, which he handed to his wife. As she took it, she smelled an indefinable fragrance rather reminiscent of olive. On the green paper wrapper was a bright golden seal with a network of tiny designs. Hsiu-erh bounded forward to seize this and look at it, but her mother promptly pushed her aside.

"Been shopping?" she asked as she looked at it.

"Er—yes." He stared at the package in her hand.

The green paper wrapper was opened. Inside was a layer of very thin paper, also sunflower green, and not until this was unwrapped was the object itself exposed—glossy and hard, besides being sunflower green, with another network of fine designs on it. The thin paper was a cream color, it appeared. The indefinable olive-like fragrance was stronger now.

"My, this is really good soap!"

She held the soap to her nose as gingerly as if it were a child, and sniffed at it as she spoke.

"Er-yes. Just use this in future . . ."

As he spoke, she noticed him eyeing her neck, and felt herself flushing up to her cheekbones. Sometimes when she rubbed her neck, especially behind the ears, her fingers detected a roughness; and though she knew this was the accumulated dirt of many years, she had never given it much thought. Now, under his scrutiny, she could not help blushing as she looked at this green, foreign soap with the curious scent, and this blush spread right to the tips of her ears. She mentally resolved to thoroughly wash herself with this soap after supper.

"There are places you can't wash clean just with honey locust pods,"[1] she muttered to herself.

"Ma, can I have this?" As Hsiu-erh reached out for the sunflower-green paper, Chao-erh, the younger daughter who had been playing outside, came running in too. Mrs. Ssu-ming promptly pushed them both aside, folded the thin paper in place, wrapped the green paper round it as before, then leaned over to put it on the highest shelf of the washstand. After one final glance, she turned back to her paper money.

"Hsüeh-ch'eng!" Ssu-ming suddenly called in a drawn-out voice, as if he had just remembered something. Then he sat down on a high-backed chair opposite his wife.

"Hsüeh-ch'eng!" she helped him call.

[1] In many parts of China, honey locust pods were used for washing. They were cheaper than soap, but not so effective.

She stopped pasting coins to listen, but not a sound could she hear. When she saw him with up-turned head waiting so impatiently, she couldn't help feeling apologetic.

"Hsüeh-ch'eng!" she called shrilly at the top of her voice.

This call proved effective, for they heard the tramp of leather shoes draw near, and Hsüeh-ch'eng stood before her. He was in shirt sleeves, his plump round face shiny with perspiration.

"What were you doing?" she asked disapprovingly. "Why didn't you hear your father call?"

"I was practicing Hexagram Boxing[2] . . ." He turned at once to his father and straightened up, looking at him as if to ask what he wanted.

"Hsüeh-ch'eng, I want to ask you the meaning of *o-du-fu.*"

"*O-du-fu?* . . . Isn't it a very fierce woman?"

"What nonsense! The idea!" Ssu-ming was suddenly furious. "Am I a woman, pray?"

Hsüeh-ch'eng recoiled a few steps, and stood straighter than ever. Though his father's gait sometimes reminded him of the way old men walked in Peking opera, he had never considered Ssu-ming a woman. His answer, he saw now, had been a great mistake.

"As if I didn't know *o-du-fu* means a very fierce woman. Would I have to ask you that? This isn't Chinese, it's foreign devils' language, I'm telling you. Do you understand what it means?"

"I . . . I don't know." Hsüeh-ch'eng felt even more uneasy.

"Pah! Why do I spend all that money to send you to school if you don't even understand a little thing like this? Your school boasts that it lays equal stress on speech and comprehension, yet it hasn't taught you anything. The ones speaking that devils' language couldn't have been more than fourteen or fifteen, actually a little younger than you, yet they were chattering away in it, while you can't even tell me the meaning. And

you have the nerve to answer 'I don't know.' Go and look it up for me at once!"

"Yes," answered Hsüeh-ch'eng deep down in his throat, then respectfully withdrew.

"I don't know what students today are coming to," declared Ssu-ming with emotion after a pause. "As a matter of fact, in the time of Emperor Kuang-hsü [r. 1875–1908], I was all in favor of opening schools; but I never foresaw how great the evils would be. What 'emancipation' or 'freedom' have we had? There is no true learning, nothing but absurdities. I've spent quite a bit of money on Hsüeh-ch'eng, all to no purpose. It wasn't easy to get him into this half-Western, half-Chinese school, where they claim they lay equal stress on 'speaking and comprehending English.'[3] You'd think all should be well. But—bah! After one whole year of study he can't even understand *o-du-fu!* He must still be studying dead books. What use is such a school, I ask you? What I say is: close the whole lot of them!"

"Yes, really, better close the whole lot of them," chimed in his wife sympathetically, pasting away at the paper money.

"There's no need for Hsiu-erh and her sister to attend any school. As Ninth Grandpa said, 'What's the good of girls' studying?' When he opposed girls' schools I attacked him for it; but now I see the old folk were right after all. Just think, it's already in very poor taste the way women wander up and down the streets, and now they want to cut their hair as well. Nothing disgusts me so much as these short-haired schoolgirls. What I say is: there's some excuse for soldiers and bandits, but these girls are the ones who are creating chaos everywhere. They ought to be very severely dealt with indeed . . ."

"Yes, as if it weren't enough for all men to look like monks, the women are imitating nuns."[4]

"Hsüeh-ch'eng!"

Hsüeh-ch'eng hurried in holding a small, fat,

---

[2] A health-building exercise.

[3] English was taught in nearly all the new schools at that time, and learning to speak was considered as important as learning to read.

[4] Because monks and nuns shaved their heads, at the end of the Ch'ing dynasty and later, conservatives laughed at the men who cut their queues, claiming they looked like monks.

gilt-edged book, which he handed to his father.

"This looks like it," he said, pointing to one place. "Here . . ."

Ssu-ming took it and looked at it. He knew it was a dictionary, but the characters were very small and horizontally printed too. Frowning, he turned toward the window and screwed up his eyes to read the passage Hsüeh-ch'eng had pointed out.

" 'A society founded in the eighteenth century for mutual relief.'—No, that can't be it.—How do you pronounce this?" He pointed to the devils' word before him.

"Oddfellows."

"No, no, that wasn't it." Ssu-ming suddenly lost his temper again. "I told you it was bad language, a swearword of some sort, to curse someone like me. Understand? Go and look it up!"

Hsüeh-ch'eng glanced at him several times, but did not move.

"That's a tough nut to crack. How can he make head or tail of it? You must explain things clearly to him first, before he can look it up properly." Seeing Hsüeh-ch'eng in a quandary, his mother felt sorry for him and intervened rather indignantly on his behalf.

"It was when I was buying soap at Kuang Jun Hsiang on the main street," sighed Ssu-ming, turning to her. "There were three students shopping there too. Of course, to them I must have seemed a little finicky. I looked at five or six kinds of soap all over forty cents, and turned them down. Then I looked at some priced ten cents a cake, but it wasn't any good, with no scent at all. Since I thought it best to strike a happy medium, I chose that green soap at twenty-four cents a cake. The assistant was one of those supercilious young fellows with eyes on the top of his head, so he pulled a long dog's face. At that those worthless young students started winking at each other and talking devils' language. I wanted to unwrap the soap and look at it before paying—for with all that foreign paper around it, how could I tell whether it was good or bad? But that supercilious young fellow not only refused, but was very unreasonable and passed some offensive remarks, at which those worthless young rascals laughed. It was the

youngest of the lot who said that, looking straight at me, and the rest of them started laughing. So it must have been some foul word." He turned back to Hsüeh-ch'eng. "Look for it in the section headed Foul Language!"

"Yes," answered Hsüeh-ch'eng deep down in his throat, then respectfully withdrew.

"Yet they still shout 'New Culture! New Culture!' When 'culture' has come to this state, how could it get any worse?" His eyes on the rafters, Ssu-ming continued, totally absorbed in his argument. "The students have no morals, society has no morals. Unless we find some way to save ourselves, China will really be destroyed . . . How pathetic she was. . ."

"Who?" asked his wife casually, not really curious.

"A filial daughter . . ." His eyes came around to her, and there was respect in his voice. "There were two beggars on the main street. One was a girl who looked eighteen or nineteen. Actually, it's most improper to beg at that age, but beg she did. She was with an old woman of about seventy, who had white hair and was blind. They were begging under the eaves of that clothes shop, and everybody said how filial she was. The old one was her grandmother. Whatever trifle the girl received, she gave it to her grandmother, choosing rather to go hungry herself. But do you think people would give alms even to such a filial daughter?"

He fixed her with his eye, as if to test her wisdom.

She made no answer, but fixed him with *her* eye, as if waiting for him to elucidate.

"Bah—no!" At last he supplied the answer himself. "I watched for a long time, and saw only one person give her a copper. Plenty of others gathered round, but only to jeer at them. There were two rogues as well, one of whom had the impertinence to say:

" 'Ah-fa! Don't be put off by the dirt on this piece of goods. If you buy two cakes of soap, and give her a good scrubbing all over, she wouldn't be bad at all!' Now what do you think, is that any way to talk?"

She snorted and lowered her head. After quite

a time, she asked rather casually: "Did *you* give her any money?"

"Did I?—No. I'd have felt ashamed to come up with one or two coins. She wasn't an ordinary beggar, you know . . ."

"Mm." Without waiting for him to finish she stood up slowly and walked to the kitchen. Dusk was gathering, and it was time for supper.

Ssu-ming stood up too, and walked into the courtyard. It was lighter outside than in. Hsüeh-ch'eng was practicing Hexagram Boxing in a corner by the wall. This constituted the "discipline" required by his father, and he used the economical method of employing the hour between day and night for this purpose. Hsüeh-ch'eng had been boxing now for about half a year. Ssu-ming nodded very slightly, as if in approval, then began to pace the courtyard with his hands behind his back. Before long, the broad leaves of the evergreen which was the only potted plant they had were swallowed up in the darkness, and stars twinkled between white clouds which looked like torn cotton. Night had fallen. Ssu-ming could not repress his growing indignation. He felt called on to do great deeds, to declare war on all the worthless students around, and on this wicked society. By degrees he grew bolder and bolder, his steps became longer and longer, and the thud of his cloth soles grew louder and louder, waking the hen and her chicks in the coop so that they squawked and cheeped in alarm.

A light appeared in the hall—the beacon that signaled that supper was ready—and the whole household gathered around the table in the middle. The lamp stood at the lower end of the table, while Ssu-ming sat alone at the head. His plump, round face was like Hsüeh-ch'eng's, with the addition of two thin lines of hair for a moustache. Seen through the hot vapor from the vegetable soup, he looked like the God of Wealth you find in temples. On the left sat Mrs. Ssu-ming and Chao-erh, on the right Hsüeh-ch'eng and Hsiu-erh. Chopsticks pattered like rain against the bowls. Though no one said a word, their supper table was very animated.

Chao-erh upset her bowl, spilling cabbage soup over half the table. Ssu-ming opened his narrow eyes as wide as he could. Only when he saw she was going to cry did he stop glaring at her and reach out with his chopsticks for a tender morsel of cabbage he had spotted. But the tender morsel had disappeared. He looked right and left, and discovered Hsüeh-ch'eng on the point of stuffing it into his wide-open mouth. Disappointed, Ssu-ming ate a mouthful of yellowish leaves instead.

"Hsüeh-ch'eng!" He looked at his son. "Have you found that phrase or not?"

"Which phrase?—No, not yet!"

"Pah! Look at you, you haven't acquired any learning, nor do you understand any higher principles—you only know how to eat! You should learn from that filial daughter: although she's a beggar, she still treats her grandmother with great respect, even if it means going hungry herself. But what do you impudent students know of such things? You'll grow up like those rogues."

"I've thought of one possibility, but I don't know if it's right . . . I think, perhaps, they may have said *o-du-fu-la*." [5]

"That's right! That's it exactly! That's exactly the sound it was: *o-du-fu-la*. What does that mean? You belong to the same gang: you must know."

"Mean?—I'm not sure what it means."

"Nonsense. Don't try to deceive me. You're all a bad lot."

"Heaven doesn't strike people when they eat," burst out Mrs. Ssu-ming suddenly. "Why do you keep losing your temper today? Even when you eat you kick the hen and curse the dog. What do children like them know?"

"What?" Ssu-ming was on the point of answering back when he saw her sunken cheeks were puffed out with anger, her color had changed, and a fearful glint had come into her eyes. He hastily changed his tone. "I'm not losing my temper. I'm just telling Hsüeh-ch'eng to learn a little sense."

"How can he understand what's in *your* mind?" She looked angrier than ever. "If he had any sense, he'd long since have lit a lantern or a torch and gone out to fetch that filial daughter. You've

---

[5] Chinese transliteration of "old fool."

already bought her one cake of soap: all you have to do is buy another . . ."

"Nonsense! That's what that rogue said."

"I'm not so sure. If you buy another cake and give her a good scrubbing, then worship her, the whole world will be at peace."

"How can you say such a thing? What connection is there? Because I remembered you had no soap—"

"There's a connection all right. You bought it specially for the filial daughter; so go and give her a good scrubbing. I don't deserve it. I don't want it. I don't want to share her glory."

"Really, how can you talk like that?" mumbled Ssu-ming. "You women . . ." His face was perspiring like Hsüeh-ch'eng's after Hexagram Boxing, but probably it was mostly because the food had been so hot.

"What about us women? We women are much better than you men. If you men aren't cursing eighteen- or nineteen-year-old girl students, you're praising eighteen- or nineteen-year-old girl beggars: such dirty minds you have! Scrubbing, indeed! It's simply disgraceful!"

"Didn't you hear? That's what one of those rogues said."

"Old Ssu!" A thundering voice was heard from the darkness outside.

"Old Tao? I'm coming!"

Ssu-ming knew this was Ho Tao-t'ung, famed for his powerful voice, and he shouted back as joyfully as a criminal newly reprieved.

"Hsüeh-ch'eng, quickly, light the lamp and show Uncle Ho into the library!"

Hsüeh-ch'eng lit a candle and ushered Tao-t'ung into the west room. They were followed by Pu Wei-yüan.

"I'm sorry I didn't welcome you. Excuse me." With his mouth still full of rice, Ssu-ming went in and bowed with clasped hands in greeting. "Won't you join us at our simple meal?"

"We've already eaten." Wei-yüan stepped forward and greeted him. "We've hurried here at this time of night because of the eighteenth essay and poem contest of the Moral Rearmament Literary Society. Isn't tomorrow the seventeenth?"

"What? Is it the sixteenth today?" asked Ssu-ming in surprise.

"See how absentminded you are!" boomed Tao-t'ung.

"So we'll have to send something in tonight to the newspaper office, to make sure they print it tomorrow."

"I've already drafted the title of the essay. See whether you think it will do or not." As he was speaking, Tao-t'ung produced a slip of paper from his handkerchief and handed it to Ssu-ming.

Ssu-ming stepped up to the candle, unfolded the paper, and read it word by word: " 'We humbly suggest an essay in the name of the whole nation to beg the President to issue an order for the promotion of the Confucian classics and the worship of the mother of Mencius,[6] in order to revive this depraved society and preserve our national heritage.' Very good. Very good. Isn't it a little long, though?"

"That doesn't matter," answered Tao-t'ung loudly. "I've worked it out, and it won't cost more to advertise. But what about the title for the poem?"

"The title for the poem?" Ssu-ming suddenly looked most respectful. "I've thought of one. How about 'The Filial Daughter'? It's a true story, and she deserves to be eulogized. On the main street today—"

"Oh, no, that won't do," put in Wei-yüan hastily, waving his hand to stop Ssu-ming. "I saw her too. She isn't from these parts, and I couldn't understand her dialect, nor she mine. I don't know where she's from. Everyone says she's filial; but when I asked her if she could write poems, she shook her head. If she could, that would be fine."[7]

"But since loyalty and filial piety are so important, it doesn't matter too much if she can't write poems."

---

[6] A woman famous for her virtue. According to tradition, she moved her home three times to avoid undesirable companions for her son.

[7] In old China, it was considered romantic for women to exchange ideas with men through the medium of poems. The fashionable courtesans could write poetry.

"Not true! Quite the reverse!" Wei-yüan raised his hands and rushed toward Ssu-ming, to shake and push him. "She'd only be interesting if she could write poems."

"Let's use this title." Ssu-ming pushed him aside. "Add an explanation and print it. In the first place, it will serve to eulogize her; in the second, we can use this to criticize society. What is the world coming to anyway? I watched for some time, and didn't see anybody give her a cent—people are utterly heartless!"

"*Ai-ya,* Ssu-ming!" Wei-yüan rushed over again. "You're cursing bald-headed thieves in front of a monk. I didn't give her anything because I didn't happen to have any money on me."

"Don't be so sensitive, Wei-yüan." Ssu-ming pushed him aside again. "Of course you're an exception. Let me finish. There was quite a crowd around them, showing no respect, just jeering. There were two rogues as well, who were even more impertinent. One of them said: 'Ah-fa! If you buy two cakes of soap and give her a good scrubbing, she wouldn't be bad at all!' Just think—"

"Ha, ha! Two cakes of soap!" Tao-t'ung suddenly bellowed with laughter, nearly splitting their eardrums. "Buy soap! Ho, ho, ho!"

"Tao-t'ung! Tao-t'ung! Don't make such a noise!" Ssu-ming gave a start, panic-stricken.

"A good scrubbing! Ho, ho, ho!"

"Tao-t'ung!" Ssu-ming looked stern. "We're discussing serious matters. Why should you make such a noise, nearly deafening everyone? Listen to me: we'll use both these titles, and send them straight to the newspaper office so that they come out without fail tomorrow. I'll have to trouble you both to take them there."

"All right, all right. Of course," agreed Wei-yüan readily.

"Ha, ha! A good scrubbing! Ho, ho!"

"Tao-t'ung!" shouted Ssu-ming furiously.

This shout made Tao-t'ung stop laughing. After they had drawn up the explanation, Wei-yüan copied it on the paper and left with Tao-t'ung for the newspaper office. Ssu-ming carried the candle to see them out, then walked back to the door of the hall feeling rather apprehensive. After some hesitation, though, he finally crossed the threshold. As he went in, his eyes fell on the small, green, oblong package of soap in the middle of the central table, the gold characters with fine designs around them glittering in the lamplight.

Hsiu-erh and Chao-erh were playing on the floor at the lower end of the table, while Hsüeh-ch'eng sat on the right side looking up something in his dictionary. Last of all, on the high-backed chair in the shadows far from the lamp, Ssu-ming discovered his wife. Her impassive face showed neither joy nor anger, and she was staring off into space.

"A good scrubbing indeed! Disgraceful!"

Faintly, Ssu-ming heard Hsiu-erh's voice behind him. He turned, but she was not moving. Only Chao-erh put both her small hands over her face as if to shame somebody.

This was no place for him. He blew out the candle, and went into the yard to pace up and down. Because he forgot to be quiet, the hen and her chicks started cheeping again. At once he walked more lightly, moving further away. After a long time, the lamp in the hall was transferred to the bedroom. The moonlight on the ground was like seamless white gauze, and the moon—quite full—seemed a jade disc among the bright clouds.

He felt not a little depressed, as if he, like the filial daughter, had become a "poor and helpless soul," forlorn and alone. That night he did not get to sleep until very late.

By the next morning, however, the soap was being honored by being used. Getting up later than usual, he saw his wife leaning over the washstand rubbing her neck, with bubbles heaped up over both her ears like those emitted by great crabs. The difference between these and the small white bubbles produced by honey locust pods was like that between heaven and earth. After this, an indefinable fragrance rather reminiscent of olives always emanated from Mrs. Ssu-ming. Not for nearly half a year did this suddenly give way to another scent, which all who smelled it claimed was like sandalwood.

HSÜ TI-SHAN
(1893–1941)

Hsü Ti-shan (pen name: Lo Hua-sheng) was only two years old when his parents left Taiwan for Fukien following the Sino-Japanese War in 1895, when the island was ceded to Japan. As a minor official and schoolteacher, his father subsequently took his family with him to Singapore, Siam, Rangoon, and Sumatra when he was not stationed in Fukien or Kwangtung. Thus Hsü Ti-shan was a much-traveled youth even before he entered Yenching University in 1918. Although his parents were originally Buddhists, he had had much contact with Christian missionaries and was converted to Christianity while at middle school. He received his B.A. degree from Yenching in 1921 and stayed on at his alma mater as an instructor. Together with Shen Yen-ping, Cheng Chen-to, and other friends, he organized the Literary Association (Wen-hsüeh yen-chiu hui), and contributed frequently to its principal organ and the leading literary journal of its time, *The Short Story* magazine (*Hsiao-shuo yüeh-pao*). He has to his credit four short story collections: *The Vain Labors of a Spider* (*Chui-wang lao-chu*, 1925); *Letters That Couldn't Be Sent Anywhere* (*Wu-fa t'ou-ti chih yu-chien*, 1928); *The Liberator* (*Chieh-fang che*, 1933); and *Letters from an Endangered Home* (*Wei-ch'ao chui-chien*, 1947).

In 1923 Hsü Ti-shan came to the United States for graduate studies at Columbia University, majoring in religion. Two years later he transferred to Oxford University to continue his studies in the history of religion, Indian philosophy, and Sanskrit. After returning to China in 1926, he joined the Yenching faculty as a professor of theology and history, but also lectured at Tsinghua and National Peking University in the years following. As Professor of Chinese at the University of Hong Kong from 1936 to 1941, he did much to promote Chinese culture on the British crown colony.

In view of Hsü Ti-shan's family and educational backgrounds, it is small wonder that many of his stories are religious fables with often exotic settings, as are our two selections, "The Merchant's Wife" (*Shang-jen fu,* 1921) and "Yü-kuan" (1939). Like several other of the author's best-known tales, these two have as their heroine a Chinese woman of humble background who takes what life has to offer with patience and sees her tribulations within a larger pattern of meaning, not readily perceivable unless one's conduct is guided by the spirit of charity or forgiveness. Thus both Yü-kuan and Hsi-kuan, the heroine of "The Merchant's Wife," would agree with Thomas à Becket when he declares in

T. S. Eliot's *Murder in the Cathedral* (*The Complete Poems and Plays* [New York, 1952], p. 182):

> Neither does the actor suffer
> Nor the patient act. But both are fixed
> In an eternal action, an eternal patience
> To which all must consent that it may be willed
> And which all must suffer that they may will it,
> That the pattern may subsist, for the pattern is the action
> And the suffering, that the wheel may turn and still
> Be forever still.

Hsü Ti-shan has as much humanitarian sympathy for tradition-bound Chinese women as Lu Hsün or any other author in this volume, but he alone embraces them with love and ennobles them with a Christian mode of understanding.

"Yü-kuan" is Hsü Ti-shan's masterpiece. If we may regard Hsi-kuan as a natural saint who accepts her outrageous fortune with hardly an evil thought against her abusers, Yü-kuan is much more stubbornly human and stubbornly Chinese in her way of thinking. Her search for disinterested goodness is a much more arduous and psychologically believable process, and she stays in our memory as an entirely credible human being. According to some recent research, Yü-kuan may have been a portrait of the author's mother.

C. T. H.

The Merchant's Wife

by Hsü Ti-shan

Translated by William H. Nienhauser, Jr.

"It's time for your morning tea, sir."

The voice of the second-class cabin attendant was urging me to get up. Since I'd been very busy yesterday before boarding the ship, my mind and body were so completely exhausted that I slept from nine o'clock straight on through until seven A.M. without stirring. When I heard the attendant's call, I got up immediately. After attending to those matters which need to be taken care of in the morning, I went to the dining hall.

By that time the hall was crowded. Everyone there was drinking tea and chatting: predicting who would be victorious in the European War, discussing whether Yüan Shih-k'ai [1859–1916] should have made himself emperor, or conjecturing whether the revolt of the Indian soldiers in Singapore was incited by the Indian Revolutionary Party. The buzzing and murmuring almost transformed the hall into a marketplace. I wasn't accustomed to it. As soon as I was done with my tea, I returned to my cabin, took a volume entitled *Miscellanies of the Western Capital,* and ran off to starboard looking for a place to sit. I was planning on an intimate conversation with the characters of the book.

As I opened it and was about to begin reading, an Indian woman, leading a child of about seven

or eight by the hand, came and sat down facing me. I had seen this woman at the Pond for Releasing Life[1] in the Temple of Supreme Joy[2] the day before yesterday. I had also spotted her boarding ship, and on board had often seen her at the rail, port and starboard, enjoying the cool air. As soon as I saw her my curiosity was stirred, for though her attire was Indian, her deportment was not that of an Indian woman.

I laid the book down and watched her furtively, pretending to be reading whenever she turned her gaze toward me. After I had done that several times, I feared she might suspect an ulterior motive and lowered my head, not daring to allow my eyes to touch her again.

She absentmindedly sang Indian songs to the child, who pointed here and there, asking her questions. As I listened to her replies, unconsciously I stared at her face again. When she saw me raise my head, she ignored the child and quickly asked me in a Southern Fukienese dialect, "Uncle,[3] are you going to Singapore too?" (She had the accent of the Hai-cheng country folk, and her tone of voice too was that of a country dweller.) She spoke slowly, syllable by syllable, as if she were just learning to speak. When she asked me this question my suspicions multiplied, and I

Professors Dennis T. Hu, Muhammed Umar Memon, V. Narayana Rao, and Seng-tong Wong have all made important suggestions and clarifications to the translator. The responsibility for any remaining infelicities or errors lies solely with the latter. In the case where Muslim terms cannot be identified, romanizations according to the Chinese renderings are provided.

The numbered footnotes were supplied by the translator, whereas the footnotes keyed with letters are the author's own.

[1] A pond where people release captive fish or turtles, often after purchasing them nearby; the practice is a Buddhist one, reflecting the Buddhist principle of respect for life.

[2] This temple is located on the island of Penang off the west coast of Malaysia.

[3] "Lao-shu" in the original, which means "Old Uncle."

answered, "I'm returning to Amoy. Have you been to our area? How is it that you speak our language?"

"Eh? I suppose since you saw that I am dressed as an Indian woman, you suspected I wasn't from the 'lands of the T'ang.'[a] To tell you the truth, my home is in Hung-chien."

When the child saw us conversing in our native dialect, he had a strange feeling. Shaking his mother's knee, he asked in Indian: "Mama, what language are you speaking? Who is he?" He had probably never heard her speak this language before, and thus felt it was strange. To learn this woman's background a little more quickly, I went on with my questions.

"Is that your child?"

She first answered the child, then turned to me and sighed. "Why not? I raised him in Madras."

The more we talked the more familiar we became, so that our initial inhibitions subsided. Once she knew my home and that I was a teacher, she stopped addressing me as "uncle" and called me "sir" instead, which was more appropriate for a man of my profession. She related to me, moreover, the general conditions in Madras. Because her experiences were out of the ordinary, I asked her to tell them in some detail. By then she was in a mood to talk, and she agreed. Only then did I put the book in my bag and with undivided attention listen to her story.

When I was fifteen I was married to Lin Yin-ch'iao of the Ching-chao area. My husband ran the sugar shop around the corner from us. Although he spent little time at home, this scarcely affected our good relationship. During the three or four years I spent with him, we never argued or had a difference of opinion. One day, he came back from the shop looking troubled and depressed. As soon as he came through the door, he grasped my hands and said, "Hsi-kuan,[b] my business is ruined. From now on I won't be going back to the shop again."

When I heard this I had to ask, "Why? Has business been bad?"

"No," he said. "No, I ruined it myself. These past couple of days some friends have been urging me to gamble with them. At first I won quite a bit, but then I lost everything—even the store's equipment and furniture. I wish I hadn't done it . . . I'm really sorry; I can hardly face you."

I was stunned for a while and couldn't find the right words to console him. I was even more at a loss for words to rebuke him.

He saw my tears stream down and hurriedly wiped them away as he went on. "*Ai*, you've never cried in my presence before. These tears you shed before me now are like molten pellets of iron dripping one by one into the depths of my heart. It really hurts me more than you. But you needn't worry too much: I'll simply look for some capital to set up business again."

Then we two sat there wordlessly staring into each other's eyes. Although I had a few things I wanted to set straight with him, whenever I looked at him, I felt as if he had a kind of demonic power that, before I could speak any thought, had long since understood it. I could only say, "From now on you'd better not throw your money away! You've got to realize that gambling . . ."

He was at home, without a job, for almost three months. It turned out that we could get along on the money I had saved, so there was no need for him to worry about a livelihood. He would be out the whole day to borrow money for capital, but unfortunately no one trusted him enough to loan him a penny. He was so desperate that he finally decided to migrate to Southeast Asia.

By the time he was ready to leave for Singapore, I had all the things he would need, including a pair of jade bracelets to sell at Amoy for travel expenses. He wanted to take advantage of the morning tide in leaving for Amoy, so the day before we were to part we talked all through the night. The next morning I saw him off onto a small

---

[a] Overseas Chinese refer to their motherland as "T'ang Shan," the lands of T'ang China.

[b] It is customary for people of Fukienese origin to address one another by adding the suffix "kuan" to the given name, whether it is a person of an older generation speaking to one of a younger, or a man and woman of the same generation addressing each other.

boat and then walked back alone, my mind troubled. I sat down at my desk thinking that most men who went to Southeast Asia never missed their homes or thought of their families, and I wondered whether he would be like them. As I was still lost in this thought, a trail of hurried footsteps stopped at the door. I recognized them as his and quickly got up and opened the door. "Did you leave something behind?" I asked.

"No," he replied. "I forgot to tell you something. When I get there, no matter what I'm doing, I'll write you. If I don't return in five or six years, you come look for me."

"All right," I said. "You had to come back to tell me this? When the time comes I'll know what I should do. It's getting late. You'd better hurry back to the boat!"

He pressed my hands, heaved a long sigh, and then turned and left. I watched him until he reached the edge of the banyan tree's shade and saw him descend the long dike, before I closed the door.

I was twenty that year when I parted from Lin Yin-ch'iao. After he left home only two letters came, one saying he had opened a grocery store in Tanjong Pagar in Singapore and that business was good. The other said he was quite occupied with business and couldn't afford to come home. For many years I waited for him to come back for a reunion, but year after year my hopes were in vain.

The woman who lived next door often urged me to go to Southeast Asia and look for him. When I gave this some thought, I realized we had been separated for ten years. To go searching for him, even if it weren't easy, would be much better than suffering alone at home. I got together the money I had saved, turned the house over to the care of a village family named Jung, and went to Amoy to take ship. Since this was the first time I had gone abroad, of course I couldn't get used to the rocking of the ship in rough seas, so when I arrived in Singapore, after what seemed to be ages, I was happier than I'll ever be again. I asked someone to take me to the Yi-ho-ch'eng Grocery in Tanjong Pagar. I can't put into words the excitement I felt. I saw that business in the shop was

furious and there was no need to wonder about the success my husband had enjoyed in those ten years, since I could see it displayed right before my eyes.

None of the employees in the store knew me, so I told them who I was and why I had come. A young clerk said to me, "The boss didn't come down today. I'll take you to his home." Only then did I realize that my husband didn't live in the shop; at the same time I guessed he had married again. If not, he certainly wouldn't have kept a separate "home." On the way I tried to sound out the clerk a bit, and it was just as I'd expected!

The rickshaw wound about through the streets and stopped at a two-story, half-Chinese, half-foreign building. The clerk said, "I'll go in first and tell the boss." I was left outside, and it was quite some time before he came back out and said, "The boss has gone out this morning and isn't back yet. His wife asks you to go in and wait a while. Maybe he'll be home soon." He took my two cloth bundles—that was my only baggage—and I followed him in.

I saw that the rooms were plushly furnished. The so-called "boss's wife" was a Malay woman. She came out and nodded perfunctorily. As far as I could see her manner was most disrespectful, but I didn't understand Southeast Asian customs, so I just returned her greeting. She was wearing huge diamonds and pearls in her hair. Among the precious stones, gold, and silver that she wore, her swarthy face was conspicuous in its unbearable ugliness. She exchanged polite pleasantries with me and had someone bring me a cup of coffee while she herself stayed to one side, smoking, chewing betel nut, and not engaging me in much conversation. I thought that was due to the uncertainties of a first meeting, and thus didn't dare ask her too many questions. After a short time I heard the sound of horses coming from the main gate straight up to the portico and guessed it was my husband returning. I saw that he was much fatter than ten years ago and sported a potbelly. He had a cigar in his mouth, and was carrying an ivory stick in his hand. As he got out of the carriage and stopped in the door, he hung his hat on the rack. Seeing me seated to one side, he was just about to ask me something when that Malay woman stepped forward and murmured a buzz of words at him. Although I didn't understand what she said, I could tell from her expression that she wasn't happy at all.

My husband turned to me and said, "Hsi-kuan, why didn't you give me any notice before you decided to come? Who made you take the trip?" I had thought that once he saw me, he would be sure to say some tender words; I had never dreamed that he'd angrily demand an explanation! Then I suppressed my disgruntled feelings and forced a smile, saying, "But Yin-ko,[4] you know that I can't write. And that letter writer in the village, Mr. Wang, often writes the wrong words for people, even to the point of getting the wrong meaning across. So I didn't want him to write for me. Besides, I'd made up my mind to come look for you, and sooner or later I still would have had to set out. Why waste all the time and effort? Didn't you say that if you hadn't returned in five or six years I should come?"

"So you came up with this brilliant idea on your own, huh?" my husband scoffed.

When he finished he went straight into the house. What he said proved that he was a different man from ten years ago. I couldn't understand the reason behind all this. Was it because I was getting old, losing my charm? But I felt that I was so much prettier than that Malay woman. Could it be an accusation of misconduct? But I had pleased him all the years we had been married and had never gone beyond my bounds. To this day I haven't been able to figure out the riddle of Yin-ko.

He put me up on the ground floor, and for seven or eight days didn't come to my room even to speak to me. That Malay woman, however, was very hospitable. She came and told me, "Yin-ko has been rather upset these past few days because you showed up. But don't worry too much about it; in a few days he won't be angry anymore. We're invited to dinner tonight. Why don't you go get dressed and we'll go together?"

These sweet words of hers completely dispelled

my former suspicions about her. I put on a lake-green cotton blouse and a bright red skirt. When she saw them she couldn't repress her laughter. I felt like a country bumpkin from head to toe and was quite embarrassed.

"That's all right," she said. "Our hosts aren't from 'T'ang lands.' They certainly won't notice whether you're wearing the latest fashions. Let's go, then!"

The horse-drawn carriage went on for some time and then passed through a grove of coconut trees before arriving at our hosts'. Just inside the gate was a very large garden, and as I followed her into the sitting room, I looked about me. They really had a strange banquet set up. All the female guests were Malays or Indians, and they were in the midst of an animated and incomprehensible conversation. My husband's Malay wife left me by myself and went over to chat with them. Before long she left with a woman. I thought they had gone for a walk in the garden, and didn't pay much attention. But after a good deal of time, when they hadn't returned, I became a little anxious and said to one of the women present, "Where did the lady who came in with me go?" Although she could get my meaning, I didn't understand a word of what she said in reply.

I sat on a cushion, my heart beating violently. A servant brought a pot of water and gestured toward the set table. I saw the others wash their hands and realized that it was a custom before eating. So I washed my hands. They showed me to a table. I didn't have the faintest idea where I was supposed to sit and simply took the place they directed me to. They prayed before they selected what food they wanted, with their hands, from the platters. The first time I picked up something to eat with my fingers, it was certainly unwieldy, but they taught me how to do it. At that time I was very troubled by the absence of that Malay woman of my husband's, so I wasn't able to concentrate on eating or socializing. After the tables were cleared, the guests kissed me with a smile and left.

---

[4] "Ko" is "brother," used here as a suffix of affection.

I too wanted to follow them out the door, but the mistress of the house told me to wait a bit. I gestured to her in mute talk, and we were dying with laughter when an Indian man in his fifties came in from outside. The woman hurriedly got up and said a few words to him, and then they sat down together. Encountering a strange man while in a foreign place, I was naturally abashed. That man walked up to me and said, "Hello, you mine now. I use money to buy you. It good you stay here." Although he spoke Chinese, his syntax, accent, and tones were all wrong. When I heard him say he had bought me, I couldn't help bursting into tears. The woman was at my side comforting me, trying to be nice about it. It was after nine, and they told me to go in and sleep, but I simply sat, fully dressed, through the night off to one side of the sitting room. How could I have done as they said?

Sir, hearing this much of my story you certainly must be wondering why I didn't choose to die. Well, I had the same thoughts then, but they guarded me like a prisoner—no matter what time it was there was someone with me. As time went on, my violent emotions subsided; I gave up wanting to die and decided to live this life of mine through and see what fate had in store for me.

The man who bought me was Ahuja, an Indian Muslim from Madras. He was a serge merchant, and since he had made a fortune in Singapore, he wanted to take another woman home with him to enjoy life. And my ill fate brought me to this chance, turning me into his foreign curio. Before I had lived a month in Singapore, he took me to Madras.

Ahuja gave me the name Liya. He made me unbind my feet and pierced a hole in my nose, hanging a diamond nose ring through it. He said that according to their customs every married woman had to wear a nose ring, since that was the sign of a wife. He also had me wear a fine *kurta*,[c] a *ma-la-mu*,[d] and a pair of *ai-san*.[e] From then on I became a Muslim woman.

Ahuja had five wives—six including me. Among those five I got along best with the third. The remainder I detested, because they often took advantage of my not being able to speak their language and made fun of me too. My small feet were naturally a rarity among them: although they couldn't stop touching them, I didn't take offense. What I hated was that they told tales to Ahuja about me and made me suffer.

Akolima was the name of Ahuja's third wife— she was the very same woman who had arranged that dinner when I was sold. She was quite fond of me, often urging me to use *surma*[f] to line my eyes, and to dye my nails and palms with balsam flowers. Muslim women use these things daily, as we Chinese employ rouge and powder. She also taught me to read Bengali and Arabic. I remembered that because I couldn't write a letter, I had given Yin-ko an excuse and ended up in this predicament. Therefore, in this period when I hadn't a single friend or relative around, I wanted to use the time to work hard at learning to read a bit. Although Akolima was not much of a scholar, she was more than good enough to be my teacher. I studied a year with her and then could actually write! She told me that in their religion there was a holy book, which wasn't readily given to women, but that later she would be sure to bring it to teach me. She always said to me, "Your fate has been such a painful one because it was predetermined by Allah. Don't keep thinking of your family! Someday it's possible that great happiness will descend upon you, and it'd be too much for you to enjoy." At that time such fatalistic words of comfort could actually raise my spirits somewhat.

Although I never felt a wife's love for Ahuja, I had to live with him as man and wife. Ah! This child of mine (as she spoke she stroked the child's head with her hand) was born the year after we arrived in Madras. I was over thirty when I became pregnant and had never in all my life experienced such pain. Fortunately, Akolima was thoughtful and often comforted me with her

---

[c] Muslim woman's upper garment.   [d] A bodice.   [e] Trousers.

[f] *Surma* is generally used only by men. It is a powder applied to an iron rod and then inserted into the eyes by the traditional Muslim vendor. It is intended as a cooling agent. Colerium, often called *surma,* is used as a sort of eyeshadow and is probably intended here.

words, distracting me from the pain of that time. Once when she saw the pain was particularly bad, she said to me, "Hey, Liya! Be strong! We don't have the fortune of the fig tree,[g] and so we can't avoid the strain of pregnancy. When you're going through painful times, appeal to Allah. If he has pity on you, he'll grant you peace." She helped me a lot when I was about to give birth. Even today I cannot forget her kindness to me.

Not more than four months after I gave birth, a disappointing turn of events distressed me: I was separated from my good friend. She didn't die, but I'll never find out where she went. Why did Akolima leave me? It's a long story, but probably it was my fault.

We had a young, eighteen-year-old widow next door to us named Honna. She had been widowed since she was four. Her mother treated her cruelly, but that wasn't enough. She told her that her sins accumulated from her past lives were great, and if she didn't pay for them through suffering, she would not be redeemed in her next life. Everything that she ate or wore was worse than others'. She often wept secretly in the back yard. Since her garden was separated from ours only by a hedge, when I heard her there, crying, I would go and chat with her, sometimes to comfort, sometimes to offer something to eat, and sometimes to give her a little money.

When Akolima first saw me help the girl, she didn't feel it was right at all. I explained to her time after time that anyone in China could receive someone's aid regardless of creed. She was influenced by me and later also showed compassion herself for that widow.

One day just as Akolima was handing a few pieces of silver to Honna through the hedge, she was accidentally seen by Ahuja. He kept quiet and tiptoed up behind her, gave her a slap and yelled, "You little bitch! You dirty sow! What are you doing here?" As he went back in, so angry that his entire body trembled, he pointed his finger at Akolima and said, "Who told you to give money to that Brahman woman? You stained your own reputation! Not just your own, but mine and that of Islam. *Mā-shā-Allāh!* [5] Take off your *burqa* [h] immediately!"

I heard clearly from inside, but thought that everything would be normal again after the scolding. Who would have known that in no time at all Akolima would come in batting tears as big as pearls from her eyelashes, and say to me, "Liya, we'll have to say goodbye." When I heard this I was shocked and asked immediately, "What do you mean? I don't understand."

"Didn't you hear him ask me to take off my veil? That means he's disowning me. I'll have to return to my family right now. You needn't feel sorry for my sake, for after a couple of days when his anger subsides, he'll probably have me come back."

I was so grief-stricken, I didn't know what to say to comfort her. We sobbed in each other's arms and then parted. Indeed, as the couplet goes, "Those who kill and burn wear moneybelts; Those who repair bridges and fix roads turn into lepers." What an apt description of human life!

After Akolima left, my desolate and sorrowful days started all over again. There were simply no feelings of friendship between Ahuja's four other women and myself. As for Ahuja, as soon as I saw that thin strip of a dark face, with a beard like the spines of a porcupine, I would be filled with loathing and wish that he would leave the next second. My day-to-day life consisted of nurturing my child; aside from that there was nothing to do. I was so frightened by Akolima's incident that I no longer dared venture into the garden for a stroll.

A few months later my painful days were about over, since Ahuja returned through an illness to

[g] This reference to the fig tree alludes to the Koran, where it is recorded that Adam and Eve, having been lured by the devil A-chatsei to eat the fruit Allah had forbidden them to, noticed immediately that their heavenly garments had vanished. They were ashamed by their nakedness and tried to borrow leaves from a tree in Eden to cover their bodies. Since they violated Allah's command, none of the various types of trees dared loan them any. Only the fig tree, moved by their pitifulness, generously loaned them a few leaves. Allah approved of this conduct by the fig tree and conferred upon it the capability of producing fruit without going through the pain of blossoming and being disturbed by the bees and butterflies.

[5] Hsü Ti-shan's original gloss for this phrase is "Allah forbid." However, it should mean "As Allah wills."

[h] A veil.

his Paradise. I had heard Akolima say before that one hundred and thirty days after a husband's death a wife became free, and could pick another match of her choosing. Originally, I wanted to wait until that prescribed day before leaving, but those four women were afraid I'd take advantage of them in the inheritance, because I had a child, so they put various pressures on me to drive me out. I still can't bear to talk about their schemes.

Honna urged me to flee to her older sister's. She told me to send a little money to her brother-in-law, and then I could take shelter with them. I'd already met her sister once, and she was a good person. When I thought about it, running away didn't seem like such a bad idea after all. Those four women were treacherous by nature, and if I'd been caught in their schemes, I'd have had it. Honna's brother-in-law lived in Arcot. I set things up with her and told her to let me know when she found a good opportunity.

A week later, Honna told me her mother had left town and wouldn't be back until late at night, and I should climb across the hedge. This wasn't an easy matter, because it must be done so that I wouldn't cause Honna to suffer afterward. Moreover, a barbed wire ran along the top of the hedge, making it difficult for me. I peered up at the jackfruit tree growing next to the hedge—one branch stretched over to her side, and the tree had grown at a slanted angle. I told her to wait until everything was quiet and then to stand ready underneath the tree.

As it happened, the room I lived in had a small door leading into the garden. That evening, when there was just a little starlight in the sky, I packed my clothes and valuables into a bag, put on two extra layers of clothing, and was just about to leave when I saw my child sleeping there. I really didn't want to take him along, but was afraid that when he woke he'd see I wasn't there and would cry. So I stopped for a moment and picked him up in my arms to let him nurse. Only when he was nursing did I truly feel that I was his mother, and although I had no emotional tie to his father, I had still borne him. Moreover, once I'd gone, he

would certainly be ill-treated. As this thought crossed my mind, tears burst from my eyes. And yet to add the burden of a child to the escape would make my task even harder. After I considered all this over and over again, I finally put him on my back and in a low voice said to him, "If you want to be a good boy, don't cry! All right? You've got to sleep quietly too." Fortunately, it was as if he understood me then, and he didn't make much noise. I left a letter on the bed explaining that I was willing to give up those possessions due me, and my reasons for running away, then went out that small door.

With one hand I steadied the child, with the other carried the bag, as I stole to the foot of the jackfruit tree. I tied the bag to a rope and slowly crawled up the tree, stopping for a moment when I reached the extended branch. Just then the child grunted once or twice. I patted him lightly and rocked him a few times, then pulled the bag up, tossing it over to Honna. I crawled over further and groped for the rope Honna had prepared for me. I grasped it tightly to me and slowly let myself down. My hands couldn't stand the friction and were cut by the rope in no time.

After I had descended and thanked Honna, I quickly left her house. Not far from Honna's gate was the Adyar River. Honna went with me to rent a boat. After she had explained things clearly, she went back. The helmsman was an old codger and probably didn't understand what Honna said. He rowed me to the Saidapet Terminal and bought a ticket for me. Since it was the first time I had taken a train, I wasn't very clear about the regulations of rail travel. When he told me to get on, I just did as I was told. Only after the train had started and the conductor examined my train ticket did I learn I had boarded the wrong train.

When it arrived at an intermediate stop, I quickly got off, intending to wait for a return train. By that time it was the middle of the night, and the people in the station said no train would be going into Madras until dawn. I was forced to sit in the transit lounge. I spread my *Ma-chih-la*[i] over me and put my hands in my pockets,

---

[i] A Muslim woman's outer garment.

pretending to sleep. At around three or four o'clock, looking up by chance, I saw a very distant gleam of lamplight through the railing. I quickly went to the platform and, pointing to the light, questioned the people standing there. There was one man who smiled and said, "This woman can't tell one direction from another. She mistakes the morning star for the headlight on a train." Taking a good look, I couldn't help laughing as I said, "I'll be darned! My eyes aren't seeing right!"

As I faced Venus, I thought of something Ako-lima had said. She once told me that that star was the transformation of a woman who had been a siren good at bewitching men. Because of this I remembered that the feeling between Yin-ko and myself had been basically good, and that if he hadn't been fooled by that foreign bitch, he never could have stood for having his beloved first wife sold off. My being sold couldn't have been completely Yin-ko's responsibility. If I could have stood those painful days in China, and if I hadn't decided to go to Singapore to rely on him, none of this would have happened. As I thought it over, I had to smile at my own impulsiveness in fleeing. I figured that since I had made it all right out of the place, what need was there to impose on Honna's sister? When I had reached this conclusion, I returned to my waiting place with the child in my arms and summoned all my energies to resolve this question. The things I'd run off with and my ready cash together were worth more than three thousand rupees. If I lived in a village, they could support my expenses for the rest of my life. So I decided on an independent life.

The stars in the sky one by one gathered in their light, until only Venus still twinkled in the east. As I looked at her, it was as if a voice beamed out from her saying, "Hsi-kuan, from now on don't take me for a woman out to bewitch men. You should know that nothing which is bright and sterling could bewitch. Among all the stars, I appear first, to tell you that darkness will soon arrive; I return last, so that you may receive the first rays of the sun on my heels. I'm the brightest star of the night. You could take me as the diligent awakener of your heart." As I faced her, I felt ex-

uberant, and can't describe the gratitude I felt in my heart. From that time on, whenever I saw her, I always had a special feeling.

I inquired about where an inn was to be found, and everyone said I'd have to go to Chinglepet to find one. So I took another train there. I didn't live in the inn for long before I moved to my own home.

That house was bought with the money I got in exchange for my diamond nose ring. It wasn't large—only two rooms and a small yard, with pineapple trees planted all around as an enclosing wall. Although Indian-style homes weren't good, I loved the location near to the village and could not afford to be bothered by appearances either inside or outside. I hired an old woman to help with the housekeeping, and besides raising the child, I was able to find time to read some Indian books.

Every day at dusk, a rather solemn song would drift to my ears. I went into the garden for a look and saw that it came from a small house opposite mine. At first I didn't know the purpose of their singing, and only later did I understand they were Christians. I met the mistress of the house, Elizabeth, before long. And I often went to their evening prayer meetings. Her family could be considered the first friends I had in Chinglepet.

Elizabeth was a most amicable woman. She urged me to attend school. Moreoever, she promised to take care of the child for me if I did. I felt that only a person completely without ambition would idle away the days, so the very next year she arranged for me to study at a woman's school in Madras. I went home once a month to visit my child. She took care of him for me very well, so that I didn't have to worry.

Since while at school I had nothing to divert my attention, my grades were very good. In this period of about six or seven years, not only did my knowledge progress, but my beliefs also changed. And since graduation I've worked as a teacher in a small village not far from Chinglepet. So that's my whole life in outline; if I were to go into details, I couldn't finish relating everything in a year's time.

Now I'm going to Singapore to look for my husband, because I want to know just who it was that sold me. I firmly believe that Yin-ko couldn't possibly have accepted it. Even if it was his idea, then someday sooner or later he'll repent.

Hsi-kuan and I had been talking for two full hours or more. She spoke very slowly, and the child bothered her from time to time, so she had not told me about her student life in much detail. Because she had talked for such a long time, I was afraid she would be tired out, and so I didn't go on asking questions. I just said to her, "That you were able to find your way in life during such a period of drifting is really admirable. If you would like me to help you look for Yin-ko tomorrow when we reach Singapore, I'd be glad to do it."

"It's not really that I'm so smart. This way was merely one opened for me by some unknown heavenly mentor. When I was in school I was moved the most by *Pilgrim's Progress* and *Robinson Crusoe*. These two books gave me much comfort and many things to learn from. Now I'm simply a female Crusoe. If you would help me search for Yin-ko, I'd be very grateful. Since I don't really know Singapore, tomorrow I'll need your—"

At this point the child began pestering her to go into the cabin and get some toys for him. She stood up, but continued speaking: "Tomorrow, I'll need your help."

I stood up and bowed as she left, then sat back down to record the conversation we'd just had in my diary, which I carried with me.

After twenty-four hours some mountain peaks appeared faintly in the southeast. All the people on the ship were very busy. Hsi-kuan too attended to packing and didn't come out on deck. Only as the ship was entering the harbor did she appear, holding her child by the hand. She sat with me on a bench. "Sir," she said to me, "I never expected a chance to see this place again. The leaves of the coconut trees are still dancing; the sea gulls above the water are still flying back and forth to welcome strangers.

"My happiness is the same as it was nine years ago when I first met them. In the blink of an eye these years have passed—like an arrow—yet I can't find any difference between what I saw then and what I see now. So the expression 'Time is like an arrow' doesn't refer to the speed at which an arrow flies, but to the arrow itself. For no matter how fast time flies, things show no change—as something attached to an arrow, although it may fly with the arrow, doesn't go through any changes at all. But though what I see today is the same, I hope Yin-ko's affections won't change as slowly as natural phenomena; I hope he'll change his mind and accept me now."

"I know how you feel," I said. "I heard this ship will moor at Tanjong Pagar. I think that when we arrive, you should wait on board at first; I'll go ashore to inquire a bit and then come back for you. What do you think?"

"This is getting to be more and more of a bother to you," she said.

I went ashore and asked at a good number of homes, but they all said they didn't know any Lin Yin-ch'iao. I couldn't find even a trace of the sign for the grocery, "Yi-ho-ch'eng." I was getting desperate, and after being on my feet for the better part of the day, a bit tired, so I went into a Cantonese teahouse to rest. By chance I picked up a clue there when I questioned the shopkeeper. According to him, because Lin Yin-ch'iao had sold his wife to an Indian, he incurred the ill-feelings of the numerous Chinese in this area. At that time, some people said it was his idea to sell her, others said it was that foreign bitch who sold her; in the end it couldn't be said for sure who did it. But his business suffered immensely because of this. He saw that he couldn't stay in Singapore any longer, and so closed his shop and moved, lock, stock, and barrel, to some other place.

When I returned and had reported all that I had learned to Hsi-kuan, and, moreover, urged her to return to China, she said, "I can never go back. With this brown-skinned child, as soon as I got home, people would shame me and laugh at me. Besides, I can't read Chinese at all. If I went, I'd just starve to death. I plan to stay in Singapore for a few days, to ask carefully about his whereabouts. If I can't learn anything, I'll return to India. Well, I've become an Indian now!"

From what I made of the situation, I truly could

not think of anything to persuade her to return to her home town, and just sighed and said, "Your life is really full of misfortune, isn't it?"

But she smiled. "Sir, in all human affairs, there is basically no distinction between the painful and the pleasurable. When you try too hard, it is painful; when you have hope, it is pleasurable. As you're actually doing something, it is painful, but to recall it is pleasurable. In other words, everything in the present is filled with suffering. The past, recollections of it, and hope are pleasant. Yesterday, as I related my experiences to you, you felt they were painful. My narration of past circumstances, displayed before your eyes, led you to feel that they were events in the present. If I recall them myself—the long separation, being sold, my escape, etc.—none of these events are without happiness. So you needn't feel sorry for me. You must be able to take things easy. I would only ask one thing of you: when you go back to China, if it is convenient, would you go to my village and let my mother know the latest news? She must be over seventy—she lives in Hung-chien. She's the only relative I have left in China. Outside her gate there is a very tall olive tree. If you ask for Mame Liang, everyone will know."

As the boat left the dock, she stood on the shore waving me off with a handkerchief. That sincere expression on her face is something I can never forget. Not more than a month after I got home I went to Hung-chien. The broken-down house under the olive tree was sealed up by old vines. Through a crack in the door I could see faintly several sets of rotting wooden ancestry tablets on the table. How could there have been a Mame Liang there?

Yü-kuan

by Hsü Ti-shan

Translated by Cecile Chu-chin Sun

It seems that it was only yesterday, but, in fact, some decades have gone by.

It was during the First Sino-Japanese War [1894–1895]. Most of the people and soldiers were addicted to opium; they became so emaciated that they hardly looked human. Even those who didn't smoke opium were as torpid as figures of clay. Guns and battleships were like funeral utensils: more decorative than useful. Although we had lost the war, not too many people seemed to mind it much, nor even to have suffered from it. There were, however, some who were directly affected. Yü-kuan's husband was one of them. He was a sailor on a battleship and was killed less than an hour after the fighting started. At that time, Yü-kuan was in a county of her native Fu-kien province with practically no savings. What her husband left her, aside from a house slightly bigger than the temple of the local deity, was a boy hardly two years old. She was only twenty-one and still young enough to remarry if she wished. But she thought remarriage would be inconvenient with the child around and that it was better that she bring up this fatherless child on her own. Should the child one day by chance get a government post and apply on her behalf for a posthumous title to honor her chaste widowhood, then after all her life would not have been a total waste.

Ever since she made up her mind not to marry again, Yü-kuan's door had remained closed most of the time. She eked out a living making embroidered tobacco bags for the Shoo-Hang shop.[1] It was impossible to get any help from her friends or relatives; she had very few to begin with anyway. What she earned was just about enough to cover food and clothing. To send the child to a tutorial class was utterly out of the question, as she could not even afford to pay for the school supplies, not to mention the ten strings of cash for tuition each year. Even if she sold the house, which she had no desire to do, she could get no more than twenty taels of silver. Her husband had a cousin, several years her senior, who came to visit her quite frequently. Every time he came, he urged her to have her husband's coffin shipped home from Wei-hai-wei. In fact, nobody knew for sure where the body was, and his request was just a way to force Yü-kuan to sell the house or her son. What he wanted most was for Yü-kuan to remarry so that he could cash in on the fringe benefits. Although Yü-kuan knew that her brother-in-law was trying to take advantage of her, she still maintained some minimal politeness to him.

Nobody in town cared a straw about what her brother-in-law's name was. Though he had attended the country school for two years and had been given a formal name, he was soon dismissed for poor academic performance. Thus acquaintances persisted in calling him by his nickname,

---

[1] "Soo-Hang" is a short form for Soochow and Hangchow, respectively in Kiangsu and Chekiang provinces. Both cities are noted for their scenic beauty, cultural heritage, textile products, and handicrafts. A Soo-Hang shop, however, does not deal in products from Soochow and Hangchow exclusively.

Fen-sao.[2] Yü-kuan was evasive each time he broached the subject of remarriage, but he did not want to give up on her yet. He told her one day point blank that should anything happen to her rather delicate child, she would probably regret for the rest of her life having wasted her youth. He also added that since she could not send the child to school, how was he expected to get anywhere? Even if she could afford the tuition, what guarantee was there that he would pass the official examination? And even if he did pass the examination, it still remained to be seen whether he could get a position in the government and let his mother enjoy her life thereafter. For Yü-kuan, these importunities were only Fen-sao's tricks to make her find someone to support her, and she regarded them as a form of curse. Whenever she thought of his coaxing and threats, she would lash out with such words as: "You heartless scoundrel, may your body rot by the roadside!" But that was as far as she could go.

Yü-kuan had given some thought to reporting Fen-sao to the county yamen[3] so that there would be a record there in case anything happened. But, on second thought, she realized that it was not proper for a young widow to present herself in a public place like that. Besides, Fen-sao's request to have the coffin shipped home was not entirely unreasonable. She herself also knew that she should find some way to have the coffin shipped back. It was, after all, not right to leave it in such a distant place. But what could she do, sheltered and weak as she was? She wasn't about to sell the house, let alone her son, and she didn't want to remarry. Though she didn't go to ask whether her husband's remains had been found, she did make up her mind that even if his clothes and hat were all that could be located, they should still be shipped back to be buried. She could not wait until her son, her only hope, grew up to help her carry out this task. She wanted to leave her home town, so she wouldn't be bothered by Fen-sao any more. But that was nothing but a dream—first of all, she did not have any money to make such a move; second, being illiterate herself, she could not teach her son to read and write on her own; third,

she might risk exploitation if she moved to a place where she did not know anybody; fourth—there were numerous other reasons against such a move. All things considered, it seemed that the best bet was still to keep her door closed and live like a snail in its shell. If no signs of danger were visible, she could open the door and put her feelers out and see what was happening; the minute she found some signs of danger, she would immediately lock herself up and curl up in her shell. Many a tear had been shed over the problem of her husband's remains. At times she would light a candle in front of her husband's tablet in the living room, praying and making wishes.

Fen-sao still came to bother her despite the closed door, thus defeating her decision to lead a snail-like existence. Courtesy demanded that she open the door whenever he came. But how could she let a man visit her frequently, being a widow and all that? True, they were relatives, and there was nothing ambiguous about the relationship. But in a society hungry for scandal, it was rather difficult to prevent the neighbors from gossiping. Though she wasn't familiar with Confucian classics like the *Book of Rites,* still she realized that such time-honored sayings as "Unmarried men and women are not supposed to be intimate" and "Brothers-in-law and sisters-in-law should be kept at a distance from one another" might prove useful on occasion. Unfortunately, these teachings did not really apply to someone like her, who was not in the gentry class. Worse still, because Fen-sao realized that she was afraid of his visits, he came even more frequently to annoy her. Eventually the neighbors believed that there was really something going on between them and gossiped about them all over the place.

On the same street there lived a "God-worshipping" woman, Chin-hsing, whom people called Hsing-kuan. Her husband's surname was Ch'en. A few months ago, he had beaten up a relative of his wife's: under threat of arrest he had escaped, and his whereabouts were unknown. The cause of all this was that after Hsing-kuan's nephew converted her to Christianity, she returned home and smashed all the sacred images

---

[2] "Dung broom."   [3] *Yamen* was the administrative headquarters of a Chinese government official.

and ancestral tablets. At this, her husband, Ch'en, naturally hit the ceiling and went to his wife's family for an explanation. He made the mistake of almost beating his wife's nephew to death. The minister of the church, who was a Westerner, decided to handle the case and insisted that the county magistrate locate the criminal and punish him severely. Now that Ch'en had fled, the case was left pending.

Nobody in the neighborhood dared touch Hsing-kuan, since she had some foreign backing from the church. But at heart people despised her for being such a shameless "rice Christian"[4] who even got her own husband into trouble. Her nephew, a pharmacist in a missionary hospital, was now regarded as a specialist in prescribing strange potions to make people destroy the sacred pictures and tablets of one's ancestors. Against all odds, Hsing-kuan had become a very fervent Christian and evangelist since her conversion. But she was not a professional missionary. She drew her income from an annual interest of about three hundred dollars from stock she owned in a pharmaceutical company in a trading port. She had moved to Yü-kuan's neighborhood only recently with her two daughters, Ya-li and Ya-yen. Ya-li was just over two, and Ya-yen was only a few months old. In the beginning, the two families did not have much contact with each other. Only lately had Yü-kuan begun to visit Hsing-kuan frequently in order to avoid Fen-sao's harassment. Yü-kuan would often come to visit Hsing-kuan, and whenever she decided to spend the whole day at Hsing-kuan's place, she would even bring her own food along with her. Being quite lonely herself, Hsing-kuan found her company welcome.

There was no furniture to speak of in Hsing-kuan's two-bedroom house, but everything in it was spic and span. In the living room there was a picture from *Pilgrim's Progress* hanging in the middle of the wall, and on the desk there was a very thick Bible with gilt edges and a black leather cover. Much of the gilt had already turned dark red, and the leather also had lost its sheen. Its dog-eared corners, as well as the slips of paper sticking out as markers, showed only too well that the owner of the book must consult it several times a day. There was also, sitting in a corner of the living room, a small organ, whose keyboard had obviously been fingered several times a day to accompany the singing of psalms. All this was new to Yü-kuan. She felt much better now that she had changed from a snail to a bird who left its nest in the morning and came back only at night. After spending some time at her neighbor's, she realized, to her surprise, that the so-called "rice Christian" was not only as kind and personable as most people, but was also a source of comfort to others. She asked Hsing-kuan one day what it was she believed in. No matter what Hsing-kuan said, she could not make Yü-kuan understand the reason why everybody was a sinner and must repent in order to gain a new life through salvation. To regard oneself as a sinner? Ridiculous! To offer one's life to complete strangers for nothing? Ridiculous! That men and all living creatures were created by God was equally ridiculous. Who ever heard of a virgin conceiving by herself? That was even more ridiculous! Yü-kuan chuckled secretly when she thought about these ridiculous stories, but she did not want to, nor could she, reason out what was wrong with them. Sometimes when Hsing-kuan was not around she would open the Bible and steal a glance or two at it. But what a pity that it was all written in a foreign language! She could not figure out how Hsing-kuan could read this foreign book, since she had never heard her speak a foreign language. She asked and was told that the Bible she saw was written in the Chinese vernacular in romanization, which one could learn to read in three days; to write in seven days; and in ten days one could express whatever one wished with it. She encouraged Yü-kuan to learn this language. For days on end, one could hear Yü-kuan read "A," "B," "C," as if it were a kind of chant. Hsing-kuan was right that it was easy to master this foreign language, because in seven days Yü-kuan could read that thick book as fast as flowing water.

There was a foreign girl who came to visit Hsing-kuan quite often. Yü-kuan had never before been within five feet of a foreigner. When oc-

---

[4] Chinese converts who go to church for the sake of getting alms rather than to worship.

casionally she saw them on the street, she would always step aside, and never did she dare look them in the eye. She was basically afraid of foreigners, and that was that. She was afraid that foreigners might cut off one's hair to make some kind of charm out of it; she was afraid that foreigners might dig out one's eyes to make drugs with; she was afraid that foreigners might hex her by making a sign of the cross on her forehead and get her to do all kinds of things to blaspheme the gods and disgrace her ancestors. One day when she was doing some needlework, the same foreign girl came again, and Yü-kuan, as expected, immediately withdrew to the back room. After the usual greetings, Hsing-kuan began to chat with the girl about the church. Yü-kuan could not understand what the foreign girl was saying, but from Hsing-kuan's responses, she knew they were talking about the pharmacy where Hsing-kuan had some shares. She heard from the foreign girl that the other church members were attacking the pharmacy because it sold morphine. The manager of the pharmacy repented at a Sunday church gathering and was willing to contribute a sum of money to build a church in the country. She had come to tell Hsing-kuan about this because Hsing-kuan was one of the shareholders in the pharmacy. As Hsing-kuan did not know much about business, all she could bring herself to say at this point was "Thank God!" As the foreign girl was leaving, she asked Hsing-kuan to help her find an amah. She would pay six hundred cash per month, including room but not board.

When Hsing-kuan returned to the room, it suddenly occurred to her that she should do her best to talk Yü-kuan into taking the job. Yü-kuan figured that she could still save two hundred cash a month if she spent four hundred on food. Besides, since her housing was taken care of, she could rent her own place out and collect at least one or two hundred cash a month. As a way of saving for her son's future educational expenses, this was far better than working her figures to the bone doing needlework for less than ten or twenty cash a day. And the most important thing was that once she started working for the foreigner, Fen-sao would not dare trouble her anymore. Before she took the job, however, she asked Hsing-kuan to guarantee that the foreign girl would not force her to drink the "mind-boggling"[5] potion, cut off her hair, or dig out her son's eyes while she was sleeping. She was still a nervous wreck after the date was set to begin her job. She feared that she could not understand the language; she feared that the foreigner might be bad-tempered. She feared this and that, and she feared everything.

The foreign girl allowed her to bring the child with her and gave them a very small room right behind the church. Her mistress's house was about fifty feet away, separated from her quarters by some trees. She could not find anybody to rent her house, but since it was close to the church anyway, she was thinking of returning there to sleep after work. But then she was afraid that Fen-sao might come to trouble her, and besides, there was nobody to take care of the boy if she left him at home. So she figured that it was better for her to have the house locked up and come back quietly on Sundays to see that everything was all right. On the first and the fifteenth of every month, she returned before dawn to clean the place and burn a stick of incense before the sacred tablets of the gods and her ancestors. Sometimes she would stand there and pray awhile. To her, this old house was like her family shrine, which made her feel secure; she was not really bothered by the fact that she could not rent it out.

Now that Yü-kuan was working for the foreigners, Fen-sao dared not bother her. For a long time they had not met, until one Sunday morning Yü-kuan came home to find him waiting at the door. He had learned from Hsing-kuan that Yü-kuan always came home around that time on Sundays. The minute he stepped inside the house, he began to harp on the sale of the house and the shipping of his cousin's coffin back. Then he asked Yü-kuan for a loan. Naturally, Yü-kuan was

---

[5] During the last days of the Ch'ing Dynasty and the early Republican years, Chinese countryfolk were suspicious of almost everything Western. They were afraid of having their pictures taken, as they thought the camera was a kind of "soul-sucking" machine. The "mind-boggling" potion referred to here is presumably Western medicine in liquid form.

not happy about his visit at all, and she used some strong words, asking him not to disturb her anymore; otherwise she would ask the church to report him to the county yamen. In the middle of this bickering Hsing-kuan came in; she took Yü-kuan's side and reproached him too. Outnumbered, Fen-sao left the house with only a bruised ego. The two women followed him out, locked the door from the outside, and went straight to the church. Fen-sao watched them out of sight and immediately came back to the front door, which, unfortunately, was securely locked. There was no way to break in because the walls on all sides were very high. The more he thought about what had just happened, the angrier he became at Hsing-kuan. He felt that Hsing-kuan should not have urged Yü-kuan to work for the church to begin with. To vent his anger, he decided to go to her house and see if there were any valuables there worth taking. He didn't expect that Hsing-kuan's place would also be locked tight. He followed the walls all the way to the back door and saw nothing but empty fields around him. He picked up a thick wire from a pile of dirt and started poking at the bolt; in a little while he got the door open and went inside. There were the two little girls sleeping in the bed and a few suitcases lying around which, again, were all locked. Since there were no valuables on the desk, he began to try the locks on the suitcases. The noise almost woke up the children; so he gave up trying. A thought suddenly occurred to him. He crept over the bed, picked up Ya-li gently and wrapped her in a small blanket. As he was picking up the blanket, he discovered two silver ingots under the sheet. What a happy surprise! He snatched them up immediately and, holding them tight against his chest, disappeared like a puff of smoke.

I

With Ya-li in his arms he reached the outskirts of the city and began to wonder what he should do with the little girl. At that time there were people who were interested in buying girls under three to be used as housemaids when they grew up. Those who had daughters liked the idea even more, since these housemaids could become part of their daughters' dowries. Fen-sao decided to sell Ya-li, but not in the immediate area. He had to go somewhere else. After he had covered some distance, he stopped by the roadside to rest awhile. He took out the ingots and enjoyed feeling their weight—about ten taels—in his hand. As he was putting the ingots back in his pocket, he saw somebody coming toward him from a distance. Fearing that he might be followed, he immediately picked up the child and began to run. After a few turns in the road, he came to a ferry about to depart and hurriedly jumped aboard. His heart was still pounding with fear when he finally made his way to a seat at the bottom of the cabin.

After many close calls, he finally got to Amoy. Carrying the baby, he really did not know what to do next. He didn't realize that without a go-between who knew all the tricks of the trade, he would not be able to sell the child himself. And he didn't want to make a scene by auctioning off the baby on the street. After a few days, he decided to go to Southeast Asia lest he be discovered.

On one misty morning, he left his inn and followed a group of foreigners out to the wharf. As this was his first voyage, he did not notice that there were many different lines at the port, nor did he know how to get on board the big ship with the other passengers. So again, indiscriminately, he got onto a small boat near the ferry and thought to himself that it must be the right one, since there were already a lot of people on board. It turned out that the ship was bound for Shanghai. As soon as he was aboard, he tried to find a place to hide. It was only after the ship left port that he learned from others that he was on the wrong ship. There was nothing he could do except bear it with patience while he tried to figure out what to do next.

For the first couple of days the sailing was smooth, but it was midsummer and inside the cabin it was unbearably hot. Ya-li's crying for Mama certainly did not make life any easier. He told people in the cabin that the child was his niece. Because his brother had passed away in

Malaysia, he had made a special trip to fetch his sister-in-law and the child back to China. Unfortunately, his sister-in-law had gotten sick on the way and died. Worse still, he had gotten onto the wrong ship. The story he told was so plausible and touching that his audience was quite moved; some suggested that since quite a number of people in Shanghai were from Ch'üan-chou and Chang-chou, the same area he came from, he should go to the Ch'üan-Chang Club House for financial assistance or help in finding a job. Seeing that his fellow travelers were not suspicious, he began to relax. After that he was often seen on deck walking with the child.

On the day before the ship reached Shanghai, an old woman servant came to Fen-sao and said that her mistress would like to have a look at the baby. Before Fen-sao got a chance to ask her anything, she had already begun to tell him that her mistress had lost a girl about half a month before. When her mistress saw his baby in the cabin yesterday, she felt very sad, and could not help crying over her own daughter. The old woman also told Fen-sao that her mistress was still crying just now and earnestly requested that the girl be taken to see her. She added that her mistress was a very kind person and would definitely give him some money for his trouble. After exchanging some information with her about each other, Fen-sao let the servant take the baby to the cabin reserved for government officials.

It was a long wait for Fen-sao. He became very nervous, and this made him perspire profusely. He went up on the deck, trying to steal a glance at the door of the lady's cabin. After a long time, the servant finally came out and told him that the minute the mistress had seen the baby, she had felt that there was an amazing resemblance to their own daughter; the nose and even the hair were exactly alike. It was really fortunate for the baby, said the servant, that the mistress took such a liking to her.

Upon hearing this, Fen-sao was shrewd enough to drag the servant to a quiet corner of the deck and ask her who her mistress was. From what she said, he realized that her mistress was the wife of

a circuit intendant named Huang. He was an expert on foreign affairs serving under the powerful imperial commissioner, Li Hung-chang. The servant urged him to ask for a high price. But he was thinking of taking advantage of the opportunity to ask for some long-term employment instead. Since it was rather inconvenient to bargain on board the ship, he arranged to meet her after the ship landed.

Ever since she had seen Ya-li, Mrs. Huang had felt much better. She could not bear to leave the child even for a minute. As soon as the ship landed, she sent somebody to take Fen-sao to a respectable inn. She rushed to the inn as soon as she had settled some business at home. Knowing that she was very anxious to have the child, and that he could definitely make a deal, Fen-sao pretended that he couldn't bear to part with her. Naturally, this made Mrs. Huang all the more anxious. As Fen-sao did not want to cut himself off completely from the Huangs, he begged her to give him a small job in lieu of cash. This did not appeal to Mrs. Huang, however, for she feared some later inconvenience. It took quite a while before both parties settled on the terms: Ya-li was to be traded for one hundred taels of silver plus a menial job for Fen-sao.

Since Fen-sao was virtually illiterate, Mrs. Huang could only recommend him to the yamen of the regional garrison as a captain of bodyguards. He changed his name and did so well in the yamen that the circuit intendant, in less than a year, recommended him for an appointment as a captain of the sentry squad. He was greatly encouraged by this promotion, and as a result he spent his spare time reading and studying. Surprisingly, he became quite good at both reading and writing in a relatively short period of time. Out of gratitude for Mrs. Huang's help, he would from time to time pay visits to the Huangs' residence in Shanghai and at the same time see how Ya-li was doing.

Ya-li turned out to be quite a delicate little lady, with a maid waiting on her all the time. There were all kinds of imported toys in her room; she had twenty or thirty dolls alone. She would take a ride with her mother every day in a Victorian-style carriage. It goes without saying that what she ate or drank was of the best quality. She had grown to be a pretty girl and was admired by all those who met her as a very fortunate girl. Mrs. Huang, who loved Ya-li as her own daughter, did not allow anyone to breathe a word that she was adopted. Mrs. Huang seemed to be fated not to have any children of her own. She had a series of miscarriages, and her last child had died only a year after it was born. When she adopted Ya-li, she went to the temple of the city god to have her fortune told. The temple keeper read the divination slip and told her it was her fate to adopt a child who would in turn herald a brother.

Mrs. Huang loved Ya-li very much, not only because she felt healthier and happier after the adoption of the baby but also because the Bodhisattva had assured her that the adoption would bring good luck. Intendant Huang did not spend much time at home, since he had to follow His Excellency Li practically everywhere he went. Aside from Mrs. Huang and the young lady, therefore, the household was all servants. Most of the servants knew that Fen-sao was the young lady's uncle, and therefore were especially polite to him whenever he came. Naturally, he was no longer called Fen-sao. For lack of something more suitable, everybody called him Captain Li. During the New Year holiday or other festivals, Captain Li would always pay his respects to Mrs. Huang. She would always remind him not to disclose his relationship with the young lady. One can well imagine that under the circumstances she didn't dare slight him.

Now that Captain Li had gotten a government job, he thought perhaps he could do something about his cousin's remains. He wrote to Wei-hai-wei, but got not a word in response. As for his sister-in-law, he did not dare write her for fear that it would bring him trouble.

Hsing-kuan, when she discovered that her daughter had been kidnapped, immediately reported it to the minister of her church. But nothing happened even after the county magistrate put up a notice promising a huge reward. The unfortunate police officer in charge of the case was given several beatings by the magistrate because he failed to produce any results. Naturally, everybody had good reason to suspect that it was Yü-kuan's brother-in-law who did it; but nobody could prove his guilt without material evidence. After several months had passed, people gradually forgot about the whole thing. Even Hsing-kuan herself was slowly coming to her senses.

As for Yü-kuan, she had felt much better since her brother-in-law disappeared. Her missionary mistress liked her very much because she was both smart and quick. Since evangelism was her business, the mistress, whenever she had time, would preach to Yü-kuan. With the prior knowledge of the Bible she had acquired at Hsing-kuan's place, Yü-kuan was always quick to get the whole point long before her mistress had finished. Her mistress was especially pleased with her competence and thoughtfulness, which set her apart from the other servants. Naturally, the evangelist was very interested in converting Yü-kuan, asking her to unbind her feet, and even promising to educate her to be a "handmaid of the Bible" if she so wished. This would not only increase her salary to more than two taels a month, but would also enable her to send her son to a missionary school without paying tuition.

After several weeks of consideration, Yü-kuan decided to accept the offer. For the time being, her mistress sent Yü-kuan's son to a minister's home to play with some foreign children, As for unbinding her feet, she knew she had to obey, although she did not like the idea much. Her program of studies, aside from the Bible, included catechism lessons, *Pilgrim's Progress* and the singing of psalms. Even though her mistress told her that the way of Heaven was bright, holy, and true, and that of men dark, sinful, and false, she still could not find her way. Nor could she find any angels. As for devils, she believed in them and trusted that she had met them in her dreams. In fact, she did not think that the way of men was as dreadful and loathsome as her mistress had described it.

II

After one year's course work, Yü-kuan became a Christian. She had her own opinion about the doctrine, although on the surface she accepted whatever she was told. Her son, now named Li Chien-teh, had already started at a missionary school. He was a very bright boy, always at the top of his class, and was well liked by his teachers. In less than two years, he learned several thousand characters and was able to speak a good bit of English. In a short while, Yü-kuan became a "handmaid of the Bible." Her job included distributing copies of the Gospels and pictures of miracles all over town as well as instructing the womenfolk in Christian doctrine. She was so eloquent and so well trained that nobody could outtalk her, despite the fact that she herself did not totally believe in what she said. But for the purpose of preaching and argument, she managed very well. She often heard the foreign ministers tell her colleagues that "To serve God, one has to sacrifice some material comfort," but she, for one, was quite satisfied with her pay. Besides, she was especially pleased with the arrangement for Chieh-teh to earn his tuition by picking up tennis balls for the foreign ministers every day after school. Besides, she no longer had to stay in the small room behind the church. She had now moved back to her own home. People in the neighborhood were somewhat afraid of her since she was a Christian under the protection of her church. The couplet on her door was now changed to a Christian one which read "Love thy neighbor as thyself; live on earth as in Heaven"; there were four characters pasted on the lintel which read "Worship the True God." While nobody knew when and where she had moved the family shrine in the living room, it was almost certain that she had wrapped up her ancestral tablets and put them in a bag and hung them somewhere under the beams of the bedroom. The door to that room was often closed, as if it were a sacred place. She would not destroy the ancestral tablets, because she believed that it would be sacrilegious to do so, and it would also bring bad luck to her son. Another such secret place in the house was underneath the kitchen stove, where she stored her silver. She and her son slept in another bedroom.

Before long, the Boxer Uprising started in the North; her city was fortunate enough to escape involvement, thanks to the local officials who asked all foreigners to move to the treaty port. Yü-kuan's foreign mistress therefore entrusted the house behind the church to Yü-kuan before she left the city. Yü-kuan did a very good job for her mistress. As a result, when the mistress returned several months later, she put more trust in Yü-kuan's ability and her devotion as a Christian. By and by, Yü-kuan became quite well known for her missionary work. But whenever she was asked, "Where does God live?"; "If God were truly kind, why would He allow devils to harm people all over and then condemn innocent victims?"; or questions about "Immaculate Conception," she could only answer, with all her eloquence, that these were mysteries beyond the comprehension and intelligence of mortal human beings. Sometimes when she had some problems with Christian doctrine, she did not dare bring them up with the foreign missionaries; when she did ask, she was not satisfied with their answers. She thought to herself, since the church was trying to teach people to do good and to lead them to the right path, who cared whether what one believed in was a son born of a virgin or a goblin who popped out of a crack in a rock? She also believed that there might have been some miracles, but that this had little to do with doing good. All these ideas she kept to herself. Outwardly, she had to pretend that she practiced what she preached: she had to oppose idolatry and ancestor worship, as well as the concept of reincarnation, dismissing such practices and beliefs as superstition. Her romanized vernacular Bible did not succeed in enlightening her very much, nor did she believe that those scholarly looking foreign missionaries really and truly believed deep down in what they preached either. But she wore a very conspicuous kind of black blouse and skirt and always carried that great big Book in one hand an an umbrella in the other. She walked like a goose with her pointed, long feet, which had to cover some ten miles a day.

Gradually she became used to walking all over town, and when she went to the country she would normally rest in the shade whenever she was tired. Later the districts she had to cover increased, and sometimes she had to stay overnight in the country when she had gone too far to get back to the city the same day. There was no fixed place for her to stay—sometimes she would stay in a church when there was one; most of the time she would stay in the homes of her Christian friends. Aside from the fact that they did not like to listen to her preaching the doctrine of repentance and worshipping the true God, people in the country were nice to her, as she was not only personable but would often bring gifts to them, such as used glass bottles, or empty biscuit boxes discarded by the foreigners, or some medicine like quinine or balsam oil.

Because of her oustanding services, she was sent to a neighboring town; she was allowed to come back home only two or three days a month. In fact, this special permission to return was granted because Yü-kuan had to come back every now and then to take care of her son, since he had to remain in the city for school. At the same time, the church could receive a monthly work report from her.

Not far from the highway, which stretched for more than ten *li*,[6] were the tombs of her husband's parents. She had been there only once, when they were first buried. But since she became a Christian, she had never gone there to pay respects. One afternoon, when she passed on this road, it suddenly occurred to her that the tombs of her husband's parents were right in the vicinity. She searched awhile and found them almost buried in weeds, which she soon asked some farmers to root out. By the time they were cleared, it was already dusk, too late for her to go back to town. At this time of day the surrounding mountains were covered with evening clouds, and homebound birds were chirping rather noisily in the forest. The paddy fields were bubbling with the sound of flowing water, and the rising mists were hovering over wildflowers, whose colors

were no longer distinguishable in the twilight but whose fragrance was still lingering in the air. With one hand holding an umbrella, the other carrying a satchel, she slowly approached a small village behind a grove. In between the village and the grove there ran a little brook. The small village was called Chin-li; it was rather sparsely populated, since most of the men had gone to Southeast Asia to make a living, and also because, since the village was right on the highway, it was a convenient place to cross not only for the regular travelers, merchants, and transients who passed by it every day, but also for soldiers and bandits. Nearly the whole village was populated by old farmers, women, and children; the rest had gradually moved out. The missionaries had bought a big, run-down house there, which was to be rebuilt into a church and a school. Yü-kuan knew that the house was bought from the contributions of the pharmacy where Hsing-kuan had some shares, so she decided to spend the night there.

The house had been bought some time ago, but construction work had not yet started; only a caretaker stayed there to look after the place. It was a huge house, with more than ten rooms, including several bedrooms, a living room, and a desolate garden. Outside the front door, there was a big fish pond whose water ran almost level with its sides. It was so quiet that the least noise could be heard clearly, such as the beating of bats' wings near the eaves, the wind rustling the weather-beaten New Year's couplets pasted on the columns, the scurrying of rats into their holes, the scraping of beetles on the windowpanes, the murmuring of the trees from the back yard, or the splashing of the fish in the pond. All these sounds in the dead of night could make one unused to them shudder and believe that ghosts did in fact exist.

The caretaker, Ch'en Lien, was in his forties. It was the first time that Yü-kuan had come here to spend the night. After he knew who she was, he began to prepare supper for her. He set the table under the melon trellis outside the door, and asked Yü-kuan to sit there instead of going inside

[6] One *li* is roughly one-third of a mile.

because he was afraid that mosquitoes might follow her into the room once the light was on. After supper, Yü-kuan began to chat with him about the history of the house and the neighboring villages. He sat on the threshold. Under the dim light from a small storm lamp hanging from the trellis, his face was blurred. He held a pipe, and his knees were drawn up against his chest. He told Yü-kuan that the house was haunted, and that was why its previous owner decided to sell it to build a big mansion outside the grove which lay opposite the brook. He also told Yü-kuan that he had been looking after the house for quite some time. When he learned that it was to be sold to the church he was going to quit, but the church begged the owner to keep him there until school started. From what he said it was obvious that he was not a Christian; in fact, it became clear that he was very much against other people taking up the religion. He was not a native of the village, but after staying there for a long time, he had become well acquainted with it. Looking after the house was a part-time job to earn him some extra money and provide a roof over his head. His regular job was selling meat, which he did by carrying baskets on his shoulders while blowing a horn to attract travelers from one village to another. Normally, by noon time, he would have sold about twenty catties of meat, and would call it a day unless there was a religious festival going on in the village. Then there would be operas staged outdoors by the villagers to express their thanks to their deities. On such occasions he would set up a stand for selling tidbits of cooked meat below the makeshift stage. Sometimes he would go to other villages and stay there for days before returning.

It was quite something for Yü-kuan to talk to a man at night, something she had not done since her husband died in the war. She was a bit carried away by this, and they kept talking until midnight, when Ch'en Lien took her to a room in the back. Then he locked the door from the outside and slept beneath the melon trellis in the yard. Thinking over what they had talked about and his blurred features under the dim light, Yü-kuan could feel the heat rushing through her body as she tossed and turned in her bed. She could not sleep at all. Her eyes were wide open as she listened to the outside noises, which frightened her more and more until she felt that the ghosts were pressing toward her. She had no way to hide herself, for the weather was warm, and she'd had no use for any blanket as she lay on the bamboo bed. She did not dare extinguish the oil lamp for fear that she might be even more frightened in the dark. Nor did she dare open her eyes again once she had them closed, for she had sensed that a big, black shadow was standing in front of her. All she could do was lie still in bed, soaked in cold sweat, without daring to make a move, even when the mosquitoes came to sting her. Finally, she decided to get up, take out the Bible from the satchel on the desk, and put it on the bed. She began to chant the Nicene Creed and the Litanies of the Lord, which made her feel much better. Before long she went to sleep with the Bible next to her, although the loud noises on all sides continued unabated. Throughout the night, she felt that the ghosts were pressing upon her, making it impossible for her to breathe. Finally, when the roosters began to crow and the color of the horizon in the east turned white, she sat up in bed. But she was still in a daze, her eyes staring at the Bible. She thought that perhaps Chinese ghosts were not afraid of the Holy Bible or foreign prayers; otherwise why hadn't there been a moment of peace last night? She got up and went to the door and saw that Ch'en Lien was already up and was boiling some water to cook breakfast for her. Ch'en Lien asked if she had slept well. Yü-kuan did not dare tell him anything except that there were too many mosquitoes. Seeing that beside Ch'en Lien's pillow there was also a little book, she asked him what it was. Ch'en Lien told her that it was the *Book of Changes* because he was afraid of ghosts. It suddenly dawned on her that Chinese ghosts were only afraid of Chinese texts.

This eventful night convinced her that ghosts existed after all. She felt somewhat feverish after breakfast. Ch'en Lien was certain that she had caught a chill during the night, but she did not think so. She looked at Ch'en Lien closely, and, without knowing what came over her, felt happy and contented. Despite the fact that Ch'en Lien was looking after her the entire morning, her temperature still didn't go down; instead there was another kind of heat burning inside her. Ordinarily, Ch'en Lien would carry his meat baskets to town at the crack of dawn, but today he was delayed, and, seeing that she was really sick, on his way to town he ordered a carriage to take her home.

After riding in the carriage for a day or so, she finally got home and rested for a few days before her temperature went down. She told no one about her illness. She thought that perhaps her sickness had something to do with the ancestors of her husband's family. They might be pestering her because she was seldom home to worship them.

When Chien-teh came home, most of the time he stayed with Hsing-kuan. Yü-kuan's house had been kept locked up ever since her transfer, except on the occasions when it was used by the Christians for social gatherings. When she went to bed at night, she tossed and turned, feeling very restless. Finally, in the dead of night, she got up and untied the bag from the beams, took out the ancestral tablets, and put them on the desk. Then, after she had changed clothes and washed her hands, she burned incense and said a prayer in front of the tablets. Although she was a Christian now, she had never changed her old habit of worshipping the ancestors because she figured if there was a life after death, there was all the more reason for descendants to worship their ancestors. She felt that the souls in Hell might not be free, but those in Heaven should have the privilege of communicating with their descendants. As for the notion that one's soul would wait around in the tomb for the Final Judgment, this was something that she could not subscribe to. Actually, she was convinced that, because no soul would know whether it was destined for Hell or Heaven until Doomsday, ghosts had to be floating all over the place. She did not tell anybody about this because it did not accord with what the Bible said or what the ministers had taught her. She also believed that all ghosts, especially the vicious ones, liked to dominate human beings; therefore it was necessary that she carry a charm book with

her to ward off the evil spirits. Granted that her ancestors might not be vicious, nonetheless she must still pay them due reverence in order to keep them contented.

After worshipping she felt much better and healthier, and from that time on she carried a copy of the *Book of Changes* in her satchel whenever she went on a trip. Occasionally, she would leaf through the pages, but to her surprise she did not understand anything, even though she did recognize some of the characters. She thought the mystery of the text lay precisely in its unintelligibility. Like most Chinese of her time, she felt that no paper with printed or written words upon it should be trampled on. For this reason, whenever and wherever she came upon a shredded slip, a torn envelope, or a crumpled letter, she would pick it up and dispose of it in a nearby furnace.

III

Several years went by swiftly. Chien-teh was now in his teens; Yü-kuan was stationed in Chin-li to take care of the church business in the neighboring villages. Chien-teh continued to live in the city and went to the church-operated school there. He usually came to Hsing-kuan's place every day after school to play with Ya-yen. Hsing-kuan was very fond of Chien-teh and thought the children were a perfect match whenever she saw them together. She told Yü-kuan what she had in mind about the young couple, but the two women were not in complete agreement. What Hsing-kuan would like Chien-teh to do was to become a doctor after seven or eight years of study in a medical school. Afterwards, he could open a pharmacy in a treaty port. She had known quite a number of doctors returning from abroad who had gotten rich this way. Some of them had earned enough to buy a lot of property in the countryside and build mansions in the city after being in practice for only two years. Naturally, she wanted her future son-in-law to invest his talent in such a promising profession, which would surely pay off ten thousand times over. Yü-kuan, however, felt differently. First of all, the ministers had hoped that her son would take up theology and become a missionary. Second, she herself still hoped that her son could get a government position; this would please her greatly, for she might thus become entitled to a small tablet, if not an arch, in honor of her widowhood. As for the first point, Hsing-kuan was of the opinion that an intelligent boy should go into medicine rather than theology. As for the second point, she reminded Yü-kuan that a Christian should not go to a regular school, since these schools required their students to worship images of Confucius and Mencius, and that would be a violation of church regulations. Moreover, Hsing-kuan added, since Chien-teh had not gone to a regular Chinese school, how could he be expected to pass the civil service examination, which was the only way to get a government post? It seemed that theoretically Hsing-kuan had the upper hand. But Yü-kuan did not believe that a pharmacy was necessarily a gold mine; she thought that as long as her son studied hard and could write good compositions, there would definitely be somebody who would recommend him for a government post. Whatever the difference of opinion, and whatever directions Chien-teh's future would take, in fact the two children were getting to be so very close to each other that finally the mothers agreed to contract a marriage for them.

By the time Chien-teh had learned how to write compositions, the civil service examination system was being abolished. This naturally disappointed Yü-kuan somewhat, but she did not give up her original hope. Chien-teh's getting a government post still remained the main obsession of her life. She heard from many sources that young students could still get the same kind of academic distinction as *chü-jen* and *chin-shih* [7] no matter where they graduated from, so long as they had spent some time studying abroad. Thus, she asked the minister to send her sor abroad; but as a condition for sending him, the minister insisted that Chien-teh study theology and return to do missionary work. This, of course, was not the kind of future she had hoped for her son. For lack of any better alternative, and as a temporary measure, she decided to put her son in a missionary school (the only institutions for Western knowledge at the time), with free tuition and room and board. She thought that in eight or ten years she could save enough to send Chien-teh abroad. She had been told that in the United States students could easily find a part-time job, and that those who worked hard enough could even send money home. So all she needed was to save about fifteen hundred dollars or so for travel expenses. Having thus decided, she went back to the country to continue her work.

Yü-kuan's savings increased as months flowed into years. As she was constantly occupied with ways and means of sending her son to study abroad, her health was seriously affected. She became absentminded, suffering from poor appetite and insomnia. One night around the time of the Ch'ing-ming Festival,[8] she received a letter that Chien-teh was seriously ill, and her heart immediately beat faster. When she finally went to sleep, after tossing about in pain, she dreamed that her husband's parents were standing in front of her in rags, looking wretched and undernourished. After she woke up, she thought about what she had dreamed and felt that her son's illness must be due to the fact that for years she had not visited their tombs to offer sacrifices. From the morning until late in the afternoon she struggled with a dilemma: now that she was a Christian, she was not allowed to offer sacrifices at the tomb. Nor could she buy any paper money to burn there. She had often advised others not to waste cash on paper money, and now it was her turn. She was greatly disturbed by this, and, out of sheer restlessness, she went outside, crossed the bridge over the little brook, and went to the grove for a walk.

Since the time when the old house was re-

---

[7] *Chü-jen* and *chin-shih* refer to successful candidates in the civil service examination system before the founding of the Republic of China. A *chü-jen* is one who has passed the provincial examination and a *chin-shih* one who has passed the examination held in the imperial capital. For readers who want to have a feeling of what the atmosphere of a traditional Chinese examination hall is like, see Yeh Shao-chün's "Horse-bell Melons" in this anthology.

[8] In the spring; see footnote 1 to "Medicine," p. 9.

modeled into a church, Ch'en Lien had not worked there as a caretaker. As usual, every morning he traveled all over town selling meat. By sheer coincidence, Yü-kuan ran into him outside the grove and began to chat with him on the bridge. Ch'en Lien was quick to discern that something was bothering her, and soon he learned about her nightmare. Ch'en Lien told her without any hesitation that it was perfectly in order for her to worship her husband's parents according to the traditional customs because her husband's parents were not Christians. He advised her that if she did not want people to know about it, she could leave in the middle of the night; that would definitely get her to the graveyard early the next morning, and in that way she could still return to the city afterward if she wanted to. He also told her that he would prepare the offerings for her, such as wine, meats, incense, and candles. Yü-kuan thought him very sympathetic and decided to leave all the preparations to him. She would meet him outside the village when everything was ready. People in the country often traveled in the middle of the night in order to speed up the journey; in fact, Yü-kuan had done it several times herself, and so nobody in the church would suspect anything unusual.

Under the silvery, moonlit sky, Yü-kuan and Ch'en Lien seemed to be the only two people left in the world. The mountains and the trees, together with their own shadows, spread an eerie quietness about them. Only the occasional barking of some dog from a distant village reminded them that they still belonged to this world. As they walked past a tree, a startled bird flapped its wings in the dead quiet of the night, frightening Yü-kuan and sending chills over her body. In order to dispel her fear, Ch'en Lien walked beside her: if he were to walk in front of her, she might not be able to keep up with him, and if he were to walk behind her, she would not dare to take one step forward on her own. Thus, they chatted as they walked side by side. Their conversation invariably centered on their own families. Yü-kuan took Ch'en Lien into her confidence, telling him she hoped her son could become somebody one day so that she could be assured a peaceful retirement. But Ch'en Lien seemed reluctant to tell her much about his family except that he was all alone, spending as much as he earned. By the time they began to talk about their own lives, the morning clouds, white as a fish's belly, had spread across the eastern horizon, and before they knew it they had reached their destination. Ch'en Lien immediately began to put the offerings on the ground and then stepped aside to let Yü-kuan pray awhile before the tombs of her husband's parents. Holding the incense sticks, she knelt down and kowtowed a few times. Before they parted company, Yü-kuan insisted that Ch'en Lien take the offerings back with him for his meals. After some protest, Ch'en Lien accepted.

Watching her receding figure, Ch'en Lien thought to himself that, after all, not all the rice Christians were bad. He admired her willpower and sympathized with her plight. He sighed unconsciously, dutifully picked up his meat baskets, and slowly began to walk toward the town.

As for Yü-kuan, she was touched; Ch'en Lien was the first man since her husband's death who was able to arouse that mysterious sensation in her whenever she thought about him. She kept thinking about him, and sometimes a smile would appear on her face, which, however, would immediately be replaced by a serious expression of misgiving. Perhaps Ch'en Lien did not like her; after all, she was as much a stranger to him as he was to her. Nevertheless, the thought "If we were husband and wife" kept coming to her on her way home, so that she even forgot why she was hurrying back home, not to mention the length of the journey. After she got to the town, she hired a carriage and continued with her fantasy until she was suddenly, as if caught unawares, brought to the front of her home. She knocked anxiously at the door. When the door opened, she was shocked to find her son, Chien-teh, standing before her because he was supposed to be sick in bed and should certainly be resting at such an hour. Chien-teh explained that he was not really sick, only feeling not very well the other day, so he had taken several days off school. But the fact was that he missed Ya-yen very much and would often make up any excuse to come home. As soon as Yü-kuan stepped into the living room, Ya-yen appeared from inside to welcome her home.

Chien-teh told his mother that had it not been for Ya-yen's company, he would have been bored to tears. Seeing that his mother was grateful for what Ya-yen had done for him, Chien-teh took the opportunity to ask his mother to set the date for their marriage. Yü-kuan was finally persuaded and gave her consent. After taking out her savings for the wedding expenses, Yü-kuan asked the church to let her come back to work in the city for a year or so.

It was a church wedding, and Yü-kuan was asked to make all the arrangements for the ceremony. The minister said a prayer to bless the newlyweds and performed all the other rituals pertaining to a Christian wedding. When Yü-kuan returned home, she expected her son and daughter-in-law to kowtow to her; but, to her dismay, they simply bent their backs a bit toward her, which was neither bowing nor kowtowing. She did not know what that was supposed to mean. It was the astute Hsing-kuan who explained to Yü-kuan that the reason they couldn't kowtow to her was that the church forbade people to kneel down to anything except the image of God. Yü-kuan was surprised to find that the church was so strict about kneeling and kowtowing. Not to worship one's ancestors was already difficult to accept; and what a shock it was that parents were not even allowed to receive the formal respects of their own children! Besides, she thought, it was really not right to omit any reference to her ancestors during the wedding ceremony. So on the morning of the fourth day, when Chien-teh and Ya-yen went out to visit friends, she very respectfully invited the ancestors down from the beams and paid homage to them, which somehow eased her conscience a bit.

IV

Things seemed to be going smoothly after the wedding. Yü-kuan was enjoying all the blessings of being a mother-in-law. Whenever she came home, for instance, she would always be served a cup of hot tea or a bowl of hot soup. Her daughter-in-law was surprisingly docile and re-spectful; everything was mother this and mother that, which naturally pleased Yü-kuan tremendously. In turn, the mother-in-law took every opportunity to sing the praises of her daughter-in-law.

But as flowers cannot stay fresh for long, in less than half a year Yü-kuan began to dislike Ya-yen. Perhaps, after all, a daughter-in-law is never the same as one's own flesh. But what caused this change of attitudes was something more specific. Chien-teh had joined the Revolutionary Party. It was Ya-yen's fault for not having dissuaded her husband from getting involved, and she hadn't even let Yü-kuan know about it. It turned out that Chien-teh had planned to go to T'ung-an with some comrades to start an uprising there in order to support the effort in Wu-han. Unfortunately this information leaked out, and more than ten of them were arrested, including Chien-teh himself. The county magistrate had already executed some of them. When the news reached Yü-kuan, she immediately went into hysterics, pleading for help from both God and her ancestors. She felt that her daughter-in-law had been really stupid not to interfere with her husband in a case involving something as serious as capital punishment. She blamed it all on Ya-yen, who could do nothing to defend herself but cry as her mother-in-law lashed out at her with both words and tears.

Yü-kuan went to see the foreign minister of her church, asking him to go to the county yamen to intercede and bail her son out. At the same time, she used a lot of money to bribe the people in the yamen. She thought that if she used enough money, definitely someone would come forward to say that her son had been charged on false grounds. Moreover, the minister's intercession would also be a move in Chien-teh's favor, because it was very difficult for the magistrate to turn the minister down, lest he get a memo from either the consul or the deputy ambassador. That was certainly no laughing matter, and the magistrate knew it. As expected, Chien-teh was released immediately after the minister's intercession, and the only ordeal he went through was an admonition from the magistrate. The minister was, of course, very happy about the verdict; he held Chien-teh in his arms for a while while praying with his eyes looking straight up at Heaven. As they stepped out of the county yamen, the minister told him not to seek after worldly fame, but to devote himself to the world beyond, and so on and so forth. Chien-teh was much moved by this, thinking that he really should do whatever the church asked him to do in return for the grace he had received from God. As for the Revolutionary Party, he really did not know why he had joined it in the first place, so that it did not matter much now if he washed his hands of it. Naturally, the minister wanted him to be a minister. Chien-teh agreed, and thus after his graduation from high school he was sent to a seminary. The minister had a few things to say to Yü-kuan on this matter. He told her not to lose hope in Chien-teh's future despite the fact that he might not be able to satisfy all her expectations. What was important for her was working toward a higher goal and striving to live in a more spiritual world.

Now that Chien-teh had gone to the seminary, Yü-kuan returned to the country to continue with her missionary work, leaving Ya-yen alone at home. Her savings had been exhausted on Chien-teh's marriage and defense. When she thought about it, all her anger was directed against Ya-yen; so when she returned home, she never stopped finding fault with her, though Ya-yen was as obliging and obedient as before. At first, Ya-yen suffered all this with forbearance, keeping her tears to herself. After a time, she lost patience, and the two started quarreling. Yü-kuan thought that the fault clearly lay with Ya-yen, and that everybody would agree with her that her daughter-in-law was not filial; she didn't realize that other people might think differently. For one thing, her son did not agree with her; nor did Hsing-kuan think that Ya-yen was to blame. What irked her son most was that whenever he came back from school, all that his mother did was complain; nothing Ya-yen said or did could escape her harsh criticism. Finally, he couldn't take it any more and asked his wife to try to ignore his mother. This infuriated his mother so much that she vented all her bitterness on him, saying that he was not much of a man to listen to his wife and

that he was conspiring with his wife to make her life miserable. What made her truly indignant was that whenever Chien-teh was at home, Ya-yen kept him in their room all day talking privately. She was either a licentious woman or a big gossip. In any case, the daughter-in-law was no good for the family. Whenever Yü-kuan became desperate, she wanted to talk it all over with Hsing-kuan to see what she would say. It did not take Yü-kuan long to realize that Hsing-kuan was on her own daughter's side. For instance, whenever Yü-kuan complained about Ya-yen's overintimacy with Chien-teh, to the point of neglecting *her,* Hsing-kuan's response was that it was only natural for young couples to be like that, since the Bible clearly stated that husband and wife should be as one; moreover, her daughter was, after all, married to a husband and not to a mother-in-law.

One day, when Yü-kuan was bothering Hsing-kuan again with the same old story, Hsing-kuan finally blew up at her and spit out something to the effect that if Yü-kuan was really jealous of Ya-yen's intimacy with her son, why didn't she consider remarrying herself?! Hsing-kuan also told Yü-kuan not to be too harsh on Ya-yen, as her daughter was pregnant, and, should anything go wrong, Hsing-kuan would never forgive her. At this, Yü-kuan flew into a rage, and, in a hysterical moment, slapped Hsing-kuan in the face. Hsing-kuan, of course, would not stand for this, and so the two women instantly came to blows.

After a few exchanges, Hsing-kuan suddenly reminded Yü-kuan that, since she was a professional missionary, she should not be as willful as she was. Yü-kuan, flushing with shame, felt as if she were being tortured by the cruelest of punishments. She sat down panting, and tears trickled down her cheeks and onto her lapel. Shame-facedly, she begged Hsing-kuan for forgiveness. Hsing-kuan said a few words of comfort, and, using her own life as an example, told her how she herself had managed to carry on after she lost her husband and her daughter. Hsing-kuan said that if one truly trusted in God and learned to be more accepting and tolerant, one would feel much better. She advised Yü-kuan not to strive so hard for selfish satisfaction, fame, or prestige.

Hsing-kuan believed that if Yü-kuan had more confidence in her children's love for her, they would then act in a filial manner.

After she left Hsing-kuan, Yü-kuan still felt very much ashamed of herself. Yet she was still puzzled by the kind of "Christian ideal" that Hsing-kuan advocated; reality was the only thing that really mattered to her. To Yü-kuan, having the respect and compliments of one's friends and relatives while living, and enjoying posthumous fame afterward, was what life was all about. Although she was supposedly treading the heavenly path, she was, in fact, looking for a worldly path that would take her to the same end. She was not sure she was on the right track. Yü-kuan was afraid that her old age might be terribly lonely and miserable, since both her son and daughter-in-law were so cold to her, and she did not believe that one could live in this big, wide world all by oneself. Of the six blessings in this world—wealth, position, fortune, longevity, prosperity, and peace—she should try to get at least one.

When Yü-kuan got back home, she went straight to bed and did not even bother to answer when Ya-yen asked if she needed anything before sleep. She slept the whole day, and in her waking moments she felt that her present job was absolutely meaningless when she reflected on her past hopes and ideals in contrast to her actual situation. In fact, she thought, her job was actually against her conscience. On the other hand, she believed that to educate her son was to follow her conscience, and that her son was in a way her "boss." It therefore followed that she had to listen to whatever her "boss" told her with all her devotion and energy, just as in any other profession where the employee had to be totally at the disposal of the boss. She was a professional woman, not a nun. But things seemed to have changed now: she no longer felt there was any meaning in her work since her "boss-son" no longer belonged to her; nor did he listen to her or need her anymore. She began to wonder if there was any real meaning in her job. She also realized that, after all, she had to think of herself first. She began to think about her late husband, and Ch'en Lien. Strangely enough, the very name of Ch'en Lien

could make her forget about all her problems, as if he were the light at the end of the tunnel which would definitely lead her out of darkness despite all the other uncertainties.

So she decided to quit her job as a missionary and live with Ch'en Lien in the village for the rest of her life. She thought that Ch'en Lien would definitely go along with her. So she wrote a letter of resignation to the church without giving any reason for her decision. The foreign woman in the church asked her to stay and also wanted to know if there was anything that Yü-kuan did not like about her present job. Yü-kuan couldn't produce any specific reason. Seeing things from a woman's point of view, the foreign lady took Yü-kuan's reticence to mean only one of two things: either Yü-kuan had been insulted by the nonbelievers in the country, or she had been raped by some tramp in the fields. If the latter were the case, there was nothing that could be done about it except silence and prayer. The foreign woman did her best to get Yü-kuan to stay on the job, at least temporarily until a further decision could be taken by the church.

Yü-kuan went back to Chin-li, intending to talk it over with Ch'en Lien. It so happened that there was a festival going on in the neighboring village, and, as usual, Ch'en Lien went there to sell cooked meat. Yü-kuan spent two good days waiting for him, during which time her mind underwent all kinds of changes.

Several days later the festival was over, and Ch'en Lien came back to the village, feeling quite pleased with himself about the money he had made. Over the years, Ch'en Lien had managed to save quite a bit of money, enough to buy a few acres of land. But instead he had put all his savings in a local banking house to earn interest. Sitting on a hugh camphor-tree root protruding from the ground and trying to figure out how much he had made during the day, he saw, to his great surprise, Yü-kuan walking toward him. The tree was not a secluded place but a favorite resting spot for the villagers. Both Ch'en Lien and Yü-kuan liked the place very much. Seeing that Yü-kuan was coming, Ch'en Lien immediately stood up and invited her to sit down for a chat. It was not long before the subject of marriage came up. For Ch'en Lien it was a big surprise that a rice Christian was willing to marry a pagan! But after Yü-kuan told him about her feelings and her situation, Ch'en Lien was somehow tempted. He told Yü-kuan that, if they decided to get married, they shouldn't stay where they were but should go to Southeast Asia to begin life anew. His savings over the years would provide enough capital to start a small business there.

Yü-kuan had never told Ch'en Lien about the bad relationship she had with her family, and there was no way for Ch'en Lien to know anything about her life either, since he had not been back to the city in more than a decade. Ch'en Lien, however, was less reticent about his life this time; he volunteered to tell Yü-kuan that he used to live in the city too. But because he had committed some crime there, he had taken refuge in Chin-li. After listening to Ch'en Lien's story, Yü-kuan thought to herself: he couldn't be anyone but Hsing-kuan's husband. Didn't he tell her that his wife's family name was Chin, and that he had two daughters? She was lost in thought and didn't utter a word. Ch'en Lien, however, thought that she was perhaps wrapped up in her own musings about their move abroad. Finally, Yü-kuan got up and told him that they should both reconsider the whole thing very carefully before reaching a final decision. Feeling somewhat lost, she went back to the church and kept debating with herself whether she should confront Ch'en Lien with the truth of the matter or simply let the whole thing drop.

Ch'en Lien had originally been very much against foreign religion, but he had gradually changed his attitude since he met Yü-kuan. Though he had no liking for the church, whenever he saw Yü-kuan he chatted with her without knowing when to stop. He confessed to her that he used to be short-tempered and had often gotten himself into fights, but since he came to live in the countryside, he had mellowed a great deal. And, since he had gotten to know Yü-kuan, he said, he had become as meek as a lamb. Nobody knew, of course, why he was attracted to Yü-kuan. He went about his business quietly and was

regarded in the village as an honest and decent man. Marrying Yü-kuan was not something Ch'en Lien dreamed about; but since it was Yü-kuan who brought it up, there seemed no reason for him not to go along with her. Yü-kuan, however, had cooled off considerably after she realized that he was Hsing-kuan's husband. But at this point she did not want to tell him about her relationship with Hsing-kuan because she was still tempted by the idea of starting a life with him in Southeast Asia.

As Ya-yen was expecting soon, Hsing-kuan was getting so excited and busy knitting and making clothes for her future grandchild that she simply did not have the time for anything else. Yü-kuan's resignation did not concern her at all. Chien-teh was home too, to take care of his wife. When the day came, a Western-style midwife was called in; this was very much against what Yü-kuan had had in mind. Yü-kuan had been thinking of calling in an old-fashioned midwife who would be much cheaper than the modern one, who used forceps and things like that. But Yü-kuan's attitude had changed drastically in recent months, and she showed no interest in anything other than waiting for the church to let her resign so that she could remarry. And so she did not interfere with the arrangement and let Hsing-kuan handle the whole thing.

The midwife had failed to deliver the baby after one whole day's labor. Ya-yen was in such pain that her whole body was drenched in cold sweat; everybody in the family was a nervous wreck. Finally, late at night, a baby boy was born, but its mother's face was chalk white. While people were busily occupied in taking care of the newborn baby, Ya-yen had quietly left this world. Yü-kuan discovered that, though Ya-yen's heart was still warm, her breath had already stopped, and she uttered a wail. Finally, after much heart-rending crying and screaming, the family began to accept the fact that Ya-yen had died. The midwife couldn't do anything about it either; all she did was mutter to herself as if half in prayer and half confessing something. Hsing-kuan completely lost control, crying frantically; Yü-kuan was simply in a daze, sitting there without saying a word. Chien-teh was all tears. He left the next morning to make arrangements for the funeral. It took the family several days to finish with the funeral and all the other related chores. Afterward, Hsing-kuan took the baby home with her.

Ya-yen's death seemed to have revived all Yü-kuan's hopes for Chien-teh. The old saying that "One mountain cannot accommodate two tigers; one country cannot tolerate two kings," was not entirely groundless. Now that there was only one woman in the house, she had the peace and quiet to think about her own life. She no longer felt the need to get married again. Instead, she felt quite content being a grandmother. She figured that it would be kind of ridiculous for her, now a grandmother, to get married even though she did not look her forty-two years. She chuckled at the very thought of getting a step-grandfather for the little baby. What she should do now, she thought, was to keep her mind on her work and her son's education. So she decided to retract her former resignation and accept the standing offer of the church to continue with her missionary work. But, on the other hand, she felt somewhat guilty about Ch'en Lien. She felt she should tell him about Hsing-kuan's present situation, but she did not know exactly what to tell him. Nor did she break the news to Hsing-kuan for fear that the latter might get jealous and say something nasty to embarrass her.

V

After Ya-yen's death, the church transferred Yü-kuan back to the city to make it easier for her to take care of her grandson. Chien-teh had now graduated from the seminary, and, as there was no appropriate job for him in the church, the principal of the seiminary, who appreciated his talents, sent him to the States for advanced studies. Occasionally, Yü-kuan would manage to send some money to him. Although financially she was worse off than before, on the whole she was much happier.

Time passed very quickly, and, before she knew it, Yü-kuan's grandson, T'ien-hsi, had gradually grown into a big boy. The church, again, sent her

back to work in Chin-li and other neighboring villages, but she no longer allowed herself to bare her feelings to Ch'en Lien as she had years ago. As for Ch'en Lien, he had also cooled off considerably because, after all, he had not been the one who had initiated the whole thing. Besides, it was so many years ago. He had now opened a small shop in the downtown area, and, except for collecting bills or placing meat orders, he seldom came back to Chin-li, much less had a chance to meet Yü-kuan.

The war in Europe affected the smooth running of the missionary work. Not only had the mission headquarters cut down on the funding, but the fighting and killing among the Christians themselves gave those who opposed Christianity a perfect excuse to resist the missionaries. Besides, all kinds of "isms" like nationalism and communism were beginning to spread from the city to the country, and their various doctrines were also beginning to be translated into action. This was a stormy time for the social system as well as a high time for new ideological waves of various kinds. Yü-kuan's very limited kind of cleverness certainly was not enough to withstand the surging torrents of the times. The elementary school teachers in the country often argued with her about religion, and sometimes she would find herself at her wit's end in a heated debate; often all she could do was close her eyes and pray. It would be an exaggeration to say that the foundation of her faith was shaken on such embarrassing occasions, because she did not have any religious foundation to begin with. She had never really been clear as to what she was asked to believe in. In fact, she was not really interested in her missionary work. She was just marking time until Chien-teh came back to give her a peaceful and comfortable life.

Chien-teh had been away for almost nine years. In postwar America, life was almost a daily holiday. He enjoyed it very much, so that when it was time for him to come back, he decided to stay on. In the last two years, he no longer asked his mother for money; he was able to make some by doing bookkeeping for a minister. Among the Chinese students abroad, he was considered by many as quite a capable person.

One evening at a party, he met a girl student,

Huang An-ni from Nanking. It was love at first sight for both of them. To Chien-teh, she looked so familiar that he felt he must have met her in a previous life. An-ni had only her mother back home; her father had left a huge amount of money deposited in the bank under their names. It was difficult to say what field she was in because she shifted her major all the time. She studied literature for a year or so, gave it up for home economics; got tired of that, transferred to painting; then dropped it for music, as she could not stand too much exposure to the sun while sketching; left music for philosophy; gave that up again to take up politics, for philosophy was too esoteric and gave her a lot of headaches. She had been in the States for quite some time now and was known in many circles. Some nasty students called her the campus butterfly. As far as she was concerned, however, she couldn't care less what people called her; she was simultaneously a butterfly, a flower, a politician, and an artist. When she posed as a flower, other people would follow her, protect her, and flatter her. Because she had changed her field so many times, her stay in the States naturally was prolonged, and before she knew it she was twenty-eight. It did not matter how long she decided to stay in the States, because money was no problem at all. Whatever comfort was available in the United States she made available to herself. She never missed anything, be it a ball game, mahjong, a dinner party, a dancing party, or a cocktail party.

Chien-teh was one of the boys she was interested in; she felt they had a lot in common. From the first time they met they had been as close as Siamese twins. One day Chien-teh got a letter from Hsing-kuan, saying that she wanted to introduce him to a relative's daughter, whose beauty would put even a goddess to shame. She hoped Chien-teh would agree to an engagement. Chien-teh showed the letter to An-ni, who didn't say anything to him for a long time. Chien-teh then knew for sure that she had really set her heart on him and so became more intimate with her.

Now, Yü-kuan had known that her son had a girl friend abroad; she was as pleased as she was anxious for his return, because this meant that he wouldn't be back soon. From time to time, she would receive letters from Chien-teh, sometimes with pictures of both him and An-ni, telling her what a wonderful girl An-ni was. She was delighted by this development, and all her unhappy memories of Ya-yen seemed to be behind her now.

For some time Chien-teh had not asked Yü-kuan to send any money, so her savings had gradually began to increase. T'ien-hsi was still living with Hsing-kuan, but her indulgence made it possible for him to play hooky all the time. He often left the house early in the morning and did not come back until school was over. Though the boy's absence was reported by his teachers, Hsing-kuan didn't pay much attention to it. Yü-kuan never really got to know how her grandson was doing at school, because her visits from the country never lasted more than ten days.

T'ien-hsi was practically a little monkey king [like the one in the novel *The Journey to the West*]. He would try everything: climbing trees, digging holes, and scaling walls, and even overturning the tiles of roofs. His teachers simply could not do anything with him. One day, with a little friend from school, he went to Hsüan-yüan Kuan, a deserted Buddhist temple in the suburbs. They climbed up to the shrine, trying to tear off the pendants from the headpiece of the statue. The deity looked quite dignified with both hands very solemnly holding a jade tablet. The two kids got up to its sleeves, and, all of a sudden, its two clay hands, with their sleeves, crushed down together. It was as if the deity suddenly had come out of its clay body to push the two sacrilegious urchins to the floor. T'ien-hsi's head hit the bars surrounding the shrine and bled very badly, while his little friend only got his skin scratched. Seeing that T'ien-hsi was seriously injured, he opened his satchel and took out some tissue paper to stop the bleeding. The tissue paper was completely soaked in red in no time, and it was not until he wrapped T'ien-hsi's head with his shirt that the bleeding stopped. Despite T'ien-hsi's wound, they were not yet ready to go home; they still wanted to fool around in the temple. Some scores of years ago it had been much frequented, but, later on, it virtually became a tomb to house the coffins of those people from other places whose bodies could not be immediately brought back to their home towns for burial because of the continuous fighting over the years. It was said that the temple was so terribly haunted by these wandering ghosts that not even beggars dared spend the night there. Except for the rectangular boxes lying all over, there was not a single soul in the temple; its windows and doors had long since been torn down by the people for fuel.

The little boy went to the back yard to see if there was anything interesting there, while T'ien-hsi nursed his head wound sitting on the threshold. Shortly afterward, a big noise exploded from the back. T'ien-hsi immediately rushed to the spot, only to find his friend lying in a pool of blood, with his eyes wide open but unable to utter a single word. T'ien-hsi was completely dumbfounded; he tried to help his friend sit up straight, but the boy had already stopped breathing. T'ien-hsi's body was stained all over with his friend's blood. Not knowing what to do, T'ien-hsi put down the dead body and sneaked out of the temple in fright.

T'ien-hsi did not dare go straight home, but waited in the grove until after sunset, when all the houses were lit up. When Hsing-kuan saw him stained all over with blood, she was shocked speechless. T'ien-hsi did not dare tell the truth but said that he fell in the street and fractured his head. Hsing-kuan gave him a severe scolding while she was busy getting water to wash him, helping him change his clothes, and feeding him. That evening, T'ien-hsi went to sleep right after eating, which was no different from what he normally did after a day's fooling around outside.

Two days later, news broke out in the city that somebody had been killed in the Hsüan-yüan Kuan Temple. This attracted a lot of spectators and newsmongers, old and young, men and women. In less than half a day, the temple was bustling with all kinds of activities, as if a fair were going on there. Vendors of all descriptions, selling peanut soup, fritters, and sesame cakes, had already lined up on the street. The gate of the temple was now guarded by a group of soldiers to prevent any loiterers from getting in. But the soldiers themselves were completely surrounded by onlookers, as if they were the main attraction. In a little while, a narrow path was cleared amid all kinds of hubbub when the county magistrate came pompously with his cane and entourage. The soldiers immediately held their guns erect, snapped to attention, and bowed to the magistrate. It was really an imposing show. Some of the onlookers were so impressed by this that they secretly wished that they could have an official examine their corpses after they died, so they could attract the same attention. The magistrate went to the back yard and covered his nose with a perfumed handkerchief; he superciliously asked a few questions to which the coroner gave a few routine answers about the circumstances of the dead person. The officers curiously looked around, and one of them spotted a coffin with its lid placed aslant on the top. He went over to the coffin, and as soon as he removed the lid, he saw that it was filled with bombs and ammunition of all kinds. In a panic, he screamed, "Bombs!" The magistrate, who was the most afraid of this kind of thing, no sooner heard "bombs" than he threw away his cane, scrambled for the gate of the temple, and rushed out. The onlookers, following the magistrate blindly, also dashed away as fast as their feet could take them. Some thought that it must have been the ghosts which had suddenly appeared in broad daylight; some thought that the county magistrate was suddenly under some kind of spell. Some took to their heels because they saw others running away.

It was not until the county magistrate was quite a distance away from the temple that some of his officers caught up with him and helped him back to his office. Then they requested that their headquarters send some troops over to inspect the temple closely. In recent months, munitions from unknown sources had been discovered in several places. Sometimes red flags painted with a hammer and sickle were found among them too. The military and administrative personnel, ignorant of the meaning of these signs, simply busied themselves with confiscating the munitions without doing anything about the rest.

Outside the temple, masses of people were gathering. Each one of them stuck up his head, looking curiously in all directions as if waiting for a miracle to take place. Suddenly, a voice of command could be heard drawing near, accompanied by marching footsteps. As soon as they saw the soldiers coming, the people hurried to make way for them. The troops entered the temple and carried away the guns and the bombs to the city.

After examining the corpse, the coroner went to the entrance of the temple and was immediately surrounded by curious onlookers asking him who the dead person was. He gave a simple description of the body, the clothes it had on, and so forth. A woman in the crowd, hearing what he said, went into hysterics. She rushed to the temple and kept mumbling "Oh, my son, my precious, my darling." She was sure that her son had been killed by a bandit and insisted that he be found. By then the soldiers had left the scene; some of the onlookers advised her to report to the county yamen immediately, and some suggested that she post a reward for the whereabouts of the murderer. In the meantime, she was crying wildly and kept muttering that she wanted to take to task the principal of her son's school. Finally, a county officer took her to the yamen and wrote a report to the magistrate on her behalf. After asking her a few routine questions, the magistrate had somebody escort her home.

The investigation which followed lasted several days and shook the whole town. Hsing-kuan was sent for by the school principal. It was only after her meeting with him that she learned of T'ien-hsi's implication in the murder at the temple. This was further confirmed by a careful cross-examination of T'ien-hsi. She immediately took the boy to the foreign minister and told him the whole story. The minister advised T'ien-hsi to report to the county yamen on his own, assuring him that he had nothing to do with this case. Hsing-kuan thought this was a good idea, and so she took her grandson to the school principal right away to ask him to vouch for T'ien-hsi's innocence before they reported to the county yamen. The principal, however, told her not to get involved with the county yamen because, once involved, it might take "two to three thousand taels' fortune" to get out of the whole thing. The best solution, accord-

ing to the principal, was to ask the minister to go to the yamen and put in a few good words for T'ien-hsi. For lack of any better alternatives, Hsing-kuan could only follow the principal's advice, and so she went back again to the minister for help.

At the county yamen, the magistrate was very polite to the minister, inviting him to take a seat in the reception room, and so forth. T'ien-hsi's small, innocent-looking face had already half convinced the magistrate that the little boy was not involved in the murder. T'ien-hsi's report of what actually happened that day made the cause of his little friend's death at least partially clear. Then the magistrate said that he would still continue his investigation in order to determine whether T'ien-hsi and his little friend were involved with the munitions in the temple. At this, the minister tried his best to affirm T'ien-hsi's innocence and promised that he would send T'ien-hsi to the yamen whenever the boy was summoned. The magistrate was finally persuaded to let T'ien-hsi go home.

Along with T'ien-hsi, the minister brought back to Hsing-kuan some really grim news he had overheard at the county yamen. It seemed that the local people were in for a big civil war, and that the antigovernment bandits were already hiding everywhere. This got Hsing-kuan really worried. After the minister left the house, Hsing-kuan immediately scribbled a few words to Yü-kuan, asking if she had any plans.

The county yamen did not get anywhere with their investigation. In the meantime, Hsing-kuan heard that the people in the streets were talking about Li Chien-teh's past involvement with the Revolutionary Party. And, if only by coincidence, some of the munitions brought to the city by the soldiers had tags with the character "Li" on them. All this made Hsing-kuan suspect that her son-in-law might really have something to do with the shipping of the munitions. While the authorities were in the process of investigating the mystery of the character "Li," T'ien-hsi was summoned several times. But they didn't find anything suspicious about the boy. In order to avoid any further trouble, Hsing-kuan, without anybody's knowledge, took T'ien-hsi with her to the treaty port one morning.

VI

The district where Yü-kuan worked was not as peaceful as it had been before. The noises of bugles and battle drums were often heard now, day and night, amid the bleatings of the sheep and calves. Curfews and martial law went into effect several times a month. Since the withdrawal of General Ch'en, the commander-in-chief, from Fukien, in the past few years it had been customary for troops to bivouac around the area. Yü-kuan, like anybody else in town, was oblivious to these changes.

From the time Yü-kuan had heard from Hsing-kuan about what had happened to T'ien-hsi, she had been thinking of going back for a visit. She waited until the end of the week, when she could be free from her missionary work in the country. She planned to get to Chin-li first and spend the night there before starting on her journey back home early the following morning. She was totally taken by surprise when she was stopped by a bunch of people before she even arrived at Ta-wang Temple. The highway had been completely blocked by a group of soldiers with red armbands, and nobody was allowed to pass. Faced with such a dead end, Yü-kuan could only turn back to a small nearby village. There was a Christian farmer there, who, because of cramped quarters, could only put her up in a hayloft. The smells of dung and of the outhouse were already too much for her, not to mention the rats of all sizes scurrying about, paying absolutely no attention to her presence. Moreover, she believed that houses with rats in them were almost always haunted. Fortunately, she had long since learned from Ch'en Lien how to ward off ghosts, and so she put both the Bible and the *Book of Changes* next to her before she went to sleep. Although she knew how to exorcise ghosts, she had no way of coping with the foul smell. It was way past midnight before she finally fell asleep.

The footsteps and gunshots she half heard in her dream finally woke her up and alerted her to the fact that a nearby haystack had caught fire. She had no time to figure out whether the fire had been caused by gunshots or by an arsonist. She immediately got up, grabbed her clothes, and rushed outside. It was past midnight, and the village was ablaze. Thinking that something terrible must have happened, she decided to hide herself under a makeshift awning near a deserted melon field. She squatted under the awning and, overtaken by fear, prayed in turn to both God and her ancestors. Cries of the villagers amid the blazing fire were heard everywhere as the red-armbanded soldiers looted the village. The villagers had over the years heard about the disruptions caused by the communists, and they also knew there were several varieties: one group was called the "local communists," the other two were "the Red Army" and "the Soviet Army." But the villagers did not know the differences among these varieties except by the different behaviors of the soldiers. The ones who kidnapped, blackmailed, looted, and burned down the village—in short, the ones who acted not unlike bandits—were invariably the local communists. The bunch who had just come were most likely the local communists, because they ravaged the place for an entire night. Yü-kuan did not dare close her eyes all night. Because the awning was bamboo in the form of an arch, one could easily see what was inside from the openings on both ends. Yü-kuan realized the danger of hiding in such a place and decided to return to Chin-li. But before she got far, she was again stopped on her way.

It was even worse this time. She was caught by the soldiers with the red armbands and black caps and was sent to another village as a prisoner. It turned out that all the women prisoners were put in one big place; among them many were Yü-kuan's acquaintances. After some days of confusion, each of them was assigned a specific job, ranging from cooking and washing to mending clothes. Yü-kuan's job was mending clothes. The soldiers seemed to have more than their share of worn-out clothes and hats whose endless mending chores were too much for Yü-kuan. There was simply not a moment when she could rest from her work; by the end of the day a tiny needle would seem to weigh as much as a copper column in her tired hand. This was the first time in her life she had really experienced the pain of physical labor. Compared to her life as a missionary, routine and monotonous, with no one supervising her or pushing her, Yü-kuan's present situation was just the opposite: she was living like a prisoner. She kept thinking about her son who was abroad and her grandson in the city. There was no way to tell when this ordeal would end. Besides a few tears, there was simply no outlet for her misery.

In the meantime, fighting had been going on for nearly two weeks, and many of the soldiers with red armbands had been killed; the rest came back to the village to pack away all their military supplies before retreating to a thick grove some twenty *li* behind the village. Men, women, and even cattle were forced to clear out, along with every single portable item. During the exodus, young men and women were dragged along with the soldiers, and cries of people mixed with those of the cows, horses, sheep, dogs, and pigs piercing through the clouds, because nobody wanted to risk the danger of journeying with these soldiers. In a short while the whole village was deserted; only a handful of old men and women remained. Even toddlers were forced to leave the place; as for infants, it was up to their mothers whether they could be carried or not. Mothers who were not able or not willing to carry their babies either left them in the village or abandoned them by the wayside. Wounded soldiers who could not walk were shot lest they be caught and tortured for information.

After having covered several *li*, the commanding officer suddenly discovered that a very important map and booklet of names and numbers had been left in the village on the dead body of one of the leaders. This very important document should never have been lost, much less allowed to fall into the hands of the enemy. The commanding officer wanted to find a man and a woman who, disguised as a couple, would go into the village to search for it. Yü-kuan had been looking for an opportunity to run away for a long time, and so she immediately volunteered for the mission; she said they should send her because she knew some shortcuts which could speed up her return a great deal. Her fellow traveler was an "old comrade" who watched Yü-kuan closely and did not let her out of his sight for one second. By way of a shortcut, as Yü-kuan had promised, they arrived at the outskirts of the village in no time. The government soldiers had not arrived yet, but across from the fence they could hear the old people left in the village already cursing the bandits and saying how, when the government soldiers came to the rescue, they would like to serve as guides to track the bandits down. Yü-kuan told her "comrade" to wait under the bamboo shade, because it would be rather inconvenient for him to get caught in the village. Originally, Yü-kuan had thought to hide herself someplace as soon as she got into the village; later on, she thought that since the man carried a gun, he might be provoked into firing if his patience were overtaxed. So she followed his instructions, and, after some search, she located the body with the number the commanding officer had given her. The document they wanted was indeed in one of its pockets. Corpses and remains of military supplies were scattered all over the streets, and all the doors in the village were bolted. She had not encountered anyone on her way there and back. After giving the document to her "comrade," she told him to leave the place as quickly as possible. For herself, she told him, she was too tired to walk now, but would follow him as soon as she recovered. The "comrade" was pleased with the document and simply took to his heels without asking any questions. Yü-kuan waited until the man was out of sight before she turned back to the village. She then thought that it was not safe there either, and so she finally decided to follow a little path along the paddy field in the direction of Chin-li.

Yü-kuan's rather long and slender feet, which had once been bound, could not walk very fast now without the support of an umbrella. Limping on the narrow path, she really looked pathetic. As she was struggling on her way to Chin-li, she was again stopped by two soldiers in gray uniforms. Without listening to her pleading, they took her to the battalion commander who, however, dismissed her with a disappointed expression. Yü-kuan could not understand what these soldiers were saying; they did not speak her dialect. Two of them took her to a big house, which she recognized was in the back yard of the community temple. The yard in the front was now guarded by a small group of soldiers. She told the two men that she used to live in the church near the end of the lane; but no matter what she said, they could not understand her. In the big room that Yü-kuan was taken to, there were already eight or nine women; some of them were crying, some simply looked dazed, some acted nonchalant. From the expressions on their faces, Yü-kuan figured that they had probably been dragged there by the soldiers to mend clothes for them.

In a war zone, if troop discipline was slack, two things became top priority. One was to make an inventory of the local food supply; the other was to make an account of the number of women available. No war could be waged without food or women. As soon as they saw Yü-kuan enter, several women in the room came over to her, crying and hoping that she could rescue them. Having worked in the region for so many years, she had gotten to know every one of them, but being a woman herself, she really did not know how she could be of much help. She remembered that, several days ago, when she was caught in the other village, she had been slapped in the face and berated as an imperialist lackey when she told them she was a Christian. Because of that terrible experience, she was now very careful about associating herself with the church. Interestingly enough, the woman who advised Yü-kuan not to give up on God during this crisis turned out to be one of those who Yü-kuan had originally converted to Christianity. This woman took out a copy of the Bible from her sleeve and gave it to Yü-kuan, saying that it was the only thing she carried with her. She asked Yü-kuan to select one or two passages for their general edification. This touched Yü-kuan deeply. So, very solemnly and carefully, Yü-kuan read a few passages from the Bible.

They had some watery congee soup for supper, and then they all sang psalms and prayed under the guidance of Yü-kuan, who also read them a chapter from the Bible. Peace and calm reigned in the entire room. In the meantime, Yü-kuan got very excited about what she heard herself saying. She told everyone to be calm and composed, giving the impression that some horrible disaster was about to occur. The more she talked, the more self-confident and fearless she became, for, after all, it was her religion that taught people to serve justice at the expense of their lives. So she prayed and sang and prayed again in such a frantic manner that one would think her audience was soon to be eaten by wild beasts in a Roman arena.

This went on for several hours, until around nine o'clock, when some of the soldiers pushed the door open and, like hungry tigers rushing toward a sheepfold, they dashed toward the women, laughing continuously as they tried to drag them out. Yü-kuan was leaning against the wall, and she screamed before the soldiers had a chance to grab her, begging all of them to stop what they were doing and, at the same time, lecturing on how all people should love one another as brothers and sisters and should be kind and gentle. Only a few of them understood Yü-kuan's dialect; most of them, however, knew something about Christian rituals, and some of them had even been to church themselves and had been exposed to the Bible and Christian doctrine. Yü-kuan asked one of the men who understood her dialect to be her interpreter, and he was able to do justice to Yü-kuan's tone of sincerity. She told them that debauchery and exploitation were the greatest human crimes. She warned them that those who resorted to force would be destroyed by force, and, at the same time, told them that these women were fearless and were prepared to sacrifice their lives when the time came. Many pious sayings flowed from her lips in a most mellifluent way.

The more she talked, the more she was carried away by her self-generated enthusiasm, which was burning brighter by the minute. Gradually the soldiers began to loosen their grips on the women. Yü-kuan then asked them to sit down to listen to what she had to say about retribution. She took the opportunity to elaborate on some old Chinese sayings, such as, "To respect one's ancestors and to be good to others is to sow the seed of good fortune for one's descendants"; "To rape another's wife and daughter will result in having one's own wife and daughter debauched by others." Some of her ideas were quite modern, such as the notion that eating and sex are instincts and that when a man is aroused, he is simply hungry for sex just as his empty stomach is for food. Yü-kuan went on to explain that there was nothing wrong with these instinctual desires, except that one should, for example, eat only what one was justly allotted. To be sure, it was wrong to kill others in order to satisfy one's hunger; to rob others of their food was just as selfish, and by no means fair or honest. She went on to elaborate on the point that it was natural for man to desire woman; but to resort to force or coercion in this regard would definitely meet with punishment.

Originally, the soldiers had come for pleasure; when they were first lectured by Yü-kuan, some of them said that they had not come here for a catechism lesson. But after listening to Yü-kuan for a few minutes, they began to take some interest and decided to sit down and listen to her and to the singing of psalms. Yü-kuan asked the women and the soldiers to call one another brothers and sisters. She also told the soldiers that they could ask these women to mend clothes for them or chat with them as long as they promised to behave themselves. She asked them to teach other soldiers what she had told them, so that the others would follow their good example.

Just at the moment when the soldiers seemed to be going through some character change, another batch of soldiers charged in, shouting that they had been waiting outside far too long. The "reformed" soldiers inside asked the new batch to sit down, but the latter refused to be so docile. The two batches almost got into a fight before the two sides decided to make peace with one another. Knowing that there was still another batch of soldiers waiting outside, the soldiers inside decided to lock the door in order to protect the women. As they had anticipated, they soon heard curses from outside as the third batch banged on the door.

The soldiers inside lined themselves up and leaned against the door to keep it from being pushed open from the outside. There was not a moment of quiet the whole night until, finally, the crowing of the roosters called in a new day. After asking the soldiers to return to their camps, Yü-kuan then asked the group leader to talk to their battalion commander, beseeching him to issue an order that there was to be no rape or rapine. This was done without too much fuss. Now that the worst was over, Yü-kuan told her women friends to rest for awhile. In addition to what she knew about the *Book of Changes* being able to ward off ghosts, she learned from this nightmarish experience that the Old and New Testaments were capable of checking the living devils. After praying for awhile to express her thanks to God, she lay down to rest.

The back door of the temple was not guarded by the soldiers as the front one was, but remained closed most of the time. The church was only a few blocks from this back door, at the end of a small lane. The general uncertainty of the situation worried Yü-kuan very much, and she couldn't get a wink of sleep. She didn't know, for instance, what she should do in the evening, if these soldiers decided to change their minds and go back on their word. Fortunately, Yü-kuan was a resourceful person, and it did not take her long to realize that she and her friends should escape to the church through the back door. A church in the countryside was as sacred as a foreign embassy; nobody dared enter without permission. So she immediately told the women about her plan to move to the church. They all got very excited and decided that Yü-kuan should open the back door of the church and then come back to fetch them. Very quietly and quickly Yü-kuan got all the women moved to the church. As soon as they got inside, Yü-kuan locked the gate. In the meantime she sent the doorkeeper of the church to the barracks to inform the soldiers of the women's whereabouts. Yü-kuan also let the soldiers know that they could still send their worn-out clothes to the church to be mended, as she had promised in the beginning.

Yü-kuan and her friends stayed in the church seven or eight days without any disturbance from the soldiers. Many of them went there, but only to chat or leave their clothes for repair. In the meantime, Yü-kuan not only missed her grandson very much but also was anxious to get back to her people, since they must have been worrying about her safety after they learned she had been taken captive by the local communists. She entrusted her duty as guardian to a staff member of the church, and bade the women goodbye. As she was leaving the village, she passed Ta-wang Temple and the sentinal at its front gate; she waved at him, and he let her pass without any trouble, knowing that she was a missionary in the community. After she crossed the bridge, the faded memory of Ch'en Lien came back to her mind again. This prompted her to go to the town, hoping she might find him there. After some inquiries, she soon learned that he had closed his meat shop and gone to Southeast Asia with all his savings during a recent communist uprising. Nobody in town knew his new address except that it was a port in Borneo. For a long time, Yü-kuan had been thinking of telling Ch'en Lien about Hsing-kuan so that they could be reunited as husband and wife. Now that Ch'en Lien had gone to Southeast Asia, she began to feel sorry for Hsing-kuan. A nameless feeling of loss accompanied her as she walked slowly on the street alone.

VII

The situation in the city was much worse than on the outskirts. Sensing the approach of war, many of the rich families had already moved elsewhere. When Yü-kuan got home and saw that the door was bolted from the outside, she went straight to the church for news of her family. The doorkeeper of the church returned the key to her and told her that Hsing-kuan had taken T'ien-hsi to a treaty port to escape the war. He also told her that people in the city said that she had disappeared, and some even said that she had been killed. At this point, there was nothing she could do but go home to rest.

In a few days, government troops had retreated to the city from Chin-li, and a few days later, they moved to another place. Without firing a single bullet, the soldiers with red armbands then oc-cupied some areas on the outskirts of the city. The change was dramatic: within forty-eight hours the whole city was flying red flags, and the streets were filled with the propaganda brigade, service brigade, protection brigade, etc. Clever ruffians and intellectual frauds were already talking about mass revolution, the *Internationale* tunelessly on their lips. Upstarts among the bandits had done away with a number of their older counterparts, which helped to placate the local people. But before long, these people were gripped by a new surge of anger and hatred when these upstarts forced them to turn in their land deeds and to listen to such strange slogans as "Organize the Masses" and "Support the Soviet Troops." Whether they were willing or not, whether they understood it or not, they had no choice but to do as they were told. On top of this, all the men in the city were assigned one kind of work or another, whose varieties were beyond one's comprehension.

The women also had their assignments. Those who could afford to run away had already left. Yü-kuan was rather calm about the situation and decided to remain in the city, waiting for her assignment. But the minute she entered the place she was assigned to, the military guard reported to the boss that she was the very fugitive from Chin-li they were looking for. Before she knew it, she was sent to headquarters for further investigation. Because of her eloquence, her punishment was reduced to parading in the street as a criminal. Her miraculous experience with the soldiers earlier made her confident in the power of God's love and protection, and so, when she heard that she was to be marched through the streets, she was unafraid. The soldiers at headquarters put a cone-shaped paper hat on her and forced her to wear a vest made from a hempen bag. On the paper hat, there was a sign of a cross which was flanked by the phrase "The Lackey of Imperialism." The same design was repeated on the vest. "The Lackey of Imperialism" was the catchword of another kind of religion of whose significance Yü-kuan was ignorant. While she was being paraded in the streets, she kept thinking that she was actually innocent, even though her religion was being insulted. Thus thinking, she was able to immerse herself in her own thoughts, and could not have cared less about the people who swarmed around her and insulted her. She figured she was now past fifty, and pretty soon when Chien-teh came home from abroad at the age of thirty-six or seven, she could enjoy some leisure and let Chien-teh take over. She was so completely carried away by her fantasy that, in a moment of excitement, she cried out "Hallelujah." The soldiers gave a start, then slapped her in the face, because they thought that she was cursing them. Recently Yü-kuan had become acquainted with this sort of physical insult, and so the slap did not seem to give her too much pain. She continued to mumble "Hallelujah" a few times.

Right before this humiliating spectacle was about to start for the second day, a special order was issued to release Yü-kuan. This, however, did not change her mood much. With swollen face and tired feet, she slowly walked home, only to find that everything had been taken away except the dry leaves and trash, which were scattered all over the courtyard. She rushed straight to the living room, and it was not until she saw the tablets still hanging from the beams that she was able to heave a sigh of relief. At the corner of the wall, only two chairs were left, with five legs between them. She then rushed to the kitchen stove, uncovered its broken lid of tile and dug out two big piggy banks, at the sight of which she was finally content. But before she could reach into the piggy banks, she suddenly fainted to the ground.

It was a long time before she gradually came to. Thirst, hunger, and fatigue weighed her down so much that she couldn't raise herself. She crawled painfully to the cistern to scoop up some water to quench her thirst. Feeling slightly recovered, she slowly walked to the rice crock, to find only a few husks on the bottom, along with a few sticks of half-dried scallion and a head of garlic hanging against the window sill. Inside the cupboard, she found a lidless biscuit box. The biscuits had been devoured by the rats; only some crumbs remained. After this meal of crumbs, however, she felt slightly better and was energetic enough to go to the stove again. She broke one of the piggy

banks, counted the money, and put it next to the stove. Then she got herself some water to wash her face before going out to get something to eat. As she went out, a letter sitting in the courtyard caught her eye. She thought it must have come from her son and was delighted. She picked it up, but before she had a chance to read it, she heard anxious cries of "Sister-in-law, Sister-in-law" outside the door.

She stuffed the letter into her pocket and hurried to the door, but the man had already crossed the threshold. He stood in front of Yü-kuan, wearing his black uniform with red armbands and holding a parcel. It was some time before she was able to pull herself together to ask him who he was and whom he was looking for. Instead of answering her question, the man walked toward the hall full of smiles, indicating that he meant no harm. He said to her that he was her brother-in-law, Fen-sao, whose official name now was Li Mu-ning. He said that he was now a rather important figure in the Soviet district government. He also told her that he had started looking for her as soon as he arrived last night. It was due to his intercession that Yü-kuan had gotten a special release that morning. Yü-kuan thanked him for his favor, but at the same time, she was full of all sorts of questions and utterly confused about the whole thing. She invited him to sit on the three-legged chair, telling him that it was the best furniture left in the house. When asked what he meant by the Soviet district government, Li Mu-ning elaborated with various fancy terms involving communism, Marxism, dialectical materialism, and many other bits of jargon. Since Yü-kuan could not follow him, it appeared to her that he must have become fairly literate or even scholarly. Yü-kuan thought that what he was talking about might be another kind of Western religion. But the fact was that, aside from the jargon, Mu-ning's knowledge of both politics and economics was miniscule. Since the two did not really speak the same language—one was too ignorant to understand and the other too incompetent to explain—they had to talk about something other than politics or economics. Mu-ning thought it would be much more down-to-earth to talk about what had happened to him in the past thirty-odd years. He had gone through a lot during those years, but before he got started on his long story, he gave Yü-kuan the little bundle that he was carrying with him. Yü-kuan was delighted to find that it contained her favorite Horse-Hoof cookies from her home town. She swallowed twenty of them in no time and was very grateful to him. She felt that her brother-in-law had become thoughtful and much more sophisticated than before. It was hard to imagine how drastically life had educated him over the years.

Yü-kuan did not dare ask him where he had taken Hsing-kuan's daughter Ya-li. Instead it was he himself who told her the whole story. He said that after he had worked for Intendant Huang a while, he had been sent to a military academy in Hopei. After graduation, he had followed a regiment commander and served for a long time under him as sentry officer. After the Revolution had begun, he had followed others to join various political parties to overthrow this and squeeze out that until, finally, his own party was overthrown. He had changed his name as often as necessary until he finally went into the mountains to join others in organizing a new government. He told Yü-kuan he had just come down from the mountains to join his comrades in Chin-li in order to leave for somewhere else. He said the name "Red Army" was most suitable to his purpose, and therefore he used it. But the real Red Army had nothing to do with the "local communists."

What had happened to Ya-li? Mu-ning was quite frank about it and told Yü-kuan practically everything. He said that shortly before the Revolution, the intendant to whom he had given Ya-li was transferred from the food bureau to a very lucrative customs bureau from which he made a fortune. From time to time, Mu-ning would visit Ya-li as her uncle. After the Revolution, the old intendant, in the wink of an eye, became something like one of the old regime of Shanghai. As for Mu-ning, he became a fast-rising star in the new regime. As a rule, the old regime, as well as the upstarts, had property in foreign concessions and fat bank accounts in foreign banks. In the beginning, Li Mu-ning had all these too, but they

were gradually dissipated after several inspections and confiscations until, finally, he decided to go back to the people and be one of them. Ya-li's foster father was fortunate enough to have lived a rather undisturbed life. Since the old couple had no children, they loved Ya-li as their own, looking after her down to the smallest detail and in every way possible. Ya-li began her school education in Shanghai. Since her adopted parents worshiped Western civilization, they insisted that she study English. Just as expected, in the girls' school run by missionaries, not only did she learn to speak English, but she learned to behave just like a foreigner with all the accompanying mannerisms and habits. She wanted to eat nothing but imported food, wear nothing but imported clothes. Everything she consumed had to be imported, as if a contract had been signed between the church and foreign business firms. The former ran the advertisements, the latter supplied the goods. Mu-ning said that before he went back to the south, the intendant had passed away, leaving a huge fortune and property to his wife, who would in time pass them on to her daughter. Ya-li went to the States to study after her graduation from the missionary school. Mu-ning had no idea what had happened to her after that. He knew only that she had not been called Ya-li since her childhood. As for the name she used in school, he could not even begin to pronounce those funny English sounds. He told Yü-kuan not to tell Hsing-kuan anything about Ya-li because Ya-li would suffer greatly if she knew about her past. He also did not want Yü-kuan to tell Hsing-kuan that Li Mu-ning was actually a new name for the old Li Fen-sao; he was apparently thinking that, once Ya-li had inherited that huge fortune, he might ask her for a handout as her uncle.

Yü-kuan asked if he was married and had any children. Mu-ning shook his head and said no; but then he corrected himself, saying that he had married when he was in Honan. Like all other women, Yü-kuan was interested in who the woman was and what kind of family she came from. Her father, Mu-ning said, had been a peasant who owed the local Catholic church some money which, with the interest, was too much for him ever to return, even if he were to sell all the twenty-odd acres of his land. The usurer was a "philanthropic" Catholic priest, who said that he would relieve the peasant of the debt if he and his entire family joined the Catholic Church. For lack of any better means of paying his debt, the farmer had become a Catholic. Since his conversion, he had felt rather sorry that he could no longer worship his ancestors in the graveyard as before. Moreover, he could not remember the words of the Lord's Prayer and often confused it with the Taoist Sun Sutra. For this he was once scolded by the priest. But to the end he never understood why the Sun Sutra could not be recited. The Holy Communion was another thing which had puzzled him greatly. He could never figure out how a thin slice of bread, which was neither sweet nor hot, could become the body of Christ after the priest had mumbled some words over it. And the mystery of thrusting that piece of bread into his mouth with his eyes closed was simply beyond him. He felt that it was a flat lie, and the whole thing made him suspect that the priest might dig out his eyes, heart, and liver after his death and turn them into medicine, or might even go as far as taking his soul. The more he thought, the more suspicious he became of the deep significance behind that cannibalistic ritual of the communion: why would the priest set him free of his debt of several hundred dollars for nothing? The more he thought, the more scared he became until, finally, he decided that it was far better to sell his daughter to pay his debt. It was not too long before the story of the old peasant reached Mu-ning's battalion. As an officer, Mu-ning could certainly afford to buy himself a wife, and the pathetic situation of the old peasant naturally hastened his decision to marry the daughter. So he gave the father three hundred dollars and got himself a wife. The peasant was grateful for Mu-ning's kindness and treated him more as a benefactor than as a son-in-law. In fact, some years after the Revolution the old man followed Mu-ning to some of the places the latter was posted and rather enjoyed his twilight years. The unexpected death of Mu-ning's wife was a fatal blow to the old man, and he died of grief soon afterward.

As Mu-ning had no children, he was all by himself now, an old widower.

Yü-kuan asked him why people in the army opposed religion and confiscated people's property. As usual, Mu-ning quoted the clichés he had learned from antireligious articles. He told Yü-kuan that people nowadays were of the opinion that Christianity was in fact based on feeble and illogical kinds of premises; its power was maintained solely by its conservative practices and rigid organization. People, as a rule, did not like to think; the easy way was to drift along on what was dictated by rules and organization, and this, according to Mu-ning, was a big stumbling block to the establishment of a modern society with a new political as well as a new economic system. Therefore it was imperative that Christianity be opposed; the fact that there were other forces involved in Christianity made the religion all the more undesirable. Although Yü-kuan did not agree with what he said, she was incapable of carrying on an argument with him. He told Yü-kuan that both he and his comrades had been planning to attack the neighboring city for a long time and that they had often shipped munitions in coffins from the treaty port to the mountains. He also said that a large number of these munitions had been recently discovered in the Hsüan-yüan Kuan temple, and, as a result, the army had lost quite a lot of military supplies. Mu-ning disclosed to Yü-kuan that pretty soon his army was going to attack another very important place, and thus he inadvertently revealed that they were unable to hold the city they were now occupying, as well as the fact that serious fighting was about to occur in a nearby area. Mu-ning then got up and bade Yü-kuan farewell, saying that he would come to visit her again soon.

After seeing him off at the door, Yü-kuan took the letter out of her pocket; it was not from Chien-teh but from Hsing-kuan, and had been sent from the foreign settlement of Amoy. She learned from the letter that T'ien-hsi had fallen down some stairs and broken his spine. The doctor said that the situation was critical, and it was hoped that Yü-kuan could come right away to help care for him. When Hsing-kuan was writing this letter, she probably had no idea of the hardship Yü-kuan was going through. Judging from the postmark, the letter was mailed on the day that Yü-kuan was arrested. Yü-kuan almost passed out again when she realized that three or four days had already passed since T'ien-hsi's accident. It was indeed true that misfortunes always travel in pairs. She did not dare blame this on God; she was positive that it was the doing of some ghosts or some evil force.

Putting everything else aside, she went straight to Hsing-kuan's place. The minute she got there, she fainted. Hsing-kuan helped her up, and, finding her weak and sick, decided to send her to the hospital.

A month slipped by, but fighting was still going on in the country. From the newspaper, Yü-kuan learned that Li Mu-ning had been killed, which made her secretly shed some tears for him. Since she had no way of getting back home, Yü-kuan decided to stay with T'ien-hsi at Hsing-kuan's place after they both got out of the hospital. It was confirmed that T'ien-hsi's spinal injury could not be cured, and he would have to wear a metal vest for support for the rest of his life. Yü-kuan's only hope at this time was a letter from Chien-teh telling her he had decided to come back. She went to the missionary office every day to find out if there was any news from her son. Nothing else could interest her now. In about two weeks, she did get news from the foreign minister that Chien-teh had already returned, but could not come back for a visit for the time being because he was working in Nanking. The minister was apparently not too happy about the news. Yü-kuan thought the church had assigned him there and was complaining that the church should have discussed the matter with her beforehand, and so forth. The minister then explained that Chien-teh's assignment in Nanking had nothing to do with the church; in fact, they were still hoping that Chien-teh could come back to take charge of the missionary work in the city. But they did not know, the minister added, who had helped him return all the money—including the interest—he had owed the church over the years. The minister

also told Yü-kuan that Chien-teh had written a very earnest letter to the church, saying that he had now changed his field of interest and that his outlook on life had changed as well. What he wanted now was to get a post in the government. But to be able to fill a government position with a degree in theology—one could not help but praise the omnipotence of Western education! Chien-teh's ambition was in fact no news to Yü-kuan, who had known about it long ago when he had first joined the Revolutionary Party. He had taken up theology to fulfill the promise he had made to the foreign minister many years ago when the latter had rescued him from arrest. Yü-kuan was secretly rather pleased to learn that her son had gotten a post in the government, as this was what she had hoped for him anyway. So when the minister complained about Chien-teh, Yü-kuan did not utter a single word to apologize for her son. Instead, she asked how much her son's salary was and what kind of job he had in the government. The minister knew only the English equivalent of Chien-teh's position, not the title in Chinese, which was a word his Chinese instructor had not taught him. Thus he was unable to describe it to Yü-kuan more than to say that Chien-teh was an official in charge of local affairs. A local-affairs official of course took care of local affairs. But what this was exactly, the minister could not explain. Finally he showed her the title as it appeared in the English letter which Chien-teh had written him.

Ever since that summer gathering, Chien-teh and An-ni had been seeing each other more often. An-ni did not want Chien-teh to go back to the old country as a missionary and had asked him many times to change his profession. An-ni was more than confident that Chien-teh could get whatever job she wanted for him, since her family could pull many strings with the government authorities. After all, some of them were still using her family's money. As long as she was willing to do the asking, she could get him any job. Fortunately, Chien-teh knew what he was capable of and wanted nothing beyond him. All he wanted was to work for a commission related to economics, with a modest salary of about two hundred dollars. This would still be two-thirds more than he could make as a missionary. But material gain was not of primary importance to him; his main concern was to obey An-ni. An-ni had such great control over him that it could suppress his love for his mother and his gratitude to the church. She returned all the money Chien-teh owed the church; not only did she pay the interest, she also contributed a huge sum of money to renovate the church. Since she was not a Christian herself, her help made Chien-teh feel even more of a ransomed slave. He thought that there was no better way to repay her kindness than by marrying her. But so far neither of them had broached the subject.

Before long, Yü-kuan was invited by Chien-teh to Nanking. She entrusted her house to Hsing-kuan and brought with her a few suitcases, the ancestral tablets, and the crippled T'ien-hsi. She thought to herself that it was completely due to An-ni that her son had gotten a government job and paid his debt, not to mention the contribution to the church. She was naturally grateful for what An-ni had done for her son. Before she ever met An-ni, she had already become very fond of her.

When Chien-teh saw T'ien-hsi wearing his steel vest all the time and noticed that he had to walk on crutches, he was extremely displeased. He was resentful that his mother-in-law had not taken good care of his son. After the many ups and downs of recent years, Yü-kuan's health had begun to deteriorate. She had developed a heart condition, so that she could not stand any rigorous exertion. Chien-teh was being especially good and respectful to his mother; he gave her all his income and let her take charge of the household. Although they could live very comfortably on Chien-teh's income, she was just as hard-working as ever, attending to every single detail in the kitchen, bedrooms, bathroom, and courtyard. In fact, she worked much harder than her two servants. In less than three months, she changed cooks six times and women servants four times. They all complained that the old lady was too demanding for them to stay on the job.

Both mother and son lived quite happily in a Western-style house. Sometimes she would think of Ya-yen when she saw Chien-teh coming home from the office. On a clear bright day, she felt somewhat sad and even shed a few tears when she thought of the few good things her late daughter-in-law had done. At the same time, she was very concerned about her son's relationship with An-ni, who was still abroad at this point. She often thought of drawing her son out on the subject, but he would never give her an exact answer. He told her only that An-ni's late father had been a government official in the Ch'ing dynasty and that there was only her mother in Shanghai; An-ni had no brothers or sisters. He also told Yü-kuan that An-ni's family had lots of property, and, in Shanghai alone, what they owned was worth a million. Naturally, Yü-kuan would have liked to have her son marry An-ni. The very thought of it would produce a smile on her face. Chien-teh told his mother that An-ni was a girl who loved freedom more than anything else. She would have come back home with him, for instance, except that her free spirit had tempted her to go to the Arctic to see the aurora. She had decided to wait until the weather became warmer, and then take a ship from Canada to get there. She would probably have to spend the winter abroad. Thus he would also have to wait until she came back to know what her plans were. In fact, there was no telling whether or not she really wanted to get married.

Another year slipped by quietly and uneventfully. Early in the summer, An-ni sent a telegram saying that she was on her way back. When the day came for her arrival, Chien-teh went to Shanghai to meet her and then stayed with her family for a few days. There Chien-teh proposed to her, and without giving it a second thought, she accepted. She went to her room and showed him the bridal veil she had gotten abroad and told him that she had been waiting for his proposal for a long time. They exchanged a few expressions of love with each other quietly, and then they sat down and discussed the date, place, and ceremony for the wedding. As a matter of course, An-ni's decisions were to be everybody's decisions. After she had finished planning all the details of the wedding, she told Chien-teh very frankly that she did not want to live with Yü-kuan, because she was an advocate of the nuclear family.

They did the whole of their wedding shopping in Shanghai. An-ni realized that the bridal veil she had bought abroad was not as stylish as the ones she saw in Shanghai. She figured that this was perhaps because she had spent too much time in the Arctic, and the veil she had bought had gone out of fashion in the meantime. She bought another one immediately. Then she insisted that Chien-teh go to the classiest tailor to have his wedding suit made. It cost him almost two months' salary. They stayed in Shanghai for some days before she finally let him go back to Nanking.

Yü-kuan was extremely happy when she learned that Chien-teh was going to marry An-ni. But at her most elated moment, Chien-teh told her that An-ni was planning to set up a separate household after their marriage. Yü-kuan was so angry that her fingertips felt numb, and the disillusionment was discernible on her face. She thought that this must have something to do with the tide of the Revolution. Formerly, she thought that the Revolution meant change of government or dress style; later, when she was more experienced, she thought it meant change of either one's husband or one's wife. But now it had come to mean something more sophisticated: it meant getting rid of one's own mother. She felt bad enough that Chien-teh probably was going to live with his mother-in-law, but she felt even more offended that her son had not consulted her on the date or place of the wedding. It turned out that the wedding date Chien-teh and An-ni had decided upon coincided with the anniversary of the death of Chien-teh's father. Chien-teh had not noticed this because he was used to the solar calendar, and besides, over the years, the anniversary had always been commemorated by Yü-kuan alone. Yü-kuan therefore asked Chien-teh to change the date, but Chien-teh said that the date was An-ni's idea because it was her birthday. As for holding the wedding in Shanghai, this was because they could have a big wedding there,

since An-ni had many friends and relatives in Shanghai. None of these explanations satisfied Yü-kuan. She sighed and cried and then went into her room muttering to herself.

The wedding was held on the date and at the place originally planned. All that Yü-kuan did on that day was cry, in the company of her husband's ancestral tablets, which she took out to the living room that day especially for the occasion. Everything seemed to have gone wrong for her. She sat transfixed in the living room feeling as though the whole world was against her.

The next day, Chien-teh came back with An-ni for a visit. He introduced her to his mother. Yü-kuan insisted that the bride wear a veil and bow to her in the most respectful manner. Her reason was that when she was a bride in the old days, she had to wear the ceremonial clothes with a phoenix design on the crown and embroidered pythons on the robe for three days. She had not bothered as much at Chien-teh's first marriage because they had not had enough money at that time to observe the rituals in all their detail; besides, Chien-teh and Ya-li had been married in the church, where the rituals were rather simple. But things had changed now. Now that Chien-teh was a government official, everything should be done in grand style. An-ni, however, didn't pay much attention to formality. As soon as she had cut the cake for the guests, she took off the veil. She would not wear it again even if she were to marry for a second time. Knowing that it would be difficult to reason with his mother, Chien-teh finally begged An-ni to obey his mother this once at least, or there would be no end to the old lady's weeping and wailing. Very reluctantly, An-ni put on a silvery gown and a white chiffon cape which trailed twice her height along the floor. But this kind of ceremonial gown was utterly unbearable to Yü-kuan, since there was nothing colorfully Chinese in what An-ni was wearing; she looked like a plain porcelain figurine in it. Nor was Yü-kuan at all happy about the white cape, since it was not a lucky color. She thought that she had seen a red cape being worn in the countryside, and felt she was justified in insisting on it. But for An-ni, it was not a problem of lucky or unlucky;

there simply was no red cape available for the wedding. Thus, in a rage An-ni stripped off the whole outfit, went straight to her room, and started grumbling in English. The mother-in-law did not eat all day; such unfilial behavior, she complained, was the government's fault, because it did not stipulate that all brides wear the customary deep red dress for weddings. She hoped that the government would issue an order to the effect that those who did not observe such a stipulation would not be considered legally married.

On the third day, the newlyweds, following the fashion of the time, were going to Lushan for their honeymoon. An-ni forced herself to say goodbye to Yü-kuan. On the day before, Yü-kuan hadn't had a chance to look closely at her; now, even though her cheeks were puffed up with anger, she took a good look at her daughter-in-law. Yü-kuan felt that An-ni looked like Ya-yen in many respects, except she was garishly made up. After they left, Yü-kuan's anger began to subside; her son and daughter-in-law were, after all, her children, and even if she did not agree with everything they did, it was not worth getting mad about. Thus thinking, she felt much better and smiles began to appear on her face. She moved out of her own room and had someone come to paint the walls, windows, and even the door, making it into a decent room for the newlyweds. She even replaced the furniture for them. However, she was still old-fashioned, and so, aside from this one room, she didn't touch the rest of the house.

VIII

Two weeks later the couple came back. No sooner had An-ni stepped in than she complained that the furniture looked too boorish, and the color of the wall was not right either. When she walked into the reception room, she found it too old-fashioned; she also found the kitchen dirty. In fact, she found nothing in the house that was right. Yü-kuan was only trying to please her daughter-in-law, but the more she did, the more complaints she got in return, until finally she decided to leave everything to An-ni. An-ni then put Yü-kuan in a small room next to the kitchen. Though Chien-teh felt uneasy about it, there was nothing he could do. After all, An-ni had already compromised a lot by letting his mother stay with them. An-ni disliked not only Yü-kuan but T'ien-hsi as well.

Meanwhile, for months Yü-kuan had been trying to find evidence to confirm her suspicion that An-ni was actually the girl Fen-sao had kidnapped years ago, in order to make An-ni realize, among other things, that T'ien-hsi was, after all, her blood relative. But she never got the courage to confront An-ni with her suspicions. Since there was no genuine affection between An-ni and Yü-kuan, sometimes they could sit in the same room for a long time without exchanging a word. An-ni was always speaking English to Chien-teh, which was totally incomprehensible to Yü-kuan. On the other hand, An-ni could not understand a single word of the dialect Yü-kuan spoke with her son. This total lack of communication naturally increased their mutual suspicion. What angered Yü-kuan most was the fact that An-ni wanted to be the boss of the family. Chien-teh used to give all his salary to his mother, but this was no longer the case after his marriage. Yü-kuan felt that while she could give in on almost everything, she wouldn't yield one inch on this matter. She didn't want to be a dependent in the house. An-ni allowed her husband to give only a little pocket money to Yü-kuan, giving the latter even more reason for Yü-kuan to feel that her son was most unfilial. She thought that, even if her son had gotten his job through An-ni, it was still outrageous for his mother to be treated like this.

After a time, An-ni began to nag her husband about moving out of the house, because it was becoming increasingly impossible for her to live under the same roof with the old lady. An-ni frequently insulted Yü-kuan by calling her an "old cockroach" in front of Chien-teh, meaning that Yü-kuan was good for nothing but consuming food and bugging people. For the old lady life in Nanking was simply a dead end. There were no friends around in this unfamiliar place to whom she could tell her grievances. When she went to church, her fellow Christians could not understand her dialect; the minister couldn't give her any advice except to try to be open-minded about things. As a result, she decided to quit the church. She thought that the God she used to believe in had gone to sleep; otherwise how could he permit her own children to behave like this toward her?

There was another thing which displeased Yü-kuan. She asked Chien-teh to apply to the government for a wooden complimentary tablet with words like "Pure-hearted and Lofty-minded" to honor her as a chaste widow. As an official, Chien-teh, though mediocre in talent, was level-headed and practical. He thought that the time for honoring virtuous widows had long since passed. So whenever Yü-kuan asked if he could pull some strings to get her the tablet, his answer was negative. This was utterly unacceptable to Yü-kuan. She did not think her son had really tried, and she could not forgive him for that. As for Chien-teh, he felt that his father, who had sacrificed his life for the country, was really somebody worth honoring; as for his mother, he felt that she did not even really fulfill her duty as a mother. The gap between mother and son became wider than it had ever been.

Life for Yü-kuan was boring. While her daughter-in-law was out, house-hunting day after day, Yü-kuan spent most of the time in her room doing nothing. She began to realize that everything that she had done for her son since her husband's death was actually out of selfish motives. Decades of missionary life could be summarized by the old saying, "A chinaware dealer who used broken bowls himself," because she herself had never benefited from what she had preached. When she thought about this, she got up from her chair as if suddenly she grasped some priceless truth. She began to realize that her brother-in-law's words to her when she first became a widow had been right. Her widowhood was nothing but vanity; her missionary work was close to hypocrisy; and her present suffering was, in fact, a natural outcome of her past deeds. She wanted to go back to the country to start a genuine missionary life. But first she must repent. She felt that she should do at least one good deed for someone. She had her mind set on something now.

On the day Yü-kuan left her son, she had nothing to say to him except that she did not regret what she had done for him in the past and that she would still have his best interests at heart in the future. Absolutely confused by her words, Chien-teh simply made some rather impatient remarks and went straight to his office. When An-ni had gone house-hunting, Yü-kuan packed a few of the ancestral tablets and quietly left for the train station with T'ien-hsi.

X

After she got back to her home town, the church again assigned her to work in Chin-li. But this time she was not going to do any preaching; she was, after all, getting too old to go from one house to another. Instead, the church asked her to be the principal of a local elementary school. She lived with T'ien-hsi and was very careful about his education. Hsing-kuan lived alone in the city, and from time to time she would invite T'ien-hsi to stay with her in the city for a few days.

Yü-kuan was very much tempted to tell Hsing-kuan about whom she suspected An-ni to be, but she decided to be quiet about it for fear that it might cause a lot of trouble. She figured that, fortunately, her brother-in-law had already died, and as long as she kept quiet, nobody would know anything about An-ni's history. Yü-kuan enjoyed her new job as a school principal very much. In nearly a year since she had taken over the job, she had stopped worrying so much. The church might not notice anything different, but Yü-kuan knew she was now taking a genuine interest in what she was doing rather than using her job as a stepping stone to something else. From time to time, Chien-teh would write to her and sometimes even send her some money, which naturally pleased her. She spent all her money on the development of the school, and all those who knew her appreciated her. But to her, all she did was simply repentance for her past sins.

A few more years slipped by in busy work. Yü-kuan's school was becoming a good one, but in the meantime, Yü-kuan's chronic heart condition began to flare up again. Finally, she decided to ask Hsing-kuan to come and help. For Hsing-kuan, this was not a bad idea at all, since she was somewhat lonely living all by herself in the city. Before she moved, Hsing-kuan left both her house and Yü-kuan's place in the care of the church and arranged that the rent go directly to the development fund of the school. For all practical purposes, one could say that the school in Chin-li was run by the two women.

Turmoils gradually subsided, and the village was restored to the peace and quiet that it had known in the old days. For Yü-kuan, the only thing missing from the scene was Ch'en Lien. Whenever Yü-kuan thought of him, she was genuinely tempted to tell Hsing-kuan about him. But she always managed to curb herself in time. Since Ch'en Lien was far away in Borneo, what good would it do for Hsing-kuan to know anyhow? Sometimes, when the early morning clouds were about to disperse or when the evening mists began to gather, she would go to Ta-wang Temple and sit on that old tree root, reminiscing about her conversations with Ch'en Lien so many years before. Despite her old age, sweet memories of the past would still bring her pleasure. She felt almost young again.

The villagers in Chin-li were grateful for Yü-kuan's work there over the years; especially they remembered her heroic protection of the captive women during the days of turmoil. So some of them decided to pool resources and celebrate her birthday as a token of their gratitude for her many years of hard work in Chin-li. In a few days even the people in the neighboring county got wind of what the villagers were planning to do for Yü-kuan. The church, seeing that everybody was so enthusiastic, had to take note of the situation and decided to have a commemorative party to honor Yü-kuan's forty years of service. The gregarious villagers were naturally excited about the coming party, and in a very short period of time they raised several hundred dollars for the occasion. Yü-kuan herself was more embarrassed than excited by the enthusiasm of the villagers, telling them not to spend so much money and energy for her sake. She told them that she had

simply been doing what she wanted to do, and that there was nothing really worth celebrating; she confessed that her past mistakes were precisely due to her greed for reward, which in the end brought her only emptiness and disappointment. She now realized, she added, that one's service was valuable only when one sought to benefit not oneself but other people. Regardless of what Yü-kuan said, the people in the village worked together, and, in a short while, the whole village was decked out for the occasion.

The minister suggested to the villagers that they should use the huge sum of money they had collected for something of lasting value. Some felt that a stone tablet should be erected in honor of Yü-kuan near the community property, and some suggested that a stone arch would be more impressive. As for Yü-kuan, she would have liked it all to be spent on the school if she could have had it her way. Hsing-kuan, who knew that Yü-kuan was not concerned about personal glory anymore, did not really try to urge her to accept either of these grandiose expressions of gratitude by the villagers. She did take the initiative to write to Chien-teh, telling him how his mother was respected and loved by the villagers and how they were thinking of honoring her for many years of service there. Chien-teh sent five thousand dollars right after he received the letter, and said that he would come with An-ni to celebrate the grand occasion.

Yü-kuan was ten thousand times happier about Chien-teh's coming than about his gift of five thousand dollars. The villagers were busy with various tasks to prepare for the commemoration party, and they unanimously decided to spend two thousand dollars to build a bridge right outside the city. There was a genuine need for a new bridge, because the only bridge over the brook, a wooden one, was in very bad condition. Moreover, the entrance to Ta-wang Temple was a place where Yü-kuan spent a lot of time; the fact that the government had given the forest area across from the brook to the school made it all the more necessary to build a bridge.

In five months the bridge was built; at the same time Ta-wang Temple was renovated, and the people in the village changed it into a local office. The bridge was fifteen feet wide and thirty feet long. It was made of cement mixed with cobblestones, and its surface was laid in granite. At the end of the bridge, there was a wide road leading straight to the forest. To say nothing of its practical function, the new bridge added much to the scenery of the surrounding area.

Chien-teh and his wife An-ni came back just before the commemoration party. Unfortunately, from overexcitement, Yü-kuan's heart condition flared up again, but somehow she managed not to let anybody know it. For Yü-kuan, An-ni's coming was a great honor, but her arrogance to Hsing-kuan, whom she met for the first time, gave people the impression that she didn't want to have anything to do with this old country bumpkin. In less than two days, An-ni had started nagging her husband about returning to Nanking.

In the eyes of the villagers, Chien-teh was an important mandarin in the capital, and so they decided to hold the commemoration at an earlier date in order to cater to his wife. Yü-kuan fainted from overexcitement several times that day. Seeing that Yü-kuan was not physically fit, Hsing-kuan insisted that she stay at home instead of going to the church for the ceremony. After the ceremony, it was Chien-teh who led the villagers at the dedication of the new bridge; after considering several names, they had finally decided to call it Yü-tse Bridge [9] in honor of Yü-kuan's kind service over the years. The occasion was marked with incredibly lively drum music, fireworks, and an opera, which added a great deal to the grandness of the atmosphere.

The next day, when Chien-teh and An-ni came to say goodbye to Yü-kuan before they went back, Hsing-kuan was there too. Hsing-kuan was most impressed by the young couple, whose presence triggered off a lot of tears because she was painfully reminded of her own daughter, Ya-yen. Again, at this point, Yü-kuan was tempted to reveal to Hsing-kuan who she suspected An-ni to be, but she was afraid that An-ni would scold her and refuse to accept the fact. Yü-kuan figured

that even if An-ni recognized Hsing-kuan as her mother, she still would not live with the two old women. So finally, with tears in her eyes, Yü-kuan sent the young couple off until they disappeared beyond the newly built Yü-tse Bridge.

But when Yü-kuan got back to school, she regretted very much that she had not disclosed the great secret in front of An-ni. When Hsing-kuan came, Yü-kuan asked her, smilingly, whom she would like to meet first if she had a choice between her husband and her daughter. Hsing-kuan did not take Yü-kuan's question seriously at all. She told Yü-kuan that it was pure fantasy on her part to conjure up such a situation. However, Hsing-kuan added, if she could but take one look at her daughter, she would be more than satisfied. As for her husband, Hsing-kuan thought that was absolutely hopeless. After chatting for some time, Yü-kuan suddenly told Hsing-kuan that she wanted to go back to the city to see her son and daughter-in-law off on their boat trip [to Nanking]. Hsing-kuan insisted on going there with her; she was worried about Yü-kuan, who looked so exhausted.

By the time the two women got to the city, Chien-teh and An-ni had already left for the harbor. Fortunately, they could still catch up with the couple—it was not departure time yet. They immediately went to the church and learned that Chien-teh and An-ni were staying at the foreign minister's place to wait for the boat. An-ni was genuinely touched when she saw them, and, for the first time, she began to appreciate Yü-kuan's love for Chien-teh. Yü-kuan told them that her health was getting worse, and that she really had no idea whether she would see them again. She hoped they would come back soon. Chien-teh was moved to tears and promised that he would visit her once a year.

That night when Yü-kuan went back to the pharmacy, she told Hsing-kuan that she had to rush through some unfinished business. Hsing-kuan kept asking her what it was about until she finally told Hsing-kuan that she wanted to go to Borneo to look for Ch'en Lien. She said that she

[9] *Yü-tse* means "kindness of Yü-kuan."

owed everything that she was today to Hsing-kuan, ever since she had worked as a maid for the foreign minister. She told Hsing-kuan that she did not realize this in the beginning; not until she got back from Nanking had she begun to think seriously about her past. Then she felt that she must do something nice to return Hsing-kuan's kindness. Hsing-kuan was naturally very happy to know Ch'en Lien's whereabouts and hoped that she could go there to look for him herself. At this point, Yü-kuan produced a ticket from her pocket, and said that she had gotten a berth that day right after she learned at the harbor that there was a ship leaving for Nanking the following day. She wanted Hsing-kuan to stay at home to take care of T'ien-hsi and the school, since only she, Yü-kuan, knew how to look for Ch'en Lien. Besides, the sea breeze would be good for her health.

Early the next morning, Hsing-kuan went to tell Chien-teh that his mother was leaving for Southeast Asia that very day for a vacation. Chien-teh didn't think this was a good idea at all, saying that his mother's heart condition perhaps could not take the sea voyage. They rushed back to the pharmacy, only to find that Yü-kuan had gone. Then they dashed to the harbor and went on board the ship, where they finally found Yü-kuan among a crowd of workers in a third class cabin. Chien-teh begged his mother to move to the first class cabin if she really insisted on going, since there was no reason at all for her to be so stingy with herself. Yü-kuan's reason, however, was that it was easier for her to make friends in the third class cabin, and besides, she did not at all

mind mixing with these people, since they were the type of people she saw every day. An-ni could not stand the cabin at all; no sooner had she put her head in than she went to a first class section. Hsing-kuan was somewhat surprised that Yü-kuan was traveling so light, with only a small bundle of bedding and a small suitcase, and so she asked Yü-kuan what the small suitcase had in it. Yü-kuan said with a smile that what she kept there was simply some old stuff she had been carrying with her for several decades: a copy of the vernacular version of the Bible, a copy of *Pilgrim's Progress,* and the unintelligible *Book of Changes.* Yü-kuan asked them not to worry about her, because everything would be all right; she would have a pleasant journey and come back safely. Pointing at Chien-teh, she turned back and told Hsing-kuan not to estrange herself from him, since he was still her son-in-law. She said she would come back when she finished her business in Southeast Asia and asked Hsing-kuan to wait for the news in Chin-li. She also said a few words to console and encourage Chien-teh before the signal sounded to hurry the passengers on board the ship.

Hsing-kuan and the others went to the sampan, and from there, they could still see Yü-kuan with her tearful face and her gray hair blowing in the wind, leaning against the rail, waving at them with her handkerchief. When they got back to shore, the ship had already started its engines, getting ready to sail toward the sea. They watched the ship for a long time, and it was not until its silhouette passed the watch tower outside the port that they turned back with tears in their eyes.

YEH SHAO-CHÜN
(*1894–*)

The son of an impoverished rent collector in Soochow, Yeh Shao-chün, also known as Yeh Sheng-t'ao, became a teacher upon his own graduation from middle school in 1911, though more as a result of economic necessity than as a career choice. Demands on his time as a conscientious instructor and, later, as a diligent editor for both the Commercial Press and the K'ai-ming Book Company in Shanghai never deterred him from devoting his remaining energies to literature. His close friend, the historian Ku Chieh-kang, encouraged him to heed the call of literary revolution in 1917, and Yeh began writing short fiction in the vernacular language. He became a member of the New Tide Society (*Hsin-ch'ao she*) in 1919 and later, in 1921, a founder of the Literary Association along with Shen Yen-ping and Cheng Chen-to.

In six short story collections, two anthologies of children's literature, one autobiographical novel (*Ni Huan-chih*, 1930), and collections of occasional essays, Yeh Shao-chün has demonstrated his indebtedness to such diverse writers as Su Man-shu, Washington Irving, and Hans Christian Andersen. At the same time, Yeh exhibits in some of his works the influence of such philosophers as Wang-Yang-ming and John Dewey. In the manner of Anton Chekhov, Yeh wrote from a dispassionate stance that often camouflaged deep personal concern and commitment. Themes which occupied Yeh's imagination include: the dilemma faced by the individual in a China of rapid social change; loneliness and alienation; problems in education for both students and teachers; women's liberation; the absurdity of superstitious beliefs and practices in an avowedly secular age; the consequences of military anarchy among Chinese warlords; and the nature of revolution itself. Through his literary career, Yeh's maturation as a short story writer is shown by the increasing use of sophisticated narrative techniques, individuated characterization, and thematic complexity. Indeed, of all the writers associated with the prestigious magazine, *The Short Story*, Yeh has perhaps best stood the test of time with works of consistently high quality.

The thrust of the story "Rice" (*Fan*, 1921), as C. T. Hsia noted, is toward the children's "final comprehension of the menace of approaching famine and death" (*History*, p. 62). Yet it is necessary to recall that, economically, the 1920s were particularly hard on teachers, with their salaries often in arrears, diverted to military budgets, or appropriated by unscrupulous school officials. As a teacher himself, Yeh Shao-chün was apparently in an unenviable position to portray the sorry predicament of Mr. Wu with dramatic authenticity.

"Solitude" (*Ku-tu,* 1923) is a story redolent with Chekhovian melancholy, displaying Yeh's ability to capture the psychological and spiritual despair of a man who finds himself aging, infirm, and alone. "Autumn" (*Ch'iu,* 1932) is another melancholic piece about a professional single woman entering her twilight years who, while "longing nostalgically for the parental roof" (*History,* p. 68), finds instead that she cannot go home again.

"Horse-bell Melons" (*Ma-ling kua,* 1923), an autobiographical story, is told from a child's point of view, but the interest it holds is decidedly as adult as Lu Hsün's "K'ung I-chi," another story that uses the consciousness of a boy to show the debilitating psychological effects which the traditional Chinese examination system had exercised on the individual. But unlike "K'ung I-chi," "Horse-bell Melons" is a warm and affectionate narrative in which the chill of the examination hall is offset by the boy's close family ties and, of course, the taste of the melons.

FRANK KELLY
J.S.M.L.

Rice

by Yeh Shao-chün

Translated by Frank Kelly

"It's time for class now! Just where is your teacher?"

The two-room schoolhouse, already many years old, listed forward in the manner of a hunchback. A muddy road that connected farm plots with the village ran right outside the front gate. The weather was the quintessence of midautumn, with white cirrus clouds drifting through a pale blue sky. The early morning sun shot onto a bank of willow trees, turning their leaves to a soft green and making them appear as they do in the light of spring. In the flat and distant fields the rice shoots and spikes seemed equally light, bending and swaying with a wave-like rhythm in the passing breeze. Farther off, the trees of the village formed what appeared to be a giant ring, stately and still, from which emanated the faint sound of a dog barking. It was, indeed, a seasonal landscape for poets!

Pity, though, that none of the inhabitants here were poets. The six or seven children in the schoolhouse were, in fact, just then in the grip of an unimaginable fear.

Autumn had brought floods with it, and the fields belonging to the children's parents were overflowing. When the water level finally merged with that of the river, the rice plants could only poke their sprouts a few inches above the inundation. The adults sighed constantly in their misery. Some even proclaimed, "The day of starvation is in sight!"

The children thought all this quite odd, and a few said, "We plant the fields. How could *we* starve?" Their parents retorted, "Don't you see

that the paddies are completely underwater, and that not even a single grain of rice has appeared?"

Other children murmured, "If so much rice hadn't been sold last year, everything would have been all right this year!" To which the adults replied, "Who was happy to sell it? A lot *you* know!"

Still other youngsters declared, "If we don't go to school, then everyone can pitch in to work the foot pumps and drain all the water out!" But their parents objected, "Where are you going to pump it? The river is at the same level as the water in the fields!"

The children were then convinced that they lacked the insight of their elders and that death by starvation was indeed staring them squarely in the face. They imagined that death would be just like sleep, something vague and darkened. Enveloped by it, you wouldn't be able to eat or play. You wouldn't even be able to move, since you would probably be tied up somehow and not know when the bonds would be loosened.

Such thoughts terrified the children because, after all, they really had no way of knowing what starvation would be like. But it was definitely coming! Unconsciously, they put aside their normal attitudes. Chasing after each other really wasn't much fun anymore, and the mighty shouts once raised in their throats now brought little joy. Instead, they sat quietly in their schoolroom, murmuring accounts of their cricket-catching experiences in voices that betrayed alarm and depression.

In a room to the left of the schoolroom was a

bed with blankets and a bare table at the head of the bed. Stacked in a corner were pots and pans, jars and cans, kindling and the like, all hidden away in darkness. Through a hole in the wall about a foot square a shaft of sunlight shaped like a rhombic prism illuminated the uneven contours of the mud floor. A length of woodboard formed a partition between the two rooms. More light entered the room to the right of this divider, although both rooms had windows that were now open. A small blackboard hung askew on the partition. Aside from a dozen or so sets of small desks and chairs and one dilapidated rectangular desk of larger size, the room was empty, and what it did contain was none too neatly arranged.

The six or seven students had been slouching in their places and turning toward each other to discuss their adventures in catching crickets. At first, their voices were only whispers, but after talking a while, they began to feel that crickets were the only things that really mattered in the world and they became excited.

One child slapped his desk, gleefully shouting, "There was this really big cricket on the side of a cornstalk. I trapped him just like this. Three other ones had been chewed up pretty good by him. He—"

Just at that moment a man appeared, striding through the door to the side of the blackboard. After an initial glimpse, the children riveted their attention on the figure and the shrill talk of crickets naturally turned to silence. They thought they knew who this person was, but they weren't exactly sure. Their parents had explained, "This gentleman has a great deal of power. He visits the yamen frequently and often discusses matters with the county magistrate. What's more, he is the man who supervises the teachers, and the teachers are afraid of him." This was the extent of the pupils' knowledge about him. Yet they did not find him very fearsome. On the contrary, they found his dazzling set of clothes quite eye-catching.

Now this man stepped into the room and glanced nonchalantly about. Suddenly, he knit his brows and his eyes darted all around, as though on a search. Appearing irritated, and in a rather contemptuous manner, he proceeded to question the students with the words that began our story.

In one hand, Mr. Wu carried a square bamboo-strip basket filled with mustard greens, beancurd, a jar of oil, and other assorted items, while his other hand held a salted fish less than eight inches in length. The teacher scurried through the mired fields, his gaunt face flushed to the nape of the neck and his listless eyes fixed on the ground before him. His breaths grew shorter and shorter until finally he started to pant.

Wu had, in fact, already been alerted. Some woman had warned him: "You had better move quickly! That superintendent of yours has arrived and I just saw him heading toward the school. His boat is moored just beyond the eastern palisade."

What fearful news this was! Wu's entire body felt racked with spasms and his mind went blank. It seemed as if he were no longer master of his rapid stride and glassy stare.

It had certainly been no easy matter for Mr. Wu to obtain his teaching position in that two-room schoolhouse. Only through the most kind efforts of an intermediary provided by a country squire was his name registered with the superintendent of schools. A slender sprout of hope was then implanted in his mind, and he eagerly awaited some good news. He had originally been a village tutor, earning in one season a salary of about fifty strings of cash. But economic responsibilities toward his family weighed heavily on his shoulders, and he realized that unless he found another position he couldn't go on. With a new prospect now open before him, how could he help hoping?

Hope he did, for an entire year, when the unthinkable happened—a letter arrived from the superintendent of schools! It invited Wu to the official's home for an interview, apparently the fruitful result of the country squire's kind intercession. Putting the letter aside, Wu picked it up again to read over and over, now convinced that his expectations had not been misplaced. He need only present himself immediately! Yet, he could not help harboring a feeling of apprehension.

Amazingly enough, it took Wu only three tries to catch the superintendent at home. Wu took an unassuming seat in the parlor and perched on its edge. By leaning forward, he was able to maintain his balance. His vision was blurred to begin with, and now, since he was looking down, he was probably unable to see clearly either the room in which he found himself or his interlocutor.

The superintendent wore an undershirt and was reclining in a rattan chair, his right hand pillowing his head and his eyes regarding Wu askance. Contemptuous thoughts suddenly welled up in the official's mind. He didn't know why, but he felt Wu was unworthy of his gaze.

"Teaching small children," the superintendent began rather reluctantly, "is not an easy task."

Beads of sweat covered Wu's face and he felt ill at ease. He agreed that teaching definitely was not an easy task and, in a trembling tone, replied, "I know."

"There is a vacancy in this county's Public School No. 2. I was thinking of having you take up the post, but . . . You've never attended teachers' college, have you?"

"No." Wu felt a paroxysm of remorse; yet the question was upon him, and he'd had no choice but to respond.

"Now that presents a problem. The students in that school are all children of local villagers. If the instructor is not familiar with teaching methods, it will simply be impossible to get results."

A period of silence followed, during which Wu could hear the beating of his own pulse. With the greatest difficulty he drew a breath and forced himself to say, "There should be some books that explain teaching methods. I could buy one and look it over. I am very eager to obtain your counsel, sir."

"We'll discuss this later." With that, the superintendent brought the conversation to a close.

After taking his leave, Wu felt that his sprout of hope had been crushed. He was filled with gloom and despair on his way home. He was extremely afraid, and thought his only course lay in presenting himself once more to the country squire with connections. Fortunately, the squire agreed to write a letter for him, and Wu was soon back in the sitting room of the superintendent.

"I had originally intended to hire a teachers' college graduate," said the official gravely, "but now, because of this letter of recommendation, I'll hire you."

"No mistake about it—I heard him clear as a bell. He just hired me," Wu said to himself. His heart fluttered and he was unable to speak. His head inclined forward naturally, bowing ever lower.

"Board of Education regulations stipulate that those who are not teachers' college graduates draw a monthly salary of six dollars. You may begin class at the school day after tomorrow."

Wu repeatedly responded "Yes," then withdrew, his new life begun.

A month later when he went to the superintendent's home to pick up his salary, he was mystified, for he received only three dollars. The remaining three would be withheld for ten days. Still, the superintendent ordered him to sign a receipt for ten dollars. Wu wondered why the figures didn't correspond, but a spirit of combined timidity and satisfaction prevented him from opening his mouth to protest.

"I'm not a teacher's college graduate, and there are lots of them out there! Besides, compared with what I was making before, six dollars make things much more comfortable." With that, he buried his suspicions in the back of his mind and left with his three dollars.

When the children heard the superintendent's question, several of them began clamoring together in response. "He's gone to buy things, like beancurd and scallions." At this, a few students stifled their laughter.

"Doesn't look proper, his not being here by this time," the superintendent muttered to himself. After a pause, he put another question to the children.

"Does he do this every day?"

"Every day it's the same. He has to eat." A child who trailed a large queue had spoken up.

Another chimed in, "My mom sometimes takes him along shopping."

"Don't believe *him*, but—"

This youngster, who sported a silver earring and a brash disposition, had not finished speaking when Mr. Wu rushed in, empty-handed, since he had probably already deposited his groceries in the cooking area. He perceived the angry mien of the superintendent, who stood beside the blackboard. Totally at a loss as to how to act, Wu fidgeted left and right, then back and forth. He ended up folding his hands and bowing his head in salutation.

The superintendent nodded curtly in acknowledgment and coldly remarked, "Starting time for class has long since passed, and you're just getting here now!"

Wu wanted to get out a few appropriate words of response but was unable to think, and the awkward position he was in elicited the squeaky laughter of his students. Prevarication, Wu realized, was impossible. He could only mumble the obvious truth in a quavering voice. "I went to buy groceries and didn't anticipate returning late."

"Buy groceries!" The superintendent's voice shrilled. "It's class time and the students are all in their places waiting for you. And you went out to buy groceries?"

"Well then, I simply won't go shopping anymore, that's all," Wu blurted out uncontrollably. The children suddenly burst out laughing, pointing at Wu and whispering to each other, "Teacher isn't going to eat anymore! Teacher isn't going to eat anymore!"

The superintendent felt that Wu was truly an incompetent teacher. The more he looked at him, the more he looked down on him. Wu had neither enthusiasm for teaching nor any sense of responsibility toward his profession. But patience overcame the superintendent as he recalled the important matter concerning which he had come.

Tired of standing and thinking to rest a bit, the official first blew the dust off an empty chair, then carefully grasped the rear hem of his long robe, for fear of soiling or wrinkling it, before he slowly sat down. Cupping his chin with his right hand, he frowned slightly but affected an air of nonchalance.

"You make for a very bad appearance here, having only these few students. In a few days, the provincial school inspector will arrive on his round. From seeing this small number of pupils,

he could infer that this was a poor school. To preserve your own sense of dignity, you need to go get a dozen or so children on loan to cover yourself. It doesn't matter from which families you choose them, just so long as you make sure they'll sit here quietly. This has nothing to do with me, but since I'm concerned about you, I thought I'd mention it."

As the superintendent finished speaking, he passed his left hand over his upper lip in the manner of an elderly man stroking his beard. His eyes were riveted on Wu.

Wu felt as though an invisible rope tightly binding his body had been almost totally loosened, and he was much more relaxed. A warm feeling of gratitude replaced fear in his heart and he became indescribably jubilant. Though he had no idea how to go about borrowing children, he did not want to ask. He merely clasped his hands upon his chest and bowed, mumbling, "Thank you for helping me out, sir. Thank you for helping me out!"

Wu was suddenly struck by a thought. "Isn't this a fine opportunity? I went twice to see him and had no luck, but now here he is at my very door!" An impulse seized him and he spoke up.

"Last month's—" But a wave of embarrassment swept over him and he swallowed the rest.

"What's that?" the superintendent snapped.

"Last month's—" But it was no use for Wu. He could not bring himself to look directly at the superintendent and, as before, he lacked the courage to continue.

"Come now, speak what's on your mind."

Wu realized that he could not remain silent, so he stiffened his resolve and said, "Would you please give me the remaining portion of my last month's salary?" He couldn't have gotten out a single word more.

"What will it be used for?"

"For food and other things."

"Haven't you just returned from buying groceries? What more can you possibly need?"

"My family—there are three more at home. How can I look after myself alone when they're all waiting for something to eat?"

The sound of the word "eat" struck the chil-

dren's ears with particular clarity. They had
forgotten everything else as they watched their
teacher and his guest talking, but they were now
reminded. The boy with the large queue tugged
at the shirttail of the pupil seated in front of him
and whispered, "Did you hear that? Teacher's
family is waiting for this man to give them food to
eat. Otherwise, they'll soon starve to death!"

But the student wearing the earring disagreed
with this conclusion and scoffed, "Teacher has
much more money than we do. When our bones
have rotted, his belly will still be bloated. How can
you talk nonsense!"

"Are we really going to die of hunger and will
our bones rot?" A tiny child, terror flashing in his
eyes, put the question.

"When you go home today there'll be nothing
to eat. Tomorrow you'll starve to death, and the
day after that your bones will rot away. They'll
become soft and squishy like mud." The youngster with the earring proclaimed his predictions
with a great sense of self-satisfaction.

The tiny child questioned no further, having already fallen prey to musings of mystery and terror.

Mr. Wu was quite put out. He had hoped that
his students would sit quietly, but here they were
not only moving about but raising a fuss as if no
one else were around. He shot them glances several times, but with no effect. The youngsters
were really slow to catch on and were completely
insensitive to Mr. Wu's feelings at this moment. If
they could only be quiet for a while! In desperation, Wu was only able to wave his hand and angrily shout, "Silence!"

Like an autumn shower coming to an end, the
patter of the children's voices thinned out here
and there until all was quiet. Every eye was on Mr.
Wu and each student sat up a bit straighter. Unable to bear the shift of their bodies, their chairs
creaked loudly.

The superintendent lowered his right hand,
straightened up and, raising his eyebrows, assumed a stern manner.

"A teacher who does not discharge his responsibilities should be punished rather severely. Today
you shall be punished by having one third of your
entire salary withheld!"

With that, he reached into his pocket and took
out a dollar, which he casually flicked onto the
desk. As it struck, its clear, ringing sound attracted the eager attention of all the children at
once. "This is what you are due," sniffed the superintendent. "Take it."

How could Mr. Wu have foreseen such a turn
of events? Though he was of a mind to argue, he
was unable even to order his thoughts, let alone
form them into words. But, after all, that object
on the desk glistening white as snow was a dollar.
Wu picked it up almost without thinking, feeling
something cold and hard in the palm of his hand.

Solitude

by Yeh Shao-chün

Translated by Frank Kelly

In the tiny parlor burned a "Shell" brand kerosene lamp, its light dim and circumscribed, its shade layered with grimy soot. Everything in the room was thus made to appear hazy and indistinct, without any clear outlines. A small boy listened to his mother tallying the household budget and muttering "So much for vegetables, so much for beancurd, so much for water . . ." The child grew drowsy, his body becoming soft and limp as he leaned against his mother's knee. The woman stopped mumbling to herself and, tenderly patting the boy's chest, asked, "Are you falling asleep?"

Just at that moment could be heard the sound of an old man coughing outside. One cough gave way to an uninterrupted series of hacking noises until his strength was finally exhausted and there remained only the sound of a slight wheezing.

The mother said to her child, "The old gentleman is back." But the little boy was off in a dreamland and perfectly oblivious to his mother's words.

After a moment, the lattice-work door that had been closed was pulled open. The creaking sound of its motion was soon followed once more by the old man's coughing and panting. He grasped the door handle with one hand to support his hunched-over frame. His wizened face had flushed to a scarlet hue, as though he were drunk. As a result of his coughing fit, his eyes glistened and droplets of tears and mucus shone in his moustache. He stood still a moment, until his breathing had almost returned to normal, before stepping across the threshold and turning to close

the door. Since this action too required expending a little more energy, he was forced to lean on the lattice work of the door and succumb to another paroxysm of coughing.

Yet at the same time, the old man's left hand was fumbling around inside his sleeve. When it had found the object of its search, he turned and called to the little child, who was still sunk in his reverie.

"A treat, son?" The old man could not have managed another word. It had taken so much of his strength to get out this one sentence that its last syllables trailed off in a pathetic gasp. Nonetheless, a gnarled and bony hand emerged quivering from his broad sleeve, and in this hand was a bright, fresh Foochow orange.

The mother nudged her child and prompted him, saying, "The gentleman has a treat for you. Do you want it or not?"

The word "treat" seemed to possess a peculiar magic power, for as soon as it penetrated the child's dreamworld, saliva began to run in his mouth, causing him to swallow again and again. He extended his tiny hand, sleepily asking, "Where? Where is it?" But the hand only ended up rubbing his eyes.

"Here it is," answered the old man as he approached the little boy. "Look, what's this?" He brought the orange before the child's eyes and doffed his winter cap with the other hand.

The child saw it quite clearly: "Red, round—I bet it'll taste great!" At the same time, he got a whiff of a delightful scent that made him salivate so fast he couldn't swallow it all. Unable to resist this temptation any longer, the boy's little hand darted toward the old man's to grab the orange.

But the old man suddenly withdrew his hand and looked at the child. Smiling an ugly smile, he said with a slightly seductive tease to his voice, "Say hello to me and I'll give it to you." He was able to formulate this relatively long sentence only because he had rested up a bit by standing still a while, allowing his wheezing and coughing to abate.

The little boy, however, paid him no mind whatsoever and, moving forward a step, stuck his hand out farther in pursuit of the retreating orange. The old man had drawn his hand back as far as he could, but, not possessing the agility of the child's, it was finally caught. Still, he gripped the orange insistently, once more assuming an air of enticement as he smiled. "Say hello to me. Just say hello to me."

The mother again tried to prod her son. "Now darling, say hello to the gentleman and he'll give the orange to you. Say 'sir' or 'grandpa.' " She looked at the child and directed his attention toward the old man with a smile, hoping that the little boy would comprehend the meaning she was trying to convey.

But the youngster missed the point entirely. One of his hands had failed in its mission, so the other was brought in as reinforcement in the attempt to pry open the old man's fingers. The old man sensed the futility of resistance and relaxed his grip, saying, "Okay, take it." He had suddenly realized that the demand he had just made of the child was meaningless and he had only gotten what he deserved. Feelings of loneliness began to layer over his heart like drifting clouds. He could only stand there, stroking his gray beard.

The victorious little boy had by this time peeled away the skin of the orange and was bringing a section of the pulp to his mouth. Tugging on his mother's sleeve, he said, "Let's go bye-bye. I want to take this to bed."

The mother, meanwhile, was a bit embarrassed by her child's words, so she made a point of scolding him. "You're such a brat! You won't say hello to the gentleman, but you'll eat his goodies! Bad enough you're eating that orange—now you want to take it to bed!"

The little boy really did not feel that there was either harshness or severity in these words, so he continued tugging on his mother to leave. He would tug a while, then relent, lifting another section of orange to his lips.

The mother, in fact, had no intention of stopping him. Now that he had become more insistent, she could only stand up and address the old man: "I wonder whether you would like to retire to your room, sir? We won't take our lamp away until you've lit your own. There's boiled water under the cozy. Please help yourself."

The old man was just then gazing at the little boy eating his orange. He noticed how smugly the victor was consuming his spoils, without paying him the slightest attention. This made the man feel extraordinarily empty inside, as if there were no substance whatever to his physical being. And when he heard his landlady urge him to retire, dejection once more welled up within him. "So even here there's no place for me. I'm only fit to be imprisoned in that cramped little world!" Thinking thus, he moved off toward the left corner of the room and removed a key from his pocket to unlock a door there.

Stooped over, applying all the strength in his wrist, and with inattentive eyes causing him to fumble fruitlessly, the old man took a long while to get the door open. But all this activity induced another severe coughing spell, preventing him from going through the door. Once again he had to lean against its frame for support.

Over half of the orange sections had by this time disappeared from the little boy's hand. Any further delay would mean that he wouldn't be able to finish them in bed, so he urged his mother to hurry.

The mother restrained him, saying, "Wait—just wait another minute!" But as her eyes came to rest on the old man's back, she frowned. "He coughs like this all the time," she thought. "Why is he finding it so difficult to bear tonight?"

The wheezing hadn't completely stopped, but as soon as it had eased up a little, the old man pushed the door open and entered his room. In the dim light that penetrated from outside, he groped about for a match. He struck one and lit a white candle, whose faint halo of light illuminated a faint round world. The objects beyond the pale of this world, however, remained tucked away in darkness as before. The old man used his sleeve to wipe away a layer of dust on a table, resulting in the formation of a few jumbled patterns all too obvious to the eye. A teacup, rice bowl, teapot, and kerosene stove were also scattered on the table top, along with the shards of some sugar cakes and the bones of a once marinated fish. The features of all these objects were revealed quite clearly.

Outside, the landlady called, "Since you have your own light, we'll go in now." And with that, the two, mother and son, could be heard moving off to their own room.

"Ah, how can I go on like this?" sighed the old man to himself, almost inaudibly, before turning to shut the door. But then he remembered that there was boiled water under the tea cozy in the outer room, so he opened the door again and groped about in the darkness until he found it. He touched the kettle and found it only luke-warm. After closing the door once more behind him, he lit the kerosene stove and placed the kettle on top of it. Soot started to spew forth, but the old man was oblivious to it, panting as he was once again. He sat down slowly on a bed that was pushed against the rear wall just beyond the perimeter of dull light.

Such had been his routine for about twenty years now. His bed was never made. When he went to sleep, he merely pulled the covers over him, and when he got up he left them in a heap. Mixed up with them were some out-of-season clothes and a few sashes, money purses, and the like that he was no longer using. With this arrangement, he could both avoid the bother of continually having to open and close his trunk and add a bit more warmth to the bedclothes. Though he eventually began to feel the physical burden pressing down on him, he still couldn't

bear to forfeit the added insulation. During the day, his bedding and mosquito net were quite discernible as being sooty black in color, and one would have found it hard to believe that their material had once been pure white. The kerosene stove was no doubt to blame for this, particularly the way the old man used it.

He sat resting and after a while began to doze, but an apprehensive heart kept him from drifting into a sound sleep. Getting up in the morning and retiring at night were the two crises he feared the most. The mere act of buttoning or unbuttoning, taking off or putting on a shirt could unleash a spasm of coughing. Only after a long pause while the fit subsided would he dare move again. And yet, still another bout could always be anticipated. He always needed a couple of hours to settle in peacefully for the night or dress himself completely in the morning. And every day of his life now, he faced these two intervals of hard labor. He was truly terrified of them, and he would have been perfectly content if sleep were totally unnecessary. But what else can one do at night except go to sleep?

The old man seemed to hear the pitter-patter of light rain and drowsily surmised that there would be more to worry about when he went out the next day. But he suddenly realized that the sound wasn't rain at all and, lifting himself up, he walked over to the table, quickly snatched up the kettle, and leaned over to blow out the stove flame. Yet the fire was not to be easily extinguished. Following the old man's attempt, the flames licked upright as before while kerosene fumes filled the room. He thought of another method and, turning the flame down very low, he blew once again, and the fire went out.

He poured himself a cup of boiled water and, lifting it with both hands, slowly began to drink from it as he leaned on the bed. His hands, now warmed, felt quite comfortable compared to his feet, which were cold as ice. The old man was over sixty years of age, his circulation increasingly poor, and the chill of a winter night wrapped itself so tightly around him that, despite his thickly padded Mongolian-style slippers, it was as though he went barefoot. But there was really no way out; sticking his feet under the covers to warm them was no easy task.

The boiled water was soothing as it slid down his throat. His coughing stopped and his breathing became regular, almost as if he weren't sick at all. He felt so content at this rare circumstance that he remained quite still in his leaning position. In truth, he was pitiable, for this cup of boiled water was the whole of his supper!

As a younger man, he had been a notorious toper. He was to be found every night at the local tavern, playing finger-guessing games with friends and consuming quantities of alcohol in the process. He would eventually return home, where his wife would already have prepared a delicious meal and decanted some vintage Shao-hsing wine. He would slowly pour the wine out for himself and either skim a few lines of a book or make small talk with his spouse before lifting the glass to his lips.

Life continued on in this way, uninterrupted, until his wife passed away. Yet he kept on drinking just as before, getting tipsy at the tavern. When his boon companions started to die off, he sent sets of mourning scrolls or packets of spirit money and each time was moved to sadness. Later on, when it got so that he hardly knew anyone among the tavern customers, he decided to invade the camaraderie of the inner room no longer, preferring instead to sit alone at the outside bar. The drinking games of the past seemed a remote dream as he sat gazing at the passersby on the street and downing his lonely wine.

In addition to his coughing spells, the old man had within the last few years fallen prey to spells of nausea. When, after a drinking bout, he went home to sleep, he would often be jolted awake in the middle of the night with unbearable churnings of the stomach. A sour-tasting, rancid liquid would then regurgitate into his mouth, and after he spit this out he would immediately be seized with an asthma-like attack. All hope of falling back to sleep had, of course, by this time disappeared. Opening his eyes, he was aware only of a limitless blackness, so impenetrable as to make him despair of ever seeing daylight again. Closing

his eyes, he was pursued by profuse unspeakable terrors and sorrows that pierced his heart. Yet he was unable to speak (and even if he could, to whom would he speak?); he could only sigh, long and deeply.

A doctor he consulted decided that the principal cause of his illness was drinking. When asked if he was urinating with any discomfort, the old man replied that he didn't urinate much at all, and when he did, the urine was cloudy. The physician then told him that it was absolutely necessary for him to forswear alcohol. The old man had himself suspected that his was a drinking ailment, but evenings still found him perched at the bar, sipping his usual libation. Yet his capacity was diminishing, and after having drunk less than half a liter he would feel quite bloated. What's more, he feared that even this much would come back up in the middle of his sleep, so he stopped drinking. But it was no use. He would still end up retching in the night.

And so it went until this winter, when a severely cold northwest wind that had been howling for two days poured misery through the old man's entire body. The taste of wine seemed to have changed. Once he got it into his mouth he couldn't swallow it. This, then, was to be the fatal farewell to his old friend of several decades!

There was no end to the vomiting, however. It didn't matter what he ate of an evening—a bowl of congee, a few sweet cakes—everything would return in the dead of night. Still, on a few occasions, he had consumed nothing at night and had somehow managed to escape the problem. Wiser for this experience, he decided to make boiled water his whole supper. He chose water over tea because he felt the latter's taste also had recently changed.

After the old man had finished his cup of water, the warm feeling in his palms gradually gave way to the cold and he had no alternative but to stand up and put the cup down. His feet were so frigid they hurt. Reflecting that sooner or later he would have to endure his nightly torture, he decided that for the sake of his feet he might as well get to bed a bit early.

Courage then welled up in him, and he moved

the candlestand to a chair in front of the bed. He sat down on the bed, steeling himself to perform the impossible. The coughing had commenced right on cue, of course, and his breath was nearly gone by the time he leaned on the bed's headboard for support. Having all the patience of a monk enduring a spiritual trial, however, the old man paused until the coughing had subsided, then undid a few buttons and got out of one sleeve of his shirt.

His clothes were covered with stains and were all either torn or had holes in several places. Ever since his wife's death, he had been buying new clothes from an apparel store. If they got stained, torn, or perforated while he wore them, he paid no attention, since he had never before mended anything. But when it got so that even he, through his tired old eyes, perceived his shabby appearance, he would go buy some new things, leaving the old for the rubbish heap.

When he lay sprawled on the bed asleep, with the covers wrapped around him, a slight snore emerged from somewhere in the old man's throat. Not having the strength to move again, he felt his body as a pile of immobile stones pressing down heavily on the mattress. With the fire now extinguished, darkness enveloped his tired old eyes but could not cloak his lonely heart. His heart was a spark about the size of a bean, flickering, flashing. Though slight, if it began to burn, it could become a flame to set the heavens ablaze. At the moment, this heart was flashing as he recalled the events of the day.

That morning, he had, as usual, struggled out of bed at the crack of dawn, knowing full well he was practically issuing a special invitation to a coughing fit. But to remain in the darkness, were his eyes open or closed, induced all the fears of incarceration, and a mere glimpse of the dawn left him no choice but to cast caution to the winds and escape.

By the time he had finished putting on his clothes, it seemed all he could do to exhale. Leaning on the bedpost, he didn't dare move, and dropped his head slowly to reduce the rate of exhalation. A gray light framed his face, and

around his eyes pale black circles were faintly discernible. If he had had a mirror with which to examine himself, he perhaps would not have recognized the person in the glass. Fortunately, he had long ago given up such vanity. In fact, he no longer even knew where the mirror was.

He rested against the bed quite a while before shuffling over to the table, where he lit the kerosene stove to boil a little water. A thick deposit of soot had collected on the bottom of the kettle and was spreading to its sides and handle. So when the old man picked it up, his fingers became part blackened, but since he never paid any attention to such things, he didn't notice it. When a slight bubbling sound could be heard in the kettle, he poured the water into a basin and perfunctorily washed his face.

Afterward, the old man put on his cap and prepared to leave. The cap was his constant companion, off his head no more than a few months a year. He continued to wear it even when the pomegranates were in bloom, and when people had just begun to wear lined coats in enjoyment of midautumn, he had long since donned the cap again. It was made of black satin, but its fringe was now almost completely frayed. Filthy, it gave off a bright oily sheen. He would slip it on carelessly, only bothering to fasten a button or two. Sometimes he'd put in on aslant, giving his countenance a tilted appearance and making the children in the alley clap their hands and laugh aloud.

The old man shut the door, locked it, and fumbled inside his coat pocket with trembling hands before going out. The main gate was already open, and at the entry stood Tailor Ting, just at that moment buttoning his coat in front of his store. He greeted the old man with his customary question: "Out for a stroll, sir?"

"Yes," came the old man's stock reply, and with persistent panting, he was off. The cold morning wind struck him in the face and cleared his breathing passages. But at the same time, his skin felt pulled taut and he was very uncomfortable about it. He was bent far over, arms held tightly against his body, hands tucked into the sleeves opposite them. In this way, his solitary, wasted body passed through the clear cold of the streets.

The old man arrived at a teahouse where only a few customers were present, all sitting in silence. When a waiter who was sweeping the floor saw the wizened figure approaching, he went to wring out two hot hand towels for him to wipe his face and then poured out a pot of boiling water which he placed on a table.

Very few people drink boiled water in a teahouse. In the morning, everyone delights in sipping a strong brew of tea that seems to impart an added zest for going about the day's activities. But since the old man's tastes had changed, he could no longer tolerate the strong bitterness of tea. Clear and flavorless boiled water had become its substitute!

And yet, where else could he go besides the teahouse? Though the world was vast, he felt that entry was barred to him everywhere else he went. Only the bed in his room and this chair in the teahouse were on relatively familiar terms with him and still permitted his companionship. As a result, he cherished these two objects with a particular fondness. In fact, it could be said that in the teahouse, the chair had become the sole object of his affections, since he had no relationship at all with the other patrons, who all ignored him.

Occasionally, a number of customers would congregate around him to chat about seasonal outings, social news, political events, and so on. This provoked an overwhelming emotion in the old man: there they were, having a good time, discussing all manner of things, as if to flaunt pride in their superiority and, in the process, ridicule his own solitude and senility. But then, past memories, permanently engraved in his mind, would one by one unfurl themselves like scrolls. Comparing present with past, the old man became even more aware that the "now" of his existence was unbearable. A long, audible sigh escaped with his wheezing breath. Though no tears formed in his eyes, there was desolation there. Yet he remained sitting in the teahouse and went nowhere else.

This particular day, the old man had had a few things to eat and had drunk two pots of boiled water. He had been watching the throng of other customers thin out. The majority were inviting each other to go gambling and fritter away the time they had so much in abundance. The rest of them were going off to attend to business. The old man was himself preparing to leave, but the worrisome question was: where to? It was the same impasse he encountered every morning just prior to leaving the teahouse.

Suddenly, he thought of his niece (the only relative he had), whom he hadn't seen for nearly three months, and decided to pay her a visit. His motive for going was naturally not limited to making a social call. He was seriously ill and had not heard a soothing word from another soul, nor had he ever complained of his condition to anyone. To him, this sort of suffering was far more intolerable than the disease itself. Now that he had thought of her, a secret anticipation ignited like fire within him. He had to go see her at once! Her home was quite a distance, and getting there on foot would present innumerable difficulties, so he opted instead to hire a sedan-chair.

His niece made a truly admirable housewife. Methodical at managing all the details of housework, she was also well-versed in social matters. She was, in short, a delight to all. The young woman was about thirty years old, but because she had never given birth and knew how to care for her appearance, she looked just over twenty. Around her cheeks there remained the rosy flush or maidenhood, and her eyes were clear and brimming with vitality. Her husband, Hua Suichih, was a middle-school teacher, and they were very affectionate with each other.

On this particular afternoon, the couple was planning to attend a friend's "cold-dispelling party" to celebrate the winter thaw. The lady of the house was just getting ready for the affair when the old man's sedan arrived. As soon as she saw how he was panting, she invited him to be seated on a sofa. The old man emitted a slightly melancholic sound, similar to that made by a baby suddenly seeing its mother.

A yearning to be soothed shone in his eyes as he said, "Haven't seen you in a long time. How've you been?" Gasping for breath, he forced himself to continue, "I'm really having a hard time of it!

There's no strength in my arms or legs and my body only seems to get heavier. I'm unable to eat anything at night; if I do, I can't keep it down. My cough has really gotten serious. It barely lets me move. It's really getting hard for me."

His niece smoothed the hair around her temples as she studied his face, seeing much there that was worrisome. But she decided to make light of it and comforted him. "Don't fret—that's nothing unusual. The weather has been cold recently and elderly people are bound to feel some discomfort. Wait until spring. It'll gradually get warmer and your health will return to normal."

These words struck him as commonplace, and he was more than a bit disappointed. He thought to himself, "Young people really don't understand the old and their suffering. Here I come right out and tell her my troubles, and she dismisses the whole situation so easily!" He felt a twinge of bitterness and reiterated his plaint. "I'm really having a hard time of it! One thing I know for sure—it's never been this bad before."

Making no effort to be any more consoling, his niece only repeated, "Don't worry, don't get upset. It'll be all right."

The old man then realized the futility of trying to rouse her sympathies and spoke of the situation no more, merely mumbling his assent. Then he leaned back on the sofa to give his mind a rest. His niece smiled at him and said, "You must have lunch here today. I'll have someone go buy a little wine and you and Sui-chih can drink together."

"I don't drink anymore—not a drop. For years and years I drank too much and now I can't handle it!" A wan smile appeared on his face.

"Surely it won't hurt to have just a touch?"

"No, really, not even a drop. All wine has changed its taste as far as I'm concerned and, try as I might, I can get none of it down. Anyway, I can't stand for it to come back in the middle of the night." He sighed almost inaudibly.

She realized that talk of drinking was only intensifying his melancholy, so she changed the subject. "Today a friend of ours is throwing a 'cold-dispelling party.' We're planning to go after lunch. Indoor games will be avilable there, a lady is going to sing, and there'll be four male and female dance teams. Toward evening, everyone will gather around the table for a 'fire pot meal'[1] and eat to his heart's content. It will be an interesting party, and everyone should have a good time, especially since the guests will be free to do as they please. We should all be like one big happy family!" She rose to open the window facing south and let in more sunlight. The old man's whole body was bathed in it.

Again he felt the subtly oppressive force in her words, causing him grief over his own decrepitude and loneliness. The old man had been no stranger to the merriment of group gatherings in the past, and listening to songs and dancing had not been dreamlike activities unknown to him. Yet now those things seemed hazy and far away, remnants of life superfluous to his present solitary and isolated existence. The young woman's conversation, then, assumed a mocking tone in his ears. He fumed inwardly: "Young people are always up to something, parties, singing, dancing—all nonsense and nothing more!" But an involuntary response then tumbled from his lips. "So, there's a party."

"Yes, and it's for couples only too, though those with children can bring them along. Another special feature."

But the old man wasn't really paying much attention, and spoke on something else with great concern. "The two of you are doing so well here, it's a shame you have no children. You wouldn't need a horde of them, mind you. One or two make all the seasons seem like spring and bring boundless zest to one's life." As he said this, he looked around the room, as if to demonstrate that if they were to take his suggestion, "zest" would cascade into and fill the room like air.

"We don't really see it that way," she countered softly. "In our view, the arrival of a child can of course be a very joyful event, involving responsibilities and emotional commitment. But we are

[1] A meal prepared with uncooked meat, poultry, and seafood sliced into thin pieces on separate dishes. On the center of a round dinner table is set a special designed *wok*-shaped charcoal broiler filled with steaming hot water. Food can be cooked rare, medium, or well-done according to individual taste in this "fire pot."

unwilling to admit to a lack in our lives just because we don't have any children at the moment. Children can be a source not only of joy but of psychological concern and physical exhaustion as well.

"What's more, children can't be companions to their parents all their lives. Of course, their winsome smiles and charm can cause a blissful oblivion, and make us feel as though we had seized a monopoly on the meaning of life. But they grow up all too quickly, making their own friends, forming their own opinions. We, then, come to be looked on as outsiders. Though they may continue to associate with us, they are merely going through the motions, conforming with the demands of propriety. I think the sorrow of losing something one has once gained is quite unbearable, and that not to have gained in the first place is much to be preferred."

Again the old man was rudely awakened, and his entire being was overcome with emotion which he had no way to express. He could only lower his eyes in silence. Actually, he had come to the same conclusion himself, and the older he got, the truer it seemed to him. To hear his niece speak as she did just then only served to recut an already deep scar in his heart. He thought to himself, "How can this be only a matter of the child's relationship to his parents? It's actually the common outlook of all younger people toward their elders. You're still a young woman, so naturally you haven't yet realized this." He didn't utter a word of this to her, however.

His niece's demeanor grew more gentle as she continued. "We don't feel anything missing right now. In fact, we feel snug and secure. My only hope is for Sui-chih and myself to remain healthy always, peacefully reaching a ripe old age. Then we will thank fate for being so good to us. I believe a human's closest and most abiding companion is one's spouse. If two people of one mind and heart bind themselves together, if they share the same interests and are approximately the same age, then there will be no danger of separation. And in one's declining years, when everyone else has disappeared, you need only consider: each has the other as lifelong companion, and compared to having anyone else, this is a full

blessing and reason for pride." At this point, she displayed a slightly self-indulgent smile. Her cherished desires had unintentionally been made known.

The old man acted as though he had seen a ghost. In a near-reclining position, he raised one hand to cover his face, knit his eyebrows tightly together, and once more emitted a sigh that was more a wheeze. His niece took this as symptomatic of the ill humor of all old people and, concluding that he had tired of the conversation, said no more, save for one solicitous question: "Would you like some tea?"

"No, no," he mumbled in refusal. How could she know of his pain? It was like a long-standing scar, constantly inflamed, given no chance to heal completely. That it was an old wound to begin with, and had been well bandaged up, almost made ignoring it possible. Now, however, an arrow had been unleashed that found its mark in that very spot. A sudden pain had shot through him, sufficient to resurrect all the hurts of the past. It was unbearable for the old man, particularly since the archer in this case was his own niece. Yet how could she have known?

In general, husbands and wives who are in love would more or less share the young woman's viewpoint. Precisely because they are in love, they wish to seek love's motivation, and this is truly a dark mystery to penetrate. Fully aware that this mystery is difficult to untangle, yet still determined to seek a simple answer, husbands and wives often resort to eternal companionship as the solution. Such had been the case with the old man and his wife. They not only thought in this way—they also voiced their feelings as proof. Unexpectedly their opinions were so similar that the then young man in his joy clasped his wife's hand as tightly as he could. But his spouse shook it free, poured out a brimming cup of wine, and smilingly presented him with it.

"As our hearts are a perfect match, I will share this cup with you in celebration!" she declared. He drew near to her to drink his half, and she then drained the remainder.

This was for him an ineradicable memory. But the young couple's wish turned out to be an empty hope, for he had barely reached middle age when his wife was taken from him. It was as though his internal organs had been crushed, and he suffered unspeakable agonies. Drinking offered little comfort, but what else could he do but drink?

So year after year he continued to drink, and each year he became more convinced that the original wish of those two hearts united as one had been full of meaning, even though it was now no longer attainable for him. This thought made the old man hate himself for having such a heavy body, unable to float airily away into the void and be transformed into immaterial specks of dust.

Now that his old sorrows had been reawakened by his niece, and at a time when his old sickness was being complicated by a new one, he was all the more distressed, reluctant even to sigh. If he were to breathe his last at this moment, would he not be better off?

His niece, however, had no inkling of any of this. Seeing that he refused the tea and seemed quite tired, she thought to let him rest a while. She herself sat in the same chair and fingered some young daffodils that were protruding a few inches out of a vase.

Silence reigned a while in the room until shattered by the sound of someone's hurried footsteps outside. Sui-chih entered the room quickly, calling out as he did, "Let's eat now!" But when his eye fell upon the old man in his reclining position, he offered a salutation.

"Ah, Uncle is here! We haven't seen you in quite a long time." With that, he removed his topcoat and scarf. There was a fresh and rosy radiance to his near-frozen face.

"I haven't been here very long. Yes, it's been an age since we last met." The old man sat up a bit, heavily exerting himself to do so, and nodded to Sui-chih, who in turn hastily responded, "Please relax—no need to sit up." By the time these words were spoken, the old man had resumed his original position, his chest heaving.

Sui-chih too sat down and listened to his wife explain the old man's situation. He could only frown in silence, since it was so difficult for him to think up comforting words to say. But when his wife had finished speaking, he forced himself to open his mouth.

"Uncle shouldn't be concerned. Just take good care of yourself and you'll be all right." Turning to his wife, he added, "We really should eat."

The old man did not respond. Either he hadn't heard the young man or he didn't know what to say.

During the meal, the old man found the rice too hard for his few remaining teeth. The soup didn't seem warm enough either, and swallowing it made him uncomfortable. His niece noticed his difficulty and, deducing that old people crave different types of food, gave him a fresh helping of softer rice and specially made a hot bowl of soup for him. It was only with this that the old man was able to force half a bowl of the rice down into his stomach.

When the meal was over, they rested a bit until Sui-chih, starting to grow impatient, addressed his wife: "Well, it's time. We really should be going." And to the old man he said, "It's unfortunate you picked a day to visit when we can't spend more time with you. We have this—"

His wife interrupted. "I've already explained to Uncle that there's this 'cold-dispelling party.' So inopportune! Otherwise, we could have talked much longer. I hope Uncle can come by this way again soon and spend an entire day with us."

As they spoke, both husband and wife wore embarrassed smiles which could also have been interpreted as disdainful.

"I have to be on my way in any case. Can't lie around here all day!" The old man responded with emotion, for he was deeply resentful at heart. His hatred, however, was directed at no one but himself. "Why did it occur to me to come here? Surely this is no place for me, and surely now I'm being chased away!" So thinking, he raised himself to a sitting position, then to a stand, and prepared to take his leave.

Sui-chih and his wife were embarrassed at this and both of them spontaneously chorused, "There's no hurry. Please stay a while longer."

"No, I really have to go. I'll come back some other day." His feet began to take those steps that were so difficult for him.

"Then we won't keep you. Please take good care of yourself." His niece bade him goodbye, purring as only a female can.

"Many thanks."

"Hire a sedan chair for your trip back," urged Sui-chih solicitously.

"Won't be necessary. If I walk slowly, it will help my circulation. If I get tired, I can stop in at a roadside teahouse and rest. Besides, I can hire a chair anytime on the spur of the moment."

The couple accompanied the old man to the door and watched his solitary form slowly recede in the soft, cold sunlight. "Poor old man," sighed the two together. They went back inside, readied themselves a bit, then went off hand in hand to the "cold-dispelling party." After a few songs and a few laughing conversations, all memory of the impression their uncle had created was erased.

The old man, meanwhile, was shuffling along the road, wheezing all the way. When a coughing fit erupted, he would stand still, patting his chest until the seizure had passed before resuming his trek. He kept reproaching himself as he walked.

"Going to visit them this time was really asking for trouble." And then the other feelings would well up again: "Everything has changed today, and none of it is right, the way I see it. All right, friends throw parties, but why must husband and wife both go together? It's only to show off that you two are a couple, a match! Isn't that going a bit too far?" As he mulled these things over, his eyes emitted a weak but angry light. It did not matter that his two relatives no longer stood before him to receive it.

He stopped for tea three times during his trip before arriving at the establishment he normally frequented. It was like homecoming after a long separation and a warm sensation took hold of him as he eased into his dilapidated old chair. Even the boiled water that the waiter served him seemed especially sweet. He was now enjoying himself in silence. The cacophony of the other patrons' voices and laughter blared out as usual, of course, and was enough to induce once more the old man's consciousness of solitude. But he had one means of escape. He was already somewhat deaf, and this condition, coupled with his deliberate disregard, made all sounds seem vague, distant, and without meaning. The old man made a valiant struggle against the feelings of indignation inside him, refusing to allow them to build into a conflagration. His eyes closed, but he did not fall asleep.

There weren't many windows open in the teahouse. The waning winter sunlight slanted westward until it rolled completely away, leaving the old man feeling even further enveloped by the gloomy cold. Exhalations of carbon dioxide and the smoke from water pipes curled upward and hung in a sedentary cloud, framing all the customers in shadowy silhouettes and making them appear as they would through a thick fog. Dim hanging lamps were lit, but they merely defined circles tinged with red in the smoky atmosphere and were powerless to penetrate the overall blackness beyond. The old man had been thoroughly familiar with this transformation for decades, so he paid it no attention now.

Though he fought the fires of indignation, he could not combat every furtive lick of flame. When these flared up, he would open his eyes and look all around him, sometimes sipping boiled water as he did so. Once, when he focused his vision, he discovered that the other customers had, to the last one, disappeared. In fact, the old man then realized, the buzzing in his ears had ceased quite a while before. The waiter was arranging the scattered chairs in a sullen manner, shoving each chair lightly with one hand and not caring if it ended up where it should be. The legs of the chairs produced a dolorous moan as they scraped across the floor. Seeing that he could stay no longer, the old man rose and left, greatly depressed. A few sharp blasts of cold air greeted him as he stepped outside, and these brought on a severe coughing seizure. This time, though, blood rushed to his face, giving it a ruddy, almost healthy appearance.

He passed a fruit store and noticed a great pile of oranges set out. Their bright color gleamed in the light of a large kerosene lamp. On a sudden impulse, the old man bought one of the oranges and shoved it into his sleeve. In winter, he himself didn't eat fruit very often because such cold substances were likely to irritate his stomach. The orange he had just purchased had, in fact, been meant to coax the landlady's little boy into calling him by his name. But he had failed!

Elderly people hold vivid recollections of youthful experiences. By contrast, the adversities of their old age make less lasting impresions. But before recent events become obliterated from their memories, they will occasionally pop back into the mind, one by one, like numerous indistinct pictures, flashing before the eyes. As he lay in bed, once more unable to fall asleep, the old man's lonely heart became completely absorbed in reviewing these pictures: "My niece treats my illness as though it were nothing; where in the world can one find any real sympathy? . . . Young people are always gadding about. When it's cold, they throw a 'cold-dispelling party'! . . . Everything has changed! Husband and wife even seek entertainment together! . . . My wife! . . .

Her face had a bluish tinge to it when she died! . . . 'Till death do us part.' How sweet those words, and yet how painful! . . . No child escorted her to her grave! . . . It's hateful that that boy refuses to say hello to me! . . . But what can I hate? For me, none of it was meant to be!"

Wave after wave of similar thoughts washed over his mind, repeating themselves endlessly. His feet felt as though they were stuck in a bucket of ice. His bed covers and clothes weighed down on him so heavily that he was unable to move, so he lay stiffly curled up. He was surrounded by a boundless darkness and stillness. It was as if that bright, bustling world had forgotten all about him.

Horse-bell Melons

by Yeh Shao-chün

Translated by Jason C. S. Wang

From my home to the square in front of the Examination Court was no more than a *li*'s[1] walk through a few deserted alleys. One section along the way was lined with scrubby mulberry trees reminding one a little of the countryside. It was a moonless night with only a few scattered stars visible, and the entire sky was glowing. In the grass under the trees the crickets were dreamily singing away in their fine choppy notes. Their chorus, however, failed to dispel the quiet of the mulberry groves.

I was carrying a light bamboo basket containing two horse-bell melons,[2] seven or eight *man-t'ou*,[3] some ham, and other refreshments like roasted watermelon seeds, peanuts, and preserved olives. But constantly on my mind were those two horse-bell melons. They were the size of rice bowls, with lovely markings on their jade-green skin. The very thought of them made my mouth water. The day before, I had told Father, "If you want me to go, you've got to let me take along two horse-bell melons." Hearing this, Father smiled and promised generously, "I don't see why not. You want

two; you shall have two." True to his word, that afternoon he brought back two horse-bell melons. He handed them to me, saying, "Better put them in your little lunch basket." I couldn't have been happier. I placed the melons in the basket gently and covered them with some paper before putting in the other things. That night, when it was time to leave I hurriedly volunteered to take the basket, leaving everything else for Chiu-fu[4] to carry.

In one hand, Chiu-fu carried a small book case containing lithographic editions of such books as *The True Meanings of the Four Books,*[5] *Essentials of the Five Classics,*[6] *A Must for Every Examinee, A Golden Guide to the Examination,* and *The Imperial Moral Teachings.*[7] It also contained other things, paper, writing brushes, an ink box, etc. At that time I had studied only the Four Books and the Three Classics.[8] I was then as now not familiar with the *Book of Documents* or the *Book of Rites.* The editions we were using were those commonly seen in private tutorial schools then. In fact, I could hardly even make any sense of the titles of those books in the book case. But I remembered that

---

[1] Roughly one-third of a mile.

[2] *Ma-ling-kua,* a type of midget watermelon, having a yellowish pulp sweeter than that of a common watermelon but not as juicy.

[3] Chinese steamed bread.   [4] Title for the brother of one's mother.

[5] The four Confucian classics to be studied by every pupil in traditional China, i.e., *The Great Learning, The Doctrine of the Mean,* the *Analects* of Confucius, and the *Mencius.*

[6] The five most important works in the Confucian canon, i.e., the *Book of Changes,* the *Book of Documents,* the *Book of Odes,* the *Book of Rites,* and the *Annals of the Spring and Autumn Period.*

[7] *Sheng-yü kuang-hsün* (The Imperial Moral Teachings), issued in the year 1724, is a work written by Emperor Yung-cheng (r. 1723–1735) of the Ch'ing dynasty. It is an amplification of the sixteen-point moral teachings first proclaimed in a decree by Emperor K'ang-hsi in 1670.

[8] *San-ching,* collective name for three of the Five Classics: the *Book of Changes,* the *Book of Odes,* and the *Annals of the Spring and Autumn Period.*

my Shu-fu[9] had said, "This year's exam will be different. There will be no searching at the entrance. You can openly take books with you to consult." With this, he picked several volumes from his bookshelves and said, "Why don't you take along these and the ones you brought to the county and prefectural exams?"[10] And so my Shen-mu[11] helped me put the books into the box. Judging from their small print and compact format, I figured that they must be some very profound stuff. The question of how to consult them never even crossed my mind.

In his other hand Chiu-fu had an official summer hat with a red tassel,[12] which also belonged to Shu-fu. Father had told me to unscrew its brass top and leave only the crown with a stick jutting out from the center. When I tried it on, the brim of the hat came down flush with my nose, blocking everything above from my view; and when my head turned, the hat would also turn around loosely. Father said, "Anyway, you'll only be wearing it for a short while on your way in. No need to be too fussy about it." And so it too was handed to Chiu-fu to carry. Where I come from, Chiu-fu has several duties that cannot be done by anyone else, namely: to hold his nephew on the occasion of his first haircut, to lead his nephew by the hand to school to pay his respects to his first teacher, and finally to accompany him to the examinations. I asked quite a few elders what was the story behind this custom, but none of them seemed to have an answer. They simply said, "It's always been that way." To this day I haven't figured out why it is so.

Walking like this in the streets at night was then a rare experience for me. The only other time I remember was coming home one night from a wedding feast given by some relatives of ours. Because we had stayed to watch the guests tease the bride, and then Father had had some wine with several people and played finger guessing games with them, it had been this late when we started home. I was holding quite a few boxes of colored wedding eggs. Father held me tightly by the right arm and led me on. Dark shadows moved past us on both sides. The lantern Father had in his other hand only dimly lit up a patch of ground around our feet no bigger than a washbasin. The ground in front of me appeared to be a void, and I hesitated to step on it with my full weight. The lantern swung back and forth, making a mysterious and lonely sound which aroused in me a vague, inexplicable fear. The road also seemed to have stretched itself. Though we walked on and on, it never seemed to end. Finally I lost all courage to walk another step. Turning around, I clung to my father's legs and said, "Carry me. I don't want to walk anymore."

This time, though I was twelve years old and had gone to the county and prefectural examinations at night before,[13] I was no more used to walking in the dark than the time coming back from the wedding feast. The sound of the insects chirping made the road seem all the more desolate, and a dejected feeling began to settle on me. The basket in my hand got heavier and heavier; its contents seemed to be growing. I thought to myself, "Wouldn't it be wonderful if an extra melon or two appeared!" As I dreamed on, I took the basket with the other hand and at the same time asked Chiu-fu, "How come we're still not there?"

---

[9] Title for the younger brother of one's father.

[10] The county and prefectural examinations were two series of tests that had to be passed before one could take the yüan-k'ao (Court Examination) described in the story. Each of these two series consisted of five to seven tests (actual number varying from region to region). The regulations governing them were fairly lax. In certain regions they could even be taken at home or in the lodgings. These two series of tests and the yüan-k'ao, which lasted only one day, comprise the three parts of the hsiao-k'ao (preliminary examinations). One who successfully passed all three parts was admitted into the local academy as a fu-sheng (associate student), and commonly referred to as a hsiu-ts'ai (literally, an outstanding talent). This, however, was not an academic degree during the Ch'ing dynasty as it was in the Sui and T'ang dynasties.

[11] Title for the wife of the younger brother of one's father.

[12] Wei-mao, a hat of plaited rattan cane in the shape of an inverted wok. Similar hats without the red tassel were worn by commoners.

[13] At these examinations the questions were usually distributed around dawn. The examinees therefore must set out from home during the night.

"We're almost there. Listen to the noise," Chiu-fu said reassuringly. I listened carefully. Indeed, there were waves of noise like the din in a tea-house, seeming to drift skyward, spreading beyond that vast, luminous curtain of pale blue. Involuntarily, our steps became quicker and heavier. Only then did I begin to hear the sound of my own footsteps. They sounded louder, and I began to feel a little tired.

After we turned a corner the scene changed: now the doors of the houses along the street were open, and had either paper lanterns or glass lamps hung over them. I could often see people going in and out of these houses. Women and children stood around chatting, laughing, and watching the excitement. Many people were passing in the street. Peddlers of refreshments and snacks had laid down their loads of delicacies and were trying to attract customers by shouting or beating their small brass gongs. I found all this peculiar. It was different from what I had seen at the county and prefectural examinations. It was rather interesting, but I couldn't find anything to compare it to. I felt something eerie about everything I saw and heard around here, and I instinctively held on to Chiu-fu's long gown.

As we walked on we came to a square which was so vast that it seemed unending. There were two enormously high flagposts, and the flags fluttering in the wind made a sound like vultures flapping their wings. In the square were countless people milling about, and I felt as if I'd been swallowed by the crowd at a temple fair. No matter which way I turned I was in danger of bumping into someone, so that I ended up circling around the same spot, tugging at Chiu-fu's gown.

Chiu-fu looked northward and said, "It's still early. This time the Hus have rented a lodging. We'll go there to rest awhile." As if hypnotized I looked in the same direction. With much difficulty I maneuvered myself to a vantage point where I could peer through the gaps in the crowd at the gate of the Examination Court. A lot of people blocked the gate and backed away only a little when no less than a dozen rattan sticks

whizzed down on their heads. From the gate hung four big red paper lanterns, whose dim yellow light barely made visible the crowns of those few crowding under them. Nothing could be seen inside the gate, as if a black curtain had been drawn over it. Suddenly I thought this place looked almost like the temple of the city god,[14] but neither as well kept nor as awe inspiring. On festive days the various activities held in front of the temple were far more spectacular, not to mention the fact that everything was in broad daylight. While I was lost in thought, Chiu-fu urged me to get moving, and so I followed him.

The lodging the Hus had rented was next to the west side of the Examination Court. It had been the bedroom of a family which had decided to make some money by renting out any available space to those who came to take the examination. The Hus had many sons, and they were accompanied by a number of relatives. They only managed to have enough places to sleep by using doors and planks covered with mats as makeshift beds. These beds took up all the space except a small area alongside the window, and on that spot they had placed a square table for a game of dominoes.

When I first entered the room, my attention was caught by the people sitting around the table. They seemed so tightly packed that not even a crisp mustard seed could squeeze through, and I could hear the sound of the tiles hitting the table. Only then did I realize what a "lodging" was like. As I looked around, I saw the beds, and before I knew it found myself sitting on one to the right. Chiu-fu said hello to the group of people, at the same time shoving the book case under the bed. Then putting the summer hat on the bed, he said, "Your basket can go under the bed too." I really didn't want to let go of the basket, and so I laid it on the bed with my hand still holding its handle, saying "I think this will do." As soon as I said this I felt very, very thirsty. My palate and tongue seemed parched. "Wouldn't it be nice to take out a horse-bell melon and eat it now?" I thought to myself. Then I thought again. It would certainly

[14] *Ch'eng-huang,* a celestial official of a city or town.

be bad manners to eat alone in front of so many people, but if I gave each person a piece there wouldn't be much left for me. Besides, Father had said that the melons were to be eaten only after I got into the Examination Court. So I had no choice but to bear the thirst, and in the candle-light I stared vacantly through the spare holes in the basket at the jade-green melons.

The domino players didn't seem to have no-ticed us. They banged on the table, cursed their luck, speculated, and yelled, and laughed just as before. Only one of them, a man with a mous-tache, looked at Chiu-fu out of the corner of his eye and asked him, "How old is our young friend?"

"Twelve."[15] Chiu-fu was now sitting on one of the beds too, stretching his tired arms.

Stroking his moustache, the man said amusedly, "A boy wonder, indeed! Have you braided some red yarn into his queue? Red yarn?"

His strange question confused me. As if I didn't know what color yarn I had used, I reached back for the end of my queue to have a look. The yarn was black; I realized that was the color I always used.

The man saw it also and observed with pity in his voice, "Why don't you use red yarn?! He's so small, and has such delicate features. He would look cuter and lovelier if you used red yarn. Who knows? The chief examiner might take a fancy to him and mark his name on the roster for special attention. Then he'd be in luck."

Another voice was heard: "He must already write very well, I presume."

"Not really," Chiu-fu replied modestly. "He began learning to write only the year before last. He can barely manage to put together a three hundred word composition. We're not holding out any hope for him this time. The idea is for him to get some experience, so that he won't get cold feet later on."

"That's the right thing to do. But still there shouldn't be any reason why he couldn't make it if the questions happen to be right for him."

I began to feel sleepy. My head was heavy and in spite of myself threatened to nod forward. In my drowsiness I heard someone ask, "What's in this basket?" I suddenly came full awake and said guardedly, "Horse-bell melons!" It was the man with the moustache who had asked the question. He had now left the people playing dominoes and was standing in front of me, smiling. He said, "You certainly know how to enjoy yourself! Others are worried, because they're afraid they won't do well on the exam, but you're bringing melons and candies with you to have a good time!"

"After all, he's only a child," I heard Chiu-fu comment.

I grew drowsy again; I leaned to one side and rested my head on the windowsill. The noise of dominoes and voices gradually faded away, leav-ing only faint traces. I felt itchy somewhere on my legs and arms; perhaps the mosquitoes were steal-ing my blood. But because I didn't have the strength to raise my arm and scratch, I had to let them be. After a while I didn't even feel itchy anymore.

When Chiu-fu woke me, the room looked quite different; people were hurriedly leaving. Some of them were putting on their long gowns, while a few others were checking the contents of their book cases. The four candles at the corners of the table had burnt down to a couple of inches; the flames were all bent to one side by the wind, and melted wax was trickling down from the candle stubs. The domino pieces were in disarray, bony side up, a cadaverous white.

A few puffs of wind brushed past me, and I suddenly felt an uncomfortable chill. At the same time I began to sense something sad and desolate about the room. I got up, grabbed the basket, and was ready to go. Chiu-fu already had the book case in his hand. He put the hat on my head and said, "The roll call has already begun. Better put it on now."

[15] To all appearances this is an autobiographical story. The locale of the story is unmistakably the author's home town, Wu-hsien of Kiangsu province. The events described here probably happened in 1903, the last year in which the civil service exami-nations were administered (they would be formally abolished in 1905). The author was then twelve years old, the same age as the boy in the story.

I followed behind Chiu-fu like a sleepwalker, and soon we found ourselves inside the gate of the Examination Court. The inner gate[16] was dark with people crowding in front of it; I could only see their backs. Their necks all stuck out, and appeared to be stretching longer and longer all the time. The red lanterns hanging from the gate swung slowly and dimly, giving out an eerie light. By this time, the lantern on the east side had burned out. There were muffled conversations mixed with shuffling of shoes. Occasionally a solemn but slightly shaky voice would rise above all these noises. It lasted three beats. I knew from my experience at the earlier two examinations that this was roll call. Once a name was called, a voice "Here!" would burst from among the crowd. Then people would begin to mill about in all directions. At the same time a deferential voice would be heard: "Sponsored by so-and-so." Chiu-fu had told me that at this important examination the sponsors[17] had to announce their own names themselves. This must be it.

Chiu-fu handed me the book case and told me to hold onto it, though he still helped me carry it with one hand. He whispered, "Listen carefully." I did as I was told, but all the names I heard were unfamiliar and none of them was mine. Now we began to feel pressure on our backs as many of the latecomers pushed from behind. We had no choice but to press against the backs of the people in front of us. So now my oversized hat was resting against the waist of the person in front of me, and tilted so much that it almost fell from my head. But I couldn't put down what I was carrying to right it, and even if my hands had been free there was no room for me to reach up. All I could do was to bend my head to keep the hat from dropping. I couldn't see anything but the waist of the man in front of me. We were surrounded by people, and my chest, my back, and my arms were all being pressed against someone around me. I felt suffocated, as if I were stuck inside a big urn—only the wall of this urn was soft.

All this jostle made me sweat profusely, and so the discomfort of the cold I had left a while before disappeared.

Suddenly anxiety welled up in my chest. My legs sensed that the basket was almost crushed flat by the mounting pressure. Would the horse-bell melons in it be squashed? If they were, I'd be left with nothing to quench my thirst the whole day. And things looked bad. My legs felt slightly moist. What else could it be but wheat-yellow, deliciously sweet melon juice! But since I couldn't so much as turn my body around, I had to put up with the churning motion of the soft-walled urn. How I wished I could lift up the basket to have a look! Then I thought regretfully: "If I'd known things were going to turn out this way I would have eaten them at the lodging. I had no idea that I was going to bring the melons all this way for them to end up crushed!" My grief at the loss was so deep that I forgot about the stuffiness of the air, and the noises around me became so faint that they seemed barely audible.

As if being called by someone in my sleep, I heard a series of sounds: a person's name, and a sort of familiar one too. Soon I realized the name was my own. Chiu-fu quickly nudged my back a few times with his elbow and said something I could not hear clearly. I hesitated a moment before I raised my voice and yelled, "Here!" The book case was suddenly heavy; Chiu-fu had let go of it. I knew perfectly well that I was supposed to walk over to pick up the examination book, how to enter the inner gate to find the assigned seat, which would begin a special day of life isolated from my family and in the midst of total strangers. But my way was blocked on all sides. The urn would not open a thread-thin crack for me. How could I get up there?! I yelled and pushed forward. Chiu-fu did the same, but it was useless. We barely managed to start a ripple in the mass of humanity and brought curses on ourselves from people around us. When I listened again they were still calling out names one after

---

[16] *Yi-men,* the name of a second gate inside the wall of a government building complex during the Ch'ing dynasty; lit. "exemplary gate," meaning the officials were fit examples for the people to emulate.

[17] *Pin-sheng,* short for *pin-shan sheng.* In each local academy there were a limited number of students chosen from those who had distinguished themselves in examinations to receive a stipend, known as *pin-shan sheng.* Only *pin-shan sheng* could serve as sponsors for the candidates in this last and most crucial part of the preliminary examination.

another. The voice was composed but slightly
trembling, just as before. As if I'd lost a treasure,
I felt a deep feeling of sadness settling on my
chest. Up to this point I had never wanted to go
in there. It was all Father and my Shu-fu's idea.
Now that I found it impossible to get in, strangely
enough, I suddenly began to feel disappointed. At
this moment my mind went blank. I didn't think
about whether we should go home straight from
there, and I didn't care about finding out if there
was some way to get in. I just stood there, disheartened. Then Chiu-fu lowered his head a little
and comforted me: "There's no hurry. Just wait.
In a little while you'll be able to get in." With that
he reached out a hand to help me carry the book
box again.

Gradually the crowd began to loosen up a little.
I turned around and even raised a hand to adjust
my hat without meeting any obstruction. But
while the noises around us seemed to have become fainter, the names of candidates and their
sponsors were becoming louder and more distinct. Later, when there were only thirty or forty
men left, I saw clearly a big table in the center,
draped in red, and a man with a black beard and
round glasses sitting behind it. He sat motionless,
like a statue. Chiu-fu nudged me. I caught on and
moved forward. Finally those thirty or forty people also disappeared inside the inner gate. Only a
few bystanders remained, who I knew did not
belong to the same class as I did. Seeing that the
place had suddenly become strangely quiet, dark,
and empty after all the excitement, I felt an inexplicable sadness in my heart.

Somehow I got an examination book from a
clerk. After taking it with the hand that was carrying the basket, I too made for the inner gate. I
had no idea of when Chiu-fu let go of the book
case or when I parted from him. I immediately
lifted up the basket and looked it over carefully by
the light, and only then I felt happy and reassured. The basket had not been crushed, and the
jade-green horse-bell melons were still intact.

Once behind the screen I was suddenly over-

whelmed by darkness. When I looked very hard I
made out a few shadowy figures standing in the
dark, and my heart gave a start. The threshold of
the inner gate had already been fitted into place.
It was high, very high. It couldn't have been lower
than my chest. Since my shoulders could hardly
support the weight on my two arms, how could I
possibly push myself up and climb over the
threshold? At a loss about what to do, I was involuntarily setting down what I was carrying when
one of the shadows began to speak: "Kid, can't
you get in? Let me carry you over." His strange
accent and playful tone frightened me somewhat.
He lifted me up by the waist effortlessly, as if
picking up a baby. When I found myself on solid
ground again, I was inside the threshold. After
the journey my loose hat fell to the ground. I
picked it up. I realized that the examination book
had gotten all crumpled up, so I spread the book
across my chest and smoothed it out with my
hand. The man handed me the book case and the
basket. As I turned around I found another mysterious scene unfolding before me. At a great distance from me stood a huge hall, so far away that
it appeared almost ethereal. There were some
dots of light there and some blurred human figures. From the examination cells on both sides of
the passageway came a humming like the sound
of swarming bees. Many small red lanterns were
hung along the eaves of the cells. From a distance
they seemed to form two dotted lines like the two
nonparallel sides of a trapezoid. The red lanterns
were not bright enough to illuminate the passageway, but fortunately, the passageway was white
with starlight, and I was able to see the serial designation on the book. It was *yin*,[18] number twelve.
So, one by one I checked the serial numbers on
the small red lanterns. I was very glad to find that
my seat was only a few lanterns away on the east. I
plucked up courage and lurched forward, only to
find that what I had seen was not the *yin* series but
the *chou*[19] series. I was very depressed, like an
exhausted traveler in the wilderness unable to
find lodging late at night.

[18] Usually each row of cells or seats was designated by a character from the *Ch'ien-tzu wen* (One Thousand Character Essay in
four-syllable rhymed lines, composed by Chou Hsing-ssu in 535–545), which every pupil had to commit to memory. The character *yin*, one of the twelve Celestial Stems, often used in other kinds of lists, is not found in this essay.

[19] *Chou*, the sixth character in the *One Thousand Character Essay*. It may easily be confused with *yin* from a distance.

After a lot of searching and delay, I finally spotted the red lantern of the *yin* series slowly turning on the west side. It was about the same distance from the big hall as from the inner gate. Feeling that I had found a home, I rushed toward it as fast as I could. As soon as I stepped inside the shed and located seat number twelve, I put down everything on the plank and took a few deep breaths. All the other seats were occupied. I paid no attention to what they looked like or what they were doing; I only knew that there were a lot of people around me and that I had become part of the crowd. Many white candles were now being lit on the wooden planks that served as desks, their flames flickering erratically. A few people who were more particular set their candles in glass globes [they had brought with them]. This made the light much steadier. I too took my candle, which was carefully wrapped in several layers of paper, out of the basket. I struck a match, lit the candle, and glued it to the plank with a few drops of wax. So I sat down, and there I was, with a small world to call my own.

"Horse-bell melon!" Suddenly the thought flashed across my mind. Hastily removing everything on top of the basket, I fetched from below a lovely jade-green melon. "Let me eat half of it now." No sooner had the thought occurred than I had pierced the melon skin with the tip of a paper knife. Once it was cut open, the bright, wheat-yellow color and the sweet smell, unique to fruits in the watermelon family, were so enticing that they made me forget everything else. First I ate the fleshy part, cutting it into squares with the knife. Then I cut the rind into pieces and chewed the pulpy linings one by one. When there was nothing left but the thin outer skin I realized that I had eaten more than I had planned to. There *was* another one. Thus, the future began to look less grim. I got up and dumped the skin into the urinal. (There was one for every dozen sheds or so. There was urine all around it—fortunately the closest one was a considerable distance from my cell.) After this, I cleaned the plank with some scrap paper, sat down as before, and watched the melted wax dripping down the candle. Then I heard faint trumpets and signal cannons in the distance. I thought vaguely to myself: "They are sealing the gates now. Too bad I can't go back to see what's going on at home. Will mother be thinking of me in bed? Has Shu-fu finished his nightcap?" Indeed, anyone used to living at home can't help thinking like this when he's away. Because I knew well enough that what I was imagining could not be what was actually happening at home, I began to feel restless.

Suddenly everyone in the shed looked toward the passageway. Automatically following their gaze, I saw a group of people rushing toward the great hall with quick and heavy steps. I was then told that the Director of Education[20] had just gone in, riding in his rattan sedan chair. A while later a few people walked slowly down the passageway carrying white paper lanterns on their shoulders. And on the lanterns were written the examination questions. Right away the human shadows came wildly alive. Layers upon layers of heads squirmed like maggots, and at the same time a muffled drone began to rise. I was too short. If I stood in the passageway I could never hope to see anything but other people's backs. So I climbed onto the plank, stood up straight, and hastily copied down the questions. My big scrawly characters filled a whole sheet of paper.

The first question was an essay on the import of a certain classical quotation, and already I was in trouble. The quotation looked unfamiliar and didn't seem to be from any of the classics I had studied. Then, as my eyes fell on the row in front of me, I saw a man pulling two or three volumes from a stack of lithographed books. The title on the spines appeared to be the *Book of Rites.* But since I had never written on any topic related to the *Book of Rites,* how would I know in which volume to look for the quotation, and how was I to write on it? However, I wasn't too worried about it. I had no intention of starting to prepare a draft immediately anyway. For the time being that could wait. It was the other horse-bell melon that occupied my mind. "I'll be able to concentrate on

[20]*Hsüeh-t'ai,* the Honorable Director of Education, short for *Ch'in-ming t'i-tu sheng hsüeh-cheng* (Imperial Commander-director of Educational Affairs of a province). The appointee to this office was in charge of not only the entrance examination to county and prefectural academies but also those of local military academies; hence the term *t'i-tu* (military commander) in the title.

the composition only after I've eaten it. The sooner I finish it the sooner I'll be able to start writing." Having convinced myself, I reached into the basket. This time I did not plan to eat only half, and so I finished it all at once. The only regret I felt while putting the last bit into my mouth was that the melon was too small. But there were still a lot of other things to distract me. Peanuts and watermelon seeds, being what they were, could not be consumed in a hurry. So I popped them one by one into my mouth to pass away the long hours. I felt terribly cold. The muscles in my arms and legs seemed to cramp, and I began to doze as my eyelids became heavy.

But before long the passageway was flooded with pale blue light. Rafters and tiles on the roofs were gradually becoming visible, and most of the small red lanterns had already gone out. In my stupor I could hear a low drone. Obviously people in the shed were already making drafts, or at least had some idea what to write, but I still had nothing on paper except for the questions copied down earlier.

"Someone back there used a false birthplace to get in!" Suddenly someone shouted, and his voice seemed to carry a note of authority. I looked in the direction of the voice. Right under the eaves of our shed stood a tall man with big radiant eyes. The muscles on his face seemed to be charged with energy. He had one hand propped against a post. His fingers were so thick and long that I couldn't remember seeing the like of them before. I was awed by his appearance, which reminded me of a statue of a youthful god I had seen in a temple somewhere.

People in the shed began to tell one another,

"False birthplace! Tu the Heavenly King is going to kick up a big row again this time!" A dozen or so people left their seats and swarmed into the passageway, asking eagerly, "Where, where?"

As soon as I heard the nickname "Heavenly King" I knew who the man was. By this time many public middle schools had already been established.[21] He was a student of a local middle school. When the date of the examination was getting near, the school authorities posted an announcement to the effect that no one enrolled in middle school was permitted to take the examination. If a student took the examination under a false name, once discovered he would be expelled immediately. Roughly it boiled down to this: a person could only follow one line of career. To pursue more than one was considered dishonest opportunism. And such loopholes had to be closed.[22] But the Heavenly King cared nothing for such regulations. He registered under a false name, and on that day he asked leave from school to take the examination. Actually he was not the only person to do this. Many of his schoolmates and students of the county elementary school also wanted to try their luck with this second career possibility.

Public school students differed from ordinary private tutorial school pupils in many ways, but most notably in these two: first, they were against superstition; and second, they believed in the new theory of "power in unity." They came as a group to the square in front of the Examination Court to take the examination and also to have a good time. And both these characteristics of theirs found an outlet on the Buddhist statues in the Ting-hui Temple[23] nearby.

[21] Reformers of the late nineteenth century like Yüan Shih-k'ai and Chang Chih-tung had long realized the inadequacy of traditional Chinese education and recognized it to be one of the causes of China's weakness. They advocated the abolition of the civil service examinations and proposed to replace them with a Western educational system. In 1898 the reform-minded Emperor Kuang-hsü decreed that all old-style schools (shu-yüan) be converted to middle schools. But a coup staged by the conservatives later the same year thwarted this attempt at modernization. Thus most Chinese middle schools were established after the reformers rose to power again in 1901 following China's humiliating defeat by the Western powers in the 1900 Boxer Rebellion. The duration of these schools was five years.

[22] The real reason to forbid students enrolled in Western-style schools to take these examinations is that if they were permitted to do so, they almost certainly would take time from their schoolwork to prepare for the civil service examination. And once they took a degree they would promptly drop out of school. If this were allowed to happen, the newly introduced Western educational system would never be able to take hold in China.

[23] An ancient temple in Wu-hsien, the author's home town, originally a part of a bigger temple called Shuang-t'a Ssu (The Twin Tower Temple) first built in the ninth century. After the eleventh century it became a separate temple.

There were eighteen gilded statues of the ar-hats,[24] which were considerably taller than a man. At the center of the rear sanctuary sat a gigantic statue of Buddha. One could only see up to its chest. Its head and shoulders rose above the ceiling and occupied most of the space of the upper floor. When I was seven or eight I once went with Po-fu[25] to see the statue, and was a little frightened by it.

I heard this was how it happened: the Heavenly King and a group of his schoolmates went to visit the temple. Naturally, some of them brought up the subject of how idols helped foster superstition. And then everyone began to feel that these man-shaped clods of clay were enemies that must not be spared. "Only by knocking them down can we rid those ignorant people of their superstition," the Heavenly King first cried out. Immediately the group shouted their assent: "If you have the courage, we'll do it together!" Facing this challenge, the Heavenly King could no longer contain himself. Right away he gave orders to look for some rope, and a roll of thick hemp rope was found somewhere. It was unraveled and cut into four or five pieces. They tied them around the waist and arms of the statue of Buddha. At the word "Go!" everybody pulled hard at the ropes as if playing tug-of-war. The statue began to creak. Then with a loud thump, the body of Buddha fell on its side; his arms were broken and his face smashed. A few planks were also knocked down from the ceiling. After this unexpected success the students' unspent high spirits were still raging. Like fierce beasts charging out from their lair, they eagerly searched for more to destroy. The eighteen statues of the arhats fell easy prey to them. Since they were now more experienced, and the new targets were smaller and lighter, the students dispatched them in no time. Finally all the arhats ended up sprawled this way and that on the floor, some with heads or limbs lost, others with their wooden frameworks or the hollows inside exposed.

There was only one sickly monk in the temple. No sooner had he heard the students, in fact illegal examinees, vandalizing the Buddha than he escaped through the back door. Later, when the police learned of this and found out who the instigator was, they took Tu away with them. But they released him soon afterward because his father was a powerful country squire. After this Tu was given the honorable title "Heavenly King." He had been known by it ever since, so that it had replaced his given name. Everyone knew who the "Heavenly King" was whenever the name was mentioned. Having heard it so often, I too was more than familiar with this heroic name. Now that the hero who bore the name was in front of me, though a little scared, I would not miss the chance to look at him. Presently he puckered his mouth, and, in an irate tone, answered those who questioned him: "In the *yang* series!" His thick eyebrows slowly rose, making his face the more fearsome. He dropped the hand that had been propped against the post, turned around briskly, and walked away. The dozen men that had gathered in the passageway followed behind him as if they were being led on a string.

My curiosity was aroused. I also got up and followed them. The Heavenly King stopped at other sheds to recruit more supporters. By the time we had reached the *yang* series, he had seventy or eighty men behind him, a powerful army indeed. Then, like a great general, he led the attack. Through the little spaces in between the crowd I was able to make out that he was standing beside someone. The side view of that person's torso was thick, and his shoulders were round and full. I could tell that he was a fat man. His slightly purplish face was not as firm as Tu's, though it was as big.

Everyone in the *yang* shed raised his head. Some of them even stood up. With the arrival of the Heavenly King's army, the rows of seats and the passageway were suddenly crammed. The mingled noises of questions asked in surprise and

---

[24] In Indian mythology there were originally sixteen arhats (meaning men who have attained Nirvana). They were Buddha's disciples who stayed in this world at the latter's command to guide the masses of people to enlightenment. During the Sung dynasty different Chinese transliterations of the same two arhats' Sanskrit names were wrongly taken for the names of two additional arhats, thus bringing the number to eighteen.

[25] Title for the elder brother of one's father.

muttered angry curses shook the air and shattered the calm. But still they all behaved themselves, not daring to talk as loud as even normal conversation. They wanted to hear whatever heroic things the Heavenly King had to say, and were afraid that if they had talked too loud they would drown out his voice.

With a lofty air, Tu the Heavenly King patted the fat man's back and asked, "What's your name? Where do you come from?"

The man bent his head lower. His body seemed to shrink, like a mouse cringing in front of a cat. He made no answer.

"Answer! Quick!" the crowd burst out shouting. Tu pulled at the man's shoulder; only then did everyone get a clear look at his reddening purplish face. Tu yelled again, "Answer me quickly! No use playing games, it's no use!"

The man's wretched face crumpled, near tears. He finally yielded to the pressure and said something in a muffled voice. I couldn't make out what he said, but I could tell that his accent was different.

"That's not true!" snapped a sharp voice. Immediately a wave of "Not true!" rose from the crowd like a surging tide. Tu then punched the man on the back. Again the man cringed like a mouse facing a cat. People had tightened the circle. Some stood right up against him, and some stood on top of the desk planks. He was totally surrounded. Although I could no longer see him, I could still hear the sound of fists falling on his back.

The man being beaten up kept his silence, and so did those doing the beating. For a while it was peculiarly quiet. I could only hear monotonous hollow thumps, one after another.

"He's got another exam book!" a hoarse voice yelled in surprise. "Aha! More! One, two, three, four, five, five exam books altogether! His last name is Lu, Ni, Yeh all at the same time! Who knows what his real name is?"

"This is too much; first using a false birthplace, then ghost-writing for other people!"

"Beat him up good, and teach him a lesson!"

"What nerve! How dare he take the exam for five different people? Is his fat body full of ideas for composition?"

"What ideas? There's nothing in him but sneaky bones. Sneaky bones that deserve a good beating!"

"Beat him." "Beat him . . ." The sound of fists pounding on the man's back became faster and heavier. He began to moan as if delirious from high fever, but he never once begged for mercy or tried to explain.

Just as someone was yelling, "We can't do what we'd like to him here. Let's take him outside and give him a decent workover," six or seven clerks and two other men dressed in official robes and hats came up the passageway. I couldn't tell the rank of those two officials, but I was certain that neither of them was the Director of Education. At the clerks' shouted command the thick layers of men parted to let them get near the beaten man. The crowd then closed in behind them. Though I tried to squeeze in, I wasn't fast enough, and so I was left out of it. I climbed onto an unoccupied seat, stood on my toes, and looked down, but it was no good, All I could see was the man's thick fat neck showing outside his collar and a length of his thick queue.

"He used a false birthplace, . . . and is taking the exam for other people! . . . He's got six exam books altogether! . . . What are you going to charge him with?" Everyone started to talk at once protestingly. Then there was an uproar. Now that restraint wasn't necessary anymore, the talking had become unusually loud, so loud that the air seemed to be expanding.

A while later the crowd again parted; the culprit everyone despised came out surrounded by those six or seven clerks. He walked as if in a daze, with his eyes fixed on the ground. In his hands he had a basket, a hat, and a few other things, and a long gown was tucked in his arm. The examination books were in the hands of one of the officials; they were important evidence.

A light hiss of disgust came from the men in the crowd. They watched the back of the fat man with contempt and then returned to their own sheds. I watched too, leaning against a porch post. I felt a little worried, wondering how they would punish the fat man. They were walking in the passageway, heading for the big hall. The sun was shining on their heads from behind the roof of a shed to the east. The fat man's head looked as if it had snapped and dropped forward. I couldn't see the back of his head or either of his ears. Only his shiny, raven-black queue was visible from behind.

When I got back to my seat, the sound of people reading their own drafts had become busy as the chirping of autumn insects. Only then I remembered there was a composition to write. But I was a little hungry, and so I took out a *man-t'ou* and made a ham sandwich. As I ate I became thirsty, and my thoughts returned to horse-bell melons. Wouldn't it have been great if I hadn't been so impatient and had saved them for now? The sun was so red. We were in for a hot day, just the kind of day for eating horse-bell melons.

By eleven o'clock I had consumed everything. Not one melon seed was left. I then began to leaf through the *Book of Rites*. When I had turned over about twenty pages or so, something suddenly flashed in front of my eyes. That sentence was familiar! I thought again carefully. Wasn't it the quotation in the essay question? I read the annotation below it and wrote down the first sentence of my essay. When I was at the private school, I had formed the habit of writing down one sentence before thinking of the next. And I would, after every three or four sentences, stop and count to see how many characters I had written. This time was, of course, no exception. After I'd written about two hundred characters, I could not continue any more. But it was clearly posted on the bulletin board: "Essays under the minimum of three hundred characters will not be considered." How could I stop when there were only two hundred characters or so! I had no idea what my writing was like, yet I strove to write up enough words just to be considered! Isn't the whole thing a bit ridiculous?

Those who had handed in their examinations early were already filing out. There were heavy noises of gates opening, the elusive sound of trumpets and drums, and cannon shots fired as signals. The oppressive heat of the afternoon and my own anxiety left me soaked in sweat. Those on their way out looked like immortals to me, free and without a care in the world.

By the time I finished adding the hundred or so characters to the first essay, hastily completed another essay three hundred and six characters long, and *copied* a passage from the *Imperial Exhortations* that we had been instructed to write out from memory, there were only two or three others remaining in the shed. It was quiet except for the chirping birds in the distance, and the passageway was becoming dark again.

Hurriedly I gathered up all my things and carried them in my hands the way I had come in. I walked alone down the passageway. The inner gate was already wide open. I first put everything outside, and then, with great difficulty, I climbed out over its tall threshold. The outer gate was also open. There were no bands playing, no signal cannons fired. All was quiet. I saw the servant of our next-door neighbor waving to me outside, and quickly walked up to him. (My parents had asked him to come and fetch me.) He took everything from me and then carried me over the threshold of the front gate. When he let me down I felt the ground as soft underfoot as if I had landed on a comforter. I looked up. The sky was dark with a tinge of yellow, unlike what I usually saw. I was terribly thirsty. I thought that when I got home I would have a good reason to ask Father to buy two more horse-bell melons for me.

Autumn

by Yeh Shao-chün

Translated by Frank Kelly

Door unlocked and pushed open—a rush of musty air. It was towards evening on a bleak autumn day, and the room's unfamiliar, nearly unrecognizable furniture seemed particularly indistinct. It took opening the two window shutters to discover that everything was covered over with a layer of grimy dust.

She stood before the mirror stand, and the face in the glass took on a spectral pallor, with gray, scar-like indentations beneath both eyes and lips that had lost the sharpness of their contours. It did not at all resemble the face she saw every day. She began to realize how tired she was, the result of a crushing crowd at the ticket window, being unable to move as she stood for three hours in the third-class coach, and, upon arrival, wading through a sea of waiting rickshaw pullers while toting a bag that wasn't really all that light. Seldom had she exerted herself so strenuously. For the past few days, she had been feeling sluggish of limb, and now the condition had been exacerbated. She wanted only to lay herself down flat and let the mattress take her full weight. She was startled to realize that it was, in fact, the autumnal equinox, and a flood of melancholy feeling followed: she was not quite forty years of age, but a calendar had already been hung about her body.

Her attention became riveted on some of the articles lying atop her dresser. A number of circular objects and a few elongated ones, all etched in sepia-like tones, lay strewn there, like skeletons in a deserted field. She remembered—that was the wild rose she had plucked beside the river the previous spring at grave-sweeping time. She'd dropped it there upon her return to the house, since she was hurrying to catch a train. A year and a half had slipped by, and now she had returned to sweep the graves again.

She cursorily brushed away the dust on top of the bed and lay down. It seemed to her quite like arriving at a lonely inn. She stared at the top of her mosquito netting and allowed depression to consume her.

A wrinkle-faced old maidservant brought a kerosene lamp into the room and placed it on a table near the window. She then turned her head and, squinting, mumbled to herself, "Ah, Young Miss is resting here." With that, she plodded heavily out of the room.

In a little while, the sound of quiet conversation drifted into the room from somewhere beyond. Though subdued, the interlocutors apparently had not fully mastered the art of controlling their vocal cords, since every syllable they spoke was transmitted to the ears of the woman lying down in the room.

"To hear the mistress tell it, she's a midwife in Shanghai."

"Ugh! What a disgusting occupation! Blood all over the place . . ."

"Never mind that. But think how low-class it sounds just to say 'midwife'!"

"And she's still single. How can someone who hasn't married yet do that kind of work? I think the situation would be very embarrassing. How can she have the face to see anyone?"

"I agree. If she wants to get married, it's going to be tough. If someone's looking for a new daughter-in-law, but you admit you're a midwife, who's going to want you?"

"And she's no spring chicken either, is she?"

"I'm not sure. I haven't heard the mistress say. To look at her, I'd guess she was thirty-five, maybe older."

The woman reclining on the bed knew that one of those speaking was the wrinkle-faced old crone who had just delivered the lamp and who was in the employ of her sister-in-law. The other was probably a maidservant for another branch of the family. Their eyes were likely fixed on the cracks in the wall of her room, hoping for a glimpse of her, disgusting, low-class, and embarrassing as she was. So she imagined them, yet did not resent them for it. What, after all, do old maidservants know? In the year since beginning her career, she had delivered no more than thirty babies, and among those parents who considered themselves enlightened, requiring the services of an obstetrician, how many were there who did not look at her askance? One could always read the question in their eyes: *You* do *this* kind of work?" The old maidservants had merely put the question into words, that was all.

But their conjecture concerning her age stung the woman a bit. She didn't herself understand why she was so annoyed by those who tried to establish how old she was. When she was in school, some of her schoolmates had put the question to her bluntly. Though she had definitely felt uncomfortable, she didn't want to make a fuss about it, and so evaded the issue by saying she could not remember. Some of her slyer classmates, however, would try to catch her unawares by suddenly asking under what animal sign of the zodiac she was born. But even then, she never slipped up. She would respond either that she was born under the zebra or under the giraffe (those things you see in pictures of an African hunt). Following such skirmishes, she would regard the questioner as a busybody without goodwill and decide the less she had to do with the person, the better.

The old maidservant had also mentioned something about its "being difficult" . . . ah, why bother about it, anyway?

So thinking, the woman rolled over to face her own black shadow on the mosquito netting.

After supper, her sister-in-law came to the woman's room to chat. Having broken the ice with some meaningless trivia, the visitor turned with some hesitation to the main topic.

She said that they had originally intended to write to her in Shanghai, but because her elder brother could not spare the time, and because she was coming home to sweep the graves anyway, she had left everything for this conversation.

She explained that a matchmaker had come to tell her that a widower named Chang was looking for a second wife. He wasn't very old—just fifty-three—and he was a bank manager, having twenty or thirty thousand to hand. He had two sons and one daughter. The daughter was the eldest and already married, and the older son was going to take a wife the following year. It really would not be a burden for her to act as stepmother for them.

Her sister-in-law wanted to ask her to make up her own mind whether or not to tell the matchmaker there was need to discuss the matter further. In her opinion, there would be no harm in giving some thought to this matter, since a match as good as this was hard to come by.

The woman had no immediate response for her sister-in-law, and this was not due to bashfulness. Before she reached the age of twenty, whenever someone had come to speak with her mother, saying such and such young master from such and such house would be a suitable match for her, she would disappear at once like a mischievous cat. During her twenty-first year, her mother and father both passed away within a short time of each other. Since then, her elder brother and sister-in-law had taken her parents' places whenever matrimonial matters came up, and she had gradually come to master the art of turning a deaf ear to such talk. Although she could not prevent her face from blushing, she no longer had to slip away. She would hear snippets of conversation containing words such as "remarry," or "new wife." When she was twenty-seven or twenty-eight, she decided not to marry, since her father's will stipulated that any daughter who remained a spinster should receive twenty *mou*[1] of land.

Still, matchmakers continued to call. Adopting the stance of a disinterested bystander, she listened to the conversations and sometimes even went so far as to ask the matchmakers questions more probing than those of her sister-in-law. It was as though the subject under discussion had nothing whatever to do with her. No one, of course, could have seen through to her heart, a bubbling cauldron in which satisfaction and jealousy were churning in a turbulent mix.

And now, hearing this talk of a fifty-three-year-old man, the woman felt as though the stiff stubble of a beard were scratching all about the area of her mouth, and this revolting, nauseating sensation spread to her cheeks and neck. A portrait of herself and the old man standing side by side flashed before her eyes. Ugh! What a vision! What meaning could it possibly have? She shut her eyes tightly for a moment before answering her sister-in-law.

"I told you long ago that I wouldn't discuss marriage. Why do you insist on bringing it up again now?"

Her sister-in-law's tone expressed the greatest solicitude. "The way we see it, you must be having a hard time trying to make it on your own working in Shanghai. But if you were to find a suitable match, life would be a lot easier."

Well, Sister-in-law had for once hit the mark—it had certainly not been easy. To protect one life while at the same time welcoming another into this world was a task that required the concentration of all one's energy. To join with a woman in labor through each stage of her struggle takes all the strength one can gather in one's arms to coordinate with her every effort. Only when the new life has finally emerged from the mother's womb can the midwife take a breath. By then, clothes are soaked through with sweat and the entire body feels as though it is no longer under one's control. But one cannot really rest at this point. There are still many details to attend to concerning the aftermath for both mother and child.

The fact that she had been able to cope with this kind of toil sometimes even surprised herself. She was aware, of course, that, as far as her physical well-being was concerned, she would only be able to bear this kind of strain for, at most, some ten more years. After all, would a fifty-year-old still have the stamina to deliver a child? And besides, there would be other perils of the profession to worry about. She had been in business just over a year and had delivered fewer than thirty infants, a situation in which she was barely making a go of it. Shingles for obstetricians hung in practically every street. And on street corner billboards, announcements for discount deliveries could often be seen hanging in rows: "Day or Night—Five Dollars—Medicine Included"; "Half Off Regular Price—Four Dollars."

Obviously the competition in the profession was no less fierce than that in the marketplace. Yet with pregnant women practically filling the streets, why should so very few of them seek her out to deliver their children? If things should go even worse for her the following year and continue to decline thereafter, then what was to be done?

When she grew aware of her family's reduced circumstances and the sudden reverses the country had suffered, she decided to take the obstetrics college entrance examination and prepared to become a career woman. But at that time she had no idea that things would turn out as they had. Even during her three years as a student, she always thought that upon her final exit from school after graduation, a world of freedom and contentment would be awaiting her. Only when she had begun work and experienced her profession at first hand did she discover what toil, both physical and spiritual, really meant. Though it was bitterly hard, she bore with it and struggled on. The future was hazy indeed, but what could one do besides struggle? This was the logic she now employed.

"The work is definitely hard, but I can take it."

---

[1] One *mou* is roughly one-seventh of an acre.

She stared at the kerosene lamp so as to avoid eye contact with her sister-in-law.

"You may be able to stand it now, but how about later on?" Her sister-in-law paused a moment, then continued: "Again I'm inclined to speak as a woman. A woman must have someone to rely on. If you were to give birth to a child or two, then wouldn't everything be taken care of?"

"I find that hard to believe," the woman replied, shaking her head. "All I can see are the inconveniences that women suffer on account of their children. All that business about feeling more secure is nothing but talk."

The sight to which she had become quite accustomed, of a mother giving birth, flashed before her: the tide of blood, the flesh being rent, the trembling and screaming as though the woman were under torture. Truly it was a sacrifice without equal! Then instantly, she thought of what she had learned in her textbooks about the age at which women were most likely to have difficult deliveries, and she seemed to see an image of herself falling into just such a perilous situation. Ah—how terrifying!

Her sister-in-law saw that her cajolery was meeting with no success, so she changed her tack. "Then again, consider this: you wouldn't necessarily have to bear children yourself. This Mr. Chang, his daughter is already married and his two sons are grown up. As a person, you are incapable of mistreating anybody, so they, naturally, would treat you respectfully and affectionately. Would this be any different from having given birth to them yourself?"

Her sister-in-law had moved to sit a bit closer to the woman and extended a hand as if she were going to tug on her sleeve. Her voice became very soft and soothing. "When you hear Mr. Chang's children calling you 'Mother,' you will certainly be happy."

"Mother!" This strange yet somehow pleasant word really made her feel so warm inside, as if she had drunk some wine or heard herself respectfully addressed as "Madam" or "Mistress." If a chubby, innocent child were to appear before her and begin tugging at her clothes with a little hand while lovingly calling out "Ma," she could proba-

bly put all thought of misery out of her mind. And failing that, even if a young married woman were to address her as "Mother," and speak with her about personal matters, she would probably feel that her life really wasn't empty . . . But instead the stiff stubble of beard was back, scratching around her mouth, and this time she seemed to see a head of gray hair, a forehead layered with wrinkles, a pair of dim-looking eyes, and a yellowish set of teeth. A wave of revulsion forced her to blurt out decisively, "Siter-in-law, please let's drop this and talk about something else!"

"Well then, I guess I'd better thank the matchmaker for the offer of her services," her sister-in-law mumbled in embarrassment. She had initiated many similar conversations in the past, and she nearly always concluded them in this way.

Her sister-in-law turned the talk to the setback suffered by her husband's stocking factory. Since there were a dozen or so similar small-scale concerns, exploring new sales opportunities was made even more difficult than borrowing money from someone. For this reason, the elder brother was preparing to shut down operations at the end of the year.

Recently, however, someone had shown up with a proposal that they reinvest in the manufacture of broadloom pongee. The prospects looked pretty good because the material could be used to make Western-style clothing and was said to sell very well. The elder brother hadn't the capital at hand, so he had it in mind to convert some land into stock. For years on end now, this land had been subjected to constant natural disasters of flood and insect blight. The harvest was poor to begin with, and this combined with the factor of taxation to reduce the worth of the property greatly. Her sister-in-law concluded by saying, "They're over there now in a preliminary meeting. That's why he hasn't made it home yet."

Suddenly, the woman's mind was pricked as though by a needle, and she thought of the terms of her father's will: a spinster daughter will receive twenty *mou* of land. She now felt as if she completely understood the motive behind her sister-in-law's solicitations this time. Anger welled up uncontrollably within her as she resolved to persist in her determination not to marry, and so put her brother's and sister-in-law's attitude toward her to the test. She also thought to press some questions on the matter, to ascertain whether or not the twenty *mou* she had coming to her was to be separated out from the land marked for conversion to stock. But then she changed her mind, deciding that since they had not raised the issue, there would be no harm in her temporarily feigning ignorance. She could argue her case with them when the time for the transaction had actually arrived. So the woman resigned herself to listening to her sister-in-law prattle on about the cost of living and other domestic matters.

She sat to the right in the cabin of a boat, near a window of translucent shell. Six or seven men sat in a circle. She and her sister-in-law were the only women and her two nephews were the only children aboard. White clouds massed over the level fields. A light breeze carried both the clear, fresh scent of grass and periodic gusts of cold. The river swirled in a lively manner beneath the boat, and the sound of human voices above it seemed rather lonely by comparison.

Contrasted with ten years before, the atmosphere surrounding the sweeping of the graves had sobered considerably. Back then, all branches of the family lived together on the estate, and on the morning of the ceremony, everyone would assemble in the main hall. It was a singularly joyous gathering.

All the women, married and single alike, would parade out in new finery, designed according to their hearts' desires. One dress would be embroidered with butterflies, another with peonies, and every conceivable variety of lace and pattern was on display. The scents of rouge and powder wafted off every face and arm, intoxicating all those present to the point of tipsy, inexpressible joy. Small children dashed in and out of the room, in a frenzy to board the boat, this one dragging Uncle, that one pulling Father. But only when everyone was present and accounted for would the party exit the house to embark.

There were three boats in all, which glided along side by side once they had maneuvered out into the broad reaches of the river. Fruits and sweets were arrayed to fill a table, and flutes and recorders joined in harmony. The sound of laughter echoed from boat to boat, back and forth. It was, in truth, a happy excursion for the entire family.

But now the family had broken up. One branch had made a killing in the stock market and, consequently, moved into a small Western-style house in Shanghai. Other branches either set themselves up in business in Shanghai or relocated in Nanking, where a few of them had assumed lower-echelon posts. Since they all took their families with them, the quarters vacated as a result were rented out to several families of a different surname.

The great hall had already become a forgotten, untended place. Several old, dilapidated chairs now sat in a most unsightly manner, covered with thick layers of dust. A bamboo pole was now often to be seen suspended across the rafters, with some child's diapers hung over it all in a row. The grandeur of the past, when the female in-laws competed with each other to be most in style or most lovely, would never again materialize in this place. For one thing, the womenfolk from the other branches of the family no longer came; only the men put in an appearance. But the spheres of activity were so diverse even among these men that, aside from the grave-sweeping ceremony, their opportunities to get together were few and far between.

Thinking about all this made the woman feel intensely lonely. Even if the past were only a dream, couldn't she be allowed to dream it once more?—her father and mother robustly alive, all branches of the family not having to eke out livings and being in one place as before, everyone going together on the joyous jaunt to sweep the graves, the three boats drifting on in a row, fruits and sweets set out in abundance, the musical blend of flute and recorder, laughter passed back and forth among the boats—how beautifully sweet was that dream!

". . . Who could have known that he would end up being swindled?" A thick-bearded cousin of hers burst in upon the woman's train of thought in a high-pitched voice, so she started to listen.

"He was told that if he put up three thousand taels as security, he could collect six percent interest on this deposit and draw a monthly salary of a hundred dollars. After the security was paid, they found one excuse after another for not being able to open for business, claiming all the time that the arrangements still had not been finalized. When this at last made him suspicious and he demanded the return of the security deposit, he was told that it no longer existed! Just imagine! A young man so incompetent in his dealings! I believed the boy completely. Who would have suspected that he'd end up throwing snow-white silver into the sea!"

She then realized that "the boy" of her cousin's story was his son, graduate of a business school.

Another cousin, a low-level bureaucrat in Nanking, removed his glasses and sniffed. "You have no choice but to take them to court."

"Naturally I want to," replied the father of "the boy," stroking his bushy beard, 'but I had trouble enough just scraping together the three thousand taels of silver! Now I've been cleaned out, and you can't sue when you don't have a cent. So today, I wanted to discuss with you the possibility of selling our estate."

At this, all those present, seemingly stunned, could only stare dumbfounded at each other for a while.

"The fact is we've all moved away, and it doesn't seem likely that we'll ever have any need to move back." Another cousin had spoken up as if to clarify the suggestion.

The woman's elder brother than interjected, "If everyone is agreed, naturally I will not oppose such a move. I can rent another place to live."

The woman felt as though the wind had suddenly been knocked out of her. At the same time, her head became so dizzy that the people in the boat, as well as the sky and fields beyond, began to swirl around in her vision. The room she had occupied from the age of sixteen on, the only world that was ever completely her own, was now about to be wrested away!

Before the family graves, she prostrated herself reverently, tears falling like rain.

On the Shanghai-bound train later on that evening, she sank back listlessly in a long narrow seat, her consciousness bombarded by thoughts in bits and snatches: twenty *mou* of land . . . a wilted wild rose . . . fifty-three years old . . . rivers of blood and the rending of flesh . . . a woman big with child knocking on her door . . .

YÜ TA-FU
(1896–1945)

Like many another eminent writer of the May Fourth period, Yü Ta-fu grew up in northern Chekiang and received his advanced education in Japan. While still a student there in 1921, he became a founding member of the Creation Society, a highly influential literary clique in the twenties, and published a volume of three stories called *Sinking (Ch'en-lun)*, which immediately established his reputation as an autobiographical writer unafraid to expose his weaknesses and fantasies. His exploration of the individual psyche as a moral theme for fiction was certainly something new, but he was not defiantly modern in the sense that he repudiated the old Chinese culture. Though far better read in Western and Japanese literature than most of his contemporaries, he shared their humanitarian and patriotic concerns, and by the middle thirties, when he had ceased to write fiction, a traditional sensibility reasserted itself in his essays and poems. Along with Lu Hsün, he is generally regarded as one of the finest poets in the traditional style among modern Chinese writers.

Yü Ta-fu's characteristics as a modern writer rooted in traditional sensibility are already apparent in his first book. There his love of nature and his proud consciousness of his own worth and the world's vulgarity, while obviously showing the strong influence of Western romanticism, are also traceable to the Chinese literary tradition. But no traditional writer, of course, could have shown such strong obsession with his own sexual frustrations and equated his personal failure with the impotence of China in quite the same fashion. The title story of *Sinking*, in particular, had a great impact on Chinese youth and is rightly considered a work of key importance for its time because of its dual concern with the emotionally charged themes of sex and patriotism. The story, of course, is not without its technical crudities and may be considered too sentimental for some tastes, but, as I have contended in *History*, "precisely because of the utter discrepancy between the excessive emotion and the trivial action, 'Sinking' has generated a kind of nervous intensity which transcends its manifest sentimentalism" (p. 105).

In 1928 Yü Ta-fu quit the Creation Society to join forces temporarily with Lu Hsün as co-editor of a literary magazine. By that time he had exhausted his vein for autobiographical fiction and came briefly under the spell of proletarian literature. But disgusted with the revolutionary antics of the League of Left-wing Writers (of which he was a founding member), he soon joined the circle of two prominent non-leftist writers, Lin Yutang and Chou Tso-jen (the younger brother of Lu Hsün), who were promoting in the early thirties a nonpolitical personal literature. A minor official in Fukien at the time the Sino-Japanese War broke out in 1937, Yü Ta-fu went to Singapore in the following year to make his living as a newspaper editor. When Singapore fell into Japanese hands in 1942, he fled to Sumatra, living there under a different name for the remainder of the war; but soon after the victory, the Japanese police tracked him down and killed him.

For Chinese and Western readers alike, Yü Ta-fu's personal life, and particularly his courtship of and disastrous second marriage to Wang Ying-hsia, have been of as much interest as his creative writings. For a portrayal of our author as an unhappy romantic see Leo Lee's *The Romantic Generation of Modern Chinese Writers*.

C.T.H.

Sinking

by Yü Ta-fu

Translated by Joseph S. M. Lau and C. T. Hsia

I

Lately he had been feeling pitifully lonesome.

His emotional precocity had placed him at constant odds with his fellow men, and inevitably the wall separating him from them had gradually grown thicker and thicker.

The weather had been cooling off day by day, and it had been almost two weeks since his school started.

It was September 22nd that day. The sky was one patch of cloudless blue; the bright sun, timeless and eternal, was still making its daily circuit on its familiar track. A gentle breeze from the south, fragrant as nectar, brushed against his face. Amidst the half-ripened rice fields or on the meandering highways of the countryside he was seen strolling with a pocket edition of Wordsworth. On this great plain not a single soul was near, but then a dog's barking was heard, softened and rendered melodious by distance. He lifted his eyes from the book and, glancing in the direction of the barking, saw a cluster of trees and a few houses. The tiles on their roofs glittered like fish scales, and above them floated a thin layer of mist like a dancing ribbon of gossamer. *"Oh, you serene gossamer! you beautiful gossamer!"* [1] he exclaimed, and for reasons unknown even to himself his eyes were suddenly filled with tears.

After watching the scene absently for a while, he caught from behind him a whiff suggestive of violets. A little herbaceous plant, rustling in the breeze, had sent forth this scent and broken his dreamy spell. He turned around: the plant was still quivering, and the gentle breeze dense with the fragrance of violets blew on his pallid face. In this crisp, early autumn weather, in this bright and pellucid *ether,* his body felt soothed and languid as if under a mild intoxication. He felt as if he were sleeping in the lap of a kind mother, or being transported to the Peach Blossom Spring in a dream,[2] or else reclining his head on the knees of his beloved for an afternoon nap on the coast of southern Europe.

Looking around, he felt that every tree and every plant was smiling at him. Turning his gaze to the azure sky, he felt that Nature herself, timeless and eternal, was nodding to him in greeting. And after staring at the sky fixedly for a while, he seemed to see a group of little winged angels, with arrows and bows on their shoulders, dancing up in the air. He was overjoyed and could not help soliloquizing:

"This, then, is your refuge. When all the philistines envy you, sneer at you, and treat you like a fool, only Nature, only this eternally bright sun and azure sky, this late summer breeze, this early autumn air still remains your friend, still remains your mother and your beloved. With this, you have no further need to join the world of the

---

[1] Italicized common words, phrases, and sentences in this translation appear in Western languages in the original.

[2] An utopia depicted by the poet Tao Ch'ien (365–427) in his poem "Peach Blossom Spring" (*Tao-hua-yüan shih*) and its more famous preface.

shallow and flippant. You might as well spend the rest of your life in this simple countryside, in the bosom of Nature."

Talking in this fashion, he began to pity himself, as if a thousand sorrows and grievances finding no immediate expression were weighing upon his heart. He redirected his tearful eyes to the book:

Behold her, single in the field,
*   Yon solitary Highland Lass!*
Reaping and singing by herself;
*   Stop here, or gently pass!*
Alone she cuts and binds the grain,
And sings a melancholy strain;
O listen! for the Vale profound
Is overflowing with the sound.

After reading through the first stanza, for no apparent reason he turned the page and started on the third:

Will no one tell me what she sings?
*   Perhaps the plaintive numbers flow*
For old, unhappy, far-off things,
*   And battles long ago:*
Or is it some more humble lay,
Familiar matter of to-day?
Some natural sorrow, loss, or pain,
That has been, and may be again?

It had been his recent habit to read out of sequence. With books over a few hundred pages, it was only natural that he seldom had the patience to finish them. But even with slender volumes like Emerson's *Nature* or Thoreau's *Excursions,* he never bothered to read them from beginning to end at one sitting. Most of the time, when he picked up a book, he would be so moved by its opening lines or first two pages that he literally wanted to swallow the whole volume. But after three or four pages, he would want to savor it slowly and would say to himself: "I mustn't gulp down such a marvelous book at one sitting. Instead, I should chew it over a period of time. For my enthusiasm for the book will be gone the moment I am through with it. So will my expectations and dreams, and won't that be a crime?"

[3] Yü Ta-fu's translation of the two stanzas is omitted here.

Every time he closed a book, he made up similar excuses for himself. The real reason was that he had already grown a little tired of it. However, a few days or even a few hours later he would pick up another book and begin to read it with the same kind of enthusiasm. And naturally the one which had touched him so much a few hours or days earlier would now be forgotten.

He raised his voice and read aloud once more these two stanzas of Wordsworth. Suddenly it occurred to him that he should render "The Solitary Reaper" in Chinese.[3]

After orally translating these two stanzas in one breath, he suddenly felt that he had done something silly and started to reproach himself: "What kind of a translation is that? Isn't it as insipid as the hymns sung in the church? English poetry is English poetry and Chinese poetry is Chinese poetry; why bother to translate?"

After saying this, unwittingly he smiled a little. Somewhat to his surprise, as he looked around him, the sun was already on its way down. On the western horizon across the great plain floated a tall mountain wrapped in its mists which, saturated with the setting sun, showed a color neither quite purple nor quite red.

While he was standing there in a daze, a cough from behind his back signaled the arrival of a peasant. He turned around and immediately assumed a melancholy expression, as if afraid to show his smile before strangers.

II

His melancholy was getting worse with time.

To him the school textbooks were as insipid-tasting as wax, dull and lifeless. On sunny days he would take along a favorite work of literature and escape to a secluded place on the mountain or by the sea to relish to the full the joy of solitude. When all was silent about him at a place where sky and water met, he would now regard the plants, insects, and fish around him and now gaze at the white clouds and blue sky and feel as if he were a sage or hermit who had proudly detached himself from the world. Sometimes, when he ran into a peasant in the mountain, he would imagine himself Zarathustra and would repeat Zarathustra's sayings before the peasant. His _megalomania,_ in exact proportion to his _hypochondria,_ was thus intensified each day. Small wonder that, in such a mood, he didn't feel like going to school and applying himself to the mechanical work. Sometimes he would skip classes for four or five days in a row.

And when he was in school he always had the feeling that everyone was staring at him. He made every effort to dodge his fellow students, but wherever he went, he just couldn't shake off that uncomfortable suspicion that their malevolent gazes were still fixed on him.

When he attended classes, even though he was in the midst of all his classmates, he always felt lonely, and the kind of solitude he felt in a press of people was more unbearable by far than the kind he experienced when alone. Looking around, he always found his fellow students engrossed in the instructor's lecture; only he, despite his physical presence in the classroom, was wandering far and wide in a state of reverie.

At long last the bell rang. After the instructor had left, all his classmates were as lively and high-spirited as swallows newly returned in spring—chatting, joking, and laughing. Only he kept his brows knit and uttered not a sound, as if his tongue were tethered to a thousand-ton rock. He would have liked to chat with his fellow students but, perhaps discouraged by his sorrowful countenance, they all shunned his company and went their own ways in pursuit of pleasure. For this reason, his resentment toward them intensified.

"They are all Japanese, all my enemies. I'll have my revenge one day; I'll get even with them."

He would take comfort in this thought whenever he felt miserable. But in a better mood, he would reproach himself: "They are Japanese, and of course they don't have any sympathy for you. It's because you want their sympathy that you have grown to hate them. Isn't this your own mistake?"

Among his more sympathetic fellow students some did approach him, intending to start a conversation. But although he was very grateful and would have liked to open his heart to them, in the end he wouldn't say anything. As a result, even they respected his wishes and kept away from him.

Whenever his Japanese schoolmates laughed and joked in his presence, his face would redden because he thought the laughter and jokes were at his expense. He would also flush if, while conversing, one of these students glanced at him. Thus, the distance between him and his schoolmates became greater each day. They all thought him a loner and avoided his presence.

One day after school he was walking back to his inn, satchel in hand. Alongside him were three Japanese students heading in the same direction. Just as he was about to reach the inn, there suddenly appeared before him two girl students in red skirts. His breathing quickened, for girl students were a rare sight in this rural area. As the two girls tried to get by, the three Japanese boys accosted them: "Where are you going?"

Coquettishly the two girls answered, "Don't know, don't know."

The three students all laughed, pleased with themselves. He alone hurried back to his inn, as if he had done the accosting. Once in his room, he dropped his satchel on the tatami floor and lay down for a rest (the Japanese sit as well as sleep on the tatami). His heart was still beating wildly. Placing one hand underneath his head and another on his chest, he cursed himself:

"You coward fellow, you are too coward! If you are so shy, what's there for you to regret? If you now regret your cowardice, why didn't you summon up enough courage to talk to the girls? _Oh coward, coward!"_

Suddenly he remembered their eyes, their bright and lively eyes. They had really seemed to register a note of happy surprise on seeing him. Second thoughts on the matter, however, prompted him to cry out:

"Oh, you fool! Even if they seemed interested, what are they to you? Isn't it quite clear that their ogling was intended for the three Japanese? Oh, the girls must have known! They must have known that I am a Chinaman; otherwise why didn't they even look at me once? Revenge! Revenge! I must seek revenge against their insult."

At this point in his monologue, a few icy teardrops rolled down his burning cheeks. He was in the utmost agony. That night, he put down in his diary:

"Why did I come to Japan? Why did I come here to pursue my studies? Since you have come, is it a wonder that the Japanese treat you with contempt? China, O my China! Why don't you grow rich and strong? I cannot bear your shame in silence any longer!

"Isn't the scenery in China as beautiful? Aren't the girls in China as pretty? Then why did I come to this island country in the eastern seas?

"And even if I accept the fact that I am here, there is no reason why I should have entered this cursed 'high school.'[4] Those who have returned to China after studying only five months here, aren't they now enjoying their success and prosperity? How can I bear the five or six years that still lie ahead of me? And how can I be sure that, even if I managed to finish my long years of studies despite the thousand vexations and hardships, I would be in any way better off than those so-called returned students who came here simply for fun?

"One may live to a hundred, but his youth lasts only seven or eight years. What a pity that I should have to spend these purest and most beautiful seven or eight years in this unfeeling island country. And, alas, I am already twenty-one!

"Dead as dried wood at twenty-one!

"Dead as cold ashes at twenty-one!

"Far better for me to turn into some kind of mineral, for it's unlikely that I will ever bloom.

"I want neither knowledge nor fame. All I want is a 'heart' that can understand and comfort me, a warm and passionate heart and the sympathy that it generates and the love born of that sympathy!

"What I want is love.

"If there were one beautiful woman who understood my suffering, I would be willing to die for her.

"If there were one woman who could love me sincerely, I would also be willing to die for her, be she beautiful or ugly.

"For what I want is love from the opposite sex.

"O ye Heavens above, I want neither knowledge nor fame nor useless lucre. I shall be wholly content if you can grant me an Eve from the Garden of Eden, allowing me to possess her body and soul."

III

His home was in a small town on the Fu-ch'un River, about eighty or ninety *li* from Hangchow. The river originates in Anhwei and wanders through the length of Chekiang. Because it traverses a long tract of variegated landscape, a poet of the T'ang dynasty wrote in admiration that "the whole river looks like a painting." When he was fourteen, he had asked one of his teachers to write down this line of four characters for him and had it pasted on the wall of his study. His study was not a big one, but since through its small window he could view the river in its ever-changing guises, rain and shine, morning and evening, spring and autumn, it had been to him as good as Prince T'eng's tall pavilion.[5] And in this small study he had spent more than ten years before coming with his elder brother to Japan for study.

When he was three his father had passed away, leaving the family in severe poverty. His elder brother, however, managed to graduate from W. University in Japan, and upon his return to Peking, he earned the *chin-shih*[6] degree and was appointed to a position in the Ministry of Justice. But in less than two years the Republican revolution started in Wuchang. He himself had by then finished grade school and was changing from one middle school to another. All his family reproved him for his restlessness and lack of perseverance. In his own view, however, he was different from

---

[4] A Japanese "high school" of the early modern period provided an education equivalent to the last two years of an American high school and the first two years of college.

[5] Celebrated in the T'ang poet Wang Po's lyrical prose composition, "The Pavilion of Prince T'eng" (*T'eng Wang Ko hsü*).

[6] See footnote 7 to "Yü-kuan," p. 62.

other students and ought not to have studied the same prescribed courses through the same sequence of grades. Thus, in less than half a year, he transferred from the middle school in the city K. to one in H. where, unfortunately, he stayed less than three months owing to the outbreak of the revolution. Deprived of his schooling in the city H., he could only return to his own little study.

In the spring of the following year he was enrolled in the preparatory class for H. College on the outskirts of Hangchow. He was then seventeen. Founded by the American Presbyterian Church, the college was notorious for its despotic administration and the minimal freedom it allowed its students. On Wednesday evenings they were required to attend vespers. On Sundays they were not allowed to go out or to read secular books—they could only pray, sing psalms, or read the Old and New Testaments. They were also required to attend chapel every morning from nine to nine twenty: the delinquent student would get demerits and lower grades. It was only natural that, as a lover of freedom, he chafed under such superstitious restrictions, fond as he was of the beautiful scenery around the campus. He had not yet been there half a year when a cook in the employ of the college, counting on the president's backing, went so far as to beat up students. Some of his more indignant schoolmates went to the president to complain, only to be told that they were in the wrong. Finding this and similar injustices altogether intolerable, he quit the school and returned to his own little study. It was then early June.

He had been home for more than three months when the autumn winds reached the Fu-ch'un River and the leaves of the trees on its banks were about to fall. Then he took a junk down the river to go to Hangchow where, he understood, the W. Middle School at the Stone Arch was then recruiting transfer students. He went to see the principal Mr. M. and his wife and told them of his experience at H. College. Mr. M. allowed him to enroll in the senior class.

It turned out, however, that this W. Middle School was also church-supported and that this Mr. M. was also a muddle-headed American mis-

sionary. And academically this school was not even comparable to the preparatory class at H. College. After a quarrel with the academic dean, a contemptible character and a graduate of H. College as well, he left W. Middle School in the spring. Since there was no other school in Hangchow to his liking, he made no plans to be admitted elsewhere.

It was also at this time that his elder brother was forced to resign his position in Peking. Being an upright man of strict probity and better educated than most of his colleagues in the ministry, he had invited their fear and envy. One day a personal friend of a certain vice-minister asked for a post and he stubbornly refused to give him one; as a result, that vice-minister disagreed with him on certain matters, and in a few days he resigned his post to serve in the Judicial Yüan. His second elder brother was at that time an army officer stationed in Shaohsing. He was steeped in the habits of the military and therefore loved to squander money and associate with young gallants. Because these three brothers happened at the same time to be not doing too well, the idlers in their home town began to speculate whether their misfortune was of a geomantic nature.

After he had returned home, he shut himself in his study all day and sought guidance and companionship in the library of his grandfather, father, and elder brother. The number of poems he wrote in his diary began to grow. On occasions he also wrote stories in an ornate style featuring himself as a romantic knight-errant and the two daughters of the widow next door as children of nobility. Naturally the scenic descriptions in these stories were simply idyllic pictures of his home town. Sometimes, when the mood struck him, he would translate his own stories into some foreign language, employing the simple vocabulary at his command. In a word, he was more and more enveloped in a world of fantasy, and it was probably during this time that the seeds of his *hypochondria* were sown.

He stayed at home for six months. In the middle of July, however, he got a letter from his elder brother saying: "The Judicial Yüan has recently decided to send me to Japan to study its judicial system. My acceptance has already been forwarded to the minister and a formal appointment is expected in a few days. I will, however, go home first and stay for a while before leaving for Japan. Since I don't think idling at home will do you any good, this time I shall take you with me to Japan." This letter made him long for his brother's return, though he did not arrive from Peking with his wife until the latter part of September. After a month's stay, they sailed with him for Japan.

Though he was not yet awakened from his *dreams of the romantic age,* upon his arrival in Tokyo, he nevertheless managed to pass the entrance examination for Tokyo's First High School after half a year. He would be in his nineteenth year in the fall.

When the First High School was about to open, his elder brother received word from the minister that he should return. Thus his brother left him in the care of a Japanese family and a few days later returned with his wife and newborn daughter.

The First High School had set up a preparatory program especially for Chinese students so that upon completing that program in a year they could enroll along with the Japanese students in regular courses of study in the high school of their choice. When he first got into the program, his intended major was literature. Later, however, when he was about to complete the course, he changed to medicine, mainly under pressure from his brother but also because he didn't care much either way.

After completing his preparatory studies, he requested that he be sent to the high school in N. City, partly because he heard it was the newest such school in Japan and partly because N. City was noted for its beautiful women.

IV

In the evening of August 29, in the twentieth year of his life, he took a night train all by himself from Tokyo's central station to N. City.

It was probably the third or fourth day of the seventh month in the old calendar. A sky the color of indigo velvet was studded with stars. The cresent moon, hooked in the western corner of the sky, looked like the untinted eyebrow of a celestial maiden. Sitting by the window in a third-class coach, he silently counted the lights in the houses outside. As the train steadily surged ahead through the black mists of the night, the lights of the great metropolis got dimmer and dimmer until they disappeared from his ken. Suddenly his heart was overtaken by a thousand melancholy thoughts, and his eyes were again moist with warm tears. *"Sentimental, too sentimental!"* he exclaimed. Then, drying his tears, he felt like mocking himself:

"You don't have a single sweetheart, brother, or close friend in Tokyo—so for whom are you shedding your tears? Perhaps grieving for your past life, or feeling sad because you have lived there for the last two years? But haven't you been saying you don't care for Tokyo?

"Oh, but how can one help being attached to a place even after living there for only one year?

The orioles know me well because I have long lived here;
When I am getting ready to leave, they keep crying, four or five sad notes at a time.[7]

Then his rambling thoughts turned to the first Puritans embarking for America: "I imagine that those cross-bearing expatriates were no less grief-stricken than I am now when sailing off the coast of their old country."

The train had now passed Yokohama, and his emotions began to quiet down. After collecting himself for a while, he placed a postcard on top of a volume of Heine's poetry and with a pencil composed a poem intended for a friend in Tokyo:

The crescent barely rising above the willows,
I again left home for a distant horizon,
First pausing in a roadside tavern crowded with revelers,
Then taking off in a carriage as the street lights receded.

[7] A couplet from a quatrain by the T'ang poet Jung Yü, entitled "I-chia pieh hu-shang-t'ing" (Bidding goodbye to the pavilion on the lake on the occasion of moving my home). We are indebted to Professor Chiang Yee for this identification.

A youth inured to partings and sorrows has few tears to
    shed;
The luggage from a poor home consists only of old
    books.
At night the reeds find their roots stirred by autumn
    waters—
May you get my message at South Bank!

Then after resting for a while, he read some of
Heine's poetry under a dim light bulb:

Lebet wohl, ihr glatten Säle,
Glatte Herren, glatte Frauen!
Auf die Berge will ich steigen,
Lachend auf euch niederschauen! [8]

But with the monotonous sound of the wheels
pounding against his eardrums, in less than thirty
minutes he was transported into a land of dreams.

At five o'clock dawn began to break. Peering
through the window, he was able to discern a
thread of blue making its way out of the nocturnal
darkness. He then stuck his head out the window
and saw a picturesque scene wrapped in haze. "So
it's going to be another day of nice autumn
weather," he thought. "How fortunate I am!"

An hour later the train arrived at N. City's
railroad station. Alighting from the train, he saw
at the station a Japanese youth wearing a cap
marked by two white stripes and knew him for a
student of the high school. He walked toward him
and, lifting his cap slightly, asked, "How do I find
the X. High School?" The student answered,
"Let's go there together." So with the student he
left the station and took a trolley in front of its entrance.

The morning was still young, and shops in N.
City were not yet open. After passing through
several desolate streets, they got off in front of the
Crane Dance Park.

"Is the school far from here?" he asked.

"About two *li.*"

The sun had risen by the time they were walking the narrow path between the rice fields after
crossing the park, but the dewdrops were still on
the rice stalks, bright as pearls. Across the fields in
front were clusters of trees shading some scattered farmhouses. Two or three chimneys rising
above these structures seemed to float in the early
morning air, and bluish smoke emanating from
them curled in the sky like incense. He knew that
the farmers were preparing breakfast.

He inquired at an inn close to the school and
was informed that the few pieces of luggage sent
out the previous week had already arrived. The
innkeeper, used to Chinese lodgers, gave him a
hearty welcome. After unpacking, he had the feeling that the days ahead promised much joy and
pleasure.

But all his hopes for the future were mocked by
reality that very evening. His home town, however
small, was a busy little town, and while he had
often felt lonely amid large throngs in Tokyo,
nevertheless the kind of city life there was not too
different from what he had been accustomed to
since childhood. Now this inn, situated in the
countryside of N. City, was far too isolated. To
the left of its front door was a narrow path cutting
across the rice fields; only a square pond to the
west of the inn provided some diversity to the
scene. Since school had not yet begun, students
had not yet returned, and thus he was the only
guest in this spacious hostel. It was still not too
unbearable in the day, but that evening, when he
pushed open the window to look out, everywhere
was pitch darkness. For the countryside of N. City
was a large plain, with nothing to obstruct one's
view. A few lights were visible in the distance, now
bright and now dim, lending to the view a spectral
quality. Up above the ceiling he could hear the
scampering rats fighting for food, while outside
the window several *wu-t'ung* trees would rustle
whenever there was a breeze. Because his room
was on the second floor, the rattle of the leaves
sounded so close that he was frightened almost to
the point of tears. He had never felt a stronger
nostalgia than on that evening.

---

[8] "You polished halls, polished men, / Polished women—to all adieu! / I'm off to climb in the mountains, / And smiling to look
down on you!" These lines form the last stanza of the Prologue to Heine's "Harzreise" (Travels through the Harz Mountains).
See Heinrich Heine, *Werke*, ed. Martin Greiner (Cologne and Berlin, 1962), pp. 767–824. The poem is a satire in the form of a
travel diary written in late 1824, criticizing the superficial polish of polite society which Heine's narrator longs to abandon for the
simple life in the mountains. The Editors are grateful to William Nienhauser for translating this poem.

He got to know more people after school started, and his extremely sensitive nature also became adapted to the pastoral environment. In less than three months he had become Nature's child, no longer separable from the pleasures of the countryside.

His school was located on the outskirts of N. City which, as has already been mentioned, were nothing but open fields offering an unobstructed vision of broad horizons. At that time Japan was not so industrialized or populous as it is now. Hence this large area of open space around the school, diversified only by clumps of trees and little knolls and mounds. Except for a few stationery shops and restaurants serving the needs of the students, there were no stores in the neighborhood. A few inns, however, dotted the cultivated fields in this mainly untilled wilderness. After supper he would put on his black serge mantle and, a favorite book in hand, take a walk in the lingering glow of the setting sun. Most probably it was during these *idyllic wanderings* that he developed his passion for nature.

So at a time when competition was not as keen as today and leisure was as plentiful as in the Middle Ages, he spent half a year of dreamlike existence in a quiet retreat, simple in its manners and uncontaminated by the presence of philistines. These happy days and months seemed to go by in a flash.

The weather was now getting milder, and the grass was turning green under the influence of warm breezes. The young shoots in the wheat fields near the inn were growing taller inch by inch. With all nature responding to the call of spring, he too felt more keenly the urge implanted in him by the progenitors of the human race. Unflaggingly, he would sin every morning underneath his quilt.

He was ordinarily a very self-respecting and clean person, but when evil thoughts seized hold of him, numbing his intellect and paralyzing his conscience, he was no longer able to observe the admonition that "one must not harm one's body under any circumstances, since it is inherited from one's parents."[9] Every time he sinned he felt bitter remorse and vowed not to transgress again. But, almost without exception, the same visions appeared before him vividly at the same time the next morning. All those descendants of Eve he would normally meet in the course of the day came to seduce him in all their nakedness, and the figure of a middle-aged *madam* appeared to him even more tempting than that of a virgin. Inevitably, after a hard struggle, he succumbed to temptation. Thus once, twice, and this practice became a habit. Quite often, after abusing himself, he would go to the library to look up medical references on the subject. They all said without exception that this practice was most harmful to one's health. After that his fear increased.

One day he learned somewhere in a book that Gogol, the founder of modern Russian literature, had also suffered from this sickness and was not able to cure himself to the day of his death. This discovery comforted him somewhat, if only because no less a man than the author of *Dead Souls* was his fellow sinner. But this form of self-deception could do little to remove the worry in his heart.

Since he was very much concerned about his health, he now took a bath and had milk and several raw eggs every day. But he couldn't help feeling ashamed of himself when taking his bath or having his milk and eggs: all this was clear evidence of his sin.

He felt that his health was declining day by day and his memory weakening. He became shy and especially uncomfortable in the presence of women. He grew to loathe textbooks and turned increasingly to French naturalistic novels as well as a few Chinese novels noted for their pornography. These he now read and reread so many times that he could almost recite them from memory.

On the infrequent occasions when he turned out a good poem he became overjoyed, believing that his brain had not yet been damaged. He would then swear to himself: "My brain is all right, since I can still compose such a good poem.

[9] From *The Book on Filial Piety* (*Hsiao-ching*), an early Confucian classic.

I mustn't do that sort of thing again. The past I can no longer help, but I shall control myself in the future. If I don't sin again, my brain will be in good shape." But when that critical moment came each morning, he again forgot his own words.

On Thursdays and Fridays or on the twenty-sixth and twenty-seventh of each month he abandoned himself to this pleasure without a qualm, for he thought that he would be able to stop by next Monday or next month. Sometimes when he happened to have a haircut or a bath on a Saturday evening or the evening of the last day of the month, he would take that as a sign of his reformation. But only a few days later he would have to resume his diet of milk and eggs.

Hardly a day passed in which he was not troubled by his own fears as well as by his sense of guilt, and his hypochondria worsened. He remained in such a condition for about two months, and then the summer vacation began. However, he suffered even worse during the two-month vacation than before: for by the time school resumed, his cheek-bones had become more prominent, the bluish-gray circles around his eyes even bigger, and his once-bright pupils as expressionless as those of a dead fish.

V

Again it was fall. The big blue firmament seemed to be suspended higher and higher each day. The rice fields around his inn had now turned the color of gold. When the chilly winds of morning or evening cut into his skin like a dagger, he knew that bright autumn days were not far behind.

The week before, he had taken along a volume of Wordsworth and strolled on the paths in the fields for a whole afternoon. From that day on he had not been able to free himself from the spell of his cyclic hypochondria. Moreover, the two girl students he had met a few days before stayed in his memory and he couldn't help blushing whenever he recalled that encounter.

Recently, wherever he went, he was uneasy. At school he had the feeling that his Japanese class-mates were avoiding him. And he no longer wanted to visit his Chinese classmates simply because after each such visit his heart felt all the more empty. Those Chinese friends of his, hard as they tried, still couldn't understand his state of mind. Before each visit he expected to win their sympathy, but as it happened, no sooner had they exchanged a few words than he began to regret his visit. There was one, however, whose conversation he enjoyed, and sometimes he told him all about his private and public life. On his way home, however, he always regretted having talked so much and ended up in a worse state of self-reproach than before. For this reason a rumor circulated among his Chinese friends that he was mentally ill. When the rumor reached him, he wanted as much to avenge himself on these few Chinese friends as on his Japanese schoolmates. He was finally so alienated from the Chinese that he wouldn't even greet them when he met them in the street or on the campus. Naturally he didn't attend any of the meetings for Chinese students, so that he and they became virtual enemies.

Among these Chinese students there was one eccentric. Probably because there was something reprehensible about his marriage, he seemed to take particular delight in malicious gossip—partly as a means of covering up his own immoral conduct. And it was none other than this eccentric who had spread the rumor that he was mentally ill.

His loneliness became most intolerable after he had cut himself off from all social contacts. Fortunately, the innkeeper's daughter held some attraction for him, for otherwise he could really have committed suicide. She was just seventeen and had an oblong face and big eyes. Whenever she smiled, she showed two dimples and one gold tooth, and quite often she put a smile on her face, confident of its charm.

Although he was very fond of her, when she came in to make his bed or deliver his meals he always put on an air of aloofness. And however badly he wanted to talk to her, he never did because he could hardly breathe in front of her. To avoid this insufferable agony, he had lately tried to leave his room as soon as she entered it. But the more he tried to avoid her, the more he longed for her.

One Saturday evening all the other students in the inn had gone to N. City to amuse themselves. For economic reasons he didn't go there. He returned to his room following a brief after-dinner stroll around the pond on the west side. But it was difficult for him to stay by himself on the deserted second floor, and soon he got impatient and wanted to go out again. To leave the place, however, meant passing the door of the innkeeper's own room, which was situated right by the main entrance, and he remembered when he returned that the innkeeper and his daughter were just having dinner. At this thought he no longer had the desire to go out again, since seeing her would mean another torturing experience.

Instead, he took out a novel by George Gissing and started to read; but before he had finished three or four pages, he heard, in the dead silence, the splashing of water. He held his breath and listened for a while; soon he started panting, and his face turned red. After some moments of hesitation, he pushed open the door quietly and, taking off his slippers, went down the stairs stealthily. With equal caution he pushed open the door to the toilet and stood by its glass window to peer into the bathroom (the bathroom was adjacent to the toilet; through the glass window one could see the goings-on in the bathroom). At first he thought he would be content with just a glance. But what he saw in the next room kept him completely nailed down.

Those snow-white breasts! Those voluptuous thighs! And that curvaceous figure!

Holding his breath, he took another close look at the girl and a muscle in his face began to twitch. Finally he became so overwrought that his forehead hit the windowpane. The naked Eve then asked across the steam, "Who is it?" Without making a sound, he hurriedly left the toilet and rushed upstairs.

Back in his room he felt his face burning and his mouth parched. To punish himself, he kept slapping his own face while taking out the bedding to get ready for sleep. But he could hardly fall asleep. After tossing and turning under the quilt for a while, he strained his ears and concentrated all his attention on the movements downstairs. The splashing had stopped, and he heard the bathroom door open. And judging by the sound of her footsteps, he was positive she was coming upstairs. Immediately he buried his head beneath the quilt and listened to the whisper of his inner voice: "She's already outside the door." He felt as if all his blood were rushing to his head. Certainly he was now in a state of unusual excitement, compounded of fear, shame, and joy, but if someone had asked him at that moment, he would have denied that he was filled with joy.

Holding his breath, he strained his ears and listened—all was quiet on the other side of the door. He coughed deliberately—still no response. But just as he was getting puzzled, he heard her voice downstairs talking with her father. Hard as he tried (he was so tense that his palms were soaked in sweat), he still couldn't make out anything she was saying. Presently her father roared with laughter. Burying his head under the quilt, he said through clenched teeth, "So she's told him! She's told him!"

He didn't get a wink of sleep that night. Early the next morning he stole downstairs to make a quick toilet and rushed out of the inn. It was not yet time for the innkeeper and his daughter to get up.

The sun was rising, but the dew-drenched dust on the road had not yet dried. Without knowing exactly where to go, he headed east and before long saw a peasant pushing a vegetable cart coming his way. "Good morning," the peasant greeted him as their shoulders brushed. This took him by surprise, and immediately his emaciated face flushed red. He wondered, "So he also knows my secret?"

After walking hurriedly with no sense of direction for a long while, he turned his head and saw that he was already a great distance from his school. The sun had now risen. He wanted to determine the time but could not do so, since he had forgotten to take his silver pocket watch along. Judging by the position of the sun, it was probably about nine o'clock. He was hungry, but unwilling to go back and face the innkeeper and his daughter, though all he had on him was twelve cents, hardly enough for a decent snack. Finally he bought from a village grocery store twelve cents' worth of food, intending to eat it in a nook, unseen by others.

He kept walking until he reached a crossroads. There were very few pedestrians on the side path running from north to south. Since the south side sloped downward, flanked by two precipices, he knew that the path had been dug out of a hill. Thus the crossroads was the tip of the hill, while the main path on which he had been walking was its ridge and the intersecting side path sloped in two directions following the hill's contour. He paused at the crossroads for a while and then came upon a large plain which, he knew, would lead to the city.

Across the plain was a dense grove where, he thought, the A. Shinto Temple was located. When he had reached the end of the path, he saw that there stood upon its left bank a parapet encircling a few cottages. Above the door of one of these cottages hung a tablet inscribed with three Chinese characters, *hsiang hsüeh hai* (sea of fragrant snow).[10] He walked up a few steps to the entrance of the parapet and with one push opened both leaves of the door. Stepping casually inside, he found a winding path leading uphill flanked by a great many old *mei* trees and knew for sure that this was a *mei* grove. He walked up the northern slope along this winding path until he reached the hilltop, where he saw stretching before him a plateau of great scenic beauty. From the foot of the hill to the plateau, the whole grove covering the surface of the slope was most tastefully planned.

West of the plateau was the precipice, which faced another across the gulf, and down below was the narrow pathway he had just traversed. Aligned on the edge of this precipice were a two-storey house and several cottages. Since all their doors and windows were tightly shut, he knew that they were restaurants and taverns, open only during the season of the *mei* blossoms. In front of the two-storey house was a lawn with a ring of white rocks at its center, and inside the ring an old *mei* tree crouched on its gnarled trunk. At the outer edge of the lawn marking the beginning of the southern slope stood a stone tablet recording the history of the grove. He sat on the grass in front of the tablet and started eating the food he had bought in the grocery store.

He sat on the lawn for a while even after he had finished breakfast. There were no human voices; only from the trees in the farther distance came the occasional chirping of birds. Gazing at the azure sky, he felt that everything around him—the trees and houses, the lawn and birds—was being equally nourished by Nature, under the benign influence of the sun. In face of all this, his memory of last night's sin vanished like a boat sailing beyond the outer rim of the sea.

From the plateau to the end of the downhill slope there were many little winding paths. He got up and walked randomly among these until he came to a cottage situated midway down the slope, surrounded by *mei* trees. Nearby on the east side was an ancient well covered with a heap of pine needles. He turned the handle of the pump several times trying to draw some water, but the machine only creaked and no water came up. He thought, "Probably this grove is open only during the flowering season. No wonder there's no one around." Then he murmured as another thought flashed upon him, "Since the grove is unoccupied, why don't I go and ask the owner if I could lodge here for a while?"

This decided, he rushed downhill to look for the owner. As he came near the entrance, he ran into a peasant around fifty years of age coming into the grove. He apologized and then inquired, "Do you know who owns this place?"

"It's under my management."

"Where do you live?"

"Over there." The peasant pointed to a little house on the west side of the main path. Following his direction, he saw the house on the far end of the western precipice and nodded to acknowledge its existence. Then he asked, "Can you rent me that two-storey house inside the grove?"

"Sure. But are you by yourself?"

---

[10] A traditional metaphor for a grove of *mei* or Japanese apricot trees.

"Yes."

"Then you might as well save yourself the trouble."

"Why?"

"Because I have had student tenants before, and they hardly stayed more than ten days before they moved out, probably because they couldn't stand the solitude."

"I'm quite different from the others. I won't mind the solitude as long as you agree to rent the place to me."

"I can't think of any reason why not. When do you want to move in?"

"How about this afternoon?"

"It's all right with me."

"Then may I trouble you to clean it up before I move in?"

"Certainly, certainly. Goodbye!"

"Goodbye."

VI

After he had moved to the *mei* grove, his *hypochrondria* took a different turn.

Over some trivial matters he had started a quarrel with his elder brother, which prompted him to mail to Peking a long, long letter severing ties of kinship. But after that letter was sent, he mused for many an hour in front of his house. He thought he was the most miserable man in the world. Actually, he was the one to blame for this fraternal split, but precisely because a quarrel of this sort is usually more bitter than a quarrel among friends, he hated his brother like a viper or scorpion. When he was humiliated, he would reason thus: "If even my own brother could be so unkind to me, how can I blame others?" After reaching this conclusion, he would review all the unkind things which he imagined his brother had done to him and declare that his brother was bad and he himself was good. He would then itemize his own virtues and list all his past wrongs and sufferings in an exaggerated fashion. When he had proved to his own satisfaction that he was indeed the most miserable of all men, his tears would course down like a waterfall. A soft voice would seem to be speaking to him from the sky, "Oh, so it's you who are crying. It's really a shame that such a kindhearted person as you should be so maltreated by the world. But let it be, since it has been decreed by Heaven, and you'd better stop crying, since it won't do your health any good." When he heard this voice, he would feel greatly relieved: there seemed to be infinite sweetness in chewing the cud of bitter sorrow.

As a means of retaliation, he gave up his study of medicine and switched to literature, intending this change of major to be a declaration of war, since it was his brother who had urged him to study medicine. Also, changing his major would delay his graduation for a year, which meant shortening his life by one year, and the sooner he died, the easier it would be to maintain a lifelong enmity toward his brother. For he was quite afraid that he would be reconciled with his brother in a year or two, and he changed his major to help strengthen his sense of enmity.

The weather had gradually turned colder. It had been a month since he moved up the hill. In the past few days dark clouds had hung heavily in the somber sky, and when the frosty northern winds came, the leaves on the *mei* trees would begin to fall.

Upon moving to his retreat, he had sold some old books to buy cooking utensils and had made his own meals for nearly a month. Now that it was getting chillier, he gave up cooking and ate at the grove keeper's house down the hill. Like a retired monk idling in a temple, he had nothing to do but to blame others and reproach himself.

One morning he got up very early. Pushing open the window facing the east, he saw a few curls of red cloud floating on the far horizon. The sky directly above was a patch of reddish silver-gray. Because it had drizzled the day before, he found the rising sun all the more lovely. He went down the slope and fetched water from the ancient well. After washing his face and hands with the water, he felt full of energy and ran upstairs for a volume of Huang Chung-Tse's[11] poetry. He

---

[11] The famous Ch'ing poet (1749–1783) is the hero of Yü Ta-fu's story, "Ts'ai-shih chi" (Colored Rock Cliff).

kept pacing along the winding paths in the grove as he chanted the poetry. Soon the sun was up in the sky.

Looking southward from the plateau, he could see, at the foot of the hill, a large plain checkered with rice fields. The unharvested grain, ripened to a yellowish gold, gave a most brilliant reflection of the morning sun against the background of a violet sky. The scene reminded him of a rural painting by Millet. Faced with this magnificence of Nature, he felt like an early Christian of Jesus' time and could not help laughing at his own pettiness:

"Forgive, forgive! I have forgiven all ye who have wronged me. Come ye all and make peace with me!"

As he was contemplating—with a book of poems in hand and tears in eyes—the beauty of the autumnal scene and thus getting lost in thought, all of a sudden he heard two whispering voices close by him:

"You have to come tonight!" It was clearly a man's voice.

"I want to very much, but I'm afraid . . ."

It was a girl's seductive voice, and he felt instantly electrified, as if his circulation had stopped. Looking around, he found himself standing by a growth of tall reeds. He was on its right and the couple was probably on its left, completely oblivious of his existence.

"You are so kind. Do come tonight, because so far we haven't . . . in bed," the man continued.

" . . . "

He heard the noise made by their sucking lips, and immediately he prostrated himself on the ground, as stealthily as a wild dog with a stolen morsel in its mouth. "Oh, shame, shame!" he cursed himself severely in his heart, "How can you be so depraved!" Nevertheless, he was all ears, listening to what they were doing and saying.

The crunching of fallen leaves on the ground.

The noise of undressing.

The man's rapid panting.

The sucking of lips.

And the woman pleading in half-audible, broken tones: "Please . . . please . . . please hurry . . . otherwise we . . . we will be seen . . ."

Instantly his complexion turned ash-gray, his eyes reddened with fire, and his upper teeth clattered against his lower. He could hardly get up, let alone run away from the scene. He was transfixed in agony.

He waited there until the couple had left before he went back to his bedroom upstairs like a drenched dog and covered himself up with a quilt.

VII

Without bothering with lunch, he slept until four o'clock—until the whole area was suffused with the late afternoon sun. In the distance a thin veil of smoke was seen floating leisurely on top of the trees across the plain. Hurriedly he ran downhill to get on the road and headed south for no apparent reason. He eventually crossed the plain to arrive at the trolley stop in front of the A. Temple. A trolley came by just then and he boarded it, without knowing why he should be taking the trolley or where he was going.

After running for fifteen or sixteen minutes, the trolley stopped and the operator asked him to change cars. So he took another trolley. Twenty or thirty minutes later it reached its last stop, and so he got off. He found himself standing by a harbor.

In front of him was the sea, lazing in the afternoon sun, smiling. Across the sea to the south was the silhouette of a mountain floating hazily in translucent air. To the west was a long dike, stretching to the middle of the bay. A lighthouse stood beyond the dike like a giant. A few tethered boats and sampans were moving slightly, while a number of buoys farther out in the bay shone red on the water. The wind carried from a distance broken snatches of a conversation, but he was unable to tell what it was about or where it came from.

After pacing aimlessly for a while on the bank, he suddenly heard something which sounded like chimes. He went over and saw that the musical signal was designed to attract customers to the ferry. Soon a steamboat came by from the opposite side. Following a middle-aged worker, he too boarded the ferry.

No sooner had he landed on the eastern bank than he found himself in front of a villa. The door was wide open, showing a courtyard neatly decorated with a lawn, flowering plants, and miniature hills made of rocks. Without finding out the identity of the place, he simply walked in and was immediately greeted by a very sweet feminine voice: "Please come in."

Taken by surprise, he stood there in a daze and thought, "This is probably some kind of restaurant, but I have heard a place like this cannot be without prostitutes."

At the thought of this he became invigorated, as if drenched by a bucketful of cold water. But he soon changed color because he didn't know what to do with himself, whether to advance or retreat. It was a pity that he had the lust of an ape and the timidity of a rabbit, which accounted for his present quandary.

"Come in. Please do come in." That seductive voice called from the hall again, accompanied by giggles.

"You devils! You think I am too timid to come in?" he said to himself in anger, his face burning hot. Stamping his feet lightly, he advanced, gnashing his teeth and clenching his fists, as if preparing to declare war on these young waitresses. But hard as he tried, he couldn't possibly erase the flushes of red and blue on his face nor compose its twitching muscles. So when he came near these girls, he almost cried like a child.

"Please come upstairs!"

"Please come upstairs!"

Bracing himself, he followed a waitress of around seventeen or eighteen upstairs and felt somewhat calmer. A few steps on the second floor and he came into a dark corridor; immediately his nostrils were assaulted by a strange mixture of the perfume of face powder and hair tonic and the special kind of bodily fragrance that distinguished Japanese women. He felt dizzy and sparks floated before his eyes, which made him reel. After

steadying himself, he saw emerging from the darkness in front of him the oblong, powdered face of a woman who asked him with a smile:

"Would you like to have a place by the sea? Or did you have a special place in mind?"

He felt the woman's warm breath upon his face and he inhaled deeply without being aware of what he was doing. But as soon as he became conscious of his action, his face reddened. With great effort he mumbled an answer:

"I'll take a room facing the sea."

After taking him to a small room by the sea, the waitress asked what kind of food he would like, and he answered:

"Just bring a few dishes of what you have ready."

"Want some wine?"

"Yes."

After the waitress had left, he stood up and pushed open the paper windows to let in some fresh air, for the room was stuffy and her perfumed presence lingered on, suffocating him.

The bay was calm. A light breeze passed by and the surface of the sea was wrinkled into a series of waves which, under the reflection of the setting sun, glinted like the scales of a golden fish.

After watching the scene from the window for a while, he was moved to whisper a line of poetry:

"The setting sun has crimsoned my seaside chamber." [12]

Looking westward, he saw that the sun was now only about ten feet from the horizon. But however beautiful the scene, his thoughts were still with the waitress—the fragrance emanating from her mouth, hair, face, and body. After repeated attempts to engage his mind elsewhere, he resigned himself to the fact that in his present mood he was obsessed with flesh rather than poetry.

Before long the waitress brought in his food and wine. She squatted by him and served him most attentively. He wanted to look closely at her and confide in her all his troubles. But in reality he didn't even dare look her in the eye, much less talk to her. And so, like a mute, all he did was

[12] Most probably, this line of verse is Yü Ta-fu's own composition.

look furtively at her delicate, white hands resting upon her knees and that portion of a pink petticoat not covered by her kimono.

For Japanese women wear a short petticoat instead of drawers. On the outside they wear a buttonless, long-sleeved kimono with a band about fourteen inches wide around the waist fastened into a square bundle on the back. Because of this costume, with every step they take, the kimono is flung open to reveal the pink petticoat inside and a glimpse of plump thighs. This is the special charm of Japanese women to which he paid most attention whenever he saw them on the street. It was because of this habit too that he called himself a beast, a sneaky dog, and a despicable coward.

It was specifically the corner of the waitress's petticoat that was perturbing him now. The more he wanted to talk to her, the more tongue-tied he became. His embarrassment was apparently making the waitress a little impatient, for she asked, "Where are you from?"

At this, his pallid face reddened again; he stammered and stammered but couldn't give a forthright answer. He was once again standing on the guillotine. For the Japanese look down upon Chinese just as we look down upon pigs and dogs. They call us Shinajin, "Chinamen," a term more derogatory than "knave" in Chinese. And now he had to confess before this pretty young girl that he was a Shinajin.

"O China, my China, why don't you grow strong!"

His body was trembling convulsively and tears were again about to roll down.

Seeing him in such agitation, the waitress thought it would be best to leave him to drink alone, so that he could compose himself. So she said:

"You have almost finished this bottle. I'll get you another one."

In a while he heard the waitress coming upstairs. He thought she was coming back to him, and so he changed his sitting position and adjusted his clothes. But he was deceived, for she was only taking some other guests to the room next to his.

Soon he heard the guests flirting with the waitress, who said coquettishly, "Please behave. We have a guest in the next room." This infuriated him, and he cursed them silently:

"Bastards! Pigs! How dare you bully me like this? Revenge! Revenge! I'll revenge myself on you! Can there be any true-hearted girl in the world? You faithless waitress, how dare you desert me like this? Oh, let it be, let it be, for from now on I shall care nothing about women, absolutely nothing. I will love nothing but my country, and let my country be my love."

He had an impulse to go home and apply himself to study. At the same time, however, he was envious of those bastards next door, and there was still a secret corner in his heart which expected the waitress's return.

Finally, he suppressed his anger and silently downed a few cups of wine, which made him feel warm all over. He got up and opened some more windows to cool himself, and saw that the sun was now going down. Then he drank a few more cups and watched the gradual blurring of the seascape. The shadow cast by the lighthouse on the dike was getting longer and longer, and a descending fog began to blend the sky and the sea. But behind this hazy veil the setting sun lingered on the horizon, as if reluctant to say goodbye. After watching this view for a while, he felt inexplicably merry and burst out laughing. He rubbed his burning cheeks, muttering, "Yes, I'm drunk. I'm drunk."

The waitress finally came in. Seeing him flushing and laughing idiotically in front of the windows, she asked:

"With the windows wide open, aren't you afraid of the cold?"

"I'm not cold, not cold at all. Who can afford to miss this beautiful sunset?"

"You're indeed a poet. Here is your wine."

"Poet? Yes, I'm a poet. Bring me a brush and some paper and I'll write a poem for you."

After the waitress had left, he was surprised at himself and thought, "How have I become so bold all of a sudden?"

He became even merrier after emptying more

cups of the newly warmed wine and broke into another round of loud laughter. In the next room those bastards were singing Japanese songs aloud, and so he also raised his voice and chanted:

Drunk, I tap the railing and feel the chillier because of
   the wine;
Rivers and lakes again turn bleak in the death of win-
   ter.
The mad poet with his profound pity for the parrot
Was spared through death—his bones buried in the
   Central Province;
The further ignominy of another talented youth
Exiled to Ch'ang-an with the title of grand tutor.
It's not too hard to try to repay a life-saving meal
With a thousand pieces of gold,
But how many could pass through the capital
Without heaving five long sighs?
Looking homeward across the misted sea,
I too weep for my beloved country.[13]

After repeating the poem several times, he fell asleep on the floor.

VIII

When he woke up, he found himself lying underneath a red satin quilt scented with a strange perfume. The room was not large, but it was no longer the same room he had occupied in the late afternoon. A ten-watt bulb suspended from the ceiling gave a dim light. A teapot and two cups were placed beside his pillow. After helping himself to two or three cups of tea, he got up and walked unsteadily to the door. As he was opening it, the same waitress who had taken care of him in the afternoon came in to greet him: "Hey, there! Are you all right now?"

He nodded and answered with a smile, "Yes. Where is the toilet?"

"I'll show you."

He followed her and again passed through the corridor, but it was now lit up and from far and near came singing and laughter and the sound of the samisen. All this helped him to recall what had happened this afternoon, especially what he had said to the waitress when in a drunken state. His face flushed again.

Returning from the toilet, he asked the waitress, "Is this quilt yours?"

"Yes," she answered with a smile.

"What time is it now?"

"It's probably eight forty or eight fifty."

"Would you please give me the check?"

"Yes, sir."

After he had paid the bill, tremblingly he handed the waitress a banknote, but she said, "No, thanks. I don't need it."

He knew she was offended by the small tip. Again red with embarrassment, he searched his pocket and found one remaining note. He gave it to her, saying, "I hope you won't scorn this paltry sum. Please take it."

His hand trembled more violently this time, and even his voice quivered. Seeing him in this state, the waitress accepted the money and said in a low voice, "Thank you." He ran straight downstairs, put on his shoes, and went outside.

The night air was very cold. It was probably the eighth or ninth of the lunar month, and the half moon hung high in the left corner of the grayish-blue sky, accompanied by a few lone stars.

He took a walk by the seashore. From afar the lights on the fishermen's boats seemed to be beck-

---

[13] Like the earlier poem intended for a friend in Tokyo, this poem is Yü Ta-fu's own composition in the eight-line, seven-character *lü-shih* style. We have expanded its second and third couplets into eight lines (ll.3–10) because otherwise these highly allusive couplets could not have made much sense to the general reader. The "mad poet" of l.3 is Ni Heng, a precocious and utterly proud scholar of the Later Han dynasty who once wrote a *fu* poem on the parrot, indirectly comparing himself to this bird of supernal intelligence forced to live in captivity. At the age of twenty-six he was executed by Huang Tsu, governor of Chiang-hsia (Central Province), one of the several patrons he had offended with his rude arrogance. "Another talented youth," in l.5 refers to Chia I, a Former Han writer of greater fame. His hopes for a political career were dashed when he was assigned, or rather banished, to the state of Ch'ang-sha to serve as its king's tutor. A few years later he died heartbroken at the age of thirty-three. Han Hsin, a prominent general under the founding emperor of the Former Han dynasty, was befriended in his youth by a washerwoman who repeatedly gave him meals when he had nothing to eat. After he had achieved fame, he sought her out and gave her "a thousand pieces of gold" (l.8). Liang Hung, a recluse of the Later Han, once passed through the national capital and composed a "Song of Five Sighs" (*Wu-i chih ko*), each of its five lines ending with the exclamatory word *i* (alas!). Emperor Su-tsung was highly displeased, and Liang Hung had to change his name and live in hiding.

oning him, like the will-o'-the-wisp, and the waves under the silvery moonlight seemed to be winking at him like the eyes of mountain spirits.[14] Suddenly he had an inexplicable urge to drown himself in the sea.

He felt in his pocket and found that he didn't even have money for the trolley fare. Reflecting upon what he had done today, he couldn't help cursing himself:

"How could I have gone to such a place? I really have become a most degraded person. But it's too late for regrets. I may as well end my life here, since I'll probably never get the kind of love I want. And what would life be without love? Isn't it as dead as ashes? Ah, this dreary life, how dull and dry! Everyone in this world hates me, mistreats me—even my own brother is trying to push me off the edge of this world. How can I make a living? And why should I stay on in this world of suffering?"

This thought gave him pause, and tears began to roll down his face, which was now as pallid as a dead man's. He didn't even bother to wipe away the tears, which glistened on his moon-blanched face like the morning dew on the leaves. With anguish he turned his head to look at the elongated shadow of his thin body.

"My poor shadow! You have followed me for twenty-one years, and now this sea is going to bury you. Though my body has been insulted and injured, I should not have let you grow so thin and frail. O shadow, my shadow, please forgive me!"

He looked toward the west. The light on the lighthouse was doing its job, now beaming red and now green. When the green beam reached down, there would immediately appear on the sea an illuminated path of light blue. Again looking up, he saw a bright star trembling in the farthest reaches of the western horizon.

"Underneath that shaky star lies my country, my birthplace, where I have spent eighteen years of my life. But alas, my homeland, I shall see you no more!"

Such were his despondent, self-pitying thoughts as he walked back and forth along the shore. After a while, he paused to look again at that bright star in the western sky, and tears poured down like a shower. The view around him began to blur. Drying his tears, he stood still and uttered a long sigh. Then he said, between pauses:

"O China, my China, you are the cause of my death! . . . I wish you could become rich and strong soon! . . . Many, many of your children are still suffering."

[14] In using the term *shan-kuei* (mountain spirits), the author must be alluding to the female deity of identical name celebrated in one of the "Nine Songs" (*Chiu-ko*). See David Hawkes, tr., *Ch'u Tz'u: The Songs of the South* (London, 1959; Boston, 1962), p. 43.

MAO TUN
(1896–1981)

A native of T'ung-hsiang, Chekiang, Mao Tun (pen name since 1927 of She Yen-ping) was born of enlightened parents who took a personal interest in his education. However, his father, who would have encouraged him to prepare for a career in science and technology, died when Mao Tun was only nine years old. Thus during his middle school years, he was free to follow his own bent for literature. At seventeen, Mao Tun enrolled in the preparatory college course at National Peking University. He completed the three-year course in 1916, at which time financial difficulties compelled him to accept a position as a proofreader at the Commercial Press in Shanghai. However, he was soon promoted to editor and translator.

Mao Tun became a founder of the Literary Association in November 1920 and served as editor of the renovated *Short Story* magazine from 1921 to 1923. During that formative period he read widely in Western literature, not only the established classics of fiction like Dickens, Maupassant, Zola, Tolstoy, and Chekhov, but also the writers of Poland, Hungary, Norway, and other small nations. After resigning as editor, however, Mao Tun became more involved in politics in the next few years. In the spring of 1926 he served as a propagandist in the Political Department of the Nationalist government in Canton. Following the Nationalist-Communist split in 1927, Mao Tun withdrew from politics and wrote three short novels—*Disillusion* (*Huan-mieh*), *Vacillation* (*Tung-yao*), and *Pursuit* (*Chui-ch'iu*)—under the collective title of *The Eclipse* (*Shih*, 1930). This trilogy about the revolutionary youth of his time was of such scope and honesty that it catapulted Mao Tun into the position of China's foremost novelist. His next major novel, *Midnight* (*Tzu-yeh*, 1933), about the financiers, bourgeois youths, and factory workers of Shanghai, is a more ambitious piece of naturalistic fiction, but less successful as a work of art. But because it interprets Chinese society in strictly Communist terms, it has been regarded by Communist critics as his masterpiece. Equally acclaimed was the so-called "Rural Trilogy" of the same period, comprising three short stories: "Spring Silkworms" (*Ch'un-ts'an*), "Autumn Harvest" (*Ch'iu-shou*), and "Winter Ruin" (*Ts'an-tung*).

During the war years Mao Tun continued to be very active, producing among other works the two novels *Putrefaction* (*Fu-shih*, 1941) and *Maple Leaves as Red as Flowers of the Second Month* (*Shuang-yeh hung-ssu erh-yüeh hua*, 1943) and the play *Before and After the Ch'ing-ming Festival* (*Ch'ing-ming ch'ien-hou,* 1945). With the establishment of the People's Republic in 1949, however, Mao Tun ceased to function as a creative writer and played the role of a leading bureaucrat in governmental and cultural organizations, including a long term as Minister of Culture (1949–65). For over a quarter of a century, therefore, Mao Tun wrote mainly reports and speeches plus some occasional criticism; in recent years, following the downfall of the Gang of Four, however, installments of his memoirs, called *Hui-i lu,* have appeared in print.

"Spring Silkworms," our choice for this volume, is generally regarded as Mao Tun's best story because it "comes nearest to transcending the inherent limitations of the proletarian genre. . . . As a Communist commentary on the Chinese scene, it shows the bankruptcy of the peasantry under the dual pressure of imperialist aggression and traditional usury, and as such the story is usually praised. Yet this standard interpretation hardly explains its strength and appeal: almost in spite of himself, one feels that Mao Tun is celebrating in his tale the dignity of labor" (Hsia, *History,* pp. 162–63).

J.S.M.L.
C.T.H.

Spring Silkworms

by Mao Tun

Translated by Sidney Shapiro

Old T'ung Pao sat on a rock beside the road that skirted the canal, his long-stemmed pipe lying on the ground next to him. Though it was only a few days after the Ch'ing-ming Festival[1] the April sun was already very strong. It scorched Old T'ung Pao's spine like a basin of fire. Straining down the road, the men towing the fast junk wore only thin tunics, open in front. They were bent far forward, pulling, pulling, pulling, great beads of sweat dripping from their brows.

The sight of others toiling strenuously made Old T'ung Pao feel even warmer; he began to itch. He was still wearing the tattered padded jacket in which he had passed the winter. His unlined jacket had not yet been redeemed from the pawn shop. Who would have believed it could get so hot right after Ch'ing-ming?

Even the weather's not what it used to be, Old T'ung Pao said to himself, and spat emphatically.

Before him, the water of the canal was green and shiny. Occasional passing boats broke the mirror-smooth surface into ripples and eddies, turning the reflection of the earthen bank and the long line of mulberry trees flanking it into a dancing gray blur. But not for long! Gradually the trees reappeared, twisting and weaving drunkenly. Another few minutes, and they were again standing still, reflected as clearly as before. On the gnarled fists of the mulberry branches, little fingers of tender green buds were already bursting forth. Crowded close together, the trees along

the canal seemed to march endlessly into the distance. The unplanted fields as yet were only cracked clods of dry earth; the mulberry trees reigned supreme here this time of the year! Behind Old T'ung Pao's back was another great stretch of mulberry trees, squat, silent. The little buds seemed to be growing bigger every second in the hot sunlight.

Not far from where Old T'ung Pao was sitting, a gray two-storey building crouched beside the road. That was the silk filature, where the delicate fibers were removed from the cocoons. Two weeks ago it was occupied by troops; a few short trenches still scarred the fields around it. Everyone had said that the Japanese soldiers were attacking in this direction. The rich people in the market town had all run away. Now the troops were gone, and the silk filature stood empty and locked as before. There would be no noise and excitement in it again until cocoon-selling time.

Old T'ung Pao had heard Young Master Ch'en—son of the Master Ch'en who lived in town—say that Shanghai was seething with unrest, that all the silk weaving factories had closed their doors, that the silk filatures here probably wouldn't open either. But he couldn't believe it. He had been through many periods of turmoil and strife in his sixty years, yet he had never seen a time when the shiny green mulberry leaves had been allowed to wither on the branches and become fodder for sheep. Of course, if the silkworm

[1] See the note to "Medicine," p. 9.

eggs shouldn't ripen, that would be different. Such matters were all in the hands of the Old Lord of the Sky. Who could foretell His will?

"Only just after Ch'ing-ming and so hot already!" marveled Old T'ung Pao, gazing at the small green mulberry leaves. He was happy as well as surprised. He could remember only one year when it was too hot for padded clothes at Ch'ing-ming. He was in his twenties then, and the silkworm eggs had hatched "200 percent"! That was the year he got married. His family was flourishing in those days. His father was like an experienced plow ox—there was nothing he didn't understand, nothing he wasn't willing to try. Even his old grandfather—the one who had started the family on the road to prosperity—seemed to be growing more hearty with age, in spite of the hard time he was said to have had during the years he was a prisoner of the Long Hairs.[2]

Old Master Ch'en was still alive then. His son, the present Master Ch'en, hadn't begun smoking opium yet, and the House of Ch'en hadn't become the bad lot it was today. Moreover, even though the House of Ch'en was the rich gentry and his own family only ordinary tillers of the land, Old T'ung Pao had felt that the destinies of the two families were linked together. Years ago, Long Hairs campaigning through the countryside had captured T'ung Pao's grandfather and Old Master Ch'en and kept them working as prisoners for nearly seven years in the same camp. They had escaped together, taking a lot of the Long Hairs' gold with them—people still talk about it to this day. What's more, at the same time Old Master Ch'en's silk trade began to prosper, the cocoon raising of T'ung Pao's family grew successful too. Within ten years grandfather had earned enough to buy three acres of rice paddy and two acres of mulberry grove, and build a modest house. T'ung Pao's family was the envy of the people of East

Village, just as the House of Ch'en ranked among the first families in the market town.

But afterwards both families had declined. Today, Old T'ung Pao had no land of his own; in fact he was over three hundred silver dollars in debt. The House of Ch'en was finished too. People said the spirit of the dead Long Hairs had sued the Ch'ens in the underworld, and because the King of Hell had decreed that the Ch'ens repay the fortune they had amassed on the stolen gold, the family had gone down financially very quickly. Old T'ung Pao was rather inclined to believe this. If it hadn't been for the influence of devils, why would a decent fellow like Master Ch'en have taken to smoking opium?

What Old T'ung Pao could never understand was why the fall of the House of Ch'en should affect his own family. They certainly hadn't kept any of the Long Hairs' gold. True, his father had related that when Grandfather was escaping from the Long Hairs' camp he had run into a young Long Hair on patrol and had to kill him. What else could he have done? It was fate! Still from T'ung Pao's earliest recollections, his family had prayed and offered sacrifices to appease the soul of the departed young Long Hair time and time again. That little wronged spirit should have left the nether world and been reborn long ago by now! Although Old T'ung Pao couldn't recall what sort of man his grandfather was, he knew his father had been hard-working and honest—he had seen that with his own eyes. Old T'ung Pao himself was a respectable person; both Ah Szu, his elder son, and his daughter-in-law were industrious and frugal. Only his younger son, Ah To, was inclined to be a little flighty. But youngsters were all like that. There was nothing really bad about the boy.

Old T'ung Pao raised his wrinkled face, scorched by years of hot sun to the color of dark

[2] In the mid-nineteenth century, China's oppressed peasants rose against their feudal Manchu rulers in one of the longest (1851–1864) and most bitter revolutions in history. Known as the Taiping Revolution, it was defeated only with the assistance of the interventionist forces of England, France, and the United States of America. The Manchus hated and feared the "Long Hairs," as they slanderously called the Taiping Army men, and fabricated all sorts of lies about them in a vain attempt to discredit them with the people.

Old T'ung Pao, although steadily deteriorating economically, is typical of the rich peasants. Like others of his class, he felt and thought the same as the feudal landlord rulers.

parchment. He gazed bitterly at the canal before him, at the boats on its waters, at the mulberry trees along its banks. All were approximately the same as they had been when he was twenty. But the world had changed. His family now often had to make their meals of pumpkin instead of rice. He was over three hundred silver dollars in debt.

Toot! Toot-toot-toot . . .

Far up the bend in the canal a boat whistle broke the silence. There was a silk filature over there too. He could see vaguely the neat lines of stones embedded as a reinforcement in the canal bank. A small oil-burning river boat came puffing up pompously from beyond the silk filature, tugging three larger craft in its wake. Immediately the peaceful water was agitated with waves rolling toward the banks on both sides of the canal. A peasant, poling a tiny boat, hastened to shore and clutched a clump of reeds growing in the shallows. The waves tossed him and his little craft up and down like a seesaw. The peaceful green countryside was filled with the chugging of the boat engine and the stink of its exhaust.

Hatred burned in Old T'ung Pao's eyes. He watched the riverboat approach, he watched it sail past, and glared after it until it went tooting around another bend and disappeared from sight. He had always abominated the foreign devils' contraptions. He himself had never met a foreign devil, but his father had given him a description of one Old Master Ch'en had seen—red eyebrows, green eyes, and a stiff-legged walk! Old Master Ch'en had hated the foreign devils too. "The foreign devils have swindled our money away," he used to say. Old T'ung Pao was only eight or nine the last time he saw Old Master Ch'en. All he remembered about him now were things he had heard from others. But whenever Old T'ung Pao thought of that remark—"The foreign devils have swindled our money away"— he could almost picture Old Master Ch'en, stroking his beard and wagging his head.

How the foreign devils had accomplished this, Old T'ung Pao wasn't too clear. He was sure, however, that Old Master Ch'en was right. Some things he himself had seen quite plainly. From the time foreign goods—cambric, cloth, oil—appeared in the market town, from the time foreign riverboats increased on the canal, what he produced brought a lower price on the market every day, while what he had to buy became more and more expensive. That was why the property his father left him had shrunk until it finally vanished completely; and now he was in debt. It was not without reason that Old T'ung Pao hated the foreign devils!

In the village, his attitude toward foreigners was well known. Five years before, in 1927, someone had told him: "The new Kuomintang government says it wants to throw out the foreign devils." Old T'ung Pao didn't believe it. He had heard those young propaganda speechmakers the Kuomintang sent when he went into the market town. Though they cried "Throw out the foreign devils," they were dressed in Western-style clothing. His guess was that they were secretly in league with the foreign devils, that they had been purposely sent to delude the countryfolk! Sure enough, the Kuomintang dropped the slogan not long after, and prices and taxes rose steadily. Old T'ung Pao was firmly convinced that all this had occurred as part of a government conspiracy with the foreign devils.

Last year something had happened that made him almost sick with fury: only the cocoons spun by the foreign-strain silkworms could be sold at a decent price. Buyers paid ten dollars more per load for them than they did for the local variety. Usually on good terms with his daughter-in-law, Old T'ung Pao had quarreled with her because of this. She had wanted to raise only foreign silkworms, and Old T'ung Pao's younger son Ah To had agreed with her. Though the boy didn't say much, in his heart he certainly had also favored this course. Events had proved they were right, and they wouldn't let Old T'ung Pao forget it. This year, he had to compromise. Of the five trays they would raise, only four would be silkworms of the local variety; one tray would contain foreign silkworms.

"The world's going from bad to worse! In another couple of years they'll even be wanting foreign mulberry trees! It's enough to take all the joy out of life!"

Old T'ung Pao picked up his long pipe and rapped it angrily against a clod of dry earth. The sun was directly overhead now, foreshortening his shadow until it looked like a piece of charcoal. Still in his padded jacket, he was bathed in heat. He unfastened the jacket and swung its opened edges back and forth a few times to fan himself. Then he stood up and started for home.

Behind the row of mulberry trees were paddy fields. Most of them were as yet only neatly ploughed furrows of upturned earth clods, dried and cracked by the hot sun. Here and there, the early crops were coming up. In one field, the golden blossoms of rapeseed plants emitted a heady fragrance. And that group of houses way over there, that was the village where three generations of Old T'ung Pao's family were living. Above the houses, white smoke from many kitchen stoves was curling lazily upwards into the sky.

After crossing through the mulberry grove, Old T'ung Pao walked along the raised path between the paddy fields, then turned and looked again at that row of trees bursting with tender green buds. A twelve-year-old boy came bounding along from the other end of the fields, calling as he ran:

"Grandpa! Ma's waiting for you to come home and eat!"

It was Little Pao, Old T'ung Pao's grandson.

"Coming!" the old man responded, still gazing at the mulberries. Only twice in his life had he seen these finger-like buds appear on the branches so soon after Ch'ing-ming. His family would probably have a fine crop of silkworms this year. Five trays of eggs would hatch out a huge number of silkworms. If only they didn't have another bad market like last year, perhaps they could pay off part of their debt.

Little Pao stood beside his grandfather. The child too looked at the soft green on the gnarled fist branches. Jumping happily, he clapped his hands and chanted:

Green, tender leaves at Ch'ing-ming;
the girls who tend silkworms
clap hands at the sight!

The old man's wrinkled face broke into a smile. He thought it was a good omen for the little boy to respond like this on seeing the first buds of the year. He rubbed his hand affectionately over the child's shaven pate. In Old T'ung Pao's heart, numbed wooden by a lifetime of poverty and hardship, suddenly hope began to stir again.

II

The weather remained warm. The rays of the sun forced open the tender, finger-like little buds. They had already grown to the size of a small hand. Around Old T'ung Pao's village, the mulberry trees seemed to respond especially well. From a distance they gave the appearance of a low gray picket fence on top of which a long swath of brocade had been spread. Bit by bit, day by day, hope grew in the hearts of the villagers. The unspoken mobilization order for the silkworm campaign reached everywhere and everyone. Silkworm rearing equipment that had been laid away for a year was again brought out to be scrubbed and mended. Beside the little stream which ran through the village, women and children, with much laughter and calling back and forth, washed the implements.

None of these women or children looked really healthy. Since the coming of spring, they had been eating only half their fill; their clothes were old and worn. As a matter of fact, they weren't much better off than beggars. Yet all were in quite good spirits, sustained by enormous patience and grand illusions. Burdened though they were by daily mounting debts, they had only one thought in their heads—if we get a good crop of silkworms everything will be all right! . . . They could already visualize how, in a month, the shiny green leaves would be converted into snow-white cocoons, the cocoons exchanged for clinking silver dollars. Although their stomachs were growling with hunger, they couldn't refrain from smiling at this happy prospect.

Old T'ung Pao's daughter-in-law was among the women by the stream. With the help of her twelve-year-old son, Little Pao, she had already finished washing the family's large trays of woven bamboo strips. Seated on a stone beside the stream, she wiped her perspiring face with the edge of her tunic. A twenty-year-old girl, working with other women on the opposite side of the stream, hailed her.

"Are you raising foreign silkworms this year too?"

It was Sixth Treasure, sister of young Fu-ch'ing, the neighbor who lived across the stream.

The thick eyebrows of Old T'ung Pao's daughter-in-law at once contracted. Her voice sounded as if she had just been waiting for a chance to let off steam.

"Don't ask me; what the old man says, goes!" she shouted. "He's dead set against it, won't let us raise more than one batch of foreign breed! The old fool only has to hear the word 'foreign' to send him up in the air! He'll take dollars made of foreign silver, though; those are the only 'foreign' things he likes!"

The women on the other side of the stream laughed. From the threshing ground behind them a strapping young man approached. He reached the stream and crossed over on the four logs that served as a bridge. Seeing him, his sister-in-law dropped her tirade and called in a high voice:

"Ah To, will you help me carry these trays? They're as heavy as dead dogs when they're wet!"

Without a word, Ah To lifted the six big trays and set them, dripping, on his head. Balancing them in place, he walked off, swinging his hands in a swimming motion. When in a good mood, Ah To refused nobody. If any of the village women asked him to carry something heavy or fish something out of the stream, he was usually quite willing. But today he probably was a little grumpy, and so he walked empty-handed with only six trays on his head. The sight of him, looking as if he were wearing six layers of wide straw hats, his waist twisting at each step in imitation of the ladies of the town, sent the women into petals of laughter. Lotus, wife of Old T'ung Pao's nearest neighbor, called with a giggle:

"Hey, Ah To, come back here. Carry a few trays for me too!"

Ah To grinned. "Not unless you call me a sweet name!" He continued walking. An instant later he had reached the porch of his house and set down the trays out of the sun.

"Will 'kid brother' do?" demanded Lotus, laughing boisterously. She had a remarkably clean white complexion, but her face was very flat.

When she laughed, all that could be seen was a big open mouth and two tiny slits of eyes. Originally a maid in a house in town, she had been married off to Old T'ung Pao's neighbor—a prematurely aged man who walked around with a sour expression and never said a word all day. That was less than six months ago, but her love affairs and escapades already were the talk of the village.

"Shameless hussy!" came a contemptuous female voice from across the stream.

Lotus's piggy eyes immediately widened. "Who said that?" she demanded angrily. "If you've got the brass to call me names, let's see you try it to my face! Come out into the open!"

"Think you can handle me? I'm talking about a shameless, man-crazy baggage! If the shoe fits, wear it!" retorted Sixth Treasure, for it was she who had spoken. She too was famous in the village, but as a mischievous, lively young woman.

The two began splashing water at each other from opposite banks of the stream. Girls who enjoyed a row took sides and joined the battle, while the children whooped with laughter. Old T'ung Pao's daughter-in-law was more decorous. She picked up her remaining trays, called to Little Pao, and returned home. Ah To watched from the porch, grinning. He knew why Sixth Treasure and Lotus were quarreling. It did his heart good to hear that sharp-tongued Sixth Treasure get told off in public.

Old T'ung Pao came out of the house with a wooden tray-stand on his shoulder. Some of the legs of the uprights had been eaten by termites, and he wanted to repair them. At the sight of Ah To standing there laughing at the women, Old T'ung Pao's face lengthened. The boy hadn't much sense of propriety, he well knew. What disturbed him particularly was the way Ah To and Lotus were always talking and laughing together. "That bitch is an evil spirit. Fooling with her will bring ruin on our house," he had often warned his younger son.

"Ah To!" he now barked angrily. "Enjoying the scenery? Your brother's in back mending equipment. Go and give him a hand!" His inflamed eyes bored into Ah To, never leaving the boy until he disappeared into the house.

Only then did Old T'ung Pao start work on the tray-stand. After examining it carefully, he slowly began his repairs. Years ago, Old T'ung Pao had worked for a time as a carpenter. But he was old now; his fingers had lost their strength. A few minutes' work and he was breathing hard. He raised his head and looked into the house. Five squares of cloth to which sticky silkworm eggs adhered hung from a horizontal bamboo pole.

His daughter-in-law, Ah Szu's wife, was at the other end of the porch, pasting paper on big trays of woven bamboo strips. Last year, to economize a bit, they had bought and used old newspaper. Old T'ung Pao still maintained that was why the eggs had hatched poorly—it was unlucky to use paper with writing on it for such a prosaic purpose. Writing meant scholarship, and scholarship had to be respected. This year the whole family had skipped a meal and, with the money saved, purchased special "tray pasting paper." Ah Szu's wife pasted the tough, gosling-yellow sheets smooth and flat; on every tray she also affixed three little colored paper pictures bought at the same time. One was the "Platter of Plenty"; the other two showed a militant figure on horseback, pennant in hand. He, according to local belief, was the "Guardian of Silkworm Hatching."

"I was only able to buy twenty loads of mulberry leaves with that thirty silver dollars I borrowed on your father's guarantee," Old T'ung Pao said to his daughter-in-law. He was still panting from his exertions with the tray-stand. "Our rice will be finished by the day after tomorrow. What are we going to do?"

Thanks to her father's influence with his boss and his willingness to guarantee repayment of the loan, Old T'ung Pao was able to borrow money at a low rate of interest—only 25 percent a month! Both the principal and interest had to be repaid by the end of the silkworm season.

Ah Szu's wife finished pasting a tray and placed it in the sun. "You've spent it all on leaves," she said angrily. "We'll have a lot of leaves left over, just like last year!"

"Full of lucky words, aren't you?" demanded the old man sarcastically. "I suppose every year'll

be like last year? We can't get more than a dozen or so loads of leaves from our own trees. With five sets of grubs to feed, that won't be nearly enough."

"Oh, of course, you're never wrong!" she replied hotly. "All I know is with rice we can eat, without it we'll go hungry!" His stubborn refusal to raise any foreign silkworms last year had left them with only the unsalable local breed. As a result, she was often contrary with him.

The old man's face turned purple with rage. After this, neither would speak to the other.

But hatching time was drawing closer every day. The little village's two dozen families were thrown into a state of great tension, great determination, great struggle. With it all, they were possessed of a great hope, a hope that could almost make them forget their hungry bellies.

Old T'ung Pao's family, borrowing a little here, getting a little credit there, somehow managed to get by. Nor did the other families eat any better: there wasn't one with a spare bag of rice. Although they had harvested a good crop the previous year, landlords, creditors, taxes, levies, one after another, had cleaned the peasants out long ago. Now all their hopes were pinned on the spring silkworms. The repayment date of every loan they made was set up for the "end of the silkworm season."

With high hopes and considerable fear, like soldiers going into hand-to-hand combat, they prepared for the silkworm campaign!

"Grain Rain"[3] day—bringing gentle drizzles—was not far off. Almost imperceptibly, the silkworm eggs of the two dozen village families began to show faint tinges of green. Women, when they met on the public threshing ground, would speak to one another agitatedly in tones that were anxious yet joyful.

"Over at Sixth Treasure's place, they're almost ready to incubate their eggs!"

"Lotus says her family is going to start incubating tomorrow. So soon!"

"Huang 'the Priest' has made a divination. He predicts that this spring mulberry leaves will go to four dollars a load!"

[3] Falls on April 20 or 21.

Old T'ung Pao's daughter-in-law examined their five sets of eggs. They looked bad. The tiny seed-like eggs were still pitch black, without even a hint of green. Her husband, Ah Szu, took them into the light to peer at them carefully. Even so, he could find hardly any ripening eggs. She was very worried.

"You incubate them anyhow. Maybe this variety is a little slow," her husband forced himself to say consolingly.

Her lips pressed tight, she made no reply.

Old T'ung Pao's wrinkled faced sagged with dejection. Though he said nothing, he thought their prospects were dim.

The next day, Ah Szu's wife again examined the eggs. Ha! Quite a few were turning green, and a very shiny green at that! Immediately, she told her husband, told Old T'ung Pao, Ah To . . . she even told her son Little Pao. Now the incubating process could begin! She held the five pieces of cloth to which the eggs adhered against her bare bosom. As if cuddling a nursing infant, she sat absolutely quiet, not daring to stir. At night, she took the five sets to bed with her. Her husband was routed out, and had to share Ah To's bed. The tiny silkworm eggs were very scratchy against her flesh. She felt happy and a little frightened, like the first time she was pregnant and the baby moved inside her. Exactly the same sensation!

Uneasy but eager, the whole family waited for the eggs to hatch. Ah To was the only exception. "We're sure going to hatch a good crop," he said, "but anyone who thinks we're going to get rich in this life is out of his head." Though the old man swore Ah To's big mouth would ruin their luck, the boy stuck to his guns.

A clean, dry shed for the growing grubs was all prepared. The second day of incubation, Old T'ung Pao smeared a garlic with earth and placed it at the foot of the wall inside the shed. If, in a few days, the garlic put out many sprouts, it meant the eggs would hatch well. He did this every year, but this year he was more reverential than usual, and his hands trembled. Last year's divination had proved all too accurate. He didn't dare to think about that now.

Every family in the village was busy incubating. For the time being there were few women's footprints on the threshing ground or the banks of the little stream. An unofficial "martial law" had been imposed. Even peasants normally on very good terms stopped visiting one another. For a guest to come and frighten away the spirits of the ripening eggs—that would be no laughing matter! At most, people exchanged a few words in low tones when they met, then quickly separated. This was the "sacred" season!

Old T'ung Pao's family was on pins and needles. In the five sets of eggs a few grubs had begun wriggling. It was exactly one day before Grain Rain. Ah Szu's wife had calculated that most of the eggs wouldn't hatch until after that day. Before or after Grain Rain was all right, but for eggs to hatch on the day itself was considered highly unlucky. Incubation was no longer necessary, and the eggs were carefully placed in the special shed. Old T'ung Pao stole a glance at his garlic at the foot of the wall. His heart dropped. There were still only the same two small green shoots the garlic had originally! He didn't dare to look any closer. He prayed silently that by noon the day after tomorrow the garlic would have many, many more shoots.

At last hatching day arrived. Ah Szu's wife set a pot of rice on to boil and nervously watched for the time when the steam from it would rise straight up. Old T'ung Pao lit the incense and candles he had bought in anticipation of this event. Devoutly, he placed them before the idol of the Kitchen God. His two sons went into the fields to pick wildflowers. Little Pao chopped a lamp wick into fine pieces and crushed the wildflowers the men brought back. Everything was ready. The sun was entering its zenith; steam from the rice pot puffed straight upward. Ah Szu's wife immediately leaped to her feet, stuck a "sacred" paper flower and a pair of goose feathers into the knot of hair at the back of her head, and went to the shed. Old T'ung Pao carried a wooden scale-pole; Ah Szu followed with the chopped lamp wick and the crushed wildflowers. Daughter-in-law uncovered the cloth pieces to which the grubs adhered, and sprinkled them with the bits of wick and flowers Ah Szu was holding. Then she took the wooden scale-pole from Old T'ung Pao and hung the cloth pieces over it. She next removed the pair of goose feathers from her hair. Moving them lightly across the cloth, she brushed the grubs, together with the crushed lamp-wick and wildflowers, onto a large tray. One set, two sets . . . the last set contained the foreign breed. The grubs from this cloth were brushed onto a separate tray. Finally, she removed the "sacred" paper flower from her hair and pinned it, with the goose feathers, against the side of the tray.

A solemn ceremony! One that had been handed down through the ages! Like warriors taking an oath before going into battle! Old T'ung Pao and family now had ahead of them a month of fierce combat, with no rest day or night, against bad weather, bad luck, and anything else that might come along!

The grubs, wriggling in the trays, looked very healthy. They were all the proper black color. Old T'ung Pao and his daughter-in-law were able to relax a little. But when the old man secretly took another look at his garlic, he turned pale! It had grown only four measly shoots. Ah! Would this year be like last year all over again?

III

The fateful garlic proved to be not so psychic after all. The silkworms of Old T'ung Pao's family grew and thrived! Though it rained continuously during the grubs' first and second moulting, and the weather was a bit colder than at Ch'ing-ming, the "little darlings" were extremely robust.

The silkworms of the other families in the village were not doing so badly either. A tense kind of joy pervaded the countryside. Even the small stream seemed to be gurgling with bright laughter. Lotus's family was the sole exception. They were only raising one set of grubs, but by the third moulting their silkworms weighed less than twenty catties. Just before the fourth, people saw Lotus's husband walk to the stream and dump out his trays. That dour, old-looking man had bad luck written all over him.

Because of this dreadful event, the village women put Lotus's family strictly off limits. They made wide detours so as not to pass her door. If they saw her or her taciturn husband, no matter how far away, they made haste to go in the opposite direction. They feared that even one look at Lotus or her spouse, the briefest conversation, would contaminate them with the unfortunate couple's bad luck!

Old T'ung Pao strictly forbade Ah To to talk to Lotus. "If I catch you gabbing with that baggage again, I'll disown you!" he threatened in a loud, angry voice, standing outside on the porch to make sure Lotus could hear him.

Little Pao was also warned not to play in front of Lotus's door, and not to speak to anyone in her family.

The old man harped at Ah To morning, noon, and night, but the boy turned a deaf ear to his father's grumbling. In his heart, he laughed at it. Of the whole family, Ah To alone didn't place much stock in taboos and superstitions. He didn't talk with Lotus, however. He was much too busy for that.

By the fourth moulting, their silkworms weighed three hundred catties. Every member of Old T'ung Pao's family, including twelve-year-old Little Pao, worked for two days and two nights without sleeping a wink. The silkworms were unusually sturdy. Only twice in his sixty years had Old T'ung Pao ever seen the like. Once was the year he married; once when his first son was born.

The first day after the fourth moulting, the "little darlings" ate seven loads of leaves. They were now a bright green, thick and healthy. Old T'ung Pao and his family, on the contrary, were much thinner, their eyes bloodshot from lack of sleep.

No one could guess how much the "little darlings" would eat before they spun their cocoons. Old T'ung Pao discussed the question of buying more leaves with Ah Szu.

"Master Ch'en won't lend us any more. Shall we try your father-in-law's boss again?"

"We've still got ten loads coming. That's enough for one more day," replied Ah Szu. He could barely hold himself erect. His eyelids weighed a thousand catties. They kept wanting to close.

"One more day? You're dreaming!" snapped the old man impatiently. "Not counting tomorrow, they still have to eat three more days. We'll need another thirty loads! Thirty loads, I say!"

Loud voices were heard outside on the threshing ground. Ah To had arrived with men delivering five loads of mulberry branches. Everyone went out to strip the leaves. Ah Szu's wife hurried from the shed. Across the stream, Sixth Treasure and her family were raising only a small crop of silkworms; having spare time, she came over to help. Bright stars filled the sky. There was a slight wind. All up and down the village, gay shouts and laughter rang in the night.

"The price of leaves is rising fast!" a coarse voice cried. "This afternoon, they were getting four dollars a load in the market town!"

Old T'ung Pao was very upset. At four dollars a load, thirty loads would come to a hundred and twenty dollars. Where could he raise so much money?! But then he figured—he was sure to gather over five hundred catties of cocoons. Even at fifty dollars a hundred, they'd sell for two hundred and fifty dollars. Feeling a bit consoled, he heard a small voice from among the leaf-strippers.

"They say the folks east of here aren't doing so well with their silkworms. There won't be any reason for the price of leaves to go much higher."

Old T'ung Pao recognized the speaker as Sixth Treasure, and he relaxed still further.

The girl and Ah To were standing beside a large basket, stripping leaves. In the dim starlight, they worked quite close to each other, partly hidden by the pile of mulberry branches before them. Suddenly Sixth Treasure felt someone pinch her thigh. She knew well enough who it was, and she suppressed a giggle. But when, a moment later, a hand brushed against her breasts, she jumped; a little shriek escaped her.

"*Ai-ya!*"

"What's wrong?" demanded Ah Szu's wife, working on the other side of the basket.

Sixth Treasure's face flamed scarlet. She shot a glance at Ah To, then quickly lowered her head and resumed stripping leaves. "Nothing," she replied. "I think a caterpillar bit me!"

Ah To bit his lips to keep from laughing aloud. He had been half starved the past two weeks and had slept little. But in spite of having lost a lot of weight, he was in high spirits. While he never suffered from any of Old T'ung Pao's gloom, neither did he believe that one good crop, whether of silkworms or of rice, would enable them to wipe out their debt and own their own land again. He knew that they would never get out from under merely by relying on hard work, even if they broke their backs trying. Nevertheless, he worked with a will. He enjoyed work, just as he enjoyed fooling around with Sixth Treasure.

The next morning, Old T'ung Pao went into town to borrow money for more leaves. Before leaving home, he had talked the matter over with daughter-in-law. They had decided to mortgage their grove of mulberries that produced fifteen loads of leaves a year as security for the loan. The grove was the last piece of property the family owned.

By the time the old man ordered another thirty loads and the first ten were delivered, the sturdy "little darlings" had gone hungry for half an hour. Putting forth their pointed little mouths, they swayed from side to side, searching for food. Daughter-in-law's heart had ached to see them. When the leaves were finally spread on the trays, the silkworm shed at once resounded with a sibilant crunching, so noisy it drowned out conversation. In a very short while, the trays were again empty of leaves. Another thick layer was piled on. Just keeping the silkworms supplied with leaves, Old T'ung Pao and his family were so busy they could barely catch their breath. But this was the final crisis. In two more days the "little darlings" would spin their cocoons. People were putting every bit of their remaining strength into this last desperate struggle.

Though he had gone without sleep for three whole days, Ah To didn't appear particularly tired. He agreed to watch the shed alone that night until dawn to permit the others to get some rest. There was a bright moon, and the weather was a trifle cold. Ah To crouched beside a small fire he had built in the shed. At about eleven, he gave the silkworms their second feeding, then returned to squat by the fire. He could hear the loud rustle of the "little darlings" crunching through the leaves. His eyes closed. Suddenly he heard the door squeak, and his eyelids flew open. He peered into the darkness for a moment, then shut his eyes again. His ears were still hissing with the rustle of the leaves. The next thing he knew, his head had struck against his knees. Waking with a start, he heard the door screen bang and thought he saw a moving shadow. Ah To leaped up and rushed outside. In the moonlight, he saw someone crossing the threshing ground toward the stream. He caught up in a flash, seized and flung the intruder to the ground. Ah To was sure he had nabbed a thief.

"Ah To, kill me if you want to, but don't give me away!"

The voice made Ah To's hair stand on end. He could see in the moonlight that queer, flat, white face and those round little piggy eyes fixed upon him. But of menace, the piggy eyes had none. Ah To snorted.

"What were you after?"

"A few of your family's 'little darlings'!"

"What did you do with them?"

"Threw them in the stream!"

Ah To's face darkened. He knew that in this way she was trying to put a curse on the lot. "You're pure poison! We never did anything to hurt you."

"Never did anything? Oh, yes you did! Yes, you did! Our silkworm eggs didn't hatch well, but we didn't harm anybody. You were all so smart! You shunned me like a leper. No matter how far away I was, if you saw me you turned your heads. You acted as if I wasn't even human!"

She got to her feet, the agonized expression on her face terrible to see. Ah To stared at her. "I'm not going to beat you," he said finally. "Go on your way!"

Without giving her another glance, he trotted back to the shed. He was wide awake now. Lotus had only taken a handful, and the remaining "little darlings" were all in good condition. It didn't occur to him to either hate or pity Lotus, but the last thing she had said remained in his mind. It seemed to him there was something eternally

wrong in the scheme of human relations; but he couldn't put his finger on what it was exactly, nor did he know why it should be. In a little while, he forgot about this too. The lusty silkworms were eating and eating, yet, as if by some magic, never full!

Nothing more happened that night. Just before the sky began to brighten in the east, Old T'ung Pao and his daughter-in-law came to relieve Ah To. They took the trays of "little darlings" and looked at them in the light. The silkworms were turning a whiter color, their bodies gradually becoming shorter and thicker. They were delighted with the excellent way the silkworms were developing.

But when, at sunrise, Ah Szu's wife went to draw water at the stream, she met Sixth Treasure. The girl's expression was serious.

"I saw that slut leaving your place shortly before midnight," she whispered. "Ah To was right behind her. They stood here and talked for a long time! Your family ought to look after things better than that!"

The color drained from the face of Ah Szu's wife. Without a word, she carried her water bucket back to the house. First she told her husband about it, then she told Old T'ung Pao. It was a fine state of affairs when a baggage like that could sneak into people's silkworm sheds! Old T'ung Pao stamped with rage. He immediately summoned Ah To. But the boy denied the whole story; he said Sixth Treasure was dreaming. The old man then went to question Sixth Treasure. She insisted she had seen everything with her own eyes. The old man didn't know what to believe. He returned home and looked at the "little darlings." They were as sturdy as ever, not a sickly one in the lot.

But the joy that Old T'ung Pao and his family had been feeling was dampened. They knew Sixth Treasure's words couldn't be entirely without foundation. Their only hope was that Ah To and that hussy had played their little games on the porch rather than in the shed!

Old T'ung Pao recalled gloomily that the garlic had only put forth three or four shoots. He thought the future looked dark.

Hadn't there been times before when the silk-worms ate great quantities of leaves and seemed to be growing well, yet dried up and died just when they were ready to spin their cocoons? Yes, often! But Old T'ung Pao didn't dare let himself think of such a possibility. To entertain a thought like that, even in the most secret recesses of the mind, would only be inviting bad luck!

IV

The "little darlings" began spinning their co-coons, but Old T'ung Pao's family was still in a sweat. Both their money and their energy were completely spent. They still had nothing to show for it; there was no guarantee of their earning any return. Nevertheless, they continued working at top speed. Beneath the racks on which the co-coons were being spun, fires had to be kept going to supply warmth. Old T'ung Pao and Ah Szu, his elder son, their backs bent, slowly squatted first on this side then on that. Hearing the small rustlings of the spinning silkworms, they wanted to smile, and if the sounds stopped for a moment, their hearts stopped too. Yet, worried as they were, they didn't dare disturb the silkworms by looking inside. When the silkworms squirted fluid[4] in their faces as they peered up from beneath the racks, they were quite happy in spite of the mo-mentary discomfort. The bigger the shower, the better they liked it.

Ah To had already peeked several times. Little Pao had caught him at it and demanded to know what was going on. Ah To made an ugly face at the child, but did not reply.

After three days of "spinning," the fires were extinguished. Ah Szu's wife could restrain herself no longer. She stole a look, her heart beating fast. Inside, all was as white as snow. The brush that had been put in for the silkworms to spin on was completely covered over with cocoons. Ah Szu's wife had never seen so successful a "flowering"!

The whole family was wreathed in smiles. They were on solid ground at last! The "little darlings"

had proved they had a conscience; they hadn't consumed those mulberry leaves, at four dollars a load, in vain. The family could reap its reward for a month of hunger and sleepless nights. The Old Lord of the Sky had eyes!

Throughout the village, there were many simi-lar scenes of rejoicing. The Silkworm Goddess had been beneficent to the tiny village this year. Most of the two dozen families garnered good crops of cocoons from their silkworms. The har-vest of Old T'ung Pao's family was well above average.

Again women and children crowded the thresh-ing ground and the banks of the little stream. All were much thinner than the previous month, with eyes sunk in their sockets, throats rasping and hoarse. But everyone was excited, happy. As they chattered about the struggle of the past month, visions of piles of bright silver dollars shimmered before their eyes. Cheerful thoughts filled their minds—they would get their summer clothes out of the pawnshop; at Summer Festival[5] perhaps they could eat a fat, golden fish . . .

They talked too of the farce enacted by Lotus and Ah To a few nights before. Sixth Treasure announced to everyone she met, "That Lotus has no shame at all. She delivered herself right to his door!" Men who heard her laughed coarsely. Women muttered a prayer and called Lotus bad names. They said Old T'ung Pao's family could consider itself lucky that a curse hadn't fallen on them. The gods were merciful!

Family after family was able to report a good harvest of cocoons. People visited one another to view the shining white gossamer. The father of Old T'ung Pao's daughter-in-law came from town with his little son. They brought gifts of sweets and fruits and a salted fish. Little Pao was happy as a puppy frolicking in the snow.

The elderly visitor sat with Old T'ung Pao be-neath a willow beside the stream. He had the rep-utation in town of a "man who knew how to enjoy life." From hours of listening to the professional storytellers in front of the temple, he had learned

[4] The emission of the fluid means the silkworm is about to spin its cocoon.

[5] May fifth in the Western calendar. Here Mao Tun probably meant *tuan-wu chieh* or Dragon Boat Festival, which falls on May fifth of the lunar calendar.

by heart many of the classic tales of ancient times. He was a great one for idle chatter, and often would say anything that came into his head. Old T'ung Pao therefore didn't take him very seriously when he leaned close and queried softly:.

"Are you selling your cocoons, or will you spin the silk yourself at home?"

"Selling them, of course," Old T'ung Pao replied casually.

The elderly visitor slapped his thigh and sighed, then rose abruptly and pointed at the silk filature rearing up behind the row of mulberries, now quite bald of leaves.

"T'ung Pao," he said, "the cocoons are being gathered, but the doors of the silk filatures are shut as tight as ever! They're not buying this year! Ah, all the world is in turmoil! The silk houses are not going to open, I tell you!"

Old T'ung Pao couldn't help smiling. He wouldn't believe it. How could he possibly believe it? There were dozens of silk filatures in this part of the country. Surely they couldn't all shut down? What's more, he had heard that they had made a deal with the Japanese; the Chinese soldiers who had been billeted in the silk houses had long since departed.

Changing the subject, the visitor related the latest town gossip, salting it freely with classical aphorisms and quotations from the ancient stories. Finally he got around to the thirty silver dollars borrowed through him as middleman. He said his boss was anxious to be repaid.

Old T'ung Pao became uneasy after all. When his visitor had departed, he hurried from the village down the highway to look at the two nearest silk filatures. Their doors were indeed shut; not a soul was in sight. Business was in full swing this time last year, with whole rows of dark gleaming scales in operation.

He felt a little panicky as he returned home. But when he saw those snowy cocoons, thick and hard, pleasure made him smile. What beauties! No one wants them? Impossible. He still had to hurry and finish gathering the cocoons; he hadn't thanked the gods properly yet. Gradually, he forgot about the silk houses.

But in the village, the atmosphere was changing day by day. People who had just begun to laugh were now all frowns. News was reaching them from town that none of the neighboring silk filatures was opening its doors. It was the same with the houses along the highway. Last year at this time, buyers of cocoons were streaming in and out of the village. This year there wasn't a sign of even half a one. In their place came dunning creditors and government tax collectors who promptly froze up if you asked them to take cocoons in payment.

Swearing, curses, disappointed sighs! With such a fine crop of cocoons the villagers had never dreamed that their lot would be even worse than usual! It was as if hailstones had dropped out of a clear sky. People like Old T'ung Pao, whose crop was especially good, took it hardest of all.

"What is the world coming to?" He beat his breast and stamped his feet in helpless frustration.

But the villagers had to think of something. The cocoons would spoil if kept too long. They either had to sell them or remove the silk themselves. Several families had already brought out and repaired silk reels they hadn't used for years. They would first remove the silk from the cocoons and then see about the next step. Old T'ung Pao wanted to do the same.

"We won't sell our cocoons; we'll spin the silk ourselves!" said the old man. "Nobody ever heard of selling cocoons until the foreign devils' companies started the thing!"

Ah Szu's wife was the first to object. "We've got over five hundred catties of cocoons here," she retorted. "Where are you going to get enough reels?"

She was right. Five hundred catties was no small amount. They'd never get finished spinning the silk themselves. Hire outside help? That meant spending money. Ah Szu agreed with his wife. Ah To blamed his father for planning incorrectly.

"If you listened to me, we'd have raised only one tray of foreign breed and no locals. Then the fifteen loads of leaves from our own mulberry trees would have been enough, and we wouldn't have had to borrow!"

Old T'ung Pao was so angry he couldn't speak.

At last a ray of hope appeared. Huang the Priest had heard somewhere that a silk house below the city of Wu-hsi was doing business as usual. Actually an ordinary peasant, Huang was nicknamed "The Priest" because of the learned airs he affected and his interest in Taoist "magic." Old T'ung Pao always got along with him fine. After learning the details from him, Old T'ung Pao conferred with his elder son Ah Szu about going to Wu-hsi.

"It's about two hundred and seventy *li* by water, six days for the round trip," ranted the old man. "Son-of-a-bitch! It's a goddamn expedition! But what else can we do? We can't eat the cocoons, and our creditors are pressing hard!"

Ah Szu agreed. They borrowed a small boat and bought a few yards of matting to cover the cargo. It was decided that Ah To should go along. Taking advantage of the good weather, the cocoon selling "expeditionary force" set out.

Five days later, the men returned—but not with an empty hold. They still had one basket of cocoons. The silk filature, which they reached after a journey of two hundred and seventy *li* by water, offered extremely harsh terms—only thirty-five dollars a load for foreign breed, twenty for local; thin cocoons not wanted at any price. Although their cocoons were all first class, the people at the silk filature house picked and chose only enough to fill one basket; the rest were rejected. Old T'ung Pao and his sons received a hundred and ten dollars for the sale, ten of which had to be spent on travel expenses. The hundred dollars remaining was not even enough to pay back what they had borrowed for that last thirty loads of mulberry leaves! On the return trip, Old T'ung Pao became ill with rage. His sons carried him into the house.

Ah Szu's wife had no choice but to take the ninety odd catties they had brought back and reel the silk from the cocoons herself. She borrowed a few reels from Sixth Treasure's family and worked for six days. All their rice was gone now. Ah Szu took the silk into town, but no one would buy it. Even the pawnshop didn't want it. Only after much pleading was he able to persuade the pawnbroker to take it in exchange for a load of rice they had pawned before Ch'ing-ming.

That's the way it happened. Because they raised a crop of spring silkworms, the people in Old T'ung Pao's village got deeper into debt. Old T'ung Pao's family raised five trays and gathered a splendid harvest of cocoons. Yet they ended up owing another thirty silver dollars and losing their mortgaged mulberry trees—to say nothing of suffering a month of hunger and sleepless nights in vain!

LAO SHE
(1899–1966)

Lao She (pen name of Shu Ch'ing-ch'un) was born into a Manchu family which had long resided in Peking. Bereaved of his father when he was a mere infant, he had a hard childhood and had to support his mother upon graduation from a normal school at the age of seventeen. He had served as the principal of a primary school and as a schoolteacher in Tientsin and managed to study for a short period in Yenching University before sailing for England in 1924 to teach Chinese at the University of London's School of Oriental Studies. During his tenure as instructor there, he wrote three novels, *The Philosophy of Lao Chang* (*Lao Chang ti che-hsüeh*), *Chao Tzu-yüeh,* and *The Two Mas* (*Erh Ma*), and had them serialized in *The Short Story* respectively in 1926, 1927, and 1929. They established his reputation as a serious novelist with a gift for comedy and a concern for the present and future of China.

Upon his return to China in 1930 until the outbreak of the War of Resistance in 1937, Lao She taught at various universities and wrote a steady succession of novels which consolidated his reputation as one of the two major novelists (the other being Mao Tun) of that period. Four of these are available in English translation: *The City of Cats* (*Mao-ch'eng chi,* 1933; *Cat Country,* tr. William Lyell), *Divorce* (*Li-hun,* 1933; tr. Evan King), *The Biography of Niu T'ien-tz'u* (*Niu T'ien-tz'u chuan,* 1936; *Heavensent*), *Camel Hsiang-tzu* (*Lo-t'o Hsiang-tzu,* 1938; *Rickshaw,* tr. Jean M. James, 1979). Of these four, *Camel Hsiang-tzu* won instant acclaim as a modern classic for its memorable portrayal of a proletarian hero doomed to failure despite his heroic efforts toward financial betterment, while *The City of Cats* has won belated recognition abroad as "the most savage indictment of China ever penned by a Chinese" (Hsia, *History,* p. 546).

Soon after the outbreak of the war, Lao She became the chief administrator of the Chinese Writers' Anti-Aggression Association and turned to various kinds of patriotic writing to rouse the nation. Years of propaganda work impaired his creative integrity, however, so that his postwar trilogy, *Four Generations under One Roof* (*Ssu-shih t'ung-t'ang,* 1946–51), despite its immense size, fell short of expectations. After 1949, Lao She wrote a total of twenty-three plays all designed to celebrate the achievements of the Chinese people under Communism. Of these, *The Teahouse* (*Ch'a-kuan,* 1957) has proven to be the most successful as theater and shown the author's undiminished command of dialogue in the Peking vernacular. Though a zealous eulogist of the Communist goverment, Lao She was not spared persecution at the onset of the Cultural Revolution. He died a victim of the Red Guards on August 24, 1966.

Though best known today as a novelist and playwright, Lao She also won much praise for his short and long stories written during the thirties. "An Old Tragedy in a New Age" (*Hsin shih-tai ti chiu pei-chü*), the novella chosen for our volume, was deservedly one of the author's favorites among his shorter fiction. It shares with the best of his early novels a deft portrayal of certain types of character, a remarkable handling of comic satire, and an able probing into generational conflict, but it also shows his characteristic weakness for melodrama, and unrealized melodrama at that. The novella would have been better without the subplot involving Ch'en Lien-po and the Chief of Police, but since the melodramatic subplot is there, the phrase "an old tragedy" may have been intended to cover the perennial tragedy of Priam even if Lien-po is hardly to be compared to Hector. That both his sons should turn out to be disappointing to Old Mr. Ch'en points to the principal meaning of the title. Had he not been the father he was, forever reminding them of their duty to be filial and to restore family glory, one would not have turned corrupt and the other would not have rebelled.

C. T. H.

An Old Tragedy in a New Age

by Lao She

Translated by Michael S. Duke

I

"Venerable Master!" Ch'en Lien-po said in a slightly tremulous voice as he knelt on a brocade cushion. He wanted to raise his head and look at his father, but he could not. He lowered his head, rested his hands on the cushion, half closed his eyes, and continued, "Your son respectfully presents you with a bit of business property!" Having said that he calmed down a little, but he could not think of another word to say. Rather like hearing the far-off sound of the wind on an autumn night, he felt an uneasy calmness fusing his elation, tranquillity, melancholy, and emotional excitement into one uncontrollable feeling. He didn't know what to do, but his arms were beginning to go numb, and he couldn't just kneel there foolishly. Might as well kowtow. After kowtowing three or maybe four times, he felt much more comfortable, as if he had once more regained his full strength. Then he dared to raise his head and look at his father.

In his eyes his father was a "holy one," a "holy one" who was directly related to him. When he worshipped the Sage Confucius, the Master of War Kuan Yü, and the other gods and saints, he felt a kind of solemnity and respectful fear, or even an attitude of insincere play-acting. But when he kowtowed to his father his awe and his emotional warmth were completely blended, with absolutely no trace of play-acting. It was as if he could feel his father's blood flowing in his body, making him pure as a newborn baby. At the same time he felt that his own abilities could repay his father's benevolence, could make the flesh and blood that his father passed on to him even more bright and glorious, and open up a fresh, bright, sweet-scented way for the Ch'en family. He was the inheritor of the past and the creator of the future. He lived up to the ancestors' expectations, and would certainly win the admiration of later generations!

As he looked at his father his heart felt somewhat fuller, he raised his right hand easily, and his whole body seemed to increase in strength. Old Mr. Ch'en—Ch'en Hung-tao—continued to sit up straight in his redwood chair, smiled slightly while glancing at his son, and said nothing. Father's and son's eyes meeting in one place had already poured out everything that was in their hearts, and there was no need to say anything further. Old Mr. Ch'en continued to sit quite straight there to savor his son's filial piety and to await the others who would come in to congratulate him. Whenever Lien-po respectfully presented him with a house, a parcel of land, or as now, a business property, first Lien-po would kowtow to his father in the sitting room and then the whole family would come in, in order by ages, to offer congratulations.

Old Mr. Ch'en had a red and open face; his long eyebrows and moustache were still black, but

Since Old Mr. Ch'en (Ch'en Hung-tao) is an old-style Confucian gentleman habitually quoting poetry or the classics to impress others, no attempt has been made to identify all his quotations. His learning is quite shallow and his memory none too good, as seen in his inability to cite the second line of Meng Hao-jan's famous poem (see footnote 2). Eds.

his hair was partly white. Because he was of a certain age his large eyes had fleshy semicircular pockets under them, and these pockets had grayish-red lines on them, giving him a rather awesome aspect. His nose was not high but broad, and the nostrils flared out. His body was tall, and his hands and feet were large. Sitting upright with his hands on his knees and his back quite straight, he looked like a small mountain—majestic, vigorous, and overbearing.

Lien-po stood at his father's side, his mouth open slightly, looking vacantly at his father's awesome but lovable appearance. He had only his father's size and lacked the bearing. He was tall and slim with a soft, serpentine waist. Whenever he walked fast he would get gooseflesh. His general appearance was like the old man's, but his complexion was not as ruddy. Although nearly forty, he still had very few whiskers and could only envy his father's long, full beard. Standing beside his father, he once more felt that vague fear that so often assailed him. He was always afraid something untoward would happen to his father, and he would not be able to handle his father's fortune and business affairs.

He semed to feel that, in terms of bearing and demeanor, in his generation the Ch'en family was rather like watered-down wine that no longer had such a rich, full flavor. In other respects he might be superior to his father, but he lacked that essential air of self-confidence and authority.

His father was his backbone and main support, like a living god who could provide unseen protection for him. It was as if only through the living presence of his father could he dare take risks, dare to grab money when offered, dare to oppose others and make them enemies, dare to be ruthless. Every time he encountered difficulties and was irresolute and undecided, he would come home for a while. His father's red face and long beard would give him courage and determination. He did not really have to discuss anything with his father; just seeing his red face was enough. At this moment when he had just presented the newly acquired property to his father, his father's good fortune could outweigh every other consideration. Even the fact that the provenance of this property was slightly illegitimate was outweighed by his

feeling of filial piety and by the rightness of his father's store of happiness.

The first one to come in to offer congratulations was Lien-po's eldest son, Ta-ch'eng—an eleven-year-old with a big head and a loud voice, a little silly because he had taken too much "cold medicine" as a small child. When the old man saw the boy enter, he considered getting up and taking his little hand, but then he thought that he should not leave his big red chair before everyone else had come in.

"Ta-ch'eng!" the old man boomed out, "what are you doing here?"

Ta-ch'eng scratched his nose and looked all around, "Ma told me to come in and tell grandpa con—, con—." The silly little fellow lowered his head, and the brocade cushion on the floor caught his eye. He immediately bent down and touched the velvet cord on the edges of the cushion and seemed to have forgotten everything else. Old man Ch'en smiled slightly, glanced at Lien-po, nodded his head several times, and said, "A silly son has great good fortune." Lien-po also smiled with him.

Then Lien-chung, the old man's second son, quietly walked in. He was only a little over twenty years old, very tall, with a fat, red face. He looked a lot like old man Ch'en, but he was slow and awkward in his movements and did not have the old man's stature or air of authority.

Without waiting for his second son to open his mouth, the old man dropped his smile and called out, "Lien-chung!"

Lien-chung's fat face changed from red to purple, and he was at a loss what to do as he averted his eyes from Lien-po.

"Lien-chung," the old man called out again, " 'The gentleman worries about the Way and not about poverty.' You need not be uneasy in the face of your elder brother's filial piety. The family that stores up goodness naturally has an abundance of good fortune. To say that your elder brother's success is due to his abilities would not be so correct as to say that it is the result of the good merit that the Ch'en family has accumulated over the past few generations. Property is hard to acquire, but even more difficult to maintain. This principle"—the old man shook his head slowly—

"is so difficult to explain! To be satisfied with 'a bowl of rice and a cup of water,' that is the Way of the sages, and I cannot expect you to live up to it. To achieve success and demonstrate your nobility, to make your family's name known, that is the Way of ordinary men. Although a fortunate fate comes from Heaven and cannot be forced, still 'you're a man, I'm a man, and a man of accomplishments works diligently.' I do not expect you to develop in the same way as your elder brother. Your talents are simply not as great as his; and besides, your mother spoiled you. If you cannot do anything on your own, I only ask that you conduct yourself on the basis of the proprieties and help your father and brother to maintain the patrimony. Your elder brother has again presented me with a piece of property today. This is really nothing. I'm not really so happy only because of this—this piece of property; but I am quite pleased. What pleases me is his filial respect." The old man suddenly turned to his grandson: "Ta-ch'eng, go call your little sister!"

Lien-chung's fat face was sweating. He didn't know what to do. While his father was talking to Ta-ch'eng, he slowly moved over behind the old man's back and began looking at a landscape painting on the wall. Ta-ch'eng had not yet shown whether or not he'd understood his grandfather's words when his mother came in leading his little sister by the hand. In old Mr. Ch'en's mind women were of no value at all. Lien-po's wife had probably been standing outside the door waiting to be called.

Lien-po's wife was thirty-four or -five years old and rather plump and prosperous looking. Ten years ago she had surely been a very pretty bride. She still wasn't bad looking now—her skin was very fine, but her youth was buried under a layer of fat. She was only plump and prosperous-looking now, and lacked real beauty or appeal. In the midst of settled ease, she had a slight air of uneasiness, and her eyes kept glancing around furtively and uncontrollably. Her plump face wore a slight smile, as if she were apologizing to someone or comforting herself somehow—like a middle-aged woman with an amiable temperament but without anything in the way of ability. As soon as she came through the door, old Mr. Ch'en stood up as if to announce that the visiting ceremony had come to an end.

"Great happiness, Grandfather!" Lien-po's wife said laughing in a halting and none too natural manner, not daring to look right at her father-in-law but uncertain where else to look.

"There's nothing to be so happy about! Nothing to be so happy about!" Old Mr. Ch'en wasn't really angry, but his face didn't show the least sign of a smile. He was like a talking machine, talking without any trace of feeling. He seemed to be expressing the principle that fathers-in-law were required to speak to daughters-in-law in that manner. "Just take good care of your husband and teach your sons well—that's women's responsibility. And don't become proud or lazy just because you're well off. Your mother's family was not very prosperous . . . eh . . . eh . . ." Apparently the old man did not want to complete his statement lest he make his daughter-in-law too uncomfortable.

Lien-po's wife's face began to redden, but then took on a vacant smile. She pulled at her little daughter, trying to make her go to her grandfather. Her grandfather saw her out of the corner of his eye, but he had no inclination to greet her. Daughters were all money-losing properties. The old man didn't want to favor his grandson, but he couldn't help not loving his granddaughter.

The old man took a few steps across the room. With each step he placed his foot firmly on the floor, making great proud strides. Placing his whole body in front of a wall mirror, he paused briefly to examine himself thoroughly, then turned about and smiled at Lien-po. "Feng T'ang ages so easily, and General Li Kuang fails to be enfeoffed in the end![1] Talent is difficult. Talent is difficult. But to find one who knows men and appreciates talent is especially difficult! I'm already over sixty . . ." The old man shook his head for a

[1] Feng T'ang served Emperor Wen (r. 179–157 B.C.) of the Han Dynasty ably, but his talent was not sufficiently recognized until the reign of Emperor Wu (r. 140–87 B.C.) of the same dynasty. By that time, however, Feng T'ang was over ninety years of age and too old to serve in any position. Li Kuang also served under Emperor Wen. In spite of his brilliant military exploits against the Hsiung-nu, however, he was never rewarded with a fief. He died by cutting his own throat in resignation.

long time before the mirror. "Having talent but no good fortune, without the least accomplishments . . ." He stroked his beard and closely examined his face in the mirror.

The old man could not help loving his own face. He was a literary man, but he had a martial appearance. He had all of the "benevolence, dutifulness, propriety, and wisdom" and the will to "maintain the Way and protect the moral teachings" of the literary man, but he also had something men of letters dare not hope for—he compared himself to the great general Yüeh Fei [1103–1131]. He was, he described himself, a ruddy-faced, long-bearded scholar chanting loudly "the great river flows east" in the manner of Su Shih. He looked down on ordinary pale-faced scholars. Only he—perfect in civil *and* military virtues—could take up the great responsibility of "protecting the moral teachings and loving the people." He was confident that his learning and spirit surpassed those of others. He understood everything and understood it in the finest and most profound way, but unfortunately he had only been a candidate for a prefectship and had never filled a real office. On this account, on the one hand he felt that his "having talent but no good fortune" was a very great loss to the world, and on the other hand he truly liked his eldest son. "Literature *and* economics"—his literary productions would without doubt be transmitted to posterity, but as for practical economics, he'd best leave that to his son.

Lien-po was now Chief of Detectives and could get his hands on a great deal of money. The old man didn't like the title Chief of Detectives, but a Chief of Detectives could hope for a promotion to Chief of Police, and Chief of Police was almost the same as the Ch'ing government's Provincial Commander-in-Chief. Then a Chief of Detectives could be considered . . . well, at least a military officer of the third rank. Since the Republican Revolution in 1911, official titles no longer carried references to the past; but one simply had to admit that an office is an office; even though some of them had lost their grandeur, there was no way to remedy the situation. And besides, officeholding would always be a case of "study well

and then serve"; no matter how the official titles changed, the principle would remain the same forever. In the old man's mind, learning was always associated with taking office, just as morality was always inseparable from personal interest. Since his son was an official, could handle money, and was a filial son, there was no way the old man could help feeling satisfied. Only when he reflected on the way that his own official career had never materialized was he slightly jealous of his son; but that sort of complaint was just the right material for traditional poetry. So he would write a few regulated poems or quatrains that were exactly "sad but not distressing."

The old man walked around the room for a while, and his melancholy gradually faded away. "Lien-po, who's coming for dinner tonight?"

"Just a few close friends," Lien-po replied with a smile.

"I don't like people to come around congratulating me!" The old man knit his brows slightly. "Our prosperity is the proper reward of a loving father and a filial son. It's a proper reward. How can they understand?"

"Just close friends, the Chief of Police, Director Wang, . . ." Lien-po knew the old man's temper was sometimes a little strange, and so he did not want to call out all the names one by one.

The old man had no further comment. After a while he said, "Don't ask Ch'en Shou the cook to prepare everything. Order a few dishes from outside, then have Ch'en Shou make a few things. That way it won't look too bad, but it will still seem like a simple family meal." The old man's eyes lit up happily as he said this. In his mind, this way of receiving guests belonged also to the realm of "practical economics."

"Why don't you just think of a few dishes right now and later drink a few cups with us?"

"All right, I'll tell Ch'en Shou. Of course I'll come out and sit with you. Lien-chung, you come home a little early too!"

II

A crescent moon hung just over the roof of the west room of the Ch'en mansion. A continuous light breeze carried the courtyard sounds and the fragrance of cassia flowers for some distance around. Three cars were parked by the main front gate. The Ch'en's three wolf dogs were lying there in front of the cars. Neither the cars nor the dogs made a sound; both just listened quietly to the laughter coming from the courtyards. It was quite noisy in the courtyards. In the south room of the outer court, the three chauffeurs, the Chief of Police's armed guards, and Ch'en Lien-po's personal detectives were busy playing cards. In the inner court they had not yet finished dinner.

Lien-po was not entertaining formally; he had just casually invited the Chief of Police, the Director of the Bureau of Health, the Head Secretary of the City Government, and their wives to come over for an evening's enjoyment. Of course, they merely offered a semblance of congratulations without actually sending presents, and so could not in good conscience demand a formal party. Most of the food was prepared by Ch'en Shou. Of the dishes ordered from outside by old Mr. Ch'en, the finest one was a cassia-flower shark-fin soup— although it was a common dish, it was quite right for the season. Ch'en Shou was a pretty good cook, and the guests were well satisfied with the meal; but old Mr. Ch'en repeatedly called him a bastard nevertheless. The old man's speech could be extremely elegant or extremely vile, depending on whom he was talking to.

The old man drank quite a lot of wine, and the bags of flesh under his eyes turned completely purple. Every time he downed a cup, he would slowly stroke his beard and look over his guests as if he were reviewing the troops.

"The old gentleman can drink up an ocean!" Everyone kept praising him extravagantly.

"Not really!" The old man was really very proud of himself, but he tried not to show it, as if he knew that cultural refinement was just another name for hypocrisy. But he was not a skinny, weak man of letters; he was perfect in both military and civil virtues, and so he couldn't refrain from demonstrating a certain flamboyant spirit. "I can always handle a few cups, ha, ha! Drink up! Drink up!" Then he would wash another one down.

Everyone seemed to fear him somewhat. Perhaps they had even richer or more illustrious fathers, but they couldn't help admiring old Mr. Ch'en's vitality and awesome bearing. They could see that if their own status were only slightly lower, surely the old man would not come out and drink with them. They understood well, and in fact often themselves employed this hypocritical method of entertaining; but they still could not help admiring the old man's verisimilitude in carrying it off, expressing the entire necessary repertoire of the Confucian literatus, the poet, the elegant scholar, and the great general in a moving, grandiose manner worthy of a fine theatrical performance.

After the dinner things were cleared away, Ch'en Fu came in and set up the mahjong table. Old Mr. Ch'en did not play, and he disapproved of others' playing, but Lien-po had to entertain, and he could not very well interfere. Seeing the card table set up, he closed his eyes for a while as if he were putting his eyeballs into those fleshy pouches for a rest. After that he had a nice long yawn. Lien-po quickly asked with a smile, "If the old gentleman is . . ."

Old Mr. Ch'en opened his eyes, dropping a big tear, and looked at everyone as if he were about to smile slightly.

"Wouldn't the old gentleman like to play a few rounds?" the guests asked.

"I'm old, and cannot do it!" The old man smiled and shook his head as if feeling deep regret and sadness. Then he sat back again for a while, and slowly rose to his feet: "I must excuse myself now. Ch'en Fu, serve the tea!" He bowed slightly to everyone, immediately rose up straight, set off in his big strides, and walked away with an air of majesty.

The men and women then split up, the men taking the east room and the women the west. Lien-po and his younger brother made up one hand, and so he let his younger brother play first.

After the games had gone on for about eight rounds, Ch'en Fu and Liu Ma served refreshments to the two rooms. Lien-po urged everyone to eat, and they all nodded their heads without taking their eyes off the tiles. Lien-po urged them again, and they all used their hands to pick up the refreshments while their eyes remained glued to the tiles. The Director of the Bureau of Health forgot all about cleanliness, and the Head Secretary of the City Government very nearly put a chip into his mouth.

Lien-chung did not eat. His eyes were fixed on the useless "blank" tile that he did not dare play. He wished like the devil that he could carve that blank tile into a one of *t'ung* or a four of *wan* with his eyes.

Lien-chung would not play that blank tile for anything, because the Chief of Police had two of them in his hand already. When Lien-po passed the refreshments, he took the opportunity to look at everyone's tiles, and he wanted to hint to his younger brother to play out that valuable tile, because the Chief of Police had already lost quite a bit of money. To have his younger brother win a little less and make the chief happy would probably not be a bad deal. But then, what if the chief got one good tile and then just kept on winning? Gambling is gambling, and there's no such thing as yielding politely. He didn't tell his younger brother. If it were only a question of one tile, he probably would not be so fierce. Play it out for the chief, make the chief happy, the chief, the chief, he just could not give in to him so easily. At this point his confidence drew on a lesson from his father: entertainment is a clever skill, and going on to the finish is the Ch'en family's spirit. Maybe in the future he would manage to be something higher than Chief of Police, but today he could and he should be the Chief of Police. He could not retreat and yield the field just because the chief had two blank tiles and needed a third to hit a jackpot. No, his younger brother's tile could not be given away as a free gift.

After a couple of more draws, the chief himself drew a blank tile and won the game on his own. Lien-chung pushed his tiles away and smiled up at his older brother. Lien-po's expression demolished his younger brother's smile.

From the moment the chief got that blank tile, his luck changed, and he immediately began making small talk: "Director, here's a 'hygienic' tile

hee, hee!" he laughed as he gave the director an unneeded nine of *wan*. After finishing eight rounds, however, everyone stood up.

"Keep right on!" Lien-po invited everyone to sit back down: "It's still early!"

The Director of the Bureau of Health, thinking of his health, wanted to go to sleep; but he also wanted revenge. Those "hygienic" tiles of the chief's had really cleaned him out. Early to bed, late to bed—what difference did it make? Was the Director of the Bureau of Health not a man with feelings to express? He finally won himself over.

The Head Secretary kept on acting humble, expressing complete humility purely for the sake of humility. He didn't want to take the lead in urging them on to continued warfare, and he could not very well suggest breaking up the game, and so he just kept on saying that he had played poorly.

They all waited for the chief's orders: "All right, let's play some more. Lien-po hasn't even played yet!"

Everyone sat down slowly, but they were all quite excited. Lien-chung did not dare sit squarely in his seat. His eyes glanced quickly at his older brother, and his heart kept beating rapidly. He glanced at his older brother, fooled around with the dice, and kept hoping Lien-po would let him play some more, even if it were only one more round. Lien-po decided to enter the fray, however, and Lien-chung picked himself up slowly like a camel being forced to its feet. No one even said, "stay around and be a dreaming fifth!" His face began to burn, but the others didn't even notice. He hated that bunch, and especially he hated his older brother, but he could not bear to leave the game. Not being able to really play, he could still satisfy his craving vicariously by looking on. He sat at Lien-po's side. After he watched a couple of plays, his eggplant-colored face slowly faded, leaving only a pair of round patches like red rouge on his cheeks, slightly silly but kind of cute.

From the beginning of the ninth round, the sound of everyone's voice and the noise of the tiles redoubled. Etiquette, culture, status, and education all seemed to have nothing to do with them, or perhaps they had never had any connection with them. The later and quieter the night grew, the more crude and boisterous they became, still keeping their entire attention concentrated on the movement of the tiles. They used the most vulgar and boisterous tones in asking for the smallest denomination of chip. Their faces lost those gentle smiles, and their eyes glowed like thieves' as they glanced around at the others' hands and hid the changes of their own emotions. Their lips were scorched by cigarettes, their noses dripped droplets of cold sweat, and their bodies emitted a moist and smelly odor.

In the west room the wives' voices were no lower than those in the east room, even somewhat shriller. They played a little more slowly, though. When the east room's ninth round began, their eighth round was not yet over. The trouble was Lien-po's wife. It was obvious that the chief's wife did not much like to play with her, and she herself didn't seem to be completely enthusiastic about the game. Without her, however, they could not make a foursome, and so there was nothing to be done about it. She played slowly, counted her points slowly, and every time she played a tile she had to smile so apologetically, so boringly, as if she had no way out. The others looked only at the tiles she played and not at her smiles. The tiles she played were always worthless. If the others took one they were not grateful, but if they could not take one they always scolded her. She didn't dare show any displeasure, and, in fact, was not used to having a temper. She just felt very uncomfortable and uneasy in her mind, ever fearing that her husband would come in and investigate her behavior—he was losing face because she played so poorly. Those three women were expert players. Lien-po's wife did not really care too much about the way they played, but she envied the fact that they could please their husbands with their skill at mahjong. The chief's "wife" was only his concubine, but she achieved real status when playing mahjong and openly looked down on Lien-po's wife.

After playing eight rounds, Lien-po's wife

breathed a little easier; but she did not dare make it clear she did not want to continue her punishment. When Liu Ma came in to serve more tea, she suddenly remembered and smiled plumply: "Liu Ma, where's the second master?"

The chief's wife and the others knew that Lien-chung was a fierce player, but they didn't object to letting him take his sister-in-law's place. If they were going to play, they might as well have a good time; besides, when they gambled, they showed pretty much of a masculine temperament anyway. As soon as Lien-chung sat down he seemed like a breath of spring, and everyone grew more animated, but also considerably less attractive. Nobody cared anymore what kind of state their facial makeup got into. The very beautiful concubine of the Chief of Police was no exception. Her face had a streak of yellow here, a blotch of white there, and looked something like faded wallpaper on a cloudy day. The room was rather damp and a little smelly.

Lien-po's wife was much more comfortable then, but still could not escape right away. She knew what her responsibility was, an extremely embarrassing and extremely unnatural responsibility that would win her neither respect nor gratitude from anyone. She felt that she was nothing, just Lien-po's wife—this title had her trapped here.

Lien-chung was certainly elated. Gambling was where his talents lay. Mahjong, cards, chess, or drawing lots—he was not only expert at all of them but also had special tricks up his sleeve. No matter how he studied, he could not learn anything else; but in games of chance one look was enough for him to understand. At home these talents never won him any praise, but out in society many people admired him as a truly clever hand. He hated old Mr. Ch'en and Lien-po, especially when the old man said, "It's all because your mother spoiled you." He had loved his mother, and he always felt that if she were still alive he would not suffer such insults and ridicule. His mother being dead, he could only be close to his older sister-in-law. "An older sister-in-law is like a mother." He very much loved and respected his sister-in-law. For this very reason old Mr. Ch'en treated him even worse. The men in the Ch'en family all regarded women with scorn; only Lien-chung was an exception, and thus the more hopeless.

Every time he played a good tile, he would have to glance up at his sister-in-law, just like a child cutely showing off to win parental praise. Though he well knew that his sister-in-law did not understand the game too well, still he would often call her over to look at his hand. In that manner his heart was comforted. His sister-in-law's smile clearly expressed that she respected the second master's skill and ability. In his sister-in-law's eyes he was Second Master and not the Ch'en family's parasite.

III

It was nearly dawn. A cool breeze blew lightly below the yet uncertain cloud cover, blew away the cassia fragrance in the courtyard, and brought in the distant sound of dogs barking. Although the breeze was clear and cool, the atmosphere was rather humid, and the grass and bushes were covered with gray dew drops. All along the foot of the wall, insects were chirping with a shrill yet melancholy sound. The Ch'en family's mahjong games were over, and everyone was washing the oil and grease off their faces with perfumed hot towels, after which they lit cigarettes and burned their already numb tongues as if to drive away the unpleasant feeling of boredom. Everyone still hated to leave the mahjong table, but they had already stopped talking about the events of the game. They were talking casually about unimportant matters, talking quite politely now as if they had begun to recover somewhat their sense of etiquette and culture. Lien-po's wife's status suddenly improved in the light of day; everyone remembered her children and inquired solicitously about them. Ch'en Fu and Liu Ma were running about bleary-eyed serving noodles in chicken broth. Everyone exchanged pleasantries, after which they closed their eyes and began gulping and swallowing. Their mouths were moving,

but their heads were dizzy, and they all stopped talking. Not until the second round of hot towels came could they finally loosen their muscles a little as they gritted their teeth to hold back yawns.

"Are you tired, Chief?" Lien-po used all his strength to overcome his fatigue.

"Tired? No! No!" The chief was wiping the back of his neck with a hot towel.

"Mrs. Ch'en, you really should rest; we've all been too impolite!" The Director of the Bureau of Health's palm was sweating as he began to plan vaguely what sort of medicine he should take when he got home.

Lien-po's wife did not say anything, but only smiled her smile.

The chief stood up and everyone began to move about preparing to say "thank you." The chief said it, and then a long string of "thank you's" rang out. Ch'en Fu quickly ran outside, the horns of the cars outside the gate blasted, the Ch'en's three wolf dogs playfully yapped, and all the stray dogs and house dogs on the block began an answering din. Everyone was still quite polite, urging one another to go through the door first, and talking a great deal in a boisterous manner. The host insisted on asking Ch'en Fu to fetch sweaters and said the weather was cold. The guests insisted on saying no, it was not cold, but were all shivering slightly. The sweaters never actually materialized, the car doors slammed shut, the horns blared out again, the cigarettes everyone was holding bobbed up and down with an orange glow . . . "thank you!" "you're welcome!" . . . everything resounded together. Ch'en Fu yelled at the dogs, the front gate closed like a thunder clap, and the bolt slipped into place. He had a couple of long, tired yawns there in the courtyard, smelled the fragrance of cassia flowers, and saw there were only a few stars left in the sky.

Just as the dew drops on the grass were turning white, old Mr. Ch'en got up. Early to bed and early to rise, diligence and frugality prosper one's family—he respected and followed the old ways. All was quiet and peaceful, and the only sounds he made carried for some distance as he slammed doors, coughed, cursed the dogs, and chanted poetry. The quieter it was, the more he loved to listen to his own voice—he was a morning bell to awaken the world.

As old Mr. Ch'en was enjoying chanting his poetry, Ta-ch'eng—because he had a poor dinner the night before—woke up and came in shouting that he was hungry. The old man was most concerned about his grandson. He called loudly for Ch'en Shou to come in and do something about Ta-ch'eng's hunger right away. Ch'en Shou had not slept all night, but when he heard the old master call him he did not dare delay even one second. "You stayed up all night, but you got some good tips." He knew that sentence was waiting for him in the old man's mouth, and there was no point in looking for trouble. Despite his dizzily throbbing head, he prepared something for the little master to eat and even pretended not to be sleepy by walking around briskly.

Hearing that his grandson had stopped calling out, the old man finally returned peacefully to chanting poems. There was nothing finer to hear than the sound of the boy's crying or laughing and the sounds of reading aloud. The Ch'en family always had both of these and the old man could not help feeling happy.

When Ch'en Shou finished feeding the little master, he still did not dare go to sleep and just walked back and forth quietly outside the old man's room. He was afraid that once he lay down he'd never be able to open his eyes again. Hearing the old man's poetry chanting drop down a register, he took some jasmine tea and refreshments in to him. On his way out he fed the dogs and then went lightly to his room and closed his eyes.

After old Mr. Ch'en finished breakfast, he went into the courtyard to look at the flowers. He did not really like flowers, but every time he saw some he had to take a look at them. At home he had to go and look at them for a while every morning and night, because poems frequently described the dew and frost on flowers. He could dislike flowers, but he could not let on that he didn't understand poetry. The autumn morning sunlight shone on the leaves so that they shimmered with golden beads. He thought he should write a poem to express his troubled heart, but in reality his heart was very comfortable and happy, and he was constantly thinking of that newly purchased store. There was no way to write a poem, but he couldn't afford to lose that certain feeling of "discontent," whether he wrote a poem or not. Without discontent one simply could not be considered a gentleman, poet, and famous scholar.

Yes, he thought, his sixty some years had passed in vain. He had a heart full of literary works that he had never been able to show off. "Without talent, rejected by the bright ruler!" He could not think of the next line of verse.[2] Tu Fu, Po Chü-i, Su Tung-p'o had all served as officials,[3] and even though they held office they were still full of grief and distress. Then what of old man Ch'en? He felt ashamed and empty! Then he recalled that new purchase. A piece of real estate that his son had respectfully presented to him, it definitely had to be managed carefully. He decided to go to the store and take a look around. He looked down on merchants, of course, but he had to help his son manage things a bit; and besides, the Way existed everywhere. Tzu Kung, a noted disciple of Confucius, was also a shrewd businessman! His dealing in money did not compromise his reputation. One should study practical intent and flexibility. He began to change his clothes. Just after he put on his shoes, Feng Yu-ts'ai, Lien-po's personal detective and the Ch'en family's butler, came in to ask for instructions.

"If you please, sir." Feng Yu-ts'ai— a little over forty, with a mouth like a freshwater gar—said quietly, "That, ah, they sent over that, ah, two small envelopes."[4]

"Why come and tell me?" The old man's eyes grew large.

"It's not that— The first master is still sleeping." The great gar mouth tried to force a smile: "I can't, I don't dare disturb him, so I . . ."

[2] The second line is: "Often an invalid, deserted by old friends." These two lines are from a poem by Meng Hao-jan (689–740), a famous poet of the T'ang Dynasty (618–906).

[3] Tu Fu and Po Chü-i are famous poets of the T'ang, and Su Tung-p'o is a poet of the Sung (960–1279).

[4] A payoff wrapped in red envelopes.

Old Mr. Ch'en was too embarrassed to think it all out, but he had to say something appropriate. "I understand; they didn't break up until dawn," he said in a milder tone of voice. "You just take the envelopes now, and give them to First Master later. I have nothing to do with it, nothing to do with it!" He walked away with his book of poems under his arm and didn't look at Feng Yu-ts'ai again.

Feng Yu-ts'ai left almost without touching the ground, like a fish that has slipped out of the net and escaped. The old man put the book down again and read, "A cool wind rises at the sky's end; What is on the gentleman's mind?" "The gentleman . . . mind . . . what . . . ?" The old man had a vague feeling of shame—not having ever been a real prefect, he did not even dare to accept an envelope. That bastard Feng Yu-ts'ai was surely laughing at him too! Presentation of "gifts" was a time-honored custom, but at what time should they be presented? Should one announce openly that he was presenting an envelope, just like the mailman calls out "here's a letter"? He could not say for certain—damned embarrassing! "Literary talents and economics"— he certainly lacked practical experience, felt empty, kept reciting, "what's on his mind?" He looked in the mirror and quoted, "I cultivate my nature amid wars and chaos, / And preserve my life among the deer." He looked more closely in the mirror to see if his old eyes had any teardrops, but there were none. The feelings of the ancient masters were sometimes hard to match!

The old man finished dressing and was just about to leave for the store, when Feng Yu-ts'ai came in again: "Sir, oh, yes, just now I forgot to tell you, Director Ch'ien sent a message asking you to go over today and talk."

"What time?"

"The earlier the better."

The old man closed his eyes, and Feng Yu-ts'ai left the room. The old man stood there savoring the awesome power of closing his eyes and began to feel that life was not really so empty. Just closing his eyes had such force. If he were a "great officer," closing his eyes just once like that would be worth so much. A pity he could only practice on a

useless bastard like Feng Yu-ts'ai. What a waste! In the final analysis his life was still not complete, and he still felt out of sorts, "just like a scholar for three months without a prince" to look up to in the old times.

He decided to visit Director Ch'ien now. He didn't take the car because he wanted to exercise his legs a bit. A slight breeze blew his beard sideways, and the tip of his beard sparkled with gold highlights under the sunlight. He straightened up his frame and gradually forgot that it was his body walking along the street; rather it was an enormous and beautiful mirror, carried along by spirit and vitality, moving down the street as an exemplary model for the masses—in the mirror was a living sage. As he walked along, he felt uneasy again, wondering if those two envelopes were checks or cash. Left to that bastard Feng Yu-ts'ai to accept . . . he wouldn't, probably he wouldn't . . . but if it were a lot of money, who could guarantee he would not take the money and run away? The depravity of the human heart nowadays, who could tell? He thought of returning, but felt too embarrassed—status and the traditional proprieties all forbade him going back. Then again this was not being overly anxious. He ought to go back! The more cultural refinement one has, the more unreliable others naturally become; and so his concern was well founded. Then should he go back? There seemed to be no way out of it!

IV

Director Ch'ien and General Wu were seated in the lounge. Director Ch'ien was once Vice-Minister of Education as well as Salt-Transportation Officer; now, however, he wanted people to call him Director Ch'ien—Director of the National Studies Academy. General Wu was a retired officer. Since he "went into seclusion," he did not look anything like a military man. With a fat neck and big ears he looked for all the world like a rich merchant. Recently he had begun to enjoy reading and study.

Old Mr. Ch'en was not really an old friend of theirs. It was only since his son was promoted to

Chief of Detectives that he had begun to associate with them. He rather admired Ch'ien Tzu-mei, Director Ch'ien, first because of his status as director, second because he really didn't know a great deal about classical studies, and third because he was a man of few words and knew how to handle money—"literary talents *and* practical economics." Old Mr. Ch'en quite magnanimously treated General Wu as a friend, primarily because he did not know a single thing and enjoyed very much asking the old man for learned instruction. The three men exchanged greetings. Director Ch'ien kept right on drawing on his water pipe with a gurgling sound, his two small eyes fixed firmly on the pipe, without saying a word. General Wu, however, wanted to talk, but did not know just what to say. He always felt uneasy in the presence of literary men. Old Mr. Ch'en could not very well begin the conversation—he had to maintain his dignity.

After they sat that way for about ten minutes, the ashes in front of Director Ch'ien's feet were piled up like a small scale model of a grave mound. He put down the tobacco pouch and lightly scratched his head with the long fingernail of his right ring finger. A slight smile seemed to shine from his small eyes like tiny spring shoots pushing up slowly out of the earth after a prolonged dormancy. He flicked the nail of his right ring finger with the nail of his left little finger and, as his small eyes saw the two nails come together, he smiled and said, "Mr. Ch'en, General Wu wants to begin his studies of the Confucian classics with the *Spring and Autumn Annals*. What do you think? I recommended he first read the *Book of Documents* as rather more basic. Of course, the *Spring and Autumn Annals* is fine, also very fine!"

" 'One thread runs through them'; the Thirteen Classics are basically a perfect circle." Old Mr. Ch'en rested his hands on his knees, looked down at his own chest, listened to his voice: "No matter where you begin or where you leave off, it's all very fine!"

General Wu looked at the two old gentlemen and thought what they said was quite meaningful, although, of course, he did not understand them

very well. He could not get a word in, and felt it best just to listen attentively. He thought to himself, "This is meaningful, profound!"

"Just so, just so!" Director Ch'ien took up the water pipe tobacco pouch again and pinched out a little tobacco without putting it in the pipe just yet. He mused for a while; "Hung-tao, is there any value in those recent researches on the *Book of Documents* in the light of oracle bones? The other day—"

"That's—"

The director nodded to yield the floor. Old Mr. Ch'en felt slightly off balance. "That's nothing but 'departing from the classic and opposing the Way.' The purpose of the classic is to transmit the Way, transmit the Way! Understanding of the Way is either deep or shallow, and thus detailed expositions are different, but this does not injure the classic text itself. But to regard the classic as a mere instrument of utility, to dissect it and hack it to pieces . . . Oracle bones! Upon my word! Ha, ha, ha!"

"A profound observation!" Gurgle, gurgle. "The other day a young man came to see me and brought up this matter. I also gave the same reply—agreement without previous consultation."

General Wu was waiting to hear the conclusion: should he study the *Spring and Autumn Annals* or the *Book of Documents?* But the two old gentleman did not discuss the matter any further. Like a pair of old fighting cocks that had just finished one round, they rested awhile and began to fight again.

Old Mr. Ch'en was extremely proud of himself. He had actually defeated Director Ch'ien. His own status and experience were far from Ch'ien Tzu-mei's, but when it came to classical learning he was certainly no weakling, not weak at all. Perhaps, then, learning was not necessarily so closely related to experience? Or maybe so-called learning was all talk, and the more learning one had, the more empty one felt? He did not dare resolve this conflict. His feeling of self-satisfaction gradually dissipated, and he wished that Director Ch'ien, or even General Wu, would talk about something else.

General Wu suddenly thought of something to

say. "Director Ch'ien, are southern women best or are northern women best?"

Old Mr. Ch'en felt as if his ears had been violently stabbed by something all of a sudden.

General Wu smiled foolishly and pulled his neck in, showing a few folds of fat.

Director Ch'ien's lips were on the water pipe; his small eyes blinked, and he tittered, "General Wu, we were discussing the Way, and you bring up women—that's wonderful revenge!"

General Wu raised his face, however. "Don't joke with me. I really want to know. You are older than I am and have wider experience . . . as for women, who doesn't like women?"

"Now, there is a question!" Director Ch'ien laughed out loud.

Old Mr. Ch'en looked at Ch'ien Tzu-mei without speaking. He certainly did not like to hear the conversation take this tack, but he couldn't offend either of them. Their status was above his, and nothing could be done about it.

"Mr. Ch'en?" General Wu continued on with his error, growing more animated all the while.

"General Wu's so naïve, so naïve! 'Food and sex are man's nature,' of course. However . . ." Old Mr. Ch'en pretended to laugh.

"Wait, General Wu, wait until we drink a few cups someday, and I'll tell you, but first you should memorize the *Spring and Autumn Annals!*" Director Ch'ien began to laugh, but still did not make much noise, rather like a dog panting.

Old Mr. Ch'en began to laugh too. Whatever the topic of discussion, he was no less knowledgeable than Director Ch'ien, he said to himself—learning, strategy—but he did in fact feel that he had just learned a trick from Director Ch'ien. The reason that literary men can control military men was right there—strategy. He knew himself, however, that he laughed rather unnaturally. He also realized if he were not there perhaps Director Ch'ien and General Wu would have begun to discuss women. He had to change the topic of conversation, couldn't let everyone sit there at a loss for words. The longer they sat that way, the more uneasy the director would feel.

"Well, Tzu-mei, did you have something serious to discuss? I've got some other affairs . . ."

"Yes, I did," Director Ch'ien remembered. "Other people cannot get up so early, and so I invited only the two of you here. The flood relief needs a great deal of money right now, and we should collect some now and send it out—there's not a minute to lose. Later on we can dicuss it with everyone else."

"Very good!" General Wu understood quite clearly and was very willing to give some money for a charitable cause. "The director can decide how much we should give!"

"Yesterday evening I ran into old Yin, and he gave one thousand. Everyone can pay what they can," Director Ch'ien said slowly.

"Well then, count me in for two thousand." General Wu stretched his legs out very far, closed his eyes, and rested, as if he were through with it.

Old Mr. Ch'en felt embarrassed. "One must not yield when asked for benevolence"; he could not lose face right there. But a mere scholar, a scholar who had never held office, how could he compete with a salt-transportation officer and a general? Of course he had a little money now, but he didn't feel rich. He always felt that he was still an impoverished scholar. It was just because he felt himself impoverished that he was able to write poetry. Furthermore, that small amount of property was all acquired by his son in difficult struggles. If he spent it so cavalierly now—even though for a charitable cause—would not that be being generous with someone else's goods? "A loving father and a filial son"—that was a two-sided proposition! It was for his son that he had cultivated these people, but before he had received anything from their association, he first had to pay out a large sum of money! His son's money. How could he face his son? Naturally, it was conceivable that by paying out a sum of money he could win Director Ch'ien's respect, and that just might do his son some good. But hope was one thing; paying out cold cash was something else again. To win their respect, he'd have to pay out a goodly sum, and he had to speak up quickly, because the director was waiting for his reaction. "Happy at the world's happiness and worried by the world's worries." He often said that, but why had he never even occupied a prefect's office?! Old Mr. Ch'en's discomfort was greater than his anxiety—he hated him-self. He stroked his beard, and his hand trembled slightly.

"A poor scholar, but then again, 'one must not yield when asked for benevolence'; I'll donate the same amount as old Yin. As long as the relief fund's not too much I guess I won't go bankrupt! Ha, ha!" Even he could hear that his laughter was shaky. He felt a little better though, like having swallowed down a bitter medicine—it didn't feel comfortable, but it reduced his discomfort and doubt.

Two thousand from General Wu and a thou-sand from Mr. Ch'en—that was no small amount. But the director didn't even raise his head. He just continued gurgling his water pipe. On the one hand old Mr. Ch'en envied the director's aplomb; on the other, he wanted to know just ex-actly how much he had donated.

"To figure out the total, Director, how much did you give?"

The director seemed not to have heard. After a long wait, still without raising his head, he said, "I mailed mine out yesterday—five thousand. The few thousand from you two gentlemen can be mailed out this morning. Is that convenient? If it's inconvenient, I can send a telegram now report-ing the amount, and we can mail it out in half a day.

"Giving us half a day's time would be good." Old Mr. Ch'en asked General Wu with his eyes, and the general nodded his assent. There was again nothing for them to talk about.

General Wu suddenly got an idea. "Hung-tao, let's go, come over to my place for lunch! Direc-tor, will you come along?"

"I cannot accompany you; I still have to locate a few friends and hurry up with the relief fund!" The director stood up: "Don't hurry, it's early yet."

Old Mr. Ch'en wanted to leave that place, but he was less than enthusiastic about going to Gen-eral Wu's for lunch. He agreed, though, without even thinking, because his mind was a little con-fused, and it would be better to have someplace to go. He felt ashamed that his mind could be so unsettled over one thousand dollars. The problem

was merely that he had never been a salt-transportation officer or a general, and so he had to forgive himself. Still, his mind was quite un-settled. By car they reached General Wu's house in a short time.

General Wu's study was large and airy as a sta-dium, but the walls were hung with paintings; there were tables and chairs everywhere, and the tables were covered with ornaments. The paint-ings and ornaments were all very expensive, and almost all were imitation antiques. People who knew were embarrassed to tell him they were fakes, but even if they told him, General Wu would not care. On rainy days when there was nothing to do, he would not look at those things but rather would compute their prices one by one. After he added up the total figure, then he would divide them into categories—so much for paint-ings, so much for bronzes, jades . . . counting back and forth that way, he could quite happily spend a whole morning or afternoon.

Old Mr. Ch'en could not comfortably say that those things were all false or that they were all genuine. He merely pointed out a few pieces that were not genuine and admonished the general, "In the future when you buy something take me with you, or else make it plain that you have the right to return it if there is cause." He felt sorry about all that money.

"Fine, I'll just invite you along. If I don't buy anything, at least we can talk for a while!" General Wu immediately thought of things to say: this house was worth fifty thousand, he only had four women left with him, originally he had had nine but he dismissed five of them in order to safe-guard his health and cultivate the Way. If he ever took military command again, he would not kill so many people—too immoral.

Old Mr. Ch'en couldn't get a word in, but he thought to himself that if he were a prime minis-ter he'd surely have to associate with generals. He was too narrow because he had never held office. A traditional literatus' or scholar's entire experi-ence came from holding office. He gradually loos-ened up a bit and began to feel that General Wu also had his likable points. His generosity, for ex-ample. As soon as the director mentioned the flood relief, he immediately offered to donate two thousand. No matter what you said, that was of benefit to the people. At least, he could not offend the general, for his son's future— King Wen's great virtue and King Wu's martial exploits were accomplished through mutual support, through mutual support!

A servant brought in a letter. General Wu accepted it and casually placed it on a Fukien lacquered table, but the servant still stood there waiting. The general glanced at the envelope and asked, "What's the matter?"

"They want the general's card. It's an important letter!"

"Find a card and ask Mr. Wang to come here!" Mr. Wang was the general's secretary.

"Mr. Wang's gone to lunch; he won't be back for a while."

The general tore open the envelope, took out the letter, and handed it right over to old Mr. Ch'en. "Please read it for me, my friend. I just hate to read letters! You there, there are cards in this drawer."

Old Mr. Ch'en took his big glasses out of his pocket and read the letter with great enthusiasm:

> I respectfully request your honor, benevolent elder brother, General Wu, to read this letter:
> I trust that this letter finds you in excellent health and the enjoyment of daily prosperity.
> Concerning the question of my nephew, about which I previously requested your assistance in person, fortunately, I recently learned that you and Vice-Minister Ch'ien Tzu-mei are very close friends. The Vice-Minister and General Ch'in are also the best of friends. If I could be so fortunate as to receive your aid in the form of communication with the Vice-Minister, then I would be prepared to offer you six thousand dollars which the two of you may divide as you please.
> Since the Vice-Minister often visits General Ch'in's home, perhaps you could just mention the affair to him at your convenience. I am certain that you will be able to inform me of your success, and I shall be eternally grateful to you.
> This matter, of course, need not go beyond the three of us.
>
> >   With my sincere best wishes,
> >   Your friend as dear as your
> >   younger brother,
> >   Ma Ying-lung

Old Mr. Ch'en's beard could not hide his smile. His status as a literary man, like the things a literary man would laugh at, came most obviously from the art of writing. What a letter! Old Mr. Ch'en would never forget that poorly written letter.

"What's the matter?" General Wu asked.

The old man felt embarrassed. Could he read such a letter right out loud for the general? The two of them were not really close friends. He thought of using his own words to translate the letter from its literary style, but there was no way to translate words like six thousand dollars very elegantly; and besides, if his language was too dignified it would be a real question whether or not General Wu could understand it. He used the vernacular language to tell the general but was afraid the general would feel uneasy. Then the general understood, however: "Just don't take in sworn brothers—that's troublesome!" His attitude was one of utter naturalness. Old Mr. Ch'en understood many things then.

V

Lien-po's wife was just then sitting by the lamp knitting woolen stockings for her silly little son. Her mouth was open slightly as she counted the stiches in a low voice. Lien-po came in. She glanced at her husband and then turned back to her work with an expression that was not quite a smile. Lien-po felt rather strange, as if he didn't recognize her. An image of her as she was when they married came to mind and the person in front of him seemed vague and unreal. He sat down in a chair listlessly and slowly. He refused to admit he detested his wife, but there was no way he could love her again. She was now only a mass of flesh, a mass of disgusting flesh! There was nothing he could say to her and nothing he could do with her.

"Are the children asleep?" He did not want to sit there foolishly.

"They just went to bed." She pointed to the west with a knitting needle. Liu Ma had taken the children to sleep in the west suite. Having said that, she continued knitting the little stockings in her hand. Almost as if concentrating, yet also as if playing, she moved her lips slightly, counting the stiches with a silly air.

Lien-po lit a cigarette and felt as if he himself were just like a smokestack—long, thin, empty, and only able to emit a little smoke. After finishing about half the cigarette, he could not take it any longer and thought about going out—he had someplace to go. He didn't move, however; having been busy all day, he did not want to go out again. He tried to see her beautiful traits; just as he found one, it disappeared again. He didn't feel like looking again. Maybe he could say something, treat her just like a "wife" and talk about the trivialities of domestic life. She did not make a sound—even when she coughed it was way back in her throat with a small muffled sound as if she feared that he might hear.

"Hey!" he burst out with a low but harsh tone, "Mute!"

"Oh!" She held her needle and yarn to her heart. "You startled me!"

Lien-po's anger arose uncontrollably. He threw the cigarette rapidly to the floor, causing hot ashes to fly up. "Shit!"

"What?" She hurriedly put her things down and prepared to rise.

He didn't say anything, but seeing her frightened made him a little more comfortable. He stamped out the cigarette with his heel.

She looked at him foolishly like a startled chicken and did not know what to do.

"Say something," he said, half annoyed and half smiling. "Knitting that fucking thing all the time! It's a long way from winter. What's the rush?"

She managed to smile weakly. "But it'll be cold soon, don't you think so?"

He really hadn't had anything to say to begin with, and now could think of nothing. When they were first married, there would have been no need to say anything more—there were plenty of things to do instead of talking. Now he had to say something. All they had left was some sort of a "relationship." Everything else was dead. All that was left was this tenuous relationship and if he didn't want to cut off that relationship, he had to

return home every day and try to think of something to talk to her about!

"Where's the second master?" He casually brought up his brother as something to talk about.

"He's probably not back yet. I don't know." She felt that she ought to say a little more. "He didn't come home for dinner; probably found a mahjong game."

"Ought to find him a wife so he won't always stay away from home." Lien-po felt somewhat better, lay down on the bed resting his head on his hands: "Who was that you mentioned the other day?"

"The Chang's third daughter. She's a little doll!"

"Oh, it doesn't matter much whether or not she's beautiful."

She felt a stab to her heart. Her own family was not as prosperous as the Ch'ens, but before she married she had been quite a beauty.

Lien-po didn't pay any attention to her. He was deeply aware of the difficulty in arranging Lien-chung's marriage. His younger brother was incompetent and relied completely on him, but his own status had not yet reached its ideal height. To make a match was very difficult: reaching too high, he couldn't make it; going too low he wouldn't accept. Even if his own status were somewhat higher, however, wouldn't his younger brother still be taking unfair advantage of him? Lien-po felt rather uneasy. For the best interests of the Ch'en family, his younger brother should marry a woman with status. But for his younger brother, it would be a case of an idiot having a fool's good fortune. The whole thing was a real pain for him as older brother! Have to go about it slowly and deliberately!

Having thus disposed of his younger brother's marriage, he began immediately to think of his own situation. As soon as he did so, he felt the room to be rather depressing. He wanted to go out, but then—

"How about if I bring Hsiao Feng [Little Phoenix] home? You'd have a companion too!"

Lien-po's wife was still smiling, the kind of smile that replaces crying. "Suit yourself."

"Don't say 'suit yourself.' Say you want it too."
Lien-po stood up. "It's not only for me. You'd
have a helper too. She's not bad."

She didn't have anything to say. Thinking back
and forth, she could only smile through the pain
in her heart.

"Say it," he said, becoming more insistent. "Say
you want it too, that's all, save a lot of fuss!"

"But shouldn't we wait until after Second
Younger Brother's marriage?"

He realized her cleverness. She did not cry and
did not argue, but merely used his younger
brother as an excuse. If she made a fuss, things
would be easier, because his father would certainly side with him. His father would not encourage him to take a concubine, but he would certainly like to have another grandson; and his wife
could not easily bear another child. "Shouldn't we
wait until after Younger Brother marries?" How
fine sounding and reasonable! What the hell was
Younger Brother to him? Husband and wife for
ten years—she just fouled up his plans! He stood
up, grabbed his hat, could not bear to stay in that
room another minute.

"Where are you going at this hour?" He didn't
answer.

VI

Under the pale moonlight, that little door covered by the shadows of the trees seemed as if it
were painted on the wall. His mouth felt dry as he
knocked lightly at the door, and he resented the
fact that he could not just stride right into the
room. He hoped Hsiao Feng herself would open
the door, but her mother came instead. The old
woman asked him something or other, but he just
mumbled a reply and made straight for the north
room. The room was very small and very clean,
with a vase of cassia flowers in the middle. She
came out from the east room: "Oh, it's you."

Her mother did not dare go in with him, but
went to the kitchen to make tea. He wanted to
embrace Hsiao Feng, but when he saw her he felt
somewhat cold. She had not put on her makeup,
her face was sallow, her eyes were rimmed with

red, and she seemed suddenly to have aged
greatly. Lien-po sat down in a chair and could not
think of anything to say.

"I'll go wash my face and be right back." She
smiled slightly and went into the eastern room
again.

Her mother brought the tea in and made small
talk, but Lien-po had no heart to listen. The old
woman's white hair was long, loose, and disheveled, and seemed to give off a white glow under
the electric light. He looked silently at her hair
and felt empty at heart.

After a short while Hsiao Feng returned. She
had powdered her face and changed her dress,
and grown a little younger in the process. Her
light green gown was printed with little flowers.
Lien-po liked the gown, but the red-rimmed eyes
and yellow face of a moment ago were still in his
mind and he felt cheated somehow. At the same
time, he did not want to leave—she still had a certain attractiveness. No matter what, he could not
return home—he could not lose to his wife. The
old woman stole into hiding again.

When Hsiao Feng was not made up she was still
not bad looking, and when she was made up she
was still not really enchanting. She had a tall and
slender figure and a long face, not dark and red
but pale, white, and clear. Her nose and eyes were
very lovely, and her teeth were bright white and
extremely pretty. She was neither healthy nor seductive, but quite lovable. She had a kind of natural aura about her, like spring mist, like autumn
waters, lightly surrounding her whole body. She
had no particularly beautiful feature, yet everywhere she was light and delicate, and her every
movement was soft and graceful. Clothes on her
body were like diaphanous clouds covering the
moon—bright, fresh, light and airy. She did not
often smile, but when she did occasionally smile
and show her pretty teeth, those were her most
beautiful moments. They lasted so briefly though,
and then were gone, leaving one to savor their
memory just as when looking at flowers one suddenly sees a white butterfly fly out and then
lightly drift over the fence.

"Why are you so late?" She handed him a cigarette and a box of matches.

"Busy!" Lien-po was much more comfortable. As he watched the blue smoke float upward, he settled his nerves—why did he love only this anemic woman? It was strange. Ever since he had had this woman, he regarded "seeking flowers and willows"[5] as a kind of social necessity only and had her alone in his heart. Why? A fragrance of cassia perfume, strong but pleasant, wafted to him through the smoke. Right, her fragrance lingered on!

"Why were your eyes red again?"

"It's nothing really." She smiled very slightly; only the corners of her eyes and the sides of her nose moved lightly, with an expression of some anxiety. "I had a slight headache and didn't wash my face after dinner."

"You quarreled again for sure!"

"I didn't want to tell you. My younger brother came back again!" She frowned.

"Where is he?" He took a long sip of tea and looked very concerned.

"He left. Mother and I used your name to frighten him off."

"He'd better not run into me, or there'll be hell to pay!" Lien-po said forcefully.

"He took mother's money too . . ." she sighed lightly and seemed regretful.

"I'll have to run him off again!" Lien-po was very determined and confident that he had such ability.

"There's no need to be so hasty, he—"

"What can he do to Ch'en Lien-po?"

"No. That's not what I meant. He's got his good points."

"Him?"

"If it weren't for him, we wouldn't have come together, would we?"

"I see what you mean. We have him to thank for being our matchmaker, ha, ha!"

"I really don't know what to do." She knit her brows again. "Mother only has this one son. She gets so angry with him but still worries about him. I suppose all mothers are like that. And I'm stuck in the middle and cannot really favor either of them!"

"Forget it! Let's talk about something else. Anyway, I can take care of him!" Actually Lien-po liked very much to listen to her complaints. It made him feel his power and status. At least it was much better than sitting dumbly at home with his wife. He thought of his wife and said, "Today I think I'll just spend the night here and not go home."

"You two were quarreling about me again too?" She wanted to laugh but could not laugh out loud.

"Because of you? We didn't really quarrel. I have my freedom. I can go out whenever I please and no one else can interfere! But I really don't like things this way. You are my woman and I should receive you into my house. It's annoying this way!"

"I think it's still better this way," she said with her head bent down.

"What?!" he asked looking straight into her eyes.

Her eyes were very soft but she still looked right at him. "It's still best this way."

"What?!" His lips were closed tightly.

"Don't you really understand?" She still looked at him as if she didn't notice that he was about to become angry.

"I don't know!" He smiled a very cold smile. "I know women are troublesome creatures. They eat off of men, drink off of men, and when they've had their fill then they deliberately anger men. My old lady doesn't want you to come, and you don't want to see her either. This I know, but what you ought to know is that what I say goes!" He straightened up his serpentine waist. She did not say anything further.

Because she had no bright future, she did not want to think of her murky past. She only hoped to make it through the day. Lying at Ch'en Lien-po's side, however, she could not sleep. Images of her past kept appearing one by one and she was helpless to drive them away. They made her weep, but it seemed that crying was the only easy thing to do.

She really was not called Hsiao Feng. She was

[5] Dallying with prostitutes.

Sung Feng-chen; Hsiao Feng was the name Lien-po gave her because with the word "Hsiao," "Little," it sounded more like the name of an "outside woman." She was a teachers' college graduate who had taught elementary school to take care of her mother. She refused to marry because her younger brother, Lung-yun, refused to take the responsibility of caring for their old mother. Her mother had endured great hardships for the sake of her two children, and since Lung-yun refused to give the old lady any thought, Feng-chen could not put aside the least duty of providing for her mother. Or perhaps it was a kind of privilege, if one considered the concept of "filial piety." For this reason she had passed up several opportunities to marry.

In the elementary school she was very popular. She had the sort of attitude and thinking that were quite lovable, and so everyone liked her. The principal was an old maid over forty years old who had managed a school for over ten years already. She was extremely incompetent and extremely opinionated and had a head of false hair. She had money, wanted to run a school, and no one could stop her. When she could not find any fault with Feng-chen, but her younger brother said Feng-chen was bad, she also thought Feng-chen was annoying. Feng-chen was afraid of losing her job. She went to the principal and told her that the principal's younger brother kept following her around and also wrote her letters, but she had paid no attention to him. The principal often fired the women teachers because they had lovers. The principal herself was an old maid and she did not countenance any romances by the women teachers under her. On this account the general public greatly respected her. Everyone seemed to believe more or less that if all principals were like her, even if the nation were ten times weaker they could still wake up one morning to find it strong again. Feng-chen understood all this, so she thought if she went and explained to the principal, the principal would handle her young brother.

But the principal told Feng-chen quite simply, "You cannot falsely accuse innocent people, and you must not seduce men! If this sort of thing happens again, well!"

Feng-chen held all her tears in her heart. She planned to resign, but had to find another job first and did not dare take any risks.

Gradually everyone learned about this situation and became indignant on Feng-chen's behalf. When the principal found out she was even angrier. At one morning's meeting, when she was admonishing everyone in most unpleasant terms, a violent-tempered student called out, "Why don't you just take care of your younger brother!" The principal laughed out loud, "Ha! I don't need to take care of my younger brother. I have to take care of the teachers first!" She then took a piece of paper from her pocket. "Just look! She accepted five hundred dollars from my younger brother and then says my brother is in the wrong. Sung Feng-chen! I treated you well, and this is how you repay a friend? You get the hell out of here!"

All Feng-chen could do was shiver. The students immediately turned on her, and some of them even spat at her. She didn't know how she walked home. When she arrived home she did not dare cry. She knew that the five hundred dollars had been taken by her younger brother, and she could not tell her mother. She could not tell her mother she had lost her job either. She merely said she wasn't feeling well and had taken a few days off. She hoped she could find another job soon. She looked up a few friends to ask them to help her find a job, but they did not seem too willing to have anything to do with her.

Lung-yun came home and told his older sister quite sincerely, "Sister, I know you can forgive me. I have my business, and I need money. Perhaps my methods are not too good, but my goal is correct. Only you can help me, in the same way that only you can take care of Mother. In order to help Mother and me, you must give up yourself, just exactly as if you had never been born into this world. You have to return the principal's younger brother's money for me, but I don't think you should go off with him. The Chief of Detectives is hot on my trail. If you could win over the Chief of Detectives, then he wouldn't grab me. Do you understand, sister? If you win him over, he'll pay back the five hundred dollars, find a position for you, and take care of Mother for you. Win him over and help protect me at least, if you can't find out anything else. I have to go now, he's right behind me! Goodbye sister! Forgive me for not being able to listen to your opinion! Remember sister, you were not even born into this world!"

She understood her younger brother's words. She understood other people. In order to do something for other people, she had to sacrifice herself.

Everything her brother said came true, except for one line: "he'll find a position for you." He did not find a job for Feng-chen, but he wanted her to sleep with him. Feng-chen did not go out of the house again, just as if she had never been born into this world. All she could do was protect her younger brother by saying that he was unfilial, stupid, undependable. She could not spy out information for him and didn't want to. She only hoped to get through the day and did not hope for anything else.

VII

Old Mr. Ch'en understood several things that day. People of ability teach other people many things. People without ability learn from others. What a shame! But one had to learn: "The gentleman is ashamed of not knowing even one thing; as long as he lives he is learning!" It was his own fault that he never held an office! Only officials can know everything. His grandfather was a provincial intendant under the Ch'ing government. His father, though regarded as "a model of virtue for the community," had never earned an official title. His father counted for nothing in the clan register and he himself was not much better, but his son . . . no, he could not rely completely on his son. He should grow stronger as he grew older. If he could not hope for merit and fame, at least he should help his son to bring his great affairs to a successful conclusion. He could not be an official himself, but could he not make good contacts with officials? In order to help his son, he would have to proceed that way. He could see that being an official brings benefits forever—the salt-transportation officer and the general continued to rake in large sums of money even after they retired. Officials always had the same ideas, always helped each other out. Sworn brothers, relatives, friends all came together in a group. New officials were the leaves and branches of old officials. Even if it was a case of "thunder and lightning striking on a clear day—ascending straight into the Heaven of success," the parvenu still had to find an old official family to marry into and create an alliance. "One man in office benefits three generations." He understood that well.

Then he thought of his second son. Usually he thought of his second son as worthless. Now he seemed like a treasure. Lien-po was unfortunately already married, but for Lien-chung there was still great hope. Perhaps General Wu had a younger sister or a daughter to give to Lien-chung? Though Lien-chung did not have a trace of ability, just how much better was General Wu anyway? He made a resolution: Lien-chung simply had to marry a woman that was worth some money; even if she was a little ugly or a little too old, it didn't matter. Lien-po was only a Chief of Detectives, so ugliness and age were only items to trade off in the negotiations—the Ch'en family's status is a little lower, but your daughter is not very attractive! What a shame that the Ch'ens had to bargain and trade off conditions with other people. There was nothing to do about it, all because Ch'en Hung-tao had great talent but no good fortune! But he had great scholars to talk and laugh with and did not associate with illiterates—what an impressive character! The old man laughed to himself.

He immediately asked General Wu, and General Wu most unceremoniously asked him how much money he was worth. The old man did not want to say, could not help but say, and even had to exaggerate things somewhat. From the point of view of his often quoted "The gentleman is anxious about the Way and not about poverty," he ought to respond thus: "I have a house with ten plus acres and eight or nine rooms." Even though that would be the purest of deceptions, it would still have the ring of poetry about it. He was not now discussing the Way, however, but practical affairs, and practical affairs could never be proper material for poetry. He had to put it a little better, or else General Wu would look down on him.

"Though we're but a humble scholarly family, we do have about a hundred thousand dollars. My late grandfather was a provincial intendant . . ." He did not want it to seem as if his son was corrupt, so he added that last bit of family history.

"Lien-po has probably got his hands on a good deal of money? The official position does not have to be high, but the appointment should be suitable," General Wu said amicably.

"Well yes, he's all right, all right!" The old man did not want to talk as openly and frankly as the military man, but did not want to talk the market down too much either.

"All right, old gentleman, just leave it to me and wait for my reply!" General Wu said in agreement.

The old man breathed a sigh of relief and felt that he really was not without practical talents. Unfortunately, he had never had any good luck with an official career, and after the happiness passed he felt a twinge of self-pity. His mouth and beard moved slightly and without any sound he recited, "To revel in wine requires a good salary; to sing wildly one must live under a sagely dynasty—"

"Hey!" General Wu slapped his thigh vigorously. "I should be beaten. How could I have forgotten? Doesn't Pao-chai have a little sister?" He looked at Old Mr. Ch'en as if the old man should know about Pao-chai.

"Which Pao-chai?" The old man had not hoped that things would develop so rapidly, and he had a vague feeling of fear.

"Why, Meng Pao-chai, a really fine fellow! That year we won a great victory at Nan-k'ou, he was promoted to brigade commander. Then later when Commander Ch'iu rebelled, he was also involved and lost his command. He didn't have much money left, just a couple hundred thousand. A first rate fellow. Let me see, he . . . he's only forty-one or forty-two, and his younger sister shouldn't be much over twenty-five or twenty-six—an 'old' younger sister. Quite suitable. Tomorrow I'll go over and see him, he's a very close friend. This is certainly a good match!"

Old Mr. Ch'en was rather flustered. If things went too smoothly, he was afraid something would go wrong. What sort of a man was Meng Pao-chai anyway? Something as important as a marriage was no casual joking matter, but General Wu's good offices could not easily be refused. How could he take back a request after just having made it? But to make a marriage alliance with a brigade commander—was his own son not Chief of Detectives? Sons and grandsons had their own good fortune. If Lien-chung had a good fate he could even marry into a much richer family. If he had a poor fate, even if he married a woman as virtuous as Ê-huang,[6] it would not help him any. A father could only do his utmost duty, and as for everything else . . . Besides, General Wu would not necessarily accomplish his task immediately. Giving it a try could not hurt anything. He nodded his assent.

After he left General Wu, he certainly felt elated. Even though they were only giving it a try, still he had to consider it a victory. If General Wu did not respect the Ch'en family, would he be a go-between for them so enthusiastically? If things did not come off this time, there would be many future chances. The Ch'ens had already broken into another circle through the old man's influence. Lien-chung was not so bad. He had a fool's good fortune. The old man would have to treat him with more consideration in the future.

Having thus disposed of his second son's affair, he remembered that thousand dollars. Telling General Wu that he had well over one hundred thousand was, well, was a little too . . . , well, it was a momentary stratagem. "A gentleman knows how to use power and succeed by changing his strategy." Although he did not have over a hundred thousand, one thousand dollars was no problem; but the director and the general did not have to take their contributions out of their own pockets—one piece of "business" would pay them three or four thousand—remember that letter! Why should he have to come up with a thousand of his own? And furthermore, who knew but that

[6]Ê-huang is the virtuous and industrious daughter of the legendary Emperor Yao (r. 2357 B.C.); together with her younger sister Nü-ying, she was betrothed to Shun (r. 2255 B.C.). When Shun was offered the throne by Yao, Ê-huang was made the queen and Nü-ying the imperial concubine.

even their contribution was nothing but a piece of "business?" Officials really knew how to handle money—literary talents and economics. Probably Lien-po also had some such talents—envelopes sent over so early in the morning. And it was not anything improper either. If one did not want it, he would only be letting others off easily. A person should not be too foolish. How could he prevent his son from knowing about that thousand dollars and still not come up with it all by himself? As old Mr. Ch'en pondered this matter with all his mental powers, he felt his life to be much more fulfilling than before.

He had been a scholar for his entire life, and now he finally understood the official world and finally had a practical problem waiting for him to find a solution. His son's extreme filial piety was a rather glorious thing, but at bottom it was empty. Even though he need not receive it with shame, still it could not really express his true abilities as a father. This time he could not ask his son for the thousand dollars, but wanted to demonstrate a trick or two of his own. At least in these two matters—Lien-chung's marriage and the donation of one thousand dollars—he was going to be responsible for them as a father should, let those youngsters see what he was made of, and prove that he was not really just a pedantic scholar.

The streets seemed to be much brighter than usual. Even the dust flying up into the autumnal sunlight seemed especially dry and clear, like tiny golden sparks drifting high up on the wind. Very thin and very high white clouds were drifting along in the blue sky, about to dissolve into the blue color, like long white threads hanging from an eagle's feathers. The old man felt slightly exhausted, but extremely happy. A few beads of sweat broke out on his forehead as he continued along, taking his great wide strides. The young people going back and forth on the street had all changed into their new early autumn clothes. Those walking alone kept looking around at each other furtively, and those walking together were holding hands or talking softly shoulder to shoulder. The old man stared fiercely at them—what a spectacle, no difference between male and female, wretched! The old man thought that if he could still be an official, he would have to eradicate

these bastards. "Love the people with virtue, regulate the people with the rites." But still, "heavy penalties when the nation is in danger"—a few of them would have to be executed! When a nation is about to decline devils will surely arise—young men and women of that sort were surely devils. Only reading the classics and revering the rites were sufficient to "regulate the nation and bring peace to all under Heaven."

But he probably had no chance of becoming an official. The best he could do was to be a gentleman who "cultivates himself and regulates his family." "Although the sages and worthies are far away, their poems and books remain, and they are far superior to the sound of the old man next door striking his chimes!" "Cultivate himself"—he had taken care of his body all his life just like preserving a precious jade. "Regulate the family"—the father is loving and the sons filial. "Without shame before Heaven and Earth, how determined and resolute is his heart!" He forgot the men and women on the street—"when my way does not prevail, I'll take good care of myself alone."

He decided to go over to the new shop and take a look. Since his son had respectfully presented him with it, he should go over there and look around before it opened and give them a little advice. "Being a merchant or being a scholar, wherein lies the difference?" Indeed, Heaven gave him his virtues and there must be a use for his talents.

The Prosperity Market was just being prepared for opening. The ornamental lintel was still sealed with yellow paper, the right corner of which was torn slightly, showing a freshly painted red character for "people" on bright black lacquer. Two large carts were parked outside the store and a gang of bare-backed men were carrying flour sacks inside, their backs covered with sweat that had soaked through the large linen clothes they had draped over themselves, and their hair and eyebrows covered with a layer of white powder. Fat mules were standing beside the carts leaning their mouths into their food bags and flailing their tails around constantly to beat off flies. The smell of flour and sweat mixed up together had attracted a great many red-headed green flies that were buzzing around like flashing lights. Things were very busy on the inside of the store too. Wicker baskets had already been put in place and had strips of red paper attached to them, young clerks were pouring various sorts of grain into them according to their labels, and sawdust was flying all over the room and had covered the freshly painted green counter with a layer of yellowish white. Every place was freshly painted, bright red and bright green, like a country bride who had done her best to make herself up but felt quite uncomfortable. Flour sacks were piled up higher than a person and still they were carrying them in, soft and labeled in green lettering like a bunch of overstuffed pillows. The most eye-catching thing in the hanging shrine was the image of Lord Kuan, God of War. His face was as red as the pair of big red candles standing in front of it, and underneath it was hung a string of cash and two or three strings of paper silver ingots.

Old Mr. Ch'en stood outside waiting for Manager Sun to come out and welcome him. The clerks and the men carrying the flour sacks did not pay very much attention to him, and his anger began to flare. "Move aside please, don't block the way!" Carrying two flour sacks they stared up at him with angry eyes.

"Call the manager out here!" old Mr. Ch'en shouted.

"Venerable Proprietor! Venerable Proprietor!" The words went around and everyone suddenly stopped working and their faces assumed an expression of respect through the sweat and flour.

The old man was somewhat more comfortable then and deliberately paid no more attention to them as he raised his head to look at the character "people" showing on the ornamental lintel.

Manager Sun squeezed out in rolly-polly fashion from behind the inner counter, the smiling expression on his face increasing as he came into the sunlight. By the time he reached the doorway his face was completely illuminated by the sunlight and also completely covered with a broad smile. His pants and shirt of Shantung silk flashed brightly in the sun, and the cloth shoes on his feet were so white that they made one suddenly feel cool.

"Please come in, please come in, sir." The manager's smile flashed at the venerable proprietor as his eyes glanced at the flour carts and his soles carefully avoided the horse piss. With a nod of his head he directed a young apprentice to go in and make some tea and prepare towels. He was not in the least hurried, but everything was done just so—a real manager. Slowly they walked toward the inner counter without saying a word. The manager's plumply smiling face turned left and right and then raised slightly and turned back slightly. The old man's eyes followed that plump smiling face and saw everything.

At the inner counter, the odors of new paint, aged Kuang-tung tobacco, horse manure from the back yard, and sawdust that wafted in from the front, all blended together to make a strong but somehow pleasing stink. The old man entered another world. That odor made him forget his former self and brought to mind many affairs that were more exciting and fulfilling than a scholar's life. His usual feelings came from books and his usual hopes and wishes came from books—they were empty, just empty. Now when he looked at a row of blue-cloth-covered account books hanging on the wall, the dark red abacus on the desk, and the big cash drawer sitting in the corner, locked with a large shiny lock and decorated with the words "attract money and receive treasure," he felt that this was a practical and promising business. This sort of business might not necessarily compare with being an official, but it was after all a great deal better than staring dumbly at books or loudly reciting "Heaven gave me virtue." This was life, action, business. Even if his son lost his job, here, here at least there was rice, flour, and money—economics!

He remembered that one thousand dollars.

"Manager Sun, let me ask you something, just for the sake of conversation mind you; what if we could get a handle on some relief supplies—this year many places are suffering from natural calamities, probably even here we will soon be receiving quite a few refugees—would we lose money handling relief supplies? Please keep in mind that this is a most charitable enterprise!"

Manager Sun could not quite comprehend the venerable proprietor's meaning, and he could only smile all the harder. "We couldn't lose money. How could we lose money?"

"Just for the sake of discussion, why couldn't we lose money?"

Smiling broadly again, Manager Sun picked up his pipe, struck a couple of matches, put them both to the tobacco, then placed the old jade pipestem to his lips and took a deep and hot drag of smoke. "How's that? It's like this: relief supplies are naturally tax free and are transported for free!"

"So what of that?" The old man closed his eyes and felt expansive.

"Naturally no one wants just to handle relief supplies. Free transportation is something that can be turned into a tidy profit." He paused a minute and, seeing that the old man said nothing, finally went on to say, "When the provisions come in and you start to distribute them, there's also money to be made."

"But that would be . . ." The old man opened his eyes wide.

"You don't necessarily have to do it that way, not necessarily. If we handled it, receiving and delivering honestly, not hurting the people, made a good name, we could establish a fine reputation just as we are opening the shop. The business is flexible and depends on how you work it." Manager Sun bit on his pipestem and looked down at his cloth shoes.

"The business is flexible," kept ringing in the old man's ears just like a fine prose essay style—"begin, elaborate, turn, and conclude."

"Have you got an in, sir?" Manager Sun asked gingerly.

"What sort of an in?"

"To handle relief provisions."

"I'll give it some thought."

"But it would take a considerable amount for payoff, though."

"There are ways, there are ways, I'll give it some thought." Old Mr. Ch'en began to feel that Manager Sun was not so annoying after all. Gen-

eral Wu and Manager Sun were neither of them as annoying as he had imagined. He was probably a bit too stuffy. The Way is enough to regulate nature, but it might also decrease one's life choices. It seemed as if he should change his ways. If he had money and status, would it not be much easier to transmit the Way? After all, T'ang and Wu were both emperors whose riches reached to the four seas, and that did not prevent their being sages. There would be nothing wrong with taking that one thousand, adding another couple of thousand to it, and using it as payoff money. If he could prosper from this piece of business, and daily take in pounds of gold, it would be worth it. He then talked the whole business over in detail with Manager Sun.

As he was leaving, Manager Sun remembered, "Oh sir, the inner counter still needs an ornamental lintel. Could you please write out some appropriate characters and tomorrow I'll go get them in person?"

"What should I write?" The old man seemed to actually respect Manager Sun's opinion.

"You can surely think of something good. I've only got a mind full of vulgar phrases!"

The old man laughed out loud and a slight breeze blew his beard sideways, shining forth some scattered golden threads in the sunlight.

VIII

"Big Sister!' Lien-chung was outside the window. "Big Sister!"

"Come in, Second Brother." Lien-po's wife came hurriedly out from the inner room. "Oh, what is it?"

Lien-chung's face was covered with sweat and his cheeks were dreadfully red. As soon as he came into the room, he collapsed into a chair as if he were about to faint.

"Second Brother, what is it? Are you sick?" She was about to go for some sugar water.

Lien-chung shook his head as he leaned back in the chair and finally recovered his breath. "Big Sister!" He cried out and then began to sob convulsively with his face buried in his hands.

"Second Brother! Second Brother! Tell me! I'm your big sister!"

"I know." Lien-chung struggled to speak up, his tear-filled eyes looking at his sister-in-law. "I can tell only you. Aside from you there's no one who treats me like a person. Big Sister, you tell me what to do!" He cleared his nose.

"Slow down and tell me, Second Brother!" Lien-po's wife's eyes were also filling with tears.

"Father has arranged a marriage for me, you know?"

She nodded her head.

"He didn't say a word about it to me. I heard about it by accident. The woman, that woman, Big Sister, she openly sleeps with the family chauffeur, everyone knows! I don't even count as a man. I'm not capable. They're only interested that her father is a brigade commander and the go-between is a general, they don't care about me . . . the bastards . . ."

"Surely Father doesn't know about her then."

"Whether he knows or not, I can't take it. But this isn't what I came to tell you. Listen, Big Sister." Lien-chung's tears gradually dried, leaving his eyes red. "I know that I'm not capable. I'm foolish, but I'm still a man. I want to run away—to starve to death or die in poverty. I'll accept my fate—and not set foot in the Ch'en's house again. It's unbearable living here!"

"We are the same, Second Brother!" Lien-po's wife said softly.

"I really want to pay them back somehow." Seeing that his sister-in-law was so sympathetic, he let her know fully and frankly everything that he was thinking. "I know all of their rotten schemes. They force merchants to send them 'gifts'—protection money. They got their hands on 'white powder,' heroin, and they use flour to cover it up and hide it. They monopolize the relief supplies racket . . . I know it all. If I blew the whistle on them, they'd be shot, shot!"

"Oh Second Brother, don't say that; it's frightening! You just run away, that's all, but don't do those things! It won't do you any good, and it would surely harm them. And me, you've got to think of me too! A woman like me." Her eyes looked all around again, terrified.

"That's right, so I didn't do it that way. I hate them, but I certainly don't hate you, Big Sister; and the children are not my enemies. I'm not crazy." Lien-chung smiled. He seemed to feel that not turning them in for his big sister's sake was a very magnanimous act. He felt better because his sister-in-law would certainly be grateful to him. "I didn't do it that way, but I thought of another way out. Originally I intended to leave yesterday and not set foot in this door again. I went to gamble, Big Sister, you know I'm a good gambler? I had it all planned. I'd gamble the whole night, win a few hundred, and then easily run far away."

"But you lost?" Lien-po's wife asked with her head bowed.

"I lost!" Lien-chung closed his eyes.

"Lien-chung, do you plan to win or to lose?" Sung Lung-yun asked.

"Win!" Lien-chung's face reddened.

"I won't gamble. How can we play if both sides want to win? I need money bad."

Then they both laughed.

"Without you we'll be short one hand." Lien-chung moved a tile around with his palms.

"If I play it can't be mahjong. Haven't got the time." Lung-yun blew a puff of smoke up toward the black ceiling.

"I could play anything with you, but these two gentlemen just have to play mahjong to get them through the night. Sit down!" Lien-chung was very anxious to start playing.

"Okay—eight rounds and not one round more?"

The other three reluctantly nodded their heads. "Sit down!" they all said together.

"First wait a minute. Take out your money and let me see it. I need money bad!" Lung-yun refused to sit down.

The other three took out their cash and threw it on the table. Lung-yun ran his hands over it a bit and said, "That's all? Play by yourselves!"

"We don't even have to use cash. Just use chips. Whoever loses can send the money over early tomorrow morning. How much do you want to play for?" Lien-chung stood up and grabbed Lung-yun by the arm.

"I need two thousand dollars bad. If you lose more than two thousand, I only take two thousand, not even a bit more. We'll clear all debts tomorrow morning!"

"Sit down then! If you lose it'll be the same?" Lien-chung knew he could win.

"That goes without saying. Let's get started!"

After playing eight rounds, Lien-chung only won on the last round. His fat hands trembled as he counted the chips and saw that he had lost fifteen hundred dollars.

"Play four more rounds?" he asked.

"We plainly agreed, eight rounds and we quit." Lung-yun was wiping his sweaty hands on his pants. "Tomorrow morning I'll go with you to pick up the money. I need it!"

"What about you two?" Lien-chung asked the other two with a pleading look in his eyes.

"You want to play again, let's play again. He's the only one ahead. I haven't won or lost."

"I lost a little too. If you want to go again, let's go."

"Let the winner decide!" Lien-chung still had courage. He knew he could turn his defeat into victory in the last half of the night. If there were no other way, he could always pull a few tricks. It looked as if he'd have to pull a few!

"I can't just keep on though, only four more rounds, that's it, get started!" Lung-yun seemed to have got the bug too.

Lien-chung's luck changed.

"Wait a minute!" Lung-yun handed a few chips over to Lien-chung. "Let's get this straight, no tricks!"

Lien-chung knit his brows tightly, but did not reply.

In the next round of play, Lien-chung won three times. Each win was substantial.

"Let's all draw our tiles and then exchange a few from each other's hands, all out in the open with no one cheating and no one being taken advantage of," Lung-yun said as he traded some of the tiles in his hand for a few in Lien-chung's hand.

Lien-chung did not dare say anything, but just stared at everyone's hands.

In the second round, however, he still didn't do

badly. He only won once, but it was a big win. He smiled as he stacked up his tiles.

"Take off your big-sleeved jacket!" Lung-yun said pointing to Lien-chung's fat face.

"What for?" Lien-chung's face tightened and his expression was ugly as he forced the words between dry lips.

"I can't go around with anyone who pulls tricks, switching tiles at will like a fairy maid picking beans!"

Wham—Lien-chung pushed aside his tiles. "Losing money is nothing, but I've got my reputation . . . I'm not playing!"

"You? You wanted to play, pick 'em up!" Lung-yun smiled coldly.

"Is it against the law not to play?"

"All right, let's not play, but the last two rounds don't count. You owe me a clean fifteen hundred."

"I don't owe you a damned thing." Lien-chung stood up.

"What? You think you can just walk out?" Lung-yung also rose to his feet.

"Kidnapping? I've seen that before!" Lien-chung thought he could scare them a little. He could not keep on playing because he could not pick up his own tiles, could not switch tiles, and did not have any assurance of winning. In a show of force, he could not match Lung-yun.

"Cut the crap. If I lose won't I fork up the money the same as you?"

"I don't have any money!" Lien-chung told the truth.

"What? You two gentlemen can go, but I have to have a few words with Lien-chung." Lung-yun turned to the other two: "You broke even and you lost a little, but it doesn't matter. See you tomorrow."

Those two put on their coats. "Goodbye."

"Sit down," Lung-yun said a little more peacefully. "Tell me what this is all about."

"It's nothing. I thought I'd win a little money for travel expenses and run far away," Lien-chung said listlessly with a disappointed smile.

"You didn't think you'd lose, and even if you lost you could use your big brother, the Chief of Detectives, to scare people."

"He's not my older brother!" Lien-chung just could not think of anything else to say. His mind was suddenly very confused, but he dare not go home for the money. To use his brother's power and authority one last time would not work because Lung-yun was not to be fooled with. Besides, Lung-yun was Lien-po's greatest enemy and it would not do to help either one of them. If Lien-po took Lung-yun in, it would mean at least ten years' imprisonment. If Lung-yun came out on top, Lien-po might just be done for. What should he do?

"Why are you in such a hurry to have the money? Couldn't you wait a couple of days?"

"I've got my reasons. When I need money I need money. You just think of a way to find the money!" Lung-yun did not give an inch.

"I told you, I don't have any money!" Lien-chung could find nothing else to say.

"Go home and get it."

"You know they wouldn't give it to me."

"Ask your sister-in-law!"

"Where would she get it?"

"How do you know she doesn't have money?" Lien-chung did not reply.

"I'll tell you what to do." Lung-yun smiled slightly. "Go home and put it to your sister-in-law straight. Tell her you lost money, lost money to me. What do I want the money for? You tell her this: Lung-yun is planning to get some money together to secretly take his sister and mother away. If you put it that way, she'll definitely give you money. Understand?"

"Are you really going to take them away?"

"That's none of your business."

"All right. I can go now?"

"Wait, wait!" Lung-yun stopped Lien-chung short. "Isn't that a big chair there? You sleep there a while and tomorrow at nine I'll let you go. I don't have to go with you. You know who I am. If you bring me the money like a good boy, that's fine; and if you take off and never come back, that's all right too. I don't like killing. I don't even want your older brother's life—but if I get mad, I

just might take a couple of shots for the fun of it!" Lung-yun patted his hip pocket.

"Big Sister, you know I can't ask my father or brother for money. You remember when I was a kid I got a beating because I kicked the ball when I wasn't supposed to? They tied me to a tree! I think if they wanted to beat me now, they would probably do it again." [7]

"You don't have to ask them for it, Lien-po's wife said very sympathetically. "How about this: I'll get together some of my jewelry so you can take care of it."

"Big Sister! I lost one thousand five hundred!"

"Second Brother!" She swallowed hard. "I don't mean to scold you, but you really had your nerve! A thousand five hundred!"

"They forced me! I usually never gamble for such high stakes, but Father and Older Brother forced me!"

"Who did you lose it to?"

"Lung-yun, he—" Lien-chung's tears welled up again. Only his sister-in-law loved him. How could he lie to her with his eyes wide open? But if he did not pay this debt, he'd be in for it. Lung-yun was no one to fool with. And if he let his father and brother find out, he'd be in deep trouble too. The only road to take was to lie to his sister-in-law—an extremely dishonorable but absolutely necessary way out!

"Lung-yun, Lung-yun"—he completely swallowed his shame and his feelings—"needed money and I also needed money, so the more we played, the higher we put the stakes."

"The Sung family are a bad lot, all of them. You simply shouldn't have gambled with him!" She did not say this completely in anger, but did express her dissatisfaction with Lien-chung.

"He said if he got hold of this money he would take his sister and mother away secretly!" Every single word burned his tongue.

"Whether he goes away or not, where are we going to find that kind of money?" Lien-po's wife became slightly mollified. "Although I can get by

---

[7] In this speech Lien-chung must be alluding to an occasion when he was caught playing ball and was beaten by his father. As an old-fashioned scholar, he believes that boys should devote themselves to their studies and refrain from playing in the field.

with this kind of life, still oil, salt, soy sauce, vinegar, and other groceries have to be paid for, and all I have is a couple of dollars on hand."

"Then find something that's worth money!" Lien-chung was becoming more and more edgy and only hoped to bring things to a conclusion as quickly as possible.

"I wouldn't dare take anything like that!" Big Sister was stumped for a moment. "I'll just do it! I don't dare take anything else, but could I dare to touch their smuggled goods? Even if he raises a fuss with me, he wouldn't dare shout it all about. And besides, I'm not afraid of fighting with him! We'll see what he can do to me! A few days ago he gave me two packages of 'white powder' to hold. It's bound to be worth quite a bit of money, but I don't know if it'll be enough to pay this debt of yours."

"Where is it? Quick, Big Sister, quick!"

IX

It was already early winter. Lien-po was taking two pots of very fine-petaled white chrysanthemums to visit Hsiao Feng. The chrysanthemums were fully open, and their long and delicate petals leaned against the wires of the pot, shaking slightly as if they were about to fall off. He ordered his driver to be careful. Those thin white petals evoked tender feelings, and he held the pot steady with his feet for fear that they would be shaken too greatly. The car drove along very smoothly, but the flowers continued to shake, and as he silently watched the jade-like petals he suddenly felt a vague uneasiness. The sun was pushing down on the hill tops.

Arriving at Hsiao Feng's gateway, he took up one pot of flowers himself and told the driver to carry the other one, carefully. The gate was not locked and he went straight in. As he set the flowers down in front of the steps, he told the driver to return at nine o'clock to pick him up.

"Why are you so early?" Hsiao Feng was already standing on the steps. "Ma, come quick and look at these two flower pots; they're so nice!"

Lien-po stood in front of the flowers with his hands on his waist, looking attentively at Hsiao Feng and then again at the flowers. " 'Opening the curtain to the west wind, she is more slender than the yellow chrysanthemums!' It should be something close to that, I guess!" he said with a smile.

"Well, it's really something that you could remember something like that," Hsiao Feng said looking at the chrysanthemums.

"All you can do today is pick out my faults, hmm?" he asked with a laugh. "As soon as I come in, you're after me for being too early, and then you say, 'it's really something' . . ."

"I thought you were very busy and couldn't come so early, that's all."

"Oh, well, you always have something to say; let's go inside."

On the table was a book with a very beautiful bookmarker lying on the opened page. He picked it up casually and remarked, "So, you're studying criminology?"

Hsiao Feng smiled. He felt as if it was the first time he'd ever seen her smile, and she appeared more beautiful than he'd ever seen her before. "I was just bored and reading it for fun. You must have memorized all this stuff, right?"

"Me? I've never read it before!" He was still looking at her face as if trying to recapture that already vanished slip of a smile.

"You never read it?"

"Books are books and practical affairs are practical affairs: real practical affairs are a matter of status and authority. You just have to be able to control things, and that's all. Think of it, if you had to carry around a library to get anything done, it'd be ridiculous! Just look at me; anything I do is all right, and I didn't have to read even one book."

"It wouldn't hurt you to read it though?"

"Who cares?! Let's have a little something to eat first. Say! I forgot I told the driver to go. Let's go out to eat. How about it?"

"There's no need. We just finished wrapping some dumplings and there are plenty for three people. I'll tell mother to go out and get you some wine. What kind of wine?"

"Er—a bottle of citron wine. But isn't it a lot of bother for your mother to go out again?"

"It's only around the corner. The wine you want, spicy pork, wine-flavored crab, white pears, and plum wine, how's that?"

"Great! 'A cup of wine to admire the flowers!'" Lien-po was extremely happy.

After dinner, Lien-po was feeling the wine a little, and easily became quite talkative. "Feng"—he took her hand—"let me tell you, I have a chance to take over the position of Chief of Police in the next few days!"

"Really, that's wonderful."

"Don't tell anyone!"

"I never go out. Who would I tell? If I told Mother, she wouldn't understand."

"Lung-yun hasn't come around?"

"Not for a long time."

"No one knows. I've got it all set up!" Lien-po looked at himself in the mirror. "In the next couple of days"—he turned around and lowered his voice—"there's going to be a blowup in town, but the Chief of Police doesn't know anything about it yet! I know, but I'm not letting on. When the thing blows up and the chief can't handle it, then I'll come along and clear it up easily because I have inside information. But I'll have to watch very carefully. When he decides to resign, I won't show myself until he does resign. I've got them by the balls, but I'll have to make sure that I'm going to be his replacement. If it's not to be me, I won't go into action!"

"But what if the city is thrown into chaos?" She frowned.

"Chaotic times produce heroes, Feng!" Lien-po was dead serious. "When a child cuts its finger, its mama worries half the day, because mama is a woman. A real man looks at the world in a different way. A crisis is only a move in a game of chess. History is the history of great men! Don't you worry; no matter how bad it gets, it won't touch you here. If need be I'll send a special detective around to guard you." His air of seriousness relaxed a bit. "You satisfied?"

She nodded her head and didn't say anything.

"There's no danger." Lien-po lit a cigarette and blew the words out with the smoke. "Nobody will notice me. I'm too small a fish," he smiled coldly, "and only an insider would know that I'm the

moving spirit behind all of them. Why, without me those directors and officers couldn't last a single day. So if for any reason things don't go just right, the higher-ups, the outsiders still won't blame me. And if things move along smoothly and just as I've planned, the people in the department won't be able to shake their heads at me! What?" He listened a minute. Outside there was the sound of a car stopping. "I told him nine o'clock. Is your clock slow?" He pointed at the small alarm clock on the table.

"No, it's just eight o'clock."

In the courtyard someone called out, "Master Ch'en!"

"Who is it?" Lien-po asked.

"The chief wants you!"

"Is that old Chu? Come on in!" Lien-po opened the door and the lamplight fell on the white chrysanthemums.

"The chief asked you to please hurry on over. Several division heads are already there."

Feng-chen pulled at him from behind. "Is it safe?"

He came back in. "It's nothing. Maybe they heard a little something, but they definitely couldn't know the whole story. I'm going. If I have time, I'll come back, but you needn't wait up after eleven." He went out in a hurry.

As soon as the car left, someone was knocking on the door again; knocking very impatiently. Feng-chen was startled. "Ma! Open the door!" She opened the door of her room and waited to see who it was.

Lung-yun came striding in in a rush.

"Ma, Sis, put on your clothes and go!"

"Go where?" Feng-chen asked.

The mother just looked at her son and did not hear clearly what he said.

"Sister, you can still make the nine o'clock train. You and Mother take off. Here's three hundred dollars, you take it, Sister. When you reach Shanghai, I'll send you more money. Right up until you find a job. In the south you're bound to find something to do."

"What about him?" Feng-chen asked.

"Who?"

"Ch'en!"

"Why worry about him? He won't be coming here again for a while."

"Is he in danger?"

"Women are all the same. You really seem concerned about him." Lung-yun laughed.

"He treats me pretty well." Feng-chen said with her head down.

"He treats himself even better! Hurry up, the train won't wait for you!"

"Just leave without taking anything?" The mother seemed to have understood now.

"Mother, I'll take good care of these things; nothing will be lost!" He was obviously kidding.

"Oh, you had better take good care of things!" Feng-chen began to cry.

"Sis, shame on you, crying for him!" Lung-yun said in a teasing tone.

"A woman's feelings for a man," she said slowly, "for a man she's lived with, if she doesn't want to kill him, then at least she must love him some!"

"Who cares about all that crap? Don't you remember you were not even born into this world? Get going, now, hurry!"

X

Old Mr. Ch'en was very pleased with himself. His second son's marriage was all nicely arranged. General Wu's secretary, Mr. Wang, acting as go-between, had set up a first-class match. The old man did not much believe in all that stuff about matchmaking and choosing an auspicious day, but since it was a first-class match, he felt that he had certainly lived up to his paternal responsibilities toward his sons.

The second thing that made him happy was that the relief provision business was being handled by the Prosperity Market, the profits being divided equally between himself and Director Ch'ien. Of course he was not as avaricious as

Director Ch'ien. He had set up that business for the sake of his sons and grandsons.

Although the third thing did not bring with it any great practical profit, it gave him great spiritual delight. Director Ch'ien had invited him to the National Studies Academy to lecture three times on the classics. His subject was "regulate the mind and cultivate the person." He had already lectured twice. No small number of people came to hear him, and most of them came in automobiles. The old man knew that his appearance and voice were enough to impress people, and furthermore, since what he had to say was in such perfect harmony with the classics and histories, even if no one came to listen he would have been happy just to listen to himself. After he had lectured twice, whenever he walked down the street, he felt that the people passing by in cars were paying special attention to him. Not only were the two essays that he had already delivered published in the local papers, but he had also received copies of two papers from Hunan that had specially reprinted them. This made the old man particularly happy. He had not been wasting his breath and strength. There must be many people who would begin seriously studying the classics because of his efforts. Perhaps if he tried a little harder, a general trend might begin that would restore the ancient morality and bring glory to the ancient culture. In that case, the old man could not believe that he had lived in vain! "Establish virtue, merit, and words." Although the old man had not yet been able to "express his loyalty to the court," still his virtue and words were already good enough to be undying. He imagined himself in the eyes of his audience as a venerable scholar and poet worthy of respect and admiration. Truly, "whenever I talk of past things to the youngsters, / they begin to realize that I am an old man of wisdom!"[8] He began to feel something in his life, both material and spiritual, and something

[8] The second line of this couplet, probably made up by Lao She, can be interpreted in various ways, and we have chosen the reading that seems to suit the context best. The ambiguity resides in the two terms *lao-tzu* and *ch'en-jen*. The former is a colloquial expression meaning "father"; thus any man, and especially an old man, can use that term in place of "I" when talking to others, especially if he is in a jocular or angry mood or wants to assert his seniority or general superiority. Lao-tzu, of course, is also the name by which the author of the *Tao-te ching* is best known. *Ch'en-jen* can mean "a man passé or out of date," "a man of the past," or "a man from the state of Ch'en." The first two characters in the line, *shih-chih*, could also mean "I begin to realize." Thus, when detached from the context of the poem from which it is taken, the couplet can be translated in many ways.

ineffable like "three thousand strands of white hair blowing in the west wind."

"Why doesn't Lien-chung ever stay home?" the old man asked Lien-po's wife as he was looking at the chrysanthemums in the yard, and she was standing there with her little daughter under the eaves.

"He probably goes to study English at night and comes in rather late." She looked far off as she lied.

"Studying English! What for? He cannot even write decent Chinese! Hey, child!" He glanced at his granddaughter: "Don't put your fingers in your mouth!" He also looked at his daughter-in-law as he gave this command.

"Big Sister!" Lien-chung suddenly ran in and, thinking his father not at home, ran straight up to his sister-in-law. When he saw his father he stopped short and did not dare move. "Father!"

The old man looked Lien-chung up and down, slowly, carefully, sternly, so that Lien-chung's heart was beating fast. Having observed him long enough, the old man took a step forward, and Lien-chung hung his head.

"Where have you been to? These days you never even come to see me, as if I were not your father! Tell me, what has your father done to offend you? I found a job for you. Could you ever earn sixty dollars a month otherwise? I made a marriage match for you. You really are not worthy of marrying such a fine girl! You don't come to see me in the daytime naturally because you have to go to work, but why don't you even come at night? I'm not dead yet! When you come through the door you just call for your sister-in-law and don't even look at your father! You're not as good as Ta-ch'eng. At least he knows enough to greet his grandfather first! You're really not a child anymore. In no time at all you'll be married and have children. Look at yourself! You don't measure up in any way!" In his anger, the old man could not think of appropriate literary phrases but had to use the vernacular, and that made him even angrier.

"Mama!" the little girl called out softly while pulling on her mother's sleeve, "Let's go inside!"

Lien-po's wife pushed her away lightly, not daring to budge.

"Father." Lien-chung still hung his head: "Elder Brother has gone to jail! You'd better go see him."

"What?"

"My brother was taken in and jailed by the police department last night at the Sung's house!"

"That's impossible!"

"It's true he didn't come home all night last night," said Lien-po's wife, beginning to worry.

"What about Feng Yu-ts'ai? Just ask him and everything will be clear." The old man still did not believe Lien-chung's words.

"Feng Yu-ts'ai was taken in too!"

"You say the police department took them in?" The old man had begun to worry too. "Taking in their own people? What for?"

"I can't tell you for sure." Lien-chung mustered up his courage to look at the old man: "It's very complicated!"

"Then set it straight, you fool!"

"Grandfather had better go and find out!" Lien-po's wife was turning pale.

"Do I know where they are?" The old man's voice was very loud. All he could do was to get angry at his family, because for the moment he had no idea what to do.

"Why don't you go see the chief? If you don't go, I'm going to!" Lien-po's wife was very anxious.

"Where would a woman like you go?" The old man's ire began to rise. "I'll go! I'll go! Indeed, 'when service is needed, the disciples should be available.' You worthless creature!" He pointed at Lien-chung as he cursed.

"Should we call a taxi?" For the sake of his sister-in-law, Lien-chung accepted the bawling out.

"Go and call one!" The old man went to pick up his hat and calling card.

The car arrived. Lien-chung helped his father in, and Lien-po's wife stood by the car door. After watching the car drive off, brother and sister-in-law slowly walked back toward the house.

"What's it all about, Second Brother?"

"I really don't know!" Lien-chung now felt at liberty to talk openly. "It was like this, Big Sister:

ever since that day when I took those two packages of stuff, I've stayed in the area. I couldn't give up my friends and couldn't bear to leave this place. I've lived here all my life! I gave those two packages of stuff to Lung-yun and he gave me a hundred dollars. I simply went back to work in the daytime, and then went to a hotel at night. Every time I thought about the marriage arrangements, I wanted to leave; but after a while I'd forgotten about it again. Luckily I knew father went to sleep early and wouldn't look for me at night. Naturally Lien-po wouldn't ask about me, because he never paid me any attention anyway. Of course I thought about coming to see you many times, because I knew you would be worried. But I really didn't feel like setting foot in this door again. As soon as I see this gate, it's as if I'm worth less than a dog. So that's how I muddled through these last few days. I wasn't really happy, but I wasn't really unhappy either, just getting by. Last night I felt bored and went for a stroll, and I went by the Sung's house at just about nine o'clock. Lien-po's car was parked there by the gate. The gate is on the north side of the road, and the car was parked up against the south wall. There wasn't even a light in the courtyard. The driver was asleep in the car, so I woke him up and asked him what time the Master arrived. He said a long time ago, but that he had just brought the car back to pick up the Chief of Detectives and had waited about twenty minutes without seeing anything. So, he'd taken a nap."

Handing the little girl over to Liu Ma, the two of them sat down on the steps in the warm sunshine. Lien-chung continued, "I pushed the gate a little, but couldn't push it open. Then I knocked, but no one answered. Strange! I waited a while longer, but still there was no activity. I asked the driver what we should do. He said they're surely sleeping inside, or else they've all gone out to the theater. I didn't dare believe him, but I didn't dare knock on the door anymore either. The driver decided just to wait there."

"Didn't you tell me that day that Lung-yun was going to take them away secretly?" Lien po's wife remembered.

"Right, I also suspected that Lung-yun had sent them away and then tricked Lien-po into going in . . ." Lien-chung did not want to continue because he felt that he ought not to be so concerned about his older brother, and that he should not frighten his sister-in-law this way. But those were certainly his feelings at the time. An older brother is still an older brother in the end, no matter how much he hated him. "I decided to go in even if I had to jump over the wall! I was just trying to figure a way, when some people came up from far away, and as they walked under the light in the alley, I could see that the one in front was old Chu, the Brigade Commander of the police department. They must be coming to find Lien-po, I thought, and so I hid behind the car so as not to let them or Lien-po see me there. When they reached the car, they started to talk with the driver. They asked him who he was waiting for, and he laughed and replied who else could he be waiting for. 'Oh, he doesn't know' old Chu said. 'You probably brought Ch'en here, went away to find a place to eat, and just now returned?' I didn't hear the driver say anything—probably just nodded his head. 'All right,' old Chu said again, 'we'll just use your car. Hsiao Feng has to go down to headquarters too!' After he said that, they began to push on the gate. It wouldn't open. They seemed pretty anxious, and old Chu climbed up on the wall; there was a small tree by the wall. In a minute, he opened the gate from the inside and they all went in. I took the opportunity to run farther away and hide in the shadows to wait. After quite a long time they finally came out, but she wasn't with them. The car drove off.

"I took the long way around going to search for Lung-yun. I searched for him until two in the morning, but couldn't find him anywhere. Then I knew things were bad. 'Hsiao Feng has to go down to headquarters too!' Has to go *too!* Didn't that mean Lien-po had already gone? If he could not even protect Hsiao Feng, then he must not be able to look out for himself either! I still didn't dare come home though, because I really didn't have any solid proof. This morning I phoned the Detective Bureau asking for Feng Yu-ts'ai, but he wasn't there. When I came home right now, he was not in his room. I'm sure he's had it too. After phoning, I was even more suspicious, but still didn't have any real evidence. I didn't dare go make inquiries at the Police Department, but I had to find out somehow. Might as well try my luck. I went to look for Manager Sun at the Prosperity Market. He had been taken in last night too, and there was a plainclothes policeman there guarding the door. The shop was open as usual, probably to prevent people from becoming alarmed, but at the same time the clerks were not permitted to leave. I pretended to ask about the price of rice, and a clever older clerk secretly told me, 'taken off in a car last night!' "

"Second Brother!" Lien-po's wife's face had no color at all, and she was in a cold sweat. "Second Brother! Your brother—" She burst into tears.

"Big Sister, don't cry! Let's just wait until Father comes back and then we'll know. It's probably nothing important!"

"He won't live, I know; those two packages of 'white powder!' " she said through her tears.

"It won't come to that! Big Sister! Let's think of something fast!"

That little simpleton Ta-ch'eng ran in with a cookie in his hand: "Uncle Fatty! You bothering Mama again? When he comes back, I'll tell Grandfather and Grandfather will spank you!"

XI

On any ordinary day, given old Mr. Ch'en's clothing and appearance, he could easily drive into the Police Station, but today there were guards posted at the gate with bayonets fixed on their rifles who halted the car as soon as it pulled up. The old man took out his calling card and said that he wanted to see the chief, but the guard on duty told him right there that the chief was not seeing anyone that day. At that point, the old man finally realized that the situation was very serious and he did not dare make a fuss, but immediately got back in the car and drove off to find Director Ch'ien. He knew the situation was serious, but could not think what sort of crime his son could have committed. His son was good in every way.

He probably had offended someone in the department, and it was only necessary to have somebody come in and patch things up for everything to be all right. And if that was not enough, he'd just have to spend a little money and send in a few gifts to butter up a few people and everything should be cleared up in a day or so. These thoughts were enough to make him feel a little more comfortable.

When he met Director Ch'ien, he told him briefly what he knew: "Tzu-mei, old friend, you know that Lien-po is a filial son, and 'there's never been a case of a filial son committing crimes against the authorities.' He could not do anything improper. As for myself, you know just as well, how many families are there like ours these days? It's probably just that Lien-po has accidentally offended someone, so I would like to ask you to mediate a bit and probably it will be easily settled."

"It's probably not too serious. This sort of infighting is a common occurrence in the official world." Director Ch'ien was still gurgling his water pipe. "I'll look into it a bit."

"It would be best if you could go with me to the Police Station, because I still don't really know what has happened. It would be best if we could see the chief and then talk with Lien-po. After that I could plan what to do."

"Let me think about it." The director kept nodding his head. "One ought not to be too hasty in these matters. Let me think about it. There must be a way."

Old Mr. Ch'en began to feel coldly disheartened. "Please Tzu-mei, can you find a way for me to see the chief? If I go alone . . . Could General Wu . . . ?"

"That's right, of course, General Wu is much closer to the authorities than I am. Of course, go and see him!"

Hoping that General Wu would do something on his behalf, old Mr. Ch'en overlooked Director Ch'ien's coolness.

When he saw General Wu, he used only the vernacular to explain why he had come, for fear that the general would not understand otherwise. General Wu very gladly agreed to go with him to see the chief.

At the gate to the Police Station, General Wu was admitted as soon as he handed in his calling card, and old Mr. Ch'en followed behind him. The chief shook hands very warmly with the general, but when he noticed old Mr. Ch'en he knit his brows slightly and nodded his head.

"Mr. Ch'en came here just now but you were probably very busy and he didn't get to see you so I agreed to come with him." General Wu said it all in one breath.

"Oh, yes of course." The chief spoke to General Wu but didn't look at Mr. Ch'en at all. "I'm sorry, but just now I had some very important business."

"Lien-po did not come home last night." Old Mr. Ch'en used every effort to repress his anger. "I heard he was locked up and I'm very worried."

"Oh, yes." The chief still spoke to General Wu. "It's only a matter of procedure, nothing very important."

"Could you tell me, Chief, what law has he violated?" The old man straightened his back and his tone of voice was cold and disrespectful.

"I'm not at liberty to say, old friend." The chief smiled coldly for a moment and turned to face Mr. Ch'en: "It's a classified matter, and a classified matter is something very difficult for friends to do anything about!"

"I appreciate the chief's information." Old Mr. Ch'en understood that it was going to be very difficult to do anything, but he could not imagine what rules Lien-po could have violated. This was certainly a plot by the chief, and he could no longer restrain his anger. "Chief, you know that Lien-po is a filial son and his father is a scholar, and he absolutely could not have done anything dishonest. The chief also has parents and children. I wouldn't dare ask an officer to reveal any secrets; it's only out of a father's love for his son that I came to plead with you in this exceptional manner, to ask you to please tell me what this is really all about! 'A scholar can face death but not ignominy'; I can forfeit this old life of mine, but I cannot bear—"

"Wait, wait, wait, old man, you're going too far!" The chief smiled a little more softly. "You cannot be with him all the time. How can you know everything he does?"

"May I see Lien-po then?" the old man asked.

"I'm really sorry!" The chief lowered his head and then immediately looked up again.

"Chief." General Wu put in a word: "Tell the old man a little, just a little. He's really very worried."

"Of course he's worried. I'm even anxious on his behalf"—the chief smiled slightly—"but in this case I can't help you even if I'm willing to."

"Is Lien-po in very great danger?" The old man's forehead was visibly perspiring.

"Probably, perhaps, maybe not. The case is just now being examined and naturally cannot be finished too quickly. As for me, in whatever area I can exert my authority, I will use every effort, every effort. The chief stood up.

"Wait, Chief, wait." Old Mr. Ch'en also got up. His face was very pale, his cheeks were sucked in, and his whiskers stood on end. "For the last time I'm pleading with you to tell me the general situation. Everybody suffers misfortune and you should not cut them off without a chance! If you mistreat a filial son, your misdeed will be infamous forever. Although I'm old and useless, I'll hound you to the end!"

"Well then, old man, if you really want to know, please wait a minute!" The chief rapped heavily on a bell. A police officer came in and stood most respectfully in front of the desk.

"Bring in the account of the charges against the Chief of Detectives, the complete file!" The chief's face was also white with anger, but he still managed to force a smile in front of General Wu.

Old Mr. Ch'en sat down and his hands trembled on his knees. In a short while the officer brought a sheaf of official papers and put them on the desk. The chief just pushed them in front of General Wu's and Mr. Ch'en's faces. The general did not move. Old Mr. Ch'en skimmed over the top few papers; very quickly skimming over them, he already saw several charges: forcing merchants to give gifts, taking advantage of women from decent families, using public business for private gain, using relief transport to ship private rice, secretly selling stolen goods, etc. The old man could not bear to read further. He rested his hands on the desk and all he could do was tremble. After shaking for quite a while, he used all of his strength to raise his head. His face suddenly became very thin and gaunt, and he spoke very slowly and in a very low voice: "Chief, Chief! Who has not made mistakes? He is not necessarily any worse than others, and these charges are not necessarily all reliable. His life is in your hands, Chief, all you have to do is be lenient! You just close your eyes, and our whole family will be eternally grateful for your mercy!"

"Wherever I can use my authority, I will spare no effort. General Wu, I'll come over to see you some other day!"

General Wu supported the old man out of the building. The general took him home and he did not say a word. Old Mr. Ch'en knew that most of those criminal accusations were true, and some of them were even things he had done in his son's name. He was still not ready, however, to admit that they were all the fault of father and son. The chief should take the major responsibility. The chief had the ability to set all of those accusations aside and not even look at them. His sense of resentment and anger was greater than his shame and his heart seemed to be on fire, but he could not say anything. He hated the fact that his power was too small and he could not immediately take care of the chief. He hated the fact that his fate was so bad. Fate brought him this calamity; not his own faults, but Heaven's mandate!

After he reached home, the more he thought, the more frightened he became. Things would not permit procrastination. He had to start doing something for his son. Fortunately, he had made friends with many powerful people. The first one he thought of was Meng Pao-chai—a new in-law would of course help out. But Meng Pao-chai had not finished his opium and, although he agreed to help, in the end he did not even move. When the old man went to see others, they all told him not to be so anxious, which was only an expression of their unwillingness to do anything. After running around until nighttime, the old man understood that the present-day lack of morality was not caused only by the young men and women on the streets! His friends in morality and duty and the people who came to hear him expound on the classics did not have the least sense of the ancient morality either. He did not have the heart to think of those things, however, because his body was exhausted and his mind was totally confused. Standing in front of the mirror, he could no longer recognize himself. His eyes were deeply sunken and the bags of flesh under his eyes had become scaly, like a pair of flattened-out beetles. He was angry, indignant, confused, bemused, and bitter. He would sacrifice anything if only he could save his son's life. His daughter-in-law was in her room crying loudly. She had taken Ta-ch'eng to see Lien-po and been unable to see him. Hearing her crying, the old man could no longer hold back his own tears. The more he thought, the worse he felt, and he too began to cry out loud.

He wanted only water and did not eat any dinner. He lay down very early, exhausted, but unable to close his eyes. Any thoughts that came to mind he forgot again in the middle. Confused and chaotic, his mind was like a film strip cut up and incomplete. Thinking until he was quite annoyed, he still did not want to rest, but kept hoping that somewhere in the farthest reaches of his mind he would find a good plan. There was no plan forthcoming and he could only call out softly, call out Lien-po's childhood name. Not until three in the morning did he finally fall into a muddled sleep; not really sleeping, but just anxiously and nervously closing his eyes as if he were floating inside a fog. It was as if he kept seeing his son coming home, as if he heard his daughter-in-law crying, and even as if he saw his long dead wife and companion. He never did open his eyes, but was blurred like a lamp wick in the wind, about to be extinguished but not yet extinguished, unable any more to shine for others.

XII

The sun had been up for quite a while, but the old man was just lying there half asleep and half awake, not wanting to see that hopeless light again. Suddenly, his daughter-in-law and Lien-chung started to wail loudly. The old man crawled out of bed, helpless and rather lonely. Without taking time to put on his long robe, he ran hurriedly in to them. His daughter-in-law had already cried until she could not breathe, and he understood. He gritted his teeth as his heart suddenly felt a hot pain and swallowed back a mouthful of paste-like stuff which had rushed up to his throat. Leaning against the doorway, he yelled out, "Lien-chung, your sister-in-law!" He squatted on the floor in a trembling mass.

Lien-chung and Liu Ma helped Lien-po's wife to her feet, but all she could do was gasp for breath.

"Father, a letter came, to pick up the body!" Lien-chung's fat face was swollen and covered with two streaks of yellow waxy tears.

"Yes! Yes!" The old man braced himself on the doorway and pulled himself up, but his arms gave way and he squatted down even lower. "You go, and use my coffin. I still have to take care of the funeral!" He sat back on the floor and wailed uncontrollably.

Old Mr. Ch'en really did send out obituary notices everywhere and gave his son a large and proper funeral. Not very many people came to pay their last respects, however, and the Meng family did not send anyone. General Wu sent a large floral wreath and Director Ch'ien sent an honorary mourning couplet, but not one of Lien-po's friends attended. The old man followed the coffin all the way to the burial ground. Just before it was lowered into the ground, the old man rapped on the coffin and said, "Lien-po, I am still hale and hearty and I will raise and educate your children!" When he finished speaking, he himself burned the mourning couplet that he had written:

A filial son and a loyal official,
    the blowup should not have touched you.
White hair under a lonely lamp:
    how could I transmit the classics
and histories to my grandsons?

After some time had passed, the true events began to become known, and people's opinions began to exhibit a certain fairness. Lien-po's crimes were indefensible, but the crime for which

he had paid with his life was illegally selling heroin—having taken it from criminals and then using flour to replace it. Naturally this was only a "criminal charge," and the real heart of the matter was that he had tried to push out the Chief of Police. Unfortunately, that was just at the time when the government had issued an order strictly cracking down on heroin, and so the chief gained the upper hand. If that order had not been issued, or if it had been in effect for some time, then not only could Lien-po's life have been spared but also the chief, in order to firm up his own position, would at least have had to appoint Lien-po to an additional position. If he could not have executed him, he would at least have had to give him a promotion; those would have been the chief's only alternatives. Neither would he have been able to disclose Lien-po's activities, because Lien-po could either aid the chief or he could mutiny—he had many contacts in the underworld who could cause trouble in the city. Everyone finally concluded that Lien-po and the chief left little to choose between them, but Lien-po's luck was bad; he deserved punishment but not execution.

Quite a few people sympathized with the Ch'en family. No matter what you said, Lien-po was a filial son; what a pity! This gave quite a boost to old Mr. Ch'en's reputation. That mourning couplet of his was already known all over the city. Even the Chief of Police did not dare to finish them off completely. Manager Sun of the Prosperity Market was soon let out of jail and the Ch'en property suffered only slight losses—"How could I transmit the classics and histories to my grandsons?"—what a powerful phrase! The chief did not dare start a family feud and sent over five hundred dollars for the children's education, but old Mr. Ch'en did not accept it.

Since the Ch'en family's property hadn't suffered any great loss, their friends and relatives gradually began to return. About six or seven months later the National Studies Academy's lecture committee once more decided to invite old Mr. Ch'en to deliver the final two lectures in his series on "regulating the heart and cultivating the person." The old man had grown somewhat thinner and slightly more stooped, but his voice was still strong. Many people came to hear him lecture, most of them wanting to see what the old father of the lately executed "filial son" looked like. When the old man mounted the podium, put on his bifocals, and held up his lecture notes with trembling hands, his long beard already had a few white whiskers, but his appearance was still quite impressive. He talked for a while with one hand resting on the lectern and one hand touching his head, and then paused speechless for a long while, as if he'd forgotten something. Suddenly, he took off his glasses and hurriedly came down off the stage. Everyone was extremely confused and they all stood up.

When those in charge of the meeting stopped him, he spoke very anxiously and in a low voice: "I'm worried and I've got to go home! My oldest, my filial son is dead. Lien-chung, although he's an unfilial rascal, must not run away again! He wants to run away, I know! He is not satisfied with the marriage match I made for him. Wants a damned free marriage! I'll go home and take a look and then come back in a while to lecture. I not only can lecture, but also can be an example in my personal actions. Don't try to stop me. I'm worried about my daughter-in-law too. Her husband has died and she's all mixed up. Keeps saying she wants to commit suicide, damned nonsense! She keeps muttering that she killed her husband—something about giving away two packages—such mixed-up gibberish! What a mess! What a mess! When will I ever be able to 'buy a straw raincoat and live in a cloudhidden city in the mountains, and play a flute by the riverside while the moonlight fills the pavilion.'" Having finished his speech, he stooped over slightly, and set off with less than totally steady strides.

Everyone jostled to get outside, and the first ones out could still make out the image of the old man's back with a few wisps of long whiskers flowing around his shoulders.

LING SHU-HUA
(*1904–   *)

In her book of childhood reminiscences, *Ancient Melodies* (London, 1953), Ling Shu-hua does not supply the year of her birth—unreliably given as 1900 in Li Li-ming's *Brief Biographies*—but is otherwise quite candid about her family background. Both her parents were Cantonese, but had lived in Peking for many years before her birth. "When my father was appointed Mayor of the capital" by the Manchu court, Ling recalls, "my family lived in the huge mayor's residence. No one can now tell how many rooms or courtyards it really contained, but I remember little children often lost their way when they walked out alone from their own courtyard. I always failed to find out exactly how many people lived in that house, because the births and deaths of my half-sisters and brothers and the number of new and old servants were never certain. Those I remember clearly were Father, Mother, Father's two concubines whom I called Third Mother and Fifth Mother—my mother was his fourth concubine. (His wife and second concubine had died before I arrived in the family.) My mother had four children, all girls—I was the youngest" (*Ancient Melodies*, p. 11). When Ling Shu-hua was five years old, her father took a sixth wife, who monopolized his favors from then on, to the chagrin of his other concubines. Her formal arrival in the mansion is recorded in the chapter called "A Happy Event," based on a short story of the same title (*I-chien hsi-shih*, 1936).

Like so many top Mandarins of imperial China, Ling's father was at once a sensualist and an elegant scholar-poet taking pleasure in painting and calligraphy. In "A Happy Event," even while awaiting the arrival of the sixth concubine, he inquires of the young heroine why she isn't painting—for long before she took up writing as a vocation, Ling Shu-hua had been painting flowers and mountains in the traditional Chinese style, and she has continued to paint even in her old age. She must have inherited from her father a fastidious taste and a genuine passion for art, but her family background tells us even more clearly why in her subsequent development as a short-story writer she showed such a strong antipathy toward the traditional mode of family life and such an acute insight into the unhappiness of women bound to that mode of existence.

As a middle school student during the initial phase of the new literary movement (1917–19), Ling Shu-hua had been so much under the influence of her father and the spell of traditional Chinese art and poetry that she found the vernacular (*pai-hua*) experiments in verse by Hu Shih and Ping Hsin (1902–   ), the first new-style woman writer to receive nationwide acclaim, quite laughable. It was only in 1925, while she was still a student in the English Department of Yenching University, that she began to assert her independence of her father, who to his dying day disdained to read anything by her in *pai-hua,* and publish her first stories in *Contemporary Review (Hsien-tai p'ing-lun).* Highly impressed by her talent, the editor of that journal, Ch'en Yuan (1896–1970), courted her, and married her in 1927. Ch'en, himself a noted critic and commentator and a prominent member of the Anglo-American wing of Chinese intellectuals, served as dean of college and professor of English at Wuhan University during the period 1929–46. As a campus wife, Ling Shu-hua continued to write short stories until the late thirties and served for three years as editor of *Wuhan Literature (Wuhan wen-i). The Selected Works of Ling Shu-hua (Ling Shu-hua hsüan-chi,* Singapore, 1960) reprints practically all her stories from three previous collections: *The Temple of Flowers (Hua-chih ssu,* 1928), *Women (Nü-jen,* 1930), and *Little Brothers (Hsiao ko-erh-liang,* 1935), plus "A Happy Event."

After Ch'en Yuan was appointed China's first delegate to UNESCO in 1946, Ling Shu-hua moved with her husband to London and became a friend of Vita Sackville-West, who provided an introduction to *Ancient Melodies.* André Maurois wrote a foreword to an album of Ling's paintings published by a French firm. She was in Singapore from 1954 to 1960 as a visiting professor of Chinese at Nanyang University and published there, in addition to her *Selected Works,* a volume of essays entitled *Dreams from a Mountain-Lover's Studio (Ai-shan-lu meng-ying;* Singapore, 1960). Following her husband's death in 1970, she has continued to live in London, though making occasional trips to China.

Our two selections, "Embroidered Pillows" *(Hsiu-chen)* and "The Night of Midautumn Festival" *(Chung-ch'iu wan),* are taken from *The Temple of Flowers,* the volume that established her reputation as the finest female short-story writer up to that time despite the greater popularity of Ping Hsin. Both stories show her "as a keen observer of the frustrations and tragedies of Chinese women in a transitional period" *(History,* p. 84) and a careful artist in her manipulation of irony and symbolism.

C. T. H.

Embroidered Pillows

by Ling Shu-hua

Translated by Jane Parish Yang

Eldest Young Mistress, her head bent over, was embroidering a back cushion. The weather was hot and humid. All the little Pekinese dog could do was lie under the table and pant, his tongue hanging out. Flies buzzed against the windows, spinning lazily in the sullen air. Perspiration trickled down the face of Chang Ma, the amah, as she stood behind her mistress waving a fan. She would blot her face with her handkerchief, but was never able to keep it dry. If she blotted her nose dry, then beads of perspiration appeared on her lip. She saw that her mistress wasn't perspiring as much as she, but her face was flushed in the heat. Her white gauze blouse clung to her damp back. Chang Ma couldn't help blurting out:

"Eldest Young Mistress, stop awhile and cool off. Master said the cushions must be sent over tomorrow, but he didn't say whether it had to be morning or evening."

"He said it was best to send them over before noon tomorrow. I have to hurry. Come closer to fan me," the young mistress answered, then, bending over, returned to her work.

Chang Ma moved to the left and kept on fanning. Examining the embroidery, she clicked her tongue in admiration:

"I used to listen to people tell stories, and I'd think that those pretty young women in the stories, so clever and bright, were just made up by the storyteller. How could I have known there really is such a young lady, as fresh and delicate as a scallion, able to embroider like this! This bird you're making is simply adorable!" A smile formed on the young mistress' mouth, then van-ished. Chang Ma, undaunted, continued enthusiastically:

"Hmm. When this pair of cushions is sent to Cabinet Secretary Pai's house and everyone sees them I'm sure the matchmakers will be coming to see you; the gate will be trampled down by the crowds. By the way, I've heard that Cabinet Secretary Pai's second son is over twenty but still hasn't found a suitable match. Oh, I see what the master has in mind: last time the fortune teller told Mistress this year your marriage star would be on the rise—"

"Chang Ma, don't talk nonsense." Eldest Young Mistress, stopping her embroidery, interrupted. Her face reddened slightly.

The room became still again. Only the sounds of the embroidery needle poking through the satin backing and the slight stirring of the wind could be heard. Suddenly a young girl of thirteen or fourteen shouted from outside the bamboo curtain:

"Mother, I'm here."

"Is that Little Niu? What did you come for in such hot weather?" Chang Ma asked anxiously. Little Niu wore a blue shirt and pants, her brow beaded with perspiration, her oval face purple in the heat. She slipped inside the bamboo curtain and stood by the door, staring at Eldest Young Mistress. She panted: "Mother, yesterday Fourth Sister-in-law told me that it took Eldest Young Mistress half a year to embroider a pair of back cushions—on just the bird alone she used thirty or forty different colored threads. I didn't believe her that there were so many different colors.

Fourth Sister-in-law said if I didn't believe it, I'd better hurry over to take a look because in two days they would be given to someone. I came into the city right after lunch. Mother, can I watch from over there?"

Chang Ma hurriedly tittered: "Eldest Young Mistress, Little Niu wants to look at your embroidery; is that all right?"

Eldest Young Mistress raised her head and looked at Little Niu. Her clothes were filthy. With a gray handkerchief held in her hand, she dabbed at the perspiration on her face; her gaping mouth revealed two rows of big, yellow teeth. Little Niu was staring straight at her. She unconsciously wrinkled her brow and said, "Tell her to go out now; we'll talk about it later."

Chang Ma knew it was because the young mistress thought her daughter was dirty that she didn't let her look. She immediately ordered Little Niu:

"Just look at the perspiration on your nose. Hurry up and wipe your face! I have water for washing your face in my room. Don't make Eldest Young Mistress faint from your stench in this humid weather."

Little Niu appeared extremely disappointed. She heard what her mother said but still didn't want to leave. Chang Ma, seeing that she wasn't going to move, gave her an angry look and said, "Go to my room and wash your face. I'll be right there."

Little Niu pursed her lips, raised the bamboo curtain, and went out. Eldest Young Mistress happened to look up out the window when she was changing threads. She saw Little Niu lifting her lapel to wipe the perspiration off her brow. Most of the lapel was soaked with perspiration. The potted pomegranate trees in the yard, afire with blood-red flowers, shimmered in the sunlight, causing her to feel the oppressive heat even more. On bending back down, she saw her own armpit was blotched with perspiration.

Two years passed quickly. Elder Young Mistress was still at home doing embroidery. Little Niu had already grown as big as her mother and had learned to wear clean clothes. When her mother

returned home for a vacation, Little Niu could unexpectedly act as her replacement.

One summer evening, Little Niu was sitting close to the lamp in one of the side rooms sewing a pair of pillow covers when she heard Eldest Young Mistress calling her. She put down her needle and thread and raced over to the main section of the house.

While she massaged Eldest Young Mistress' legs, she rambled on about this and that: "Eldest Young Mistress, yesterday my godmother gave me a pair of pretty pillow covers. On one side is a kingfisher, on the other side is a phoenix."

"You mean each bird has only one side?" Eldest Young Mistress appeared to mock her.

"There's a long story behind these pillow covers. I even had a fight with my godsister over them. It was Second Sister-in-law Wang who gave them to my godmother. She said they were cut from two large back cushions which has been soiled. They were gorgeous when new. One was embroidered with lotuses and a kingfisher, the other with a phoenix on a mountain of rocks. The very first day someone sent them to her old grandfather, they were placed on chairs in the parlor to use as back cushions. That same night a drunk guest vomited all over a large part of one of them; the other one was pushed off onto the floor by someone playing mahjong. Someone used it as a footstool, and the beautiful satin backing was covered with muddy footprints. When the young master saw them he told Second Sister-in-law Wang to take them away. Later my godmother asked Second Sister-in-law Wang for them to give to me. That night when I got them, I looked at them for a long time. They're simply adorable. More than forty different colors of thread were used on the tail of the phoenix alone. The eyes of the kingfisher looking at the little fish in the pond are embroidered so true to life—they really sparkle. I don't know what kind of thread was used."

When Eldest Young Mistress heard this, her heart suddenly leaped. Little Niu went on talking:

"It's really too bad, such a beautiful thing ruined. When Godmother saw me yesterday, she told me to cut off the dirty part and sew a pair of pillow covers. How could I have known Godsister would be so stingy, saying whenever I see something nice that Godmother has, I think of a way to get it."

Eldest Young Mistress didn't pay attention to the quarrel. She thought back to two summers ago when she had embroidered a pair of exquisite pillow cushions—there were a kingfisher and phoenix on them. When it was too hot then during the day to work the needle, she had often waited until evening to embroider. After she had finished, her eyes bothered her for more than ten days. She wanted to see how this bird compared with the one she had done. She ordered Little Niu to bring that pair of pillow covers to her immediately.

Little Niu brought her the pillow covers, saying: "Eldest Young Mistress, just look, such a nice background of indigo cloud satin all dirtied up. The bird is said to have been raised in relief but now it's already been trampled and it's caved in. Look! The crest of the bird, its beak—the colors are still bright and glossy. Second Sister-in-law Wang said that the kingfisher's eyes used to have two real pearls sewn into them. The lotus has been stained and has turned gray now. The lotus leaves are too big; this part can't be used as part of the pillow cover. There's a little flower beside the mountain of rocks."

Eldest Young Mistress just stared at the two pieces of embroidery. She didn't hear what Little Niu said toward the end. She began to recall that when she had made the crest she had had to embroider it, then take it out, altogether three times. Once her perspiration had discolored the delicate yellow thread. She didn't discover it until she was

through embroidering. Another time she used the wrong color of green for the rock. She had mistaken the color while embroidering at night. She couldn't remember why she had taken it out the last time. For the light pink of the lotus petals, she didn't dare just take up the thread after washing her hands. She had sprinkled her hands with talcum powder before touching it. The large lotus leaf was even harder to embroider. It would have been too uninteresting to use only one color of green so she had matched twelve different colors of green thread to embroider it. After she had finished the pair of cushions and sent them to Cabinet Secretary Pai's house, many relatives and friends offered flattering words and her girl friends made jokes at her expense. When she heard these remarks, she would redden and smile faintly. At night she dreamed she would become spoiled and proud, wearing clothes and jewelry she had never worn before. Many little girls would chase after her to take a look, and envy her. The faces of her girl friends would radiate jealousy.

That was pure fantasy, she had realized soon enough. She didn't wish to think about it anymore and have it upset her. But now she had run into the embroidery again, and one by one her old thoughts returned.

Little Niu, seeing her silent, her gaze fixed on the pillow covers, said, "Eldest Young Mistress, you like them too? This lifelike embroidery is simply adorable. Why don't you start a pair like these tomorrow?"

Eldest Young Mistress didn't hear what Little Niu had said. She could only shake her head in reply.

The Night of Midautumn Festival

by Ling Shu-hua

Translated by Nathan K. Mao

On the night of the Midautumn Festival, the moon had just risen gracefully above the rooftops; in the clear sky no trace of a cloud could be seen. The roofs and the courtyards seemed to be sheeted in hoarfrost, and the trees and the shrubbery, far and near, covered with thin sleet. From time to time the smoke of incense swirled and the scent of fruits and delicacies emanated from the reception room.

Ching-jen had just paid his respects to his ancestors.[1] Still wearing an outer jacket and a skull cap,[2] he paced the reception room and smilingly watched his wife put away articles of worship as she gave orders to the cook: "Later, when you serve dinner, no need to heat the fish again; add some cooking wine to the chestnut chicken and stew it again; also add some sugar to the vegetable dish and stew it some more. The 'Together Duck' is a little tough. Simmer it some more."

"That's right, simmer the 'Together Duck' some more. Could we also add some slices of bamboo shoots to it?" Ching-jen asked his wife, walking up to her. From his beaming face he was quite pleased with her arrangements.

"All right, add some bamboo shoots; fish out the ham bones; make sure the soup doesn't get too greasy."

The cook received her orders and left the room, her arms full of bowls.

Ching-jen sat in a big chair and took off his cap.

As he relaxed against the chair's arm, he closed his eyes momentarily. The dress she had on this evening, he realized, was the same one she had worn on the third day of their honeymoon in the spring. It was made of bluish-green silk, with embroidered golden green floral sprigs on its shoulders, sleeves, and hem. Because she had been quite active during the day, she didn't look as pale as usual; her cheeks were lovely, rosy through her light rouge. She was exceptionally beautiful this evening, he thought; if he were a European or an American, he would, at this moment, passionately hug and kiss her. But the Chinese usually do not indulge in such open demonstrations of affection between husband and wife.

"What do you want to drink, rice wine[3] or grape wine?" she asked, walking up to him with a pleasant smile.

In a euphoric mood, he didn't quite hear what she had asked. But vaguely aware that she must be referring to either food or drink, he replied: "Whatever you like."

"I know nothing about drinks. Let's invite someone to drink with you. How does that sound?"

"Tonight, I just want to drink with you and no one else." With his eyes half closed, he smiled, hinting that she should sit by him.

"I get tipsy with two little cups. But you, even ten cups don't affect you." She had taken his hint

---

[1] Presumably before a small wooden tablet inscribed with ancestors' names.
[2] Traditional Chinese costume worn on formal occasions. The jacket has wide sleeves.
[3] *Hua-tiao,* a type of rice wine produced in Chekiang province.

and sat on a chair to the left of him. Her roundish chin, accentuated by affectionate dimples, appeared especially charming.

Unable to restrain himself, he held her hand, smiled, and said: "I want you to get drunk. This is the first Midautumn we've spent together. It's a festival of family union, and people should be together. Pity that Mother isn't here. She'd enjoy the dishes you cook." Reminded of the loneliness that his mother and sister in the country must be feeling on this festival day, he felt a little downcast. "Mother used to say that if the family stayed together for the Midautumn dinner, they wouldn't be separated for a year. Let's step outside and have a look at the moon before we eat." Together he and his wife went into the courtyard.

At dinner, the second dish had just been served; his wife was still sipping her first cup of wine, and he was about to toast her when Old Tung the doorkeeper rushed in. "Sir, telephone from Mason Lane. The doctor said that your foster sister is failing fast, and they want you there immediately."

"Which doctor said that?" His face turning pale, Ching-jen rose from the table.

"They didn't say which doctor. They hung up right away; they probably used someone else's phone." Old Tung left the room.

"Why is Foster Sister failing so fast? Didn't Dr. Wang say the other day that she could be cured? I didn't think it was so critical," the wife commented, a touch of frost moving over her face.

"I'd better get a good doctor or two to look at her. It's a pity her parents-in-law are too stingy to spend money on her treatment," he said, getting up from the table and preparing to leave.

Although his wife was disconcerted, she was unwilling to see him leave right away, for the "Together Duck" had not been served. If they didn't eat it, she reasoned, the "Together Dinner" would not be complete and might portend some catastrophe. So she quickly pulled him down, saying: "Have some rice before you go. You must eat the rice tonight."

Very much aggrieved, Ching-jen remembered the way his foster sister had looked the last time he saw her. Her thin face was ashen, and her listless and teary eyes had stared fixedly at the top of the bed-net. Though he was in no mood to eat, he nonetheless realized that he must eat the Midautumn dinner. So he yelled: "Bring the rice. Get the rickshaw ready. I'll leave presently."

A servant brought the rice. Quickly he mixed it with some fish broth and swallowed it down in a hurry.

"Where's the duck? Master is almost done with his dinner." The wife became impatient, worried about his leaving without eating the duck.

When the duck was served, he was already rinsing his mouth and hastily putting on his outer jacket. Quite displeased, she looked at him piteously and the rosy hue on her cheeks faded as she said: "Eat a piece of this 'Together Duck' before you go. How can you not eat a piece on this festival day?" She chose a fat piece and put it on his small serving plate.

"No time to eat. She's dying and waiting for me. How can I eat any more?"

Her feelings were hurt. Still afraid that not eating the "Together Duck" would bring misfortune, she pleaded with him in a whisper: "If you don't eat the 'Together Duck,' it will bring bad luck. Ching-jen, you must eat this piece."

Ching-jen felt he must eat. So he sat down and put the piece into his mouth. It was extremely greasy; he spat it out and hurriedly swallowed a mouthful of rice. He rinsed his mouth again and sipped a mouthful of tea.

He walked to the hall outside. "Is the rickshaw ready?" "It's been ready for some time. They called again and urged you to hurry. They said your foster sister wanted to speak with you."

"Tell them I'm on my way." He stepped quickly into the rickshaw, and the puller dashed away.

It was nearly midnight. The moon hung in the middle of the sky; its clear, faint light shone on the windows and made everything look dismal. Sitting by a window in the bedroom, the wife was wrapped in thought. As her thoughts turned to the evening's dinner, she shivered, as if the demon of bad fortune were pushing around that small piece of uneaten duck and deliberating on what to do with Ching-jen.

She seemed lost in a dark, dim forest, engulfed

in terror, chill, and worry. She prayed for a man to console her, to take her hand and take her out of there. She thought that if she could only hold quietly to a dear one's hand—of course, the first person that came to mind was Ching-jen—she'd be free of her worries and fears.

Good. Ching-jen was home. She hurried into the courtyard to greet him. "How was it? Nothing serious, I hope."

Ashen, his eyes red-rimmed, he ran into the reception room and flopped on the guest couch, speaking huskily: "Why do you ask? If I had been there five minutes sooner, I'd have seen her before she died. All because you insisted on my eating that bowl of rice, I was delayed for ten minutes. It's such a pity that in this capital she had only her foster brother, yet she couldn't see him before she died . . . Her death is so sad." His voice was hoarse. It was as if he saw his newly dead sister again—her emaciated face, her dim and tear-filled eyes, her disheveled hair, her body covered by a white bedsheet with yellow paper money[4] strewn over it, and a lone pair of flickering candles on the floor, between which was a cluster of burning incense sticks. The more he thought about her, the sadder he became. He heaved a long sigh.

"*Ai,* we really didn't do right by her. It's bad enough that she was widowed a year after she was married, not to mention that she didn't have any children; she couldn't even see her only foster brother before she died. It's all because you forced me to eat that bowl of rice. Chang Ma said that she asked people to look for me just moments before she died. *Ai,* I didn't do right by her."

To begin with, she regarded death as a taboo subject on a festive day like this. As Ching-jen continued to berate her, she became somewhat piqued. Nevertheless she restrained herself, saying merely, "Don't keep blaming me. It's better not to see a dead person on a festival day."

The word "better" unexpectedly provoked him. Strongly resentful of her air of impatience he said indignantly: "I never thought a young woman like you could be so cold-hearted. She died all alone,

yet you say it was better not to see her. What's 'better' about it?" His grief had turned to anger. For the first time since his marriage, he felt his wife was wrong. After saying this, he stretched out his foot and violently kicked his shoe upward. The heavy shoe accidentally knocked a vase from a small tea table and shattered it into many pieces.

Dumbfounded by his show of temper, the wife had been considering a rebuttal to air her grievances; then, when she saw how he knocked over the vase—another bad omen—instantly, grief and anger took complete control of her. "What's the matter with you? Are you determined to give me a hard time tonight?" she cried. "On this festival day you were unwilling to eat your rice and now you broke the vase. What future is there for us? I might as well—"

She sobbed loudly. Ching-jen had never expected her to be so upset. Already depressed, he felt only more annoyed. "I didn't break the vase on purpose. Why do you, on this festival day, curse about not having a future? And that 'I might as well'—what about it? Why don't you finish what you were trying to say?"

She was crying, her tears soaking her white muslin handkerchief. Haltingly she went on: "What does it matter what I said? It's a festival day and you're deliberately picking on me."

As his wife used a fresh handkerchief to wipe off her tears, he noticed how unsightly her swollen nose was. How her lips, which he had considered pretty, looked purplish without the lipstick, dark and contorted from crying. He also noticed how slanted her plain eyes really were, a flaw he had failed to notice before because he was in love with her. Suddenly he remembered what his mother used to say: "Slanted-eyed women are the most difficult to handle." This was the first time in his married life that he had become aware of her ugliness.

"Who's giving you a hard time? Damn it, I can't reason with women." In a state of despair and melancholy he walked into the courtyard and gazed at the round bright moon, which seemed to be snickering at him. Unconsciously he heaved a

[4] Paper money for the dead to use in the nether world.

long sigh. After pacing around the courtyard a few times, he felt the cold dew dampening his lined jacket and headed toward the bedroom.

His wife was still sobbing. Showing no patience with her, he crawled into bed.

All night long sleep evaded him. He stole a glance at his wife and noted that her lips were green and her eyes swollen from crying. He felt sorry for her, yet he hated her. He decided not to speak to her. It was nearly dawn. Watching her resting on the tiny couch, he fell asleep.

No sooner had he fallen asleep than his foster sister appeared in a dream, wearing the same clothes she had seven years ago when they lived in the same house in the country. As she smiled and beckoned him, he awoke with a start. His mind replayed the scene where she sat on his bed and cared for him in his mother's place during a bout of malaria. He was averse to taking quinine pills, which he considered unsanitary; and she, with tears brimming in her eyes, had fed him sugar water and coaxed him into taking them. As he drank the last mouthful, his lips accidentally brushed against her smooth, scented hand. Instantly feeling an indescribable, sweet sensation, he sniffed hungrily at her hand. She reddened, and he smiled and lay down again. From that time on, she looked a little embarrassed when she saw him, but she also seemed more concerned about him. She had been promised in marriage to a Feng family when she was still a child. When she married into that family the following year, she was grief-stricken, and he shared her grief. Within a year she was widowed. For five years he hadn't seen her, until last spring in the capital. As he reminisced to this point, unknowingly he again sighed.

"I didn't do right by her! I wasn't there when she died. Will she forgive me?" He crawled out of bed. The white light of dawn slid across the window curtain; it was six thirty in the morning.

He was rather sulky, vexed by his quarrel with his wife the night before. When he saw her cover her eyes with her sleeves in her sleep, he felt sorry for her, but he was also convinced that he had been in the right. He walked to the tiny couch and started a conversation. "Go sleep in the bed. How can you sleep here?"

His wife was silent. He stepped out of the bedroom, hurriedly put on his clothes, and left for his foster sister's home to make the funeral arrangements.

It was ten in the evening when he completed all the arrangements for burial clothes and coffin. Since the Feng family couldn't spend much, and since he felt his sister deserved a decent burial, he spent more than two hundred dollars from the profits he made in his own shop on the funeral. For the coffin alone, he deposited more than a hundred and sixty dollars as down payment; still the man in the coffin shop made clear that the coffin was not of the best quality.

Home in his courtyard, he muttered, "At least I've done my best" as he felt the empty wallet in his pocket.

His wife's hair was uncombed, her eyes puffed, and she seemed oblivious to the world around her. Leaning on a bedpost, she was talking to her personal maid.[5] When he entered the room, they immediately stopped talking.

Trying to make conversation, he sat down on a chair and sighed: "Well, I'm finally done with the funeral arrangements."

"Have you had dinner, sir?" the servant asked, offering him a cup of tea.

"Well, more or less. I couldn't really eat while I was busy making funeral arrangements. Have you all eaten?"

"We waited until nine thirty. Missy had only a tiny morsel," the servant replied. After a short pause, she went on: "Did you see the two bills on the desk, sir? They said you promised to settle the accounts today."

"Damn! I forgot that the money I spent today was to pay those bills. What do I do?" Ching-jen twisted a short strand of hair on his forehead, looking a little worried. Turning to his wife, he asked: "Have you spent the hundred dollars I gave you two days ago? Let's use that money to pay the bills."

---

[5] A maid who had been with her before her marriage; probably someone who had taken care of her since childhood.

"Didn't I show you an account of how I spent the money yesterday? You didn't look at it yesterday, and now you demand the money. I've never wasted a penny of yours. I don't have a foster brother to give me money or worry about me."

With a bellyful of grievances, the wife had been waiting for this chance to express them. She became garrulous.

"My God you're strange. What evil spirit's possessed you these last two days? All you want to do is argue with me. What kind of talk is that, a foster brother giving you money to spend? She's dead now; stop saying such nasty things. I really have to get away from you."

"I knew a long time ago that you didn't care for me. I'd better go back to my mother's. Why do you have to pick on me? You embarrassed me on the festival day. What did I ever do to deserve that?" Still sobbing, she yelled, "Yang Ma, pack up; we're going to my mother's. My family can afford to feed one extra mouth. I'm not—" Weeping, she stood up and began to pack.

That evening, the wife tearfully returned to her mother's and stayed there for three days. Ching-jen's friends urged him to bring her home. Still feeling upset, however, he did not go. Every evening he and a few acquaintances, whom he normally didn't often see, visited pleasure haunts, went to the Peking opera, and followed fashionable ladies in the streets; sometimes he had simple dinners in small restaurants and drank *pai-kan* wine,[6] and when he was drunk, he shouted bravos at entertainers in opera houses and frequently got home at one or two o'clock in the morning.

A month went by. Ching-jen's mother-in-law had heard a great deal about Ching-jen's escapades and became worried for her daughter. On the day of the Double Ninth Festival,[7] she brought her daughter back to him. Though husband and wife no longer quarreled, there had been erected between them a chilly stone tablet on which was inscribed: "You are mere dinner partners who share the same quilt."

By now Ching-jen was familiar enough with the pleasure dens. In the spring of the second year, he upgraded his dissipation by becoming a regular patron of an establishment in Stone Alley. By the Midautumn Festival of the second year, he had sold his grocery store and used half the money to pay off debts at the Pao Ch'eng Jewelers and Lao Chieh-fu Silk and Brocade Shop for two of the establishment's girls.

In the second month of the second year, his wife miscarried a seven-month-old boy with handsome features. The miscarriage was caused by her frequent bouts of anger during pregnancy, which in turn had damaged the embryo, the doctor said. Because of this, the wife lay sick for three months, growing haggard in appearance. She had aged considerably. Ching-jen was often not at home, and he slowly realized that she was very ugly. When spoken to, he would seldom bother to respond to her.

In the third year, Ching-jen's mother came from the country to visit him. She saw how addicted Ching-jen was to pleasure, how the family's grocery store was gone and the deed of the remaining paper shop was mortgaged, though he still ran the business. When her son would not listen to her, she blamed her daughter-in-law's stupidity. Had her daughter-in-law attended to his needs properly, she reasoned, her son would not have squandered the family fortune. Hence, every day she cast unpleasant looks at her daughter-in-law from morning to night.

On the night of the third Midautumn Festival, the wife hid in the kitchen, silently wiping her tears and watching the hearth fire. She dared not cry out loud. The same evening, Ching-jen suddenly remembered the death of his foster sister three years before. To his mother he blamed his wife for everything. And since the foster sister had always been a favorite of hers, the mother, after hearing the story, scolded the wife severely.

Toward the end of the eighth month, Ching-jen's wife miscarried another boy at six months. Because the boy's nose was not fully formed, and he had only one ear and a few fingers, everyone

---

[6] A type of liquor made from sorghum.

[7] Also known as Ch'ung-yang Festival; takes place on the ninth day of the ninth month by the Chinese calendar. This day is traditionally celebrated by climbing mountains.

called it a freak. The doctor, upon examining it, said that the deformities were caused by syphilis.

On Midautumn Festival of the fourth year, Ching-jen's reception room was full of spider webs. When the moon climbed up over the roof ridges, one could see shadows of dark bats flying and fluttering their wings under the moon. From a small room by the kitchen came the voices of two women. One was Ching-jen's wife, the other probably her mother.

"*Ai,* do you have to move out the day after tomorrow?"

"Of course, without delay. We were supposed to hand over the house tomorrow. Fortunately, when I begged them they allowed me to stay here for one extra day."

"Are you certain that Ching-jen won't come to get you?"

"No, he won't. Last night Second Master Wang told me that he's moved to the *san-pu-kuan* area." [8]

"*Ai,* who would have thought that the family could fall to such a sad state!"

"No, I guess no one could. But, Mother, this is probably my fate." She blew her nose and sobbed: "On the first Midautumn Festival after my marriage, he and I quarreled. He had a piece of 'Together Duck,' which he spat out. At the time I was rather uneasy about it. Later, when his shoe knocked over an offering vase[9] I knew for sure it was a bad omen."

"It's the will of Heaven. Who can avoid these catastrophes? I think you'd better be more cheerful, try to be good, and wait for your next life."

After the old woman had said all this, she coughed a few times and started to blow her nose.

It was after two in the morning; the weak oil lamp in the tiny room was near death, and darkness blackened the paper windows. There were still two or three moths ramming themselves against the windows. A little later the light died; moths fell into the chill frost, turned dewy white, and went to meet their Creator. Heavy breathing, mingled with intermittent *ai-yo ai-yo* sounds, emanated from the tiny room. The noises of moths plunging against the windows still lingered.

As usual, the moon slowly spread a thin layer of cold frost on the courtyard and covered the treetops in the forest with silvery sleet. Fatigued, the bats went into hiding. In the moonlight, the spider web along the big pillar, blown by a gentle breeze, reflected a faint silken ray.

---

[8] An area beyond the jurisdiction of the French, Japanese, or Chinese authorities located between the French and Japanese Concessions in Tientsin.

[9] A vase used in religious ceremonies honoring departed ancestors.

JOU SHIH
(1901–1931)

On February 7, 1931, five young Communist writers—Jou Shih, Hu Yeh-p'in, Feng K'eng, Li Wei-sen, and Yin Fu—along with eighteen other Party members were executed in Lunghwa, Kiangsu, on charges of conspiracy against the Nationalist government. Though they were all writers of small talent, they have been assured posthumous honor in Chinese Communist literary history as the Five Martyrs. The real story of the betrayal of these twenty-three by their comrades is fascinatingly told in Tsi-an Hsia's *The Gate of Darkness* (Seattle, 1968), which also discusses the personalities and literary works of the five minor authors.

The oldest of the five, Jou Shih (pen name of Chao P'ing-fu) was a native of Ninghai, Chekiang. Under the guidance of two teachers at the First Normal School in Hangchow, the famous writers Chu Tzu-ch'ing and Yeh Shao-chün, he showed an early interest in literature and wrote a number of poems as a member of the Morning Light Society (Ch'en-kuang she). Upon graduation in 1923, he taught in a primary school for two years and then went to Peking, where he attended classes at the National Peking University as an unregistered student. In 1926, after less than a year's stay in the capital, however, he had to resume his career as a teacher in his home town to provide for his family. He was promoted to director of education of Ninghai in the following year, but as a consequence of his increasing involvement in radical politics, he lost his position in 1928 and fled to Shanghai.

While in Shanghai, Jou Shih renewed his acquaintance with Lu Hsün, whose lectures he had attended in Peking. The senior writer took a paternal interest in the youth and entrusted to him various editorial duties in connection with his magazines. In 1930 Jou Shih joined the Communist Party as well as the League of Leftwing Writers, not knowing that his political and literary career would be so soon terminated.

Almost identical in content, *Jou Shih: Selected Works* (*Jou Shih hsüan-chi*, Peking, 1951) and *Fiction by Jou Shih: A Selection* (*Jou Shih hsiao-shuo hsüan-chi*, Peking, 1954) exclude all his translations and the bulk of his creative writings. The two major items preserved therein are an autobiographical novel entitled *February* (*Erh-yüeh*, 1929) and the story chosen for this volume, "A Slave-Mother" (*Wei nu-li ti mu-ch'in*). The latter, especially, shows our author at his best as a writer of "sobriety and restraint" who maintains "a plain flawless style" even in the telling of a shocking story (*The Gate of Darkness,* p. 194), and has deservedly become a favorite piece for anthologists in China and abroad.

C.T.H.
J.S.M.L.

A Slave-Mother

by Jou Shih

Translated by Jane Parish Yang

Her husband was a fur trader who collected furs and cow hides from hunters in the country and sold them in the larger seaport. Sometimes he also did a little farmwork in mid-June, helping others transplant rice seedlings. He could plant each row in a very straight line. If there were five workers in the rice paddy, he'd be the one to stand in the lead position to set the standard. Still, his financial situation was never good. Debts piled up year after year, and so he began to smoke, drink, and gamble. He turned into a cruel and violent man, and became even poorer. People wouldn't agree to lend him even the smallest amount of money.

After an illness, his whole body became a withered sallow color, his face as amber as a brass drum; even the whites of his eyes turned yellow. People said he had jaundice. The children all called him "Yellow Fatty." One day he said to his wife: "There's no other way out. If things continue like this, we'll have to sell even the small frying pan. I've been thinking. I should find some way to make use of you. What good is it for you to starve along with me?"

"Make use of me?" she stammered in a low voice. His wife was sitting behind the stove, holding her son to her breast. The child had just turned three but was still nursing.

"Yes." Her husband's voice had been listless since his illness. "I've already pawned you . . ."

"What?" His wife nearly fainted.

The room became still for a moment. He wheezed: "Three days ago, Wang the Wolf came here and spent half the day trying to get his loan back. I left with him and walked down to Nine Acres Pond. I didn't want to live anymore. I just sat under a tree, that one you can climb up and in one leap jump off into the pond. I thought about it but didn't have the energy to do it. An owl was hooting into my ear. It took away all my courage and I got up and returned home. But on the way back I ran into old Granny Shen. She asked me, "What are you doing out so late?" I told her, and asked her to lend me some money, or at least get a girl in someone's family to lend me some clothes or jewelry to pawn for a while. Otherwise Wang the Wolf's green, wolfish eyes would be gleaming in my house every day. But she just smiled:

" 'What are you still keeping your wife at home for? And look at yourself, you look so sick and shrunken too.'

"I stood in front of her with my head down, not saying anything. She said, 'You have only one son, of course you can't give him up, but your wife—'

"I thought then: 'Can it be that she wants me to sell my wife?' And she continued: 'But your wife—although she's your formal wife—when you're poor, it can't be helped. What are you keeping her at home for?'

"Then she spoke right out: 'There's this *hsiu-ts'ai*.[1] He's already fifty but doesn't have a son, and wants to buy a concubine. His first wife won't let him and will only allow him to get one on loan

[1] The lowest degree conferred upon successful candidates under the former civil service examination system.

for a few years. He told me to go look for a likely person, about thirty, who's raised two or three sons. Quiet, honest type, willing to work and be submissive to his first wife. This time it was the *hsiu-ts'ai*'s wife who asked me. If I could find someone who fit those conditions, they'd be willing to put up eighty to a hundred dollars. I've been looking around for such a woman for a long time but haven't found anyone.' She said since she had run into me just then, she started to think about you. Everything about you fits the description. She asked me my opinion. I cried, but she pressed me and I agreed."

He hung his head, his voice feeble, then abruptly stopped. His wife was simply stunned. She couldn't say a word. After some moments of silence, he continued:

"Yesterday old Granny Shen went to the *hsiu-ts'ai*'s house. She said he and his wife were most satisfied. The price was one hundred dollars for a period of five years, unless you can produce a son in three. Old Granny Shen also decided on a date—the eighteenth of this month, five days from now. Today, she went to get the written agreement."

By this time, his wife was trembling all over. She gasped, "Why didn't you tell me earlier?"

"I was pacing the floor before you all day yesterday but just couldn't bring myself to tell you. But after giving it some thought, I realize that unless I use you as a way out, there *is* no way out."

"It's final, then?" Her teeth chattered.

"Everything except the contract."

"What rotten luck! Is there really no other way out? Ch'un-pao's Dad?"

Ch'un-pao was the name of the child in her arms.

"Rotten luck indeed. I thought so too. We're poor, but if we don't want to die, what else can we do? This year I don't think I can even plant rice seedlings."

"Have you given any thought to Ch'un-pao? He is only four years old. How can he do without a mother?"

"I'll take care of him. He's weaned."

He seemed to be getting angry, and walked outside. She began to cry.

She remembered back to what happened exactly a year ago: she had given birth to a girl. She lay on the bed as if she were dead. In death, however, she would at least have been whole, but then her limbs and body seemed ripped apart. The newly born girl lay on a pile of dry grass on the floor crying in a loud voice, her feet drawn in and hands in tight fists. The umbilical cord was wrapped about her body, and the placenta was fallen to one side. She wanted to gather her strength to get up and wash her, but when she raised her head, her body was still frozen to the bed. She saw her husband, this cruel, hard man, face beet-red, carry a bucket of boiling water over to the little girl. She used the very last strength she could muster to scream at him: "Wait! Wait!" But this man, who had been cruel even before he got sick, didn't allow her a moment's discussion. Without a word in reply, he picked up the loudly screaming little girl, this newborn life, in his coarse hands, like a butcher holding a lamb to be slaughtered, and tossed her in the boiling water. Besides the sound of water splashing and the hissing of the boiling water as it touched her skin, there was no sound. She wondered, why didn't the child scream out? Was the girl willing to be wrongly put to death without so much as a cry of protest? Oh, she realized now, that was because she had fainted then. She had fainted away as if her heart had been gored out.

As she thought back over it, her tears finally dried. "Oh, this wretched life!" She sighed softly. Ch'un-pao stopped sucking her nipple, looked up at his mother's face, and cried, "Mama, mama!"

The night before her departure, she chose the darkest corner of the house to sit in. An oil lamp was lit in front of the stove, the light flickering like a firefly. She held Ch'un-pao in her arms, her head pressed against his hair. Her thoughts seemed to have drifted far away, but she couldn't be sure where. Then slowly they returned, back to her field of vision, back to her child. She whispered softly to him:

"Ch'un-pao, my precious!"

"Mama!" The child gurgled, still sucking her nipple.

"Mama has to leave tomorrow."

"Eh?" The child didn't seem to understand, but instinctively buried his head in her breast.

"Mama won't be coming back, not for three years."

She wiped her eyes. The child stopped sucking and asked, "Where is mama going? To the temple?"

"No, thirty *li* away from here, to a family named Li."

"I want to go too."

"Ch'un-pao, you can't go along."

"*Wa!*" protested the child, and suckled a little milk.

"You stay at home with papa. Papa will take care of you. He'll sleep with you and take you out to play. Now you have to be a good boy and listen to what papa tells you. In three years . . ."

She didn't finish. The child, on the verge of tears, said, "Papa will hit me!"

"Papa won't hit you anymore." She stroked the child's right temple with her left hand. His father had struck him there with the handle of a hoe three days after he killed the newly born baby girl. The wound, once swollen, was now more or less healed.

She seemed to have more to say to the child, but her husband came in the door. He walked over to her, a hand in his pocket, and pulled out something, saying, "I've already got seventy dollars of it. They'll pay the other thirty ten days after you get there."

After a pause, he added, "They agreed to send a sedan chair." After another pause, he continued, "They also promised to feed the carriers breakfast before sending them over in the morning." After that he walked away from her and went inside. That evening, she and her husband didn't eat supper.

The next day, the spring rains fell.

The sedan chair would arrive early, but she didn't sleep at all that night. She mended the few articles of clothing Ch'un-pao had. Spring was almost over and summer soon to come, but she even took out his ragged padded jacket that he wore in winter, intending to give to her husband. The man, though, had gone to bed. She sat by his side, thinking to say something to him, but as the long night slipped away, not a word was said. When she had gotten up her courage to call to him a few times, she mumbled something indistinctly, the sound beyond his hearing. She then gave up and lay down to sleep. Just when her thoughts had quieted down and she was about to fall asleep, Ch'un-pao awoke. He poked her, calling "Mama, I want to get up." While dressing him, she said, "Ch'un-pao, you be good at home, don't cry or your father will hit you. From now on, Mama will always buy candy to bring home to give you, so don't cry."

The young child didn't know what grief was. He opened his mouth and began to sing. She kissed him and said, "Don't sing now, you'll wake up Papa."

The sedan carriers sat on stools by the door, talking among themselves. After a moment, old Granny Shen from the neighboring village arrived. The shrewd old matchmaker entered the house, and brushing raindrops from her clothes, announced: "It's raining. A good omen that your family will flourish from now on."

The old lady bustled around the room, then sidled up to the child's father. She was trying to get payment for her trouble, since it was through her efforts that he was offered such a favorable contract.

"To tell the truth, father of Ch'un-pao, with another fifty dollars the old man could have bought a concubine," she said.

She turned around to hurry the woman. The woman was holding Ch'un-pao, sitting there with no intention of moving. The old lady raised her voice. "The sedan-carriers have to make it home for lunch. Hurry up and get ready!"

But the woman just looked at her, as if to say: I don't want to go. Let me stay here and starve.

The words were stuck in her throat, but the old lady understood them. She walked up to her, smiling broadly.

"You're really a naïve woman! What can 'Yellow Fatty' give you? Those people over there have more food than they can eat, more than two hundred *mou* of land. They're very well off. The house is theirs; they have hired hands to raise cattle. Ta-niang[2] has a good temperament, she's very polite to others. Whenever she sees someone, she gives that person food to eat. And the old man—really, he's not so old—he has a fair complexion, no beard. Because he reads so much, his back's a little hunched, but he is such a gentle person. There's really no need for me to tell you. You'll see for yourself and you'll know I'm not making up anything."

The woman dried her tears, and almost to herself said: "Ch'un-pao. How can I leave him like this?"

"Don't worry about him." The old lady put a hand on her shoulder, moving her face close to them. "He's already four years old. As the old saying goes: 'A child of three, from the mother's free.' He can live without you. If you're lucky and raise a son or two for the old man over there, then everything will be fine."

The sedan-carriers outside were calling that they had to be on their way, jabbering, "She's not a bride; what's all the crying about?"

The old woman pulled Ch'un-pao out of her arms, saying, "Now let me take care of Ch'un-pao." The little child cried and thrashed about, but the old woman finally got him outside the door. As the woman entered the sedan chair, she turned toward her husband and the old woman: "Take the boy inside. It's raining."

Her husband, his head propped in his hands, sat motionless and silent.

The two villages were thirty *li* apart, but the second time the sedan chair was set down, they were there. The light spring rain blew in the covered sedan chair and wet her clothes. A woman in her early fifties, with a plump face and crafty eyes, came to greet her. She thought: this must be Ta-niang. But she only gazed at her in some embarrassment without greeting the elderly lady, who cordially helped her out onto the steps. A rotund man with a long thin face appeared. He looked her over carefully, then, face wreathed in smiles,

asked: "Here so early? Your clothes got all wet."

The old woman, as if she hadn't heard what he said, asked, "Is there anything else inside?"

"No," the young woman replied.

Several women from the neighborhood stood outside the gate and peeked in after they had gone inside the house.

She didn't know why, but her mind was on her own home, and she couldn't stop thinking of Ch'un-pao. Obviously she should be happy for the beginning of the three years she was to spend here. This household, and the husband who had obtained her on loan, were much better than her own, and the *hsiu-ts'ai* turned out to be as friendly as he was said to be. He spoke in such a soft voice. Even Ta-niang was not what she had imagined. She was attentive and friendly in her discourse, speaking of her life with her husband, from the beginning of their happy marriage thirty years ago to now. She had been pregnant once, fifteen or sixteen years ago, and gave birth to a son. According to her, he was a beautiful and intelligent child, but died of smallpox before he was ten months old. She hadn't had another child. The old woman implied that she had wanted her husband to take a concubine, but somehow this had never materialized. Perhaps it was because he cared for her too much to take another woman, or a suitable one was not available. Anyway, Ta-niang was not clear on this point, and the situation had remained unchanged until now. What was clear was that Ta-niang's speech had made the young woman sad, bitter, happy, and depressed in short turns, good-natured as she was. In the end, the old lady told her what she hoped for. Her face turned red with embarrassment, but the old woman went on:

"You've had children of your own and of course you know. You certainly know more than I do about it."

Then she left.

That evening, the *hsiu-ts'ai* also told her all about the family, either to impress her or to flirt with her. She sat by a dresser of red wood and had her eyes fixed on it, because it was something she didn't have in her other house. The *hsiu-ts'ai* sat down in front of the dresser and asked:

"What's your name?"

She didn't reply and without smiling, arose and walked over to the bed. The *hsiu-ts'ai,* following her, asked with a smile: "Are you shy? Ah, you must be thinking of your husband! But I'm your husband now." He spoke lightly, and took her sleeve. "Cheer up a bit. You're thinking of your child too, aren't you? But—"

He didn't finish, but gave a laugh and took off his outer robe.

She could hear Ta-niang outside the room cursing someone in a loud voice, though she couldn't tell whom she was cursing. It could either be the cook or herself. Since Ta-niang must resent her, she felt herself to be the object of the curses. The *hsiu-ts'ai* called from the bed: "Come to bed. She's always nagging like this. She used to be very fond of one of the hands, but because he likes to talk to Mrs. Huang in the kitchen, she's always cursing her."

The days passed. The memory of her former home faded. Her present life became more familiar to her. Even so, sometimes the sound of Ch'un-pao's crying echoed in her ears. She dreamed of him several times too. But such dreams became fewer and fewer as her duties increased. She knew the old woman was jealous and suspicious. Outwardly she acted generously, but her jealousy made her behave like a spy, monitoring her husband's every movement and gesture. Sometimes when the *hsiu-ts'ai* returned home, if he happened to meet the young woman first he would of course talk to her first. Then the old one would suspect him of giving her something special. That very evening she would call him to her chamber and lecture him harshly. "Are you bewitched by that fox?" "Go weigh yourself, you old bag of bones! Still acting so shameless at your age!" The younger woman had heard words like these on more than one occasion. After that, whenever she saw the *hsiu-ts'ai* coming home and Ta-niang wasn't sitting next to her, the young

woman would hurriedly evade him. Even if she were there, she would still try her best to stay away from him, though she was careful to make her exit as natural as possible, so that others would not notice her, for fear that Ta-niang would explode and say she intentionally humiliated her. After that, she was burdened with more and more of the housework, her position no better than a maid's. But she was a rather clever woman. Sometimes when the old woman changed her clothes, she would wash them for her. Then Ta-niang would say: "Why should you wash my clothes for me? Even your own clothes you should have Mrs. Huang wash for you." But almost immediately she would say: "Younger Sister, you'd better go out and take a look at the pigpen. Why are those two pigs oinking so? They might still be hungry. Mrs. Huang never feeds them enough."

After eight months, that next winter, her appetite changed: she had no taste for rice, and she wanted fresh noodles or sweet potatoes. But after a few meals, she was tired of these too and wanted won-ton dumplings. If she ate too much, she would vomit. In addition she craved pumpkins and plums. But those wouldn't be in season until the sixth month and were extremely scarce. Where could they be found? The *hsiu-ts'ai* knew what this change meant. He went around with a smile on his face all day. He made an effort to get whatever was available. He himself went to buy oranges, and asked others to bring back tangerines. He would pace back and forth under the veranda murmuring to himself. When he saw her milling rice for New Year's with Mrs. Huang, he'd tell her to rest before she had gotten even three pecks ready. "Stop and rest. The hired hand can do it. Everyone wants to eat glutinous rice cakes."

Sometimes in the evening, when others were talking, he'd be off by himself with a lamp reading the *Book of Songs:*

Kuan-kuan cry the ospreys
On the islet in the river.
The modest, charming young lady
Is a good match for the gentleman.[3]

---

[3] Adapted from James Legge's translation; *The Chinese Classics* (Taipei, 1972), vol. 4, p. 1.

Then the hired hand would ask, "Master, you're not going to sit for any examination; what are you reading that for?"

He would stroke his clean-shaven lips and reply with pleasure: "That's right. Do you know what life's pleasures are? 'Candles lit on the wedding night, success in the imperial exam.' You know what that means? These are the happiest moments of one's life. I'm already past that. But I have something even better."

Everyone except his two wives would laugh.

The old woman was really annoyed by all this. At first, she was delighted by the news of the pregnancy, but when she saw how the *hsiu-ts'ai* went to such lengths to please the younger woman, she then loathed her own barrenness. Once, in the third month of her second year there, the young woman felt sick and headachy, and slept for three days. The *hsiu-ts'ai* wanted her to rest and often came to see if she needed anything. The old woman was furious. She accused her of pretending to be sick and nagged her about it for three days. At first she maliciously ridiculed her, saying she had begun putting on airs the minute she arrived—her back was sore, or her head hurt—affecting the pose of a real concubine. She said she didn't believe she'd been so pampered at her own house. Rather, she must have been more like a mangy bitch. Belly pregnant with pups, she still had had to scurry around begging for food before giving birth. But now because "that old thing"—the name Ta-niang used to refer to her husband—fawned over her, she was acting spoiled.

"Who hasn't raised a son?" she was once heard saying in the kitchen to Mrs. Huang. "I've been pregnant myself—what's so difficult about it? And besides, right now that thing in her womb is still just a name in the King of Hell's record book.[4] Who can guarantee that it is a boy and not a scabby toad? Only after that baby worms its way out for me to see can she put on airs in front of me. Right now it's no more than a bloody hunk. Don't you think she's acting up a bit too early?"

That evening the younger woman had gone to bed without eating supper. When she heard the oblique curses and mockery, she began crying softly. The *hsiu-ts'ai*, dressed and sitting in bed, broke into a cold sweat and began to tremble when he heard what Ta-niang had just said. He wanted to fasten his robes and get up again and give Ta-niang a sound beating— grab her by her hair and thrash her to vent his rage. But for some unknown reason he didn't seem to have the strength; even his fingers were trembling, his arms limp and sore. He sighed, "*Ai*, I've been too good to her. We've been married for thirty years and I've never hit her. I've never even so much as grazed her skin with my fingernail. No wonder she's become as difficult as Her Majesty the Empress."

Saying this, he crawled over to the young woman's end of the bed, drew close to her side, and whispered in her ear: "Don't cry, don't cry. Let her screech. Really, she's like a hen without a womb, so she can't stand seeing others hatching eggs. If you can give me a son, I'll give you two jewels—I have a blue jade ring and a white jade . . ."

He didn't finish what he intended to say, as he could no longer bear to hear Ta-niang's mocking laughter reverberate outside his door. He hurriedly disrobed and, slipping under the covers, pressed his head to her breast:

"I have white jade . . ."

Her belly grew larger day by day, to the size of a bushel basket. The old lady finally hired a midwife, and openly began making baby clothes from some patterned cloth.

June was spent in hope, the hottest month in the lunar calendar when summer neared its end. At the beginning of autumn, cool breezes swept over the village.

One day, their hopes reached a climax. The atmosphere in the house became agitated. The *hsiu-ts'ai* was unusually nervous, pacing back and forth in the courtyard. He held an almanac in his hand,

---

[4] A superstitious belief in the operation of reincarnation which holds that until a child is born, his or her "soul" is kept in the King of Hell's register.

as if he were memorizing it, mumbling over and over *wu-ch'en, chia-hsü,* and the year of *jen-yen.*[5] At times he glanced anxiously in the direction of the room with closed windows. In this room lay the mother in labor, moaning in a low voice. Then he looked up at the sun obscured by banks of clouds, walked to the door, and asked Mrs. Huang, who was standing at the door:

"Well? How's she doing?"

Mrs. Huang gave a silent nod, then after a pause, added: "Any minute now."

Then he again took up his almanac and paced back and forth on the veranda.

This went on until dusk. When kitchen smoke rose into the air and lamps lit up in the houses like spring flowers bursting into bloom, the child arrived. It was a boy.

The child screamed loudly inside the house. The *hsiu-ts'ai* slumped in a corner, so happy that he almost cried. No one felt like eating dinner. Before the plain dishes on the table, Ta-niang announced to everyone:

"Keep it a secret for a while so the little cat won't run into bad luck.[6] Should anyone ask, say it's a girl."

They all nodded, smiling contentedly.

One month later, the child's soft, white face shone in the autumn sunlight. The younger woman nursed him while the neighboring women gathered around to look. Some praised his mouth, others praised his ears, still others praised the child's mother, saying she was stronger than before and her complexion fairer. Ta-niang appeared as protective and doting as a grandmother, saying, "That's enough for now, don't make him cry."

The *hsiu-ts'ai* racked his brains to think of a name for the child, but couldn't come up with an appropriate one. The old lady wanted to choose a character from the sayings "Longevity, wealth, and prominence" or "Fortune, prosperity, longevity, and happiness." Still the best was "Longevity"

or a synonym like "Ch'i-i" or "Peng-tsu."[7] But the *hsiu-ts'ai* wouldn't have it, feeling they were too vulgar, names anyone might choose to use. So he paged through the *Book of Changes* and the *Book of History* in search, but half a month passed, then a whole month, and he still hadn't found a suitable name. The name should bring fortune to the child on the one hand and signify his getting a son late in life on the other, so it wasn't an easy task.

One day, as he was holding the three-month-old child, he leafed through his books looking for a name. He wore a pair of glasses and held the book in the lamplight. The child's mother sat woodenly to one side, lost in thought, when she suddenly blurted out:

"I was thinking, wouldn't it be better to call him 'Ch'iu-pao'—Autumn Treasure?" Everyone turned to look at her and listened in silence. "Wasn't he born in autumn? Treasure of Autumn—let's call him Ch'iu-pao."

"That's right." The *hsiu-ts'ai* immediately followed up: "I've been trying to think of just such a name. I'm over half a century old—truly in the autumn of my life. The child was born in autumn. Autumn is the season when everything comes to maturity. Ch'iu-pao is truly a good name for him! And doesn't the *Book of History* have it: 'Then there was Autumn'? Now I truly have my 'autumn'!"

Then he praised the child's mother, saying it was really useless being a bookworm like himself because intelligence was innate. His praise made the woman feel uncomfortable sitting there. She lowered her head and smiled sadly with tears in her eyes. She thought to herself: "It was only because I was thinking of Ch'un-pao, my Spring Treasure."

Ch'iu-pao, growing up into a lovely child, wouldn't leave his mother's side. He had unusually large eyes and never tired of gazing at strangers. However, he could immediately recog-

---

[5] The *hsiu-ts'ai* is figuring out the possible time and date of the child's birth in terms of the Decimal and Duodecimal cycles in the Chinese calendar.

[6] It used to be a superstitious practice in China to give an extremely precocious boy, or as in the present case, a much hoped-for child, a name such as "pig," "dog," or "cat" so as to ward off the jealousy of the gods.

[7] Ch'i-i lived to be a hundred; Peng-tsu is the Chinese Methuselah.

nize his mother from a distance. He clung to her all day long. Although the *hsiu-ts'ai* loved him more than she did, he didn't like his father. Ta-niang, on the surface, loved him as if he were her own son, but the child's large eyes gazed at her as if she were a stranger in his odd untiring way. He clung closer to his mother as the days of her leaving drew near. Spring overtook winter, summer came close upon the spring, and soon everyone became aware of the fact that the mother's three-year contract was about to expire.

The *hsiu-ts'ai*, because he loved the child, first broached the subject with Ta-niang. He wanted to take a hundred dollars and buy her outright. But his first wife answered:

"If you want to buy her, then poison me first!"

When the *hsiu-ts'ai* heard that, he was so angry he snorted and couldn't speak for a long time. Later, he forced a smile and said: "Think about the child's not having a mother . . ."

The old woman scoffed in a shrill voice: "Oh? I'm not good enough to be his mother?"

The child's mother wrestled with her conflicting feelings: on the one hand, the thought "three years" always went through her mind. Three years would pass quickly, in spite of the fact that she had become like a maid in the *hsiu-ts'ai*'s household. The Ch'un-pao of her imagination was as lively and lovable as the Ch'iu-pao before her. If she couldn't give Ch'iu-pao up, how could she give up Ch'un-pao either? But on the other hand, she really wanted to stay in this new home forever. She figured that Ch'un-pao's father probably wouldn't live very long because of his illness. He would probably live three to five more years. In that time, she could beg her second husband to let Ch'un-pao come stay with her. Then Ch'un-pao could be with her.

Once she sat on a bench in the corridor, crumpled with fatigue. In the rays of the early summer sun, it was easy for her mind to wander. Ch'iu-pao slept in her arms, still sucking her nipple, but she felt as if Ch'un-pao were also standing by her side. She reached out her hand to embrace Ch'un-

pao, at the same time wanting to speak to her two sons, but there was nothing there.

Instead, in a doorway farther down the hall stood the old woman, with her benevolent face and fiendish eyes. Her gaze was fixed on the younger woman. Immediately, wakened from her reverie with a start: "I think I'd better leave this place as soon as possible. She watches over me like a spy." But no sooner had the child in her arms started to cry than she was brought back to the reality before her eyes.

Sometime later, the *hsiu-ts'ai* modified his plan. He wanted to call old Granny Shen over and have her talk to the young woman's husband and ask if he would be willing to accept thirty, at the most fifty, dollars to renew the contract for another three years. He reasoned with Ta-niang: "When Ch'iu-pao reaches five, he could then be separated from his mother."

Ta-niang was saying her Buddhist rosary.[8] Thus, amid the "Amitabha Buddha, Amitabha Buddha" incantations, she answered, "Her first child is still at home; you ought to let her be reunited with her first husband awhile."

The *hsiu-ts'ai*, lowering his head, mumbled incoherently, "Just think, when Ch'iu-pao is only two years old he'll have lost his mother . . ."

This time the old woman put her beads aside and said, "I can raise him. I can take care of him. Are you afraid I'll harm him?"

When he heard the last sentence, the *hsiu-ts'ai* hurriedly departed. But the old woman would not stop, and kept on saying:

"This son was born for my sake. Ch'iu-pao is mine. I didn't have any children and that cuts off your family line, but I still eat at your family table. You've really become bewitched, you're muddled in your old age, for you can't think straight at all. How many more years do you think you can live? So why drag her around by your side? Place her spirit-tablet beside mine in the ancestral temple? No way!" The old woman had more venomous remarks for him to hear, but the *hsiu-ts'ai* hurried out of earshot.

---

[8] The Pure Land practice consists of repeated chanting of the name of Amitabha, the Buddha of compassion; the prayer beads are used to keep track of the number of recitations.

That summer, a boil appeared on the child's head, and sometimes he had a slight fever. The old woman prayed to the Buddha constantly and tried to obtain some Buddhist medicine to put on the boil, or force down his throat. The child's mother didn't think it was urgent and didn't want to upset him and make him cry himself into a sweat. Once, she had no sooner secretly disposed of the medicine he barely touched than the old woman was heard to sigh audibly and complain to the *hsiu-ts'ai:*

"Just look at her. She doesn't care one bit about the child's sickness. She even says he hasn't gotten any thinner. Love in the heart is the deepest, love for appearance's sake only is false."

The young woman could only keep her tears to herself. The *hsiu-ts'ai* remained silent.

On Ch'iu-pao's first birthday, the family celebrated with a noisy all-day banquet. Thirty or forty guests came. Some gave presents of clothing, others birthday noodles or lions made of silver bullion to hang around his neck. Still others gave the child a gold-plated God of Longevity to pin on his cap. The guests brought their presents tucked in their sleeves. They came with best wishes for the child's future success and long life. The host was radiant with joy, as if his cheeks reflected the glowing clouds at sunset.

But on precisely that day, just when they were beginning the evening banquet at dusk, a guest arrived. He came out of the fading sunlight and walked toward them in the courtyard. Everyone fixed his gaze on him: a gaunt and haggard man from the country, unshaven, and with patched clothes. He had a package tucked under his arm. The host, startled, went to greet him, asking where he was from. He answered haltingly, as if he had a lisp. The host was perplexed for a moment, then understood. He was the fur trader. The host said softly, "But why did you bring a present? There was no need to do that!"

The guest, looking about timidly, replied, "Of course I should . . . I've come to wish the baby long life . . ."

His voice trailed off. He took the parcel from under his arm and opened it. With trembling hands, he unwrapped two or three layers of paper and took out four inch-square silver-plated brass letters, "Longevity Comparable to the Southern Mountains."

Ta-niang went over, eyeing him carefully with an air of disapproval. But the *hsiu-ts'ai* ushered him to the table as the guests whispered among themselves.

After two hours of meat and wine, the guests became reckless and impetuous. They played the finger-guessing game, shouting at the top of their lungs and shoving a large bowl of wine back and forth to punish the loser by making him take a drink. Their clamor nearly toppled the house over. The fur trader, though he had drunk two cups of wine, was the only one who remained in his place. The others didn't invite him to join in. Their enthusiasm waning, the guests hurriedly wolfed down a bowl of rice and, having exchanged pleasantries, faded off by twos and threes out of the lantern light.

The fur trader continued to eat until the servants came to clear the table. He then retreated to a dark corner of the veranda, where he came across his pawned wife.

"What did you come here for?" The woman asked pathetically.

"Why would I want to come? I had no choice."

"Then why did you come so late?"

"Just where do you think I got the money for the present? It took all morning running here and there to beg for a loan. Then I had to go into town to buy the gift. I got tired and hungry. So I came here late."

The woman changed the subject and asked, "Where's Ch'un-pao?"

The man hesitated, then replied, "It's because of him that I've come."

"Because of him?" the woman echoed in alarm.

The man slowly explained, "Ever since summer, Ch'un-pao's been getting very thin, and he got sick in the fall. Where could I get the money to take him to a doctor and buy him medicine? Now he's really sick, and if we don't do something for him, he'll surely die!" After a moment of silence, he continued, "I've come to borrow some money from you."

The pain was like having cats clawing at her heart, ripping it apart and devouring it. She wanted to cry but she didn't dare, because it was the occasion when others had come to celebrate Ch'iu-pao's birthday. She held back the tears and said to her husband, "Where would I get any money? They only give me twenty cents a month for pocket money. Since I've no need for it, I spend it on the child. So what can we do?"

They fell silent. Then the woman asked, "Who's taking care of Ch'un-pao now?"

"A neighbor. I want to go home tonight. I'd better be going." He wiped away his tears as he spoke. The woman then said, sobbing: "Wait a minute. I'll see if I can borrow some money from him."

She walked off.

Three evenings later, the *hsiu-ts'ai* suddenly asked her, "What happened to that blue jade ring I gave you?"

"I gave it to him that night. He pawned it."

"Didn't I lend you five dollars?" the *hsiu-ts'ai* retorted angrily.

The woman, hanging her head, paused, then answered, "Five dollars wouldn't have been enough."

The *hsiu-ts'ai* sighed. "No matter how good I am to you, you're always more attached to your former husband and son. I originally wanted to keep you for another two years, but now I think you'd better leave next spring!"

The woman was so shocked that she couldn't even cry.

Several days later, he spoke to her: "That ring is an heirloom I wanted you to pass on to Ch'iu-pao. Who'd have thought you'd immediately take it out and pawn it? It's lucky she doesn't know or she'd carry on for three months."

The woman became thinner and more sallow by the day. Her listless eyes stared blankly ahead of her, and her ears rang with mockery and abuse. She often thought about Ch'un-pao's illness. She tried to find out if any friends were coming through from her home town or if there were any passersby going in that direction. She hoped to hear the news that Ch'un-pao had regained his health, but she heard nothing. She wanted to borrow two dollars and buy some candy to send there, but there weren't any travelers going there.

She often stood along the road near the main gate holding Ch'iu-pao in her arms, looking down the road where people would be coming or going toward her home town. This made Ta-niang very uncomfortable and she often reminded the *hsiu-ts'ai:* "She doesn't want to stay here. She can hardly wait to run home."

For several nights she suddenly cried out in her sleep holding Ch'iu-pao. Ch'iu-pao was frightened and began to cry. The *hsiu-ts'ai* questioned her closely: "What's the matter with you? What is it?"

She made no answer, only hummed and patted Ch'iu-pao. But the *hsiu-ts'ai* continued, "Did you dream that your other son died, so you cried out? You even woke me up."

The woman immediately said, "No, no . . . but there seemed to be a grave mound in front of me."

The *hsiu-ts'ai* was silent. The sad image once more floated before her eyes: she was approaching a grave.

At the end of winter, the birds announcing the spring and hastening her departure were already chirping under her window. First the child was weaned, and then the Taoist priests came to say a service to insure the child's safety through this critical situation. Thus the eternal separation of the child and his real mother was decided once and for all.

That day, Mrs. Huang privately asked the first wife, "Shall I call the sedan-carriers to take her home?"

The first wife was saying her Buddhist rosary. She replied, "Let her walk. The fee would have to be paid when she arrived there. Where would she get the money? I hear her own husband doesn't even have any rice to eat. She needn't act like she's rich. It's not too far. I've walked thirty or forty *li* myself, and her feet are bigger than mine. She can make it in half a day."

That morning when she dressed Ch'iu-pao, tears streamed down her face and the little child called out to her, "Auntie, Auntie." (The old woman wanted him to call *her* "Mother," so she only permitted him to call the younger woman "Auntie.") She answered him in a choked voice. She wished to say something to him like "I'm leaving you, my dear son. Your mother will be nice to you. You want to be nice to her too when you grow up. Don't think of me anymore." But she couldn't say the words. She knew, of course, that a child a year and a half old wouldn't understand.

The *hsiu-ts'ai* quietly approached her from behind and slipped two strings of cash under her arm, saying in a low voice, "Here's two dollars. Take it with you."

The woman buttoned up the child's clothes and stuffed the money in an inside breast pocket. The old woman entered the room, and when she saw the *hsiu-ts'ai* leave it, she told the woman, "Let me hold Ch'iu-pao, or else he'll cry when you leave."

The woman didn't answer, but Ch'iu-pao wasn't willing to let the old woman hold him. He struck her over and over in the face. Finally, in anger, she blurted out: "All right, then! Go eat breakfast with him. Give him to me when you're finished."

Mrs. Huang pressed her to eat more, saying, "You've been this way for half a month now. You're thinner now than when you came. You ought to go take a look in the mirror. Today you'd better eat a whole bowl. You still have to walk thirty *li*."

She replied indifferently, "You're really nice to me."

The sun was already high and the weather was good, but Ch'iu-pao wouldn't leave her side. The old woman brutally snatched him out of her arms. Ch'iu-pao kicked her in the stomach with his tiny feet, scratched at her head with his tiny hands, and screamed at the top of his voice. The woman, standing behind them, said, "Let me wait until after lunch."

The old woman turned around and replied coldly, "Pack up your things and be off with you! You have to leave sooner or later anyway."

She gradually walked out of range of the child's screams.

While she packed her things, her ears rang with the sound of her child's crying. Mrs. Huang stood off to one side, comforting her and watching what she was putting in her pack. She finally tucked the old bundle under her arm and left.

When she went out the main gate, she could hear Ch'iu-pao's cries; after she had slowly walked three *li*, she could still hear him crying.

The road, bright in the warm sun, stretched out before her, as endless as the sky. When she reached a river, she wanted to stop all her weary steps in life by throwing herself into the clear mirror-like waters. However, after resting a while on the riverbank, she continued on her way, moving her shadow along.

The sun had already passed the meridian when an old farmer in one of the villages told her she still had fifteen *li* to go. She said to him, "Uncle, please call a sedan chair for me. I can't walk any farther."

"Are you sick?" The old man asked.

"Yes." She sat in the roadside pavilion at the entrance to the village.

"Where are you from?"

The woman paused, then replied, "I'm going there. This morning I thought I could walk there myself."

The old man, pitying her, didn't ask anything more, but found two sedan-carriers for her. The sedan chair didn't have a cover, as it was spring planting time.

About three or four o'clock in the afternoon the coverless sedan chair passed into the narrow, dirty little village lane. Sprawled in the sedan chair was a middle-aged woman with a withered face the color of a dried and yellowing vegetable leaf. Her sunken, dispirited eyes were closed. Her breaths came faintly. Passersby stared at her with pitying looks. A gang of children chased after the sedan chair, as if some rare occurrence had happened in the isolated little village.

Ch'un-pao was one of the children following behind the sedan chair. He raced after it shouting, as if herding pigs. But once the chair turned the corner, continuing in the direction of his house, he stuck out his hands in amazement. When the sedan chair arrived at the door to his house, he froze in his place and stared at it from afar. He leaned against a pillar and faced the sedan chair. The other children timidly circled it. The woman got out. Her dazed eyes didn't at first recognize that the seven-year-old child before her, wearing ragged clothes, with tousled hair, the same size as three years ago, was her Ch'un-pao. Suddenly she cried out in a loud voice, "Ch'un-pao!"

The children all started involuntarily. Ch'un-pao was so frightened he ducked into the house where his father was.

The woman sat in the dim house for a long time. She and her husband didn't exchange a word. Night fell. He raised his head to her and said, "Make dinner."

The woman had no choice but to get up. She slowly looked around in the corner, listlessly replying to her husband, "The rice jar is empty."

The man laughed bitterly. "You act as if you're still living with the gentry. The rice is kept in that cigarette box over there."

That evening, the man said to his son, "Ch'un-pao, go sleep with your mother."

But Ch'un-pao stood by the stove and cried. His mother approached him saying, "Ch'un-pao, my precious."

But when she reached out to touch him, he dodged away from her. The father then said, "You've forgotten your mother that quickly? I'll beat the daylights out of you."

She lay on a filthy, narrow bed, eyes wide open. Ch'un-pao, like a stranger, lay sleeping beside her. In her dulled numb mind, it was as if her lovable Ch'iu-pao, plump and fair, were restlessly tossing and turning by her side. She reached out to hold him, but it was Ch'un-pao who was beside her.

Ch'un-pao had already fallen asleep. She turned over and held him close to her. The child, breathing evenly, his face buried in her bosom, reached out to stroke her breasts.

The long night, silent and cold as death, seemed to drag on endlessly.

SHEN TS'UNG-WEN
(1902–)

Called "Little Miao-tzu" (Miao being the varied, colorful ethnic minority scattered through southwestern China) by many of his discerning critics, Shen Ts'ung-wen indeed shows the local color of his place of origin, Western Hunan, with strength and fidelity. Equally well captured in Shen's writings are the joy and the dramatic display of emotion in a world that is at once primitive and overdeveloped to the point of decay. The primitive comes from the rural roots of the border towns between large counties, where the way of life of indigenous minority groups continues to dominate. Overdeveloped are those institutional features superimposed from outside and above: multilayered government bureaucracy without a central government, soldiery without a national army, customs and mores of cityfolk that seem so very irrelevant to the lives of the frontier—not marginal—people.

It was a storyteller's unsatiable desire to weave everything he touches into a tale that drove Shen to creative writing. He was touched by the growing wave of social consciousness, and his stories reflect a good deal of sympathy for the exploited, but he stayed far away from championing a revolution. The onrush of translations from Russian and European literature affected him, but he struggled with his own vocabulary, groped for his own style, and finally found both. And when one reads Shen's twenty-odd collections of short stories and full-length novels, one is inevitably won over by his breadth and depth, by the finesse of his characters. Then one proceeds to forget the occasional lapses into verbosity in some of his less mature works.

The selections in this anthology come close to representing Shen's multifaceted best. "Pai-tzu" (1928) is a worthy specimen of a story rooted in the rural; the young boatman laughs, chatters, and dances in rhythm with the boat, and the boat with the river, until the story crests in a dramatic sexual rendevous with a village woman. Theirs is the primitive rhythm unsoiled by the overdeveloped, superimposed culture. Shen's soldiering experience reveals itself in "Three Men and One Woman" (San-ke nan-tzu ho i-ke nü-jen, 1936), where the real works its way into legend, and the macabre (in the eyes of the superimposed culture) becomes human and credible. The school teacher in Shen collaborates with the foot soldier in him to create "The Lamp" (Teng, 1930), which was written, as the author said in an end note, "because of a dream." The quartermaster-cook's simple devotion speaks eloquently for a whole nation's tradition, and the ending only accentuates Shen's delight in storytelling. "Quiet" (*Ching,* 1932), written in memory of Pei-sheng, the son of the author's elder sister, reveals the impressionistic beauty of a world divided between pastoral serenity and wartime realities. In "Hsiao-hsiao" (1929) C. T. Hsia sees a simple farm girl "inviolable in the strength of [her] animal purity. . . . situated in a primitive society in which a kind of corrupted Confucian ethic still governs" (*History,* p. 202); but neither the unexpected penalty for innocence nor her family's censure can do her any permanent damage.

After 1949 Shen made one abortive attempt to adapt his writing to suit the needs of the time, and then promptly turned to research in the material culture of ancient China as the chief curator for the National Palace Museum. The success of his second career as a research scholar and the nostalgic explanation of his farewell to creative writing have been recorded in an interview with him in *The Chinese Literary Scene* (New York, 1957).

KAI-YU HSU
J.S.M.L.

Pai-tzu

by Shen Ts'ung-wen

Translated by Kai-yu Hsu

Arriving in Ch'en-chou, the boat docked at the riverside. It was ready for the passengers to go ashore, over a gangplank, a single-board affair with one end over the gunwale of the boat and the other end resting on the stone steps of the bank. It sagged and swayed as one walked over it, but one by one the shore-bound managed to swing their way across.

Too many boats crowded together along the bank, too many masts lined up, some tall, others short, but all pointing at the sky. From a distance, all the rigging seemed tangled, but actually it was not.

On the bow and stern of every boat stood men dressed in blue or black shirts and pants with long tobacco pipes in their mouths. Their forearms and shanks, exposed, had long black hair that would remind a child of the fabled hairy demons scurrying around in haunted caves. Or one might be reminded, by the sight of these hairy limbs, of the Mercury-like nimble-footed heroes in folktales. And one could be right, for these characters could very well be just those heroes: when the rigging got stuck in a pulley up on the mast, one of them would instantly seize the opportunity to show off his gymnastic agility by slithering up the mast—who said all he had was on his shanks? There must be a pair of hooks somewhere on his feet—in a flash up the smooth vertical mast, twenty, thirty feet high where the rope was stuck. Just to show again that there was nothing to it, he would sing a bawdy song as he straightened out the tangled rigging. A few boats away another nimble-footed sailor was doing exactly the same

thing to impress the spectators, and the two gymnasts would keep up a duet, singing and singing, on and on.

Other crew members stood around, cocking their heads to watch the performance and shouting encouragement from time to time. Any one of them could repeat the same feat at any time, if the helmsman would simply nod in his direction. But the boss picked one, and all the rest fought the itch in their fingertips, helpless because only one could climb up to be the hero of the moment, to sing bawdy songs to tease the women in the next boat. Helpless, but one could always get even this way:

"Sonny, you watch, you're going to fall and smash yourself to pieces the next minute!"

"Hey, kid, see if you can keep singing after you've dropped dead!"

Lots of kidding, lots of laughter, but all for the fun of it.

The one up there kept singing, and louder too. Singing "One Pretty Flower" a moment ago, now he switched to "My Many Buddies," aiming at his admirers below. And the "many buddies" kept looking up at the singer, all smiling, all in good humor.

Some other boats were hard at work. There, many suntanned faces and suntanned bodies were busy, with the same hairy hands and legs, rolling black metal drums off the boats. The drums rolled along the gangplanks and, wobbling a bit, tumbled to rest on the muddy shore. More freight crates came pouring forth: square bundles of textiles tied with metal strips, round bundles of dried kelp and dried squid and herb medicines. Like the passengers, these bundles had stayed packed together on board for a couple of weeks, and now were due to be liberated ashore. The passengers got off the boat, each seeking his own way home, or his own inn, and managing his own room and board; the freight bundles one after another tumbled into the arms of a troop of big-footed village women who carried them to the warehouses.

In the midst of these quick-tempoed activities there were also those of leisure, perhaps most un-hurried leisure, removed from all these noises but near enough to hear the songs from up the masts. They were leisurely but their hearts were a-flutter, and they had the singers with them the moment the songs hushed and red lanterns rose to where the singers had been. Red lanterns heralded the arrival of evening, and evening brought a magic world to the riverside.

The rain came, and the wind stirred. Shelters went up and men sat underneath listening to the sound of wind and rain. With its roaring waves, the river had become a crazy man. However tightly squeezed together, the boats could not stop themselves from rocking. But it did not bother the boatmen; they were indifferent, their life had separated them from the likes and dislikes of those land-based people. (If a moon appeared, it would be different, just as the river had a dif-ferent interest under the setting sun or with the morning dew.) Anyway these boatmen paid no at-tention to the weather. Their moods, if they had to be divided into categories, could be arranged into two or three. A meal of beef would cause a mood among them different from a meal of pick-led cabbage; these fleet-footed heroes preferred beef. In a similar way they preferred docking their boats at a riverport to just anywhere along the way.

The rain had been falling for a while. The muddy river bank had become slippery, hard to stand on, but just the same the boatmen one by one went ashore to the waterfront street.

Pai-tzu was one of them. He was tireless climb-ing the mast and singing during the day, and never seemed tired out at night either. Like every one of his buddies he filled his money belt with coppers and stepped on the gangplank. He walked along the muddy bank, with no moon or stars above, only the fine rain sprinkling over-head. His feet churned the mud and the mud climbed up his legs; he couldn't walk as fast as he wanted to. He headed toward a little red light in the upstairs window of a building fronting the river. Under that light there was something that made Pai-tzu's heart sing.

There were many such little red lights, each of them shining on a boatman or a crowd of them. The feeble light of the lantern could hardly fill the tiny room, and yet joy filled the breast of every boatman there to the bursting point. Every eye was half-closed, as the songs and laughter poured forth from every throat, overflowing the room, spilling into the street, over the bank onto the boats where those without the necessary money stayed behind to listen, and curse. They could not go ashore, but their hearts went, sway-ing and swinging over the gangplanks, onto the street, following their past experiences toward one or another familiar upstairs room facing the river.

Wine, tobacco, and women—what a romantic would brag about in this world—were the boat-men's regular fare, although the wine burned their tongues, the tobacco smoldered like rice straw, and the women . . . Just the same, every heart pounded violently, every head became giddy, and every mouth, which ordinarily oc-cupied itself with pickled cabbage, pumpkins, or half-rotten beef, or dirty jokes, suddenly turned to honey under the magic of the moment. Every mouth somehow could find sweet nothings from a hidden storage place deep down in the heart to offer to the woman before him, and could find its way onto the cheeks, lips, feet, and other parts of the woman before him, in however clumsy a way. These men drowned themselves in the air of gai-ety, and for the moment they forgot the whole world, including their own past and future. The women helped them, replacing their poverty, hard life, and expectations with excited intoxica-tion, like wine, like tobacco. Over each of these women a crowd of boatmen dreamed their dreams, most realistic and courageous dreams, ready to shower on her all the money and all the energy they had saved up for a month. They asked for nobody's sympathy; they were not at all sorry for themselves.

If they had a moment to reflect on their lives in a different setting, perhaps they would still feel satisfied. They had few tears to spare, but they had lots of fun.

Pai-tzu finally reached his happiness.

He pounded his fist on the door and, in a boatman's habit, whistled at the same time.

The door loosened. With one of his muddy legs still outside the threshold Pai-tzu found himself clutched in a pair of bare arms, and a cheek, warm and wide, pressed itself against his sunburned but newly shaven face.

The hair oil smelled familiar. The embrace, though he couldn't have described it a moment before, felt equally familiar the moment it happened. And that cheek, soft and powder-scented, was waiting there for him to lick and suck. It was only a swift moment before he turned and caught a wet tongue between his lips. He nibbled on it.

She wiggled, and scolded him:

"Damn you! I thought you had been washed into the lake by the urine of those cheap women in Ch'ang-teh!"

"I'm going to bite your tongue off!"

"I'm going to bite your . . ."

He got inside the door. Under the red lantern light she looked at him, with an adoring smile. He stood a head taller. He stooped to gather her waist to him, as though gathering up the lines of the boat. She leaned forward.

"I'm sick of rowing. I want to push a wheelbarrow."[1]

"Push your mother's!"[2] she said, one hand busy searching his pockets, tossing everything she found onto the bed, naming them one by one: "A jar of cold cream, a roll of paper, a handkerchief, another jar—hey, what's in this jar?"

"Guess!"

"Guess your mother's! You forgot to bring me face powder?"

"Look at the label on the jar! Open it and see!"

She couldn't read. On the label she saw two pretty girls. She opened the jar under the lantern and took a sniff which made her sneeze. He was delighted. He snatched the jar and laid it on a bench, and, grabbing the woman, rolled with her onto the bed.

The lantern light shone on a collection of muddy footprints on the floor.

The rain came down thick and heavy now.

Songs mingled with curses and laughter continued in the air. With only a thin layer of unpainted board as the partition, one could hear even a drag on a tobacco pipe on the other side. But everybody was too busy to eavesdrop.

The muddy footprints dried and became better defined on the floor as the lantern shone on the pair who lay across the bed.

"Pai-tzu, you're a bull!"

"If I didn't show you, you wouldn't believe how well-behaved I was downriver."

"Well-behaved, huh! I dare you to swear you're pure enough to enter the temple of the Heavenly Ruler!" she said.[3]

"Swear your mother's! You're the one who believe in swearing. I don't."

There was truth in the woman's saying that Pai-tzu was a bull. The bull was now panting, relaxed, like a bundle of muddy lines from the boat coiling listlessly on the edge of the bed. He clenched the two fat breasts, bit them, then bit her lower lip, her shoulder, her thigh . . . Yes, this was exactly the same Pai-tzu who had sung his songs on top of the mast.

Lying on her back, she watched his every motion, a satisfied smile on her face.

A little later they put a tray of opium smoking paraphernalia between them and started working on the pipe.

She deftly rolled the opium paste on a stick, while softly humming the folk song "Meng-

[1] A pun that suggests a sexual intercourse position.   [2] "Your mother's": common swearword.

[3] T'ien Huang ("Heavenly Ruler") is the head of the family of fabulous sovereigns who succeeded P'an Ku, the creator of the universe in Chinese mythology.

chiang's Lament at the Great Wall." Pai-tzu was the king, sipping tea and puffing on the opium pipe.

"Woman, let me tell you," he said, "those girls downriver are really good-looking. I die just thinking of them!"

"Why don't you die right there! Why'd you come back here again?"

"They won't look at me even if I offer them my life!"

"So, my turn comes only because they won't even look at you?"

"Your turn? You— Tell me how many men you've had before it's my turn? Tell me, how many?"

With a grimace she fitted a bean of baked opium paste on the pipe and pushed the pipe into Pai-tzu's mouth to shut him up.

Pai-tzu drew on the pipe, then asked again, "Let me ask you, who was here with you yesterday?"

"Who your mother's! I've been waiting for you, counting the days. I figured that stinking corpse of yours would—"

"If I really got lost over the Blue Surf Rapids, you'd be happy, wouldn't you?"

"Yeah, I'd really be overjoyed!" She was getting angry.

He liked to tease her, making her mad. When he saw her pull a long face he pushed the opium tray aside. Without the barrier between them the scene quickly changed. In less than a minute he had his muddy legs stretched over the edge of the bed, and clutching these legs were a pair of tiny feet sheathed in red silk slippers.

An unabashed exertion, a divine wrath—a resumption, a fresh beginning.

Under pouring rain Pai-tzu walked along the muddy shore. In his hand was a lighted torch—a section of old, discarded bamboo-woven cable that had been used to pull the boat when going upstream. The light probed three feet of darkness around him, and picked out the silvery streaks of rain. He walked through these streaks, his feet splashing in the muddy water. His business ashore finished, he was returning to his boat.

It rained hard, yet he was not in a hurry, per-haps because he didn't want to slip and fall, also perhaps because he had with him something to shelter him from—no, better say, to make him forget about—the rain.

His heart warmed to the recollection of what lingered before his eyes. He recalled all that lingered before his eyes, and then the rain over his head and the mud under his feet did not invite his attention.

Was she sleeping now, or tumbling with another man in that same unpainted wooden bed? Who could tell? And he was not about to let it bother him. He retained her in his memory, every small detail: the curves, the undulations, the most private and secret— He felt he could touch her even if there were a thousand miles between them, and he could tell the size and contours of every part of her body. Her laughter and her movements clung to his heart like so many leeches, and that was enough. That was more than enough, more than made up for his month-long labor, thirty days of hot sun and hard rain, even with his gambling losses all tossed in, and perhaps even with the fun expected on his next downriver trip tossed in—still he'd be ahead. It would be another two weeks or a month on this trip, but he would work happily for all those days, eat and sleep happily for all those days. Tonight he had had a feast of satisfactions, and what he had tonight could easily last one, even two months; surely he would return to her before that.

His money belt was empty, but it was worth every copper. Besides, he had put away a bit to reserve for gambling on board. What did he get for his money? He didn't want to try figuring that one out. He had no interest in figuring out how money came to him and how it went away. Even if he did, sometimes, think about it, he would always conclude that he was ahead.

He hummed the tune of "Meng-chiang's Lament at the Great Wall," and then the tune of "Two Lovers Playing Dominoes." He reached the gangplank and carefully stepped on board. His humming stopped abruptly before he got to "Eighteen Ways of Touching Her" because the boss's wife was there, breast-feeding her child.

Pai-tzu heard her softly talking to the child, and the sounds of the child's sucking.

The boats calling at the Ch'en-chou port belonged to different guilds, each having its own fixed docking place for the vessels. As soon as each boat unloaded its cargo, it had to be on its way again. This time Pai-tzu got ashore only twice, then the boat promptly left with him on board.

Hsiao-hsiao

by Shen Ts'ung-wen

Translated by Eugene Eoyang

Just about every day around the twelfth month,[1] the folks at home seem to be blowing the bamboo pipes for a wedding.

Following the pipes a gaily decked bridal palanquin appears, gliding forward on the shoulders of two bearers. The girl is shut up tight inside, and even though she is wearing a festive gown of greens and reds—something she doesn't get to wear every day—she can't help sobbing to herself. For, in her heart, a young woman knows that becoming a bride and leaving her mother to become, in time, someone else's mother, means having to face a host of new and unexpected problems. It's almost like entering a trance, to sleep in the same bed with someone you hardly know in order to carry on the ancestral line. Naturally, it is somewhat frightening to think of these things, so if one is inclined to cry in such a circumstance—as so many before have cried—is it any wonder?

There are, of course, some who don't cry. Hsiao-hsiao did not cry when she got married. She had been orphaned, and had been sent to an uncle on a farm to bring up. All day long, carrying a small, wide-brimmed bamboo hat, she was to look for dog droppings by the side of the road and in the gullies. For her, marriage meant simply a transfer from one family to another. So, when the day came, all she could do was to laugh about it, with no sense of shame or fear. She was scarcely aware of what she was getting into: all she knew was that she was to become someone's new daughter-in-law.

Hsiao-hsiao was eleven when she married, and Little Husband was hardly two years old—almost ten years younger, and not long ago suckling at his mother's breast. When she entered the household she called him "Sonny," according to local custom. Her daily chore was to take "Sonny" to play under the willow tree in front of the house or by the stream; when he was hungry, to give him something to eat; when he fussed, to soothe him; to pluck pumpkin blossoms and dog-grass to crown Little Husband with, or to soothe him with kisses and sweet nothings: "Sonny, now there, hush, there, there." And with that she would kiss the grimy little face: the boy would break out in smiles. In good spirits again, the child would act up once more, and with his tiny fingers, he would paw at Hsiao-hsiao's hair—the brown hair that was untidy and unkempt most of the time. Sometimes, when he had pulled too hard at her braid, the knot of red wool would come loose, and she would have to cuff him a few times: naturally he bawled. Hsiao-hsiao, now on the verge of tears herself, would point to the boy's tear-drenched face and say: "Now, now, you naughty thing, you'd better quit that."

Through fair and foul, every day she carried her "husband," doing this and that around the house, wherever her services were needed. On occasion she would go down to the stream to wash

---

[1] References to "months" in this story allude to the lunar calendar; when the term is converted into months in the solar calendar, the name of the month—December, January, etc.—will be given. The twelfth month is roughly February.

out clothes, to rinse out the diapers, but she found time to pick out colorful striped snails to amuse the boy with as he sat nearby. When she went to sleep she would dream dreams that a girl her age dreams; she dreamt that she found a cache of copper coins at the back gate, or some other place, and that she had good things to eat; she dreamt that she was climbing a tree; she dreamt she was a fish, floating freely in the water; she dreamt she was so light and lithe that she flew up clear to the stars, where there was no one, but all she could see was a flash of white and of gold, and she cried aloud for her mother—whereupon she woke up, her heart still thumping. The people next door would scold her: "You silly thing! What were you thinking of?

Those who do nothing at all but play
Wind up with bad dreams at end of day."

When she heard this, Hsiao-hsiao made no response, but merely giggled to herself, thinking of the good dreams that her husband's crying sometimes interrupted. He would sleep by his mother's side, so that it would be easier for her to breast-feed him, but there were times when he had too much milk or was colicky. Then he would wake up in the middle of the night crying, and Hsiao-hsiao would have to get up and take him to the bathroom. This happened often. Her husband cried so much, her mother-in-law didn't know what to do with him, so Hsiao-hsiao had to crawl out of bed bleary-eyed and tiptoe in—brushing the cobwebs out of her sleepy eyes—to take the boy in her arms, and distract him with the lamp or the twinkling of the stars. If that didn't work, she'd peck and whistle, make faces for the child, blather on like a baby—"Hey, hey, look—look at the cat"—until her husband broke out in a smile. They would play like this for a bit, and then he would feel drowsy and close his eyes. When he was asleep, she'd put him back to bed, watching over him awhile, and, hearing in the distance the insistent sound of a cock crowing, she couldn't help knowing about what time it was when she huddled back in her tiny bed. At daybreak, though she had had a sleepless night, she would flick her eyes open and shut to see the yellow-and-purple sunflowers outdoors shifting forms before her very eyes: that was a real treat.

When Hsiao-hsiao was married off, to become the "little wife" of a pint-sized little child, she wasn't any the worse for wear; one look at her figure was proof enough of that. She was like an unnoticed sapling at a corner of the garden, sprouting forth big leaves and branches after days of wind and rain. This little girl—as if unmindful of her tiny husband—grew bigger day by day.

To speak of summer nights is to dream. People seek the cool of the evening after summer heat: they sit in the middle of the courtyard, waving their rush-fans, looking up at the stars in the sky or the fireflies in the corners, listening to the "Weaver Maid" crickets—on the roofs of the pumpkin-sheds—clicking away interminably on their "looms." The sounds from near and far are intertwined like the sound of rain, and when the hay-scented wind falls full on the face, that is a time when people are of a mind to tell jokes.

Hsiao-hsiao grew very tall, and she would often climb the sloping sides of the haystack, carrying in her arms her already sleeping husband, softly singing self-improvised folk melodies. The more she sang, the drowsier she felt—until she too was almost asleep.

In the middle of the courtyard, her in-laws, the grandparents, and two farmhands sat at random on small wooden stools.

By Grandfather's side there was a tobacco-coil, whose embers glowed in the dark. This coil, made of mugwort, had the effect of repelling long-legged mosquitoes. It was wound around at Grandfather's feet like a black snake. From time to time, Grandfather would pick it up and wave it about.

Thinking about the day in the fields, Grandfather said: "Say, I heard that Old Chin said that, day before yesterday, there were a few co-eds passing through town."

Everyone roared with laughter.

And what was behind the laughter? Everyone had the impression that co-eds didn't wear braids: wearing the hair in the form of a sparrow's tail made them look like nuns, and yet somehow not like nuns. They wore their clothes in the manner of foreigners, yet they didn't look like foreigners. They ate, behaved in such a way . . . well, in a word, everything seemed out of place with them, and the slightest mention of co-eds was cause enough for laughter.

Hsiao-hsiao didn't understand much of what was going on, and so she didn't laugh at all. Grandfather spoke again. He said:

"Hsiao-hsiao, when you grow up, you'll be a co-ed too." At this, everyone laughed once more.

Now, Hsiao-hsiao was not stupid when it came to people, and she figured this wasn't flattering to her, so she said:

"Grandpa, I won't become a co-ed."

"But you look like a co-ed. It won't do if you don't become one."

"No, I certainly won't."

The bystanders mined this for a laugh and egged her on:

"Hsiao-hsiao, what Grandpa says is right. It's not right if you don't become a co-ed."

Hsiao-hsiao was flustered and didn't know what was going on.

"All right, if I have to, I have to." Actually, Hsiao-hsiao had no idea what was wrong with being a co-ed.

The whole idea of co-eds would always be thought of as queer in these parts. Every year, come June, when the start of the so-called "summer vacation" had finally arrived, they would come in small groups from some outlandish metropolis, and, looking for some remote retreat, they would pass through the village. In the eyes of the local people, it was almost as if these people had dropped down from an altogether different world, dressed in the most bizarre ways, their behavior even more improbable. On the days these co-eds passed through, the whole village would come up with joke after joke.

Grandpapa was an oldtimer from the region, and, because he was thinking about the carryings-on of the co-eds he knew in the big city, he thought it was funny to urge Hsiao-hsiao to become one. As soon as he made the crack, he couldn't help laughing, but he also had in mind the way Hsiao-hsiao felt, and so the joke wasn't totally innocuous.

The co-eds that Grandfather knew were of a type: they wore clothes without regard to the weather; they ate whether they were hungry or full; they didn't go to sleep until late at night; during the day they worked at nothing at all, but sang and played ball or read books from abroad. They knew how to spend money: with what they spent in a year, you could buy at least sixteen water buffalo. In the capital cities of the provinces, whenever they wanted to go anywhere, they'd never dream of walking, but would climb instead into a big "box," which took them everywhere. In the cities there were all sorts of "boxes," big and small, all motorized. At school, boys and girls go to class together, and, when they get acquainted, the girls sleep overnight with the boys, with no thought of a go-between or a matchmaker, or even a dowry. This is what they call being "free." They sometimes serve as district officials, and bring families to their posts; their husbands are called "Masters" still and their children "Little Master." They don't tend cattle themselves, but they'll drink cow's milk and sheep's milk like little calves and little lambs; the milk they buy is canned. When they have nothing better to do, they go to a theater, which is built like a huge temple, and take from their pockets a silver dollar (a dollar of their money can buy five setting hens hereabouts). With this they purchase a piece of paper in the form of a ticket, which they take inside, so that they can sit down and watch foreigners performing shadow-plays. When offended, they won't curse at you or cry. By the time they are twenty-four, some still won't marry, while others at thirty or forty still have the cheek to contemplate marriage. They are not afraid of men, thinking men can't wrong them, for if they do, they take the men to court and insist that the magistrate fine them. Sometimes they spend the fine themselves, and sometimes they share it with the magistrate. Of course, they don't wash clothes or cook meals, and they certainly don't raise hogs and feed hens; when they have children they hire a servant to look after them for only five or ten dollars a month so that they can spend all day going to the theater and playing cards, or reading all those good-for-nothing books.

In a word, everything about them is weird, totally different from the lives of farmers, and some of their goings-on are not to be believed. When Hsiao-hsiao heard her grandfather saying all this, which explained everything, she felt vague stirrings of unrest, and took to imagining herself as a "co-ed." Would she behave like the "co-eds" Grandfather talked about? In any case, there was nothing frightful about these "co-eds," and so these notions began to occupy this simple girl's thoughts for the first time.

Because of the picture that Grandfather had painted of the "co-ed," Hsiao-hsiao giggled to herself for some time. But when she had collected herself, she said:

"Grandpa, when the 'co-eds' come tomorrow, please tell me. I want a look."

"Watch out, or they'll make a maidservant out of you!"

"I'm not afraid of them."

"Oh, but they read all those foreign books, recite scripture, and you're still not afraid of them?"

"They can recite the 'Bodhisattva Kuan-yin Dispels Disaster' sutra or 'The Curse of the Monkey Sun' for all I care. I'm not afraid."

"They'll bite people, like the officials; they only eat simple folk; they munch even the bones and don't spit up the remains. Are you sure you're not scared?"

Hsiao-hsiao replied firmly: "No, I'm not scared."

At the time, Hsiao-hsiao was carrying her husband, who, apparently for no reason, broke out of a sound sleep crying. Daughter-in-law used the tones of a mother and, half in reassurance, half in remonstrance, said:

"Sonny, sonny, you mustn't cry, the voracious co-eds are coming!"

Her husband continued to cry, and there was no choice but to stand up and walk him about. Hsiao-hsiao carried him off, leaving Grandfather, who went on talking about other things.

From that moment on, Hsiao-hsiao remem-bered what "co-ed" meant. When she dreamt, she would often dream about being a co-ed, about being one of them. It was as if she too had sat in one of those motorized boxes, though she felt they didn't go much faster than she did. In her dream, the box seemed to resemble a granary, and there were ash-gray mice with little red, piggy eyes, darting all over the place, sometimes squirming through the cracks, their slimy tails sticking out behind them.

With this development, it was only natural that Grandfather would stop calling her "Little Maidservant" or "Hsiao-hsiao" and would call her "Little Co-ed." When it caught her off guard, Hsiao-hsiao would turn around involuntarily.

In the country, one day is like any other day in the world: they change only with the season. People waste each day as it comes, in the same way that Hsiao-hsiao and her kind hang on to each day: each gets his share, everything is as it should be. A lot of city sophisticates while away their summers in soft silk, indulging in good food and drink, not to mention other pleasures. For Hsiao-hsiao and her family, however, summer means hard work, producing ten catties or more of fine hemp and twenty or thirty wagons of melons.

The little daughter-in-law Hsiao-hsiao, on a summer day, must tend to her husband as well as spin four catties of hemp. By August, when the farmhands harvest the melons, she would enjoy seeing piled high in rows on the ground the dust-covered pumpkin melons, each as big as a pot. The time had come to collect the harvest, and now the courtyard was filled with great big red and brown leaves, blown from the branches of the trees in the grove behind the house. Hsiao-hsiao stood by the melons, and she was working a large leaf into a hat for her husband to play with.

There was a farmhand called Motley Mutt,[2] about twenty years old, who took Hsiao-hsiao's husband to the date tree for some dates: one whack with a bamboo stick, and the ground would be covered with dates.

"Brother Motley Mutt, no more, please. Too much and you won't be able to eat them all."

---

[2] *Hua-kou*, literally "piebald dog." The phrase is both appellation and description.

Despite this warning, he didn't budge. It was as if, on account of the little husband's yen for dates, Motley Mutt wouldn't listen. So, Hsiao-hsiao warned her little husband:

"Sonny, sonny, come over here, don't take any more. You'll get a bellyache from eating all that raw fruit!"

Her husband obeyed. Grabbing an armful of dates, he came over to Hsiao-hsiao, and offered her some.

"Sis, eat. Here's a big one."

"No, I won't eat it."

"Come on, just one."

She had her hands full: how could she stop to eat one? She was busily putting the hat together, and wished she had some help.

"Sonny, why don't you put a date in my mouth?"

Her husband did as he was told, and when he did he thought it was fun, and came out with a laugh.

She wanted him to drop the dates so that he could help her hold the hat together while she added a few more leaves.

Her husband did as he was bidden, but he couldn't sit still, all the while singing and humming. The child was always like a cat, prone to mischief when in a good mood.

"Sonny, what song are you singing there?"

"Motley Mutt taught me this mountain song."

"Sing it properly so that I can follow."

Husband held on to the brim of the hat, and sang what he could remember of the song.

"Clouds rise in the skies, clouds become flowers:
Among the corn stalks, plant beans for ruth;
The beans will undermine the stalks of corn,
and young maidens choke off flowering youth.
Clouds rise in the skies, one after another
In the ground, graves are dug, grave upon grave;
Fair maids wash bowls, bowl after bowl,
And in their beds serve knave after knave."

The meaning of the song was lost on husband, and when he finished, he asked her if she liked it. Hsiao-hsiao said she did, asking where it came from, and even though she knew that Motley Mutt had taught him the song, she still wanted him to tell her.

"Motley Mutt—he taught me. He knows lots of songs, but I . . . gotta grow up before he'll sing them."

When she realized that Motley Mutt could sing, Hsiao-hsiao said: "Brother Motley Mutt, Brother Motley Mutt, won't you sing a proper song for me?"

But that Motley Mutt, his face was as coarse as his heart: he had a touch of the vulgar about him, and, knowing that Hsiao-hsiao wanted a song, and sensing that she was about at the age to understand, he sang for her the ballad of the ten-year-old bride married to the one-year-old groom. The story says that as the wife is older, she can stray a bit because the husband is still an infant, not yet weaned, so leave him to suckle at his mother's breasts. Of course, Little Husband understood nothing at all of this song; Hsiao-hsiao, on the other hand, had but an inkling. When she had heard it, Hsiao-hsiao put on airs, as if to indicate she understood it all. Affecting outrage, she said to Motley Mutt:

"Brother Motley Mutt, you stop that! That song's not nice."

But Brother Motley Mutt took exception: "But it *is* a nice song."

"Oh, no it isn't. It isn't a nice song."

Motley Mutt rarely said much: he had sung his song; if he had offended anyone, he wouldn't sing again, that's all. He could see that she understood a little of what he sang, and was afraid that she would tell on him to Grandfather, and then he'd really be in for it, and so he changed the subject to co-eds. He asked Hsiao-hsiao if she had ever seen co-eds exercising in public and singing Western songs.

If Motley hadn't brought this up, Hsiao-hsiao would have long ago forgotten all about co-eds. But now that he mentioned it, she was curious to know if he had seen any lately. She was dying to see them.

While he was moving the melons from the shed to a corner of the courtyard wall, Motley told her stories about co-eds singing foreign songs—all of which he had originally heard from Grandfather. To her face, he boasted of having seen four co-eds on the main road, each with a flag in her hands, marching down the road perspiring and singing away just like soldiers on parade. It goes without saying that all this was some nonsense he had cooked up. But the stories inflamed Hsiao-hsiao's imagination. And all because Motley characterized them as instances of "freedom."

Motley was one of those clownish, leering, earthy types. When he heard Hsiao-hsiao say (with a measure of admiration): "My, Brother Motley, but you have big arms," he would say: "Oh, but that's not all that's big!"

"You've got such a large build."

"I'm big all over."

Hsiao-hsiao didn't understand this at all; she just thought he was being silly, and so she laughed.

After Hsiao-hsiao had left, carrying her husband off, a fellow who picked melons with Motley, and who had the nickname "Mumbles" (he was not much given to talk),[3] spoke out on this occasion.

"Motley, you're really awful. She's a twelve-year-old virgin, and she's still got twelve years before her wedding!"

Without so much as a word, Motley went up to the farmhand, slapped him, and then walked to the date tree to pick up the fruit that had dropped off.

By the time of the autumn melons harvest, one could reckon a full year and a half that Hsiao-hsiao had been with her husband.

The days passed—days of frost and snow, sunny days and rainy days—and everyone said how grown-up Hsiao-hsiao was. Heaven kept watch over her: she drank cold water, ate coarse gruel, and was never sick the year round; she grew and blossomed. Although Grandmama became something of a nemesis, and tried to keep her from growing up too fast, Hsiao-hsiao flourished in the clean country air, undaunted by any trial or ordeal.

When Hsiao-hsiao was fourteen, she had the figure of an adult, but her heart was still as blithe and as unschooled as that of a child.

When one is bigger, one gets a heavier burden of household chores. Besides twisting hemp,

spinning thread, washing, looking after her husband, she had odd jobs like getting feed for the pigs or working at the mill, flossing silk, and weaving. She was expected to learn everything. It was understood that anyone who could make an extra effort would fit in a few chores to be done in their own quarters: the coarse hemp and spun silk that Hsiao-hsiao had gathered in two or three years were enough to keep her busy for three months at the crude shuttle in her room.

Her husband had long ago been weaned. Mother-in-law had a new son, and so her five-year-old—Hsiao-hsiao's husband—became Hsiao-hsiao's sole charge. Whatever happened, wherever she went, her husband followed her around. Husband was a little afraid of her in some ways, as if she were his mother, and so he behaved himself. All in all, they got along pretty well.

Gradually, as the locality became more progressive, Grandfather would change his jokes to: "Hsiao-hsiao, for the sake of freedom, you ought to cut off your braids." By this time Hsiao-hsiao had heard this joke; one summer she had seen her first co-ed. Although she didn't take Grandfather's ribbing too seriously, she would nevertheless (whenever she would pass by a pond after he made his crack) absentmindedly hold up her braid by the tip to see how good she would look without a braid, and how she would feel about it.

To gather feed grass for the pigs, Hsiao-hsiao would take her husband up on the dark slope of Snail Mountain.

The child did not know any better, and so whenever he heard singing, he would break into song. And no sooner did he open his mouth than Motley would appear.

Motley began to harbor new thoughts about Hsiao-hsiao, which she gradually became aware of, and that made her nervous. But Motley was a man, with all the wiles and the ways of a man, strong of build, and nimble-footed, who could divert and charm a girl. While he ingratiated himself with Hsiao-hsiao's husband, he found ways of sidling up to Hsiao-hsiao and of disarming her suspicions about him.

But what is a man compared to a mountain?

---

[3]*Ya-pa,* literally "mute," a derisive appellation, referring to his customary inarticulateness.

With trees everywhere, Hsiao-hsiao would be hard to locate. So whenever he wanted to find Hsiao-hsiao, Motley would stand on a rise and sing in order to get a response from the little husband at Hsiao-hsiao's side. As soon as Little Husband sang, Motley, after running over hill and dale, would appear face-to-face before Hsiao-hsiao.

When the little child saw Motley, he felt nothing but delight. He wanted Motley to make insect-figures from grass, or to carve out a flute for him from bamboo, but Motley always came up with a way to send him off to find the necessary materials so that he could sit by Hsiao-hsiao and sing for her those songs that would bring her guard down and produce a blush on her cheeks. At times, she was worried that something might happen, and she wouldn't let her husband go off; at other times it seemed better to send the boy-husband off, so that he wouldn't see what Motley was up to. Finally, one day, she let Motley sing his way into her heart, and he made a woman of her.

At the time, Little Husband had run down the mountain to pick berries, and Motley sang many songs which he performed for Hsiao-hsiao:

"Pretty maid, an uphill path leads to your door;
If others have walked a little, I've walked more.
My well-made sandals are worn out, walked to shreds;
If not for you, my pretty, then who for?"

When he had finished, he said to Hsiao-hsiao "I haven't slept a wink because of you." He swore up and down that he would tell no one. When she heard this, Hsiao-hsiao was bewildered: she couldn't help looking at his brawny arms, and she couldn't help hearing the last thing he said. Even when he went to the outhouse, he would sing for her. She was disconcerted. But she asked him to swear before Heaven, and after he swore—which seemed a good enough guarantee—she abandoned herself to him. When Little Husband came back, his hand had been stung by a furry insect, and it was swelling up: he ran to Hsiao-hsiao. She pinched his hand, blew on the sting, and sucked on it to reduce the swelling. She remembered her thoughtless behavior of a moment ago, and she was dimly aware that she had done something not quite right.

When Motley took her, it was May, when the wheat was brown; by July, the plums had ripened—how fond she was of plums! She felt a change in her body, so when she bumped into Motley on the mountain, she told him about her situation, and asked what she should do.

They talked and talked, but Motley had not the faintest idea of what to do. Although he had sworn before the very heavens, he still had no idea. He was, after all, big in physique, but small in courage. A big physique gets you into trouble easily, but small courage puts you at a loss as to how to work your way out.

After a while, Hsiao-hsiao would finger her snake-like black braid, and, thinking of life in the city, she said:

"Brother Motley, why don't we go where we can be free in the city and find work there. What do you say?"

"That won't do. There's nothing for us there."

"My stomach is getting bigger. That won't do either."

"Let's find some medicine: there's a doctor who sells the stuff in the market."

"You'd better find something quick. I think—"

"It's no use running to 'freedom' in the city. Only strangers there. There are rules even for begging your bread; you can't go about it as you please."

"You're really worthless, and you've been awful to me. Oh, I wish I was dead."

"I swore never to betray you."

"Who cares about betrayal; what I need is your help. Take this living thing out of my belly right away! I'm frightened."

Motley said no more, and after a little while he left. In time, Little Husband came by from a spot where he was gathering red fruit. When he saw Hsiao-hsiao sitting all alone in the grass, her eyes red from crying, Little Husband began to wonder. After a while he asked:

"Sis, what's the matter?"

"It's nothing. I've got a cobweb in my eye. It smarts."

"Let me blow it away."

"No, don't bother."

"Hey, look at what I've got."

He took out of his pocket little shells and pebbles he had snatched from the nearby brook. Hsiao-hsiao looked at them, her eyes brimming, and managed a laugh: "Sonny, we get along so well. Please don't tell anyone else I've been crying. They might get upset." And indeed, no one in the family got wind of it.

Half a month went by and Motley, taking all his belongings with him, left without so much as a word. Grandfather asked Mumbles (who roomed with Motley) whether he knew why Motley had left. Had he merely drifted off into the hills, or had he enlisted in the army? Mumbles shook his head, and said that Motley still owed him two hundred dollars; he had gone with not so much as a note when he left. He was certainly a no-good. Mumbles spoke his mind, but gave no indication where Motley might have gone. So the whole family buzzed about it the whole day, talking about this departure until nightfall. But, after all, the farmhand had not stolen anything and had not absconded with anything; so after a while, everyone forgot all about him.

Hsiao-hsiao, however, was no better off. It would have been nice if she could have forgotten Motley, but her stomach kept on getting bigger and bigger, and something inside began to move. She felt a sense of panic, and she spent one restless night after another.

She became more and more irritable: only her husband was aware of that, because she was now always harsher on him.

Of course, her husband was at her side all the time. She wasn't even very sure what she was thinking herself. On occasion she thought to herself: what if I were to die? Then everything would be all right. But then, why should I have to die? She wanted to enjoy life, to live on.

Whenever anyone in the family mentioned—even in passing—her husband, or babies, or Motley, she felt as if a blow had struck her hard on the chest.

Around October she was worried that more and more people would know. One day, she took her husband to a temple, and, making private vows, she swallowed a mouthful of incense-ashes. But as she was swallowing her husband saw her, and asked what she was doing. She told him this was

good for a bellyache. Of course she had to lie. Though she implored the Bodhisattvas to help her, the Bodhisattvas did not see it her way; the child in her grew and grew just as before.

She went out of her way to drink cold water from the stream, and when her husband asked her about it, she said that she was merely thirsty.

Everything she could think of she tried, but nothing could divest her of the awful burden which she carried within. Only her husband knew about her swelling stomach; he did not dare let on to his mother and father. Because of the disparity in their ages and their years together, her husband regarded her with love mixed with fear, deeper even than his feeling for his own parents.

She remembered the oath that Motley swore, as well as what happened besides. It was now autumn, and the caterpillars were changing into chrysalises of various kinds and colors all around the house. Her husband, as if deliberately taunting her, would bring up the incident when he had been stung by the furry insect—that brought up unpleasant memories. Ever since that day, she had hated caterpillars, and whenever she saw one she had to step on it.

One day, word spread that the co-eds were back again. When Hsiao-hsiao heard this, her eyes stared out unseeing, as if in a daze, her gaze fixed on the eastern horizon for some time.

She thought, well, Motley ran away, I can run away too. So she collected a few things, bent on joining the co-eds on their way to the big city in search of freedom. But before she could make her move, she was discovered. To the people of the farm this was a grave offense, and so they tied her hands, put her away in a shed, and gave her nothing to eat for a whole day.

When they looked into the causes for her thwarted attempt at escape they realized that Hsiao-hsiao, who in ten years was to bear a son for her husband to continue the family line, now carried a child conceived with another. This produced a scandal that shook the household, and the peace and tranquillity in the compound was totally disrupted. There were angry outbursts, there were tears, there were scoldings: each one had his own complaint to make. Hanging, drowning, swallowing poison, all these the long-suffering Hsiao-hsiao had considered desultorily, but in the end she was too young, and still wanted to hold on to life, and so she did nothing. When Grandfather realized the way things were, he hit upon a shrewd plan. He had Hsiao-hsiao locked up in a room with two people to stand guard; he would call in her family to ask them whether they would recommend that she be drowned, or that she be sold. If it was a matter of saving face, they would recommend drowning; if they couldn't bear to let her die, they would sell her. But Hsiao-hsiao had only the uncle, who worked on a nearby farm. When he was called, he thought at first he was being invited to a party; only afterwards did he realize that the honor of the family was at stake, and this put the honest and well-intentioned fellow at a loss as to what to do.

With Hsiao-hsiao's belly as proof, there was nothing anyone could say. By rights, she should have been drowned, but only heads of families who have read their Confucius would do such a stupid thing to save the family's honor. This uncle, however, hadn't read Confucius: he couldn't bear to sacrifice Hsiao-hsiao, and so he chose the alternative of marrying her off to someone else.

This also seemed a punishment, and a natural one at that. It was normal for the husband's family to be considered the injured party, and restitution was to be made from the proceeds of the second marriage. The uncle explained all this carefully to Hsiao-hsiao, and then was just about to go. Hsiao-hsiao clung to his robe and would not let him leave, sobbing quietly. The uncle just shook his head, and, without saying a word, left.

At the time, no reputable family wanted Hsiao-hsiao; if she was to be sent away, someone would have to claim her, and so for the moment she continued to stay at the home of her husband. Once this matter had been settled, no one, as a rule, made any more fuss about it. There was nothing to do but wait, and everyone was totally at ease on the matter. At first, Little Husband was not allowed in Hsiao-hsiao's company, but after a while they saw each other as before, laughing and playing like brother and sister.

Little Husband realized the situation about Hsiao-hsiao being pregnant; he also understood that, in her condition, Hsiao-hsiao should be married off to someone living far away. But he didn't want Hsiao-hsiao to be sent away, and Hsiao-hsiao for her part didn't want to go either. Everyone was in a quandary as to what to do, though the force of custom and circumstance dictated what had to be done, and there were no two ways about it. Lately, if one asked who was making up the rules and the customs, whether the patriarch or matriarch, no one could rightly say.

They waited for a prospective husband: November came with still one in sight. It was decided that Hsiao-hsiao might as well stay on for the New Year.

In the second month of the new year, she came to term, and gave birth to a son, big-eyed, with a large round head, a sturdy build, and a lusty voice. Everyone took good care of both mother and son; the customary steamed chicken and rice wine were served to the new mother to build up her strength, and ritual paper money was burned to propitiate the gods. Everyone took to the baby boy.

Now that it turned out that the child was a boy, Hsiao-hsiao didn't have to be married off after all.

When, years later, the wedding ceremony for Hsiao-hsiao and her husband took place, her son was already ten years old. He could do half a man's work, he could look after the cows and cut the grass—a regular farmhand who could help with the chores. He took to calling Hsiao-hsiao's husband Uncle: Uncle would answer, with never a cross word.

The son was called "Herdboy." At the age of eleven, he was betrothed to a girl six years older. Since she was already of age, she could lend a helping hand and be very useful to the family. When the time for the bamboo wedding pipes to be sounded at the front door came, the bride inside the sedan chair sobbed pitiably. The grandfather and the great-grandfather were both beside themselves.

On this day, Hsiao-hsiao had lately given birth (the child was already three months old), and when she carried her newborn babe, watching the commotion and the festivities by the fence under the elm, she was taken back ten years, when she was carrying her husband. Now her own baby was fussing, so she sang in low tones, trying to soothe him:

"Now, there, there, look! The pretty wedding-sedan is coming this way. Look at the bride's lovely gown! How beautiful she looks! Hush! Hush! Don't act up now. Behave yourself or Mommy will get angry. Look, look! The co-eds are here too! One day, when you grow up, we'll get you a co-ed for a wife."

The Lamp

by Shen Ts'ung-wen

Translated by Kai-yu Hsu

A girl dressed in green dropped in to see him one day. She noticed a lamp on his desk; it was an old contraption, but polished to a high shine. She wanted to know why all that care was lavished on an old lamp. He told her the story behind it:

Two years ago I came here to teach a few hours at the college. The usual two-room arrangement received me, with the front room a sort of combined living room–study, and the bedroom in the back. It was May.

For reasons I never knew for sure, the lights were completely unpredictable. Often in the evening when dinner was laid out on the table, and I had barely made out the colors and shapes of what was there, and I was just about to offer a few not-too-dishonest compliments to the cook, the light would go out and spoil everything, including the act of downing the dinner. At other times the light would quit almost as if on purpose just as I was getting ready to do some work after dinner, or just as friends dropped in for a chat. Once a friend was trying to decipher a scroll written in the Chang style of cursive calligraphy, and another time when he and I were debating the authenticity of a seal affixed to another scroll, again the light failed. The friend lost his customary gentility and burst out in a stream of curses at the power company.

Some people must have actually complained to the power company after about two weeks of this off-again on-again lighting. The reply from the company, printed in the local paper, blamed it on the weather. The company thus denied any re-sponsibility, but the price of tapers in the neighborhood stores jumped by five coppers a package. I learned from the cook about hoarding and market speculation of this kind among the people of Shanghai. The cook, who had taken over the management of my little household, had the same story to tell every evening when he came in to put the dinner on the table, and lit a small candle just in case the lighting played tricks on us again.

The cook, my own steward and house manager, was middle-aged, and honest to a fault. When young he had followed my father on trips to the northwest and northeast, crossing the frontier into Mongolia and west to Szechwan Province. Then he traveled a lot alone, in Yunnan and Kwangsi provinces in the Southwest. In our home town he had tended the grave of my grandfather for years. A year ago he had joined the Northern Expedition troops and had gone to Shantung. Near the city of Chinan he had witnessed the soldiers' brutality against defenseless civilians. He was then the quartermaster of a company under the Seventy-first Regiment, and one evening, with machine guns threatening to fire all around him, somehow he managed to sneak away, to lose himself in the dark. Of course, he left behind everything he could call his own. He found his way to Nanking, drifting around all alone for a while before he learned my present location from an old acquaintance. He wrote and asked to come and "serve" me. I told him it was all right for him to visit me and be my guest for some days, but getting him a job would be another and very difficult matter. I told him how simply I lived, and promised him some help, but not a whole lot, when he wanted to go home after staying with me for a while.

He came, in a worn gray cotton military uniform at least two sizes too small, looking as though it had been issued three years before when the Northern Expedition Army first marched through Hunan Province. He carried a small bundle—his traveling pack. A thermos bottle dangled on a sling like a tourist's binoculars. A toothbrush peeped out from his jacket pocket. In the bundle, in the typical foot soldier's fashion, he had stuck a pair of chopsticks made of boxwood. Yes, he was an ideal companion, a companion I had been hoping for day and night for a long time. Everything about this man fitted my expectation—his whole outward appearance and everything hidden beyond the appearance, particularly that simple, kind heart of his. I understood him thoroughly without any need for words.

His arrival opened the floodgate of things we wanted to talk about together. He wanted to cover all the topics in one sitting, from my grandfather all the way down to the grandson which my father had yet to see but had talked about with this old soldier lots and lots of times. He never got tired of talking about my family, nor did he ever finish telling of his own experiences, being a man of around fifty who had walked about half of China's immense landscape, seen with his own eyes the Boxer Rebellion of 1900 and the revolution of 1911, been through an untold number of battles, crossed an equal number of mountains and rivers. He had tasted all kinds of exotic food, slept in all kinds of strange beds. Who could resist the endless tales stored in his memory? Quickly I became addicted to hearing him spin his yarns. I asked him about one thing after another whenever I could find a moment to do so.

For sixteen dollars a month the landlady's maidservant, the cook, had been serving me two meals a day. The menu was left entirely in the hands of that woman from north of the river. It didn't take her long to discover that I wasn't too particular about food, so she served me a dish of beans one day and a dish of small, hard-shelled clams the next, and pretty soon my diet contained not much beyond these two alternating dishes. When a meat dish was due, she never forgot to add some sugar to it; neither would she alter her way of cooking fish—just steaming it over the rice and serving it with a few drops of soy sauce. My old soldier friend during the first couple of days acted like a guest, then he couldn't stand it anymore. On the third day, without telling me what for, he asked me for some money. That evening at mealtime, to my surprise, he presented dinner in his well-disciplined, respectful manner, in his well-worn soldier's uniform. He acknowledged with a broad grin that he had tried out his cooking, and declared that he would henceforth make it his regular job. This old soldier's personality and the flavors of the food he cooked brought forth a strong nostalgia for my old army life, which dominated our dinner conversation that evening. I resumed my reading of student papers after dinner; the light, as usual, was out. The feeble candlelight must have added something to my appearance at the desk, something related to my military past perhaps, for he returned, quietly opened my door, and snapped to attention with a crisp, "Reporting for duty, sir!" "What is it?" I asked. He carefully walked over with a slip of paper, an account of the day's expenses. I nearly burst into scolding over this uncalled-for bureaucratic behavior, but I held myself back with a chuckle, recalling his lifelong career as an army quartermaster. Instead, I said, "Why all this bother?"

"I must make everything clear," he said. "I want you to know. If we cook our own meals, we don't need to spend more than sixteen dollars a month for both of us. Every day they serve you only clams, and every day they give you leftover rice, and for that you pay them sixteen dollars just for your board alone!"

"But wouldn't it be too much work?" I said.

"Too much work? Cooking meals is nothing compared to carrying rocks up from a river bed. You're really still a young master of the old type; you know nothing about working with your hands."

I stared at his open, honest face, unable to think of anything to say. From that moment on the old soldier took on the duties of my cook.

Now that he was in the city, I wanted to get him some decent clothes. I asked him what kind he liked, but he wouldn't say. One day he learned that I had received a good lump sum of money; he asked me for ten dollars.

That evening he brought home from God knows where two military uniforms, with a pair of used boots complete with cavalry spurs. He was beyond himself with joy when he showed me his purchases. I said, "You don't need to wear these here. You're not on active duty. Why don't you do as I do, and wear a long gown?"

"I'll always be an army man," he said. That's how, as I said at the beginning of the story, I got a military officer for a cook.

The power failures worsened, now often lasting for hours at a stretch, and a candle became indispensable at mealtime. From somewhere the old soldier managed to secure for me an old lamp, which he polished to a gleam, its wick carefully trimmed into a rounded crown. Knowing him, I did not want to suggest that using kerosene lamps in a place like Shanghai was a bit odd; furthermore, I really could use one. It would free me from the tricks of the fickle electricity. I let the lamp stay on my table. At night, under the yellowish light that shone from the crystal-clear glass chimney, and with such a classic old soldier on duty nearby, I dreamed of the ancient temples where my regiment had been billeted, and the roadside inns in tiny villages. That was a world with which I used to be intimately familiar, and which now seemed so remote because of my current commitment to city life. Such reminiscence invariably made me restless with my present life. Just what does it all mean to me, I would ask myself. Every day I ascended the podium, looking hypocritically serious. I talked about this and that, making nonsense and telling lies, quoting from one book after another. After a while I caught the spell myself, feeling that I was actually developing the subject into something really serious, only to be startled by a noise from the audience, and to discover that one of the seniors ready to graduate at the end of the semester had fallen sound asleep right under my nose. I would lose my train of

thought. Back in the faculty lounge, a crowd of well-educated gentlemen would remark to me, "What wonderful weather. You must be inspired to write another story!" They might be proud of such a remark, and thought they were the epitome of academic wit. But I couldn't get interested in those flat faces in front of heads that knew only how to eat well, sleep well, and guffaw at silly jokes. Speechless, I would retreat from the lounge into the bright sun outside. But there invariably a crowd of students came up and besieged me with questions, all kinds of questions, as though my teaching a few hours here had obligated me to respond to their desire to know all the fine details of a writer's life, and once their desire was satisfied by some idle chatter they would have learned as much literature as they were supposed to know. Then I would return to my two-room apartment and drop into the chair in front of my table cluttered with manuscripts and books and magazines. I would fight strenuously to gain a few inches of space on the table, where I would spread out the students' papers to read, line by line. The first piece repeated "love has broken my heart" five times. The second piece repeated it seven times. The third piece talked about revolution, full of blood and tears, but not without love, naturally. The pile of student homework would be reduced by only a fraction when daylight would start to fade, the three daughters of the widow across the alley would turn on their gramophone, and out would fly the shrill notes of their favorite Italian love song. And suddenly I felt wronged. Why, here I could do nothing, absolutely nothing. I was a village product. This world was not mine. Weary of city life, and weary of life itself, I felt driven to think of leaving all these amenities behind—at least I would be better off if I returned to the butcher's life of a tax collector, paid 140 coppers a month; a tax collector who could sit in the village militia office, listening to the frogs croaking in the rainwater puddles in the yard, and practicing calligraphy modeled on some ancient master's with a "champion" brand brush.

Then I would notice this kerosene lamp, and the old soldier's face under the lamplight, and his slightly stooped shoulders that expressed so very well the classical style of life that typified my old home town; I would forget the day's frustrations and fatigue, forget the chaos in front of me. My interest in this old soldier's spirit would instantly return and arouse me.

"Well, do you know any army songs?" I joked with him.

"Of course I do. I just don't know any of those foreign songs," he said.

"Just as well you don't know any foreign songs. You know folk songs?"

"Depends on which folk songs you mean."

"Are there different kinds of folk songs? 'The Clouds Rise in the Sky, One Piling on Top of the Other,' and, 'The Clouds Rise in the Sky and the Clouds Bloom . . .'—they're all good folk songs. I didn't understand them when I was little, but later when I served in Commander Yang's guerrilla unit, we ate dog meat and sang dirty songs to our hearts' content. We were happy as gods."

"We would have been embarrassed to sing those songs," he said. "A regular army soldier can't get out of line."

"Then I must have been miles out of line. But I often think of my fellow soldiers, the ones who had barely grown up, just barely cut the cord. In such beautiful weather I wonder if some of them are still singing those songs."

"The good things are gone," he said. "Good people and the good life—all gone. Maybe it's fate. Take this lamp, for instance. Years back when I stayed in the countryside with the Old Master, this was the only kind of lamp we had."

The disappearance of kerosene lamps plunged the old soldier into a spell of deep sighs, like an old country gentleman moaning over the passage of time.

So we talked, and so the magic of a familiar voice and atmosphere lured me on to lose myself in reverie over an old world in which everything called to me and moved me. But then the land-lady's clock in the corridor would strike nine, and the old soldier would abruptly end our conversation, even if I yelled at him to stay put. Time was up. He would glance at my bedroom, snap to attention, give me a military salute, bid me good-night, and go off to his bed in that closet-like en-

closure downstairs. Why? He must be worried about keeping me up too late, keeping me from doing my work, and for that he would hold even his favorite topic until the next day. Ironclad army rule: no conversation after 9:00 P.M., and no exceptions! Every time he left a new emptiness would grip me, and I would feel restless, unable to concentrate on my work.

I had been writing stories about village life, mostly about how economic needs effected change in that pattern of living. But now, with the old soldier pouring out from his treasury over fifty years' worth of fascinating real experiences, I couldn't write fiction anymore, not even a short story. How could I capture on paper this simple but beautiful soul, with the kind of simplicity he deserved? Whenever I watched him or listened to his voice I was instantly struck by the flatness of the characters I had portrayed in the past. How little I really knew! Those eyes of his, sad, but never without a gleam of hope for the future, seemed to be saying something beyond words; his eyes left me speechless. He would be talking about the war, about how innocent people had their houses burned, or how a cow was taken from a farmer's and driven back in triumph to the army camp; then suddenly he would recall something which would make him pause. I suspected that there was much more to the story but that he had run out of words, and had to remain silent. He stared at me, and perhaps satisfied that our feel-ings were in harmony, he would smile, almost ten-derly, then nod, then change the subject, or sing a few lines of a folk song. He could not see that I was really shaken at such moments. In his every movement I saw so many of his rural fellow-coun-trymen, all uneducated, but at the same time all so very good and honest. Time had uprooted the peace-loving soul of an old eastern race, and thrust it into a world of wars with which it had no empathy. Life had compromised itself, with a touch of melancholy and much restraint, in order to survive in this new world, but its dreams retained the lights and colors of a bygone world. I felt like crying.

His presence disturbed me. Sometimes I had to complain and send him away. He would quietly fade, like a fish into the deep, which made me feel worse. So I asked him, "Would you like to go to the theater?" And I dug out two dollars for him, urging him to spend them in any theater he chose. He stared at me for a moment, accepted the money, and left. I listened to him leaving, and later I heard him return around 10 o'clock. I thought he must have been to the theater, or had a drink somewhere, or enjoyed himself in a gambling joint. The next day, a steamed chicken appeared on the lunch table. I didn't dare ask him how the chicken got there; instead we exchanged an understanding smile. I knew the language of his eyes. "You should have a drink," I could only say; "you can drink quite a bit, can't you?"

"I got some," he said. "The stuff they sell around here is all cheap hard liquor. I searched around and finally got some rice wine from a fellow-townsman's place." He seemed embarrassed to bring up the subject of drinking, but now that I had mentioned it first, he rushed downstairs to bring up half a cup of wine and the bottle along with it. "You drink a cup," he said, "but don't overdo it." I drained the cup he handed to me. When he took back the empty cup, he refilled it for himself, downed it, smacked his lips, again a wordless smile, then returned his bottle downstairs. The following day we had another chicken. Chickens cost a dollar apiece in Shanghai.

The college lay outside his concern, though he did ask me once about the future of its graduates; he wondered if every one of them would later be appointed a mayor. He also wondered about my salary, and if it would be affected whenever war flared up, as the army pay had been. His curiosity about the college graduates was prompted by his wish to know how many future mayors would have been my students, and he wanted to know also if I was paid enough, and if so, if I was paid promptly. He worried about me, about my life. At first he went along with my way of living; then he seemed to have discovered additional duties toward me, and started questioning me about every aspect of my life. Unlike the prejudiced, stubborn elders in my family, this old soldier would not criticize me right and left, but his gentle sighs and

smiles were eloquent, which upset me. Still, I couldn't bring myself to hit him or even scold him for his negative comments on my way of life. What he disapproved of most was my wifeless status.

When he touched upon this last thing in my life, at first I pretended not to understand what he was driving at, and changed the subject to talk about our army life and the local customs in different places. He rapidly made a nuisance of himself, an honest but earnest nuisance, until I had to tell him straight out that I could do nothing about my bachelorhood because I had neither the qualifications of an accomplished gentleman nor those of a carefree student. Why should I waste my time thinking about it? That, however, made it worse, for from that time on he seemed to have taken the responsibility upon himself, and started watching over my women visitors like a foxhound. Now, every time a woman showed up, whether a friend or a student, this old soldier would quietly appear with a plate full of fresh fruit, which he presented to the visitor with exaggerated courtesy. Next he would retire beyond the door to eavesdrop. When I saw my visitor off, he would act as though he just happened to be outside my door looking for something, and he would pump me for information about the visitor, for clues to my own attitude toward her, and even offer comments on the manner, speech, and personality of the woman guest. He quoted his fortune-teller's handbook to elaborate on a theory of the signs of intelligent and good-natured women, or of women destined to bear many children. He would go on until my impatience was showing. He thought he was very clever; he thought he had fooled me, and that I couldn't detect his secret wishes for my life. I knew all along what was happening, but I didn't know what to do about the bother he had created. I could never hate him; explanations would not reach him; consequently I could only try to dodge the subject.

In his touching naïveté, this old soldier tried an untold number of ways to help me get a woman. He wanted to be the chief usher at my wedding, to stand in front of the fashionable hotel-restaurant in his newly acquired woolen uniform and greet all the guests on my behalf. He wanted, also, to take care of my son, who would be dressed in a way befitting the offspring of a great general; he would go for walks in the park with this child in his arms. His dream went further; he dreamed of riding on the first horse to dash into my home town and proclaim the great news of my triumphant return, with my wife, children, money, and lofty titles. He would be the first to answer questions from friends and relatives who came to greet me; briefly dismissing these questions, he would gallop away toward my old home where my old mother would receive the first word of my return from this old soldier. He would startle the whole town with the news he bore! Ten years ago and more he had had such a dream fixed on my father, but my father had returned from the Northwest and Mongolia with only the desolation of deserts in his hair and a backache from a wound incurred fighting horse thieves, plus failing health that came with his years, to live out his remaining life as a colorless army doctor. Next, the old soldier had pinned his hopes on my brother, but my brother brought home an uncouth manner which he had learned from the Manchurian troops, a stoic patience from the wild Northeast, and a knowledge of the metropolitan life in Shanghai—all these he packed away into the obscure life of a painter, which he became in my home town. Then there was my younger brother, whom the old soldier considered his real buddy, though he had never met him. My younger brother mingled together experiences of blood, sword, and revolution acquired in Kwangtung province, fought in the many battles throughout Yüeh-chou, Wu-ch'ang, Nan-ch'ang, Lung-t'an—cities in Central China—as a petty officer in the army. He survived, but his wavering thought over a life snatched from fate's jaws, and his crowded memories of shouting, running, dying, and decay—foolish acts of men in this age—drove him home to pass his waning days in lonely repose with a sinecure job. Now the old soldier had to turn to the useless me for his selfless and sincere hope. He thought that what I was doing was superior to all my father and brothers had done, in bringing glory to my home town and surprise and envy to my fellow townspeople.

He created a mirage in his head, and placed me in the middle of it. Before him, I felt ashamed and sad, but I could not bring myself to smash his dreams, since I felt I had no right to.

But how was I to live in peace with him now? What I did was too far removed from his expectations. I came to dread our encounters. I could tell him that the world was treating me all right, but I was only writing a few stories and teaching a few classes. But on his part he only noticed the impressive visitors coming to my house, including those pretty young women, so pretty that they seemed to be made of powder and cream. He looked at the surface, and what he saw of me perpetuated his dream. He tried to be very patient with me, maintaining his role as my servant, but every day his sympathy over my bachelorhood mounted. The difference between his world and mine was too much for him to grasp. How could I explain all this to him? At times I felt I should hit him hard.

In those days the one visitor who came most often was a woman in blue; she seemed to be dressed in blue all year round, and only blue suited her. We were very close; her ideological inclinations and her interest in writing gave us much to talk about together. My old soldier watched us secretly for days and weeks, and concluded all by himself that this woman was for me. He took it upon himself to act as my mother. He stuck around whenever she showed up, hinting broadly that I should introduce him to her. Before her his manner was a bit stiff, almost bureaucratic, but always correct. I told her about the old soldier's good intentions, his honesty and fascinating life experience. By and by a sort of friendship developed between them, which made him determined to see me live with the woman. His heart, toughened by all those years of living with hunger, cold, and near-death, literally melted when he thought of me and that woman together. He made me feel that if we didn't end up as man and wife it would be an unpardonable crime on my part. He had even discussed this with me seriously, the disapproval plain on his face.

In the beginning this soldier was reluctant to talk with the woman. When she asked him about this or that, as if she were urging him to tell her his life stories, he always appeared somewhat ill-at-ease and bashful, and responded stiffly to her questions. But by and by familiarity increased, and he eventually went so far as to talk with her about my life! He asked the woman to make me live as befit my station, eating and dressing better and working less hard. He put the point across diplomatically by referring to how my father lived, how good my family was; he gently hinted to the woman how nice it would be for her to marry into my family. He knew he was exaggerating, but he eyed me to stop me from interrupting. When he felt the woman had been persuaded, he would feel very pleased with his performance, and proceed downstairs to prepare some refreshment for me and my guest.

He saw me writing letters home; he asked me if I was telling my mother about a certain girl who was very, very . . . He meant to say "very close to me," or "very suitable for me." But as soon as he saw my frown, he would immediately utter some subdued sounds, as if clearing his throat, apparently suggesting "I'm only joking; I don't mean any offense; please don't take it seriously . . ." And he would step away from me to occupy a far corner of the room, as if he feared that I would really throw my ink bottle at him.

However, on every other occasion he would always drag that woman in blue into our conversation.

What could I do about all this? I could imitate neither my younger brother, who stuffed horseshit into the mouth of a talkative orderly, nor my father, who dismissed such a person with irrelevant remarks. I could only smile a pained smile whenever I saw this old soldier of mine. I maintained this approach constantly, whether he talked about his own life or about my future aspirations. He was not to be silenced at anybody's request. Even if he lost his voice altogether, his every gesture and every motion would never fail to remind you that he was scheming, out of perfectly good will, something and everything for your sake. He wasn't much of an actor. As I saw through his transparent techniques, I could only be deeply touched.

One day the woman in blue came to call while I was out. My old soldier talked a great deal with the visitor. (From the way he looked afterward I knew that when he spoke with her he must have assumed the kind of amiable politeness very much befitting a servant before the mistress of the house.) Not knowing how soon I would be back, she left. After my return I was discussing the visitor with the old soldier when the woman in blue came again. It was dinner time. The old soldier was visibly pleased when he heard that she was to stay for dinner. Before long he brought up an unusually impressive meal. I don't know where he had picked up such delicacies—he had learned that she would not use hot peppers, and so the fish that night was cooked sweet-sour, unlike his usual style, which was highly spiced.

The main dishes over, without my asking the old soldier brought in apples for dessert. He filled the teacups with water freshly boiled over an alcohol burner. He lingered for quite a while, seeing to it that everything was in order, before he retreated downstairs to have a drink, I was sure, in glee. He must have been dreaming of seeing his master and mistress together. In his wine cup he must have already seen his young master in a miniature dress uniform, like some of the foreign children we often saw on the boulevards, swaggering along, with tiny leather boots on his tender, white feet. The old soldier himself would follow behind, walking slowly like a dignified officer. Just because of my visitor's presence, the old soldier indulged in unrestrained dreaming. He could hardly know that my guest was there that evening to tell me about her wedding, planned for the following month, with her fiancé waiting in Peking. Somehow the old soldier must have overheard, out of context, the word "wedding," and he took it as a prophecy assuring him a place in his vision.

She left, and I was leaning on the table, my joy over her good news mixed with a tinge of unnamed regret. That good man, who had had a bit too much to drink—a wine-flushed face—appeared unsteadily before me.

"You had quite a bit to drink, didn't you?" I said. "How did you manage to get such good food today? The guest said she had never tasted anything like it."

"I'm happy today." He broke into a fawning smile when he heard my compliments.

"You should be happy!" I said.

"Why should I? I don't understand it. I just know I've never been as happy as today. I finished half a bottle!"

"All right, that's all right. We'll go get some more tomorrow. You're here, and I can't offer you much else. At least I can let you drink all you want," I said.

"I've never had this much to drink all at once. You said I should be happy. Why should I? I've been unhappy most of the time. I think of Old Master and what happened to his life, I can't feel happy about that. I think of the Master, your elder brother, and the way he is now, I can't feel happy either. I think of the Third Master, your younger brother; I've heard a lot about him. They say he's a leopard, he's got guts and he's got ambition. I want to go fight in his unit, go rush the enemy with him, gun in hand, crawl over the obstacles, yell 'Kill!' and thrust my bayonet right through the chests of those guys. I want to ask him how to handle a grenade with seven seconds' delay action. But the ones with him are a stinking rotten heap now, just piled up together out there. They say everyone from the Fourth Class of the Whampoa Academy died during the Dragon Pool campaign, and two months later when people passed by, the stench was still unbearable. Lucky for him, he got out of that alive, and he still could go boar-hunting on horseback. That's a hero for you, but I can't be happy thinking about him either, because he didn't make division commander. And you, you're not strong at all. Why don't you—"

"Why don't you go right to bed," I said. "I have some work to do. I don't feel like talking."

"You don't want to tell me. You treat me like a stranger. But I'm an old horse, got a horse's long ears. I heard it and I know I'm going to be invited to a wedding banquet. Such an important thing you don't want to tell me. I'm quitting! I'll leave tomorrow!"

"What *did* you hear? What am I hiding from you?"

"I know, I know, but I ask you . . . You don't know how I feel right now."

He really started crying, an old soldier like him, crying like a child. But I knew his tears were those of joy. He still thought I was going to marry the woman who had just left the room. He thought he was about to have a mistress in the house, and he just couldn't hold back the tears of happiness. Busy wiping his cheeks with his big hairy hands, he was equally busy asking me what day it was going to be, and whether or not to inquire from Wu, the blind fortune-teller, about a lucky date. It wouldn't hurt to observe convention a bit, he thought. He even urged me to send a telegram to my folks at home some two thousand miles away. He praised my choice of a bride, saying that he was sure the woman would please my mother very much.

I had to tell him now, though in a quiet and gentle voice. He gaped, but he listened without interruption, and he believed me, perhaps too much, so that my white lie failed to work on him. I said, just to make him feel better, that I had another girl in mind, who looked, and was, very much like the woman in blue. He listened, then tears welled up in his small eyes, and he cried again. His big strong frame seemed suddenly shrinking, shriveling.

The clock in the corridor struck ten.

"Let's go to sleep. Let's talk about it tomorrow," I said.

He seemed to have awakened to his situation only this minute. He quickly mumbled apologies about having had a bit too much to drink and swore never to do it again. He asked me if I would like some freshwater perch for dinner the next day. I said nothing. He looked around awkwardly for a moment, picked up the lacquer plate full of apple peelings, and tiptoed out, quiet as a fish. He closed the door behind him and crept down the stairs. I sat there, depressed, thinking my confused thoughts about the complications of feeling between one person and another. At midnight, I was still sitting up; then I heard very soft footsteps on the stairs, approaching my door and halting there. "I've finished my work and am ready to go to bed now," I said. There was no answer. A little later I opened the door and looked out. He had gone.

He changed. He bought no more wine. When

asked he would say the kinds of drink sold in the market were all adulterated stuff, not worth it. Women ceased to be a subject in our conversation; he had completely lost interest in my female guests. The optimism about my life and work had left him; he could note only my frustration, and he was no longer ready to mention his expectations for me when I refused to start the conversation. He was trying to relocate his dream, to rechannel it in a new direction. And it seemed to be even more unrealistic because he pretended to be cheerful when I knew well that his optimism had drastically diminished. He gave up scolding me for not saving for a family of my own, and for not taking care of my comfort and appearance.

We understood each other better now. I continued in my solitude regardless of the changes in season and weather, unwilling to resume a connection with this world. As to the old soldier, because he had gotten from me some ideas totally unnecessary to him, there was no way of finding an excuse to put back together his shattered dreams. His loneliness was more pitiful than mine. In the past it was he alone who brought up speculations about a happy life ahead, and he had refused to be discouraged in spite of my denial. But later it was I who was required to validate the basis for those dreams, to tell him how they could be accomplished and how satisfaction could be brought about, in order to help him hold on to them.

The woman in blue came once again to say goodbye before her wedding in Peking. My old soldier friend this time only added one extra vegetable dish when he realized who my dinner guest was, and the way he presented the dish was less than hospitable. I saw it, and it gave me a small measure of mischievous satisfaction to see him punished, because it had been his stubborn imagination that had created the whole comedy about me and this woman. For a moment I forgot that I owed him some sympathy.

Never again did the woman in blue appear in my apartment, which was just as well, and I didn't tell him anything about her arrest in Tientsin along with her fiancé. The old soldier never asked about her again, and I knew he somehow included me in his resentment against women.

We had agreed to go back to our home town together at the beginning of the summer vacation in July. I had not seen my birthplace for over eight years now, and he for over six. But come June, skirmishes broke out in Fukien. He asked me for some travel money, saying he wanted to visit Nanking. Since he had become more irritable, and his argument with the landlady's maid over her theft of our food had become almost a daily routine, I let him go to Nanking. And he promptly disappeared.

I would not want to think of him as dying on a battlefield. He must be still living, like many others, still serving as a quartermaster stationed with his army outfit in an old temple somewhere. Early each morning he must go to the market with the cook to shop for food; he would wander into the familiar rice store to indulge in desultory conversation for a while, then stroll over to the riverside to watch the boats for a while. At night he would sit on an ammunition box to work out the day's expenses with the platoon leader under an oil lamp. He would scribble figures on a piece of unbleached toilet paper, and he would argue over the tiny discrepancy of one or two coppers to the point of swearing, passionately defending his honesty and integrity. Later, wrapped in his torn, worn cotton quilt on a hard bed made of rough boards, he would dream of having a drink with the local tax inspector, or of going down to the countryside to catch bandits, or of eating a steamed goose at the house of a rich landlord where he had happened to drop by. A man like him should live the way he did forever in this world—or at least twenty more years in the country of China. Lack of news about him did not worry me at all.

The lamp remained on my table. I lit it in preference to the electric bulb whenever I sought to relive a chapter of my life that had long gone, whenever I wanted to write about that past and yet familiar world. For under the lamplight my room would change its complexion, and I would once more see the wine-flushed face of the old soldier, and below it his military uniform—a character from a frozen past, an eighteenth-century butler of the old estate, and from his eyes would flow eloquent, wordless language that perpetually stirred my memory.

He finished telling the story. The girl in green sighed and walked over to the table. Touching the lamp with her delicate hands, she was surprised to discover that there was still kerosene left in it after two years. But then, he had just said that at night under the lamplight he would be able once again to see the old soldier and hear his voice. She said, as though really curious about the whole thing, she would like to see it tried at night, to see if she too could encounter that old quartermaster sergeant; she seemed to have become really interested in him.

Night came. Light rather feebly radiated from the lamp in his room. The flame in it flickered slightly while emitting a whispering sizzle. For those accustomed to a 50-watt bulb, under the lamplight everything in the room looked gloomy and blurred. They sat in two small armchairs, while he again returned to the subject of the lamp. He told her where the old soldier used to stand and how he looked when he talked, and in the old soldier's hands how sparkling the glass chimney of the lamp always looked, against such a messy desk strewn with books and paper. Finally he pointed at her chair as the very same one where the woman in blue used to sit.

She smiled, then another gentle sigh. A little later she said with a tinge of regret in her voice, "That old soldier, he must have died by now."

"Yes, he must have died," he said. "He must have also died in the mind of that lady in blue. But in your mind he is alive; he must be still very attractively alive in your mind, right?"

"Too bad I can't meet him."

"I'm sure he is equally sorry not to meet you!"

"I really would like to meet him, to get to know him and talk with him, to . . ."

"What's the use? Wouldn't that cause trouble for everyone involved?"

She felt that there were things about which one should blush.

Silence reigned over the two people under the lamplight.

Some days later, she came again, but this time suddenly dressed in blue. He understood that must be an effort on her part to complete the story about the lamp for them. Sharing a wordless excitement about what they were doing, which seemed calculated to make the old soldier happy, they embraced and kissed, but not without some awkwardness. She felt the light in the room and asked about the lamp, wondering why it was not on the table. He smiled.

"Is the light too glaring now?"

"Not exactly. I want that old quartermaster sergeant to see how another woman in blue fits in this room," she said.

He savored this last remark and made ready to go downstairs for the lamp.

"Is it kept downstairs?"

"Yes."

"Why did you put it downstairs?"

"The night before last the bulb burned out. I borrowed the lamp from the landlady. I can just go and get it again."

"The lamp belongs to the maid?"

"No. I believe I told you that the old soldier bought the lamp!" Then he added, with some insistence, "You know very well that it was bought by the old soldier himself!"

"Ah, that was a white lie, wasn't it?"

"If a lie turns out to be more beautiful than truth, why not? . . . And, isn't there a woman in blue here now?"

"Yes there is another woman in blue, but she surely is not going to make the old soldier happy," she said.

"I agree, because if such an old soldier really ever lived, he should deserve punishment," he said.

"You're a bad boy; you told me a tall tale, didn't you?"

"But there *is* a servant in the picture. He is very solicitous about his master's well-being. The master need only tell a lady visitor about his servant; that's enough to get her interested in the master and sympathize with him. So, this bad boy is . . ."

She burst out laughing, and they agreed to go to Soochow and Nanking together the following week. He further promised her that the trip would be expressly to find out what had happened to the old quartermaster sergeant.

Quiet

by Shen Ts'ung-wen

Translated by Wai-lim Yip and C. T. Hsia

Extremely long, the spring days. The long, long bright days. In a small town, old people either warmed themselves in the sun or dozed off; the young, having nothing else to do, would fly kites from sun terraces or open ground. Up in the sky the white sun and clouds moved very slowly, and whenever a kite had freshly broken away from its owner, here and there people would lift their heads to peer into the sky. The little children would shout the loudest, waving their hands and stamping their feet, hoping that this ownerless kite would fall into their courtyard or its thin string would get tangled on the forked laundry poles erected at the corners of their terrace.

Yo-min, a girl about fourteen with a pale, undernourished-looking little face and wearing a new knee-length blue gown, was watching such a kite from the sun terrace above the back part of her house. She saw it gliding down obliquely above her head; the broken end of its string caught between the roof tiles of the house next door. A fat woman on the sun terrace over there poked at the string with a bamboo pole, hoping to get the kite. Meanwhile Yo-min heard some noise behind her: a little boy on all fours was climbing the stairs. Soon a small head rose above the top rung of the staircase. With bright, lively eyes the boy looked furtively around without going farther up, calling out quietly to the girl:

"Little Auntie, Grandma is asleep now. Can I come up for a minute?"

Yo-min, upon hearing the voice, immediately turned her head. Looking at the boy, she reproached him softly:

"Pei-sheng, you ought to be spanked. Why climb up again? Aren't you afraid of being scolded when Mommy comes back?"

"Little Auntie, I only want to play a tiny bit. Please don't say anything. Grandma is sleeping." The boy repeated his request humbly, his voice weak and tender.

After knitting her brows to scare him a little, the girl walked over to help him climb up to the terrace.

This sun terrace, like all such terraces in the town, was nothing but the flat portion of the housetop sparsely fenced with a number of laths. These laths, usually old and rickety, were stuck into a wooden framework around the terrace. The two now leaned against the mildewed railing, rotting and about to collapse, and counted the kites of various sizes in the blue sky. Directly below the railing sloped the roof proper, with its loosely spaced tiles. Since there had been several days of spring rain, some patches of the roof were overgrown with green moss. The roofs of the houses on the same row were contiguous, and each terrace faced others on its left and right. On some terraces clothes and bed sheets were hung high up on bamboo poles to dry, and they fluttered in the breeze like flags. Facing the front of the house was a stretch of the stone wall surrounding the city; from the terrace one could see the new sprouts of the grapevines with roots in the stone crevices. Behind the terrace a limpid stream flowed softly. On the other bank was a broad meadow, like a big green carpet embroidered with variegated flowers. Beyond the meadow, one could see in the distance a number of vegetable plots and a small, red-walled nunnery. The peach trees by the hedges of the plots were in luxuriant bloom, as were those in the Buddhist convent.

The sun was quite warm, and the scene extremely quiet. The two said nothing to each other, but gazed at the sky and then at the stream. Its water was not so green as it would be in the morning and evening. Some patches looked blue and some patches directly under the sun were silver. Across the stream, one section of the meadow was filled with rape, now bursting into a shimmering gold. Another section was striped with pieces of white cloth, brought here to dry by men from the dyer's shop in the town. These were spread out in great lengths, the two ends of each piece weighted down with big rocks. Elsewhere, three people seated on boulders were flying kites. Among them was a young boy who, a reed pipe in his mouth, was blowing out various bridal tunes. In addition, five unattended horses, three white and two light brown, were grazing and moving about at ease.

Seeing two of the horses starting to run, Pei-sheng cried out in glee, "Little Auntie, Little Auntie, look!" Little Auntie looked at him and pointed her finger downward. The boy understood and hurriedly put his palm over his mouth so as not to disturb the people downstairs. Looking at Little Auntie, he shook his small head as if to say, "Don't talk, don't talk. Don't let them know."

Both gazed at the horses, the lawn, and the other sights, the boy delirious with joy and the girl lost in thought over recent events that already seemed so remote.

They were refugees here. This place was neither their home nor the destination of the journey. With Yo-min on the trip were her mother, sister-in-law, elder sister, sister's son Pei-sheng, and the maid Ts'ui-yün—all of them women except for the four-year-old boy. Not at all sure of what they were doing, they had boarded a small sailboat and sailed for fourteen days. When the boat arrived here, they should have changed to a steamship, but when they inquired for news they learned that Wuchang was still under siege and that no ship or train bound for Shanghai or Nanking could proceed from there. This news

proved that what they had heard up north was not true. Thus stranded, they found it impractical to return home, since this would mean running into more expense, more trouble, and possibly danger. So at Mother's suggestion they moved into this house as their temporary quarters, sent back to I-ch'ang the soldiers that had escorted them, and wrote letters to Peking and Shanghai in the expectation of getting replies.

After they had settled here, Mother and Sister-in-law longed only for a messenger from I-ch'ang, and Sister for letters from Peking, but Yo-min herself centered her thoughts on Shanghai. She hoped only that the letter from Shanghai would arrive first so that she could go back to school. To go to I-ch'ang to live with her father, a military representative in the Ministry of War, and her big brother, an army officer, would not be half so good as living with her second brother, who was a teacher in Shanghai. But Wuchang had been under siege for a month and was not yet taken. Who could tell when the Yangtze would be reopened for commercial travel? Forty days gone already. Accompanied by the maid Ts'ui-yün, she went every day to stand before the local daily's office building by the city gate and read the newspaper posted on its bulletin board and then hurried back to relay all the news to Mother and Sister. Then from these items of news they each tried to find cause for comfort or hope. Sometimes they exchanged the good dreams they had had the night before, trying self-deceptively to read into them all kinds of auspicious signs.

Mother had always been sickly. Since arriving here, for over a month she had waited in vain for any message from the people she had written to. The money she had taken along for the journey was dwindling fast. Her ill health, aggravated by these worries and also by the hardships endured on the voyage, had naturally worsened. Yo-min frequently thought, "If we can't sail in another fifteen days, I'll go to the Kuomintang School for Cadre Training." At that time there were indeed many girls around the age of fourteen enrolled in the Kuomintang School. So why shouldn't a colonel's daughter, who didn't have to pay one cent to get into the school? After six months she'd be a graduate assigned to serve at various places and receive a monthly salary of fifty dollars. Naturally, all these were things she had learned from the newspapers and had kept in her own mind, without daring to bring them out before her mother.

While she was thus thinking of getting a copy of the school's bulletin, and thinking of her chances, Pei-sheng heard his grandmother coughing (all along his keen ears had been listening for her movements, for if she knew upon waking that he had surreptitiously gone up to the terrace, she might scold him again for not heeding her warning against the danger of falling into the gutter and breaking his small hands), and he pulled at Yo-min's gown and whispered:

"Little Auntie, help me down. Grandma is awake!" The boy only knew how to climb, and could not get down the stairs without help.

After Yo-min had taken the boy downstairs, she found Ts'ui-yün washing clothes in the courtyard, and so she squatted down beside the washtub and helped the maid rub some of them. But she soon found the work dull and said, "Ts'ui-yün, you're already too busy here. Let me hang these for you on the terrace." She grabbed some clothes that had been wrung out and went up on the terrace again. In no time she had them on the bamboo poles.

Because the section of the small river observable from the terrace was quite far from the bridge, there was a ferryboat there for public convenience. This ferryboat, however, was as narrow as a bench and usually beached on the shore, since it served few passengers besides the men from the dyer's shop going to the lawn to dry cloth and a few laborers crossing the river to carry back loads of topsoil. Very often the boat saw no business for half a day. Right now, the ferryman was sound asleep on a big rock in the middle of the meadow. The sunlit boat, weather-beaten and bleached to a grayish-white color, also seemed listless as it floated on the water, moving and rocking ever so slowly with the breeze.

"Why is everything so quiet?" thought Yo-min to herself, even though a fair distance across the river some boatwrights were driving nails, *bing-bang, bing-bang*, into the sides of a boat, and the

itinerant peddler of sewing goods was rattling his small drum in a nearby hamlet on the opposite bank. The ceaseless banging and rattling vibrated in the air, making her feel the more keenly the quietness of the town.

After a while, from the convent with the blooming peach trees emerged a young nun in a black cowl and a gray cassock, a new bamboo basket in her hand. With brisk steps she crossed the big meadow toward the riverside and stopped at some distance to the left of the ferryboat. Squatting on a rock, she slowly rolled up her sleeves and took time to look around and watch the kites before taking out, unhurriedly, a large bunch of green vegetables from the basket and rinsing them clean one by one in the flowing water in front of her. Thus stirred, the water sparkled with sunlight. Then, a little later, from the bank along the edge of the town came a countrywoman. She called the ferryman, wanting to cross the river. It took the ferryman some effort to punt the boat over and then ferry the woman to the other side of the river. For some reason Yo-min couldn't know, the ferryman yelled at the woman as if they were in a quarrel. But the woman said nothing in return and went away. Soon after, there appeared on this side of the river three men, each carrying on his bamboo pole two large empty baskets. They called the ferryman from the bank, and the ferryman punted as slowly as the last time. On this trip a dispute broke out among the three countrymen. The ferryman, however, said nothing, and no sooner had he reached the bank than he nailed his pole into the sand. Soon the six baskets were seen in a line disappearing toward the edge of the big meadow.

At this point, the young nun had finished washing the vegetables and was now pounding a garment or a piece of cloth with a pestle. After several vigorous poundings, she shook it in the water a few times and then started pounding it again. The sound of the pestle bounced against the city wall, giving rise to ringing echoes. Later the nun, probably intrigued by the echoes, stopped pounding and called out loudly: "Ssu-lin, Ssu-lin." The other side responded: "Ssu-lin, Ssu-lin." Not long after, from the nunnery came the loud call of another woman, "Ssu-lin, Ssu-lin," followed by some indistinguishable words. It must be that she was asking whether Ssu-lin (apparently the young nun's name) had finished her errand. The latter, her work done and now tired of playing by the waterside, picked up her basket and went back, deliberately stepping in the empty spaces between the pieces of white cloth being sunned.

After Ssu-lin was gone, some vegetable leaves drifting slowly by the ferryboat reminded Yo-min of how very happy the young nun had appeared to her a moment ago: "The young nun must have hung the clothes on the bamboo poles by now! . . . must be massaging the abbess's back with her fists under that blooming peach tree . . . must be intoning Buddha's name while teasing a kitten with her hand . . ." All these things she had imagined amused her very much, and made her smile. She even tried to mimic the young nun by calling out softly, "Ssu-lin, Ssu-lin."

Thinking thus of the nun's happiness, of the water in the river, of the flowers in the distance, of the clouds in the sky, and then of her mother sick in bed, Yo-min, almost without knowing it herself, felt somewhat lonely again.

She remembered the magpies[1] chattering for a long time on the terrace this morning, and since the mailman usually came by this time, perhaps she might as well go down to see if there were any letters from Shanghai. As she reached the edge of the staircase, she saw Pei-sheng on all fours on the lowest step, trying to climb up again without making any noise. The boy too must be quite lonesome.

"Pei-sheng, you bad boy. Mommy will be back in a minute. Don't come up again."

When Yo-min got down from the terrace, Pei-sheng pulled at her, wanting her to bend her head until her ear was close to his little mouth. Then he whispered, "Little Auntie, Grandma is spitting that again . . ."

Yo-min went into Mother's room and found her lying still on the bed, like a dead person, breathing calmly but weakly. Her thin, narrow face was a mask of fatigue and anxiety. Mother had apparently been awake for some time, and upon hearing footfalls in the room she opened her eyes.

"Min-min, see for me how much water is left in the thermos bottle."

While Yo-min was pouring out hot water to mix with Coacose[2] for the patient, her eyes fell upon Mother's emaciated face and small nose.

"Mother, it's an extremely nice day today. From the terrace one can already see the peach blossoms in full bloom in the small nunnery across the river," said Yo-min.

The patient said nothing in reply, but smiled a little. Remembering the blood she had coughed up a while ago, she stretched out her emaciated hand to touch her own forehead and then muttered, "I don't have fever, do I?" So saying she looked at Yo-min and smiled tenderly—a smile so helplessly pitiable that the girl sighed, almost inaudibly.

"Is your coughing better today?"

"Better now. It doesn't matter, and doesn't really hurt me. I was not careful this morning and ate some fish, which made my throat burn a little bit. It doesn't matter."

While talking with her mother, the girl thought of going over to inspect the small spittoon near the pillow. The patient, knowing what she intended to do, said, "There's nothing." And then: "Min-min, stand there and don't move. Let me see. You've grown taller again this month. Almost a full-grown person now!"

Yo-min smiled bashfully. "I don't look like a bamboo, Mama, do I? I am afraid it's not pretty to grow so tall at the age of fifteen. People will laugh at a tall girl."

Then a pause during which Mother seemed to have recalled something.

"Min-min, I had a good dream. I dreamed that we were already on board ship. The third-class cabin was shamefully overcrowded. I was very uneasy, but I thought to myself that in a few days when we arrived we should be able to rest for half a month or so."

---

[1] The Chinese traditionally regard the magpie (*hsi-ch'üeh*) as an auspicious bird. Hearing its chatter in the morning has led Yo-min to think that she will receive good news during the day.

[2] We have translated the term *K'u-a-k'o-ssu* as a trade name, Coacose. It is probably a cocoa-flavored preparation like Ovaltine.

In fact she had invented the dream and, her memory being so poor and disorganized, she was telling it for the second time.

Seeing her mother's small waxen face, Yo-min forced a smile, saying, "Last night, I really dreamed that we were in a big ship and Cousin San-mao came to meet us. But he also seemed to be the man from the Fortune Hotel whose job it was to welcome its guests at the pier. He gave each one of us a copy of the tourist guide. This morning the magpies chattered for quite a while. It seems that it should be time for the mail to arrive now."

"If not today, it should be arriving tomorrow."

"Maybe he'll come himself."

"Didn't it say in the paper that the Thirteenth Division in I-ch'ang is being transferred?"

"Could it be that Papa has already set out?"

"If he's coming, he should first cable us."

Thus saying this and that in a deliberately optimistic vein, each tried to beguile the other into a better mood. Contrary to their words, the girl was actually saying to herself, "Mama, what can we do now that you are so ill?" and the patient to herself, "It's really rotten to go on being ill like this."

Meanwhile, just back from the fortune-teller's place north of the town, Sister and Sister-in-law were talking in whispers in the courtyard. Yo-min moved to the door and assumed a cheerful voice as she said, "Sister and Elder Sister-in-law, a while ago there was a kite whose broken string got tangled between the roof tiles. The woman next door wanted to drag it down, waving a bamboo pole. Instead of getting the kite down, she broke many tiles. Isn't it funny?"

Sister said, "Pei-sheng, you must have gone up with Auntie to the sun terrace again. You might break your leg and go lame and in the future become a beggar."

Pei-sheng was squatting beside Ts'ui-yün and helping her wash the vegetables when he heard his mother. He didn't dare reply but looked at Little Auntie with a furtive smile.

Smiling back at Pei-sheng, Yo-min started walking past the courtyard and she pulled Sister toward the kitchen, telling her in a low voice,

"Sister, it seems that Mama has spat blood again."

"What are we going to do?" Sister said. "There should be mail from Peking by now."

"Have you got the fortune teller's tally with you?"

While getting out the tally slip and handing it to Yo-min, Sister beckoned the squatting Pei-sheng over. Pei-sheng went to his mother and embraced her with his small arms, saying, "Mommy, Grandma coughed up blood again. She hid it under the pillow."

"Pei-sheng, I told you not to go into Grandma's room and disturb her, understand?" said Sister.

Pei-sheng, as if he really understood, said, "Yes, I know." and then: "Mommy, Mommy, the peach flowers across the river are all in bloom now. Can you let Little Auntie take me to the sun terrace to play for a while? I'll be good."

Sister put on an angry face: "No. After so much rain, it's very slippery up there," and then: "Why don't you play in your own room? If you go up to the terrace, Grandma will scold Little Auntie!"

The boy walked past Little Auntie, squeezed her hand, and obediently went into his own little bedroom.

Ts'ui-yün had by then finished rubbing and rinsing the laundry. Yo-min, helping her wring the clothes dry, said, "Next time let's wash the clothes by the river. It is much more convenient. There are scarcely any people using the ferry. It should be quite all right for me to go there." Not saying anything in reply, Ts'iu-yün bent her head and let a smile appear on her blushing face.

The patient in her room had a fit of coughing. Sister and Sister-in-law went in to see her. Ts'ui-yün had already wrung the clothes dry and was about to go up to the terrace. Yo-min looked at the shadows cast by the sun in the courtyard for a while, and then, walking over to the patient's room, she looked inside the partly open door. She saw that Sister-in-law was cutting out clothes patterns from paper while Sister, seated on the edge of the bed, was trying to inspect the little spittoon. Mother wouldn't let her at first, stopping her with her hands, but eventually Sister saw its contents and repeatedly shook her head without making any comment. The three of them all wore forced smiles and tried deliberately to lighten their present burden of sorrow by changing their topic of conversation and recalling some event of the distant past. They ended up in a discussion about sending out letters and telegrams. Yo-min, without knowing why, felt an acid sorrow seeping through her heart. Red-eyed, she stood in the courtyard, biting her lips as if angry with someone. Then, after a while, she heard Ts'ui-yün calling her from the terrace:

"Miss Min, Miss Min, come up quickly. See the bride on horseback. She's about to ferry across the river."

A minute later, Ts'ui-yün called out again:

"Come, come quick and see. A tile-shaped kite has broken loose. Come, come, it's right above my head now. Let's catch it."

Yo-min lifted her head and saw even from her limited view of the sky in the courtyard a high-flying kite reeling like a drunken patrolman. She could even vaguely see a portion of the white string waggling in the sky.

Not to watch the kite nor to see the bride, Yo-min nevertheless went up on the terrace after Ts'ui-yün had come down. Leaning, as usual, by the railing, she viewed everything both distant and near, and her heart began to calm. She did not leave the terrace until after she had seen the men from the dyer's shop folding up the cloth into squares like beancurd cakes and placing them neatly on the lawn, and had further watched smoke rising above the tiled roofs of the nunnery and of other houses, near and far.

Down from the terrace, she peeped into the patient's room, finding all three, Mother, Sister, and Sister-in-law, asleep. She then walked into Pei-sheng's room. He too had dozed off for a time, sitting on the floor beside his little velvet toy dog. She walked into the kitchen. Ts'ui-yün, sitting on the bench by the stove, was stealthily applying Peerless Brand tooth powder to her face as if it were facial powder. Probably afraid that she might startle the complacent maid, Yo-min hurried to the middle of the courtyard.

At this moment, she heard knocking at a neighbor's door, followed by a brief exchange between someone asking a question and another answering. A strange thought occurred to her: "Who is asking whom? Could it be that Papa and Big Brother have arrived, and are asking for the correct house number?" Such a thought made her heart pound with excitement, and she hurried to the door. Should there be a knocking or pulling at the string of the doorbell, it would have been the expected ones from afar.

But everything soon lapsed into silence.

Yo-min smiled aimlessly. Under the slanting sun a part of the wall and the laundry stand on the terrace cast their shadows on the floor of the courtyard just as elsewhere a paper flag cast its shadow on the tomb of the man the women here were expecting—Yo-min's father.

Three Men and One Woman

by Shen Ts'ung-wen

Translated by Kai-yu Hsu

Because it's raining, my friends insist that I tell stories about the rain. This is one of the least exciting of them. If it fails to move you, that's only because it is all too real. We all know that beautiful things are often unreal; we find examples in the rainbow in the sky, and in our dreams at night.

Nobody knew why it must rain whenever the troops were to move on.

We couldn't find a reason for this. Perhaps only the quartermaster at regimental headquarters could figure it out, since without rain the foot soldiers would not wear out too many pairs of straw sandals, but the moment it rained, the expense for straw sandals would immediately skyrocket. Perhaps marching the troops in the rain was profitable for the quartermaster—we were not very clear about it. As usual, the matter seemed complicated to us, and as usual even the regimental commander did not know much about it because he wore leather boots, not straw sandals. Anyway, every time the troops were to move on, the timing seemed to correlate with the rain. We'd been lucky that way all year.

Even in the rain soldiers had to fight battles; we had no complaint about marching in the rain. Since the rain was erratic, we had been completely outfitted with oilcloth and raincoats. The mess sergeant and his staff, preceding us, never found an excuse in the rainy weather to be derelict about meals. Our battalion commander on horseback was never afraid of catching malaria with his uniform totally soaked in the rain. We marched through bamboo groves, or waited under a shed on the river bank for the ferry boat to take us across; the view was much more attractive than usual because of the rain.

The rain made everything muddy, but the walking wasn't bad on the long slippery road. The rain had reduced the distance we were supposed to cover in a day. It had also given us an excuse to stop at a house where there was a young woman, to joke with her a bit, laugh a bit, and ask her for a few palm peelings with which we could wrap our feet. The rain had made us relax a bit, enough to wash our feet in the same basin as the battalion commander. For an ordinary private to wash his feet in the same basin as the battalion commander was a liberty, against military discipline. It was a rare thing to happen in our time.

Our battalion marched for four days before we reached our destination. The weather was fascinating. As soon as we got there, the rain stopped and the sun came out. People could say the sun was deliberately giving us a hard time, which might well be true, but we were not going to bother about it. We were there to take over garrison duty from another unit that had just left. They had been doing things that made little sense; now we were to continue the same nonsense.

While the afterglow was still bright our battalion settled down. Another battalion also stopped there, but only overnight; the following morning they would have to march further to a village some fifty *li* away. They had already found billeting in the small inns and some villagers' houses, while we were still hunting for a place to spend the night. According to assignments made in advance, our company was to stay at the family shrine of the Yangs. But no one in our company knew where to locate this Yang family shrine. We could only fire questions blindly at any soldier from another company who happened to be walking around.

It turned out that there were two Yang family shrines. The one we succeeded in locating, after much fumbling, didn't seem to be the right one. It was too small and dilapidated. Our company commander was not amused; his noble feet were not about to move another step. He said that since that place was unoccupied, we might as well rest there and then dispatch some of us to investigate further. We had all walked the whole day. We saw that many other comrades were already relaxing in villagers' houses, were washing feet in large wooden tubs, and were carrying dried fish into the various kitchens. They all seemed to have assuaged their hunger and fatigue. Only we were still walking about like homeless souls. Now that we had also found a place, and it would soon be dark, we didn't mind what we had found. We stacked our rifles on the porch outside the temple building. Many of us sat down around the stone lions and started taking off our knapsacks and other burdens.

A young bugler got a gourd full of liquor from nobody knew where. He greedily sneaked over to the corner of the walls where he proceeded to drink from the gourd. His comrades saw him and rushed over to snatch his gourd, which was soon smashed in the struggle and all its contents spilled on the damp ground. The bugler felt desperate, started cursing his comrades, and tried to chase after them and beat them up.

The company commander heard the commotion. He thought of the proper use for a bugler and immediately ordered him to signal regimental headquarters. The young bugler climbed up on top of the stone lion and, with one hand securing him to his perch and the other holding his short copper bugle, blew a message of inquiry. The tune sounded touching in the evening breeze.

A glorious sunset spread all over the sky, against which rose columns of cooking smoke that floated gently over the roofs. Many young women, surprised and curious looks on their faces, stood under the eaves of distant houses to watch the activity. They wore newly laundered blue cotton dresses, the fronts covered with embroidered aprons, small children huddled in their arms.

The bugle at regimental headquarters responded. Our company commander wanted to know if his superior approved our stay at the Yang family shrine, but the answer coming through the bugle calls was not very clear. Our bugler had to purse his lips to repeat for the third time his performance with the copper instrument.

Two dogs sauntered over from the southern end of the street. They stopped before a small group of people, like twin children, both with neat white coats, intelligent looking eyes, and stout bodies. The animals too seemed to know something was happening in front of the temple, and they wanted to come over for a look.

The well-fed pair of dogs sparked our imaginations: encountering a fat dog would usually call forth murderous impulses which were most difficult for us to suppress. But one more thing attracted our attention: the voice of a girl calling "Blanchi, Blanchi"—a clear but delicate voice. Called twice, the dogs looked at us for a moment, then turned and ran away, apparently knowing they were not supposed to linger.

It was getting dark, and the clouds turned deep crimson.

Suddenly there was an accident among us. We had all sat down to rest, but the young bugler, who had marched a whole long day with us, still had to climb up on the stone lion to sound his bugle time and again. Somehow his legs went to sleep. When he jumped down from the height, they were not there to support him, and he fell, breaking both his ankles. He couldn't walk like the rest of us; he couldn't even get up by himself.

He had come from the same town as I did. We had grown up together in the same village compound, gone swimming in the same river in the summer, passed many a long day together picking mushrooms in the same woods. It was only right that I should take care of him now.

There was no way out for this young man of twenty, cursed by a misfortune that condemned him forever to his station of bugler. The company commander, being another fellow townsman, did not dismiss him, but he could no longer seize an opportunity to enroll in a cadre training school to prepare for promotion, like every other normal bugler. He no longer qualified for combat against the bandits and things of that sort. He could no longer, like every other young soldier, climb over an adobe wall at night to keep an appointment with a local girl. All in all, in this accidental fall he had smashed beyond repair all his human rights and privileges.

As a fellow townsman I took particular care of him. I was a squad leader then. I took him into my own tent-like shelter. Every morning at the crack of dawn he would get up as usual, put on his uniform and spruce himself up neatly before going over to the stone steps in front of the temple to blow reveille. Ten minutes later he would do the roll-call signal. At eight it was the fall-in for drill, and two hours later, the fall-out signal ending the exercise. All these and many other bugle calls he had to do every day without fail. Even though for half a month we were not ordered to drill at all, the bugler still did his part, blowing all those signals, and each time he went out to do his duty I had to help him walk; when I was busy, the job of helping him would fall on one of the cooks.

We all hoped that he would quickly recover. The battalion surgeon even gave a guarantee to this ill-starred young man, whose legs were treated for a long time with blood-letting, massage, and cauterization. Then they were placed in pine-wood braces. Days passed, and all the treatments produced no visible results. We were getting discouraged, but he remained confident.

He said he would get well soon, and then he would remove the braces and start chasing rabbits in the field again. Hearing this, the old army doctor just smiled, because he knew that the young bugler could never hope to do such things again. And yet, since the medical profession dictated that he behave this way, and since the law permitted people like him to lie, the doctor continued to promise him all kinds of improvement which sometimes went unrealistically far beyond even his dream of chasing rabbits.

Two months later, the young man showed no improvement. The swelling had gone down, the danger of blood poisoning was over, and he no longer need worry about getting his injury infected again, but he was permanently crippled. He could do his duties without physical support, and he stayed on in my shelter. A strong bond of friendship had grown between us.

The village where we were stationed was not very populous, and had a special character when compared with other frontier towns of Hunan Province. There were only four large streets meeting at the center of the village, where stood a drum tower that overlooked the whole village. As in every other town, there were medicinal herb stores and opium shops, gambling joints and drinking taverns. Each day I spent most of the time with the crippled bugler; we went out together, drank together, and shared the proceeds in any game of chance.

If we weren't ordered to move on, this young man still had his share of the blessings of a soldier's life. He could still do some of the things every soldier did. When he wanted to go to visit young women, they didn't dare offend him. When he sat down at a gaming table to play twenty-one for 50-coin stakes, nobody felt right about cheating him. In playing the bugle, those who were not his match in the past, didn't try to out-play him now. Because of his misfortune, we were all willing to bend over backwards to help him.

But he had changed. Ordinarily, a bugler would be addicted to his bugle, carrying it with him everywhere he went. He would also be a nimble-footed fellow active in all sorts of things. At dawn he would climb to the top of the hill or the city wall near the camp to practice his bugle. At night he would play it under moonlight in response to other buglers in the distance. On market days he would parade through the marketplaces in his best uniform, along with other horn-blowers from nearby companies. As they showed off before the local people, lucky things might happen; one of those women with clean foreheads and shining black eyes, half hidden behind the side doors of their houses, just might take a liking to him. If he had been completely free to move about, he could have taken his bugle up to play on the mountain; many children would have gathered around him to admire and to be awed by the art of this great man. Then he would have been able to establish some sort of contact with them which gradually would lead to friendship.

But all these amenities due to a bugler were now over for our young friend. What was left was his duty, pure and simple. Formerly very active, always looking for things to do, he became sullen, looking pathetic. Since his legs were crippled, the company commander called him a cripple in front of everybody. A convenient mark of distinction had been added to this formerly very normal bugler; now they called him Crippled Bugler. Even the cooks of our company somehow felt they had acquired the privilege of looking down on him; they talked about him behind his back and amused themselves by imitating his awkward movements.

He continued to perform his bugler's duties, blowing the signals at the prescribed hours, until a newly recruited young assistant had sufficient training to do the same signals tolerably well. Then the crippled bugler stopped being so punctual about his services.

Every day he and I went to the southern street to sit on the long bench of a beancurd shop and watch the young proprietor making his commodity. Across the street was the town's post station, which was also the town's most impressive looking house. From where we sat we could see through the store front the many scrolls of painting and calligraphy hung on the glossy yellow wall. The two white dogs I saw on the day of our arrival belonged to this house. They stationed themselves in front of the house and greeted all familiar people with their antics. The moment they heard someone summoning them, they would rush back into the house, disappearing behind the door into a courtyard where a goldfish tank stood.

Were we there all day long just for that bowl of free bean milk, or in order to swear brotherhood with the young proprietor?

There was another reason for our visits. However, we were two soldiers, one a cripple, the other a mere squad leader who, to be sure, could step forward to do the roll call during an assembly, enjoy special status of a sort among his buddies as well as before the officers as a potential officer himself, and hold the privilege of calling his squad cook any and all kinds of names to vent his own frustration. Once outside the camp, though, what status could he retain? There were twelve squad leaders in a company, thirty-six in a battalion, over a hundred in a regiment. The squad leader's insignia on someone like me only added a bit of responsibility while taking away much of the advantage and privilege of indulging oneself available to a plain private. If you knew the responsibilities of a squad leader or platoon leader in combat, you would pity him. When I went out there to the beancurd shop, I didn't go as a squad leader; rather I was taking a liberty open only to plain soldiers. We never refused to accept that bowl of bean milk offered by the youthful bachelor proprietor, but that was not what we were there for; we had our eyes on those two white dogs and their mistress. It's really a case of "a toad with scabies wishing to eat the meat of the heavenly goose," I suppose.

She was a divine creature! I had never seen anyone like her in my life. I had seen many concubines of divisional commanders, and I had seen many girl students. The former were either prostitutes or came to look like it on becoming concubines. The latter were robust, so much so that they frightened us. They raced, played ball, and did many other things beyond our imagining; they had turned themselves into water buffaloes. They were neither graceful nor dainty. But this one, I really could not say what, to our taste, was so perfect about her, except that in all honesty I felt she was a beautiful flower, an angel on earth.

We observed military discipline, but when we went there we observed our instinctive desires. We dared not step out of line in this town, and yet we went to sit in that beancurd shop every day, making desultory conversation with the young proprietor or helping him push the millstone, transfer bean milk to the cooking pot, or wrap beancurd. All the while we hoped to catch a glimpse of that face as she stepped out the door for a moment. Often we caught sight of a corner of her white dress next to the goldfish tank in the courtyard by the inner door of the house across the street. Our hearts would skip a beat and our pulses would quicken a pace. Every day we schemed to buy things to feed the dogs and befriend them. In the beginning the beasts seemed to have sensed our ulterior motives; they would only sniff at our offerings and quickly turn away. Later we let the beancurd shop proprietor toss the food to them, and they ate it, after studying the proprietor carefully as though to make sure the food wasn't poisoned.

Why we wasted so much thought on such a hopeless situation was beyond our comprehension. Our position being what it was, even if we succeeded in making friends with the dogs, we could not hope to get close to their mistress. Her family ran the postal service, which ranked them as the only gentry family in town. The head of the family chaired the town's chamber of commerce, and his store functioned as the cashier's office for all garrison troops stationed there. He entertained a lot, receiving all people of consequence, such as the regimental commander, the battalion commander, and their immediate staff. Normally the staff officers from battalion headquarters would drop in at the store to have drinks and play mahjong or cards with the head of the family.

The beancurd shop proprietor told us that she was the youngest daughter in the family, aged fifteen. Even after we had realized the hopelessness of our situation, we kept sitting there every day, waiting for this family treasure of a young girl to come out. If we only had one look at her, that would make our day. Or even if we only heard that delicate voice calling her dogs, that too would give us ample comfort. Often we found ourselves gazing at the goldfish tank because when a corner of white or green dress flashed by we would know that she was playing there in the courtyard.

By and by the dogs became our friends. With only a little hesitation, they would come over to the shop to play with us. We liked them, but at the same time we hated them, because no matter how much they seemed to be involved with us they would spring away the instant they heard their mistress's voice. However, we had to admit that those two dogs were really friendly and in-

telligent. All dogs regarded soldiers as their enemies to be sneak-attacked or avoided at all costs. But these two had really become our friends.

The beancurd shop proprietor was young and strong and reticent. He worked cheerfully at his daily routine and dealt with all kinds of customers. At night he closed his shop and went to sleep. He seemed to do nothing besides operating his shop and he never went anywhere. At first we couldn't even discover when he ate his meals or left his shop to buy beans. He was short on words, but not to the extent of ignoring his customers. When we asked him about something his response was never terse.

Once we treated him to drinks, but when we went to pay we were told that the beancurd shop proprietor had already taken care of it. But the next time he let us pay for him.

He came from the countryside, that much we learned about him. From time to time his relatives from the country would come to see him at the shop; they didn't look too poor. In his hands the beancurd business was good, and he said he was sending all he earned back home. When asked if he was saving all his money for a bride, he only smiled. He had a good singing voice, better than those in our unit. Though illiterate he somehow managed to recognize the few words on the Chinese chess pawns and become very good at that game. We never saw him keep any account books, and yet he made no mistakes in collecting late payments or handling his finances, by sheer memory or some mnemonic device. He treated us as friends, neither suspecting nor flattering us on any occasion. We went to his shop to see the young girl, but if we hadn't had such a compatible friend in him we wouldn't have gone there every day, rain or shine.

In the shop my crippled companion and I talked about the young lady. At times we could not avoid saying certain coarse and silly things, or we would do silly things with the two dogs. The young proprietor only smiled, and in that smile we sensed a secret.

I asked him, "Why do you smile? Don't you admit that she's a beautiful girl? Don't you agree that these two dogs are luckier than we?" As usual he would not respond to these questions. Even if he did, he would still be smiling in that bashful way which was a bit feminine.

"Why are you still smiling? You country bums don't understand beauty. You must be fond of ones with huge breasts and bottoms, sows and water buffaloes, because they're big and fat and they fit you. That's because you don't know a beautiful girl when you see one; you don't recognize beautiful things."

Sometimes the crippled bugler would say, "Son-of-a-bitch, what good luck!" And he would purposely embarrass the proprietor by asking him if he wanted to be a dog so that he could have a chance to be close to the young lady every day.

And the young proprietor would blush, and apply himself more attentively to his millstone, smiling all the while.

Who knew what all this meant? Why should anyone insist on knowing what all this meant?

One could say that our days passed merrily, because besides going to the shop to have a pleasant time, drink some of his bean milk, and peep at that beautiful girl, we also often went to the open field to watch executions. Every fifth day was a market day when our regimental headquarters would pick a few bandits arrested with clear evidence of their crimes to be executed on the edge of the town as a public display. When we were stationed at Huai-hua, every time our company was assigned the guard duty at a public execution, one platoon would be detailed to escort the criminal, with the bugler, playing his instrument, marching at the head of the column through the main streets. Upon arriving at the final approach to the execution ground, the guards would break into double time and the bugler would play "assault" to heighten the tension and excitement. After the event, the troops going back to camp would march slowly through the same main streets with the bugle playing a triumphal march. All these were now beyond our crippled bugler. Now the regimental commander's bodyguards, who protected him on raids against bandits, had the sole privilege of executing criminals. We could only watch the heroic processions and witness the comedy of bloodshed, and I myself could no longer

exercise my squad leader's authority to lead the parade down the streets with the doomed under escort in our midst. But this was not necessarily our loss. Indeed it could be our gain, for security over an execution was no longer our responsibility; hence we could feel free to walk over to the execution ground to view the severed heads and the ashen gray, stiff bodies, and we could linger there as long as we wanted—no need to hurry back.

Once we dragged the beancurd shop proprietor along with us just because ordinarily he hadn't the guts to watch this sort of thing. When we arrived at the blood-stained ground, there were four bodies sprawling in the dirt, all naked to the waist, just like four dead pigs. Quite a few little soldiers in their oversized uniforms, looking utterly mischievous, were poking bamboo sticks into holes in the corpses where their throats had been. A pack of starving dogs had gathered around, sitting on their haunches to observe with concentration all the strange proceedings before them.

The crippled bugler asked the beancurd shop proprietor if the sight made him afraid. The young rustic's response was the same smile, so kind and at the same time so mystifying. It made us feel happy about our friendship, just like hearing the voice of that young girl, which made us feel that our lives had been fulfilled.

Our days passed easily because we were very happy.

Before we knew it, we had spent half a year in the beancurd shop watching the young lady.

We had become even more familiar with the beancurd shop proprietor, and thoroughly acquainted with the two dogs. Whenever there was a chance we would take them with us to play at the camp, at the riverside, and their mistress would not object.

We stopped talking nonsense and harboring silly designs on the young girl because we knew it was a hopeless case (the beancurd proprietor's confidence in us had let us learn from him a lot of things). Yet we continued to go to the shop and give him a hand with this and that. By then we had a thorough knowledge of the process of making beancurd. We could tell the grade and quality of the beans as well as judge whether the bean milk had been cooked at the right temperature. We also got acquainted with many local customers, who enjoyed talking with us and making friends with us. When our fellow soldiers came to buy beancurd, the proprietor would give them a better deal, or even decline payment. We wove our lives into the beancurd business, and the two white dogs stayed closer and closer by us. Though the young girl's voice still could get the dogs away from us, sometimes our whistle would also bring them back, running to us from their house.

Often we saw one, then another, young officer in well-pressed woolen uniform, his fair-complexioned face showing a hint of a blush, his chest up and out as he walked, march through the inner door of the house across the street, at every step tapping the stone pavement with his spurred, long black-leather boots; we would speculate what could be happening there, and such speculation would fill us with envy. Having seen a bit of the world before, I could take such blows and still find other consolations, but our crippled bugler was staggered. I saw him shake his clenched fists at the backs of those young officers who had just visited the house opposite. I also heard him talking with the beancurd proprietor about things which had escaped my notice.

Once we both had a bit too much to drink in a small restaurant. Feeling uninhibited, I said something like this to the cripple:

"You're crippled, friend; old pal, you're crippled! A girl from that kind of family'll only marry a battalion commander. Go look at our reflections in the water, you'd know we haven't got a chance. Who are we anyway? Four dollars a month; the troops pull out, we march in mud; we settle down at camp and it's drills and roll-calls; at night we sleep on straw pads feeding bedbugs. Our mouths're meant for tough old horsemeat[1] and sour greens; only cold rifle barrels under our hands . . . We're young, yes, but what good's that? We're dogs and we're pigs, just all lined up in formation. Why do we get such wild ideas about this girl? Why don't we face up to our limitations?"

I was really drunk; I didn't watch my language. I just went on and on, not realizing what I was saying, dressing down this friend who ordinarily took advice very well. It seemed that I also used many metaphors referring to his crippled legs. We were alone then. A bit later, I couldn't tell why my friend was suddenly transformed from his usual self into a mad beast swooping down on me. We grappled together, tearing at each other's ears. It was a good, honest fight. Both being drunk, we cursed and argued, making very little sense. Some other soldiers passed by and, hearing a racket they could tell was from their buddies, came in to separate us. They succeeded after much trouble.

We got back to camp, and then neither of us could stop throwing up. Around midnight the alcohol had worn off and thirst drove us out to the water tank. Quantities of cold water in our gullets sobered us somewhat, and we vaguely recalled what had happened earlier that evening. We both fell to crying. Why should we fight? What had made us hate each other that much? What was there that had to be handled in that way? We wrapped ourselves in our newly issued padded cotton uniforms and went out to the courtyard to look at the moon, which was almost down past the horizon. It looked like the face of the dead. The sky was busy with falling stars that cut threads of brilliant light. Roosters were calling everywhere. When we first arrived here, when our friend broke his ankles, it was still April. Now it was October.

The following morning, we looked at each other's swollen faces and felt very embarrassed. People at camp knew about our fight; some of them were afraid we might fight again. They didn't expect that we two would have forgotten all about what had happened to us while drunk the night before. No, we did not try to dismiss the whole thing from our minds. On the contrary, because of it our friendship seemed even stronger.

---

[1] The original has "beef," which could be either old cow's or old water buffalo's meat. In either case it must have been meat from an old, possibly sick, dying, or even dead animal. In the China of those days, beef was rarely eaten, possibly because the cow was such a useful animal for farming.

We continued to go to the beancurd shop. The proprietor thought something drastic had happened to us, since there were gashes on our swollen faces, and at first he was very surprised. It made us laugh when we looked at each other.

Finally I told the proprietor the whole thing before he could figure out what really had happened. I told him that I vaguely remembered having talked a great deal of nonsense, calling my friend a crippled dog, and that somehow we got tangled together. Fortunately both of us were drunk; we fought hard but our alcohol-weakened muscles kept us from breaking each other's heads.

The girl came out at that moment to stand near the front door. Her two dogs fawned and jumped around her, their red tongues licking her dainty hands.

We three men stopped talking to gaze at her. She also seemed to have noticed something amusing on our faces that was quite unusual. She smiled at us, showing no fear or suspicion. But that smile also seemed to say that she knew what had caused our nonsense the night before.

I was very depressed because that young girl did not take us seriously. Perhaps in her little heart she thought we came here every day only because we joined the proprietor in his business to make some money. I looked at the bugler; he also seemed extremely depressed. Everybody had known about his crippled foot,[2] which made him look inferior even to me. That gave me a basis for concluding that he must be feeling very low.

As to the beancurd shop proprietor—I couldn't tell if it was intentional—he started at that very moment to lift the millstone to inspect the axle, thus showing his handsome, muscular forearms. The same thing had happened, it seemed to me, twice before. At least one other time when a similar opportunity occurred, this youthful, honest, and simple man inspected his millstone in exactly the same manner.

I wanted to ask him about it, but there was no appropriate opportunity for the question.

A moment later she had disappeared behind the inner door, a double door painted green and adorned with gold leaves. Like a falling star, a glowing rainbow, she disappeared after what seemed to be only a glimpse. Each of us recorded on our hearts a flash of light. I was just about to smile an understanding smile at my crippled friend when he suddenly said:

"Second Brother,[3] your curses were right last night! We are dogs and pigs! We're dirty toads in the gutter . . ."

He looked so heartbroken that I felt I had to say something to comfort this unfortunate cripple. I said:

"Don't put it that way; that's not what a man should say. We have our ambitions, with them we can do anything. Every skyscraper starts from the level ground. Some day we'll be presidents or generals. What's so precious about a woman?"

He said, "I don't reckon on becoming president; that's too hard. Only this foot of mine, his mother's![4] Only this foot of mine . . ."

"Who's stopping you from having your life? Your foot can be taken care of some day. You can still look forward to the company commander's recommending you for cadre school. Then like all those students you can earn your position in the world on your own strength."

"I'm worse than a dog. Right now I'm thinking, if my foot gets fixed up I'll ask the company commander to reenlist me as a regular soldier. Then I would work hard on the drill ground all day and every day . . ."

"Bit by bit you'll get there," I said. Turning to look at the proprietor, who had replaced the millstone in position and had again started pushing and pulling the long wooden shaft, I added, "For us life is really like turning this millstone, totally meaningless. What do you think?"

This man seemed to think that what I had just said didn't fit me; neither did it fit his life. As he would on another occasion and another subject, he gave me the same smile.

---

[2] Earlier in the story, the injury supposedly affects both the bugler's legs or feet. Here the original refers to one leg. Presumably, one of the legs is healed.

[3] This is the first appearance of this form of address. Among friends who feel as close to each other as sworn brothers, the use of such kinship terms is customary.

[4] "His mother's": common swearword.

It dawned on me that all three of us were equally in love with that girl.

On October 14 I was sent to deliver a document to general headquarters seventy *li* away. That plus some other assignments kept me at Shih-men for a day. Two more days passed en route.

Upon returning to camp I first dropped off the reply at regimental headquarters to report "mission accomplished." The six dollars I collected as a special reward for this assignment made me feel very good. I wanted to see if anyone in our company was making a trip to my hometown who might bring four dollars out of the extra pay to buy pork to cure for the winter. The first one I ran into was the cripple. Before I opened my mouth he said:

"Second Brother, that girl died!"

"What?"

I couldn't believe it. Slowly I bent down to remove my sandals. The cripple, standing in front of me, said again, "The girl died," which forced me to take it seriously. I sprang up straight the moment I got the message clearly, and grabbed the man by his collar, demanding to know if it was true. He told me to listen for myself, because at that very moment funeral music was coming from a distance, and a *so-na*[5] was sending forth its sad, tremulous, shrill notes. With one foot bare and the other still in the wet straw sandal, I dragged the cripple along and we ran toward the beancurd shop like a couple of fire fighters. I was oblivious of his bad foot and of the stares of the passersby. Before we reached the shop it had become clear to me that the sounds of the *so-na,* gong, and drum were coming from the house across the street from the shop. A chill seized me; my head felt as if it had just received a heavy blow; something was rumbling in my ears. I thought: this is strange, this is really strange . . .

Quietly I sat on the bench in the beancurd shop and accepted a bowl of warm bean milk from our friend. In front of the house across the street many people had already gathered. Strips of white funeral cloth hung over the doorway. Lots of children in white turbans were buying snacks near the door. Next to the goldfish tank in the courtyard beyond I could see someone bending over a pair of long tongs with which he handled the burning paper money for the dead. Flames shot up and ashes flew to the sky.

I knew that everything was real. My whole body was twitching, but I laughed.

I looked at the beancurd proprietor, who did not seem his usual carefree self. Obviously he also had felt a severe blow which he could hardly bear. He turned his face away, pretending he didn't see me. I looked at the bugler again; somehow he was disgusting at that moment. I couldn't tell why I was so annoyed at that crippled man. I felt like hitting him, but could never bring myself to do such a silly thing.

Later I inquired and found out that the girl had committed suicide swallowing gold the day before.[6] Why? Who else was involved? I didn't know; it's not clear to me even today. (Many people died that way; and the survivors thought little of it.) The girl's death took something away from each of us—something we had never mentioned before, but now we had the courage to admit it. At first we mentioned it in sorrow, but soon all of us were laughing, and when we were about to part, we came close to jovially slapping each other on the back out of a mutually shared joy.

It was difficult to tell why we were so cheerful. Perhaps each of us knew that the girl was like a pot of flowers that belonged to none of us. At first the breaking of the flower pot brought us a measure of unavoidable grief. Then we talked about how the numerous flower pots were long kept in the possession of many rascals, and how all flower pots sooner or later fell into the possession of someone powerful and rich; yet this one broke and fell to the ground. At that we naturally seemed to feel a measure of comfort.

However, after returning to camp we felt awful. Our lives had been dashed to pieces. From that moment on, our hearts would never again skip a beat, nor would we go crazy about certain dreams.

[5] A wind instrument that looks like a stubby clarinet.

[6] It is a folk belief in China that one can kill oneself by swallowing gold. Chapter 69 of *The Dream of Red Chamber* (*Hung-lou-meng*) describes in detail how Second Sister Yu selects a chunk of gold from her belongings which she swallows (with difficulty because of the size) and dies.

There would forever be something amiss in our lives—a patched tear perhaps. Invisible though it might be, our lives could never be whole again.

In reality whether such a girl was alive or dead had nothing to do with us. Even if she were alive, the moment we received orders to move on to another duty station, that would be the end of all our hopes. Even if we were staying on much longer, with one of us a cripple and the other a squad leader, what chances were there for two bums like us? Besides making friends with the two white dogs, what grand schemes could we entertain?

The next day we woke up very early. Sitting on our bunks we faced each other, wordless. We each seemed to be trying to place ourselves in a broader context, to free ourselves from the siege of memories. Both were irritable, and yet neither understood why suddenly we had become so bad-tempered.

"Why are your eyes swollen, you stupid bum?!"

The bugler did not retaliate against my ridicule; he only looked at me, pathetically.

I said, "You don't mean to tell me that you want to cry over her like a bereft son now that she is dead?"

He stayed that way; he seemed to want to use silence as the advocate for his conscience and make me notice his behavior.

I understood that, but I did not wish to forfeit my opportunity to make fun of him.

"Cripple, you're really an ugly toad, feeding on vermin while hoping for something beyond your station."

At long last he said, but gently: "Second Brother, tell me, do dead people ever come back to life?" This silly remark provoked me to another long spell of tongue-lashing.

When we returned to the beancurd shop again, the house opposite had become desolate—only some white paper money for the dead left in front of the door. Our young friend the proprietor sat on the bench holding his head in his hands. People came to buy beancurd; he asked them to help themselves by scooping up the beancurd with a knife. He livened up a bit when he saw us coming. Apparently he wanted to hide his wound from us

with the same smile, and his smile proved the good health and kind heart he retained.

"What's the matter? Headache?"

"Buried. They buried her. Early this morning."

"They buried her early this morning?"

"They left before sunrise."

"What have you got that made you so unhappy?"

"Nothing. Nothing at all."

After this he hurried to pick up the bowls to serve us bean milk.

Something sad and chill weighed on our hearts as we sat in that shop gazing at the house opposite. After sitting there for a while, we left the shop and walked over to a local woman's place to play cards. There we learned that the girl was buried in Catfish Village two *li* away.

I didn't know why every time I saw the long face of the bugler I felt like scolding him and hitting him. The cheerless look of this man seemed to insult my secret devotion to that young girl. The way he held himself seemed a direct insult to me. I couldn't bear sitting at the same table playing cards with him. I went back to camp and plunked myself down on the straw pad.

The cripple didn't return to camp that night. He had told me that he didn't want to go back to camp that night, and I had thought that he would spend the night at that local woman's place, which was nothing unusual. The following day I didn't feel like going out either; instead I stayed in bed. By afternoon my head had started to feel feverish and something was wrong all over me. My appetite was gone. After gulping down some sweetened ginger-herb tea, I pulled the quilt over my head to induce sweating. When I woke up soaked in perspiration, it was already late afternoon.

I crawled to the back of the main hall which housed the Yang family altars to relieve myself. It had just cleared after the rain, and a touch of sunlight lingered on the corner of the roof, leaving a patch of deep yellow there. Fleecy clouds in the sky were baked into colorful ribbons by the sunset. The evening view, including the threads of cooking smoke that rose around and above the roofs, and the sounds of roosters and dogs, and of the bugles from the camps, all reminded me of the things that had happened on the day of our arrival. I thought about the fate of my ill-starred friend, and the events in our lives; it made me sad and despondent. A question was sealed in my heart about this strange thing called life which I could not explain. My thought, of course, was still rather simple, certainly not complicated at all.

I went back to sleep; I didn't feel like eating, or talking, or even thinking. I stayed that way, not knowing how long I had slept, still with the quilt over my head. I heard the muffled sounds of the soldiers playing cards and quarreling upstairs. I seemed to be seeing many people. Another moment I seemed to be on the march, going somewhere, and then having arrived there. Things of the past returned to my mind, and I was seeing once again the look of the bugler when he fell and broke his ankles. I woke up feeling someone sitting next to me. I tossed away the quilt only to realize that the lights had gone out. The faint light from the oil lamp in the hall sketched the silhouette of someone sitting next to me.

"Hey, Cripple, is that you?"

"Yes."

"Why didn't you come back until this minute?"

He hid his face in the darkness and made no sound. Having slept a long time and sweated profusely twice, I was dizzy and couldn't tell what time it was. I asked him, but he seemed not to hear me. He didn't stir.

Some minutes passed before he said, "Second Brother, my ancestors must be looking after me and Heaven must have blessed me, or else the sentry's rifle shot would have gotten me."

"Didn't you know the password?"

"How could I have known the password?"

"Is it past midnight now?"

"I don't know."

"Where have you been tonight? Why didn't you come back until this hour?"

Silence seized him again. I saw the kerosene lamp some soldiers had set on the rice barrel for me. It was lighted, though the wick had been turned down. I asked the bugler to turn it up a bit. He did not move. I asked him again.

As brighter light shone on him I saw the bugler with mud all over him, dirty and haggard. His face bore multiple scratches and bruises; he must have just come from a fight with somebody. I was so stunned that, staring at him, I didn't know how to ask him where he had been or what he had done during the past twenty-four hours. I myself was none too clear about anything at that moment. In my hallucination I had just seen him fall off the stone lion and break his ankles. Now I didn't know for sure whether I was in a dream.

Gently he said in a whispering voice, "Second Brother, Second Brother, I don't know who robbed that grave."

"Whose grave?"

"It must have happened only a while back. I saw it very clearly." He spoke very stubbornly, which made me suspect that he had lost his mind.

"Listen, whose grave are you talking about? Where is it? How did you know?"

"Why shouldn't I know? I heard that the long-hair [7] was buried at Catfish Village. I wanted to go see. I went there once yesterday; it was still in good shape. I went there again tonight. I remembered the way very well. That grave had been robbed, and I don't know who did it."

Either I was going crazy, or he must be. Now that I knew which grave he was talking about I jumped up like a perfect madman. "You went to her grave, didn't you? What's on your mind? You—beast!"

My friend was not disturbed at all. He said, again quietly and a bit mysteriously, "Yes, I went to her grave, yesterday and again today. I wasn't going to do anything bad, I swear. Old Lord Heaven above be my witness. I didn't bring any tools. Last night I saw the dirt mound, a perfect dirt dome. But tonight it all changed. I could swear I saw the same grave I had seen the night before, but it had changed. I don't know who did such a thing, digging her out of her coffin and carrying her away."

As I heard this shocking story, suddenly I thought of a person. I did not mention him because he only flashed across my mind and as rap-

[7] Lit., "big-pigtailed."

idly disappeared from my awareness. I was wondering if the girl had come back to life, struggled out of her entombment, and at this moment might already be back home talking with her parents; or if her death were a hoax, which would explain the hurried burial, only to be rescued by someone else and escorted away; or perhaps it was all a mistake on the part of my crippled friend whose confused mind erased his memory of the direction and location, so that his two visits led him to two different places, which gave rise to his false discovery. I resorted to all kinds of imagined possibilities to explain it because I thought this story could not be completely true.

I asked him why he went to the grave. He turned timid, thinking that I suspected him of knowing about the whole thing, or at least about the real culprit. Swearing by all gods in heaven he repeated seven times his declaration of innocence that he had no intention of stealing her corpse. His consistent explanation was that he had brought with him no iron tool with which the grave could be dug open. He argued over and over, and when he finished he looked scared because he marked my sullen face. If I hadn't expressed my confidence in him at that very moment, he could easily have gone mad and strangled me right there.

The shock had taken care of my sickness. Now I was busy figuring out how to handle this friend who was on the verge of madness and who, the next moment, would definitely go mad. I kept saying things to comfort him, inventing many absurd stories to soothe his broken heart. He calmed down somewhat. The peak of his excitement over, he mumbled the same coarse, dirty words while admitting to me that he really had harbored that intention because he heard some people say that the female victim of suicide by swallowing gold could come back to life if she were hugged and loved by a man within seven days of death. My friend went on to tell me that when he went to the grave for the first time, he was only thinking that he might hear her call for help from within her coffin, and he would then act like a knight-errant and rescue her. The second time, however, he had heard the theory about reviving a dead girl

within seven days of her death, and hence went there prepared to dig her out without waiting for any call for help. But one look at the mound told him that it had completely changed. The lid of the coffin was thrown to the side and the empty wooden box held its mouth wide open ready to swallow somebody. My friend jumped down into the coffin to inspect it. Nothing was there but a few pieces of clothing. Someone must have done it shortly before—digging open the grave and carrying away the girl's body.

No longer would he invoke the gods to bear false witness for him. He told me honestly in detail what had happened. After that I could think of nothing further to say to comfort him. Still, I could not believe it all. In my mind I figured that all of us were living in a dream, and even if we were not wholly dreaming, the following morning the bugler would regret what he had just confessed. After all, it is true that his kind of desire was humanly uncontrollable, but when translated into real action it would still be inadmissible in this world. And if he regretted his confession to me, he could very well kill me to erase what he had just said. I thought of what precautions I should take, but this bugler had already melted, become like a woman with his strength gone out of him, and now the only thing he could do was express his regret.

A question presented itself to us: how were we to handle this case now? Should we report it to our superior, or should we let the mystery go on? We discussed this question for a while. Our simple reasoning led us to conclude that we had no right to involve ourselves with this discovery; we might as well wait until the next morning when we could go to the beancurd shop to take a look. The bugler had walked a lot during the night; his crippled foot was long worn out. That plus the long hours of conversation with me sent him to sleep. However, I had slept the whole day and now could no longer fall asleep no matter how hard I tried. Under the lamplight I looked at that battered, miserable face, and the muddy body below it. I turned off the light and sat next to him to wait for dawn.

It was quite late when we arrived at the beancurd shop, but the young proprietor was not there to open the door. What I had thought about the night before again flashed across my mind. The door was locked from the outside; obviously the proprietor was not sleeping late or running into any trouble inside. What I had imagined threatened to become a reality, and that scared me. I dragged the bugler and ran back to camp where I described my guess to him, who himself had had such a wild idea. Not convinced, he went out alone for quite a while. He said he had gone to another family to seek information and learned that the young proprietor had left his beancurd shop the night before.

For three days we didn't dare go out; we stayed on our straw pads playing dominoes. Later, news began to circulate in the camp that, as though riding on invisible wings, rapidly reached every ear: "The new grave of the daughter of the chamber of commerce president was robbed almost as soon as she was buried, and someone stole her body." Another bit of news said, "Somebody found the young girl's body in a cave about half a *li* away from the grave. She lay completely naked on a stone ledge. Wild blue chrysanthemums were scattered all over her body and on the ground."

Human ignorance embroidered these news

items, turning the obscene into the divine.

But we were dumbfounded at the news. We knew what our other friend had done.

We never again went back to the beancurd shop to sit on that bench, drinking the bean milk made by that young friend; we never again laid eyes on that friend, so youthful and honest. As to that crippled fellow townsman of mine, he remains a bugler in the Forty-seventh Company. He is still crippled, but he would never mention the incident to anyone. He himself is guiltless, but what another young man did left him melancholic all his life.

What do I think of the whole incident? With my melancholy I don't make good company for young people. I didn't get along too well in the army. So I came to the city, but the city doesn't seem to suit me either, although now I don't know where next. I am forever restless because the past returns to haunt me often. To each his own destiny; this I know. Some things of the past perpetually gnaw the inside of me. When I talk about them you would think they are only stories. Nobody can understand how a person feels who lives day after day under the weight of hundreds of stories like this one.

TING LING
(*1907–*)

A native of Liling, Hunan, Ting Ling (pen name of Chiang Ping-chih) was bereaved of her scholarly father in 1911 and entrusted to the care of her mother's family for several years while her mother went to school to prepare herself for a teaching career. Ting Ling was as independent as her mother and left for Shanghai in 1921 to attend a very liberal girls' school. She subsequently studied at the Communist-affiliated Shanghai College for a few months and early in 1924 left for Peking, where she soon became friends with Shen Ts'ung-wen and with Hu Yeh-p'in, who was to become her husband.

The three were all young and impecunious authors, but Ting Ling enjoyed far greater luck than her husband when her first stories, such as "The Diary of Miss Sophia" (*Sha-fei nü-shih ti jih-chi*, 1927), were accepted by *The Short Story* magazine and published to instant acclaim. Nevertheless, the couple remained poor, and following the failure of two literary magazines which they launched with Shen and a period of sojourn in Tsinan, where Hu served as a school-teacher, they went to Shanghai in May 1930 and soon became members of the League of Leftwing Writers. Hu Yeh-p'ing also became a very active member of the Communist Party, and on February 7, 1931, he suffered the same fate as Jou Shih as one of the Five Martyrs executed by the Nationalist police.

Ting Ling, who had become a Communist in early 1933, was herself arrested on May 4, and lived on parole for about three years in Nanking. After regaining her freedom, she undertook a long journey and arrived in Yenan at the end of 1936. "When I Was in Hsia Village" (*Wo tsai Hsia-ts'un ti shih-hou*, 1940) and "In the Hospital" (*Tsai i-yuan chung*, 1941), included in this volume, are among the best stories Ting Ling wrote during her Yenan period. The latter story could hardly please the Communist authorities for its exposure of corruption and bleak poverty in Yenan and its sympathetic treatment of a heroine who receives undeserved censure for her attempt to correct medical abuses; but it was only after the publication of an editorial by Ting Ling on March 9, 1942 and a spate of critical articles by Yenan writers soon afterward that Mao Tse-tung felt compelled to convene the Yenan Forum on Literature and Art in May of that year to reimpose discipline on all writers and artists. Ting Ling was secretly punished at that time, but her case was not publicized. After a period of inactivity, she participated in land-reform work in 1946 and wrote a novel of documentary realism called *The Sun Shines Over the Sangkan River* (*T'ai-yang chao-tsai Sang-kan-ho shang,* 1949), for which she won the Soviet Union's Stalin Second Prize for Literature in 1951.

In 1957, however, Ting Ling became a chief target of vilification during the Anti-Rightist Movement, and a number of her works, including our two stories, were exposed as "poisonous weeds" (*tu-ts'ao*). The author herself, after serving as a charwoman in the Peking headquarters of the Writers' Association, was sentenced to penal servitude in the northern wilderness of Manchuria. It is only recently that she has been rehabilitated, an old woman ravaged by malnutrition and cancer but still determined to write.

J.S.M.L.
C.T.H.

When I Was in Hsia Village

by Ting Ling

Translated by Gary Bjorge

Because of the turmoil in the Political Department, Comrade Mo Yü decided to send me to stay temporarily in a neighboring village. Actually, I was already completely well, but the opportunity to rest for a while in a quiet environment and arrange my notes from the past three months did have its attractions. So I agreed to spend two weeks in Hsia Village, a place about ten miles from the Political Department.

A female comrade from the Propaganda Department, who was apparently on a work assignment went with me. Since she wasn't a person who enjoyed conversation, however, the journey was rather lonely. Also, because her feet had once been bound and my own spirits were low, we traveled slowly. We set out in the morning; but it was nearly sunset by the time we reached our destination.

The village looked much like any other from a distance, but I knew it contained a very beautiful Catholic church that had escaped destruction and a small grove of pine trees. The place where I would be staying was in the midst of these trees, which clung to the hillside. From that spot it would be possible to look straight across to the church. By now I could see orderly rows of cave dwellings and the green trees above them. I felt content with the village.

My traveling companion had given me the impression that the village was very busy, but when we entered it not even a single child or a dog was to be seen. The only movement was dry leaves twirling about lightly in the wind. They would fly a short distance, then drop to earth again.

"This used to be an elementary school, but last year the Jap devils destroyed it. Look at those steps over there. That used to be a big classroom," my companion Ah Kuei told me. She was somewhat excited now, not so reserved as she had been during the day. Pointing to a large empty courtyard, she continued: "A year and a half ago this area was full of life. Every evening after supper the comrades gathered here to play soccer or basketball."

Becoming more agitated, she asked, "Why isn't anyone here? Should we go to the assembly hall or head up the hill? We don't know where they've taken our luggage either. We have to straighten that out first."

On the wall next to the gate of the village assembly hall many white paper slips had been pasted. They read "Office of the XX Association," "Hsia Village Branch of the XX Association," and so on. But when we went inside we couldn't find a soul. It was completely quiet, with only a few tables set about. We were both standing there dumbly when suddenly a man rushed in. He looked at us for a moment, seemed about to ask us something, but swallowed his words and prepared to dash away. We called him to stop, however, and made him answer our questions.

"The people of the village? They've all gone to the west door. Baggage? Hmm. Yes, there was baggage. It was carried up the hill some time ago to Liu Erh-ma's home." As he talked he sized us up.

Learning that he was a member of the Peasant's Salvation Association, we asked him to accompany us up the hill and also asked him to deliver a note to one of the local comrades. He agreed to take the note, but he wouldn't go with us. He seemed impatient and ran off by himself.

The street too was very quiet. The doors of several shops were closed. Others were still open, exposing pitch-black interiors. We still couldn't find anyone. Fortunately, Ah Kuei was familiar with the village, and led me up the hill. It was already dark. The winter sun sets very quickly.

The hill was not high, and a large number of stone-cave dwellings were scattered here and there from the bottom to the top. In a few places people were standing out in front peering into the distance. Ah Kuei knew very well that we had not yet reached our destination, but whenever we met someone she asked, "Is this the way to Liu Erh-ma's house?" "How far is it to Liu Erh-ma's house?" "Could you please tell me the way to Liu Erh-ma's house?" Or, she would ask, "Did you notice any baggage being sent to Liu Erh-ma's house? Is Liu Erh-ma home?"

The answers we received always satisfied us, and this continued right up to the most distant and highest house, which was the Liu family's. Two small dogs were the first to greet us. Then a woman came out and asked who we were. As soon as they heard it was me, two more women came out. Holding a lantern, they escorted us into the courtyard and then into a cave on the side toward the east. The cave was virtually empty. On the *k'ang*[1] under the window were piled my bedroll, my small leather carrying case, and Ah Kuei's quilt.

Some of the people there knew Ah Kuei. They took her hand and asked her many questions, and after a while they led her out, leaving me alone in the room. I arranged my bed and was about to lie down when suddenly they all crowded back in again. One of Liu Erh-ma's daughters-in-law was carrying a bowl of noodles. Ah Kuei, Liu Erh-ma, and a young girl were holding bowls, chopsticks, and a dish of onions and pepper. The young girl also brought in a brazier of burning coal.

Attentively, they urged me to eat some noodles and touched my hands and arms. Liu Erh-ma and her daughter-in-law also sat down on the *k'ang*. There was an air of mystery about them as they continued the conversation interrupted by their entry into the room.

At first I thought I had caused their amazement, but gradually I realized that this wasn't the case. They were interested in only one thing—the topic of their conversation. Since all I heard was a few fragmentary sentences, I couldn't understand what they were talking about. This was especially true of what Liu Erh-ma said because she frequently lowered her voice, as if afraid that someone might overhear her. Ah Kuei had changed completely. She now appeared quite capable and was very talkative. She listened closely to what the others were saying and seemed able to grasp the essence of their words. The daughter-in-law and the young girl said little. At times they added a word or two, but for most part they just listened intently to what Ah Kuei and Liu Erh-ma were saying. They seemed afraid to miss a single word.

Suddenly the courtyard was filled with noise. A large number of people had rushed in, and they all seemed to be talking at once. Liu Erh-ma and the others climbed nervously off the *k'ang* and hurried outside. Without thinking, I followed along behind them to see what was happening.

By this time the courtyard was in complete darkness. Two red paper lanterns bobbed and weaved above the crowd. I worked my way into the throng and looked around. I couldn't see anything. The others too were squeezing in for no apparent reason. They seemed to want to say more, but they did not. I heard only simple exchanges that confused me even more.

"Yü-wa, are you here too?"

"Have you seen her yet?"

"Yes, I've seen her. I was a little afraid."

"What is there to be afraid of? She's just a human being, and prettier than ever too."

At first I was sure that they were talking about a

[1] A *k'ang* is a brick structure from four to six feet wide and about two feet high from the ground built along the side of a room in parts of northern China. It is used for sitting and lounging upon during the day and sleeping at night. In cold weather a fire is built within it.

new bride, but people said that wasn't so. Then I thought there was a prisoner present, but that was wrong too. I followed the crowd to the doorway of the central cave, but all there was to see was more people packed tightly together. Thick smoke obscured my vision, so I had no choice but to back away. Others were leaving by now too, and the courtyard was much less crowded.

Since I couldn't sleep, I set about rearranging my carrying case by the lantern light. I paged through several notebooks, looked at photographs, and sharpened some pencils. I was obviously tired, but I also felt the kind of excitement that comes just before a new life begins. I prepared a time schedule for myself, and was determined to adhere to it beginning the very next day.

At that moment there was a man's voice at the door. "Are you asleep, comrade?" Before I could reply, the fellow entered the room. He was about twenty years old, a rather refined-looking country youth. "I received Director Mo's letter some time ago," he said. "This area is relatively quiet. Don't worry about a thing. That's my job. If you need something, don't hesitate to ask Liu Erh-ma. Director Mo said you wanted to stay here for two weeks. Fine. If you enjoy your visit we'd be happy to have you stay longer. I live in a neighboring cave, just below these. If you need me, just send someone to find me."

He declined to come up on the k'ang, and since there was no bench on the floor to sit on, I jumped down from the k'ang and said, "Ah! You must be Comrade Ma. Did you receive the note I sent you? Please sit down and talk for a while."

I knew that he held a position of some responsibility in the village. As a student he had not yet finished junior high schoool.

"They tell me you've written a lot of books," he responded. "It's too bad we haven't bought them. I haven't seen a single one." As he spoke he looked at my open carrying case that was lying on the k'ang.

The topic of our conversation turned to the subject of the local level of study. Then he said, "After you've rested for a few days we'll definitely invite you to give a talk. It can be to a mass meet-

ing or to a training class. In any case, you'll certainly be able to help us. Our most difficult task here is 'cultural recreation.' "

I had seen many young men like him at the Front. When I first met them I was always amazed. I felt that these youth, who were somewhat remote from me, were really changing fast. Changing the subject, I asked him, "What was going on just now?"

"Chen-chen, the daughter of Liu Ta-ma, has returned," he answered. "I never thought she could be so great."

I immediately sensed a joyful, radiant twinkle in his eyes. As I was about to ask another question he added, "She's come back from the Japanese area. She's been working there for over a year."

"Oh, my!" I gasped.

He was about to tell me more when someone outside called for him. All he could say was that he'd be sure to have Chen-chen call on me the next day. As if to provoke my interest further, he added that Chen-chen must certainly have a lot of material for stories.

It was very late when Ah Kuei came back. She lay down on the k'ang but could not sleep. She tossed and turned and sighed continuously. I was very tired, but I still wished that she would tell me something about the events of the evening.

"No, comrade," she said. "I can't talk about it now. I'm too upset. I'll tell you tomorrow. Ahh . . . How miserable it is to be a woman." After this she covered her head with her quilt and lay completely still, no longer sighing. I didn't know when she finally fell asleep.

Early the next morning I stepped outside for a stroll, and before I knew it I had walked down to the village. I went into a general store to rest and buy red dates for Liu Erh-ma to put in the rice porridge. As soon as the owner learned that I was living with Liu Erh-ma his small eyes narrowed and he asked me in a low, excited voice, "Did you get a look at her niece? I hear her disease has even taken her nose. That's because she was abused by the Jap devils."

Turning his head, he called to his wife, who was standing in the inner doorway, "She has nerve, coming home! It's revenge against her father, Liu Fu-sheng."

"That girl was always frivolous. You saw the way she used to roam around the streets. Wasn't she Hsia Ta-pao's old flame? If he hadn't been poor, wouldn't she have married him a long time ago?" As she finished speaking, the old woman lifted her skirts and came into the store.

The owner turned his face back toward me and said, "There are so many rumors." His eyes stopped blinking and his expression became very serious. "It's said that she has slept with at least a hundred men. Humph! I've heard that she even became the wife of a Japanese officer. Such a shameful woman should not be allowed to return."

Not wanting to argue with him, I held back my anger and left. I didn't look back, but I felt that he had again narrowed his small eyes and was feeling smug as he watched me walk away.

As I neared the corner by the Catholic church, I overheard a conversation by two women who were drawing water at the well. One said: "She sought out Father Lu and told him she definitely wanted to be a nun. When Father Lu asked her for a reason she didn't say a word, just cried. Who knows what she did there? Now she's worse than a prostitute . . ."

"Yesterday they told me she walks with a limp. Achh! How can she face people?"

"Someone said she's even wearing a gold ring that a Jap devil gave her!"

"I understand she's been as far away as Tatung and has seen many things. She can even speak Japanese."

My walk was making me unhappy, so I returned home. Since Ah Kuei had already gone out, I sat alone in my room and read a small pamphlet. After a while I raised my eyes and noticed two large baskets for storing grain sitting near the wall. They must have had a long history because they were as black as the wall itself. Opening the movable portion of the paper window, I peered out at the gray sky. The weather had changed completely from what it had been when I arrived the day before. The hard ground of the courtyard

had been swept clean, and at the far edge a tree with a few withered branches stood out starkly against the leaden sky. There wasn't a single person to be seen.

I opened my carrying case, took out pen and paper, and wrote two letters. I wondered why Ah Kuei had not yet returned. I had forgotten that she had work to do. I was somehow thinking that she had come to be my companion. The days of winter are very short, but right then I was feeling that they were even longer than summer days.

Some time later the young girl who had been in my room the night before came out into the courtyard. I immediately jumped down off the *k'ang*, stepped out the door, and called to her, but she just looked at me and smiled before rushing into another cave. I walked around the courtyard twice and then stopped to watch a hawk fly into the grove of trees by the church. The courtyard there had many large trees. I started walking again, and on the right side of the courtyard picked up the sound of a woman crying. She was trying to stop, frequently blowing her nose.

I tried hard to control myself. I thought about why I was here and about all my plans. I had to rest and live according to the time schedule I had made. I returned to my room, but I couldn't sleep and had no interest in writing in my notebook.

Fortunately, a short while later Liu Erh-ma came to see me. The young girl was with her, and her daughter-in-law arrived soon after. The three of them climbed up on the *k'ang* and took seats around the small brazier. The young girl looked closely at my things, which were laid out on the little square *k'ang* table.

"At that time no one could take care of anyone else," Liu Erh-ma said, talking about the Japanese attack on Hsia Village a year and a half before. "Those of us who lived on the hilltop were luckier. We could run away quickly. Many who lived in the village could not escape. Apparently it was all fate. Just then on that day our family's Chen-chen had run over to the Catholic church. Only later did we learn that her unhappiness about what was happening had caused her to go talk to the foreign priest about becoming a nun. Her father was in the midst of negotiating a marriage for her with the young proprietor of a rice store in Hsi-liu Village. He was almost thirty, a widower, and his family was well respected. We all said he would be a good match, but Chen-chen said no and broke into tears before her father. In other matters her father had always deferred to her wishes, but in this case the old man was adamant. He had no son and had always wanted to betrothe his daughter to a good man. Who would have thought that Chen-chen would turn around in anger and run off to the Catholic church? It was at that moment that the Japs caught her. How could her mother and father help grieving?"

"Was that her mother crying?"

"Yes."

"And your niece?"

"Well, she's really just a child. When she came back yesterday she cried for a long time, but today she went to the assembly in high spirits. She's only eighteen."

"I heard she was the wife of a Japanese. Is that true?"

"It's hard to say. We haven't been able to find out for sure. There are many rumors, of course. She's contracted a disease, but how could anyone keep clean in such a place? The possibility of her marrying the merchant seems to be over. Who would want a woman who was abused by the Jap devils? She definitely has the disease. Last night she said so herself. This time she's changed a lot. When she talks about those devils she shows no more emotion that if she were talking about an ordinary meal at home. She's only eighteen, but she has no sense of embarrassment at all."

"Hsia Ta-pao came again today," the daughter-in-law said quietly, her questioning eyes fixed on Erh-ma.

"Who is Hsia Ta-pao?" I asked.

"He's a young man who works in the village flour mill," replied Liu Erh-ma. "When he was young he and Chen-chen were classmates for a year. They liked each other very much but his family was poor, even poorer than ours. He didn't dare do anything, but our Chen-chen was head over heels in love with him and kept clinging to him. Then she was upset when he didn't respond.

Isn't it because of him that she wanted to be a nun? After Chen-chen fell into the hands of the Jap devils he often came to see her parents. At first just the sight of him made Chen-chen's father angry. At times he cursed him, but Hsia Ta-pao would say nothing. After a scolding he would leave and then come back another day. Ta-pao is really a good boy. Now he's even a squad leader in the Self-Defense Corps. Today he came once again, apparently to talk with Chen-chen's mother about marrying Chen-chen. All I could hear was her crying. Later he left in tears himself."

"Does he know about your niece's situation?"

"How could he help knowing? There is no one in this village who doesn't know everything. They all know more than we do ourselves."

"Mother, everyone says that Hsia Ta-pao is foolish," the young girl interjected.

"Humph! The boy has a good conscience. I approve of this match. Since the Jap devils came, who has any money? Judging from the words of Chen-chen's parents, I think they approve too. If not him, who? Even without mentioning her disease, her reputation is enough to deter anyone."

"He was the one wearing the dark blue jacket and the copper-colored felt hat with the turned-up brim," the young girl said. Her eyes were sparkling with curiosity, and she seemed to understand this matter very well.

Such a figure began to take shape in my memory. When I went out for my walk earlier that morning I had seen an alert, honest-looking young man who fit this description. He had been standing outside my courtyard, but had not shown any intention of coming in. On my way home I had seen him again, this time emerging from the pine woods beyond the cave dwellings. I had thought he was someone from my courtyard or from a neighboring one and hadn't paid much attention to him. As I recalled him now, I felt that he was a rather capable man, not a bad young man at all.

I now feared that my plan for rest and recuperation could not be realized. Why were my thoughts so confused? I wasn't particularly anxious to meet anybody, and yet my mind still couldn't rest. Ah Kuei had come in during the conversation, and now she seemed to sense my feelings. As she went out with the others she gave me a knowing smile.

I understood her meaning and busied myself with arranging the *k'ang*. My bedroll, the lamp, and the fire all seemed much brighter. I had just placed the tea kettle on the fire when Ah Kuei returned. Behind her I heard another person.

"We have a guest, comrade!" Ah Kuei called. Even before she finished speaking I heard someone giggling.

Standing in the doorway, I grasped the hands of this person whom I had not seen before. They were burning hot, and I couldn't help being a bit startled. She followed Ah Kuei up onto the *k'ang* and sat down. A single long braid hung down her back.

In the eyes of the new arrival, this cave which depressed me seemed to be something new and fresh. She looked around at everything with an excited glint in her eyes. She sat opposite me, her body tilted back slightly and her two hands spread apart on the bedroll for support. She didn't seem to want to say anything. Her eyes finally came to rest on my face.

The shadows lengthened her eyes and made her chin quite pointed. But even though her eyes were in deep shadow, her pupils shone brightly in the light of the lamp and the fire. They were like two open windows in a summer home in the country, clear and clean.

I didn't know how to begin a conversation without touching an open wound and hurting her self-respect. So my first move was to pour her a cup of hot tea.

It was Chen-chen who spoke first: "Are you a southerner? I think so. You aren't like the people from this province."

"Have you seen many southerners?" I asked, thinking it best to talk about what she wanted to talk about.

"No," she said, shaking her head. Her eyes still fixed on me, she added, "I've only seen a few. They always seem a little different. I like you people from the South. Southern women, unlike us, can all read many, many books. I want to study with you. Will you teach me?"

I expressed my willingness to do so, and she quickly continued, "Japanese women also can read a lot of books. All those devil soldiers carried a few well-written letters, some from wives, some from girl friends. Some were written by girls they didn't even know. They would include a photograph and use syrupy language. I don't know if those girls were sincere or not, but they always made the devils hold their letters to their hearts like precious treasures."

"I understand that you can speak Japanese," I said. "Is that true?"

Her face flushed slightly before she replied, in a very open manner, "I was there for such a long time. I went round and around for over a year. I can speak a fair amount. Being able to understand their language had many advantages."

"Did you go to a lot of different places with them?"

"I wasn't always with the same unit. People think that because I was the wife of a Jap officer I enjoyed luxury. Actually, I came back here twice before. Altogether, this is my third time. I was ordered to go on this last mission. There was no choice. I was familiar with the area, the work was important, and it was impossible to find anyone else in a short time. I won't be sent back any more. They're going to treat my disease. That's fine with me because I've missed my dad and mom and I'm glad to be able to come back to see them. My mother, though, is really hopeless. When I'm not home she cries. When I'm here she still cries."

"You must have known many hardships."

"She has endured unthinkable suffering," Ah Kuei interrupted, her face twisted in a pained expression. In a voice breaking with emotion she added, "It's a real tragedy to be a woman, isn't it, Chen-chen?" She slid over to be next to her.

"Suffering?" Chen-chen asked, her thoughts apparently far, far away. "Right now I can't say for certain. Some things were hard to endure at the time, but when I recall them now they don't seem like much. Other things were no problem to do when I did them, but when I think about them now I'm very sad. More than a year . . . It's all past. Since I came back this time a great many people have looked at me strangely. As far as the people of this village are concerned, I'm an outsider. Some are very friendly to me. Others avoid me. The members of my family are just the same. They all like to steal looks at me. Nobody treats me the way they used to. Have I changed? I've thought about this a great deal, and I don't think I've changed at all. If I have changed, maybe it's that my heart has become someahat harder. But could anyone spend time in such a place and not become hard-hearted? People have no choice. They're forced to be like that!"

There was no outward sign of her disease. Her complexion was ruddy. Her voice was clear. She showed no signs of inhibition or rudeness. She did not exaggerate. She gave the impression that she had never had any complaints or sad thoughts. Finally, I could restrain myself no longer and asked her about her disease.

"People are always like that, even if they find themselves in worse situations. They brace themselves and see it through. Can you just give up and die? Later, after I made contact with our own people, I became less afraid. As I watched the Jap devils suffer defeat in battle and the guerrillas take action on all sides as a result of the tricks I was playing, I felt better by the day. I felt that even though my life was hard I could still manage. Somehow I had to find a way to survive, and if at all possible, to live a life that was meaningful. That's why I'm pleased that they intend to treat my disease. It will be better to be cured. Actually, these past few days I haven't felt too bad. On the way home I stayed in Chang-chi-ai for two days and was given two shots and some medicine to take orally. The worst time was in the fall. I was told that my insides were rotting away, and then, because of some important information and the fact that no one could be found to take my place, I had to go back. That night I walked alone in the dark for ten miles. Every single step was painful. My mind was filled with the desire to sit down and rest. If the work hadn't been so important, I definitely wouldn't have gone back. But I had to. Ahh! I was afraid I might be recognized by the Jap devils, and was also worried about missing my rendezvous. After it was over, I slept for a full

week before I could pull myself together. It really isn't all that easy to die, is it?"

Without waiting for me to respond, she continued on with her story. At times she stopped talking and looked at us. Perhaps she was searching for reactions on our faces. Or maybe she was only thinking of something else. I could see that Ah Kuei was more troubled than Chen-chen. For the most part she sat in silence, and when she did speak it was only for a sentence or two. Her words gave voice to a limitless sympathy for Chen-chen, but her expression when silent revealed even more clearly how moved she was by what Chen-chen was saying. Her soul was being crushed. She herself was feeling the suffering that Chen-chen had known before.

It was my impression that Chen-chen had no intention whatever of trying to elicit sympathy from others. Even as others took upon themselves part of the misfortune that she had suffered, she seemed unaware of it. But that very fact made others feel even more sympathetic. It would have been better if, instead of listening to her recount the events of this period with a calmness that almost made you think she was talking about someone else, you could have heard her cry. Probably you would have cried with her, but you would have felt better.

After a while Ah Kuei began to cry and Chen-chen turned to comfort her. There were many things that I had wanted to discuss with Chen-chen but I couldn't bring myself to say anything. I wished to remain silent. After Chen-chen left, I forced myself to read by the lamp for an hour. Not once did I look at Ah Kuei or ask her a question, even though she was lying very close to me, though she tossed and turned and sighed all the time, unable to fall asleep.

After this Chen-chen came to talk with me every day. She did not talk about herself alone. She very often showed great curiosity about many aspects of my life that were beyond her own experiences. At times, when my words were far removed from her life, it was obvious that she was struggling to understand, but nevertheless she listened intently. The two of us also took walks together down to the village. The youth were very good to her. Naturally, they were all activists. People like the general store owner, however, always gave us cold, steely stares. They disliked and despised Chen-chen. They even treated me as someone not of their kind. This was especially true of the women, who, all because of Chen-chen, finally developed some self-respect and perceived themselves as saintly pure. They were proud about never having been raped.

After Ah Kuei left the village I grew even closer to Chen-chen. It seemed that neither of us could be without the other. As soon as we were apart we thought of each other. I like people who are enthusiastic and lively, can be really happy or sad, and at the same time are straightforward and candid. Chen-chen was just such a person. Our conversations took up a great deal of time, but I always felt that they were beneficial to my studies and to my personal growth. As the days went by, however, I discovered that Chen-chen was not being completely open about something. I did not resent this. Moreover, I was determined not to touch upon this secret of hers. All people have things buried deeply in their hearts that they don't want to tell others. This secret was a matter of private emotions. It had nothing to do with other people or with Chen-chen's personal morality.

A few days before my departure Chen-chen suddenly began to appear very agitated. Nothing special seemed to have happened, and she showed no desire to talk to me about anything new. Yet she frequently came to my room looking disturbed and restless, and after sitting for a few minutes, she would get up and leave. I knew she had not eaten well for several days and was often passing up meals. I had asked her about her disease and knew that the cause of her uneasiness was not simply physical. Sometimes, after coming to my room, she would make a few disjointed remarks. At other times she put on an attentive expression, as if asking me to talk. But I could see that her thoughts were elsewhere, on things that she didn't want others to know. She was trying to conceal her emotions by acting as if nothing was wrong.

Twice I saw that capable young man come out of Chen-chen's home. I had already compared my impression of him with Chen-chen, and I sympathized with him deeply. Chen-chen had been abused by many men, and had contracted a stigmatized, hard-to-cure disease, but he still patiently came to see her and still sought the approval of her parents to marry her. He didn't look down on her. He did not fear the derision or the rebukes of others. He must have felt she needed him more than ever. He understood what kind of attitude a man should have toward the woman of his choice at such a time and what his responsibilities were.

But what of Chen-chen? Although naturally there were many aspects of her emotions and her sorrows that I had not learned during this short period, she had never expressed any hope that a man would marry her or, if you will, comfort her. I thought she had become so hard because she had been hurt so badly. She seemed not to want anything from anyone. It would be good if love, some extraordinarily sympathetic commiseration, could warm her soul. I wanted her to find a place where she could cry this out. I was hoping for a chance to attend a wedding in this family. At the very least I wanted to hear of an agreement to marry before I left.

"What is Chen-chen thinking of?" I asked myself. "This can't be delayed indefinitely, and shouldn't be turned into a big problem."

One day Liu Erh-ma, her daughter-in-law, and her young daughter all came to see me. I was sure they intended to give me a report on something, but when they started to speak I didn't allow them the opportunity to tell me anything. If my friend didn't confide in me, and I didn't ask her about it directly, then I felt it would be harmful to her, to myself, and to our friendship to ask others about it.

That same evening at dusk the courtyard was again filled with people milling about. All the neighbors were there, whispering to one another. Some looked sad, but there were also those who appeared to find all this exciting. The weather was frigid, but curiosity warmed their hearts. In the severe cold they drew in their shoulders, hunched their backs, thrust their hands into their sleeves, puffed out their breath, and looked at each other as if they were investigating something very interesting.

At first all I heard was the sound of quarreling coming from Liu Ta-ma's dwelling. Then I heard Liu Ta-ma crying. This was followed by the sound of a man crying. As far as I could tell, it was Chen-chen's father. Next came a crash of dishes breaking. Unable to bear it any longer, I pushed my way through the curious onlookers and rushed inside.

"You've come at just the right time," Liu Erh-ma said as she pulled me inside. "You talk to our Chen-chen."

Chen-chen's face was hidden by her long disheveled hair, but two wild eyes could still be seen peering out at the people gathered there. I walked over to her and stood beside her, but she seemed completely oblivious to my presence. Perhaps she took me as one of the enemy and not worth a moment's concern. Her appearance had changed so completely that I could hardly remember the liveliness, the bright pleasantness I had found in her before. She was like a cornered animal. She was like an evening goddess. Whom did she hate? Why was her expression so fierce?

"You're so heartless. You don't think about your mother and father at all. You don't care how much I've suffered because of you in the last year." Liu Ta-ma pounded on the *k'ang* as she scolded her daughter, tears like raindrops dropping to the *k'ang* or the floor and flowing down the contours of her face. Several women had surrounded her and were preventing her from coming down off the *k'ang*. It was frightening to see a person lose her self-respect and allow all her feelings to come out in a blind rage. I thought of telling her that such crying was useless, but at the same time I realized that nothing I could say now would make any difference.

Chen-chen's father looked very weak and old. His hands hung down limply. He was sighing deeply. Hsia Ta-pao was seated beside him. There was a helpless look in his eyes as he stared at the old couple.

"You must say something. Don't you feel sorry for your mother?"

"When the end of a road is reached one must turn. After water has flowed as far as it can, it

must change direction. Aren't you going to change at all? Why make yourself suffer?"

The women were trying to persuade Chen-chen with such words.

I could see that this affair could not turn out the way that everyone was hoping. Chen-chen had shown me much earlier that she didn't want anyone's sympathy. She, in turn, had no sympathy for anyone else. She had made her decision long ago and would not change. If people wanted to call her stubborn, then so be it. With teeth tightly clenched she looked ready to stand up to all of them.

At last the others agreed to listen to me, and I asked Chen-chen to come to my room and rest. I told them that everything could be discussed later that night. But when I led Chen-chen out of the house, she did not follow me to my room. Instead, she ran off up the hillside.

"That girl has big ideas."

"Humph! She looks down on us country folk."

"She's such a cheap little hussy and yet she puts on such airs. Hsia Ta-pao deserves it . . ."

These were some of the comments being made by the crowd in the courtyard. Then, when they realized that there was no longer anything of interest to see, the crowd drifted away.

I hesitated for a while in the courtyard before deciding to go up the hillside myself. On the top of the hill were numerous graves set among the pine trees. Broken stone tablets stood before them. No one was there. Not even the sound of a falling leaf broke the stillness. I ran back and forth calling Chen-chen's name. What sounded like a response temporarily comforted my loneliness, but in an instant the vast silence of the hills became even deeper. The colors of sunset had completely faded. All around me a thin, smoke-like mist rose silently and spread out to the middle slopes of the hills, both nearby and in the distance. I was worried and sat down weakly on a tombstone. Over and over I asked myself, "Should I go on up the hill or wait for her here?" I was hoping that I could relieve Chen-chen of some of her distress.

At that moment I saw a shadow moving toward me from below. I quickly saw that it was Hsia Ta-pao. I remained silent, hoping he wouldn't see me and would continue on up the hill, but he came straight at me. At last I felt that I had to greet him and called, "Have you found her? I still haven't seen her."

He walked over to me and sat down on the dry grass. He said nothing, only stared into the distance. I felt a little uneasy. He really was very young. His eyebrows were long and thin. His eyes were quite large, but now they looked dull and lifeless. His small mouth was tightly drawn. Perhaps before it had been kind of cute, but now it was full of anguish, as if trying to hold in his pain. He had an honest-looking nose, but of what use was it to him now?

"Don't be sad," I said. "Maybe tomorrow everything will be all right. I'll talk to her this evening."

"Tomorrow, tomorrow—she'll always hate me. I know that she hates me." He spoke in a sad low voice that was slightly hoarse.

"No," I replied, searching my memory. "She has never shown me that she hates anyone." This was not a lie.

"She wouldn't tell you. She wouldn't tell anyone. She won't forgive me as long as she lives."

"Why should she hate you?"

"Of course—" he began. Suddenly he turned his face toward me and looked at me intently. "Tell me," he said, "at that time I had nothing. Should I have encouraged her to run away with me? Is all of this my fault? Is it?"

He didn't wait for my answer. As if speaking to himself, he went on, "It is my fault. Could anyone say that I did the right thing? Didn't I bring this harm to her? If I had been as brave as she, she never would have— I know her character. She'll always hate me. Tell me, what should I do? What would she want me to do? How can I make her happy? My life is worthless. Am I of even the slightest use to her? Can you tell me? I simply don't know what I should do. Ahhh! How miserable things are! This is worse than being captured by the Jap devils." Without a break he continued to mumble on and on.

When I asked him to go back home with me, he stood up and we took several steps together. Then he stopped and said that he had heard a sound coming from the very top of the hill. There was nothing to do but encourage him to go on up, and

I watched until he had disappeared into the thick pines. Then I started back. By now it was almost completely dark.

It was very late when I went to bed that night, but I still hadn't received any news. I didn't know what had happened to them.

Even before I ate breakfast the next morning I finished packing my suitcase. Comrade Ma had promised that he would be coming this day to help me move, and I was all prepared to return to the Political Department and then go on to XX. The enemy was about to start another "mopping-up campaign," and my health would not permit me to remain in this area. Director Mo had said that the ill definitely had to be moved out first, but I felt uneasy. Should I try to stay? If I did, I could be a burden to others. What about leaving? If I went would I ever be able to return? As I was sitting on my bedroll pondering these questions, I sensed someone slipping quietly into my room.

With a single thrust of her body Chen-chen jumped up onto the *k'ang* and took a seat opposite me. I could see that her face was slightly swollen, and when I grasped her hands as she spread them over the fire, the heat that had made such an impression on me before once again distressed me. Then and there I realized how serious her disease was.

"Chen-chen," I said, "I'm about to leave. I don't know when we'll meet again. I hope you'll listen to your mother—"

"I have come to tell you," she interrupted, "that I'll be leaving tomorrow too. I want to leave home as soon as possible."

"Really?" I asked.

"Yes," she said, her face again revealing that special vibrancy. "They've told me to go in for medical treatment."

"Ah," I sighed, thinking that perhaps we could travel together. "Does your mother know?"

"No, she doesn't know yet. But if I say that I'm going for medical treatment and that after my disease is cured I'll come back, she'll be sure to let me go. Just staying at home doesn't have anything to offer, does it?"

At this moment I felt that she had a rare serenity about her. I recalled the words that Hsia Ta-pao had spoken to me the previous evening and asked her directly: "Has the problem of your marriage been resolved?"

"Resolved? Oh, well, it's all the same."

"Did you heed your mother's advice?" I still didn't dare express my hopes for her. I didn't want to think of the image left in my mind by that young man. I was hoping that someday he would be happy.

"Why should I listen to what they say? Did they ever listen to me?"

"Well, are you really angry with them?"

There was no response.

"Well then, do you really hate Hsia Ta-pao?"

For a long time she did not reply. Then, in a very calm voice, she said, "I can't say that I hate him. I just feel now that I'm someone who's diseased. It's a fact that I was abused by a large number of Jap devils. I don't remember the exact number. In any case, I'm unclean, and with such a black mark I don't expect any good fortune to come my way. I feel that living among strangers and keeping busy would be better than living at home where people know me. Now that they've approved sending me to XX for treatment I've been thinking about staying there and doing some studying. I hear it's a big place with lots of schools and that anyone can attend. It's better for each of us to go our own separate ways than it is to have everyone stay together in one place. I'm doing this for myself, but I'm also doing it for the others. I don't feel that I owe anyone an apology. Neither do I feel especially happy. What I do feel is that after I go to XX I'll be in a new situation. I will be able to start life fresh. A person's life is not just for one's father and mother, or even for oneself. Some have called me young, inexperienced, and bad-tempered. I don't dispute it. There are some things that I just have to keep to myself."

I was amazed. Something new was coming out of her. I felt that what she had said was really worth examining. There was nothing for me to do but express approval of her plan.

When I took my departure, Chen-chen's family was there to see me off. She, however, had gone to the village office. I didn't see Hsia Ta-pao before I left either.

I wasn't sad as I went away. I seemed to see the bright future that Chen-chen had before her. The next day I would be seeing her again. That had been decided. And we would still be together for some time. As soon as Comrade Ma and I walked out the door of Chen-chen's home, he told me of her decision and confirmed that what she had told me that morning would quickly come to pass.

In the Hospital

by Ting Ling

Translated by Gary Bjorge

I

December was almost gone. The season's first snow had fallen, and creeks and rivers were covered with ice. The wind blowing across the harvested hills made a rustling sound over the reed thatching of animal shelters and moaned before it rushed off along the bottom of the watercourse. A pheasant hiding in the thick grass arranged its feathers and squeezed into what was either a crevice in the rocks or a hole in the ground. Sunlight shining on frozen piles of cattle and horse dung made a foul stench. A few flies crawled over them listlessly.

Twilight came swiftly to this scene. In all its vastness it closed in from every side, dropping down icily from the distant hills, sweeping in silently from the barely visible horizon. Birds shivered. Dogs pulled their tails closer to their bodies. Men returned to their homes, to those cave dwellings that were their only shelter.

While this was happening, a young woman in a gray cotton military uniform came walking along the road near the watercourse, following a man wearing a sheepskin greatcoat. The woman was very nimble, and this, along with the fact that she was wearing male clothing, made her look like a young boy. She deliberately wore a pleased expression. Opening her small black eyes wide, she looked happily at the bleakness on every side.

"I haven't had any work experience, so I'm sure I'll be giving you a lot of trouble. I'll have to keep asking for your help to make sure everything is all right. You're an experienced revolutionary, Section Chief Li. Are you from the Hupei-Honan-Anhwei area?"

By now she was very good at this tone of voice. She felt that no matter what organization she went to, the first task was to establish good personal relationships with the maintenance personnel there. In school she had used this flattering tone of voice every time she went to the kitchen to draw water or to the communication section to pick up a letter. She had also used it whenever she replenished the lamp oil or went to get charcoal. But she didn't strike one as being the least bit ingratiating, just lighthearted and relaxed.

Section Chief Li, the man walking in front of her, looked exactly like a general in his old sheepskin greatcoat. He had that not too demanding yet not too relaxed manner of a typical administrative section chief. Sometimes such fellows appeared rather slow-witted, but at other times they seemed very intelligent. If their personnel committed errors they could use the most vulgar of soldiers' swear words. But they were also capable of unobtrusively sending a few chickens, some eggs, or some roasted pumpkin seeds to secretaries-general or directors. These were small matters, though. Li's work with the masses was good, so there was no cause for any suspicion or jealousy.

As they crossed from the far to the near side of the valley and passed through the watercourse, they caught a glimpse of a man dressed in white. Apparently trying to console herself, the woman heaved a heavy sigh and said, "What a lovely, quiet place for convalescing."

The woman did not dare view this place too optimistically. Yet, neither did she dare think that this life would be too terrible. Despair and frustration were what she feared, and so whatever mishaps came her way, she always tried her best to interpret them in a generous light. That afternoon she had not been herself, but she had still managed to present a resolute front.

Following along behind the administrative section chief, she went into a courtyard and then entered the cave where she would be living. It was the exact opposite of what she had been hoping for. Too big, it didn't get enough sun, and was sure to be damp. As she stepped into the broad center of the cave, a frightful chill stole up on her from all sides. Where the weak rays of the setting sun shone upon the black dirt walls a layer of cold, mournful, lonely light seemed to be floating in the air. It was as if she had been placed in a world that was dark, yet translucent. She seemed to have left reality. Then she saw her small leather carrying case and her bedroll lying bleakly on the cold ground.

Section Chief Li was a kind-hearted man, and he began making up her narrow-legged bed. But when he shook out her quilt, which was no thicker than a pancake, he could not restrain himself. "Your quilt is so thin!" he exclaimed. Even among the troops he had seldom seen one so flimsy.

She glanced around the large cave, a twinge of uncertainty pulling at her heart. Yet, not wanting to ask for anything from someone else, she said simply, "I don't mind the cold that much."

Opposite her bed was another one that was already neatly made up. Li told her that it was for a nurse who was the wife of a Dr. Chang. This news shattered her dream of living the kind of quiet, clean, orderly life that comes from living alone. Struggling to comfort herself, she responded, "If I'm to live in such a large cave, I ought to have a roommate."

At that moment the administrative section chief did something that brought the whole bed down. Quickly he strode out of the cave, probably in search of a hatchet. The young woman squatted down on the floor to see about repairing the bed herself. As she looked around for a tool to use, an old pine table in front of the window caught her eye. If it hadn't been leaning against something it never would have stayed up. Next to the table two benches lay haphazardly on the ground. It seemed as though the furniture in this recently opened hospital was just remnants and cast-offs dragged in from all over.

How was she to pass this boring time, now that the section chief was gone? There was nothing better to do than stroll out into the courtyard. In the courtyard were a manure pile and a haystack so close together that one could not find room to step between them. Two women completely covered with chaff were kneeling in the hay. One held a lever shears, the other grasped the bundles, and with undivided attention they cut the hay and mixed it [with cowdung to make fertilizer].

The young woman stood to one side and watched them for a while. Then she asked in a friendly way, "How are you, neighbors?"

"Fine," the two women answered. Stopping their work, they stared at her curiously until one of them finally remarked, "Ah, another one come to have a baby." This woman had short hair that was sticking out in all directions. In the midst of that straw-like chaos was a pale face that looked like a piece of worn cloth. Her listless eyes had no more expression than a fish's.

"No, I'm not here to have a baby. I'm here to deliver babies," the young woman replied. As with any woman who had never married, when she was mistaken for an expectant mother rather than a midwife, she felt a disgust so great that she was on the verge of vomiting, as if she had just swallowed a fly.

By now faint pale-yellow lamplight was shining out of the three caves which faced eastward, and the bawling of a newborn baby could be heard. This gentle, comforting cry of a small life was most familiar, and brought a limitless freshness to her breast. She opened her mouth slightly, raised her eyebrows, and as she faced the rooms with the lighted lamps, said lovingly, "Tomorrow. Tomorrow I start."

While she had been walking outside, the glow of twilight had descended. The grove of trees along the watercourse was an indistinct blur. The distant hills wore a belt of gray, and above them colored clouds drifted across the sky. Although there was no wind to speak of, the air was bone-chilling. She had to return to her room.

She was startled to see that a lamp had already been lit in her room and she ran back quickly. When had the administrative section chief come back? Perhaps her bed had been repaired. When she entered the room, however, she saw only a female comrade in black clothing sitting on the bed that was already made up. She had lit the hempseed oil lamp and was polishing her shoes. The benches had been placed one on top of the other, and the lamp sat on top of them.

"Are you Lu P'ing, the doctor that just arrived?" the woman in the room asked as openly and as naturally as if she were accustomed to seeing her every day. She cast a casual glance her way and then returned to polishing her shoes, continuing to hum a strange song. She paid no heed whatever to the joy that the newly arrived Lu P'ing was showing. She answered her questions and comments with commonplace expressions. She was like an experienced traveler. She didn't care whether or not there was someone sleeping in the bed opposite hers. If someone different came along it was all the same. Nothing could excite her interest. After a final look at her shoes she pulled back the quilt, but did not go to sleep. Instead, she sat there inside the covers with her back against the wall and began to sing a song from northern Shensi.

Lu P'ing once again picked up the wooden bed supports. She knocked and pounded, but no matter what she tried they could not be set right. Finally, she had no choice but to spread her bedroll on the floor and resolve that she would somehow get through this one night. She too took a seat inside her covers, and aimlessly took the measure of Dr. Chang's wife.

Dr. Chang's wife was really very pretty, wasn't she? Her head and face were properly formed. Her black hair was neither too thick nor too thin. Her eyes, ears, nose, and mouth were all just right. Her neck and shoulder blades fit together well. Maybe she would be a good subject for painting on canvas. Yet, she seemed to have no emotion. There was neither gentleness nor ferocity about her. There was nothing about her to indicate intelligence, but neither did she appear to be stupid. She had answered several of Lu P'ing's questions, had spoken in some detail, and had even raised certain questions of her own. But there was no way of telling whether she enjoyed this or really found it all unpleasant.

Suddenly it was as if Nurse Chang had been jabbed by a needle. She leaped out of bed and rushed out of the room. Lu P'ing heard her push open the door to the next room, say a few words, and go in, obviously in high spirits. Her quilt, which had stirred up quite a breeze as she rushed out, now lay mostly on the floor.

Once again Lu P'ing was alone. Her quilt was hard to wrap up tightly. The lamp was running out of oil and the remaining light was cold and cheerless. Rats were beginning to come out. At first they stayed under the bed opposite her, but as time passed they came over and jumped on top of her quilt. She curled up inside her covers, not daring to take off her clothes. The cold made it hard to fall asleep, and many things kept coming into her mind.

Thinking about what had happened just that afternoon could have occupied her for the whole dark night. With all her power she comforted herself, encouraged herself, and scolded herself. Once again she constructed a new tower of hope. She tried to fall asleep within that tower, but in the cattle shelter across from her cave the cattle were endlessly chewing hay and constantly kicking something or other with their hooves. After a while Lu P'ing opened her eyes to find the room pitch black. The lamp had failed some time before, and by now the rats were even braver. They were coming up to her head!

Much later Lu P'ing heard the door of the adjoining cave open and the doctor's wife come storming back. She opened the door with a crash, bumped into one of the benches, and stepped on her quilt. "Those dog-fucking, mother-fucking administrators!" she cursed loudly. "So stingy with the oil! As soon as it's lit, it's gone. The rotten mother-fuckers!" She spit out these extreme vulgarities one after the other in a familiar manner. She had learned them well from the soldiers. However, even as she swore it did not appear that she was really angry or that her words were really meant to be obscene.

Lu P'ing didn't make a sound, but as she moistened her lips she tasted something deeply satisfying. As for the nurse, she began snoring rhythmically as soon as she laid her head on the pillow.

II

Lu P'ing had graduated from a school of obstetrics in Shanghai in accordance with her father's wishes. She had felt after the first two years of study that she was not cut out to be an obstetrician. She had more enthusiasm for literature. There were even times when she felt a hatred of all doctors. However, she still completed four full years of study. The Japanese attack on Shanghai on August 13, 1937 brought her into the war, and she went to serve in a battle hospital. She patiently bathed the wounded soldiers and changed their dressings. She wrote letters home for them and often ran off to get something they needed. She looked after them like a mother or a girl friend, and they relied on her as if she were too. After their wounds healed, she felt happy for them. When they left some talked about seeing her again, and she did receive a number of letters of appreciation. But then there would be no more news. As this happened she would quietly gather in her lonely feelings and turn them toward the new arrivals. For almost a whole year she lived this drifting life. She endured a great many hardships before she turned away and ran off to Yenan, where at last she became a student at Resistance University.

At Resistance University Lu P'ing experienced a change of heart. She applied herself diligently to reading a variety of books that she had never come in contact with before. She studied public speaking. She seemed to see her future as that of a vigorous political worker. She was very young, only twenty years old, and felt confident about her own intelligence. She was satisfied with this life and where she was going. She was careful with her time and didn't waste her feelings on those who wouldn't reciprocate.

After living at Resistance University for a year Lu P'ing became a member of the Communist Party. At the same time the director of the Political Department sought her out and told her that the needs of the Party dictated that she leave her studies and go to a recently opened hospital some twenty miles from Yenan. He also told her that medical work should become her vocation, her means of making a lifelong contribution to the Party. Lu P'ing argued against this. She said her character was not suited to such work. She said she would do anything else, no matter whether it was important. She even cried. None of her arguments, however, could sway the director in his determination. Since she could not overturn the decision, there was nothing to do but obey. The Party branch secretary came to discuss this matter with her, and the cell leader talked with her for a full day. Lu P'ing did not care for all this talk. She understood all the reasons for the action. It was just that they wanted her to cut away the bright future that she had been dreaming about for the past year. They wanted her to return to her old life. She knew that she could never be a great doctor. She was nothing more than an ordinary midwife. Her presence, she felt, would probably not make any difference at all.

Lu P'ing was a person full of illusions who had the endurance to break out of the circumstances of her life. But now the iron hoops of "Party" and "needs of the Party" were around her. Could she go against a Party directive? Could she ignore these iron hoops, these bonds that she herself had put on? There was nothing to do but go, but she agreed to only a year. Then she swept away her old mood and went out happily to meet her new life. Had not Lenin said, "Being unhappy is the greatest insult to life?" That was how Lu P'ing came to the hospital.

The hospital's superintendent was a Szechwanese of peasant stock. After joining the revolution he had served long in the military. Medical work was completely foreign to him. He welcomed Lu

P'ing as if he felt that female comrades needed no respect or politeness, and read her letter of introduction as indifferently as he would look at a hay purchase receipt. After taking a long look at her, he declared, "Well, very good! You'll be staying here." He indicated that he was too busy to talk longer with her and suggested that she look for the political adviser in the room across the hall. Having said that, he didn't look at her again. He just sat there, not lifting a finger to do anything.

The political adviser, Comrade Huang Shou-jung, looked like a company commander in the Youth Corps of the Eighth Route Army.[1] He was cautious, but he also loved very much to talk. His clothes were neat, and he exuded a sense of sincere youthful enthusiasm. He was somewhat shy, but he tried to act with great dignity.

Huang Shou-jung told Lu P'ing about the hospital's problems. First, they had no money. Second, they had just moved into the area, and because they hadn't yet established a good relationship with the masses, it was difficult to mobilize people. Third, there weren't enough doctors. Finally, those in charge of things had all come from other areas and were hard to deal with. Huang also told her about his past, how he had once served as political adviser to an army company. How he wished he could return there!

After she left the political adviser's office, in the course of the day Lu P'ing met several of her colleagues. Lin Sha, a woman in the chemical analysis laboratory, gave her a hostile glance right at the start. Lin Sha had thin, slanting eyes that closed into half circles when she laughed. The corners would drop, the lids would puff up slightly, and a delicate, enticing brilliance would reveal itself. She seemed to be waiting to be loved, asking people, "Look! Aren't I pretty?" But when she looked at Lu P'ing there was only disdain in her eyes, as if to say, "Humph! Where did they drag in this midwife from? She looks like a pauper!" Lin Sha's face had many expressions. Sometimes she was like a flower smiling. At other times she was like a cold star in the dead of night. She carried herself well when she walked and spoke in a slow rhythm that was haughty but attractive. Lu P'ing could do nothing but smile inanely at her, at the same time thinking, "Why should I fear you? How dare you get arrogant with me? I'll make you sit up and take notice!" Lu P'ing believed she could do it, and she wanted to very much.

One of Lu P'ing's former classmates at Resistance University, Chang Fang-tzu, was in the hospital working as a cultural instructor. Lu P'ing had never felt anything special for this girl, who liked so much to sing songs in front of others. Chang Fang-tzu was very good at frittering away her days. Her character was gentle, and she would never refuse any kind of arms extended to her. Yet, she had few friends. This was not because she was peculiar, or anything like that. Rather, it was because she seemed to lack any backbone at all. Like a rotting piece of cotton cloth, she had no strength, and could not hold the interest of others. When Lu P'ing first caught a glimpse of her former classmate, a wave of happiness rose up in her heart. But as she looked again at that vulgar, flat face, her heart became calm and cool as if it had just sunk deep into the ocean.

Lu P'ing's next stop was the director of obstetrics, Dr. Wang So-hua. Dr. Wang's wife, a pediatrician, had the air of a woman completely immersed in her church. She looked at everything around her as a white man regards a colored man. She was like an immortal banished to this mortal world, at once compassionate and condescending. Her husband, however, made a more favorable impression on Lu P'ing. He was a middle-aged man with an air of the gentry about him. His complexion was ruddy, his voice clear, and he maintained a constant level of satisfaction toward his work. Although Lu P'ing recognized in him a variety of the vain manners cultivated by the bourgeoisie, she also noticed that he was energetic and had some real enthusiasm for what he was doing. Lu P'ing did not particularly care for this kind of person. Neither did she need such a

[1] To present a united front during the War of Resistance against Japan, the Communist Party reached an agreement with the Kuomintang and reorganized its troops in August 1937, under the command of Marshal Chu Teh. It was known as the Eighth Route Army.

person for a friend. But as far as work was concerned, she would be happy to cooperate with someone like this. However, sitting there with that icy wife of his on one side made her so nervous that she did not dare stay too long. Although Dr. Wang's manner was friendly and open, she still felt some inexpressible pressure.

These various matters disturbed and worried her, but after a night's sleep, Lu P'ing brushed them off like dust from her sleeve. Having made a reasoned assessment of the whole situation, she bounced back again with great vitality. She felt that she had enough energy to take on any challenge, and called to herself, "Let my new life begin!"

III

Every morning after breakfast, when there was nothing special to do, Lu P'ing made a round of the five obstetrics wards without waiting for the head doctor. The great majority of patients were women from northern Shensi, with a scattering of students from a number of places. All of them welcomed her warmly. Each one looked at her with careful eyes. They called her name cordially and asked questions about their illnesses. At times, as women are prone to do, they showed a flare of temper. But all of them entrusted their hopes to Lu P'ing.

At first, one might find such trust and confidence exciting as well as flattering, except for certain things that went on day after day. For one thing, the women didn't do as she told them. They seemed afraid of becoming sick, but they didn't care about cleanliness. They used unsterilized paper, refused to let the nurses bathe them, and less than three days after giving birth they would begin to creep quietly out of bed and go to the toilet by themselves. They were a stubborn lot. They had all become mothers, but they wanted others to treat them like children.

Every day Lu P'ing repeated her requests to them. At times she pretended to be angry, but the rooms remained as dirty as before. The nurses in attendance were uneducated, and everything was just piled in corners. The laundry men did not come regularly, and used cotton and gauze could be seen all over the courtyard. Since flies that had not yet died of the cold were finding nourishment there, Lu P'ing had no choice but to put on her face mask, wrap a towel around her head, pick up a broom, and sweep out the courtyard herself. Some patients, a few passersby, and even a nurse or two often stood by and watched. But it wasn't long before they returned the courtyard to its original appearance without the slightest thought of remorse.

Besides the wife of Dr. Chang, the wife of a business manager in some other organization was also working in the hospital. Both of them were nurses in the obstetrics ward. Having studied nursing for some three months, they were able to recognize a number of characters and about a dozen names of Chinese medicines. However, they had no interest in nursing and didn't really know what they were doing. Yet, they had to work. A new fear was pressuring them. Groups of female students were coming to Yenan from other parts of China, and divorce cases were rampant. Of course, there were instances of women who had really awakened and were willing to work hard to achieve independent lives. But for the most part there was only fear and confusion.

These two wives really put on airs, especially the wife of the business manager, who was twenty-six or twenty-seven years old. This woman wore a Sun Yat-sen style of uniform that she had made herself, and placed the kind of hair clips used by young maidens in her thinning hair. Thinking herself attractive, she strutted arrogantly about the courtyard with her stomach bulging. These two women had no desire whatever to serve others. They were lazy. They were dirty. They showed enthusiasm only when they were patching their shoes and socks or starching their clothes.

Lu P'ing had no choice but to put pressure on them, and when that failed to get results, she had to do their work for them. Because she was apprehensive about their performance, she watched them sterilize instruments and checked on them as they bathed and changed the babies and made cotton balls and gauze rolls. Since she didn't want those who were sick or near term to suffer pain, she personally changed the dressings for several who had had operations or who had infections. This kind of habitual moral sense was not in vogue, and more than a few people looked down at her. However, she had developed the habit as a very young child.

Lu P'ing was always a little happier in the afternoon. Or, to put it another way, she became happier if there were no women in labor and her time was comparatively free. She would attend meetings and bring up many ideas that she had written down the night before. She was enthusiastic enough, but she had little understanding of the ways of the world. She was forever talking, arguing, or reiterating the unreasonable things that she had seen each day. Lu P'ing didn't realize what the expressions meant which she saw on the faces of other people. She brought up all sorts of things that many others did not dare or did not wish to mention themselves. She did receive some support. A few doctors and nurses often sought her out for a talk. The patients were especially supportive. They had heard that she was looking out for their welfare and was arguing with many people about improving their treatment. They all had great sympathy for her. Lu P'ing, however, had by now become the "little eccentric" of the hospital, and there was no doubt that the majority considered her unusual.

As a matter of fact, Lu P'ing's ideas had already been accepted by everyone as good. It was not completely impossible to implement them either. It was just that they were too new and different. In comparison with the life that had become normal, they seemed peculiar. Still, the main argument against Lu P'ing's ideas was a lack of personnel and materials.

Lu P'ing cared nothing for such reasons. Whenever someone entered the obstetrics ward she would point out problems, exclaiming, "Look! The equipment is so poor. The only syringe has a bent needle, and the doctors and the hospital superintendent just tell us to learn how to use bent needles. The rubber gloves are torn, though there's no use talking about them. They can't very well be repaired. But it *would* be possible to burn

an extra two or three catties of charcoal. How can a room be good for expectant mothers and newborn babies when it's this cold?" She would take people through the patients' rooms and let them see why nurses who lacked an education were unsatisfactory. By her description, the patients' lives were like a form of punishment. Lu P'ing wanted the patients to have clean quilts and clothing, a warm room, nourishing food, and an ordered life. She requested picture books, magazines, and papers for them. She wanted informal social discussion groups, small recreational meetings in the evening, and more. All who heard her speak listened with great enthusiasm, but later they never reacted with more than a laugh.

Lu P'ing was not completely without support, though. She did have two close friends. She and a girl named Li Ya had established a solid friendship in their very first conversation. This young assistant in the surgery department was also from the South, but she seemed to be tougher, less complicated, and more experienced than Lu P'ing. Together, they discussed the past, present, and future, especially the future. They wove the same kinds of beautiful fantasies. They discussed everyone in the hospital, and were surprised to find their ideas so similar. They never, however, stopped to analyze why this was so.

Besides Li Ya, Lu P'ing had become friends with Cheng P'eng, a doctor in the surgery department who often wrote short stories and plays. In the operating room, however, he was a tight-lipped professional. He forbade any extra moves and had a strict look that actually frightened people. He hardly spoke at all and used his hands instead to get his message across. In leisure conversation, however, there was no stopping him. He had a great knack for describing things in detail.

Whenever Lu P'ing was worn out by her work, or whenever she felt inexplicable pressures from her job or her surroundings, she was always overwhelmed by an indescribable feeling of despondency. However, when these two friends came by she was able to pour out her feelings. She could be more pointed and even exaggerate a little, because she did not need to fear that they would misunderstand her, twist her words, fault her, or betray her. Her vexations would dissipate, and they would begin to plan how to improve the hospital environment and make their work more relevant to actual conditions. Both of her friends cautioned her about getting too excited. Excessive zeal untempered by reason, they warned, would end in nothing.

The three of them also discussed the latest hospital gossip—for instance, who was Lin Sha finally going to fall in love with? Would it be the superintendent of the hospital, the director of surgery, or perhaps someone else? None of them liked it when the stories going around the hospital became too numerous or malicious, and at times they suspected that someone was deliberately trying to damage the authority of the superintendent. In fact, they frequently wound up defending both him and Lin Sha, even though in their hearts all three of them disliked this woman, with her phony cordiality, and none of them felt any respect for the superintendent. This was especially true of Lu P'ing, who always felt that she needed to guard herself against Lin Sha, though she couldn't explain why.

One of the biggest stories circulating through the hospital was about Chang Fang-Tzu, whom the political adviser's wife had slapped in the face. She had also complained directly to the Ministry of Health, with the result that Chang Fang-tzu was transferred to a dispensary at an army base. Meanwhile, everyone in the hospital was speculating that she wouldn't last long there either, because the same thing was likely to happen again. Since all the people in the hospital were being kept very busy, were constantly being exhorted to improve their skills, and had so many meetings to attend, it's a good question why everyone still had so much free time to talk about things like: Who's in love with whom? Who is and who isn't a Party member? If a person isn't a member of the Party, why not? There must be a problem there!

By this time Lu P'ing herself was the topic of idle chatter, no longer because of her various suggestions. She had said many things about the hospital system and its operation, and from the start there had been those who accused her of wanting to run things, of being a zealot, and of

loving to be the center of attention. But that kind of criticism had gradually become routine, and no one paid much attention to it. Even if Lu P'ing's remarks did make people react, they weren't beyond forgiveness, and were certainly insufficient cause for spreading spiteful gossip about her. Now, however, the situation was different. For some reason or other, people were pointing at her behind her back. Even the patients lying in bed picked up various rumors and began to steal glances at her with eyes full of curiosity.

As sensitive as Lu P'ing was, she didn't get the slightest hint of what was going on. She continued eagerly taking care of the expectant mothers and infants. For the sake of their smallest needs she argued with the administrative section, the business section, the secretary-general, and even with the hospital superintendent himself. Wearing only a short cotton garment tied tightly about her, she ran from one place to another in the cold wind. Her face became swollen with cold. The skin on her heels cracked open. But Lu P'ing never grumbled. The nights were the worst of all. Most of the time she could not get a full night's sleep because a woman had waited until night to give birth. There were times when she was called at midnight. The two nurses were easily frightened and were afraid to go out in the dark alone. It was left to her to go through the bone-chilling night to fetch water from the kitchen. In the delivery room, a small brazier of burning charcoal notwithstanding, her hands were often stiff with cold inside her rubber gloves. She would be extremely nervous, but she dared not let it show. If there were no complications she would handle the delivery herself. The doctor-in-charge lived quite far away, and she didn't want to rouse him on such cold nights.

Lu P'ing's enthusiasm for service extended beyond her own work. She wanted experience in other skills too. Thus, if she had the good fortune to be free when Cheng P'eng was operating, she always went to observe. In her opinion surgery was of the utmost necessity in time of war, and if she really had to do medical work—if there were no other choice—then being a surgeon would be far preferable to being a midwife. If she were a surgeon, she could go to the Front. She could busily rush through the forest of guns and the rain of bullets. Yes, she had always wanted to be on the move.

Lu P'ing was forever dissatisfied with the present. Recently she had heard that Cheng P'eng was about to perform a major operation. She was now in the midst of ensuring that she wouldn't miss this opportunity.

IV

Thoughts of what Li Ya had told her the evening before awakened Lu P'ing before dawn. Of course, the combination of her thin quilt and the especially cold temperatures that occurred just before sunrise often woke her up. Today, however, she couldn't go back to sleep.

The pale light coming through the paper window illuminated everything in the cave. Lu P'ing looked enviously at Dr. Chang's wife sleeping on the other bed. She always slumbered peacefully through the whole night like a child who had exhausted himself playing during the day. She and Lu P'ing were among the youngest in the hospital. Lu P'ing's work was tiring, but all she needed was a good night's sleep. She recalled that in the past she would sometimes wake up at night, but she would always feel so drowsy that after turning over she would fall right back to sleep.

Being unable to sleep, however, did have its advantages. As Lu P'ing stared at the plain white window paper, she thought of many things. They were unimportant things, things that otherwise she would not have had time for, but thinking of them gave her a great deal of pleasure. Her mind went back to the southern plains with their green grass. She thought of the streams, the villages, all the great trees that she couldn't name. She thought of the courtyard in her old home and of her mother, brothers, and sisters. Did cooking smoke still rise over the rooftops? Was the house still there? What had happened to all those people? She recalled her childhood friends and wondered whether they had gone away. Lu P'ing had heard that some of her friends had joined the guerrillas, and for a moment she dreamed of

doing that someday. In her reverie she took a deep breath of air scented by wildflowers, grass, and trees. The old folks at home embraced her. How she longed to be able to see her mother again. It would soon be three years since she had left home. She was tougher now, but in a secret spot she still felt a need for her mother's love and comfort.

Outside the window snowflakes silently floated down, covering the path that had been swept clean yesterday. A chorus of roosters nearby and from a distance could be heard, ushering in a new day. As the sound of trumpet practice carried faintly into the room, Lu P'ing's thoughts turned again to the question, "How can the operating room be satisfactory without a coal stove?" She was annoyed with the hospital superintendent. All he understood was enduring hardship. He didn't understand that certain basic conditions had to be met in medical work. Lu P'ing was also angry at the director of surgery. Why didn't he insist that a coal stove be installed? Cheng P'eng ought to say something too. That was their responsibility. If they failed once or twice, they should try again! Very upset, Lu P'ing crawled out of bed, quietly started a fire, lit the lamp, and wrote an entreating letter to the superintendent. She also wrote a note to Li Ya telling her to go out and do some talking in favor of the idea. She said that she herself would not be able to get away from the obstetrics ward all morning. By the time Lu P'ing finished it was broad daylight and she was getting nervous. She hoped that no one would go into labor that afternoon. She was happily looking forward to seeing the operation.

Li Ya neither came to see Lu P'ing nor returned her note. She was busy preparing all the things that would be needed that afternoon in the operating room. If even a single item was missing, and it affected the patient's life, the responsibility would be hers alone. Because of this, she had to arrange the entire room, sterilize everything, and put everything in order for easy use. She apportioned the work between the two nurses and told them which areas should be given special attention. She dared not take a single thing for granted.

Cheng P'eng came by once to check things over. "Have you seen Lu P'ing's letter?" Li Ya asked, handing him the note she had received that morning. "I think that no matter what we do, it's impossible to take care of this today. It's so late. That's why I haven't done what she suggested. However, if it is too cold, we could delay the operation for a few days. It's your decision."

Cheng P'eng folded the note and returned it to Li Ya without a word. Wrinkles creased his brow as he walked over to inspect the scalpels and scissors that had been laid out. The delicate metal instruments had a harsh cold shine, but to him they were familiar and dear. After looking them over he nodded to Li Ya, as if to say, "Very good." At times like this their relationship was strictly professional; he ordered and she obeyed. He didn't permit her the slightest trace of the mischievousness she displayed when they were acting as friends. Finally, on his way out, he said, "Please have everything ready by two o'clock. And light one more brazier. The patient cannot wait for me to install a stove."

Immediately after lunch, Lu P'ing rushed over to the surgery department building. By now Li Ya was infected with Cheng P'eng's silence and seriousness, and all she told Lu P'ing was that the patient could not wait for a stove to be put in place. Then she noticed that several people were already in the operating room, and suddenly felt a certain pressure in the atmosphere. Without saying another word she walked over and put on her sterilized cap.

A small piece of shrapnel from a bomb that had exploded two months earlier was lodged in the patient's abdomen just below his ribs. Twelve fragments had already been removed, and only this fragment remained. They had tried to find it once before without success. This would be the second attempt.

Because of the nutritious diet he had had recently, the patient seemed fairly strong. He walked into the operating room on his own, and decided to have his appendix out too. However, as soon as he sat down on the edge of the table, the color drained from his face. There was fear and weariness in his eyes as he looked at this group of people dressed in white. His voice quivering, he stammered out the question, "How many hours?"

"It'll go very fast," someone replied, but Lu P'ing knew that doctors never tell patients the truth.

For convenience, Cheng P'eng wore only a wool shirt under his gown. Li Ya also went without a cotton jacket. Everyone's actions were as sincere and as careful as if they were conducting a religious ceremony. The patient lay down and they bathed him with a medicinal lotion. Lu P'ing could see an old wound—an inch-long scar. Cheng P'eng motioned to her and she realized he wanted her to help the nurses measure out the drops of anesthetic. The odor of chloroform immediately entered her nostrils, but it didn't matter. She received only a slight whiff, while the patient, who had been counting, quickly fell silent.

Lu P'ing watched as Cheng P'eng plotted, cut, and folded the skin back in a well-practiced manner. With pieces of gauze he swiftly wiped away the blood that was flowing out, and changed instruments in rapid succession. Li Ya handed him each one without the slightest confusion. The knife blade cut in for an inch and a half, and the doctor gently drew out some red things and some other things that were bluish-green. Pushing his forceps into the incision, he felt around for that single piece of steel that was hidden so deeply inside.

In spite of the three braziers full of charcoal, the room was still extremely cold. Lu P'ing worried constantly about the anesthetized patient, whose internal organs were exposed. Afraid to take her eyes off him for an instant, she kept a steady watch on his breathing and his reactions.

Once again the doctor pressed downward, listened, and folded open several more things that were all twisted together. A slight wisp of steam floated upward from the incision. Almost half an hour had gone by. Lu P'ing cast a worried glance in Cheng P'eng's direction, but he didn't even look at her. He was pulling the scalpel upward and beginning to search nearer the ribs. Blood still flowed at times, but Cheng P'eng wiped it away as he had before. By now the patient's face was paler. Lu P'ing was afraid that he was getting cold, when suddenly she herself began to feel dizzy.

The door to the operating room was tightly closed and three braziers of charcoal were burning brightly inside. Lu P'ing looked at the time and really began to get nervous. Three-quarters of an hour had passed. There were seven people shut up in this unventilated room. How could they stand it?

At last the piece of steel was plucked out with the tiniest forceps. It was the size of a grain of rice. Only a small area of flesh around it had given way to pus. With this work done Cheng P'eng went about cutting out the appendix. Lu P'ing's head was swimming, but somehow she held on. Li Ya, however, suddenly fell against the operating table and became still. She had been in the room too long; carbon dioxide had taken its toll.

"Carry her out into the cold courtyard," Cheng P'eng told the two nurses, and in an instant the other two doctors assumed her responsibilities. As Lu P'ing watched Li Ya being carried out like a corpse, tears welled up and filled her eyes. She didn't know whether Li Ya would live or die. All she could think about was going with her to see how she was. But she also realized that she was handling another person's life. She couldn't leave.

Cheng P'eng's movements became more rapid, but before he had finished, Lu P'ing couldn't stand any longer and began to moan. "Help her to the door and leave it open a crack," Cheng P'eng said.

Lu P'ing lay down just outside the doorway, and as her mind cleared a bit she waved her hand and shouted, "Go back in! Go back! He can't do it all himself!"

Left alone outside the door, Lu P'ing thought of going to see Li Ya. She began to crawl away from the operating room, but the two nurses who were returning pulled her back to the door and left her there. She didn't move. Snowflakes flew onto her face. Shivers ran up and down her body. Her teeth chattered. Her head seemed about to burst.

Lu P'ing didn't know how long she had been asleep when she heard some people walk past and realized they were carrying the patient back to his room. She thought of how late it was and how she ought to be going back to her room to sleep. However, she also thought again of going to see Li Ya. What if something happened to Li Ya? "Oh, she's so young!" she thought.

The cold wind had already made her mind clear, but a strange sense of exhilaration and weakness controlled her. She rushed unsteadily across the snow-covered ground. The wind howled around her. Dusk was falling. Melting snow and tears mixed together and covered her face. "Is this how she's to give up her life?" she cried out. "Her mother doesn't know anything about what's happening!"

Lu P'ing couldn't find Li Ya, so she ran back to her own cave. She knew full well that she needed to sleep and sleep, but something was crushing her. She had to scream . . .

While Lu P'ing shivered under three or four quilts, patients crowded into her room and made guesses about what was wrong with her. At eleven o'clock Cheng P'eng came to see her and gave her a sedative. That afternoon his head had been as dizzy as hers, but he had somehow kept control and finished the operation. Then he had gone to a deserted, snow-covered slope and had sat there for an hour while his head cleared. After this he had come back, drunk some hot water, and gone to see Li Ya. She was sleeping soundly. After eating a little more he had brought the medicine and come to see Lu P'ing.

Knowing that a friend was beside her made Lu P'ing feel weaker than ever. She was unable to keep from crying. She just wished that she could see her mother. If she could collapse on her mother's breast and cry her heart out, everything would be all right.

Cheng P'eng did not leave until he had helped Lu P'ing take her medicine. Even she herself had no idea when she finally fell asleep, and the next day she was still in bed when Li Ya came to see her. She told Li Ya that she seemed to have lost interest in everything. All she felt like doing was lying in bed and not moving.

V

Lu P'ing stayed in her room as if she were ill, but gossip about her flew in all directions throughout the hospital. No two stories were alike. Some said she was in love with Cheng P'eng, had gone crazy that night, and was still suffering from lovesickness. Others said that the Party would not endorse their love because Cheng P'eng was not a Party member and his background was unclear.

Lu P'ing could not possibly pay attention to such things. Her mind was in a state of utter confusion. The reality of life was too frightening for her. She wondered why so many people had walked by her prostrate body that night without a single offer to help. She thought about the willingness of the hospital superintendent to endanger patients, doctors, and nurses in order to save a little money. She examined her daily life and wondered what use it was to the revolution. The revolution was for all mankind. Why, then, were even the closest comrades so lacking in love? Lu P'ing was unsure of herself. She asked herself if her support of the revolution was wavering. Once again the nervous exhaustion that she had suffered in the past took hold of her. Night after night she suffered from insomnia.

Meanwhile, people in the Party branch were criticizing her. Labels such as "petty bourgeois mentality," "intellectual heroism," and "liberalism" were pinned on her. The general conclusion was that her sense of Party loyalty was weak. The superintendent of the hospital called her in and gave her a talking to. The patients cooled in their attitude toward her and said she was loose.

Lu P'ing felt that yes, she should struggle. But against whom? Against everyone? If she didn't fight this out with them she should leave. It wasn't right to stay here and upset people. Yet, where could she go? She wished with all her might that she could stand up and go somewhere she wanted to. She was seeking the determination she had felt when she arrived. But everything was moving in the wrong direction. All she could do was sit in her cave all day, frowning and brooding.

Cheng P'eng and Li Ya wondered why she had suddenly become so weak. They came by often to talk with her and tried to ease her frustration. This, however, led to more gossip, and finally even the political adviser came to believe the rumors. He told her formally that love could not be permitted to obstruct one's work.

Such talk left Lu P'ing feeling shocked and insulted, but it also stirred her anger. As if seeking revenge, she looked everywhere for weak points to attack. She criticized everything. Every day she thought about how she could assail the others and bring them down. She believed firmly that truth was on her side.

A new strength seemed to be supporting Lu P'ing. Whenever she had a free moment she went to as many rooms as possible, gathering comments to use in support of her accusations. One day she went to room number six, where a malaria patient with no feet was staying. Without waiting for her to speak he motioned for her to sit down, and with a sense of closeness that one finds among kin, said, "Comrade, I've been in the hospital for two weeks, and ever since I first heard people talk about you I've been wanting to meet you. You've come at just the right time. Please don't be polite, for you'll have to excuse me for talking to you like this. I have to lean on something, since both my feet are gone."

"Why is that?"

"The medical work was poor and unskilled. For no good reason they sawed off both my feet."

"When did this happen?"

"Three years ago. At that time there were many nights when I considered killing myself."

Lu P'ing was at a loss as to how to comfort him. "I really can't stand any more of this. What kind of monstrosity is this hospital?"

"Comrade, now . . . now things are better. Come here and look at how few lice I have on my body. When I came here before because of my feet, the lice almost ate me up. You say that the hospital superintendent is no good, but do you know anything about his background? He was an illiterate peasant! The political adviser was a young herdsboy, and he grew up in the military. How much can he know? Yes, they're all unsatisfactory, but who can take their places? I tell you that their superiors are no different. Your knowledge is greater than theirs! You are more able to assume responsibilities than they are. However, oil, salt, firewood, and rice have to be obtained from somewhere. Can you make them? The work style must be changed, but is it so easy? You're a good person. You have a fine character. I could see it in your face the moment you came in. But you don't have an overall strategy. You're too young. Don't be impatient! Go slowly. If you have any problems come and talk them over. And by the way, making formal accusations is good too. It always serves some purpose." He chuckled as he looked at Lu P'ing's astonished expression.

"Who are you? How can you see everything so clearly? If I'd met you earlier, things would be different now."

"Everyone understands this. Go and ask the cook. Who do you think told me these things? Who do you think told me about you? They know everything. You should talk things over with them more often. Don't just look to a few people. If you do, your energy will drain away and it won't be easy to keep going in the midst of fierce self-struggle."

Lu P'ing felt that this man was really unusual, and she didn't leave. He talked to her about many things as if she were his younger brother or sister, including what seemed to her the cruel struggles of life. He explained, encouraged, and patiently taught her. She learned that he had been a student and had gone to the Soviet Union. Now, because he was crippled, he was editing popular readers for the soldiers. She shed tears for him, but he seemed to be detached from his own situation.

After a few days the Ministry of Health called Lu P'ing in for a discussion. She didn't make any accusations. Instead, after she explained herself several times and was thoroughly investigated, she had the good fortune of being understood. Moreover, her request to continue her studies was approved.

When Lu P'ing left the hospital the ice had not yet begun to melt, but the sting was already gone from the wind that touched her face. As she went away her heart felt as though it were really springtime. She was reluctant to leave Li Ya and Cheng P'eng, but there was nothing she could do but pass on to them what the man without feet had told her.

A new life was beginning for Lu P'ing, but there would still be trials ahead. People, like iron, must pass through numerous tempering fires before their real worth can be proven. A person matures amidst hardship.

PA CHIN
(*1904–*)

Li Fei-kan's pen name, Pa Chin, was formed of syllables from the names of two anarchists, *Ba*kunin and Kropot*kin*. Born into a large landowning family in Chengtu, Szechwan, he was very much the darling son of his mother. An extremely sensitive child who was first exposed to suffering and death when he witnessed the killing of his favorite rooster for a family meal, Pa Chin considered himself driven since childhood to serve the insulted and the injured. He confides in the preface to a 1936 collection of his stories:

> I am not an artist. People say that life is short and art is long. But I think there is something which has a more perennial value than art. That thing enthralls me. For it I am willing to forsake art without any compunction. What is art if it cannot bring some light to the masses and strike a blow at darkness? [Quoted in Hsia, *History*, p. 237]

Pa Chin's desire to "strike a blow at darkness" led him to speak frankly during the Hundred Flowers campaign in 1957, a brief period of literary freedom. He was subsequently criticized and silenced. In spite of his great popularity and international renown, he was further persecuted by the Gang of Four during the Cultural Revolution. Though even today his works are considered restricted by his class and his times, there is little doubt that he is being rehabilitated as one of the great humanitarian writers modern China has known.

Excluding translations, Pa Chin's works from 1927 to 1946 total fourteen volumes, collected as *The Works of Pa Chin* (*Pa Chin wen-chi*, Peking, 1958–1962). To the Western reader, Pa Chin is chiefly known by two novels in English translation: *The Family* (*Chia*, 1933) and *Cold Nights* (*Han-yeh*, 1947).

Of the four stories included in this anthology, "Nanny Yang" (*Yang sao*, 1931) is decidedly autobiographical. Pa Chin's memory of Nanny Yang is later "movingly embodied in the death scene of the maidservant Ch'ien-erh in the novel *Autumn* [*Ch'iu*, 1940]" (Hsia, *History*, p. 239). "The General" (*Chiang-chün*, 1933) has a touch of exoticism, since the general and his wife are not Chinese but Russian refugees in Shanghai. "Sinking Low" (*Ch'en-lo*, 1934) bespeaks Pa Chin's abhorrence of those academic intellectuals who advocate pacifism in the face of Japanese aggression, bury their heads in idle research, and encourage their students to study abroad. "Piglet and Chickens" (*Chu yü chi*, 1942), taken from the collection *Little People and Little Events* (*Hsiao-jen hsiao-shih*, 1945), is a jewel of a story that shows the author's marked maturity as a compassionate realist during the forties.

J.S.M.L.

Nanny Yang

by Pa Chin

Translated by Perry Link

—La morto de la servistino [1]

Every evening when the nine o'clock gong had sounded, Elder Brother and I would close the volume of *Pai Hsiang's Lyric Primer* which Mother had copied down for us to read.

"Tell Nanny Yang to take you to bed," Mother would say. Then we said goodnight to her and, with sleepy eyes, walked from her room.

"Nanny Yang, we want to go to bed." Usually Elder Brother was first to call her.

"Coming!" her gentle voice would bounce back, usually with the same word every night. Then, very quickly, Nanny Yang's large frame would appear before us. Her eyes smiled at us. She would lead us away with her big, rough hands, one of us on each side. She would talk to us as we went, leading us straight to our room.

Our room was also her room. She slept in the same room because we were afraid of ghosts. Besides, we were still very young and had to be taken care of in everything. There were two beds in the room: one was for Elder Brother and me to share, the other for Nanny Yang. Both bedspreads were perfectly clean. She was extremely fond of cleanliness, and kept the room and its beds in tidy order. She wouldn't let us spit on the floor; nor could we roughhouse on the beds during the day. Twice she caught us playing shadow puppets on the lowered mosquito net, and on

those occasions she grew angry and bundled us down from the bed. When I saw her grab hold of Elder Brother and get ready to slap his palms, I scurried off to safety. Before long, though, my curiosity brought me back. I began peering stealthily through the doorway and saw Elder Brother standing next to the table with rice cakes in his hands, munching away. Nanny Yang was only making our beds! As I gazed at the rice cakes, their flavor returned in my memory. I crept slowly into the room until I was right in front of Elder Brother. Noiselessly, I just stared at the few strips of rice cake in his hands. Elder Brother laughed complacently in my direction, then took a couple of strips and pressed them into my hand. I quickly stuffed them in my mouth, chewing laboriously. But Nanny Yang had already spotted me.

"You're back?" she asked with a smile. "Would you like some rice cakes?"

Without answering her, I just nodded my head fearfully, mouth still moving.

"Hold out your hands and let me hit them," she threatened, still smiling.

Instead of extending my hands, I did the opposite—hid them behind my back. But I didn't run away, either.

"All right, I'll let you off this time, but you can't

[1] This epigraph in Esperanto appeared in the original. Pa Chin was interested in Esperanto in the late twenties. The closest we could reconstruct it in French would be "La mort de la servitude" (the death of servitude). Or, in Italian, "La morta della servitù" (the dead woman of servitude). We are grateful to Professor Fannie J. Lemoine of the University of Wisconsin, Madison, for this information.

fool around on the bed anymore. If I catch you again, you'll get a spanking." She gave me a pat on the head as she said it, then went and opened the doors of the wardrobe and took a slab of rice cake out of a porcelain jar and handed it to me. Then she led Elder Brother and me out of the room.

We liked her in spite of these punishments she administered. This was not only because the punishments were followed by rice cakes, but because they occurred very seldom; unless we did something wrong, Nanny Yang was never cross with us. Most of the time she was extremely warm. Next to our mother, we loved her most.

Every night she would lead us into our room, and sometimes would even play with us for a while. She knew all kinds of ways to amuse children. Otherwise she would just tell us to stand aside while she spread out the bedding, then would help us get undressed, first Elder Brother and then me. When she had tucked us into bed and was about to let down the mosquito nets, we would often raise a great cry for her to stay behind and tell us a story or two. Sometimes we wouldn't go to sleep until we'd heard a story and were happy with it. Other times our eyelids fell as the story progressed, and we had no idea what she was talking about. Immortals, righteous swordsmen, goblins, what have you—they all became the same to us.

From the time we came to the county seat with our father, who was the magistrate, this was the way we always went to bed at night. Things went on pretty much like this for most of a year. During this time we could not, of course, be without our mother; yet neither could we be without Nanny Yang.

The situation suddenly changed, however.

One night, after the usual closing of *Pai Hsiang's Lyric Primer,* Mother did not say, "Tell Nanny Yang to take you to bed now." Instead she told Elder Sister to lead us out, and she herself followed us into our room. She watched while Elder Sister tucked us into our bed, then, telling us to sleep tight, lowered the mosquito nets and left.

That night the other bed's mattress, quilt, and mosquito net had all been switched. It was Elder Sister who slept there.

Mother's footsteps could no longer be heard, and the stillness in the room was broken only by Elder Sister's coughing. Her voice was as familiar to us as Nanny Yang's, but still we lay under the blanket and stared blankly at the top of our mosquito net. Then we turned our heads to look at each other. We didn't say a word. We were both thinking of Nanny Yang. This night really was different from other nights: first, we had no rice cakes to eat; second, there was no story. All because Nanny Yang was ill.

"Where is Nanny Yang sleeping?" I asked myself. I thought I could hear her moans, but I still couldn't tell where she was sleeping. There was no answer to this question until the next day.

Behind our room was a big lawn, which I could see whenever I opened the window. A few rows of mulberry trees were planted along the two sides of the lawn, leaving in the middle a wide promenade which reached to the fourth residential hall. On the two sides there were stone steps atop which lay a row of three connected rooms. These rooms were dark for lack of sunlight. The three nearer my room were normally used for storing old furniture, and the ones across from them were bedrooms for the amahs and maids. At that time we had, in addition to Nanny Yang, three other amahs, a wet-nurse in charge of Ninth Younger Sister, and a young maid named Fragrance, all of whom Mother had brought from Ch'eng-tu. At present, Nanny Yang had one whole room to herself within that row of three.

The room was visible from my window, but not clearly so, because it was blocked off by the big, wide leaves of the mulberry trees. That was before Mother had started raising silkworms, so the mulberry leaves were of no particular use to us and nobody picked them. We did get berries, though, which would fall one by one from the trees around late spring and early summer. Some of them would break apart when they hit the ground and ooze with shining, deep purple juice. But others lay there in perfectly good shape. After school Elder Brother and I often went mulberry-picking with Fragrance, picking out the nicest berries and popping them in our mouths. We would hold out the fronts of our loose gowns to cradle berries in our laps, and always came away with a full load. We would keep a few for ourselves, but give all the rest to Nanny Yang for wine-making. How fresh and delicious those ripe mulberries tasted!

Every time we called Nanny Yang into our room and showed her pile after pile of deep purple mulberries, she made a surprised face and exclaimed, "So many! Such good ones!" She would hold a few to her nose and sniff them, then put them into her mouth. "Delicious!" she would say, showing her teeth in a broad smile and reaching for a few more to put into her mouth. Elder Brother and I, and she and Fragrance, would gather around the table eating mulberries. All our hands turned bright red from the juice. When the berries were almost gone, Nanny Yang would stand up and with a clap of her hands say, "Okay, that's enough. No more eating!" Lifting the flap of her gown to wipe her mouth, she would go and open the doors of the wardrobe, take out a wine bottle, and put the remaining mulberries into it. If one bottle wasn't enough, she would go get a second. Each bottle had been more than half filled with a white-colored wine.

We watched her very closely as she did all this. We were no less fascinated than when listening to Mother's recitals from *Pai Hsiang's Lyric Primer*. "How is Nanny Yang's wine doing?" we often wondered. Before long we could observe her taking the wine bottles out and rubbing her hands over them, or shaking them up. The white-colored wine turned purple. Later on we would see her, in the evening, pour herself a little cup of wine. She would hold the wine and savor it slowly, telling us a story at the same time.

We listened to the stories very carefully, of course. But at the same time, our eyes would come to rest on the wine cup. When we saw that purple liquid (how rich and appealing the color was!), we couldn't help recalling its much paler color before the mulberries had been put in. The change not only stirred our curiosity; it also brought a marvelous new zest into our lives. How we longed to taste a bit of the liquid in that cup.

That bouquet, that color—their attraction was overwhelming! I keep saying "we" here because Elder Brother and I shared all these feelings at the time.

These impressions were to stick in my mind for a long time; even much later, when fully grown, I was to be unable to forget them completely. But it was all over and done with now, because fall had come, only one bottle of mulberry wine was left in the wardrobe, and Nanny Yang lay ill in bed in the women servants' quarters.

One day after school Elder Brother tugged at my sleeve and said, "Let's go see Nanny Yang." Without the slightest hesitation I followed. We ran to the third residential hall, then rapidly into Nanny Yang's room.

Quite to our surprise, we found that there was no other person in that dark room, nor was there the slightest sound. Nanny Yang lay very still on a low bed, the lower portions of her body covered by a thin quilt on which brownish stains were apparent. One side of the bed's mosquito net had been let down and dropped to the floor. Not far from the bed there was a little stool on which rested a bowl of thick, black herb medicine, already cold. Two flies were crawling up the side of the bowl.

Not a sound came from Nanny Yang as we drew near the bed. Soon we could see her face, and it was white as paper. She lay curled up, disheveled hair piled atop her head, eyes closed. There was a yellowish ring around her mouth, which opened slightly as she exhaled. This mouth was the only sign of life in her. One of her arms extended from under the quilt to grasp the edge of the bed. But all motion had left that yellow, scrawny hand.

I began to have my doubts. I couldn't believe the person sleeping here was our own Nanny Yang. My child's mind just couldn't understand how, in such a few days' time, a lively human being could be transformed into the likes of this. No trace of the lively, robust Nanny Yang could be found anywhere on this body. To believe this really was Nanny Yang would be to suspect that the whole past had been nothing but a dream world. How could that mouth—so drawn that it couldn't even cover its own teeth—have recounted all those memorable stories? How could that scrawny, helpless hand have so often caressed us, and spanked us, and given us rice cakes to eat?

As these thoughts occurred to me, Elder Brother decided to break the silence. "Nanny Yang! Nanny Yang!" he cried, rubbing at her hand. My mind stood still. I stared at her face with every ounce of concentration.

Very slowly a sound began coming from her nose. The hand that had been clutching the edge of the bed gently relaxed. Her body shifted, ever so slightly, and some inarticulate sound came from her mouth. Then her eyes slowly opened, closed again, then reopened wider than before. As her gaze fell upon Elder Brother and me, her lips moved slightly, as if she were about to smile. When I knew she saw us, I joined Elder Brother in calling to her.

She smiled, although her smile was different from what it had always been. Slowly she raised her hand to caress Elder Brother's head, and said, "You've come. Do you still think about me? I haven't seen you for quite a few days . . . Wonder what kind of a total mess your room must be in! Who's there to look after you these days?" Her voice, though it did slightly resemble her normal one, was nevertheless quite different from it. How faint and feeble it now was! It actually sounded more like sighing.

Elder Brother answered her. "Our room's very neat. Elder Sister takes care of us. She stays with us at night, and Mommy takes care of us too."

"Good, I'm relieved then. You don't know how much I've been worrying about you! I often wonder what's become of you, now that you don't have me around." She smiled faintly again. "The rice cakes in the wardrobe must be all gone by now. Go tell Mommy, and get her to buy some more for you."

A most peculiar feeling suddenly came over me. I fondly grasped her hand, and even though the hand was cold as ice, I held tightly to it. It was as if I were clinging to a close relative and I didn't want her to leave.

Her gentle gaze shifted toward my face. There was a smile in her eyes, but it was several mo-

ments before she said anything. "Fourth Little Master, are you still as naughty about your school-work these days?" I wanted to talk, but couldn't get anything out. She went on, "You're so nice—you still care about me. I'm not too sick; in a few days I'll be all right."

Suddenly her eyes turned away from us. She seemed to catch a glimpse of the medicine bowl on top of the little stool. She frowned, then smiled again. "Look how bad my memory is! This bowl of medicine probably got cold a long time ago, and I've forgotten to drink it." As she spoke she started to prop her body up and reach for the bowl.

Elder Brother restrained her. "Don't get up, Nanny Yang," he said. "I'll bring it to you." He went and took the medicine bowl in his hands. "It's cold, you don't want to drink it. I'll get somebody to go heat it up." As he spoke he turned to leave.

"So what if it's cold? It's all the same in the stomach. You mustn't bother anyone. They'll think I'm making a special case of myself!"

She spoke excitedly to Elder Brother, her face turning red, as she struggled to prop herself up. She was waving to call him back.

Elder Brother headed back with the medicine bowl, spilling some of its contents on the way. When he neared the bed Nanny Yang snatched it from him. Then she lowered her face and gulped down the medicine. As we listened to the gulping noise, it almost seemed we could watch how the medicine passed through her esophagus and into her stomach.

She downed the medicine all at once, then lifted her head. She was still red in the face, with some medicine dregs clinging at her mouth's edges. She handed the bowl to Elder Brother, wiped her mouth with her hand, and heaving a long sigh, slumped back listlessly. She looked completely exhausted.

She closed her eyes, and did not open them to look at us after that. A faint snoring issued from her nose, and the portion of her bosom which lay outside the quilt began to rise and fall. The color gradually faded from her face, though a few dregs of medicine remained on her cheeks. I thought how lucky it was there was no mirror in the room, so that she couldn't see her own face.

We stood there for quite a while without observing any movement from her. I felt we had lost our Nanny Yang again. Added to the fear which this thought brought upon me was the fearful, gloomy aura which now seemed to descend over everything in the room. Gradually, before my very eyes, Nanny Yang's face began to change. I saw the face of a goblin: the long, disheveled hair, the pallid, meager face, the high cheekbones, and big, blood-red eyes—this was just like the goblins' faces in the stories Nanny Yang used to tell.

"Let's go!" I said in terror, clutching Elder Brother's sleeve. We left very quickly, as if escaping a demon's den.

After that day, we never again spoke of going to see Nanny Yang. Of course I missed her, but the person I missed was the lively, healthy Nanny Yang, not the Nanny Yang whose face had become like a goblin's. Even though several people told me that the Nanny Yang who was sleeping in that dark room was the same Nanny Yang who used to sleep in our room, I still could not forget that goblin face. Whenever I remembered it I would be afraid to go to the dark room again. I would tell myself, "Nanny Yang has gone away someplace. She's returned to her home. She's not in this yamen. She will come back. Before long she'll come back."

Elder Brother disagreed with me. "Nanny Yang is in this yamen," he said. "She's sick, and she'll get better soon. She can't go home—she doesn't have a home any more." Elder Brother was, after all, older than I was, and he knew a bit more. It was news to me that Nanny Yang had no home; the very idea that a person could be without a home was something I had no way of comprehending at the time.

But enough of all this. Nanny Yang never did return to our room. I only heard others speak of her illness, but I never clearly understood what kind of illness it was. The days passed one by one. Nanny Yang remained ill. We could often hear her groans when we walked across the courtyard behind the third residential hall.

"I guess that's our Nanny Yang groaning," I couldn't help thinking. But I would always resist the conclusion: "It must be a goblin—Nanny Yang would never groan like that." Weird screeches now punctuated the groans, making them unlike those of an ordinary invalid.

More than a month passed, and things didn't get any better. Our Nanny Yang never came back, but the patient in the dark room began emitting heart-rending screams. When this happened I decided once and for all that they were indeed the cries of a goblin, not of an invalid. Besides screeching the goblin sometimes talked. All I could make out was "My Little Mao! Give me back my Little Mao!" I knew that Little Mao was her son; she had often compared us to him. She also said things like "If Little Mao were living he'd be seven this year."

No matter how firm my judgment that the invalid was a goblin, people still kept calling her Nanny Yang. Whenever they mentioned her their faces turned solemn and terrified. Several times I heard Mother sigh and say, "Heaven is so blind; how can such a good person as Nanny Yang come down with an illness like this!" But I still didn't know what illness it was she suffered from. And Mother instructed me not to go peeking in from beneath Nanny Yang's window: by this time none of the amahs or servants dared enter Nanny Yang's room unless they absolutely had to, but they made a practice of huddling beneath the window and peeking through the cracks in the window paper. Mother was afraid I would join them. In fact, though, I was afraid of peeking, even when the occasion arose as Elder Brother and I sometimes passed through the courtyard behind the third residential hall on our way to play in the haystack behind the fourth residential hall.

"Nanny Yang is not going to recover," Mother tearfully told Father one day. "Let's get her a really nice coffin. These years she's been with us she's treated our Third and Fourth so well—almost as if they were her very own." Her words suddenly made me cry. It was the first time I understood what death meant.

More than ten days later, though, Nanny Yang still had not died. She was still in that dark room talking loudly, or laughing, or screeching. She was saying more things now. Besides her Little Mao, she spoke also of "goblins," "spirits," and "the Great Jade Emperor"—but she was not telling stories.

"Third Little Master! Fourth Little Master! Go look, quick! Nanny Yang is eating lice!" One afternoon when Elder Brother and I got out of school we met Fragrance. Wonder showed in her happy face as she spoke to us.

"I saw her unbutton her clothes to hunt lice. When she got one she tossed it in her mouth and bit down with all her might. You could hear the 'pop' when she bit it open. Then she caught several more in a row and put them in her mouth. She was laughing all the time. She even took off her smelly footbinding rags and chewed on them." Fragrance imitated Nanny Yang's gestures as she spoke. "I don't want to look; I'm busy," I said, and ran away toward Mother's room. Without a word I threw my head into Mother's bosom and burst into tears. My head was filled with footrags and lice. Our Nanny Yang, who so loved cleanliness, was eating lice and chewing on footrags. I couldn't imagine it, or even mention it. Mother spent quite a long time comforting me.

From then on Nanny Yang ate lice and chewed footrags every day. Of course she still screeched, and still railed against people. At first there were some who found her eating of lice and chewing of rags amusing, but within a few days people would just knit their brows, or shake their heads and walk away, whenever it was mentioned. No one stood beneath her window to peek any more.

Everybody knew that medicine could no longer help, that there was no point in waiting for our inexpert doctor to refer the invalid to other "experts" for better treatment. In Kuang-yüan county, so poor that most of its residents had to eat cornmeal instead of rice, there simply were no expert doctors. "Heavens! Isn't there some way to let her die sooner, so she won't suffer this living torture?" everybody was saying. Eventually a yamen guard suggested we administer poison. But no one dared agree with him, even though everyone hoped she would die soon.

Finally, the doctor didn't come any more.

Nanny Yang continued eating lice, chewing footrags, screeching and railing. Any two people meeting in the yamen would ask each other, "Hasn't she died yet?" When the answer came, "She hasn't," everyone's expression would turn gloomy, as when hearing unfortunate news.

That the good intentions of so many people should lead them to hope for another person's death—the death not of a person they hated but of one they loved—was something beyond the understanding of a child like myself. And I'm afraid it's probably something I won't understand even when I'm forty or fifty.

Finally, though, everyone's wish came true. One winter day just before noon, just as we were eating lunch, an amah came running, out of breath, to say, "Amah Yang is dead." Her expression was happy, as if reporting good news.

"Thank Heaven and Earth!" said Mother, putting down her chopsticks. Everyone at the table heaved a long sigh, as if a protracted worry had been blown away by a breath of fresh air. No one felt death to be a frightening thing. But no one felt like eating, either, and we all put our chopsticks down. The next thing I noticed was tears welling in Mother's eyes.

Some years later Mother occasionally brought up details of Nanny Yang's life: she had had an orphan son named Little Mao, who was born two or three months after his father died. Having lost her husband, Nanny Yang suddenly had no means of support, and so it was that, only a few days after Little Mao was born, she had come to the city to look for work as a wet-nurse in the wealthy households. Her own son she entrusted to some country people, to whom she sent a small subsidy every month. But even though she sent money, Little Mao was never well cared for. One morning when Little Mao had just turned three, he somehow fell into a stream and drowned. Nanny Yang never even got to see the child's corpse. Later she came to our house as an amah. She was here a total of four years. She was still under thirty when she died.

That's the little bit of information I have been able to gather about Nanny Yang.

The General

by Pa Chin

Translated by Nathan K. Mao

"Get out of my way; it's my damn lousy luck to see you again tonight," Feodor Nietkov said and then cursed as his right foot kicked a scrawny dog huddled against a wall. At first curled into a lump, when kicked the dog uttered a piercing cry, stretched itself, and limped into a narrow side street, leaving the quiet pavement to Nietkov.

"Here in your country nothing is right; even the dogs won't bite, they're so meek!" Nietkov had often said huffily to a plump Chinese waiter. Almost every night he would come into the small café, drink wine until he had spent all the money he had with him, and then leave in a half-conscious stupor. He felt at home there. He spoke freely to the Chinese waiter, on all subjects. "This isn't really cold; here in your country, it's never actually cold. In our country, your nose would freeze in the winter." He was forever making self-satisfied statements like this to the Chinese waiter. The Chinese always listened to him with a happy look; in this great city the waiter seemed to be the only one who respected him and believed what he said. "You people are no good, no good for anything," he would say and angrily curse the waiter whenever he felt annoyed over a slight.

He left the café, and after a dozen steps, a gust of wind hit his face, like a needle pricking his nose. But immediately the painful sensation was gone. Swaggering, he said obstinately: "This is nothing, nothing. Over here winter isn't cold at all; even the wind is meek" He imagined himself in his own country, where the winter would really be something to be feared! The wind whirling in the sky could carry people away with it and the

blustery snow would have the strength to force a horse and carriage backwards! He remembered one occasion when he was with the general—the famous Prince Tsubetskoi. One night, he and the general were hurrying to St. Petersburg in a snowstorm; on the way the groom grew numb with cold and the horses, running wild in the snowstorm, almost crashed the carriage against a hillside. It was thanks to him that the horses were stopped. Fighting both the snowstorm and the horses was by no means easy, but he had succeeded. When they reached an inn, the general happily patted him on the shoulder and said: "Friend, you're really something. You should get the Cross of St. George!" The general even shook hands with him! Later, he was promoted to first lieutenant. Yes, the general would have been pleased to promote him further. There was even the prospect of becoming a general himself. But soon the world changed and everything was finished. The general died in battle. From then on, so many things happened, one right after the other like scenes on a stage; the changes came so rapidly that he had wondered if he were dreaming. Finally he drifted to China—this place where nothing was any good—and was forced to stay. He had settled down and, almost without realizing it, spent several years here; now it was as if he had chains on his legs, and could not move on even if he wanted to.

"This place—China—is like a desert, a huge and lonely desert where there isn't one live human being!" Walking on the quiet pavement and looking at the dim street lights shivering in the chilly wind, he could not help thinking of his own country. Despite himself, he sighed.

A black automobile raced up from behind, swerving past him like a snake. The lights dazzled his eyes, swirling; they seemed all around him. He didn't feel strange, only his head was a little heavy and his heart a little warmed. He thought he had heard someone calling him "General" and he had vaguely responded.

He had become accustomed to being called General in this place. At first he had called himself that; later others called him General, half in jest. The Chinese waiter had always addressed him as General. Perhaps that stupid, honest man really believed he was a general. Weren't his manners like those of a general? Every time the waiter called him General, he thought proudly: "Which of your generals can be compared to me? If they can be generals, why not I?" When he raised his wine glass to drink, he looked scornfully at the café's furnishings; with a smug feeling in his heart he came to believe he really was a general.

But when he left the café and took an honest, inward look at himself, his pride crumbled as if someone had stripped away his official rank. In front of the café neither automobile nor carriage waited for him, only a long straight pavement. To go home, he must walk down this one, take two turns and two other streets. It wasn't far, and every night he stayed at the café until it was very late before he went home. He said he was going home; but judging from his expression it didn't look as if he wanted to. He was willing to talk to the Chinese waiter about everything, but when the word "home" was mentioned, he clammed up.

A general without an automobile, a carriage, attendants, or a mansion. What sort of a general was that? Sometimes he felt the lack of trappings; then naturally he thought of a mansion. "Now the general returns to his mansion," he had said unashamedly to the waiter, having had his fill of wine. Then he threw his shoulders back and walked out.

After a while he felt the wind cooling his face a little, when suddenly the word "home" came into his head as if blown into it by that same wind. Im-

mediately, he visualized the reality: a sparsely furnished room on the second floor of an apartment building owned and managed by Chinese. That was his mansion. In that room, he lived with his wife Anna. He was almost fifty; Anna was younger. He had married her when he was a first lieutenant. She was the daughter of a junior officer, and had all the virtues common to Russian women. They had lived together now for nearly twenty years; they had never been separated. She was a very understanding wife. So it was hard to understand why, whenever she was mentioned, he seemed so uneasy, so frightened. He knew the reason, though he was unwilling to disclose it to anyone.

"Is she really my wife?" he would ask himself every time he entered the alley and saw his home in the distance. A few times he had stood before its rear entrance not daring to ring the doorbell, and only after some hesitation did he stretch out his hand. The doorman let him in; once inside, he climbed the stairs with difficulty, and took out his key to open the door. Their room, as usual, was empty, and only the smell of cosmetics awaited him.

"That's life. A general's wife must attend parties every night," he would mutter to himself while switching on the light, pacing to and fro, touching the table and the bed at random. He recalled vividly that a long time ago, in St. Petersburg, Prince Tsubetskoi had often allowed his wife to mingle with the guests all night long, while the general himself was busy attending to other matters. "Yes, all generals are like this, all like this."

Though he told himself this, his heart was not satisfied. He didn't believe what he said, but there was no time to think about it anymore. He fell on his bed and went to sleep almost immediately.

When he awoke the next morning, there was still no sign of Anna. She had not yet come home; there was no one to take care of him; he had to look after himself. Later, Anna came home. She fixed them lunch and also gave him a little pocket money.

"Anushka, you're ravishing," he said, upon seeing his wife's powdered face.

"Fedya, I won't let you say that. You're a heartless scoundrel!" Smiling, she walked over to him and let him kiss her.

"I won't say it again. But when I see you at home, I can't resist saying such things." He accepted her kiss half-apologetically, as if he thought she was doing him a favor.

"You've been drinking again, Fedya, I know. You're a lush, always spending your money on liquor," she scolded him good-naturedly.

"Don't say that, Anushka. In St. Petersburg, we drank champagne all the time," he replied pleadingly. Of course, this was an exaggeration. In St. Petersburg, he drank champagne only occasionally; what he drank all the time was vodka.

"St. Petersburg—that was a long time ago. Now we're in China. In China everything's cold, life is cold," she said slowly, her smile vanishing. She sat down on the old sofa, her eyes fixed on a picture on the wall in which she saw their life in St. Petersburg.

When he realized his wife was unhappy, he went to comfort her. He sat on the arm of the sofa, put one hand around her neck and said, still apologetically: "It's all my fault. You're unhappy because of me. Please forgive me."

She leaned against him, not answering. After a while she sighed and said: "The past is a dream that will never return."

"Anushka, are you reminiscing about St. Petersburg? Don't torture yourself with memories," he said, pitying her. He really loved his wife, just as much as ever.

"I can't take this life much longer. I want to go back; I must go back. You don't care for me; all you care about is drinking; you can't do anything but take money from me," she said to him, half in anger and half in tears, her shoulders shaking.

He was used to hearing these words and knew his wife's temper. If she had been abused the night before, she would turn her anger on him when she came home. But her temper tantrum amounted to no more than a few words of chiding or of clamoring to go back home. He could take all that without too much trouble. As these scenes increased, however, he too felt he couldn't take it

much longer. The humiliation gave him more and more pain.

"Anushka, you must wait a little while longer. For my sake, please be patient. We'll find something; life will be better." At first he had used these words to comfort her, but then even his heart rebelled and he realized the words meant nothing.

"A change for the better. I'm afraid that will always be a dream! If we go on living here the torment will kill me! I don't dare think about the future. I don't know how many days there will be after today . . ." She began to sniffle, but was trying, trying hard, not to cry.

His heart softened; his pride flew away, and only distress remained. Then he asked her: "Was the man nice to you last night?" Asking the question seemed to put a knife blade through his heart; the pain made him grit his teeth.

"Nice? I never met a nice man. That beast last night had had a lot to drink. He was brutal. I had to let him maul me all night and he bit my arm raw," she said, rubbing her left arm. She unbuttoned her blouse to let him look. Not far below the shoulder were several purplish rows of teeth marks, distinctly visible against her white arm.

He had seen many wounds, even some that had proved fatal. Yet these seared him like flame too bright to watch with open eyes. Distantly he heard a woman's voice pleading: "Please think of another way for me. I can't take this life any longer." He tried his best to restrain the tears, but they conquered him and flowed freely. Helplessly, he cried on her arm.

His wife stopped complaining and soon stopped crying, gently fondled his hair, and said: "Don't be a baby. Look, you're staining my clothes. I believe you—our life will get better." Having first chided her husband, now she was trying to comfort him. The tears had ended the argument.

Then the husband promised: "I won't drink anymore." The two would become friendly, share some intimate words, do some chores together, or maybe go out to a restaurant for dinner. But, of course, not to the one where the husband went drinking every night. If they stayed home for dinner, the wife would tell a few jokes about American sailors, and the husband would listen with a smile. They knew how to enjoy their time together. By the time the wife was ready to go out in the evening, he would have received a little pocket money and her admonition: "Don't go out to drink! Just stay home and have a good time." She would always say that to him, like a mother admonishing a child. But she knew that he would go to the café half an hour or so after she had left the house.

At first, he didn't intend to go to the café; he told himself: "I must obey her this time." He would sit in their room and start reading from an old Bible, trying to get some comfort out of it. For all those years, that Bible, as well as his wife, had accompanied him in his wanderings. He believed in God, and knew if he lost the ability to face life, he could ask God to help him.

Then he read: "the Son of Man shall be delivered unto the chief priests, and unto the scribes; and they shall condemn him to death, and shall deliver him to the Gentiles: And they shall mock him, and shall scourge him, and shall spit upon him, and shall kill him: and the third day he shall rise again."

What kind of words were these! He could not continue. He thought: "What is the use of reading this over and over again? Only the Son of God could suffer all this and yet rise again. We mortals couldn't rise again. They mock me, spit in my face, scourge me, abuse me until I die. But after I die, I won't rise again. What's the good of believing in God?" And now his wife's powdered face seemed to appear on the page he had been reading. He turned the page but still could not see the words, only his wife's face. He couldn't sit still anymore. He closed the book, put on his hat and coat, and went off to the café.

He entered the café and the affable Chinese waiter, as usual, came over to greet him, called him General, and brought him wine. After a glass he began to talk casually with the Chinese. Slowly his courage and his pride returned and he began to behave as if he really were a general.

"In our country everything was good. You don't

understand. In the general's mansion in St. Petersburg . . ." he said airily. But the mansion had not been his, but Prince Tsubetskoi's. At the time he had been only a first lieutenant. He remembered it all clearly as if it were happening now. At that ball, that very evening, he and Anna fell in love. The lights in the hall were bright as day. Wearing medals and a splendid uniform, the general had a roundish face, with a pencil-thin moustache on his upper lip. Didn't the general's face look very much like his own now? There were so many guests; most of them were his superior officers and his colleagues; there were so many wives and daughters, all wearing beautiful dresses. The music was starting; many couples began dancing. He put his arm around Anna's waist. She was young and beautiful, and smiling radiantly at him. Colleagues were envying him. Look, wasn't that Boris? Winking at him? Boris, come, have a glass? Nikolai, with a glass in his hand, was gesturing to him, congratulating him. He was smiling, he was drunk.

"General, have another bottle of wine." The Chinese waiter's rasping voice drove away all those people. He opened his eyes wide and saw a picture of the Kazan Church in St. Petersburg hanging on the wall, nothing else. He sighed and said: "Good, give me another. I'm drunk anyway."

He closed his eyes awhile; then opened them and saw the waiter filling his glass. As he stared at the wine, his eyes lost focus and a young woman's face appeared in the glass. The face kept getting larger and larger; he seemed to have returned to the ball.

He took Anna onto a balcony overlooking the garden. The time was autumn, and it was a moonlit night. From the balcony one could see the ripples in the Neva River and the moonlight quietly reflected in the ripples. Bewitching music floated out from the hall. It was then that he declared his love for her. The beautiful maiden was shaking like a slender white poplar in his arms. She accepted his love and, for the first time, his kiss. How lovely is first love! He felt that moment marked the beginning of his ambitious plan to conquer the world.

"Life is beautiful after all," he was moved to say. All of a sudden, the scene before him changed. In front of him stood the waiter, smilingly asking: "General, are you drunk? It's really cold out. Will you have another bottle?"

Music, moonlight, the ball—all had disappeared. Only this small deserted café and a stupid Chinese waiter. "This isn't cold. In your country here, it's never cold at all," he had wanted to say stubbornly but was overcome by another thought. So he changed his mind and said: "No more. I'm drunk, drunk!" He suddenly felt old.

"General, is the earth in your country all black?" The waiter asked with interest, even though Nietkov had become taciturn.

He answered vaguely, still seeking the face of the young maiden in his memory.

"I ask because of one of your fellow countrymen. He often brought a bag with him when he came here. He sat by himself and after he ordered a cup of coffee, he'd empty out the stuff in his bag—guess what he had filled the bag with, General?" The Chinese waiter suddenly broke into laughter. The waiter was damned ugly with the features of his fat face all squeezed together.

He didn't answer, allowing the waiter to continue:

"Dirt, all black dirt. He emptied the dirt out on the table and cried, looking at it. One time I asked him what it was. He gave me a strange answer and said 'It is black soil, the black soil of Mother Russia.' He had taken it out of the country with him. That man was really dumb!"

Grain by grain, pile by pile, the black soil stretched before his eyes, forming a wide expanse of grassland. Quietly, firmly, continuously, it produces everything. Numberless human shadows moving on the plain, quiet and firm and diligent—these scenes were all familiar to his eyes. He was moved to say:

"Mother Russia. We're all her children. We're all like that." Then he stood up, paid his bill, and walked out. As he left, he heard not the voice of the Chinese waiter but that of his wife Anna:

"I want to go back, I must go back."

Out on the quiet street he thought again of Neva Avenue, for that was where the general's mansion was. But now everything was ruined.

"Finished . . . Everything was destroyed in the war," he sighed to himself. He imagined he could see the general lying in a pool of blood; he seemed to see others setting the general's mansion aflame. The fire was raging; it burned away his career.

He heaved a long sigh, and a few tears fell from his eyes.

"Now I'm beginning to understand . . . We're all one family. All of you can see how I've been mistreated here, how I've been insulted!" After a while he seemed to be pleading with someone. He thought with regret: Why shouldn't he go back? What was the good of suffering here?

He thought of his wife. "Why shouldn't I go home early? I deserve to suffer, but I shouldn't ruin Anna as well." Lost in self-recrimination, he thought he saw in the sky that beautiful, innocent face of long ago. The face came closer and slowly transformed itself into Anna's powdered face today. "She'd done nothing wrong. I'm the cause of her suffering. All her suffering is on account of me. Nietkov, you're a beast!" His face burned and his head felt heavy. He threw his hat on the ground and, in despair, tore at his hair.

"I want to go back, I must go back," a woman's pleas echoed loudly in his ears. He seemed to see his wife crying in the arms of that brutal American sailor. The sailor, with a red face, red nose, and a mouthful of sharp teeth, was forcing himself on her, fondling her, biting her arm, leering lustfully—exactly as she had described it. A man's and a woman's voices blasted in his eardrums.

"I want to go back, I must go back." Frantically, he covered his ears and ran. He saw nothing in front of him except a face, the tear-stained face of a powdered woman whose small quivering mouth muttered: "Pity me, save me!"

Then he collided with something. He fell to the ground and lost consciousness. When he opened his eyes, people were standing around him in a circle. A Chinese constable opened a notebook and asked him his name.

"They call me general, General Nietkov . . .

Neechevo.[1] Don't let Anna know. I'd go with you . . . *Neechevo* . . . I just had a little to drink. I'm not drunk at all. *Neechevo* . . . ," he said with an effort. He felt very tired and wanted to shut his eyes. He seemed to see Anna, Anna struggling with that American sailor, and the sailor lying on top of her. Quickly he opened his eyes and looked around. But Anna was not with him. He couldn't move his body. He just lay there. He said: "Take me to her, take me to Anna! I must tell her I've decided to go back home." And then he slowly closed his eyes.

But he spoke in Russian. And no one understood him.

[1] *Neechevo,* Russian for "it's nothing" or "it doesn't matter."

Sinking Low

by Pa Chin

Translated by Perry Link

—*Enablsmig* [1]

"Don't fight evil." He often said this in his advice to me.

"He," of course, did have a name, and a well-known name at that. But I feel it's quite enough just to use "he." I am no worshipper of celebrities—so why should I publicize his name?

"What use is your individual dissent? Whatever is going to happen, is going to happen anyway. And things that have already happened you can't recall. So it is with the Japanese seizure of Manchuria.[2] Don't you think we're better off spending the time on our own work?"

He would talk to me like this, in measured tones, sitting on the sofa and leisurely stroking his moustache. Just what he meant by one's "own work" is something he never explained. When I asked he gave only vague answers. On one occasion he did let it slip that he was currently working on his "own work." But that was only once, for later he even modestly denied he had ever said such a thing.

I was a slow-witted young fellow. I may not have admitted it, but he, anyway, already had that impression. I knew this from two or three occasions when he regretfully told me that he once had a first-rate student named Yen, who was as good as Yen Hui, one of Confucius' famous disciples. But unfortunately, he had died young. Since then he had had no other worthy disciple. There was one Fang Yün-hsien, who was just getting ready to take the Boxer Indemnity Examination to study in England.[3] He was all right, but not quite up to snuff. As for me, I was far, far from adequate.

Be that as it may, he was still very nice to me. He still often used all the great wisdom at his command to advise me, to discourse with me, and to inform me most sincerely about all kinds of things.

He had quite a few friends, but they didn't go see him much. I doubt anyone went more regularly than I. There were some young students who sought him out for instruction at his house, but after one visit they seldom returned. I didn't know the reason for this. Several times it occurred to me that I too was young—so why did I still keep on seeing him? Was it because he was nice to me? Or because I was particularly curious? There had to be some explanation.

He had an attractive wife, who was younger than himself. She was his second. This, by the way, was nothing extraordinary: many eminent

[1] This epigraph appears in the original. The Editors were not able to identify its source.

[2] In 1931. In 1932 the Japanese set up a puppet regime called "Manchukuo" (lit. the "country of Manchuria").

[3] After the Boxers were defeated by the eight powers (England, the United States, Germany, France, Russia, Japan, Italy, and Austria) in 1901, the Ch'ing Government agreed to pay indemnities, to establish an autonomous extraterritorial legation quarter in Peking, and grant the right of foreign troops to maintain open communications between Peking and the sea. Later, some Western countries (notably the United States and England) returned the indemnity funds to China for educational purposes. It is estimated that "by 1915, more than 1,200 Chinese students were studying in schools and colleges in the United States" (Chow Tse-tsung, *The May Fourth Movement* [Cambridge, Mass., 1964], p. 26).

scholars and professors had younger wives, and he was no exception. Feelings between him and his wife weren't especially good, but they weren't especially bad, either. Though I never saw them quarrel, I always had the impression that there was no real warmth between husband and wife. They were courteous to one another, but at the same time distant. True, he had been wildly infatuated for quite some time, back when he was chasing this girl student of his who was now his wife. Things had long since returned to normal. He was her husband, secure in the knowledge that he had observed all the legal requirements. And he remained an eminent scholar and professor.

His wife liked to dance. There was a time when he did a lot of dancing too, but now he was seldom seen in those dancing halls where the upper-class Chinese were wont to go. His wife still went quite often, though; when he stopped taking her she began going in the company of another friend, a famous history professor who had studied in America on a government grant. Come to think of it, this professor was his student too, having been in his class for half a year.

"Don't fight evil . . . Everything that exists exists for a reason. So does the existence of [the puppet regime in] Manchuria. Sometimes 'evil' is inevitable, but after a while it will just fizzle out by itself. You only waste your time if you want to fight evil. You should do something more realistic. All your ranting and raving about rebellion is simply empty talk. Moreover, it's really not your business. You youngsters are just too frivolous—simply impossible!"

Even though I could still contain myself pretty well, sometimes my anger would burst its bounds. "And what have you done that's so realistic?" I would rudely snap. "I suppose *you* never waste your time!"

He did well in controlling himself. Not angered in the least, he answered with a hint of smug mockery: "Me? I've done a great many things! I read books. I read and think about questions day and night. I work harder than any of you!"

I believed him. He had a house like a palace

and a luxurious and comfortable study where he was free to close himself in for the whole day. His book collection, which of course was large, was displayed in one glass cabinet after another in both his spacious living room and his study. Every one of the books, moreover, was exquisitely bound and designed, including quite a number of English as well as Chinese titles.

"Take my advice, and do more reading. That's more important. It won't do to skimp on studying. People who bury their noses in books are just what China needs these days. She has no need for those youngsters who go around shouting 'down with this' and 'down with that.' Look at me: I've read quite a bit and still thirst for more—so how can a young man like you get by without books? The recovery of Manchuria, like anything else, will depend upon study." There was a tinge of arrogance in the way he lectured me thus.

Whenever he mentioned studying, I was better off with my mouth closed. He had read so many books, and what I had read did not even amount to 10 percent of the books in his collection—in fact, one percent would be a more realistic estimate. Having listened to his lecture on national salvation through study, I couldn't help regarding him with admiration. It amazed me that such a small and slender frame could hold so many books.

"We must be tolerant, and must respect others. There's no such thing as absolute evil. We should respect every kind of person here in China: everyone's efforts make a contribution. Everyone should stay in his proper station and give all his attention to his own work. That's why you should study hard. Leave other things alone. Don't you plan to take the Boxer Indemnity Examination to study in England or America after you graduate?"

Having listened to his admonitions, I took my leave and went home. I walked into my rooming house, and as I opened the door to my room and took a look around those cramped, clammy quarters, all of a sudden the English phrase *Boxer indemnity student* [4] crossed my mind (I had once heard an Englishman use this term contemptuously). Somehow I was suddenly overwhelmed

---

[4] English in the original.

with a feeling of uneasiness. And he wanted this to be my ideal! Everything he said was now beginning to repel me. I looked at my little bookcase, and there were only thirty or forty tattered books in it, some of which were borrowed from the library. How could I compare with him? My environment was so unlike his.

"What's environment?" he had often said, trying to encourage me. "Hard study can overcome anything. The palace of learning is open to rich and poor alike."

He made it all sound so wonderful. Everything he said sounded wonderful. But he never gave any consideration to whether or not he was being realistic. Once outside his main gate I would begin to doubt the validity of his statements; and by the time I got back to my room, my respect for him would begin to waver.

Several times I pronounced a solemn resolution to close my door and read: but my room was not his study. Even with the door closed I would continue to daydream about the world outside. When I closed my book to think something over, my mind would strike out on its own, ever farther and more boldly, until I had just about overturned his whole body of thought. I didn't want to get anywhere near the palace of learning.

To be quite frank, I was losing respect for him day by day. For many days—no, for over a month—I stayed away from his place. Then a letter came from him.

The style of his letter also had something unique about it. Not only the style, but even the language and ideas seemed as if they were copied from books a few hundred years old. He wrote a lot of nice-sounding words, but it all boiled down to one thing: why hadn't I been to see him for so long?

Out of curiosity, and perhaps for some other reason too, I went to see him that afternoon. His servant, who had always been very polite to me, let me enter without prior announcement.

All kinds of flowers were blooming in the courtyard, with a lattice for grapevines in the middle. Appearances had changed somewhat during my month's absence. In one corner of the living room his wife and the history professor were tête-à-tête. She was beautifully dressed, probably because they had just returned from going out, or were just on their way out.

They didn't notice me, and I quickly withdrew. I didn't want to disturb them, knowing how the history professor worshipped her. It was rumored that he had written her quite a few English poems; some even said they were having a Platonic affair. It was all possible, in fact quite natural. The history professor was young, handsome, and carried himself in a pleasant way. They really matched each other. I'm afraid even he, the husband, wouldn't be able to contradict me.

I went directly to his study. He was sitting comfortably on the sofa with a string-bound book [5] in his hands, his head bobbing up and down as he softly intoned its words.

"Ah, you've come!" He put down his book and greeted me with a smile. Judging from his manner, he seemed happy that I had come.

"It's been more than a month—you must've made great progress in your studies. You must've read quite a number of books."

I told him quite frankly that over the past month or so I hadn't even read three books from cover to cover. He looked nonplussed.

"Then what have you been doing with yourself? It's really pitiful the way you young people squander your valuable time."

I hadn't seen him in over a month, had come this time only because of his letter, and still he jumps right in and talks to me like that! I couldn't say I was pleased.

"What about you?" I shot back at him halftauntingly.

"Me? I just bought a really good volume of Ming essays." Seeming not to notice the disrespect in my remark, he proudly picked up the book and pointed to it as he spoke. "This is a rare book. The Ming essayists are really superb, especially in their attitude toward life. You must read this book," he said as he handed it to me.

I took the book and flipped through a few pages. It was the diary of somebody named Yüan.[6] I didn't give it a second thought, but just

---

[5] Chinese old-style binding. [6] Presumably Yüan Hung-tao (fl. 1592).

shook my head disdainfully and handed it back to him without a word.

He shot me a glance, obviously perceiving my attitude. But even though he was upset with me, he still appeared patient and forgiving. "Why is it you young people feel superior to everything that comes along?" he said in his typically benign way, but this time with a touch of reproach. "The fact is, you people just can't compare [with these writers of the past]. You seldom have the chance to read a good book like this. I give it to you, and you won't even take a good look. This kind of attitude simply won't do!"

Of course my attitude was far different from that of a Ming dynasty person. I knew that. I also knew that I could not be patient and forgiving.

When he saw that I remained silent, he assumed he had already convinced me. So he said with renewed enthusiasm: "I also bought a Sung porcelain vase. Genuine Sung porcelain. Too bad such things are beyond you."

He didn't show me the vase because he knew I couldn't appreciate its value.

"Young people should work hard! Our ancestors have left behind so many treasures—what a shame if succeeding generations can't appreciate them! That's why I urge you to work hard! There's no end to learning! What can you young people do if not study?!" He went on preaching at me with great clarity and confidence, ponderously stroking his moustache all the while.

Formerly I had been all ears for this kind of stuff, but lately it had begun to make me uncomfortable. Especially now that my disposition had undergone some changes, I just couldn't take it anymore. My head was already reeling with Ming this and Sung that, and it made me angry: why did he have to go out of his way to pick on me? I began to understand why it was that young people seldom went to his house more than once.

"Sir!" I blurted impatiently. "I'm only twenty-two years old, you know."

"Twenty-two is precisely the time for hard work. Youth is a most precious period in life." He went on instructing me in his same patient, good-humored way. It seemed he didn't understand me at all.

"And why should I get all bothered about Ming dynasty books or what some piece of Sung porcelain is worth? That stuff's only for your kind!" Now I was speaking very disrespectfully.

He knew what I meant immediately. His facial color changed convulsively—now red, now white. His eyes glowered furiously from beneath his wide-rimmed spectacles, and his breathing turned heavy. His mouth fell open one moment and closed the next, as if he wanted to get something out but couldn't.

To see an advocate of tolerance lose his temper this way brought me a strange inward elation. Originally it had been my idea to walk out at this point, but now I felt like staying to subject his tantrum to a cruel scrutiny. I was aware that the tantrum of a tolerance advocate was like a Ming period book: a rare sight.

He was struggling with himself, and finally heaved a sigh. "Go away," he said, waving his hand at me.

Instead of leaving I sat down right opposite him. I was now, if anything, even more dispassionate in my scrutiny of his countenance. I had an idea, and a cruel one at that.

After waving two or three times and realizing it was no use, he joined me in silence. His hand fell softly to his side and his eyes slowly regained their warmth. The expression on his face changed from rage to remorse.

"It's not so easy to be forgiving, is it?" I said to myself with some sarcasm. My eyes continued to bear down on him.

"Let's drop the subject. You young people are ruthless; you won't give an inch. Let's just say you won this time. But you'll live to regret it some day, and you'll see that I was right." He was actually admitting defeat. I was glad I had beat him.

How could I have the patience to listen to him? I was completely involved with other ideas, and now I had lost all respect for him.

"Remember what I'm telling you. Someday you'll see. I was just like you when I was young, and now I realize those first mistakes. You'll regret them too someday. I tried to help but you let me down." He was making one last-ditch effort to get me to understand.

Then I remembered. I'd been told there was indeed a time when he wrote essays urging people not to accept the way things were, not to remain silent in the face of evil, to throw their string-bound books into the toilet and sell their antiques to foreigners. He was also credited with a number of other radical views. At that time, moreover, he was writing in a completely different literary style. People had indeed told me all this, but I had found it hard to believe. I had taken it all with a grain of salt because it seemed so far-fetched, considering the way he was now. Time does bring changes in people, of course; but I couldn't believe a person could change into his exact opposite in just ten years or so. Now, though, everything was confirmed by his own words. How could he have taken such a giant step? It was an astonishing feat—simply incredible! And now he wanted me to come along and repeat the astonishing feat!

I was peering at his face as if trying to solve a riddle. I was looking for some trace of his youthful self. A roundish bald head, a pair of big, wide-rimmed spectacles, a moustache across the lip, and an egg-shaped face that bore no expression other than complacence and satisfaction. All this told me only one thing: indeed everything that exists exists for a reason.

I then felt as if my body were suddenly stretching out to be much taller than his. My eyes shot down on him from above. "You yourself no longer have a reason for existing," I was thinking.

"Why are you looking at me like that? Are you analyzing me?" He had suddenly noticed my gaze and inferred my thoughts from it. He looked increasingly uncomfortable.

I nodded my head with an air of intransigence.

"You're really strange," he ventured. "I've never seen a young person like you. You respect nothing! You believe in nothing!" Then he added, more emphatically, "You snub your nose at everything! You don't accept anything!"

I didn't quite understand his point, but could already see that my general attitude was annoying him. It was also helping him to realize some things which he had never gotten into his head.

"You're not at all like a Chinese, not at all!" he said, wagging his head in vexation.

I was greatly interested to see that I had dispelled his complacency and satisfaction and that he was speaking in a kind of annoyed tone he had never used before.

"You're entirely ignorant of Chinese history. You're entirely ignorant of the treasures our ancestors have left us. Your ideas are peculiar, most peculiar. You're not one of us." He toiled with his words, while behind those wide-rimmed spectacles his eyes were rolling in pain. His face had turned red in agitation. He seemed more animated than usual. But I also noticed a shadow creep across his brow. That book by Yüan So-and-so dropped silently to the floor and landed near a spittoon, but he didn't even notice.

"Would you like to know about my ideas?" As my courage continued to increase my questions grew more provocative. I had the impression that if he knew what my current ideas were, he would be even more bewildered and hurt.

"No! No!" he cried, hands waving. He had suddenly realized my question's import, and his eyes beseeched me to desist. He lay down on the sofa, despondent, appearing thoroughly frail and weak. Thinking to myself that this man still had a trace of humanity in him, I stood up to leave him alone.

When I reached the door I encountered his wife—arm in arm with the history professor, laughing and chattering, strolling out of the house. An automobile was waiting out front, and as soon as they had entered it drove off.

As I stood in the doorway my thoughts again came to rest upon him in the study. It felt strange that we had actually had a talk like that.

During the next few days I would have entirely forgotten about him, if not for the fact that he and his wife had their names in the paper. He had given a lecture on Shakespeare at some university, saying how great Shakespeare was, and how, since this Englishman's death, there had been no one who could hold a candle to him. The following day he had lectured at another university extolling the virtues of the Kung-an and Ching-ling schools of writing in the Ming dynasty.[7]

---

[7] "Kung-an" is the home town (in modern Hupeh) of the three Yüan brothers, Tsung-tao, Hung-tao, and Chung-tao, all noted essayists of the late Ming period. The "Ching-ling" school of essay writing is represented by Chung Hsing and T'an Yüan-ch'un, contemporaries of the Yüan brothers. Ching-ling is also in modern Hupeh.

There was even more news about his wife: items like performing on the piano at a charity-sponsored variety show, or being asked by some VIP to be hostess at such-and-such a garden party banquet for foreign guests, or accompanying some famous litterateur from abroad on his visit to such-and-such ancient remains during his sight-seeing tour.

These bits of news set me wondering about the couple's married life. One had to admit this was an interesting subject, yet after a while I found it somewhat frivolous. Wasn't it he who said everything that exists exists for a reason? Why should I poke my nose into their private life?

I went right on casting his advice to the winds. Night and day I wasted my time, intemperately pursuing all those things that were not my "own work."

One morning I read in the English newspaper about the *Boxer Indemnity scholarship students* who were going overseas. That evening, quite by chance, I met him and his wife while passing by an opera house. They were just getting out of their car. The big sign board at the entrance to the opera house announced: "Ch'eng Yen-ch'iu featured in The Red Duster Girl." Apparently he was taking his wife to the opera again.

He called to me, so I had to stop and say hello to him.

"Did you know that Yün-hsien left for overseas study today? Yün-hsien always worked hard, and now it's paid off. Someday you can have a go at it too." He was affable, and very happy, because Yün-hsien was a favorite student of his who kept in touch with him even after graduation. I had once met Yün-hsien at his house; the two of them were cast of the same mold.

When I saw how cordially he spoke, as if he'd completely forgotten the events of our last meeting, I decided to be polite and perfunctory as well. I greeted his wife, and just at that moment the history professor showed up to sidle her into the opera house. He, though, stayed at the door waiting for my response.

"What have you been reading these days? Are you still squandering your time away?" he asked in the same cordial manner.

Just as I was about to say something, a strange feeling suddenly took hold of me: it's hard to say whether it was pity or disgust. I lost all control of myself. "Do you realize," I barked at him, "how many more years the Chinese people have to shoulder the Boxer Indemnity? That's what I've been studying these days!"

His face immediately changed color. For a moment he seemed to hesitate, but then he turned and went inside without another word to me. I think what I said hurt him deeply.

I stood at the entrance to the opera house, chuckling derisively. I was thinking what a good time he must be having inside, all on the pretext of studying Chinese culture. I had heard it was Ch'eng Yen-ch'iu who starred in the one-act play "My Dear Husband" by Ting Hsi-lin.

I did not follow up this incident with a visit to his house. Looking back on it, though, I have occasionally felt that I treated him a little too harshly. He never intended me any harm, after all.

One day another letter came from him. Quite unlike his earlier ones, it was a short note which seemed to express genuine feeling. He sounded melancholic and depressed, and hoped that I wasn't purposely keeping my distance, but would drop by to see him once in a while.

I threw the letter into my wicker wastebasket without a second thought. But a few days later, when I happened to be passing by his front gate, I did go in.

He had no classes that day, and was lying in his pajamas on the small sofa in his study. He was holding a little English book in his hands and seemed to be reading it rather inattentively.

"How nice of you to come." His lips performed a weary smile as he turned the book over on the sofa's armrest. A glance told me it was an English translation of Chekhov's short stories.

Noticing my glance toward the book, he started explaining: "I've been reading nothing but Chekhov these days. When I read him a number of years ago I found him dull; but now I find him very good indeed. These really are fine stories. You might take a look at them too."

I shuddered. A feeling of pity welled in me as I recalled the Chekhov stories I had read, stories which had managed only to arouse my terror and disgust. I couldn't stand the stuff! It was full of all kinds of spineless, fate-driven fools. The two volumes of Chekhov I had bought ended up as firewood in my stove.

I sat down and was just about to say something when I was suddenly gripped by an indescribable feeling of hatred. "You probably enjoy Chekhov," I charged, "because you're just like those characters he depicts." I was unable to keep the malice out of my voice.

He nodded his head without thinking; then, realizing what I meant, shook it sideways. "No, no!" he said, with apprehension and suspicion in his eyes, as if I had exposed some unpleasant secret of his.

"So not even you would want to be a Chekhovian character?" I deliberately kept the pressure on him.

"What do you mean by that?" he asked, making every effort to stifle his agitation.

"You retreat to this snug room all day, serenely discussing the treasures our ancestors have left behind, or some event of a few centuries ago, believing that everything that exists, etc., etc.—isn't this right out of a Chekhov story?"

He had run out of replies. An expression of pain contorted his face. He cast his eyes downward and stared at the floor, as if trying to escape my notice. After quite some time he raised his head and gave me an exhausted, despairing look. "Maybe you have a point," he said, his voice like a groan. "I'm finished. People like me are finished."

Setting aside all his favorite topics—like Sung porcelain vases, like the diary of Yüan So-and-so, like Shakespeare, like essays in the *Kung-an* and *Ching-ling* styles, like the Ming literati's approach to life, like his beloved "Boxer Indemnity"—this time, for once, he had spoken the truth. He had admitted that he was finished. A feeling of solemnity and mild sorrow took hold of me, as if I were standing before a coffin which had just been sealed.

"I couldn't see, couldn't see . . . being in this study I couldn't see anything." He spoke in an earnest, low voice, but with great difficulty, as if locked in struggle. Some illusion may have been appearing in his mind at that moment, because a rather peculiar look came into his eyes. He raised

his right arm feebly and pointed at his beautiful book cabinets. "It's all because of them! They're all I ever saw! I only knew . . . I only saw the past. I'm surrounded by the past . . . by the dead . . . speaking dead people's talk . . . which I'm repeating . . ." His voice grew more like wailing as he continued; more than that—and quite to my surprise—I saw teardrops falling from the corners of his eyes. He didn't wipe them as they rolled down his cheeks. This was the first time I had ever seen him weep. My heart softened, and I began to feel sorry for him.

"Well . . . can't you change your environment?" I asked sympathetically. I took it for granted that since he knew he had made the mistake, it would be relatively easy to correct it.

"Change my environment? You think it's that easy?" he said painfully. "I'm rooted in this environment. I'm finished. You're more fortunate than I. I have no choice but to live in this kind of environment. Day by day I sink deeper and deeper. Once sunk, I can't—"

He suddenly closed his mouth, as if a great effusion of grief had clogged his throat. He began faintly gasping for breath, a look of utter despair and helplessness in his eyes. The tears continued to stream down his cheeks; those which rolled into his mouth, which was alternately opening and closing, he swallowed.

The room grew completely silent. No sound came in from the courtyard, nor any breeze. The stillness was fearsome. It was as if all activity had finally ceased, as if the world had fallen into a state of rest which foreshadowed its imminent end.

I was sitting opposite him. The sounds of his panting leapt straight across at my heart. There were no other noises to obstruct them, and it seemed this world contained only his panting, only the helpless panting of one despairing man. How very frightening! The atmosphere was growing unbearably heavy. Moment by moment it bore down and pressed in, until I began to feel difficulty breathing. I could even hear my own heartbeat, as the room came to resemble an ancient tomb. I thought of how he buried himself here day after day, listening to his own heartbeat and reading the works of those rotten scholastics. How could he have stayed alive? I no longer could har-

bor the slightest doubt about his future. A firm
voice sounded in my head like a command: he is
finished, irretrievably finished.

He was unable to speak, and I was silent as well.
I knew there was no use in any more talk. I very
much wanted to leave, but made no move to do
so. I felt as if I were waiting for the arrival of
some agonizing disaster.

A moment later a vibration stirred the air. The
sound of a car horn broke the unbearable stillness. Inside the room we could hear very clearly
as the car approached the main gate and pulled to
a halt. I knew his wife had returned, but he continued to lie listlessly on the sofa as if he hadn't
heard.

The sounds of two pairs of footsteps and two
people chatting now reached my ears. A moment
later his wife walked in, dressed in the latest style
of 1934 and beaming with happiness. She was followed by the famous history professor.

When he saw his wife come in his expression
changed at once, and next his manner. He
greeted her with a smile. She was a star at the
social graces, and could use them on her husband
as well as anyone. In a very few words she had
him pacified and contented, even talking and
laughing. I had no time to watch such antics, so
took the chance to excuse myself and leave.

I thought of him after returning home and felt
I could see his face before me, sinking, sinking—
until it sank from view at the bottom of an abyss. I
could remember only one thing he said: "I am
finished."

As far as I was concerned he had ceased to
exist, so I never went to see him again. I further
believed that, with the exception of his obituary, I
would never again have news of him from another source.

In a few days, though, I was taken aback to see
in the newspaper that he was lecturing at a certain
university on the Ming literati's approach to life.
A few days after that I learned that he and another Shakespeare expert were jointly organizing
a group to translate the complete works of Shake-

speare. Following that, I saw he'd written an article called something like "Ch'eng Yen-ch'iu-ism," [8]
and two or three months later the advance publication notice of the works of Yüan So-and-so,
which he had punctuated, appeared in the newspapers. Another six months later I heard someone say he'd been made an honorary member of
such-and-such a government ministry. It was
probably the Education Ministry, but I wasn't listening carefully. It seemed from this that he was
probably doing his best to keep on floating upwards, while in reality he only kept sinking, sinking deeper and deeper.

The newspapers carried a large number of
stories about his wife, and her picture frequently
appeared in the magazines captioned with a few
editorial comments. The final piece of news was
about her splitting up with her husband. She was
accompanying the famous history professor on his
travels in America. It was the history professor's
year of leave from the university, and he had it all
arranged to go to Harvard University to lecture
on Chinese history.

I knew these events would leave him deeply
shocked. But I couldn't care less about it. To me
he had become like a person from another world.

One more thing, though, was to take me by
surprise. Less than ten weeks after his wife left for
America he sent an announcement of his engagement to another woman. Stranger still, within two
more months the newspapers carried his obituary.
All this came so incredibly quickly, so suddenly!

The newspaper ran many articles mourning
him, and a good number of periodicals came out
with special issues, including all kinds of photographs. These articles left the general impression
that every literate human being worshipped him.
All were agreed that his death was an immense
loss to Chinese culture. Even people who didn't
know him wrote his life's story like an elegy.

But me, even though I too heaved a sigh at his
death, I never felt the slightest loss at it. In fact I
congratulated myself: that voice saying "Don't
fight evil!" had died with him forever.

---

[8] Ch'eng Yen-ch'iu, a famous Peking opera singer.

Piglet and Chickens

by Pa Chin

Translated by Anita M. Brown and Jane Parish Yang

Outside the window, as the sun shone brightly through the green leaves of the gently swaying trees, I noticed the dark shadow of a small insect on the back of a fully open leaf. A bright spot passed in front of my eyes. A small white butterfly which had been perched in a tree flitted by, disappearing into the blue sky that silhouetted it. My eyes were still following its outline when the eaves of the house blocked my view. A little sparrow peeped out over the eaves, but immediately drew its head in and hopped away. As the tips of the trees began to sway heavily, I felt a slight coolness permeating my room. Directly in front of my window was a pumelo tree with several fruits the size of bowls hanging from its branches. The weather was already burning hot, even though it wasn't yet time for the pumelos to be ripe. Absently, I rubbed my forehead with my hand and found it covered with beads of sweat.

It was about nine in the morning, the most peaceful time in the compound. In the house around this time every day I could read for two or three hours. Thus morning was my favorite time. Although it was hotter than usual, I still felt tranquil.

This was my home, even though I no longer was familiar with the place. After being several thousand *li* away for over ten years, I had returned home less than a month ago. The house had five rooms including a main wing and side wings with over ten people living in them. There was a reception room in the middle of the house which served as both living and dining room. It was not overly crowded, but at the same time not particularly comfortable either. During the day everyone was gone, some to school, others to work at the office, leaving me at home all alone to lounge around like a guest. Other than visiting a friend or relative occasionally, reading, writing, or just chatting to those at home, I had nothing to do. I think that "leisurely and peaceful" is the perfect description of my life at that time.

I heard a sound of leather shoes on the stone path rise, then gradually disappear. I knew who it was and scowled. The reaction may have been unconscious but it certainly was not unfounded. I raised my head and gazed out the window at the blue sky and green trees in anticipation.

"Shit! What bastard is spreading nonsense about me again? It's not illegal to raise pigs! With the cost of living going up the way it is, who isn't looking for a little spare cash? Raising pigs is a business too!" bellowed a voice as clear and crisp as if it belonged to a seventeen- or eighteen-year-old girl. Without looking, I knew it was Widow Feng, in her early thirties. More than an hour ago I had seen her standing next to the pumelo tree in the courtyard. She wore a contented smile as she watched a little black pig, with up-turned mouth, wallowing in the mud, and five small yellow chickens leisurely pecking away at insects. As her eyes followed the movements of the pig and the chickens, she mumbled under breath. A *ch'i-p'ao*[1] of black silk covered her short, plump body.

[1] A tight-fitting sheath with a high mandarin collar and side slits.

Her dark yellow face was flat and round, with narrow lips exposing two rows of snow-white teeth. I chuckled to myself, thinking that this person under the pumelo tree with the pig and chickens made a very fine painting. Almost as if she felt me watching her, she suddenly turned her back to me and walked away, slightly embarrassed.

A good many squabbles occurred in our compound on account of that pig and those chickens. About twelve or thirteen days ago on Ch'ing-ming Festival[2] morning, the son of the tenant who lives in the left extension chased the little chickens into the outhouse. The widow then began to jump up and down in the courtyard, cursing the Wang boy in a shrill voice. As usual, her tirade opened with, "You son-of-a-bitch" and "your mother's!"[3]

"You son-of-a-bitch, every goddam day stirring up my chickens. You're never happy until you've scared a few to death. What have I ever done to you? You just love to play? Fine. But why don't you go somewhere else? Why keep coming to my place? Do you really think I'm afraid of you? Just wait until your father comes home and then I'll settle the score. You son-of-a-bitch, you bastard. Just wait and see how I get even with you. One of these days you'll know what sort of a person I am!"

"You get even with me? Go ahead! As if I were afraid of you, you old hag! I don't give a damn who the hell is messing around with your chickens. You'll come to no good end slandering people like that."

"You're cursing me? If it wasn't you, you son-of-a-bitch, then who was it? And if you weren't bothering my chickens, why would I scold you? You say I'll come to no good end, but you're the one who's going to drop dead! Fuck you."

"Come on, come on. I'm waiting. Drop your pants, and then we'll see who's afraid of whom!"

Widow Feng was in such a frenzy that she was kicking her legs about. Neither was willing to relent, and their language became even more offensive, so much so that I couldn't bear to listen any longer. After another half hour or so of bickering back and forth, the Wang kid seemed to lose the battle and slipped away. Widow Feng victoriously cursed on for a while, and then the compound quieted down.

After lunch I went outside and saw the chickens scratching leisurely about under the tree. As I passed by the small separate courtyard on the side of the alley, the door to the house was wide open and inside a mahjong table was set up. Among the four women players was that same middle-aged woman who had fought with the kid just a while ago. As if she had a perfect hand, she broke into a smile accompanied by happy chuckles. When I returned home in the evening, those same four ladies were still glued to the mahjong table. The only difference was that a fifty-watt lamp had replaced the sunlight.

There was another time when two of the chickens had run into my house looking for food, but my youngest nephew chased them out. Widow Feng had just come from the right wing and saw what was going on. Grumbling on the stairs, she began to raise her voice and gave the chickens a piece of her mind.

"You don't have any sense of shame. You have food in your own house, but you won't touch it. Instead, you go out looking for strange things to eat. When people throw you out you don't even dare open your mouths to say anything. You're really good for nothing."

Not a soul responded. I told my nephew not to pay any attention to her. In his room he cursed her awhile, then buried his head in his books.

However, she continued her harangue. "You take a beating and can't make a sound, you cheap critters. If you run into someone's house again tomorrow, if they don't beat the shit out of you I will."

Still, nobody paid her any mind, and so she declared herself victor. About half an hour later, I saw her sitting at the mahjong table again, pouting and looking unhappy.

The next day when the little chickens came over to our house as usual, my nephew was not in. I let them roam around freely and peck. Widow Feng happened to be talking to someone in the com-

[2] See footnote 1 to "Medicine," p. 9.   [3] A profanity.

pound and should have seen the little chickens entering my house. But instead of breaking her chickens' legs, she left, still talking and laughing.

Another time, a chicken was missing and no one knew whether it had run off somewhere or, as she said later, it had been killed by the Wang kid. Or it could have drowned in some ditch. At any rate, she never found it. At dusk she just stood in the compound yelling, "You son-of-a-bitch, you son-of-a-turtle, you stillborn child, you chicken thief, you mother-fucker, if you take one bite your belly will burst and you'll die of poison. You'll choke to death on it, and when your stomach, bowels, heart, and liver rot out I'll throw them to the chickens and dogs to feast on. You'll die a horrible death."

Nobody said anything. I stood deliberately under the window watching her rant and rave. She was wearing a striped undershirt with black silk pants. Her hands danced about, and she stamped her feet, while her white teeth made her dark yellow complexion even darker.

"Whoever stole my chicken should have guts enough to stand up for himself instead of hiding behind his mother's petticoat. My chickens aren't easy to swallow. You take one bite and you and your family will never have offspring."

" 'Old Dame Wang Curses the Chicken,' live at the Szechwanese opera," said my nephew with a soft chuckle as he came up next to me. I also found it hard not to laugh.

She kept up her tongue-lashing for a whole hour. At about ten the next morning, she stood in her doorway and was at it again, using almost the same language as before, but with some new additions.

"So you stole my chicken because you think I'm easy to bully, huh? Tomorrow, when I get to the bottom of this, I'll either beat the shit out of you or throttle you, you dead son-of-a-turtle. You'll never see old age! *Ai,* if life wasn't such a struggle, who'd be willing to be bothered raising chickens? You little thing, giving me such a hard time, you short-lived . . ."

"Whom are you referring to? Make that a little clearer," the Wang kid interrupted coldly as he walked out of the house. He was not more than

eleven or twelve years old, with a long, thin face, slightly high cheekbones, and a protruding chin.

"Who else? Yes, I'm pointing my finger at you, you dead son-of-a-turtle! So what? Fuck your mother, fuck your ancestors," she countered, her feet kicking and face purple, screaming as if she were about to pounce on him. But she and the kid were still separated by the courtyard between them.

"If you're accusing me, then say it right out; don't beat around the bush," said the child with the air of an adult, pointing his finger. "So you're bringing up my mother and my ancestors again, eh? I think you've gotten so used to being fucked that you can't talk about anything else. Who gives a damn about your chickens? If you're afraid someone will steal them, take them to bed with you."

On hearing this, the woman became even more enraged. This time she actually jumped into the courtyard, but checked herself after only three or four steps. Saliva sprayed from her mouth as she sputtered, "Okay, you've cursed me. I'm not going to argue with you, you dead son-of-a-turtle. I'll just wait until your mother comes home and have her straighten this out for me. Your father must have fucked the brains out of your mother, otherwise how could she have given birth to a short-lived son-of-a-bitch like you?"

A heated battle of words ensued. The language became so foul that I didn't want to listen anymore. The only thing I could do was to sacrifice my reading time and go out to visit a friend.

All this happened two days ago.

The pig was a new addition, so no major argument had occurred over it yet. However, I had heard complaints about it quite a number of times. With the arrival of the pig the whole place seemed a little dirtier and the people of our compound all appeared disgruntled. Some just grumbled about it, including my nieces and nephews, but no one had protested to Widow Feng yet. This time she suddenly broached the subject herself, probably because she had heard something said. However, the whole thing had nothing at all to do with me, so I just ignored it.

"Widow Feng, you've really figured it all out, raising both chickens and pigs," an old lady said in an envious voice. "Today the price of pork went up to over eight dollars a catty."

"Mrs. Yen, you don't know. Just talking about raising pigs and chickens gets me all upset. Day after day I worry and don't sleep well at night. One moment that son-of-a-turtling yellow weasel will come drag my chickens away, the very next the pig will run into trouble. I don't know how many fights I've had with that son-of-a-bitching Wang kid over these little chickens. It's really, really frustrating. It's not that I've nothing to do after filling my stomach, it's just that the cost of living is too high. Otherwise why would any son-of-a-bitch want to raise chickens and pigs?" Widow Feng said this with a smile, as if she were perfectly content with her pig and chickens.

"Isn't that the truth! For over two months I haven't smelled the faintest whiff of lard, not to mention chicken. Even eggs are selling for a dollar apiece. It's really enough to scare a person to death," old Mrs. Yen sighed.

"That's right. Things are getting more expensive every day," Widow Feng replied. Then she volunteered, "When they lay eggs, I'll give you some."

"I don't deserve it," old Mrs. Yen thanked her, and after a pause, continued; "By that time, who knows how much they'll cost apiece."

"Who could know," chimed in Widow Feng.

"I heard that in Kunming Indanthrin[4] has dropped to a dollar a foot," Mrs. Yen announced as if reporting some important news.

"How could that be? You can't believe everything people say! Around here Indanthrin only goes up, almost twenty dollars now," added Widow Feng loudly.

While they were talking three little chickens, one after the other, hopped into our house and to my disbelief meandered leisurely around the room.

"Look at that, they're running off to someone's house again. You can't teach them anything. Mrs. Yen, you wouldn't believe how much I've worried over those chickens. Just talking about them makes me sad. You all know I'm a mahjong addict, but these past few days I haven't even touched a tile."

"So that's it. I thought it was a little strange that I haven't seen you playing at the Changs' recently. I can't believe you've given it up? And I hadn't heard anything about your having a fight with anyone. So that's what it was all about. Certainly, playing mahjong is a pastime, but raising chickens is not only a pastime but also a good business," Mrs. Yen said patronizingly. She then rambled on to add one more flattering sentence: "Really, you're the capable one around here, Widow Feng."

"Come on, Mrs. Yen, you're making fun of me. How in the world can I be called capable?" said Widow Feng in mock astonishment. "To tell you the truth, in times like these, I have no alternative but to come up with some way to earn a little spare cash. If I had to depend on what my husband left, how could I survive? Mrs. Yen, just think about it, when I first moved in here the rent was five dollars. Now, it's gone up to fifty dollars and I hear it's going to go up even more."

"I heard that your landlady, Mrs. Fang, is very well off. She has several houses, and since hers is a small family, I don't know why she's still so greedy about the rents. The rents never stop going up!"

"The more money one has, the meaner one gets. These few broken-down rooms leak the minute it rains, and tiles break loose as soon as the wind blows. If it hadn't been so hard to find a place to rent in wartime, I'd have moved long ago and wouldn't have to put up with that old hag anymore," Widow Feng said angrily.

"Hold it now, look who's coming. Mrs. Fang is coming," Mrs. Yen gave a low warning.

"Well, speak of the devil! If she didn't have something up her sleeve she wouldn't be coming around here. You can be sure she's up to no good," Widow Feng mumbled.

---

[4] Indanthrin is a brand name for a German-made color-fast blue cloth similar to the American-made denim. It was very popular in Shanghai during the war years, and, judging from this story, it was also well regarded in the interior.

Before long, the overbearing, high-pitched voice of a woman was heard: "I say, where did the pig come from? My house is not a pig pen. Whose pig is that? Get it out of here."

Her voice was ahead of her entrance. I heard her say: "Widow Feng, you haven't gone out visiting today?"

Widow Feng answered with a couple of polite sentences, whereupon her landlady again called out, "Widow Feng, do you know who's raising that pig? Pigs cannot be raised in my house! Things are getting stranger and stranger nowadays—raising pigs in a courtyard! I won't have it!"

"Mrs. Fang, how would I know? I'm hardly ever around," Widow Feng said evasively.

"I simply hate pigs. They're not only filthy and ugly, but they wander around everywhere, ruining everything. I don't mind renting for a low price, but if they mess the house up, where's the money to fix it going to come from?" the landlady complained. "These days it's just not worth renting out houses. What can one do with that measly amount of money? It isn't enough to buy a few catties of meat, or even a peck of rice. So why should I rent out a perfectly good house to be ruined by someone raising pigs?"

"Mrs. Fang, you shouldn't upset yourself. I haven't ruined your house at all. I'm the kind of person who loves cleanliness. When I live in a rented house, I take care of it as well as if it were my own. When my husband was around, he used to praise me for this good habit of mine." Widow Feng covered up with tact and logic.

"Well then, I really should thank you, Widow Feng," Mrs. Fang replied sarcastically.

At that moment the crisp voice of a child cut in: "Widow Feng, your pig ran into our house again this morning."

"You devil! Who asked you to open your big mouth?" Widow Feng cursed resentfully.

"So it is your pig, Widow Feng. But didn't you just say that you didn't know anything about it?" Mrs. Fang asked in surprise. I could tell from her tone of voice that she wasn't happy.

"So what if it is mine? I haven't broken any fucking laws. With things getting so expensive, who doesn't want to make some extra money?

That's what I call economics. If government workers can raise pigs, why can't a widow like myself?" Widow Feng answered, suddenly changing her tone as if she had arrived at a point where covering up was no longer necessary.

"The house is mine, so if I say you cannot raise pigs, then you cannot."

"But I'm the one who pays the rent, and if I want to raise pigs, it's my own business. What can you do about it?"

"I heard you. What can I do about you? I'll kick you out, that's what!"

"I won't go! I can pay the rent and I don't owe you a penny. So what grounds do you have for evicting me?"

"Okay. So you can pay, eh? Let me tell you then. Beginning next month, the rent goes up one thousand dollars. If you want to stay here, then stay. If not, then move. I have nothing more to add, except that if you don't get that pig out of the house, the rent will go up another fifty dollars. I've made my point clear, and if you don't do as I say, don't blame me later when I take action."

"You're just jacking up the rent at will. I won't pay any attention. What right do you have to raise the rent? I'm not that easy to bully around. I won't add another penny to my rent and I won't move either, so let's see what you're going to do about it."

"I won't waste another word on you. When the time comes I'll get someone to come collect it. The house is mine, and I can raise the rent as much as I want. Whether you want to stay or not is up to you. Nowadays, with the cost of living so high, this trivial amount is simply not enough. If I don't raise the rent, what am I supposed to live on?" Mrs. Fang spoke forcefully. Without waiting for Widow Feng to answer, she turned her head toward the Wang kid and said, "Wang Wen-sheng, now remember to tell your mother that beginning next month, the rent is one hundred dollars higher and the security deposit is one thousand dollars more. Don't get that confused. I have to be going now."

She turned and left. Widow Feng mumbled, cursed behind her back, "You old bat, you cheap hussy. You're almost fifty years old; what's the use of trying to paint yourself up? The most you can manage is to bewitch your old man. Don't think you can get any respect from me. My money is for raising my pig, not to support a bitch like you. So quit putting on airs. Maybe tomorrow a bomb will drop right on your house. See who gets the last laugh then."

"You want her house bombed? What good would that do you?" Wang Wen-sheng said, reveling in her misfortune.

"Who's talking to you? You son-of-a-bitch! It's all your fault!" Widow Feng suddenly cursed shrilly. "You sure know how to bad-mouth a person. But don't think you'll get any reward. Isn't your rent going up too? Don't think you can curry the old hag's favor that quickly! You shameless son-of-a-turtle."

After this the feud broke out again between adult and child, and continued for more than twenty minutes. As for the three chickens that were in my house, having played enough, they slowly filed out.

It seemed that Widow Feng had gone out for a while, since I didn't hear her voice at all for the greater part of the day. There was only a bee buzzing back and forth by the window. The sky was exceptionally blue and the leaves on the trees were strikingly lustrous. It all made me a little drowsy.

Around noon I took a long nap, but was awakened by the sound of "move along, move along." As I went outside, I spotted Widow Feng bending over, herding her pig. She wore a contented smile as she gazed lovingly at the little pig. Actually the pig was not all that small. It was already as large as an average-size dog. It had a gray coat and an upturned mouth, and it waddled heavily from side to side.

In the evening, I talked with my nieces and nephews about Widow Feng. It was already past ten o'clock when suddenly I heard sobs from the right wing. I knew they came from Widow Feng.

"The weasel's come to carry off her chickens again," my youngest nephew said with a happy smile.

The same evening, Widow Feng flew into a rage over that weasel three times. One of the times

seemed to be in the middle of the night and awakened me with her carrying on.

About ten o'clock the following morning, Widow Feng and the Wang kid were in the compound speaking loudly. This time they were not swearing at each other, but on the contrary, her tone was considerably more cordial.

"Wang Wen-sheng, I beg of you. Please don't bother my chickens anymore. Just be good for once. All I have left is this one chicken and it really hurts me even to talk about it. It's been so hard just getting them to this point. Last night every other one of them was dragged away by the weasel and only this one is left. I'm really distressed. How can you keep on tormenting me? I've never done anything to you . . ."

The apologetic oration, delivered in a plaintive tone, satisfied Wang Wen-sheng. He smiled and without answering, just kept on playing. His mother worked outside the city, coming home only two days a week. His father was a government employee who had to be at work at seven in the morning and didn't return home until after five in the evening. There was no one to discipline the child, only a deaf maid sixteen or seventeen years old looking after him.

When Wang Wen-sheng finally disappeared, Widow Feng, in a low voice, let loose one sentence: "May that short-lived animal die a miserable death!" The deaf maid stood in the doorway giggling, unable to hear what had been said.

After a while, Widow Feng went inside. The Wang kid leaped happily back into the compound. Suddenly he climbed up a tree and, sitting on one of the branches, contentedly hummed a wartime song, while the little black pig waddled back and forth down below. The solitary little chicken was listlessly pecking the ground for food.

A clear sound broke the quiet: "Widow Feng, my mistress invites you to hurry over." This was the voice of the maid from the small house on the separate courtyard.

"Okay, I'm coming," answered Widow Feng from within the house. In a short time she came out, neatly dressed. She looked at the pig and chicken, and also at Wang Wen-sheng sitting up in the tree. Then, feigning a smile, she said to him, "Wang Wen-sheng, would it be too much trouble for you to keep an eye on my pig and chicken so they don't run off somewhere? When they get bigger I can sell them and invite you over for a special snack."

"Okay!" Wang Wen-sheng nodded curtly. He gazed at Widow Feng's disappearing shadow, and as before, leisurely hummed a tune. But once her shadow had vanished from sight, he blurted out disdainfully, "Hunh, if that pig of yours can grow up, then my name isn't Wang! Who gives a damn about your food? You bitch."

In a flash he jumped down from the tree. As his body twisted, one leg collapsed under him when he hit the ground. Fortunately he landed on his hands. As he got up, he saw the deaf maid standing by the doorway laughing. Snatching up a handful of dirt he threw it at her, but she managed to dodge it. Irritated, he cursed her: "Damn your ancestors! You stupid laughing bitch!"

The compound quieted down again. As I looked out from the window, not a shadow of a person could be seen. The pig was lying under a tree while the chicken walked listlessly about.

I had not yet removed my face from the glass when I saw Widow Feng swagger into view. Her whole body appeared to be vibrating to the sound of her clopping shoes.

"Now that pest's gone, we can have some peace and quiet around here," she said to herself. Suddenly with a note of astonishment, she added, "The pig looks a little weak today. He couldn't be sick, could he?"

As she was speaking she moved toward the courtyard, looking at her pig with much concern. There followed the sound of "move along, move along," as she hastened it forward. More than ten minutes passed before she entered the right wing of the house. Soon after she came out again, and hurried out of the compound. At the last moment she turned her back for one last look at the courtyard.

Three days later—actually, I don't recall whether it was three or four days—at two o'clock in the afternoon, I returned home drenched in perspiration. Not a cloud was visible in the sky and the sun was burning down on my head.

When I got inside the main gate, I bumped into Landlady Fang, who was on her way out, seething with anger. The sweat pouring down her face had streaked her makeup, leaving blotches here and there, baring all her wrinkles. Her long hair, which had been set with a curling iron, lay disheveled along the nape of her neck. (At a glance you could tell that her hair had just recently been curled. The day before yesterday I overheard my nieces talking about the price of having a set—one hundred and fifty dollars!) Her portly body was clothed in a *ch'i-pao* of the latest style. She wore a cheap perfume (although these days it can no longer be called cheap). As its smell rushed toward me, I thought to myself: "She's really an old witch!" Following behind her was a solid middle-aged man in a short Chinese jacket.

Widow Feng, her collar open, sat down in her doorway and cried, "You bitch, you whore, pay me for my pig! Pay me back for that pig . . . You think I'm such a pushover. If anything happens to my pig . . ."

I couldn't help chuckling at this point, but she didn't hear me.

"I want a life for a life. You think because you have money you can do anything. I live in your house, but I pay for it. I haven't broken any law raising this pig!" There ensued a long stream of profanities.

Old Mrs. Yen and Mrs. Chang, the one with the small house on the separate compound, stood to one side discussing this event. During the conversation they faulted Mrs. Fang for a few things, but in general their tone was temperate. From their conversation I learned that Mrs. Fang had sent a servant to talk things over with Widow Feng. The talk failed, and there was a big scene. Mrs. Fang's servant, on her instructions, had given the little pig a few kicks. When these two ladies had finished their conversation, they approached Widow Feng and bent down to comfort her.

Mrs. Yen intoned slowly: "Widow Feng, take it easy now. People who have both money and power, like her, can we afford to provoke them? Besides, it's such a trivial thing. Pigs have always been hard to raise. For the past couple of days, it's appeared so weak and droopy, as if it were sick.

The way I see it, if you hurry up, you can still sell it and get some money back."

"No! No! I'll raise him just to spite her! I'm not afraid of that old hussy! The most that can happen is that I'll have to move!" wailed Widow Feng stubbornly. Not long after, she stopped crying. She turned toward her two friends and broke into a tirade of complaints, interspersed with a string of profanities. After listening to their words of consolation, she left with them.

The compound was very still. Though no wounds could be seen on its body, the pig was lying on the ground as if in a stupor. Suddenly it opened its eyes and gazed at me with a pitiful and helpless look.

I went inside to my brother and sister-in-law, who had returned from the country. They were discussing the rent increase with my nieces and nephews. The landlady had just been here to announce it formally, her tone a little warmer than we would have expected. She said she would only add fifty dollars to the rent and three hundred dollars to the security deposit. For Widow Feng she had set harsher terms. As a result a heated argument ensued which almost culminated in these two women hitting each other. The little pig had been beaten during their argument. If it had not been for Mrs. Chang's intercession, the matter would never have been settled so simply.

After about an hour, my youngest nephew came in and whispered to me, "Uncle, come quick, look, Widow Feng's giving her pig a bath. It's really too funny!"

I followed him outside and stood under the window. The tree trunk didn't block my view. Widow Feng had pulled up the front flap of her *ch'i-pao* and was squatting on the ground. With brush in hand, she wetted it from a basin next to her and scrubbed the pig. The pig grunted weakly, while Widow Feng lovingly consoled it.

That evening as my brother, sister-in-law, and myself were going out for tea, we saw Widow Feng bending over her pig and carefully ushering it into the pen. (I really should explain here that the pig pen was behind Widow Feng's house and was reached by a small lane.) The little pig lay on the ground as if it were unconscious, moving only

slightly. Mrs. Feng displayed an amazing degree of patience. From beginning to end, she gently swung her hands and softly called to the little pig.

On the following day I did not see the little pig come out at all. After another day had passed, at about noon, I heard Widow Feng talking with old Mrs. Yen.

"Today he's even worse. He can't get up at all and hasn't eaten a thing. All he does is roll his eyes around. I look at him and he gazes at me, his eyes brimming with tears. It pains me to see him like that. Animals are just like people. They have feelings too, and can understand, except that they can't speak it." Widow Feng sounded melancholy and anxious.

"I think most probably he was hurt, and the internal injuries are serious. You should apply a little salve and see whether that works," offered Mrs. Yen.

"If only he could talk, everything would be all right. I just don't know where it hurts him, so I can't do anything for him. Worrying doesn't do any good. Mrs. Yen, could you please ask around for me and see if anyone can come up with some way?"

The conversation that followed was interrupted by my nephews and nieces. They raced in and called me to lunch. Widow Feng continued talking, but it was impossible for me to hear clearly any longer.

That very same day, before dark, the pig died. I saw Widow Feng sitting all by herself in the doorway crying bitterly, and knew the pig was gone. She was no longer quarreling and her voice had quieted down. She buried her head in her hands, desolate cries alternating with plaintive murmuring.

No one paid any attention to her. At first Wang Wen-sheng and his deaf maid, a smirk on their lips, watched her for a while. He held a green pumelo as large as a rice bowl in his hands, which he had probably just picked from the pumelo tree I had seen him climbing earlier. Later on he coerced his maid into playing catch with the pumelo and they didn't pay any more attention to Widow Feng. Those two were not the only ones who had come to see the excitement, but after a while, the crowd dispersed. The cover of night obscured any shadow of her. The dark engulfed any sound from her.

This night, as usual, was driven out by the rays of the morning sun. Thereafter, I often saw Widow Feng in the courtyard scattering feed for her only surviving little chicken. Sometimes she would also feed the swallows who had flown out from under the eaves of the house and were pecking for something to eat. Gradually the chicken grew larger. It leisurely hopped back and forth in the yard, but always seemed a little lonely.

After a few more days had passed, toward the end of the month, Widow Feng moved out. I did not see her move, nor do I know where she moved to, but I did hear that she had directed the cart hauler herself. She didn't have very much, but she still had to make three trips. Judging from this, her new residence seemed to be somewhere in this vicinity. Nobody offered to help. She didn't have a single close friend, but that was quite understandable.

My youngest nephew told me about her moving. The most fascinating thing to him was the way she sat in the rickshaw holding the little chicken against her breast as if she were embracing a child.

On the morning of the second day after Widow Feng had moved, the landlady came over to take a look at the empty house and instructed the servant who accompanied her to sweep it out. That very same afternoon, a young married couple moved in. The man was a native Szechwanese and the woman spoke Shanghainese. She was as beautifully dressed as she was good-looking. It seemed that this couple were newlyweds, being quite devoted to each other. Every day around evening, after the husband returned home from work, the compound rang with laughter and singing like silver bells.

Rumor had it that these newlyweds were relatives of the landlady. For this reason, the number of visits the landlady paid to our compound increased. Thereafter, it goes without saying, the stairs in the courtyard were all extremely clean, without any trace of pig or chicken tracks.

However, as usual, my house still leaked when it rained, and when the wind was strong, tiles came tumbling down, sending sand and dust flying all around.

CHAO SHU-LI
(1906–1970)

In 1946 Chou Yang, chief spokesman for the Communist Party's position on literary matters, heralded Chao Shu-li's fiction as "marking the successful realization of Mao Tse-tung's principles on literature and art." For years after this Chao Shu-li represented the Maoist ideal of a creative writer: with his unimpeachable background in the impoverished hinterlands of China, he wrote vividly of the peasants' awakening to socialism in a style largely free of the Western influences which had dominated Chinese fiction since 1918.

Chao Shu-li was born in 1906 in Chin-ch'eng, a village at the foot of the T'ai-hang Mountains in the province of Shansi. As a child, he worked on his father's farm, herding cattle and collecting manure, but found time to participate in a local folk music group as well, where he learned the techniques of traditional storytelling. With his father's encouragement, Chao Shu-li entered the Ch'ang-chih Fourth Normal School in 1925, but soon became involved in the anti-warlord movement among the students, resulting in a brief imprisonment. After his release, he taught for a time at his village primary school, and continued his work with local theater troupes and his various political activities. After the outbreak of the War of Resistance against Japan, the Communist Eighth Route Army consolidated itself in the T'ai-hang District in which Chao's village lay. The T'ai-hang base, as a major wartime center, was one of the few to establish a printing press. Chao Shu-li was a major contributor to the local wartime journals, and even undertook the editorship of his own small newspaper, *New Masses* (*Hsin ta-chung*).

Chao Shu-li's first story, *The Marriage of Hsiao Erh-hei* (*Hsiao Erh-hei chieh-hun*), a simple tale discrediting superstition and advocating free choice of one's marital partner, was published by the T'ai-hang New China Press in 1943. The story promptly won the praise of the border-region commanders, and sold thirty to forty thousand copies in Shansi alone. Chao's second story, *The Rhymes of Li Yu-ts'ai* (*Li Yu-ts'ai pan-hua*, 1943), was even more warmly received. It is the story of a village balladeer who uses colloquial rhymes to educate and encourage the villagers in their struggle against government corruption, and its composition incorporated many of the folk techniques the author had learned in his youth.

Changes in Li Village (*Li-chia-chuang ti pien-ch'ien*), Chao Shu-li's first novel, was published after the Japanese surrender in 1945. It also concerns the fortunes of a Shansi village as the peasants, led by the Communist Party, appropriate political power from the despotic landlords and officials. After the success of this work, Chao continued to write short stories, focusing more and more on the heroic characteristics of the peasants. Thus the hero of "Lucky" (*Fu-kuei*, 1946), included in this anthology, overcomes the oppression he has suffered at the hands of the old society, and discovers in himself heroic powers of will.

These early works were highly praised for their direct, colloquial prose, and the judicious employment of techniques from traditional fiction. Traditional devices include careful integration of descriptive passages into the narrative, straightforward introduction of character and situation at the opening, use of "hooks" (brief breaks in the narrative) to entice the reader's attention, and marked variations in narrative density.

The subjects of Chao Shu-li's stories were drawn from the conflicts he confronted in his political work in rural China. *Sanliwan Village* (1955), his second novel, was in fact the product of extensive field work, and reflects his personal involvement in the political processes he chronicles. It documents the conversion of dissenting farmers to the advantages of collectivization, and its publication coincided with Mao Tse-tung's appeal for the development of cooperatives in 1955.

Though Chao Shu-li continued to write into the sixties (including the novel *Sacred Fountain Cave* [*Ling-ch'üan-tung*], 1959, and many short stories), and held several powerful positions in Chinese literary associations, his works were increasingly subjected to ideological criticism after 1962. His stories were said to lack the spirit of "romantic realism," and to focus too heavily on "middle characters" whose ideological position could not be clearly identified. This criticism culminated in his denouncement as a counterrevolutionary in January 1967, at the height of the Cultural Revolution. Recent Communist sources hold Lin Piao and the Gang of Four responsible for his death in 1970.

MARSTON ANDERSON

Lucky

by Chao Shu-li

Translated by Cyril Birch

Lucky's name stank worse than dogdirt in the village. They said his biggest problem was that he couldn't keep his hands to himself. Whoever's yard he walked into, they would keep a careful eye on him until he'd gone out the gate again, and then breathe a sigh of relief. If he walked across anyone's field, they would have to look out for any pipe or jacket left against the dike. Anyone who noticed something missing from his house would make sure he took a casual stroll round Lucky's place, and if somebody's ox disappeared he would see first of all whether Lucky was at home . . .

And yet everyone felt that for certain things you couldn't do without him. When there was a death in the family, it was Lucky they'd get to dress the corpse. If a child died, it was Lucky who did the "seeing off."[1] And when it came to a real funeral, you couldn't manage without Lucky to help bear the coffin and dig the grave.

Work in the fields was something Lucky knew from start to finish. He could tackle half as much again as anyone else—only no one could manage to keep him at it; as soon as he had a couple of coins in his pocket, he'd be off gambling. Sometimes a dike would fall in, leaving a big gap, and then even if you had to pay him double you'd

have to ask Lucky along for a few days' work—when he mended a gap, it wouldn't fall in again in a hurry. But all the time he was with you you'd have to be careful for fear he would make off with some tool or other as the fancy took him.

Later Myriad Wang, the head of his clan, wanted to have Lucky buried alive because he was working as a hired musician at funerals. So he ran away, and it wasn't until last year that he came back, after the Japs had surrendered and the Eighth Route Army[2] had been in his village for a month or more.

When our area cadres first arrived in Lucky's village they saw that he was very poor and wanted to discover the roots of his poverty. But as soon as they started questioning the villagers, every one of them said he was a scoundrel and best left alone, and only after a good many honest citizens, sons of toil and suffering, had "turned over"[3] did the area cadres begin slowly to find out the details of his past.

I

When Lucky was eleven his father died. His mother made her home her whole life, weaving

---

[1] The background of this story as in most stories by Chao Shu-li, is in the rural area of Shansi province where the people live in extreme poverty. Lucky's role in "seeing off" (*sung-sung*) a dead child is made clear in the last part of the story when an old woman offered to pay him to bury her grand-daughter. No coffin was used, just a strip of old straw matting to cover the child before depositing her in a hole.

[2] See footnote 1 to "In the Hospital," p. 283.

[3] "Turn over" (*fan-shen*) in Communist terminology means getting one's grievances redressed and wrongs righted. Apparently Lucky had been falsely accused by the villagers the cadres talked to earlier, and his defenders could be found only among the "sons of toil and suffering."

cotton cloth from homespun thread to bring up
her son. Lucky was a good boy, smart, capable,
and handsome. By the age of eleven or twelve he
could hoe seedlings, and at fifteen or sixteen he
was the equal of a grown man at manual work, except for the heaviest loads. It was just about this
time that his mother had him betrothed to a girl
of eight. This girl was called Silver Flower. She
came from a very poor home, her father and
mother had died some time ago, and her big
brother and his wife couldn't afford to raise her.
So as soon as the match was arranged she was sent
over to Lucky's home as a "live-in bride," a girl
who because of her poverty is brought up in her
fiancé's home. But Silver Flower never suffered
any ill-treatment after she entered her new
home—Lucky's mother was an understanding sort
of woman, and what's more she had never had a
daughter, and so she treated this girl as her own
flesh and blood.

The village had its own concerts, and Lucky
learned how to sing opera—when he was smaller
he did walk-on parts, then when he grew up he
sang the leading male roles, and sang them very
well. On the Lantern Festival[4] a year after Silver
Flower arrived, she went to see the play, and
when Lucky made his entrance all the other children gathered around her and cried, "Look,
Silver Flower, that's your bridegroom coming on!"
She felt very awkward and embarrassed when
they said this, but later she got used to it, and
then they didn't bother to say it anymore.

The first few years when Silver Flower went to
see the play she was just a child watching the fun,
but when she was a few years older she began to
see something in it. It wasn't that she understood
the play; it was seeing her own man, when he was
dressed up, handsomer than anybody else—every
time the village gave its own concert in the temple, however busy she was, she always wanted to
go have a look, but for fear of a scolding from her
foster-mother she would only watch until Lucky
left the stage and then she would go back home.
Once Lucky was on right through to the last
scene, and she got back too late to cook the sup-

per. Her foster-mother gave her a scolding, but in
private Silver Flower only smiled to herself. Nobody else noticed, but up on the stage Lucky saw
what was in her mind, and because of this he
didn't blame her even for being late with supper.
He only said with a gentle smile, "Couldn't you
have tried to get back earlier?"

II

When Lucky was twenty-two his mother fell ill;
whatever she ate only came up again. She knew
she would never get better, and the woman next
door said they should not delay with the funeral
preparations. Lucky had the doctor in several
times to look at her, from the Myriad Cures herb-
shop. She swallowed a few doses of medicine, but
to no effect.

One day Lucky's mother said to the neighbor:
"It looks as though this illness of mine is all that's
needed to finish me. They always say, 'If you get
through the fall you won't see summer; if you get
through summer you won't last the fall.' It's the
seventh month now, and it won't be long before
we see the autumn out, but I don't think I'll be
able to last out the winter."

The neighbor cut her short: "Sister, don't let
your thoughts run away with you. Which of us
who eat grain to live can escape trouble?"

"I'm well aware what this illness of mine is like,"
said Lucky's mother, "and I'm not afraid of dying.
I don't think because I've lived fifty or sixty years
I should never die. I've just one thing on my mind
that's not settled: I don't want to leave her half-
way up the slope, that bride of Lucky's that I've
brought up from a child. I don't want to die without seeing them married. The girl's fourteen now.
I'd like to get her hair put up for her wedding
while I've still got eyes to see with, and then for
good or ill I'll have done my duty by her. It's only
that we're a small family, too few to manage, so I
must ask you if you'll kindly lend a hand when the
time comes."

The neighbor agreed with every word, asked

---

[4] Falls on January 15 in the Chinese calendar.

what the date was to be, and promised to give her all the help she could.

The day Lucky and Silver Flower were to be married was the twenty-sixth of the seventh month. Silver Flower's big brother came to give the girl away. They took her next door to dress her and do her hair and seat her in the sedan chair. They carried her in a circle through the village, then brought her back to the same court-yard. Getting out of the chair, she went into the rooms on the west side, Lucky's place. In the main room sat the guests from the bride's family, there to give the bride away. The clan leader, Myriad Wang, was asked to play host. Lucky's mother feared that beancurd and noodles wouldn't be good enough, and so she killed a chicken specially to make a four-dish "firepot."[5]

For good or ill the thing was over and done with. Lucky and Silver Flower had seen a lot of each other from childhood. They got on very well together, and Lucky's mother was completely happy about it.

As she had foreseen, however, as soon as the harvest was in and the weather grew colder her illness worsened. Even though she started wearing her padded jacket in the ninth month, she couldn't keep out the cold; as soon as she ate any-thing the pain came, and when the pain came she vomited. Dark circles formed around her eyes and her cheekbones protruded under the skin.

The woman next door said to Lucky: "I don't think there's anything to be done about that illness of your mother's. You ought to get things ready." Lucky too had seen this coming. He went off to look for Myriad Wang.

"Everything is all ready for you," said Myriad. His "Myriad Cures" was an herb shop and general store as well, and he had a few willow coffins in stock waiting for use. But it didn't matter what you bought; as soon as you went above a certain figure you had to write out an agreement for him. Myriad often gave his own children a little ser-mon: "How much cash do you expect to make from a year of nothing but ordinary trade? It all depends on the loans you put out; money makes money a lot faster than men can."

They managed to get the harvest in, but before they had finished cutting up the straw for feed, Lucky's mother died. Silver Flower was an inexpe-rienced child; she could do nothing except cry. Lucky himself was only twenty-two; he was a bit more use than she was, but by the time he had hired the men to carry the coffin and got the di-viner in, he had no thought for all the things that had to be done at home. It was good that they had the neighbor to help Silver Flower make the mourner's hats and white shoes, and prepare the funeral meal of noodles with a pot of stew. In the end they got through all the fuss and worry of a funeral.

What with taking a wife and arranging a fu-neral, Lucky owed Myriad Wang between ten and twenty dollars for cloth and other things, and with the coffin as well it was thirty dollars altogether. Lucky wrote out an agreement.

III

The little family owned two-thirds of an acre of land and had no other prospect of income. Lucky was fearful of never being able to repay Myriad Wang, and so he worked half time as a laborer for him in the year that followed. Silver Flower had began to learn spinning before her tiny arms could properly reach the wheel, and though she was only fifteen she was already a good spinner. The two of them got up every morning and each set to work without needing any prod from the other.

Myriad employed four laborers altogether, but the old foreman said you should count Lucky as two, for whatever work it was, just mention it and he knew what needed doing. Ten or more years ago the foreman had been a good worker. Now he was getting on and couldn't hold his own with Lucky on the heavy jobs, but he really knew his stuff and Lucky learned a lot from him.

The trouble was, Lucky had used up the house-hold stock of grain on the wedding and the fu-neral the previous year; so this year he had to borrow as soon as the farm work started and go

[5] See footnote 1 to "Solitude," p. 101.

on borrowing right up to reaping-time. When the work was over, in the tenth month, Myriad reckoned up the loan on the basis of the spring prices. Lucky's wages paid that off, and all he owed was ten dollars eighty cents interest on the thirty dollars. The thirty on the IOU grew to forty, and Myriad let him off the eighty cents, since Lucky was both his own kin and his own laborer.

From this time on it was as though Lucky had both legs stuck in quicksand and was being sucked down deeper and deeper. By the fourth year the loan capital had snowballed to between ninety and a hundred dollars. When the reckoning came in the tenth month, Lucky handed his wages to Myriad together with the grain surplus from his two-thirds of an acre, but it still wasn't enough.

On the tenth of the first month Silver Flower had her first baby. Her only relative was her brother's wife, and it being the first month she had visitors to look after and couldn't come to help Silver Flower. So Lucky had to stay home and boil up rice-water for her to drink.

All the grain had gone to Myriad Wang to pay the interest, and when New Year's was over they had nothing left to eat. Although Silver Flower had just had her baby they could only afford a fistful of rice to boil up a broth. There was no other rice for Lucky, besides what was needed for the soup, so all he could do was swallow a couple of mouthfuls of the sediment left in the bottom of Silver Flower's soup pan and call that a meal. It hurt Silver Flower inside to see that he hadn't eaten solid food for two days and was just drinking these dregs, and she caught at his arm and cried.

IV

On the fourteenth the drama troupe were putting on a play in the temple, and they sent a man along to give Lucky a call. Lucky just at this time was crazed with hunger, and he had to turn them down: "The baby's only three or four days old. I can't leave them home with nobody to look after them."

They managed to get through the day, but they really needed him for the evening. Time and again they sent people to fetch him but he

wouldn't come. Still, the audience wouldn't have anyone else taking his part. A few said, "His own village gives a play and he puts on airs like this! Bring him along if you have to carry him!"

Lucky's neighbor heard them from up in the gallery and shouted down at once, "You don't realize, any of you! It's not that the lad's putting on airs; he hasn't a thing in the house to eat! He hasn't had a square meal for three or four days. All he's had is a little leftover broth of his wife's. How do you expect him to sing for us?"

There was a babble of voices from both stage and audience: "Why didn't he say so earlier? And the first month, too—there's nobody who can't spare a wheat cake for him."

"The boy's too thin-skinned," said the neighbor. "He can't face the shame. I took him a cake and he didn't want to accept it!"

From the village clubroom Myriad called out, "Send for him again. Explain that when he comes he can have a few fried cakes in the marquee; the club will pay!"

So they took the problem as settled, and when the club had forked up a few coins and his actor friends had sent him a wheat cake or two he was provided for during the three days the plays lasted.

What was more, the club had a rule; every year when the plays were over in the first month they gave expense money to the actors. It wasn't much—they would only get twenty or thirty coins each—but Lucky was one of the principals and got thirty.

It was still the old society at that time, and in the first month the village was never free from gambling. Just as Lucky came out of the temple with his thirty cents on the morning of the seventeenth, he was stopped by a crowd of young fellows, all fond of a game, wanting him to try his luck.

He felt uneasy and was for hurrying back to look after Silver Flower, but they wanted him to stay. Some of them said he was tied to his wife's apron strings, some of them said he couldn't bear the thought of losing thirty cents—there were some nasty things said: "Does your life depend on thirty cents?" "Can't you sweet-talk your wife a bit when you get home?" In the end he felt it wouldn't be right not to stay, and started throwing his money in with the others. He was a smart lad and knew the ropes. As a boy he had usually played a game or two with the other children when the first month came around. It was only these last few years he hadn't played, when things had not gone right for him. Playing with these young fellows for a while, he cleaned them all out, and when he counted up he had won a whole dollar and more.

V

When he reached home Silver Flower said, "The foreman has just been for you, to start work. He said the fifteenth of the month has already gone, and spring's been early this year. He says to start work right away."

"Whether I work or not, I get nothing for it!" said Lucky in reply. "I work half my time as a hired hand and I get a dollar fifty a month from him; I owe him ninety dollars, so he makes three sixty a month out of me. I lose two dollars a month or more for the privilege of slaving for him! When are we going to be able to pay him off?"

"If you don't work for him, won't it mean owing him even more?" asked Silver Flower.

"It would leave me a bit of time, and I could earn something to live on as a carrier."

"But then," Silver Flower went on, "even if you earn money that way won't it still go to him? How can we go on like this?"

"It's been no use for a long time now—have you only just found that out?" said Lucky.

His thoughts ran on: if he worked for him he couldn't go on, if he didn't work for him he couldn't go on—either way it was hopeless. Why should he be bound hand and foot like this to another living creature? "I'll work no more for him. I'll go get in a couple of sacks of rice and then we'll see." He told Silver Flower what he had decided, and then slung a sack over his shoulder and went off to market.

Passing the doorway of the first gaming-house at the edge of the village, he could hear something going on inside. He turned aside to look in,

and it was the young fellows of the day before. One of them came running up to drag him in: "I don't like the way you play! What a rotten trick yesterday to run off the minute you started winning!"

"You'd lost all your money. What were you going to use for stakes—promises?"

He turned away as he spoke and made for the door, but the other youth hung on to him like grim death, dragging him back with one hand, the other hand jingling the coins in his own pocket: "There's no catch to it! Here's some more for you to win—if you're clever enough!"

Lucky couldn't tear himself away, so he played with him for a while but without winning or losing much. At this point a burly newcomer appeared, pushed his way through to the table, and threw down a silver dollar for his stake. None of the young lads dared play for a stake like that, and slowly they backed away until only four or five remained. Lucky was just getting ready to leave too when the man who had dragged him in began to tease him: "You can handle me, Lucky, but when a big fellow turns up he puts an end to your show!"

Lucky couldn't stand being told he was not as good as somebody else. He worked off his annoyance by playing another round, and as luck would have it he threw a red and raked in the silver dollar. The other man pulled two more out of his money belt, put them down, and told Lucky to throw. Lucky didn't like to say the stake was too high. He gritted his teeth and threw again—and won again. The other man started getting excited and put down another five dollars. His nerves tingling, Lucky threw again—two reds and a "skin"; the dice went to the other man. The foreman came for him again at this point to start work, and he said, "Wait a bit and we'll see. I haven't decided yet whether I'm going to keep on for him!"

The young man standing behind Lucky's back turned to the foreman and added, "Can't you see what's happening? One win and it's a few months' wages; go down once and it's like being laid off for months. How can you expect him to care about a dollar-fifty a month pay?" The foreman left without a word.

Not long after this a boy came running in

shouting, "Quick, the headman is on his way to arrest anyone caught gambling!" One word, and the whole roomful, players and spectators alike, disappeared in every direction. By the time Myriad Wang walked into the courtyard there was not a soul to be seen.

When Lucky got back home that night with the rice he had bought, Myriad sent the foreman for him, gave him a good tongue-lashing, and badgered him into continuing as a hired man. "All right," said Lucky, "I'll stay, but only if you'll lend me grain for the year's food."

Myriad totted it all up: "The crops he gets from two-thirds of an acre aren't enough to pay off his interest. If on top of this he borrows my grain, what is he going to pay me back with? If I don't reckon the grain in with what he already owes me, and make him pay interest on both, I'd do better to hire another man altogether." He told Lucky, "All right, we can arrange that, but you're still seven dollars short on last year's interest. If you're not going to work for me you'll have to produce that now."

"You might as well have my land straight off!" was Lucky's reply. "Whichever way I farm it I can't get enough for what you want."

It was just as simple as that. A day or two later Myriad sent his men along with a load of manure.

It had taken Lucky the last few years to get his paths and dikes neat and straight, and now someone else was doing the planting there. If he didn't see it he didn't get mad, and so he never felt like going down to the fields anymore. But the fields were very near, and he could never leave the house without seeing them. This was how he started to turn up more often at the gaming tables—whether he played or not he'd go just the same to cheer himself up. As the days went by they couldn't do without Lucky. If they hadn't enough players for a game they'd send for him to make up the number.

VI

From this time on Lucky began to spend less and less of his time at home. At first he idled about the village, but later on a bunch of young wastrels led him off to other villages. Sometimes he went a good distance and it would be two or three months before he came back. The woman next door said to Silver Flower, "You speak to him the next time he comes back! If a man goes on long enough idling and drifting he'll never be able to settle down to hard work again."

Once Silver Flower did speak to him about it, but he replied, "Whether you work or not it's all the same; you get damn all out of it either way."

When he had some money he would often buy something good to eat for Silver Flower and the boy. If he was cleaned out he wouldn't come back to sponge on her even if it meant starving for days on end. He would often say his job wasn't a proper one and he didn't want his wife and his child to be ruined because of him. Silver Flower knew he was unhappy, and the times when he came back she would see that he got his own way. She knew she couldn't depend on him to keep her. All she could depend on was her own two hands to feed herself and the boy. She hadn't the money to buy her own cotton to spin and weave into cloth; she had to go out to work for other people and make a bit of money that way.

One winter, not long before Silver Flower's second baby was due, she had earned a roll of cloth. She could have used it for herself, but was saving it to exchange for rice to make some rice broth, when Lucky chanced to come back. He had lost all his money and his padded jacket as well, and all he had to wear in these winter months was an old tattered tunic. Silver Flower couldn't abide the thought of it, and made the cloth up for him to wear.

Silver Flower had her second baby on the twentieth of the twelfth month. It was the same as the first time. There wasn't a grain of rice in the house, she had nothing to make rice broth with for herself, the little three-year-old boy kept crying with hunger, and Lucky too felt his stomach rumbling for lack of food. "Get a pint measure," Silver Flower urged him, "and go borrow a pint of rice from round the front there. Tell them I'll do some spinning for them in a couple of days."

Lucky went off, but a year or two of knocking about had given him a bad name. They suspected he was up to no good and put him off by saying they hadn't any rice milled. When he returned, he heard the young woman crying across the way. A minute later, her mother-in-law lifted the curtain and called out softly, "Come here a minute, Lucky!" Lucky went over to her, and she said, "There's a little job you might do for me, I don't know whether you'd be willing . . ." Lucky asked her what it was. Her little granddaughter had died, and she wanted Lucky to "see her off." Lucky had never done anything like this before, it was so sudden he thought the old woman was trying to insult him. He felt like answering, "How dare you ask me to do this sort of thing?", but he didn't say that. The old woman noticed his hesitation and went on, "Will you do it or not? Come on! What are you afraid of? Isn't it better than cadging rice?"

He saw the force of this: he'd got to the state where he wasn't worth a pint of rice; what right had he to stand on his dignity? He walked inside without replying, and when he came out again a little later he had a strip of old straw matting rolled up in a bundle under his arm. For fear of coming across anyone he knew he made his way through the back alleys. He met nobody inside the village, but when he came out into the fields and glanced back he saw a group of people at the edge of the village staring at him and clucking away to each other. He couldn't make them out clearly or hear exactly what they were saying, but he could hear Lucky this and Lucky that. By this time he could hide neither himself nor his matting bundle, nor could he throw it away half way to his destination. All he could do was take to his heels.

He earned two pints of rice for this, but by doing it this once he had made it his trade. From then on if anyone's child died they sent for him, and it became a popular taunt among the kids: "You're no good! We'll get Lucky to carry you off under his arm!"

They didn't want Lucky for the play in the first month of the new year; they felt it was a disgrace to be seen with him and got a new singer in his place.

VII

When a man has sunk until he's lost his pride he's not too particular when something presents itself. At his wits' end from hunger in summer and early autumn, he took to stealing a pumpkin here and a turnip there, if he was caught hardening his face under curses, cowering under a beating—as long as he could get something in his belly he stopped bothering about his pride.

Then one year, toward the end of autumn, a relative of the clan arrived with the news that Lucky had stolen some carrots from a man in his village. He had been fined twenty dollars and put in the village jail. The news reached Silver Flower's ears, and she went to plead with Myriad Wang to get him off. What this relative had really come for was to find out whether Lucky still had any possessions. If he had then they could get Myriad to settle the score for Lucky; if not then they must prepare to send him off to the district court. Myriad reflected that although he had taken over Lucky's two-thirds of an acre, there was after all no sort of binding agreement, and moreover with two rooms of a house still in Lucky's possession twenty dollars presented no problem and the matter could soon be settled. "You go back home," he said to Silver Flower. "This business involves the whole family. We must all stick together, but when you get a young fellow like that what can you do about it?" Myriad agreed to put up the money and Lucky was freed and brought back, and the title deeds for the land and the house were made over to Myriad for good.

After the deeds had been made over, Myriad talked things over with the members of the family proper and decided this wastrel who disgraced them all should be taught a lesson. More than twenty of the Wangs foregathered that evening. They trussed Lucky up against the pagoda tree by Myriad's gate, and Myriad himself gave the order, "Flog him!" Lucky was flogged with wet hemp lashes until his body was one great red weal. He squealed like a stuck pig, and Silver Flower never left off beseeching Myriad for mercy, down on her knees in front of him.

It took Lucky a month to recover from the injuries of the flogging, during which time he ate up the couple of pecks of rice that Silver Flower had managed to save over the last six months.

VIII

When the wounds had healed, Silver Flower said, "You mustn't go running off again after this. Aren't you afraid of what they'll do to you?"

"If I don't go what do we eat?" was his reply. Silver Flower could think of no way out, and said nothing, only wept.

He went off again that winter. This time it was better than ever; in less than a month he was back, all his clothes new, and he had already sent her five dollars. When Silver Flower asked where it had all come from he said, "Don't ask that," and so she didn't ask again but spent the money on rice and a change of clothing for the children.

When the people of the village noticed Lucky's children with new clothes and reflected how long it was since Silver Flower had been to anyone's house for a loan of rice, they were certain that Lucky had done something serious this time. Anyone who was missing some money or an ox suspected it was Lucky's doing.

In the first month of the new year they buried one of the rich city gentry, and Myriad Wang received an announcement of the funeral. He went into the city to join the mourners, and when he heard the hired musicians singing at the funeral feast he thought one of them sounded like Lucky. As the banquet was nearing its close the two musicians came around collecting from the guests, and Myriad saw that Lucky was one of them. Lucky saw Myriad and hurriedly turned his face away.

When the funeral was over each made his way home. Lucky had no sense that he had done anything bad, he had just been earning a few dollars, but Myriad was feeling that this scoundrel Lucky must be got out of the way at all costs.

That evening Myriad called together all of the Wang family who had any standing whatsoever and addressed them: "This— this Lucky has lived long enough! The latest is that he's working in the town as hired musician at funerals. If people out-side the clan hear of this, how will we ever be able to face them again? A common ancestral line, a common burial ground—if we of the Wang clan get this muck smeared on us, none of us will ever be clean again! Think, all of you, think what the—what the devil we are going to do about this!" The people of the district were always very concerned to keep their family escutcheons unspotted. Hired funeral musicians they called "bastard" or "son-of-a-turtle," and what Myriad said got them all worked up—some of them shouted "Beat him to death!"; some of them shouted "Bury him alive!"

You can't keep a thing secret where a lot of people are involved. One way or another the woman next door got to hear of it and passed the word to Silver Flower. Silver Flower told Lucky at once, and he ran off in the night.

There was no word from him then for another seven or eight years, and Silver Flower just carried on looking after the two youngsters. When the elder boy was fourteen he was set to tending cows for a neighbor, and the other children often mocked him as "turtle-spawn."

Less than a year after Lucky left, the Japs occupied the area. People urged Silver Flower: "Why don't you find another man? What hope have you of Lucky ever doing you any good?" But she wouldn't take their advice. Then they would say, "Is there no other man in the world that you have to stick to that thieving bastard of a gambler?"

"You don't know the whole story," she would reply. "He's not a bad man, that husband of mine."

When the area cadres had found out all the details of Lucky's past they went along for a chat with him, taking with them the chairman of the Farmers' Committee. "We've settled up with Myriad Wang," said the chairman. "Wherever he has forcibly taken possession of someone else's goods he has had to restore them, but you are one of the ones he has swindled, and you haven't 'turned over.' Our village cadre talked this over yesterday with the comrade from Area, and they propose to give you an acre of the temple land to farm. What do you think about it?"

Lucky jumped to his feet and cried, "None of that matters! I want nothing else but to get Myriad Wang in front of everybody, make an accusation against him and clear myself, and get rid of all this damned rage I've been bottling up." The area cadre and the Agricultural Committee chairman agreed to this.

In the evening, using the time usually devoted to the winter evening school, the chairman of the Farmers' Committee announced the purpose of the meeting. Some of the old diehards were very displeased about holding a meeting with a cad, but it didn't concern Lucky whether they wanted it or whether they didn't. He started off: "Gentlemen, I've been back half a month now, and I've been very keen to find someone to have a good chat with, but everyone has been avoiding me like the plague because I'm a cad—as soon as I stop somewhere on the street everybody moves to the other side. My apologies! Tonight I have come to ask advice from the head of my clan, Myriad Wang, and I would like all of you to stand by and listen. Don't be afraid! The lousy old system of things has been over and done with for a long time now in the liberated areas, and although this area is only newly liberated it'll soon be the same here. Mr. Myriad, sir! I'll still call you 'sir'! I'm afraid that now this cad of a nephew of yours has come back you'll have to put up with a little embarrassment from him. Now this account of ours is very clear and straightforward; what I owed you was thirty dollars and a little over two hundredweight of grain. What I've paid you is a house, two-thirds of an acre of land, and five years' labor as a hired hand. But you needn't be afraid, I'm not trying to get you for all this. I just have a great desire to hear you say whether I really am at bottom a good man or a bad man?"

Myriad sat for a while in uneasy silence, looked at the crowd, looked at Lucky, and said, "This is spite, nothing else. If you've got anything against me let's have it straight out. I've made amends to all the people I've taken things from in the past. There's only you left. Can't we clear things up? Though I've no land left, they've let me keep my shop."

"Uncle," said Lucky, "this is not spite. I don't want anything back from you, I only want you to say what sort of a man I am! If you won't say I'll tell you myself: when I was small no one could call me bad. Right up until I was twenty-seven, I never did a rotten thing."

"That's right! That's true enough!" said many of the older people at this.

Lucky went on, "It was after then I went to the bad. Gambling, thieving, singing at funerals as a 'bastard,' I've done every shameless thing a man can do. I know it was wrong, there's nothing glorious about these things. I've already been all through a self-examination, elsewhere. But . . . what you used to mean by a good man in those days was completely beyond me. On the plan you'd laid down for me, I worked for you as a hired hand for half the year, then on top of that I farmed my own two-thirds of an acre; at the end of the year we reckoned up, I gave you my wages and the crop from my land to pay off the interest, and my wife and children went hungry. Year after year, and the end was the grave. Now just think, why should I want to be a 'good man' on that pattern? I gambled because I was hungry, I stole because I was hungry, I sang at funerals as a 'bastard' because I was hungry. And why was I hungry? Because my mother needed a coffin from you and ten dollars worth of odd things. For fear of not being able to pay you off I worked five years as a laborer, but it didn't make up for what I owed, so in the end I handed my two-thirds of an acre over to you—and that's when I really went hungry! I began going to the bad when I was twenty-eight. For six years I led a rotten life, and which of you can count all the floggings, the cursings, the tears, the hunger? Right up to this year everyone is still saying I'm a bad lot—you avoid me on the street, you call my children "turtle-spawn"—uncle, this is what your grace and favor have done for me. Fortunately, I managed to prevent your burying me alive. I ran off to Liao county to beg, and I went on gambling and stealing there. It was only because the Japs came and people didn't bother about music at their funerals that I didn't sing as a bastard again. Then later the district became an Eighth Route Army base against the Japanese, and the Resistance government reformed all the vagrants, idlers, and petty thieves, and put me in with a refugee group to reclaim hill land. From that time on I had land to farm again, a house to live in, food to eat—the only thing was I didn't dare come back to my wife and children in their distress! I haven't made a fortune in these seven or eight years, but I've bought an ox and piled up a cellarful of grain and another big cellarful of potatoes. I really came back this time to take my wife and my children back there. I had no idea of settling my account with you. But then after I got back I saw that nobody dared say a word to me. I don't know whether they were scared I would rob them or afraid of being contaminated with my corruption. I didn't like the idea of going off like this under a cloud of mystery, and God knows how long it would go on for, this rotten name I've had, and so I thought of asking you to explain it all to everyone here, uncle. Let's see what sort of a man I really am after all. I went to the bad—all right, you tell me then, who should take the responsibility?"

CHANG T'IEN-I
(1906–   )

Chang T'ien-i was the most brilliant and powerful short story writer of the thirties. During a decade remarkable for the abundance of talented story writers, none could match him for the economy of his comic art, the depth and range of his satiric representation. Gentry, bourgeoisie, and proletariat alike are grist to his satiric mill, and his grasp of the essential meanness of the human soul and of the deep animosity existing between different social classes is astonishing. His world, therefore, is filled with snobs and malcontents, abject underlings and ambitious schemers intent on getting ahead, and every kind of oppressor abusing his power and position to inflict pain on his inferiors out of sheer malice. Though a Marxist and a member of the League of the Leftwing Writers, Chang T'ien-i was too much of a realist fascinated by the ugly social phenomena of his time to observe in his best stories the required leftist formulas of protest and rebellion.

Though his birthplace was Nanking, Chang T'ien-i is the scion of an eminent Hunanese family of scholar-officials. His mother was a noted poet and one of his sisters became in time a famous educator on good terms with the Nationalist government, but Chang stuck to his nonconformist path and after middle school supported himself as a government clerk, army officer, reporter, and schoolteacher. His varied experience in these jobs must have given him special insights into many walks of Chinese life.

"The Bulwark" (*Ti-chu*, 1936) and "Midautumn Festival" (*Chung-ch'iu*, 1936), the two stories in this anthology, are among Chang's best. The former depicts with robust humor the old-style, hypocritical Confucian gentleman earlier satirized by Lu Hsün in "Soap." Huang Yi-an, the hero of "The Bulwark," is like Ssu-ming of "Soap" a hypocrite with a lascivious turn of mind, pretending to moral rectitude and complacently disapproving of modern tendencies. But whereas Ssu-ming is merely aroused by a beggar girl in her imagined state of nudity, Huang Yi-an is arbitrarily disposing of his daughter's future for his own advancement. He is thus more of a sadist, and the undertones of cruelty in the story are characteristically Chang T'ien-i's own. As applied to Huang, the Chinese title *Ti-chu*—a proverbial metaphorical term for an upholder of orthodoxy and morals in a depraved age—is clearly ironical.

"Midautumn Festival," about a landlord's deliberate postponement of dinner so as to humiliate his hungry brother-in-law, is almost without a parallel in modern Chinese fiction for its haunting evocation of cruelty and abjectness. Chang T'ien-i takes full command of the dramatic situation occasioned by the postponement of the festival dinner and squeezes from it every possible drop of irony without extending overt sympathy to the poor relative.

During the thirties Chang T'ien-i also wrote four novels, of which the third, *The Strange Knight of Shanghai* (*Yang-ching-pang ch'i-hsia*, 1936), is immensely comic and deserves an English translation. Author of many pre-1949 stories about children in either realistic or fantastic settings, Chang has specialized in juvenile literature since the early fifties.

C.T.H.

The Bulwark

by Chang T'ien-i

Translated by Nathan K. Mao

Lying sideways on the bed in his cabin, the venerable Mr. Huang Yi-an was reading a book. His right leg was on top of his left, the toes spread wide apart. His left hand was rubbing at the athlete's foot between his toes.

The characters in the book were rippling like shadows in water.

"Why isn't she back yet? That stupid girl!"

Over the rims of his reading glasses he stared at the cabin door. The first class deck was noisy; a few waiters were shouting excitedly: "Gentlemen, watch out, watch out."

Somewhere people were laughing boisterously and talking about women, and from time to time the *tzu, tzu, tzu* sounds of opium smoking could be heard. The opium combined with the fishy stench of the ship produced a peculiar odor. "Damn it all," he cursed.

He sniffed at the fingers of his left hand, then drew on his socks and walked to the door on his "Double Bridge" brand slippers.

This time he must call Mei-tzu[1] back in! A decent man couldn't let his young daughter run wild. How would it look to others?

Impatiently he pulled open his cabin door about half a foot. With the look of a man facing a duel to the death, he thrust his long face out to appraise the situation. His gray eyes, like those of a dead fish, peered into the lobby around the rims of his glasses.

His daughter was chatting with a fat woman, in exactly the same position as before. Her blouse still unbuttoned, the fat woman was nonchalantly feeding her baby with a fleshy breast. Her face wore a tiny smile as if her ample breasts were a legitimate source of pride.

The old man by the door now knew the woman had switched from one breast to the other. He had taken a peep twice before but seen only her right breast. So they were both equally fair!

A few men were laughing and muttering to one another, occasionally eyeing the women; a young man sitting on a bunk never took his eyes off the woman. His mouth was wide open, as if he wanted a mouthful from the nursing woman.

The only exception was a middle-aged man lying on a bed. He was holding a little book to read in one hand and, legs crossed, scratching his crotch with the other.

"The guy must have jock itch," Huang Yi-an thought to himself. "Huh. The swine! And that shameless fat woman should be arrested by the police!"

He closed the door, sucked in his stomach, and returned to his bunk.

The ship splashed through the water. Below, the engine room was making such thumping noises that a person felt as if his heart were being pounded on.

Someone laughed loudly; the noise seemed to have come from the next room, and was followed by more *tzu, tzu, tzu* sounds.

[1] Miss Huang's formal name is not given in the story. She is referred to by her father as "Chen-mei-tzu," literally "Virtuous Maiden"; in the translation "Mei-tzu" ("Maiden") is used for convenience.

The old man suddenly thought of the guy with the jock itch. What had he been reading? Why was he so absorbed in his reading? No doubt about it, must be pornography. Even the cover looked like it.

With renewed misgivings he pulled the door open. Scowling, he stuck his head out through the crack between the half-open door and the door-post, looking like a prisoner with his head locked in a cangue.

When his daughter accidentally met his eyes, he immediately signaled with his chin to return her to the cabin.

His face long, he asked her: "Who was the woman you were talking to?"

"A schoolmate's sister-in-law."

"Don't talk to her! Do you understand? She can't be a good woman. One must be careful in one's associations. One must! Don't you see?"

Mei-tzu shot a glance at him and sighed.

He sat on the bunk and removed his shoes. Thrusting out his lower lip, he intoned: "It's not that I enjoy criticizing you. As your father, naturally I want my daughter to be good, above criticism by others. You see, if that woman had any sense of decency, how could she unbutton her blouse in front of all those men? If no distinction is drawn between men and women, are they not like animals? However the world changes, 'propriety' must be observed. And that's the way it should be."

He took off his socks. His right middle finger rubbed between his toes and then he smelled his finger. "For example, even in the privacy of one's own room one still must behave properly, not to speak of . . ."

A loud voice from the next room interrupted him. "Oh, yeah, that woman's called 'Three Open Gates.' Her mouth is good . . ." A fit of giggles seeped through the thin wall.

A tremor went through Huang Yi-an. Holding his chest high, he pretended not to have heard anything. He cleared his throat, pulled a long face, and resumed his talk. From the corners of his eyes he watched his daughter closely as if

guarding a treasure. He felt all those degenerates should be locked up! "That's it. I should submit a proposal to the provincial governor. I'm sure it would be accepted," he thought to himself.

The young lady sat quietly, with her right elbow resting on her leg while her hand supported her chin. She stared at the porthole as if lost in thought or reverie.

In contrast with the river, which resembled rice-flour in color, the paddy-fields on the shore were so temptingly green that one might wish nothing better than to take a nap there. In the sky the floating white clouds had blended into one mass with the distant hills. One could almost touch them merely by stretching out a hand.

Inside the ship, however, only Huang Yi-an's deep, hoarse voice could be heard, sometimes mixed with a noise of sniffing.

He was talking about himself. Whenever he lectured his children, he used himself as an example. He put down his well-rubbed left foot and began to rub his right. After kneading his fingers for a while he rattled on. The reason he had recognition in his home town was not because he was rich, not because his family received annually three hundred piculs of grain as rental, not because he was a *hsiu-ts'ai*[2] and had studied law; it was because his moral conduct was different from others'. "Humph! The new trend, the new trend! Fortunately they have finally come to realize their folly and understand that managing a family, running a nation, and bringing peace to the world are greatly dependent upon traditional learning. Even Magistrate Yao wants me to lecture on the classics. You can see from that, can't you? I only want you to take after me a little bit; if only you wouldn't be influenced by fads, then I'd be content. I don't want you to become a sage. I just . . ."

The rest of his words were drowned out by laughter from the next room. He knit his eyebrows. With his finger suspended in the air half-way to his nose, he continued: "Mei-tzu, did you hear what I just said?"

Startled, Mei-tzu turned toward him, as if just

[2] See footnote 10 to "Horse-bell Melons," p. 107.

realizing that her father had been speaking to her.

The old man heaved a sigh and shook his head. "It's best not to say anything; there's no one listening anyway. Of late, officials seem to be treading the right path; they even invited me to give lectures on morals. But my own flesh and blood simply ignores me."

He sniffed his finger again. With his eyes closed, he drew a deep breath as if he wanted to enjoy to the full the pleasure of the moment, so that he wouldn't be troubled by unpleasant thoughts. A moment later, unable to remain quiet, he continued: "You're sixteen already, and you don't seem to know a thing. All you have to do is ask your mother. She and I have been together for more than thirty years, and we have never had one flippant conversation. Come to think of it, your mother has never appeared before strange men. Propriety is the basis of human conduct, and this is especially true for women. Do you understand?"

Exhaling, he leaned against the wall and picked up his book. "Pour me a cup of tea." Without lifting his eyes, he moistened his fingertips and leisurely turned the pages. As he took the cup from her, he looked at her face and felt a ticklish sensation in his heart. His child, after all, was quite pretty; he was certain that the wedding plans he had in mind for her would work out and that thenceforward he would be a relative of Commissioner Yi. Like a connoisseur he sipped his tea and smacked his lips. In a much softened tone he said to her: "Mei-tzu, let me tell you something. I don't mean to ask you to inherit all my morals. Yet one must . . . Oh, yes, one must . . . if only . . ."

He stopped for a moment. Inching his body forward a bit, he then told his daughter confidently that if she could pay attention to proper behavior, even generals and ministers would be interested in her and ask for her hand in marriage.

After saying all this, he felt somewhat relieved and leaned back more comfortably against the wall. Though his eyes were fixed on his book, he could not concentrate. His thoughts drifted to the good days ahead of him and he felt buoyant with expectations.

The girl was still sitting quietly, casting her gaze at the sky outside the window as if she were determined to seek illumination from the outside world.

"Didn't you bring any books with you?" he asked.

She raised a guilt-ridden face and shook her head. Then, apparently wanting to prove that she also had some serious work to do, she picked an unfinished sweater from a small basket and began to knit. From time to time she seemed to be in a trance. She stared straight ahead, as if listening to the engine and to the splashing of the water, while at the same time she appeared equally attentive to the din of human noises.

Huang Yi-an cleared his throat and swallowed. His hands scratched frantically between his toes; he let the book lie on his stomach. The wrinkle on his left cheek pulled his mouth sideways, and a glistening drop of saliva hung on his lower lip.

The noises from the next room became increasingly louder, as if they were deliberately meant to be heard by the people in this room. "Then you must be greater than Hsiao Chiang-ping!"[3] "What? What? I only said . . ." After moments of babbling, there was a loud laugh.

The old man in Cabin Number Seven pulled a long face and quit rubbing his toes. "Damn it," he said to himself. "Who are those ruffians? Huh, 'Hsiao Chiang-ping' indeed!" He stiffened his neck and assumed a dignified pose. He didn't stir except to watch his daughter from the corners of his eyes. Thank God, she was ignorant of what they were saying.

Somewhere a mosquito hummed with a quivering rhythm. Meanwhile, the *gung, gung, gung* sounds from the ship were keeping time with the vibration of the mosquito's hum.

Precisely at that moment, someone uttered "Oooh" in the next room. It seemed to be a woman's scream, soon followed by giggles, as if a woman's laughter had been muffled.

Huang Yi-an tensed, feeling as if a soft hair-

---

[3] A fictitious character known for sexual prowess.

brush were brushing his insides. He straightened his legs, then bent them again. He sighed and sucked in a breath between his flushed cheeks, while eyeing his daughter.

The sixteen-year-old concentrated on knitting her sweater. Her hands moved deftly, showing no interest in the strange chatter of the next room. Apparently she had neither heard nor seen that type of thing in school.

"Yet that woman is something else . . ." He again thought of those thick nipples and imagined what it would be like to touch them, how they would swell to his touch. Now he was unsure whether he should report her to the police, although he was entitled to do so.

He still had the book and pretended to concentrate, moistening his fingertips with saliva and flipping the pages. But the long characters in the Sung calligraphic style all looked ugly to him, and none made any sense at all.

A current of warmth flowed through his body and his toes itched. He stole a glance at his daughter and, after clearing his throat, looked at her again.

This time the father's and daughter's glances met. He said sullenly: "If you're knitting, then put your heart in it. Why look around?"

Outside a waiter was yelling something at the top of his lungs, almost drowning out other human noises. Someone in a thin voice was humming a tune, inviting one to visualize the seductive way the singer must be twisting her body. But in a moment this sexy tune was cut short by a coarse voice. Apparently there was quarrel over there. Maybe it was a squabble over women. Oh, what a God-forsaken place! Never a moment of peace on the ship.

No sooner had the quarrel ended then the ship's whistle blew, interminably. The blast seemed to be an outburst of long-suppressed lust suddenly coming into the open. The noise entered his head and ran through his body, making him shake all over. His ears rang with the noise long afterward.

His eyes half closed, and feeling vexed, he grunted like a frog caged in an urn. With his mind distracted, he became all the more sensitive to the rocking of the ship. From next door came more *tzu, tzu, tzu* sounds of opium smoking. And the noises came in such intensity that one couldn't help suspecting that someone was gasping for breath while being held down.

Casually, he glanced at his daughter out of the corner of his eye. Maybe this young girl knew everything; perhaps it was only because she was in the presence of her father that she seemed so innocent. There was a sudden tightening in his chest. He glared at her unrelentingly.

The noises from the next room increased in volume. Certainly the people in the room must be worldly wise, with some social standing; they must also have liked certain books. A while back they had talked about a "monk" who could be large and small at will and made references to a dildo[4] made of precious metal. Then the man with the hoarse voice spoke in a carefree tone: "This book really has much to offer. It represents experience. No mistake about it. The woman I met was an expert at 'blowing the flute.' "[5] Another man in a deep voice corrected the first speaker's use of the technical term and said it was not called "blowing the flute." Then an argument ensued.

On this side Huang Yi-an pursed his lips. "Bullshit! They haven't even read the book. What nonsense!" he muttered to himself. "But that woman must be the one they called 'Three Open Gates.' "

After gazing at the wall for a second or so, he looked again at Mei-tzu. Since she was sitting by the porthole, what he saw was a bent silhouette, yet he imagined that her face was flushing, her eyes glistening and moist.

"Huh-hnnh," he coughed loudly, deliberately pulling a long face. Mei-tzu was so startled by the noise that her body trembled. From what he had observed of his daughter, the old man deduced that she must be guilty. Feeling suddenly sick to his stomach, breathing unevenly, his eyes nearly popping out, and glaring at Mei-tzu with mounting rage, he decided to give her a thorough lecture and a good scolding. Yet he was tongue-tied.

"Mei-tzu! . . . You! *Hmm,* damn it all. This, this

[4] The Chinese original is *t'o-tzu,* literally a device to "hold things up."   [5] Conventional Chinese euphemism for oral sex.

. . . I'm telling you . . . Don't you remember? A person, a person . . ."

He opened and shut his mouth, his sparse moustache twitching a few times, and after he coughed once, the words burst forth from his throat: "A person shouldn't listen to things that aren't proper."

The daughter gaped at him, her eyes wide open.

"Don't just look at me!" The old man forced these words out from between his teeth. "A person must constantly search his soul and see if he has done anything improper. If he listens to the improper, he himself will become improper. Don't you see?"

Mei-tzu was speechless with amazement: "What? What did I listen to?"

"What did you listen to? The next room, the next room. I think you . . ."

The father stared at his daughter for a while before heaving a long, despairing sigh. He then looked at his own feet, at the ceiling and, in spite of himself, at her again.

She was still staring at him. As if he had been offended, he said fretfully: "If you didn't, you didn't. If you have faults, you must correct them; if you don't, you should try to be better. Why don't you resume your work?"

Mei-tzu dropped her eyelids, and he seriously attempted to read his book. He moistened his fingers with lots of saliva and noisily leafed through the pages. His fingers were shaky and tasted of salt.

The ribald chatter, however, continued to penetrate the gray wall of his cabin undiluted. A man whose voice resembled a martial character's in the Peking opera began to extol the "virtues" of a certain middle-aged woman, but he was soon interrupted by laughter.

Huang Yi-an scowled. Damn it! Who is that woman, and what happens to her later? he wondered.

He lowered his book just enough to glance at his daughter's face. The light outside the window reflecting on her hair made it shine like silver threads.

The men in the next room became more explicit in their descriptions of women, although their expressions, compared with the crude ones of field hands, were more restrained. The talk captivated him, in spite of himself.

"Damnation!" Huang Yi-an's upper lip quivered. Those people were obviously well educated, for their conversational art was so clever that it made such racy talk irresistible.

Sometimes the words came haltingly, like broken threads, and other times in rapid succession like cricket sounds. Once in a while a word or two had him spellbound. Meanwhile he sighed and glared at his daughter. He was warm and sweating. He raised his book high to cover his face, worried that his flushed cheeks might reveal his impropriety to his daughter.

The middle-aged woman they had just referred to—what had happened to her later? he wondered. How could they have the story without an ending? Those idiots should be shot! Why must all this happen when he was traveling with his daughter?

He had thought the second class section might be too unruly, with people from all quarters of life; yet, he found the first class section equally disorderly. Maybe the people were just making up tall tales. Otherwise, why wouldn't there be conclusions to their stories?

He hadn't finished a single page; he was shaking. Biting his lower lip, he tried hard not to drool. He was seriously thinking of jumping out of his bunk, to run a few steps, skip a few times, and roll on the floor. Then he mused that if he were going to roll on the floor, he might as well do it on the bunk. "*Ai,* even if sages Chu Hsi and Ch'eng Yi[6] were alive today, they too would, *ai,* feel like this."

Angrily he threw his book aside. Wrinkles to the left of his chin twitched, as he chewed at his lip. His legs bent and his hands rubbed between his toes frantically, as if rushing to finish some

---

[6] Famous commentators of the Sung Dynasty noted for their exposition of the classics, and for their advocacy of moral propriety.

task. He worked so hard that he didn't have time to sniff his fingers.

Saliva fell from his lips. He glared at his daughter protectively, afraid that the dropping saliva might give her improper or indecent thoughts. Unconsciously he hummed a tune; a spicy feeling in his throat made him feel good. The young girl cast a glance at him. It was apparent that his excitement had aroused her attention. Then, as if wanting to avoid his stern gaze, she turned to look at the wall.

Suddenly Huang Yi-an ceased his hand movements. "Ridiculous! This is simply ridiculous! All right, I'll just go and take a look." Very quickly he removed his glasses, put on his socks, and felt for his shoes on the floor, legs dangling.

As he opened the door, he assumed a dignified manner and walked with measured steps. His protruding stomach and his hunched back formed his body into an S shape. His tightly shut mouth gave him an air of great determination. He decided to barge into Cabin Number Six with a stern look to stop that immoral chatter. Those idiots should be hanged, couldn't they see he had his sixteen-year-old daughter in the next room? If they had some education, they ought to have heard the name of Huang Yi-an—a Neo-Confucianist, a bulwark in a period of tumult, a relative of Commissioner Yi.

He walked with a limp, pain jabbing him between the toes.

"If they don't heed my warning," he thought, gritting his teeth, "then I can't afford to be polite. I have to report them to the police, charge them with the corruption of morals. And that's a serious offense!"

He concentrated all his strength on his right hand, wanting to pull open the door to Number Six with force. His eyes were sparkling. One could tell at a glance from the deep horizontal creases on his forehead that he had inherited the moralist tradition of the sages of the Southern Sung period.

A waiter with a load on his back walked toward him, muttering: "Gentlemen, watch out, watch out." But Huang stood by the door of Cabin Number Six in a dignified pose and did not stir.

The waiter's load brushed against him and knocked his head against the wall, thus straightening his S shaped body. "Hey, you, you!" Huang stared at the waiter's back and suddenly shivered. The crude waiter made him think of these low-class morons—as if a newly healed wound had been torn open. Now everything seemed to be on the right track, except that lowly herd, he thought. He had always guarded himself against them, wary of them. Gritting his teeth, he yelled: "I'll have you hanged!"

He felt that was the cleanest way to handle the likes of him. They did not deserve his edification; only the educated class was worthy of his attention. He watched the waiter disappear around a corner; he then resumed his original dignified posture, thrusting his stomach out.

Gently he touched his forehead and knit his eyebrows. It seemed as if he were on his way to his disciples to recount to them how these scoundrels had mistreated him.

The door creaked. Presently he removed his hand from his forehead and cleared his throat, apparently having decided that since the educated class were easier to deal with, he might as well vent his full indignation on them. "You must all be severely penalized! I'll send you to a magistrate's court and you'll get a flogging. Humph, what do you think you are?" he told himself silently.

Suddenly the door opened and a dark shadow leered at him from the crack. Startled, Huang Yi-an moved his left leg back, so that his two feet were positioned like a capital V. A strong opium smell penetrated his nostrils, sending him into a dream-like state. His body seemed to be floating in the clouds. The merry noises seemed amplified. As he stepped inside the door, the noises subsided, as if swept away by a mild breeze.

Sunlight filtered through the porthole into the smoke-filled room, which reflected a streak of white light. None of the faces was distinguishable except for the one standing by the door facing the light, glaring at him with bloodshot eyes.

On the table were displayed some wine cups and a mound of cooked food wrapped in lotus leaves. A fanciful thought flashed through his mind—he was almost sure that there must be an ox organ[7] cooked in cassia bark somewhere.

On the bunk to the right a bald man was smoking opium, and reclining beside him was a big fellow watching listlessly. Amid the opium smoke the two stared at Huang spitefully. Their eyebrows were knit tight, as if they resented the glare of the opium lamp.

Huang Yi-an raised his head and surveyed the room. Nonchalantly he pursed his lips, cleared his throat, and then slowly opened his mouth.

The big fellow sat up on his bunk. Suddenly he raised his eyebrows in excitement and called out happily: "So, it's you, Yi-weng!"[8]

After a moment of silence, the one standing by the door gently closed it, but it produced a loud noise nonetheless.

Huang Yi-an was stupefied. He narrowed his eyes and then opened them wide in order to size up the occupants of this room. He felt his insides sinking and his skin itching. He did not know whether he was pleased or disappointed at this sudden turn of events.

"What?" he murmured, "Oh, it's President Hsiao of the Society."

"Ha, ha, what a coincidence, what a happy coincidence indeed!"

President Hsiao's large frame glided off the bunk; the light of the opium lamp flickered. With studied casualness he greeted his friend before loudly introducing him to everyone in the room.

It turned out that all those characters were members of the Confucian Classics Study Society. In the manner of a shopkeeper boasting of his wares to customers, the President, with a radiant look and choosing his words carefully, proceeded to introduce Huang to his members: "He too is a classics expert, very well known in his home town." Almost immediately after he broke into somewhat mystifying laughter.

Huang stared at the wall for a moment, licked his lips, and wanted to tell them that District Magistrate Yao had invited him to interpret the classics, and that the provincial governor was also an admirer of his. Moreover, he thought he would tell them these things in a loud voice. He cleared his throat. But just then his friend made him sit down and said: "Since we all have similar interests, we should feel free to say whatever strikes our fancy. Ha, ha, ha, but, by the way, how did you know I was here?"

After scanning the people in the room, Huang forced a smile on his face. Sitting on the edge of a chair and obsequiously inclining his body toward Hsiao, he stammered: "I . . . well, originally I didn't know President Hsiao was here."

"Wonderful, wonderful. Really, it's been more than a year since I saw you," the President said, and cackled like a hen.

The rest of the people seemed to know that the newcomer was not too important, for they soon resumed sipping their wine. One loudly smacked his lips, as if to arouse the others' appetite for the wine. They continued their chitchat without paying attention to Yi-weng.

In a friendly and yet distant tone President Hsiao asked Huang how he had been, and if anything new had happened in his home town. At the same time he was as much concerned with what the others were saying. From time to time he cut into their conversation, laughing freely.

"Oh, that's right," he said, his eyebrows raised, "Yi Lao-erh[9] told me that you're going to be a relative of Yi Lao-wu."[10]

Blushing, Huang replied, "Yes, yes. As a matter of fact, I'm taking my daughter to him to let him have a look. In the next room . . ."

"What a coincidence . . . What? You heard about the whore who continued to receive customers at sixty? Ha, ha, ha, oooh, very nice. You

---

[7] Believed to have aphrodisiac effects for males.

[8] *Weng* is a polite form of address among middle-aged men of some social eminence.

[9] Literally, "Lao" ("old") "erh" ("second") is the second son or daughter in the family. In the present context, it is a reference to the older brother of Commissioner Yi.

[10] Lao-wu ("old fifth") is Commissioner Yi, the fifth in the family. By referring to Commissioner Yi as "Lao-wu" in the familiar form of address, President Hsiao wanted to impress upon Huang Yi-an his close relationship with the Commissioner and his family.

heard what we said? Is that how you knew I was here? Right?"

"I . . ." Huang lowered his voice, looking at the wall again. "My daughter is on the other side. I'm afraid that she might overhear. This is, well, a little inconvenient."

Unexpectedly President Hsiao burst out laughing. He slapped Huang on the shoulder and the latter almost fell at the impact. *"Ai-ya,* Yi-weng, you're too much!" He was laughing hard, almost breathless. Rubbing his eyes, he said: "We're all friends. Why such worries? Really, my friend, you've no need to worry. To give you an example, the magicians' public performances are really for the benefit of the audience; they don't play the same tricks on their own partners, do they? So why play games among ourselves? Am I right? Ha, ha, ha."

Huang joined in the laughter. Mouth twitching and looking at the wall, he wondered what his daughter was doing. He tried hard to make himself look as natural and as carefree as possible. Still, he couldn't help feeling sorry for himself for having brought Mei-tzu along on the trip.

Hsiao turned toward the others and, with the approval of his roommates, he stood before Huang. Holding in his stomach, he declared: "I'm always a blunt person and I like to tell it like it is. That year—" he turned in another direction: "What? Oh, that's right. Everyone called her 'pisspool.' Oh, oh, that type, that type is . . ." He made a funny face, patted Huang's shoulder with his right hand, and continued: "That type—ah, Yi-weng is the expert among us. Ha, ha, ha."

Huang was embarrassed, sweat visible on the tip of his nose. He stammered: "I— It's not true."

"Come, don't be polite. Let's have it. You're the expert in this area. I know you, you've tried all the exotic kinds. Ha, ha."

After this endorsement by the president, members clamored to hear about Huang's most exciting sexual escapades and his special amatory talents. They offered him a drink in ritual acceptance of him as a friend. One man announced that since they had similar interests they should be friends immediately.

Their president laughed heartily in agreement and clapped his hands hysterically.

As if someone were tickling him, Huang Yi-an tittered, his eyes forming two slits, his face compressed, and his body bent forward in the shape of a big dried-up shrimp.

He played coy for ten seconds or so. Giving President Hsiao a knowing look, he nodded a few times and whispered: "All right, all right, I'll tell you all." Then he looked around the room and wiped the saliva off his chin. His upper lip twitching, unsteadily he walked on his toes to the door. Then turning his head around, shrugging his shoulder, eyes slanting, he again whispered with a smile: "Wait for me a minute. Be patient."

Once outside the door, he thrust out his stomach. A limp feeling pervaded him; he felt he was floating in the clouds. His excitement was akin to that of an explorer finding some lost treasure. Lifting his head high he glared at the waiters milling around in the lobby and uttered a contemptuous "Humph." Vaguely, he felt he had become more resourceful and had much greater confidence in his ability to handle these low-class morons.

With a steady hand he pulled open the door to Cabin Number Seven. His face long, his eyebrows knitted, he said to his daughter: "Mei-tzu, go to your schoolmate's— Go to the woman and spend some time with her."

The girl looked at him in surprise. She seemed to be debating whether to take her knitting with her. A moment later she sighed and left the room empty handed.

His gaze followed her motion, and stood to watch her for a while. After taking one angry look at a waiter, he turned his eyes on the middle-aged man lying on the bed. That man was still holding a book with one hand and scratching his crotch with the other. Finally, he glanced sideways at the bosom of the fat woman. The woman had buttoned up her blouse and was playing with her child. When she saw Mei-tzu, she greeted her with a smile. On one of her ample cheeks a dimple emerged.

Huang Yi-an felt he had lost something; then

he said to himself calmly: "*Mm*, it's better this way, otherwise it would be . . ."

A smile flashed on his face. He was certain that woman was a lush, since she had a flushed face, bloodshot eyes, and a sleepy look.

A military policeman walked by him. He quickly put on a stern countenance and smacked his lips.

With square steps he walked toward Cabin Number Six. His chin raised high, he looked at the end of the passageway.

Then he gently pushed open the cabin door. Human noises welled up; then the door was shut.

After two minutes a tittering laughter burst out.

Midautumn Festival

by Chang T'ien-i

Translated by Ronald Miao

The wine and dishes were already neatly arranged on the table.

K'uei Ta-niang[1] shifted a chair slightly. In an earnest voice she called to the guest: "Third Uncle, please sit over here!"

Third Uncle crinkled his thin, jaundiced face into a smile. His tongue flickered over parched lips, but his body betrayed not the slightest movement. He merely cast a wistful glance at K'uei Ta-yeh.[2]

K'uei Ta-yeh had no intention of sitting down to the feast. He was strenuously lecturing on ingratitude:

"I don't get it . . . I really don't! The human mind these days is really odd! It used to be that tenant farmers acted like tenant farmers. They showed respect for the landlord . . . didn't dare fart! At New Year's they'd send over chicken and meats . . . at least there they showed proper manners! But look at how they treat us now! Here we're celebrating our festival and they don't give a damn! Very few send gifts, and only a few come to pay their respects. None of them stop to think where their food comes from!"

"Yes . . . yes . . ." Third Uncle stared foolishly at his host and gave a faint nod. K'uei sighed and stood up, his short, dwarfish body like an upright jar. Third Uncle felt a little easier. His sight remained riveted on his host, as if to draw him to the table.

The eight-year-old young master of the house allowed his body to lean forward. Surreptitiously, his eyes swept over the plates of food. K'uei Ta-yeh, however, paid no heed to any of this. He continued to tell everyone just how strange the world had become. Leaning his face toward Third Uncle, he compared the world to a house: the walls were collapsing yet there was no one to make repairs.

"It's really outrageous. When a house leaks, for example . . . by the way, Third Uncle, when you first built your house, why didn't you open more windows to the south?"

Third Uncle couldn't imagine why anyone would ask such a question. He ventured: "What? Yes, of course." Now this house had originally belonged to Third Uncle. He then mortgaged it to K'uei for one hundred dollars. When the time came he was unable to redeem it, and so it reverted officially to his younger sister's husband. The incident was eight years in the past.

Third Uncle was the kind of person who had no interest in things of the past: right now he gazed expectantly at what they were going to eat. His empty stomach rumbled. He hadn't the slightest idea of how to respond to K'uei Ta-yeh's question. Luckily, the latter dropped the subject. After some further grumbling, he concluded:

"I don't mind telling you, Third Uncle, that there are a lot of things I don't find pleasing!"

"Yes, yes." Third Uncle's dry, wrinkled face smiled politely as he sighed in sympathy. At that, K'uei shifted his round body near the table.

"Well, at last," Third Uncle thought, drawing a

[1] Title for the wife in the household. [2] Lit. "Great Master," the head of the household, here used as a proper name.

deep breath. His little nephew lunged forward, quickly seizing a chair. The boy's eyes were fixed on the food; his hands gripped the edges of the table. Third Uncle also considered sitting down. His eyes grew larger, his knees shook slightly. As the steamy aroma rose to his nostrils, saliva suddenly formed under his tongue.

K'uei Ta-niang stared at him apprehensively. Although she addressed him as Uncle, he was, in fact, a first cousin on her father's side. Now she was afraid that her family might lose face before her husband. She was convinced that when a man was poor he would show it in unbecoming speech and expressions. "Ah, why did you squander a whole family fortune in the first place?" she complained silently.

This Third Uncle had now become a pathetic bachelor, taking temporary quarters upstairs in the eastern part of the city temple. He muddled through his days, sometimes eating and sometimes not. Most people spent Midautumn Festival with their families, but he was an old man all by himself. For seven or eight years he had received no word from his only son, who was off somewhere. Taking pity on him, K'uei Ta-niang took the matter up with her husband. In a manner that was half politeness and half condescension, they had invited Third Uncle to spend the Midautumn Festival with them. Now the woman glanced at her husband, taking note of his attitude by observing his facial expression. Suddenly, with quick steps, he rushed to the child and raised one palm, *slap!*

"This little devil! So big, and so stupid! Grownups haven't come to the table and there you are! Will you starve if you wait a little longer? You, you!"

Slap! Slap!

Third Uncle, the guest, quickly composed himself and stood still. Stealthily he retreated a few steps as if he had no intention of ever sitting down. As he did so, he swallowed back the saliva that had seeped through his lips.

"Such a big boy, and still no manners!" K'uei Ta-niang knit her brows. She dragged the little boy off and at the same time said to her husband, "Really, why make such a fuss? Couldn't we have a peaceful dinner?"

"What? What did you say?"

Third Uncle started to fidget, occasionally shifting his body and waving his right hand in an empty gesture. He wanted to put in a word, but he didn't dare. With a wry face and an imploring look, all he could do was mumble: "Oh, well—"

The sky just then grew as overcast as K'uei Ta-yeh's face. Ash-colored clouds drifted from east to west. The withered leaves in the courtyard, swept up by the wind, were rustling impatiently.

Third Uncle shivered. His spine felt as if glued to a cold plate of steel. After taking a quick look at what was laid on the table, he felt an uncontrollable, crazy urge—he wanted very much to take the pot of warm wine and in one gulp to pour it down his throat.

K'uei Ta-yeh was jumping heatedly up and down, as if he wanted to match heights with Third Uncle. His eyes bulged, and a hail of words poured fast and furious from his mouth.

"Bastard! Bastard! These are terrible times, terrible. What a fine son you've raised! And people say I'm lucky to have two sons. Just look at our eldest. Look how he treats me! Others remember that midautumn is a time of reunion. Our eldest doesn't even come home!" His wife interrupted gently: "His school doesn't let out for the holidays. Why blame him?"

"Why not blame him? He's the one who wanted to enter that damn school in the first place!"

Third Uncle sat down on a chair. His whole body grew lax. Suddenly he felt his stomach contract tightly; then he felt it gradually expand. The dishes of food had ceased to give off steam. Only a gust of air would waft a rich, oily aroma to him. Eyes half closed, he drew in a deep breath: his intestines began to tremble. Suddenly he felt as if some painful event of his life had gripped him, and all he wanted to do was to burst into a loud wail.

The boy had long since controlled his sobs. He clung to his mother's side, chewing on his index finger. Not once did his eyes leave the table. He seemed unaware that he was the cause of his father's furious outburst. Others too would find it hard to believe that K'uei was really angry at his son. Clearly, K'uei Ta-yeh's remarks had now taken a new turn. He began to mutter about things that he was in the habit of repeating every day.

"I work like a cow all year round to earn forty or fifty piculs of grain from rented land. And what do you know, I'm treated just like a cow or a horse! Of course I make money for you people to enjoy. But you at least should show a little conscience." As soon as his eyes fell on Third Uncle, the latter would give a start. Third Uncle straightened up, offering him a quick "Yes, yes."

The host folded his hands behind him and paced back and forth. There was a rasping noise from his mouth, like the sound of wind cutting through withered trees. "The world has changed completely!" With such earnest words did old K'uei warn his family. "If we go on like this, the end will surely come . . . the grain harvest is never enough . . . there is never enough money . . . and man's heart is wicked." At that, he sighed.

The guest, feeling as if he had been unjustly wronged, asked himself: "Why does he choose to complain just before a meal?" As for K'uei Taniang, she behaved as if she hadn't heard a thing. She stared at the floor and from time to time her eyebrows arched slightly. Everything had become very still; even Third Uncle's faint breathing could be heard clearly. Slowly she raised her eyes and observed him: the jutting bones in that miserable face caused her to shudder. Her husband tugged his own sleeves and said loudly:

"Other people have relatives, and they rely on their relatives for help. Me? Every relative uses my money and sponges on me. I really don't understand it. I really don't!" He glanced at Third Uncle, who snorted gently.

"Sponge on him?" Third Uncle thought to himself, confused. He recalled that old K'uei had never given him anything. On the contrary, when *he* still had property he had been generous: without a thought he had given away a bamboo-covered hillside to his sister's husband. Since youth he and K'uei had been schoolmates and good friends. He had acted as the marriage go-between for K'uei and his sister. But now he said nothing. His lips quivered slightly as his gaze reverted to the table. Again he felt his stomach tighten.

K'uei sighed, grumbling over the misery of his lot. People did everything to use him and eat off him. And who knew whether someone hadn't already made off with his money to act the stupid philanthropist! "No matter how you look at it, I've been taken advantage of. Isn't that nice?"

"Now you're exaggerating!" his wife cut in finally. In the same breath she asked: "Which relative has 'sponged on' you? Who's taken your money to act the foolish philanthropist? Really, you're getting upset over nothing!"

"What? What?" Whenever his wife interrupted him he would resort to such a trick. Unable to go on, he would jump up and smack the tea table.

Third Uncle lifted a hand painfully, as if he wanted to sneeze but couldn't. "Well, in fact . . ." His mind went blank. His tongue was numb.

K'uei apparently wanted to continue. He waved his fists in the air, his mouth open. But as he was about to speak his tenant farmer Foolhardy hurried in. His large buck teeth flashed in a grin; his hands were clutching a capon. Angry that his speech had been interrupted, K'uei glared at the intruder. "It's really good of you to remember that today is Midautumn Festival!" he blurted.

"What can we do? Right now, we, well, you know very well, K'uei Ta-yeh, not only are we on the point of starving; worse still, we're up to our necks in debt!"

Third Uncle wanted to stand up, but he sank down again. His body felt like wax exposed to the scorching summer heat. Yet his finger tips grew cold. Sweat gathered in his palms. For the life of him he couldn't see why he had been invited to spend this holiday—it must be a trap! His stomach tightened. Bubbles of saliva filled his mouth; secretly he swallowed. With a shaking hand he clutched at his throat. The room seemed to revolve, yet there was K'uei firmly planted on the ground and about to shout something. "That son-of-a-bitch!" Third Uncle thought. In his bewilderment, he saw K'uei take up a steelyard to weigh the capon. A flurry of ear-piercing cries filled the room.

"Not even three catties! Not even three!" There followed shouts of "sponging!" "I'm just an ox, a horse!" "Everybody takes my money—no conscience!"

Third Uncle opened his mouth as if to speak, but something seemed to be stuck in his throat. The smile suddenly disappeared from Foolhardy's face. With a strained expression he asked:

"What are you talking about? When have we ever taken your money? Sure, we've borrowed money from you, at 8 percent interest. We're even mortgaged to you. But when in God's name have we ever sponged on you?" Discretion was not one of this farmer's virtues.

Third Uncle's body was visibly shaken, as though something tightly fastened had been suddenly released. He couldn't help feeling a sense of relief: the pleasure was like draining a glass of good wine. He blinked, and then took a long look at the coarse face of the tenant farmer. But in spite of himself, he felt a chill creep down his spine, and in a flash he had returned to his senses. The corner of his mouth curled into two folds. Half in contempt, half in anger he blurted out between his teeth:

"How dare you! How can you treat your landlord like this?" Even though he was poor and starving, he had still been a member of an honored and respected family. He still wore the long gray gown befitting a gentleman, even if he didn't have a short jacket underneath.

The volume of K'uei's voice overwhelmed his words. K'uei was jumping about with the steelyard in his hand, as if he wanted somehow to strike Foolhardy's head. From his lips poured a volley of bitter curses, but not to the extent of demeaning a man of his status. After hopping about for a while, he finally hoisted the steelyard and aimed at his target.

The young master cried out in fright. K'uei Ta-niang ran over to restrain her husband. At the same time, she looked imploringly at Third Uncle. Although he tried his best to stand up, his thighs collapsed under him. Again he struggled to rise, but his legs gave no support. He swooned and quickly leaned against the incense table. The flames from the two red candles danced. "Ah-h-h . . ." came his hoarse voice. His vision blurred.

Completely losing control of his temper, Foolhardy seized the steelyard in one hand. Spitting flecks of saliva he shouted: "Well said! Well said— the money you've earned! Whore mothers!

Money *you've* earned." It seemed now that they would fight it out.

Third Uncle huddled against the incense table, not daring to move. Eyes half shut, his mind revolved in a daze. Foolhardy's coarse voice swelled and stuck in his ears.

"I won't rent your land! I quit! Send a middleman over and give me back my rent!" So shouting he grabbed the capon and marched off.

"What? That idiot's taking his gift back?"

K'uei Ta-niang for the moment would rather go against her husband than let Foolhardy go. "Don't go! Don't leave! Everything can be settled. K'uei Ta-yeh always gets riled, don't you know that by now?" Then, anxiously to Third Uncle: "Reason with him!"

The dazed guest awoke with a violent start. For the sake of his sister and her husband he had to think of something, of course. Like a little boy first learning to walk, he threw caution to the winds and bounded to the door.

"Hey, hey, you there! . . . He won't listen; he's gone! Oh, no!" His hands gripped the door as if he felt suddenly nauseous. Up and down heaved his thin, flat chest as he gasped for breath. Sweat on his face gathered and dripped from the end of his chin.

K'uei's anger had again shifted its target. His squat, bucket-like legs jumped and stamped. His right fist alternately pounded the tea table and his own chest.

"I just don't understand it! I just don't! My relatives and friends know only how to take advantage of me. When there's food, they come running. When there's a problem, they fold their hands and look on. Such wonderful relatives— wonderful!"

Third Uncle clenched his teeth. He could not stop their chattering. He shot a glance full of hatred at his sister's husband. Still, Third Uncle said nothing. He didn't want to talk back. Only the relatives of this house had anything to do with him; if they cut him off, it would end his sole chance at a livelihood! His only hope of existence was for this household to take pity on him. Leaning motionless against the lintel, he let his legs tremble.

K'uei Ta-yeh continued to stare at him. Not for

a second did his mouth stop moving. Like some creature with inborn docility, Third Uncle never once answered back. Besides, in view of the trouble which Foolhardy had just stirred up, if he did make any complaint, he would appear to be siding with the tenant farmer. Thus he blinked his quivering eyelids and looked away.

The dinner table seemed to jump. In a bowl of stewed pork in the right-hand corner, a cube of fatty meat giggled, as if it possessed some inner resilience; it threatened to leap out of the dish at any time. The wine pot tottered. Third Uncle thought he spied something spilling out of the mouth of the pot. His lips turned pale. In the meantime, K'uei's harangue went on in fitful bursts.

"Spongers! . . . fine relatives! . . . Just want to eat and drink—wonderful, wonderful!"

But now these sounds gradually receded for Third Uncle. He seemed to be hearing them from the other side of a city wall. In a few moments even these faint sounds could no longer be heard.

K'uei Ta-niang sighed. She was afraid that her husband would say something even more unpleasant to a member of her family. Gently she prodded Third Uncle. "You'd better go home now."

Third Uncle swayed a few steps. The courtyard began to roll and pitch like a ship, ever faster and harder. In a moment even the sky was overturned. His legs no longer supported him. He tripped and fell fainting to the ground.

The withered leaves in the courtyard made a swishing sound; listening to them was like hearing wine being poured into a cup.

HSIAO CHÜN
(*1908–*   )

Hsiao Chün has the distinction of being the author of the first modern Chinese novel to be translated into English. His *Village in August* (*Pa-yüeh ti hsiang-ts'un*), translated by Evan King, was published in 1942. Though widely praised as the first anti-Japanese novel upon its publication in Chinese in 1935, the novel was soon proscribed by the Kuomintang censors. A popular success with the reading public, *Village in August* was based on the author's own experiences as a guerrilla fighter and underground activist in Northeast China (Manchuria) in the early thirties. The mixed theme of war and romance signaled the beginning of a new trend in fiction writing.

Hsiao Chün (pen name of Liu Chün) was born in Liaoning on July 3, 1908. He is probably the most famous of the "Northeastern Group of Writers" (*tung-pei tso-chia*). By his own accounting, his origins were decidedly proletarian, and his youth was spent in a number of varied and at times unusual pursuits, culminating in a stint as a junior officer in a militia unit stationed around the city of Shenyang (Mukden). He began writing fiction and verse just prior to the Mukden Incident, September 18, 1931, a date generally regarded as the opening of hostilities with Japan. Soon thereafter he met and began living with Hsiao Hung. They traveled together to Tsingtao and then to Shanghai, where they came under the wing of Lu Hsün and the influence of the League of Leftwing Writers.

Following the publication of *Village in August,* his first novel, Hsiao Chün published three volumes of short stories, essays, and poetry: *Goats* (*Yang,* 1935); *On the River* (*Chiang-shang,* 1936); and *The Story of a Green Leaf* (*Lü-yeh ti ku-shih,* 1936). At the same time he was working on a second and much more ambitious novel entitled *The Third Generation* (*Ti-san tai*). Part I and most of Part II of this novel were serialized in the Shanghai monthly *The Writer* (*Tso-chia*) in 1936; it appeared in book form the following year. Hsiao Chün devoted most of his creative energies over the ensuing decade and a half to an expanded version of this novel.

In 1954 *The Past Generation* (*Kuo-ch'ü ti nien-tai*) was published. Totaling 1,100 pages, it was the first of a planned but never completed trilogy that was to be a historical novel set in Manchuria, a work of massive proportions. From 1937 to 1953 Hsiao Chün published only a record of his travels and several essays.

Hsiao Chün's association with Lu Hsün, the popularity and importance of

Village in August, and his open advocacy of the Communist revolution made his enthusiastic welcome in Yenan in 1940 a foregone conclusion. But his stay in the Communist stronghold, with all its promise, was fraught with troubles owing to his abrasive, arrogant nature. He also invited trouble by writing an article about Party attitudes toward the individual "comrades." Entitled "Love and Patience Among the Comrades" (*T'ung-chih chih "Ai" yü "Nai"*), this article, together with other pieces by several Yenan writers, prompted Mao Tse-tung to call the famous Yenan Forum on Literature and the Arts in 1942. Party policy on literature and the arts was from then on codified, and Hsiao Chün, along with Ting Ling and other dissenters, was censured. He published virtually nothing for the three remaining years of his stay in Yenan.

In 1945 Hsiao Chün was sent back to his native Northeast, where he founded and ran the Party-sponsored *Cultural Gazette* (*Wen-hua pao*). This turned out to be his undoing. Finding himself totally at variance with Party policies and attitudes vis-à-vis land reform and human rights, he began writing a series of trenchant editorials attacking the Soviet and Chinese functionaries for their mismanagement. A survivor of the first literary rectification campaign in 1942, he was now the central figure in the second. In 1946, as criticism of him mounted, the newspaper was shut down and he was sent to work in a Northeast China coal mine, from which he did not emerge until 1951.

Following his release and the publication of *The Past Generation* and a reprint of *Village in August,* Hsiao Chün wrote and published a proletarian novel entitled *Coal Mines in May* (*Wu-yüeh ti k'uang-shan,* 1955). Yet it too backfired: it was quickly and vigorously attacked as a "poisonous weed" for its neglect of the role of Chairman Mao and the Party in the advances made in coal production. It was also faulted for its transparent satire. Hsiao Chün disappeared from the public eye and was rehabilitated only after the fall of the Gang of Four in 1976. He is at the time of this writing busy with his autobiography and with materials on Hsiao Hung and Lu Hsün.

"Goats," the title story of Hsiao Chün's first story collection, appeared in the October 1935 issue of the magazine *Literature* (*Wen-hsüeh*). It bears witness to its author's potential as a writer of moving, sophisticated stories, a potential he did not fulfill often enough. It is also a showcase of his humanist convictions. Hsiao Chün perceived the incarceration of a patriot in his own country for political reasons as the ultimate injustice and a national disgrace. Although there is no evidence that he ever suffered from such a fate himself, he must have had in mind his friends or acquaintances who had.

HOWARD GOLDBLATT

Goats

by Hsiao Chün

Translated by Howard Goldblatt

I

The iron bars over the window divide the sky's vista into rectangular sections. The colors of these sections often vary; in the mornings and evenings they are most often a reddish-brown or a pale or even a deep yellow. But when the color is the red of a delicate rose or the blue of a flawless piece of crystallized jade, that's when it's most fascinating. Through any one of the sections the panorama is all red or all blue. But this isn't common; usually the view is of clouds—ashen and dark like smoke—and of fog, with a texture somewhere between the two. There they lie suspended, as if pasted up in the sky, and even the wind seems unable to disperse them. And the ocean too seems fused to them, being swallowed up . . . eroded.

Off in the distance the broad expanse of ocean is dotted by the swells of island-groups and by scattered and unimposing islets. These islets seem covered with a stunted growth of fleece, with no trace of anyone ever having lived there. They are nothing more than medium-hued islands in miniature. There are some, as I look at them from here, that fail to fill up even one of the squares in my window. If someone wanted to paint a seascape, the scene in one of these openings would be ideal. Sad to say, I'm not an artist, and besides there aren't any brushes or palettes here.

Steamships, whether leaving or entering, must all pass along the foot of a continuous row of mountains. The ships appear even greater in size against the mountain backdrop, which at the same time gives proof that they are definitely not just anchored out there, but steadily moving on . . .

The strait off to the left resembles the leg of a woman stretching far out into the middle of the ocean. The crests of the waves are often a frenzy of excitement with almost ghastly white caps of foam; when winds come up, every billowing wave breaks up and erupts into a surging pillar of water a dozen feet high, only to come crashing down pell-mell over the surface, one following closely upon another. Where the waves are the loftiest and most numerous I have yet to see a single bather or fisherman; even casual visitors are seldom seen there.

And the strait off to the right, what does it look like? Is it much the same as the one on this side? This is something I just don't know. That's because my room has only two windows, one in the front and one directly opposite at the rear. Nothing but mountains can be seen through the window at the back, and as for the one in front, I have to look past the barred opening in the door and the passageway that runs by, and so whatever view that angle allows, that's how much I can see. If it weren't for those iron bars and the door, I could, of course, stick my head through and then draw it back once I had looked at as much of the view as I wanted. Frequently I try to see if I can make something out from the reflection on the window, which is thrust open, but the glass is so filthy that it looks like a dull and opaque piece of board. What good then are any such attempts in here?

Behind me now are a summer and an autumn of looking within the same angle at this small slice of sea and hillside. Each day the worn portions of the floor planks become imperceptibly paler and sink deeper; they form a neat, broad strip from this corner to that one. Little remains of the heels of my shoes, and I haven't paid any notice to where the shreds of leather and wood that are worn off have disappeared to.

I eat. I sleep. I wear out the floor, my shoes, and my allotted span of youth and life . . .

The swallows like to soar casually in the clear sky at dusk, looking like so many small, angular black specks, while sea birds circle as they climb and descend. At first I was jealous of these feathered creatures, and if I were a hunter armed with a bird gun, in my state of mind at that moment I would shoot down every one of them without mercy. Was this their way of showing off in front of us humans? Or what? But now it's different; I feel as though they should be this way, that they have the freedom and privilege of being as they are. Now I regard them with complete tranquillity, and if at times fewer of them come, I have an empty, lonely feeling, as if things are not as they should be.

On the hill at the rear the leaves on the trees have become sparse. The smell of goat and pig dung and other odors that float up from below aren't as strong as they used to be.

At sea the islets used to be a luxuriant green, arched like the backs of small mice. Now they have lost their sheen, and their dreariness is revealed as though, stripped of hair and skin, they were helpless before the onslaught of ocean waves surrounding them. The sailing ships can now no longer trail their long and steady shadows across the ocean's surface as they could in the summer. These days the weather sometimes turns stormy and ships begin to roll and toss.

Each day at the fixed time come the sounds of leg-irons and of steel doors opening and closing from down the passageway. The men on their way out to work and the men returning from their work all pass by my door and, as is their habit, hurriedly throw wolfish glances toward the opening in the door, baring yellowed or blackened teeth. I know that they are begging for my cigarette butts. The cigarette butts are here all

right, but even though there are plenty and I have no use for them, the guards will not permit me to give them away. As they passed by my door the scant slice of ocean view that I have is blocked out. Fortunately the guards don't allow them to stop; if one of them should tarry a moment, he has the "privilege" of being given a boot in the rear.

A strapping young man, the last one to appear, passed in front of my door, gazing off with an unfamiliar and childish look. I knew he was a newcomer, as he didn't have the greedy look of those others who begged for the cigarette butts.

"Is he new?" I asked a guard walking by.

"Brought up from below—came only three days ago."

"What's he here for?"

"Theft."

The guard seems to treat every matter as commonplace; there's nothing that can capture his interest, and I have never seen any notable change of expression on his face—is it made of stone? Or carved out of wax? His lips are pursed and completely colorless. The area around his nose is bowl-shaped, with the two lines coming down from the base and forming deeply etched arcs. His mouth is encompassed by these arcs just as if it were enclosed in a pair of algebraic brackets. Similarly his forehead and brows are artlessly creased with the same kind of irregular, curved wrinkles.

Right below my floor the semi-subterranean rooms are identically equipped with passageways, and they also have doors with openings and iron-barred windows. They differ in that one can't see the ocean from there—they are set up for prisoners who have just arrived.

"He's quite a robust fellow, eh!" I said, partly to myself, with a ringing sigh of resignation.

"Robust? Hah! We've had stronger ones than him before! What is he, after all . . . a thief—a goat thief."

The guard faced me, slowly exposing his darkened teeth, and continued:

"Just wait and see . . . robust? Hah!"

In the evening a couple of Russian children were sent into my room, each of them holding on for dear life to the end of a loaf of bread which he clasped to his breast, even though so little of the bread remained you could only call them empty crust ends. Then too, they had a military canteen and an unbearably soiled pulp magazine.

The guard explained to me that these were two youngsters who had wanted to flee to their own country, but they had neglected to buy boat tickets and were delivered here last night by someone from the boat.

"The prisoners here are really detestable. During the night they filched these two Russky kids' bread and nearly ate it all . . . detestable!"

The guard locked my door and left, his voice trailing off as he walked away. The two children uneasily scrutinized every nook and cranny, and in a moment they began to get restless and started scurrying about like mice, all the while gnawing away at what remained of their loaves of bread.

They sized me up from all angles and finally, after they had talked it over between themselves repeatedly, in a more relaxed manner they put their canteen, their magazine, and their bread crusts down on my small table.

"You must be a teacher."[1]

The children probably thought that I didn't look as though I was in prison as a thief or a heroin user—a teacher wouldn't filch their bread and eat it—perhaps because they had seen the few sheets of newspaper on my bed. In here, anyone able to get a newspaper must probably be a teacher.

"I'm a lawbreaker too."

At first the children didn't understand what I was saying and just stood there staring at me blankly. They had begun by questioning me in a broken Shanghai patois, and at this point I felt it best that I explain my meaning to them in Russian.

"I am a person who has committed a crime too. Do you understand? A person who has committed a crime!"

"You are a criminal too? Like them?" The elder of the two pointed downward—meaning the prisoners below us. The smaller one merely opened wide his eyelashes, leaving the pupils of his eyes, deep gold with a touch of brown, completely isolated from either eyelid, solidly suspended there in the surrounding pale blue of the whites.

"Just like them . . . like a thief or a robber . . ." I said to them with a smile. Do I look nice when I smile? I don't have the slightest idea. There's no mirror here for me to look at myself, but I seemed to detect that it may have made them even more uneasy. I scratched my itching scalp with my fingers, and something came down with the scaly white flecks—they were strands of my hair. Lately these superfluous hairs seemed to be shedding more easily, and my forehead, which was not normally very extensive, now seemed a bit broader, with more smooth surface.

"Are you a thief too?"

The boys didn't trust me anymore. Once again they, the older one leading the younger, picked up all their things from my table—magazine, the bread crusts, and the canteen—with the intention of going over to open the door.

I didn't stand in their way, for I knew there was no need for me to do so. I remained seated in the room's lone chair gently twisting a fallen strand of hair around my fingers, and for some unknown reason felt content.

They yelled and kicked the door with their feet and together turned their eyes up toward the rectangular opening in the door.

A face like a carved bust appeared at the opening and blocked out every bit of light that had been coming through.

"What the hell are you doing?" The guard's eyes shone and every deeply etched wrinkle on his face quivered slightly. The children were struck dumb; they merely pointed to me and to their crusts of bread.

"He won't steal your bread. Now if you cause any more trouble, I'll—"

The guard deliberately swung his thick rattan rod past the opening in the door a couple of times. The children came back and looked me

---

[1] The term *hsien-sheng* (teacher) could also mean a gentleman, a member of some privileged class.

over again, while the guard availed himself of the moment to throw me a smiling glance. Then he walked away.

"Why don't you sit down, kids. I wouldn't take your bread away from you."

I went over and tugged on their arms, but they steadfastly shied away with hopeless looks on their faces. In the younger one's eyes I could already see some moisture welling up. The older one, however, looked as though he knew what to do, and he asked me:

"Are you really not a thief? You won't steal our bread and eat it?"

"Not even a little bit. Why, I could give you something to eat!"

"Then why are you in here? This is a bad place; there are all kinds of people here! Why are you here too, huh?"

How could I answer this child? Even I was at a loss to find a reason for my being here. I stroked the hair of the younger one and said:

"I like to watch the ocean from here!"

"Watch the ocean?" His eyes began searching for the sea. "Watch the ocean from this opening?" He bounded over and, standing on tiptoe, looked toward the sea. "I can't see it!"

"Sure you can."

I led them over and brought the chair for them to stand on; the little one started shouting:

"Morye! Morye!" [2]

Just then there was a steamship heading out to sea, a long trail of smoke stretching out behind it; perhaps it was the very ship that had brought me back to my homeland. It couldn't know that a passenger it had once carried was just then looking at it through a small opening like this, watching its comings and goings as it navigated freely.

From somewhere the children turned up the red-tipped matches I use to light my cigarettes. They withdrew into a dark place and began striking them against their wet, sticky palms, letting off a phosphorescent glow. They roared with laughter.

At night the sea is sheer darkness, deep and somber, while the stars in the sky are kept apart by the window's iron bars. Compared to the daytime, the sound of the ocean's crashing waves is clearer and a little more violent.

The children slept on my bed. I listened to the mixed sounds of their snoring and to some indistinct and disconnected murmurings in their sleep. As usual I walked along my regular path, from this corner over to that one . . .

I picked up the magazine with the unbearably soiled cover from the table and casually flipped through the pages; there were both words and pictures. The names of some of the people pictured were familiar, but others were completely unknown, and none of them had any connection whatsoever with my thoughts of the moment.

Like a blade of grass that has been existing for a long, long time in a cave with no wind or rain, no sunlight . . . no thoughts . . . The arrival of these two children today seems to have destroyed me, destroyed my serenity! My thoughts began to revive, like those of a pent-up animal.

II

The fetid smell of goats that gently floats up through the window at the rear is disquieting. I look out through the iron bars at those few suffering goats sleeping, without change, cuddled up at one corner of the enclosure; they are already just a blur of white. The bleating sounds these past few days have been neither as regular nor as loud and shrill as they were. I no longer see the goat with the long beard and solid, twisting horns sniffing and chasing the tail of his already pregnant fellow prisoner as he did when he first came out. All day long he just sleeps there softly, bleary-eyed. Occasionally he stands up, but only when someone has thrown something edible into the enclosure, and then he goes and clashes with his pregnant fellow prisoner. When he does so his earlier good-natured way of sniffing and chasing the tail of his fellow prisoner changes completely.

[2] Ocean or sea.

For by that time he has already become cruel, and sticking his neck out in an exaggerated manner, he tosses his horns in a threatening gesture toward her. Often his fellow prisoner is thrown to the ground, exhausted; baring her teeth, she bleats dispiritedly as her exposed belly is wracked with spasms.

It has been three days since the children left me—no, I can only say, since they left this room. When they found out that they were going to be released, and moreover, that they could board a ship returning to their homeland and would be given back the five dollars that had been confiscated, they were so happy they nearly took wing! They danced around me and kicked over my chair; they shredded my newspaper into confetti; they whistled, sang, and then recited poems of their homeland by Tolstoy, as well as the poems of Pushkin and Lermontov. They flipped through the torn magazine about a thousand times and pointed things out to me:

"Look here, this is Moscow! We're going to see Moscow! Look! All of this is our homeland—all of it! There are airplanes there, and cannons . . ." They shook their heads fitfully and pointed out some enlargements to me. The children simply went berserk, and I was fired by their happiness to the point where my eyes were a little moist. I felt a soreness in my nostrils that is impossible to describe, but all the time I was smiling. Only when the guard's face appeared in the door's opening did the children finally settle down.

"Are you two really going home? Don't you think about your mama and papa?"

I took hold of one hand of each child and sat on the bed. I liked the younger one better, and I was already aware that he wasn't the other one's younger brother—they were just friends. He was only eleven, three years younger than the older boy.

"No," the older one answered. The younger one remained silent; he just kept his eyes glued on his companion and listened to him speak. The older one pulled his arm back from me, clenched his hand into a fist, and pounded it on his knee.

"We have a country . . . why does everyone want to mind our business? Everyone minds our business! Wherever we go there is always someone. In Shanghai it was the French; then we came here and it was the Chinese . . ." I knew that the child's past anger was rekindled, and I said:

"Why did you break the law? If you commit a crime, someone will make you his business! My boy, no matter who it is, they can all make you their business."

"What! Break the law! Smashing a pane of glass—is that breaking the law? For that they can keep us a day and a night with nothing to eat or drink, and take away our freedom! They can lock us up in a dark room like that—a stinking room! Didn't we drink wine before that? That wine was given to us by Papa and Mama . . ."

On the second day the children were staying in this room with me they told me the reason they just had to return to their own country. They had gotten drunk in Shanghai while celebrating a holiday and had broken some glass in a shop. Their parents wouldn't accept responsibility and make restitution, so they were held in custody in the police station for a day and a night.

"Our five dollars that was impounded at the dockside detention center, will they give it back?"

"Yes, they will," I answered them without any hesitation.

"They will!" They couldn't speak more than a few sentences without anxiously asking about their five dollars. One after another they asked:

"They'll return it? They won't confiscate it?"

"They'll give it to you for sure. Your money isn't stolen goods; they probably won't confiscate it."

"That's right, we got that money from Papa. That day . . . he was drunk . . . there was only five dollars in his pocketbook . . ."

"You had money, so when you went aboard the ship why didn't you just buy a ticket? Why let them bring you here?"

"Why should we buy a ticket? If we had used the money to buy a ticket, then there wouldn't have been any money for food and lodging. A ship that big and the two of us being so small, what difference could it have made to have two more people on deck? They wouldn't even let us

rest on our haunches there on deck . . . they
wanted to hit us or throw us overboard . . ."

"Your parents will be looking for you; the people here will send you back to Shanghai."

"Papa and Mama won't be looking for us . . .
will they really send us back from here?"

"Perhaps not, it's hard to say."

"Well, if they want to send us back, then we'll
jump into the ocean. We want to return to our
homeland . . . we'll return home! We've seen it in
the movies, and we've seen it in magazines; in the
winter there's snow as white as silver . . . and ice-
skating . . . and no foreigner to bully us . . . no
foreigner would dare stick his nose in our business there."

They were so excited they didn't know what to
do. They haphazardly flipped through their magazine, reading and pointing things out to me. I
looked and listened while I tried to calm myself
down.

They recited the poems and songs they could
recall, especially the younger one, and when he
began to chant Pushkin's "My Nurse," I was
moved to the point that I could no longer hold
back my tears.

"Children, listen to me . . ."

Softly I too recited for them all the poems that I
knew and could remember. But the children
couldn't understand their meaning. I explained
them and at the same time said:

"In your homeland all these are very popular
poems."

The children—the younger one, that is—
draped himself around my neck.

"We are friends!"

The elder one gave me a slice of what remained
of their crusts of bread and said:

"We begged this bread from someone on the
road, but it was taken and eaten up by the fiends
below."

Now the children have left me.

Were they sent back to Shanghai? Or have they
really returned to their fatherland? I spent a
whole day gazing out through the openings between the bars, gazing at the sea, at the sky, at
every ship headed north . . . I didn't know which
ship carried them or what their situation was at
the time. Were they in the hold or were they
above deck? If they spotted this prison where they
once stayed, this almost black building, would
they wave their hands or shout a farewell toward
me—no, I should say, toward the whole prison?
That was too much to hope for!

When the children left me they kissed my hand
and again asked me:

"Why is it that you've come to this place? When
will you leave? We're returning to our homeland,
but this is your homeland; you don't have to return home like we do!"

"*Ai!* Once I've seen my fill of the ocean, then I'll
leave here."

Every time the children asked me why I had
come here, I would say—usually with a laugh—
that I came to look at the ocean, and if they asked
when I would leave, I would say:

"Wait until I've seen my fill of the ocean, then
I'll leave here.

"Will you remember our names? I'm called
Kolya; I'm fourteen years old."

"I'm Alyosha; eleven years old . . . sir."

"I'll remember it all . . . my dear friends."

I could only see them as far as the threshold of
the iron door, and I shook hands with each—little
Alyosha was actually crying. The noise of the iron
gate being locked cut short the sounds of their
goodbyes and their shadows; it also severed our
earthly ties.

It's now nighttime, and I'm still looking at the
ocean, still listening to its breathing and to the
repeated blaring of the beacon horn. Occasionally
I get a real whiff of the damp, fishy smell of the
fog that floats over from the ocean.

I was glancing over the words of the poems
they had written down in a rather untidy hand on
the newspaper for me.

As you would lovingly cherish an infant, I
began to cherish my own heart, to cherish my
somewhat untamed emotions.

I'll just have to be patient—like the goats.

The man snoring in the room next to me was
awakened by the guard's cursing. I knew it was
the robust goat thief.

"You bastard, you! Is this what happens to you when you go to sleep?"

When the goat thief passes in front of my door he no longer has that stupid, faraway look, but is always smiling . . . smiling. At first I saw him as a guileless lad, full of youth and life.

"You should go to sleep now, sir."

"Um-hmm."

The guard's eyes appeared at the rectangular opening of my door, his whole face outlined behind the opening; his face was shiny and sallow and the door was black . . . His eyes began probing the room, glancing here and there, and he said:

"This place of yours is really too comfortable; one person in a single room, with a bed and a chair too. In a room like this, when we're crowded, at the very least we would damn well stuff forty or fifty . . ."

When he had gone away from the ocean-viewing opening in my door, I thought about what he had said, and examined this room that I now occupied alone. It was a box of about three or four cubic meters, I guess, constructed of concrete, stone, and iron. Up to now I had overlooked the fact that I was actually receiving kid glove treatment. I should have been grateful, at least I should have been grateful for that much. If my heart wasn't forged of concrete, iron, and stone, I should stamp onto it this piece of "gratitude."

III

Besides looking at the ocean, watching the goats out beyond the back window, and reading with great care every insignificant word in the newspaper—besides walking from this corner to that corner and wearing out my shoes on the graying path, I have now begun to pay some attention to the goat thief.

"There's frost!" he informed me one morning as he passed by my door. He was right; as I looked out the window, the leaves of the trees on the hillside all appeared drab and somber. The tips of the hair on the goats in the enclosure had also taken on a damp appearance.

"Is it cold? Outside?" I asked.

"Hah!" He moved his bare feet up and down on the pavement and wrapped his arms around himself; his eyes were darting back and forth uneasily.

"Sir, they want cigarette butts. Do you have any? Hurry . . . the guard will be coming out . . ."

I passed the cigarette butts that I had already gotten together to him through the opening, and he disappeared like a fox. But from somewhere near the door I heard the guard call him to a halt:

"What's that you're holding in your hand?"

"Nothing." His voice was gloomy—childish and very guttural.

"Open your hand . . . what's this?"

While he was being beaten he never uttered a sound; he merely panted like an ox.

"You can't give these things to them anymore. Don't spoil them with treats like that . . . it'll lead to a beating every time." The guard showed me the cigarette butts he had seized and continued:

"That young guy is a damned fool. He doesn't smoke himself, but he comes and begs for cigarette butts for others . . . don't give them any more . . ."

"There's frost on the ground, and a cigarette or so in the morning makes it a little easier to warm up for work." I forced a smile into my eyes, knowing full well that this explanation would serve no purpose.

"You're really most considerate! If you were the warden here, the prisoners would turn the place upside down. That would never do! All this is the talk of a bookworm. *Ai yo!*"

I saw those dozens of cigarette butts that I had so diligently collected disappear through my ocean-viewing window. As he threw them out I could still see them turning, end-over-end, as if they were flying way off in the distance to the horizon.

I knew that they were carrying earth from somewhere to fill in a mountain gully of dirty water in the courtyard. After they had it filled in, I was told, they were going to construct a new prison building on the site.

"The goat had a kid! My goat had a kid!"

In the morning the goat thief once again appeared at my door. I wasn't fully awake yet. Cupping his hands into the shape of a horn, he spoke to me in a low, thick, raspy voice:

"The goat had a kid—my goat."

"Last night?"

"Just before dawn this morning—everyone's watching! You can see it through your window too. The big one is going to die!"

I had lost some sleep during the night because of the goat's cries, but it never occurred to me that she was giving birth. I looked out through the window, but the view, as always, wasn't very clear. I asked the guard:

"I would like to take a walk in the courtyard, is that all right?"

The wrinkles on the guard's face expanded slightly; he didn't answer, but went ahead and opened the door for me.

"You can't take too much time, you know."

"I know."

My eyes, which had long been denied the sight of the sun, and my nose, long a stranger to the smell of mud, didn't feel natural now; I was rather like a mole that has lived only in the sunless lower strata of the earth. The vast sky, the unrestricted expanse of ocean, the limitless canopy of floating white clouds, the group of men in the midst of carrying earth under the hot sun . . . it was as though we had all forgotten each other, and the memories were only then coming back to me.

That gully, it stayed just as greedy, just as sunken in, and the men looked like ants, crawling back and forth. The guards had rifles on their backs, and they dragged their rattan canes along the ground, casually chatting with one another and yelling curses at the loafers.

Following the line of the base of the wall, I searched out the enclosure near my back window.

The goat with the horns was moving his mouth, and his chin whiskers moved lightly in harmony with it. He seemed to be protecting his fellow prisoner, and he looked at me with a blank stare in his eyes. The little kid was sleeping next to its mama, its felt-like hair not yet completely dry.

Inside the enclosure, on several of the rails there was some blood and sweat that had nearly turned black—in the places that had been kicked in and smashed, one could still discover blood that hadn't completely soaked in.

The belly of the mother which had just given birth seemed to have become uncommonly concave, uncommonly out of balance. That part of her body didn't look like a belly at all, but a rising and falling pit. Even the energy to lick her kid clean appeared to be lacking.

During his rest period the goat thief walked over to where I was standing. I was just then looking over beyond the wall, where my wife was being held prisoner.

"The little kid won't make it—there's no milk for it. The big ones won't make it either—there's no grass for them to eat. All they have to eat is their own dung . . . I stole them all . . . all of them . . ."

His compassion for the goats—the goats he had stolen—seemed excessive, as if he were somehow unaware that they were stolen from someone else. He had already broken the law—he was a thief; what he took had become stolen goods, and stolen goods should be confiscated and made public property. I understand the law—laws always so prescribe. Maybe he was still young and didn't know as much as I did.

"They're stolen goods. You can't count them as yours. They are in the public domain."

"Wouldn't it be great if they let me take them home! I guarantee I'd fatten them up. Keep them here and they'll all starve to death, including the kid . . . They said that anything stolen that's living is just turned over to this place. The ducks, when they're hungry they eat pebbles; pigs and goats, when they're hungry they eat their own dung . . . Where our village is there are hills and a stream with water you can drink . . ."

At the base of the wall one can often find faded shreds of clothing on the tops of which are layers of white specks. Everyone knows that those are lice which have starved to death.

"They've made rags of our clothes."

I noticed the ghost-like faces of smiling men behind the iron bars; they were there behind every opening, smiling, smiling. My whole body was agitated by the smiles on their faces, and I could feel the pounding of my heart. I wondered if when I smiled I looked like these fellows whose destiny I shared. I thought back to the first time I smiled at the two children. What was the look that had come into their eyes? They were startled!

"When I'm shackled with manacles and leg irons . . . if I have lice . . . all I can do is rip my clothing. Look! That's how I lost this piece."

The goat thief passed up his rest time and just walked around and around the outside of the enclosure talking to himself; then, after a moment, he came back and talked with me. He pointed to his own neck, showing me how the collar of his undershirt had already disappeared because of the lice.

"Why is your padded gown so short?" I noticed he had put on a padded gown today, but it only reached to slightly below his knees, and then the sleeves, they looked even less becoming. They only came down to just below his upper arms, and his chest was completely exposed.

"Oh this? This is my mother's. She was afraid I would be cold. My mother sent it along to me." As he said this he kept trying to pull the sleeves down further. He had an embarrassed, hard-to-describe look on his face, and his head hung down as he looked once again at his bare feet.

"Your mother is still living?"

"I . . . if I didn't have a mother, I wouldn't be a thief now . . . I must send this padded gown back to her! I'm young—what's a little cold weather to me! Here, feel my arm!"

He stuck out a muscular arm for me to see. I was startled to see that he had such a beautifully formed arm—it could easily be taken for an artist's plaster-of-paris mold. If he had been born into high society, he would have made an excellent athlete; now he is a goat thief.

The earth-filling work began again.

I returned to my own window and observed the others' flurry of activity; I said to the guard:

"I'll pitch in and carry some earth, all right?"

"You?" he said incredulously. "Not you!"

"Why not? I'm not exactly weak!" To prove my strength, I bared my arm and thrust it toward

him—an arm turned so white it would shock someone to see it. The guard's flabby jowls quivered momentarily:

"Strong as you may be, it's still no good! Our orders from above are that you are to receive special treatment . . . it's only the thieves . . . they have to work . . . now, your case . . . Why don't you rest a little?"

As always, he locked my door. As was my custom, I looked out from behind the barred window at the ant-like human figures and at the goats inside the enclosure—for the first time I saw that the goat was actually searching out and eating his own dung—at the leaves on the hill at the rear, at the grass, and at the distant mountains bathed in the colors of late autumn. I am separated from all this . . . cut off . . . I very much regret that I'm not a goat thief . . . some kind of thief . . . I am immersed in a colorless, sweet, poisonous liquid! I suppose I'll turn into a lifeless skeleton of rickety bones. My skin . . . my hair, turning so white, and shedding . . . dissipating my strength and flow of blood like this . . . this exquisite punishment . . . this . . .

The goat thief had taken off his padded gown; contrasted with the collarless undershirt, his neck showed up even stronger and longer. Because of all the energy he was exerting with his shoulders his veins bulged out clearly. He still stood out from the crowd, strong, tall, and big, not in the least destitute-looking . . . not looking at all like a thief.

Under midday rays of sunlight evenly spread everywhere the men's shadows grew shorter, and there was no wind. I could not bear the ocean's panting through the window in front. Because of the distance it was hard to tell whether the slanting sails and masts were entering or leaving on the sea, whose surface glittered as though covered with a layer of floating mercury.

The goat munched on his own dung, his whiskers moving unconcernedly. The other one was still there with the skin of her belly listlessly rising and falling—quite possibly even a little more slowly. The little kid resembled a blind puppy, nudging and pushing between its mother's legs with its greedy little mouth.

IV

An event that smacked of revolt occurred—it was just a few days after the she-goat and her kid died.

The morning that the kid and its mother died the goat thief came and reported to me:

"They're both dead! My goats! The big one and the small one . . . look! They're still lying in the enclosure." As he was reporting this news to me I saw that he didn't have his normal expression of childish delight, but had begun to look like an old man—exceedingly slow! He kept nervously rubbing his nose with his hand. I said:

"It's just as well they died. Sooner or later they would have died anyway. So what good is there in feeling sad?"

"I stole them . . . all for my mother's illness, to buy medicine . . . but mother didn't die after all." He shook the padded gown that he was wearing, and then said:

"No one ever comes to see me. If someone came, they could take the padded gown back for Mother. It's getting cold, and Mother's getting on in years. She can't do without a padded gown."

He raised his eyes and gave me a bleary look, and then as usual went out to carry more earth.

He was right. The weather was getting cold, and the time was already here when you could no longer get by in the morning without padded cotton clothing. I said:

"Then what will you wear?"

"Me? I'm young!" He seemed just then to be reminded of his youth and his strength, and with a shrug of his shoulders he walked off.

At noontime I got special permission for a twenty-minute stroll, and again I sought him out; he pulled me by the hand over to the skylight of a semi-basement room at the end of the building and pointed for my benefit.

"What is it?" I didn't bend over right away. He shot a furtive glance all around, then bent over and said:

"A man . . ."

With a confused and strange feeling I followed his lead and looked inside. The man didn't appear very clearly at first, nothing more than an object shaped like a human body lying stretched out on the ground. On top of that, the natural darkness of the room made it look even more gruesome, like a thing carved out of bone. Only with some effort could I make out his facial features.

"Oh!" I had never been so startled before, and I had never before been able to make the sound I had just uttered. But now I found myself holding on tightly to the neck of the man on his haunches next to me; he forced my hands away with an apprehensive laugh:

"They put all the dead ones in this room—the dead ones from upstairs, them too . . . I once carried earth with him . . . he was a pickpocket . . . young!"

After the goat thief went back to carry more earth I was occupied fully twenty minutes of my stroll time with this event. I had nothing on my mind, so quietly, and for no particular reason, I just leaned on the near side of the enclosure and watched that window at a distance. At the base of the wall the shreds of cloth had increased, and there were new lice, all swollen and frantically crawling around the pieces of cloth—probably not much time had passed since they had left some human body. I was seized by the rank odor of the goats; the dead mother and her kid were still sprawled out in the enclosure, as insidious flies swarmed noisily around their mouths and eyes. The older goat's eyes were still open, and her ceramic-like eyeballs partially jutted out, but were devoid of any luster, even though the sun was shining brightly in the sky above. There was nothing unusual about the kid—its head was pillowed on one of its mother's legs; there were still some remnants of peach-red moisture around its small tapered mouth and its fleece looked as though it had never even had a chance to fluff up.

The billy goat no longer shook his whiskers, no longer moved his mouth. He slept flatly there in the muck of his own dung and urine, his coat all smeared with mud. Yet there was no change in that bright clean, curving pair of long horns. Perhaps, like a warrior who loves his sword, he loved his horns and would not willingly let them be stained by anything. I had often seen him test them by scraping them on the enclosure rails.

"Psst . . . psst . . . sir! Give us a length of wire, how 'bout it? We're being throttled to death!"

The sound came to me from behind—it was a raspy voice like that of a mute. Up there on the other side of the iron bars I could see the outline of bobbing faces with lips puckered out. I was a little frightened; I had no idea what kind of request this was.

"Wire! Sir! Give us a piece of wire . . . you're on the outside . . ."

From where I don't know, the guard's stick smacked against the iron bars and the shadowy faces dispersed in alarm, then disappeared completely.

"They're back again asking for cigarette butts, I suppose?"

"No, they wanted a length of wire!" I answered the guard without a second thought. I never guessed that one sentence could startle him like that.

"They wanted wire? Which one?"

His eyes lit up and I sensed that this was a rather serious matter. From behind the window I heard the faint *shhh, shhh* sounds of someone trying to stop me from saying anything.

"I didn't get a good look . . . what difference does it make?" I said.

"Oh, you must be kidding! Your stroll hour is over . . . you can't stand here any longer. And from now on, no more hanging around under this window. Go!"

I walked away from the window, and as I was nearing the last window I again heard a *shhh* sound.

"Shhh! Sir! Do you have wire? Cigarette butts . . . ?"

The fingers of a manacled hand were thrust out, making a hurried, nervous scissoring motion. I could only shake my head and nod in the direction of the guard who was at that moment hitting the bars of the windows and cursing at the top of his voice:

". . . I'll flay your hides! So, you want wire . . . you want a revolt! I'll flay your hides, that'll do it!" He was cursing to himself, for he got no response, though there was a slight echo—perhaps that was

his voice resounding off the stone wall on the slope of the hill. He looked as though he was born to be a guard—a natural. When he cursed people out he did so with unbroken eloquence; not the slightest inadequacy could be found that would make him ill-equipped for this occupation. He was fat and he had the typical face of a guard, oily and glistening, like some kind of congealed, opaque yellow lard on top of which were crudely etched several superfluous wrinkles. These guards . . . their youth, their strength, all used up in this cursing. It seems as though they are spending their entire lives on this prison, despising man's nature, despising everything outside this prison— that is, everything outside the range of their authority. Their occupation has made them the kind of men they are, given them this cruelness of soul and visage.

Yet the guard assigned to me today was a particularly pleasant older man, one whose appearance didn't seem to fit a man whose job it was to watch over us each and every day.

"You're five minutes over," he said, pointing to a dirty old horseshoe-shaped watch on the small table.

"Just this once—I won't go over again." Ordinarily I seldom pass the time of day chatting with people like the guards. But today, for some unknown reason, I had a desire to talk with this older guard.

"Have you eaten?" I asked him as he was locking my door.

"Yes, I have . . . it's not enough time for a stroll, is it?"

He rattled his keys but didn't leave right away. We took advantage of the hole in the door to look at each other and impart our facial expressions. I could hear that the cursing downstairs had not yet stopped, and it came in through every window like a radio broadcast warning. I asked the old guard:

"He hasn't let up at all with his cursing, has he?"

"*Ai!*" Simply and without expression he asked:

"Is it again on account of the prisoners' disturbance? They forever take great delight in cursing people out . . ."

He wasn't looking for an answer from me but was looking for one from himself.

"They take advantage of their own youthful strength . . . They all love to cuss people out . . . when I was young I was the same."

I was no stranger here, and certainly this wasn't the first incident of verbal abuse, but the cursing had never gone on this long before.

When the time had come for me to take my stroll the following day, the door remained locked. I wondered if my twenty-minute stroll privilege had been cancelled. Perhaps because of what happened yesterday.

Looking out the back window, I could see the earth movers doing their work as usual, only I couldn't see that exceptionally tall goat thief who normally stood out in a crowd.

What could be the matter with him? What could be the reason for his not working today as usual?

I felt like seeking out the guard and asking why my twenty-minute stroll had been cancelled, but I didn't know if he was sitting there in his place. I'm afraid that even if my head were half its present size it would still be difficult to poke it out through the hole in the door. I yelled for the guard:

"Guard!"

"What is it?" The guard appeared in front of my eyes.

"How about it, aren't you going to open the door and let me go out today?"

"Today . . . warden's orders . . . for the time being we can't let you out. You know . . . that incident yesterday . . ."

"What incident?" I was in a dream.

"Yesterday noon, downstairs, what was it the prisoners wanted from you?"

"They wanted a piece of wire."

"Right, and the disturbance was caused by that piece of wire. So today you can't go out and walk about at will."

I wanted very much to prove to him that I hadn't given in to their request, so I said:

"I certainly didn't give it to them. What was it they wanted the wire for?"

"Hm! How could we let them have wire in here? That would lead to a prison rebellion!"

"Then just forget it! How come I'm still not permitted to go out?"

"For your information, you didn't give them any wire, but someone got some in for them."

"Who?"

"Who else would do a stupid thing like that? Who but that ignorant, good-for-nothing goat thief?" The old guard seemed grieved and threw open his hands in disappointment.

"He brought some wire in? What happened? What kind of disturbance did he cause?"

"Not a very big one. Before going to sleep at night they pried open all the shackles and irons . . . had a comfortable sleep . . . when daylight came they still hadn't got up."

Owing to my anxiety to know how the goat thief was being dealt with, my heart was beating so fast it could no longer keep its balance. At the same time I understood the reason why I didn't see him today among the crowd of men carrying earth in the courtyard. My desire to stroll outside was forgotten.

"What will happen to the goat thief?" I asked.

"Naturally he'll have to spend some time in the 'black hole.'" The old guard calmed down and said, as though he had a premonition: "Those in the 'black hole' get their share of troubles. There are three of them in there now—with him it makes four—one has already been there twenty days . . . he's nearly finished."

"How did they know it was that big guy, the thief, who got the wire in?"

"That's easy! All you need to do is start the beatings and the prisoners themselves will confess."

Before he left the old guard said with a smile:

"As for you, tomorrow you can probably take your stroll."

The dead goats inside the enclosure were gone. The lone billy goat trailed along the enclosure stretching out his neck, and occasionally he gave a cry. The leaves of the hilltop trees were getting sparser by the day, while each day the gully that was being filled in got shallower.

Once again an intimacy formed between me and the sea that was visible through the rectangular openings in the window at the front. The sea's color had become more turbid—like that of thick ink. Seeing the ocean, I thought again of the two Russian children.

Even though my wife and friends were also imprisoned in those other prison buildings, I had no thoughts for them. I thought most often of other things.

When night came I was no longer blessed with peaceful sleep. Each image that appeared, every thought I had, troubled me; this was something that had never before happened in all the months I had been here.

The hardest of all to bear has been the vision of the face in the morgue. Last night it came to torment me and tonight it returned to plague me again. The more I try to suppress it the clearer it becomes—and the more real. Its protruding teeth seem about to engulf me; in fact it's as though I have already fallen victim to their bite. I am in the midst of struggling to break out through the cracks between the teeth. Its eyes aren't gentle like the dead goat's[3]—its ugly face resembles nothing more than a clay idol's in an old temple, the face of the Buddhist Ruler of Demons. It seems to begrudge its own death, to be full of hatred and a will to struggle, filled with a hankering and an unsatiated, boundless hope for the mortal world . . . or perhaps it is filled with abhorrence, and that alone!

Reading the poems that the children left behind for me, or a newspaper, or whatever books there were here, regardless of whether it was in a poem, or in the newspaper, or on each page of every book . . . this detestable image of a face possessed it all! I thought of every method imaginable but could not drive it away. On the contrary, it spread out even larger and appeared as a strange and confused painting.

A great many cigarette butts had accumulated, which I arranged into several pyramids and lined up on the table corners. But each time the men passed in front of my door they scurried by like mice, and in their eyes were the harried looks of

rodents. If one of them dropped back a little or yearningly rested his eyes a bit too long on my door, the loud threatening voices of the guards could be heard. Though time and again I held all the cigarette butts in the palms of my hands for them to see, there wasn't one who dared openly come and take them as the goat thief had done. Once I even called out to one of them:

"Hey! Cigarette butts. Do you want them?"

At that moment the guard may not have been in his seat, or maybe he was dozing . . . this time the man hastily stuck his hand, bony and black like a raven's claw, in through the opening.

"Hurry, mister, hurry!"

"What about the goat thief?"

"Don't know. Mister, hurry. There's someone walking outside."

His hands full, he went away with as many as he could possibly carry. Then there were the scattered few that had fallen to the ground, but those he just left behind.

What the occasion was I can't remember. The goat thief passed again in front of my door; I saw him, but I could only see his silhouette. I was startled, thinking I must have been mistaken. But then I recognized that padded gown. What was different was that his nose, cheekbones, and jaw all jutted out sharply. His neck stretched out long, with exaggerated veins. The strong body of a few days ago that had presented such a contrast to the padded gown that covered it seemed to have been removed, and now the padded gown fitted him quite well.

During my midday strolls I was no longer allowed to pass under the wall of that building, even though the windows outside the iron bars had long since been nailed up and sealed. I walked up near the goat thief. It seemed that he was avoiding me, as his eyes fluttered up and then down. The other prisoners also seemed to be keeping their distance from me.

"Hey, big fellow! Are you working today?" I forced a smile.

---

[3] Here the author uses the term *mien-yang*, which means "sheep." This is the only such instance, whereas the term for "goat" (*shan-yang*) is used elsewhere throughout.

"Yes, I'm working today . . . let's not talk! The guards won't allow it!"

Having been informed of this, I felt somehow weak. I could only look out rather uncertainly at the almost completely filled-in gully in front of me; basket after basket of dirt and rocks, clumps of grass and roots of trees . . . I knew that soon this mountain gully would be filled up to the brim, and then atop it they would start laying a stone foundation and then a new prison building.

A pickpocket was brought into my cell in the evening. Inasmuch as a large group of heroin users had been apprehended, every cell was completely filled.

The pickpocket was incredibly cheerful and completely familiar with the people here. He was still young, certainly not more than eighteen, with cheerful and lively airs. As he was thrust into my room the guard gave him a kick in the behind.

"Wow, what a spacious room!" He looked up and down, like he was searching for some trace that he may have left behind on the walls of my room. He called out:

"Look! I've stayed in this cell before!" He pointed with his hand to a small hole in the wall and showed me a spot where the traces of blood from bedbugs were most plentiful.

"You must be an old-timer here!"

"I won't kid you . . . not really so old . . . this makes my sixth time."

I began to find myself interested in this little thief. No one introduced us—still we very quickly became good friends. He never did ask me my name nor I his. In here that kind of protocol doesn't seem necessary; besides, we all have our numbers.

He wasn't even eighteen, yet he had already been in here six times; no wonder he was so familiar, so relaxed and lighthearted. In the evening, to my amusement, he told me a number of things of which I was ignorant. His pleasant-sounding voice drowned out the regular breath-like sounds of the ocean, the panting of the goat under the window, and the snores from the adjoining cells . . . it even blocked out the image of the face on the corpse in the morgue that disturbingly kept me awake night after night. His stories unfolded like a whole motion picture in front of my eyes. He began by telling me how he had come to be a thief in the first place.

". . . my mother died when I was three years old. I've supported myself by stealing ever since—up 'til now . . ."

"That scar, how did you get it?" I asked, having noticed that on the right side of his forehead there was a long scar where no hair grew.

"This scar?" Without being aware of it, he rubbed it. The scar resembled a crescent moon crudely laid out on the young man's forehead.

"I got this scar when I fell while jumping off a train. At the time my only thoughts were of running . . . dammit! It didn't hurt at all, but later I felt something dripping from my head, and then I discovered it was blood. A few days and it was all healed up." He gave it another pat with his hand and said: "Having this sure makes it tough! Everyone can recognize me. Lots of times I go without a haircut just to cover it up . . . if it hadn't been for this tell-tale scar I wouldn't be back in here now!"

"What! You mean they all recognize that scar?"

"They all recognize it. The moment I came here the guards all yelled out: 'Scarface, you back again!' They all call me Scarface."

"What are you in for this time?"

"I stole a foreigner's watch and overcoat."

Without any urging from me he started right in telling his story.

"For several days I hadn't been able to steal a thing, and my money was all gone. I just had to steal something. One evening there was this foreigner—well, after all he was a foreigner . . . I can't tell the difference between the English devils, the big-nosed Russians, or the American asses—anyway, I spied that big watch of his—it looked just like a KR watch—and the collar of his overcoat wasn't bad—made of otter; probably it wasn't very cold that day, and he had opened the front of his coat—the lining was most likely real fur, but I wasn't sure—and I thought to myself, if I could lay my hands on that you can bet I'd try it on first—how classy that would be! I was still wearing these clothes at the time." With his hand he lifted up his undershirt, then tugged his torn and ragged pant leg and said: "The night winds these days are really murder! And that day . . . it was drizzling off and on. A place like this near the ocean, it's no picnic . . ."

He hesitated for a moment and cocked his head as though something were gnawing at him; he kept his eyes fixed on me.

"Listen . . . this ocean; I tell you it's no picnic . . . what time is it now? . . . making all that noise . . ."

The voice of the ocean was truly loud and re-sounding. The winds knifed in through the holes in the window, and there was no way a person could stop shaking. He said:

"It was a drizzly day . . . my belly was empty . . . no money to buy a cup of wine . . . my ciga-rettes were gone . . . I swore that if I made a good haul this time I could lay off all this winter. I couldn't take my eyes off him—I'm talking about the foreigner—no matter how I tried I couldn't stop my teeth from chattering. I watched him enter the courtyard and I followed in right after him . . . The gate watchman was dozing off, giv-ing me a real good opportunity. Some days earlier I had noticed this dirty pig. He lived there all by himself . . ."

The night winds that floated in through the cracks in the door were unbearable. I wanted to call out to the guard, but it was already too late at night and he wouldn't be very happy about get-ting up to close the outside window for us. Still, we couldn't just go on enduring it, so I took all the accumulated newspapers, books, and even the magazine the two Russian children had left be-hind for me, and stuffed up all the cracks—the wind could no longer pierce in dauntlessly, and the sounds of the ocean seemed much further away. We laughed contentedly, laughing at this plan which was of our own making. In times of urgent need people often become much cleverer.

"I followed him . . . kept following him . . . I got a good vantage point where I could see his room clearly, and I hid myself in a corner where I wouldn't be noticed—behind a trash can—and from a distance I kept my eye on his window. I sized up the situation; if the door was locked, then

what would I do? Would I run the risk of break-ing a leg if I jumped down from that window? Or else . . . Meanwhile I was waiting for night to fall. The rumblings of my stomach and my body's tremblings were real; but, afraid . . . I wasn't all that afraid. If a thief can't control himself or is faint-hearted, how can he possibly make it? The rain began falling more and more heavily and I could barely make out the sound of a door open-ing. The bobbing and weaving silhouette of a man appeared in the window.

"It was then at least ten o'clock. In other rooms there were record players and there were radios . . . someone was trying to sing along with a record . . . it sounded terrible—like the cries of a cat in heat. I couldn't wait any longer; if I waited any longer the whole thing would fall through. Once he—this goddamn pig—went to bed and locked the door . . . it would be the end of every-thing! I summoned up all the ability I had, and faster than a shot, before he even returned from the toilet, I had already safely lodged myself under his bed where I could look out, facing the door, and watch that grubby swine. Then if he discovered me, I could immediately use the blan-ket that hung down from the bed to cover his head and get away. At the time I was using the hanging blanket to conceal myself. I still couldn't stop shivering, so I chewed on my own sleeve. The sleeve had a horrible taste—all salty and bitter—and I wanted to vomit! I lightly rubbed the blanket with one hand; it was a really good blanket—it had a wonderful feel, warm, soft and velvety . . .

That grubby swine, it was like he was com-pletely in a dream world. When he returned he didn't so much as open his eyes; he merely felt around for the key in the door lock, gave it a turn, and jumped right into bed. As he did so the bedsprings gave me a knock in the head. I had al-ready fixed in my mind the location of the watch and the overcoat—the overcoat was hanging on a clothes rack in the corner of the room and the watch was on a small bedside stand, its pure gold casing glistening under the lamp, while it kept running with a loud ticking sound . . . I figured that this watch would go for twenty or thirty dollars at least and the overcoat would be a good item too. Naturally, there were quite a few other things in the room that would have brought a good price, but I didn't pay any attention to them. I waited until I heard the swine's grunting snores; at the same time I could hear the sharp tap of a woman's heels in the hallway outside, as well as the laughter of some men . . .

"I crawled out, and in a flash the little treasure was in my hand. I listened for its ticking sound—there was no mistake—and a feeling of fulfillment came over me. Holding my shoes by my teeth, I started crawling over to the clothes rack . . . naturally, the overcoat found its way into my hands too. My only thoughts were of how I should go about getting out of the room . . . just then that grubby swine spoke out in Russian:

" *'Poshol, durak!'* [4]

"I had already grabbed the end of the key, but I didn't dare turn it at once; I just held it tightly, for all I was worth. By then I no longer had cold shivers, but had broken out in a sweat.

"After a brief pause his snores began again and I knew that grubby swine had been talking in his sleep. I finally very cautiously opened the door and removed the key. Then I locked the door from the outside so that in case he woke up suddenly I could still get away. Wouldn't you know it . . . that grubby swine had no idea what was going on . . . what annoyed me was that the hallway was too bright, so I had to take a big chance—I was already wearing the overcoat . . . it was much too warm. I held the watch tightly in one hand, while in the other hand I carried my shoes. I had forgotten, I should have taken a pair of shoes along while I was at it. How could shoes like these go with such a coat?

"I stayed there behind the trash can squatting on my heels until the following morning. The young gate watchman came out half-dressed, opened the main gate, and hurried on back—I suppose to get some more sleep. Before anyone came out to sweep up the trash area I turned up the otter-skin collar of the overcoat in a dignified manner so that it covered my face, and just like

that I stepped out right through the main gate."

He took a deep breath. He didn't seem as thin or sallow as he was when he came in that day. The scar on his forehead glistened against the lamplight. He looked every bit a child, with his thin neck and lanky body—there was just no flesh and muscle on his bones.

"First thing after coming out I had to find a place to hide my watch . . ."

"Where did you hide it?"

"I can't tell you that . . . anyway, we can't have anything on us . . . I put my watch in the crack of a wall."

"How did you run afoul of the police?"

"That was after I had the watch hidden. I ran into an undercover man who knows me, and he wanted to give me five dollars for the overcoat.

" 'Scarface, how's business?' he asked.

" 'I'm looking forward to your patronage, sir!'

" 'You haven't paid me your respects for some time now. Where did you come across this? The color of the fur isn't bad!'

" 'Um-hmm.'

" 'How much do you want?'

" 'At least twenty dollars.'

" 'Five dollars. Why don't you just leave it here with me?'

" 'No. Not enough.' I tapped my foot as an expression of my dilemma.

" 'Scarface, you sure are greedy!'

"Well, he left. I knew then that I had offended him, but I didn't regret it. Because in the past they had chewed up some of my buddies without mercy. They would work like fiends to get their hands on a little something and then these guys would want to buy it up . . . just buy it up. I've suffered at their hands as much myself . . . but this time I had planned on making it for the winter. Naturally, the next day I was arrested, but then I'd known all along that was coming . . . I didn't have any of the money on me that I had made from the sales . . . this time they couldn't seize any loot . . ."

Finally he said:

"The Ruler of Demons doesn't care if his sub-

---

[4] "Get out, you fool!"

jects are skin and bones. The people who live off
thieves are worse than the thieves themselves. We
get our hands on some small thing or other and
they always manage to make it theirs! If not . . ."

V

The goat thief was dead.

Looking in through the window of the morgue
I could clearly see his long body stretched out on
the ground, and next to it, all crumpled up, was
that ill-fitting padded gown with its graying cotton
oozing out here and there like intestines.

Late autumn weather was already upon us.

The morning of the previous day he had passed
by my door being dragged along by several
guards. I was just then watching the ocean and
the clear autumn sky from behind the passageway. He was still alive then, and still speaking
clearly; he was struggling to get free, resisting
having to go downstairs and resisting having to go
see the doctor.

As he neared the opening of the stairwell his
pants slipped down, and along with them down
came—in mixed colors—a mess of excrement that
dripped all over the floor. His hand had a death
grip on the bannister of the stairs, and his ribs
and spine were bent and protruding, giving him
the appearance of some kind of canine animal.
The flesh on his wrists was gone; only bones and
veins remained. He was no longer the same goat
thief I had seen that first time.

"You son-of-a-bitching filthy pig . . . my shoes
and socks are all dirty!"

"Wrench his hand loose, push him downstairs!"

In full sight of us all, a guard began raining
blows on him with his stick where the ribs and
thigh bones stuck out. Then another fat guard
wrenched his fingers free . . . the sounds the
goat thief made weren't clear anymore, but were
like the death rattle from the throat of a dying
man . . . a hoarse cry.

Finally even this hoarse cry died out in the stairwell. He bumped all the way as he rolled down
the stairs.

The smell that his excrement left behind
floated back and forth in the passageway.

Now, looking at his corpse through the window
of the morgue, what I remember most clearly
must be that same padded gown . . . he had said:

"This is my mother's . . . I should mail it back
to her . . ."

Now his mother's padded gown will serve as his
burial clothing.

It was about a week earlier that the goat in the
enclosure had died. At that time the thief had
passed in front of my door and said softly:

"Mister, my billy goat has died too."

At that moment, as he passed in front of the
door, I became aware that his eyes had already
taken on the dull look of a dead fish. His beard
and face were a contrast of deep black and ghostly
white. As he walked his steps were unsure, his
shoulder blades stuck out precariously, and the
back of his skull jutted out.

Each day, along with the others, he had been
there filling in the foundation of the planned new
prison building—they were in the process of piling rocks up on the foundation. The men were
busy as usual and the foundation was already secure and level and sturdy.

I began increasing my pacing from one corner
of the room to the other—that pale gray path
grew even deeper, while the soles of my shoes had
worn through; as for the heels, the outsides were
worn all the way down to the shoe lining. I was
convinced that on my feet, before long, even the
lining would soon be wasted away—just be swallowed up.

As the goat neared his end there was no more
of his own dung. For two whole days he simply lay
there stretched out, and then he finally died. Before he died there were some people who threw
bits of food to him, but what good were they
then? By that time he had no more need of food.

Like the female before him, the goat's eyes took
on a peaceful look . . . and he was finished.

The ocean is the same as always, the sky is the
same as always, and my vantage point of both the
sky and the ocean is the same as always—
everything is painted with early winter colors.

I no longer take pleasure in my noonday strolls. I've grown to detest all those things in sight out there—the animal enclosure, the cell windows, and the new prison building under construction. Even the window through which I could see the scenery on the hill at the rear, I've sealed up; all that remains is the slice of ocean in front of me.

Once I received a letter from the two Russian kids. They said they had already reached Harbin, had received entry from their country, and were about to strike out across Siberia and return to their homeland. In the letter they wrote:

"Mr. ——, haven't you had your fill of the ocean yet? Wishing you good health."

Yes, my dear little friends, I'm still watching the ocean, watching the same slice of ocean . . . I'm healthy . . .

I shook my head, and some strands of hair fluttered down onto the letter; this time I was truly smiling.

WU TSU-HSIANG
(1908–   )

Chang T'ien-i was one of the many who began to receive critical attention in 1928–1929; during the early thirties, an even larger number of fiction writers emerged, and several of them continued to be productive until the Cultural Revolution of 1966. But in the three or four years before the outbreak of the Sino-Japanese War in 1937 the most brilliant of that group was Wu Tsu-hsiang, a native of southeastern Anhwei who began to write even while a student of the Chinese Department at Tsinghua University. He wrote about his home region with an unobtrusive sympathy for the poor and downtrodden and a deep-seated disgust for the oppressors. But whatever his personal feelings, he records the manners and speech habits of peasants and gentry with equal accuracy and thus achieves an unsentimental realism rare among leftist writers. Unfortunately, he wrote little; except for his patriotic novel *Mountain Torrent* (*Shan-hung*, 1942), practically all his best work is contained in *The Stories and Essays of Wu Tsu-hsiang* (*Wu Tsu-hsiang hsiao-shuo san-wen chi*, Peking, 1954), which includes, in addition to four hitherto uncollected pieces, the bulk of *West Willow* (*Hsi-liu chi*, 1934) and *After-Dinner Pieces* (*Fan-yü chi*, 1935). A professor of Chinese at National Peking University, he has for the past three decades specialized in literary research and criticism.

Whatever the name of the village, "Young Master Gets His Tonic," "Let There Be Peace," and "Fan Village," our three selections, all take place in a rural region where the peasants, if not already starved to death, are destitute. They have three choices: to engage in any available additional work or business to stave off hunger, borrowing money from local usurers to meet emergencies; to go to the cities, usually Shanghai, to get employment as coolies or factory workers; or to turn to theft and banditry. Because even the better-off villagers feel the impact of this rural bankruptcy and live in fear of the bandits, they become more mean-spirited than they would be in normal times and cling to money as their very life. They would not even part with it to save their own kin. One after the other, the shops are closing, leaving their employees totally uncared for; the gentry families are leaving for the cities, and their discharged servants also face a bleak future. Whereas young women in the cities can always turn to prostitution to relieve their hunger, village women do not have this option. Only the lactating mothers can sell their milk to augment their income, though their own babies suffer pangs of hunger and may even die of starvation. Because the peasants out of habit turn to the gods for help when everything else has failed them, the local temples and nunneries are thriving as usual, but for those who have seen through their hypocrisy and quackery, the monks and nuns are objects of hatred. In such a rural environment, only the few spoiled scions of the richest landowning families can still have good times in Shanghai while remaining utterly callous to the misery of those who literally sustain them with their own milk and blood.

Our three stories all gauge the human cost of this rural plight, and yet each story is distinct from the others in narrative technique and thematic emphasis. In "Let There Be Peace," the author assumes the storyteller's role and even begins with a storyteller's formula *hua-shuo* (now it is told), understandably omitted from James Shu's translation. The story of Wang Hsiao-fu and his family is told to illustrate the destitution of Feng-t'an Village as a whole. Thus, the ironic title notwithstanding, "Let There Be Peace" properly focuses on the unrelieved suffering of the Wang couple as they undergo a series of humiliations without being able to save their young and old from death or sickness. Though the peasant couple in "Young Master Gets His Tonic" are almost equally helpless and the husband certainly suffers a worse fate than Wang, their story, nevertheless, is told in the first person by the young master as a series of highly amusing episodes to underscore his utter lack of humanity. By this use of Swiftian irony, the author invites us not so much to commiserate with the peasant couple as to share his disgust with the young master and the landlord class he represents.

The peasant couple in "Fan Village," also facing starvation, show greater defiance in fighting for their survival and personal integrity. Quite unlike the other two couples, who expect no succor from their relatives or neighbors, Hsien-tzu Sao and her husband can turn to her mother for help since she is relatively well off. But she refuses to lend a hand even after her son-in-law is imprisoned. In focusing on the clashes between daughter and mother, "Fan Village" achieves in the end a moral dimension of meaning that one rarely finds in stories about peasant destitution written in the thirties. Rightly regarded as Wu Tsu-hsiang's masterpiece, "Fan Village" is in narrative form a series of sharply visualized scenes where the characters disclose themselves through dialogue.

C. T. H.

Young Master Gets His Tonic

by Wu Tsu-hsiang

Translated by Cyril Birch

I'm a country boy. My thanks to Yama, Lord of the Underworld, for bringing me into the world in a family that amounted to something, so from the moment I popped forth it was "Young Master" this and "Young Master" that. Sit all day with my hands tucked cosily in my sleeves, I'd still get something nice to eat. Since there was someone else to bother about all those things people have to bother about to stay alive, I was only too happy to escape from that barbarous, boring place and take my station with the smart set. I'm quite a passable individual by this time: nice pale complexion, nice pale hands, stylish dress, stylish conversation too, and not a dance hall or a movie theater that I'm not perfectly at home in.

I was very young when I left home—must be ten years now. We have a lot of land and property back there which makes it impossible for the family to move out; then there is my mother, a *grande dame* of the old school, who objects to moving her old bones elsewhere for fear of becoming a "lonely ghost" when she reaches the shades. So she prefers to stay on in the country, never stirring out of the old mansion that has been handed down for two or three centuries, and this is quite a nuisance because I have to make an annual trip home to visit her. Out of regard for my mother's feelings I do go back every year for a short stay. This year the whole region was plagued with bandits, but I still risked it and managed to get home safe and sound under the protection of four stout militiamen my uncle sent to escort me.

From boyhood on I've remained a typical "young master," my delicate constitution a frequent prey to sickness. Once I grew up I developed as well that kind of fashionable sickness which gives you headaches and cold sweats. Then in Shanghai last summer I was out for an airing with Miss Tenderness Lu and got into a bad car smash. I lost a great deal of blood, and though they gave me a blood transfusion my health really suffered. Now I'm thinner than ever. My mother, her maternal instincts undiminished, began prattling away: "Young Master's run down, he needs a tonic."

Now I'm no simpleton, I'm fully aware of the benefits of a tonic. In the city it was the simplest thing in the world to take a tonic. Things like pasteurized milk or even Kepler's Cod Liver Oil and Malt: pleasant-tasting and did you good. But back in the village: hopeless! These country people eat porridge and rice and beyond that they've simply no idea what one might take: where would one find cod liver oil? As for milk, these country cows are like the country people, all they're good for is careering up and down a field, neck hunched, head down, dragging a clumsy plough. How can they compare with city cows that live in luxury just like city people, lying about in sheds with just the right temperature, just the right ventilation, making their milk?

"Kuan-kuan, how would it be if we hire a wet-nurse and get some mother's milk for you?" said my mother.

I laughed: a grown man five feet tall, cuddling up to a woman's bosom sucking tit! Nothing wrong with that, mark you: but these country women aren't quite your city girls! All these women can offer you is a weatherbeaten brown complexion and a stink of sweat from head to foot. They've no notion of caring for their skin until it's white and soft, and doing it up with perfume and scented powders from Paris ready for you to kiss and fondle!

I frowned and shook my head.

"Why are you shaking your head?"

"I'd be embarrassed."

"What's there to be embarrassed about?" My mother laughed as she corrected my misunderstanding. "Silly boy, we're not going to make you go and suckle for yourself the way you did as a baby. We'll have her squeeze into a cup so you can drink it!"

This clever idea had never occurred to me. I was amazed, and asked: "'You mean it's like cow's milk, you can squeeze it out and drink it?"

"Of course! But it's ten times better for you than cow's milk!"

"Let's give it a try, then."

My mother was delighted and sent out word at once. The very next day a wet-nurse of around thirty was led in by one of the servants whose nickname was Auntie Iron Plantain. Auntie Plantain came in first, cradling in her arms a little baby boy with a huge plump head; the wet-nurse followed. The wet-nurse was your standard type of village woman: top-heavy on her thin legs, a tangle of dry-looking hair like a sparrow's nest; tiny feet with swelling arches jammed crookedly into "stub-fronted" clogs; lackluster eyes, snub nose, dun-colored lips crusted with some sort of grayish crud at the corners of her mouth; and with all this, naturally, a dried-up complexion and a rancid sweaty smell. She had on an oversized, tatty old blue cotton jacket, and her big breasts bounced in their hiding place as she waddled forward, up and down in rhythm with every step.

My mother told her to sit down and she did so, blushing. When the maid poured tea she scrambled to her feet again, took the cup in both hands, opened her mouth and murmured with a shy smile, "Too kind of you, miss."

"No need to be formal," said my mother. "Our

Young Master—I'm sure Aunt Plantain must have mentioned it—he grew too fast and didn't get enough milk when he was small. He's too frail altogether and we're looking for someone to give a drop of milk for him. You seem like a healthy woman, and well-behaved too. I'm very glad. I just wonder if your milk is all right?"

Auntie Iron Plantain slid both hands under the baby's arms and dandled him in the air, then came up to my mother and said in a grating voice like a man's, "Ma'am, don't take any notice of this girl's dirty looks—see what good rich milk she has for babies. Now then, just look at this little turtle's spawn. No more than a few months old and he's real Li K'uei!"[1]

The little beggar clenched a pair of little fists like dumplings and stuffed them into a dimpled mouth with toothless pink gums. Mother pinched his cheek, and the firm, fat brown flesh quivered and shook. There were more bands of firm fat flesh at his chin and his wrists.

"How many months old?" Mother asked.

The wet-nurse had been watching her brat and smiling. When she heard my mother's question she pursed her lips and then said, soft and slow, "Seven months. A year old come September."

"Nothing wrong with your milk, to judge by the baby."

"Unbutton yourself so madam can have a look." Auntie Plantain was only too anxious to please.

I was lying on the couch enjoying a cigarette. The wet-nurse turned her dull gaze bashfully in my direction; presumably she felt awkward about unbuttoning in front of me.

"Trouble-making bitch!" said Auntie Iron Plantain. "You think our Young Master's never seen anything like these goddam gourd-shaped tits of yours before? Nearly thirty, already dropped a couple of little turtles, and still pretending to be godalmighty shy!"

The wet-nurse, red-faced, looked timidly across again to where my mother had been sitting, but mother had already walked over to her. There was nothing for it: shyly she undid her buttons.

Her breasts, nipples jutting, really were the size

[1] Bandit-hero of *The Water Margin* and other tales, whose build and role correspond roughly to Little John's in the Robin Hood legends.

of a pair of giant pumpkins hanging off a trellis. Clusters of dark brown freckles mottled their slopes, and a network of blue veins spread back to her chest like rivers on a map. With the air of a customer carefully discriminating between various wares my mother inspected them closely. She reached out her fingers and gave a little tweak, whereupon a white milk like liquid beancurd came spurting out. Aunt Plantain wetted her finger, tasted it, smacked her lips and said, "Sweet and fresh, no wonder her brat's growing like a little pig! Just taste it and see, ma'am."

"I can see it's good from the color, no need to taste it. Very well, Aunt Plantain, you can settle the payment with her."

Aunt Plantain instructed the wet-nurse: "We'll leave it up to you. Just give us a fair price."

"I couldn't say. My mother-in-law said to ask the lady to give what she thinks is right. I know madam wouldn't cheat us."

"Well, that's sensible talk." My mother settled comfortably into a chair. "The usual rate when we hire a wet-nurse to live in and look after the baby is three dollars a month. In this case I only want you to come and give a cupful twice a day. Your own little one can suckle as before . . . You needy people, I know how hard things are for you, I'll let you have a dollar fifty a month."

"Just come twice a day and you get a whole silver dollar and a half every month—that's a smart piece of business for you! If only that luckless old man of mine weren't in his coffin, I'd quit service and sit at home making milk to sell and take it easy all my life!"

My mother laughed as Aunt Plantain bellowed away. The wet-nurse shyly ran the tip of her tongue around the crusted corners of her mouth, and said with a slow smile: "Madam is a real saint of mercy. Heaven grant the master will rise to the highest office in the land, and we'll all come and share the crumbs from his table. But ma'am, you don't realize, it's not easy for us to get by in times like these. Too many to feed at home, and my father-in-law a cripple and getting on in years; and the little one's daddy . . ."

"Get on with your job and give your milk. When you've done that you can go on with your

song of woe!" This was Aunt Plantain, croaking like a frog as she went to fetch a lidded tea bowl.

The wet-nurse blushed, hurriedly took the bowl, and began to unfasten again the buttons she had just done up. With her right hand she heaved out her left tit, rolled the nipple in her fingers, and squeezed it at the bowl. I heard a crisp swoosh, and the white milk came jetting out in streams.

I watched, intrigued, from across the room. This wet-nurse was as clumsy as any cow, but she was smarter than a cow when all was said and done. When a cow's made its milk it needs someone to come along and squeeze it out to sell, while the cow itself just goes on sticking its head in the manger and chewing its cud. But this cow of a wet-nurse had the ability to squeeze it out with her own fingers and then sell it to feed both herself and her family. People are smarter than cows when all's said and done, I said to myself.

"I didn't think to ask: who've you got at home?" my mother said sympathetically.

Aunt Plantain butted in: "I'm sure you'll remember them when I tell you, ma'am. Her father-in-law is that should-have-died-already old Ch'en with the paralytic leg; her husband's that Young Baldy that gave the blood for the master when he was in the hospital after his accident in Shanghai last year."

"Oh yes, that tenant who used to work the three acres over at Poplar Bank by West Village, and then gave up his rental year before last?"

"That's who it is, that good-for-nothing."

When she mentioned old Cripple Ch'en and Young Baldy the two of them came back to me. Of all the tenants we had, Cripple Ch'en was the biggest nuisance. All the rest would make their payments as agreed in good white rice; his alone would turn up in poor quality grain in baskets of every size and shape. Of his thirty piculs rent a year he'd be short scores of catties that never did reach us. If you pressed him or threatened to rent to someone else, he'd come crawling up like a snail, dragging his bad leg, a mournful expression on that miserable face of his, and start buttering up my mother or my uncle. He could talk your head off: how the rain hadn't fallen right, and how many bugs there'd been; how Poplar Bank was too far from the river, and the land too steep to get water up to it properly; what a world it was, land tax, poll tax, militia assessments, too much to manage; and then himself a cripple and only one son, a man had only one pair of hands, and wages too high for him to afford a laborer. He'd plead with my mother, a drop of coarse gruel for the half-dozen mouths waiting at home, for pity's sake, it would be such a good deed she'd be doing, none greater. My mother is all compassion and he would soon have her all softened up, every time. Until, year before last, a drought interfered with the harvest, and then he came up short fully one half of his rent. My uncle blew up, said he was resisting payment, defying the law, wanted to haul him before the county magistrate and jail him. Every word my uncle said made perfectly good sense: he said we all had the same sky over our heads, we all had to get by with the same sort of harvest conditions. How come every other tenant's fields get even rainfall, water everywhere, it just happens to be your land that misses it? How come no locusts in anyone else's fields, it's just your land they come to? Militia assessments, poll tax, land tax, it's the same for all the other tenants, and they all have to hire laborers to work their land, how come they can manage it and every year it's just you we hear weeping and wailing and bemoaning your fate? My uncle said, it's all right there in the deeds; "so many piculs of good white rice to be delivered annually without fail, regardless of pests, blight, flood, or drought. In the event of nonpayment, delay, or shortfall, fully accept obligation of court process for recovery. . . ." And your own thumbprint right there. You must understand the law and not go breaking it, accept your lot and be content. It was cast-iron logic, and for all his cunning, the old cripple could do nothing but stand there staring with his eyes brimming tears, not a word in reply. Then his only hope is to go to my mother, ask her to put in a word for him, don't let them file a complaint with the county magistrate. My mother's the kindest-hearted old lady you'll ever meet. She saw the state he was in and had the idea of laying in a little store of blessing for her descendants, and told my uncle not to prosecute. She said what did a few piculs of rice one way or the other matter to us? Let him off his past debts too, get another tenant in his place and cut free of these tangles and tendrils for the future or we'll just go on to-ing and fro-ing and never get clear.

Cripple Ch'en's son, Young Baldy, was drifting around Shanghai last year; it was myself that rescued him and brought him back. This was what Aunt Plantain was just referring to:

It was last summer in Shanghai, and I'd just fallen in love with Tenderness Lu. She was a taxi dancer at the Luna Dance Hall, with a skin like ivory. Her dark eyes sparkled, full of love and passion. She knew songs in English, and she could write a letter in the new vernacular style. You'd never find anything in the world to compare with that slender, alluring body of hers.

It was one evening, there'd been a tea-dance at the Luna. I was really in the mood and I'd danced a dozen sets in a row with Tenderness. The dance ended but I was still in the swing of it. No more band, so we turned on the phonograph and I got Tenderness Lu to teach me the tango. We went on having fun until nearly dawn. It had been hot as blazes for days, not a breath of air. The thick smoke puffed straight up from the mill chimneys and never stirred, just hung there in a black fog right across the city, made you feel even more like your chest was stuffed with cotton; even electric fans weren't much use. Tenderness Lu couldn't stand the heat any longer and wanted a ride in a motorcar to get some air. We got in the car and I urged the driver to go full speed so that the wind roared and beat all over us. Tenderness Lu snuggled her face against my chest and her hair, with all its fragrance, whipped against my cheek. I was like drunk, like crazy, I thought up something to say to her like in those writers people go for: "I want you and me to die together. If only this car now could be like the ones I've kept seeing in the papers the last day or two, hit a telegraph pole or flip over into the river, and then we'd die holding each other like this, with smiles on our lips, so sudden we'd never feel it. Wouldn't it be wonderful!" I was kidding, I didn't realize it was a prophecy. I don't know whether the driver was drunk or drowsy, he came to a bend of the riverbank and the whole car just overturned and landed in a ditch by the side of the road.

It was a really sad thing to happen: my darling Tenderness Lu had internal injuries. She was bleeding from mouth and nose and died on the way to the hospital. I was unconscious for thirty minutes and more, the back of my head lacerated by shards of glass, and I only came to when they gave me a shot to stimulate my heart. The driver was the only lucky one. He got off light with just a broken right hand. What with the medical costs and the compensation to Tenderness Lu's family, the accident cost us close to ten thousand, and I came in for a lot of grumbling and lecturing from my uncle and my mother.

I'd lost a lot of blood and been very upset. I was really down in body and spirit, and a couple of weeks in the hospital brought hardly any improvement. When my uncle came up from the country with the money, he saw how badly I was hurt and had an anxious talk with the doctor, insisting I be given the best and fastest treatment. It was a foreign doctor and he said I ought to have a blood transfusion. I'd no idea what this blood transfusion thing was supposed to be and didn't want to let them. The foreign doctor was very nice and friendly. He spoke Shanghainese with a thick Foreign Settlement accent: "Blood transfusion very good, very good. Not hurt at all. Just like mosquito bite, nothing more."

"But what kind of medicine is it you inject me with?"

"We use someone else's blood to supplement your own." My uncle, after all, knows more about things than I do.

"Whose blood? You mean you can buy it?"

"What a young innocent, a real young gentleman!" The foreign doctor clapped his hand on my shoulder. "If there's one thing China has plenty of it's paupers. They don't have the ability to earn money for themselves, but their stomachs won't let them off, they have to eat just the same. Either they sell their blood or put up with an empty belly. Haven't you seen them? When you're a little better go look outside the door: those raga-

muffins of beggars who line the benches day after day both sides of the hall, they're all here to sell blood."

I laughed for sheer joy. What a wonderful world it is; if you have the money there's nothing you can't buy.

"But this Shanghai's a filthy place," the doctor went on, wrinkling his prominent nose and shaking his head. "Take blood from ten of these deadbeats and you'll find nine of them impure. It's infected, contaminated. No use, no use."

My uncle's got brains, and he's been around; he said this matter wasn't one to be handled any old way. Here in Shanghai every street and alley bristles with V.D. notices, every sidewalk has its low-class whores, "pheasants." None of these men selling their blood can afford to take a wife; you can imagine what kind of low conduct they get up to. Then, once contaminated blood of that sort is injected into your veins, there's no way of getting it out again. As my uncle was speaking, suddenly a thought struck him, and he told us of a man from our own village he'd come across at North Station yesterday afternoon when he got off the train. This man's blood would surely be more dependable. I asked who it was, and my uncle said it was this Young Baldy, Cripple Ch'en's son.

"What's a fellow like that doing, trotting up to Shanghai to see the world?"

"What indeed! Tried to bum five dollars from me the moment he saw me. But he's getting what he deserves, this fellow. Told me after we canceled their tenancy last year he couldn't make a living in the village, but he heard from a traveling cloth-peddler about how many mills there were in Shanghai, high wages and the work not too hard. So his eyes sparkle and like an idiot he comes hightailing it to Shanghai with the cloth-peddler. Well, this peddler did help him get a job as a laborer in a mill across the river, wages thirty cents a day. But the bastard was out of luck, five months later the mill shuts down. He said the mill failed, it was losing money, something about competition with the Japanese mills, but how can you believe that sort of crap. Anyway, he'd lost his job, lost touch with his peddler friend, didn't know another soul in Shanghai, and no way to get back to the village. But he's a slick customer, he goes and stands guard outside the North Station every day, on the lookout for someone he knows from the village traveling through."

"Did you give him the money? If you did, he'll have left Shanghai by now."

"Fat lot a youngster like you knows of the ways of the world! It was someone else brought him to Shanghai. Why should I present him with five dollars for no reason at all? And how should I know whether it was a true story he was telling me or a pack of lies?"

I was on edge and pressed my uncle to go hunt him out right away. My uncle told the doctor he could find a reliable donor, someone he knew; was it all right?

"Very good, very good. As it happens the hospital hasn't received any good blood the last couple of days. Bring the man here and I'll examine him, see whether we can use it."

My uncle was gone for a while and when he got back there was Young Baldy Ch'en with him. I remembered Young Baldy the moment I saw him. Somewhere over thirty, a few straggly hairs the color of straw across his scalp, slant eyes. He had on a dirty white jacket and pants. Bare-chested, feet bare inside a pair of sneakers that gaped open at the toe. He looked a bit thinner than before, but still strong as a water buffalo with his rippling muscles. He came in, greeted me, and stood with his slit eyes taking in everything in the room.

The doctor didn't want him in the sickroom and ordered him straight out for a blood test. When the doctor came back he kept exclaiming, "Jesus Christ," absolutely delighted, congratulated my uncle on his perspicacity, said the man's blood was terrific and exactly the type for me, God was looking after me. But he said I was still too frail to accept too large a transfusion. Three quarters of a pint would be plenty.

The usual price when the hospital bought blood was ten dollars a pint. But it was quite common for a donor to get the feeling that some sick person had a desperate need for his blood, and then he'd hang back to boost the price. Young Baldy was as sly as his father. He'd seen how my uncle

had come searching for him at North Station, and heard the doctor say his blood was terrific when he took the test. So now he seized his chance, tried to rip us off by asking my uncle twenty dollars for his three quarters of a pint.

"You scoundrel, you don't realize when people are doing you a good turn!" My uncle got mad with him. "Our Young Master only threw this deal your way because he felt sorry for you, drifting about like this away from the village. And now you try to swindle us! All right, let's see you try! But be careful you don't trip yourself—what do you think all those poor slobs waiting outside the door are there for? Think we can't buy blood any time we want?"

Young Baldy put his head back and sighed, as if he felt he'd no room to maneuver. He asked me to put in a good word for him, see whether he couldn't give a bit extra. All I wanted was to get my health back and not have to go on cooped up in this hospital that was driving me crazy. I asked my uncle to give him fifteen dollars, since he was a man from our village after all.

The doctor drew the blood (keeping it safe in a bottle that had medicine in it to stop it cooling or clotting), and that evening he gave me my transfusion. It really didn't hurt much. Only, about ten minutes later I started sweating and shivering as if I'd caught malaria; I shook so much the bedsprings were twanging away. I got scared.

"I've been tricked!" I yelled shakily. "The doctor didn't test it properly, Young Baldy's blood is infected, it's got to be!"

The doctor and the nurses explained calmly and quietly that this was the inevitable consequence of a transfusion and that it would clear up in a little while. I lay dozing all night, and next day the fever had subsided, but I still felt achy all over and completely listless.

I stayed three months in the hospital until my health and spirits were completely restored, whereupon my uncle pressured me into going back home for a few months more.

My mother asked sympathetically: "Where is your husband now?"

"He came back from Shanghai last year," the

wet-nurse replied, changing over to her right breast and continuing to press and squeeze. "But how can people of our sort support a man, ma'am, who has nothing to do all day but eat? His parents were at him all the time. He sat around at home a couple of weeks, then he got together with some of our neighbors and they all went off. They said they were heading for the provincial city to join the army. But they'd no money to get there. Been gone seven or eight months now, not a word, I don't really know where he can be."

"A low-down daddy like that, better off dead for all his brat can expect from him!" This was a bellow from Aunt Plantain as she planted a series of lip-smacking kisses on the kid's face. Then she went on to the kid: "Don't copy that precious pa of yours! When you grow up you want to be a real water buffalo, get on with your job and put up with it, earn some money to look after your ma."

The wet-nurse had given a bowlful and was worrying about getting cussed out by her mother-in-law for being home late, so she took her child up in her arms and went straight off. My mother told her to drink a lot of soup. If she drank soup it would be good for her milk. She said too we wouldn't worry about an extra mouth to feed, it was all right for her to come and eat her meals every day at our house. The wet-nurse smiled and came out with all kinds of blessings and benedictions.

Aunt Plantain heated up the milk over some boiling water and brought it me to drink. You don't need to put sugar in mother's milk, it's really sweet; and there's no unpleasantly strong flavor to it at all. In the city you pay four dollars a month for a pint of regular milk a day, and most of it's watered down with beanjuice, it's not a patch on this mother's milk.

I drank a couple of bowls of milk every day. The wet-nurse never missed coming twice a day to our house for her midday meal and her supper. She'd eat her meal and then give her milk, and when she'd given her milk she'd hurry off again back home. The milk really was good stuff. After a month or so my appetitite had improved by leaps and bounds and my cheeks were fuller and pink with health. I wasn't used to living in a bor-

ing, barbaric place like this and thought of taking a trip or two; but there were troubles with bandits all over the county, and although every town and village of any size had raised its own militia, they hadn't been able to root the bandits out and get rid of them completely. Because of this my mother didn't feel comfortable about letting me risk it outside, but said I should use this time to keep on with the milk for another month or two and really get my strength back. And it would be no easy business getting milk if I went away.

Speaking of bandits, the talk has been scarier than ever this last month. A month ago the bandits on Seven Stars Ridge joined forces with another bunch; they've collected over five hundred men and all the guns and ammunition they need. They wrote a letter to the county seat demanding thirty thousand dollars to be handed over in full within a week; otherwise they'd launch an immediate attack on the county town and plunder every village they came to. When word of this got out, the militias in every town and village started pooling their defense plans and posting sentries night and day along all the highways. Anyone whose movements were suspicious was picked up for interrogation.

My uncle is a militia commander and has been at work from morning to night in his headquarters. I've been bored sitting around the house, so every day I've been over there for a chat and to learn what's happening. The best is when they arrest someone whose movements are suspicious and have him up for questioning, that's fun. The headquarters is located in our ancestral shrine in the village. The last couple of days all the commanders have been getting together for a bit of company and to talk things over.

"A comet appeared in the sky in the first half of the year. I knew it was an omen of great disorders." This was one of the militia commanders. "They say these bandits are in touch with the extremists. If we don't find some way to exterminate them pretty soon, we'll have a fine situation when the time comes they start spreading their wings!"

"Perhaps it's our own time of reckoning. Like the ancients said, calamity can't be avoided, everything's a matter of fate. No need to look: just tell me of any village, any town that isn't going down-hill from one day to the next? Nine out of ten families too poor to eat, seven or eight out of every ten businesses failing and closing down. If this isn't fate what is it?" An old fellow, stroking his beard: what he said made good sense.

The most novel argument came from a distant cousin of mine who is a partner in a business in the city and just recently came back for a summer break: "Everything around here going downhill from one day to the next has nothing to do with fate. If you ask me, it's because we've been cheated out of all our money by the foreigners. I can remember when we were small, there wasn't a household in the village that didn't spin its own yarn and weave its own cloth. There wasn't a household that didn't light its lamps with bean oil. Or take smoking: you lit your pipe with a flint and a twist of paper; when did you ever see anybody strike a match and light up a cigarette, a Player's or a Capstan Navy Cut? We made our own things for our own use, and the money went back and forth from one hand to the next among ourselves. And nobody had to worry in those days where his next meal was coming from. But then it all changed: you spun your yarn, wove your cloth, no place to sell it. Everybody knows a calico dress or an imported cotton suit is both cheaper and smarter. A bean-oil lamp isn't bright enough, you have to fill up with Mobil kerosene. All these things are foreign invented, foreign manufac-tured, ways they've thought up to cheat us Chi-nese out of our money; and once they've made off with your money there's no way to get it back—how are you going to stop the country from get-ting poorer? And then you talk about fate! And recently worse than ever: your farmer's hard at it year-round, pays his rent, pays his assessments, pays his taxes, and ends up empty-handed for all his efforts, if he wants a bowl of coarse gruel it's no easy thing to come by. When it comes to trade, it's just not possible anymore. Anyone with any money in the countryside is off to the city. Every-body knows the city's where all the fun and excite-ment are nowadays. Who's going to put up with living in the countryside when he could be riding in cars or watching movies? Just take this cousin

of mine here, nothing but Shanghai this, Shang-hai that from morning to night, no patience to live at home!"

"Don't drag me into this." I was blushing and laughing. "How about yourself? Don't you prefer living in the city?"

"That's just it!" My cousin went on: "The rich are off to the city to see the world, middle-class people are getting more hard-pressed every day; what's left but a bunch of poverty-stricken beggars? Nothing but what they stand up in, work all day for a mouthful of gruel—what kind of money have they got to buy anything with? You say the businesses shouldn't be closing down. Who are they going to trade with? All right, so the peasants leave the farms, the tradesmen, shop-keepers, assistants, not a scrap of business for any of them in the interior. Let's say they all move into the city. The city's just the same, there's more unemployed in the city even than in the interior. If these people don't turn into robbers and ban-dits, what else is there? So what's fate got to do with it?"

"You can talk 'til you're blue in the face, you can't get away from fate," the old man argued. "Otherwise, how is it the foreigners never used to be able to cheat us Chinese out of our money, it's just right now at this moment they can manage it? What's this if it isn't fate?"

"Because it used to be that we Chinese closed our ports and kept ourselves to ourselves, don't you see?" My cousin was a good one in an argu-ment. "Foreigners never used to be allowed into China. Then we were defeated in one war after another, and the foreigners came in, and can't you see how China's gotten poorer from one day to the next ever since?"

"But they say the foreigners are in a hopeless mess as well! Wasn't it in the papers a few days ago, how many million unemployed in America, how many million more in Japan? It's fate and the foreigners can't escape it any more than China can! What I say is, when you get right down to the root of it, it's nothing but fate!"

To tell you the truth, I haven't the slightest in-terest in this kind of discussion. What I was hop-ing for was that the militiamen guarding the highways would pick up a few more suspicious characters; I really enjoy watching the interrogations. Like one time, they brought in a troupe of acrobats from Shantung, five of them, two of them girls. The tale was they were expert cat burglars because they could somersault over the highest wall. They were questioned over and over and no one was willing to let them go, but since we couldn't prove they were lookouts for the bandits, we couldn't just execute them on the spot. In the end we had to send them off to the county seat to get rid of them.

Then a thing that really surprised us happened one noontime. That was when a bunch of militiamen from Hsüeh Family Village, ten miles away, suddenly marched in with Young Baldy Ch'en as their prisoner.

The men carried a message from the guard commander at Hsüeh Village. The message said that this Baldy Ch'en they'd arrested, not only were his movements suspicious, they'd searched him and found an important communication, sewn into the waistband of his trousers, from the Seven Stars Ridge bandits to the Phoenix Mountain bunch (the gist of it was to set the date for the attack on the county seat), clear proof he was acting as a messenger for the bandits. On examining him they'd discovered he was from our village so they were forwarding him to our village headquarters for disposal of the case.

It gave me a start, I can tell you.

Young Baldy looked better than the last time I saw him, and as soon as he saw my uncle and myself he started protesting mightily—he'd never been a bandit, he'd started up as a peddler over at North River. He hadn't been home for a long time and so he'd come back especially to see how things were going, but he'd been arrested for no reason when he got to Hsüeh Village. The trousers weren't his, he'd switched by mistake with somebody else at an inn. If there was a message sewn into the waistband he knew nothing about it. However, the Hsüeh Village men insisted that the road he was on wasn't the one to our village, it was the road to Phoenix Mountain. There was no question but that he was carrying messages for the bandits and no need for further interrogation.

"I always knew you'd come to no good!" my uncle railed at him. "Nothing but sly tricks, you and your old man, when you were tenants on our land; and you tried to swindle us when we were in Shanghai last year! Well, there'll be no end to our problems unless we deal with a scoundrel of your sort properly!"

Everybody was in agreement. You could tell this turtle's-spawn was a real criminal; just look at his slant eyes and his villainous expressions! You had to make an example of him, kill one to warn a hundred, or there was no justice.

They did the job with amazing speed. They tied Baldy's hands behind his back right away and hauled him off to the South Village riverbank. He kept a set face throughout, watching us with his staring eyes, no fear at all, he even asked permission to go back home to see his parents and his wife and kids, but of course he didn't get it.

Because the idea was to set an example, my uncle proposed that he not be shot but beheaded, short and sweet, with a sword. They picked one of the militiamen who was a pork butcher to act as executioner. This fellow had a face that was all black pockmarks. He'd drunk a bellyful of hot sorghum liquor and marched behind Young Baldy with a great old-fashioned saber clutched in his fist; a vicious-looking face with his eyes bloodshot from the drink. But he didn't look as terrifying to me as Young Baldy did. One look at Young Baldy's expression and you couldn't help shivering.

The riverbank was packed.

They marched Young Baldy up to the riverbank; my uncle ordered the executioner to kick him to his knees. But the executioner couldn't manage it with kicking, so he gave him a wild shove with his hand and sent him sprawling among the rocks. Young Baldy wasn't going to give up while he still had breath; he deliberately stuck his head and neck against a big boulder and wouldn't be prized loose from it.

The executioner was helpless, he just stood there with both hands gripping the saber's hilt, he couldn't stop shaking, no way he could bring the saber down. Until my uncle went over and bawled him out furiously: then he hacked away three or four times like splitting firewood, turning the edge of his blade until it looked like a row of fangs.

The onlookers were solemn and silent, except for a few urchins who clapped their hands and yelled.

A few of the hacks had got to Young Baldy. His blood was spattered all over the jumbled rocks. He lay there stiff and motionless, and the executioner staggered off supported by some of the other militiamen, when suddenly the corpse struggled up, raised its arms, and began to scream in a wild shrill voice like some evil demon. Everybody ran off in terror as far as they could get, stumbling and shrieking. My uncle's lips went bloodless, his face turned green, he dragged me away with him and we kept tripping and falling. It was only a handful of the bolder ones among the farmers there who went up and helped him. I was terrified out of my wits and clung to my uncle's hand, wouldn't let go.

"Imagine this fellow joining the bandits!"

"Must be one of those stars of retribution, come down on earth in human form! Way he carried himself, you've got to say he was a real desperado!"

Tongues were wagging all the way back, everybody chipping in. My uncle did nothing but damn the executioner and the militiamen for a pack of shitheads; but after a while he managed to joke out of it: "You wouldn't get a cent for this son-of-a-turtle's blood now, and last year he was asking twenty dollars a pint!"

But when Uncle and I got back to militia headquarters we saw my wet-nurse coming out the door, weeping and yelling, her hair streaming: "'My husband's no bandit, my husband's no bandit!'"

She stood like a crazy woman, head back, mouth wide open, bawling at the top of her voice: "A wrong to blacken Heaven! A wrong to blacken Heaven! We paid our share for this militia, paid our money and then you come killing us! Heaven is dark and blind to my wrong!"[2]

Still yelling, she went waddling off in the direction of the riverbank. A crowd of children and womenfolk followed along behind to see what would happen. Aunt Iron Plantain pushed through them, caught up with her, grabbed hold of the still screaming wet-nurse and started berating her in her man's voice that grated like a frog's: "What's wrong with you, woman, your brains full of shit? That man of yours deserved slicing to death—they did him a favor cutting his head off! Why don't you get back and squeeze your milk for our Young Master, instead of wailing your goddam funeral cries like you'd run up against the Demon Fiveways![3] You . . ."

[2] The wet-nurse's cry gains an epic dimension by recalling an ancient image of injustice that we find often, for example, in Yüan plays: the magistrate's court trapped beneath an overturned bowl which shuts out the light of Heaven, and with it all justice and human decency.

[3] A malevolent spirit in old folk belief who specialized in taking possession of women.

Let There Be Peace

by Wu Tsu-hsiang

Translated by James C. T. Shu

There was a temple in Feng-t'an Village. Pressed on by a dense grove of big trees on the hill slope behind it, the temple towered above the fields. Despite its drab, dilapidated look from long years of neglect, its imposing structure still carried an awe-inspiring dignity: the flying eaves on the four corners, delicately upturned, were spread horizontally like a gigantic claw of a deified genie; the finial in the center of the temple ridge, rising above the sky-piercing trees on the slope, looked like the genie's cap, visible from dozens of miles away. The finial was a massive ancient vase of fine red cinnabar, with three square spears shooting up from its mouth. The top, bottom, left, and right of the halberd were each decked out with a character wrought in metal, and the four characters read: "Let There Be Peace."

The supplication engraved in those four characters had not gone completely unheeded: Feng-t'an Village had seen many a peaceful day. Even in recent years—not to mention the remote past— the villagers had constant reports of battles fought here and there, hundreds and thousands of people killed by foreign cannon, about such and such number of Chinese slaughtered by foreigners, so many revolutionaries and extremists arrested or executed somewhere, other places fallen into the hands of the Japanese devils; yet all this had nothing to do with their village. Many neighboring county seats, towns, and villages had time and again experienced ravage and rape by the soldiers who passed through, attacks and kidnappings by large and small bands of robbers; but Feng-t'an

Village, tiny and tucked away in a valley, had been exempted from such horrors.

Life in Feng-t'an Village had always been peaceful, maybe owing to the potency of the gods it worshipped, maybe to its favorable geomantic location. Everybody seemed to believe that the peace of the village was a blessing from its temple. So the villagers entrusted their kind and sorrowful hearts to the temple. Sometimes they went sleepless, worrying about the food supply or debts; sometimes, awaking from a dream, they heard the shrill song of an owl and their bodies froze in fear, sensing that something ominous was about to take place. But as soon as they heard the wind blowing through the metal bells on the eaves of the temple, making a gong-like music, low and dignified, they would heave a long sigh, remembering that the temple was keeping all evil forces under control, and feel somewhat relieved. Sometimes they sighted a comet in the sky. They went wild-eyed with panic and their teeth chattered until their jaws hurt, sensing an impending catastrophe. But as soon as they saw the "Three Spears on a Vase" on top of the temple reflecting a whole sky of stars, dazzling in its red-gold splendor, so mysterious and so powerful, they were reassured that the temple was protecting their village, and calmed down a bit. Their belief was not without some ground. Legend had it that once, when the doors and walls of the temple were painted red, the village suffered from continual fires; when they were painted white, the village repeatedly had plagues. The legend dated back to the prosperous days of the village; whether it was true, none of today's villagers could say one way or another. But the following was a fact witnessed by everyone: the walls of the temple, currently painted blue, were drab, cracked, and very much run-down; the village had become equally drab and run-down, and its inhabitants ragged and ungainly.

Not until recent decades had the lives of the Feng-t'an villagers gradually turned from affluence and contentment to poverty and sorrow. At present, the situation was very bleak. The yarn the village women spun and the cloth they wove had long since found no buyers in town. The spinning wheels and the weaving looms gathered dust that was inches thick. They were either shunted to the corners or burned as firewood. As for the fields, they had suffered from floods and droughts year after year because the waterways and dikes hadn't been repaired. The crop produced could hardly be sold even dirt cheap. The town factory that used to buy cocoons had gone out of business four or five years earlier, and the village simply stopped bothering about cocoons in spring and summer—in fact, some households followed the example of neighboring villages in cutting down the mulberry trees and planting instead opium, beans, or corn. The few villagers who used to work as clerks in town all came back home, sad-faced, to be supported by their mothers or wives. However, all the Feng-t'an villagers—whether farmers, who were in the majority, or the jobless former clerks who were in the minority—were good-natured. Be kind and generous, work hard, keep your place—all the precepts handed down from their ancestors had become second nature to them. They entrusted their fates to the temple, kept their place, worked as hard as they could, and drank the little thin porridge they could get or went without. So, while bandits ravaged the neighboring villages, Feng-t'an Village, poor as it was, after all was peaceful. Whenever the villagers saw those four words on the "Three Spears on a Vase" on top of the temple, their sorrowful souls found consolation.

But now a shocking incident had taken place. It concerned the household of Wang Hsiao-fu.

Of the row of old tiled houses directly facing the temple across the fields, the one in the center with the tallest roof-ridge belonged to the family of Wang Hsiao-fu. He was in his thirties, being one of hundreds of men in the prime of life in the village. He had a straight nose, dull eyes, and a small bony face. His expression was like a monkey's: sad all the time. His clothing and demeanor were almost reduced to those of a beggar, but the slight hunch of his shoulders and back, the craning of his neck, and the sluggish movement of his limbs still bespoke the posture of a clerk with a formal apprenticeship.

He had worked as a clerk for twenty-three years in the town five miles from the village. He started as an apprentice in a store when he was eleven. His daily work was to serve tea to the boss and the manager, sweep the floors, dust the counters, clean the smoking pipes, twist paper into spills,[1] empty the urinal, carry the merchandise, run errands, be a whipping boy to the boss, the manager, and even the cook. Just like a small beast of burden, he busied himself with such things every day, without a word of gossip, without one second of malingering. Generosity, filial piety, diligence, frugality—all the character traits of the Feng-t'an villagers could be found in him. Twice a month his boss gave him five coppers for a haircut, but he managed to put off the haircut to every other month. The money thus saved, together with the twenty to forty coppers he earned from tips at festivals, he sent to his mother through a villager whom he knew well. At the end of his three-year apprenticeship, he became a clerk. Within a few years he had won his boss's trust and approbation and was promoted to manager. He made forty or fifty dollars a year.

During this period, he had many simple, beautiful daydreams. After his mother had gradually set aside enough of his money, he thought, he would open a small store. He wouldn't overprice the goods as his boss did, and he wouldn't use so many clerks and managers. He was sure he could

---

[1] Used to light candles, tobacco in a pipe, etc.

handle all kinds of chores, large and small; he would lower prices, making only such profit as he could feel at ease about and which the gods and the Bodhisattva wouldn't disapprove of. After he became rich, he would buy some land for his sons to farm, but he would have one of them learn how to manage a store. He would buy his father and mother a geomantically auspicious grave site and marry his sons to frugal, diligent women. He would give out alms to the helpless, poor orphans, and widows of his village. He would repair the temple that affected the rise and fall of Feng-t'an Village, so that his village would become prosperous again.

But all these beautiful daydreams, as well as his hard work, could not stave off the decline of his village and his family. His father, who had spent his whole life as a hard-working farmer, died very early, and except for three old tiled buildings inherited from his ancestors, he had not left any property. By the time Wang Hsiao-fu was promoted to clerk, glazed cotton cloth and printed calicos, which were at once pretty and inexpensive, were in vogue in the town and the village. His mother's spinning and weaving job had ended, and a clerk's annual salary usually came to a mere dozen dollars. Even in the best year, one could not make more than twenty dollars. After he paid for one or two necessary items of clothing, the remainder of the wages was only enough to help his mother make ends meet. Wasn't the mother just as eager to save some money for the son? But one had to eat when hungry, dress when cold. No matter how hard they tried to tighten their belts, mother and son were empty handed at the end of each year. After he became a manager, he had a higher salary. The mother had put together eighty dollars after four or five years of rigorous saving. She married him off. His wife was only a little short-tempered, a little wily and, in his eyes, not "straight" enough. But she was an ideal wife as far as diligence and tolerance for hardship went. Following the marriage, he had children. Pretty soon things got very bad. By and by, it was difficult to collect all the debts owed to the store. Then circulation of money became slow, and business went sluggish and shrank. His wages

were cut, and the bonus—well, better not mention it. Many of his colleagues were laid off, for the boss wanted to decrease the staff in order to cut down on expenses. Because he was the one most trusted by the boss, he was lucky enough to keep his livelihood—what could he complain about? By this time he already had two children. His growing family could barely live on his meager income; he could only dream about saving money as he lay in bed.

By and by, he watched all his beautiful yet modest plans, like a rainbow, slowly dispersing. But he didn't lose heart. He still expected the store to revive and prosper so that his dream could come true one day. Things were getting worse and worse, however. Business was getting even more sluggish. Each year would see more of the big stores close. A manager of a certain store was kidnapped by bandits while he was on a buying trip in some city; a certain store was looted by soldiers; a certain store lost several thousand dollars of its capital; a certain stockholder sued to withdraw his holdings; a certain boss took his own life—news like this bombarded one's ears every day. The store he worked for showed no signs of recovery. On the contrary, its staff had decreased from two dozen to a dozen, then to four; its annual transaction of twenty to thirty thousand dollars had shrunk so much that it could scarcely keep going. Then last year the boss was suddenly arraigned in the county court. A large old store that had boasted very substantial capital finally met the same fate as many other stores: its merchandise was sealed and put away; its door was tightly closed and plastered, as was customary, with a transverse strip of paper with the words "Property Transferred" on it.

Like a man who, at a time of rampant epidemics and deaths, clings to an ailing relative on whom he depends, he had entertained the impossible hope that one day the store would bottom out, so that his family would have something to hold on to, so that he could go on dreaming his beautiful dreams. Yet the relative had died after all. He lost all that he could fall back on—as well as those simple, beautiful daydreams of yesterday. He knew very well what a miserable lot awaited a man without any savings nowadays. To try for another job as a clerk—that was a ridiculous fantasy. A small business of one's own—you couldn't borrow a few dollars' capital from any source. He had seen how many a man in the prime of life, both in the town and the village, was reduced from a respectable clerk, manager, or small-store owner to a thief or a beggar; or was forced into exile and ended up as a soldier or a bandit. On the day he left the store for good, he fell on the counter and cried his heart out like a child. It was understandable. The counter was the very one at which he had stood for well over twenty years, whose smooth, mirror-like old surface he had leaned on, touched, and wiped for more than twenty years! Here he had made many beautiful plans. Here he had spent the best of his youth working hard. Now he had to leave, with empty hands, as he had first come, and with a heart full of apprehension and despair.

Of those from his village who had worked for the store, some managers and five or six clerks, he was the last to leave for home. He was not at all to blame for losing his job. Even though his mother and wife were awfully sad, all they did was cry together a few times—they could not bring themselves to complain or reproach him.

His mother was almost seventy years old. She was so far-sighted her eyes were little better than a blind man's. As for her bound feet, seven or eight of the toes had been damaged by frostbite. Still, she never idled away her time. Every day she would totter around to collect a little firewood in the hills and gather some rags. His wife was expecting for the third time. Though big with child, she kept working as hard as ever. She had cleared a piece of land behind the house and grown four or five plots of winter cabbage; she had also succeeded in soliciting needlework from the town. She was certainly able: in addition to cooking and doing laundry, she could manage to finish a pair of shoes in two days and manure four or five plots of vegetables in half a morning. However, times were just too bad. Vegetables usually sold for only a dozen coppers—and they had to be taken to town to be sold. The fee charged for the labor of making a pair of shoes fell to only forty or fifty

coppers, and it was not easy to get even this work. It simply wouldn't do to rely solely on her, a mere woman, to make money to feed the family's half-dozen hungry bellies. Some former colleagues had discussed with Wang Hsiao-fu going off together to work in some big city. For a while the idea had fascinated him. But after some deliberation, he decided it was after all not the right thing to do. Even though he could hardly imagine what it was like in a big city, he had heard often enough about the unceasing slaughter and the battles there, about the police, soldiers, and foreigners arresting or killing people at will. Those of his village who had headed for a big city either were never heard from or came back wretched and miserable within two or three months. And he also knew what happened to people who had become thugs or bandits. He dearly loved his mother, his wife, his children, his village, and himself. After a lifetime of hardship, all his mother had left was one son. He shouldn't leave her alone. Of his children, the older one was about twelve, the younger one was only six, and yet another one was still inside his wife. He couldn't tear himself away from the young ones. To know his place and to be blameless in the eyes of the gods and the Bodhisattva, to be a filial son and a responsible father—all this had always been the credo of his life. To leave young and old, leave this home, leave one's native place for an inscrutable, strange, and frightening city? At the moment Wang Hsiao-fu wouldn't do it even in his dreams.

"I don't know anybody there; besides, I don't have the money for the trip." Thus Wang Hsiao-fu declined to join his colleagues, his small eyes staring dully.

Thereafter he managed to forget his status as a respectable manager and started a humble new life as a peddler. He tried his hand at a variety of small businesses that did not require capital. He climbed to the hills to pick wild bamboo shoots and bracken leaves, or to dig for roots of kudzu vine. He always made for the hills at dawn, carrying a bag of rice crust. In the afternoon he returned from the hills, bringing along whatever he had found to hawk in town. Early on he would

feel extremely ashamed. He was terrified of running into familiar faces, and most afraid of those
who would, through an impractical sense of pity,
extravagantly praise the life he had left behind.
He hid half of his face in a worn-out hat, covered
his toes with rags before putting on straw shoes
(for his first and second toes were close together,
a sign of the feet of a clerk who once wore stockings and cloth leggings), and walked with his head
lowered, looking at the ground. He felt uneasy
every time he heard his own sad, tuneless hawking. By sunset, when he had made a few dozen
coppers and bought some rice, he would start on
his way home. The distant sight of the "Three
Spears on a Vase" above the trees on the slope
and the gong-like melody of the metal bells made
him feel sure that the gods and the Bodhisattva
had taken note of his principled life; besides, the
very idea that he would get home shortly, his wife
would make porridge out of the rice he had
bought, and the whole family would go to bed
after drinking their fill, noisily and yet without a
word, brightened his heart.

But this kind of business was for spring only. It
was over as soon as summer came along. He then
had the worst time, unable to find any kind of
work and forced to live parasitically off his wife,
mother, even children.

The new business his mother and older son
took up was selling twisted dough fritters. This
was a trade for old people and children: in recent
years those who plied it were so numerous that
they were not far from being beggars. After they
got the fritters from the stand in town, they would
visit home after home, rattling off a long string of
solicitations, in hope of winning a bit of pity.
Those who did not eat them or had just had some
still might buy a fritter or two. After a morning's
peddling, they would have sold forty or fifty fritters and have made a profit of a dozen to twenty
coppers. When Wang Hsiao-fu saw his mother
and child, sweaty and red in the face from exposure to the fierce, scorching sun, tottering back
home with one or two catties of rice, and when he
drank the thin porridge made out of this rice, his
heart bled with frustration.

"I'm in my thirties—a man in the prime of life.
But I can't support my mother, wife, and children. On the contrary, I allow myself to be supported by my mother and son, who work like
horses," he thought to himself.

Several times he worked up his courage to go to
farmers to inquire whether they needed a temporary hand. But it never came to anything. In recent years the price of rice kept falling and the
harvests were generally bad. Landlords tried hard
to raise the rent, passing taxes on to the tenants.
The latter could not stand it anymore. Some of
them broke the lease and managed to find other
jobs. Those who failed to do so and reluctantly
went on farming would rely only on the labor of
the family, hustling and bustling day and night.
They definitely could not afford to use hired
hands. The small landowners who were better off
did hire short-term laborers during the busy season. However, if they had to pay two or three
dimes a day, they would prefer seasoned farm
hands. Who needed a greenhorn like himself who
had attempted a new trick in mid-life?

"You're a respectable manager. How can you
work in the fields? You must be kidding?" His inquiries invariably elicited such a taunting wise-
crack.

One day he went to town, hoping to chance
upon some kind of chore. He inquired in the few
stores which were still in business whether anyone
needed a laborer to go down to the river and
move cargo. He inquired at several fresh-food
stalls whether they needed someone to carry fish
or fruit. After asking at several places in blushing
embarrassment, he finally came upon an acquaintance who told him that someone was going to cut
down mulberry trees to make a clearing to grow
opium, and that he had better hurry to inquire;
he might have this job all to himself.

"I'm only asking for a dime and a half a day.
Only a dime and a half. Please do me a favor and
go talk to them for me," Wang Hsiao-fu kept imploring the man, his eyes glittering, wishing he
had already landed the job.

The man told him the place and the name of
the person, wanting him to ask for himself. Wang
Hsiao-fu hesitated, feeling uneasy. He was afraid
that if he walked straight into the home of a com-

plete stranger, he might be embarrassingly rejected.

His face strained with a broad smile, he said, "My friend, I'm only asking for a dime and a half. Other people ask for two dimes, three dimes. I want only a dime and a half. If you can get me the job, I'll treat you to cigarettes. I'll be grateful for the favor."

"*Ai-yi!*" The man became impatient, knitting his brows, and said scornfully, "You're being too insistent. One has to find one's own food; do you really expect other people to find it for you and serve it to you in bed?"

That silenced him. He worked himself up and rushed to the place without stopping, only to find a laborer stepping out from the side door of the mulberry garden, carrying bamboo baskets with a full load of gravel. He wiped away the sweat all over his face, aware that this excitement had come to nothing. He felt so vexed that he could hardly talk.

He asked the laborer, "Are you cutting mulberry trees for them?"

"Mm, I am." The laborer, a stranger from some other vicinity, was fierce-looking and unfriendly in his manner, blinking ominous eyes.

Wang Hsiao-fu felt very uneasy. The idea of a job in town going to a stranger outraged him. He quietly stood aside, watching the laborer carrying the gravel to a refuse pile, dumping it, and coming back. Then a respectable-looking gentleman appeared from the garden gate, holding a hookah, as if to supervise the work. He figured it must be the master.

"Sir," he asked after some hesitation, "how much do you pay this laborer?"

"Two dimes, and meals too." The gentleman stirred the ashes on the paper spill a little and answered with a smile.

He was very kind. Wang Hsiao-fu felt a glimmer of hope. He approached him and whispered, "I'm only asking a dime and a half, a dime and a half."

Wide-eyed, Wang Hsiao-fu was waiting for the gentleman to reply when all of a sudden he heard behind him the snapping sound of a coolie-pole. The gentleman, shaken, pulled him aside. When he looked around, he saw the laborer fiercely raising his coolie-pole and aiming at him, cursing, "You son-of-a-bitch!"

Wang Hsiao-fu hastened to hide himself behind the gentleman and succeeded only after he had been hit heavily on the left arm.

"You've gone berserk!" The gentleman checked the angry laborer. "I've already hired you; of course you're to do the whole job. What did you hit him for? Go back to your digging. Go back to your digging. Quick!"

"I was only asking, and you became so violent! Unless you're a bandit you—" Wang Hsiao-fu argued, his dull eyes staring, one of his hands holding the injured arm.

"Good fellow, leave quickly. Those strangers can be unreasonable and fierce," said the gentleman with a smile, waving the paper spill in his hand.

As he walked dejectedly, Wang Hsiao-fu's mind was preoccupied. The laborer was also poor, even though he was a stranger. Out of desperation, Wang Hsiao-fu was trying to steal his means of living. It was an immoral scheme. It was unprincipled. He had been very much outraged, but after this thought, he was no longer angry.

Once he found a job with a fresh-food stall to dig for arrowroots in a pond. The pond was on the premises of a residence in town. When he approached the door of that residence, he saw an old woman, carrying her basket of fritters, in a state of panic and trepidation. She was rushing unsteadily from the door on her walking stick as if in a desperate effort to save her skin. Meanwhile she was yelling pleadingly, "I'll never come again! I'll never come again! *Ai—ai*, I—I—I—"

The young master rushed out after her, waving a broom in his hand and cursing in seeming jocularity, "You old thing that refuses to die! If you ever come again I'll break your feet! My nephew got a fever from eating your fritters, and you still come to bother us every day!" Wang Hsiao-fu was stunned, then realized it was his mother. She was gasping hoarsely, almost out of breath. She looked wretched and pitiful, just like a wounded old dog. Spurts of something burning hot seemed to cover his whole face. His eyes saw a confusion of stars. He immediately dropped the baskets on his shoulder and went forward to hold his mother steady, meanwhile saying to the young master, "Young Master, she's an old woman, an old woman in her seventies. She can't take the beating!"

"Since she won't listen to what I've got to say, I have to beat her."

Wang Hsiao-fu looked at the young master, who appeared naughty and undisciplined; he knew that there was nothing he could do. Without a word, he supported his mother and walked away. While his mother, leaning on her walking stick and propped up by him, was tottering along, she turned around and remarked in the direction of the door of the house, "It was only because I didn't have other means of making a living. I didn't—didn't mean to do any harm to your little baby. The old lady of your house is a nice person—a very nice person. She never drove me away. Only because—only because—"

The young master stood at the door a while and then strode into the house, whistling. Wang Hsiao-fu, supporting his mother, walked her a little distance and then asked, "Did he hit you anywhere?" He tried to say something more to her but couldn't.

"How come I came across you? He only tried to drive me away. He didn't beat me. I'm all right. You can go ahead with your own business." His mother pursed her creased mouth a little, twitched her nostrils, and held up the hem of her garment to wipe her eyes. She was shedding tears.

As for the older boy, who was twelve, even though he had a scabby head and was too thin to look human, he was in his small way proud and eager to prove himself. On the days when his business of selling fritters did not go well, that is, when the money he made in a morning was not enough to buy a catty of rice (which cost ten or eleven coppers), he would refuse to go home. Enduring hunger, ignoring his rumbling stomach or the hunger-sweat that broke out all over his face and body, he persistently carried his basket, walked from one end of town to the other, in his torn, over-sized adults' shoes picked up from some trash pile, and hawked his fritters with all the strength that remained, forcing open a mouth that was dry, cracked, and inflicted with white, dirty pus at both corners. Only after it was past noon and he was certain that there could not be any more business would he go home, his tiny, greasy, scabby head bobbing at every step like a sick calf's, his hands holding tight the coppers or a paper bag of rice, his nose buzzing with the sniveling of thick snot. On several occasions, what with excessive hunger and drinking too much cold water from ditches, the stubborn boy would throw up water on arriving home, while his eyes went dully white and his small face changed from purplish to livid. His grandmother would fuss around the house. Wang Hsiao-fu would only stare at the monkish face and knead the cleft of his upper lip, shouting, "Little Pigtail, Little Pigtail" (that was the name of the child with scabies). Only Grandma knew what to do. She knew it was "hunger-cholera." She would grease the mouth of a bowl with vegetable oil and vigorously scrub the child's back with it, cursing all the time, "You devil! You devil!" or "You goblin! You goblin!" While she was cursing and scrubbing, his back would gradually turn purplish. After the "devil" or "goblin" groaned a few times and threw up a few mouthfuls of thin saliva, he would be able to walk over to the stove and eat a couple of bowls of rice crust softened in boiled water. Afterward, he would wipe the cold sweat from his brow and the runny mucus from his lips, take up the portable covered basket, and brave the fierce sun to pick fresh water snails.

All this was not lost on Wang Hsiao-fu. It went without saying that he was agonized at the thought of all the principles of life he used to believe in. In fact he had vaguely foreseen all this immediately after he lost his job. It was now utterly hopeless, utterly irrevocable. He could only sigh long and deeply, and on occasion, talking to himself, make some slips that revealed his self-condemnation, his apology to his mother and children, ridden with guilt and shame. In any case, no sooner had he opened his mouth than his wife began to put him down. So he would prefer to sit silently on the threshold, holding his head in his hands and staring at the words on the "Three

Spears on a Vase" of the finial of the temple, lost in deep, idle thought, all alone.

His wife gave birth to a girl in early June. The newborn baby of course added to the problems of the family. Whenever his wife was overtaxed with work, she would take her spite out on that small baby, who could only open her mouth wide and bawl all the time. "You little devil! Why didn't you die the moment you came into this world! What wrong did I do you in a previous life! . . . Why won't the King of the Underworld send for you! If he won't, I'll kill you and devour you—kill you and devour you!" She would curse like this through gnashed teeth, thumping the baby on the ground, the bed, or in the cradle, as if she would not feel relief until she actually thumped her to death. His wife had always been a little irascible all right, but she had never abused a baby by yelling such curses. When this happened, Wang Hsiao-fu sometimes could not refrain from saying something: "Little Pigtail's mama, even a humble baby girl counts as a soul—the gods and the Bodhisattva too keep an eye on her. It's all because I'm out of luck—there's nothing we can do. What good can come from your resentful and spiteful curses? She was reborn into this world to live, not to die!"

Grandma too advised her, "You need to learn to be more patient. The poorer we become, the more we should cherish our children. All our ancestors were known to be generous, and they treated girls no differently from boys. They're all your flesh and blood. You must be patient."

Both her mother-in-law's and her husband's advice was weak and absolutely of no practical use. It was June, sultry and sweltering. Chores such as washing clothes and boiling water piled up much more than usual. The new baby meant countless breast-feedings and diaper-changings each day. The little time left was often insufficient to get the needlework done in time, the work she was commissioned to do for the townspeople. Busy often until midnight, she found sweat hardened into whitish frost in her hair and on her torn blouse, her whole body a briny mess of cracked flesh, aching, itching, and stinking in a way unbearable even to herself. But she could not find time to take a bath. She worried about tomorrow's salt, tomorrow's rice—about the unending days of pitch-darkness yet to come. Thus when the innocent baby's pointless tantrums fanned her anxiety like a flame, she needed an outlet for her frustration. She began to treat the baby with loving care only when it reached one month of age and she finally was able to find a lucrative job of an unusual sort in town. The job was the result of much deliberation with her mother-in-law and husband, of a dozen days' hustle and bustle on the part of every one, and, finally, of the recommendation of an acquaintance. But the baby was getting skinnier and sallower each day.

The lucrative job was none other than selling her own milk. Initially she had planned to give up her new, unwanted "money-losing commodity"[2] for adoption, and she herself would find a job in town as a wet-nurse, so that she could make a couple of dollars a month without having to feed an extra mouth in the family. As a rule in the hill counties, if you gave away your daughter to someone as his "adopted" daughter-in-law, he would have a maidservant to order around after only a few years of inconvenience. When she reached a certain age she could be whisked out of the kitchen to have her face "brightened,"[3] to get dressed up in red, and to worship Heaven, Earth, and the ancestors. Consequently she would become the official daughter-in-law. One didn't have to defray the mammoth expenses of a formal wedding. Since it was such a good deal, everybody used to look on the practice favorably. But in recent years things had changed tremendously. After having asked many people to inquire for her in the villages in the vicinity, Wang Hsiao-fu's wife was unable to find a single family that wanted an adoption. Nowadays women of the hill counties all felt the need to stay free to work for a living; they would rather save their milk to exchange for some cash in order to meet the immediate

---

[2] A vulgar epithet for a daughter; she will need a dowry but is not expected to support her parents.
[3] That is, to have the downy hair on her face shaved. A girl was considered marriageable after this "rite of passage."

needs of their families. Their sons were just children. To have daughters-in-law—well, let the future take care of itself; right now none could afford to worry about it. But Wang Hsiao-fu's wife
was quick in coming up with ideas. She was quite
healthy, not easily overcome by hardship; and she
had plenty of milk. If she was unable to give away
her "money-losing commodity"—so be it.
Through an acquaintance she found clientele for
her milk by retail. There were two customers. The
first one was a gentleman in his forties who, because of excessive preoccupation with family finances, had recently developed an illness that
caused him to cough blood. He was following his
physician's order to have a bowl of mother's milk
a day. The second one was a baby boy scarcely a
year old. His mother had just died. A very weak
baby, he needed to continue on mother's milk.
Since his family could not afford to hire a wet-
nurse for him, they had to buy two goblets of
mother's milk each day as a supplement to porridge and rice soup. Early every morning she
went to town carrying her baby child, got milked,
and rushed right back home to cook, wash, and
do needlework. She made two dollars and forty
cents a month from the two places: a dollar in one
and a dollar forty in the other. She would get paid
every few days. On some opportune occasions she
might even have her breakfast at one of her em-
ployers' homes. With such a big income, life for
her family eased up a little. Grandma was asked
not to sell twisted fritters in town anymore.

However, most of the baby's daily fare had been
snatched away from her. When it was her turn,
what she had in her mouth was often a dried-up
teat, hardly giving off a mouthful of milk in spite
of strenuous sucking. Therefore Grandma set
about stuffing her with a hodge-podge of food
that she herself happened to be eating, such as
porridge, rice, vegetables, or what not, just to
keep her from crying. It did not take long, with
things going on like this, for the baby to grow
skinny and sallow—only her belly became bigger
and firmer.

Wang Hsiao-fu should not have let his wife take
this lucrative job, but he did not stand in her way.
Every day to be lived from the very moment one
opened one's eyes. Every member of the family,

himself included, had an empty, starved stomach
that needed to be filled. He was a man in his
prime, but he was in every sense a parasite. All
that he could do was sit on the threshold all day
long and, with his head in his hands, stare blankly
at the finial of the temple. As his mother was so
senile and so feeble, it was more than clear that
she could barely handle the selling of twisted fritters anymore. Which one should he save: his
mother, who had been through a lifetime of hardships, or the innocent baby? In any case he was totally lacking in ideas—not in a position to come up
with any. He could no longer afford to care about
all those principles of conduct he had set for himself. His sensitivity was growing duller too. Every
day, as usual, he would eat the three meals of porridge or dried rice served him. It was his wife's
blood, his baby's flesh, but he could not bring
himself to think about that. His heart was gradually becoming a lump of lead, weighty, murky,
and dark. For some time now he had rarely had
any kind of response or feeling.

It was another year of drought. The better part
of June passed without a drop of rain. Many of
the tenant farmers, beset with the fatal double
onset of decline in the amount and in the price of
the crops, gave up their tenancies and switched
jobs to become cargo-carriers or sedan-carriers, or
to try their uncertain hand at a small business
after putting up a little money. Among them was
Wang Hsiao-fu's nextdoor neighbor Ah-fu. He
had turned twenty or so acres of fields back to his
landlord. He then hired himself out to a sedan establishment in town as a carrier, so as to earn his
own keep. His wife used the little pin money she
had saved to start a small rice-cake stall at the
edge of town, availing herself of her adroitness to
make and sell glutinous rice cakes. In this way she
kept her soul and body—and those of her two
children—together. For those farmers, especially
Ah-fu's family, Wang Hsiao-fu and his wife had
not sympathy but admiration. Even though they
had fallen on bad times as well, they had the
strength and stout physique common to farmers
and were able to carry or shoulder heavy things.
As soon as they quit farming, they worked at carrying a sedan or shouldering commodities on a
long trip and at least managed to earn their daily

bread themselves, instead of living off their wives and children. Wang lacked the strength and the capability. Every day Ah-fu's wife had to work like a horse at her cake stall, but she did make enough to buy food for her children. It was, however, beyond Wang Hsiao-fu to raise some capital to buy apparatus, glutinous rice, and sesame, even though it meant only a few dollars. Because of this, his wife took to making nagging insinuations. He, of course, never talked back, since he was aware that she had a really hard time and he could never be of any help. Only Grandma would come forward to say something on his behalf. She would say: "Above everybody's head hovers a certain Fate, and it is all planned by the gods and the Bodhisattva. Why all this fuss? Little Fu[4] isn't a good-for-nothing. He's only out of luck."

Grandma had scarcely enjoyed a few days of leisure at home after she quit selling twisted fritters when she came down with an illness. It was an endemic disease that came with autumn. A couple of days' diarrhea gradually developed into dysentery: urgency in the intestines, pressure around the posterior, and dashing to the thatched outhouse countless times a day. She was able to hold on in the beginning but was overcome after three or four days. She would lie in bed all day long, without a groan, her whole body scorching with fever. His expression hopeless, Wang Hsiao-fu was compelled to go to the pharmacy in town and, after some groveling, brought the warm-hearted physician home to diagnose. The physician called it "sunstroke induced by humidity," and, lest nothing be done about it, he prescribed some medicine for "dispelling the fever and ventilating the breath." Of course nothing resulted from the prescribed medicine after it was served a few times, except that the Wangs ended up owing several dimes to the pharmacy.

But Wang Hsiao-fu would not give up. He could still go to the gods and the Bodhisattva for help. One day he bought an incense stick and went to the temple to beg for a "divine prescription." After he had kowtowed, he wrapped the in-

cense ashes up with a piece of yellow-dyed paper. Now that he had his "divine prescription," the next thing for him to do would be to ask the Bodhisattva about what was yet to come. He fetched the lot-sticks container from the shrine table, knelt down once more, and shook the container with great care. The shaking went on a long while, and sure enough, the Bodhisattva revealed his power: unexpectedly, out of the container two bamboo lot sticks fell. After a moment's hesitation, he picked up both and, following the numbers on them, he went to the shrine table to check out the divination slips.

One read: Lot 76, Middle-Fortunate

Floating clouds lock up the moon of Heng-o;[5]
The sky is overcast and blurry.
Suddenly a rising wind clears all up:
Mountain scenes and lake views return
To what they should be.

The other one read: Lot 123, Low-Low

The treasure stumbled on in the dream vanishes upon
    waking:
Blame the fact that Mount Wu[6] is but an illusion.
If you are asking about marriage, ailment, or litigation,
Be sure to seek another exit.

Wang Hsiao-fu had had two years of schooling. Even though he couldn't make out the whole meaning of the two divination slips, he did get a general impression. One said approximately that despite the bad luck he was currently in he would be able to get out of it soon; the other obviously portended mishaps. But which one was genuine? It was such a serious matter to determine that he had to ask for help from the resident temple keeper.

"Sir, could you tell me which is the genuine one? I was given these two slips by the Bodhisattva."

"The one that first touched the ground, of course." The old man, sitting next to the street

<hr>

[4] An intimate title for Wang Hsiao-fu, considered proper only when used by his parents or those of his parents' generation.
[5] Or Ch'ang-o, a lady in Chinese mythology who stole the elixir of immortality and fled with it to the moon.
[6] A mountain in the east of Szechwan, which has mythic significance because, as the legend has it, King Huai of Ch'u once dreamed of having a love affair with the Goddess of Mount Wu.

and catching the fleas in his cloth stockings, asked throatily, "What do you want to know about?"

This caused Wang Hsiao-fu's grim, dejected face to shine in relief. He told the temple keeper about his mother's illness, among other things. Life had always been hard for her, he said, and it was too much that she still had to suffer so in her old age. The gods and the Bodhisattva should take pity. As soon as he got out of his predicament he would do his best to express his filial piety, so that his mother could enjoy a few easy days. The temple keeper held the first slip in his hand, squinted his small eyes, groaned, nodded, and remarked in measured tones, "Take it easy. Don't worry."

Carrying the "divine prescription" with him and repeatedly reciting the verse lines of the divination slip in silence, Wang Hsiao-fu hurried home, crossing the uniformly dry and grayish-brown fields in big strides. He had not looked so cheerful for years.

But he was to be surprised to find out that the temple keeper was wrong. What came to pass was predicted in the second slip. On arriving home, he found that his mother was in bed, her torso held up by his wife while the two children, who surrounded her, were yelling, "Grandma! Grandma!" Grandma strained her small eyeballs of deathly paleness and panted hoarsely, deeply, making no answer. The way it looked, she was on her last legs. Helter-skelter, he dissolved the divinely prescribed medicine in "yin-yang water" (half hot water and half cold), as it should be prepared. By the time it was to be served, his mother's jaw had already clamped shut. The two spoonfuls of medicine that were fed to her with great difficulty flowed out again, trickling down the corners of her mouth. Even the "divine prescription" could not help. His mother twisted her nose and upper lips, contorted her face, and, leaving a heap of excrement on the bed, departed for a better world.

Wang Hsiao-fu fell on her slender body, which was as thin as a bamboo rod, and abandoned himself to cries that sounded like the howl of a mountain monkey at midnight. As his cries continued into the evening, his voice turned hoarse. The neighbor Ah-fu's wife came over to console him.

"These days life is very much a punishment for a seventy-year-old. It won't do to keep crying. You should pull yourself together and take care of what comes next."

"Mother did not live out her time! Mother got that disease because she had to sell twisted fritters in June! Why didn't the gods and the Bodhisattva protect her?" He sounded like a dolt, if not a child.

But Ah-fu's wife was right. What good was it to cry and cry like a child? He had to take care of this unexpected expense. But where to get the money?

The next day, husband and wife went to kneel down before her client, the master who coughed blood, begging for help. It was the only solution the wife came up with after a night's thinking. Prevailed on by their importunity, the master agreed to be a guarantor so that they could borrow from a woman usurer. The woman was a widow in her fifties. She had about a hundred dollars of savings, which she jealously guarded. She was relentless and heartless toward her poverty-stricken debtors: if one was just a few days behind in paying the interest, she would come, on her walking stick, right into his house and press for it unrelentingly. Wang Hsiao-fu had taken out a loan of eight dollars, at the interest rate of twenty coppers per dollar.

"You should consider your ability. My money is my blood. I'm never touched with pity. You need the right kind of stomach for this slice of meat. Oh well, I like to make every thing clear in the beginning. I'll get my interest money by deducting it from the old master's milk payment. I have to. It is he who guarantees for you. Otherwise I'd never lend money to people like you, who are turnips without roots."

Husband and wife wiped away their tears and of course thanked her, keeping to themselves the pain they felt.

After Grandma was buried, Little Pigtail, the older child with the scabby head, fell ill. His illness was the same as Grandma's. Wang Hsiao-fu was utterly numbed. He no longer felt much shame or pain over the fact that his wife labored all day long and his children were so piteously sick. It was a mere seven or eight months that he had been out of work, but he had had too many sad, intolerable experiences. They had become like heavy black lead, sinking one lump after another down to the depths of his mind, or deposited in his nerves. His former credo appeared vaguer and vaguer. Sometimes he would sweep away the obnoxious excrement his older son left all over the house. Sometimes he would sit on a low stool, holding the ghost-thin baby, making dabs at her eyelashes to clear away the thick mucus, unfeelingly massaging her belly, which grew bigger and harder each day, or looking at her open mouth, sniveling feebly like a kitten. Sometimes he would follow his old habit, sitting on the threshold, holding his head in both hands, dully staring at the finial of the temple that faced him, and remaining immobile, mute for the better part of a day. Some time later, chestnuts and hawthorn berries were ripe. He finally had business on his hands. Still, every day his monkish face remained glum, and his staring eyes glassy. He acted only out of instinct. His brain was like a thick sheet of black paper or a knotted mass of floss silk, unresponsive and incapable of thinking.

The older child never got over his dysentery, but his appetite stayed pretty much the same as when he was well. This tallied well with one proverbial saying of the village: "No one dies of hunger who has typhoid fever; no one dies from eating who has diarrhea." As for the baby girl, she was getting worse each day. Early on, she would whimper like a kitten. Later, her tiny face was swollen like yellow wax, and her skin and flesh dried up and wrinkled like the crumpled paper made from mulberry bark. One afternoon when Wang Hsiao-fu arrived home after having sold wild nuts in town, his wife was sitting on the threshold with the baby on her lap, sobbing audibly. With a glassy stare, he walked over like a zombie and, without expression, asked slowly in a low, thick voice, "Already very bad?"

His wife shook her head, bawling even more heartbrokenly. He nevertheless showed no signs of sorrow. He did not shed tears. He only touched the small corpse with a hand that seemed seized with cramp, silently walked over to the corner to fetch a hoe, tucked it under his armpit, took the baby from his wife's hands, and with his eyes staring like a stray ghost's, totteringly made for the hills.

The death of the girl brought to the parents not pity and sorrow but anxiety and despair. Two days before she breathed her last breath, the child was already unable to suck the teat. When Wang Hsiao-fu's wife found her milk getting thinner and thinner, she desperately went around trying to find families that needed a wet-nurse. There were families that needed one, but as soon as they learned that her milk was being fed to a dying baby, they all refused to hire her. Even the two families that had been patronizing her let her go around this time. After it went on like this for a few days, her milk all turned into colorless liquid and finally dried up.

What was happening was plain to everybody. The woman usurer was anxious. Every couple of days she would walk on her stick to Wang Hsiao-fu's home. At first she would speak in the manner of the needy, which she customarily affected when pressing her debtors for money: "Hsiao-fu, I would like to borrow some money to buy a little rice."

Later on she would not be so indirect: "I'm a widow. I've none to fall back on. My money is my blood, my life. It can't be helped. You have to return my money even if it means you have to gouge your flesh. Otherwise you'll have to kill me!"

With each sentence, she struck the ground with her stick. Her face was so rigid that it couldn't be carved with an ax. The way she looked sent shivers through Wang Hsiao-fu and his wife.

As usual the couple knelt down to implore her, but it came to nothing. The woman had made it clear beforehand that she was not to be touched by pity. Consequently, whenever they were unable to pay the interest with the earnings from the wife's needlework or her peddling of vegetables, they would have their old clothes, torn bedding, and even the rice about to be cooked taken away.

One day, inspired by who knows what, the wife suddenly came up with an idea about their house. It occurred to her that even though you could not sell those three run-down buildings as they were, you might be able to get some money by tearing them down and selling the tiles and bricks at a low price. The idea was just great. Besides the fact that the bricks and tiles could sell for money, there was a secret hope that made one's heart palpitate: according to the previous generations, their ancestors used to possess such great abundance of gold and silver taels—too abundant to be conveniently deposited—that they made a practice of burying them underground or inside the walls.

"I should have thought of this long ago," the wife reproached herself.

First they tore down the gate-wall. The two gloomy hearts were filled with the expectation of encountering excitement and surprise. Their dry and bitter eyeballs protruded, their expressions turned solemn and tense, their hands shook, and their breath came in gasps. Each time a layer of bricks was torn off, and the dirt and gravel inside the bricks fell tumbling down, their hearts would leap to the throat, to the mouth. Meanwhile, their four hands were busy scraping open the rubble. It went on like this well into the afternoon. They were more exhausted than they had ever been before.

"We'd better take the bricks first and go see if anyone wants to buy them," said the wife, dabbing at the grime and sweat smeared on her face.

Wang Hsiao-fu arranged the bricks into piles, tied them up with straw ropes, and carried them to town. He started hawking them on the desolate street. People on the street all looked at him, surprised by his stray-ghost manner. A few children followed at his heels, laughing mischievously. Every time he came across someone with whom he had slight acquaintance he would ask slowly in a gloomy, low voice as if talking in his sleep, his eyes staring: "Old brother, do you know of any house that needs repairing?"

"You're really strange! Those aren't one of the seven daily basics,[7] so why are you carrying them around and hawking them?" someone gibed.

"Mr. Chao's house next to the Ch'ang-fa Inn at the end of West Street has a wall that's caved in.

You should go and ask," another one told him.

When he heard this, vigor surged up in his fatigued body. He bent his shoulder and carried his loads all the way to the end of West Street. The wall facing the gate of Mr. Chao's house had indeed caved in. Bricks had dissolved into powder and fallen everywhere. He knocked hesitantly at the door. It was Mrs. Chao who opened it.

"M— M— Mrs.," he stuttered. "Someone said you need bricks and tiles."

"None of that."

"This wall— My bricks are really cheap!"

"In these times, the—" Mrs. Chao changed her tone in the middle of her speech, "you young people don't want to do honest work but instead tear down houses every day in order to sell bricks."

With a bang she shut the door.

Wang Hsiao-fu's enthusiasm was so dampened that his tired body became utterly paralyzed. He sat down on his brick piles, wiping away his sweat. Meanwhile the Ch'ang-fa Inn right next to Mr. Chao's house was crowded with townspeople with a variety of antiques in their hands, soliciting with great insistence an out-of-towner who was collecting antiques and scrolls. Tired out, Wang Hsiao-fu sat a while. He noticed that the out-of-towner, wearing broad-rimmed eyeglasses and with a vest of ebony brocade open on the chest and a bronzed face furrowed with deep wrinkles, was knitting his thick, black eyebrows and carefully scrutinizing the antiques one after the other. He went over some calligraphy scrolls, paintings, and old-style ink-slabs, and he set them aside without exception, shaking his head. Finally, when it came to two flower vases of a fine red color, he promptly made a bid of six dollars.

Like an ailing cow, Wang Hsiao-fu was carrying back home the loads of bricks intact. As he came close to the temple, he raised his head and saw the finial that stood in dazzling splendor, reflecting the westerly sun. It then came back to him that the crown of the temple was a rare treasure! Since childhood he had heard this passed around among the villagers: it was one of the three vases kilned of the bodies of the thirty-six generals ex-

---

[7] The proverbial seven daily necessities of a household are firewood, rice, oil, salt, soy sauce, vinegar, and tea.

ecuted by Emperor T'ai-tsu of the Ming Dynasty: somehow it turned up in Feng-t'an Village and was used to crown the temple.[8] It was this precious vase that protected Feng-t'an Village from evil spirits and brought about its erstwhile prosperity and peace. The villagers often saw it glow in the darkness of night, reddening half the sky! His neighbor Ah-fu, for one, saw it one night when he was pedaling for irrigation water. A wicked idea flashed through Wang Hsiao-fu's head. All the veins and arteries in him, which had been tired, cold, and hard, began to beat rapidly. He felt a confusion, a kind of anxious fear that he had never felt before. It seemed to him that something horrible but hard to pinpoint was about to descend on him and his village. Without knowing it, he dropped his load and entered the temple. He knelt down and piously worshipped the Bodhisattva for a long while. His mind, troubled by fear and anxiety, gradually became tranquil.

Days passed with the usual numbness of feeling. The woman still dropped in from time to time. Every time she came, the couple would exhaust their vocabulary imploring her to take the bricks and tiles which had been torn down in place of the money they owed, capital and interest. (The front wall and the rear wall of their house had been completely demolished; still standing were the walls on the left and the right sides, which they shared with their neighbors.) At first the woman absolutely refused to listen to them, saying that what she had lent was in hard cash—how could these bricks and tiles, which one might not want to have for free, be used to pay the loan? Later, when she noticed that there was not anything better left, she decided to come to terms with her bad luck and ordered Wang Hsiao-fu to carry for her all the bricks and tiles torn from the two walls. Meanwhile she cursed viciously. Therefore she seldom showed up to press for her money.

When winter arrived, Wang Hsiao-fu had to stop plucking and selling wild fruits, and the nee-

dlework his wife took in suddenly decreased because it was the end of the year. At the time, the entire family often went without eating a grain of rice all day long. They had to go to the hills to pick pine nuts to be cooked into thin porridge or use old vegetable leaves to make soup. The older child, who was ill, would purse his mouth, grimace, and sob mutely. Sometimes, Wang Hsiao-fu's wife would curse him, calling him "dead ghost" or "living ghost." Sometimes she would go with her husband to steal a few red sweet potatoes or turnips from other people's fields for him to eat. Hardest to endure was each and every lengthy cold night. The front and the rear of the house were unsheltered; the bone-biting wind blew in freely through windows and doors. As all the cotton quilts had been taken away by that woman in lieu of interest, the four members of the family had to curl up their heads and hands, burying themselves under the straw. They all looked like hedgehogs. All night long they coughed like a broken bamboo tube. At midnight when the two children found the cold intolerable, they would cry like wronged ghosts in shrill, tremulous voices, which would continue until dawn.

In the daytime, since Wang Hsiao-fu had nothing better to do, he would follow his wife's suggestion and do some hoeing in front of the house, behind the house, under the floor, in the backyard garden—everywhere, hoping that at one stroke of the hoe he would hit a slab of granite or uncover something like an earthen jar, and find heaps upon heaps of ingots of gold and silver.

It was a snowy day. The scabby-headed older child, who had been reduced to thin bamboo sticks after three or four months of chronic dysentery, was cold and hungry, and cried hoarsely all day long. He no longer could take vegetable-leaf soup. Even his neck had gone limp.

"I want a little rice porridge, a little rice porridge," he said, sobbing hoarsely, his deep-set eyes closed, his mouth fluttering open.

That same evening, at her home, Ah-fu's wife,

[8] Emperor T'ai-tsu (1328–1398), founder of the Ming dynasty, is known for putting to death many of his subordinates. Reference to the three vases has no historical basis. However, it was a folk belief in ancient China that precious metal molten with human flesh and blood would take on some magical qualities. Some of the "precious swords" in China were reportedly forged in this manner.

who attended to a rice cake stand in town, all of a sudden bawled and shouted as if demented, "It's breaking my heart! It's breaking my heart! It's killing me! It's killing me!"

She walked back and forth, crying and yelling, clapping her hands, and stomping her feet.

Some of her neighbors who heard the noise came over to inquire, hunching down to keep their heads and hands warm. Ah-fu's wife told them what was the matter. After she had finished her business in town and, with her child, braved the snow to go back home, she noticed upon arriving that the door of her house, which she herself had locked, had been unbolted and pushed awry. After she checked inside the house, she found a used cotton quilt and half a jar of rice missing.

"That half jar of rice came from months of scraping and pinching. It was set aside for the end of the year to be used to pay the rent I owed my landlord! A landlord that never lets up on us! Heartless thief! My quilt—all that was left of our property was that used quilt! My child can't stand the cold! Heartless thief! Why did you make away with rags from the body of a beggar? What a wicked heart!"

Thus Ah-fu's wife clapped her hands, stomped her feet, cried, and shouted like a madwoman, without the slightest idea what to do. Those who had come to inquire, some pitying her and some outraged over an incident of a type so rare in the village, urged her on: "Sister Ah-fu, you shouldn't let it go. You must report to the night watch booth for further investigation. Humph! A thing like that can never be allowed to happen in our village!"

Thereupon Ah-fu's wife started out unsteadily, shouting and crying all the way to the night watch booth of the village. The leader of the watch went over to look for clues only once, and by the next day he already discovered the stolen goods at Wang Hsiao-fu's home. The quilt was hidden underneath the floor; the rice was gone.

Some said, "I never expected you to do this kind of thing too!"

Some said, "A good rabbit doesn't eat the grass by its lair. Little Fu, you must have been spellbound by a ghost!"

Some said, "These days, which of us doesn't eat one meal and skip two? One can only leave himself to the guidance of the gods and the Bodhisattva. If everyone acted like you, the world would be upside down!"

Some said with a sigh of sympathy, "Ai, he was forced to do it; he couldn't have helped it."

Ah-fu's wife, sitting on the threshold with the quilt in her lap, was wailing, "How could you bring yourself to steal from me! My rice was saved by scraping and pinching to pay the farm rent I owed my landlord! What a wicked heart! You've got to pay me back, pay me back!"

The faces of Wang Hsiao-fu and his wife were pale. They neither retorted nor begged. It was not until Wang Hsiao-fu was stripped to the waist, his hands tied behind him, and hung from a tree in the fields that his wife started jumping around and bawling like a boar.

The cowhide whip hit the naked scrawny back, leaving a bloody stripe at each stroke. At first Wang Hsiao-fu, like a wounded wolf, screamed in a loud, husky voice, trembled, and struggled: later, as he gradually lost his voice, he merely opened his mouth wide, panting laboriously, his eyes glazed over, his face contorted and ugly, only a vestige of the human form remaining.

When he came to, he found himself at home in bed. His wife was sitting beside him, moaning like a ghost, "How are we to live? How?"

He felt a heart-piercing pain all over his body. But his mind was getting clearer: he realized what he had done, what kind of person he had become, and in what a situation his family found itself. He vaguely thought of his past, of his future. He felt he no longer could stay in this village.

With some effort he sat up. He reached out his hand to touch his older child. The child curled up his skinny body and hid himself under the straw, sniveling and coughing. The second child, snuggled close to Wang Hsiao-fu's feet, was making an unpleasant snoring sound.

"Give me something to eat! Give me something to eat!" the younger one yelled, moving his mouth and sqirming his tiny body.

Wang Hsiao-fu sighed and lay down again, thinking of numerous disquieting matters. He thought of his colleagues who invited him to go

together to some city to make a living last year
. . . of the precarious situation in a strange city
. . . of the possible treasure of gold and silver
buried underground or hidden somewhere inside
the walls, of . . .

"To the big city! To some big city!" He muttered to himself as if talking in his sleep.

He endured the pain and struggled with his
rigid body to get himself up, and got out of bed.
The window was filled with a silvery radiance. He
dragged himself out of the house. Outside, the
uneven snow-covered ground reflected a crescent
moon; the air of night was all-pervasive. For a
while he crouched, dragging himself along. He
crawled on, unable to find a piece of land which
he had not already turned over. A death-like
quiet prevailed in the village. He could vaguely
hear his wife sobbing, as if a ghost were moaning.

"To some city! To some city! Travel expenses!
Travel expenses! Travel expenses!" He muttered
to himself as if still dreaming.

He heard the intermittent ringing of the metal
bells. He raised his head and saw the crown of the
temple. The four black characters, "Let There Be
Peace," countered by the snow and the moon,
stood out most clearly. The ancient vase of fine red
cinnabar, as usual, was sending out golden-red
rays of dazzling brightness, invincible power
inherent in it.

Suddenly he recalled the out-of-towner in the
Ch'ang-fa Inn at the end of West Street, vest open
on his chest, broad-rimmed eye glasses, bronzed
face. He seemed overcome by a demonic power.

He did not in the least know how he had managed to cross the field at his snail's pace and climb
up the hill slope; nor, holding onto the trees on
the slope, how he had got atop the wall of the
temple and reached the rooftop. He got his panting and groaning under control. He crouched in
one sloping furrow between the rows of tiles, and
touched the "Three Spears on a Vase" with his
fingers.

There was no telling how much time had
elapsed before he tore down the engraved brick
and tiles which were firmly attached to the bottom
of the vase. Then with one hand grasping the
mouth of the vase and the other holding its body,
he mustered all the strength left in him to jiggle it
back and forth, while swaying his body. Finally
the entire "Three Spears on a Vase" came off and
landed in his arms.

In a twinkling, he saw golden stars dancing, saw
the Bodhisattva in the shrine, saw many of his ancestors, many steel whips and many majestic steel-
blue or bronzed faces. Suddenly the world was
turning upside down. He felt his body float up in
the air and then float down from the clouds. A
whole sky of golden stars was circling the four
white, glowing characters, "Let There Be
Peace"—red, green, five-colored characters—flitting and chasing, circling each other.
Suddenly, a loud explosion, and utter lucidity before him! He saw his mother, his daughter, his
wife, and his two sons. They were racing in the
clouds. Gradually, what had been before him
turned into a deep, black hole. He had eight, ten,
numberless heads afloat in the air.

Finally, like an insect, he flew into the black
hole.

Fan Village

by Wu Tsu-hsiang

Translated by Russell McLeod and C. T. Hsia

I

On a sunny day in the eighth month the lonely fragrance of *kuei* blossoms[1] floated about a village with a single row of thatched huts.

This was Fan Village, and people from the various hamlets and small towns of the southwestern district[2] had to pass through here to get to the county seat or beyond the county seat to the port city. A long line of some thirty or forty huts faced a road to the east, paved with loose stones. Large cracks were visible on the low, earthen walls of most of these huts. Some walls managed to stand because they were propped up with fir logs, though large chunks of mud had already fallen from others. Some huts even had rotten rafters and ceilings, as if they were no longer inhabited.

Booths made of straw and logs lined the main road, one before each thatched hut. In the bright sun the straw roofs of booths and huts alike appeared dark gray. The straw ropes binding the thatch that should have assumed a pattern of rhomboid checks were now loose or broken, and most of the fir logs serving as pillars no longer stood straight. Inside each booth were heaps of straw, some seeming to have fallen from the roof and some gathered from the fields to serve as

mattresses for beggars fleeing an area of famine. A few benches and tables made of thin planks, thickly covered with dust and decrepit beyond use, lay about in the straw.

A woman emerged from one of these thatched huts and leaned against a pillar of the booth in front. She had a blade of dogtail grass in her hand, and was picking her teeth with it while at the same time gazing up and down the road.

The woman, probably twenty-five or twenty-six years old, looked strikingly haggard with her disheveled black hair and a square black headache plaster on one of her temples. Below her coarse, plucked eyebrows was a pair of diffident and bloodshot eyes which were probably infected. They were staring hard, even though it seemed to require some effort on her part to keep them open. She wore a knee-length coat of glazed cotton, patched in several places but freshly laundered.

Shading her forehead with one hand, she squinted her eyes in a long stare, gazing for a while at the southern stretch of the road and then turning around to gaze toward the north. In both directions the road twisted and turned to a mountain slope, with not a single traveler in sight.

All of Fan Village was dead still, except for

---

[1] "Probably the most popular autumn-blooming tree in China is the Kuei Hua, *Osmanthus fragrans*. It is a small-or-medium-sized tree, with thick, dark, shining evergreen leaves that are ornamental all year round. . . . The individual flowers, or florets, are small, yellow or white, and somewhat insignificant, but they are produced in such lavish profusion that they virtually cover the entire tree and therefore present a beautiful sight when in full bloom. They also have a pleasant perfume that pervades the air to great distances." H. L. Li, *The Garden Flowers of China* (New York, 1959), p. 151.

[2] Of Anhwei Province.

someone in a neighborhood hut continually pounding sandals into shape with a mallet, and a baby crying now and then.

A light breeze carried the lonely fragrance of the *kuei* flowers to the woman's nostrils. Raising her head, she looked through a hole in the roof at the tall tree and saw its blossom-laden branches shimmering with a pale golden light. She then looked again at the long row of tumbledown huts and at the booth floor heaped with straw until finally she threw away the blade of dogtail grass she had been holding in her mouth and breathed out a long sigh.

"Is everybody dead?" she mumbled softly to herself, beginning to recall the bustling Fan Village of several years ago.

In those years each booth contained neat rows of boards and benches, and a wooden table straddled the threshold of each hut. On this table were yellow bamboo chopsticks in a bamboo container, a stack of earthenware bowls with the right amount of tea leaves inside each, packs of Player's and Capstan Navy Cut cigarettes, plates of soybeans cooked with red peppercorn, fried freshwater fish, sautéed leeks, and other dishes. On the stove of each house were two or three steaming kettles, their lids jumping, singing like broken-voiced opera singers in the role of the flirt. As for the passing travelers, some carried loads on a pole, some were chair-bearers, some pushed wheelbarrows, and some drove animals, and still others were the owners, clerks, and managers of shops. They brought big lots of salt, sugar, kerosene, piece goods, and other foreign commodities from the port city to the various villages and small towns of the southwestern district, or transported local products such as rice, cotton, silk, and cocoons to the port city. Group after group, they passed in a continual stream from dawn to dusk. She and the neighbor women in charge of the booths, both married and unmarried, all wore freshly laundered and starched coats and trousers of glazed cotton and had aprons of patterned cloth tied around their waists. With flushed cheeks, beads of perspiration covering their noses, they carried the water kettle or the rice bowls, busy as butterflies in springtime, darting from

booth to stove, from this table to that, and all the time smiling pleasantly and chatting with their customers.

After being served attentively by her or the other booth keepers, those travelers would stamp dust off their feet, blow their noses, and put on smiles indicative of their present contentment and temporary relief from fatigue. And once on the road, they would again hear the sound of singing in the fields from near and far. Her husband and the neighbor menfolk were singing airily in the "Flower Drum" style as they worked in the fields.

After the fall harvest or during the first month of the year, when there was no work to be done in the fields, these men would customarily set up a simple stage in the grain-drying area behind the huts, and with a few simple costumes plus gongs provided by this house and drums by that, and the clothes, jewelry, and cosmetics of their mothers and wives, they would for a number of nights give expert performances of such familiar pieces as *The Seventh Celestial Maid Descends to Earth, Ts'ai Miao-feng Leaves the Inn, A Gift of Fragrant Tea,* and *Chu Ying-t'ai.* The families and relatives of these actors, people from nearby villages (including the very old and the very young), and travelers staying overnight at the booths, all watched intently. At amusing moments they would laugh loudly and at sad moments they would draw up a corner of their clothing to wipe away tears. When it came time for group singing, they would sing in unison from before, behind, and even atop the stage.

"Hsien-tzu." A short figure waddled down the road from the north, a fat old woman over fifty. In one hand she held a stick which she used as a cane and over her shoulder she carried another stick with a large bundle of clothes at the end of it.

Hearing the voice, the young woman was suddenly roused from her deep thoughts. She turned her head toward the northern stretch of the road and saw her own mother. "Mother," Hsien-tzu said lazily, "what are you doing back home again?"

The old woman walked into the booth, pulled

up a bench from the pile of straw, and placed her
bundle on the ground. As soon as she sat down on
the bench, she unfastened her headband[3] and
fanned her fat, wrinkled face with it, saying, panting a bit.: "What am I doing back home? I came
home for support in my old age! Mother[4] is about
to starve to death!"

"It will never be your turn to starve."

"You unfilial bitch! What do you think happened to Mother? The master was afraid of the
bandits, so the whole family moved to Shanghai!
The bandits wrote to the county yamen demanding fifty thousand dollars in ten days, fifty thousand . . . *Ai-ya,* still this hot in the eighth month!
Not even the weather is right!"

As she spoke, she put the headband on the
bench, lifted the corners of her jacket with both
hands, and flapped it. "Still no business here?
How about Kou-tzu?[5] How much paddy did he
thresh?"

"Everybody is dead. Even the ghosts avoid us."

"And Kou-tzu? How much paddy did he
thresh? Enough for the rent?"

"How much did he thresh? Don't ask. Even if
we were starving to death, we wouldn't ask you
for a copper. Don't worry!"

"You unfilial bitch. What do you take Mother
for? You think I'm loaded? How much money do
you think I've got?"

"I don't care how much you've got."

Listening to her daughter's words, the mother
had the sensation of swallowing several cold
stones. She looked at the cold, hard face and felt
this was not the time to speak of her own misery.
She blew her nose and said with a sigh, "Aren't
you going to pour a bowl of tea for me?"

Another figure approached on the northern
stretch of the road, a long skinny body wearing a
full, long-collared frock. Her bound feet, encased
in round-toed shoes, looked like a pair of small
breams, and she limped with each step she took.

The dragon-headed cane in her hand gave forth a
series of crisp sounds as she tapped it against the
stone pavement. Her round, clean-shaven head
swayed in the sunlight.

The old woman recognized Sister Lien, a nun
from the Kshitigarbha Convent at Mount Sunset.
She stood up and waved, calling, "Sister Lien,
coming from the city?"

"From the city . . . What a wonderful scent
from the *kuei* blossoms!" She stood still, fingering
her prayer heads with her left hand as she spoke.

"Have you heard the news? The bandits wrote a
letter to the county yamen demanding fifty thousand in ten days, fifty thousand! This road is hard
to walk on, though you're strong enough to manage. Rest awhile."

"Are you still helping out at Mr. Chao's at West
Gate? Come back to see your daughter?"

"That's right. Please have a seat, Sister Lien."
As she spoke, she moved to let Sister Lien sit
down on the same wobbly bench. "Altogether I've
worked there for nine years. Now Mr. Chao's
whole family has moved to Shanghai. Moved to
Shanghai. Left yesterday. The master didn't want
to part with me and I didn't want to leave him.
T'ai-t'ai[6] wanted to take me along to Shanghai.
With that brood of mine, big and small, how
could I go? Drag these old bones to a strange
place? Make a lot of bother for Mr. Chao? I
thought it over and decided not to go. The third
master of the Yuan-k'ang-hsiang store at East
Gate said he'd hire me. I went today to inquire,
but they said they weren't hiring. Bandits, bandits.
Every family has felt the pinch."

"You haven't done badly. It's time for you to return home and look after your old age."

"Sister Lien, what are you saying? Look after
my old age? Do I have that kind of good luck? I'm
looking out for the old age of my children and
granchildren instead. And yet I have a daughter
who's always vexing me, all the time."

---

[3] *Pao-t'ou.* Author's note: "A piece of black silk in several folds. A son would donate money to the Kshitigarbha convent and
have this piece imprinted with a Buddhist seal. He would then give it to his mother to wear around the area where her hair
touched the brow, and she would still wear it when she was laid in her coffin. This fillet has the supposed power of redeeming its
wearer's sins and reducing her punishment in Hell. Most grandmothers in that part of the rural country, whether of the gentry
or peasantry, wear it."
[4] *Niang.* In some parts of China it is customary for a woman to refer to herself thus when talking to her children.
[5] Hsien-tzu's husband is called Kou-tzu (Dog).   [6] Mistress of the household.

"How many sons? I should remember."

"Three useless hulks, eight small ones. The past few years our rice crops have been sold at a loss and there haven't been any buyers for our silk cocoons. The eldest went to the city to be a militiaman, thanks to Mr. Chao's kindness. The second and third worked in various goods stores in town; one by one they lost their jobs and came home! This family of starving bedbugs, what can they do but suck blood from my old corpse? And still I have a daughter vexing me with her red eyebrows and green eyes!"

"Miss Hsien [7] has a rather bad temper." The nun spoke in a lowered voice. "The last time I ran into you here I noticed the expression on her face. It really wasn't the kind of expression to greet her mother with. It was nasty, really nasty. But you gave her suck; it's no wonder you're so attached to her."

"It wasn't this way before." The answer came in a similar whisper. "Last year Kou-tzu, my son-in-law, couldn't pay the rent on his farm. The landlord called the district office to send a couple of men to dun him. They wanted to arrest him. Hsien-tzu came to the city to beg from me, saying there hadn't been any business in the tea booth lately and they didn't have a cent. And she asked me to lend her the money for rent. See how simple she made it sound! I'm not a city magistrate—where would I get the money to lend her? The past few years there's been no demand for cocoons. Didn't everybody stop raising them when they saw which way the wind was blowing? But the two of them buried their brains in dung, still wanted to go on raising them. Said they were going to raise them precisely because the others weren't. Stupidly thought they'd make a lot of money. Raised no fewer than ten big trays. The few mulberry trees they had couldn't supply enough leaves. When it came time for the third molting and the silkworms were just about grown they ran out of leaves. Came calling on me again for money to buy leaves. If there's no business in your booth and you don't have the mulberry leaves or the money, how can you raise silkworms, Sister Lien?"

"Young people are always rash."

"I can't help that. You make a mess of things and you clean it up yourself. I didn't care—well, really it's not that I didn't care, but how could I? What about the rest of my family, more than ten, more than ten mouths to feed? Is my old corpse the only one that should die?"

"Um-hmm, isn't it so though." The nun pursed her wrinkled lips, continuously nodding her shaven head. "After all, the ones living with you demand more of your attention."

"She buried her brains in dung, said I had money to join credit unions but no money to lend her. Damn it, do I go around joining credit unions? How many credit unions have I joined? It just happened that some years ago Mrs. Chang's husband died and she didn't have money to bury him. I had to heed T'ai-t'ai and so I joined Mrs. Chang's five-dollar-a-share ten-member union. [8] We throw dice twice a year to determine who'll get the money each time. Once in the third month and once in the ninth. This is the fourth year. I've done nothing but pay so far; my turn hasn't come up yet. The way it looks, I'll be the last person in the group to get hold of the money. A few years back everybody had some money; that's when I joined. I wanted to sell out, I wanted to get a substitute. I begged people as if they were my grandfather and mother, but who's going to substitute for you? People were actually begging you to substitute for them, to join their groups! For two years I've been borrowing money to pay. It was last spring that I borrowed five dollars at your convent so I could pay. She saw the money and wanted me to turn over the loan to her to buy mulberry leaves. I've paid four long years into this thing, why shouldn't I continue? Should I just forfeit everything I've paid in? She hated me, took me for a rich person, took me for a millionaire, as if I had ingots of gold and silver hidden away and wouldn't get them out to help her. I've slaved till my hair is white—have I been a thief? Robbed people? Does money grow out of my skin? Well, things are dandy now! The master's gone. Gone! We're all the same now, all going to starve to death. She's seeing this happen with her own

---

[7] *Hsien ku-niang*, which has the force of "Miss Hsien" and emphasizes her status as a daughter. *Ku-niang* is a young lady.

[8] Almost certainly Mrs. Chang (Chang Sao-tzu) was a fellow servant in the employ of Mr. Chao.

eyes!" As the old woman spoke, her feeble eyes
were filling with tears, so she placed a shaking
hand inside her coat and fumbled for a while
until finally she pulled out a handkerchief to wipe
her eyes.

"Married-off daughters are like water poured
outside the door. All a mother can do is sigh.
Where is she?"

"Inside making tea. Seeing how I've walked
more than ten *li* and sweated buckets, she didn't
even offer me a bowl of tea. I had to beg—beg for
it myself."

"People's hearts have changed greatly. The
Bodhisattva Kuan-yin appeared to me in a
dream; did you hear about it? It happened last
month. The Bodhisattva had a steel whip in her
hand and a furious look on her face, I've never
seen her that furious before. When I saw the steel
whip in her hand, I knew it was a bad augury. She
was carrying a steel whip in the year of the Republican Revolution too. Amitabha, have mercy,
have mercy!" The nun assumed a grave and
frightened look, pursing her mouth so that it was
surrounded by wrinkles. At the same time she was
telling her beads and sighing.

"Oh, what did the Bodhisattva say?"

"The Bodhisattva pointed her steel whip toward
the northwest and didn't say anything for a long
time. I was kneeling, not daring to raise my head.
How would I dare to? After a long, long time she
spoke. Her voice was like a brass gong—it's not
like that usually. She said the end was coming:

Of the white-haired half may be spared;
Of the black-haired none shall be spared.

Only these two sentences; then nothing for a long,
long time. I kept begging her to save the sinning
souls." At this point she took in a deep breath and
then exhaled.

Riveting her eyes on the shaven head, the old
woman also straightened her back and sighed,
asking, "What else did the Bodhisattva say?"

"As a matter of fact, three days after the vision,
the bandits at Five Dragon Mountain started up.
You've just asked if I knew the bandits wanted
fifty thousand. Of course I knew! If I hadn't told
Mr. Chao, you think he would have decided to
move away? What even the Bodhisattva can't tol-

erate is that men's hearts have changed greatly.
From the fourth of the tenth month the sky will
darken for seven days."

"The Bodhisattva said so?"

"Say, who's there? Is that Sister Lien talking?"
Hsien-tzu Sao, her eyes squinting, stuck her head
out of the thatched hut. There was no expression
on her face as she spoke.

"Sister Lien's telling about a dream in which the
Bodhisattva warned her of the calamities to come.
Hsien-tzu, come and listen."

"Rich people are afraid of the calamities. Not
us. If the sky fell down, those taller than we, better off than we, would bear the crash first. You
had better make plans." She went inside again.

"Listen to that!"

"Oh, my." Sister Lien shook her head continuously, grunting her disapproval.

"Hsien-tzu, Hsien-tzu, still no tea?" the old
woman called out in a loud voice.

Hsien-tzu Sao came out carrying an earthenware pot and two large bowls and plunked them
on the ground. "Dying of thirst, eh?" she said sarcastically, rubbing her eyes. "Guzzle it down, guzzle all you want."

The old woman exhaled deeply, bent down,
and picked up the bowls. First she poured a bowl
for the nun and then one for herself. She drank
one bowl and then a second.

"Sister Lien, a person like me drags on year by
year, day by day. When you really think about it,
you don't harbor any hopes. People say, 'Raise
children to provide for old age; store grain to
guard against famine.' Me, right now, I'm—"

"What happened?" Hsien-tzu Sao waved toward
the southern road and called aloud, "He still
won't lower the rent?"

The man approaching was naked above the
waist. A blue towel was thrown over his shoulder
and his black cotton trousers were rolled up above
his calves. Although his build was muscular, his
triangular face was sensitive and good-looking,
the face of a good female lead in Flower Drum
operas.

"Is it Kou-tzu?" The old woman, who had just
dashed the remains of her tea onto the floor,
asked, empty bowl in hand, "What's he been up
to?"

Saying nothing, Kou-tzu came steadily closer. His sweat-covered face was stiff as a wood carving.

"Kou-tzu," the old woman said, "Things are just dandy for Mother now! Mr. Chao has gone, his whole family moved to Shanghai. We're all going to starve now, all going to starve! The bandits demanded fifty thousand. They wrote to the county yamen."

Still making no reply, Kou-tzu wiped his sweaty face with the blue towel, then removed the hempen sweatband from his forehead and squeezed it with both hands. As the sweat dropped on his bare feet, he stamped them a couple of times so that a small cloud of dust flew up. Then he turned and walked into the hut.

"Still won't lower the rent? Did you find a rice dealer?" Hsien-tzu Sao asked, standing close behind him.

"Rice dealers indeed! They're all cannibals!" Kuo-tzu yelled inside the house.

"A dollar sixty? Still just a dollar sixty? The same price as the miller in the city offered?"

"Still want to get rich, don't you? A dollar sixty! Dream on!"

The nun stared vacantly for a long while, then grasped her cane and stood up. "The sun is setting. Still three *li* of mountain road to go. Men's hearts have changed greatly. Amitabha, have mercy, have mercy."

"You're leaving?" the old woman asked.

The nun staggered slightly as she took the first step. Using her cane to steady herself, she turned her head and said, "You rest here and take your time. I'm slower than you." She then hobbled out of the booth.

For a while the old woman stared blankly into the pitch-black hut. Finally she bent her back, groped inside her bundle on the floor, pulled out a few red candles and a cake of soap, and slowly made her way into the house.

The house was low-ceilinged and very dark. Only the small round window in the east wall let in a ray of dim light. When she first entered, a green haze seemed to float before her eyes and she couldn't tell where anyone was. Then gradually she made things out. Kou-tzu was squatting

on the sill of the door dividing the kitchen from the bedroom, holding his head in his hands, while Hsien-tzu was standing by the stove, using a gourd ladle to pour water into a wooden tub.

"Hsien-tzu, Hsien-tzu. I asked for a few of Mr. Chao's altar candles. They're going to melt. Put them in a cool place." She walked over to the large water jar and placed them in a corner by its side. "This cake of Sunlight Brand soap is also a gift from T'ai-t'ai."

"Keep it for yourself."

"I've got some. Now really, what's eating you, Kou-tzu? Still not enough to pay the rent this year?"

Silence.

"Still not enough, Hsien-tzu?"

"Our 6⁴/₅ *mou* of land have yielded twenty-five piculs of rice. A few days ago he asked the miller, who would only give him a dollar sixty a picul. Today he asked a rice dealer, who wouldn't pay even a dollar sixty. Just paying back what the miller has advanced us in foodstuffs will take thirty dollars. We might as well pay out our lives to the landlord. He's hard as iron and won't give up half a penny that's due him. If we harvest one grain, he wants that one grain. Three stewards stood guard over the threshing. All our rice is being held at the mill."

"Which one?"

"What do you ask that for? Fu-feng-t'ai—isn't it another one of your Mr. Chao's concerns? Every one of the heartless lot is a Yama! In the spring they measure the rice out and sell it to us for two fifty or two sixty. Now when we want to pay our debts, they'll only allow one sixty. Not even one sixty! They kill us without seeing any blood!" At this point she carried the tub into the bedroom, saying, "Take your bath."

"No use tilling the fields any more, Kou-tzu," advised the old woman. "Better quit—right now."

"Mother's![9] Your father[10] wants to kill people! He'll start at Fu-feng-t'ai!" shouted Kou-tzu as he stood up and walked to the back room to take his bath.

"It's true. Farming is impossible. How many in this village of yours are still farming?"

---

[9] "Mother's," "his mother's" (*ta-ma-ti*), and "grandmother's" are all common expletives.

[10] Meaning himself. In many parts of China a man may call himself "your father" (*lao-tzu*) in front of others when he is angry.

"If we don't farm, what will we do? What will we eat?" Hsien-tzu smiled coldly. "Such nice comforting words! We're not like your old ladyship. We—"

"Quit farming and turn bandit!" came a voice from the back room. "I've heard Ch'en Pien-tan say that Lao-ssu and Lao-san next door and the wheelbarrow pushers Hsiao-san-hua and Ta-mao-tzu have all gone to the Five Dragon Mountain. Your father will go there too. If you don't kill people, they'll kill you. That's what it comes to!"

"Watch what you're saying!" Hsien-tzu eyed her mother.

The old woman stood stiffly for a moment and sighed once again. As she walked outside, she said, "I'm going. Everything's dandy now! We're all going to starve to death."

II

Under a darkened sky the hills all around the village were wrapped in fog. A drizzle of oxhair-like rain floated everywhere. As a gust of cold wind blew in their direction, the trees around the thatched huts all rustled. The withered *kuei* flowers, now drenched with rain, scattered to the ground through holes in the thatched roofs of the tea booths.

Inside one booth huddled beggars in unbelievable tatters, sitting or lying about on the straw. They were refugees from famine. Some of the women, bare-breasted, sat with their legs crossed in the straw. They were trying to straighten the filthy rags piled around their feet while allowing their children to crawl from the ground to their breasts and suck at them. Others held chipped clay jars filled with grains which had been left in the fields after the harvest and stuffed them into their mouths by handfuls. They wrinkled their eyebrows in distaste as they licked or chewed the grains. Some of the men sat on the ground piling sticky mud onto pieces of broken pottery while others used molds to cast crude human figures in mud, drying them in rows at the foot of the wall.

Still others, holding with one hand a bamboo stick with a bundle of straw tied to its end, were inserting into the straw human and animal figures made of coarse red and green paper. Those children who were not around their mothers were either stretching their ugly, dirty faces in loud howls, crawling about in the wet dirt, or picking up fallen *kuei* flowers and stuffing them one by one into their mud-covered mouths.

A woman pushed out of her hut a beggar with a baby fastened with straw ropes to her back and holding in both hands a broken pottery bowl filled with muddy grain.

"Trying to steal, are you?" said the woman as she closed the door of her hut.

The beggar gave a bitter smile and then spoke sullenly in a strange dialect, "Your grandmother's! The straw won't burn. What's wrong with my using your stove for a while?" Following the complaint, she bent her head into the bowl, licked up a few grains with her tongue, and started chewing them slowly.

From afar came bugle notes that were sadly out of tune: "Di di di daa-daa daa-de-da."

After some time a column of men came winding down the mountain slope on the southern road. They approached slowly, their discordant footfalls reverberating through the surrounding countryside. These men, about forty or fifty of them, all wore ill-fitting gray cotton uniforms. Their leggings were carelessly done and their straw sandals and ankle socks were all encased in mud. Each carried a gun awkwardly on his shoulder: either a rifle, a locally made hunter's shotgun, or a "mountain-crossing dragon" over ten feet long.[11] Behind them rode a bespectacled officer of around forty in a neat Sun Yat-sen uniform properly decorated with a cartridge belt in front. He sported the kind of moustache that distinguished the man on a package of Jintan pills[12] and held an open umbrella in one of his white-gloved hands. His chest stuck out and, as he rode, the saber on his right clinked against his leather boot and iron stirrup. He looked very imposing, as if he were a great general.

---

[11] *Ku-shan-lung*, a Chinese-made gun normally requiring two men to carry it. A Chinese foot is about fourteen inches long.

[12] Jintan, a Japanese-made nostrum, was highly popular in China until the middle thirties. On its package appeared a man's face distinguished by heavy moustache with pointed ends which curved upward.

A standard-bearer preceded the troops. Since the flagpole was heavy and long, he rested its lower end against his belly to help him propel it. But the work was obviously too strenuous for him and he perpetually grimaced, revealing one side of his teeth. The flag was soaked through with rain, but when an occasional gust of wind forced its folds to open slightly, one could still read some black characters against their white background: Third Detachment of the People's Militia, X X County.

"Halt! At ease!" The officer gave a shrill command as he approached the tea booths.

Several haggard women came out of the huts and stood in their doorways staring. The beggars in the particular tea booth described earlier all stopped what they were doing and looked with frightened eyes at the troops.

When the officer reached that booth, he closed his umbrella and dismounted. He stood facing the beggars, his right hand on the saber at his waist and his countenance stern. After a few moments, he raised his left hand to gesture, and spoke out in poor Mandarin:

"You, listen well. You, all have homes. You, all have. Now we, in this area, things are very difficult. Very, unpeaceful. You, should, all have been informed. You, must, within three days, leave, this area. Three days, three days. Understand? In three days, leave, this area. Other groups, we have told also. No exceptions, all have to leave. Outside people, we, cannot allow, to stay."

He turned and looked at the village women watching the scene. Changing to local dialect, he asked, "Any men in your houses?"

"They aren't home," the women answered.

"Any guests staying in the booths?"

"No guests. Where would any guests come from? These past two years—"

"All right. Listen carefully. If you should have any customers who look the least bit suspicious, you must report to our office immediately. The area is not peaceful. We've already made plans. Just go about your work, don't be alarmed."

Everybody was silent.

Outside the tea booth a short militiaman emerged from the column of troops "at ease" in the rain. He held in his hand a "mountain-crossing dragon" almost thrice his own height. Walking hesitantly to the door of a hut, he put a forced smile on his face and called in a low voice, "Hsien-tzu!"

Hsien-tzu Sao was at first startled by the comic distress of the man who called her, but when she realized it was her elder brother, she laughed. "Congratulations! What a nice job you've got!"

"I don't drill good. I just can't. We've been on patrol since yesterday afternoon. We left the city at East Gate . . . What about Kou-tzu? Heard he had trouble—"

"Fall in!" the officer howled.

"Di di di di di," the tuneless bugle began blowing on cue. The short man raised his "mountain-crossing dragon" and tiptoed away like a deer.

When the ranks had formed, the stern officer again shouted an order, opened his umbrella, and mounted his horse to close up the rear. The troops now straggled off toward the north.

There was an outcry among the beggars. Some yelled, "His mother's!"

"Aren't you going to move out?" the woman in the doorway of the hut asked.

"Move his mother's!"

But Hsien-tzu Sao had no heart for conversation with the beggars. Her brother's cryptic message had frightened her like a clap of thunder, making her stream with sweat. Full of misgivings, she closed the door and walked into her house.

But no sooner had she crossed the threshold of her bedroom than she ran insanely out of her hut in three big steps. She dashed through the booth and yelled, out of breath, in the direction of the northern road: "Brother, brother!"

"Di di di daa-daa daa-de-da!"

The tuneless bugle notes were already far away: the straggling troops had almost approached the mountain slope.

Hsien-tzu Sao stared for a long time at the troops, her haggard face gradually turning ashen. She felt as if her heart were scurrying inside her chest like a little mouse and her feet trampling on cotton.

She rubbed her sore eyes a couple of times to compose herself. After a while she returned to her house, closed the door, and sat down on the doorsill of the back room. Resting her right elbow on her knee, she placed her right palm on the temple covered with a headache plaster. Her head was swimming as if it had received a sudden blow. Slowly she recalled the events of a few days ago.

That day at dusk a big, rough-looking fellow with long hair walked into her hut. He held a reed torch, and its bright flame revealed a ferocious, drunken face.

"*Ai-ya,* isn't it Old Pien-tan?" she asked, startled.

"Where's Kou-tzu?"

"Gone to the city. Back any time now."

"What, hasn't had his supper yet?"

"Maybe he'll have supper in town."

"Did you know I was supposed to meet him? We have business."

"He didn't say anything. What business?"

"Tell you later."

Before long her husband pushed open the door and walked in. Both men took handfuls of soot off the bottom of a cooking pot and smeared their faces with it.

"What are you two planning to do?" Her teeth were chattering.

"None of your business."

"Kou-tzu, you mustn't do it. You—"

"I've got to try this," her husband replied calmly.

"You can't. I won't let you go." She grabbed at his belt.

Her husband gave her a push, and the two men pulled the door open and rushed out.

That night she didn't sleep at all.

Around midnight she heard a tapping at the door. She opened it, and there stood her husband: on his blackened face his lips were stained purplish-red with blood from his gums. Violently shaken, he staggered into the back room.

"Thought it was going to be a big haul. Mother's!" He ejaculated the words with trembling red lips, panting hard. At the same time he fumbled in the money belt at his waist until he had extracted eight silver dollars, two bank notes, and a gold bracelet. These he threw on the table.

"My God! Whose house?"

"Mount Sunset . . . What sharp eyes! She recognized me as soon as she saw me. Then she yelled and grabbed me."

"Recognized you?" she cried, opening her eyes wide.

"Hush! Old Ch'en landed a blow right on her chest and threw her over on the front steps. To make sure she was dead, he grabbed a bronze incense burner and bashed her head in."

"My God!" She couldn't contain another cry.

"Shut up, I said. You're asking for your own funeral, really asking for it!"

Outside someone pushed the door open and walked in.

"Anybody home?"

Suddenly wakened from her confused train of thought, Hsien-tzu Sao raised her head and got up from the doorsill.

"Who is it?"

"It's me, ma'am."

The person came closer, beaming with a smile that revealed two gold teeth. He wore an old lined jacket of silk and held an umbrella upside down. The rubber galoshes on his feet glistened. His lean face was a long rectangle and the top of his head was flat. When Hsien-tzu Sao realized that it was the assistant deputy from the county yamen, her heart instantly jumped to her throat.

"Wang Ch'i-yeh." [13]

"Yes."

"What is it, Ch'i-yeh?" Hsien-tzu asked casually, forcibly controlling herself.

"Nothing—I must attend to a small matter at Fen-chieh Ferry. The road is bad. Came in for a bowl of tea."

"You haven't been out this way for a long time."

"Not so long, really. Last time I passed by, I was serving a summons on a tenant farmer. It was getting late, and so I didn't stop here for tea."

"It's really embarrassing. I haven't brewed the tea yet. No business, Ch'i-yeh."

"I'm in no hurry. Just take your time."

"All right. What was the tenant's trouble?" As she spoke, she went to the stove to boil water.

[13] Meaning "Your honor, Mr. Wang VII."

"Same old thing. Right now everybody is hard up, and for farmers the suffering's even worse. The harvest wasn't good, and the price for rice in the husk is getting lower and lower."

"You're so right."

"The farmers' lot is hard, but the landlords have a difficult time too. Taxes are too heavy. The price for rice in the husk goes down, but the land and other taxes stay high. It's hard for both sides."

"That's right. How did the case finally end?"

"The usual way. The tenant owed two years' rent—naturally, it wasn't that he wouldn't pay, he just couldn't. He was lucky to have a large family, but there were too many mouths to feed. And the landlord couldn't let him go. You don't pay one year, you don't pay the second year—why does the landlord own the land? Isn't that so?"

"That's right."

"The magistrate is a good-hearted man, easygoing about everything. Only had him beaten a few strokes and locked up in the Third Ward.[14] I saw how pitiful he was, getting on in years. He was an old man, that tenant."

"Yes."

"I'm no good at working for the yamen. Heaven didn't intend me for the job, I'm too softhearted. Most of the routine cases, if I can help a man, I do. What are we born for? I have no choice but to work in the yamen, but I'm not good at it. I always want to help the poor."

"Ch'i-yeh, you're a good man."

"You say so, but other people are different. They curse me behind my back. So it's hard to be a good man too. I told his family to bring a bit of money to thank the fellows at the jail. The fellows all heeded my words, and when they could, they released him. The rent was an easy matter. I told him to pay it back little by little. But he had to pay it."

"You're certainly right."

"Isn't Kou-tzu home? This year's harvest wasn't too bad?"

"He's gone to the city. He went day before yesterday. Didn't you see him, Ch'i-yeh?" As she spoke, she felt as if her insides had been scalded with boiling water. She tried to throw some tea leaves into the tea bowl, but they scattered all over the stove.

"If the harvest is good, that's all that matters." The deputy seemed not to have heard her, following his own train of thought. "If business is a little slow in the booth, it doesn't matter. The bowl may be empty, but there's something in the pot. That's all you need."

"What do you mean, Ch'i-yeh? We till about six and a half *mou*, and last year we had to borrow to pay the rent. This year—"

"You didn't have to borrow?"

"Didn't have to borrow!" Hsien-tzu Sao's heartbeat quickened and her eyes widened as she spoke. But she calmed down right away, saying, "Yes, all in all it was a little better than last year."

"Kou-tzu is very capable. I really like him for that."

"That's kind of you, Ch'i-yeh."

"Not so. I really liked him best in *The Seventh Celestial Maid Descends to Earth.* That, that singing of his and that acting were so great. And that figure of his—ma'am, when he disguised himself, he carried it off better than you could have. I'm not being partial. And he hasn't sung for some years now."

"How true."

"That year in the first month I heard you people were going to stage an opera and I came especially to see it. It turned out to be *The Seventh Celestial Maid Descends to Earth.* Lao San next door played Tung Yung. When he sold himself to bury his father, his filial heart moved Heaven itself. And Kou-tzu as the Seventh Maiden—[15] Ma'am, I tell you it's no wonder you two are so much in love. I love him too. Ha, ha, ha!"

"Ch'i-yeh is joking."

"No, I'm not. I would really love to see it again."

---

[14] The misdemeanor ward.

[15] The story of Tung Yung and the celestial maiden has enjoyed immense popularity in the regionally diversified theater of traditional China. One ballad version of the story appears in Arthur Waley, tr., *Ballads and Stories from Tunhuang* (New York, 1960), pp. 155–61.

"This once-busy Fan Village is deserted now, Ch'i-yeh. All we can do is have him give a performance for you to watch by yourself."

"That's why I was saying all this in a joking way. If the singers were all here, you still couldn't put on the play. The whole area is in a state of emergency. The past two days the rumors have really been flying, ma'am."

"That's right. I hear that Five Dragon Mountain has sent another letter to the county yamen."

"Surely not just Five Dragon Mountain? Even in the southwestern district there have been several robberies lately."

"Really?" Hsien-tzu Sao, just getting calmer, was once again jolted. Steam rose to her face as she lowered her head to pour boiling water into the tea bowl. She placed it before the deputy, saying, "Your tea, Ch'i-yeh."

"Much obliged." The deputy threw away his cigarette butt and blew on the tea leaves floating in the bowl.

Hsien-tzu Sao again sat down on the doorsill, watching the deputy's embarrassment with a fixed stare.

"Several robberies, and then there's a murder."

"Murder?"

"So recent and you've heard of it already? The county yamen has just learned about it. They plan to examine the corpse tomorrow."

"Who said I knew? Nobody told me anything about it."

"I'm sure you know the accused. He's the peddler Ch'en Pien-tan. Long hair, big fellow—that one. He always carries hundred-catty loads and more. Remember the man?"

On a sudden, uncontrollable impulse Hsien-tzu Sao got up without knowing what she was doing, and then she sat down again. She wanted to say something, her lips trembled, but no words came out.

"I never thought that man would do something like this." The deputy went on speaking slowly, his eyes following her. "Hard to blame him, though, the times are so bad. Who would set his mind on doing wrong? You just can't help it. This time we've got the stolen goods and the criminal. Caught him day before yesterday. Day before yesterday."

Seeing that Hsien-tzu Sao had buried her face in her hands, he drank some tea, heaved a deliberate sigh, and continued:

"He was too hasty and overbold, didn't know how to take proper precautions. He took a gold pin—actually it wasn't gold, just gold-plated—and wanted to get some money for it in the city. It was dark and the militiaman at the city gate wouldn't let him pass. He thought it was like any other day and it wouldn't matter if he started an argument with the militiaman. But that militiaman was a guard from the yamen, an old hand at catching criminals. This was bound to be bad luck. If it had been a local militiaman, the matter would have ended there. The old hand wanted to search him. One was afraid of being found out and wouldn't submit, while the other thought, 'You won't let me search you. Then I must.' So Ch'en Pien-tan was taken to the station. The search was made and the pin was found. There were five one-dollar Shanghai bank notes too." He took another sip of tea. "They asked him, 'Where did you get this gold pin and the money?' The fellow is a numbskull. He can carry a hundred-catty load, strong as an ox, really a Li K'uei,[16] completely straightforward and not a trick in his head. The first question stumped him. He couldn't answer. They held him at the station. The next day—that was yesterday— they sent him to the yamen. At first he wouldn't talk. Didn't talk even when they pressed his thighs between rods. But when they brought out the red-hot chains, he had to talk."

Hsien-tzu Sao had said nothing for a long time. Suddenly she put her hands to her face and wailed.

"What's this, what's this, ma'am? I understand! He made a false accusation. I understand, I understand, ma'am." The deputy feigned a serious expression as he spoke. He walked over to comfort her. Hsien-tzu Sao paid no attention. Like a small child, she bobbed back and forth, slapping her knees and howling.

[16] A strong-bodied, simple-minded hero in the novel *The Water Margin*.

"*Ai-ya,* this is my fault."

Hsien-tzu Sao wailed for a while, then suddenly stopped. She picked up a corner of her jacket and dabbed her eyes. Sucking air through her mouth, she tried to stifle her sobs. "Ch'i-yeh, Ch'i-yeh," she cried out twice, and then resumed her grievous sobbing.

"I understand, I understand, He was scared stiff and so falsely accused your Kou-tzu."

"Ch'i-yeh, Ch'i-yeh, I just have to beg you to get us out of this." As she sobbed these words, her lower jaw moving up and down, she went over and knelt before the deputy.

"What's this, what's this, ma'am? Do you want me to die of embarrassment? Get up now, get up. I want to live a couple more years." As he spoke, he pulled Hsien-tzu Sao up by both arms and guided her back to the doorsill. "Ma'am, would I want you to beg me? We've known each other for years, Kou-tzu is my friend. If I wanted you to beg, I wouldn't have come in person to your house today."

Hsien-tzu Sao, still shaking with sobs, kept blowing her nose.

"Kuo-tzu was most wrongly accused, that I know. Let me finish so you people won't have to suffer a false charge without knowing the whole story. That Ch'en Pien-tan told the truth, saying that the things were from the Kshitigarbha Convent at Mount Sunset. His Honor brought the gavel down with a bang and said, 'Rubbish! A gold pin and bank notes in a convent?' His Honor is a good man. How could he know that the convents around here all own some land and have some money on hand? This Sister Lien was really capable. Saved incense money and loaned it out at big compound interest. Don't laugh at me, ma'am, for telling you this, but the year before last when I needed money to tide me over the New Year I took two of my daughter-in-law's rings and pledged them for seven dollars at her place, and it was only this past spring that I got them back. Ch'en Pien-tan told about Sister Lien of the convent, told everything, everything. They asked him who was his accomplice. That was when he in-

volved your Kou-tzu. And as luck would have it, Kou-tzu was settling his account at Fu-feng-t'ai and he had no way of knowing that a false charge would come flying down on his head without warning. Don't worry, ma'am, just don't worry at all. They didn't open the inquiry yesterday. He's in the, the—"

"Where is he?" she asked anxiously. She had stopped crying.

"There's some difficulty here. If he were in the Third Ward, I'd take care of everything and there'd be no problem."

"The First Ward?"[17]

"Murder. Robbery. Of course he's in the First Ward. That's why I am not exactly in the know. Tough, really tough. The whole thing is in the hands of the keeper of the First Ward. He's a Shantung man, very stern and strict. It's because it doesn't do any good to have a helpless friend like me that I came here to talk it over with you. We've got to think of a plan."

Hsien-tzu Sao held her face in her hands and began wailing again. Stumbling over, she knelt at the deputy's feet and sobbed, "Ch'i-yeh, Ch'i-yeh, please think of something for me. I beg you, Ch'i-yeh, Ch'i-yeh."

"*Ai-ya,* ma'am, what are you doing? *Ai-ya, ai-ya!* Get up quick, get up now."

"Ch'i-yeh, Ch'i-yeh," she wailed, getting up unsteadily.

"Ma'am, this is no time for crying. Sit down, sit down. Let's take our time and figure this out. We've to think of something. Kou-tzu and I are just like real brothers. I've got to help him; why should you need to beg? I want to do everything I can myself. I'll tell you how matters stand: Ch'en Pien-tan confessed, implicated, yes, implicated Kou-tzu. His Honor issued a warrant on the spot. Two of my colleagues stupidly went right out into the street to search for him without even consulting me. They found him right at Fu-feng-t'ai. Found him, didn't even tell me about it, and took him straight to the First Ward. By the time I found out about the whole thing, the rice was cooked already. I was worried, I thought, 'A

[17] The felony ward.

murder charge is really serious. It will be too much of an ordeal for Kou-tzu. I've got to do the best I can.' So I went to see the head of the First Ward. He knows I like to meddle and help people. So he gave me a scolding and flung my request thirty-eight hundred *li!* My face fell too. I only cared about justice, I had no ulterior motive, ma'am, and so I wasn't afraid of him. I said, 'This man is a very close sworn brother of mine, a very upright man. If you're really going to give him the works, then punish me first.' The warden was a good fellow after all. When he heard me talking like that, he calmed down, saying, 'If that's how things are, we're all friends and I'm willing to help.' So it looks as if we could cover up and keep this thing from being exposed. Looks as if we could do it. But although the warden was willing to help, those shrimps under him wouldn't go along. So I went and tried to soften them. I said, 'This man is my sworn brother, very close to me. Give me face and do it for my sake.' But being what they are, those fellows don't see very far. It was the same old thing: wanted me to pay them off. Mother's, this yamen routine is always a big headache. I said, 'I can't do that! This sworn brother of mine is a peasant. The crops have been bad the past two years and there's no business in his wife's tea booth. You all know this. Where do you expect me to get money from? Aren't you deliberately pushing him to the wall?' "

"How much, Ch'i-yeh?" Hsien-tzu Sao asked impatiently.

"We can't just agree to what they want, ma'am. There are altogether fifteen or sixteen men under the warden. If you give each man ten dollars, you'll have to ask the God of Wealth to come down to help you. Can't be done! Right now, I can't agree to what they want. Kou-tzu, Kou-tzu—"

As the deputy spoke, he turned his head toward the round hole in the wall and looked at the sky. Suddenly he said, "*Ai-ya,* I'm going to be late! How come it's getting dark already? Looks as if it's going to rain harder too. I've still got to get to Fen-chieh Ferry, more than ten *li* of mountain road. I can't stay. Well, ma'am, you just borrow what you can and see how it turns out. Try your mother, she has ways and means. Whatever you

get, let it go at that. Give it to me. I'll use my influence and try to reason with them. Years ago things were easy. In the past few years the fellows at the yamen have really been ducks stranded on a dry bank. It won't do not to give them something."

Toward the end of his speech the deputy got up, took his umbrella, and walked a couple of steps. Then he turned around again and said, "Don't worry, ma'am. I'll be there at the trial and do my best. He won't be tortured. And I'll think of a way to cover up for him, you can be sure of that. Be patient, don't worry, don't get upset."

Hsien-tzu Sao, gritting her teeth, stared at his receding back. After a long while she staggered to the back room and flopped on the bed. She covered her face with both hands and wailed convulsively.

III

The *kuei* blossoms had bloomed and fallen the third time. Leaves from the trees were falling now too. It was already the middle of the ninth month.

The fields were redolent with the scents of wild flowers and grasses, and the wind blowing in one's face carried the promise of chill weather. The warm sun shone on the dingy, ramshackle huts of Fan Village, but the tea booths were now busier than usual.

Among the boards and benches lying about in the straw, those still serviceable had been pulled up and made to stand. Around one set of board and benches rested wayfarers of both sexes, forming two groups. They all had fair-complexioned though worried-looking faces. Sedan chairs and baggage were crowded into the tea booths. Several booth keepers, their haggard faces now looking somewhat more cheerful, were once again busily running back and forth with their teakettles.

A short-haired girl in a blue cotton gown bent her head, stamped on the chestnut burrs on a short broken branch, then picked them up and peeled them with her fine white hands. She smacked her lips as she ate the nuts and said to the worried-looking woman next to her, "Mom, these chestnuts are sweeter than the ones sold by vendors near our house. Try them and see."

The woman forced a smile and said to another woman opposite her, "This daughter of ours doesn't know the first thing about life. Other people's hearts are filled with worries, but hers? She's not at all worried, she's very happy. All the way here she insisted on getting down from the sedan chair to pick those chestnuts."

"How old is she? Schoolgirls in the early teens or younger are all like that. And you can't blame them: in a world like this it's better to maintain good cheer. Getting worried and upset, what's the use? Now, can you believe it? We haven't brought along a thing. A big house left for a servant to look after. Can't bear to think of it, T'ai-t'ai, can't bear to think of it. If I had my way, I wouldn't leave. Even if I were to die, it would be better to die at home. One cannot escape fate."

"That's how I feel. Her father forced us to leave. I said, 'Why should I leave? If you want to, you take her and hide for a while. I'll watch the house. What am I afraid of, an old person like me? I'm not afraid. Bandits are also people.' "

"Where are you going?"

"Where is there to go? First, we thought we'd go to the port city. But we haven't got the money for that. The best thing we can do now is go to her nurse's home at the Water Bamboo Mountain. And you?"

"My cousin's home. As soon as the rumors got bad, she sent word for me to come. I—"

"Ai-ya, Mrs. Yü of the Episcopal Church is coming too," the girl shouted and left off stamping chestnut burrs under her feet to greet her.

Two sedan chairs approached from the north. A small American flag sticking out from the door of the first chair flapped in the wind. When the chair reached the tea booth, a woman in her early forties, with bobbed hair and a small crucifix hanging on her chest, stepped down. A schoolteacher in her early twenties got down from the second chair. When the girl saw her, she skipped forward and called with warmth, "Ai-ya, Miss Liu!"

"Pao-chen!" The schoolteacher held her hand.

"How is it over there, Mrs. Yü?" a woman stood up and asked.

"Still camped at Green Maple Ferry, determined to stay on. Our minister told us just as we were leaving, T'ai-t'ai. Our minister said the militia here is no good. He phoned the yamen in the provincial capital and the yamen ignored him."

"If worst comes to worst . . ."

Another woman who had been silent so far began to weep, covering her eyes with a handkerchief and sniffling continuously. A young man next to her patted her back and urged her to have a sip of tea. Several other ladies became upset too, and they sighed with reddening eyes.

"Mrs. Yü, where are you two going?" asked the girl.

Mrs. Yü was about to reply when a male servant with hair combed in the Western style came up to her with a vacant stare and whispered something in her ear. She changed color instantly and walked over to the schoolteacher.

Covering her nose and mouth with a handkerchief and squinting her eyes in disgust, the schoolteacher was surveying the piles of dirty straw and spitting out one mouthful of saliva after another.

"The refugees made them so, really filthy," a booth keeper said apologetically. "The militia tried to drive them off many times, but with no success. During the day they all hide in the hills and find wild stuff to eat. At night they come back here again to sleep."

"Miss Liu, I want to talk to you," Mrs. Yü called. She murmured to the schoolteacher for a moment.

With a flustered look, the schoolteacher called to the booth keeper who had just taken the bowls to make tea, "No tea, please." Then she called to the chair-bearers, "Let's go. Hurry."

The manservant also joined in hastening the chair-bearers. The girl stood before the schoolteacher, nonplussed. Looking up, she blinked her unbelieving eyes and asked, "Miss Liu, what is it?"

"Not too long ago," the schoolteacher said in a low voice, "not too long ago . . . All of you'd better leave too. Tell your mother to leave with us, don't stay here any longer."

At a distance Mrs. Yü was whispering something to the weeping woman. Suddenly the woman jumped up from the bench, quickly grabbed the purse on the table, and said in alarm, "Really? Really? It happened here? Here?"

"Three *li* from here. The Kshitigarbha Convent on Mount Sunset."

Thus talking, all got up and started to leave. A woman who found her sedan chair at the rear of the procession called excitedly, "Mrs. Yü, please wait for me. I need your protection."

Mrs. Yü was already seated in the chair, but she complied gladly and called her manservant to straighten the American flag at the front of her chair.

"Mrs. Yü, go on ahead, our chairs will follow yours," another lady called out.

"Sure, sure," replied Mrs. Yü.

In a while the sedan chairs and loads of baggage were all gone, and Fan Village was once again desolate.

Several booth keepers were clearing away the tea bowls and collecting the coins from the tables. One woman holding a small child in her arms looked toward the north and said to another, "This bandit trouble has brought us a little business."

"What business? There's just this much each morning. Once the sun passes that post, no one comes. Yesterday was like that too."

So talking, the booth keeper noticed a short, fat old woman entering the booth on the south side. She greeted her happily: "What's new, Auntie?" She twisted her mouth in the direction of a closed door to her right. "She didn't come out to do business."

"Now what am I supposed to do?" the old woman said, frowning. "At first Ch'i-yeh told her to collect a few dollars and that would cover it— nothing important. Day before yesterday, Hsien-tzu came to see me and said that because the situation in general was getting worse the yamen was going to try the case right away and be very strict about it, allowing no chance for bribery. Since there's no chance for bribery, well, one might as well just accept one's fate."

"I hear the First Ward wants a lump sum."

"Dream on! Where to get a large sum like that?

Hsien-tzu still vexes me with her red eyebrows and green eyes, believing I'm loaded, a millionaire, no less. Damn it! Am I a magistrate? Does money grow out of my skin? Without fear of Heaven or law, they acted shamelessly and made this trouble. What am I supposed to think up now? Mr. Chao and his whole family left for Shanghai; otherwise I could go with her to beg Mr. Chao. What am I supposed to do now? You know what? Day before yesterday, Hsien-tzu came and gave me an ultimatum. She put it eloquently: Kou-tzu's life is in my hands now. If I want him to die, he'll die; if I want him to live, then he'll live. What words were these, I ask you! Did I tell him to rob people? Did I tell him to kill? They make me so angry it'll be the death of me."

"It can't be helped, Auntie. They really love each other too much."

"Love! A son-in-law like that has totally shamed me. It's not because I want to be hard-hearted that I say even if he got off scott-free I wouldn't have anything to do with him. Guilt by association, you know."

"Hmm!" The booth keeper reddened and said with a sarcastic smile, "But that's how the world is today. There are lots of men like Kou-tzu."

Not knowing what to make of the remark, the old woman continued, "I kept telling Hsien-tzu, 'Listen to me, listen. You're still young. A live tiger doesn't have to keep company with a stone lion.' "

The booth keeper turned her head and walked into her house with the tea bowls. The old woman made a wry face and refrained from further speech. Picking up her cane, she left the booth for the northern road.

"Auntie," called the booth keeper with a child in her arms. "Aren't you going inside to see her? She hasn't eaten for several days."

Upon hearing this, the old woman turned and said, "I'm not going in. I've still got a little business in town. I'll see her when I get back."

"The rumors from town are very bad. Since day before yesterday there've been several hundred people passing here to get away from the trouble. Today was the worst. Since daybreak group after group—altogether seventy or eighty of them—

passed through here. I hear they're only a little over thirty *li* from the city."

"Really?" The old woman's face looked distressed. After musing for a while, she quickened her steps and hobbled on, saying, "I'll hurry then, I'll hurry."

"Auntie, wouldn't it be better not to go?"

But the old woman was already out of earshot.

The booth keeper who had gone inside before came out again and said with a sneer, "What are you calling her for? You're so worried about her—would she listen to you?"

"What could be so important that it kept her from paying a visit to her daughter in distress?"

"It's her turn to get the credit union money today. Isn't fifty silver dollars more important than her daughter and son-in-law?"

"Oh, today's the fifteenth of the ninth month. No wonder she's so anxious."

"You're so right!"

"But if she gets the money, I wonder if she'll be willing to lend it to Hsien-tzu?"

"Farts! Didn't you hear her talking just now? Said a son-in-law like that is better off dead. Said that even if he gets released she won't have anything to do with him. Said Hsien-tzu should remarry. Her son-in-law isn't even dead yet and she tells her daughter to remarry. A procuress for a mother!"

While the booth keeper was talking, a yellow leaf from the *kuei* tree whirled down through the roof of the booth and rested on her neck. She was startled at first, thinking it must be a caterpillar, and brushed at it quickly with her hand, but when she found it was a yellowed leaf she placed it between her lips and held it there. There were many things she badly wanted to tell Hsien-tzu Sao, and so she looked in through a crack in the closed door, pushed it open, and walked in.

The sun was about to set in the western hills. The *kuei* trees over the tea booths glowed yellow in the light of the setting sun. It seemed as though their half-bare branches had once again burst into blossom.

Along the northern road group after group came with agitated steps. Some carried cloth bun-

dles on their backs, some held rattan baskets, and some led children by the hand. Still others shouldered two baskets, one at each end of a carrying pole. Of every such pair, one basket usually contained a child sitting among bundles and chewing on a piece of puffed rice candy or some such sweetmeat.

Group after group, they passed the tea booths without stopping, heading south in a state of turmoil.

Among them an old woman supported by a cane walked into a booth and raised her head to look at the late sun hanging over the western hills. The sun had already turned pink, and the clouds around it were especially dazzling in their orange and crimson colors. Some blue birds flew serenely in the sky, calling out blithely once or twice, and then disappeared among the mountain clouds.

The old woman paused for a while, panting, She adjusted her headband, walked over to a hut, pushed the door open, and walked in.

The room was so dark that she could not see her hand in front of her face.

"Hsien-tzu, Hsien-tzu!"

There was no answer.

"Hsien-tzu, Hsien-tzu!"

"Hmm?" The noise came from the back room.

"Mother has come to see you. Did Ch'i-yeh come?"

"Hunh!" was the reply.

"Have you eaten anything? I'm worried and come especially to see you." She groped her way into the back room.

"Hunh! I suppose you came from the city?"

"That's right. I went to ask around . . ."

"Hunh! Congratulations, Madame, on getting the credit union money!"

"Don't talk about that. I'm really worried sick."

"Hunh!"

"Have you heard? It's bad: the militia retreated—retreated twenty *li*. The militia's not very brave, can't face real fighting. The city's deserted. Even the magistrate has left. How could I get that money? I put it out for nothing. Mother put the money out for nothing, Hsien-tzu."

A snort could be heard from the bed.

"If the bandits really get into the city, you don't

have to worry, Hsien-tzu. They usually break open the jail first. Our Kou-tzu will be saved then."

"Hunh!"

"But I'm afraid, afraid—Hsien-tzu."

"Hmm."

"Afraid— there's such a rumor—afraid that the militia will retreat to the city and hold it and the bandits won't get in for a while."

"Won't that be good?"

"I'm afraid for your elder brother, your elder brother—" Sensing the inappropriateness of her thought, she heaved a long sigh. After a pause, she asked, "Where is the kerosene lamp?"

Getting no answer, the old woman sat quiet and sighed deeply several times. She then got up and groped around the stove until she reached the water jar and found the altar candles where she had placed them during an earlier visit. She took one and returned to the other room.

"Where are the matches? Under your pillow?"

The old woman went to the bedside, felt about the straw pillow dampened with tears until she found some matches by its edge. She struck a match and in the candlelight saw her daughter lying on her side on the wooden bed, her face to the wall. She put the matches back by the pillow.

"It's late. I'm going to sleep here tonight. To-morrow I'll go and ask around for news." There was a long pause. "I'm really useless now. Just walk a few *li* and I'm all aches and pains. Where should Mother sleep, Hsien-tzu?"

As she spoke she looked at the red altar candle in her hand: some wax was dripping from its tip onto her finger.

"Where are your candleholders, Hsien-tzu?" She wiped her fingers against the edge of a bench. "In the clothes cabinet?"

She went over to search the cabinet standing next to the wall. There were none in the upper drawer. But she found in a corner of the lower drawer the pair of small pewter candleholders that had been part of her daughter's dowry. She took out one and closed the cabinet door. She then removed the wax stub from the iron spike of the holder, stuck the candle on it, and placed the light on the table.

After sitting abstractedly for a while, she felt her headband once and again breathed out a weary sigh. She got up, opened the cabinet, and took out a quilt and bed pad from its upper drawer. These she lugged to a small bamboo cot, on which she arranged them. She then took off her clothes, blew out the candle, and lay down on the cot.

In a short while the fat old woman was fast asleep.

Hsien-tzu Sao lay on her bed listening to her mother's snoring, her own head aching with a dull pain. Half awake and half dreaming, she thought confusedly of several things. Right in front of her eyes she saw Kou-tzu's sensitive, good-looking face and his bare, strong upper body. Now he was in her own glazed cotton jacket, performing moving scenes from Flower Drum operas on a stage erected on the grain-drying area; in another second he was working in the fields with his head and back bent humming a Flower Drum tune. His face appeared careworn as he returned from the landlord's in the city, and then it appeared covered with soot, blood streaming down his teeth. She also visualized Wang Ch'i-yeh's embarrassment during his recent visit and remembered what the booth keeper next door had told her earlier in the day her mother had said. She saw the magistrate's cruel, fat face, saw Kou-tzu's corpse befouled with blood.

She tossed and turned for a long time and thought again of the things she had pondered innumerable times before.

Her mother's heavy snoring assailed her ears continually, making her feel as if her heart were on fire. She turned over and looked through the window in the south wall at the brilliant white moonlight outside.

She sat up slowly. Her head was numb and heavy. She held it in her hands and closed her eyes to rest for a moment. Then she felt around for the matches near the pillow and lit the altar candle on the table.

Her mother slept on the bamboo cot, huddled up like a giant rabbit. Her exposed hands held the headband on her brow, while her face was buried under one arm.

A thought suddenly leapt into Hsien-tzu Sao's mind. With the eagerness of one delving into a mystery, exposing a dark secret, or baiting an offensive animal, she picked up the candleholder and walked stealthily to her mother's side.

Her mother's clothes were thrown over the quilt. She felt in a pocket and pulled out a dirty handkerchief and bunch of keys. Disappointed, she put them back in the pocket and turned her attention to the headband guarded by her mother's hands.

She lightly removed one of the hands, which made her mother stir a little. She then gently touched the headband and felt a stack of crisp bank notes under its several layers of pleated silk.

Her heart pounded, sending upward a rush of uncontrollable anger. Gritting her teeth, she pulled hard with her left hand at the headband. But before it could be pulled off, her mother awoke in a fright, desperately seized the hand with both hands, and cried out, "Oh! Oh! My headband, my headband! You're stealing my headband!" Thus screaming, she flopped about like a fish and pulled at the offending hand so frantically that the candleholder in Hsien-tzu's other hand was violently shaken. Molten wax spilled upon the old woman's face and body and the quilt, but she held on to her daughter with all her strength, determined not to release her grip. Hsien-tzu Sao pulled backward and the candle fell from the pewter holder to the floor.

Instantly the room turned dark, even though a sliver of moonlight coming through the window in the south wall illuminated the shaking candleholder in Hsien-tzu Sao's hand. She saw the sharp iron spike on the holder. In a flash she was holding it upside down and with savage strength she was repeatedly thrusting its point into her mother's head.

Her mother gave two shrill cries and then fell by the edge of the bed, silent and motionless.

Hsien-tzu Sao held the headband in her hands, stupefied for a moment. Then her whole body began to shake violently.

Though in a daze, she was vaguely aware of the still flickering candle at her feet. She picked it up and touched it to the straw mattress of her own wooden bed and to the quilt and pad . . . Breathing hard, she wrapped the headband tightly around her hand, opened the door, and ran out of the hut.

Outside it was bright as day. There were only piles of straw in the tea booth; all the beggars had rushed to the city. Like someone possessed of a devil, Hsien-tzu Sao ran swiftly along the road toward the north.

Just as she approached the mountain slope, she ran into a man with a clean-shaven head who grabbed her by the arm.

"Where are you going, Hsien-tzu?" The voice was very familiar.

Hsien-tzu Sao blinked her wild eyes, looking at the man's face—a handsome, familiar face. "You, you, you—ah, it's you! Has the city really . . ." She panted, thinking she was in a dream.

Frantic gong beats had started up in Fan Village. Tongues of fire, leaping out from the roof of the hut, were already licking that majestic *kuei* tree.

CH'IEN CHUNG-SHU
(*1910–*)

Ch'ien Chung-shu became a literary success very early in life. From his primary school days in his native county of Wusih, Kiangsu, to his B. Litt. degree from Oxford, he was a boy wonder whose learning and genius shone forth time and again. He was blessed with a scholarly family background, a photographic memory, and a keen critical appreciation for the arts and letters. To this was added constant self-application. Soon after graduating from the Department of Western Languages and Literature, National Tsinghua University, Ch'ien won his scholarship to study in England. By the time he emerged from Oxford, he was a formidable and recognized scholar of both Chinese and English literature. His command of other European languages, especially German, French, and Italian, was proficient enough to allow him to do scholarly research in the original languages.

After returning to China in 1937, Ch'ien taught in a number of universities, among them his alma mater Tsinghua, National Southwest Associated University, and Chinan University. At various times he performed the editor's task as well, working on journals such as *The China Critic, Tsinghua Weekly (Ch'ing-hua chou-k'an), Quarterly Bulletin of Chinese Bibliography,* and *Philobiblon: A Quarterly Review of Chinese Publications.* His own published writings took many forms. In both Chinese and English, Ch'ien's critical essays and review articles well demonstrated the depth of his insight into the humanities. These discourses, varying in subject matter from poetry, drama, aesthetics, translation, to cultural differences and misconceptions, graced the pages of *T'ien Hsia Monthly, Crescent (Hsin-yüeh), The Observer (Kuan-ch'a),* and other periodicals. The erudite volumes *On the Art of Poetry (T'an-i lu,* 1942) and *An Annotated Selection of Sung Poetry (Sung-shih hsüan-chu,* 1958), Ch'ien's major contributions to literary criticism, have won accolades from scholars, and remain to this day highly respected works. Some of Ch'ien's own poems written in the Sung style have been published, but have not been anthologized.

What has most endeared Ch'ien to (and at times alienated him from) the educated reading public is undoubtedly his creative prose work. Ten vignette-satires, collected under the title *Marginalia of Life (Hsieh tsai jen-sheng pien-shang)* were published in 1941, followed in 1946 by a collection of four short stories, *Men, Beasts, Ghosts (Jen shou kuei). Fortress Besieged (Wei-ch'eng),* a widely acclaimed satiric novel completed in 1947, is now available in an English translation. Regrettably, he could not write any more fiction after the establishment of the People's Republic in 1949.

However, for over thirty years Ch'ien Chung-shu had devoted himself to the writing of a monumental work of classical and comparative philology in four volumes, entitled *Kuan-chui pien* (1979). Whereas *On the Art of Poetry*, formidable as it is, covers only classical *shih* poetry and poetic criticism of the T'ang and after, this new magnum opus of over a million words studies eight pre-T'ang classics, including *The Book of Changes* and *The Book of Songs*, and two gigantic compilations of respectively all pre-T'ang prose and all pre-Sung fiction. Ch'ien explores this vast body of work with the assured command of a comparatist who has read and remembered all the Western classics of philosophy, literature, and literary criticism. The last Chinese scholar to show this kind of intellect and erudition was Chu Hsi of the Sung dynasty, the Thomas Aquinas of China.

Our two selections, "The Inspiration" (*Ling-kan*) and "Souvenir" (*Chi-nien*), are from *Men, Beasts, Ghosts*. Whereas the first story travels into an imaginary nether world and the second is a slice of mundane life in this one, both carry the marks of Ch'ien Chung-shu the archcynic. The heroine Man-ch'ien's attempted conquest of T'ien-chien in "Souvenir" is no less vainglorious than the Writer's greed for fame and fortune in "The Inspiration." Indeed, it is hardly vainglory alone that afflicts the latter. The Writer is a repository of all the less honorable human qualities which plague the intellectual circle. Much of the plot rests, of course, on the fact that the Writer is miserably far from being a person worthy of that name. His misadventures thus tell a whimsical tale of judgment day, from which emerges a caricature of the composite villain in China's community of letters. The unabashed levity and wordplay, so characteristic of Ch'ien, make the story delightful reading.

There is no similar trace of the absurd, or even any touch of the comic, in "Souvenir." Again an exploration of human frailties, the second story is a serious study of the vanity of those new to the game of love. Man-ch'ien especially is insecure and conflict-ridden. Her sufferings arise from her self-deceit and other weaknesses, as the conqueror in the end becomes the conquered. Worse yet, the "souvenir" that T'ien-chien has left her will stand as a permanent reminder of her humiliating defeat. But T'ien-chien himself is no victor in the end. In this masterly treatment of life's ironies, everyone loses.

DENNIS T. HU

The Inspiration

by Ch'ien Chung-shu

Translated by Dennis T. Hu

There was once a famous writer, but strangely enough we do not even know his name. Not that he had not taken a name, or had done away with it; nor was it that he had somehow remained anonymous, or perhaps had something about him so peculiar that it defied naming. The reason was simple enough: the ring of his fame was too deafening for us to clearly hear the name. There have been cases similar to this one. An envelope addressed to "The Greatest French Poet" would be delivered by the postman, without a doubt in his mind, to Hugo.[1] Likewise, the telegraph company was sure to route a telegram for "The Greatest Living Italian Writer" to D'Annunzio,[2] making it absolutely unnecessary to specify name and address. This writer of ours was even better known than that, for his was a name that needed no written or spoken forms. The name was completely obscured by the reputation, as it were. Whenever one mentioned "writer," the reference was understood to be made to him.

Being a genius, the Writer was prolific. But like all artists, he suffered labor pangs with each act of creation. Fortunately, writing was after all not quite the same as childbirth. Difficulty in delivery did not cost him his life, and his fecundity was a burden only to his readers. He penned numerous poems, novels, prose pieces, plays, and song-poems, thereby moving, inspiring, influencing countless secondary schoolchildren. In foreign countries, the sales of a literary work are dictated by the taste of the middle class. But China, this good old country of ours, is truly a cultured land, alive with the spirit of classical tradition, a country where it is not material wealth that matters. That was why the value of a work rested, instead, with the standards and wisdom of the secondary-school student. After all, the only ones willing to spend their money on books and on subscriptions to magazines were those who were still in middle school: adolescents with unthinking brains, crazy about speeches and lectures, eager to worship great men, and full of the unwondrous sorrows of young Werther. As for university students, they had authored books themselves, and were hoping to sell their own products. Professors, of course, would not even bother with books, writing only forewords for others, and expecting complimentary copies in return. Those more senior in position despised even forewords, limiting themselves to gracing the cover designs of friends' works with their calligraphy; meanwhile, books would of course be respectfully dedicated to them.

This Writer of ours knew only too well where the key to his success lay, seeing that secondary schoolchildren would make great customers. It was thus no surprise that his works would be collectively titled *For Those Who Are No Longer Children But Have Yet to Grow Up,* or, alternatively, *Several Anonymous, Postage-Due Letters to All Young People.* "Anonymous" because, as mentioned before, nobody knew his name, and "postage-due" because the books had to be paid for out of the young readers' pockets. The Writer was able to disguise

---

[1] Victor Marie Hugo (1802–1885).   [2] Gabriele D'Annunzio (1863–1938).

his ignorance by making it look like profundity, pass off shallowness as clarity, and speak with the voice of a radical who proceeded with caution and good sense. The volume of his production was such that he became an unavoidable author, whose works you would run into wherever you went. Customers of food stalls, of peanut hawkers, and of street-corner stands selling pan-fried cakes, regularly received his novels or plays in loose, torn-out pages, thereby unexpectedly acquiring spiritual nourishment. Thus, his contribution to the literary world, a matter of popular recognition at first, eventually won official endorsement. He had become a nationally certified talent. The government commissioned a panel of experts to have his masterwork translated into Esperanto, so that he could compete for the Nobel Prize in literature. As soon as this was announced, one fan wrote the "Readers' Forum" of a newspaper:

It is about time the government took this action. One need only consider how many characters figure in his works. Put together, they are sufficient to colonize a totally uninhabited island. Now that the nation's population has been depleted by the war, there is no more appropriate time than now to encourage accelerated growth. By the sheer quantity of production, therefore, the Writer deserves official honors, and should be recognized as a model to be emulated by all.

It was most unfortunate, however, that Esperanto did not always mean *espérance,* the hope that very name stood for. Although the Nobel judges had no trouble with English, French, German, Italian, Russian, Greek, and Latin, not one among those moldy relics of another age could handle Esperanto. No matter how they wiped and cleaned their *pince-nez,* they just could not decipher the masterpiece that our Writer had submitted for consideration. After a great long while, one of them, a Sinologist senior both in years and standing, finally saw the light.

"That's it, that's it!" he proclaimed, "This is Chinese, what they call Latinized Chinese. We've mistaken it for some European language—no wonder we didn't know what it is!"

This eased the committee's anxieties, and they heaved a collective sigh of relief. The one who was seated next to the Sinologist asked him, "You somehow should know Chinese. So what does it say?"

"My dear venerable sir," comes the solemn reply, "It is through specialization that learning ascends to its pinnacle of excellence. My late father devoted his entire life to research on Chinese punctuation, and I spent forty years studying Chinese phonology. But your inquiry just now lies in the area of Chinese semantics, quite outside my specialization. Whether the Chinese language does carry meaning is a topic I should not blindly pass judgment on before I have obtained unimpeachable evidence. This stance of mine, my dear sir, you would not want to question, I am sure."

The chair, noticing that the Sinologist was not at all amicable, quickly put in, "I don't think we even have to bother with these works, since they don't conform with our regulations to start with. According to our eligibility requirements, only works written in a European language qualify for consideration. Now, since this is written in Chinese, let's not waste any more of our time on it."

The other old fogies indicated their unanimous agreement, noting at the same time their admiration for the Sinologist's scholarly circumspection. He himself, however, was quite humble about it, insisting that he was nowhere close to the American ophthalmologist who won that year's Nobel Prize in medicine. The doctor, he explained, specialized only in the left eye, and did not treat any malfunctioning of the right. Now, that was the true specialist. It was in such an atmosphere of graciousness and mutual respect that these senior citizens pleasantly parted company. That was just too bad for our Writer and his one full day of hoping. The announcement of winners plunged the entire Chinese population into righteous wrath, not to mention our Writer himself, who was driven to a state of despair. Earlier, quite a few of his fellow writers, their green pupils seeing red, had armed themselves with mental notes, waiting for the moment he was declared Nobel laureate to attack his works in public. With one voice they were to assert that such recognition was unwarranted. These same people now all turned sympathetic, and were loud in their lamentations. Perhaps because of the cleansing effects of the tears of commiseration they shed, their sight and their pupils returned to normal; indeed, their eyes were now awash with the kind of luster that takes over the sky after a rainstorm has subsided.

One newspaper ran an editorial admonishing the Swedish Academy for its ungratefulness. Was it not true that Nobel made his fortune on gunpowder, which was invented by none but the Chinese? Therefore the prize should have been intended for the Chinese, a point the administrators would do well to keep in mind in the future. What a shame that the Sinologist on the selection committee had not yet begun his research on the semantics of Chinese, thus allowing this forceful essay to escape his attention. Another paper was quite imaginative in its attempt to comfort our Writer. It actually offered him congratulations. He had been a successful author all along, the paper argued, and now he could legitimately be conferred the additional titles of the wronged genius and the overlooked, unsung, but truly great artist. The paper went on to say, "There is no more unlikely pairing than success and injustice; yet he has now attained it. What a rare and enviable turn of events!" Still another paper made a concrete suggestion:

While there is much to be gained in the policy of securing foreign loans, to accept a foreign prize would be shameful. In order to recapture the respectability the country has lost, we should establish China's own literary award as a protest against the Nobel Prize, and so as to save the right to criticism from falling into foreign hands. The most important of eligibility requirements for our prize would limit the medium used to Chinese dialects, with the stipulation that admissible also as Chinese dialects are English as spoken by residents of Hong Kong and Shanghai, Japanese as spoken in Tsingtao, and Russian in Harbin. Once this prize is established, the Nobel would cease to be a unique attraction. Western writers would be diligent in learning and writing Chinese, in the hopes of winning our prize money. China's culture of five millennia would therefore penetrate the West. Since the Nobel Prize is supported by private funds, our prize should follow the same format. It would only be appropriate, may we suggest, that our great Writer implement the above proposal by way of retaliation, and start an endowment fund with his royalties and fees.

In addition to practical-mindedness, the editor of a fourth paper demonstrated much psychological insight. He agreed that the literary arts ought to be encouraged, adding only that those who were willing to contribute funds to that cause should themselves be honored too. Therefore, as an incentive for the rich to make grants, some honor had first of all to be bestowed upon selected men of wealth. Since this was to be no more than a gesture, the amount of their cash prizes did not have to be substantial. The wealthy surely would not mind. "Would our great Writer," he concluded by asking, "be willing to set an example for others to follow by making the first contribution?" Who could have guessed that all this goodwill and kind suggestions would only drive the Writer to his deathbed?

He took the confirmed announcement of winners so hard that he fell sick, his misery and bitterness reduced but slightly by the outrage and support of the population. While awaiting articles rallying to his defense to appear in the papers, he made plans to dictate an interview the next day, to be transcribed for publication. It had always been the practice that news stories about him were, without exception, sent in by himself. In them, he would often insert some minor factual errors, in order to create the false impression that the piece was written by someone else. This also gave him the bonus of having a correction appear in the next issue, thus ensuring that his name would see print twice for one iota of trivia. It so happened that while he was making these plans, those editorials came to his attention one after another. The first one alone was enough to send him into a rage. "Missing the Nobel Prize means a loss in personal income," he reasoned. "The minute lofty things like the country, the people, and so on, got dragged into the show, I myself would be crowded out of it!" Then he noted that the heading of the second editorial was congratulatory, and got furious enough to tear the sheet in two. Suppressing his anger as best he could, he went on to the third editorial; by the time he had finished reading it he felt nothing but icy-cold water being poured on his head. The moment he was through reading the fourth, he passed out.

That night, quite a few visitors gathered at his bedside, including journalists, fans, and representatives of various organizations. Other than the reporters, who were busy scribbling in their notebooks items that would make a good article, carrying some title such as "Profile of the Writer Indisposed," everybody was nervously gripping his handkerchief to wipe away his tears. All knew that this was the last they would ever see of the Writer. Several young, sentimental females were in fact worrying that one handkerchief might not be enough. The men's mandarin gowns had flowing sleeves that would come in useful in such an emergency. But the girls' sleeves, so short that they barely covered their armpits, would not be of any help. Looking up to find all those people standing at his side, this Writer of ours found the scene matched quite well the scenario for his dying moments that he had fantasized about. The only thing that irked him was that he was no longer master of his mental powers or organs. He could not recall in totality, nor could he properly deliver, the farewell speech he had long ago prepared for the world. At long last, a few words managed to dribble from his lips: "Don't collect my writings into a volume of complete works, because—" Perhaps this line was too long, or at least what was left of his life was too short. He could not make it to the end of the sentence. Many in the audience pricked up their ears like terriers, only to let them droop, like a hog's, in disappointment a while later. Once outside his room they enthusiastically debated the reason behind the Writer's last words. Some said he had written so much that it was simply impossible ever to make any collection a complete one. Others conjectured that since additional hundreds and thousands of novels, plays, and songs had been planned, what little there was in print would hardly be representative. This controversy between the two schools soon grew into the most intriguing chapter in Chinese literary history.

During the memorial service for the Writer, a literary critic passionately intoned, "His spirit shall endure. His masterly creations shall never perish, for, indeed, they are his most valuable legacy!" Privately, though, one young reader commented,

somewhat in relief, "He's physically too dead to keep putting out new books, that's for sure! It wouldn't have taken too much longer for me to go broke." The fact was, he had to pay for all the books out of his own pocket, whereas that critic's entire collection was of course autographed, complimentary copies.

Meanwhile, in that other world of the deceased, the spirit of our Writer soon found that afterlife was not quite as bad as one might have expected. For one thing, the release of mental tensions was like shedding a heavy overcoat at the moment a person was about to be smothered, stifled. Together with those fleas which had established themselves in the seams, whatever ailments had previously plagued him were gotten rid of too. He was dead, there was no question about that, but he had been wondering what it would be like after death. "For people who have made my kind of contributions to culture and society," he pondered, "Heaven should have sent its welcoming party to receive me long ago. Could it be true that Heaven is nothing more than a product of superstition? Maybe it doesn't exist at all? Even if that's the case, they should rush to build one just to accommodate me!" But then it also occurred to him that staying in Heaven all the time was bound to be mighty boring too. Unless it was the Heaven out of Muhammad's design, a place where one had possession of seventy-two beauties, all with large black eyes, who could be converted back to the virginal state at will. One also found swans and plump ducks, their meat roasted to tender perfection, with the skin still crisp, flying in the air, all rushing into one's mouth to be eaten. "Now, that would be quite something, wouldn't it?" The Writer was lost in thought. "What a shame that overworking has given me heartburn and ulcers! Too much of that roasted stuff might just do more harm than good. There won't be bottles of Heartburn Relief, Ulsooth, or Clear-It hanging from the swans' necks. There's no chance that Heaven will be stocked with all these innovations of modern medicine. That supply of seventy-two women is somewhat overabundant too; it's going to take a while to sample the charms of all of them. Surely, the playboy Don Juan boasted an unprecedented 2,594 mistresses. But such an impressive record has got to be the result of unremitting efforts of a lifetime, plucking flowers and accumulating experience in illicit love. To take on seventy-two females all at the same time is something even Don Juan couldn't have handled. If their looks are all different, it could very well happen that some of these lovers are favored over others, because of the peculiarities of personal taste. This will certainly lead to a war of jealousies. How could a person who cannot cope with two arguine females handle seventy-two of them? This is not even taking into account the fact that they have the traits of India's preserved vegetables, liable to turn from a sour taste to hotness enough to burn your system. But legend has it that these seventy-two houris—'hot ones' would have been more appropriate—are all from the same mold, with the same black hair, dark eyes, serpentine waists. In short, all their features are identical. Sticking with one woman is boring enough, so just imagine this one woman made into seventy-two copies through the magic of multiplication . . ."

Our Writer was so scared that he had to change his line of thought. "When it comes to falling in love, most men of letters indulge in it out of vaingloriousness, out of the desire to impress people with the mesmerizing effects a genius has on the opposite sex. The lovers of the literati are just like the new cars and mansions of the rich: they serve to generate envy and not to fill any dire needs of their owners. If every man ascending to Heaven has now six dozen women to his name, nobody could use this as a means to show off the grandeur of his sexual style. But, to collect materials for lyrical poems or confessions, this would no doubt be a superb opportunity. The thing is, do they read at all in Heaven? Well, maybe a climate for reading could be fostered after my arrival? In that case I might as well bring along a few volumes as gifts." So thinking, our Writer sauntered into his study.

As soon as he stepped inside, he felt he was treading on something funny. The floor was like an empty stomach about to cave in under a load of rocks; and yet it was swallowing air, struggling to buttress itself. It turned out that there were so incredibly many of his own works on the shelves that the ground could not carry their weight any longer. It started to come apart. Before the Writer could leap to save his books, the ground split open with a loud crack. There, off the shelves and down the gaping hole, his books, big ones and small ones, fell helter-skelter. The Writer lost his balance himself, and, engulfed by that torrent of collapsing books, fell straight down. Curled up though he was, with neck tucked in, he could not help being the target of all those books, hurting him in the head, bruising his shoulders, and lacerating his skin. Only then did he realize firsthand the impact of his works. It was too late to regret that he had not had the self-discipline to write fewer books, and each one several tens of thousands of words shorter. After an intolerably long time all those books had finally found their way past him. Bearing the marks and scars from this attack, he trailed the books, drifting down into the bottomless darkness. He was becoming more and more scared. This way, sooner or later he was going to pass through the center of the earth, no doubt, and bore straight through the globe! All of a sudden the geography he learned in primary school came back to his mind. "The other side of this shell is nothing but the Western Hemisphere, and the Western Hemisphere is where the American continent lies. For all writers of the old continent, America is the treasure island, where the unsuccessful turn successful, and the successful reap. So every writer should visit, make lecture tours, and create a market for his works there. In that way they would also be relieving somewhat the Americans' burden of gold dollars and at the same time recovering some of our country's financial loss resulting from the importation of American goods. Falling all the way to America—that would be fantastic! A perfectly straightforward, effortless, yet refreshing experience, sparing that motion-sickness business on board a ship or an aeroplane." With such thoughts on his mind, the Writer found his spirits soar higher with each inch his body dropped. He was so thankful that Providence was after all what it was, and his ceaseless toils of a lifetime were not about to go unrewarded. The reward of being a good writer, so it appeared, was not to ascend to Heaven, but to descend to America. The saying "slipping to fall, falling upon the best of fortunes" had all but come true.

As he was thus comforting himself, he suddenly hit bottom. It did not hurt, amazingly enough. He got up to find himself inside a huge room, with maps hanging on the walls. He did fall in through the ceiling, but since it was his books on the floor that he had landed on, the cushioning effect saved his bones. Just a moment ago he was regretting the volume of his works, but now he was only too happy to discover the benefits of numerous and voluminous writings. "But what now? I've smashed someone's roof!" As if in answer, the books he was standing on suddenly started to push upward, tripping him. At the same time a great many uniformed people rushed in through the door, and pulled him down the mound of books. Shoveling, kicking the books aside, they managed to clear them out of the room. Then they helped a person, wearing a huge beard, and bruised black and blue by the books, up on his feet. Now that the decor and appointments in the room came to full view, our Writer began to realize that it was an elegant private office that he was in. Some of the uniformed men were now busy patting the dust off the bearded person, setting his clothes straight, giving them a tug here and a pull there, while the rest went about tidying up the place, putting overturned desks and chairs right side up again. Finding himself in such grand surroundings, the Writer was quite ill-at-ease. He knew this person he had just knocked down must be some dignitary or other.

The bearded man was surprisingly polite to him. He bade him sit down, at the same time ordering his men to leave the room. Not until now did the man's moustache catch the Writer's attention. It circled his lips, continued all the way down to the chin as a massive beard. The growth was so black and thick his mouth could hardly be seen even when he spoke. His words, coming through his curly grove, seemed somehow dyed with the color of that beard, every one of them dark. They also appeared to have grown hair of their own, brushing about a listener's ears until they itched.

"Oh, my! Your works really weigh as if they were gold, my dear sir!" The man sat down himself as he spoke, massaging the swollen parts of his head, a weak smile curtailed by that mouthful of whiskers that screened his lips. Our Writer, seeing that the man did not give him a hard time, and thinking that he had praised his works for being worth their weight in gold, felt instantly emboldened.

"They aren't really so expensive," he said, visibly arrogant, "Maybe I should first ask whether this is America—quoted in American dollars my prices don't come out to be very high at all."

"No, this isn't America. To get there you've got to keep going for quite a while yet. You see, the Eastern Hemisphere is where you've fallen from, sir. Despite the weight of your genius, you haven't made it all the way through the earth, since the western half of the earth's shell is fortified by those skyscrapers of America, structures of steel and reinforced concrete. But your works have had a tremendous impact on the center of the earth, I'm sure, and San Francisco and other places like it may very well have experienced earthquakes of several minutes' duration."

"Where am I then?" The Writer asked, almost cutting him short.

"This, indeed, is what the world's legends used to call Hades," came the quiet reply; the chill in his tone cooled the dark gloom of his words to freezing point.

"This is ridiculous!" The Writer jumped up in shock and consternation. "I'm darned sure the way I led my life doesn't call for such rewards—being sent to suffer in Hell!"

The bearded man waved his hands, motioning for calm, and asked him to sit down. "That you don't have to worry about, sir. Hell has already been moved to the human world. See, you've been so busy writing you don't seem to be very well informed about the current state of the world. Oh, well, I don't blame you for that."

The Writer realized that it must be Pluto himself before him. "No wonder he has the liberty to sport such a flamboyant beard!" So he hurriedly stood up again. "Your Netherly Majesty, I beg your forgiveness—" bowing so low as he spoke that he was about to split his ass, exactly as the French slang has it.

"I'm afraid you're mistaken, sir," the man chortled. "And you must excuse me for not being able to return your greeting, as my back is still aching a little from the burden of your books, and I'll just have to take your bow remaining in my seat. But although this place formerly was indeed Hades, I certainly am not any abdicated emperor of a fallen dynasty, nor am I a newly appointed director of some memorial palace museum. One would think that with the abolition of the monarchy, palaces should be converted into repositories for antiques. But then all antiques in the eighteen levels of Hell are torture equipment. Humanity has progressed in many respects through the last thousand years or two, except for the cruelty toward its own kind. That hasn't become any more refined or exquisite. Take for instance the extracting of confessions by brute force inside intelligence agencies, and the punishment of prisoners of war in concentration camps: they share the virtues of being simple, homespun, and effective. Thoroughly in the time-honored savage tradition. If you look at China, it's only in the brutality of various forms of torture that you can still see the essence of her culture. You know, pumping water down the nostrils, poking a red-hot branding iron in the armpits, tightening up the hand with wooden pins stuck between one finger and the next, and similar features of the indigenous culture. So those torture instruments in Hell, far from being antiques that had outlived their usefulness, were all called to active service in the human world. Anyway, this place is the Public Administration for Chinese Territorial Production. And yours truly happens to be its Administrator."

The Writer was beginning to regret his unduly courteous bow, and was getting embarrassed. But the man's last line made his interest surge again. "What I am is a prodigy," he mused, "and this man here deals in products—the two words even alliterate. What perfect partners we're going to make!" So he asked, "Products of the land are of course valuable commodities, but this is right in

the center of the earth—who's going to do business with you here? Oh, wait a minute, I get it. Everything's been wiped clean off the face of the earth by those corrupt officials. And in these times of war, people all over are digging tunnels as shelters from air attack. Since you businessmen will go to any length to make money, you figured that you might as well do what everybody else is doing, and so bored your way underground here to open up shop. Right?"

The Administrator replied in a matter-of-fact tone, "Are you trying to say that we're about to make products out of Chinese territory, to be put on the market? Well, well, there would be a lot of potential customers, certainly, but who could afford the price of this priceless land? If I were the typical businessman, I'd hold firmly to a policy of tangible profits. In other words, I'd never close a deal at below cost, nor would I accept bad checks. That's why the China deal will never be closed, and for the same reason I wouldn't be offering China for either retail or wholesale, as those foolish politicians are doing. I'm afraid you've totally misunderstood our name. We are in fact the agency in charge of the production of newborns within Chinese territory. You see, although Hell has relocated to the human world, human beings are still destined to die, and their reincarnation, the introduction of the soul to its next life, the business of karma and such, all have to be properly taken care of. We are here to make assignments for anyone to be born in China, and that includes males, females, and animals."

"Why 'Public Administration' then?"

"The 'Administration' part is simply handed down from tradition. Aren't there such agencies as the Reward and Commendation Administration, and the Punitive Administration, in the world of Hades? My title is therefore naturally 'Administrator,' and not 'President,' as you might expect for a business concern. As for 'Public,' all that does is to give the idea that the affairs of our organization are open to public view, that we are absolutely free from corruption. Everything's fair and square; we don't make unjust assignments, and we don't allow one single soul to be born into

THE INSPIRATION

the wrong family. This thick black beard of mine veritably symbolizes the spirit of our Administration."

"I see the double meaning," said the Writer, over-eagerly. "Since those who grow beards like yours must be old enough to be grandfathers, your beard, Mr. Administrator, must be the symbol of grand justice."

"Now, now, sir, your sharp mind has flown off at a tangent again! Well, maybe this weakness is just common to all you men of letters. It doesn't take a beard for a person to be called 'grandfather,' you know—look at those eunuchs of various dynasties in our history. You must also be aware that the insignia of high justices in the West is nothing but the silvery *white* wig. I assume that you're familiar with all those bestsellers on Chinese civilization made for the export market; they're so popular in the human world. Anyway, our country, people, customs, mentality, are, by their accounts, all direct opposites of Westerners', isn't that true? We're an Oriental race, and so they'd just have to be Occidental. We're Chinese, and they'll always stay foreign. When we beckon, our fingers point down, but somehow when they do it the fingers have to point upward. We kneel to worship, but when they greet you in salute, quite on the contrary, they raise a hand. Foreign men, before their marriage, kneel in front of their lovers to propose, whereas for their henpecked Chinese brother, it's after the marriage that he kneels, in front of his wife. These, and many other things—it's all so strange. If you extrapolate from this, since we value face, Westerners must be shameless. In mourning we wear white, but they wear black; so it's obvious that if their impartial officials wear white wigs on their heads, their counterparts in our culture should try to grow natural, black, beards on their chins. This is the only way we can avoid letting down those who make comparisons of Eastern and Western civilization, and not disrupt the theories they have developed. And then, of course, it also makes a statement. That is, aside from this beard, which does stay forever pitch-black, there's nothing in this wide world that's allowed to be a deal in the

dark, so to speak." The Administrator's beard flew about with every word he spoke, making his delivery a forceful and impressive one indeed.

At this moment, our Writer was busy taking stock of his own situation. "Those who are fair are also the most obnoxious and unsympathetic. If it's left to this fellow's disposition, there's just no hope of getting to America. I'd just as soon clear out while I still can." Thus, he put a smile on his face and stood up to take his leave.

"It was very inconsiderate of me today, to have allowed my bookcases to fall down here, damaging your office, and also to have taken all this precious time from your office hours. I am really sorry about all this. But I have learned a great deal through our chance meeting, sir; it was such a pleasure. Someday when I write my memoirs, I'll make a point of saying a lot of good things about your Administration. For now, I shouldn't linger any further, though. Would you be kind enough to have your men bring in my works that have landed here just now, so that I could autograph a few to be presented to you? They should make good souvenirs. Besides, books carrying my signature are sure to fetch a handsome price from collectors of later generations, so please take this as restitution for my having smashed your roof."

"Oh, that's quite all right, don't you worry about that. But now that you've come, I'm afraid you can't leave so easily." The Administrator was fingering his beard peacefully in his seat.

"Why not?" the Writer shot back, fuming. "I just don't believe your people could have the guts to keep me here. Don't you know I'm a genius? And I didn't make this mess on purpose either. My fall is entirely an accident, entirely unintentional."

"There's no such thing as an 'accident' in the world. It's just a planned occurrence in disguise, masked. People of the human world upon their deaths all end up here, taking their own ways in coming. Indeed, the routes they take are governed by a fair enough principle: 'To your own designs you shall fall victim, and victim you shall be.' In simpler terms, whatever it was that you did for a living would be the very cause of your own undoing, sending you to report to me here. See, you're a writer, so the books you've written bored their way through the ground, taking you along with them. Just this morning a sanitary engineer's soul arrived. Could you believe how he got to this place? One way or another he fell into the toilet, and some unthinking fool flushed him all the way down here! This roof of mine does get broken once in a while, or at least damaged enough to leak, and I myself will sometimes get hit on the head, or splashed all over with dirty water. But then if you're in public service, you simply can't afford to be concerned about that."

"Well, what are you going to assign me to be then?"

"Oh, that I'm still trying to decide. In your lifetime you consumed an enormous quantity of ink. I could very naturally make you a squid in your next life, keep spitting it back out. But then you also wasted a lot of paper, and for that you ought to be reincarnated into a sheep, to make its skin available for paper manufacturing. And presumably you've also worn out countless brush tips. So I should turn you into a rabbit, mouse—or maybe that same sheep would do. What a shame that you're a writer of these new times; a brush in your hands is just about as well handled as chopsticks in a foreigner's grip. What you use most often are nibs inserted into holders, and the platinum-tipped fountain pens. I'm not too sure which animals produce metal. So I may just have to make you a ranking government official, from whose heart and countenance one could scrape off iron or steel. As for platinum, well, don't we have that handy stereotype, the platinum blonde? Finally, considering the way you make a game of hiding yourself behind all those pen names, you should in your next life be made a fugitive from justice constantly under the pressure of creating aliases. The problem is, you have only one afterlife, and just couldn't be woman, man, fish, rabbit, and so on, all at the same time! So . . . so—Hey, you aren't going to be able to just run away! There're a lot of people waiting for you outside; they have accounts to settle with you yet."

Our Writer, finding the Administrator's talk getting more unsavory by the minute, had pulled open the door and was ready to make a run for it. Now stopped by his words, he turned around and sneered at him. "What? Settle accounts with me? Aha, Mr. Administrator, didn't you make a fool of me just now for being unaware of the current world situation? I'm throwing that right back at you. You think geniuses of today are the same old down-and-out Bohemians, dreamers who know nothing about financial management. You think of them as long-haired artists with a string of creditors at their heels. You're showing residual symptoms of an infection known as romanticism; you're totally out of touch with reality, I'm afraid! We're not idiots, you know. We do realize the importance of personal finances in daily living. In fact, as if we weren't smart enough, we hire lawyers and managers to safeguard our interests. Royalties and fees that come to substantial amounts we invest in business partnerships. Of course, there are those cultural personalities who are nothing more than cultured paupers, but I'm not one of them. To tell you the truth, at the time I died, I left royalties on several novels, and income from performance rights to several plays, unclaimed. There were some thousands of shares I haven't had the time to sell, and dividends from one corporation not yet cashed. I may have a lot of collecting to do, but certainly no creditors to settle accounts with me! Who're you trying to fool?"

"Sir, your ability to grasp reality—of the marketplace, that is—has never been doubted. The crowd outside hasn't come here to clear financial accounts, but to file charges against you."

"What 'charges'? It couldn't be anything more serious than calumny, plagiarism, and immoral influence. If a man of letters gets sued, it's got to be for one of these three reasons." The Writer was well aware of the fact that a literary figure who was never involved in a lawsuit, never jailed or put under house arrest, could not, like a socialite never having been a principal in a divorce case, ever make a name.

"They are suing you for murder and robbery"—the last three words coming out of the Administrator's lips crisp and cold, as if they had been forged out of steel.

The Writer was scared stiff. His past, decades of it, instantaneously flashed past his mind in uncompromising detail. Yet there was nothing in his earthly existence that even came close to such heinous crimes, only that for a while his writings did promote revolution. "Well, maybe a handful of foolhardy young men," the Writer pondered, "who could not resist the instigation did really pitch in everything they had, blood and neck included. So this means a sinful debt, I suppose. But at the time my wife wanted to have children, and I wanted to buy life insurance for myself— and all this takes money. If, in the interest of my well-being and my wife's and children's, I did write stuff that indirectly cost a life or two, that isn't any big deal. Besides, those fools with their blood boiling in their guts were too ready to die for their cause to regret it and demand settlement." The Writer regained his nerves. With a sneer he pushed open the door of the office. But before he had taken a full step outside, he found himself bombarded from all directions by shouting and yelling.

"Give me back my life!"

"My life! I want it back!"

The throng completely packed the courtyard, overflowing out the main gates, actually. Only the uniformed men at the steps were keeping them from getting up to the corridor and rushing the office. The Administrator, patting the Writer on the back, spoke from behind him: "Well, since things have already come to this pass, you'll just have to face their questions." He walked him outside the door.

Catching sight of the Writer, the crowd stretched out their hands, jostling to come up close, shouting, "Give me back my life!" However, despite their numbers, their collective voice was but weak and lifeless. Each was able to contribute only a wisp of sound, one not cohering with any other to form the stentorian roar it should have been. On taking a better look, the Writer found that the people came in all shapes and ages, and counted among them rich and poor, male and female. What they did have in common was a look of sickliness. They were in fact so emaciated that even the shadows they cast were blurred ones. From the way they exerted themselves in their movements one could see their dire lack of strength. The arms they managed to stretch out were all trembling, not unlike a voice shaken by anger and sorrow, about to lose control any second. They also reminded one of the strands in a spider's web hung between two twigs. "With such a crowd, what do I have to be afraid of?" the Writer concluded. "And then there're even old grannies with bound feet, kids no older than five, effete women with whatever seductive vitality they had almost totally drained from them. None of these could be among the martyrs who took to revolution under my influence. Unless . . . unless these are lives taken by those revolutionary heroes, and are now tracing the responsibility to me. If you look at that old lady, you can tell at one glance that she has to have been a stubborn mother, a prime target for family revolution. Well, this type deserves what they got! They asked for it. Since I'm in the right, I have nothing to fear." Clearing his throat, he took a dignified step forward, and announced, "Quiet down please, quiet down. I'm afraid you folks have been mistaken. I frankly don't even know a single one of you."

"But *we* know *you!*"

"Oh, that's not surprising. The fact that people whom a person doesn't know do know about him is just a reflection of his fame. So, even though you may know me, that's not saying an awful lot. The problem is, you see, I don't know you."

"What? You don't know us? What a bluffer! We're the characters in your novels and plays. Now you do remember, don't you?" They were edging closer, craning their necks, turning their faces up to him so that he could take a better look. And they went ahead all at the same time to identify themselves.

"I'm the heroine in your masterpiece *Longing for Love*."

"I'm that country bumpkin in your *Chips Off the Emeralds*."

"I'm the genteel young lady in your famed *Dream of a Summer's Night*."

"I'm the grandmother in your fascinating *Fallen*."

"I'm the well-bred daughter of that distinguished family in *The Thug*."

"Remember your much admired work *Embraceable Me*? Yes, I am that intellectual who lost his directions in the crossroads of the '-isms.' "

"I'm the spoiled brat born into the country squire's family in your own favorite, the novel *The Nightmare of the Red Chamber*."

His memory now refreshed, the Writer responded, "Very well, we're all one family. What's going on here then, would you mind telling me?" Actually, deep down he was beginning to have a vague understanding of their intentions, which, like something which had been drifting in the depths of the sea, started to show up under sunlight.

"We're here to demand our lives. The way you portrayed us in your works was so dull and lifeless! Our every act and speech was just like a puppet's; we were just too far from being vivid characters. You created us, but didn't give us life. So you should reimburse us now!"

A woman among them, with ill-defined features, broke in, "You remember me? I guess only the way I dress can to some extent show what kind of a character I was supposed to have been in your book. You were going to depict me as a *femme fatale*, the ruin of countless youths who otherwise had the most promising of futures. But what really became of me under your pen? I was neither a woman who looked like a human being, nor a human being who was like a woman. I didn't have the personality to support any clear, sharp image at all. You said I had 'watery,' not 'liquid,' eyes, and that my gaze was so 'pointed' that it could pierce the soul. My God, how could anyone even think of such lines? My eyes, sharp and dripping wet, had to be frozen spikes on the eaves during a spring thawing. You wanted to make me a metropolitan temptress, draining the mental and physical energies of men. But on your pages I wasn't given one breath of life—I wasn't concrete enough to be a sponge! I was more like a piece of worn and tattered blotting paper. You

described me as a person who spoke 'frankly and boldly,' yes, 'frayed and broken' is how I'd describe the voice I have now. You've made a total waste of my life. Now what are you going to do about it?"

A well-dressed, elderly gentleman next to her spoke up too: "In your work I got old as soon as I was given life." He was gasping between his words. "That I don't mind, but an old man should act his age. With my kind of health, and with all those years behind me, should I be fancying a concubine? Isn't that asking for trouble? You scoundrel, you not only denied me life, but also made a mess of my second life—my reputation. And I couldn't even risk my life to get even with you, since I never had one. But now our paths have finally crossed. Let me first wrest out of you the life that's due me, and then risk it to—" Choking with excitement, the old man could not even go on.

"Mister, you've said enough. It's my turn to ask him something." A swarthy man, patting him on the shoulder, interrupted. He turned to the Writer, "Hey, you recognize me? I'm one of the uneducated slobs you created. You must think I look the type—wearing the short vest, sleeves rolled up, pounding my chest all the time, with *I*'s, *me*'s, and swearwords crowding my speech. Incidentally, you claimed that I use gutter language, but since I was in the habit of bringing other people's mothers into my talk, wouldn't that be just perfectly homey, and nowhere near the streets? Anyway, you wanted to make me a slob, but I don't feel myself one at all. Swollen and bloated sounds more like it, and maybe that was what you had in mind. I might as well have been soaked in water, made completely strengthless. Since I'm uncivilized, I think I'm expected to give you a couple of slaps on the face first, before we even start to settle accounts. But then if you slap me back, I won't even have enough in me to fight you. What a shame!"

It was a good thing the Writer had not portrayed a slob that was true to life, otherwise he would be in for a sound beating. At the moment, however, he was really too harried to indulge in this kind of self-comfort, for the characters were now all clambering forward to speak to him. Some of them appealed to the Administrator directly, urging him to hand down a verdict without further delay, complete with the proper sentence.

"Although this case we have at hand is not exactly a phonograph record," the Administrator grinned, "we've still got to listen to both sides, right? Eh, Mr. Writer, what do you have to say in answer to their charges?"

The Writer rose to the occasion. He faced the crowd at the foot of the steps: "What you've just said is not entirely groundless, but how else would you have existed if it were not for me? Since I am your creator, I must be considred a forefather. 'Of all under the Heavens, parents are the ones who make no mistakes': that's how the ancient saying goes. In other words, one should be ever mindful of and respectful to one's origins. So stop giving me trouble." While the Administrator was snorting at this, twisting his moustache, a male character yelled in outrage.

"In the book you made me start a family revolution because of my ideological beliefs, driving my own father to his death. How come you're talking about filial piety all of a sudden?"

"If you're my father"—a female character picked up the questioning, a smile forming at the corners of her lips—"where then is my mother?"

Another man, sobbing uncontrollably, put in, "All I know about is motherly love. Exalted, unadulterated motherly love. While in your work I never felt the slightest need for any fathers."

Then it was a middle-aged man: "Even a father who is supporting his children doesn't necessarily win their sympathy. You're supported *by* us, so why should you be let off easy? You made us all lifeless in your works, but out of that you gain your livelihood. Isn't this both murder and grand larceny? At the very least it is criminal intent on an estate. And that makes *us* your ancestors."

The old man nodded in total agreement. "Well said, well said!"

"Yes, here I am, one of his ancestors!" chimed in the slob.

"Ancestors?" the metropolitan temptress protested. "I'd hate to be that. And there are cases in which the old live on the young. Don't you see all those young girls sacrificing their bodies for their fathers? There're lots of those around all right."

An unexpectedly loud voice boomed forth from the middle of the crowd: "I for one certainly am not a product of your making!" This one drowned out all the other voices, mere whispers compared with it.

The Writer looked up, and could not be more delighted. For it was nobody but his best friend back in the world of humans. He was a forerunner in publishing and related business fields, a cultural entrepreneur who had died just a few days before the Writer did. Son of a *nouveau riche* family, he had since his younger days been a man of principle. The principle, as it turned out, was not to spurn the family's quick yet sizable fortune, but rather a deep regret over there being no history to their standing. Their wealth was, one might say, glittering so badly that it hurt the eyes, stinking so much that it was an offense to the sense of smell. There was no touch of class to it. His father shared these misgivings, and made every effort to give the family name the ring of long-established status, much like one who, wearing a gown made of a down-home fabric, crumples it on purpose to reduce somewhat its feel of the countryside, and the rustling noise it makes. To further his goal, the father wanted all along to have his children marry into the families of gentry who had fallen into humble circumstances, or those of corrupt bureaucracy. The son, on the other hand, devoted all his time and energy to playing the Bohemian poet, singing in praise of alcohol, opium, sluts, intoxication, and sin in general. His only problem was that he was unfamiliar with the intricacies of Chinese tones as used in classical poetry; consequently the verse he was capable of making up was not in quite as archaic a style as he would have liked. Knocking around in life thus, he made it with a number of women, and as for the tobacco and alcohol he consumed, their brands could well form a League of Nations inside him. So he had to be intoxicated. But he failed to commit any sins at all, other than producing some free verse that he freely borrowed here and there.

One day while eating out with his mistress, he suddenly noticed how lipstick always got swallowed with the food a woman ate. Naturally, then, after the meal her lips would be robbed of color, and she had to put on lipstick again. This stirred his inherited business instinct, emerging as if awakened from a dream, as if it were a snake coming out of hibernation. From the next day on, he exchanged Bohemian living for entrepreneurship, starting a factory with money his father had made. The first thing rolling off the lines was Vitamstick, a new product so great that only his advertising chief's catchy sales slogans could do it justice: "For Both Beauty and Health—What Else?" "Never Before Have Kisses Been So Nutritious." That last line was actually the caption to a picture showing a young man dressed as a Taoist priest embracing a girl not unlike an unshaven nun. So this scene was supposed to be Chia Pao-yü of *The Dream of the Red Chamber* tasting rouge. Another line was: "What Fulfilling Love!"—this one being caption to a picture of a fat man gleefully holding the hands of a woman with pouting lips. Her gesture was meant to focus attention on the thick layer of blood-building Vitamstick on them. The chemical composition of this particular lipstick was no different from others for cosmetic use; all our entrepreneur did was concoct a name. The result turned out to be so appealing to the mentality of the masses that he multiplied the capital his father gave him several dozen times. He kept at it, coming up next with products such as Intellegrowth, an ointment that promised to stimulate the growth of both hair and intellect, canned Diet-Rich Chicken, which promised not to put weight on slim misses, and Cod Liver Gum.

At forty, having made enough money, he thought of old times, and his youthful hobby of patronizing the literary arts came back to him. Since drama was the genre that appealed best to both the learned and the popular taste, he, with a sustained effort, advocated a movement for "healthy drama," in much the same spirit he had earlier pushed his new products. He thereby succeeded in rallying quite a few writers to his camp. He figured that comedies made one laugh, and laughing was undoubtedly good for health. But then unrestrained laughing would add wrinkles to the face, and a mouth wide open invited germs. Besides, that would also lead to cramps of the stomach muscles, dislodged jaws, and a host of other unhealthy conditions. Thus the kind of comedies he promoted abided by the rule of only causing the audience to chuckle. As for tragedies, he thought them good for health too. Everyday functioning of any opening on the physical body meant one form of elimination or another. However, the modern man, raised in a mechanized culture, lacked the normal range of human emotions. This resulted in insufficient elimination from the eyes. The moderate quantity of tears that tragedies made one produce would do the job of preventing diseases which were to the eyes as constipation or gas were to the digestive system.

By that time our Writer had already made his name, and was in the process of turning out scripts from all his novels. These plays of his all satisfied the conditions set for the healthy theater, except that they were not totally in line with the entrepreneur's original intents. But the Writer's reputation was so imposing that it amounted to a threat, a terror. No reader of his dared not rave about his works along with others. To do otherwise would be to risk being criticized as deficient in the appreciative faculties, and not good enough for works of literature. At performances of his tragedies, the audience had the urge to laugh. But cowering under his fame, they did not dare laugh out loud; every one of them hid his reactions from the person in the next seat, smothering his chuckles with the handkerchief which was brought along for tears. Of course, nothing could have been more in keeping with the spirit of the healthy theater than this. When it came to his comedies, there was not one single soul that was not bored. But who had the guts to stand up and leave? Who wanted to be branded an unknowing fool? So everybody just settled on making himself comfortable, and dozed off. Sleep was of course an important part of healthy daily living. Thus, between the entrepreneur and the Writer they had a great act going, they themselves forging a strong friendship out of it. On the former's fiftieth birthday, our Writer even took the trouble to solicit essays for an anthology in commemoration of the occasion.

Now, seeing it was none but the entrepreneur talking to him, our Writer became very much heartened, and beckoned him. "You appeared at just the right moment! Come help me argue my case!"

"Argue your case!" the entrepreneur scoffed, "I'm here to settle accounts with you myself."

The Writer was dumbfounded. "Good heavens! Since when have we become enemies? Remember your fiftieth birthday? Didn't I guest-edit a special section in the papers in your honor? Remember the congratulatory essay I wrote in the vernacular language—practically singing in exultation? Who could have known that you would have too much to drink that night, and die of some acute illness! I wasn't at your deathbed, and that has been bothering me ever since. So we should only be overjoyed at this chance meeting today. Why have you turned so hostile and ungrateful?"

"Pooh! It's precisely at your hands that I died. We have no more friendship to speak of! That special edition of yours was just special perdition. Your commemorative essay was closer to a funeral oration. And you call that 'exultation'? Execution, that's what it was! You aren't even aware yourself, aware of how destructive you could be. Your pen is nothing but a cutting edge, your ink poison, and your paper might as well be a death warrant issued by Pluto himself. It's not just those characters in your works that were like puppets, or dolls made out of clay, none showing a sign of life; even living human beings, once described or written about by you, have their lives and blessings terminated. If you hadn't written that essay, I would have had several more years' life to enjoy. Just think, your tone was so reverent in that article, practically trembling with respect and awe, that it read like a bereft son's memories of his father. Or at least an epitaph commissioned for a princely sum. How could I take this kind of overdone adulation? You were using up all my good fortune. And I've been waiting here for no reason other than to get even with you."

Just then, as the Writer listened to this dressing down, an unpleasant idea suddenly came into his mind and lodged there like some hard food particle in the stomach resisting digestion. "Didn't I, just before my death, complete an autobiography, with the intention of publishing it as soon as I got the Nobel Prize? According to the entrepreneur, whomever my pen lands on dies. Well, then, if that's the case, I didn't die of frustration over not getting the prize, but because of a fatal autobiography. Hell, I should have known better! Having such a murderous pen, I should have used it to produce propaganda for the war against Japan. It could have rivaled the atom bomb! Why, why an autobiography, of all things? I have nothing but regret now. But wait a second. Am I silly! The mistake having been made already, the thing to do now is to turn it to my advantage. So first let me use it to get rid of this bunch of devilish creditors."

"If what he said is true," the Writer declared to the crowd, "my crimes have already caught up with me, and I'm suffering my just deserts. I have paid for my acts with my own life: didn't I write an autobiography, and wasn't that suicide? Let's consider this matter settled then; we don't owe each other a thing anymore."

But they protested in unison, "You aren't going to get off so easy! Your death is not suicide. Let's just suppose you loved to eat, and feasted on globefish. If you got poisoned and died from it, that doesn't mean you had in any way grown tired of living, and killed yourself as a result. The motivation behind that autobiography of yours was to blow your own horn. It's just that you never did know you could be slain by your own pen—that knife of a pen! No matter what, we're going to get our lives back from you. Our lives back from you!"

The Writer started to panic, wringing his hands and pacing back and forth, muttering, "The way it goes, you're going to end up getting *my* life!"

"I think I'm ready to hand down the verdict now," the Administrator announced, "I intend to assign you, in your next life, to be—"

"Mr. Administrator," the Writer interrupted, bowing, "could you let me say one word, before you go on? In my last existence I really suffered everything that could be suffered in a literary life.

I've therefore been dreaming of glory and riches, the good life, for my coming incarnation. Now of course I've given up all those wild thoughts. I fully realize how serious the sins I've committed are, but I'm appealing to you to consider my past good deeds as mitigation of my wrongs, and exercise leniency in your sentencing. Why don't you, as punishment, simply designate me a writer again in my next life?"

"A *writer,* again?" The Administrator was quite taken aback. "Aren't you afraid of another crowd demanding their lives of you in the future?" The reaction of those gathered below was a similar one, all staring at the Writer in disbelief.

"Oh, I'll just translate," he explained. "No more creative writing. That way my life won't be in much danger, I'm sure. Besides, I'll translate literally, definitely not trying anything that is even close to free translation—just to make sure that the liveliness of the original is not lost. And also to prevent myself from being hauled into some foreign court. Take for example that classic American historical novel. I vow I'd faithfully render its title as "Swept Off by the Storm"; Dante's masterpiece would be entitled "The Heavenly Father Joking." In the same vein, I could give Milton's epic the interpretive title "A Blindman's Song on the Fall of Soochow and Hangchow," but I promise I won't do that, although the old saying does claim that Soochow and Hangchow are paradises on earth, and Milton had indeed lost his eyesight. And whenever I have a problem translating, I'll just follow those celebrated examples of transliteration: *yu-mo* for *humor,* *lo-man-ti-k'e* for *romantic,* and so on. Since the whole thing would then be, one might say, spelled out in Chinese, how much closer could the reader get to reading the original? That's like taking out a life insurance policy for the characters in the work.

"Or, if you're not happy with that, I won't even do translations, but just stick to playwriting, and specialize in historical tragedy. There's plenty to work on. Well-known figures such as Lord Kuan, General Yüeh Fei, Consort Yang, Lü Chu, Chaochün, etc. Historical figures are quite dead to start with, and on top of that, tragedies should of course entertain a lot of deaths. That makes

deaths here doubly warranted, so there couldn't possibly be any charges of my being a murderer. There's a third possibility too. I can retell Shakespeare. The venerable Bard came to me once in a dream, complaining that the characters in his plays lived way too long. After these endless centuries, they had become plain sick and tired of living life, were more than happy to put an end to it all, and just drop dead. So he asked me to do an act of charity, to send them off to a painless, natural death. He added this was what that foreign culture of theirs called 'mercy killing.' Before he left, he complimented me, saying I was a young man to be reckoned with, even bowing to me, and repeating his words of appreciation."

"I have my own good idea," the Administrator said. "All of you listen very carefully. His intention in writing an autobiography was not suicide, true, but he didn't write the congratulatory essay with intent to kill either. The effects of these two events could be considered to have cancelled each other out; hence there's no debt outstanding between him and the entrepreneur. But as for his depriving the characters in his works of lives, he should have to pay for that. It wouldn't be a bad idea at all to make him, as penalty, a character in a novel or play of some other writer's, and let him have his own taste of being suspended between life and death. The problem is, there're so many writers of this sort that I don't know who to send him to. Oh, I've got it! Yes! In the human world isn't there a young man currently planning to write an epoch-making mixed-genre work? He'll be adopting the syntax of those causeries written in the style of collected sayings, using the rhythm, meter, and form of modern poetry, and as a result come up with a novel in five acts and ten scenes. He has the paper all ready now; the only thing he's waiting for is inspiration. Let's, when the propitious, receptive moment comes, smuggle a spirit into his mind. The Administrator turned to our Writer: "Sir, no one could be a better choice for the hero in this work we're talking about, since you're a genius, and that successor of yours is, as chance would have it, going to portray nothing but a genius's sense of life."

One of the Writer's characters, in a hoarse

voice, asked from down in the crowd, "Mr. Administrator, did you say 'sense of life' or 'sex life'? If that fledgling author is to focus on the latter, wouldn't that be too easy"—he pointed at the Writer—"on this common enemy of ours?"

The Administrator smiled. "Relax, relax, don't you worry about it. Our Writer's mantle must have fallen on this young man. As soon as a person ends up in his work, the character will have a hard time telling whether he's dead or alive, much less living life."

"We have no objections then!" There was rejoicing and jubilation. "Long live the fair Administrator!"

Our Writer made his final protest in despair. "Mr. Administrator, I've already dropped all consideration of my own interests, and am prepared to take the rough with the smooth myself. That kind of graciousness I do have. But at least you should have some respect for the literary arts. This youngster is waiting for a stroke of 'divine inspiration,' not 'ghostly intervention.' How could you send my ghost to cast an evil spell on him? I can take whatever hard times you give me, but if you're going to play a malicious joke on the arts, which should be held in the highest respect, I'm just not going to go along with you. Should the Writers' Association ever find out about this, they'll surely issue a public statement of protest."

" 'A genius is but the most inspired of ghosts.' You more than rate it. Everything's going to be all right, just take it easy."

The Writer had long since tossed out the window all the Chinese classics he once owned, thread-sewn spines, traditional bindings, and all. Thus, taking the Administrator's archaic phrasing as a sign of erudition, and thinking his claim must therefore have been based on the great books—little knowing that the line had just been invented on the spur of the moment—the Writer was reduced to silence. Thereupon, amid the jeering and ridicule of the crowd, his spirit was escorted on its way by a uniformed elf.

Now, the fledgling author had been waiting for his inspiration for three solid years. The reams of paper he had stocked up had by now appreciated to more than ten times their original value. But his inspiration just would not come, no matter what. Perhaps it got lost somehow, or it had altogether forgotten where he lived. Finally, the enlightening thought occurred to him one day that to write a maiden work, he should seek it through a maiden. It was therefore no coincidence that just as the elf was bringing the Writer's spirit over, the young man was in the process of exploring, with the principles of the experimental sciences as his guiding light, and his landlord's daughter as fellow investigator, the secrets of life. The elf happened to be quite a gentleman, and looked away. At this crucial juncture our Writer made up his mind instantaneously. He decided that anything was better than getting dispatched to the young man's mind and ending up coming out of his pen. So, while the elf's back was turned, in a swish he scurried into the girl's ear. Indeed, since at that time the couple was one inseparable body all tangled up, only her ears allowed unimpeded entry. Thus it was that the Writer personally, but unknowingly, gave substance to the explanation medieval Christian theologians had offered for the conception of the Virgin Mary. That is, the female aural passage was a passage to conception.

From that moment on the young author-to-have-been was permanently deprived of the character that would have appeared in his work, but the girl richer by a baby. He had no choice but to marry her, and the book was never to be. Whatever writing ability he had was henceforth put to use in keeping the daily accounts of his father-in-law's grocery store. One comfort he did find, however. In traditional Chinese bookkeeping, a new line was very often begun before the previous one was completely filled. And that approximated the visual appeal of modern poetry. The language of accounting, moreover, was neither the literary idiom strictly, nor the vernacular, for which reason such writing rightfully belonged in the genre of collected sayings, wherein a cross between the literary and the vernacular was the norm.

The elf, on his return, was severely reprimanded by the Administrator. Only then did he realize that to be a subordinate meant one could not afford to play gentleman. To serve a superior well and conscientiously, one simply could not let this matter of honor bother the conscience.

Later, it was reported that the baby boy started grinning right from the moment of his birth. And whenever he saw his father, his smile would wax triumphant. The relatives all agreed that the baby had to have been blessed with good fortune of the highest magnitude. But so far, nobody could tell whether or not he would grow up to be a writer.

Souvenir

by Ch'ien Chung-shu

Translated by Nathan K. Mao

Although this was a city surrounded by one mountain after another,[1] spring, like raiding enemy planes, entered it without the least difficulty and arrived sooner there than any other place. Sad to say, the arid mountain region was not suited to a luxurious growth of flowers and shrubs. Though spring had arrived, it had no place to take up lodging. Nevertheless, spring managed to create a vernal atmosphere in this mountain city with no other help than the fermenting effect of a damp and stuffy Lantern Festival[2] and of a few ensuing sunny days. The air of such bright, cloudless days was heavily laced with the busy dust of this mountainous region. Illuminated by the twilight of the setting sun, it imparted to the spring atmosphere a ripe yellow hue. They were the kind of days when one could dream while awake, become drunk without drinking. A wonderful season it was!

From a street where the twilight still lingered, Man-ch'ien turned into an alley deserted by the sun. The early evening chill of spring alerted her to the fact that without realizing it she had reached her home. She had no idea how she had come home, but she knew her legs were very sore. The uneven gravel road hurt her feet and made her worry about her high heels, the last luxury she had bought two years ago when she passed through Hong Kong on the way to the interior. She was a little rueful that she had not allowed T'ien-chien to hire a rickshaw for her. But after

what had happened today, could she continue to accept his gallantry? Wouldn't that indicate tacit approval of what he had done? He was just the type to interpret it that way.

Engrossed in thought, after wearily passing a few homes near the entrance to the alley, Man-ch'ien saw the mud wall which circled her own courtyard. In this area, where there was a shortage of brick and tiles, mud walls were common. But contrasted with the neighbors' brick and stone walls, this mud one was unsightly and had brought lots of embarrassment to its mistress. When Man-ch'ien first looked at the house, she was reluctant to rent it because of that ugly wall. Sensing her displeasure, the landlord offered to reduce the rent. It was precisely because of the wall that the deal was made. But only recently had she made her peace with the wall and become willing to accept the protection it offered.

Her husband, Ts'ai-shu, not only accepted but also endorsed, bragged about, and praised the crude mud wall. That is, he was unwilling to accept it but used words to camouflage his true feelings. Whenever he had friends visiting him for the first time, Man-ch'ien heard Ts'ai-shu say gleefully, "Its appearance is plain and simple, especially appealing for city-dwellers long accustomed to Western-style homes. I took an immediate liking to it. There are so many kids who play in the alley, and my neighbors' white-washed walls are filled with their pencil scrawlings and pictures.

[1] Presumably Chunking, the wartime capital during the Sino-Japanese War (1937–1945).
[2] The fifteenth day of the first lunar month.

But my mud wall is dark and coarse—the kids can't do a thing to it. After the last bombing raid, the police told everyone to paint their walls black. Our neighbors, terrified of bombs, scurried around getting their walls painted. But mine was naturally camouflaged already, which saved me a lot of trouble. Otherwise we would have had to hire people to paint it black. The landlord certainly wouldn't have refunded the money for the job, so that we would have had to pay for it ourselves. And, shortly after the neighbors' walls were painted black, the kids went at it again and criss-crossed drawings in white chalk. It was just like setting up a big blackboard for the kids. It really wasn't worth the trouble." At this point, Ts'ai-shu's guests would politely join him in laughter. And if his wife were waiting on the guests, she, out of a sense of obligation, would smile too.

What Ts'ai-shu neglected to mention was that the kids, unable to write on his wall, had scrawled all over his front door many *Hsü Residence*'s of different sizes, more or less in the manner of the two ideograms Ts'ai-shu had written on a red piece of paper pasted at the top of his door. This was a fact that his guests would politely refrain from mentioning.

Man-ch'ien pushed open the door. The maid, a native of the area, asked gruffly in a loud voice, "Who is it?"

Man-ch'ien entered and asked casually, "Has the master come home yet?" The reply was negative. Of course, she had expected that answer, but today she felt relieved. She was timorous, afraid that her husband had come home before her and would ask where she had been, and as yet she had not found the most succinct and effective lie to tell him. Lying to his face seemed much more difficult than being unfaithful to him. She knew very well that because of air raids at noon, offices opened at three in the afternoon and her husband would not be home until well after dark. But one could never tell—what had happened to her a while ago was a complete accident. Yes, indeed, the meeting she had with T'ien-chien this afternoon had gone beyond the expected. She was totally unprepared for what had happened. Yes, she had encouraged T'ien-chien to admire her, but it

had never occurred to her that he would take the initiative and force her. She had only hoped for a tender, subtle, delicate emotional relationship with him, one ornamented with complications, filled with doubts and uncertainties, without verbal commitments or traces. In short, she wanted this relationship merely to enable them to touch each other's souls with remote antennae. For a woman like Man-ch'ien, that was the most interesting form of recreation, and also the safest, with her husband a convenient buffer to prevent her and her lover from overstepping the bounds.

But who could have known that T'ien-chien would be so bold and direct? The substantial, physical love he had offered only frightened her, and somewhat disappointed her, since what she had obtained was more than she had hoped for—like someone with a weak stomach filled with greasy food. Had she known him to be that aggressive, she would not have gone to see him, or at least she wouldn't have gone out without first changing her undershirt. The thought of her old undershirt, which should have been washed, still made her blush, even at this moment; in fact, this thought embarrassed her more than what had taken place.

Home. After walking through a small courtyard and through the room that served as both living and dining room, she entered her tiled bedroom. The maid went back to the kitchen to prepare dinner; like all household help from the countryside, the maid had no idea that now the mistress was back it was time to bring her mistress tea. But Man-ch'ien at this time was too exhausted to speak to anyone. Her heart confused, she was unclear about what to think. Here and there, certain parts of her skin, such as her face and lips, that had been kissed by T'ien-chien seemed to retain some lingering impressions. Each place seemed to have a mind of its own, briskly alive, standing out from a feeling of general fatigue.

The room, with its old-style framed windows, had been dark for some time. Man-ch'ien preferred the darkness, as if under the cover of night, her conscience would not be laid bare as a snail without a hiding place after it leaves its shell. So she did not turn the light on. In truth, the lights in the interior of China were only a shade better than darkness; the gleam they provided was so insubstantial that it seemed as if the color of night had been diluted with water. After she settled down in a chair, the heat generated from walking surged out of her body. She felt she just couldn't believe what had happened; it would only be likened to a relief carved on the surface of a dream.

She wanted to lie down in bed, with her clothes on, for a little rest. But she was, after all, a woman. Tired as she was, she took off her street chothes and put on her housedress before she lay down. Her fur coat was shedding, and the color of her flannel-lined ch'i-p'ao [3] was no longer fashionable. Ever since last summer, this place had been busy. Along with government offices evacuated to this city were numerous stylish married and single women, who dazzled the natives. What Man-ch'ien had from her innermost underwear to her overcoat was what she had bought for her wedding, and she wouldn't have minded having some new clothes. But her dowry had been spent long since, when she and her husband fled their home; what Ts'ai-shu earned was barely enough for monthly expenses, and there wasn't any money left for her to indulge in clothes. She was sympathetic to her husband. She never asked him for money for clothes, and she kept her yearnings to herself. Yes, in more than two years of married life, she had not had it easy; Man-ch'ien had to grin and bear the hardships of life with her husband, using her pride to sustain love, and never complaining to anyone. A wife like that had certainly done right by her husband.

It should be said, however, that her husband had not done right by her. Before their engagement, Man-ch'ien's mother insisted that Ts'ai-shu had cheated her of her daughter, and she blamed her own husband for having introduced Ts'ai-shu to her daughter. Some of Man-ch'ien's girl friends had also commented that, despite Man-ch'ien's shrewdness, Man-ch'ien had made a foolish mistake on such a vital matter as choosing a mate.

But what mother doesn't object to her daughter's choice of a mate? What woman doesn't disparage a friend's lover behind her back? At college, every young person, besides aspiring to a degree, must also aspire to a lover. In colleges that require students to live on campus, the distance between men and women is greatly reduced. Without the factor of their families, when men and women meet, they get to know each other. Thus this type of contact leads to what the families would call a mismatch. Moreover, love, as legend has it, is blind. It opens its eyes only after marriage. However, many students do not regard love as blind. They want to be loved, offer their love, beg to be given some residual love. But love seems to see them as totally unlovable and ignores them altogether. This proves that love is still blind, too blind to see their lovable traits. Thus coeducation not only increases the number of married couples through freedom of choice, but also leaves behind many rejects from the love game, especially old maids. At least the old maids, unlike Man-ch'ien, had not been willing to be mismatched.

Man-ch'ien was somewhat lethargic, and her image of herself was of a poised, refined young woman from a good family. Her long eyelashes, her egg-shaped face, her pale complexion, and her slim figure all contributed to creating an impression of gracious aloofness in her. She was especially known among her classmates for her love of art, and this caused her admirers to detect an indefinable elegance about her. Some men might consider her beauty too pure and lacking in sensuality, but her detractors, so vulgar in taste, would never have attracted the attention of her curved, slightly nearsighted eyes in the first place. By exploiting her inborn bashfulness, she developed self-appreciation. Some people called her arrogant, but arrogance in a woman makes her fascinating to a man's spirit, just as wantonness in a woman is a challenge to a man's body. Thus, though Man-ch'ien was perhaps not as elegant as she perceived herself to be, she did have a few suitors. She was slow by nature, and her attraction for men was low-key and cumulative. Her ad-

---

[3] See footnote 1 in "Piglet and Chickens," p. 313.

mirers were schoolmates of many years. Precisely because they had been together for so long, she was used to their ways and bored with them. None of them could arouse a fresh reaction in her. Until the year of her graduation from college, she had no lover. When she was bored and low in spirits, there was an emptiness in her heart which no one could fill. It must be said that she had failed to benefit from the opportunities of college coeducation. At this time, Ts'ai-shu appeared, seemingly from nowhere.

Ts'ai-shu was the son of an old friend of Man-ch'ien's father. Because of the political situation, Ts'ai-shu had transferred to Man-ch'ien's school from a college in the south. In view of Ts'ai-shu's family's straitened circumstances, Man-ch'ien's father had invited Ts'ai-shu to stay with them before school started; he even set up a couch for Ts'ai-shu to use on weekends and holidays, the idea being to give Ts'ai-shu a home away from home. Years of education in the city had not eradicated Ts'ai-shu's rusticity or his childishness. His naïve rudeness, his unsophisticated civilities, and his native smartness made him look ridiculous and yet charming. Ever since the day when Man-ch'ien's father told her to take Ts'ai-shu to register at school, Man-ch'ien had vaguely felt that she was much more experienced than this big, newly arrived country boy, and she relished the joy of being a competent sister. On the other hand, Ts'ai-shu felt strongly for her from the start and stayed at her home frequently. They became very good friends, almost as if they were of the same family. In his company, she forgot her usual reticence, partly overlooking the fact that he was, potentially, an attractive man. She felt toward him like a comfortable foot that has forgotten that it still has a shoe on, a feeling she never had with other men. What was at first companionship gradually turned to love, not passionate love, but a slowly and steadily growing intimacy. It was not until her girl friends began to tease her that she realized how much she really liked Ts'ai-shu.

When her parents found out about this, they quarreled with each other, and Ts'ai-shu was too scared to come spend the night with them anymore. The mother blamed the father; the father scolded the daughter and blamed the mother; father and mother joined in scolding Ts'ai-shu and in counseling their daughter, pointing out that Ts'ai-shu's family was poor and his prospects dim. Man-ch'ien shed some tears, but her parents' chiding stiffened her resolve, like a piece of hemp rope that has become wet and so become stronger. At first her parents forbade her to see him; later they prohibited an engagement; they hoped time would erode her love for him. But love, like a habit, takes a long time to grow, and, like illness, even more time is needed to be rid of it. So, after two years, Man-ch'ien remained steadfast in her love for Ts'ai-shu, who, of course, took everything in stride. It was because of the opposition of friends and relatives that their relationship, not nurturing itself as much as it should, began to turn into a unified force against outsiders and an alliance against snobbery. They had waited a long time when the war suddenly broke out, and political uncertainties easily divide families.

War, which traditionally produces many widows and widowers, ironically became the catalyst for Man-ch'ien and Ts'ai-shu's marriage. Her parents felt they had done their best by her and should stay out of her affairs. So Man-ch'ien and Ts'ai-shu were married without too much ceremony, as they blandly listened to the usual wedding benedictions and to such clichés as "lovers eventually get married." Soon afterward Ts'ai-shu and his fellow employees were evacuated to this city.

Purchasing items hard to come by in the interior, packing their luggage, looking for cheap transportation and lodging, buying or renting furniture, hiring a maid, and returning courtesy calls to the wives of Ts'ai-shu's colleagues took up a lot of their time before they settled down. After the wedding they were so busy they had little time to savor any sweetness. Man-ch'ien, who had never paid any attention to domestic chores, now had to worry about daily necessities such as fuel, rice, oil, and salt. She was not extravagant, but she came from a respectable family. Ts'ai-shu's income was limited, and they felt the pinch even though prices in the interior at first were low. People had not become accustomed to poverty since it was the first year of the war; Man-ch'ien and her husband were just poor enough to want to hide theirs, and could manage to get away with their pretenses. It was really hard on Man-ch'ien. For this Ts'ai-shu was both sympathetic and apologetic. Husband and wife both wished the war would end soon so they could lead a better life.

It was not long before Man-ch'ien discovered that Ts'ai-shu was not an aggressive or enterprising person. He would do no more than go to work at his square desk in the office. Even if the war came to an end, his prospects would not improve. His ignorance of the ways of the world made her feel vaguely the absence of anyone to support her. It intensified her fear that she alone had to take care of them both; that she would always have to be a gentle, protective mother to him. All the luxuries associated with being a woman—playing coy, being naughty, and throwing temper tantrums—were denied her, just like the luxury goods in the world. Ts'ai-shu himself was a child; he could not accommodate wanton coyness.

Except for some activities in the morning, there really wasn't much for Man-ch'ien to do at home. After lunch Ts'ai-shu would go to work; the maid would be washing clothes in the courtyard, and she would be sitting leisurely in the center of the room, gazing at the sun climbing the wall—a regular diet of ennui and silence which she could share with no one. She did not care to gossip with the wives of Ts'ai-shu's colleagues. In the same city lived a number of friends whom she had known before she got married. Those who were men, she felt it would be improper for her to associate with anymore. As for the women, some were married, and those who were single had jobs or were preparing to get married—all of them were busy with what they were doing. And, because she was trying to save money, she had few activities, and so her friends increasingly dwindled in number. Only in the evenings or on weekends would a few of Ts'ai-shu's friends occasionally stop by. She felt no desire to cultivate the friendship of those that didn't come to see her. She loved to read, her only regret being that there were few new books she could buy in the interior.

The few old and tattered foreign novels she borrowed were not enough to fill up the hours in the day, nor the gaps in her soul. Knowing she must be bored, Ts'ai-shu had suggested she take walks by herself. Out of extreme boredom she went to the movie theater once. She did not go to see the movie per se, but to see what constituted a movie in the interior. It was a bizarre old foreign film, and the long benches in the movie theater were crowded with local moviegoers. Whenever a kissing scene appeared on the screen, the audience would clap their hands and yell, "Good, how about another one?" After chatting with her husband a bit after coming home from the movie, she went to bed, but was deprived of sleep by the fleas she had picked up at the theater. From then on, she was afraid to go to the movies.

In this manner two years went by. And there was no sign of a baby. Every time the wives of Ts'ai-shu's colleagues saw her, they would say, "Mrs. Hsü, you should have a baby by now!" Because Man-ch'ien was a woman with a modern education and a knowledge of science, the old-fashioned wives speculated wildly as to why she wasn't pregnant. They would say with a meaningful smile, "Don't you know modern women love comfort?"

The previous spring enemy planes had bombed the city for the first time. Some houses were destroyed, and, as usual, some common folk who were not worth bombing got killed. But this was enough to frighten the citizenry of all social classes of the city. Even the most naïve aborigines knew that bombers were not hens laying eggs in the sky, and they no longer dared gaze at the sky from the streets, clap their hands, and make noises after the air raid sirens had sounded. Air raid precaution measures suddenly became a matter of supreme concern; in editorials and readers' correspondence columns local papers repeatedly stated the area's importance for the War of Resistance in the interior and called for air protection. Protection by the air force, detractors argued, would only make the city a military target and induce the enemy to bomb; but such views were not expressed by the papers. After the summer, the city had its air force academy and its airport expanded, and the people began to get used to seeing their country's planes flying in the sky.

One day late in September, Ts'ai-shu came home to say that an acquaintance who was distantly related to him had moved to town. Earlier that day a cousin from the air force academy had visited Ts'ai-shu in his office. This cousin had been a brat who refused to pay attention to schoolwork, so Ts'ai-shu told his wife. Not having seen his cousin for six or seven years, Ts'ai-shu said he could barely recognize him. He was big and tall now, but just as naughty and flippant as ever. He added that the cousin, after learning Ts'ai-shu was married, had joked that he would like to "get acquainted" with Man-ch'ien in a couple of days.

"Should we invite him for potluck?" asked Ts'ai-shu casually. Without much enthusiasm, Man-ch'ien replied, "We'll see. Those guys in the air force are accustomed to good food and fun. He may not think much of our inviting him to dinner. While you'll have spent lots of money, he may not appreciate the dinner, or, worse yet, he may feel he's been imposed on. Why bother? If you invite him for only a so-so dinner, you'd be better off not inviting him at all. Most likely he just said he'd like to visit you. So long as he has seen you, that will probably be the end of it. Someone like that probably won't spend the time to find your house."

In view of his wife's disdain for the whole matter, Ts'ai-shu lost half his excitement. Quickly he said, "We'd better wait. He said he would come. He asked for my address. He also said that he has heard you were beautiful and gifted, with both 'talent and looks,' and that he must see you. He had a good laugh with me about it."

"Humph. Please ask him not to come. I'm old and ugly, nothing more than your housekeeper. If he sees me, wouldn't we be embarrassed?"

"Come on, come on," Ts'ai-shu comforted his wife, fondling her hair. "If you saw him, you'd certainly like him. He's talkative, funny, affable, and kind." Then he changed the subject, wondering why his wife should turn so caustic when she was told she was both pretty and talented. In truth, Ts'ai-shu was born to be a subordinate or

assistant who would only be allowed to take orders and would only be good at that. As he never heard any complaints from his wife, who appeared complacent, he had taken her for granted. Now he was astonished, but dared not ask any questions. Hurriedly, he finished his dinner and dropped the matter.

It would be Sunday in a few days; Saturday night Ts'ai-shu remembered that T'ien-chien might show up the following day, and he told his wife. On Sunday she bought a little more food than usual, preparing for T'ien-chien to come to lunch. Since T'ien-chien had not committed himself to coming, they prepared just a bit more than usual, so that if T'ien-chien showed up, he would not get the impression that they had prepared a special meal for him. They also supervised the maid, who swept the living room and the courtyard more thoroughly than usual. As husband and wife made preparations, they laughed to each other, stating that they really shouldn't make too much of this, because the guest, if he showed up, was no one very important. Despite all that was said, Man-ch'ien put on a traditional Chinese dress, which she would hardly wear every day. She also put on a little more rouge, and even applied some lipstick, something she seldom did.

Shortly before noon, there was no sign of T'ien-chien. The maid, famished herself, urged them to eat. Since they had no choice, husband and wife sat across from each other and began to eat. An even-tempered man, Ts'ai-shu said smilingly to his wife, "He was never that firm about coming. We were the only ones who were certain. Let's consider today a treat for ourselves. Lucky we didn't spend too much. The courtyard hasn't been cleaned like that for some time. I wonder how the maid usually sweeps it?"

Man-ch'ien said, "It isn't a question of the money, but rather of all the planning that went into it. A fine Sunday has been spoiled by him. If he was coming, he should have said so; if not, he should have made himself clear. He was noncommittal, and we've been kept busy for him. Only someone as naïve as you would take a casual remark as a solemn promise."

Her unpleasant expression made Ts'ai-shu say

quickly, "Even if he comes, we won't entertain him. That boy's been inconsiderate since childhood. After lunch we can take a walk in the park. Since the weather is so nice, you won't have to change your clothes."

Man-ch'ien assented; in her heart she judged T'ien-chien to be genuinely disgusting.

Another week and more went by, during which time T'ien-chien did not come. After Ts'ai-shu got home one day, he mentioned that he had seen T'ien-chien with a young woman. "He was very vague about the whole thing; he didn't introduce the girl. Must be some new girl friend of his. That kid is too much. The girl looks all right, except for the way she dressed. Too provocative—definitely not a native of this area. When he heard we'd been waiting for him to come to lunch, he apologized. He said he had intended to come but couldn't because something else came up. He said he'll visit us in a few days, and he wanted me to send his regards and his sincere apologies to you beforehand."

"Come here in a 'few days'? How many days then?" Man-ch'ien asked coldly.

"Let him come whenever he likes; we don't have to make any preparations anyway. He and I are relatives, and there's no need for formality. I think he's madly in love right now, and it's likely he won't have time to come in the immediate future. I'm afraid we're getting old. For example, when I saw the young couple together today, I wasn't jealous at all. For some reason I felt them naïve enough to be pitied. There are so many ups and downs awaiting them; they have yet to be fooled and manipulated by fate; for us married folks, life has settled down—like a boat that has entered its harbor and no longer fears the storm. Though we've been married for only two years, we can consider ourselves an old married couple."

Man-ch'ien smiled and said, "Don't say us, just you!"—a line she borrowed from the novel *The Gallant Ones*,[4] in which Thirteenth Sister speaks it to a "faceless" woman. Man-ch'ien and her husband had borrowed and finished reading that novel, and they had appropriated expressions

from it to tease each other. When Ts'ai-shu saw his wife being both naughty and teasing, he begged for a kiss. Intoxicated with his own passion, he did not sense her indifference.

For better than half the night, Man-ch'ien could not fall asleep. The snores of a tired Ts'ai-shu did not relieve the tense vibrations which permeated her whole body. Quietly she lay there wondering why at such a young age she should be so tired of love. No, not only of love, but of everything. She had been married for only a little over two years, but the marriage was as stale and as boring as if she had been married a lifetime. "For us married folks, life has settled down," was what he had said. Yes, the truth was that since meeting Ts'ai-shu she had never experienced any fluctuations in her feelings. The fear of outside forces' interfering with their love affair did once exist, but there had always been sufficient mutual confidence and assurance. Groundless suspicions, deliberate misunderstandings, and other assorted delicate torments associated with romance were wholly outside her experience. There never was any bitterness, spiciness, sourness, or harshness, but always the taste of clear tea.

Her relationship with him now was like fresh boiling water poured over old tea leaves—the tea gets weaker after each infusion. Days went by as if she had not lived them, eventlessly, as if time bore no relationship to her. Soon she would be thirty—the way she aged, it really wasn't worth it. It would be better if she did have a baby, to reduce some of the emptiness of life; she might as well make up her mind to being a mother. In the beginning she had a faint hope of getting a job so she could be part of society and not confined to her home. She was unwilling to lose her role outside the family after she got married. At first she feared a baby would be a hindrance to love and she'd rather not have one. Then she didn't know if Ts'ai-shu would want a baby; she was afraid he couldn't afford it. When would this dreadful war come to an end?

Man-ch'ien rose late. When she got up, Ts'ai-shu had left for work. She had not slept for the

---

[4] *Erh-nü ying-hsiung chuan,* a novel by Wen K'ang (fl. 1821). Thirteenth Sister is among the major heroines in the novel.

better part of the night; her head felt heavy and her eyelids too weighty to lift themselves, and she was afraid to take a good look at her long, sallow face in the mirror. After washing her face and rinsing her mouth, she had little energy for anything else. No one would come this morning, and she was too lazy to tidy herself up. After resting a bit she felt better. The maid had gone to the market and returned. Donning her plain green cloth apron, she helped the maid prepare lunch. While they were in the midst of this, they heard a knock on the front door; she wondered who could be visiting at that hour. The maid ran to open the door. Suddenly she remembered that she had not combed her hair, had not made up her face, and that she smelled of grease. She definitely could not receive a visitor, and she was sorry she had not told the maid so. She heard the maid running all the way to the kitchen yelling, "Madam, madam," and saying that a man surnamed Chou, who said he was a relative of the master, had come to visit master and mistress and was standing in the courtyard. The maid wondered if she should invite the guest in.

Man-ch'ien knew the caller was T'ien-chien. Flustered and annoyed by the maid's garrulousness, she did not know what to do. Scolding the maid, her first thought, would not help matters. Should she go out to greet the guest? She felt ashamed of her condition, and since this was their first meeting, she did not want to be embarrassed. If she were to put on some makeup and receive him, she must go to the bedroom and to go to the bedroom she must pass the courtyard, which was right outside the kitchen. Not wanting to be seen in her condition, and there being no chance to make up, she was forced to tell the maid to inform the guest that the master wasn't home but would be informed of his visit and that the master would return his visit shortly. The maid answered in a loud voice, and left.

A wave of shame overtook Man-ch'ien, and she didn't trouble to find out if the maid had relayed the message correctly. She felt she had been less than civil to her guest, who certainly knew she had been hiding in the kitchen, unwilling to come

out. Perhaps he would have forgiven her for her less-than-neat appearance and for not having had time to make up properly. Yet, it was truly disgraceful that the cousin's so-called talented and beautiful wife was unable to receive her guest because she smelled of kitchen smoke. Really it was T'ien-chien's fault. Of all the times he could have called, why did he choose that time to come, and so abruptly? While she fumed, the maid came back to tell her the guest had said he'd come again on Saturday afternoon. Man-ch'ien, full of frustrations, scolded the maid for having yelled at the top of her lungs when a visitor called. The maid, peeved, threatened to quit. This only exasperated Man-ch'ien more. When her husband came home for lunch, she told him what had happened in the morning and blamed him for having a mischievous troublemaker from God knew where for a cousin.

Even though husband and wife said they didn't want to go out of their way to entertain T'ien-chien, Ts'ai-shu brought some pastries when he came home around noon on Saturday. And after lunch, Man-ch'ien herself spent some time making herself presentable. The last time she had made herself up, she merely wanted to show her respect for her guest; good manners dictated that she not be seen with her hair uncombed and her face unadorned. But this time, it was completely different, for she was still subconsciously very much affected by the shame and embarrassment she had felt two days ago when she couldn't see T'ien-chien. Though T'ien-chien had never seen her, she felt he must have an image of her as a smoked-up, greasy, untidy woman working by the stove. So today she must pay extra attention to her appearance to restore her tarnished reputation. Unconsciously, she put powder on her face in a more obvious way, to appeal to someone with T'ien-chien's crude sense of aesthetics.

A little after three, T'ien-chien came, with some gifts. On meeting him, Man-ch'ien was pleasantly surprised. It seemed T'ien-chien was not the slick, crude young man she had expected to dislike. Like all air force personnel, T'ien-chien was tall and strong, but his facial features were finely chiseled, and his manner of speaking seemed more refined than Ts'ai-shu's. What was more, his suit was well tailored without giving the impression of being either out of or at the vanguard of fashion. Even during their first meeting, his words of courtesy toward her seemed affectionate, and one could tell he was experienced in social relations. Of course, Ts'ai-shu had much to say to him, but she could tell he didn't want to spend all his time talking about his past with her husband and ignoring her. From time to time he broadened the conversatfion deliberately so as to involve her in it. Yes, the facts wouldn't allow her to dislike T'ien-chien, unless she was offended by his frequent, sly glances at her. One time, when he was gazing at her, she was looking at him at the same time; she blushed instantly and her eyes blurred like a mirror someone had fogged with hot breath. But then he gave her a candid smile and casually asked what she did for recreation.

What a smart man T'ien-chien was! Since T'ien-chien's gifts to them were quite expensive, husband and wife felt they had to invite him to eat with them the next evening. The long-scheduled dinner had to be given after all.

The next day Man-ch'ien was busy all afternoon until she felt she could trust the remaining work to the maid, and then went to her room to change. T'ien-chien came shortly, and since Ts'ai-shu had not yet returned from visiting a friend, the job of entertaining the guest fell on Man-ch'ien alone. Trying to be calm, she searched the fringes of her brain for things to say. Fortunately, T'ien-chien was a good conversationalist. Whenever she, in embarrassment, ran out of things to say, he would subtly touch on something else as if erecting a floating bridge to connect the ever-widening cracks, so linking the threads of conversation. She realized that he knew her predicament and was sympathetic. As she pondered this she felt the situation was a bit amusing, and she also felt grateful toward him.

T'ien-chien said he wanted very much to try Man-ch'ien's cooking, but he feared that would give her extra work, and hence he felt a conflict in himself. He added that he enjoyed cooking too and would demonstrate his culinary skills some time.

Man-ch'ien smiled. "It's lucky I didn't know you were so talented. I don't know much about cooking. Next time, if you come here to eat, I won't dare prepare dishes for you—I'll just have to serve you plain rice."

T'ien-chien had the ability to make new acquaintances feel like old friends; and his enthusiasm was so infectious that it made social intercourse easy. Without being aware of it, Man-ch'ien relaxed.

When Ts'ai-shu came home, he saw his wife and cousin in a happy mood, and his wife with some animation in her gentleness. He knew that her prejudices against his cousin had all dissolved and was very pleased. When they sat down to eat, the three cast formalities aside—especially Man-ch'ien, who had never known being a hostess could be so easy, and entertaining a guest so relaxing.

T'ien-chien told them about many of the things he had done before coming to town; he also said that a man from the same province had recently prepared a room for him at his house, and that sometimes when it was too late to return to the academy he would stay there.

Ts'ai-shu then thought of T'ien-chien's woman companion and asked, "I imagine you must have quite a few girl friends. Who was the one I saw you with the other day?"

Taken aback for a moment, T'ien-chien asked, "Which day?"

Man-ch'ien interrupted wickedly: "What he meant was 'Which one?' I think he has girl friends with him every day, and he doesn't remember them all."

T'ien-chien laughed, looking at her. "Now I can see for myself you've got a sharp tongue, Piao-sao,[5] but frankly, I don't remember."

Making a funny face, Ts'ai-shu said, "Don't play dumb. It was the day I met you around Chung-

---

[5] A polite title for an older cousin's wife.

shan Road. She was round-faced and wore purple. With all the evidence, aren't you going to confess?"

"Oh, that one," T'ien-chien said. "That's my landlord's daughter."

Man-ch'ien and Ts'ai-shu thought they would hear more about this, but their guest paused and had no more to offer, as if a torrent of words ready to flow had been dammed and reclaimed by silence.

Unable to bear the suspense any longer, husband and wife commented simultaneously, "No wonder you want to live with her family!"

To explain himself, T'ien-chien said, "It's like this. My landlord is an old lady, her nephew and I were very good friends when I was in Szechwan. When I came here, her nephew wrote me a letter of introduction, and it happened that she had a lot of space, and she let me have one spare room. She has a son and a daughter. The son still goes to school, and the daughter, who graduated from college this past summer, works as a clerk in some office. She's quite pretty and knows how to apply cosmetics and dress herself up. She loves fun so much that her mother can't do much about her." He stopped at this point; then he added, "Many colleagues from the air force academy go out with her. I'm not the only one."

A clerk himself, Ts'ai-shu realized that she was a "flower vase."[6] Before he could say a word, Man-ch'ien's laughter exploded like bubbling water as she said, "You could call that girl an aircraft carrier." Ts'ai-shu laughed involuntarily. T'ien-chien seemed momentarily stunned by the remark, but he quickly regained his composure and started to laugh too.

Man-ch'ien was quick tongued. After having made the remark, she was sorry she hadn't weighed her words before uttering them. As she looked at T'ien-chien she saw that his smile was perfunctory at best, and was doubly unhappy that she might have offended him. After all, that girl might be his girl friend; she felt she had spoken much more than usual, and her garrulousness had caused a gaffe. As she mulled this over, she

lost her enthusiasm, and watched what she was saying. At the same time she noticed that T'ien-chien had become inhibited. Maybe she was just being too suspicious.

The only one who remained unruffled was Ts'ai-shu; he kept talking about this and that and eased the discomfort between host and guest. The dinner seemed interminably long. When it was finally over, T'ien-chien said goodbye to Ts'ai-shu and Man-ch'ien, thanking her again and again, and praising her excellent cooking. She, of course, knew this was his social routine, but from his repeated thanks she could see his respect for her and felt somewhat pleased. As she and her husband saw T'ien-chien out of the courtyard, her husband said, "T'ien-chien, if you don't mind this place being shabby, just drop in and visit us when you have the time. In any case, Man-ch'ien is home most of the time, and she's bored. You two can talk."

"Of course, I'd love to come. But I'm afraid people like me are so crass that we aren't qualified to speak to Piao-sao." Though a smile lessened the severity of his tone, his reply implied hostility and challenge. Fortunately, the dark night by the front door concealed their faces and allowed Man-ch'ien to blush in safety.

Assuming a normal tone of voice, Man-ch'ien said, "I'm afraid you aren't willing to come. If you came, I'd be more than pleased. I've been a housekeeper for so long that I can only talk about homemaking. What's more, I've never been a good conversationalist."

"Don't be polite, either of you," Ts'ai-shu interrupted. Thus, amid abundant "Goodbyes," and "Take cares," T'ien-chien left them.

Two days later, in the afternoon, Man-ch'ien was just planning to knit something new from the yarn she had unraveled from an old sweater, soaked, and hung out in the sun to straighten, when suddenly she heard T'ien-chien coming. She felt that he had come especially for her that day, because he knew it was too early for her husband to have returned from work. This knowledge made her very constrained and ill at ease.

[6] Term for any female employee who didn't type, did little work, but looked pretty.

She said hello, she asked how he had found time to come, and then she couldn't think of another word to say. The friendliness of two days past seemed to have disappeared.

Spying the yarn on the dining table, T'ien-chien smiled. "I came especially to give you a hand," he said. Hoping to ease her own unnatural reserve, Man-ch'ien suddenly became unusually bold and said, "You came at the right time. I was worried because there was no one to help me with this. Ts'ai-shu's wrists are clumsy and he can't do this properly. Now I have a perfect chance to try you out, though I'm afraid you may not have the patience. First let me separate the yarn."

So one stretched the yarn in both hands, while the other wound it into separate balls. Even when they said nothing to each other, the yarn maintained a continual contact between them and spared them the trouble of looking for things to say. When two or three balls of yarn had been wound, Man-ch'ien, afraid that T'ien-chien might have become bored, suggested he quit, but he refused and continued helping her until all the yarn on the table had been wound up. At this point he rose, commenting that he hoped his wrists and patience had passed her test. He said he must leave and couldn't wait for Ts'ai-shu to come home.

With great sincerity, Man-ch'ien apologized. "I've put you through too much! I'm afraid you'll be scared to come back again after this punishment."

T'ien-chien only smiled.

After that time, T'ien-chien would come to sit for a while every three or four days. Man-ch'ien noticed that, except for one Sunday when he invited her and her husband out to a restaurant, T'ien-chien had never come on a Sunday. When T'ien-chien came, Ts'ai-shu was usually at work. She knew that T'ien-chien enjoyed her company, and his affection for her subconsciously improved her own self-image. Besides adding a bit of mild excitement to her humdrum existence, his interest also restored her shaky self-confidence—proving that she had not passed her prime, and that life had not completely eroded her charms.

To prove to a woman that she is attractive,

there is no better way than wooing her. For single girls in their prime, this type of proof is due recognition of their desirableness; for those who are married and approaching middle age, this proof is not only solace, but also must be considered a compliment. Those women who, when young, set the highest standards in selecting their beaux, frequently lower their standards when they find themselves at the twilight of their emotions. Persons who never could have become their husbands now have a chance to be just that.

Man-ch'ien had already reached a stage in life when she needed proof and compliments. She was certain she and T'ien-chien would never fall in love—at least she would not love him with any passion; she was not worried about the future. She had a husband—that was her best security, the best defense against T'ien-chien. Her own marriage marked a line in her friendship with T'ien-chien, one that neither was to cross. T'ien-chien was truly a likable person. She kept that knowledge to herself, unwilling to give him any more definite signs of her liking by calling him "lovable." No wonder Ts'ai-shu said T'ien-chien was a lady's man. When Man-ch'ien thought of T'ien-chien's girl friends, an inexplicable annoyance surfaced. Maybe he considered her one of his many girl friends. No, she would never consent to be that type of girl friend, and he would not treat her like that. He had never treated her flippantly, in a materialistic manner; his frequent visits with her fully showed his capacity for quietness. After T'ien-chien had visited her a number of times, she was often tempted to ask him if what her husband had said of him, that he was "madly in love," was true, but she was afraid to betray her secret, her vague sense of jealousy, by her tone or choice of words. So she held herself back. This was also a secret she wanted to keep from her husband. Hence she never breathed a word to Ts'ai-shu about T'ien-chien's frequent visits. Gradually she developed a routine. Every other day she prepared (never admitting she hoped) for him to visit her. After lunch she would apply light makeup to her face. Despite their familiarity with each other, whenever she heard him come in she became excited, and it required tremendous effort on her part to dispel the involuntary flush on her face before she came in.

In this way a new meaning seemed to enter her life. A month or so later it was winter, the best season in the mountain-circled city. Day after day of brilliant sunshine dazzled newcomers to the city, who could not believe that the weather could be so beautiful, particularly those people who had been used to dramatic seasonal changes. Daylight emerged in a tender, rosy morning ray and disappeared in the rich yellow of evening, completely different from the winter in the north, which carried with it chilly gusts of wind. Because the city was located at a high altitude, it was said that a thin layer of fog surrounded it in winter and thus diminished the possibility of its being attacked by enemy planes. The streets, as a result, were thronged with more shoppers than before.

As usual, one day T'ien-chien came to visit Man-ch'ien. After sitting for a while, he said he had to leave. When she asked him why he was in a hurry, since it was still early, he replied, "The weather is too nice to be true. How can you stay home doing nothing? Why don't you take a walk with me?"

The question put Man-ch'ien in a dilemma. If she said she was willing to be bored at home, she would be telling an obvious lie. There wasn't even enough truth in it to fool herself. On the other hand, to stroll with T'ien-chien in public, she felt, would be improper and might cause gossip. Wary of this, but unable to tell him her true feelings, she replied weakly, "If you're bored, please suit yourself."

T'ien-chien seemed to understand her. In a half serious and half joking tone he said, "It's not me. It's you who must be feeling bored sitting here all the time. I have lots of activities. What's wrong with going out together? Would Ts'ai-shu think I've abducted you?"

Man-ch'ien was in more of a dilemma. Ambiguously she murmured, "It's not like that. You just go ahead. I won't keep you."

Knowing that he could not force her, T'ien-chien left. After he left Man-ch'ien felt disappointed for a while, with the knowledge that she really had wanted him to stay. It was only a little after three o'clock, a long time before evening—a stretch of time lay in front of her as impassable as a desert. At first time had passed in blocks, but once T'ien-chien left, the hours, minutes, and seconds, as if removed from their spines, loosened into countless tiny bits and pieces. No event could serve as a thread to string them together. She was used to lonely afternoons, but she couldn't bear this one. She thought she really should have gone out with T'ien-chien because she needed small items like toothpaste and a toothbrush. Though he was not her husband, she could justify the trip as business, which would soothe her conscience and provide an excuse to anyone who asked. No one could say she had asked him to accompany her, nor gone along just for the sake of accompanying him.

The next day the weather became even more beautiful. The events of the previous day had left a residue powerful enough to vibrate in her heart, and Man-ch'ien could not sit still at home. In the morning there were some household chores for her to do, and because of air raids, stores and shops would not be open until three in the afternoon. Not having been out for a few days, she noticed some new stores which copied the style of the stores in Shanghai and Hong Kong. Standing before a new drugstore and looking at the sample goods advertised in the windows, she pondered what to buy. Suddenly she heard a man's voice behind her. It was T'ien-chien's. Eyes fixed on the windows, she blushed; her vision blurring, she could not tell what she was looking at. Her heart felt as if it were being pummeled, and for a moment she hadn't the nerve to turn and call him. Then as she began to turn, she heard a woman talking and laughing with him. Involuntarily she stopped herself. After the footsteps had passed her, she turned around and saw him and the woman enter the drugstore. Though the woman's face was partly blocked by him, she did get a rear view of the woman, a woman shapely enough to make a spectator want to run ahead and catch the front view. Man-ch'ien, awaking from a dream, realized the woman must be the "aircraft carrier." All of a sudden she lost her courage to enter the drugstore and quickly left the place as if she were avoiding them. She no longer had any desire to buy sundries. Her heart and feet were as heavy as lead, and she could not walk home. So she hired a rickshaw.

Once having settled down, she fully comprehended how much anguish she had felt. She knew she had no reason to feel that way, but who could argue with a person's heart? She didn't hate T'ien-chien, but she felt uneasy, as if she realized the happiness of the past month really amounted to nothing. No, it did not amount to nothing. If it did, she wouldn't be feeling the way she did. She yearned to see him at once to calm her much-confused soul. What she had witnessed that day she could not fully accept, and she wanted him to prove to her that what she saw was an illusion. All in all, she felt he must explain things to her. Would he come that day? Probably not. The next day? The next day seemed so far away. She really could not wait that long. Also at the same time she felt conscience stricken, afraid that her husband might notice her agitated state.

That evening when Ts'ai-shu came home, she was an unusually concerned wife, and she asked him this and that. Meanwhile, she valiantly tried to prevent her vexations from intruding into her consciousness and from making her answers to her husband appear incoherent. After they went to bed, dreading insomnia, she concentrated with all her might on removing thoughts of T'ien-chien, or at least putting them aside. She did not want to think of them now; it was like putting fish and meat in a refrigerator overnight in hot weather.

The next day when she awoke, the agony of the evening before had slipped away with sleep, and she felt very silly for having exaggerated matters. What did it matter to her that T'ien-chien had gone out with some woman? After all, he would be coming to see her soon, and she could subtly tease him on that. But as soon as noon passed, her heart fluttered, and she became fidgety, eagerly awaiting him.

T'ien-chien did not appear that afternoon, nor the next day. In fact, he didn't come even on the fifth day. He had never stayed away for this length of time since they had come to know each other. Then a thought occurred to Man-ch'ien: "Maybe, through some uncanny telepathy, he has become aware of my attitude toward him and is afraid to come anymore. But how could he know my mind?" In any case, it was better to abandon hope, never to expect to see him again. Having tasted the ironic paradoxes that life offers, she knew how God fools everyone. To turn hope into reality, she concluded, the first thing to do was to stop yearning and prepare herself for a surprise later. This "abandoning of hope" lasted three days, during which period there was no trace of T'ien-chien. It seemed that God did not care to correct any error that had been made, pretending not to know that her "abandoning of hope" was only a debased form of hope, and allowing her to be confirmed in her disappointment.

During those eight days Man-ch'ien seemed gravely ill and had aged mentally ten years. All the emotions that accompany love she had tasted in a double dose. Her weary body and mind were as tense as ever. Like an insomniac, the more exhausted she was, the tauter the nerves became. Several times she wanted to write T'ien-chien, having drafted the letter many times in her mind, but her pride prevented her from doing so; the thought "maybe he'll show up today or tomorrow" stopped her from writing. In her husband's presence, she tried her best to appear normal, but this required a lot of energy and effort. Therefore, she wanted her husband to stay out of the house, so she did not have to expend energy on him. But once he left the house, alone with herself, she felt defenseless and besieged by vexations. It was literally impossible for her not to think of the matter. Whatever she was doing, she inevitably thought of T'ien-chien—she was like a cow pulling a grinder around the mill. In these eight days the physical separation between her and T'ien-chien enhanced their mental affinity. Previously she had been unwilling to think of him and forbade herself to think of him. Now she not only missed him, she also hated him. The last time he said goodbye to her, they had been on speaking terms, but during these eight days it was as if her heart had been fermenting and made her feelings for him stronger. Her attempt to turn despair into hope had failed. It was so unfair that he had obtained her affection without wooing her. She blamed herself for being weak; she must discipline herself into not wanting to see him. At the most she'd see him once more. She must be cool to him, and so let him know she didn't care whether he came or not.

Another day passed. After lunch Man-ch'ien was washing her nylon stockings, which could not withstand the maid's crude hands: a conclusion Man-ch'ien had drawn from past experience. At this time the maid told her she was going out. Her hands covered in soapy water, Man-ch'ien did not rise to latch the door, merely telling the maid to close it. Meanwhile, Man-ch'ien thought that Christmas would come in a few days, followed by the New Year's, and she wondered if she should send T'ien-chien a Christmas card—just a card with nothing else on it. Then she hated herself for being a fool, for not being able to forget him, for wanting to retain some contact with him. A little later, after washing the stockings and drying her hands, she was about to latch the door.

Then the door creaked open. When she saw it was T'ien-chien she felt so weak that she almost could not stand still. Dazed, she watched him close the door behind him and heard him laugh on his way in, yelling "Why was the door left open? Are you home alone? I haven't seen you for a few days. How've you been?"

The tension she had been under the last eight days was suddenly released. She discovered that the bitter tears she had stored up within her were now threatening to pour out. Her intention of giving him a perfunctory smile failed to materialize. Lowering her head she said in a hoarse voice, "What a rare visitor!"

T'ien-chien sensed something unusual in the situation. Stupefied for a moment, he kept staring at her. Suddenly a smile emerged, and he walked toward her, whispering, "You seem unhappy today. Whom are you mad at?"

For some reason none of the vituperative words she had prepared for him could come out. She felt the weight of silence on her increasing every second. With considerable effort she finally blurted out, "Why did you bother to come? Such beautiful weather! Why didn't you go out with your girl friend?" After she said these words, she felt as if she had suffered many grievances, and it became even more difficult for her to hold back her tears. She thought to herself, "What a disaster! Now he sees through me!"

In her confusion, she discovered T'ien-chien cupping her neck with his hands and gently kissing her eyes. He murmured, "Silly child! Silly child!"

Instinctively Man-ch'ien struggled free of his hands and ran to her room, saying repeatedly, "Go away! I don't want to see you today. Go away this instant!"

T'ien-chien left. But what happened that day completely changed his attitude toward Man-ch'ien. In his recollections of his dealings with her over the past month or so, he saw a fresh meaning which had wholly escaped him before. Looking back, he understood what had always made him come to see her. Like a lamp on a ship's stern, his reflection suddenly lit up the path it had sailed. At the same time, he thought he had the right to request something of her, and had even the obligation to conquer her. Though he had no idea how far he'd like to go with her, his male ego told him he must pursue his course until she frankly and uninhibitedly admitted he was her lover.

As for Man-ch'ien, she knew her secret had been compromised. There was no retreat. Her only regret was that she had allowed him so much leeway, allowed him to think everything would come so easily. Therefore, she decided she must be cool to him, to discount the degree of intimacy between them, so that he would not take her for granted or at face value. She hoped this strategy of reverse psychology would lead him to beg sincerely for her love. Only in this manner could she have vengeance for what happened today, and so even the score with him. Her only worry was that he wouldn't come the next day. And when he did show up the next day, she had told her maid in advance that she was not well and so forced him to come some other time.

T'ien-chien assumed that Man-ch'ien was truly

ill, and in his concern, immediately bought two small baskets of Chungking tangerines and had a special messenger deliver them. Since it would not be appropriate to write a note, he attached his name card to the gift. A day later he sent a Christmas card and an invitation asking Man-ch'ien and her husband to Christmas dinner.

The reply was in Ts'ai-shu's name, but the writing was apparently Man-ch'ien's. It said simply, "We dare not refuse your dinner invitation. Let us thank you in advance. See you on that day."

T'ien-chien thought about this carefully and concluded that Man-ch'ien had implied she did not want him to see her. People who are capable of defending themselves don't shut their doors to callers. He thought he must behave with the magnanimity of a victor, as there was no present need to impose himself on her.

On Christmas evening T'ien-chien and Man-ch'ien met. Maybe it was because her passion toward him had cooled, or maybe she was emboldened by the presence of her husband; to his surprise, she was very calm. Many a time he had hoped to discover their mutual secret revealed either in her face or in her eyes, but he couldn't find any indication of it. The dinner went smoothly, but he was nonetheless disappointed. Then the New Year holidays came around and Ts'ai-shu remained at home. T'ien-chien went to visit Man-ch'ien once, but he had no chance to talk to her. Moreover, she seemed rather distant toward him and left the room a few times under false pretenses. At first he thought her behavior was due to her bashfulness and was a little pleased. But then, when she seemed to be so totally indifferent to him, he felt uneasy.

Ts'ai-shu went back to work after the holidays. T'ien-chien visited Man-ch'ien again. Like severed silk, their friendship of before could not be joined again. Her stern looks made him feel restrained, and he experienced the vexation of having something slip through his fingers. He could not decide what approach to use with her: to remain cool and detached or be rude and passionate. Watching her knit a sweater with her head bent, the uncontrollable slight blush on her face, her

long eyelashes covering her eyes like a lampshade over a lamp, he was tempted to kiss her. He walked toward her. Her bent head appeared even more flushed.

"You shouldn't be mad at me anymore," he said half-questioningly.

"I mad at you? No such thing," she replied, trying to appear calm.

"We get along quite well. Why must we hide our secrets and not say what's in our hearts?"

She was silent, mechanically knitting with increased speed. Edging toward her, he put his hands on her shoulders. She struggled free and knit at a furious pace. In a low but commanding voice she said, "Go away. There'll be a scandal if the maid sees us."

He had no choice but to release her. In an aggrieved tone, he said, "I know I am not welcome anymore. I've come too often and become a pest. Please forgive me this time; I won't be a nuisance anymore." As he was saying that, he realized he had been extreme in his choice of words. If she did not respond to what he said, he had allowed himself no room for other maneuvers, and he must consider the whole matter a complete fiasco. But Man-ch'ien continued to knit, giving no response. The few minutes that went by in total silence were nearly as painfully long as several lifetimes. Knowing he could not force anything from her, he was so exasperated that the following exploded from his throat: "Okay, I am going now. Never will I come again . . . and you just leave me alone too."

As soon as that was said, he went to fetch his hat. Suddenly, Man-ch'ien raised her head. With a bashful smile she looked at the fiery-tempered T'ien-chien and said, with her head lowered again, "See you tomorrow then. I plan to go shopping. Would you have time to come with me tomorrow after lunch?"

T'ien-chien was bewildered for a moment before he realized he had won. He was so ecstatic that he wanted to jump up and down; he felt he must kiss her to mark this moment of triumph. Then he realized she wouldn't dare to do such a thing, and he must be wary of the maid. As he left her, he was very happy, thinking another romance of his had borne fruit, except he had not celebrated this victory with a kiss, as was his custom. And that must be considered the only flaw in an otherwise perfect victory.

This feeling of something less than perfection persisted and increased in the three or four weeks that followed. Even though T'ien-chien and Man-ch'ien became closer, he discovered that she was always evasive about physical intimacy. Not only did she seem to make few demands on him, but also she would not try to please him. Even when there were opportunities for embraces, he had to struggle with her in order to kiss her. The kisses were never passionate, full, or harmonious.

Not endowed by nature with stimulating or intoxicating sexual charm, Man-ch'ien was not easily aroused or carried away. During courtship she was always a cool and reserved woman. Her low-key approach, ironically, stimulated T'ien-chien greatly. Her indifference seemed to imply a contemptuous challenge to his passion; it stirred up even greater desire in him and intensified his temper. The situation was like the spilling of a drop of cold water on a stove of burning coal, creating a *shee* sound and rising steam. Every time she rejected him, he invariably lost his temper and was on the verge of asking her if she ever allowed her husband to be intimate with her. But he thought such a question would only imply he was obsessed with sex and was too vulgar. He firmly believed that as there was a code of honor among thieves, that there were ethical rules governing extramarital relations. It seemed to him that a husband had the right to question his wife about her relationship with a lover, but never vice versa—the lover inquiring into his mistress's relationship with her husband.

After several rejections, T'ien-chien gradually realized that his time and energy had been wasted. His efforts in keeping up appearances and his careful calculations to prevent suspicion by Ts'ai-shu and others had all come to nought. He, in fact, had obtained nothing; it was like receiving an empty box by registered mail. This type of romance he could not drop and yet it was exasperating and boring. Something must come

out of it! He must find or make an opportunity to capture her body and soul. A few days after the Lantern Festival, his landlady's family would be going to the country for a few days, and taking the initiative, he told the landlady he would watch the house for her. He planned to invite Man-ch'ien over, and if he failed in this attempt, he decided that he'd end all dealings with her. It would be far better to break off the relationship than to keep it going in a lukewarm and noncommittal manner.

Who could have known that he would break the ice today? His passion temporarily weakened Man-ch'ien's stubborn resistance. As if affected by his passion, she seemed to warm to him considerably. Their romance could be considered complete and concluded at this point. Nonetheless, T'ien-chien experienced the emptiness one usually feels after having achieved a goal. The restraint that Man-ch'ien exercised during her indiscretion seemed to suggest that she had not treated him fairly. So, in a way his success could be viewed as another failure. Because he was not happy with this outcome, he ended up feeling guilty for having cheated Man-ch'ien and grievously wronged Ts'ai-shu. Since there were attractive women available, why must he dally with his Piao-sao? However, her abrupt departure afterward and her unwillingness to listen to his explanations and apologies made it easier for him to get himself out of this mess. He could now cast her aside completely on the pretext that he had affronted her and felt too ashamed to see her. And if she should seek him out in the future, he would think of some way to handle her then.

Without giving any thought to the future, Man-ch'ien ran home in one breath and collapsed on the bed. As sober as if she had just been splashed with ice water, she knew that she did not love T'ien-chien. She had desired him before because of her pride, which now had vanished without a trace. The romantic tryst of a moment ago left its ghostly shadows, which seemed imprinted with a thin impression of T'ien-chien. Those disgusting, lingering sentiments! When would they completely fade away? When Ts'ai-shu comes home in a while, how can I face him? she wondered. That night, Ts'ai-shu did not detect anything strange about his wife.

Man-ch'ien was worried that T'ien-chien would come back to her, just like a bad habit that was difficult to break. But fortunately he didn't show up for several weeks. Since he had had her once, he had obtained the right to have her again. If she were alone with him, she simply would not be able to cope with him. She knew he was a gentleman who would not betray her and would help her keep their secret. But what if the secret bore some kind of fruit that would be impossible to cover up? No, absolutely impossible! Could such a coincidence happen in this world? She was sorry she had been foolish, and she hated T'ien-chien for his impudence. She did not dare think about the subject any further.

The weather continued to be unbearably pleasant. It was as if Man-ch'ien's heart was a tree hollowed out with worms and unable to show any sign of growth. But also for this reason she was spared the usual vexations that came to her each spring.

One day right after lunch, Ts'ai-shu was about to take a nap when suddenly air raid sirens were sounded, destroying the calm of that pleasant day. The streets were filled with commotion. Because the city had not heard any sirens in three months, everyone panicked. The Chinese fighter planes climbed into the sky, and the clouds were filled with the sounds of their engines as they flew away toward the city's outskirts. The old maid, carrying a satchel on her back, demanded a few dollars from Man-ch'ien and breathlessly ran to the air shelter trench behind the alley for protection. Before she left, she said, "Madam, you and the master had better hurry up."

Lazily lounging in bed, Ts'ai-shu told his wife that it was most likely a false alarm and he saw no need to fight the crowd and dust in any air raid trench. Like many people, Man-ch'ien had the peculiar notion that even though many had died in the bombings, she herself would never be among the victims. Her husband had often quoted her as saying, "The chances of being bombed to death are just as slim as winning the first prize in the aviation lottery drawings." A while later the second air raid warning siren was sounded, and the siren, with its long wails, was like a huge iron throat spewing cold air toward the blue sky. When the neighborhood sank into an eerie silence, Ts'ai-shu and his wife became terrified. At first they had been too lazy to move; now they were too scared to move. Man-ch'ien stayed in the courtyard by herself. Holding her breath, she gazed at the enemy planes which entered air space above the city with a contemptuous ease, as if taunting the anti-aircraft guns.

The sound of the machine guns was like that of a stutterer—unable to express his meaning to the sky; or like phelgm stuck in the throat, unable to come out. Suddenly Man-ch'ien felt weak all over, not daring to stand or look anymore. Quickly, she ran toward her bedroom. As she was about to step into the house, a noise constricted her heart and dragged it along to the abyss. As her heart began to sink, another explosion followed, lifting her heart from its depths and leaving her eardrums ringing with sound. The windows shook uneasily within their frames; the lidded cups on the tea tray clanked against one another and made their own music. So frightened was she that she fell into a chair and held her husband's hand. Whatever resentments she felt against him all vanished so long as he was close to her now. Her head seemed to have been packed with the commotions of the whole sky. The noises of machine guns and of bombs, distinct from those of the airplanes, created havoc in her mind. She could not dispel them.

No one knows how long it was before calm was restored. The birds in the trees, after what seemed a long period of silence, began to chirp. The blue sky acted as if nothing had happened, and one lone Chinese fighter plane suddenly flew overhead. Everything was over. Some time later, the warning was lifted. Though there were no immediate stirrings in the neighborhood, the city seemed to be coming back to life. The old maid returned with her satchel, and then Ts'ai-shu and his wife went to the main street to find out what had happened.

There was more activity than usual in the

streets, people gathering to read the notice written on a strip of red cloth which had just been posted by the Air Raid Prevention Committee: "Six enemy aircraft bombed the city at random. Our casualties were extremely light. After a crushing counterattack from our planes, one enemy plane was shot down, and the rest fled the province. Another enemy plane was seriously damaged and was forced to land somewhere in the outlying area. We are still searching for it." Ts'ai-shu and his wife read the notice and simultaneously said that they would be able to get more definite information if they saw T'ien-chien. Then Ts'ai-shu rather casually asked his wife why T'ien-chien hadn't come to see them for some time.

At that point in time T'ien-chien and his plane had gone down in the rubble some forty miles from the city. He had obtained his cruel peace. A man who had been active in the air all his life could find rest only underground.

This news came to Ts'ai-shu and his wife three days later. He shed some tears, which were mingled with pride for being a relative of the dead. For the first time Man-ch'ien felt T'ien-chien was truly pitiable; her feelings of pity were exactly those an adult has toward a naughty child sound asleep. T'ien-chien's good looks, his ability, decisiveness, and smoothness were terribly attractive to women when he was alive, but in death all his qualities had now been shrunken, softened, jabbed through by death, as if they were those of a child and couldn't be taken seriously. At the same time she felt the relief of having been set free. What about the secret she had with him? At first she did not want to think about this, something she'd like to keep a secret even from herself. Now, the secret, having suddenly lost some of its repugnancy, was transformed into a souvenir worthy of being kept and preserved. It was like a maple leaf or lotus petal to be folded in a book, to be allowed to fade in color with time. But every time you open the book, it's still there, and it makes you shiver unintentionally, as if a part of Man-ch'ien's body had been contaminated by death, as if a part of her body had been snatched away by T'ien-chien and had died also. Fortunately, this part of the body was far away from

her, like a shell that has left its cocoon, like hair or nails that have been cut and no longer hurt or itch.

Soon, various city groups sponsored a memorial service for T'ien-chien, at which the remains of one enemy plane were displayed. Ts'ai-shu and his wife attended the service. The sponsors had asked Ts'ai-shu to give a talk or be responsible for some program, as was appropriate for the relative of the deceased. But Ts'ai-shu staunchly refused to do anything. He did not care to appear in public on account of the deceased and was unwilling to publicize or cheapen his personal grief in an exhibition of public emotions. This attitude increased Man-ch'ien's respect for him. After some hullabaloo, T'ien-chien's name, along with his corpse, became cold and was forgotten. It was only after two or three weeks that T'ien-chien's name was mentioned again between husband and wife. It was right after dinner, and they were chatting in the bedroom.

Ts'ai-shu said, "All the symptoms are unmistakable. Since we're destined to have a child, there's no way to run away from it. We should have a child; you shouldn't hate having one. We can afford a child at the moment; maybe the war will be over before your delivery date. If that's the case, all the more reason for us not to worry about it. I say, if you have a boy, we should call him T'ien-chien, in memory of our friendship with him during those few months. What do you say?"

Man-ch'ien was looking for something; she walked to the window, she pulled open the desk drawer, and, with her head lowered, fingered through all the items in it. Meanwhile she said, "I don't want to. Didn't you see the 'Aircraft Carrier' during the service? Tears and mucus all came out and she was dressed like T'ien-chien's widow. You know what kind of person T'ien-chien was. The two must have known each other very well. Who knows if she hasn't borne a child for him? Let her have a kid to honor him. I wouldn't want to. And let me tell you something else. I will not love this baby, because I've never wanted it."

As usual, Ts'ai-shu made no comment on what his wife had said. His wife's last sentence increased his alarm, as if he were responsible for the child. Leaning against the back of the chair, he yawned and said, "I'm tired. Oh well, we'll see. What are you looking for?"

"Nothing in particular," Man-ch'ien answered ambivalently. Closing the drawer, she said, "I'm tired too. I've got a slight temperature, but I haven't done anything today, have I?"

Indolently Ts'ai-shu looked at his wife's still slim figure, and his eyes filled with infinite tenderness and affection.

HSIAO HUNG
(*1911–1942*)

Hsiao Hung's popularity as a writer has grown considerably in recent years. Her highly evocative writing style, masterful recreations of life in Northeast China (Manchuria), and accent on the viewpoints of women are drawing readers and critics to her work in increasing numbers.

Hsiao Hung (her real name was Chang Nai-ying) was born in 1911 to a landlord family near Harbin in Heilungkiang, Northeast China. Hsiao Hung's world view was largely formed by a generally unhappy and lonely childhood. This can be seen in accounts written by friends about her personal life as an adult in one of China's most turbulent eras, and in the bittersweet reminiscences she later wrote of her home and family.

Hsiao Hung's rise to eminence on the Chinese literary scene dates from her first, and in the eyes of some critics, finest novel *The Field of Life and Death* (*Sheng-szu ch'ang*). Published in December 1935, shortly after the publication of Hsiao Chün's *Village in August,* it was acclaimed as a major literary and political event, for it deals with the issue of Japanese aggression in Northeast China and the burgeoning attempts to resist by Chinese peasants. The novel was published mainly through the efforts of Lu Hsün, who, in effect, became Hsiao Hung's patron as well as her close friend and surrogate father.

From 1936 to 1940, the early years of the Sino-Japanese War, Hsiao Hung continued the vagabond, somewhat Bohemian existence that characterized most of her adult life. Her literary output over these years was limited to several small volumes of short stories and essays. But even with this small output and the mediocre quality of much of what she wrote, her reputation continued to grow.

In 1940 Hsiao Hung, who had since taken leave of Hsiao Chün and was now sharing her life with Tuan-mu Hung-liang, flew from the wartime capital Chungking to Hong Kong. She lived in the British Colony for the remaining months of her life. She died in a hospital on January 22, 1942, slightly over a month after Hong Kong fell to the Japanese, at the age of thirty. During her refuge in Hong Kong, she produced three novels, one of which had been begun during her final year in Chungking.

The first and last of the three, entitled *Ma Po-lo* and *Ma Po-lo II*, were the first two volumes of a projected trilogy, a humorous satire set in Tsingtao, Shanghai, and the interior just prior to and during the early war years.

Tales of Hulan River (*Hu-lan-ho chuan*), the first draft of which was completed prior to Hsiao Hung's departure from Chungking, was the last of her novels to be published (posthumously in 1942). It is generally acclaimed to be her masterpiece. It is a moving and highly artistic reminiscence of the author's Manchurian home. Hence, only after the national wartime emotions had cooled did this novel begin to enjoy the acclaim and popularity it rightly deserves.

"Hands" (*Shou,* 1936), the story of Wang Ya-ming, a disadvantaged girl with an indomitable spirit and totally disarming ways, is far and away the best and most artistically executed of Hsiao Hung's short stories. Like so much of what she wrote, this story probably has a great deal of autobiographical transference, although that is not the only reason it succeeds so admirably.

"The Family Outsider" (*Chia-tsu yi-wai ti jen,* 1937), while of a totally different type, spotlights a character who suffers much the same fate as Wang Ya-ming. Yu Erh-po is unquestionably based upon a real member of the author's family, though it is uncertain to what degree the incidents and descriptions in the story belong to real life. This story, written in Japan in 1936 during Hsiao Hung's brief stay there, was the foundation upon which her autobiographical novel, *Tales of Hulan River,* was formed.

HOWARD GOLDBLATT

Hands

by Hsiao Hung

Translated by Howard Goldblatt

Never had any of us in the school seen hands the likes of hers before: blue, black, and even showing a touch of purple, the discoloring ran from her finger tips all the way to her wrists.

We called her "The Freak" the first few days she was here. After class we always crowded around her, but not one of us had ever asked her about her hands.

Try though we might, when our teacher took roll call, we just could not keep from bursting out laughing:

"Li Chieh!"

"Present."

"Chang Ch'u-fang!"

"Present."

"Hsü Kuei-chen!"

"Present."

One after another in rapid, orderly fashion, we stood up as our names were called, then sat back down. But when it came Wang Ya-ming's turn, the process lengthened considerably.

"Hey, Wang Ya-ming! She's calling your name!" One of us often had to prod her before she finally stood up, her blackened hands hanging stiffly at her sides, her shoulders drooping: Staring at the ceiling, she would answer: "Pre-se-nt!"

No matter how the rest of us laughed at her, she would never lose her composure, but merely push her chair back noisily with a solemn air and sit down after what seemed like several moments. Once, at the beginning of English class, our English teacher was laughing so hard she had to remove her glasses and wipe her eyes.

"Next time you need not answer *hay-er*," she commented. "Just say 'present' in Chinese."

We were all laughing and scuffling our feet on the floor. But on the following day in English class, when Wang Ya-ming's name was called we were once again treated to sounds of *"Hay-er, hay-er."*

"Have you ever studied English before?" the English teacher asked as she adjusted her glasses slightly.

"You mean the language they speak in England? Sure, I've studied some, from the pockmarked teacher. Let's see, I know that they write with a *pun-sell* or a *pun,* but I never heard *hay-er* before."

" 'Here' simply means 'present.' It's pronounced 'here,' 'h-e-r-e.' "

"She-er, she-er." And so she began saying *she-er.* Her quaint pronunciation made everyone in the room laugh so hard we literally shook. All, that is, except Wang Ya-ming, who sat down very calmly and opened her book with her blackened hands. Then she began reading in a very soft voice: *"Who-at . . . deez . . . ah-ar . . ."* [1]

During math class she read her formulas the same way she read essays: $2x + y = . . . x^2 = . . .$"

At the lunch table, as she reached out to grab a *man-t'ou* [2] with a blackened hand, she was still occupied with her geography lesson: "Mexico pro-

---

[1] "What . . . these . . . are . . ."   [2] Chinese steamed bread.

duces silver . . . Yünnan . . . hmm, Yünnan produces marble."

At night she hid herself in the bathroom and studied her lessons, and at the crack of dawn she could be found sitting at the foot of the stairs. Wherever there was the slightest glimmer of light, that's where I usually found her. One morning during a heavy snowfall, when the trees outside the window were covered with a velvety layer of white, I thought I spotted someone sleeping on the ledge of the window at the far end of the corridor in our dormitory.

"Who's there? It's so cold there!" The slapping of my shoes on the wooden floor produced a hollow sound. Since it was a Sunday morning, there was a pronounced stillness throughout the school; some of the girls were getting ready to go out, while others were still in bed asleep. Even before I had drawn up next to her I noticed the pages of the open book on her lap turning over in the wind. "Who do we have here? How can anybody be studying so hard on a Sunday!" Just as I was about to wake the girl up a pair of blackened hands suddenly caught my eye. "Wang Ya-ming! Hey, come on, wake up now!" This was the first time I had ever called her name, and it gave me a strange, awkward feeling.

"*Haw-haw* . . . I must have fallen asleep!" Every time she spoke she prefaced her remarks with a dull-witted laugh.

"*Who-at . . . deez . . . yoou . . . ai,*"[3] she began to read before she had even found her place in the book.

"*Who-at . . . deez . . .* this English is sure hard. It's nothing like our Chinese characters with radicals and the like. No, all it has is a lot of squiggles, like a bunch of worms crawling around in my brain, getting me more confused all the time, until I can't remember any more. Our English teacher says it isn't hard—not hard, she says. Well, maybe not for the rest of you. But me, I'm stupid; we country folk just aren't as quick-witted as the rest of you. And my father's even worse off than me. He said that when he was young he only learned one character—our name Wang—and he

couldn't even remember that one for more than a few minutes. *Yoou . . . ai . . . yoou . . . ah-ar . . .*" Finishing what she had to say, she tacked on a series of unrelated words from her lesson.

The ventilator on the wall whirred in the wind, as snowflakes were blown in through the window, where they stuck and turned into beads of ice. Her eyes were all bloodshot; like her blackened hands, they were greedily striving for a goal that was forever just beyond reach. In the corners of rooms or any place where even a glimmer of light remained, we saw her , looking very much like a mouse gnawing away at something.

The first time her father came to visit her he said she had gained weight: "I'll be damned, you've put on a few pounds. The chow here must be better'n it is at home, ain't that right? You keep working hard! You study here for three years or so, and even though you won't turn into no sage, at least you'll know a little somethin' about the world."

For a solid week after his visit we had a great time mimicking him. The second time he came she asked him for a pair of gloves.

"Here, you can have this pair of mine! Since you're studyin' your lessons so hard, you oughta at least have a pair of gloves. Here, don't you worry none about it. If you want some gloves, then go ahead and wear these. It's comin' on spring now, and I don't go out much anyway. Little Ming, we'll just buy another pair next winter, won't we, Little Ming?" He was standing in the doorway of the reception room bellowing, and a crowd of his daughter's classmates had gathered around him. He continued calling out "Little Ming this" and "Little Ming that," then gave her some news from home: "Third Sister went visitin' over to Second Auntie's and stayed for two or three days! Our little pig has been gettin' a couple extra handfuls of beans every day, and he's so fat now you've never seen the like. His ears are standin' straight up. Your elder sister came home and pickled two more jars of scallions."

He was talking so much he had worked up a

---

[3] "What . . . these . . . you . . . I."

sweat, and just then the school principal threaded her way through the crowd of onlookers and walked up to him: "Won't you please come into the reception room and have a seat?"

"No thanks, there's no need for that, that'll just waste everyone's time. Besides, I couldn't if I wanted to; I have to go catch a train back home. All those kids at home, I don't feel right leavin' 'em there." He took his cap off and held it in his hands, then he nodded to the principal. Steam rose from his head as he pushed the door open and strode out, looking as though he had been chased off by the principal. But he stopped in his tracks and turned around, then began removing his gloves.

"Daddy, you keep them. I don't need to wear gloves anyway."

Her father's hands were also discolored, but they were both bigger and blacker than Wang Ya-ming's.

Later, when we were in the reading room, Wang Ya-ming asked me: "Tell me, is it true? If someone goes into the reception room to sit and chat, does it cost them anything?"

"Cost anything! For what?"

"Not so loud; if the others hear you, they'll start laughing at me again. She placed the palm of her hand on top of the newspaper I was reading and continued: "My father said so. He said there was a teapot and some cups in the reception room, and that if he went inside the custodian would probably pour tea, and that he would have to pay for it. I said he wasn't expected to, but he wouldn't believe me, and he said that even in a small teahouse, if you went in and just had a cup of water you'd have to pay something. It was even more likely in a school, he said. 'Just think how big a school is!' "

The principal said to her, as she had several times in the past: "Can't you wash those hands of yours clean? Use a little more soap! Wash them good and hard with hot water. During morning calisthenics out on the playground there are several hundred white hands up in the air—all but yours; no, yours are special, very special!" The principal reached out her bloodless, fossil-like transparent fingers and touched Wang Ya-ming's blackened hands. Holding her breath somewhat

fearfully, she looked as though she were reaching out to pick up a dead crow. "They're a lot less stained than they used to be—I can even see the skin on the palms now. They're much better than they were when you first got here—they were like hands of iron then! Are you keeping up with your lessons? I want you to work a little harder, and from now on you don't have to take part in morning calisthenics. Our school wall is low, and there are a lot of foreigners strolling by on spring days who stop to take a look. You can join in again when the discoloring on your hands is all gone!" This lecture by the school principal was to bring an end to her morning calisthenics.

"I already asked my father for a pair of gloves. No one would notice them if I had gloves on, would they?" She opened up her bookbag and took out the gloves her father had given her.

The principal laughed so hard at this she fell into a fit of coughing. Her pallid face suddenly reddened: "What possible good would that do? What we want is uniformity, and even if you wore gloves you still wouldn't be like the others."

The snow atop the artificial hill had melted, the bell being rung by the school custodian produced a crisper sound than usual, sprouts began to appear on the willow trees in front of the window, and a layer of steam rose from the playground under the rays of the sun. As morning calisthenics began, the sound of the exercise leader's whistle carried far into the distance; its echo reverberated among the people in the clump of trees outside the windows. We ran and jumped like a flock of noisy birds, intoxicated by the sweet fragrance that drifted over from the new buds on the branches of the trees. Our spirits, which had been imprisoned by the winter weather, were set free anew, like cotton wadding that has just been released.

As the morning calisthenics period was coming to an end we suddenly heard someone calling to us from an upstairs window in a voice that seemed to be floating up to the sky: "Just feel how warm the sun is! Aren't you hot down there? Aren't you . . ."

There standing in the window behind the budding willows was Wang Ya-ming.

By the time the trees were covered with green

leaves and were casting their shade all over the compound, a change had come over Wang Ya-ming—she had begun to languish and black circles had appeared around her eyes. Her ears seemed less full than before and her strong shoulders began to slump. On one of the rare occasions when I saw her under one of the shade trees I noticed her slightly hollow chest and was reminded of someone suffering from consumption.

"The principal says my schoolwork's lagging behind, and she's right, of course; if it hasn't improved by the end of the year, well . . . *Haw-haw!* Do you think she'll really keep me back a year?" Even though her speech was still punctuated with that *haw-haw*, I could see that she was trying to hide her hands—she kept the left one behind her back, while all I could see of the right one was a lump under the sleeve of her jacket.

We had never seen her cry before, but one gusty day when the branches of the trees outside the windows were bending in the wind, she stood there with her back to the classroom and to the rest of us and wept to the wind outside. This occurred after a group of visitors had departed, and she stood there wiping the tears from her eyes with darkened hands that had already lost a good deal of their color.

"Are you crying? How dare you cry! Why didn't you go away and hide when all the visitors were here? Just look at yourself. You're the only 'special case' in the whole group! Even if I were to forget for the moment those two blue hands of yours, just look at your uniform—it's almost gray! Everybody else has on a blue blouse, but you, you're special. It doesn't look good to have someone wearing clothes so old that the color has faded. We can't let our system of uniforms go out the window because of you alone." With her lips opening and closing, the principal reached out with her pale white fingers and clutched at Wang Ya-ming's collar: "I told you to go downstairs and not come back up until after the visitors had left! Who told you to stand out there in the corridor? Did you really think they wouldn't see you out there? And to top it all, you had on this pair of oversized gloves."

As she mentioned the word "gloves" the prin-

cipal kicked the glove that had dropped to the floor with the shiny toe of her patent shoe and said: "I suppose you figured everything would be just fine if you stood out there wearing a pair of gloves, didn't you? What kind of nonsense is that?" She kicked the glove again, but this time, looking at that huge glove, which was large enough for a carter to wear, she couldn't suppress a chuckle.

How Wang Ya-ming cried that time; she was still weeping even after the sounds of the wind had died down.

She returned to the school after summer vacation. The late summer weather was as cool and brisk as autumn, and the setting sun turned the cobbled road a deep red. We had gathered beneath the crab-apple tree by the school entrance and were eating crab-apples when a horsecart from Mount Lama carrying Wang Ya-ming rumbled up. In the silence following the arrival of the cart her father began taking her luggage down for her, while she held onto her small washbasin and a few odds and ends. We didn't immediately make way for her when she reached the step of the gate. Some of us called out to her: "So here you are! You've come back!" Others just stood there gaping at her. As her father followed her up to the steps, the white towel which hung from his waistband flapping to and fro, someone said: "What's this! After spending a summer at home, her hands are as black as they were before. Don't they look like they're made of iron?"

I didn't really pay much attention to her iron-like hands until our post-autumn moving day. Although I was half asleep, I could hear some quarreling in the next room:

"I don't want her. I won't have my bed next to hers!"

"I don't want mine next to hers either."

I tried listening more attentively, but I couldn't hear clearly what was going on. All I could hear was some muffled laughter and an occasional sound of commotion. But going out into the corridor that night to get a drink of water, I saw someone sleeping on one of the benches. I recognized her at once—it was Wang Ya-ming. Her face was covered with those two blackened hands, and her quilt had slid down so that half was on the ground and the other half barely covered her legs. I thought that she was getting in some studying by the corridor light, but I saw no books beside her. There was only a clutter of personal belongings and odds and ends on the floor all around her.

On the next day the principal, followed closely by Wang Ya-ming, made her way among the neatly arranged beds, snorting as she did so and testing the freshly tucked bedsheets with her delicate fingers.

"Why, here's a row of seven beds with only eight girls sleeping on them; some of the others have nine girls sleeping in six beds!" As she said this she took one of the quilts and moved it slightly to one side, telling Wang Ya-ming to place her bedding there.

Wang Ya-ming opened up her bedding and whistled contentedly as she made up the bed. This was the first time I had ever heard anyone whistle in a girls' school. After she made up the bed she sat on it, her mouth open and her chin tilted slightly higher than usual, as though she were calmed by a feeling of repose and a sense of contentment. The principal had already turned and gone downstairs, and was perhaps by then out of the dormitory altogether and on her way home. But the old housemother with lackluster hair kept shuffling back and forth, scraping her shoes on the floor.

"As far as I'm concerned," she said, "this won't do at all. It's unsanitary. Who wants to be with her, with those vermin all over her body?" As she took a few steps toward the corner of the room, she seemed to be staring straight at me: "Take a look at that bedding! Have a sniff at it! You can smell the odor two feet away. Just imagine how ludicrous it is to have to sleep next to her! Who knows, those vermin of hers might hop all over anyone next to her. Look at this, have you ever seen cotton wadding as filthy as that!"

The housemother often told us stories about how she had accompanied her husband when he went overseas to study in Japan, and how she should be considered an overseas student also. When asked by some of the girls: "What did you study?" she would respond: "Why study any particular subject? I picked up some Japanese and

noticed some Japanese customs while I was there. Isn't that studying abroad?" Her speech was forever dotted with terms like "unsanitary," "ludicrous," "filthy," and so on, and she always called lice "vermin."

"If someone's filthy the hands show it." When she said the word "filthy" she shrugged her broad shoulders, as though she had been struck by a blast of cold air, then suddenly darted outside.

"This kind of student! Really, the principal shouldn't have . . ." Even after the lights-out bell had sounded the housemother could still be heard talking with some of the girls in the corridor.

On the third night Wang Ya-ming, bundle in hand and carrying her bedding, was again walking along behind the white-faced principal.

"We don't want her. We already have enough girls here."

They started yelling before the principal had even laid a finger on their bedding, and the same thing happened when she moved on to the next row of beds.

"We're too crowded here already! Do you expect us to take any more? Nine girls on six beds; how are we supposed to take any more?"

"One, two, three, four . . ." the principal counted. "Not enough; you can still add one more. There should be six girls for every four beds, but you only have five. Come on over here, Wang Ya-ming!"

"No, my sister's coming tomorrow, and we're saving that space for her," one of the girls said as she ran over and held her bedding in place.

Eventually the principal led her over to another dormitory.

"She's got lice, I'm not going to sleep next to her."

"I'm not going to either."

"Wang Ya-ming's bedding doesn't have a cover and she sleeps right next to the cotton wadding. If you don't believe me, just look for yourself!"

Then they began to joke about it, saying they were all afraid of Wang Ya-ming's black hands and didn't dare get close to her.

Finally the black-handed girl had to sleep on a bench in the corridor. On mornings when I got up early I met her there rolling up her bedding and carrying it downstairs. Sometimes I ran into her in the basement storage room. Naturally, that was always at nighttime, so as we talked I kept looking at the shadows cast on the wall; the shadows of her hands as she scratched her head were the same color as her black hair.

"Once you get used to it, you can sleep on a bench or even on the floor. After all, sleep is sleep no matter where you lie down, so what's the difference! Studying is what matters. I wonder what sort of grade Mrs. Ma is going to give me in English on our next exam. If I don't score at least sixty I'll be kept back at the end of the year, won't I?"

"Don't worry about that; they won't keep you back just because of one subject," I assured her.

"But Daddy told me I only have three years to graduate in. He said he won't be able to handle the tuition for even one extra semester. But this English language—I just can't get my tongue right for it. *Haw-haw* . . ."

Everyone in the dormitory was disgusted with her, even though she was sleeping in the corridor, because she was always coughing during the night. Another reason was that she had begun to dye her socks and blouses right in the dormitory.

"When clothes get old, if you dye them they're as good as new. Like, if you take a summer uniform and dye it gray, then you can use it as an autumn uniform. You can dye a pair of white socks black, then . . ."

"Why don't you just buy a pair of black socks?" I asked her.

"You mean those sold in the stores? When they dye them they use too much alum, so not only don't they hold up, but they tear as soon as you put them on. It's a lot better to dye them yourself. Socks are so expensive it just won't do to throw them away as soon as they have holes in them."

One Saturday night some of the girls cooked some eggs in a small iron pot, something they did nearly every Saturday, as they wanted to have something special to eat. I saw the eggs they cooked this time when they took them out of the pot. They were black, looking to me as if they had been poisoned or something. The girl who carried the eggs in roared so loudly her glasses nearly fell

off: "All right, who did it! Who? Who did this!?"

Wang Ya-ming looked over at the girl as she squeezed her way through the others into the kitchen. After a few *haw-haw's* she said: "It was me. I didn't know anyone was going to use this pot, so I dyed two pairs of socks in it. *Haw-haw* . . . I'll go and . . ."

"You'll go and do what?"

"I'll go and wash it."

"You think we'd cook eggs in the same pot you used to dye your stinky old socks! Who wants it?" The iron pot was hurled to the floor, where it clanged in front of us. Scowling, the girl wearing glasses then flung the blackened eggs to the floor as though she were throwing stones.

After everyone else had left the scene, Wang Ya-ming picked the eggs up off the floor, saying to herself: "Hm! Why throw a perfectly good iron pot away just because I dyed a couple of pairs of socks in it? Besides, how could new socks be 'stinky'?"

On snowy winter nights the path from the school to our dormitories was completely covered by a blanket of snow. We just pushed on ahead as best we could, bumping our way along, and when we ran into a strong wind we either turned around and walked backwards or walked sideways against the wind and snow. In the mornings we had to set out again from our dormitories, and in December it got so bad that our feet were numb with the cold, even if we ran. All of this caused a lot of grumbling and complaining, and some of the girls even began calling the principal names for placing the dormitories so far from the school and for making us leave for school before dawn.

Sometimes I met Wang Ya-ming as I was walking alone. There would be a sparkle to the sky and the distant snow cover as we walked along together, the moon casting our shadows ahead of us. There would be no other people in sight as the wind whistled through the trees by the side of the road and windows creaked and groaned under the driving snow. Our voices had harsh sounds to them as we talked in the sub-zero weather until our lips turned as stiff and numb as our legs and we stopped talking altogether, at which time we could hear only the crunching of the snow beneath our feet. When we rang the bell at the gate our legs were so cold they felt like they were about to fall off, and our knees were about to buckle under us.

One morning—I forget just when it was—I walked out of the dormitory with a novel I wanted to read tucked under my arm, then turned around and pulled the door shut tight behind me. I felt very ill at ease as I looked at the blurred houses off in the distance and heard the sound of the shifting snow behind me; I grew more frightened with every step. The stars gave off only a glimmer of light, and the moon either had already set or was covered by the gray, dirty-looking clouds in the sky. Every step I took seemed to add another step to the distance I had yet to go. I hoped I would meet someone along the way, but dreaded it at the same time; for on a moonless night you could hear the footsteps long before you saw anyone, until the figure suddenly appeared without warning before you.

When I reached the stone steps of the school gate my heart was pounding and I rang the door bell with a trembling hand. Just then I heard someone on the steps behind me.

"Who is it? Who's there?"

"Me! It's me."

"Were you walking behind me all the time?" It gave me quite a fright, because I hadn't heard any steps but my own on the way over.

"No, I wasn't walking behind you; I've already been here a long time. The custodian won't open the door for me. I don't know how long I've been here shouting for him."

"Didn't you ring the bell?"

"It didn't do any good, *haw-haw*. The custodian turned on the light and came to the door, then he looked out through the window. But he wouldn't open the door for me."

The light inside came on and the door opened noisily, accompanied by some angry scolding: "What's the idea of shouting at the gate at all hours of the night! You're going to wind up at the bottom of the class anyway, so why worry about it?"

"What's going on! What's that you're saying?" Before I had even finished, the custodian's manner changed completely.

"Oh, Miss Hsiao, have you been waiting there long?"

Wang Ya-ming and I walked to the basement together; she was coughing and her face, which had grown pale and wrinkled, shivered for a few moments. With tears induced by the cold wind on her cheeks, she sat down and opened her school book.

"Why wouldn't the custodian open the door for you?" I asked.

"Who knows? He said I was too early. He told me to go on back, saying that he was only following the principal's orders."

"How long were you waiting out there?"

"Not too long. Only a short while . . . a short while. I guess about as long as it takes to eat a meal. *Haw-haw.*"

She no longer studied her lessons as she had when she first arrived. Her voice was much softer now and she just muttered to herself. Her swaying shoulders slumped forward and were much narrower than they had been, while her back was no longer straight and her chest had grown hollow. I read my novel, but very softly so as not to disturb her. This was the first time I had been so considerate, and I wondered why it was only the first time. She asked me what novels I had read and whether I knew *The Romance of the Three Kingdoms*. Every once in a while she picked the book up and looked at its cover or flipped through the pages. "You and the others are so smart. You don't even have to look at your lessons and you're still not the least bit worried about exams. But not me. Sometimes I feel like taking a break and reading something else for a change, but that just doesn't work with me."

One Sunday, when the dormitory was deserted, I was reading aloud the passage in Sinclair's *The Jungle* where the young girl laborer Marija had collapsed in the snow. I gazed out at the snow-covered ground outside the window and was moved by the scene. Wang Ya-ming was standing right behind me, though I was unaware of it.

"Would you lend me one of the books you've already read? This snowy weather depresses me. I don't have any family around here, and there's nothing to shop for out on the street—besides, everything costs money."

"Your father hasn't been to see you for a long time, has he?" I thought she might be feeling a little homesick.

"How could he come? A round trip on the train costs two dollars, and then there'd be nobody at home."

I handed her my copy of *The Jungle,* since I had read it before.

She laughed—*"haw-haw"*—then patted the edge of the bed a couple of times and began examining the cover of the book. After she walked out of the room, I could hear her in the corridor reading the first sentence of the book loudly just as I had been doing.

One day sometime after that—again I forget just when it was, but it must have been another holiday—the dormitory was deserted all day long, right up to the time that moonlight streamed in through the windows, and the whole place was extremely lonely. I heard a rustling sound from the end of the bed, as though someone were there groping around for something. Raising my head to take a look, I noticed Wang Ya-ming's blackened hands in the moonlight. She was placing the book she had borrowed beside me.

"Did you like it?" I asked her. "How was it?"

At first she didn't answer me; then, covering her face with her hands and trembling, she said: "Fine."

Her voice was quivering. I sat up in bed, but she moved away, her face still buried in hands as black as the hair on her head. The long corridor was completely deserted, and my eyes were fixed on the cracks in the wooden floor, which were illuminated by moonlight.

"Marija is a very real person to me. You don't think she died after she collapsed in the snow, do you? She couldn't have died. Could she? The doctor knew she didn't have any money, though, so he wouldn't treat her . . . *haw-haw*." Her high-pitched laugh brought tears to her eyes. "I went for a doctor once myself, when my mother was sick, but do you think he would come? First he wanted travel money, but I told him all our money was at home. I begged him to come with me then, because she was in a bad way. Do you think he would agree to come with me? He just stood there in the courtyard and asked me: 'What

does your family do? You're dyers, aren't you?' I don't know why, but as soon as I told him we were dyers he turned and walked back inside. I waited for a while, but he didn't come back out, so I knocked on his door again. He said to me through the door: 'I won't be able to take care of your mother, now just go away!' So I went back home." She wiped her eyes again, then continued:

"From then on I had to take care of my two younger brothers and two younger sisters. Daddy used to dye the black and blue things, and my elder sister dyed the red ones. Then in the winter of the year that my elder sister was engaged her future mother-in-law came in from the countryside to stay with us. The moment she saw my elder sister she cried out: 'My God, those are the hands of a murderess!' After that, Daddy no longer let anyone dye only red things or only blue things. My hands are black, but if you look closely you can see traces of purple; my two younger sisters' hands are the same."

"Aren't your younger sisters in school?"

"No. Later on I'll teach them their lessons. Except that I don't know how well I'm doing myself, and if I don't do well then I won't even be able to face my younger sisters. The most we can earn for dyeing a bolt of cloth is thirty cents. How many bolts do you think we get a month? One article of clothing is a dime—big or small—and nearly everyone sends us overcoats. Take away the cost for fuel and for the dyes, and you can see what I mean. In order to pay my tuition they had to save every penny, even going without salt, so how could I even think of not doing my lessons? How could I?" She reached out and touched the book again.

My gaze was still fixed on the cracks in the floor, thinking to myself that her tears were much nobler than my sympathy.

One morning just before our winter holiday Wang Ya-ming was occupied with putting her personal belongings in order. Her luggage was already firmly bound, standing at the base of the wall. Not a soul went over to say goodbye to her. As we walked out of the dormitory, one by one, and passed by the bench which had served as Wang Ya-ming's bed, she smiled at each of us, at the same time casting glances through the window off into the distance. We scuffled along down the corridor, then walked downstairs and across the courtyard. As we reached the gate at the fence, Wang Ya-ming caught up with us, panting hard through her widely opened mouth.

"Since my father hasn't come yet, I might as well get in another hour's class work. Every hour counts," she announced to everyone present.

She worked up quite a sweat in this final hour of hers. She copied down every single word from the blackboard during the English class into a little notebook. She read them aloud as she did so and even copied down words she already knew as the teacher casually wrote them on the board. During the following hour, in geography class, she very laboriously copied down the maps the teacher had drawn on the board. She acted as though everything that went through her mind on this her final day had taken on great importance, and she was determined to let none of it pass unrecorded.

When class let out I took a look at her notebook, only to discover that she had copied it all down incorrectly. Her English words had either too few or too many letters. She obviously had a very troubled heart.

Her father still hadn't come to fetch her by nightfall, so she spread her bedding out once again on the bench. She had never before gone to bed as early as she did that night, and she slept much more peacefully than usual. Her hair was spread out over the quilt, her shoulders were relaxed, and she breathed deeply; there were no books beside her that night.

The following morning her father came as the sun was fixed atop the trembling snow-laden branches of the trees and birds had just left their nest for the day. He stopped at the head of the stairs, where he removed the pair of coarse felt boots that were hanging over his shoulders, then took a white towel from around his neck and wiped the snow and ice off his beard.

"So you flunked out, did you?" Small beads of water were formed on the stairs as the ice melted.

"No. We haven't even had exams yet. The principal told me I didn't need to take them, since I couldn't pass them anyway."

Her father just stood there at the head of the stairs staring at the wall, and not even the white towel that hung from his waist was moving. Having already carried her luggage out to the head of the stairs, Wang Ya-ming went back to get her personal things, her washbasin, and some odds and ends. She handed the large pair of gloves back to her father.

"I don't want them, you go ahead and wear them!" With each step in his coarse felt boots, he left a muddy imprint on the wooden floor.

Since it was still early in the morning, few students were there looking on as Wang Ya-ming put the gloves on with a weak little laugh.

"Put on your felt boots! You've already made a mess of your schooling, now don't go and freeze your feet off too," her father said as he loosened the laces of the boots, which had been tied together.

The boots reached up past her knees. Like a carter, she fastened a white scarf around her head. "I'll be back; I'll take my books home and study hard, then I'll be back. *Haw . . . haw,*" she announced to no one in particular. Then as she picked up her belongings she asked her father: "Did you leave the horsecart you hired outside the gate?"

"Horsecart? What horsecart? We're gonna walk to the station. I'll carry the luggage on my back."

Wang Ya-ming's felt boots made slapping noises as she walked down the stairs. Her father walked ahead of her, gripping her luggage with his discolored hands. Beneath the morning sun long quivering shadows stretched out in front of them as they walked up the steps of the gate. Watched from the window, they seemed as light and airy as their own shadows; I could still see them, but I could no longer hear the sounds of their departure. After passing through the gate they headed off into the distance, in the direction of the hazy morning sun.

The snow looked like shards of broken glass, and the further the distance, the stronger the reflection grew. I kept looking until the glare from the snowy landscape hurt my eyes.

The Family Outsider

by Hsiao Hung

Translated by Howard Goldblatt

I was crouching up in the tree, becoming increasingly frightened now that the sun had set. The leaves of the tree rustled around me, while all I could see of the passersby on the street was their black silhouettes. The doors and windows of the buildings in the compound were now nothing but black holes, and on top of the wall beside me a stray cat ran back and forth screeching. I slid down from the tree, and though the rear door of the house was open, I didn't dare go in until I had checked to see if Mother was asleep. As I drew up next to her window I heard the rustling of a sleeping-mat inside.

"You wretched little brat, how dare you come back here!"

I turned on my heel and slipped away along the wall that ran past the side wing of the house, then stood for a while in the grass in the middle of the compound, for some time unaware that I had broken off some blades of grass and was chewing on them. All the insects that I knew so well during the day had stopped chirping; there were other kinds making noises now that it was nighttime, and the sounds they made were more subdued, crisper, and more prolonged. The grass I was standing in was as tall as I was, and smooth to the touch; a light melodic rustling sound fell on my ears, but so softly that I wasn't sure if I was actually hearing it or not.

"Scat, go away . . . always jumping and crowding around. Who wants you?"

My uncle, Yu Erh-po, had returned, and I could hear his shouts at the dog continuing all the way to the side room of the house. I also detected the familiar slapping sounds of his shoes with their worn-down heels. Then I heard creaking sounds from the door of the side room.

"Has Ma gone to sleep?" As I parted the grass and emerged from the clump I saw that the paper window in the side room where Yu Erh-po lived was lit up from inside as if by flames. I pushed open his door and stood in the opening.

"Aren't you in bed yet?"

"Not yet," I said.

He was standing in front of the lighted stove. Skewered on the tip of a poker was an ear of corn.

"Haven't you had dinner yet?" I asked.

"What dinner? Who would leave any dinner for me?"

"I haven't eaten either," I said.

"Haven't eaten—why not? After all, you're a member of the family." His neck was even redder than it usually was after he'd been drinking, and his bulging veins looked like the small branches burning in the stove.

"Go on now, go to bed!" I didn't really believe he was saying this to me.

"But I haven't eaten either!" I looked at the roasting corn, which was beginning to turn brown.

"So why didn't you get to eat?"

"Ma beat me."

"Beat you? Why'd she do that?"

There is a difference in the warmth felt in the hearts of adults and children; here I was on the verge of tears, and there was a trace of a smile on his lips. Still, he was the only one who seemed to be on my side—he was certainly better than Mother. I immediately began to feel some regret. I found myself standing beside him clutching some sticks of firewood, grasping them very tightly, for a long time unwilling to let them go. Since I didn't dare look him in the face, I kept my eyes fixed on his waist or on the pile of firewood at his feet, and I was moved to say:

"Erh-po, the next rainy day we have I won't tease you with 'When it rains there are bubbles [on the pond], and only a turtle wears a straw hat.' "

"So your Ma beat you, did she? Well, you probably deserved it."

"Huh?" I said. "Look, she made me go without dinner!"

"Made you go without dinner. You, you do everything you're told, don't you?"

"Look, I was crouching up in the tree, and she came at me with a poker. Look here, she broke the skin on my arm." I dropped the firewood and rolled up my sleeve to show him.

"So the skin's broken. Why did she poke at you? Was there a reason or wasn't there?"

"Because I took some *man-t'ou*." [1]

"And you still wonder why. You're quite the one! This is the first time I've seen a seven-year-old girl who's a thief already, who even steals from her own family and gives the stuff away!" He removed the ear of corn from the poker. Since the fire was still burning, I could see his whiskers clearly sweeping back and forth across the ear of corn.

"I only took three—not many . . ."

"Um!" He glanced at me sideways and seemed about to say something, but he didn't. He just kept his whiskers moving over the corn.

"And I didn't get any dinner, either," I said, biting my fingernails.

"You didn't eat because you didn't want to. You're a member of the family!" As if throwing food to a dog, he tossed half an ear of corn at my feet.

One day I noticed my mother's head lying on her pillow with her hair all rumpled, so I knew

she was fast asleep. I took the egg basket from the foot of the wooden stand and ran out to join the neighbor kids, who were all waiting for me inside the empty millshed at the rear of the compound. I moved along the wall without incident, then called out softly to the kids, who reached through the window and pulled the basket inside. One of them, who was bigger then the rest of us and whom we all called Little Elder Brother, hunched his shoulders and gaped when he saw the eggs. The little mute girl, Ya-pa, showed her exceptional delight by snorting: "Ah, ah!"

"Hey, quiet down a little! Sister Hua's mother will skin her alive!"

We closed the window, then started a fire right on top of the millstone; smoke began to billow up from the burning twigs and dry grass, as rats scurried back and forth beneath the millstone. The windmill stood at a corner of the wall, its big wheel covered with spiderwebs. At the foot of the bolting frame there was a layer of powder from several kinds of grains, which in turn was covered with the dried-up carcasses of all kinds of insects.

"Now, let's divide 'em up, so many for each of us, and everybody cooks his own."

Our faces turned red as the bonfire blazed up.

"Okay, let's cook 'em! Go ahead and put 'em in . . . three apiece."

"But there's one left over; who gets that?"

"Ah, give it to Ya-pa."

She took it and went "Uh, uh."

"Quiet down, don't make so much noise! Don't mess up our chance to get somethin' to eat!"

"Now you got an extra egg, so next time don't scold us with that sign language of yours! Huh? Ya-pa!"

When the eggshells began turning brown, we were so excited we almost lost our heads and started screaming.

"Hey! Hey! They're almost ready!"

"Get ready. They'll be ready to eat soon."

"My egg's bigger than anyone's, big as a duck's egg."

"Shhh, quiet down. Hua's mother is probably awake after all this."

From the other side of the window came some

---

[1] Chinese steamed bread.

scraping sounds, which we immediately knew were being made by the big white dog as he scratched at the mud on the wall facing. But we also thought we heard my mother's voice. It *was* my mother calling me! Just as the eggshells were beginning to crack and split, her shouts pierced through the paper covering of the window. When she stopped, I gingerly eased myself out the window and walked along very slowly, pretending I was still half asleep; by the time I was standing right in front of her, no matter what I did I couldn't stop my heart from pounding.

"Ma, what're you calling me for?" I'm sure my face was pale and drawn.

"Just a minute." She turned and went back as if she were looking for something.

I thought she must be going to get something to hit me with, and although I felt like running away I forced myself to stand there and wait.

"Here, take this child out and play with her," she said as she handed my baby sister over to me.

I could barely hold her—I was sweating all over.

"Go on! What are you waiting for?" In fact, the noise from the millshed couldn't travel this far; Mother went over to her mirror and began combing her hair.

I walked by an oblique path to the locked door at the front of the millshed, where I told the kids: "Nothing's wrong, it's okay. Ma doesn't suspect a thing."

I was a few steps away from the door when a strange aroma rushed my way, spreading throughout the entire compound. By the time I got back to the house and put my baby sister down on the *k'ang*,[2] that aroma filled the whole room.

"Which family is frying eggs, I wonder? They sure smell good." Mother's high nose reflected in the mirror gave me a fright.

"They're not frying the eggs, they're roasting them! I'm sure of it! Ha! You can smell the eggshells. I wonder who . . . what stupid housewife is *roasting* her eggs? You can smell them a mile away."

"Maybe it's them over at Wu Ta-shen's," I said

as I watched the smoke coming out the window of the millshed beyond the vegetable garden. When I ran back there, though, the fire was completely out. The other kids crowded around me, nearly brushing up against my hair.

"Ma kept asking, who was roasting eggs? Who was roasting eggs? I told her it must be them over at Wu Ta-shen's. Ha! Is this Wu Ta-shen's? Why, it's just a pack of little devils."

We burst out laughing, then we jumped down from the millstone, but that was only the beginning; the others began chasing rats in the millshed after I told them that my mother had gone out to do some gossiping, taking the baby with her.

"Who's in there?" We knew at once it was Yu Erh-po tapping on the windowsill.

"If you want to come in, just climb up," someone in the group answered him. "What are you yelling for?"

At first he couldn't see anything but just stood and waved his hands outside the window. Then he said:

"What have we here?" He sniffed the air deeply a couple of times: "Something's going on here; where's that odor coming from?" He climbed up to the windowsill, and when that short, sturdy body of his jumped in through the window, it was as if the millstone had hit the floor with a resounding thud. He took a couple of turns around the millstone, sniffing the air as he walked, the red whiskers above his upper lip twitching continually and making it look as if he had an autumn caterpillar squirming above his mouth.

"Have you been making a fire? Here, look at the ashes on the millstone. Hua-tzu, this is your doing! If I don't tell your mother . . . All day long you keep leading that bunch of wild brats into trouble." As he was about to climb back up to the window he suddenly spied the basket: "Who brought this out? Isn't this our egg basket? Hua-tzu, you've stolen something again, haven't you? Without your mother's knowledge!"

As he picked up the basket to go, we poked fun at his straw hat, saying, "It looks like a little earthenware bowl, or a water bucket."

[2] See footnote 1 to "When I Was in Hsia Village," p. 269.

But that night I got a beating, after which I slunk over to one of the window ledges and licked away my tears.

"Yu Erh-po, Tiger Yu, that good-for-nothing, crummy old man." I kept crying and muttering my contempt for him. But before long I had forgotten all about it, and I was soon back with the other kids undoing his waistband, running behind him with a staff, pushing his brimless straw hat off his head, twittering and teasing him just as we did the big white dog in the compound.

Toward the end of fall there was a long lonely spell: cold winds filled all the dark, empty buildings; the tall grasses which grew in the compound dried up and crumpled to the ground; white frost covered all the vegetable stalks in the garden behind the house; the branches of the old elm tree which stood beside the wall waved their few remaining leaves in the wind; the sky looked gray and the clouds shapeless; there was occasional drizzle and once in a while a light flurry of fine snow.

Feeling a little weary, and wanting to explore, I fixed a trunk and a cupboard as stepping blocks and climbed up into the attic space over the room where we stored our old things. It was dark up there; I experienced feelings difficult to describe. I rubbed up against a small wooden chest, picked it up, and carried it back to the opening of the attic. With the aid of the light coming in through the opening I looked at it and found it secured with a shiny little brass lock. I held it next to my ear and shook it, then tapped it with the palm of my hand—a hollow rattle sounded inside. Very disappointed to discover that I couldn't open the chest, I put it back where I had found it and moved on to a place even further in, and much darker, where I crawled around searching for something else. It was impossible to stand in the pitch black space with its uneven footing, so I just crawled around, and whenever my fingers touched something I picked it up and felt it. My hand bumped a small glass jar, which I also carried back to the spot where the light shone in, and what I found filled me with delight—the jar was full of dried black dates. I didn't waste another minute, but holding tightly to my precious find, I

started to climb down. However, just as the tip of my foot reached the top of the trunk I quickly snaked my body back in through the opening and remained crouched just inside the attic for some time.

There was Yu Erh-po, trying to open up the very trunk I had used as a stepping block. After watching him work on the lock for a long time, I noticed that he was biting on something that he held in his hand. He cocked his head, and his teeth made clicking sounds; after he bit whatever it was, he gave it a twist with his fingers and tried it on the lock of the trunk. The last time he did it the brass lock gave a metallic twang, and I realized that what he had been twisting was a piece of wire. He took off his hat and tucked that little bent tool inside it.

He rummaged through the contents of the trunk a number of times; in it were some red seat cushions, a blue embroidered apron made of coarse material, some embroidered women's shoes, and a tangled ball of multicolored silk threads. Resting at the bottom of the trunk was a brass wine decanter, dark yellow. After a while he grabbed hold of the trunk with his sinewy arms and shook it.

It struck me that he was going to move the trunk away, and if he did that how was I going to get down? Several times he picked it up, but he always set it back down again, until I was on the verge of calling out to him. After a moment he took off his waistband, bent down and laid it out on the ground, and placed the seat cushions on top of it one by one, after which he tied a knot in the waistband and cinched up the cushions. Panting heavily, he tried to lift them all up. Why didn't he hurry up and get out of here? I thought of Ya-pa and some of the other kids, and in my mind's eye I could see them eating the things I had found, which filled me with a sense of proud delight.

"Hey there, here . . . here are some nice, oily black dates." I had already thought out exactly what I wanted to say to them. Meanwhile the dates glistened in front of my eyes, all smooth and shiny, and it seemed as if they were already dancing around in my throat.

He didn't move the trunk after all, but began

locking it up again. Then he stood the brass wine decanter on top of the trunk and walked off. As I stretched my body as far as I could, so that the soles of both feet were planted firmly on top of the trunk, I felt soreness in my chest where I had held the glass jar so tightly against it. Yu Erh-po walked back in, and the first thing he did was pick up the bundle of seat cushions next to the door. Then he came over to get the brass wine decanter he had placed on top of the trunk; when he had picked it up and tucked it inside his clothes up against his belly, he noticed someone standing in the corner of the room—me. A broad grin quickly spread across his face, the likes of which I had never seen on him before—every tooth in his mouth was exposed, and his lips seemed to be spreading out as if nothing could stop them.

"You won't tell?" Large beads of sweat dotted his forehead.

"Tell what?"

"Don't tell, that's a good child." He patted my head.

"Then will you let me take this glass jar with me?"

"Go ahead!"

He wasn't even looking as I also snatched up five *man-t'ou* from the basket next to the door and ran out.

On the day Mother said some things were missing, I was standing right beside her.

"I don't know anything about it," I said.

"That's strange. It was clearly locked; where did the key come from?" As she said this, she pointed her sharp chin belligerently at the others in the family. The young cook with the crooked neck said:

"Hmmm! Who could it have been?"

"I don't know anything about it," I said again, although in my mind the images were as clear as ever: there was Yu Erh-po tying up the seat cushions in his waistband and putting the brass wine decanter against his belly, smack up against his skin; it almost felt as if he were inside me gnawing loudly on that piece of wire. My ears were warm and flushed, so I shut my eyes for a moment, but when I opened them again I was still looking right at that open trunk.

"I don't know anything about it," I said for the third time.

Finally I said: "I didn't see anything."

After a while Mother found a piece of wire and tried for a while to make a sort of key out of it, but was unable to bend it.

"Not like that. You have to use your teeth, like this: bite it and then give it a twist. Bite it again . . ." Look out! If I were to let my tongue start moving, I might blurt it all out. I realized I was already making the motions with my hands; so I kept my mouth shut tight and put my arms behind me, keeping my eyes on the others.

"This is really strange; we're not talking about little things. So how could they have been taken out of the compound? Unless it was at night, but even then a thief wouldn't have been able to get away with them." My mother's pointed chin frightened me. As she spoke she pushed on the window with her hand:

"Aha! The stuff was taken out through the front door. Look! This window hasn't been opened all summer. Look here, this slit we sealed up last fall is still intact." Then she pushed me away with her hand: "Look out, you're going to trip me. Move over!"

She took another look around the room: "You don't believe me; well, there are only a few places that stuff could have gone to, and I think I have part of the answer. If you don't believe me, we'll just see. We can't let this happen. In the spring a brass chafing pot turned up missing. Everyone said it had just been misplaced, and would be found sooner or later; or they said it might have been lent out. Whoever heard of such a thing! It was sold to pay gambling debts long ago! We treat him like a member of the family, though he still complains that we don't. All right. Before long he'll be taking the very roof beams from the house!"

"Ah, ah!" The cook took hold of his apron and wiped the corners of his mouth with it. His crooked neck looked like a bent candle wick. After Mother and the others had left I remained standing there.

At dinner that night the cook asked Yu Erh-po: "They say you don't eat mutton, but how about sheep's intestines?"

"No, I can't eat them either," he said into his ricebowl.

"Then I should tell you, Master Yu, that there's a piece of sheep's intestine in these fried hot peppers."

"Why didn't you say so before? . . . this . . . this—" He put down his chopsticks, moved his neck, which was turning red again, and turned his head round very, very slowly, like an earthenware vase slowly being rotated.

"I'm a coarse man; all my life I've eaten everything . . . except that . . . I don't . . . eat . . . the flesh of . . . a sheep . . . don't wear . . . sheepskin hats . . . don't wear . . . sheepskin . . . clothes . . ." He drew out each word in a slow monotone as he continued:

"Next time, Yang An, I'm telling you, whatever you're cooking—I don't care if you're frying vegetables or just making soup—if there's any sheep's . . . um, let me know first. I'm not that greedy an eater! I don't mind what I eat. Even plain pickled vegetables are all right, so long as I can be spared anything from the body of a sheep!"

"But Master Yu, let me ask you something: what sort of wine decanter do you use when you drink wine? Does it have to be a brass one?" Yang An's chin was raised high in the air.

"Aren't all wine decanters the same?" He put his chopsticks down again, picked up the pewter decanter beside him and rapped it on the table a couple of times. "What about this one? It's a pewter decanter, but it's the wine I drink; and the taste of the wine has nothing to do with the decanter . . . humph! And it's not . . . when I was young I always liked this pewter decanter . . . polished it up all nice and shiny."

"Tell me, Master Yu, how are brass wine decanters?"

"Nothing wrong with them, since they can be polished brighter than any other kind."

"Right, brass decanters are the best after all. Ha, ha-ha." The cook started laughing, and as he was filling my rice bowl he laughed so hard he nearly dropped it.

Mother bit a hot pepper and blew out sharply to cool her tongue, so that several grains of rice landed on my hand.

"Humph! Yang An, you're laughing at me because I don't eat mutton, but I really can't eat it. You see, when I was only three months old I lost my mother. I was raised on sheep's milk, and if I hadn't been, how could I have lived these sixty-odd years?"

Yang An slapped his knee. "You're really a man of conscience; you've never done anything to anyone in bad conscience, have you? Say, Master Yu—"

"You young people, you don't believe in this, and that's no good. A man has to keep in mind where he came from; he can't turn his back on the past and repay kindness with evil—a man has to repay kindness with kindness. You'll find that in all the stories that are told. For example, a sheep took the place of my mother; if not . . . if not, could I have lived these sixty-odd years?" He straightened his back and pushed away the plate of fried hot peppers and sheep's intestines with his chopsticks.

After dinner he left the table, his brimless straw hat clutched in his hand, and walked off along the brick path, the heels of his shoes dragging along behind the toes. His feet looked like two pieces of grimy wood, and steam seemed to be rising from the cooking-pot shape that was his head.

Mother joined the cook in a hearty laugh: "A brass wine decanter, aha! And some seat cushions . . . you ask him whether he knows anything about them." The scar on Yang An's neck seemed larger than usual to me.

I was a little frightened of my mother; she picked up a fat drumstick with that bony hand of hers and raised it to her mouth, exposing all her teeth as she tore off a piece of meat.

On another occasion when Mother beat me, I ran to the tree and climbed up it, but since there were hardly any leaves on the branches to shield me, the little stones that Mother was hurling struck painfully all over my body, like sharp awls.

"If you climb any higher . . . if you climb *any* higher, I'll get a long pole and drag you down from there!"

The tree trunk around which my arms were tightly wrapped seemed to shudder slightly as she said that; by then I had already reached the top of the tree and was about to climb out onto one of the branches.

"You little monkey, you little monster, I'll fix you one of these days!" She paced back and forth under the tree and did not throw stones at me for some time.

It had been several days since I last climbed the tree, and I experienced a strange sensation; as I looked out all around me it seemed that I was higher than everything else in the world. The people and carts out on the road, the neighboring buildings, all were below me; I was even level with the pole holding the bean-sprout seller's sign over on the back road.

"You wretched little brat, are you going to come down from there or not?" Mother said "wretched little brat" so often it was just like my name. "Well? Yes or no?" As long as she couldn't get her hands on me, I wasn't all that frightened of her.

At a moment when she was off guard, I jumped from the tree to the top of the wall. "Ha! Now look where I am!"

"That's a good child; are you going to climb the pole in front of the Temple of the Patriarch next?" It wasn't my mother who answered me, but someone standing on the other side of the wall.

"Hurry and get down from there before you cave in the top of that wall. I'll go tell your mother to come give you a beating." It was Yu Erh-po.

"I can't come down. You see, look over there. Ma's over at the base of the tree waiting for me."

"What for?" He walked in through the wooden gate.

"She's going to beat me!"

"Beat you for what?"

" 'Cause I wet my pants."

"How disgusting! You ought to be ashamed of yourself, a seven-year-old girl still wetting her pants. Are you coming down or not? You're caving in the wall!" He was snorting like a pig.

"Grab her and pull her down; today I'm going to show her just who I am!"

As Mother said this, Yu Erh-po began rolling up his trousers.

"What's he doing?" I thought to myself.

"All right! Little Hua-tzu, now you're going to

see where your antics will get you. Just you wait."

As I watched him climb up into the lowest fork of the tree, I was on the verge of tears and my throat seemed to expand.

"I'm going to . . . I'm going to tell . . . I'm going to tell . . ."

Mother didn't seem to understand what I was saying, but Yu Erh-po stopped where he was and remained crouching there at the large fork in the tree.

"Come on down, that's a good child; nothing's going to happen. Your mother won't hit you; hurry down from there. Tomorrow after breakfast I'll take you to the park so you won't be around the house, where you'd wind up getting beaten." He put his arms around me and carried me down from the top of the wall to the tree, and from there to the ground. I rubbed the tears away as I heard him say:

"That's a good child; tomorrow we'll go to the park."

The next morning I waited for him at the main gate, but when he did walk toward me there was no talk of, "Come on, let's go!" So I chased after him, tugging on his belt when I caught up.

"Didn't you say you were going to take me to the park today?"

"What are you talking about? What park? You go on and play, go on now!" He kept his eyes straight ahead as he walked, not even glancing at me. It was as though what was said yesterday had come from someone else's mouth. I just hung onto his belt, so he twisted his body as if he were shaking off some kind of insect, trying to get free of me.

"Then I'll tell, I'll tell that the brass wine decanter . . ."

He glanced around him, then said with a sigh: "Well, shall we go, you little blackmailer?"

He didn't look at me once as we were walking, nor did he give a second's thought to how captivated I was by a little rubber man in one of the shop windows. I couldn't even look at it too long, for by the time I turned my head back, he had walked a long ways down the road. When he got to the little wooden bridge at the entrance to the park, I ran past him.

"Here we are! We're here!" I was so happy I spread my arms out wide and felt as if I could fly.

The bare trees and cool arbors were all there before me beckoning. The minute I walked through the entrance my ears were assailed with the sounds of cymbals and drums coming from a circus, an almost deafening din that nearly made me lose my sense of direction. I was leading Yu Erh-po along by the little round gourd on his tobacco pouch. As we passed by a white canvas tent I heard some voices inside:

"Are you afraid?"

"Nope."

"You've got the nerve to do it?"

"I've got the nerve."

I didn't know where Yu Erh-po was headed.

We had already passed by vaudeville shows, Western peep-shows, monkey acts, dancing bears, and puppet shows; from that point on there wasn't a thing left to be seen. The layer of leaves on the ground got thicker until the path under our feet was completely covered. "Erh-po, aren't we going to watch the circus?" I let go of the little round gourd on his tobacco pouch and moved away from him a little, watching the expression on his face: "They have a tiger in there; I've seen it, but I've never seen the elephant. Somebody said this circus has three elephants, a big one and two small ones. The big one . . . the big one . . . well, somebody said that his trunk—just his trunk alone—is longer than the poker we use for the fire at home." His expression didn't change at all. I ran from his left side over to his right, and back again to his left: "Is that right? Yu Erh-po, is that right, huh? Did you ever see it?" Since I was walking backwards all this time, I tripped over an exposed tree root and fell to the ground.

"Watch where you're going!" He didn't move to help me, so I picked myself up.

At the far end of the park there was a little tea shop, where I figured he was heading because he was thirsty. But he didn't enter the tea shop; instead he went around to the rear where there was a small shed made of grass mats. He took me in with him, and although it was very dark inside, I could see a man at the far end making some gestures and striking something made of bamboo. As soon as Yu Erh-po entered he moved over to one side and sat on a long bench, while I stood just in front of him. Even after I'd been standing there so long my legs were growing numb I still had no idea what that man was doing. He was wearing a pigtail, just like a girl, and he stuck out one leg like a shadow boxer, drew it back, then pushed out one hand; he kept it up as he walked around in a circle, after which, *bang!* he struck the piece of bamboo. It didn't look like a Chinese opera performance, nor a monkey show, but more like the routine of a patent-medicine peddler, though no one was buying any patent medicine.

I soon grew tired of watching what was happening in front of me, so I began looking around—there wasn't another child in the place. As soon as a vacant spot opened up on the bench in front, Yu Erh-po led me up there, where we both sat down, though I couldn't stop fidgeting for thinking of that elephant.

"Erh-po, let's go and see that elephant, okay? Let's not watch this."

"Quiet down," he said. "Just sit there and listen."

"Listen to what? What is it?"

"He's telling the story from *Romance of the Three Kingdoms* where Kuan Kung kills Ts'ai Yang."

"What's a Kuan Kung?"

"Kuan Lao-yeh. Haven't you ever been to the Kuan Lao-yeh Temple?"

Then it came to me: in the Kuan Lao-yeh Temple, he was the one riding a red horse.

"Oh yeah! Kuan Lao-yeh rides a red—"

"Just listen." He cut me off.

I listened for a while, but still didn't understand anything, so I turned around and sat facing the rear, where I saw a blind man whose eyes were coated with white film, and a man with only one leg who was holding a cane in his hands. The man sitting next to me had his arm wrapped in a cloth sling fastened around his neck. When the sounds *Bang! Bang! Bang!* resounded from the piece of bamboo, I noticed tears running down Yu Erh-po's face.

I was determined to see the elephant, so on our way back I stopped in front of the white tent and refused to walk any further.

"If you want to see it, wait until after lunch. We can come back." Yu Erh-po walked slowly away from me: "Let's go home and eat lunch, then we can come back and see it."

"No! I'm not going to eat, I'm not hungry. I'll go home after I've seen it." I tugged on his tobacco pouch.

"They won't let just anyone go in, you have to buy a ticket. Can't you see that doorkeeper standing over there?"

"Then what's to stop us from buying a *ticket!*"

"Where's the money going to come from? Two people's tickets would cost several dozen strings of cash."

"I noticed that you had some money—didn't you just give some to that man in the tent?" I was clinging to his body.

"I only gave him a few coppers! That's all I had; there's no more."

"I don't believe you; I saw a whole lot!" I stood on tiptoe and felt around in his lapels and even poked my fingers into the inside pockets.

"You see, that's all there is! I don't have any more, and I have no way to make money. There's just enough to gamble a little once a month or so; sometimes I win a little, but I also lose a lot of the time. Um-hmm." He looked down at the five or six coppers I held in my hand.

"Now do you believe me, child? I simply don't have any more, and won't have . . ." He kept talking as we crossed the wooden bridge, while the clamor and noise from the circus troupe followed us as we walked. There was a lottery stand on the other side of the bridge surrounded by a bunch of kids. Yu Erh-po laid down a couple of coppers for me, so I pulled a slip of paper from the wire loop, and when I dipped it in the bowl of water a bright red "5" suddenly appeared.

"What number is it?"

"Can't you see? It's a '5'!" I nudged him with my elbow.

"How could I tell? I can't read a word, since I never spent a single day in school."

On the road home I ate all five of the candy balls I had won.

The next time I saw Yu Erh-po steal something must have been during the following summer,

since the purslane flowers were a fiery red, and the tall grasses in the compound, which grew much faster than I, rose above my head; bees, dragonflies, and other kinds of insects that I didn't recognize were there in profusion. There was another special kind of grass on which light purple flowers bloomed, row after row standing there so tall that the buds looked like countless little flags waving atop the grassy field.

After lunch I waited for some friends to come over, but not a single one showed up. So I ran over to the grain storeroom, where I had seen Mother go in with a large platter early in the morning. "Hah!" I thought, there must be something of interest on that platter. She had hidden it skillfully; instead of placing it in the rice cupboard or in one of the huge grain bins, she had hung it by a rope from the rafters. As I was looking at that intriguing platter I heard what sounded like mice scurrying around inside one of the bins, either there or inside the wall. Whatever it was, I could hear scuffling noises, then after a while some panting sounds—could it be a weasel? Somewhat timidly I gave the bin a couple of hits with my hand and the noises stopped for a moment, but then the sound of panting began again, a gurgling, raspy sound, seemingly emanating from a pair of froth-filled lungs. I was losing patience:

"Get out of there, whatever you are!"

Yu Erh-po's chest and red neck emerged from the bin. I imagined at first that I was witnessing some kind of puppet show, but then the sun's rays streaming in through the skylight proved me wrong—there was Yu Erh-po's long, pointed nose jutting out, stained a golden red by some liquid inside the bin. His chest underneath the white cotton undershirt was heaving uncontrollably, like waves tossing in a rain storm. He didn't utter a sound, but just stood there dumbly, like a frightened billy goat.

My playmates and I amused ourselves catching beetles and dragonflies, something we never tired of doing. Wild grasses, wild flowers, wild insects—at one time or another they all wound up in our hands, and it was like that from dawn to dusk. On nice clear evenings I went by myself into the clump of tall grass, where fireflies flitted to and fro, and where there was a constant murmur of insects in the tall grass, which cast evening shadows as it waved in the wind. Sometimes I stamped down the grass in one spot and lay down on top of it so that I could look up at the sky and the stars I loved so much. I had heard people talk about the ocean, and I envisioned it as about the same as my sky.

One evening at dinnertime I returned to the house from the clump of grass carrying some little boxes filled with insects, and as I passed by the grain storeroom I was startled to see Yu Erh-po standing inside, his bluish lips and pale sunken eyes framed by the outline of the broken window.

"There isn't anyone in the compound, is there?" he asked in a throaty, sickly voice.

"Yes, there is; Ma's on the steps smoking."

"Okay. Go on!"

There wasn't a trace of a smile on his face; he seemed pale and his hair looked like the fur on the stray cat that ran back and forth on top of the wall.

Crouching on the bench at Yu Erh-po's place at the dinner table was a little spotted dog with a curly tail and a brass bell around his neck, which really made him look adorable as he frolicked on the bench. Mother threw him a piece of meat. Then the crooked-necked cook picked a big bone out of the soup pot, which the spotted puppy chased frantically after jumping to the ground, the bell ringing out crazily. My little sister banged happily on her rice bowl with her chopsticks, the cook wiped his eyes with his apron, and Mother knocked over the soup bowl.

"Hurry . . . hurry and get a rag; hurry, it's spreading." Although she tried to cover her mouth with her hand, she still spit out rice grains as she spoke.

After the cook had cleared the dinner table he lit the kerosene lamp, and I sat on the threshold of the door looking out into the garden. The pale yellow light from the lamp silhouetted my head and shoulders, so that each time I raised my head to wipe the sweat off my brow, my shadow moved in concert with it. The evening breezes penetrating my cotton undershirt felt like cool, blue river water washing over me; the strains of a stringed instrument, the *hu-ch'in,* floated over from the grain shop on the street behind the house, and with the distant echo, sound came simultaneously from the east and the west. Flowers that were yellow during the day looked white, and those which were red now looked black.

The fiery red blossoms of the purslane plants too had become black, while the tiny flowers on the wild purslanes growing at the foot of the wall had completely disappeared from sight. Perhaps Yu Erh-po had trampled on those little flowers, since he pressed himself up against the wall as he walked by. I followed him with my eyes, watching him as he went out the garden gate. He was totally unaware that I had come out and was following him. I was curious; what was he going to do with that thing he had stolen? He couldn't eat it, and it surely wouldn't be any fun to play with.

By the time I had reached the gate, he was already across the bridge, heading east on the wide, brightly lit road leading up to the tall hill. I imagined that the walls and gates standing along either side of the road in the moonlight were temples. Still watching the small round sack flung over Yu Erh-po's back, I began to hear dogs barking in the distance in the direction he was heading.

The third time I saw him steal something, or maybe it was the fourth—anyway it was the last time—he was carrying our large bathtub on his shoulders as he cut across the garden, knocking down some dragon-head flowers as he went. Seemingly without a care, he walked with the loudly clanging tin bathtub over his head. It looked like a large piece of gleaming silver, and the sparkles which danced off it seemed scary to me, so I moved over beside the wall where I just stood like a simpleton.

I wondered if Mother would give him a beating if she caught him. I also felt some respect for him: would I have the nerve to steal something like that someday? But then the thought struck me: "Why steal something like that? Since it's so big, no matter where I put it, Mother'd be sure to find it." But Yu Erh-po just kept walking along with it over his head, looking like the big snake in the storybook.

After that I never saw him steal anything again, but I did see some other things, even more risky ones and more often. Like, once in the tall grass when I had just caught a dragonfly by the tail, *ker-plunk*, something like a big boulder came hurtling over the wooden wall, scaring the dragonfly off. I no longer dared to go over by the wooden wall to catch crickets in the evenings either, because I never knew when Yu Erh-po might come crashing down. After the loss of the bathtub Mother started locking all three of the outside gates, so among all the kids who played around there I always caught the fewest crickets, and I began to resent Yu Erh-po.

"You're always jumping over the wall, and I can't catch any more crickets!"

"Don't jump over the wall, that's easy to say, but who's going to open the gate for me?" His neck was sticking straight out.

"Yang An will open it, won't he?"

"Yang . . . An . . . hah! You're all part of the family and you can give him orders, but I . . ."

"Don't you know how to yell? Call him, and then if he doesn't hear you, what's to stop you from beating on the gate?" I was swinging my arms as I talked.

"Hah! Beat on the door . . ." His eyes were fixed on the ground in front of him.

"If he doesn't hear you beating on the door, then what's wrong with kicking it?"

"Kick a locked gate; what good would that do?"

"So there's no way but to climb over the wall, right? Then can't you do it gently, instead of scaring people out of their skins?"

"How can I do it gently?"

"Like when I jump down from the wall; no one hears a sound, because I crouch as I hit the ground, with my arms up in the air." I did a practice jump there on the level ground to show him.

"I could do that when I was young, but now that I'm old there's no way! My old bones are hard! I'm sixty years older than you; how can you compare the two of us?"

A wry smile appeared at the corner of his mouth. He held his tobacco pouch with his right hand and with his left stroked the ears of the big white dog standing next to him; the dog began to lick his hand. But I still didn't believe him; how could someone's bones be hard or soft? Weren't bones just bones? A pork bone was too hard for me to bite, and so was a mutton bone, so how could my bones be any different than his?

From then on, whenever I came across some bones I tried banging them against each other, and whenever I was with a playmate who was either older than I or a year younger, I invariably wanted to try an experiment. What sort of experiment? Well, we doubled up our fists and banged our knuckles together to see how much softer or harder they were. But I could never see much of a difference. If we hit a little harder it just hurt more. The first person I tested was Ya-pa, the caretaker's daughter. At first she wasn't willing, but I said to her:

"You're a year younger than I am, so let's give it a try; the smaller someone is, the softer the bones, so let's see if yours are softer than mine."

When we did, the knuckles on her fist turned red, so I thought: "Hers must be softer than mine." But then I looked and saw that mine were all red too.

One time Yu Erh-po fell off the wall and bloodied his nose.

"Hah! I wasn't careful enough; one leg was dangling down, and the other was still hung up on the wall . . . hah! I tumbled head first."

He seemed to be mocking himself; since he didn't use his sleeve or anything else to wipe off the blood, to look at him you would have thought that it was someone else's nose that was bleeding. He stood up straight and walked off toward the side room, the blood continuing to stream profusely down the front of his clothes. His hand was bloodstained by now and dangling at his side, never moving up to stop the flow of blood. The cook, standing in the middle of the compound, cocked his head to one side and said:

"Master Yu, that's nice young blood you have there. I think even if you fell a couple more times it still wouldn't hurt you much."

"Hah! Little smart aleck . . . everybody starts

out from youth and keeps on going! There's no need for you to be so sarcastic, your time will come one of these days." There was still a smile on his bloody mouth.

After a while Yu Erh-po appeared in the doorway of the side room, bare-chested and bare-shouldered, with a piece of something stuffed up each nostril.

"Old Yang— Yang An, do you have a shirt I can wear? This one will be dry tomorrow, and then I'll take yours off. Since the sleeve on my other one is torn, I've ordered a lined jacket made, but I haven't found the time to go and get it." He was shaking out the garment he had just washed.

"What'd you say?" Yang An seemed almost to be shouting: "You haven't found the time to fetch the lined jacket you ordered? Our Master Yu sure is a busy man! His clothes are made, but he doesn't have the time to go get them. Master Yu is truly *The Master,* and one of these days he'll be needing a valet."

I had climbed a ladder up to the roof over the side room in order to get a better view of a squabble that had erupted out on the street, but the wind up there was so strong I came down shivering. Yu Erh-po was standing under the eaves still half naked, that wet garment of his hanging on a line and flapping in the wind. About the time the lamps were being lit I went back into the house to put on something warmer, and to my surprise there was Yu Erh-po sitting alone at the dinner table drinking wine, and even more strangely, there was Yang An pouring out some soup for him.

"I can pour it myself! You go on and rest." Yu Erh-po and Yang An were vying over the soup spoon. As I walked over to take a look I even saw a plate with two slices of meat on it next to the wine decanter. Yu Erh-po was wearing Yang An's short black jacket, his belt cinched up almost around his chest. He had never worn clothes that small before, and he didn't look to me at all like Yu Erh-po, although just who he did look like I couldn't say. He was chewing on something, which made the plugs in his nose move and twitch.

As a rule only Father sat alone at the dinner table under the overhead light, eating his meal after returning home in the evening; for Yu Erh-po this was unheard of, so I stood watching. Looking like a skinny doubled-over beetle, Yang An ran to the living room door:

"Come on and take a look!" He cocked his head: "Everyone says he doesn't eat mutton . . . doesn't eat mutton, eh; his stomach's so small, I'm afraid it's about to burst. He's already finished three big bowls of mutton soup . . . finished them . . . ha-ha-ha." He chuckled quietly, gestured with his hands, and then let the door curtain drop back into place.

On another occasion, when it wasn't even mutton soup but was made from beef stock, as soon as Yu Erh-po picked up his spoon, Yang An said:

"Mutton soup . . ."

He put down his spoon. Then as he picked up some fried eggplant with his chopsticks, Yang An said to him:

"Fried sheep's liver and eggplant."

He rinsed off his chopsticks, then went to the cupboard and took out a plate of pickled salted vegetables, but before he had gotten them back to the table, Yang An said:

"Sheep—" He didn't finish.

"What do you mean, sheep?" Yu Erh-po stood looking at him.

"Sheep . . . sheep . . . um . . . it's, uh, salted vegetables . . . ahhh! I mean there's clean salted vegetables, and then there's unclean."

"What do you mean, unclean?"

"Well, I sliced the vegetables with my mutton knife."

"You can't do that to me, Yang An!" Yu Erh-po walked away from the table and flung the plate on top of it. The table was so slippery the plate bounced around before bumping into another plate and coming to rest.

"You there, Yang An, don't go taking advantage of people. You're not a member of the Chiang family; just like me, you're an outsider here! Young people have to try to do good things . . . shouldn't act like this. Some day you'll have your own posterity."

"Ha! Posterity? My line is going to die with me.

But your not eating sheep's intestines is as phony as the fish smell of pastry fish frying at the dough shop. You don't eat sheep's intestines but then you go ahead and eat mutton; stop putting on that act." Yang An was so angry his neck stiffened a little.

"You hare-brained queer! God damn it, what are you getting so huffy about?" Yu Erh-po stood up and walked toward him.

"Master Yu, don't get yourself so worked up, you'll make yourself sterile that way. Listen to me, we're both a couple of poor working stiffs; it was just a joke, all in fun." The cook snickered: "There wasn't any sheep's intestine in it; I was just having some fun; don't take it all so seriously."

Yu Erh-po stood there like a statue. "I don't get angry at other things, and I'm not afraid of a little joke, but here I draw the line—this is more than a joke. The year before last I ate some without knowing it; then when I found out, I was ill for over half a month. A boil had developed here on my neck before I got better. Eating a piece of mutton didn't hurt me, but thinking about it made me uneasy, as if I had gone against my own conscience. If I hadn't done something against my conscience— But I did, and I couldn't bear my feelings of regret. And that's why I don't eat mutton." He took a drink of cold water, then lit his pipe.

One after the other the rest of us began leaving the table.

From then on Yu Erh-po's nose often had plugs of some sort stuck up it. Later he began complaining of a sore back, then of sore legs. Walking across the compound, he was no longer as erect as before—sometimes there was a pronounced lean to his body, and sometimes he was seen walking with his hand holding onto his belt. When the big white dog trailed along behind him, jumping back and forth, he tried to avoid it:

"Go on, go on!" He pulled his hand up inside his sleeve, which he flapped in the air behind him.

But then he started cursing even smaller things; like, when he stubbed his toe on a piece of brick he sat on the ground and held the piece of brick down tightly with his hand, as if he suspected it

had deliberately moved over in front of his foot. Or if there were birds flying overhead and droppings landed on his sleeve, he would shake it off, turn his head toward the sky, and tell the birds, who by then had flown off already:

"You dirty . . . hah! You sure know how to aim, bang on to my sleeve. What are you, blind? If you have to drop something, drop it on someone who's wearing silk or satin! Drop it on me and you just waste . . . you bunch of crippled beggars . . ."

He would wipe his sleeve clean, take another look at the sky, and continue on his way.

There were no longer any crickets to be found at the foot of the wooden wall, though Yu Erh-po evidently had stopped climbing over it. When the cook went out in the morning to fetch water, Yu Erh-po went out the gate behind the water bucket, then headed toward the well and sat down on the old millstone beside it. Almost every day, when I took the key out to open the gate and let my playmates in, he called out from there on the millstone:

"Hua-tzu, wait for me." He looked like a duck waddling along. "I'm really having my problems; I could see . . . I could see the kids coming this way, but I couldn't catch up with them."

As soon as he came in the gate he sat down on a wooden wine cask off to the side. One foot had a sock on it, but the toes of the other were wrapped with a piece of hemp. He loosened the hemp wrapping, and underneath the piece of cloth covering his swollen toes (which looked like little eggplants), a piece of skin was rotting away. Then he wrapped the foot up again with the cloth.

"My luck this year has all been bad . . . one problem after another." He reached up and removed a piece of hemp he'd been holding in his mouth.

After that, whenever I let my playmates in, it wasn't Yu Erh-po who called out to me, but me who called out to him, because if I closed the gate and then he walked up to it from outside, I was the one who had to go back and open it for him. Not only did he sit there on the millstone, but gradually he even took to sleeping there. He slept as if he were in a coma. Once a brightly colored duck stretched its neck out and pecked him on the soles of his feet, but he didn't wake up, and his feet stayed stretched out just where they were. With the sun's rays dancing off the millstone, it looked like he was sleeping on a large round mirror.

One day some of the kids and I were throwing stones and dirt at each other, running out of the gate and over to the well where there was plenty of ammunition. I stuffed my pockets full of stones and crouched behind the millstone, doing battle with the rest of the kids. *Pow! Pow!* The stones fell on the millstone, raising a cloud of dust. Yu Erh-po, his eyes still closed, suddenly grabbed his tobacco pouch:

"You little bastards, what's going on? How dare you come . . . how dare you climb up . . ."

He struck out to his left and right, and after we had all gathered around him, he finally sat up.

"Damn it, I was having a dream . . . dogs all over that road. And even the mongrel pups were coming at me. I finally drove them all off with the bowl of my pipe." He rubbed his knuckles as a smile spread across his face: "I'll be damned, it sure was life-like; I dreamt about getting bitten by a pack of dogs, and now that I'm awake I can still feel the pain."

It was obvious that our stones were responsible, but he said it was the "mongrel pups," and the whole affair both alarmed and delighted us. When we left him we scattered like a flock of chickens, shouting and spreading our "wings."

He yawned, making sounds like a donkey braying; we turned back to see him facing the sun, his open mouth making swallowing motions.

One drizzly morning as Yu Erh-po was sitting out on the millstone, Yang An carried his bucket out several times to fetch water, and the last time he locked the gate behind him.

"These past few days Master Yu has changed a lot," he said. "The way he looks now, I'm afraid we'll be carrying him into the temple before many more days have passed."

I looked out to the west through the crack in the gate, but I couldn't see Yu Erh-po clearly—he just looked like a haystack soaking up the rain.

"Yu Erh-po, it's time to eat!" I tried calling out to him, but the only answer I got was an echo from my own voice: "Yu Erh-po, it's time to eat!" Then I put my mouth right up against the crack in the gate, but again the only answer I got was my own echo. A rainy day always seemed more like nighttime to me, like an empty bottle that whistled with every puff of wind.

"Don't worry about that one," Mother said as she opened the window. "He's just looking for trouble. These last few days your father has been thinking of a way to fix him."

I knew what that "fix him" meant: when you hit a child it's called a "beating," but when you hit an adult it's called "fixing him." Once I had seen our caretaker "fix" Yu Erh-po over a game of cards, but I had never seen Father do it.

Mother said to Yang An: "These last few years my husband has just ignored him and has never once raised a hand against him, but the man's insufferable arrogance is getting worse and worse. The no-good loafer won't be happy until someone fixes him."

The more Mother used the words "fix him," the more frightened I grew; where would he "fix him"? In the middle of the compound? That isn't where the caretaker did it—that time it happened on the *k'ang* in the side room. Maybe that's where it would happen this time too! Would he use the fireplace poker? That's what the caretaker had used. Then I recalled that once little Ya-pa had had her finger stepped on by the caretaker and nearly got it broken; it still wasn't very straight.

As he knocked on the gate Yu Erh-po called out:

"You big white . . . big white, you don't have an ounce of decency. One of these days you'll . . ." When the dog jumped down off the wall, Yu Erh-po said: "Go on, get out . . . Open the gate! Isn't there anyone inside?"

Just as I was about to run over there, Mother put her hand on my head and stopped me: "Don't be in such a hurry! Let him stand there awhile; he's not the one who's feeding you."

The noise from the gate grew louder, and he seemed to have started kicking.

"Isn't anyone there?" He was almost shouting.

"There's someone here all right, but no one to wait on you, you useless old fool!"

I don't know whether or not Yu Erh-po could hear what Mother was saying, but a furious storm of noise erupted at the gate: "Are you all dead in there? Is everyone inside dead or something?"

"Don't you start acting like a madman. Who are you cursing at? Have we treated you badly or something?" Mother was shouting from the kitchen. "Whose food have you been eating half your life? You give it some thought when you can't sleep; if you had any self-respect you wouldn't be here eating our rice. What right has a beggar to complain that the food is spoiled?"

There was no answer. A rumbling noise came from beyond the wall, and when we saw him he was already standing on this side.

"I— I want to say— Sister-in-Law, I was talking about Yang An. I wasn't talking about anyone in the family; it's true I'm useless, but you needn't grudge a bowl of rice." Even though a fight was about to break out, or so I thought, there was still a smile on his face as he said: "If my brother were here I could settle this with him."

"Your brother? Do you think he would stoop to settling the matter with you?!" Mother stepped back and pushed me away.

"Wouldn't stoop to settle the matter with his elder brother, hah! One day we'll just see about that. One day when my brother isn't in school, then we'll have this out." He stood there huffing, his brimless hat that looked like an earthenware bowl cutting across his forehead. As he walked across the compound each footstep left a deep impression in the mud.

"That wretched devil just won't die! Even with his foot rotting off, he still manages to jump over the wall!" It seemed that Mother wanted him to hear this.

"Ah, Sister-in-law, you're talking about your elder brother, humph, humph! How can you talk to me like that? Me die . . . you shouldn't curse me like that; we're all raised by our parents and eat the same food as we grow up." He jerked open the door of the side room as if it were made of stone, but he didn't go inside. "I've lived here with you for more than thirty years, and what have I ever done to you? You check your conscience; I've never trampled down a single blade of your grass . . . ai! Sister-in-law, this year— I can't express it. No way at all. How can you tell what's in a person's heart?"

I slid down and hopped across the compound to the side room, my hands full of persimmons, where I found Yu Erh-po in front of a warm fire. He was sitting there as straight and motionless as the empty urn just inside the door.

"Scram, you little witch! What do you want? Your whole family are rats," he said. I just stood in the doorway, without even going inside, and that's the sort of abuse he greeted me with. No wonder Yang An said that Yu Erh-po had changed, I thought to myself. Even when he was using abusive language he uttered strange expressions I didn't really understand; what did "rats" have to do with me? Why bring them up? I was still in the doorway when he said:

"Bastard kid . . . hare-brained queer . . . wretch . . . cur . . . not a human being . . . haven't got what it takes to be a person." He rambled on, one curse after another, and I don't remember what all he said.

Just like he usually did, I took off my shoes and put them on the floor, soles together, then sat on them.

"You're quite a kid; whatever someone else does, you do the same thing. You see a gourd and right away you paint a calabash. A good pair of new shoes, and you sit right on top of them." He looked at me with those eyes of his like the small pits on carelessly fired urns.

"What about you then?" I put my hand out near the fire.

"I sit on— Just take a look at my shoes; it doesn't make any difference if I sit on them or not, because they're beyond repair! I've already worn these for two years." He took his shoes out from under him, put them up near the fire, and looked at them for a long time. Suddenly he got angry: "You folks, you live in a paradise. When I was your age I didn't have any shoes—where would I have gotten them? Out herding pigs with nothing but a little whip—out in the morning with the rising sun, back with the setting sun, only a couple of rice balls to take along for lunch. But look at the rest of you—*man-t'ou* and grain flowing all over the compound! If I went out and swept the compound I could pick up quite a few. When I was young I never touched even a crumb of *man-t'ou!* Now even the dog turns up his nose at them."

If no one cut off this monologue of his, he could keep it up forever: he talked about the years when he was growing up, then about the clay pot on the stove, and from the clay pot he returned to his youth and the rice balls he had had to eat. I knew the whole routine, and I was sick of hearing it, so I went up to the stove and started roasting my persimmons to see how they would turn out.

"Go on, get out of here; I never saw a brat like you. A person can't even warm himself at a fire; you'll wind up putting it out. Go on, go roast them somewhere else!" he shouted as he watched the fire.

I put on my shoes and bolted out the door; since it remained open, his abuse continued to ring out loudly:

"You little witch, what the hell do you think you're doing? Your whole family is nothing but a bunch of rats!"

Just like the eggplants in the rear garden, Yu Erh-po was grayish and pale, but the older the eggplants got, the quieter and calmer their appearance, as if they were completely resigned to their fate. Yu Erh-po, on the other hand, railed from one end of the compound to the other, hurling abuses at everything from the yard broom to the water barrel, and eventually even his own straw hat: "Bastard . . . what kind of trash are you? You just get away from me . . . no damn human feelings! You don't make it any cooler in the summer and don't add any warmth in the winter."

Eventually he put his hat on anyway and followed Yang An's water bucket out the gate to the well, but instead of sitting down on the millstone, he followed the water bucket right back.

"Bastard . . . you're not even a beast with that black heart of yours," he yelled to the pig along the base of the wall, then turned around and spotted a flock of ducks: "One of these days I'm going to kill you all . . . day in and day out, *quack, quack, quack;* God damn it, if you were human beings you'd be a lazy bunch of bums. Kill you all . . . don't figure yourselves lucky, just eat, eat, eat, . . . get nice and plump . . ."

The sunflower seeds in the rear garden were all ripe; the heavy heads of the flowers seemed about to make their bodies snap in two. Some of the corn stalks stood there with nothing but green leaves on them, while on others a few ears of corn hung here and there. As always, the cucumbers were spread out over the trellis, their brownish skins all spotted and cracked. Some were girded with red bands, having been selected by Mother for seeds to be used next year. The same was true for the sunflowers; red strips of cloth were hanging from many of their necks. Only the aging, pale gray eggplants were left undisturbed on branches; since only black seeds were inside, the children wouldn't eat them, and so the cook didn't bother with them. But the red persimmons quickly assumed their scarlet coloring, one after another, cluster after cluster, resembling nothing so much as the sound of clothes being beaten with mallets, coming at you endlessly from all directions.

One crisp, early morning, to the sound of clothes being beaten, Yu Erh-po collapsed in the compound. All of us children gathered around him, as did many of the neighbors, but when he began to pick himself up, the neighbors backed away and cleared a path for him. He ran back, then fell to the ground again; Father didn't seem to have done much at all—he merely gave Yu Erh-po a knock on the head. This scene repeated itself several times, with Yu Erh-po looking something like a coiling-worm flailing around on the ground. Father was as efficient as a machine. He still had his reading glasses on, standing with his legs apart, and each time Yu Erh-po came over to him, I saw the corner of the sleeve of his white satin gown move gracefully:

"Yu Erh, you no-account bastard, all day long

all you do is shout abuses. You have enough to eat and drink. What the hell else do you want, you son-of-a-bitch?"

Yu Erh-po didn't make a sound in reply. After falling to the ground once more, he struggled back to his feet, walked up to where Father was, and was promptly knocked to the ground once again. By the time he had fallen to the ground yet another time, the neighbors had stopped gathering around him. All this time Mother was standing on the steps; Yang An watched from beside the pile of firewood, holding a bamboo broom in front of him; and the old granny from next door was just on the other side of the gate, the blue flowers in her hair tossing in the wind. Then there was the caretaker, and little Ya-pa, plus some people I didn't recognize, all standing over near the wall. Eventually Yu Erh-po's head was pillowed in his own blood, and he got up no more; the hempen wrapping from around his toes was lying beside him, and there was nothing left of the little round gourd from his tobacco pouch but a clutter of shreds to his left. A rooster crowed, but then scrambled off into the distance; only some ducks came over to peck at the blood on the ground. I could see one with a green head and another with a spotted neck.

By the time winter arrived the elm tree had shed all its leaves; as it stood there alone, every gust of wind from the west struck it with full force. So every night as I listened to the whistling of the steam kettle on the stove I looked out the back window at that big tree—all white, it seemed covered with a layer of goose feathers, even the smallest branch looking thicker than usual. In the daytime rays of the sun the elm took on a sparkle, like the glints of light dancing on the roofs or the ground.

We first busied ourselves with making snowmen until we tired of that, then switched to having the dog pull us on a sled. Every single day there was a rope fastened around the big white dog's neck. We used a sled that Yang An made for us, but instead of pulling us along the roads, the dog always ran toward his doghouse or the kitchen. After we hit him often enough, he began to get used to it,

but still he often just ran around in a circle, sooner or later dumping us all in the snow. And every time he did this we simply didn't feed him for a whole day, and we even put a muzzle over his mouth. But he never learned to accept this punishment, running around and making an awful racket, and pawing at the snow-covered ground, so we always wound up tying him to the hitching post.

Once, for some unexplained reason, Yu Erh-po untied the dog with violently shaking hands. Then he led him over to the side room, as if he were leading a horse. After a while he came out, followed by the dog, on whose back was piled a number of things: a straw hat, a brass water jug, an oil cup for a lamp, a square pillow, a fan made of rushes, a round basket—he looked like a little cart used on moving day. Yu Erh-po carried his bedding under his arm.

"Erh-po, are you going home?"

He kept mumbling, "Let's go, let's go," and I thought "let's go" must mean "go home."

"I— um—" The snow on the ground was spotted with all the pieces of cotton that were falling out of his bedding, a bunch of black ash-like flecks bouncing around on top of the snow. Before he had reached the gate the dog stopped abruptly, and even though Yu Erh-po hit him, he seemed unable to get him to move anymore:

"So you're not going to go! You . . . big white . . ."

I fetched the key and opened the gate for him. At the edge of the well all the stuff on the dog's back flipped over; the little round basket, the brass water jug, and all the other things ended up on top of the millstone.

"Yu Erh-po, are you going home?" If he wasn't planning on going home, then why take all this stuff with him?

"Um, I . . ." By then the dog had run a long ways off. "This isn't my home, but I don't have a home anywhere else either. Come on," he called out to the dog, "you don't have to carry anything; just come here." He spread open his arms as if he was going to embrace the dog. "I wanted to wait until spring came, but there's no way." When he picked up the brass water jug and all the rest of the stuff, I thought for sure he was leaving. I looked at the main gate way off in the middle of all that snow. But he turned around and headed back toward the wooden gate, walking like someone carrying a water barrel on his shoulders, wobbling from side to side.

"Erh-po, did you forget something?"

The only answer I got was the *clang-clang* of the brass rings on the water jug. Was he going after the dog? I was growing more and more interested in the whole episode, so I left my playmates and followed along behind him. When he reached the doorway of the side room he walked in, without, it seemed, even noticing the muzzled dog.

What was it he had forgotten? But rather than fetch anything, he just sat down on the edge of the *k'ang,* that whole pile of junk still resting on his back or hanging down in front of his chest. As he began to talk, I instinctively drew closer.

"Hua-tzu, close the door and come here!" He pushed all the stuff off his body. "Come here and take a look!"

What was I supposed to be looking at?

He lifted up the grass sleeping mat and grabbed a handful of something.

"Just look at this." He threw some kernels of grain to the ground: "It's clear as can be that this was meant to drive me away. Though nobody cares about my aching back and legs, at least I could be thankful for this warm bed! Now they say they're out of rice, and since this grain is still wet, they put it here under my mat to dry out for a few days. It's been more than ten days already . . . more than an inch thick . . . but the heat can still reach the top if there's a fire going. *Ai!* I'd better wait until spring comes. These clothes are no good for cold weather."

He picked up the broom and swept the frost and snow off the windowsill, then swept the wall.

"See all this; if it were sugar I could eat without spending any money!"

Finally, after he lit a fire and put a pile of firewood and dry grass beside the opening beneath the *k'ang,* frost and ice began dripping off his beard as it melted; tears were running down my face, as both of us were engulfed in the smoke belching out. He told me he had been bitten by a wolf when he was seven, and at eight had lost a toe when he was kicked by a donkey.

"Tell me the truth, have you ever seen a tiger in the mountains?" I asked.

"No, that I've never seen," he said.

"How about an elephant?"

He didn't answer my question, but said that he had herded draft oxen for a few years and pigs for several more.

"I lost my mother when I was only three months old . . . my father when I was six months old . . . lived with my uncle for the first seven years, until just about your age now."

"What about when you were just about my age?" My interest began to wane as he moved away from the subject of wolves and tigers.

"When I was about your age I started herding pigs for people."

"You were just about my age when the wolf bit you, weren't you? After that did you ever dare to go back up the mountain again?"

"Dare? . . . hah! In your own home you're a pampered child, but when you live in other people's homes, you have to be an adult. No, I didn't dare. Sure I was afraid. I cried over it, and suffered a few good beatings too."

"Were you only bitten once by a wolf?"

He dropped the subject of wolves altogether and began talking about other things: how during such-and-such a year he had worked for someone feeding their horses; how my grandfather had brought him back home; then there was something about the cherry blossoms during the month of May. Then: "The last few years I've been giving some thought to taking a wife."

I could tell that he was starting in on his regular routine so I bolted out of the room and stood in the middle of the compound. I couldn't see a thing out of my smoke-filled red eyes, from which tears were still streaming, but Yu Erh-po just lay down beside the pile of firewood and began to weep softly.

I walked up toward the main house, the sun at my back and the ground sparkling around me, surrounding me with its glitter; it was there in front beckoning me, and behind me driving me forward. I stood on the steps and looked around at all those pure white, sparkling rooftops and the glittering tree branches. It looked as if dozens of trees carved out of white coral were standing amid the cluster of buildings.

The louder Yu Erh-po's weeping grew, the lovelier all my surroundings seemed to me. How close they all were: the snow was under my feet, and all those rooftops and tree branches were my neighbors! And though the sun was rather far away, still it came to shine down on my head.

In the spring I entered one of the neighborhood elementary schools.

I didn't see Yu Erh-po any more after that.

TUAN-MU HUNG-LIANG
(1912–)

Few Chinese leftist writers of the thirties and forties can compare with Tuan-mu Hung-liang for intellectual breadth or stylistic virtuosity. We can safely say, therefore, that he maintained a higher average of overall achievement during those two decades than any of his fellow Manchurian writers; on the other hand, he never did make full use of his remarkable intellect and literary gifts to create a work of magnitude that truly moves the reader.

Tuan-mu Hung-liang (pen name of Ts'ao Ching-p'ing, also known as Ts'ao Chih-lin) comes from a landowning family in West Liaoning which had for generations dominated the fertile plains around its principal city, Ch'ang-t'u. As a precocious boy, he was fond of reading the forbidden novels in his father's library and was particularly taken by the classic *Dream of the Red Chamber,* truly identifying with that work's author and his own namesake, Ts'ao Hsüeh-ch'in. By the time that he was a middle school student in Tientsin, his intellectual horizons had widened to include a passionate interest in contemporary Chinese literature and in Western literature, music, and cinema, along with an increasing commitment to the kind of leftist patriotism then fashionable among youths of literary bent. Following the Mukden Incident of 1931, Tuan-mu, then a senior at Nankai Middle School, was expelled for urging all-out resistance to Japanese aggression as a student leader.

In the spring of 1932 he enlisted in General Sun Tien-ying's army and moved about for some months in the Jehol-Chahar region. That fall he entered Tsinghua University as a freshman, majoring in history; by then he was already an important enough member of the League of the Leftwing Writers to be assigned the responsibility of editing several of its magazines. In the summer of 1933 he moved to Tientsin to live with his eldest brother. All the League journals had folded, and he was in a state of acute depression. However, a letter from Lu Hsün suddenly gave him new energy, and from August to December he completed, at the age of twenty-one, a massive autobiographical novel, *The Korchin Banner Plains* (*K'o-erh-ch'in-ch'i ts'ao-yuan*). But since it was the very first experimental novel in modern Chinese, its publication was unfortunately delayed until 1939.

After playing an active role in the student demonstrations of December 1935 in Peking, Tuan-mu finally left for Shanghai early in 1936. He became nationally famous that same year when his first short stories appeared in leading magazines such as *Literature* (*Wen-hsüeh*). From 1936 to 1940 he wrote three novels—*The Sea of Earth* (*Ta-ti ti hai*, 1936), *The Great River* (*Ta-chiang*, afterword dated 1939), and *A Fluffy Tale of the New Capital* (*Hsin-tu hua-hsü*, 1940)—and turned out three story collections: *Hatred* (*Ts'eng-hen*, 1937), *Fengling Ferry* (*Feng-ling tu*, 1939), and *Scene in Chiang-nan* (*Chiang-nan feng-ching*, 1940). Along with *The Korchin Banner Plains*, these remain his best-known works, mainly because their publication coincided with a period of patriotic pride when people were eager to read about Chinese heroism against the Japanese and their puppets in Manchuria and elsewhere. However, his 1940 novel, *A Fluffy Tale*, as a satire on the Chungking government, was already symptomatic of the author's and the public's growing cynicism about the war effort.

Tuan-mu's more diversified output from 1941 to 1949 includes, in addition to short stories and essays, two novelistic fragments, some remarkable memoirs, a quintet of plays based on *Dream of the Red Chamber*, a dramatic adaptation of *Anna Karenina*, and a study of the mythological content of the *Shan-hai ching* entitled *The Earliest Treasury* (*Tsui-ku-ti pao-tien*). Because of its inaccessibility, this large body of work has received no attention from Western scholars until recently.

During the fifties Tuan-mu Hung-liang wrote very little beyond a few librettos of Peking or regional operas, which are unworthy of his talent. He became an invalid in 1963, which has further curtailed his activities. Possibly for that reason, he was not attacked during the Cultural Revolution, though the completed manuscript of one novel called *The North* (*Pei-fang*) was lost or destroyed during that period. A lifelong student of *Dream of the Red Chamber*, he has been writing since the downfall of the Gang of Four a biographical novel about Ts'ao Hsüeh-ch'in, the first volume of which appeared in 1980.

Everything Tuan-mu wrote before 1949 is of some interest, but measured against his own ambition to become China's Tolstoy or Balzac, his career has been disappointing, since his most sustained creative effort remains his first novel, which, for all its faults, must be ranked among the greatest novels of modern China. His later novels do not command comparable interest, though they invariably contain passages of magnificent prose capturing a sensuous awareness of the variegated landscape of China. For Western readers with no Chinese, therefore, his short stories are much more satisfactory, especially the early ones about Manchuria and Inner Mongolia collected in *Hatred*. "The Faraway Wind and Sand" (*Yao-yuan ti feng-sha*) and "The Rapid Current of the Muddy River" (*Hun-ho ti chi-liu*), chosen for this anthology, are the best heroic tales in that collection. The former is the only story Tuan-mu has written utilizing his experience as a volunteer in Sun Tien-ying's army; we know from his other writings it was part of General Sun's job to seek the surrender and cooperation of bandits in the common cause against the Japanese. The first-person narrator of this story, presumably an inexperienced soldier like Tuan-mu himself, shares with us his admiration for at least one such bandit. "The Rapid

Current of the Muddy River" tells of hunters driven to patriotic resistance by the impossible exactions of the Manchukuo police. It has a more poetic setting than the bleak terrain of the other story, and contains an idyllic tale of young lovers. Like Hsiao Chün, Tuan-mu Hung-liang celebrates the hunters, bandits and guerrillas as the heroes of a newly awakened China ready for total resistance against the Japanese.

C.T.H.

The Faraway Wind and Sand

by Tuan-mu Hung-liang

Translated by Clara S. Y. Sun and Nathan K. Mao

By the last days of April, it would be the tail end of a joyous spring in other places. However, in Josutu League, the spring breeze is still hidden behind the violent storms coming out of Siberia. Here one can neither smell the moist fragrance of the cherry orchard nor expect to hear the tuneful and charming melodies of the bird-walker's songbird in the air.[1] Instead, he sees only yurts and hears the sounds of the herding of horses—the crisp barrages of snapping whips and their resounding echoes from the valleys. The neighs of the horses are like the sounds of swimming dragons: "*Hwee, tuoo . . . awl-oo, awl-oo.*" Travelers from afar may not recognize these sounds as horses' neighs, and might think they come from strange beasts in the wilderness. How can horses make a noise such as *awl-oo, awl-oo?* But truly, it is nothing less than the neigh of a horse. A horse makes this sound when it is trembling under the whip, or when it is reminiscing about a former mate in the clear, windy, moonlit night, its front hooves digging into the dirt beneath its feedbox.

It can well be said that horses' neighs are the only sound heard beyond the Great Wall. For unlike the sparrow hawks, gray hawks, and buzzards, which make all sorts of pretty chips and chirps on catching their prey, the grassland hawk is as proud as the great eagle. He is always floating leisurely in the blue sky like a piece of solitary cloud or a mysterious witch murmuring her incantations.

The yellow goats are exquisite creatures. Their delicate legs are fragile as tender bamboo shoots, and now and then their thin round ears perk up to listen to noises from afar. Nervous and vulnerable, they would run off at the slightest stirring of the grass or the wind. Their speed was astounding. In the twinkling of an eye, though the sand, the distant mountains, and the old paths remained where they were, a whole herd of goats would have run away, while a few forlorn whistles of wind adorned the distant skies.

These were our companions during our expedition.

There were also the homely larks with dirt-colored feathers, and other larks in the same family with a crest like a hero's plume, sadly calling out in the vastness. Don't think that these larks could sing the eloquent songs of their city cousins who live in gilded cages in bird shops. No, in this desolate, hungry land, they could never sing like that. They chittered and twittered, and when mounted troops passed by, they weren't too eager to fly away. It's as if they had never seen strangers before.

These were the only friendly creatures to greet us in the great vastness.

We had started the journey early the preceding morning, while there was still moonlight. At Chengs' Cave I deliberately ate a little more of the fried buckwheat noodles than I wanted, and now my stomach was upset. We had not stopped to eat

---

[1] In China, bird-lovers used to take their singing birds in covered cages for a walk. Each type of bird required its own style and rhythm of "walking." Sometimes the birds were taken to the woods to learn songs of other birds. [Translators'/editors' notes are keyed with numbers; the footnotes keyed with letters are the author's.]

all the day, and as it drew to a close, the hawks, which had been circling over our heads, began winging homeward. We whipped up our horses and rode on without knowing where we would spend the night.

Suddenly someone called out: "We're lost." Having endured cold, hunger, wind, sand, wading in the water, and trudging over mountains, we were overcome with weariness, and for what? Just to get lost?

My horse's girth seemed loose again. I dismounted to cinch it tighter. It really shouldn't be tightened any more. I felt guilty treating my curly dapple this way, my horse-raising experience having taught me that such handling could cripple it. Nonetheless I grit my teeth, pulled the girth in another inch, and then lightly patted the horse on the neck. Ever since I got the horse, in a less than honorable way, its fate and mine had merged into one. Indignantly, it neighed once to the sky while its front hooves pawed the ground, spraying my boots with sand and pebbles.

Double-Sting Scorpion jumped down from his horse and silently examined the ground, trying to find the footprints of any cart-drivers who might have passed through before us. There were no footprints, nor goats' droppings. If droppings were found, it would be pleasant and comforting news for everyone; for then we could be sure that there were homes nearby where we might find shelter, in a goat's pen at the very least.

Scorpion was looking at the gorge in front of us. Chia Yi, the one who first realized that we were lost, said: "There's a mountain stream ahead. We've been riding in a gully!"

This was really exasperating! What kind of guide was Scorpion? "I knew it all along. All I needed was one look at that face with its pigskin-glue color, and I knew he didn't have any magi's treasure to deliver. Sure as hell, I didn't expect him to know the damned road," Coal Blackie said to me hoarsely, not worrying that Scorpion might hear him. Every pimple on his face lit up and became as red as the red lily.

Scorpion didn't hear what Blackie had said—definitely, he didn't! Imperturbably, he picked up

a stone from the gully, rubbed away the old horse manure and turned the egg-shaped stone over and over again. Eroded by the wind and rain, its top surface was rough-textured, but the bottom was smooth. He finally threw it away and dug in the cracks among the rocks for a long time.

"He expects to find rotten clams in there! If there are rotten clams, then no doubt it must be a gully," Ch'en K'uei said to me.

Scorpion dug for a long time but found nothing—except for a white shell. And when he pressed it between his thin black fingers, it crumbled to powder. He got on his horse and lifted himself high in the saddle to have a look at the area. Beyond the hill it was bright and clear, but there were no mountain ranges nearby. He sniffed; the air was arid and heavily permeated with the smell of sand and dirt.

"Let's go! Dragon Gate Pass is right ahead," he said decisively. That would be too good to be true. We were in fact as far away from the pass as the North and South Poles are from each other. Who could believe him?

"You son-of-a-bitch, all you think about is 'jumping the Dragon Gate!'[a] 'Dragon Gate Pass,' indeed, 'Dragon Gate Pass'—it's in a gorge?! Have you ever gone through here before?" asked Blackie in a voice reeking of Shantung garlic which gave added spice to his agitation and hatred. We all agreed with him. Ch'en K'uei glanced at me with eyes full of doubt.

Scorpion said calmly: "Comrades, let's hurry, we'll be there once we pass this hill." He spurred his horse lightly. It started off, seemingly annoyed.

Blackie uttered a long and lethargic sigh. "Uhhh." He took out his Mauser, emptied it, and then put the bullets back in. Deliberately he cocked the gun. I saw a bloodthirsty look in his eyes, and a chill went down my spine. I wanted very much to warn Scorpion not to ride in front of us, and to watch for Blackie's dirty tricks.

Leading the party, Scorpion's small horse was puffing and white steam was coming out of its nostrils. Suddenly it stumbled.

On both sides were narrow gorges, in which

---

[a] "Jumping the dragon gate" is slang for sexual intercourse.

were a few small elm trees. Here and there, protected from the wind, a grass shoot could be seen in the dirt-filled cracks among the rocks, a sign of spring. But there was not a single flower or singing grasshopper. Except for the sound of hooves, there was only the eerie silence.

Blackie cleared his throat and sang hoarsely:

Buckwheat roll, a good handful, *ai-oh!*
One roll, one flower, *ai-yoo!*
Flower crowns the roll, *ai-yoo-yoo!*
Roll drops in the center of the flower,
ai-yoo-yoo! [2]

What ugly verses had he conjured up to reveal his dirty mind!

His big lips drooped to one side; his bushy beard, as disorderly as a pile of bricklayer's hemp,[3] nearly covered up his nose. His eyes squinted so hard they seemed to be just two slits. The crow's feet at the corners of his eyes quivered repeatedly, and his nostrils twitched violently. His features, slanted to one side, were mean looking. On his left temple was a large scar. It seemed as if he looked at people with that scar rather than with his eyes. The scar had a dark red shine to it.

He suddenly grinned at me. After chewing his beard with his big yellowish front teeth, he spat on the ground. "Hey, hey you, . . . hee, hee." His eyes were full of wild crassness and his face twisted lewdly.

We rode on in silence.

Blackie was not in our unit. Scorpion was one of us—our captain, in fact. His face was greenish, his body blue-green, and for all I knew, his blood might have been green as well. Some said he was an old junkie, a heroin addict; however, no one had any proof that he had ever taken heroin. Others said he had to eat a scorpion every night or he couldn't sleep well. His body, it was said, contained the "five venoms"[4] and whenever he went near a snake it would coil itself up. Once we were on night-guard duty at Willow Barrel Valley.

In the middle of the night, he got up and struck a match. I said to him: "Hey, don't, the enemy will see us!" He said: "Oh, I caught a scorpion." Though I didn't believe what people said about him, his answer really threw me that time. I didn't know whether to laugh or cry.

There was something extraordinary about Scorpion. He was not a perfect marksman, but he could, if necessary, trick the enemy and guarantee him a sad ending. This was how he went about it: he would turn his horse, pull his Mauser out from his armpit and shoot it while turning from one side to the other. The pistol was almost as effective as a hand-held machine gun. Then he would take one foot out of the stirrup and slip down to hide himself along the horse's belly. Thus he would flee. What's more: with his two hands he could simultaneously load the chambers of two pistols. Holding them below the ribs on each hip, he forced the shell out of one chamber with the muscle between his thumb and index finger, while at the same time reloading the second chamber. This trick was deadly, and it was why he was known as "Double-Sting Scorpion." As for the blue-green color of his face, that was because of the "red caps"[b] who, when he was twelve, forced him to drink kerosene four times. Probably that had upset some balance in his physiology.

With a man like that as captain, one could be sure that things would always be under control and never get out of hand. Who wouldn't feel proud to be led by him? Nonetheless, we couldn't admire that blue-green face. It looked just like a centipede's. Besides, he was, after all, responsible for having led us in the wrong direction!

Blackie was the number two chieftain of a newly converted group. Previously he had committed many atrocities on the defense front. He had been, however, enlisted by our commander and had become one of us. In fact, we were now going with him to Pala Gully, his old hideout, to look up his Big Boss and to finalize the enlistment negotiations.

---

[2] Sexual images are apparent in the last line of his "verse."

[3] Chinese bricklayers used to mix cut-up pieces of hemp twine one to two inches long with clay and lime to make plaster, which was used as mortar or to cover surfaces of walls and roofs.

[4] Venom of scorpions, centipedes, snakes, lizards, and toads.

[b] Japanese soldiers.

"Fuck that cock-sucker! Is this your Dragon Gate Pass?" Blackie shouted.

We were at the end of the gorge, and sure enough, instead of Dragon Gate Pass in front of us there was a big river. It flowed past the mouth of the gorge and cut across our path.

"This is the damned Dragon Gate River!" Blackie roared like thunder. It looked as if he were going to shoot Scorpion.

"Look to the west!" said Scorpion calmly and pointed in that direction. We shifted our gaze from the dazzling torrent of water toward the west.

Longevity Peach Mountain! Dragon Gate Pass!

At once everyone came alive. Ch'en K'uei, goading his horse, was the first to gallop westward.

"That's what they call Dragon Gate Pass. Look how gorgeous it is!" Catching up with me from behind, Chia Yi explained: "That's Longevity Peach Mountain. The King of Wu's Reviewing Stand is up there.[c] Down there is Self-Sacrifice Cliff. Once there was a filial daughter who vowed that if her mother's life were spared, she would die in her mother's place. She sacrificed herself here. On the side of the cliff you'll find very large characters carved, each measuring a *mou:*[5] "The Citadel of Defense," and "The Gate to All Roads." They were written by Yang Hung, the marquis of Ch'ang Ping." Much impressed by what he said, I urged my horse forward.

When we reached midstream, the horses drank with gusto. We tried to force them on, for after galloping on the road, they should not be allowed to drink their fill. But the horses didn't seem to realize this, for they stubbornly sank their necks deep into the water.

Longevity Peach Mountain was of dark blue granite that looked metallic. Thousands upon thousands of mountain swallows were nesting on the rocks and chirping.

When we came close to the mountain, the light was blocked by the wings of the swallows and it was therefore shaded. They returned to the rocks and then flew away again, chirping noisily. We couldn't tell what the birds were doing and why they wouldn't quiet down.

I strained my eyes searching for the inscription: "The Citadel of Defense." Sure enough, I found it. The holes which the masons had drilled to hold the scaffolding still remained on the sides of the characters. One could imagine what a gigantic task of carving it must have been. *Howl . . . ool . . .* a gust of black sand came up suddenly, as if ordered by the devil. It blinded our eyes. Quickly we covered our faces with our hands, trying as much as possible to avoid the sand.

The characters which read "The Gate to All Roads" were smaller in size than those which said "The Citadel of Defense," and the calligraphy was not exceptionally good. There were plenty of other verses written by regional commanders and frontier officers. We couldn't read them all; in any case, they weren't legible. The Statue of Self-Sacrifice was a gold figure sixteen feet high, sitting on the blue rocky cliff. At one time it had been securely enshrined in a brick niche; but as a result of earthquakes and storms, the bricks hardly existed anymore.

"Charge through!" Scorpion shouted.

As soon as we turned into the gorge, there was a gust of powerful wind—*whoosh*, the sound of grains of black sand striking against one another, fighting, *whoosh, whoosh, whoosh . . .* At a time like that even having ten faces wouldn't help. The lashing pain was enough to make you scream, but you couldn't, because your mouth was stopped by the whipping wind—*gailo, gailo*—and you were like a goldfish that had drunk nitric acid.

Whoosh . . . The whirling black sand sounded cruel and beast-like. Whoosh . . . *whoo, whoo . . .* the wind with its awesome power sounded like a cheering bugle during combat.

We didn't have face masks. Under the dual onslaught of wind and sand, we were completely at the mercy of the elements.

Nonetheless, we got through. Our eyelashes were thickly crusted with yellow sand particles, but we dared not brush them off with our hands for fear of getting the sand into our eyes. We

---

[c] This is incorrect. The King of Wu could not have come here to review his troops.

[5] About one-seventh of an acre.

gently flicked the lumps of sandy mud from the corners of our mouths, spat on the ground and massaged our stiff, sore cheeks.

My curly dapple sneezed loudly, brushing and dusting its body with its tail.

"It's easier to go to Heaven than to pass through the Dragon Gate Pass!" Ch'en K'uei said to me, gaping.

Blackie's beard, a natural mass of bricklayer's hemp, was now full of sand, dirt, and moisture. It could have been used for plastering walls. "Son of a bitch," he said, fiercely chewing his beard. The sand and dirt that had gathered on his beard must smell like cocoa powder.

After Longevity Peach Mountain, the going would be easier. We were filled with awe and relief and dreamed of what it would be like to eat again. But, oh God, not fried buckwheat again!

Our captain did not seem happy, and his face was still frowning; just as gloomy as his mood, the day was getting darker. Suddenly, small mud huts appeared before us.

"Chia Yi, go in there and check it out; see if there's any lodging. Case the place good."

Chia Yi made a gesture with his mouth and tightened his knees; his horse flew forward.

On the mud wall were few black lopsided characters that read "Mule, Horse, Camel, Inn." After the word "Feed," the plaster had fallen off and the words were no longer legible.

We all dismounted happily, found the trough, and tied up the horses.

Speaking in a literate manner but in the native dialect, the innkeeper greeted us. Reluctantly he put on a welcoming air.

With him was a middle-aged woman, well over forty, probably his wife, who had on the tight-fitting quilted vest worn by the peasant women of Suiyuan and Chahar. She was breast-feeding a child, and her arms and breasts were exposed. When she saw us approaching, she hurriedly ran inside, carrying the child under one arm. The child screamed like a stuck pig.

I asked Chia Yi: "When you first went in there, why didn't she run away?" Smiling, he said: "She

thought I was a country bumpkin, quite different from you lordly soldiers."

"Oh, so there's a piece of juicy meat here! . . . Hee . . . hee . . . ," said Blackie, fixing up his saddle, and patting his horse's stomach. He shot an ugly, wicked smile toward me and his face appeared even more crooked. "Do you have any soybeans?" he shouted.

Soybeans?

The innkeeper bowed several times. "Sir, we don't have any. Really, we don't. If we did, you wouldn't have to ask; we'd have offered them. We've good feed, specially good mixed feed. We depend on your patronage." He turned to call inside: "Erh T'ou!" A small thin boy ran out, his long hair[d] flying in the air. Wearing pants made of flour sacks, he peered at us with black eyes.

"Go and walk these horses for the officers! You, sirs, would you like to go inside and rest?" We stared at one another, realizing that we were being treated as and mistaken for bandits.

When the boy took my horse, he exclaimed involuntarily: "Hey, what a good horse!" Then he gave me a childish smile. When my curly dapple heard this, the sorrows it had gone through on the long journey surfaced. Like a warrior filled with lamentation and indignation, it neighed wildly again and again. It was spring, and my horse must have felt extremely lonely too. I smiled back at the boy. On his white pants one could still see the characters for "All Taxes Exempted" in green ink.

At this moment, the innkeeper, who had already received one slap in the face from Blackie, said: "We really don't have any meat. Even with money, meat is not obtainable. Eggs we have. Yes, we have, sir, we do. Didn't I say we do?" He had also been kicked by Blackie, for his long gray gown showed the dusty boot prints.

"Hey, comrade!" said Scorpion, his eyes glinting. "We shouldn't be too demanding. We'll just have to change our habits a little."

"Shit! He shouldn't have lied to us," said Blackie, shrugging his shoulders. "Hey you, bring some fried eggs and be generous with the oil." He

---

[d] His hair is about four or five inches long; it is difficult to tell whether it is kept for growing a pigtail or it is the remains of a cut-off pigtail.

was the only one who ate fried eggs at supper. None of the rest of us wanted eggs.

It was getting dark, and from afar came the sounds of people calling their horses: "Yo-ho, yo-ho, yo-ho, whoo, whoo, whoo."

We decided to spend the night there, so we went to bed and put aside our fears and worries. Some of us took off our boots and brushed the sand off the bottoms of our feet. Just then Blackie began hitting someone again. I went out to look and discovered he had found half a liter of soybeans somewhere, so the innkeeper was again out of luck. "You mother-fucker, this is the only way to deal with you! Go roast them." Roasting the beans for the horses? My heart was filled with gloom. How could they enlist soldiers like him? He should have been shot years ago.

Blackie came in, fuming. Lying on the *k'ang*[6] he told Chia Yi about the joys of looting.

"Hell, once I hacked off ten hands, got five pairs of gold bracelets—five pairs of them. Hell, five broads too! First raped them, and then knocked 'em off!"

"Chia Yi, go feed the horses," said the captain. Chatting spiritedly, Chia Yi had not expected the captain to cut short his fun. Unhappy with the order, he went out reluctantly.

Obviously, the captain wanted to break it up. Bushy Beard's lips drooped to one side, his eyes slanting. He looked at the captain hostilely as if about to say: "Who do you think you are?" He was boiling with rage; even the tips of his moustache were shaking.

"Go to sleep right now. Chia Yi take the first watch, Ch'en K'uei the second." Scorpion issued the orders. Pointing at me he said: "You take the third. I'll take the fourth. Two hours to each watch."

"Hit the sack? Like hell I will!" Blackie said spitefully, half to himself.

"The sky is getting cloudy," Chia Yi said upon coming in.

Whether he was kidding or not, no one paid any attention to him. Everyone was thoroughly exhausted. We all went to sleep; soon we slept so soundly that we didn't even turn over.

"You've got the first watch," Blackie said to Chia Yi, making all kinds of noise, laughing and chattering.

Gradually, I couldn't hear anything clearly anymore. But the innkeeper's voice seemed to be coming from the next room. I heard a sigh, followed by "Twenty *li*[7] . . . You're too suspicious . . . Don't be afraid . . ."

"But we . . . better leave." Those were the whispers of the innkeeper and his wife. Soon I fell asleep.

Someone shook me. I thought it was my watch. I woke hurriedly out of a sound sleep. "Listen!"

A child was crying in the next room. "Screw your ma! You're not gonna spoil my fun!" Then there was silence.

Ch'en K'uei said to me sadly, "This is terrible. How could we have enlisted him? The commander saw only the machine guns he has. What will this look like? I bet his Big Boss is even worse. He's fooled us from the start." I was silent, trying to locate Ch'en K'uei's face in the dark.

A moment later Blackie came in, walking unsteadily as if he were drunk. "Hey, Chia Yi, go quickly, go!" But Chia Yi was snoring like a pig in deep sleep.

Blackie struck a match to light his cigarette and he saw the two of us. "Ha, ha, ha, ha" he laughed loudly, revealing his feeling of sexual satisfaction. With his chin hanging down and his mouth wide open, he was swallowing saliva. "You two schoolboys, go satisfy your hunger. Go!"

His big head nodding up and down, he finally fell asleep. His snores sounded like the first thunder of early spring. In his throat a glob of phlegm went up and down as he breathed, sounding like the opening and closing of a bellows.

Dawn was misty gray. "Get up, saddle the horses!" Scorpion called. We hurriedly got up and washed our faces while our captain settled accounts with the innkeeper, who thought we were playing games with him. His whole body trembled in fear at the connotations of "settling accounts," which could mean kidnapping, extortion, or even taking a person's life. When he saw that the captain really meant to pay him, he stuttered: "That's

---

[6] See footnote in "When I Was in Hsia Village," p. 269.

[7] One *li* is about a third of a mile.

all right; anything you care to give will do!" His face was pale with fear, apprehensive that the man before him might flare up at any moment. He took the money. With tears streaming down his cheeks, he quickly turned away.

By noon we reached the Gully of Peace; both riders and horses were again exhausted. Of course, there was no place there to eat or rest.

We slowed the horses, but nobody had any idea what we should do. Scorpion coiled his whip around his wrist. His lips moved as if he was going to say something. I thought he was going to tell us where we should stop, but he said nothing, and his horse walked even slower than ours. "Hey, hey, you fools!" said Blackie, unfastening his wide belt and taking out a fried buckwheat roll and devouring it greedily. "You shitheads! What are you trying to prove? You even paid the innkeeper before leaving? Where did the money come from? Isn't it from robbery anyway? You hypocrites, shit! After you leave, you think he's gonna say you were good guys?" His saliva and pieces of the roll spat out as he spoke and he looked very proud of himself. "Why'd I come? No grub—that's why I thought I'd join you. And you, you sons-of-bitches, like blind cats stumbling on a dead mouse, start this talk about reenlisting. Just scratching your own itch . . ."

Ch'en K'uei looked at me and said: "That guy is really—"

"Look here! The bills you gave the innkeeper— here they are!" Tossing the roll of green bills in one hand, he chanted with disdain: "Suckers, my God, big suckers, bigger than the sky itself!"

I remembered that when we left the inn he had said he needed to go to the toilet and had joined us later, obviously hurrying. That was when he had robbed the innkeeper. He made our painstakingly established discipline seem a trick twice as shameful.

Ch'en K'uei's face turned white. He motioned to Scorpion, who was riding behind him, and stretched out his thumb and middle finger. Each vein on his hand stood out distinctly.

"He's going to finish him off," I thought.

Suddenly Blackie saw Ch'en K'uei's gesture. He stared straight at Ch'en K'uei, the scar on his temple got redder, and his eyes shot an oblique look at Ch'en, while his fingers slowly gripped his pistol.

Swish! A sharp crack rang out, and Blackie's pistol dropped to the ground. Scorpion coiled his whip again and tucked it in his belt, while Ch'en K'uei dismounted and picked up the pistol. "Take off his bandolier. Give him five bullets and his pistol," our captain ordered. Blackie looked at Scorpion out of the corners of eyes full of hate. Blood dripped from his injured hand. He waved the hand in all directions; the drops fell everywhere and covered the rear of his horse with peach colored spots.

"Spread out!" the capitan commanded. He rode in the rear, sniffing at the air. His eyes lit up alertly.

Suddenly a shrill sound whistled past the ears of my horse. We all took out our guns. My curly dapple courageously perked up its ears.

"Take to the hilltop!" commanded the captain. We quickly spread out.

"Man the area!" He examined our position and motioned to me. I understood and moved out rapidly about ten feet.

Scorpion looked over the deployment; then he fired a shot in the air and called out something. There was no reply from the other side. A moment later, a few men came out of the bushes. They were sizing us up. Finally a big man came up to take a closer look. He threw down his weapon, motioned with his head to the others, and then said: "Friends, keep your mouths shut." Our band of cavalry passed. Down the slope they fired three friendly shots and we responded with three shots in salute.

Our hunger, after this exciting episode, had long been forgotten. We only felt empty inside, having passed the point of hunger.

"Be careful. This is a major road leading to Dragon Fort, too dangerous. We'll take a shortcut by way of a small path, the Four-Lane Gully," said the captain.

We turned our horses toward a small path, hoping to go faster. My curly dapple smelled a mare's scent on the ground. He made a big deal out of it and neighed long and loud. In the distance we heard another horse sympathetically answering mine; probably a lovesick mare.

I was annoyed, but the harder I hit my horse the louder it called. A yellow goat rushed out. Our captain yelled: "Hind leg!" Bull's eye! As he raised his hand he fired his gun. The yellow goat rolled over once on the ground, and then lay motionless. I got off the horse to pick it up. Right on the knee of its hind leg was a layer of sand sticking to the blood.

Another shot rang out; another goat, I thought. But the company was spreading out. Sensing trouble, I left the yellow goat, got into my saddle and moved to one side. Something must have gone wrong ahead.

A man rushed out; then he turned back in a flash. What group did he belong to? Blackie might know; after all, his group often hung out around here. Up front, another volley of shots was fired. This was puzzling, for hadn't we made it clear that we didn't mean to be unfriendly? So why did they shoot at us without even asking questions? We ought to have shown them our strength, and hadn't. In the meantime, another shower of shots was fired, followed by quietness.

"Two mountains stay apart, but two people will bump into each other eventually. If you come from someplace, announce your name. Even a cock crows[8] before fighting," Blackie roared abruptly.

After a long interval, the opposite side bellowed bluntly: "The King of Hell!"

What kind of name was that? It sounded like a name from *The Water Margin*. "The King of Hell." We exchanged glances, but no one had ever heard that distinguished name before. We decided this must be a group of blockheads.

"Daredevil Shih Hsiu!"

"Shih Pu-ch'üan!"

"Shih Kan-tang!"

With all these rocks[9] being thrown into our eardrums simultaneously, we were dumbfounded.

I recalled the "Energizer" vendors at the mar-

ketplace of White Horse Fort who received accolades from the audience for chopping stone slabs apart with their hands. The slabs had actually been soaked in vinegar to soften them. After their act, the vendors went around trying to sell their "Energizer" drug. But the audience was only interested in the stone-splitting act and no one was buying any. For the audience knew that as long as they didn't have enough food to eat, no "Energizer" would ever turn their hands into knives or saws. It must be those same vendors who, unable to sell their drug, had changed their line of business and come here. They were green at this trade, unfamiliar with even the most basic rules of first encounter.

"Friends, when we bump into each other like this, the rules of the game mean more than Heaven's ordination. If you're friends, let us pass," Blackie responded in a splendid series of catchwords.[10]

"If you know the rules, pay the tribute: five saddles and some shells." From the opposite side these words came flying back.

"Shells we have! But we hand them out one at a time, through a gun barrel. Friends, have you ever heard of Coal Blackie? How long have you been at this trade?" Obviously, things had gone drastically wrong. *Bang*, a shot came from the opposite side.

Ch'en K'uei gathered all the horses together and led them to the rear. We all hit the ground ready to fire. The opposition apparently hadn't heard of Blackie before, and without the least courtesy, delivered a volley of shots.

Blackie was first on the line. When the opposition was not intimidated by his name, his anger immediately flared. His three eyes—the scar on his temple could be counted as one—opened wide as brass bells. He stretched out his hand to the captain asking for bullets. We knew we were deadlocked. Scorpion occupied the number two

---

[8]*Ming* ("call"), and there is another *ming* that means "name." There was a tradition that parties involved in combat must first announce their names.

[9]*Shih* means stone or rock.

[10]The exchange between Blackie and his "friends" here and below is conveyed in the supposed passwords of the bandits; since they are all untranslatable, no attempt has been made to reproduce them in English. Their meanings, however, have posed no problem thanks to the notes provided by the author.

position, not far from Blackie, and the two of them were in close and urgent consultation. A common enemy was at hand.

With one shot, Blackie brought a man down. He turned his head, tipped his face, and smiled foolishly at Scorpion. Scorpion hit one too. The opposition was indeed a "rocky group," hard and stubborn, with no intention of pulling back. Their shooting was intense. Because they had lost the first round, their anger was fully aroused.

Continuously, bullets streaked over my head. Their sad, piercing whistles suggested chanting or groaning. There were splashes of bright sparks where they ricocheted off the rocks.

Chia Yi fell down and lay still; he still had his hand on the trigger and a last shot came out of the barrel, after which he was silent forever.

Barrages of shots kept going. Eventually we couldn't hold out any longer. Ch'en K'uei had quietly brought the horses closer. Scorpion crawled to Chia Yi to pick up Chia's pistol.

In a situation like that, nothing was more unfortunate than to be driven into a confrontation. But this often happened because there were so many greenhorns in the trade. Before they familiarized themselves with the rules, they carried on much as they pleased. This cost many needless casualties on both sides. But we soon discovered that our speculation had been incorrect. Our adversaries weren't greenhorns, they were wearing armbands—the kind of armbands we hated the most—those of regular soldiers! The lackey of the lackey.[11]

There were so few of us left, we decided to get out.

"You go, I'll hold out." Scorpion waved his thin blue-green hand and ordered us to hurry. I was sad and worried about him; meanwhile, I mentally said farewell to the dead Chia Yi.

Ch'en K'uei almost made it onto his horse, but fell back down. His horse stood stock still, waiting for its master to try again to step into the stirrups. Blackie jumped off his horse, ran to Ch'en K'uei,

and put a hand over Ch'en K'uei's heart. Then he tied Ch'en on the horse's back; he turned his head to look at Chia Yi's body. His face twitched violently and he looked as if he couldn't bear it anymore. He raged: "I'm not leaving." Scorpion's blue-green face seemed to fill with venom as he cursed: "Bastards, run! What're you waiting for?"

Blackie abruptly put Ch'en K'uei's bandolier around his own waist. Then he slapped Ch'en's horse hard; with blood from its master dripping off its back, the horse galloped quickly away.

Blackie turned to me and smiled pleasantly. Before I could fully understand what he meant to do, he jabbed my horse on its butt. My curly dapple at once ran after the horse in front. I tried my best to pull at the bit, but it just reared briefly and then its four hooves galloped on faster than ever.

The sound of firing became louder. It was clear that the enemy was coming closer. I could now hear the sound of machine guns, and was afraid that our side could not hold out any longer. I tried with all my strength to tighten the rein and stop my horse; in the dusky wilderness, strong winds carrying coarse sands blasted at me. Finally I was able to turn the horse and charge back.

A moment later I saw two horses stampeding, each with a corpse on its back. My curly dapple could not help letting out an angry cry; it pursued the other two horses so quickly I felt we were plunging through the clouds. The black sands of Dragon Gate Pass seemed to be blowing eastward and passing by my ears.

Suddenly one corpse stood up and waved to me with both hands. Truly a most painful and sad sight.

"Follow me quickly!" It was the firm, sonorous voice of our captain. He spoke as he did when he was alive. But he had already—

Then I suddenly remembered that this was another of his famous tricks, feigning death. A ray of light flashed over my eyes. My horse was already close to his. I thought that the other corpse would suddenly sit up too, but it didn't.

---

[11] The soldiers were lackeys of Manchukuo government officials who, in turn, were lackeys of the Japanese imperialists. For explantation of the term Manchukuo, see footnote 2 to "Sinking Low," p. 305.

The Rapid Current of the Muddy River

by Tuan-mu Hung-liang

Translated by Margaret M. Baumgartner and Nathan K. Mao

On the left bank of the Muddy River was the White Deer Forest . . . When the sparrows arrived, the birdseed [1] was thoroughly ripe. The ramie stood still, dry and motionless; big leaves flashed brilliantly in autumn gold. Tasting of sadness, the rushes, though unwilling to be blown away by the wind, would soon be dispersed however their fate dictated. The unruly husks of the balsam, whose branches were like running wax, had burst open at random, casting brownish kernels over the ground.

The sun was gentle and bright, the sky high, and the air dry. Not a thread of shade anywhere; the reeds whistled in the wind. On the prairie deer bleated.

Thrusting into the sky, the aspen, bright and shining, manifested the prairie's majestic beauty in the clear air. In the breeze it gave a throaty male sigh, or else it remained still, seeming lonely in its gentle quietude.

No singing grasshoppers were in sight, nor croaking toads. Near a freshwater well came the sounds of a revolving pulley and a faint splash of water dripping from the soaked rope of a willow bucket. Chirping and twittering, sparrows flew, from time to time stealing crops from the fields or else hiding in the dense foliage of the aspen and peering down as they heard the shouts of the crop-watchers.

In the houses under the trees, the large Ma-ha fish, strung together on grass ropes, stunk of sea salt; fresh red persimmons hung under the eaves.

The yellow mottled gourds, picked by busy girls and arranged in a red net, were so much shinier than lemons. Rocking to and fro in the wind, they were pleasant to behold. In the forest a fertile and springy earth exuded the smell of fermentation when the unpicked tart fruit had dropped to the ground and the aphids had secreted their honeydew.

At this time Elder Ts'ung's little house was very quiet. Only a bluebottle fly or two leisurely buzzed in the air; his dog, in heat, had gone to meet its mate.

It was nearly dusk. Shui-ch'in-tzu had not yet returned to help her mother cook. As usual, the mother quietly murmured: "That crazy girl," more in love than in complaint. The thought of her lovely daughter—whose little red mouth would pout in protest against her affectionate chiding—brought a smile to her face.

The meal was almost ready. She wiped her hands on her apron and felt the mung-bean and rice gruel. Afraid it might still be too warm when her husband returned, she added another ladleful of cold water. Standing by the doorway and cupping her hands to her cheeks, she called out: "Shui-ch'in-tzu, come home, time to eat." In her own pleasant manner, she repeatedly called for her daughter.

Shui-ch'in-tzu, clasping a large squash under one arm, had wrapped a large bunch of thorn apples in the fold of her jacket. Like a little swallow in flight, she came running. The squash

---

[1] *Su-tzu,* a kind of grain similar to millet, used mainly for birdfeed. [Translator.]

slipped out of the cradle of her arm, and when she bent over to pick it up, the thorn apples scattered over the ground. She became excited. "Look, you called for me in such a big hurry; now the thorn apples are everywhere."

The mother came running with vigorous steps. Asking who gave them to her, she picked up the thorn apples and some grass in her dustpan. "Come quickly. I've boiled two salted duck eggs for you. If you're hungry, don't wait for Papa. Go ahead and eat."

The daughter, who was about to fuss over the thorn apples, quickly arranged her two braids and ran swiftly toward the house on hearing of the eggs.

"Ma, Brother Chin Sheng is really great at knife-throwing. Mama, he can throw like this on a large elm tree, like this." Shui-ch'in-tzu dipped her fingers in the gruel and wrote on the table the characters for "small," "mouth," and "wood." Her mother, whose curiosity had been aroused, moved closer to her and examined with narrowed eyes the characters she wrote on the table but failed to see what they were. "Afterward, he used his left hand and threw three knives all at once. In the 'mouth' character he added a dot; in the 'wood' character he added a line. Ma, you don't believe this, but it is all true." At first, the mother had been affected by the daughter's glow of youthful rapture, but as her daughter chattered on and on about things like throwing knives and shooting guns, she soon lost interest.

"Ma, really, he says if I put my head against a tree, he could nail twenty-one knives on the four sides of my head and it wouldn't hurt."

Her mother cried out: "Nonsense! That young idiot doesn't know what danger he is putting you into. Did you actually let him do it?"

"No, Ma," the daughter answered calmly, "but even if I really let him, I believe I wouldn't be hurt."

"Garbage! He doesn't know what he's doing. That young thug thinks of every way to fool you. I wouldn't forgive him!"

In a bouncing gait, the daughter left to feed her bird. Hopping out of its cage, the tame little bird pecked and ate the kernels from her fingertips. Afterward, cocking its little head, it closely examined its mistress' face. She felt the impertinent gaze and couldn't help becoming embarrassed. "Why are you staring at me like that too?" she wondered, and started reminiscing with a sweet smile on her face.

"Ma, come and have a thorn apple."

"Have you had enough to eat? I'll wait until your father comes back and eat with him."

"I'm almost full. I'll wait until Pa comes back too; then couldn't I eat again?"

"Ah, still so spoiled. When a girl is near eighteen, she becomes unruly, and after this year, you'll be eighteen, but still you . . ." The mother sighed and squeezed a thorn apple.

"Ma, look at the white seeds and pulp. He climbed up a tree and shook it, and I just picked them off the ground."

"Nonsense! Now, are you telling me that thorn apples grow on a tree?"[a]

"Sure, Ma, I mean the big one on the South Mountain."

"From now on, you shouldn't see Chin Sheng again." Becoming serious, the mother hesitated for a while and repeated her command: "Remember! Listen to your mother. You aren't permitted to be with him from today on!"

Her daughter's eyes widened. The mother chose a large bright thorn apple, squeezed out the seed with her hand, and ate it.

"Ma, why?"

"You just remember what I said, that's all."

"No, Ma, tell me . . . tell me . . ."

"Don't nag, I have to fix supper; your father's coming home soon and he'd be angry."

It was dusk. The autumn sun draped a passionate red curtain across half the sky. The twilight, piercing through the deep forest, did not lengthen the tree shadows but had subtly erased them. Like a reflection in a mirror, the forest at this moment looked dim, distant, and transparent. Yet hardly a moment later, the forest was enveloped in darkness. A lone star emerged above the

---

[a] Thorn apples grow on shrubs. [Author's note.]

high mountain; fireflies flashed in the grass; shades of the day gradually yielded to darkness. In the mountain hollows came human noises. It was time for the hunters to come home.

After sitting dully for a while, the daughter pleaded with her mother dejectedly: "Ma, do tell me the reason."

"You see, the older you get, the more childish you become." The mother mildly reprimanded her daughter's persistence.

"Ma, I have to know," the daughter insisted stubbornly. Her eyes moist with tears, she evidently had done some hard thinking.

The mother seemed confused, trying to sort out her thoughts, while the daughter waited anxiously for a reply.

"You should know."

"No, I never do," the daughter complained, as if she had been wronged.

"What's your name?"

Mentally the daughter answered that it was Ts'ung.

"Our name isn't in the *One Hundred Family Names*." The mother made a pious gesture. "We are fugitives from the law." The daughter innocently raised her troubled face, listening attentively. The mother lowered her voice: "Our ancestor was Chin. A subject of the great Ming dynasty, he was an eminent scholar. When the Ming perished, the Ch'ing asked him to surrender and offered him a high office to win the support of the people. When the emperor gave him a red tasseled cap and all sorts of hat ornaments as well as court sleeves, boots, and pearls,[2] he compared them to the furs of animals. One day as he went to the palace wearing his court pearls, he crawled on his knees. When the emperor gave him permission to sit down, he insisted on crawling; then the emperor asked him why he didn't get up and he replied: 'I am wearing the clothes of a wild beast and I'm having an audience with the king of wild beasts. Hence I must crawl.' On hearing that, the enraged emperor decreed that he and his nine clans be executed. Fortunately, a distantly

related grandmother, having foreseen his refusal to surrender to the Ch'ing and the subsequent dire consequences, including the annihilation of the family, had escaped beforehand with many others of the family. When a group of Ch'ing soldiers gave chase, our branch of the family hid amid a cluster of trees and escaped to safety. From that time on, we changed our name to Ts'ung.[3] You know our ancestor was strong-willed. If he had given in, he would have been a first-rank official, and your father wouldn't have to spend his whole life as a hunter, would have some leisure time in his old age, and certainly wouldn't have to go out early and return late every day."

"Ma, I heard the same story from Aunt Chang once. I didn't believe her then. Ma, such a good story. Why didn't you tell me this before? Ma, I'd rather have Father be a hunter all his life than—"

"Shoo, it's easy to talk. Your father isn't what he used to be in the past. *Ai,*" her mother chided her gently.

"Surely, Ma, our ancestor was strong willed. During the Ch'ing he didn't surrender. Now isn't the Ch'ing here again?[4] We still won't give in. Am I right in what I said, Ma?"

The mother looked sorrowful. "But, Ma—" the daughter was about to say something else. The mother turned to face her. After a little hesitation, the daughter sheepishly asked: "But what's all this got to do with Chin Sheng?"

Abruptly the mother turned around. "Because he is also named Chin!"

The daughter then realized the implication; ruefully, she murmured: "No wonder he said he's also named Ts'ung." Yet a moment later, hope again lit up her face. "Ma, we're more than five generations removed in blood relationship. Besides, many people are named Chin, including many Koreans and Mongolians."

"How shameless!" Trembling, the mother turned away and resumed her work.

Shui-ch'in-tzu's face suddenly lost its color. Her mother's every syllable was like a thousand-pound

---

[2] Manchu court paraphernalia.   [3] *Ts'ung* means a cluster of trees or plants.
[4] Possible reference to the Manchukuo; see footnote 2 in "Sinking Low," p. 305.

blow, hitting her face, her eardrums, her heart, and the deep recesses of her soul and splintering her into pieces. Every object in the room seemed to have lost its attraction. The canary was asleep; the hunting weapons stood up like a net ready to trap her; the guns that were lined up appeared to be glinting at her, and the big deer's head on the wall stared at her fixedly. She felt a sudden terror—the whole room dissolving into ashes and dust lightly settling down, sinking. She hid her face in the grass-colored leopard skin, and darkness quietly entered the room.

The father was coming home; from a distance came the sound of his Russian boots. Shui-ch'in-tzu trembled at the slightest of noises. The early evening brought with it the howls of various wild animals. Awkwardly, the mother welcomed and chided the father at the same time: "You came home so late. I'm starved." As she was chiding him, she carried his backpack in.

There hadn't been much of a catch, only a little deer, which she threw into a corner, as if she hadn't seen it, and began to put rice in the bowls. "You must be hungry, *ai, ai,* coming home so late." Elder Ts'ung lit his pipe and glanced at the bowl of rice gruel. Instead of eating, he began to smoke, deep in thought. His wife had a mouthful of rice, but noticing that he wasn't eating, she put her bowl down. "Here is melon fried chicken." She tried to whet his appetite with a smile.

"Mm," he grunted and scanned the room. It was very dark and he could not see anything. Impatiently he took off his Russian boots. Spotting the leopard skin in a corner, he fiercely threw them at that unlucky object to vent his frustration, both boots hitting his daughter.

If it had been any other time, she would have bellowed in pain or simply thrown herself on her father's bosom and shed a few spoiled tears. But she said nothing; she bore the pain; in fact, she was bearing a pain far greater than that.

The mother was busy getting the squash porridge, commenting on its creaminess and sweetness. But as she was about to pour it into a little green bowl, her husband was already taking big bites of melon and noisily downing the gruel. Pleased with what she saw, she too ate heartily.

Her eyes explored the dark. "Shui-ch'in-tzu, why don't you come and eat a little with Father? There's still one salted duck egg left." There was no answer, for the mother was old and unable to make out where her daughter was, since mountain folks usually ate without light. In the direction of her gaze, the father looked into the darkness and asked: "The child hasn't eaten?" Shaking her head, the mother replied: "She's pouting." He smiled, while Shui-ch'in-tzu's tears fell. Worried that her strict father might, in a moment, discover her whereabouts, she quietly got up and closed the door behind her.

She picked up her legs and ran. Unmindful of either time or direction, she ran until exhaustion overcame her. She found a chunk of white rock to sit on; all around her mushrooms exuded soft fragrance. Without anyone to give her either understanding or sympathy, she sank completely into desperate loneliness. Ahead was a strong midstream current. When its water splashed on the rocks, it produced a loud hollow sound, like that of a bronze bell. Not far in the distance was the Muddy River. Amid the bleatings of deer from afar and the hooting of owls from the depths of the forest, she gathered courage and ran toward the river bank.

The moon was up. In the moonlight water drops looked silvery and fresh. There was neither mist on the river nor a cloud in the sky: it was a sweet evening. A cool breeze emitted a wet fragrance; squirrels hopped among tree branches; the Milky Way was almost visible. Though the water of the river was muddy and its murmurs melancholic, it looked attractive in the moonlight. The red sandstone river bank, the yellow earth of the river bed, the whitish water droplets, and the greenish mist covered the height and loftiness of the northern country; a patch of frost flowed into the vastness. How charming! What a night! But Shui-ch'in-tzu was so depressed. In the distance she heard her mother calling for her from high ground. Still pouting, she waited until there wasn't the slightest sound in the air before going home.

Her father had already built a bonfire, and was smoking by it. Holding a piece of green willow over it, her mother tried to bend the wood enough to make it into the frame for a muck basket; the wood crackled. "Our quota is thirty?" the mother asked sullenly. "This isn't winter. How could you hunt without snow? What if you can't deliver?" The old man made no reply. He slapped his pipe to knock the ashes out and refilled it. "Definitely execution?" the mother continued to query the father.

"Of course," the old man answered finally. "I heard this imperial concubine was brought by some bastard to pay tribute to the Court, and she'll be received formally into court on October first. They gave us twenty-five days to deliver five hundred fox pelts in five colors: one hundred red, one hundred yellow, one hundred white, one hundred black fox; for the blue pelts we may substitute purple sable.[5] Since we only have the fire fox and the grass fox in this area, we have to contribute only two hundred red and yellow pelts, and they made no specific demands for sables. If this were winter, our quota of thirty would not be too bad, but where do I get them in the off season? It's really murder. Everything is for show. I don't know what traitor suggested getting fox pelts to match the auspicious colors of the flag. What stinking dog-fart! In the old days the hunting season had its own specific time determined by the planets, to correspond with national events. There was never such a thing as hunting for fox at this time of year. Since we're doing things against nature, how can we expect to have good game?"

"Thirty, really thirty, within twenty-five days? That means more than one a day. Where are you going to get them? In the last few years the mountains have been exhausted." Full of worries, the mother wiped her hand distractedly on her apron.

Emerging from the darkness, the daughter sat down quietly on one side of the bonfire, staring at the unsettled flames. As she noticed the daughter's haggard look, the mother became grieved, thinking: "It's all because I've spoiled you. You can't take one harsh word, and if there should be

more difficult times ahead, how are you going to face them?" In poor humor, she chided her daughter: "When and where did you run off to? I yelled for a long time and you didn't answer. Because of this, your father has kept scolding me!"

The father looked at his daughter's face and sat affectionately beside her. "Shui-ch'in-tzu, don't you be stubborn, and don't hold any grudges. Help me set traps and mix explosives tomorrow. Today is the eighteenth; by the thirteenth of next month we must deliver two hundred pelts. Probably from now on, foxes in the White Deer Forest will become extinct. But extinction is only a small matter, for if we don't deliver, the purchasing agent will consider us anti-Manchu for not having worked hard enough. He would think that we deliberately bring a bad omen to the imperial concubine on her wedding day. Then your father's old life will end, and there won't be time for you to be angry with him, even if you wanted to." As he mentioned the imperial concubine, he spat out large amounts of saliva on the ground, as if these two words were particularly filthy.

The daughter, having heard what he said, became terrified, threw herself on his bosom, and wept. After a while she fell asleep. "*Ai,* why do you feel so hurt? Your mother must have used you to let off some steam," he murmured, as he watched his daughter sobbing in her sleep. Irritated with his wife, he bellowed: "What exactly did you say to her? The older you get, the less sense you have." He then fondly carried the daughter into the house.

Early the next day, life in this little thatched hut was filled with tension and excitement: the father fixing the traps, the daughter mixing explosives, and the mother grumbling. Adroitly, Shui-ch'in-tzu broke mung-bean bowls into pieces, so that the shards would have ample sharp edges and points to break any fox's neat little legs. Carefully, she mixed the powdery phosphorus, placed it in a dark dry place, and prepared the sulfur. By evening the father had fifteen traps. Using a pair of pinchers, the mother handed partially roasted chicken meat to the father, who used it for bait.

[5] The flag of the Manchukuo had these five colors.

In the dim firelight the father called softly for his daughter. She hopped forward like a small bird, carrying five traps on her back, and silently walked into the forest with him. They planned to place the traps late at night in places where the foxes roamed, yet without the knowledge of other hunters who might steal the traps. Around the graveyard they placed five. The father hammered on each of the wedges once more; finally pleased with his work, he led his daughter to the foot of South Mountain.

The daughter seized this opportunity to speak to her father. "Brother Chin Sheng, couldn't . . . he help out? He throws knives very well."

"Can knives cut off one single hair from a fox's tail? Huh?" the father pointed out her ignorance.

"He also knows how to use clubs the way the Mongolians hunt the fox."

"Hunt. He also has time to play his flute." The rough wrinkles on the father's face convulsed, crudely twitching his beard. Without blushing, the daughter said firmly: "I'll go and talk with him."

The next day at dawn, father and daughter went to pick up the traps. Nine animals had stepped into the explosives but one had been stolen by someone else. Of the eight that had been struck, only five were foxes and the other three were miserable weasels. The father was very happy; he had already fulfilled one-sixth of his obligation. The explosives having dried, they finished setting the traps. On the fox-run in the forest, they laid down phosphorous-sulfur bombs and also made markers warning people to stay away from the area.

"Thirty is nothing," the daughter said, thinking of yesterday's catch and sizing up the day's arrangements. She giggled foolishly before her worried father.

At five in the morning, in the middle of a strange dream, she was awakened by her father. That night they had unexpectedly trapped five, all of which were fire fox. "Father, I wasn't wrong. Thirty is nothing."

"We'll see," he said worriedly, exhaling a long breath. "It's hard to say. Tomorrow we'll go to the valley of East Mountain and smoke them out. You and your mother repair the nets." The mother

also seemed somewhat happy. Weaving the nets with her daughter, she told her a few fairy tales.

But on the morning of the third day, five traps had been stolen. That evening, aside from two bobcats that had been blown to pieces, they had not caught anything. The father was very angry that his fellow hunters had been so dishonest; but when he thought of the trouble and possible execution that faced all of them, he only shook his head, sighed, and determined to hunt for more. At the very least he must have more than thirty. During the day they used smoke, nets, guns, and clubs; at dusk they set down traps, explosives, and nets; at night they had a newly added chore—to guard the traps from theft. The father saw his overworked daughter becoming thinner and the fox pelts slowly accumulating.

Yet the situation worsened as the days went by. It seemed as if the foxes had tacitly agreed among themselves that they would rather starve than venture out to hunt for food. Elder Ts'ung's family, to encourage the foxes to leave their dens, flogged chickens late at night and sprinkled boiled chicken water everywhere, hoping to whet the foxes' appetite. When every family imitated this same procedure, the forest was filled with hens screeching for life and other noises of fright and terror. "Cry as much as you can; then it'll be our turn," said a sorrowful Elder Ts'ung as he heard the noises.

By the twenty-second day, Elder Ts'ung had twenty-two pelts. Taking his daughter by the hand, he laughed heartily: "Shui-ch'in-tzu, I won't be seeing you for a while. In the three remaining days, we must hunt for three foxes each day. Only three days, and we can't even get hold of one single fox hair, let alone get three of them."

Shui-ch'in-tzu was irritated with Chin Sheng. The day before she had run to his home three times and couldn't make him do anything. He just made a reed flute and blew on it. "When he sees Papa dead, he'll be sorry!" She was heartbroken. She thought of something. "Papa, wouldn't it be better for us to buy some to meet the quota? It would have been so good if we hadn't sold those ten last year." She was very worried.

"Buy?" The father did not say much else; he

knew the inflated prices of fox pelts. Patting her head, he teased her affectionately: "Unless we sell you in exchange for the fox pelts." From the other side of the room, the mother came out with her usual banter: "She's a lively little fox all right—" and then she checked herself.

Outside a gust of wild wind blew down many leaves at random. As a gale arose from the northwest, everything appeared gloomy. The water of the Muddy River, day and night, flowed continuously. Meanwhile Shui-ch'in-tzu stood up, having decided to look for Chin Sheng, for she was still angry with him. The father carefully re-counted the fox pelts in the room, hoping to find one or two extras that might have been mis-counted. Twenty-two, still only twenty-two. Carry-ing his gun on his back, he went to look for Li Chao to see how he had been doing. Li, the biggest hunter in the area, was given a quota of fifty fox pelts.

Elder Ts'ung came face to face with Chang Teh. "Uncle, you going hunting?" asked Chang, while holding five grass foxes in his hands.

"I'm on my way to see Li Chao. I don't think I can meet my quota. How about your quota of ten pelts?"

"Uncle, I have exactly ten, just enough!"

Elder Ts'ung's heart sank. "Any extra?"

"None. If I catch any in the next three days, I'll give them to you for free, Uncle." Elder Ts'ung did not know what made him want to cry, but he said quickly: "I'm on my way, I'm going" and walked down the mountain in confusion.

The people at Li Chao's house were busy and noisy. When they saw Elder Ts'ung, they sur-rounded him. "How are you doing? We heard you haven't done badly." "Not bad." The old man threw his cap on a *k'ang*-bed.[6] "Twenty-two." Li Chao shook his head and knew from experience that the remaining eight, no matter what, would not be caught. "You have all you need?" asked Elder Ts'ung resentfully. The beautiful fox pelts hanging on the beam under the eaves made him feel deeply jealous. "So you've all you need," he was almost shouting, for from Li's nonchalant

manner he was sure that Li had met his quota.

Li Chao, stroking his goatee, appeared very wily as he asked: "What's our family's quota?" Then he smiled and winked at this eldest son, Li Sen.

"Fifty," answered Elder Ts'ung straight-forwardly.

"Ha, ha, ha, ha . . . Fifty! Good. Mr. Agent-in-Charge, I wish to deliver fifteen, would that be all right? Sir, I did everything I could to catch these fifteen; I really can't deliver any more, because the mountains have been hunted clean. 'Blow your mother's fart, can the foxes be hunted clean? You resist on purpose, you insist the superiors shouldn't assign you to hunt for pelts and destroy your source of livelihood! Is the imperial con-cubine unworthy to have your fucking foxskins? This is a royal occasion, yet you dare to cause trouble deliberately. You're obviously against the Manchu government. Men, arrest this little bas-tard.' Ha, ha, ha, ha, big brother, you think I have met my quota? Ha, these four belong to Li Ta-t'ou, those twenty-five belong to Yang San-ch'iang, and the other thirteen to Chao Yüng-lu. Here are the fifteen caught by the three of us: fa-ther and sons, three master marksmen. Ha, ha, ha, ha!" Li Chao looked up at the sky, laughing wildly and patting Elder Ts'ung on the shoulder. "How many did you catch?"

Elder Ts'ung reluctantly raised his head. "Didn't I say twenty-two?" Narrowing his eyes to slits, he stared at Li worriedly.

"Great! Good for you! The three of us are just good-for-nothing bums, for you alone caught twenty-two!"

"That's nothing to brag about. Short ten and short one is all the same. It all amounts to the same fate."

"*Ai*," responded Li Chao painfully, inhaling his pipe forcefully. He had stopped laughing.

"We still have three days. Everybody should work harder and see if we can get a few more. Now all together we probably have approximately one hundred forty or fifty." Wu Lao-t'ou, sitting at the head of the *k'ang*, slowly voiced his prudent advice.

---

[6] See footnote 1 in "When I was in Hsia Village," p. 269.

"No way. If we get one more, you must be the one who gives birth to it!" replied Yang San-ch'iang bluntly.

"Well, if we beg him, maybe . . ."

"You senile old fool. He may forgive you, but he may not let your head stay."

"Well, what to do then?"

Really what alternative was there? They discussed the matter until dark without any satisfactory result. Their tongues were so dry that they could almost be ignited.

Finally Elder Ts'ung, with a heavy heart, trampled through the tall weeds and returned home, without any solution. Everything was finished. His steps were a little unsteady, as his Russian boots, like ghosts, dragged him backward along the road. He did not know how he got home.

As soon as he reached the front of his house, Shui-ch'in-tzu flew toward him like a butterfly, put her arms around his neck and was so ecstatic that tears flowed. "Papa, nine, Papa, nine of them!" He did not comprehend what she said, gently unclasped her hands, and walked sadly into the house. "Papa, Brother Chin Sheng is here. Brother Chin Sheng helped us catch nine." The mother rubbed her eyes with her hands; every wrinkle on her face seemingly had been smoothed. "Nine, twenty-two, one extra!"

A stone dropped to the ground. Brother Chin Sheng was like a piece of sculpture made of pear wood. The bridge of his nose was thin but prominent; his dark hair was slightly curly; his mouth often revealed a cynical smile. Standing in the dim house, he was busily putting the fox pelts in order. Elder Ts'ung, noticing his handsome physique, was quite pleased. Quickly he walked toward the young man, yet suddenly he assumed an air of indifference. "Nine fox pelts?"

"Nine, Papa, nine, all of them fire foxes. The down and hair are of the same length," the daughter answered pleasantly, her eyes filled with pride as they shifted from her father to her mother.

"Uncle, yesterday I went to Black Smoke Mountain and there they couldn't deliver three hundred either. They caught thirty-some black sable, but not even one single hair of a purple sable." Smoking his pipe, Elder Ts'ung sat in silence, while the young man continued: "There they planned not to deliver. They were holding a meeting to find out what to do. Anyway the agents, those pigs, won't let us off easily, so everyone thought of resisting."

"Those sons of bitches, let them have my fart. No, I won't deliver. What good would that do even if I met my quota? Wouldn't everybody still be killed?"

A gust of wind blew in many leaves through the window, the inside of the room sinking into a whirlpool of death. The daughter, who at first had so many things to say, was now deeply troubled. "But Papa, but—"

The father appeared to be in no listening mood. "Chin Sheng, go tell every hunter to meet at Li Chao's house."

The mother ran in from outside, happily wiping her hands on her apron. "I cooked some venison for you. You two have a drink. *Ai, ai,* if not for Chin Sheng's nine fox pelts . . . He really is a good boy. Isn't there one extra? Quickly give it to Old Wang. I feel sorry that his quota is three and as of now he hasn't caught one. You people are really lucky that once you started, you got so many."

"Uncle, I'm going now," said Chin Sheng, walking toward the door.

"We'll go together," Elder Ts'ung said.

Shui-ch'in-tzu gave Chin Sheng a forlorn look but made no attempt to stop them from leaving. "Mama," she called and then stopped. The bowl of venison that the mother had just brought in was completely spilled over the table. The happy feeling of a moment ago had now dissolved into confused panic. Even thirty fox pelts would not save them. When the others could not meet their quota, it was useless for one family to do so. By the time the old woman realized the seriousness of the situation, the two men had long disappeared, leaving behind them the feeling of emptiness.

The forest in the night was intriguing. The haughty, slender aspen was waving as if in dance. The oak had a self-regarding propensity for solitude. When the wind blew, it still maintained its elegance and only swung slightly like ripples in water. Wolves howled and wild cats screamed to each other in fright; leaves fell and died in solitude. When the birds dreamed of hunters aiming at them, the birds also cried out noisily in fright. The moon on the tenth day of the month was not full, dragging a thin mist across the tips of the tree branches in the forest. A mysterious lightness was everywhere, especially when the moonlight spread like sleet on the surface of the Muddy River. It was quiet, fragrant, and cool. A stork whistled for a long time before disappearing into the reeds; a pelican flew out, holding a fish in its mouth. With the current sliding by, fishes jumped into the light; the reflections of the trees in the waves were like green-colored, woven silk. Once in a while a hunting dog barked far away; then there was the sound of a gunshot. Yet the moon forever maintained its unruffled curtain of night, and the Muddy River seemed as tranquil as ever.

In the forest two people walked silently, their heavy footsteps trampling the dry grass and making a crackling sound. Not far from Li Chao's house human voices rose and fell. Elder Ts'ung turned and looked at Chin Sheng; the two simultaneously quickened their pace.

"For them it's orgies; for us it's survival. For a Japanese whore they want five hundred fox pelts in five colors. Where can you get pelts to match the right colors? Do we owe the pelts to them, or do they deserve the pelts? When they say one word, our heads roll. Do the foxes hide in our crotches that we can just deliver them whenever we choose? Today, he marries this whore and demands five hundred pelts; tomorrow he'll get a Korean bitch and ask for another five hundred; the day after, he'll get tired of her and get a Russian—screw his ancestors—another five hundred. Why should their orgy concern us? If we don't deliver, we'll be executed! Are our heads that cheap? Fathers and brothers, we, the one hundred and twenty hunting families in the Black Smoke Mountain area, have decided that first, we refuse to submit any fox pelts. Second, we will defend ourselves and resist the agents, and third, all the hunters will join the Fifth Route Peo-

ple's Revolutionary Army. Fathers and brothers, our fate is joined, our bitterness is identical, our enemy is the same. While our enemy wants us to die together, we demand to live together. Fathers and elders, on this point, we are in agreement. Let us rise up and go forth, and let those bastards see the strength of us poor mountaineers! We, men of the the White Deer Forest, are not filling for their cakes!"

"Wait a minute, wait a minute." It was a different, raspy voice. "Everyone should stay calm. In my opinion, when he talks of execution, he probably just wants to terrify us, perhaps not really to kill us all. When the time comes, if we plead for mercy and tell them our true situation, they'll probably—"

"Comrades, what we want now is to be masters of our fate! It isn't that when they retreat a step, we advance a step; or when they gain a step, we retreat a step. Nor should we kowtow to them and wait for them to chuck our chins. We must save ourselves, each one to manage his own destiny. We don't want any 'perhaps,' 'not really,' or 'probably.' What we want is survival and to be in charge of our own fate."

"We shouldn't act impetuously. If we do, the troops will come; we can't fight them. By then if we ask for forgiveness, it will be too late."

Chin Sheng pushed himself forward in the crowd. It was Wu Lao-t'ou nervously talking. Chin Sheng rushed forward, pushed the old man down onto a wooden stool, opened his mouth and said very loudly: "Why do we want to ask for mercy? We, men of the White Deer Forest, have never asked for mercy from anyone. Now as matters have come to this, we don't care if that Manchu ham, that rack of skin and bones, is or isn't going to marry that whore; nor should we give a damn if that fat pig, the agent-in-charge, has faked an imperial edict and profits from it. The truth is that the foxes have been cleaned out, that on both banks of the Muddy River our chief livelihood is fox hunting. At the end of this winter, you'll be lucky to see a fox hair. What will we have to live on? This year the fox pelts are expensive, but once they're all gone, we'll be gone with them. I think it's the agent-in-charge, that fat pig, who's cheating us of our pelts. All the stories about the imperial concubine are just bullshit."

"Yeah, he's cheating us, that's for sure. The people in the city haven't heard anything about any imperial concubine. And there's nothing in the papers." "We don't know if there is a wedding or not. He's simply taking advantage of the ignorance of us mountain folks. He thinks we'll believe everything he tells us. Those bastards!" The crowd became visibly agitated. "We won't deliver. No! Fox pelts are our life. If we give them up, we'll have to eat snow to survive this winter. With the pelts we can go anywhere to sell them. Why let him have the benefit, that bastard?"—so said Yang San-ch'iang.

Li Chao, upon seeing Elder Ts'ung getting up from his seat, walked to him and sought his opinion: "What do you think?" But when Elder Ts'ung asked Li Chao the same question, Li, stroking his goatee, smiled pleasantly. "What else but to rise up!" Walking in a bouncing gait, Li had the forthrightness of a Northeasterner. Elder Ts'ung frowned in a pensive mood. Standing by a tall imposing tree, he asked anxiously: "Who's the commander of the Fifth Route Army?" "General So-and-so." Still deep in thought was Elder Ts'ung.

"I think everyone's opinion has already been clearly expressed many times. Now, to sum up: those who intend to join the Fifth Route Army, please raise your hands! That's to say, if you intend to save your own lives, please raise your hands!" someone finally said. Like an aspen forest, the hands rose. But as Elder Ts'ung excitedly lowered his hand, he seemed to hear a faint voice. "Papa, if you go, the Japanese soldiers will come, and what will I do?" Violently shaking his arm, he muttered: "Don't worry, don't worry." His mind was troubled as he walked homeward, afraid to face his own daughter.

Mother and daughter were leaning on the door, awaiting him. The old woman walked vigorously toward him. Solicitously she asked: "Are you going to stand up and fight?" The daughter, weakly planting her head on his chest, also inquired: "Is it right, Papa?" He brushed her soft

face with his old beard. When the three finally, in their clumsiness, reached the door of their house, Shui-ch'in-tzu noticed how her father's color had changed. Letting out a hysterical cry, she ran toward the forest. The mother, her gaze disapprovingly trailing her daughter's vanishing shadow, muttered: "We must do it and you'd better join them. We've suffered enough, we might as well see it through this time." Tears welling in her eyes, she continued: "Take off your chaps and I'll mend them for you. I'll finish sewing your fur mittens tonight." Meanwhile she thought of cutting several extra pairs of mittens and of mending the wool socks for his Russian boots.

At this time two young lovers on the bank of the Muddy River were struggling and trembling over the conflicts of life and death, love and hate. "You must go; there's no reason for you to stay here. I can protect myself. I can use some charcoal to blacken my face," Shui-ch'in-tzu said nervously. The young man was silent.

The half moon set quickly; shadows on the surface of the water broadened; the mist slowly thickened. The two, forgetting their usual tenderness, continued to argue heatedly. Chin Sheng still wouldn't go. The young man threw the rock in his hand into the water, stood up, and ran away, leaving behind him the indistinct words, "I can't go." Shui-ch'in-tzu frowned, twisted her fingers, and stamped her feet on the sticky, slippery green moss.

The next day she rose early and looked for Chin Sheng. She did not care about how the others were going, about planning their defense, the security of their families, or the transport of fox pelts to Ch'ang-ch'un. She didn't care about any of that; she only looked for Chin Sheng everywhere.

Toward evening she dragged her weary body home; on the way home she met Yang San-ch'iang and learned that Chin Sheng had been sent as a representative to Black Smoke Mountain. Lying on the *k'ang,* she was both sad and happy, though she was not certain if he had decided to leave with the rest or not. She then thought, though it would be good that he go, what would she do if she were left alone? She decided not to think about it anymore, not to think about it. She fantasized being a general capable of protecting herself. Her ancestor was a man of principle; so must her lover be. The water of the Muddy River flows year after year; the water of the Muddy River is a good witness. She almost swore by the river water: "We will cleanse the water of the Muddy River with blood." She felt faint and weak, pretending to be asleep—to avoid her mother's endless consolations. Her eyes, blurred with tears, glistened in the dark.

The father was polishing his gun; the mother was sewing fur mittens. He wiped the hammer, the firing pin, the trigger, the grip, the safety, the mainspring, the barrel, and the chamber of the gun with oil. Expressionless, he had nothing to say to the mother. Several times she tried to speak but she controlled herself, unwilling to burden him with questions. Shui-ch'in-tzu thought that Chin Sheng would certainly come back early next morning. Perhaps he was on his way now. As soon as she heard the first cock crow, she decided that she would go to see him and bid him farewell. Dizzy, weary, and sad, she was sleepy; the entire world was quickly sealed in by darkness.

Early in the morning, the whole mountain was enclosed in an ominous silence. On ordinary days there would have been chimney smoke everywhere, but there was none, only the fog and the haze. On the prairie all that remained of the sedge grass was one solitary stalk, tall and busy, emitting thick moist air. Humidity congealed thickly around it, unpleasant and still, then floated upward. By this time the morning light had penetrated the mountain valleys; the smell of corn and buckwheat was in the air. A turtledove, nesting in a large oak tree, flew haltingly out once and then returned to nap.

The rolling hills and the crescent-shaped mounds were shrouded in mist. In the wild fields on the mountain slopes, the plants that had been weighed down by dewdrops now gradually sprang back. Water drops fell on the soil and awoke the preying mantis. After napping under the leaves,

the mantis groggily extended its spindley legs. The Muddy River flowed on rapidly, as if its water would flow away completely before the sun appeared on the horizon. Every heart was panting for the fate of the White Deer Forest. Every tongue was debating the correct course to take, waiting for the "Fat Pig" to arrive, ready to let him know how sharp was the sword that was hungry for his blood. Shui-ch'in-tzu was waiting to see Chin Sheng for the last time.

Patrols filled the reeds along the Muddy River; troops of men and horses gathered at South Mountain. The suicide squads hid in the houses. There was no news of Chin Sheng.

The sun rose higher on the horizon. On the prairie a white horse descended from the misty hills, bringing a message from the Black Smoke Mountain. It warned of the imminent arrival of a raiding troop. Fat Pig had already arrived at Black Smoke Mountain. The people there had welcomed him, lit incense, exploded fireworks, kowtowed, and paid other respects. In the house explosives had been buried beforehand and the house was surrounded by the suicide squad. Suddenly the blast! "Mr. Agent-in-Charge is now filing his grievances with the late Emperor Ch'ien-lung," concluded the messenger farcically. "Fellow comrades, if there is food and drink, please bring me some; in a moment, we'll be crawling on the stomach."[b]

A vengeful wind swept over the entire mountain range, the distant trees, the prairie, the forest. Every one awaited a greater victory. Shui-ch'in-tzu was waiting for Chin Sheng.

"Go back, go back!" Elder Ts'ung warned the inquiring women and children who had come out from the thatched houses. Putting his gun under his armpit, he headed for the river bank. "Is there any news?" the old man asked when he met Wang San-ch'iang. "The reconnaissance man on the front hasn't reported. I don't know if he's been captured. Another man has been sent. The areas around the Black Smoke Mountain and the Wild Pheasant Forest are already in combat. You can hear the fighting on the mountain top ahead."

---

[b]To fire a gun or rifle is "crawling on the stomach." Ready for combat.

"Hunh," the old man responded and soon disappeared into the reeds. The whole forest was quiet. Some time before noon a rumbling sound came from the South Forest, along with the barking of a wounded dog. Then, there was silence. The birds flew for a while, chirping and twittering, and then retreated in fright. A moment later from the Muddy River came the sounds of battle cries and one or two gunshots.

Shui-ch'in-tzu was especially weak today; she had searched for Chin Sheng since dawn of the day before. His whereabouts remained unknown. She felt he should see her at least one more time before going off to battle, but there was no sign of him. Perhaps she would never see him again. Was his voice among the battle cries, she wondered. She did her best to sharpen her hearing in order to hear the sound of her lover's voice.

Suddenly from outside the window arose the chaotic pounding of a horse's hooves. The mother, who had been listening to the distant sounds with her ear to the floor, now quickly got up. She grabbed a hunting gun and stood guard by the window, and at the same time her lips motioned her daughter to hide behind a large trunk. The horse galloped closer; the mother shot her gun; there was knocking on the door. "Shui-ch'in-tzu, Shui-ch'in-tzu," was the hurried call. The mother threw down her gun and hurriedly went to open the door. "*Ai, ai,* I thought it was someone else. You scared me to death." The daughter, realizing who it was, jumped out. The gunshots told her that the war was on and yet he had come back for her. She forgot that for two days and a night she had worried herself to death about him, eagerly awaiting his return, hoping to see him one more time. Now that he had returned, a feigned anger showed on her face, she behaving in front of her mother as if she had been humiliated. Her elderly father was now at the front fighting with all he had. She again remembered how Chin

Sheng had said: "I can't go." His words were not those that the men of the White Deer Forest swore by. Her tears fell. With a pale face she had pleaded and coaxed him—you should go. Innocently, her eyes drooped, praying for his safe return.

Chin Sheng's face reddened, he stammering: "I was sent to the Black Smoke Mountain, because the two sides had mixed groups of troops. To avoid any misunderstanding, I was dispatched there to coordinate activities, so I went!"

"That was very good," the woman answered in a cool manner.

"This is the wood-handled knife that I've brought for you." He fetched it from his pocket, a knife he had thrown for ten years. Once he threw it at a white fox and the fox took it into its den; two years later he retrieved it at the den's entrance. Actually he had a number of knives, whose function, however, had been taken over by bullets. He carried only this one with him.

He jumped on the horse, and after one backward glance, disappeared. The mother flattened her ear against the ground and listened for the sound of hooves to determine if Chin Sheng had left and if the gunshots were getting closer. Spurts of shots and battle cries rose again and again. She listened intently with all her imperfect hearing to judge the situation, for in this forest she had invested everything she had. Lying prostrated on the floor, she suddenly screamed: "Shui-ch'in-tzu, Shui-ch'in-tzu, the charcoal, the charcoal!" Shui-ch'in-tzu only held on to the wooden knife handle with a determined expression on her face, as if she had never thought of blackening her face with charcoal. Ahead of her she seemed to see the water of the Muddy River rushing to huge waves.

"No, Mama, give me the gun! Give me the gun!" Passionately she stuffed the knife into the folds of her jacket.

LU LING
(1913-   )

During the war years (1937–1945), the critic Hu Feng (1904–   ) was the leader of a leftist faction resolutely opposed to the literary policies enunciated from Yenan by Chou Yang and Mao Tse-tung. Mainly stationed in the Nationalist interior, that faction consisted of young writers who contributed regularly to Hu Feng's magazines *July* (*Ch'i-yüeh*) and *Hope* (*Hsi-wang*) and shared the same fate of imprisonment or worse (with the exception of one turncoat) when Hu himself was purged in 1955 after one last desperate attempt to dispute the literary infallibility of Chou and Mao. Lu Ling, the most talented and productive novelist of that faction, also exemplifies best Hu Feng's idea of a subjective writer who celebrates primitive and defiant energy battling unavailingly against the forces of darkness.

A native of Kiangsu, Lu Ling (pen name of Hsü Ssu-hsing) never finished high school and worked for a period of time in Szechwan first as a factory hand and then as a clerk in the same factory. This plus comparable experience elsewhere (for we know very little about his early life) accounts for the large number of factory workers and miners in his early fiction. He began to contribute to *July* in 1940, and his early stories, when collected under the title of *The Blessings of Youth* (*Ch'ing-ch'un ti chu-fu*), made his reputation. But it was the short novel, *The Hungry Kuo Su-o* (*Chi-o ti Kuo Su-o*, 1943), that created a sensation. For one thing, it was most probably the first genuine proletarian novel in modern Chinese literature, in the sense that, quite unlike the "proletarian" writers of the twenties and thirties, Lu Ling had lived the life of a factory worker and knew how such workers felt, talked, and lived. For another, the character Kuo Su-o, with her unashamed craving for sex and life, was a new type of heroine, at once an earth goddess of fierce sensuality and the worst victim of feudal society on record, one whose eventual punishment for the crime of adultery is truly too horrifying to read. Hungry for food, Kuo Su-o is also hungry for love, life, and justice, as are the two heroes in the novel. But they each fight alone, not united against their exploiters, which exemplifies a major weakness of Lu Ling's fiction in the eyes of the orthodox Communist critics.

Upon completing *The Hungry Kuo Su-o* in 1942, Lu Ling turned to his next major effort, a 1,400-page novel with a cast of over seventy characters. Part I was completed in 1943 and Part II in 1944, but the two-volume set of *The Children of Wealth* (*Ts'ai-chu ti erh-nü-men*) was not published until 1948, when most readers were too much victimized by runaway inflation to buy new books. And since the next year ushered in the new Communist era, with its own priorities in book publication, this novel was most probably little read despite Hu Feng's proclamation in its preface that it was the first modern Chinese novel to deserve the designation "epic."

During the forties, in addition to the three works already mentioned, Lu Ling turned out *The Snail's on the Thorn* (*Kua-niu tsai ching-chi shang*, a novella), *Waste Land on Fire* (*Jan-shao ti huang-ti*, a novel), *Skylark* (*Yun-ch'üeh*, a play), and three story collections. He remained quite active during the early fifties, writing reportage, short stories, and plays about the Korean War. But even as these works were being published, he received increasingly harsh attack in the press until he was purged. Like other members of the Hu Feng group, Lu Ling has only recently regained his freedom.

Some critics in the forties saw traits in Lu Ling's work that justify a comparison with D. H. Lawrence. Though the early Lu Ling is a rather turgid writer, stylistically far inferior, the two do share a lyrical, mystical regard for nature, an attentiveness to the darker forces inside us that prompt us to behave irrationally, and an insistence on the ultimate separateness of male beings from female. "The Coffins" (*Kuan-ts'ai*), an early story from *The Blessings of Youth*, focuses mainly on the meanness, rapacity, and animalistic energy of the feuding Wang brothers and their wives. The injured and insulted couple, Li-sao and her husband, play a smaller role and may appear baffling unless we see them as Lawrencian characters. Fighting her oppressors in her own timid way, Li-sao prefigures the more memorable Kuo Su-o.

C. T. H.

The Coffins

by Lu Ling

Translated by Jane Parish Yang

I

It was a well-to-do household, what rural folk call a country squire's home. It was two *li* from Lai-lung-ch'ang, situated on a steep slope overgrown with shrubs and weeds. The more level ground on the slope was walled in with pieces of slate piled up to form a barrier. The side of the mountain that had been cleared to grow vegetables overlooked a vast stretch of rice fields. Its old-fashioned watchtower stood erect and ungainly. Surrounding the tower and the cluster of low tiled houses beneath it was a plastered brick wall built along the contour of the uneven slope. The wall spread out from the compound to embrace greedily the expanse of land at its back. Five years ago that vacant land did not belong to this household. Now, planted as a vegetable garden, it gave forth vegetables and fruits in abundance with no recollection of the previous owner. Five years ago the former owner's whole family had died in a few days of an unknown illness, with the exception of a seven-year-old half-witted girl who drifted away to the mining district some ten *li* or so away. Half a month after the unfortunate incident, the heads of this household, Wang Te-ch'üan and his younger brother Wang Te-jun, announced to the neighbors a fabricated version of the earlier history of this fertile plot of vacant land. They did so in order to convince the others and above all

themselves of the land's novel history. At the same time, they quietly went about repairing the back gate and enlarging the wall.

From that time on, the household prospered. Prior to this incident, if Wang Te-ch'üan and Wang Te-jun had cared to remember, they had experienced fifteen years of poverty, hardship, and misfortune. They had both been young, only around twenty then; but in those days, being young or being old really made no difference, for they had to endure the same fate. Year after year of famine, bandits, and civil war devastated the village and completely destroyed the people's livelihood. Their father, a cruel, snobbish, and dissipated widower all his life, followed his sworn brothers of the clandestine Society of Brothers[1] to other provinces and didn't once look back at the family he had left behind. He died in a distant province. A younger brother, dreaming a hopeless dream, left home to join the army at that time. He traveled to lands they had never even dreamed of. He didn't write one letter to them.

But the two brothers, Te-ch'üan and Te-jun, having married, couldn't bear to leave their homeland to drift hopelessly elsewhere; so they stubbornly chose to stay with their disasters and indigence. Wang Te-ch'üan ran a dry goods store in Lai-lung, earning barely enough to feed his family. His younger brother raced wildly all over the neighboring towns collecting payments for

---

[1] *Ko-lao hui*, a secret society that flourished in the late Ch'ing period, initially founded with the express purpose of overthrowing the Manchu government. Its members were still active during the early Republican era.

loans and extorting other loans. Sometimes he also peddled sundries got on credit to help make ends meet.

But now, the days of privation had passed like the bad dream of a day long ago. Te-ch'üan and Te-jun didn't dwell on the past. Their sons and daughters were growing up to the age when they could put their hopes on them. They enjoyed the power and glory that comes with wealth. Their destitute neighbors, hoping to borrow ten or twenty dollars, often respectfully approached them to receive their disdain. Even those women who in the past had looked down on them, or the lower river people who had fled here because of the war, now came to pay their respects to their wives so that they could borrow some furniture or the grindstone. They would chatter excitedly on and on about the once-rich, extravagant world they had never known which had been destroyed in the fires of war.

Te-ch'üan was a hard-working, cautious man. He kept the interests of his family in mind at all times, bustling around until he was exhausted. People could watch him during this time strutting solemnly, straining to pull a huge, dry, tangled earth-colored tree stump toward home. It looked like the head of some monster, jerking violently as it was wrenched up onto the steps and emitting a hideous cry, unwilling to advance any further. He'd be forced to modify his imposing rigid posture and raise his arms up to embrace it. Other times he'd carefully roll up his sleeves and hack away with a broken bamboo staff in the back yard to loosen up bean stalks that someone had drenched with water. This kind of physical labor made him happy, strengthening his cool pride, and caused him to look down on the rest of the world, despising those who didn't labor or who labored on worthless tasks. His younger brother, in his eyes, was lazy and insolent, one of the ones whom he despised.

But Te-jun had equal disdain for his elder brother. He disapproved of his brother's cunning and stinginess and his cruelty to the tenants. He thought he hardly possessed any human qualities. On the other hand, Wang Te-jun lived a dissolute life of his own, indifferent to criticism. He operated an opium den in his back room. He sold vegetable oil, *t'ung* oil,[2] and other commodities that were easily salable. When he bargained with his customers, he raised his voice rudely and wouldn't let them argue. Everyone who had dealt with him in the past marveled that such a dissipated man still had so much energy!

Their wives proved to be perfect matches for them. Te-ch'üan's wife was plump and beady-eyed with a double chin, and had the kind of face described by her fellow villagers as "prosperous-looking." She was as crafty as she was proud. Te-jun's wife was a shrew, dissolute and malicious. The two women often quarreled. When they did, Wang Te-ch'üan's wife always first snorted a deep "humph" in her irritating sort of way and slapped the table with her fleshy palms. The object of her scorn, Te-jun's wife, would then let loose a torrent of abuse from the back of the house in her high-pitched, excited voice. She accompanied her complaints with a rhythmic slapping of her hands together as if she were beating time to a melody. Then Te-ch'üan's wife would coolly walk into the house and, without making a sound, begin to mend clothes or twist hemp into thread.

The back room where Te-jun lived was crowded every night with opium smokers. The store owners and landlords who came here brought their thick phlegm, quiet anger, and cynical smiles with them. They talked business and relayed gossip on whose daughter was sleeping with whom. At such times, because Te-jun's wife didn't trust their plump maid Su-fen to prepare the midnight snack for the smokers, she had to busy herself in the kitchen. She joined excitedly in the conversations, cursing Wu-erh's wife for cutting the squares of beancurd too small, as she plucked feathers from the chicken submerged in a pot of hot water. Her children welcomed this

---

[2] *T'ung,* a general term for paulownia or phoenix tree. *T'ung* is a special kind of tree whose seeds contain 30 to 40 percent oil content, used mainly for making lacquer.

time of night because they could get a little spending money and, led by the oldest, Hei Wa-tzu, they would go down to the stand on the corner to buy peanuts to eat. They acted as if it were some kind of festival, yipping like puppies and turning somersaults on the ground.

Late at night, when the younger brother's guests were about to leave and sometimes a second group was coming, the older brother would just be finishing going over the account books. He would lock the drawer, carefully wiping clean the white lacquered surface after recording the day's creditors or the merchandise to be bought for the following day. As he left the store for home, he would be deep in thought and walk dumbly along the dark road, lightly sucking on his long pipe. He would hold his head low, his left hand repeatedly tugging at his sleeve, like a man in winter afraid of the cold—an old habit. His gaunt, sheeplike face was every now and then revealed by the flash of the pipe. It was an expressionless face with insolence frozen on it.

By the time he neared home, at the point where the stubby watchtower became visible out of the shadow of the surrounding trees, from force of habit he would take the pipe out of his parched mouth and a contented smile would come to his lips. But strangely, as soon as he entered the gate, he would become displeased and begin to seethe inside. Hearing the persistent low buzzing noise coming from the back room where his younger brother's patrons were, he would angrily spit out a wad of phlegm onto the ground. But if it fell onto the path, he would ruefully return to press it into the earth under the sole of his cloth shoe.

Though he despised his brother as much as the spit in the road, he still went over to the opium den every evening to chat with the guests, sometimes even buying a turn at the opium pipe himself, doing what a respected head of a family ought to do.

This prosperous household would not retire until well past midnight every night when the neighbors had long since gone to sleep. At that time even the low, dull, and monotonous sound of soybeans being ground in the house of Wu-ehr-sao,[3] who stayed up the latest, had been swallowed up by the silent night. At that time, the household's gate would open and guests, their cheeks aglow, would patter down the path lighting their way with paper lanterns. Following the lanterns' dim light, they would disappear into the fields, scattering life's fatigue behind them.

II

Wang Te-ch'üan arose early and inspected their possessions in the courtyard. Having finished, he passed through the watchtower, preparing to go out to the back yard to count the oranges on the trees. But a weak cry caused him to stop in the filthy corridor.

He saw the maid, Li-sao, the wife of a tenant carpenter, squatting down, one hand gripping a bamboo basket at her feet which was full of corn, the other hand raised high, covering her eyes. Her hair was disheveled, the back of her shirt ripped into shreds. The shreds lightly fluttered back and forth as she cried.

He stamped his feet angrily. Li-sao turned around and hurriedly scrambled to her feet, turning her tear-stained, swollen face to him.

"What are you up to this early in the morning?"

"Master—"

"Where did you get this corn?" He pulled up his sleeve and bent over to grab a fistful. He tossed the shiny, dark yellow corn in his palm. "These aren't bad, huh?"

"I bought them by the river, Master," Li-sao stuttered as she wiped away her tears.

"What? This early and you've already gone to the river and back? Thirty *li*?"

"I went last night."

"Nonsense. How much was this a bushel?"

"Only sixty-five." A satisfied smile appeared on the poor woman's face. "At the market it sells for ninety."

Te-ch'üan glared at her, then laughed uncomfortably.

---

[3] Lit., the wife of one's older brother; often used, as here, as a polite or convenient title for a friend's wife.

"Bring me two bushels tomorrow."

The woman sucked in her breath and was silent.

"What are you crying for?" The master had just remembered his original question.

"Me?" Li-sao began to cry again, but then stuck out her lip, and contained herself. "I didn't have anything to eat at all yesterday. I can't move this bushel any further."

"What about your old man? He's building a house. Why hasn't he come back?"

The woman stared dumbly at the master with frightened bloodshot eyes. "The army took him away." She screamed, "Master, lend me twenty dollars, huh?"

When Te-ch'üan heard money mentioned, his beady eyes bulged angrily. The carpenter Li Jung-ch'eng owed him a year's rent. Even though she was working for them for two years as a laborer, that still wouldn't pay off the debt. Besides, he even let them live in the basement of the watchtower.

"And where would I get the money, Li-sao?" he said, then spoke to her in a low voice. "You hurry up and tell Li Jung-ch'eng to come back here! This can't go on much longer. I don't have any money, I'm a poor man too."

He was moved by his own mention of poverty, and took the occasion to air what was bothering him. His face paled uneasily, his lips trembled. But he saw immediately that this woman had simply not paid any attention to what he had said. She stupidly raised her eyes toward the golden oranges on the tree in the back yard, glittering in the bright autumn sunlight.

"Master," she began again, screwing up her puffy face, mechanically pleading with him. "Rescue my husband."

"Humph. What a joke. What can I do about important government matters like that? Those thieving army brigades."

Li-sao no longer looked at him, but raised the basket and continued on to the watchtower. She went blindly about her chores: gathering firewood, emptying the corn into the pot, crying all the while. She was a woman given to daydreaming. Even when hard labor made her tired and

weak, and despair blinded her to the events around her, she had only to stare off into space and she would begin to daydream.

She would dream the steamboat in the river was heading for the flourishing city and taking those lovable country folk with it. And the one who stood out from them all was her bad-tempered, cowardly husband. She dreamed they were on a battlefield, an endless plain bathed in blood. Overhead, planes circled like eagles. But suddenly the dry grass scorching her hands brought her back to reality. She rubbed her eyes and leaned down to press her swollen face near the opening of the stove to blow weakly at the fire.

Te-ch'üan yelled toward the stone house from the back yard: "Li-sao, hurry up and finish eating. You have to cook the hog's feed. Your pot—"

He grumbled to himself as he walked to the orange grove, raised up his long pipe, and counted the oranges.

"One, two, three, four, five, six, seven, eight . . . fifteen altogether. Those sons-of-bitches are hiding behind the leaves!" He laughed happily, exposing his yellowed teeth. But having counted three times, he was still five short.

"It must be that little half-breed Hei Wa-tzu who did it! Little bastard—who knows whose bastard he really is? 'Not teaching the son is the fault of the father,' " he reflected angrily, sighing and squinting into the lovely autumn sun. Hei Wa-tzu was Te-jun's eldest son, thirteen this year. He had a special talent for swiping oranges. By Te-ch'üan's count, he had already stolen forty-two and they weren't even ripe yet.

That made Te-ch'üan angry. No doubt about it, he owned this line of orange trees. Like everything else he owned, they had a history behind them that he prized. Two years ago, because of the war, people from other provinces had fled here. Houses were built up on the opposite slope. When they built brick kilns on the slope, he moved the trees to his house. Before that, these large young trees had stood guard on the slope as if they were its brothers. The kiln's owner wanted to chop them down. When he found out about it, he thought it would be a pity, so he took the matter up with his family. "Whoever moves these six trees home can have the oranges when they bear fruit. They're certain to bear a crop." He had spoken solemnly, pulling at his left sleeve: "Those lower river people are too stupid, they don't understand at all. But I'm thinking of planting them in the back yard of the house. They'll be sure to bring us prosperity." But the main object of this proposal, his younger brother, coolly rolled his eyes in disgust. Growing angry, Te-ch'üan immediately took some laborers over to move the trees home. He swore that even if they never bore fruit, he wanted to take care of them, to cultivate them for timber and make up for this insult. But the second year they gave him hope, bearing twelve small green oranges. He had won. He watered and fertilized them and dug up the ground himself, and this year all at once they began to thrive, bearing more than a hundred oranges. But Te-jun's wife and children picked them to eat when they were still green. It was as if these six beautiful trees had originally been growing on the common ground between the two houses and had been cultivated by the sweat of both men, as if Te-ch'üan's words in the past had never been spoken.

He once again memorized the number of oranges—altogether sixty-three. Then, deep in thought, wearing a troubled expression on his face because of Li-sao's early morning crying, he returned to the house for breakfast.

There he ran into his younger brother, who had just gotten up. Te-jun, his shirt thrown over his shoulder, abruptly spit on the ground and rushed past him toward the door as if he were a wooden post. Grunting an acknowledgment of his presence, the younger brother stood in the doorway, pulled down his pants, and urinated freely onto the steps.

Te-ch'üan stood stiffly behind him and looked on.

"Hei Wa-tzu stole some more oranges. And they were ripe ones too." [4] As his brother turned around, he blurted out these words, though he had originally intended to add a word of admonition. Moreover, he felt rather embarrassed that his voice had sounded so feeble and submissive.

Thus his earlier distressed, rigid expression immediately returned to cloud his features.

The sockets of his younger brother's eyes still betrayed darkish lines from the debauch of the previous night. He appeared sullen and dazed, acknowledging his brother's words only with an abrupt snort. As his brother was about to speak again, he brushed past him and headed into the small yard, his shirt unbuttoned and his breath offensive.

"Mother's! [5] Bring me some water!"

Standing beside the rock cistern, he shouted back toward the house.

Te-ch'üan was stunned. During breakfast, his silent, angry face made his wife and children uneasy. Finally, he told his wife about the incident concerning the oranges. His wife listened, responding only by setting down her bowl to wipe her mouth. Then, picking the bowl up again, she began eating without changing her expression, as if she were telling him this incident wasn't worth disturbing their meal over. But when he related what had gone on with Li-sao, she wrinkled her brow.

By the time Te-jun was eating breakfast, his older brother had already walked down to the stone-paved road, tugging continuously at his sleeve (as if he were using the cuff to aid in his meditation), and headed for town. The younger brother ate a huge amount. He worked his square dark mouth up and down as he noisily chomped and gulped his food. His red tongue sprayed spit as he licked the bowl and then his own lips, like a wild beast gnawing at a bone. Underneath the table, his legs tensed and shook from the physical pleasure of his eating. Hei Wa-tzu, fearful that his father's knuckle would fall on his head, uneasily shifted himself to the far end of the bench. His father really had eaten too much, but still looked over the dishes on the table in his insatiable manner and plucked up a large hot pepper, dipped it in fermented wheat sauce, and stuffed it in his mouth. Finally, he squinted his sore, tired eyes and spoke to Hei Wa-tzu.

"So, you dog, you stole—oranges again!" He

---

[4] Earlier, the oranges in Wang Te-ch'üan's opinion "weren't even ripe yet." Here they became "the ripe ones." Wang is apparently twisting the facts to emphasize that what Hei Wa-tzu had stolen was worth money.

[5] A profanity.

stuck out his chest and burped, "Mother's. I'm full."

Hei Wa-tzu suddenly understood him, and stared excitedly at him, a beastly grin on his face.

"Hurry and eat!" The mother rapped the child's skull with her chopsticks. "Those oranges don't just belong to them, anyway," she shouted at Wang Te-jun. "Why can't we eat them? Don't try to put on airs with us!" She stuck out her lip, laughing disdainfully at the elder brother's stinginess.

"Of course we can eat them." Te-jun smiled contentedly, and opened his oily yellow eyes, now kindling with desire. "Well, you watch out! I'll screw the brains out of you tonight!"

"Fart!" The woman giggled excitedly, then raising her voice, yelled toward the back room: "Su-fen, you're as lazy as a pig. Come clear off the table!"

"Women must always act like women. You insolent slut!" The man stood up, stretched, then yawned. "What's all the fuss over a few orange trees, anyway? They aren't worth a damn! That old bag of bones, he's so cheap he won't even spend money to buy salt! I just can't stand—" He stopped, and looked up at the dazzling sky overhead. "I hope the Jap planes won't be coming again today. Oh, I've got something to tell you." He bent over, covered his hairy mouth with his hand and drew near her ear. "Old Li was dragged off to join the army."

The woman put on a serious expression for a moment, and then burst out into a gale of laughter. "Ha! Taken away! Then that bastard won't get his goddam rent money!" He licked her smelly ear; she raised up her hand to slap him, laughing uncontrollably. Hei Wa-tzu, confused, stared at them.

After a while, he picked up a thick staff and slowly walked to the back yard to begin his day's work. He walked slowly under the autumn sun, lazily heading wherever his feet took him. He had things to do in any direction he might go. There were quarrels, newly minted gossip, and the unsavory village news awaiting him everywhere he might go.

His wife, having given the maid instructions, hurried after him.

After husband and wife had gone, the plump maid Su-fen sneaked out to the back yard, grasping her belly as she went, and quickly ran through the sun-soaked yard to the basement of the brick tower. Li-sao's corn wasn't ready yet. She should have ground the corn first, but she had absent-mindedly just dumped the corn whole into the pot. Not knowing quite what to do with the tough kernels, she was becoming desperate.

Su-fen went in and excitedly called to her, "Li-sao, are you all right?"

Li-sao stared at her in hate, wearily shutting her eyes, and then cried out, "I ate some stones, I'm going to die. Die!"

Plump Su-fen sighed, retreated a step, then advanced toward her three steps. Taking a bundle wrapped in leaves out of her dirty apron, she opened it. A warm heap of rice topped with pickled vegetables appeared before the starved woman's eyes.

"Eat it," Su-fen urged happily.

Li-sao threw up her hands, thrashing at the air. "Aren't you afraid they'll find out?" she said, and was about to continue but her mouth was filled with rice. She wolfed it down like a wild woman.

Having finished, she stared absently at her companion. She shouted, then wept. "Have you eaten, Su-fen? I ate your breakfast. And I used to hate you too."

"I've eaten," the plump young girl replied, rubbing her coarse hands together uneasily, her face flushed with happiness. "Really. I've already eaten. I just finished. I have to go hoe the beans now. I've already eaten." She gestured with her hand, then quickly left the house.

III

Wang Te-ch'üan always attended to his affairs carefully and steadily. If he weren't going every day to take a look at his lands, he would be going to town to take care of business. His circumstances began to improve. He was glad that his ventures were all succeeding. The month before he had bought three hundred catties of vegetable oil. Just within the past two weeks the price had shot up dramatically. So he managed the business with greater care and on harsher terms. He would stand adamant over even ten cents in bargaining with the housewives from other provinces and the wives of the workers in the brick factory and coal mines. In mid-October he hired a reliable young distant cousin to be his clerk and relieve him of petty chores. He then spent some of his time in an old rattan chair at home, sunning himself and puffing on his water pipe. This was what he had dreamed of for many years: to become celebrated as a powerful master with time on his hands, the respected elder of his household. But he was unable to savor it for very long. It made him restless. He had to go twine hemp into rope or count the heaps of toilet paper or else he would feel uncomfortable, as if he had become ill. On his thin yellow face there always appeared a look of helpless stupidity. Worries he had brought upon himself plagued him, making him struggle without dignity like a carp trapped in a muddy pool of water. His stubbornness and pride separated him from his neighbors. His neighbors looked down on him for leading such a wretched existence when in fact he could afford to live a better one.

As for his younger brother, though it seemed as if he hadn't a care in the world, he ran into some trouble during this time too. The local authorities carried out strict searches and the tiny opium den was threatened. His voice wasn't raised quite so loud anymore. He didn't know for what reason, but many times when he quarreled he didn't win. As he walked along, he appeared lost in thought, but this meditation was more real than his older brother's. In sum, even if he were to be defeated, like a smuggler shot down on the border, he still wasn't as pitiful as his older brother, a man inside his own home frightened by his own shadow.

But half a month passed and nothing out of the ordinary happened. Everything went along peacefully as before.

One evening, Wang Te-jun's opium-smoking patrons had just left when a strong wind came up. It was like a mouth of iron teeth gnawing at the rafters, causing the watchtower and other buildings to shake. Te-jun was a heavy sleeper; if he weren't slapped on the head, he would never wake up. But Te-ch'üan wasn't the same at all. When the strong wind arose and rattled the door just once, he couldn't sleep. He lit a lamp and went outside, protecting the flame with his hand, looking all around, as he thought he had heard a swishing noise of somebody walking. He saw nothing. But as he was looking around, his hardened heart was secretly opened a bit by the severe, forbidding scene impressed upon him. In the cold night, he gained a fresh perspective on all about him, suddenly parted from his worries and the muddled state of his whole life. But as he hunched over and took another look, everything that carried the record of his hard, bitter life came back to him again, speaking to him without words: the old, worn table said, "Since the day you were married, I've been here. I was made by that pock-marked carpenter who was later killed." The black lacquer plaque inscribed with the words "Prolific writings" and "Gathering herbs," hanging on the left wall of the main hall, said: "Your grandfather, your grandfather." The broken stone cistern in the yard also spoke with similar words. Even the black brick building standing out above the fence and the huge *t'ung* tree at its back, screeching in the gale, angrily yet sorrowfully wept: "We've been here for two hundred years. Two hundred years! Your life will never get better. You're going to lose everything!"

The master was stunned. The dark, dusty furnishings, the sturdy old trees—they could live for so many years! But in this ceaselessly changing world, he went blindly on with his business, vainly wearing down his life, not giving them a minute's notice. Yet they were the real rulers!

He grew frightened. A gust of wind blew out the lamp. He leaned against the doorway in remorse, pitifully muddled sounds coming from his lips.

He didn't know why, but putting down the extinguished lamp, he passed through the small patio, opened the gate, and walked down the steps into the big yard. Then he thought he heard a rustling noise from the corner of the yard that the gusts of wind were covering up. He walked nearer. The sound wasn't his imagination. He saw a black shadow darting around like a dog. The wind blew open his shirt. He suddenly trembled with fear.

"Who is it?" he called out sharply. Hearing this

sound, like someone believing in his own uprightness, he grew more courageous and slowly crossed the yard toward it.

The black shadow emitted a piercing screech and, standing up, turned into a human form. He immediately recognized the hapless Li-sao. He stepped closer, and discovered an overturned basket to one side. But he didn't speak at first (if he had been his younger brother, he would have immediately become furious and begun beating her). He only bent down to investigate. In the basket and spilled over the ground were pieces of coal stolen from a pile at the base of the wall, plus several sticks of kindling.

He fingered the coal, sternly questioning Li-sao. "Just what are you doing?"

"It's for the stove," the unfortunate woman cried out in reply.

"I just bought it today. Forty-eight dollars' worth!" He pointed to the wall, his voice harsh. "How could you?"

A gust of wind struck his face, forcing him to close his mouth. "How could you take these for fuel?" he shouted, shielding his mouth with his hand.

Li-sao trembled all over like a reed. Her initial cries of terror changed to mournful sobbing, and spreading out her hands, then drawing them together, she knelt before her master.

"Save me! Forgive me! This coal . . ." She clutched his gown and wept, her weeping and pleading meant not so much to obtain his forgiveness as to change her hopeless pain into an ardent outpouring of grievances.

Wang Te-ch'üan was shaken, but he immediately recovered, extracted himself from her grip, and retreated a step. Crying upset him, making him lose his composure. Another strong gust of wind hit the wall of the house, as if whistling up the muzzle of a hidden gun.

The gust passed, and his anger rose. He began his examination.

"Why were you stealing coal? Answer me! Stand up!"

Li-sao weakly scrambled to her feet and stood woodenly before him, silent for a long time. "Uh, uh, ah, ah, . . . oh," her tongue clucked indistinctly. She then took the master completely by surprise by screaming at him as if she had just awakened from a nightmare: "Master, I'm so scared that Old Li's been shot. I had a dream, got up, and wanted to take a little coal, so I went out. I don't know. The wind was so strong!"

"Nonsense, you witch!" Wang Te-ch'üan shouted back.

"I was freezing to death. I got sick from the cold. I wanted to start a fire." She lied calmly, as if she believed it herself.

Her tone of voice infuriated Te-ch'üan. When angered, he tended to panic and not know what to do next. Finally, he picked up a piece of wood from the ground and aimed at the thief's shoulders.

The servant woman, struck by the stick, began to cry and fled toward the stone house. Te-ch'üan slowly pursued her, as if he were chasing a dog who had no hope of escape. He went right into the house.

"What do you have to say for yourself?" He ground his teeth and whined, "You stole from me, you lawless creature!" His eyes darted around the room, searching for something he could take away with him. It wasn't good moral conduct to beat a defenseless woman in the middle of the night, so he thought he might as well take away her only new gown. He inched over to the corner of the room, took the blue gown off the hook as if he were removing his own garment, and stuck it under his arm. But at that very instant, the frightened Li-sao, coiled in the other corner, madly sprang at him. She clutched him tightly, silently trying to win back her last possession. When she couldn't rip it from his grasp, she began to butt him with her head and bite him. They tugged at the blue gown for a minute until Te-ch'üan, overcome with fear, let go. He scurried out of the house as she stooped to pick up a broken bowl to throw at him. As he ran up the steps to the main house, he could hear the bowl crash behind him in the yard.

"She's mad—mad!" He shrank back, rubbing his chest.

The strong wind whistled overhead, then whooshed down to earth. The stone house shook violently, and rattled tiles off the roof. A splitting sound pierced the silence. A huge branch from the *t'ung* tree outside the wall crashed to the ground. Wang Te-ch'üan, terrified, clutched at his head, and gazed back at the stone house. The wind died down. The heavens appeared calm and ashen. The sky was larger than just a second before. The shattered trunk of the *t'ung* tree, bereft of leaves and tall branch, rose silently into the sky.

The master of the household fled inside the house.

Early the next morning, his serenity regained, he quietly stole out the back door.

The *t'ung* tree, having lost one of its main branches, seemed to have had its arm chopped off. The branch was attached to the main trunk by only a large strip of whitish bark. The dark luxuriant leaves and tiny brown nuts were scattered on the ground, rustling in the cool morning breeze. A section of rotted wood had fallen on the vegetable garden, one end thrust in a puddle of water as if searching for a little moisture.

At first Wang Te-ch'üan had been bitter and depressed, thinking it a bad omen. But later he came to feel quite lucky, since if the hollow branch had fallen on the other side, it would have crushed the wall and pigpen. In the end, he suddenly discovered an unsuspected usefulness in this section of wood; he was overjoyed and completely forgot about the unpleasantness of the night before.

He rubbed the sleep out of his eyes, set his jaw firmly, and raced around the snapped-off branch. He measured its length and width with his water pipe.

"This is mine!" he thought to himself gratefully, because he was sure that his younger brother wouldn't have thought of it. "Rotten"—he ripped off the rotting bark—"but this is mine. It doesn't matter that it's rotten."

He had many reasons he couldn't put into words that proved the branch was his. Then he thought of its use: the village and countryside had been in need of some medium-priced coffins lately. This section of wood was enough to enclose eight corpses, and enough to earn him a thousand dollars.

That afternoon three carpenters came, took the wood, and began sawing away at it. But, hearing the low whining sound, he slipped back into that pitiful worrying he was subject to. His high spirits vanished. When it was turning into reality, when the captivating notion of hope turned into a weary progression of reality under the ashen sky, the ominous shadow that had come the night before reappeared to him. His mind became fuddled; he felt hollow inside, dejected. What was there to get excited about? The branch had fallen over. It belonged to him. Of course it should be made into coffins!

Besides, gripped by that stark impression, he didn't dare tell his shrewd wife what had happened that night. He only informed her dispiritedly that to make coffins from such a piece of timber was a worthwhile venture. But her attitude in the matter, like her attitude toward anything that was an actuality and taking place before her, was to treat it as nothing especially interesting. Nothing seemed to startle her or pierce her cold, indifferent heart. When she heard the carpenters were coming, she only raised her head slightly from her bent-over position winding hemp thread. In a low voice, she slowly instructed her children to tell them to return all the excess wood scraps and pieces and not let anyone else get them.

IV

During all this Te-jun and his wife appeared magnanimous, as if nothing had happened they should feel wronged over. They spent the whole afternoon roaming around outside. Even Hei Wa-tzu had run off somewhere. He hadn't stolen any oranges that day, nor did he come near the bustling scene where the coffins were being made.

This silence perplexed Te-ch'üan. He now felt he had no good reason to keep this piece of timber all to himself, but he hadn't the courage to make acknowledgments that worked to his own disadvantage. He began to hate Te-jun, blaming his vacillation on his brother's silence. The wood was his; yet his brother's long silence made him feel as if it weren't rightly his. Rage blinded him.

But the incident that occurred the next day was especially infuriating.

After breakfast he had planned to go to town. Just outside the gate, however, he saw Te-jun and his three hired hands sawing down the old walnut tree. He stopped short and, white with rage, crossed over to where they were.

The younger brother wore a small felt cap, and snuffled through his nose. He spoke to the workmen in a hoarse but happy voice: "This would cost three hundred dollars in the market."

Te-ch'üan shouted at him, "What are you doing? That's a lucky tree!"

The younger brother turned around, glanced disdainfully at his brother, took his hand out of the pocket of his long gown, and bent over to blow his nose.

"It's to make a coffin." He spoke, holding his nostril. "The wood is excellent."

"Well, that's just fine, brother." The older brother smiled uncomfortably. "Let's go into the house. I have something to discuss with you."

"Make it tomorrow."

The older brother motioned at the sky with his water pipe, staring at him gravely. "You should have at least told me before you started."

"Tell you? Your wood is white and rotten!" The younger brother laughed. "This one's mine—red wood and fragrant!"

"You're just trying to make trouble!"

"Oh, so you can commit arson but I can't light a lamp, huh? Let's divide the household," Wang Te-jun replied, and leaped onto a nearby rock.

Te-ch'üan considered this bitterly as he watched them saw through the slowly canting old walnut tree. Like a scrawny puppet's, his arm tensed and his body jerked. He screamed passionately, "You loafer! You good-for-nothing! Are you out of your mind? You want to divide the household, huh? Just what kind of a household do you have? And do you know what kind of a family we are? Have our ancestors mistreated you in any way?"

He bowed curtly, then raised his poor head, tears welling in his eyes.

But Te-jun, whiskers bristling with rage, chanted piously: "Ancestors! Ancestors like hell! I know as much as anyone what is right and what is wrong, and I can tell you that we're all evil men!" He was shaking. "Who did that *t'ung* tree belong to? And you made it into coffins!"

"The storm blew it down!"

"The ancestors sent that storm to test your resolution!" The older brother trembled. The younger brother continued to shout. "I'm a common man, straightforward through and through. I've never harbored an evil thought, but if you want to fight, here are two fists to meet you . . ." He stared at his fists, his face contorted. "I can't stand your goddam crooked ways! You bastards have no sense of what's fair. Shameless bastards." He jumped down from the rock and turned toward the hired hands: "Go ahead and cut it down!"

The walnut tree swayed and crashed to the ground. Te-ch'üan returned home in a daze.

"Coffins! Coffins! Ancestors! Coffins!" he mumbled, heading toward the yard, but then he stopped abruptly. The workmen were ruining the timber. "Be more careful. Make sure you don't waste anything." He pointed at a piece of rotten wood and shouted angrily. "You can patch this up. Just plane the top!"

Without finishing, he ran blindly into the house and settled into the old rattan chair. He sighed.

"I won't give in. This is terrible, terrible." His fear turned into the bitterness of defeat. He hung his head. "Damn if I don't . . . No, I'm still going to do it. I'll get another carpenter. I'm not that easy to push around!"

Li-sao came in. She put her hands in her pockets and stopped short. "Master!" she called out happily.

Te-ch'üan looked at her in surprise. He asked sharply, "And what are you so happy about?"

"Old Li's come home."

The master got stiffly to his feet, reflected a moment, then demanded, "What did he come back for?"

"He knocked on the door just as the sun was coming up. Master—" She hesitated.

Te-ch'üan quickly remembered he could dispense with hiring another carpenter. "Tell him to come here right away!" He showed his teeth as he smiled, and gestured to her.

She sighed and wiped away her tears, gazing steadily at him. "His back's sore and swollen, and his chest hurts. He's sick."

"Then why did he come back?" Te-ch'üan asked sharply.

"He escaped from the city." The woman smiled timidly, almost obscenely trying to curry favor. "He wants to borrow twenty dollars from you."

"Rubbish!" Te-ch'üan replied. His neck swelled and he stretched it, as if something were hard to swallow. He just stopped himself from calling her a shameless bitch. "Tell Old Li to come here," he croaked finally.

Li-sao retreated, hanging her head.

Wang Te-ch'üan sat quietly in the rattan chair and began to smoke. After his quarrel with Li-sao, the regimen of daily life was helping him conquer the confusion in his mind. He could think about things, returning to more normal worries. The way of life before him still seemed gray and desolate. His brother the opium den owner and the thick smoke blown from the mouths of his customers quickly vanished.

"This doesn't make any difference. Wait and see," he thought. "It shouldn't bother me that he's taken advantage of me. He won't be able to live a good life. He won't make it. He sure won't," he mused bitterly, seeking a victory in his own mind. "You're not going to succeed! But me, why, tomorrow I'll put Old Li to work. That's it. Put him to work!"

Wang Te-jun's walnut coffins, altogether four of them, were ready in two days. His courageous wife ordered Hei Wa-tzu to collect the wood scraps. He cleaned out the work area with unusual alacrity and thoroughness. As soon as a piece fell from one ax, he would race over and snatch it up, oblivious to the sharp blade. At the same time, he kept a sharp eye on the other ax.

The coffins were laid out between the watchtower and the wall, so that the yard shrank in size and seemed at once an industrious and a gloomy place. Wang Te-jun's coffins, exactly as he had boasted, were a reddish color. Wang Te-ch'üan's were a sickly white, and, because the wood wasn't all of a piece, they appeared pocked all over. The coffins stood bloodthirstily gaping at the sky, yawning like weary beasts, guarding this special corner of the yard.[6]

V

Li-sao's husband, the carpenter Li Jung-ch'eng, had been seized by two soldiers as he ran down a hill to relieve himself near the construction site in a village ten *li* away. He planned his escape even as he was forced to go with them, but was shot and wounded in the stomach by the soldiers. After one month, he did succeed in fleeing the town.

He was an ill-tempered, ornery creature with strong but formless desires, lacking in willpower. He was also in poor health. Despite his wound, he had been crazy enough to make the hundred-*li* journey home in one effort, unwilling to rest along the way. When he reached his poor but well-loved dwelling, he was half conscious and could move no further. Li-sao happily lay down next to him and spent the whole night murmuring, "Thank the Buddha, he's come back. He's come back."

The next day she somehow managed to borrow a few dollars, but the carpenter ranted and raved so much that the Taoist priest, who was acting as doctor, was frightened away. He told her not to bother with doctors. All he needed was some liquor to mix herbal medicines with and he'd be fine. He was sure he wasn't really seriously ill, just chilled from the cold. Li-sao knew her husband's temperament and didn't tell him Wang Te-ch'üan wanted him to get to work right away. She spent the whole day slipping off to run errands for him, going into town, asking around to find out if he was in danger of being caught. The carpenter was paranoid, imagining that the whole world was against him and out to get him, even though his own courage and foolhardiness had enabled him

---

[6] Lit., the coffins have their "fierce foreheads protruding, their sharp chins held high—the kind of gesture that belongs to the most bloodthirsty of men." For the sake of clarity, the editors have recast this sentence.

to escape when the violent world tried to attack him.

This evening, he seemed almost well, and took a stroll in the yard. But he returned in a hurry.

"Coffins? Which bastard do they belong to? They're opening up a coffin shop?" He asked his wife.

She answered him in a tone calculated to please him. She told him about the *t'ung* tree's being blown over, the brothers' quarrel. Finally, she mentioned that Wang Te-ch'üan had humiliated her.

She sat down, placed her hands on her knees, and thought back on it. That stormy night had made a deep impression on her, but she couldn't put it into words. In trying to describe it truthfully, she became more and more mixed up. "I said, I'd come to get a little coal to make a fire. I'd been thinking. You always liked a good fire." She glanced at her husband. "Then Wang Te-ch'üan came. I knelt down and begged, but he beat me. The wind was so strong. You were still in the city then, right? Ah. He tried to steal my clothes. I fought back with all my strength. I threw a bowl at him and he ran away. Right then the wind blew the big tree down—bang! There it went." She looked outside and began to cry. "It was so awful! I was left all alone with no one to help me."

The carpenter became agitated. He looked at her amazed, then yelled out, "What did Wang Te-ch'üan do? Speak clearly."

"He beat me up!"

"Say that again. He did what?" The carpenter was enraged, his teeth showing. "I wasn't here and look what you were doing! You ugly old bat. You witch! And if I had been killed, then what?"

Li-sao cried weakly. The carpenter, blindly jealous, sprang at her and beat her. But she didn't resist. Later, the stupid man pulled a bottle of wine out from under the bed and, drinking heavily, fell down beside the bed to sleep.

She covered him up and dumbly sat beside him, staring at the lamp. Late in the evening, she stole outside.

She had to get something to make sure she and her crippled husband could survive. The day before she had stolen some coal and had taken four eggs from Wang Te-ch'üan's chicken coop. She had also picked six oranges, and sold them that very noon. This success encouraged her, made her intoxicated with her own power. This evening, she had even bigger plans.

But Wang Te-ch'üan had removed all the coal. There was nothing left in the yard except the coffins and some scraps of rotten wood. The opium den had closed for the night. The door to the master's main house was tightly locked. She felt lost. Sighing sadly, she looked at the sky, engaged in idle thought. Behind the watchtower, in its huge dark shadow, the solitary trunk of the *t'ung* tree rustled in the wind. A crow stirred on its branch, cawing bleakly, and then, after madly beating its wings, quieted down. A few bright stars flashed in the pitch-black sky. Not far away was the ponderous shadow of the mountain range that separated this land from the rest of the world.

The woman just stood there in a trance, dreaming that she was in another world, a world of which she had absolutely no knowledge, that faraway world of extravagance and the world of war and destruction, or in fact, dreaming of a world beyond man. In that world carpenters were of course in demand to build houses, but there, carpenters weren't poor or ill-tempered. There was also a Li-sao in that world, but one that didn't have to feed the pigs or hoe the garden. In the hell of her fantasy, there would be two ghosts dragged before the magistrate; one would be the scrawny diabolical Wang Te-ch'üan, the other the thief Li-sao. Wang Te-ch'üan would be sentenced to boil in oil in a cauldron. Li-sao would be sent to the village of the vicious dogs.

She felt this punishment was meted out fairly. Since her marriage to Li Jung-ch'eng, she had become a sinful woman. She felt that poverty was enough proof of one's sins. Therefore she thought back to her golden childhood and began to sob quietly. Everyone had forgotten that she was once a landlord's daughter. It caused her to wonder, without any way of knowing, if that simple, quiet, chaste, dreamy life still existed in this unfortunate world of man since she had become Li Jung-ch'eng's woman. She found it hard to explain, but she fervently hoped that kind of dreamy life didn't exist anymore!

The rigid line of coffins beckoned to her. She sprang at them, gripping one of the inside ones, and butting against it with her head.

"Nothing is mine, not even you coffins," she cried. "I'm ugly, poor, dressed in rags; I steal. That dog-fucker Wang Te-ch'üan—a whole year's rent. A whole year, a whole year [we still owe him]."

Later, growing tired, she fell asleep. When she awoke and was more clear-headed, she discovered herself outside the main gate. Before her spread the pitch-black fields, without a trace of light or human sound. She groped forward blindly, not knowing where she was headed or what she was doing. In front of the dark shadow of a low tiled house she suddenly became frightened and immediately halted and crouched down.

"Something's wrong," she thought.

Just then, the loud noise of a stool overturning erupted from the house. She backed into a ditch along the field, and heard a man's voice suddenly explode in anger: "I'm going, so what are you going to do about it?"

The feeble voice of a woman was heard: "Really, why do you have to—"

"I want to go. I want to. If you don't believe me, just ask Mother. I'm not going to waste my life out here in the country."

Before the shouting had subsided, a hen clucked uneasily and scurried out from under a fence. Li-sao crawled over to it.

"They're making such a racket even the chickens have run away!" she thought.

She lunged at the chicken and grabbed it securely by the throat.

"Ha! A chicken!" She fled, clutching the hen to her breast. "Why didn't it go back to its coop? They were making too much noise. A chicken! Ha! A chicken!"

Inside the stone house, Li Jung-ch'eng sat up in bed, his bloodshot eyes wide open. Seeing her come inside, he suddenly leaped out of bed.

"What are you carrying? What is it?" he yelled wildly.

Li-sao lovingly held the hen out to him as she approached the bed. "The Wus over there are fighting again. It's really a shame. The chicken ran away. Look—"

"What! You shameless slut. You stole a chicken!" The carpenter trembled, his face contorted in pain. Then he lurched at her crazily, cruelly kicking at her stomach. She fell and rolled on the floor. The hen escaped from her grasp and ran wildly around the room, screeching and flapping its wings.

On the floor, her eyes were open wide in pain, as if not comprehending why the world was so cruel and unfeeling. The carpenter began to rant and rave. Then, becoming ill, he fell back onto the bed in a spasm. She sat on the floor, staring dumbly at her husband as he thrashed the air with his legs. She felt a rare sense of satisfaction. But she then screamed and, kneeling by the side of the bed, cradled his dizzy, foul-smelling head in her lap, just as she had held the stolen hen a moment ago.

VI

The two brothers began to scurry around trying to sell the coffins. Te-ch'üan was less active about it, thinking that even if the coffins remained unsold, by next summer they were certain to increase in value. But Te-jun took a completely different approach. Excitedly he raced around the streets of the town as if he couldn't afford to fail. He pretended not to hear the criticism of his neighbors. If he couldn't help overhearing their remarks, his only response was a random cursing. His desire to defeat his older brother was greater than anything else. He seldom gave much deliberation to anything. Even if sometimes he had his plans well thought out, he might change them on impulse and carry them out haphazardly. Selling coffins was no different.

An old lady who worked as the cook at the lime kiln got sick and died. Te-ch'üan naturally took an interest in her. He raced over to inquire what she had died of and stood silently for a long time under the rush awning where the body lay. His expression was a bit worried and a little disappointed, because he felt this old lady wasn't the kind of person who could afford one of his coffins. Then he left, feeling restless at first, but soon consoled himself with the thought that coffins needn't be sold immediately, and at the same time began to look for something else to occupy his mind.

Just at that time, however, one of Te-jun's coffins sold for two hundred and fifty dollars. The buyer was a stone mason whose wife had died of the plague. At first he had chosen one of Wang Te-ch'üan's, figuring that they were a little cheaper. But Te-ch'üan's fat wife coldly set the price at three hundred dollars. Te-jun then got friendly with the stone mason and lowered his asking price to two hundred and fifty dollars. In addition, he happily pointed out that his brother's were all made of rotten wood patched together. So he was victorious. Te-ch'üan's wife was furious. At the same time, on orders from his mother, Hei Wa-tzu came to steal the ripe oranges off the orange trees. She therefore ordered Li-sao to knock all the oranges off the branches.

An abundant harvest—the sign of the impending storm was hung out for all to see!

Wang Te-ch'üan, this soft-spoken and calculating man, became so angry that his face turned white. It was all right if his coffins didn't sell, but not if they were rejected because the wood was said to be rotten and patched.

He rushed over to the cistern in the small courtyard and called his brother in an unnaturally high-pitched voice.

"You calling me?" His brother shouted, and strode out of the house.

"Hunh. Yes, I'm calling you."

Wang Te-jun opened his dark purplish mouth and yawned, then pushed up his sleeve as he took a look around him. Te-ch'üan began to tremble.

"Come over here!" He threw back his shoulders with an air of sternness. "I have something to ask you."

"You asking me or my prick?"

"I'm asking you," the brother replied timidly, almost in tears. He screwed up his courage and shouted: "You really know how to insult your older brother. Why did you say my coffins are 'patched together'?"

"They're rotten."

"Nonsense. Don't you have any respect for human relationships?"

The younger brother jumped and wildly leaped about, ranting: "You're mad because I was the one who sold a coffin. But I didn't break any law! Save your own to sleep in later."

The older brother tried to calm himself. Raising his water pipe in his hand, he waved the other man back with it, yelling, "Now cool down and listen. To tell you the truth, neither of us is too clean. You'd better understand this: if I were you, I'd be careful about my opium den!"

"What? What did you say? Say that again!" the younger brother cried, then panting, stood with his hands hanging at his sides, as if hypnotized by his own anger.

"You're running an opium den!" This time the shout sounded like wailing.

Te-ch'üan's fat wife, standing by the square frame door, raised her hand and screamed at her little daughter: "Get inside!" The little girl ducked her head [and walked inside]. The fat woman edged out, her nose wrinkled up.

Te-jun jumped up like a firecracker. The fat woman rushed over wordlessly, a raised club in her hand. But almost immediately she dropped it and dragged at her husband.

Wang Te-ch'üan pitched forward onto his brother's chest, his collar torn off by the huge hand of his opponent, while his left hand was being nervously tugged at by his wife. He leaped about, grunting like a pig.

The beast-like Wang Te-jun couldn't endure this sound. He suddenly felt smothered. Shaking his shoulders, he bared his teeth and snorted. With one stroke he knocked Wang Te-ch'üan into the mud.

VII

Without having to get involved himself, Te-ch'üan bribed a butcher to tell the authorities about Te-jun. The director of Internal Security, wearing a new square cap and a gray canvas overcoat, selected a bright clear afternoon to pay a visit. He wore a contented smile. An autumn fly buzzed around his nose. Mechanically he raised a hand to grab at it but, missing it, angrily shook a fist in the direction of flight. Just at this moment Li-sao passed by and observed his strange action. He felt his dignity had been compromised and became angry with himself.

This was a stifling, lazy day. Wang Te-ch'üan was sitting in a chair with his thin head collapsed on his shoulder, saliva dribbling out of his mouth as he dozed. The insistent, angry footsteps of the director woke him up.

"Oh, Mr. Director. Have a seat." He raised his drowsy head, waved his hand, and called to him confusedly, "Here, have a smoke?"

He offered the water pipe but the director walked past to the small courtyard.

"Is Lao-erh [7] at home?" he asked softly.

"Yes," Wang Te-ch'üan answered, playing with his left sleeve. He appeared abstracted, overcome by a nameless regret. But soon anger welled up in him.

Heavily he plunked himself back down into the rattan chair and listened to the voices coming from the back yard. In the beginning, it was Te-jun's wild hoarse shouting, followed by the low whisper of the director. In the end, Te-jun's high-pitched voice began to curse, as he pounded on the table. Then, two short laughs, and all was silent.

Te-ch'üan, attracted by the voices, had gotten up and slipped in the mud. It's easy to get sleepy and muddle-headed in the autumn afternoon.

"Stupid! Really stupid of me," he reflected bitterly. "What kind of a director is this man anyway? He seemed to be here this afternoon for nothing else but to buy a coffin! And now the price seems to have been settled."

Te-jun and the young official who was supposed to investigate the opium den emerged from the back of the house. The two of them looked very solemn, paying no attention to him. Clearly enough, he had lost.

Afterward, Te-jun's pugnacious wife walked to the cistern and glared at him, full of hate. She waddled along holding her stomach, flaunting a large ornamental pin in her hair, with a frantic expression on her face. She began to laugh peevishly in her cruel, sarcastic way. She stopped laughing. Her half-closed eyes were brimming with tears. She gazed into the sunlight as if listening to something. The look on her gaunt, powdered face was one of worry. She heaved a deep sigh, as if her heart had found gratification in this ancient house.

But then, suddenly, her face lit up and turned savage, her eyes were riveted on Te-ch'üan.

"You dog-fucker! You put all the blame on us because you couldn't sell your own coffins!" She ranted on, clapping her hands. "Not only do you want to keep all the oranges for yourself, you wouldn't even let anyone else touch the wood!" She wailed. "If you have any guts, go report us to X——!" [8]

Wang Te-ch'üan jumped up, his limbs gyrating like a puppet's. "What did you say? What?"

But Te-jun's wife ignored him, and remembering something, swiftly ran out of the yard. He stood there pale and drawn, uncertain what to do next, forgetting even to lower his outstretched arms.

Finally, he grasped a teacup and, as Li-sao had done to him in the past, viciously flung it after her. "So it's come to this! You can't bully me. I'll get back at you!" he screamed as the cup shattered.

His fat wife dragged him away. "Are you crazy?"

"I'm going to get even with them!"

"Oh, forget it. It's not worth the fuss."

Wang Te-ch'üan struggled out of her hold and scrambled out past the main gate. But he was stopped at the steps of the courtyard by the carpenter Li Jung-ch'eng. "What the hell are you doing?" he yelled.

The carpenter glared at him coldly, drew back, and replied weakly, "We're moving."

"Then come up with three hundred dollars."

The carpenter, his face pale, swayed painfully as if he were about to topple over.

"You've got no conscience," he whispered. Then, forgetting everything, he exploded in

[7] See footnote 9 in "The Bulwark," p. 342.   [8] The original has three X's.

anger, wildly thrashing his arms and jumping up two steps. He wheezed, "You've gotten enough out of me. Too much out of me. We can't go on living like this!"

"Shut up!"

"You're not human. You even tried to steal my wife, steal my wife's clothes—" He glared at him, panting painfully. "You're all beasts."

Te-ch'üan retreated a step and raised his water pipe, but the carpenter, his body in convulsions, toppled over like a felled tree, already unconscious. His head hit a coffin with a heavy thud. White bubbles gurgled out from his mouth and nostrils, covering his face.

"Li-sao! Li-sao!" Te-ch'üan called out, terrified.

Li-sao ambled over from the back yard, then, seeing her husband, raced to his side. She grabbed a handful of grass from the bottom of the fence and stuffed it in his mouth [to keep the bubbles from coming out], then stood up, folding her arms about herself.

"You, take him—carry him back inside," Te-ch'üan ordered anxiously.

The woman raised her eyes to him in a hateful stare as if saying, "As simple as that."

"I can't move him," she answered somberly. "Shit! Everyone saw what happened. Master, lend us a little money," she threatened clumsily. "Then it'll be all right."

As the master was about to explode in anger, Te-jun rushed over to the steps and shouted in his face, "Well, this is just fine. Come inside and we'll talk this over. You *are* my elder brother, aren't you?" He pointed toward his brother's nose, then turned and hurried inside.

The elder brother followed. As soon as he stepped aside, Li-sao bent over her writhing husband and began to wail. Her cries so disturbed Te-ch'üan that he almost stumbled over the doorstep.

The younger brother appeared in the main hall and called his brother's name haughtily. He flung a sharp knife into the table.

"Let's settle it with this," he roared, kicking over a stool. "But first pay back the three hundred dollars your hireling owed me."

The elder brother patted his chest, as if to point out his advanced age.

"The first account to settle is the three hundred dollars I loaned to that blasted carpenter of yours. The second is the favor I did you back before the war. Do you remember how I saved you once?"

Wang Te-ch'üan stole a glance at the knife, and struggled to reply. "You? Saved me?"

"Cut out the bullshit! Let's get it over with!" Wang Te-jun's voice ripped through the air, his mouth open wide, teeth flashing. "Outside," he roared at his brother who was trying to reach the table with his thin hand. "I'm going to give you a coffin today."

The fat woman rushed in.

"You're drunk, brother." Te-ch'üan stretched out his hand once again. "Listen to me, brother— Get out of here, woman, you hear?" He barked at his wife.

"We'll see." The younger brother wrapped his pudgy hand around the knife handle.

"What are you two up to?"

"Let's not do anything foolish. There must be a way out. Let's sit down and talk it over." He pulled on the corner of a stool, trying to sit down, but his younger brother motioned with his hand, and he withdrew and straightened up. "Have I ever owed you anything? What is it that we can't talk over?" He paused, wheezing. "Anyone who flashes a knife is a guilty party. And besides, I'm your elder brother."

"We'll see!" The younger brother thumped the table, reaching for the knife.

"You're overreacting!" he shouted lamely, retreating. "You're a disgrace to the family. I'll have the authorities shoot you!"

The younger brother brandished the knife, aimed, and lunged madly at him, pinning him down with one hand. The fat woman screamed, "Help! Help! Save him!"

"We'll see. We'll see." He rapped his brother's head with the knife, and at the same time, twisted his body to free himself from his sister-in-law, who was clutching his arm. He wanted to shove her to the floor, but her intervention had concealed his cowardice, making it possible for him to yield according to her wish, and at the same time holler even more fiercely. Wang Te-ch'üan thrashed around blindly, but was finally reduced to tears under the threat of the gleaming blade.

The fat woman knelt before Te-jun. "There's nothing we can't talk over."

"No way." He flashed the knife.

"Help!" Te-ch'üan wailed.

Te-jun's wife yelled excitedly and rushed inside. She threw herself at the three people, and held tight to her husband's shoulder. As soon as Te-jun's hold on him loosened, Te-ch'üan rolled on the floor and crawled under the table. Even the arbitrator, Te-jun's wife, was pushed down by her ferocious husband and the four of them fell together in a heap.

By the time Te-ch'üan and his wife had escaped to their own house, Te-jun's wife had already begun cursing them. She herded Hei Wa-tzu over to the cistern and pelted their house with rocks and sticks.

The next day they invited all the relatives from the Wang clan for a feast at the expense of Wang Te-ch'üan. The purpose of the gathering was to divide the household. By the time the last portions of the property were divided up, the two brothers had become most meticulous. Each brother was to share half the mountain slope and half the courtyard, to be partitioned by a back fence. The six orange trees were divided up, half to each household. The damaged *t'ung* tree which had lost its branch in the violent storm was given to the younger brother.

VIII

Li Jung-ch'eng died that very night. In the household Li-sao's desolate wails woke only the fat maid Su-fen. Though Wang Te-ch'üan had awakened, owing to the unfortunate events of the day he had no heart to pay any attention to it. Her sobs lengthened and became more heart-rending, permeating the autumn night and the fields, causing uneasiness among the neighbors. "Don't you know that Li Jung-ch'eng is dead?" they whispered. "Yes, and to tell the truth, it's a real shame." But in no time they went back to sleep. Who had the energy to pay heed to anyone else? Their own bitter cups were full enough!

Early the next morning the unfortunate woman, her eyes swollen from crying, went to see Wang Te-ch'üan. She kowtowed to him and begged him to give her a coffin. This caused Wang Te-ch'üan some anguish, for he too had suffered, but it didn't change his habit of not giving alms.

He ended up by shouting deliriously and beating her off with his water pipe. Therefore the body of the carpenter was wrapped in reeds and carried up the mountain.

Everyone thought Li-sao would become demented, but she didn't. The very next day—that is, the first day after the households were divided—she went back to work to pay off last year's rent. She was still lazy and dirty, and still went out at night to steal, then hurry to the river to buy corn. Except for her reticence, she was the same old Li-sao. But in the middle of the twelfth lunar month, she underwent a change. During the day, she wasn't to be found at home. Furthermore, she wore the blue cloth gown that didn't have a hole or patch in it. Wang Te-jun's wife found out everything and happily reported it to all: Li-sao was living with a worker at the lime kiln.

Wang Te-ch'üan beat her up savagely, confiscated all her belongings, and drove her away.

No one cared what happened to her. Even the death of the unfortunate carpenter had long been forgotten. The only remaining mark of his existence was the entry in the ledger that he still owed three hundred dollars. In the remote mountain valley, the households continued their existence according to long-established patterns. Dividing the household property and quarreling hadn't changed their life at all. Te-jun's tiny opium den flourished. When winter approached, his wife was seen wearing a red woolen jacket, the kind worn by women in the cities. Te-jun himself wore a long leather gown lined in satin and a Turkish cap and carried a red lacquer cane. This couple strutted along the street victoriously, talking and shouting in the bitter mountain wind with even more abandon.

Te-ch'üan, though unable to forget his humiliation over the oranges and his feud over the coffins, regained his wooden dignity. But he still was a perpetual worrier, never satisfied. His wife was the same. Almost every day, passing the new construction site, they would hoist several pieces of wood onto their shoulders, or the two of them would lift a section together, quietly, haughtily, and carry it back home. They seemed to be showing the world that no one valued property as much as they, and they were the true protectors of property. Not long afterward, their back yard was piled high with timber, molding in a great pile.

As for the coffins, neither the red nor the white ones had much hope of being sold before the spring plague came. They turned black from the dampness of winter and filled with sludge. They warped all out of proportion. When an old lady came to inquire about the price, Wang Te-ch'üan lowered his price to one hundred and fifty dollars, but they still couldn't be sold.

"I can't go any lower. This is an honest price," he said, shaking his head while tugging at his sleeve. "This price isn't enough to cover labor. Food is expensive these days. It takes fourteen working days for a carpenter to make a coffin. You can figure out how much it costs yourself."

"Holy Buddha, you've got to have a conscience—" the old lady sighed, closing her dry, dusty eyes.

EILEEN CHANG
(*1921–*)

Eileen Chang was the most gifted Chinese writer to emerge in the forties, and certainly the most important. Though she is the youngest writer represented in this anthology, her career has spanned nearly four decades. In terms of what she could have achieved in the last two decades if she had retained the creative exuberance of her youth and her sheer zest for life, her career may be regarded as somewhat disappointing. Nevertheless, her permanent status in Chinese literature is assured, and her influence on the younger Chinese writers in Taiwan and America has been as salutary as the influence of Lu Hsün on the fiction writers of the twenties and thirties. No Chinese author of recent years can yet boast of so rich an oeuvre, including not only her brilliant short fiction but also a novel of classic stature, *The Rice-Sprout Song (Yang-ko)*.

A native of Shanghai, Eileen Chang (Chang Ai-ling) comes from a distinguished family. Her grandmother's father was the statesman Li Hung-chang, and her grandfather was Chang P'ei-lun, the chief political casualty of the Sino-French War of 1884 but nonetheless an earnest official in his youth and a classical scholar. Her father, however, was a domestic tyrant, and Eileen Chang suffered greatly in her youth. She studied at the University of Hong Kong until Pearl Harbor and then returned to Shanghai to begin her literary career. All her *Collected Stories (Chang Ai-ling tuan-p'ien hsiao-shuo chi*, Hong Kong, 1954; Taipei, 1968) and many of her essays date from the period 1943–1947. In 1952 she left the mainland for Hong Kong, where two novels appeared: *The Rice-Sprout Song* (1954; English version, 1955); and *Naked Earth (Ch'ih-ti chih lien*, 1954; English version, 1956).

Eileen Chang arrived in the United States in 1955 and has since lived a most secluded life. In the sixties she produced two versions of a novel based on her story "The Golden Cangue" (*Chin-so chi*, 1943)—*The Embittered Woman (Yüan-nü*, Taipei, 1968) and *The Rouge of the North* (London, 1967)—as well as a revision of a novel first serialized in the forties, newly titled *Half a Lifetime's Romance (Pan-sheng yüan*, Taipei, 1969). Two unfinished stories dating from the forties are included in a collection mainly of essays entitled *As Seen by Eileen Chang (Chang k'an*, Hong Kong and Taipei, 1976).

I have maintained in *History* that "The Golden Cangue" is "the greatest novelette in the history of Chinese literature" (p. 398). Certainly, beside it, even the finest traditional vernacular tales of comparative length and scope (such as

"The Pearl-sewn Shirt" or "The Oil Peddler") appear victims of the storyteller's conventions in their occasional adulteration of moral and psychological reality, while none of Eileen Chang's successors have yet told an essential truth about Chinese civilization in a novella of equal weight and terrifying power. In *History* I commented on the story as follows:

> Eileen Chang has evinced an unerring knowledge of the manners and mores of the decadent upper class throughout the story and has studied the heroine's life in terms of an unflinching psychological realism; but what elevates this perception and this realism into the realm of tragedy is the personal emotion behind the creation, the attitude of mingled fascination and horror with which the author habitually contemplates her own childhood environment. In *The Golden Cangue* Eileen Chang has found a perfect fable to serve as the dramatic correlative of her emotion, and the result is an overpowering tragedy embodying an acute moral vison, uniquely her own. [p. 407]

The reader who finds the novella interesting should by all means read *The Rouge of the North.*

"The Golden Cangue," a modern work of striking originality, is nevertheless deeply indebted to *Dream of the Red Chamber* for its style and boudoir realism. Eileen Chang, who knows this novel by heart, has written a valuable textual study called *Nightmare in the Red Chamber (Hung-lou meng-yen,* Taipei, 1977).

C.T.H.

The Golden Cangue

by Eileen Chang

Translated by the author

Shanghai thirty years ago on a moonlit night . . . maybe we did not get to see the moon of thirty years ago. To young people the moon of thirty years ago should be a reddish-yellow wet stain the size of a copper coin, like a teardrop on letter paper by To-yün Hsüan,[1] worn and blurred. In old people's memory the moon of thirty years ago was gay, larger, rounder, and whiter than the moon now. But seen after thirty years on a rough road, the best of moons is apt to be tinged with sadness.

The moonlight reached the side of Feng-hsiao's pillow. She was a slave girl brought by the bride, the new Third Mistress of the Chiangs. She opened her eyes and saw her own blue-white hand on the half-worn blanket faced with quilted Korean silk. "Is it moonlight?" she said to herself. She slept on a pallet on the floor under the window. The last couple of years had been busy with the changing of dynasties; the Chiangs, coming to Shanghai as refugees, did not have enough room, so the servants' quarters were criss-crossed with people sleeping.

Feng-hsiao thought she heard a rustle behind the big bed; somebody must have gotten up to use the chamber pot. She turned over and, just as she thought, the cloth curtain was pushed aside and a black shadow emerged, shuffling in slippers worn down in the back. It was probably Little Shuang, the personal maid of Second Mistress, and so she called out softly, "Little Sister Shuang."

Little Shuang came, smiling, and kicked at the pallet. "I woke you." She put both hands under her old lined jacket of dark violet silk, worn over bright oil-green trousers. Feng-hsiao put out a hand to feel the trouser leg and said, smiling:[2]

"Colorful clothes aren't worn so much now. With the people downriver,[3] the fashion is all for neutral tones."

Little Shuang said, "You don't know: in this house we don't keep up with other people. Old Mistress is strict. Not even the young mistresses can have their own way, to say nothing of us slave girls. We wear what's given us—all dressed like peasants." She squatted down to sit on the pallet and picked up a little jacket at Feng-hsiao's feet. "Was this newly made for your lady's wedding?"

Feng-hsiao shook her head. "Of my clothes for the season, only the few pieces on view are new. The rest are just discards."

"It's really hard on your lady that this wedding happened to run into the revolution."

Feng-hsiao sighed. "Don't go into that now. In times like these one should economize, but there's still a limit! That wedding really had no style. She didn't say anything, but how could she not be angry?"

"I shouldn't wonder Third Mistress is still un-

[1] To-yün Hsüan (Solitary Cloud Studio) was famous for its fine red-striped stationery, popular down to the thirties.
[2] *Hsiao tao* ("said smiling"): standard formula phrase in traditional Chinese fiction.   [3] On the lower Yangtze.

happy about it. On your side the trousseau was passable, but the wedding preparations we made were really too dismal. Even the year we took our Second Mistress it was better than this."

Feng-hsiao was taken aback. "How? Your Second Mistress . . ."

Little Shuang took off her shoes and stepped barefoot across Feng-hsiao to the window. "Come and look at the moon," she said.

Feng-hsiao scrambled quickly to her feet. "I was going to ask you all along, your Second Mistress . . ."

Little Shuang bent down to pick up the little jacket and put it over her shoulders. "Be careful you don't catch cold."

Feng-hsiao said smiling as she buttoned it up, "No, you've got to tell me."

"My fault, I shouldn't have let it out," said Little Shuang.

"We're like sisters now. Why treat me like an outsider?"

"If I tell you, don't you tell your lady, though. Our Second Mistress's family owns a sesame oil shop."

"Oh!" Feng-hsiao was surprised. "A sesame oil shop! How on earth could they stoop so low! Now your Eldest Mistress is from a titled family; ours can't compare with Eldest Mistress, but she does come from a respectable family."

"Of course there was a reason. You've seen our Second Master, he's crippled. What mandarin family would give him a daughter for wife? Old Mistress didn't know what to do, first was going to get him a concubine, and then the matchmaker found this one from the Ts'ao family, called Ch'i-ch'iao[4] because she was born in the seventh month."

"Oh, a concubine," said Feng-hsiao.

"Was to be a concubine. Then Old Mistress thought, Second Master wasn't going to take a wife, and it wouldn't do for the second branch to be without its proper mistress. Just as well to have her for a wife so she would look after Second Master faithfully."

Feng-hsiao leaned on the windowsill, musing. "No wonder. I'm new here, but I guessed some of it."

"Dragons breed dragons, phoenixes breed phoenixes—as the saying goes. You haven't heard her conversation! Even in front of the unmarried young ladies she says anything she likes. Lucky that in our house not a word goes out from inside, nor comes in from outside, so the young ladies don't understand a thing. Even then they get so embarrassed they don't know where to hide."

Feng-hsiao tittered. "Really? Where could she have picked up vulgar language? Even us slave girls—"

Little Shuang said, holding her own elbows, "Why, she was the big attraction at the sesame oil shop, standing at the counter and dealing with all kinds of customers. What have we got to compare with her?"

"Did you come with her when she was married?"

Little Shuang sneered. "How could she afford me! I used to wait on Old Mistress, but Second Master took medicine all day and had to be helped around all the time, and since they were short of help, I was sent over there. Are you cold?" Feng-hsiao shook her head. "Look at you, the way you've pulled in your neck, so cuddly!" She had hardly finished speaking when Feng-hsiao sneezed. Right away Little Shuang gave her a push. "Go to bed, go to bed. Warm yourself."

Feng-hsiao knelt down to take her jacket off. "It's not winter, you don't catch cold just like that."

"The window may be closed but the wind sneaks in through the crevices."

They both lay down. Feng-hsiao asked in a whisper, "Been married four, five years now?"

"Who?"

"Who else?"

"Oh, she. That's right, it's been five years."

"Had children too, and gave people nothing to talk about?"

"Well—! Plenty to talk about. The year before

---

[4] The old phrase *ch'i-ch'iao,* clever seven, refers to the skill of the Weaving Maid, a star that is reunited with the Cowherd, another star, across the Milky Way every year on the seventh of the seventh moon.

last Old Mistress took everybody in the house on a pilgrimage to Mount P'u-t'o. She didn't go because it was just after her lying-in, so she was left home to look after the house. Master-in-law[5] called a bit too often and a batch of things was lost."

Feng-hsiao was startled. "And they never got to the bottom of it?"

"How could they? It would have been embarrassing for everybody. Anyway, one day the jewelry would have gone to Eldest Master, Second Master, and Third Master. Eldest Master and Mistress couldn't very well say anything on account of Second Master. Third Master was in no position to, he himself was spending money like water and borrowed a lot from the family accounts."

The two of them were talking across a gap of ten feet. Despite their efforts to keep their voices down, a louder sentence or two woke up old Mrs. Chao on the big bed. She called out, "Little Shuang." Little Shuang did not dare answer. Old Mrs. Chao said, "Little Shuang, if you talk more nonsense and let people hear you, be careful you don't get skinned tomorrow!" Little Shuang kept still. "Don't think you're still in the deep halls and big courtyards we lived in before, where you had room to talk crazy and act silly. Here it's cheek by jowl, nothing can be kept from other people. Better stop talking if you want to avoid a beating."

Immediately the room became silent. Old Mrs. Chao, who had inflamed eyes, had stuffed her pillow with chrysanthemum leaves, said to make eyes clear and cool. She now raised her head to press down the silver hairpin tucked into her bun and the chrysanthemum leaves rustled with the slight stir. She turned over, her whole frame pulled into motion, all her bones squeaking. She sighed, "You people— ! What do you know?" Little Shuang and Feng-hsiao still didn't dare reply. For a long time nobody spoke, and one by one they drifted off to sleep.

It was almost dawn. The flat waning moon got lower, lower and larger, and by the time it sank, it was like a red gold basin. The sky was a cold, bleak crab-shell blue. The houses were only a cou-

ple of storeys high, pitch-dark under the sky, so one could see far. At the horizon the morning colors were layers of green, yellow, and red like a watermelon cut open—the sun was coming up. Gradually wheelbarrows and big pushcarts began rattling along the road, and horse carriages passed, hooves tapping. The beancurd soup vendor, flat pole on his shoulder, slowly and swingingly hawked his wares. Only the drawn-out last syllable carried, "Haw. . .O! Haw. . .O!" Farther off, it became "Aw . . . O! Aw . . . O!"

In the house the slave girls and amahs had also got up, in a flurry to open the room doors, fetch hot water, fold up bedding, hook up the bed-curtains, and do the hair. Feng-hsiao helped the Third Mistress Lan-hsien get dressed. Lan-hsien leaned close to the mirror for a careful look, pulled out from under her armpit a pale green blossom-flecked handkerchief, rubbed some powder off the wings of her nose, and said with her back to Third Master on the bed, "I'd better go first to pay my respects to Old Mistress. I'd be late if I waited for you."

As she was speaking, Eldest Mistress Tai-chen came and stood in the doorway, saying with a smile, "Third Sister, let's go together."

Lan-hsien hurried up to her. "I was just beginning to worry that I'd be late—so Eldest Sister-in-law hasn't gone up yet. What about Second Sister-in-law?"

"She'll still be a while."

"Getting Second Brother his medicine?"

Tai-chen looked around to make sure there was no one about before she said, smiling, "It's not so much taking medicine as—" She put her thumb to her lips, made a fist with the three middle fingers, sticking out the little finger, and shushed softly a couple of times.

Lan-hsien said, surprised, "They both smoke that?"

Tai-chen nodded. "With your Second Brother it's out in the open, with her it's kept from Old Mistress, which makes things difficult for us, caught in between—have to cover up for her. Actually Old Mistress knows very well. Deliberately pretends she doesn't, orders her around and tor-

---

[5]*Chiu-yeh,* lit., Master Brother-in-law, in this case Second Mistress's elder brother.

tures her in little ways, just so that she can't smoke her fill. Actually, to think of it, a woman and so young, what great problems could she have, to need to smoke that to take her mind off things?"

Tai-chen and Lan-hsien went upstairs hand in hand, each followed by the slave girl closest to her, to the small anteroom next door to Old Mistress's bedroom. The slave girl Liu-hsi came out to them whispering, "Not awake yet."

Tai-chen glanced up at the grandfather clock and said smiling, "Old Mistress is also late today."

"Said she didn't sleep well the last couple of days, too much noise on the street," Liu-hsi said. "Probably used to it now, making up for it today."

Beside the little round pedestal table of purple elm covered with a strip of scarlet felt sat Yün-tse, the second daughter of the house, cracking walnuts with a little nutcracker. She put it down and got up to greet them. Tai-chen laid a hand on her shoulder. "Sister Yün, you're really a devoted child. Old Mistress had a fancy for sugared walnuts yesterday, and you remembered."

Lan-hsien and Tai-chen sat down around the table and helped to clean the walnut meat. Yün-tse's hands got tired and Lan-hsien took the nutcracker as she put it down.

"Be careful of those nails of yours, as slender as scallions. It would be a pity to break them when you've grown them so long," said Tai-chen.

"Have somebody go and get your gold nail sheath," Yün-tse said.

"So much bother, we might as well have them shelled in the kitchen," said Lan-hsien.

As they were talking and laughing in undertones, Liu-hsi raised the curtain with a stick, announcing, "Second Mistress is here."

Lan-hsien and Yün-tse rose to ask her to sit down but Ts'ao Ch'i-ch'iao would not be seated as yet. With one hand on the doorway and the other on her waist, she first looked around. On her thin face were a vermilion mouth, triangular eyes, and eyebrows curved like little hills. She wore a pale pink blouse over narrow mauve trousers with a flickering blue scroll design and greenish-white incense-stick piping.[6] A crepe handkerchief made of lavender silk was half tucked around the wrist in one narrow blouse sleeve. She smiled, showing her small fine teeth, and said, "Everybody's here. I suppose I'm late again. How can I help it, doing my hair in the dark? Who gave me a window facing the back yard? I'm the only one who got a room like that. That one of ours is evidently not going to live long anyway, we're just waiting to be widow and orphans—whom to bully, if not us?"

Tai-chen blandly said nothing. Lan-hsien said smiling, "Second Sister-in-law is used to the houses in Peking. No wonder she finds it too cramped in here."

Yün-tse said, "Eldest Brother should have gotten a larger place when he was house-hunting, but I'm afraid that for Shanghai, this counts as a bright, airy house."

Lan-hsien said, "That's so. It's true it's a bit crowded. Really, so many people in the house—"

Ch'i-ch'iao rolled up her sleeve and tucked the handkerchief in her green jade bracelet, glancing sideways at Lan-hsien, and said smiling, "So Third Sister feels there're too many people. If it's too crowded for us, who have been married for years, naturally it's too crowded for newlyweds like you."

Before Lan-hsien could say anything, Tai-chen blushed, saying, "Jokes are jokes, but there's a limit. Third Sister has just come here. What will she think of us?"

Ch'i-ch'iao patted her lips with a corner of her handkerchief. "I know you're all young ladies from respectable homes. Just try and change places with me—I'm afraid you couldn't put up with it for a single night."

Tai-chen made a spitting noise. "This is too much. The more you talk, the more impertinent you get."

At this Ch'i-ch'iao went up and took Tai-chen by the sleeve. "I can swear—I can swear for the last three years . . . Do you dare swear? You dare swear?"

Even Tai-chen could not help a titter, and then she muttered, "How is it that you had even two children?"

Ch'i-ch'iao said, "Really, even I don't know how the children got born. The more I think about it the less I understand."

---

[6] So called because the piping is rounded and narrow.

Tai-chen held up her right hand and waved it from side to side. "Enough of such talk. Granted that you take Third Sister as one of our own, and feel free to say anything you like, still Sister Yün's here. If she tells Old Mistress later, you'll get more than you bargained for."

Yün-tse had walked off long ago, and was standing on the veranda with her hands behind her back, whistling at the canary to make it sing. The Chiangs lived in a modern foreign-style house of an early period, tall arches supported by thick pillars of red brick with floral capitals, but the upstairs veranda had a wooden floor. Behind the railings of willow wood was a row of large bamboo baskets in which dried bamboo shoots were being aired. The worn sunlight pervaded the air like gold dust, slightly suffocating and dizzying when rubbed in the eyes. Far away in the street a peddler shook a rattle-drum whose sleepy beat, *bu lung dung . . . bu lung dung,* held memories of many children now grown old. The private rickshas tinkled as they ran past and an occasional car horn went *ba ba.* Because Ch'i-ch'iao knew that everyone in this house looked down on her, she was especially warm to the newcomer. Leaning on the back of Lan-hsien's chair, she asked her this and that and spoke admiringly of her fingernails after giving her hand a thorough inspection. Then she added, "I grew one on my little finger last year fully half an inch longer than this, and broke it picking flowers."

Lan-hsien had already seen through Ch'i-ch'iao and understood her position at the Chiangs'. She kept smiling but hardly answered. Ch'i-ch'iao felt the slight. Ambling over to the veranda, she picked up Yün-tse's pigtail and shook it, making conversation. *"Yo!* How come your hair's so thin? Only last year you had such a head of glossy black hair—must have lost a lot?"

Yün-tse turned aside to protect her pigtail, saying with a smile, "I can't even lose a few hairs without your permission?"

Ch'i-ch'iao went on scrutinizing her and called out, "Elder Sister-in-law, come take a look. Sister Yün has really grown much thinner. Could it be that the young lady has something on her mind?"

With marked annoyance Yün-tse slapped Ch'i-

ch'iao's hand to get it off her person. "You've really gone crazy today. As if you weren't enough of a nuisance ordinarily."

Ch'i-ch'iao tucked her hands in her sleeves. "What a temper the young lady has," she said, smiling.

Tai-chen put her head out, saying "Sister Yün, Old Mistress is up."

They all straightened their blouses hastily, smoothed the hair in front of their ears, lifted the curtain to go into the next room, curtsied, and waited on Old Mistress at breakfast. Old women holding trays went in through the living room; slave girls inside took the dishes from them and returned to wait in the outer room. It was quiet inside, scarcely anybody saying anything; the only sound was the rustle of the thin silver chain quivering at the top of a pair of silver chopsticks.

Old Mistress believed in Buddha and made it a rule to worship for two hours after breakfast. Coming out with the others, Yün-tse managed to ask Tai-chen without being overheard, "Isn't Second Sister-in-law in a hurry to go for her smoke? Why is she still hanging around inside?"

Tai-chen said, "I suppose she has a few words to say in private."

Yün-tse couldn't help laughing. "As if Old Mistress would listen to anything she had to say!"

Tai-chen laughed cynically. "That you can't tell. Old people are always changing their minds. When something's dinned into your ears all day long, it's just possible you'll believe one sentence out of ten."

As Lan-hsien sat cracking walnuts, Tai-chen and Yün-tse went to the veranda, though not specifically to eavesdrop on the conversation in the main chamber. Old Mistress, being of an advanced age, was a little deaf, so her voice was especially loud. Intentionally or not, the people on the veranda heard much of the talk. Yün-tse turned white with anger; first she held her fists tight, then flicked her hands open forcibly and ran toward the other end of the veranda. After a couple of steps she stood still and bent forward with her face in her hands, sobbing.

Tai-chen hurried up and held her. "Sister, don't be like this! Stop it. It's not worth your while to heed the likes of her. Who takes her words seriously?"

Yün-tse struggled free and ran straight to her own room. Tai-chen came back to the living room and clapped her hands once. "The damage is done."

Lan-hsien hastened to ask, "What happened?"

"Your Second Sister-in-law just told Old Mistress, 'A grown girl won't keep,' and Old Mistress is to write to the P'engs to come for the bride right away. What kind of talk is that?"

Lan-hsien, also stunned, said, "Wouldn't it be slapping one's own face, for the girl's family to say a thing like that?"

"The Chiangs will lose face only temporarily, but not Sister Yün. How can they respect her over there when she gets married? She still has her life to live."

"Old Mistress is understanding, she's not likely to share that one's views."

"Of course Old Mistress didn't like it at first, said a daughter of our house would never have such ideas. So *she* said, '*Yo!* you don't know the girls nowadays. How can they compare with the girls when you were a girl? Times have changed, and people also change, or why is there trouble all over the world?' You know, old people like to hear that sort of thing. Old Mistress isn't so sure anymore."

Lan-hsien sighed, saying, "How on earth did she have the gall to make up such stories?"

Tai-chen rested both elbows on the table and stroked an eyebrow with a little finger. After a moment of reflection she snickered. "She thinks she's being especially thoughtful toward Sister Yün! Spare me her thoughtfulness."

Lan-hsien grabbed hold of her. "Listen—that can't be Sister Yün?" There was loud weeping apparently coming from a back room and the rattle of brass bedposts being kicked and a hubbub of voices trying to soothe and reason to no avail.

Tai-chen stood up. "I'll go and see. That young lady may be good-tempered, but she can fight back if she's cornered."

Tai-chen was gone when Third Master Chiang came in yawning. A robust youth, tending toward plumpness, Chiang Chi-tse sported a big shiny three-strand pigtail loosely plaited, down his neck. He had the classic domed forehead and squarish lower face, bright chubby red cheeks, glistening dark eyebrows, and moist black eyes where some impatience always showed. Over a narrow-sleeved gown of bamboo-root green he wore a little sleeveless jacket the color of sesame-dotted soy paste, buttoned across with pearls from shoulder to shoulder. He asked Lan-hsien, "Who's talking away to Old Mistress in there?"

"Second Sister-in-law."

Chi-tse pressed his lips tight and shook his head.

"You've had enough of her too?" Lan-hsien said, smiling.

Chi-tse said nothing, just pulled a chair over, pushed its back against the table, threw the hem of his gown up high and sat astride the chair, his chin on the chair back, and picked up and ate one walnut meat after another.

Lan-hsien looked at him out of the corners of her eyes. "People shelling them the whole morning, was it all for your sake?"

Just then Ch'i-ch'iao lifted the curtain and came out. The minute she saw Chi-tse she circled over to the back of Lan-hsien's chair, put both hands around Lan-hsien's neck and bent her head down, saying with a smirk, "What a ravishing bride! Third Brother, you haven't thanked me yet. If I hadn't hurried them to get this done for you early, you might have had to wait eight or ten years for the war to be over. You'd have died of impatience."

Lan-hsien's greatest regret was that her wedding had happened in a period of national emergency and lacked pomp and style. As soon as she heard these jarring words, her narrow little face fell to its full length like a scroll. Chi-tse glanced at her and said, "Second Sister-in-law, a good heart is not rewarded as of old. Nobody feels obliged to you."

"That's all right with me, I'm used to it," said Ch'i-ch'iao. "Ever since I stepped inside the Chiang house, just nursing your Second Brother all these years, watching over the sickbed day and night, just for that alone you'd think I'd done some good and nothing wrong, but who's ever grateful to me? Who ever did me half a good turn?"

Chi-tse said smiling, "You're full of grievances the minute you open your mouth."

With a long-drawn-out groan she kept fingering the gold triad [7] and key chain buttoned on Lan-hsien's lapel. After a long pause she suddenly said, "At least you haven't fooled around outside for a month or so. Thanks to the bride; she made you stay home. Anybody else could beg you on bended knee and you wouldn't."

"Is that so? Sister-in-law never asked me, how do you know I won't?" he said smiling, and signaled Lan-hsien with his eyes.

Ch'i-ch'iao doubled up laughing. "Why don't you do something about him, Third Sister? The little monkey, I saw him grow up, and now he's making jokes at my expense!"

While talking and laughing she felt bothered; her restless hands squeezed and kneaded Lan-hsien, beating and knocking lightly with a fist as if she wished to squash her out of shape. No matter how patient Lan-hsien was, she could not help getting annoyed. With her temper rising, she applied more strength than she should using the nutcracker, and broke the two-inch fingernail clean off at the quick.

"*Yo!*" Ch'i-ch'iao cried. "Quick, get scissors and trim it. I remember there was a pair of little scissors in this room. Little Shuang!" she called out. "Liu-hsi! Come, somebody!"

Lan-hsien rose. "Never mind, Second Sister-in-law, I'll go and cut it in my room." She went.

Ch'i-ch'iao sat down in Lan-hsien's chair. Leaning her cheek on her hand and lifting her eyebrows, she gazed sideways at Chi-tse. "Is she angry with me?"

"Why should she be?" he said, smiling.

"I was just going to ask that. Could I have said anything wrong? What's wrong with keeping you at home? She'd rather have you go out?"

He said, "The whole family from Eldest Brother and Eldest Sister-in-law down want to discipline me, just for fear that I'll spend the money in the general accounts."

"By the Buddha, I can't vouch for the others

but I don't think like that. Even if you get into debt and mortgage houses and sell land, if I so much as frown I'm not your Second Sister-in-law. Aren't we the closest kin? I just want you to take care of your health."

He could not suppress a titter. "Why are you so worried about my health?"

Her voice trembled. "Health is the most important thing for anybody. Look at your Second Brother, the way he gets, is he still a person? Can you still treat him as one?"

Chi-tse looked serious. "Second Brother's not like me, he was born like that. It's not that he ruined his health. He's a pitiful man; it's up to you to take care of him."

Ch'i-ch'iao stood up stiffly, holding on the table with both hands, her eyelids down and the lower half of her face quivering as if she held scalding hot candlewax in her mouth. She forced out two sentences in a small high voice: "Go sit next to your Second Brother. Go sit next to your Second Brother." She tried to sit beside Chi-tse and only got onto a corner of his chair and put her hand on his leg. "Have you touched his flesh? It's soft and heavy, feels like your feet when they go numb . . ."

Chi-tse had changed color too. Still he gave a frivolous little laugh and bent down to pinch her foot. "Let's see if they're numb."

"Heavens, you've never touched him, you don't know how good it is not to be sick . . . how good . . ." She slid down from the chair and squatted on the floor, weeping inaudibly with her face pillowed on her sleeve; the diamond on her hairpin flashed as it jerked back and forth. Against the diamond's flame shone the solid knot of pink silk thread binding a little bunch of hair at the heart of the bun. Her back convulsed as it sank lower and lower. She seemed to be not so much weeping as vomiting, churning and pumping out her guts.

A little stunned at first, Chi-tse got up. "I'm going, if that's all right with you. If you're not afraid of being seen, I am. Have to save some face for Second Brother."

Gripping the chair to rise, she said, sobbing,

[7] A toothpick, tweezers, and earspoon.

"I'll leave." She pulled a handkerchief from her sleeve to dab at her face and suddenly smiled slightly. "You're so protective of your Second Brother."

Chi-tse laughed. "If I don't protect him, who will?"

Ch'i-ch'iao said, walking toward the door, "You're a great one to talk. Don't try to act the hypocrite in front of me. Why, just in these rooms alone . . . nothing escapes my eyes—not to mention how wild you are when you get outside the house. You probably wouldn't mind even taking your wet-nurse, let alone a sister-in-law."

"I've always been easygoing. How am I supposed to defend myself if you pick on me?" he said smiling.

On her way out she again leaned her back against the door, whispering, "What I don't get is in what way I'm not as good as the others. What is it about me that's no good?"

"My good sister-in-law, you're all good."

She said with a laugh, "Could it be that staying with a cripple, I smell crippled too, and it will rub off on you?" She stared straight ahead, the small, solid gold pendants of her earrings like two brass nails nailing her to the door, a butterfly specimen in a glass box, bright colored and desolate.

Looking at her, Chi-tse also wondered. But it wouldn't do. He loved to play around but had made up his mind long ago not to flirt with members of the family. When the mood had passed one could neither avoid them nor kick them aside, they'd be a continual burden. Besides, Ch'i-ch'iao was so outspoken and hot-tempered, how could the thing be kept secret? And she was so unpopular, who would cover up for her, high or low? Perhaps she no longer cared and wouldn't even mind if it got known. But why should a young man like him take the risk? He spoke up: "Second Sister-in-law, young as I am, I'm not one who'd do just anything."

There was a sound of footsteps. With a flip of his gown he ducked into Old Mistress's room, grabbing a handful of shelled walnuts on the way. She had not quite come to her senses, but when she heard someone pushing the door she roused herself, managing the best she could to hide behind the door. When she saw Tai-chen walk in,

she came out and slapped her on the back.

Tai-chen forced a smile. "You're in better spirits than ever." She looked at the table. "My, so many walnuts, practically all eaten up. It couldn't be anybody but Third Brother."

Ch'i-ch'iao leaned against the table, facing the veranda and saying nothing.

"People had to shell them all morning, and he comes along to enjoy himself," Tai-chen grumbled as she took a seat.

Ch'i-ch'iao scraped the red table cover with a piece of sharp walnut shell, one hard stroke after another until the felt turned hairy and was about to tear. She said between clenched teeth, "Isn't it the same with money? We're always told to save, save it so others can take it out by the handful to spend. That's what I can't get over."

Tai-chen glanced at her and said coldly, "That can't be helped. When there're too many people, if it doesn't go on in the open it will go on in the dark. Control this one and you can't control that one."

Ch'i-ch'iao felt the sting and was about to reply in kind when Little Shuang came in furtively and walked up to her, murmuring, "Mistress, Master-in-law is here."

"Master-in-law's coming here is nothing to hide. You've got a growth in your throat or what?" Ch'i-ch'iao cursed. "You sound like a mosquito humming."

Little Shuang backed off a step and didn't dare to speak.

Tai-chen said, "So your brother has come to Shanghai. It seems all our relatives are here."

Ch'i-ch'iao started out of the room. "He's not allowed to come to Shanghai? With war inland, poor people want to stay alive too." She stopped at the doorstep and asked Little Shuang, "Have you told Old Mistress?"

"Not yet," said Little Shuang.

Ch'i-ch'iao thought for a moment and went downstairs quietly, since she didn't have the courage after all to go in and tell Old Mistress of her brother's arrival.

Tai-chen asked Little Shuang, "Master-in-law came alone?"

"With Mistress-in-law, carrying food in a set of round two-layered wooden boxes."

Tai-chen chuckled. "They went to all that expense."

Little Shuang said, "Eldest Mistress needn't feel sorry for them, What comes in full will go out full too. To them even remnants are good, for making slippers and waistbands, not to mention round or flat pieces of gold and silver."

"Don't be so unkind. You'd better go down," Tai-chen said smiling. "Her family seldom comes here. Not enough service and there'd be trouble again."

Little Shuang hurried out. Ch'i-ch'iao was cross-examining Liu-hsi at the top of the stairs to see if Old Mistress knew. Liu-hsi replied, "Old Mistress was at her prayers, Third Master was leaning against the window looking out, and he said there were guests coming in the front gate. Old Mistress asked who it was. Third Master looked hard and said he wasn't sure that it wasn't Master-in-law Ts'ao, and Old Mistress left it at that."

Fire leaped up in Ch'i-ch'iao as she heard this. She stamped her feet and muttered on her way downstairs, "So—just going to pretend you don't know. If you were going to be so snobbish, why did you bother to carry me here in a sedan chair, complete with three matchmakers and six wedding gifts? Ties of kinship not even a sharp knife can sever. Even if you aren't just feigning death today but really are dead, he'll have to come to your funeral and kowtow three times and you will have to take it."

Her room was screened off by a stack of gold-lacquered trunks right inside the door, leaving just a few feet of space. As she lifted the curtain, she saw her brother's wife bent over the box set to remove the top section, containing little pies, to see if the dishes underneath had spilled. Her brother Ts'ao Ta-nien bowed down to look, hands behind his back. Ch'i-ch'iao felt a wave of acrid pain rising in her heart and could not restrain a shower of tears as she leaned against the trunks, her face pressed against their padded covers of sandy blue cloth. Her sister-in-law straightened up hastily and rushed up to hold her hand in both

of hers, calling her Miss over and over again. Ts'ao Ta-nien also had to rub his eyes with a raised sleeve. Ch'i-ch'iao unbuttoned the frog fastenings on the trunk-covers with her free hand, only to button them up again, unable to say anything all the while.

Her sister-in-law turned to give her brother a look. "Say something! Talking about Sister all the time, but now you see her you're like the gourd with its mouth sawed off."[8]

Ch'i-ch'iao said in a quavering voice, "No wonder he has nothing to say—how could he face me?" and turning to her brother, "I thought you would never want to come here! You've ruined me good and proper. Just like that you walked away, but I couldn't leave. You don't care if I live or die."

Ts'ao Ta-nien said, "What are you saying? I expect it from other people, but for you to talk like this! If you don't cover up for me you won't look so good either."

"Even if I say nothing, I can't keep other people from talking. Just because of you the anger is making me sick. And after all this, you're still trying to gag me!"

Her sister-in-law interposed quickly, "It was his fault, his fault! Miss has been put upon. However, Miss hasn't suffered just on that account alone—be patient anyway, there'll be happiness in the end." The words "However, Miss hasn't suffered just on that account alone" struck Ch'i-ch'iao as so true that she began to weep. This made her sister-in-law so nervous she immediately raised her hand and waved it rapidly from side to side, murmuring, "Be careful you don't wake Ku-yeh."[9] The net curtains hung still on the big dark bed of purple cedar over on the other side of the room. "Is Ku-yeh asleep? He'd be angry if we disturbed him."

Ch'i-ch'iao called out loudly, "If he can react like a human being it won't be so bad."

Her sister-in-law was so frightened she covered Ch'i-ch'iao's mouth. "Don't, Ku-nai-nai![10] Sick people feel bad when they hear such talk."

[8] An idiomatic expression in Chinese meaning unable to say anything.
[9] Honorific for the son-in-law of the family, here Ch'i-ch'iao's husband.
[10] Honorific for the married daughter of the house.

"He feels bad and how do I feel?"

Her sister-in-law said, "Is Ku-yeh still suffering from the soft bone illness?"

"Isn't that enough to bear, without further complications? Here the whole family avoids mentioning the word tuberculosis—actually it's just tuberculosis of the bones."

"Does he sit up for a while sometimes?"

Ch'i-ch'iao started to chuckle. "Huh huh! Sit up and the spine slides down, not even as tall as my three-year-old, to look at."

Her sister-in-law ran out of comforting words for the moment and all three were speechless. Ch'i-ch'iao suddenly stamped her feet, saying, "Go, go, you people. Every time you come I have to review once more in my mind how everything has led to this, and I can't stand the agitation. Leave quickly."

Ts'ao Ta-nien said, "Listen to a word from me, Sister. Having your own family around makes it a little better anyhow, and not just now when you're unhappy. Even when your day of independence comes, the Chiangs are a big clan, the elders keep browbeating people with high-sounding words, and those of your generation and the next are like wolves and tigers, every one of them, not a single one easy to deal with. You need help for your own sake too. There will be plenty of times when you could use your brother and nephews."

Ch'i-ch'iao made a spitting noise. "I'd really be out of luck if I had to rely on your help. I saw through you long ago—if you could fight them you'd gain more credit and you'd come to me for money; if you're no match for them you'd just topple over to their side. The sight of mandarins scares you out of your wits anyway: you'll just pull in your neck and leave me to my fate."

Ta-nien flushed and laughed sardonically. "Wait until the money is in your hands. It won't be too late then to keep your brother from getting a share."

"Then why bother me when you know it's not in my hands yet?"

"So we were wrong to come all this distance to see you!" he said. "Come on, let's go. To be perfectly frank though, even if I use a bit of your money it's only fair. If I'd been greedy for wedding gifts and asked for another few hundred taels of silver from the Chiangs and sold you for a concubine, you'd have been sold,"

"Isn't a wife better for you than a concubine? Kites go farther on a longer string; you have big hopes yet."

Ta-nien was going to retort when his wife cut in, "Now hold your tongue. You'll meet again in days to come. One day when Ku-nai-nai thinks of you she'll know she has only one brother."

Ta-nien hustled her into tidying the box set, picked it up, and started out.

"What do I care?" Ch'i-ch'iao said. "When I have money I won't have to worry about your not coming, only how to get rid of you." Despite her harsh words she could not hold back the sobs that got louder and louder. This quarrel had made it possible for her to release the frustrations pent up all morning long.

Her sister-in-law, seeing that she was evidently clinging to them a little, cajoled and lectured and succeeded in pacifying her brother, and at the same time, with her arm around her, led her to the carved pearwood couch, set her down, and patiently reasoned with her until her tears gradually dried. The three now talked about everyday affairs. It was more or less peaceful in the north, with business as usual at the Ts'aos' sesame oil shop. Their present trip to Shanghai had to do with their future son-in-law, a bookkeeper who happened to be in Hupeh when the revolution started. He had left the place with his employer and finally come to Shanghai. So Ta-nien had brought his daughter here to be married, visiting his sister on the side. Ta-nien asked after all the Chiangs of the house and wanted to pay his respects to Old Mistress.

"Just as well if you don't see her," said Ch'i-ch'iao. "I just had an argument with her."

Ta-nien and his wife were both startled.

"How can I help myself?" Ch'i-ch'iao said. "The whole family treading me down. If I'd been easy to bully I'd have been trampled to death long ago. As it is, I'm full of aches and pains from anger."

"Do you still smoke, Miss?" her sister-in-law said. "Opium is still better than any other medicine for soothing the liver and composing the nerves. Be sure that you take good care of your-self, Miss. We're not around, and who else is there to look after you?"

Ch'i-ch'iao went through her trunks and took out lengths of silk in new designs to give to her sister-in-law, and also a pair of gold bracelets weighing four taels, a pair of carnelian hairpins shaped like lotus pods, and a quilt of silk fluff. She had for each niece a gold earspoon and for each nephew a miniature gold ingot or a sable hat, and handed her brother an enameled gold watch shaped like a cicada. Her brother and sister-in-law hastened to thank her.

"You came at the wrong moment," Ch'i-ch'iao said. "When we were just about to leave Peking, what we couldn't take was all given to the amahs and slave girls, several trunkfuls they got for nothing."

They looked embarrassed at this. As they took their leave, her sister-in-law said, "When we've got our daughter off our hands, we'll come and see Ku-nai-nai again."

"Just as well if you don't," Ch'i-ch'iao said, smil-ing. "I can't afford it."

When they got out of the Chiangs' house her sister-in-law said, "How is it Ku-nai-nai has changed so? Before she was married she may have been a bit proud and talked a little too much. Even later, when we went to see her, she had more of a temper but there was still a limit. She wasn't silly as she is now, sane enough one minute and the next minute off again, and al-together disagreeable."

Ch'i-ch'iao stood in the room holding her elbows and watched the two slave girls, Little Shuang and Ch'iang-yün, carrying the trunks be-tween them and stacking them back one by one. The things of the past came back again: the ses-ame oil shop over the cobbled street, the black-ened greasy counter, the wooden spoons standing in the buckets of sesame butter, and iron spoons of all sizes strung up above the oil jars. Insert the funnel in the customer's bottle. One big spoon plus two small spoons make a bottle—one and a half catties. Counts as one catty and four ounces if

it's somebody she knows. Sometimes she went marketing too, in a blouse and pants of blue linen trimmed with mirror-bright black silk. Across the thick row of brass hooks from which pork dan-gled she saw Ch'ao-lu of the butcher shop. Ch'ao-lu was always after her, calling her Miss Ts'ao, and on rare occasions Little Miss Ch'iao,[11] and she would give the rack of hooks a slap that sent all the empty hooks swinging across to poke him in the eye. Ch'ao-lu plucked a piece of raw fat a foot wide off the hook and threw it down hard on the block, and a warm odor rushed to her face, the smell of sticky dead flesh . . . she frowned. On the bed lay her husband, that lifeless body . . .

A gust of wind came in the window and blew against the long mirror in the lacquered scroll-work frame until it rattled against the wall. Ch'i-ch'iao pressed the mirror down with both hands. The green bamboo curtain and a green and gold landscape scroll reflected in the mirror went on swinging back and forth in the wind—one could get dizzy watching it for long. When she looked again the green bamboo curtain had faded, the green and gold landscape was replaced by a pho-tograph of her deceased husband, and the woman in the mirror was ten years older.

Last year she wore mourning for her husband and this year her mother-in-law had passed away. Now her husband's uncle, Ninth Old Master, was formally invited to come and divide the property among the survivors. Today was the focal point of all her imaginings since she had married into the house of Chiang. All these years she had worn the golden cangue but never even got to gnaw at the edge of the gold. It would be different from now on. In her white satin blouse and black skirt she looked rouged, from the eyes rubbed red to the feverish cheekbones. She lifted her hand to touch her face. It was flushed but the rest of her body was so cold she was actually trembling. She told Ch'iang-yün to pour her a cup of tea. (Little Shuang had been married long ago; Ch'iang-yün also was mated, with a page.) The tea she drank flowed heavily into her chest cavity and her heart

---

[11] A familiar form of address, as to a child of the family.

jumped, thumping in the hot tea. She sat down with her back to the mirror and asked Ch'iang-yün, "All this time Ninth Old Master has been here this afternoon, he's just been going over the accounts with Secretary Ma?"

Ch'iang-yün answered yes.

"Eldest Master and Eldest Mistress, Third Master and Third Mistress, none of them is around?"

Ch'iang-yün answered yes.

"Who else did he go to see?"

"Just took a turn in the schoolroom," said Ch'iang-yün.

"At least our Master Pai's studies could bear looking into . . . The trouble with the child this year is what happened to his father and grandmother, one after the other. If he still feels like studying, he's born of beasts." She finished her tea and told Ch'iang-yün to go down and see if the people of the eldest and third branches were all in the parlor, so she would not be too early and be laughed at for seeming eager. It happened that the eldest branch had also sent a slave girl to inquire, who came face to face with Ch'iang-yün.

Ch'i-ch'iao finally came downstairs, slowly, gracefully. A foreign-style dining table of ebony polished like a mirror was set up in the parlor for the occasion. Ninth Old Master occupied one side by himself, the account books with blue cloth covers and plum-red labels heaped before him along with a melon-ribbed teacup. Around him, besides Secretary Ma, were the specially invited *kung ch'in*, relatives no closer to one than to the other, serving more or less in the capacity of assistant judges. Eldest Master and Third Master represented their respective branches, but Second Master having died, his branch was represented by Second Mistress. Chi-tse, who knew very well that this day of reckoning boded no good for him, arrived last. But once there he showed no anxiety or depression: that same plump red smile was still on his cheeks, and in his eyes still that bit of dashing impatience.

Ninth Old Master coughed and made a brief report on the Chiangs' finances. Leafing through the account books, he read out the main holdings of land and houses and the annual income from each of these. Ch'i-ch'iao leaned forward with hands locked tight over her stomach, trying hard to understand every sentence he uttered and match it with the results of her past investigations. The houses in Tsingtao, the houses in Tientsin, the land in the home town, the land outside Peking, the houses in Shanghai . . . Third Master had borrowed too much from the general accounts and for too long. Apart from his share, now canceled out, he still owed sixty thousand dollars, but the eldest and second branches had to let it go, since he had nothing. The only house he owned, a foreign-style building with a garden bought for a concubine, was already mortgaged. Then there was just the jewelry that Old Mistress had brought with her as a bride, to be divided evenly among the three brothers. Chi-tse's share could not very well be confiscated, being a memento left by his mother.

Ch'i-ch'iao suddenly cried out, "Ninth Old Master, this is too hard on us."

The parlor had been dead quiet before; now the silence sawed straight into the ears, like the sandy rustle of a movie with a broken sound track grating rustily on. Ninth Old Master opened his eyes wide to look at her. "What? You wouldn't even let him have the bit of jewelry his mother left?"

" 'Even brothers settle their accounts openly,' " Ch'i-ch'iao quoted. "Eldest Brother and Sister-in-law say nothing, but I have to be tough-skinned and speak out this once. I can't compare with Eldest Brother and Sister-in-law. If the one we lost had been able to go out and be a mandarin for a couple of terms and save some money, I'd be glad to be generous too—what if we cancel all the old accounts? Only that one of ours was pitiful, ailing and groaning all his life, never earned a copper coin. Left a widow and orphans who're counting on just this small fixed sum to live on. I'm a crab without legs and Ch'ang-pai is not yet fourteen, with plenty of hard days ahead." Her tears fell as she spoke.

"What do you want then, if you may have your way?" said Ninth Old Master.

"It's not for me to decide," she said, sobbing. "I'm only begging Ninth Old Master to settle it for me."

Chi-tse, cold-faced, said nothing. The whole roomful of people felt it was not for them to speak. Ninth Old Master, unable to keep down a bellyful of fire, snorted: "I'd make a suggestion, only I'm afraid you won't like it. The second branch has land and nobody to look after it. The third branch has a man but no land. I'd have Third Master look after it for you for a consideration, whatever you see fit, only you may not want him."

Ch'i-ch'iao laughed sardonically. "I'd have it your way, only I'm afraid the dead one will not. Come, somebody! Ch'iang-yün, go and get Master Pai for me. Ch'ang-pai, what a hard life your father had! Born with ailments all over, went through life like a wretch, and for what? Never had a single comfortable day. In the end he left you, all there is of his bone and blood, and people still won't let you be, there're a thousand designs on your property. Ch'ang-pai, it's your father's fault that he dragged himself around with all his illnesses, bullied when he was alive, to have his widow and orphan bullied when he's dead. I don't matter—how many more scores of years can I live? At worst I'd go and explain this before Old Mistress's spirit tablet and kill myself in protest. But Ch'ang-pai, you're so young, you still have your life to live even if there's nothing to eat or drink but the northwest wind!"

Ninth Old Master was so angry he slapped the table. "I wash my hands of this! It was you people who begged and kowtowed to make me come. Do you think I like to go around looking for trouble?" He stood up, kicked the chair over and, without waiting to be seen out of the room, strode out of sight in a gust of wind.

The others looked at one another and slipped out one by one. Only Secretary Ma was left behind busily tidying up the account books. He thought that, with everybody gone and Second Mistress sitting there alone beating her breast and wailing, it would be embarrassing if he just walked off, and so he went up to her, bowing repeatedly, moving his hands up and down in obeisance, and calling, "Second Mistress! Second Mistress! . . . Second Mistress!" Ch'i-ch'iao just covered her face with a sleeve. Secretary Ma could not very well

pull her hand away. Perspiring in his despair, he took off his black satin skullcap to fan himself.

The awkward situation lasted for a few days, and then the property was divided quietly according to the original plan. The widow and orphans were still taken advantage of.

Ch'i-ch'iao took her son Ch'ang-pai and daughter Ch'ang-an and rented another house to live in, and seldom saw the Chiangs' other branches. Several months later Chiang Chi-tse suddenly appeared. When the amah announced the visit upstairs, Ch'i-ch'iao was secretly worried that she had offended him that day at the family conference over the division of property, and wondered what he was going to do about it. But "an army comes and generals fend it off"; why should she be afraid of him? She tied on a black skirt of iron-thread gauze under the Buddha-blue solid gauze jacket she was wearing and came downstairs. When Chi-tse got up, all smiles, to give his best regards to Second Sister-in-law, and asked if Master Pai was in the schoolroom and if Little Miss An's ringworm was cured, Ch'i-ch'iao suspected he was here to borrow money. Doubly on guard, she sat down and said smiling, "You've gained weight again lately, Third Brother."

"I seem like a man without a thing on his mind," said Chi-tse.

"Well, 'A lucky man need never be busy.' You're never one to worry," she said smiling.

"I'd have fewer worries than ever if I sold my landed property," he said.

"You mean the house you mortgaged? You want to sell it?"

"Quite a lot of thought went into it when it was built and I loved some of the fixtures; of course I wouldn't want to part with it. But later, as you know, land got expensive over there, so the year before last I tore it down and built in its place a row of houses. But it was really too much bother collecting rent from house to house, dealing with those tenants; so I thought I'd get rid of the property just for the sake of peace and quiet."

Ch'i-ch'iao said to herself, "How grand we sound! Still acting the rich young master before me when I know all about you!"

Although he was not complaining of poverty to

her, any mention of money transactions seemed to lead them onto dangerous ground, and so she changed the subject. "How is Third Sister? Her kidneys haven't been bothering her lately?"

"I haven't seen her for some time," Chi-tse said smiling.

"What's this? Have you quarreled?"

"We haven't quarreled either all this time," he said, smiling. "Exchange a few words when we have to but that's also rare. No time to quarrel and no mood for it."

"You're exaggerating. I for one don't believe it."

He rested his elbows on the arms of the rattan chair, locking his fingers to shade his eyes, and sighed deeply.

"Unless it's because you play around too much outside. You're in the wrong and still sighing away as if you were wronged. There's not one good man among you Chiangs!" she said, smiling, and lifted her round white fan as if to strike him. He moved his interlocked fingers downward, with both thumbs pressed on his lips and the forefingers slowly stroking the bridge of his nose, and his eyes seemed brighter. The irises were the black pebbles at the bottom of a bowl of narcissus, covered with cold water and expressionless. It was impossible to tell what he was thinking. "I should beat you," she said.

A bubble of mirth came up in his eyes. "Go ahead, beat me."

She was about to hit him, snatched back her hand, and then again mustered her strength and said, "I'd really beat you!" She swung her arm downward, but the descending fan remained in midair as she started to giggle.

He raised a shoulder toward her, smiling. "You'd better hit me just once. As it is, my bones are itching for punishment."

She hid the fan behind her, chuckling.

Chi-tse moved his chair around and sat facing the wall, leaning back heavily with both hands over his eyes, and heaved another sigh.

Ch'i-ch'iao chewed on her fan handle and looked at him from the corners of her eyes. "What's the matter with you today? Can't stand the heat?"

"You wouldn't know." After a long pause he said in a low voice, enunciating each word distinctly. "You know why I can't get on with the one at home, why I played so hard outside and squandered all my money. Who do you think it's all for?"

Ch'i-ch'iao was a bit frightened. She walked a long way off and leaned on the mantelpiece, the expression on her face slowly changing. Chi-tse followed her. Her head was bent and her right elbow rested on the mantelpiece. In her right hand was her fan, whose apricot-yellow tassel trailed down over her forehead. He stood before her and whispered, "Second Sister-in-law! . . . Ch'i-ch'iao!"

Ch'i-ch'iao turned her face away and smiled blandly. "As if I'd believe you!"

So he also walked away. "That's right. How could you believe me? Ever since you came to our house I couldn't stay there a minute, only wanted to get out. I was never so wild before you came; later it was to avoid you that I stayed out. After I was married to Lan-hsien, I played harder than ever because besides avoiding you I had to avoid her too. When I did see you, scarcely two sentences were exchanged before I lost my temper—how could you know the pain in my heart? When you were good to me, I felt still worse—I had to control myself—I couldn't ruin you like that. So many people at home, all watching us. If people should know, it wouldn't matter too much for me, I was a man, but what was going to happen to you?"

Ch'i-ch'iao's hands trembled until the yellow tassel on the fan handle rustled on her forehead.

"Whether you believe it or not makes little difference," he said. "What if you do believe it? Half our lives are over anyway. It's no use talking about it. I'm just asking you to understand the way I felt; then my suffering on your account wouldn't be totally in vain."

Ch'i-ch'iao bowed her head, basking in glory, in the soft music of his voice and the delicate pleasure of this occasion. So many years now, she had been playing hide-and-seek with him and never could get close, and there had still been a day like this in store for her. True, half a lifetime had gone by—the flower-years of her youth. Life is so devious and unreasonable. Why had she married into the Chiang family? For money? No, to meet Chi-tse, because it was fated that she should be in love with him. She lifted her face slightly. He was standing in front of her with flat hands closed on her fan and his cheek pressed against it. He was ten years older too, but he was after all the same person. Could he be lying to her? He wanted her money—the money she had sold her life for? The very idea enraged her. Even if she had him wrong there, could he have suffered as much for her as she did for him? Now that she had finally given up all thoughts of love he was here again to tempt her. His eyes—after ten years he was still the same person. Even if he were lying to her, wouldn't it be better to find out a little later? Even if she knew very well it was lies, he was such a good actor, wouldn't it be almost real?

No, she could not give this rascal any hold on her. The Chiangs were very shrewd; she might not be able to keep her money. She had to prove first whether he really meant it. She took a grip on herself, looked outside the door, gasped under her breath, "Somebody there!" and rushed out. She went to the amahs' quarters to tell P'an Ma to get the tea things for Third Master.

Coming back to the room, she frowned, saying, "So hateful—amah peering outside the door, turned and ran the minute she saw me. I went after her and stopped her. Who knows what stories they'd make up if we'd talked, however briefly, with the door shut. No peace even living by yourself."

P'an Ma brought the tea things and chilled sour plum juice. With her chopsticks Ch'i-ch'iao picked the shredded roses and green plums off the top of the honey cake for Chi-tse. "I remember you don't like the red and green shreds," she said.

He just smiled, unable to say anything with people around.

Ch'i-ch'iao made conversation. "How are you getting on with the houses you were going to sell?"

Chi-tse answered as he ate, "Some people offered eighty-five thousand; I haven't decided yet."

Ch'i-ch'iao paused to reflect. "The district is good."

"Everybody is against my getting rid of the property, says the price is still going up."

Ch'i-ch'iao asked for more particulars, then said, "A pity I haven't got that much cash in hand, otherwise I'd like to buy it."

"Actually there's no hurry about my property; it's your land in our part of the country that should be gotten rid of soon. Ever since we became a republic it's been one war after another, never missed a single year. The area is so messed up and with all the graft—the collectors and bookkeepers and the local powers—how much do we get when it comes our turn, even in a year of good harvest? And these last few years it's been either flood or drought."

Ch'i-ch'iao pondered. "I've done some calculating and kept putting it off. If only I'd sold it, then I wouldn't be caught short just when I want to buy your houses."

"If you want to sell that land it had better be now. I heard Hopeh and Shantung are going to be in the war again."

"Who am I to sell it to in such a hurry?"

He said after a moment of hesitation, "All right, I'll make some inquiries for you."

Ch'i-ch'iao lifted her eyebrows and said, smiling, "Go on! You and that pack of foxes and dogs you run with, who is there that's halfway reliable?"

Chi-tse dipped a dumpling that he had bitten open into the little dish of vinegar, taking his time, and mentioned a couple of reliable names. Ch'i-ch'iao then seriously questioned him on details and he set his answers out tidily, evidently well prepared.

Ch'i-ch'iao continued to smile but her mouth felt dry; her upper lip stuck on her gum and would not come down. She raised the lidded teacup to suck a mouthful of tea, licked her lips, and suddenly jumped up with a set face and threw her fan at his head. The round fan went wheeling through the air, knocked his shoulder as he ducked slightly to the left, and upset his glass. The sour plum juice spilled all over him.

"You want me to sell land to buy your houses? You want me to sell land? Once the money goes through your hands what can I count on? You'd con me—you're trying to con me with such talk— you take me for a fool—" She leaned across the table to hit him, but P'an Ma held her in a desperate embrace and started to yell. Ch'iang-yün and the others came running, pressed her down between them, pleaded noisily. Ch'i-ch'iao struggled and barked orders at the same time, but with a sinking heart she quite realized she was being foolish, too foolish. She was making a spectacle of herself.

Chi-tse took off his drenched white satin gown. P'an Ma brought a hot towel to wipe it for him. He paid her no attention but, before sauntering out the door with his gown on his arm, he said to Ch'iang-Yün, "When Master Pai finishes his lesson for the day, tell him to get a doctor for his mother." Ch'iang-yün, who was too frightened by the proceedings not to say yes, received a resounding slap on the face from Ch'i-ch'iao. Chi-tse was gone. The slave girls and amahs were scolded and also hurriedly left her. Drop by drop, the sour plum juice trickled down the table, keeping time like a water clock at night—one drip, another drip—the first watch of the night, the second watch—one year, a hundred years. So long, this silent moment. Ch'i-ch'iao stood there, holding her head up with one hand. In another second she had turned around and was hurrying upstairs. Lifting her skirt, she half climbed and half stumbled her way up, continually bumping against the dingy wall of green plaster. Her Buddha-blue jacket was smudged with patches of pale chalk. She wanted another glimpse of him from the upstairs window. No matter what, she had loved him before. Her love had given her endless pain. That alone should make him worthy of her continuing regard. How many times had she strained to repress herself until all her muscles and bones and gums ached with sharp pain. Today it all had been her fault. It wasn't as if she didn't know he was no good. If she wanted him she had to pretend ignorance and put up with his ways. Why had she exposed him? Wasn't life just

like this and no more than this? In the end what was real and what was false?

She reached the window and pulled aside the dark green foreign-style curtains fringed in little velvet balls. Chi-tse was going out the alley, his gown slung over his arm. Like a flock of white pigeons, the wind on that sunny day fluttered inside his white silk blouse and trousers. It penetrated everywhere, flapping its wings.

A curtain of ice-cold pearls seemed to hang in front of Ch'i-ch'iao's eyes. A hot wind would press the curtain tight on her face, and after being sucked back by the wind for a moment, it would muffle all her head and face before she could draw breath. In such alternately hot and cold waves her tears flowed.

The tiny shrunken image of a policeman reflected faintly in the top corner of the window glass ambled by swinging his arms. A ricksha quietly ran over the policeman. A little boy with his long gown tucked up into his trouser waist ran kicking a ball out the edge of the glass. A postman in green riding a bicycle superimposed his image on the policeman as he streaked by. All ghosts, ghosts of many years ago or the unborn of many years hence . . . What is real and what is false?

The autumn passed, then the winter. Ch'i-ch'iao was out of touch with reality, feeling a little lost despite the usual flares of temper which prompted her to beat slave girls and change cooks. Her brother and his wife came to Shanghai to see her twice and stayed each time not longer than ten days, because in the end they could not stand her nagging, even though she would give them parting presents. Her nephew Ts'ao Ch'un-hsi came to town to look for work and stayed at her house. Though none too bright, this youth knew his place. Ch'i-ch'iao's son Ch'ang-pai was now fourteen, and her daughter Ch'ang-an about a year younger, but they looked only about seven or eight, being small and thin. During the New Year holidays the boy wore a bright blue padded gown of heavy silk and the girl a bright green brocade padded gown, both so thickly wadded that their arms stuck out straight. Standing side by side, both looked like paper dolls, with their flat thin white faces. One day after lunch Ch'i-ch'iao was not up yet. Ts'ao Ch'un-hsi kept the brother and sister company throwing dice. Ch'ang-an had lost all her New Year money gifts and still would not stop playing. Ch'ang-pai swept all the copper coins on the table toward himself and said, smiling, "I won't play with you anymore."

"We'll play with candied lotus seeds," Ch'ang-an said.

"The sugar will stain your clothes if you keep them in your pocket," Ch'un-hsi said.

"Watermelon seeds will do. There's a can of them on top of the wardrobe," said Ch'ang-an. So she moved a small tea table over and stepped on a chair to get on the table to reach up.

Ch'un-hsi was so nervous he called out, "Don't you fall down, Little Miss An, I can't shoulder the blame." The words were scarcely out of his mouth when Ch'ang-an suddenly tipped backward and would have toppled down if he had not caught her. Ch'ang-pai clapped his hands, laughing, while Ch'un-hsi, though he muttered curses, also could not help laughing. All three of them dissolved in mirth. Lifting her down, Ch'un-hsi suddenly saw in the mirror of the rosewood wardrobe Ch'i-ch'iao standing in the doorway with her arms akimbo, her hair not yet done. Somewhat taken aback, he quickly set Ch'ang-an down and turned around to greet her: "Aunt is up."

Ch'i-ch'iao rushed over and pushed Ch'ang-an behind her. Ch'ang-an lost her balance and fell down, but Ch'i-ch'iao continued shielding her with her own body while she cried harshly to Ch'un-hsi, "You wolf-hearted, dog-lunged creature, I'll fix you! After all the teas and meals I've served you, what ground have I given you for complaint? How could you take advantage of my daughter? You think I can't see what's in your wolf's heart and dog's lungs? Don't you go thinking if you teach my daughter bad things I'll have to hold my nose and marry her to you, so you can take over our property. A fool like you couldn't think of such a trick, it must be your parents who taught you, led you by the hand. Those two wolf-hearted, dog-lunged, ungrateful, old addled eggs,

they're determined to get my money. When one scheme fails they try another."

Ch'un-hsi, staring white-eyed in his anger, was about to defend himself when Ch'i-ch'iao said, "Aren't you ashamed? You'd still answer back? Get out of my sight; don't wait for my men to drive you out with rods." So saying, she pushed her son and daughter out and then left the room herself, supported by a slave girl. Being a quick-tempered youth, Ch'un-hsi rolled up his bedding and left the Chiang house forthwith.

Ch'i-ch'iao returned to the living room and lay down on the opium couch. With the velvet curtains drawn it was dark in the room. Only when the wind came in through the crevices and moved the curtains was a bit of sky hazily visible under hems fringed with green velvet balls. There was just the opium lamp and the dim light of the stove burning red. Having had a fright, Ch'ang-an sat stunned on a little stool by the stove.

"Come over here," Ch'i-ch'iao said.

Ch'ang-an didn't move at first, thinking her mother would hit her. She fiddled with the laundry hung on the tin screen around the stove and turned over a cotton undershirt with little pink checks, saying, "It's almost burned." The shirt gave out a hot smell of cloth fuzz.

But Ch'-ch'iao, not quite in the mood to beat or scold her, simply said matter-of-factly, "You'll be thirteen after the New Year, you should have more sense. Although Cousin is no outsider, men are all rotten without exception. You should know how to take care of yourself. Who's not after your money?" A gust of wind passed, showing the cold white sky between the velvet balls on the curtains, puncturing with a row of little holes the warm darkness in the room. The flame of the opium lamp ducked and the shadows on Ch'i-ch'iao's face seemed a shade deeper. She suddenly sat up to whisper, "Men . . . leave them alone! Who's not after your money? Your mother's bit of money didn't come easy, nor is it easy to keep. When it comes to you two, I can't look on and see you get cheated. I'm telling you to be more on guard from now on, you hear?"

"I hear," Ch'ang-an said with her head down.

bound feet

One of Ch'i-ch'iao's feet was going to sleep, and she reached down to pinch it. Just for a moment a gentle memory stirred in her eyes. She remembered a man who was after her money.

Her bound feet had been padded with cotton wool to simulate the reformed feet, half let out. As she looked at them, something occurred to her and she said with a cynical laugh, "You may say yes, but how do I know if you're sensible or silly at heart? You're so big already, and with a pair of big feet, where can't you go? Even if I could control you, I wouldn't have the energy to watch you all day long. Actually at thirteen it's already too late for foot-binding, it's my fault not to have seen to it earlier. We'll start right now, there's still time."

Ch'ang-an was momentarily at a loss for an answer, but the amahs standing around said, smiling, "Small feet are not fashionable anymore. To have her feet bound will perhaps mean trouble when the time comes for Little Miss to get engaged."

"What nonsense! I'm not worried about my daughter having no takers; you people needn't bother to worry for me. If nobody really wants her and she has to be kept all her life, I can afford it too."

She actually started to bind her daughter's feet, and Ch'ang-an howled in great pain. But then even women in conservative families like the Chiangs' were letting out their bound feet, to say nothing of girls whose feet had never been bound. Everybody talked about Ch'ang-an's feet as a great joke. After binding them for a year or so, Ch'i-ch'iao's momentary enthusiasm had waned and relatives persuaded her to let them loose, but Ch'ang-an's feet would never be entirely the same again.

All the children of the Chiangs' eldest and third branches went to foreign-style schools. Ch'i-ch'iao, always purposely competing with them, wanted to enroll Ch'ang-pai in one. Besides playing mahjong for small stakes, Ch'ang-pai's only love was amateur Peking opera clubs. He was working hard day and night training his singing voice, and was afraid that school would interfere with his lessons, so he refused to go. In desperation Ch'i-ch'iao sent Ch'ang-an instead to the Hu Fan Middle School for girls and through connections got her into one of the higher classes. Ch'ang-an changed into a uniform of rough blue "patriotic cloth" and in less than six months her complexion turned ruddy and her wrists and ankles grew thicker. The boarders were supposed to have their clothes washed by a laundry concession. Ch'ang-an could not remember her own numbers and often lost pillowcases, handkerchiefs, and other little items, and Ch'i-ch'iao insisted on going to speak to the principal about it. One day when she was home for holidays, in going over the things Ch'i-ch'iao found a sheet missing. She fell into a thundering rage and threatened to go to the school herself the next day to demand satisfaction. Ch'ang-an in dismay tried just once to stop her and Ch'i-ch'iao scolded, "You good-for-nothing wastrel. Your mother's money is not money to you. Did your mother's money come easy? What dowry will I have to give you when you get married? Whatever I give you will be given in vain."

Ch'ang-an did not dare say anything in reply and cried all night. She could not bear to lose face like this in front of her schoolmates. To a fourteen-year-old that seems of the greatest importance. How was she to face people from now on if her mother went and made a scene? She would rather die than go to school again. Her friends, the music teacher she liked, they would soon forget there was a girl who had come for half a year and left quietly for no reason. A clean break—she felt this sacrifice was a beautiful desolate gesture.

At midnight she crawled out of bed and put a hand outside the window. Pitch-dark, was it raining? No raindrops. She took a harmonica from the side of her pillow and half squatted, half sat on the floor, blowing it stealthily. Hesitantly the little tune of "Long, Long Ago" twirled and spread out in the huge night. People must not hear. Strictly controlled, the thin, wailing music of the harmonica kept trailing off and on like a baby sobbing. Short of breath, she stopped for a while.

Through the window the moon had come out of the clouds: a dark gray sky dotted sparsely with stars and a blurred chip of a moon, like a lithographed picture. White clouds steaming up underneath and a faint halo over the street lamp showing among the top branches of a tree. Ch'ang-an started her harmonica again. "Tell me the tales that to me were so dear, long, long ago, long, long ago . . ."

The next day she summoned up enough courage to tell her mother, "I don't feel like going back to school, Mother."

Ch'i-ch'iao opened her eyes wide. "Why?"

"I can't keep up with the lessons, and the food is too bad, I can't get used to it."

Ch'i-ch'iao took off a slipper and slapped her off-handedly, with its sole, saying bitterly, "Your father wasn't as good as other people, you're also not as good? You weren't born a freak; you're just being perverse so as to disappoint me."

Looking down, Ch'ang-an stood with her hands behind her back and would not speak. So the amahs intervened: "Little Miss is grown up now, and it's not convenient for her to go to school where there're all sorts of people. Actually, it's just as well for her not to go."

Ch'i-ch'iao paused to reflect. "At least we have to get the tuition back. Why give it to them for nothing?" She wanted Ch'ang-an to go with her to collect it. Ch'ang-an would have fought to the death rather than go. Ch'i'ch-iao took two amahs with her. The way she told it when she returned, although she did not get the money back, she had thoroughly humiliated the principal. Afterward, when Ch'ang-an met any of her schoolmates on the street, she reddened and paled alternately. Earth had no room for her. She could only pretend not to see and walk past them hastily. When friends wrote her, she dared not even open the letters but just sent them back. Thus her school life came to an end.

Sometimes she felt the sacrifice was not worth it and was secretly sorry, but it was too late. She gradually gave up all thought of self-improvement and kept to her place. She learned to make trouble, play little tricks, and interfere with the running of the house. She often fell out with her mother, but she looked and sounded more and more like her. Every time she wore a pair of unlined trousers and sat with her legs apart and the palms of both hands on the stool in front of her, her head tilted to one side, her chin on her chest, looking dismally but intently at the woman opposite and telling her, "Every family has its own troubles, Cousin-in-law—every family has its own troubles!", she seemed the spit and image of Ch'i-ch'iao. She wore a pigtail and her eyes and eyebrows had a taut expressiveness about them reminiscent of Ch'i-ch'iao in her prime, but her small mouth was a bit too drawn which made her look older. Even when she had been younger, she did not seem fresh, but was like a tender bunch of vegetables that had been salted.

Some people tried to make matches for her. If the other side was not well off, Ch'i-ch'iao would always suspect it wanted their money. If the other side had wealth and influence, it would show little enthusiasm. Ch'ang-an had only average good looks, and since her mother was not only lowborn but also known for her shrewishness, she probably would not have much upbringing. So the high were out of reach and the low Ch'i-ch'iao would not stoop to—Ch'ang-an stayed home year after year. But Ch'ang-pai's marriage could not be delayed. When he gambled outside and showed enough personal interest in certain Peking opera actresses to attend their performances regularly, Ch'i-ch'iao still had nothing to say; she got alarmed only when he started to go to brothels with his Third Uncle Chiang Chi-tse. In great haste she betrothed and married him to a Miss Yuan, called Chih-shou as a child.

The wedding ceremony was half modern, and the bride, without the customary red kerchief over her head and face, wore blue eyeglasses and a pink wedding veil instead, and a pink blouse and skirt with multicolored embroidery. The glasses were removed after she entered the bridal chamber and sat with bowed head under the turquoise-colored bed curtains. The guests gathered for the "riot in the bridal chamber" surrounded her, making jokes. After taking a look, Ch'i-ch'iao came out. Ch'ang-an overtook her at the door and whispered, "Fair-skinned, only the lips are a bit too thick."

Ch'i-ch'iao leaned on the doorway, took a gold earspoon from her bun to scratch her head with, and laughed sardonically. "Don't start on that now. Your new sister-in-law's thick lips, chop them up and they'll make a heaping dish!"

"Well, it's said that people with thick lips have warm feelings," said a lady beside her.

Ch'i-ch'iao snorted; pointing her gold earspoon at the woman, she lifted an eyebrow and said with a crooked little smile, "It isn't so nice to have warm feelings. I can't say much in front of young ladies—just hope our Master Pai won't die in her hands." Ch'i-ch'iao was born with a high clear voice, which had grown less shrill as she grew older, but it was still cutting, or rather rasping, like a razor blade. Her last remark could not be called loud, but it was not exactly soft. Could the bride, surrounded by a crowd as she was, possibly have registered a quiver on her severely flat face and chest? Probably it was just a reflection of the flames leaping on the tall pair of dragon-and-phoenix candles.

After the Third Day Ch'i-ch'iao found the bride stupid and unsatisfactory in various things and often complained to relatives. Some said placatingly, "The bride is young. Second Sister-in-law will just have to take the trouble to teach her. The child is simply naïve."

Ch'i-ch'iao made a spitting noise. "Our new young mistress may look innocent—but as soon as she sees Master Pai she has to go and sit on the nightstool. Really! It sounds unbelievable, doesn't it?"

When the talk reached Chih-shou's ears, she wanted to kill herself. This was before the end of the first month, when Ch'i-ch'iao still kept up appearances. Later she would even say such things in front of Chih-shou, who could neither cry nor laugh with impunity. And if she merely looked wooden, pretending not to listen, Ch'i-ch'iao would slap the table and sigh, "It's really not easy, to eat a mouthful of rice in the house of your son and daughter-in-law! People pull a long face at you at the drop of a hat."

One night Ch'i-ch'iao was lying on the opium couch smoking while Ch'ang-pai crouched on a nearby upholstered chair cracking watermelon seeds. The radio was broadcasting a little-known Peking opera. He followed it in a book, humming the lyrics word by word, and as he got into the mood, swung a leg up over the back of the chair rocking it back and forth to mark the rhythm.

Ch'i-ch'iao reached out a foot and kicked at him. "Come Master Pai, fill the pipe for me a couple of times."

"With an opium lamp right there why put me to work? I have honey on my fingers or something?" Ch'ang-pai stretched himself while replying and slowly moved over to the little stool in front of the opium lamp and rolled up his sleeves.

"Unfilial slave, what kind of answer is that! Putting you to work is an honor." She looked at him through slitted, smiling eyes. All these years he had been the only man in her life. Only with him there was no danger of his being after her money—it was his anyway. But as her son, he amounted to less than half a man. And even the half she could not keep, now that he was married. He was a slight, pale young man, a bit hunched, with gold-rimmed glasses and fine features meticulously drawn, often smiling vacantly, his mouth hanging open and something shining inside, either too much saliva or a gold tooth. The collar of his gown was open, showing its pearly lamb lining and a white pajama shirt. Ch'i-ch'iao put a foot on his shoulder and kept giving him light kicks on the neck, whispering, "Unfilial slave, I'll fix you! When did you get to be so unfilial?"

Ch'ang-pai quoted with a smile, " 'Take a wife and the mother is forgotten.' "

"Don't talk nonsense, our Master Pai is not that kind of person, nor could I have had a son like that either," said Ch'i-ch'iao. Ch'ang-pai just smiled. She looked fixedly at him from the corners of her eyes. "If you're still my Master Pai as before, cook opium for me all night tonight."

"That's no problem," he said, smiling.

"If you doze off, see if I don't hammer you with my fists."

The living room curtains had been sent to be washed. Outside the windows the moon was barely visible behind dark clouds, a dab of black, a

dab of white like a ferocious theatrical mask. Bit
by bit it came out of the bottomless pit. It was long
past midnight, and Ch'ang-an had gone to bed
long ago. As Ch'ang-pai started to nod while rolling the opium pills, Ch'i-ch'iao poured him a cup
of strong tea. The two of them ate honeyed pre-
serves and discussed neighbors' secrets. Ch'i-
ch'iao suddenly said, smiling, "Tell me, Master
Pai, is your wife any good?"

"What is there to say about it?" Ch'ang-pai said,
smiling.

"Must be good if there is nothing to criticize,"
said Ch'i-ch'iao.

"Who said she's good?"

"Not good? In what way? Tell Mother."

Ch'ang-pai was vague at first but under cross-
examination he had to reveal a thing or two. The
amahs handing them tea turned aside to chuckle
and the slave girls covered their mouths trying
not to laugh and slipped out of the room. Ch'i-
ch'iao gritted her teeth and laughed and muttered
curses, removed the pipe bowl and knocked the
ashes out with all her strength, banging loudly,
Once started, Ch'ang-pai found it hard to stop
and talked all night.

The next morning Ch'i-ch'iao told the amahs to
bring a couple of blankets to let the young master
sleep on the couch. Chih-shou was up already and
came to pay her respects. Ch'i-ch'iao had not slept
all night but was more energetic than ever and
asked relatives over to play mahjong, women of
different families including her daughter-in-law's
mother. Over the mahjong table she told in detail
all her daughter-in-law's secrets as confessed by
her son, adding some touches of her own that
made the story still more vivid. Everybody tried to
change the subject, but the small talk no sooner
started than Ch'i-ch'iao would smilingly switch it
back to her daughter-in-law. Chih-shou's mother
turned purple. Too ashamed to see her daughter,
she put down her mahjong tiles and went home in
her private ricksha.

Ch'i-ch'iao made Ch'ang-pai cook opium for
her for two nights running. Chih-shou lay stiffly
in bed with both hands on her ribs curled upward
like a dead chicken's claws. She knew her mother-

in-law was questioning her husband again, although Heaven knew how he could have anything
fresh to say. Tomorrow he would again come to
her with a drooling, mock-pleading look. Perhaps
he had guessed that she would center all her
hatred on him. Even if she could not fight tooth
and nail, she would at least upbraid him and
make a scene. Very likely he would steal her
thunder by coming in half drunk, to pick on her
and smash something. She knew his ways. In the
end he would sit down on the bed, raise his shoulders, reach inside his white silk pajama shirt to
scratch himself, and smile unexpectedly. A little
light would tremble on his gold-rimmed spectacles
and twinkle in his mouth, spit or gold tooth. He
would take off his glasses . . . Chih-shou suddenly sat up and tore open the bed curtains. This
was an insane world, a husband not like a husband, a mother-in-law not like a mother-in-law.
Either they were mad or she was. The moon tonight was better than ever, high and full like a
white sun in a pitch-black sky, not a cloud within
ten thousand *li*. Blue shadows all over the floor
and blue shadows on the canopy overhead. Her
feet too were in the deathly still blue shadows.

Thinking to hook up the bed curtains, Chih-
shou reached out groping for the hook. With one
hand holding the brass hook and her face snuggled against her shoulder, she could not keep the
sobs from starting. The curtain dropped. There
was nobody but her inside the dark bed; still she
hastened to hook the curtains up in a panic. Outside the windows there was still that abnormal
moon that made all one's body hairs stand on
end—small white sun brilliant in the black sky. Inside the room she could clearly see the embroidered rosy-purple chair covers and table cloths,
the gold-embroidered scarlet screen with five
phoenixes flying in a row, the pink satin scrolls
embroidered with seal-script characters em-
bellished with flowers. On the dressing table the
silver powder jar, silver mouth-rinsing mug, and
silver vase were each caught in a red and green
net and filled with wedding candies. Along the
silk panel across the lintel of the bed hung balls of
flowers, toy flower pots, *ju-yi*,[12] and rice dump-

---

[12] Lit., "as you wish." An odd-shaped ornamental piece, usually of jade.

lings, all made of multicolored gilded velvet, and dangling underneath them glass balls the size of finger tips and mauvish pink tassels a foot long. In such a big room, crammed full of trunks, spare bedding, and furnishings, surely she could find a sash to hang herself with. She fell back on the bed. In the moonlight her feet had no color at all—bluish, greenish, purplish, the tints of a corpse gone cold. She wanted to die, she wanted to die. She was afraid of the moonlight but didn't dare turn on the light. Tomorrow her mother-in-law would say, "Master Pai fixed me a couple more pipes and our poor young mistress couldn't sleep the whole night, kept her light on to all hours waiting for him to come back—can't do without him." Chih-shou's tears flowed along the pillow. She did not wipe her eyes; rubbing would get them swollen and her mother-in-law would again say, "Master Pai didn't sleep in his room for just one night and Young Mistress cried until her eyes were like peaches!"

Although Ch'i-ch'iao pictured her son and daughter-in-law as a passionate couple, Ch'ang-pai was not very pleased with Chih-shou and Chih-shou on her part hated him so much her teeth itched to bite him. Since the two did not get along, Ch'ang-pai again went strolling in "the streets of flowers and the lanes of willows."[13] Ch'i-ch'iao gave him a slave girl called Chüan-erh for a concubine and still could not hold him. She also tried in various ways to get him to smoke opium. Ch'ang-pai had always liked a couple of drags for fun but he had never gotten into the habit. Now that he smoked more he quieted down and no longer went out much, just stayed with his mother and his concubine.

His sister Ch'ang-an got dysentery when she was twenty-four. Instead of getting a doctor, Ch'i-ch'iao persuaded her to smoke a little opium and it did ease the pain. After she recovered she also got into the habit. An unmarried girl without any other distractions, Ch'ang-an went at it single-mindedly and smoked even more than her brother. Some tried to dissuade her. Ch'i-ch'iao said, "What is there to be afraid of? For one thing we Chiangs can still afford it, and even if I sold

[13] A standard reference to a house of pleasure.

two hundred *mou* of land today so the brother and sister could smoke, who is there who'd dare fart about it? When the girl gets married she'll have her dowry, she'll be eating and drinking out of her own pocket, so even if her husband is unhappy about her smoking he can only look on."

All the same, Ch'ang-an's prospects were affected. The matchmakers, who had never come running to begin with, now disappeared altogether. When Ch'ang-an was nearly thirty, Ch'i-ch'iao changed her tune, seeing that her daughter was fated to be an old maid. "Not married off because she's not good-looking, and yet blames her mother for putting it off, spoiling her chances. Pulls a long face all day as if I owed her two hundred copper coins. It's certainly not to make myself miserable that I've kept her at home, feeding her free tea and rice!"

On the twentieth birthday of Chiang Chi-tse's daughter Ch'ang-hsing, Ch'ang-an went to give her cousin her best wishes. Chiang Chi-tse was poor now, but fortunately his wide social contacts kept him more or less solvent. Ch'ang-hsing said secretly to her mother, "Mother, try to introduce a friend to Sister An, she seems so pathetic. Her eyes reddened with tears at the very mention of conditions at home."

Lan-hsien hastily raised her hand. "No, no! This match I dare not make. Stir up your Second Aunt, with her temper?"

But Ch'ang-hsing, young and meddlesome, paid her no heed. After some time she by chance mentioned Ch'ang-an's case to her schoolmates, and it happened that one of them had an uncle newly returned from Germany, a northerner too, even distantly related to the Chiangs, as it turned out when they really investigated his background. The man was called T'ung Shih-fang, and was several years older than Ch'ang-an. And Ch'ang-hsing took matters into her own hands and arranged everything. Her schoolmate's mother would play hostess. On Ch'ang-an's side her family was kept as much in the dark as if sealed in an iron barrel.

Ch'i-ch'iao had always had a strong constitution. Thus, when Chih-shou got tuberculosis, naturally

Ch'i-ch'iao thought her daughter-in-law disgustingly affected, making much of herself, eating this and that, unable to stand the least fatigue and seemingly having a better time than usual. Finally, out of spite, she got sick too. At first it was just weak breath and thin blood, but even then it sent the entire household into a spin, so that they had no time for Chih-shou. Later Ch'i-ch'iao got seriously ill and took to her bed and there was more fuss than ever. Ch'ang-an slipped out in the confusion and called a tailor to her Third Uncle's house, where Ch'ang-hsing designed a new costume for her. On the day of the dinner Ch'ang-hsing accompanied her in the late afternoon to see the hairdresser, who waved her hair with hot tongs and plastered close-set little kiss-curls from the temple to the ears. Upon returning home, Ch'ang-hsing made her cousin wear "glassy-green" jadeite[14] earrings with pagoda-shaped pendants two inches long and change into an apple-green georgette gown with a high collar, ruffled sleeves, and fine pleats below the waist, half Western style. As a young maid squatted on the floor buttoning her up, Ch'ang-an scrutinized herself in the wardrobe mirror and could not help stretching out both arms and kicking out the skirt in a posture from "The Grape Fairy."[15] Twisting her head around, she started to laugh, saying, "Really dolled up to look like the celestial maiden scattering flowers!"[16]

Ch'ang-hsing signaled the maid in the mirror with her eyes and they both laughed. After Ch'ang-an had finished dressing, she sat down straight-backed on a high chair.

"I'll go and telephone for a taxi," Ch'ang-hsing said.

"It's early yet," said Ch'ang-an.

Ch'ang-hsing looked at her watch. "We're supposed to be there at eight. It's now five past."

"It probably wouldn't matter if we were half an hour late."

Ch'ang-hsing thought it both infuriating and laughable for her cousin to want to put on airs.

She opened her silver mesh handbag to examine its contents. On the pretext that she had forgotten her compact, she went to her mother's room and told her all about it, adding, "T'ung is not the host today, so for whom is she putting on airs? I won't bother to talk her out of it. Let her dawdle until tomorrow morning, it's none of my business."

Lan-hsien said, "How silly you are! You made the appointment, you're making the match, how can you not be responsible? I've told you so many times you should have known better, Little Miss An is just as petty as her mother and not used to company. She'll make a spectacle of herself, and she's your cousin, after all. If you lose face you deserve it—who told you to get into this? Gone crazy from having nothing to do?"

Ch'ang-hsing sat pouting in her mother's room for a long while.

"It looks as if your cousin is waiting to be pressed," Lan-hsien said smiling.

"I'm not going to press her."

"Silly girl, what's the use of your pressing? She's waiting for the other side to telephone."

Ch'ang-hsing broke out laughing. "She's not a bride, to be urged three, four times and forced into the sedan chair."

"Ring up the restaurant anyway and be done with it—tell them to call. It's almost nine. If you wait any longer it's really off."

Ch'ang-hsing had to do as she was told and finally set out with her cousin.

Ch'ang-an was still in good spirits in the car, talking and laughing away. But once in the restaurant, she suddenly became reserved, stealing into the room behind Ch'ang-hsing, timidly removed her apple-green ostrich cape, and sat down with bowed head, took an almond and bit off a tenth of it every two minutes, chewing slowly. She had come to be looked at. She felt that her costume was impeccable and could stand scrutiny but her body was altogether superfluous and could as well be shrunk in size and put away if she knew how to do this. She kept silent throughout the meal.

[14] The most valued kind of jadeite, translucent and dark green in color.

[15] A short musical by Li Ching-hui, a most popular choice for school productions during the twenties and thirties.

[16] T'ien-nü san-hua (The celestial maiden scatters flowers) is the title of a Peking opera made popular by Mei Lan-fang. It is based on an episode from the Vimalakirti Sutra.

While waiting for the dessert, Ch'ang-hsing pulled her to the window to watch the street scene and walked off on some pretext, and T'ung Shih-fang ambled over to the window.

"Has Miss Chiang been here before?" he said.

"No," Ch'ang-an said in a small voice.

"The first time for me too. The food isn't bad, but I'm not quite used to it yet."

"Not used to it?"

"Yes, foreign food is more bland, Chinese food is more greasy. When I had just come back friends and relatives made me eat out for several days running and I easily got an upset stomach."

Ch'ang-an looked at her fingers back and front as if intent on counting how many of the whorls were shaped like "snails" and how many "shovels."

Out of nowhere a little neon sign in the shape of a flower bloomed on the windowpane, reflected from the shop opposite, red petals with a green heart. It was the lotus of the Nile set before the gods and also the lily emblem of French royalty . . .

Shih-fang, who had not seen any girls of his homeland for many years, was struck by Ch'ang-an's pathetic charm and rather liked it. He had been engaged long before he went abroad, but having fallen in love with a schoolmate he violently opposed the match. After endless long-distance negotiations he almost broke with his parents, who for a time stopped sending money, causing him much hardship. They finally gave in, however, and put an end to his engagement. Unfortunately his schoolmate fell in love with somebody else. In his disappointment he dug in and studied for seven, eight years. His conviction that old-fashioned wives were best was also one made on the rebound.

After this meeting with Ch'ang-an, they were both interested. Ch'ang-hsing thought she should finish her good deed but, however enthusiastic, she was not qualified to speak to Ch'ang-an's mother. She had to beg Lan-hsien, who refused adamantly, saying, "You know very well your father and your Second Aunt are like enemies, never see each other. Although I've never quar-

reled with her there's no love lost. Why ask to be cold-shouldered?"

Ch'ang-an said nothing when she saw Lan-hsien, merely shed tears. Lan-hsien had to promise to go just once. The sisters-in-law met and after the amenities Lan-hsien explained the purpose of her visit. Ch'i-ch'iao was glad enough when she first heard of it.

"Then I'll leave it to Third Sister," she said. "I haven't been at all well, I can't cope with it, will just have to trouble Third Sister. This girl has been a dead weight on my hands. As a mother I can't be said not to have done right by her. When old-fashioned rules were in force I bound her feet, when new-fangled rules were in force I sent her to school—what else is there? A girl I dug out my heart and liver to train, as it were, she shouldn't have no takers as long as she's not scarred or pock-marked or blind. But this girl was born an Ah-tou[17] that isn't worth supporting. I get so angry I keep yelling: 'Oh, for the day that I shut my eyes and go!'—her marriage will then be in the hands of Heaven and left to fate."

So it was agreed that Lan-hsien would ask both sides to dinner so they could look each other over. Ch'ang-an and T'ung Shih-fang met again as if for the first time. Ch'i-ch'iao, sick in bed, did not appear, so Ch'ang-an got engaged in peace. At the dinner table Lan-hsien and Ch'ang-hsing forcibly took Ch'ang-an's hand and placed it in T'ung Shih-fang's. Shih-fang put the ring on her finger in public. And the girl's family gave gifts in return, not the traditional stationery but a pen set in a velvet-lined box plus a wristwatch.

After the engagement Ch'ang-an furtively went out alone with T'ung Shih-fang several times. The two of them walked side by side in the park in the autumn sun, talking very little, each content with a partial view of the other's clothes and moving feet. The fragrance of her face powder and his tobacco smell served as invisible railings that separated them from the crowd. On the open green lawn where so many people ran and laughed and talked, they alone walked a porch that wound on endlessly in silence. Ch'ang-an did not feel there

---

[17] The inept heir of Liu Pei, founder of the Shu Han kingdom during the Three Kingdoms period.

EILEEN CHANG

was anything amiss in silence. She thought this was all there was to social contact between modern men and women. As to T'ung Shih-fang, from painful experience in the past he was dubious anyway of the exchange of thought. He was satisfied that someone was beside him. Formerly he had been disgusted by the character in fiction who would say, when asking a woman to live with him, "Please give me solace." Solace is purely spiritual but it is used here as a euphemism for sex. But now he knew the line between the spiritual and physical could not be drawn so clearly. Words are no use after all. Holding hands for a long time is a more apt consolation, because not many people talk well and still fewer really have anything to say.

Sometimes it rained in the park. Ch'ang-an would open her umbrella and Shih-fang would hold it for her. Upon the translucent blue silk, myriad raindrops twinkled like a skyful of stars that would follow them about later on a taxi's glistening front window of crushed silver and, as the car ran through red and green lights, a nestful of red stars would fly humming outside the window and a nestful of green stars.

Ch'ang-an brought back some of the stray dreams under the starlight and became unusually silent, often smiling. Ch'i-chiao saw the change and could not help getting angry and sarcastic. "These many years we haven't been very attentive to Miss, no wonder Miss seldom smiled. Now you've got your wish and are going to spring out the Chiangs' door. But no matter how happy you are, don't show it on your face so much—it's sickening."

In former days Ch'ang-an would have answered back, but now that she appeared a transformed person she let it go and concentrated on curing herself of the opium habit. Ch'i-ch'iao could do nothing with her.

Eldest Mistress Tai-chen, who had not been present when Ch'ang-an got engaged, came to the house to congratulate her some time afterward. Ch'i-ch'iao whispered, "Eldest Sister-in-law, it seems to me we still have to ask around a bit. This is not a matter to blunder into. The other day I heard something about a wife in the country and another across the seas."

"The one in the country was sent back before marriage," said Tai-chen. "The same with the one overseas. It's said that they were friends for several years; nobody knew why nothing came of it."

"What's so strange about that? Men's hearts change faster than you can say change. He didn't even acknowledge the one who came with the three matchmakers and six gifts, not to say the hussy who has no formal status. Who knows whether he has anybody else across the seas? I have only this one daughter, I can't muddle along and ruin her whole life. I myself have suffered at the matchmakers' hands."

Ch'ang-an sat to one side pressing her fingernails into her palm until the palm reddened and the nails turned white from the strain. Ch'i-ch'iao looked up and saw her. "Shameless girl, pricking up your ears to listen! Is this anything that you should hear? When we were girls we couldn't get out of the way fast enough at the very mention of marriage. You Chiangs had generations of book learning in vain, you may have to go and learn some manners from your mother's family with their sesame oil shop."

Ch'ang-an ran out crying. Ch'i-ch'iao pounded her pillow and sighed. "Miss couldn't wait to marry, so what can I do? She'd drag home any old smelly stinking thing. It's supposed to be her Third Aunt that found him for her—actually she's just using her Third Aunt as a blind. Probably the rice was already cooked before they asked Third Aunt to be matchmaker. Everybody ganged up to fool me—and just as well. If the truth came out, where should the mother and brother look?"

Another day Ch'ang-an slipped out on some excuse. When she got back she was going to report every place she had been before Ch'i-ch'iao had even asked.

"All right, all right, save it," Ch'i-chiao barked. "What's the use of lying to me? Let me catch you red-handed one day—humph! Don't think that because you're grown up and engaged I can't beat you anymore!"

"I went to give Cousin Hsing those slipper patterns, what's wrong in that?" Ch'ang-an was upset. "If Mother doesn't believe me, she can ask Third Aunt."

"Your Third Aunt found you a man and she's

the father and mother of your rebirth! Never seen anybody as cheap as you . . . Disappears in the twinkling of an eye. Your family kept you and honored you all these years—short of buying a page to serve you, where have we been remiss, that you can't even stay home for a moment?"

Ch'ang-an blushed, tears falling straight down.

Ch'i-ch'iao paused for breath. "So many good ones were turned down before and now you want to marry a ne'er-do-well! If he's any good, how did he live to be thirty-something, cross oceans and seas over a hundred thousand *li,* and never get himself a wife? Aren't you slapping your own face?"

But Ch'ang-an remained obdurate. Both parties being none too young, several months after the engagement Lan-hsien came to Ch'i-ch'iao as Shih-fang's deputy and asked her to set a date for the wedding.

Ch'i-ch'iao pointed at Ch'ang-an. "We won't marry early, won't marry late, has to choose this year when there's no money at hand. If we have a better harvest next year, the trousseau would be more complete."

"Modern-style weddings don't go in for these things. Might as well do it the new way and save a little," Lan-hsien said.

"New ways, old ways, what's the difference? The old ways are more for show, the new ways more practical—the girl's family is the loser anyway."

"Just do whatever you see fit, Second Sister-in-law, Little Miss An is not going to argue about getting too little, is she?" At this everybody in the room laughed; even Ch'ang-an could not help a little smile.

Ch'i-ch'iao burst out, "Shameless! You have something in your belly that won't keep or what? Can't wait to get over there, as if your eyebrows were on fire. Will even do without the trousseau— you're willing, others may not be. You're so sure he's after your person? What vanity! Have you got a pretty spot on you? Stop lying to yourself. This man T'ung has his eyes on the Chiangs' name and prestige, that's all. Your family sounds so grand with its titles and its eminent generals and ministers; actually it's not so at all. It's been strong outside and shriveled up inside long since, and for

these last few years couldn't even keep up appearances. Moreover, each generation of your family is worse than the one before, no regard for Heaven and earth and king and parent anymore. The young masters know nothing whatsoever and all the young ladies know is to grab money and want men—worse than pigs and dogs. My own family was a thousand times and ten thousand times to blame in making this match—ruined my whole life. I'm going to tell this man T'ung not to make the same mistake before it's too late."

After this quarrel Lan-hsien washed her hands of the match. Ch'i-ch'iao, convalescing, could get out of bed a bit and would sit in the doorway and call out toward Ch'ang-an's room day after day, "You want strange men, go look for them, just don't bring them home to greet me as mother-in-law and make me die of anger. Out of sight, out of mind, that's all I ask. I'd be grateful if Miss would let me live a couple of years longer." She would arrange just these few sentences in different orders, shouted out so that the whole street could hear. Of course the talk spread among relatives, boiling and steaming.

Ch'i-ch'iao then called Ch'ang-an to her, suddenly in tears. "My child, you know outsiders are saying this and that about you, have smirched you till you're not worth a copper coin. Ever since your mother married into the Chiang family, from top to bottom there's not one that's not a snob. Man stands low in dogs' eyes. I took so much from them in the open and in the dark. Even your father, did he ever do me a good turn that I'd want to stay his widow? I stayed and suffered endless hardships these twenty years, just hoping that you two children would grow up and win back some face for me. I never knew it'd come to this." And she wept.

Ch'ang-an was thunderstruck. Never mind if her mother made her out to be less than human or if outsiders said the same; let them. But T'ung Shih-fang—he—what would he think? Did he still want her? Was there any change in his manner last time she saw him? Hard to say . . . She was too happy, she wouldn't notice little differences . . . Between the discomfort of taking the cure and these repeated provocations Ch'ang-an had had a hard time but, forcing herself to bear up, she had endured. Now she suddenly felt as though all her bones were out of joint. Explain to him? Unlike her brother, he was not her mother's offspring and could never thoroughly understand her mother. It would have been all right if he never had to meet her mother, but sooner or later he would make her acquaintance. Marriage is a lifelong affair; you can be a thief all your life but you can't always be on guard against thieves. Who knew what her mother would do? Sooner or later there would be trouble, sooner or later there would be a break. This was the most beautiful episode of her life; better to finish it before other people could add a disgusting ending to it. A beautiful, desolate gesture . . . She knew she would be sorry, she knew she would, but unconcernedly she lifted her eyebrows and said, "Since Mother is not willing to make this match I'll just go and tell them no."

Ch'i-ch'iao was still for a moment and then went on sobbing.

Ch'ang-an paused to collect herself and went to telephone T'ung Shih-fang. Shih-fang did not have time that day, and arranged to meet her the next afternoon. What she dreaded most was the night in between, and it finally passed, each minute and every chime of the quarter hour sinking its teeth into her heart. The next day, at the old place in the park he came up smiling without greeting her; to him this was an expression of intimacy. He seemed to take special notice of her today, kept looking into her face as they walked shoulder to shoulder. With the sun shining brightly she was all the more conscious of her swollen eyelids and could hardly lift her eyes. Better say it while he was not looking at her. Hoarse from weeping, she whispered, "Mr. T'ung." He did not hear her. Then she'd better say it while he was looking at her. Surprised that she was still smiling slightly, she said in a small voice, "Mr. T'ung, I think—about us—perhaps we'd better—better leave it for now. I'm very sorry." She took off her ring and pushed it into his hand—cold gritty ring, cold gritty fingers. She quickened her pace, walking away. After a stunned moment he caught up with her.

"Why? Not satisfied with me in some way?"

Ch'ang-an shook her head, looking straight ahead.

"Then why?"

"My mother . . ."

"Your mother has never seen me."

"I told you, it's not because of you, nothing to do with you. My mother . . ."

Shih-fang stood still. In China must her kind of reasoning be taken as fully adequate? As he hesitated, she was already some distance away.

The park had basked in the late autumn sun for a morning and an afternoon, and its air was now heavy with fragrance, like rotten-ripe fruit on a tree. Ch'ang-an heard, coming faintly in slow swings, the sound of a harmonica clumsily picking out "Long, Long Ago"—"Tell me the tales that to me were so dear, long, long ago, long, long ago . . ." This was *now*, but in the twinkling of an eye it would have become long, long ago and everything would be over. As if under a spell Ch'ang-an went looking for the person blowing the harmonica—looking for herself. Walking with her face to the sunlight, she came under a *wu-t'ung* [18] tree with a boy in khaki shorts astride one of its forked branches. He was rocking and blowing his harmonica, but the tune was different, one she had never heard before. The tree was not big, and its sparse leaves shook in the sun like golden bells. Looking up, Ch'ang-an saw black as a flood of tears fell down her face. It was then that Shih-fang found her, and he stood quietly beside her for a while before he said, "I respect your opinion." She lifted her handbag to ward off the sun from her face.

They continued to see each other for a time. Shih-fang wanted to show that modern men do not make friends with women just to find a mate, and so although the engagement was broken he still asked her out often. As to Ch'ang-an, in what contradictory hopes she went out with him she herself did not know and would not have admitted if she had known. When they had been engaged and openly going out together she still had had to guard her movements. Now her rendezvous were more secret than ever. Shih-fang's

[18] See footnote 2 to "The Coffins," p. 511.

attitude remained straightforward. Of course she had hurt his self-respect a little, and he also thought it was a pity more or less, but as the saying goes, "a worthy man needn't worry about not having a wife." A man's highest compliment to a woman is a proposal. Shih-fang had pledged himself to relinquish his freedom. Although Ch'ang-an had declined his valuable offer, he had done her a service at no cost to himself.

No matter how subtle and awkward their relations were, they actually became friends. They even talked. Ch'ang-an's naïveté often made Shih-fang laugh and say, "You're a funny one." Ch'ang-an also began to discover that she was an amusing person. Where matters could go from here might surprise Shih-fang himself.

But rumors reached Ch'i-ch'iao. Behind Ch'ang-an's back she ordered Ch'ang-pai to send T'ung Shih-fang a written invitation to an informal dinner at home. Shih-fang guessed that the Chiangs might want to warn him not to persist in a friendship with their daughter after the break. But while he was talking with Ch'ang-pai over two cups of wine about the weather, current politics, and local news in the somber and high-ceilinged dining room, he noticed that nothing was mentioned of Ch'ang-an. Then the cold dishes were removed. Ch'ang-pai suddenly leaned his hands against the table and stood up. Shih-fang looked over his shoulder and saw a small old lady standing at the doorway with her back to the light so that he could not see her face distinctly. She wore a blue-gray gown of palace brocade embroidered with a round dragon design, and clasped with both hands a scarlet hot-water bag; two tall amahs stood close beside her. Outside the door the setting sun was smoky yellow, and the staircase covered with turquoise plaid linoleum led up step after step to a place where there was no light. Shih-fang instinctively felt this person was mad. For no reason there was cold in all his hairs and bones.

"This is my mother," Ch'ang-pai introduced her.

Shih-fang moved his chair to stand up and bow. Ch'i-ch'iao walked in with measured grace, resting a hand on an amah's arm, and after a few civilities sat down to offer him wine and food.

"Where's Sister?" Ch'ang-pai asked. "Doesn't even come and help when we have company."

"She's going to smoke a couple of pipes more and then she'll come down," Ch'i-ch'iao said.

Shih-fang was greatly shocked and stared at her intently.

Ch'i-ch'iao hurriedly explained, "It's such a pity this child didn't have proper prenatal care. I had to puff smoke at her as soon as she was born. Later, after bouts of illness, she acquired this habit of smoking. How very inconvenient for a young lady! It isn't that she hasn't tried to break it, but her health is so very delicate and she has had her way in everything for so long it's easier said than done. Off and on, it's been ten years now."

Shih-fang could not help changing color. Ch'i-ch'iao had the caution and quick wits of the insane. She knew if she was not careful people would cut her short with a mocking, incredulous glance; she was used to the pain by now. Afraid that he would see through her if she talked too much, she stopped in time and busied herself with filling wine cups and distributing food. When Ch'ang-an was mentioned again she just repeated these words lightly once more, her flat, sharp voice cutting all around like a razor blade.

Ch'ang-an came downstairs quietly, her embroidered black slippers and white silk stockings pausing in the dim yellow sunlight on the stairs. After stopping a while she went up again, one step after another, to where there was no light.

Ch'i-ch'iao said, "Ch'ang-pai, you drink a few more cups with Mr. T'ung. I'm going up."

The servants brought the soup called *i-p'in-kuo*, the "highest ranking pot," and changed the wine to Bamboo Leaf Green, newly heated. A nervous slave girl stood in the doorway and signaled the page waiting on table to come out. After some whispering the boy came back to say a few words into Ch'ang-pai's ear. Ch'ang-pai got up, flustered, and apologized repeatedly to Shih-fang, "Have to leave you alone for a while, be right back," and also went upstairs, taking several steps in one.

Shih-fang was left to drink alone. Even the page felt apologetic. "Our Miss Chüan is about to give birth," he whispered to him.

"Who's Miss Chüan?" Shih-fang asked.

"Young Master's concubine."

Shih-fang asked for rice and made himself eat some of it. He could not leave the minute he set his bowl down, so he waited, sitting on the carved pearwood couch. Flushed from the wine, his ears hot, he suddenly felt exhausted and lay down. The scrollwork couch, with its ice-cold yellow rattan mat, the wintry fragrance of pomelos . . . the concubine having a baby. This was the ancient China he had been homesick for . . . His quiet and demure well-born Chinese girl was an opium smoker! He sat up, his head in his hands, feeling unbearably lonely and estranged.

He took his hat and went out, telling the page, "Later, please inform your master that I'll thank him in person another day."

He crossed the brick-paved courtyard where a tree grew in the center, its bare branches printed high in the sky like the lines in crackle china. Ch'ang-an quietly followed behind, watching him out. There were light yellow daisies on her navy blue long-sleeved gown. Her hands were clasped and she had a gentle look seldom seen on her face.

Shih-fang turned around to say, "Miss Chiang . . ."

She stood still a long way off and just bent her head. Shih-fang bowed slightly, turned, and left. Ch'ang-an felt as though she were viewing this sunlit courtyard from some distance away, looking down from a tall building. The scene was clear, she herself was involved but powerless to intervene. The court, the tree, two people trailing bleak shadows, wordless—not much of a memory, but still to be put in a crystal bottle and held in both hands to be looked at some day, her first and last love.

Chih-shou lay stiffly in bed, her hands placed palms up on her ribs like the claws of a slaughtered chicken. The bed curtains were half up. Night or day she would not have them let down; she was afraid.

Word came that Miss Chüan had given birth to a son. The slave girl tending the steaming pot of herb medicine for Chih-shou ran out to share the excitement. A wind blew in through the open door and rattled the curtain hooks. The curtains slid shut of their own accord but Chih-shou did not protest anymore. With a jerk to the right, her head rolled off the pillow. She did not die then, but dragged on for another fortnight.

Miss Chüan was made a wife and became Chih-shou's substitute. In less than a year she swallowed raw opium and killed herself. Ch'ang-pai dared not marry again, just went to brothels now and then. Ch'ang-an of course had long since given up all thoughts of marriage.

Ch'i-ch'iao lay half asleep on the opium couch. For thirty years now she had worn a golden cangue. She had used its heavy edges to chop down several people; those that did not die were half dead. She knew that her son and daughter hated her to the death, that the relatives on her husband's side hated her, and that her own kinfolk also hated her. She groped for the green jade bracelet on her wrist and slowly pushed it up her bony arm, as thin as firewood, until it reached the armpit. She herself could not believe she'd had round arms when she was young. Even after she had been married several years, the bracelet only left room enough for her to tuck in a handkerchief of imported crepe. As a girl of eighteen or nineteen, she would roll up the lavishly laced sleeves of her blue linen blouse, revealing a pair of snow-white wrists, and go to the market. Among those that liked her were Ch'ao-lu of the butcher shop; her brother's sworn brothers, Ting Yü-ken and Chang Shao-ch'üan; and also the son of Tailor Shen. To say that they liked her perhaps only means that they liked to fool around with her; but if she had chosen one of these, it was very likely that her man would have shown some real love as years went by and children were born. She moved the ruffled little foreign-style pillow under her head and rubbed her face against it. On her other cheek a teardrop stayed until it dried by itself: she was too languid to brush it away.

After Ch'i-ch'iao passed away, Ch'ang-an got her share of property from Ch'ang-pai and moved out of the house. Ch'i-ch'iao's daughter would have no difficulty settling her own problems. Rumor had it that she was seen with a man on the street stopping in front of a stall where he bought her a pair of garters. Perhaps with her own money, but out of the man's pocket anyway. Of course it was only a rumor.

The moon of thirty years ago has gone down long since, and the people of thirty years ago are dead, but the story of thirty years ago is not yet ended—can have no ending.

Selected Bibliography
of Modern Chinese Fiction

Prepared by
Howard Goldblatt and George Cheng

The following bibliography of modern Chinese fiction up to 1949, while not intended as a comprehensive listing, includes the major works in English, most of which are available in college and university libraries. Contained in this bibliography are book-length studies, articles, books that deal in substantial part with modern fiction, anthologies of short stories, pertinent reference materials, and the names of journals and periodicals that regularly publish studies or translations of modern Chinese fiction. Works dealing exclusively with premodern or post-1949 fiction are not included, nor are book-length translations of novels or anthologies of stories by a single writer; these are listed in Gibbs and Li, *A Bibliography of Studies and Translations of Modern Chinese Literature (1918–1942)* and Yang and Mao, *Modern Chinese Fiction: A Guide to Its History and Appreciation.* Annotations are given for many of the works cited.

The bibliography is divided into five sections:

1. Studies of individual works or authors.
2. Histories, period studies, and background works.
3. Anthologies of translations.
4. Reference works.
5. Periodicals.

Studies of Individual Works or Authors

Chang, Jun-mei. *Ting Ling: Her Life and Her Work.* Taipei: Institute of International Relations, 1978. 170 pp.

Chua, Siew-teen. "Special Features of Lu Hsün's Short Stories." *Journal of Nanyang University* (1974–75), 8–9(1):84–109.

Doležalová, Anna. "Two Novels of Yü Ta-fu—Two Approaches to Literary Creation." *Asian and African Studies* (1968), 4:17–29.

Feuerwerker, Yi-tsi. "Ting Ling's 'When I Was in Sha Chuan (Cloud Village),' Archives." *Signs: Journal of Women in Culture and Society* (1976), 2(1):255–79.

Galik, Marian. *Mao Dun and Modern Chinese Literary Criticism.* Weisbaden: Franz Steiner Verlag, 1969. 185 pp.

A well-researched and highly informative study of Mao Tun, the foremost prac-
titioner of realism in the May Fourth period.

Goldblatt, Howard. *Hsiao Hung.* Boston: Twayne Publishers, 1976. 161 pp.

A study of the life and works of one of modern China's most important female
novelists and a member of the Northeastern (Manchurian) Group.

Hanan, Patrick. "The Technique of Lu Hsün's Fiction." *Harvard Journal of Asiatic Studies* (1974), 34:53–96.

An innovative and highly significant methodological study of Lu Hsün's stories.

Hu, Dennis T. "A Linguistic-Literary Approach to Ch'ien Chung-shu's Novel *Wei-
ch'eng.*" *Journal of Asian Studies* (1978), 37(3):427–43.

Kao, George, ed. *Two Writers and the Cultural Revolution: Lao She and Chen Jo-hsi.* Hong
Kong: The Chinese University Press, 1980. 212 pp.

Includes three studies of Lao She and translations of two stories, partial translations of two novels, and a retranslation of the final two chapters of *Rickshaw Boy,*
which were altered by the original translator, Evan King.

Lang, Olga. *Pa Chin and His Writings: Chinese Youth Between the Two Revolutions.* Cambridge: Harvard University Press, 1967. 402 pp.

A comprehensive study of the life and thought of modern China's former devo-
tee of anarchism and popular novelist. Although social and intellectual history is
the author's primary concern, the subject's literary works are introduced and analyzed in detail.

Lee, Leo Ou-fan. "Literature on the Eve of Revolution: Reflections on Lu Xun's Leftist
Years, 1927–1936," *Modern China* (1976), 2(3):277–326.

Liu, Chun-jo. "People, Places, and Time in Five Modern Chinese Novels." In *Asia and
the Humanities,* ed. Horst Frenz. Danville, Ill.: Interstate Printers and Publishers,
1959; pp. 15–25.

—— "The Heroes and Heroines of Modern Chinese Fiction: From Ah Q to Wu Tzu-
Hsü." *Journal of Asian Studies* (1958), 16(2):201–11.

Lyell, William A., Jr. *Lu Hsün's Vision of Reality.* Berkeley: University of California
Press, 1976. 355 pp.

An introduction and analysis of Lu Hsün's short stories, treated chronologically.
Includes translations of two obscure, previously untranslated stories.

Mao, Nathan K. *Pa Chin.* Boston: Twayne Publishers, 1978, 170 pp.

A study of Pa Chin's literary achievements. Includes a biographical sketch.

Munro, Stanley R. *The Function of Satire in the Works of Lao She.* Singapore: Nan Yang
University, 1971.

Nieh, Hua-ling. *Shen Ts'ung-wen.* New York: Twayne Publishers, 1972. 139 pp.

A sympathetic study of the life and works of one of China's most important
short-story writers.

Pickowicz, Paul G. "Lu Xun Through the Eyes of Qu Qiu-bai." *Modern China* (1976),
2(3):327–68.

Průšek, Jaroslav. "Lu Hsün's 'Huai Chiu': A Precursor of Modern Chinese Literature."
Harvard Journal of Asiatic Studies (1969), 29:169–76.

Semanov, V. I., *Lu Hsün and His Predecessors,* tr. and ed. Charles I. Alber. White Plains,
N.Y.: M. E. Sharpe, 1980. 175 pp.

A perceptive analysis by a Soviet scholar of Lu Hsün's fictional technique in
comparison with late Ch'ing fiction.

Shih, Vincent Y. C. "Lao She A Conformist? An Anatomy of A Wit under Constraint."

In *Transition and Permanence: Chinese History and Culture,* ed. David C. Buxbaum and Frederick W. Mote. Hong Kong: Cathay Press, 1972; pp. 307–19.

Slupski, Zbigniew. *The Evolution of A Modern Chinese Writer.* Prague: Oriental Institute, 1966. 168 pp.

An excellent examination of the novels and stories of Lao She from the structuralist perspective.

Vohra, Ranbir. *Lao She and the Chinese Revolution.* Cambridge: Harvard University Press, 1974. 199 pp.

A biographical and critical study, focusing more on the sociological aspects than the literary.

Yang, Richard. " 'Midnight': Mao Tun's Political Novel." In *China's Literary Image,* ed. Paul K. T. Sih. Jamaica, N.Y.: St. John's University, 1975. 156 pp.

Histories, Period Studies, and Background Works

Birch, Cyril. "Teaching May Fourth Fiction." *Modern Chinese Literature Newsletter* (1976), 2(1):1–16.

Chow, Tse-tsung. *The May Fourth Movement: Intellectual Revolution in Modern China.* Stanford: Stanford University Press, 1970. 486 pp.

An indispensable research tool for anyone seeking an understanding of May Fourth literary activities. A research guide is available in a companion volume.

Doleželovà, Anna. "Subject Matters of Short Stories in the Initial Period of the Creation Society's Activities." *Asian and African Studies* (1970), 6:131–44.

Galik, Marian. "On the Study of Modern Chinese Literature of the 1920's and 1930's: Sources, Results, Tendencies." *Asian and African Studies* (1977), 13:99–123.

Goldman, Merle. *Literary Dissent in Communist China.* New York: Atheneum, 1971. 343 pp.

Part of this work deals with pre-1949 literary dissent in both Kuomintang and Communist Party areas, some of which involved novelists included in the present anthology, most notably Ting Ling and Hsiao Chün.

——, ed. *Modern Chinese Literature in the May Fourth Era.* Cambridge: Harvard University Press, 1977. 464 pp.

A selection of seventeen papers presented at a 1974 conference on modern Chinese literature. The collection is divided into three parts: "Native and Foreign Impact," "The May Fourth Writers," and "Continuities and Discontinuities." Part Two includes studies on Lu Xun (Lu Hsün), Mao Dun (Mao Tun), Ding Ling (Ting Ling), and Yu Dafu (Yü Ta-fu). Although the quality of the essays varies, the collection constitutes one of the major critical works in the field.

Gunn, Edward M. *Unwelcome Muse: Chinese Literature in Shanghai and Peking 1937–1945.* New York: Columbia University Press, 1980. 330 pp.

A splendid study of literary activities and writers in occupied China, a subject generally shunned by Chinese scholars.

Hsia, C. T. *A History of Modern Chinese Fiction.* 2d ed. New Haven: Yale University Press, 1971. 701 pp.

The standard history of modern Chinese fiction in English.

Hsia, Tsi-an. *The Gate of Darkness: Studies on the Leftist Literary Movement in China.* Seattle: University of Washington Press, 1968. 266 pp.

A pioneering work on leftist literary activities. The two chapters on Lu Hsün, particularly "Aspects of the Power of Darkness in Lu Hsün," are especially relevant to the study and appreciation of modern Chinese fiction.

Lee, Leo Ou-fan. *The Romantic Generation of Modern Chinese Writers.* Cambridge: Harvard University Press, 1973. 365 pp.
A pioneering study of romanticism in modern China. The unique position of the literati (*wen-jen*) is analyzed in depth.

Malmqvist, Göran, ed. *Modern Chinese Literature and Its Social Context.* Stockholm: Nobel Symposium, 1975. 217 pp.
Includes one essay of direct relevance to modern Chinese fiction, "On the Social and Literary Context in the Chinese Literature of the 1920's and 1930's," and several of related interest.

McDougall, Bonnie S. *The Introduction of Western Literary Theories into Modern China, 1919–1925.* Tokyo: The Centre for East Asian Cultural Studies, 1971. 368 pp.
Important for gaining an understanding of Western literary influences on modern Chinese writers. An extensive bibliography and a glossary of Chinese names and terms add to the book's value.

Průšek, Jaroslav. *The Lyrical and the Epic: Studies of Modern Chinese Literature,* ed. Leo Ou-fan Lee. Bloomington: Indiana University Press, 1980. 268 pp.
Includes nine papers by Průšek and his celebrated exchange with C. T. Hsia on the "scientific" study of modern Chinese literature.

——, ed. *Studies in Modern Chinese Literature.* Berlin: Akademie-Verlag, 1964. 179 pp.
A collection of essays by Průšek's students on Lao She, Pa Chin, Ping Hsin, and others. Průšek's long introduction remains one of the standard critiques of modern Chinese literature.

Schwartz, Benjamin I. *Reflections on the May Fourth Movement.* Cambridge: Harvard University Press, 1972. 132 pp.
Although primarily a work of intellectual history, some of the essays (such as "The Romantic Temper of May Fourth Writers" by Leo Ou-fan Lee) deal with literary topics.

Tagore, Amitendranath. *Literary Debates in Modern China, 1918–1937.* Tokyo: The Centre for East Asian Cultural Studies, 1967. 280 pp.
A detailed study of three major literary debates (1928–1930, 1935–1936, 1936–1937). Includes an introduction to the most important literary societies, and an analysis of the effects of the debates. A bilingual bibliography and index enhance the book's usefulness.

Ting, Yi. *A Short History of Modern Chinese Literature.* Port Washington, N.Y.: Kennikat Press, 1970. 310 pp.
A reprint of the 1959 Foreign Languages Press English version of this study of modern Chinese literature. The most revealing aspect is the doctrinaire Marxist literary approach of the author.

Anthologies of Translations

Berninghausen, John, and Ted Huters, eds. *Revolutionary Literature in China: An Anthology.* White Plains, N.Y.: M. E. Sharpe, 1976. 103 pp.
An anthology of stories and essays, spanning five decades, from pre-May Fourth

literature to proletarian writings of the 1960s. Preceded by an informative introduction by the editors and includes translators' introductions to each piece. Stories by Ye Shaojun (Yeh Shao-chün), Zhang Tianyi (Chang T'ien-i), Ding Ling (Ting Ling), and others.

Birch, Cyril, ed. *Anthology of Chinese Literature.* New York: Grove Press, 1972. Vol. II, 476 pp.

Hsia, C. T., ed. *Twentieth-Century Chinese Stories.* New York: Columbia University Press, 1971. 239 pp.

An excellent selection of stories by Yü Ta-fu, Shen Ts'ung-wen, Chang T'ien-i, Wu Tsu-hsiang, Eileen Chang, and others.

Hsu, Kai-yu, ed. *Literature of the People's Republic of China.* Bloomington: Indiana University Press, 1980. 976 pp.

Isaacs, Harold R., ed. *Straw Sandals: Chinese Short Stories, 1918–1933.* Cambridge, Mass.: MIT Press, 1974. 444 pp.

More than twenty stories by predominantly leftist writers, such as Lu Hsün, Yü Ta-fu, Yeh Shao-chün, Ting Ling, Mao Tun, and others. Preceded by a Foreword by Lu Hsün, a long introduction by the editor, and biographical sketches of the authors.

Jenner, W. J. F., ed. *Modern Chinese Stories.* Oxford: Oxford Paperbacks, 1970. 271 pp.

Stories by Lu Xun (Lu Hsün), Mao Dun (Mao Tun), Zhang Tianyi (Chang T'ien-i), Ai Wu, and others, a few of which are reprints.

Munro, Stanley R., tr. *Genesis of a Revolution: An Anthology of Modern Chinese Short Stories.* Singapore; Heinemann Educational Books (Asia), 1979. 202 pp.

Stories by Ba Jin (Pa Chin), Bing Xin (Ping Hsin), Ding Ling (Ting Ling), Lao She, Mao Dun (Mao Tun), Shen Congwen (Shen Ts'ung-wen), Wu Zuxiang (Wu Tsu-hsiang), Ye Shaojun (Yeh Shao-chün), Yu Dafu (Yü Ta-fu), and Zhang Tianyi (Chang T'ien-i).

Snow, Edgar, ed. *Living China: Modern Chinese Short Stories.* Westport, Conn.: Hyperion Press, 1973. 360 pp.

Reprint of the 1937 John Day edition. The earliest anthology of modern Chinese stories, it includes stories by Lu Hsün, Jou Shih, Mao Tun, Ting Ling, Pa Chin, Shen Ts'ung-wen, T'ien Chün (Hsiao Chün), Yü Ta-fu, Chang T'ien-yi, and others. Includes a brief but informative essay by Nym Wales, "The Modern Chinese Literary Movement."

Wang, Chi-chen. *Contemporary Chinese Stories.* Westport, Conn.: Greenwood Press, 1976. 242 pp.

A reprint of the 1944 Columbia University Press edition. Includes stories by Chang T'ien-i, Lao Hsiang, Lao She, Pa Chin, Shen Ts'ung-wen, Mao Dun (Mao Tun), Yeh Shao-chün, Lusin (Lu Hsün), and others. Includes "Notes on the Authors."

—— *Stories of China at War.* New York: Columbia University Press, 1947; reprint, Westport, Conn.: Greenwood Press, 1975. 158 pp.

A sequel to *Contemporary Chinese Stories.* This volume includes stories from 1937 to 1942—stories on various aspects of life in wartime China by Tuan-mu Hungliang, Chen Shou-chu, Mao Dun, Pien Chih-lin, Ping Po, Yao Hsüeh-yin, Yang Shuo, Pai P'ing-chieh, King Yu-ling, Li Wei-t'ao, Lao She, Chang Tien-yi, and Kuo Mo-jo.

Yuan, Chia-hua and Robert Payne. *Contemporary Chinese Stories.* London: Noel Carrington, Translantic Arts, 1946. 169 pp.

Reference Works

Boorman, Howard L., and Richard C. Howard, O. Edmund Clubb, and Russell Maeth, eds. *Biographical Dictionary of Republican China.* New York: Columbia University Press, 1966–79. 5 vols.

    Lists approximately 70 literary figures. Their major works and studies are included in vol. 4. The fifth volume is an index to the other four.

Chu, Pao-liang. *Twentieth Century Chinese Writers and Their Pen Names.* Boston: G. K. Hall, 1977. 366 pp.

    An invaluable, meticulously researched reference tool listing approximately 7,500 pen names on more than 2,500 writers.

Gibbs, Donald, and Yun-chen Li, comps. *A Bibliography of Studies and Translations of Modern Chinese Literature (1918–1942).* Cambridge: Harvard University Press, 1975. 239 pp.

    A comprehensive bibliography of translations and studies of modern Chinese literature in Western languages, primarily English. An indispensable research tool. Divided into four parts: Part I lists English language periodicals and anthologies. Part II lists books and articles on modern Chinese literature. Major authors' studies and translations are listed in Part III. Unidentified authors and their works are listed in Part IV. Appendices list conference papers, unpublished works, and Chinese works consulted.

Gibbs, Donald A., comp. *Subject and Author Index to Chinese Literature Monthly (1951–1976).* New Haven: Far Eastern Publications, Yale University, 1978. 173 pp.

    Chinese Literature, which commenced publication in 1951, is the major vehicle for translations of Chinese literature, including modern. Includes studies and author information. Published monthly by the Foreign Languages Press, Peking. This index is complete and conveniently organized.

Hinrup, Hans J., comp. *An Index to 'Chinese Literature' 1951–1976.* London and Malmo: Curzon Press, 1978. 231 pp.

    Indexes *Chinese Literature* by ten broad subjects: contemporary literature, classical literature, theatre, music, film, art, cultural policy, biographical notes, history and foreign. It has an alphabetical index.

Klein, Donald W., and Anne B. Clark, eds. *Biographic Dictionary of Chinese Communism, 1921–1965.* Cambridge: Harvard University Press, 1971. 2 vols.

Schyns, Jos., et al. *1500 Modern Chinese Novels and Plays.* Hong Kong: Lung Men Bookstore, 1966. 465 pp.

    A reprint of the 1948 Catholic University Press (Peiping) version. Prepared by a Jesuit priest, this work introduces nearly 1500 novels and collections of short stories by modern Chinese writers. Intended as a guide to youth, it takes the form of a Catholic Index. The body of the book is preceded by "Present Day Fiction and Drama in China" by Su Hsüeh-lin and "Short Biographies of Authors" by Chao Yen-sheng (includes approximately 200 biographies, each with a detailed list of works and translations by the author-subject).

Although there is a significant number of errors and much dated material, this work has not yet been superseded.

Shulman, Frank J., and Leonard H. O. Gordon. *Doctoral Dissertations on China: A Bibliography of Studies In Western Languages, 1945–1970.* Seattle: University of Washington Press for the Association for Asian Studies, 1972. 317 pp.

Lists 2,217 dissertations by subject and period. Shulman edited the supplement, *Doctoral Dissertations on China, 1971–1975* (Seattle: University of Washington Press, 1978. 329 pp.), which lists 1,573 dissertations by subjects.

Tsai, Meishi. *Contemporary Chinese Novels and Short Stories, 1948–1974: An Annotated Bibliography.* Cambridge: Harvard University Press, 1979. 408 pp.

A reference work divided into four parts. Part I: Index of authors. Part II: Authors and their works. Part III: Index of titles. Part IV: Subject index of selected topics. The most useful feature of this work is the synopses of the stories and novels provided by the compiler.

Tsien, Tsuen-Hsuin, and James K. M. Cheng, eds. *China: An Annotated Bibliography of Bibliographies.* Boston: G. K. Hall, 1978. 604 pp.

Lists 2,500 bibliographies concerning China, mainly in English, Chinese, and Japanese, with some in European languages. It includes separate works, bibliographies in periodicals and serials, bibliographic essays, surveys of literature on specific periodicals of subjects. Chapter XVII, Section G, lists 50 major reference works on modern literature.

Yang, Winston L. Y., and Nathan K. Mao. *Modern Chinese Fiction—A Guide to Its History and Appreciation.* Boston: G. K. Hall, 1981. 240 pp.

The first section contains essays on pre- and post-Communist Chinese fiction from 1917 to the present and Taiwanese fiction from 1949 to the present. The second lists 450 English-language translations, dissertations, and articles, with annotation.

Periodicals

Asian and African Studies. 1965– Bratislava: Department of Oriental Studies of the Slovak Academy of Science.

Chinese Literature: Essays, Articles, and Reviews. 1979– (Twice yearly.) Edited by Eugene O. Eoyang and William H. Nienhauser, Jr. Department of East Asian Languages and Literature, Van Hise Hall 1220, University of Wisconsin, Madison, Wisconsin 53706.

Chinese Studies in Literature: A Translation Journal. 1980– (Quarterly.) M. E. Sharpe, Inc., 901 N. Broadway, White Plains, N.Y. 10603.

Issues edited by guest editors. Each issue concentrates on special topics, trends, or movements in the field of modern Chinese literature.

Journal of Asian Studies. 1941– (Quarterly.) Association for Asian Studies, Inc., 1 Lane Hall, University of Michigan, Ann Arbor, Michigan 48109. Indexed: *Bibliography of Asian Studies. Humanities Index. MLA Bibliography. Social Science Citation Index.*

A leading American journal in the field. It contains articles in the areas of Asian history, humanities, and the social sciences.

Modern Chinese Literature Newsletter. 1973– Edited by Michael Gotz and William Mac-

Donald, published and distributed by the Center for Asian Studies, University of Illinois at Champagne-Urbana. Indexed: *Bibliography of Asian Studies.*

Renditions: A Chinese-English Translation Magazine. 1973– (Quarterly.) Edited by George Kao and Stephen C. Soong. Chinese University of Hong Kong, Translation Centre, Shatin N.T. Hong Kong. Indexed: *MLA Bibliography. Bibliography of Asian Studies.*

Articles on and translations of Chinese literature. A high-quality translation journal.

Chinese Literature. 1951– (Monthly.) Edited by Mao Tun. Guozi Shudian, P.O. Box 399, Peking 37, People's Republic of China. Indexed: *Bibliography of Asian Studies, MLA Bibliography.*

A monthly literary magazine containing stories, poems, prose, and literary criticism. This is the only English-language monthly dealing with Chinese literature.

Literature East and West. 1953– (Quarterly.) Modern Language Association of America, Oriental-Western Literary Relation Group, Box 8107, University Station, Austin, Texas 78712. Indexed: *MLA Bibliography.*

Occasionally has articles on and translations of modern Chinese fiction.

Tamkang Review. 1970– Edited by Hwang Mei-shu. Graduate Institute of Western Language and Literature, Tamkang College of Arts and Sciences, King-hua Street, Taipei, Taiwan, 106, Republic of China. Indexed: *MLA Bibliography, Bibliography of Asian Studies.*

Contains articles on Chinese and comparative literature.

Notes on the Editors

Joseph S. M. Lau received his B. A. in English from National Taiwan University in 1960 and Ph.D. in Comparative Literature from Indiana University in 1966. He taught Chinese and Comparative Literature at the University of Wisconsin, Madison, before returning to Hong Kong to teach English at Chung Chi College, the Chinese University of Hong Kong, in 1968. He was Senior Lecturer in English at the University of Singapore from 1971 to 1972.

His English publications include *Ts'ao Yü: The Reluctant Disciple of Chekhov and O'Neill* (Hong Kong, 1970) and *Chinese Stories from Taiwan: 1960–1970* (New York, 1976), of which he is the editor. Professor Lau is also the co-editor of *Traditional Chinese Stories: Themes and Variations* (New York, 1978). With Professor C. H. Wang of the University of Washington, he is preparing a comprehensive anthology of Taiwan literature from 1662 to the present time.

Dr. Lau is at present Professor of Chinese at the University of Wisconsin, Madison. He is a member of the editorial board of *Chinese Literature: Essays, Articles, Reviews* (CLEAR), as well as an editor of the Chinese Literature in Translation Series for Indiana University Press.

C. T. Hsia is Professor of Chinese at Columbia University. He did his undergraduate work in China and received his Ph.D. in English from Yale University in 1951. A bilingual author, he has published two major works in English: *A History of Modern Chinese Fiction* (New Haven, 1961; 1971); and *The Classic Chinese Novel* (New York, 1968; Bloomington, 1980). His critical writings in Chinese are now collected in four volumes: *Love, Society, and the Novel* (Ai-ch'ing she-hui hsiao-shuo, 1970); *The Future of Literature* (Wen-hsüeh ti ch'ien-t'u, 1974); *Humane Literature* (Jen-ti wen-hsüeh, 1977); and *Chinese Literature: The New Tradition* (Hsin-wen-hsüeh ti ch'uan-t'ung, 1979).

Professor Hsia is also the editor of *Twentieth-Century Chinese Stories* (New York, 1971) and *The Diary of Hsia Tsi-an* (Hsia Tsi-an jih-chi, 1975). Of his numerous English articles, the following four are easily accessible: "Time and the Human Condition in the Plays of T'ang Hsien-tsu," in *Self and Society in Ming Thought* (Wm. Theodore de Bary, ed., New York, 1970); "The Military Romance: A Genre of Chinese Fiction," in *Studies in Chinese Literary Genres* (Cyril Birch, ed., Berkeley, 1974); "The Scholar-Novelist and Chinese Culture: A Reappraisal of *Ching-hua yüan*," in *Chinese Narrative: Critical and Theoretical Essays* (Andrew H. Plaks, ed., Princeton, 1977); and "Yen Fu and Liang Ch'i-ch'ao as Advocates of New Fiction," in *Chinese Approaches to Literature from Confucius to Liang Ch'i-ch'ao* (Adele A. Rickett, ed., Princeton, 1978).

Leo Ou-fan Lee received his B.A. in Western Languages and Literature from National Taiwan University in 1961. He has pursued graduate studies at the University of Chicago and Harvard University, where he received his M.A. in Regional Studies (East Asia), and his Ph.D. in History and Far Eastern Languages in 1970. His dissertation was published in 1973 by Harvard University Press under the title *The Romantic Generation of Modern Chinese Writers*.

Professor Lee has taught at Dartmouth College, the Chinese University of Hong Kong, and Princeton University, and is currently Associate Professor in the Department of East Asian Languages and Cultures at Indiana University. Besides a number of articles and reviews, both in English and in Chinese, on modern Chinese literature and history, he has completed a book-length study of Lu Hsün and is doing research on the subject of late Ch'ing popular literature. Professor Lee is a member of the editorial board of *CLEAR* and an editor of the Chinese Literature in Translation Series for Indiana University Press.

Notes on the Translators
and Contributors

Marston Anderson, the contributor of the biographical sketch on Chao Shu-li, received his B.A. from the University of Minnesota, Minneapolis in 1973, and an M.A. from the University of California, Berkeley, in 1977, with a thesis on the fiction of Wu Tsu-hsiang. At present, he is working on a doctorate in Comparative Literature, University of California, Berkeley. He is doing research on the writers of the thirties, such as Wu Tsu-hsiang, Chang T'ien-i, Ai Wu, and Sha T'ing.

Margaret M. Baumgartner is currently a graduate student in the Department of Linguistics at the University of Wisconsin, Madison. Her area of specialization is psycholinguistics with an emphasis on reading, speech perception, and child language acquisition. She also teaches English as a Second Language in the English Department. She has a M.A. degree in Linguistics from the University of Wisconsin.

Cyril Birch was born in Bolton, Lancashire, England, in 1925, and educated at Bolton School and the School of Oriental and African Studies, University of London (B.A., Modern Chinese, 1948; Ph.D., Chinese Literature, 1954). He served in the British Army from 1943 to 1947, returning to the School of Oriental and African Studies in 1948 to teach as Lecturer in Chinese until 1960. In that year he joined the faculty of the University of California at Berkeley, where he is now Professor of Chinese and Comparative Literature. He has served as Chairman of the Department of Oriental Languages and as Associate Dean of Instruction in the College of Letters and Science at Berkeley.

He has traveled in India (1944–1945), Hong Kong (1950–1951), Japan (1964), Taiwan (1970; 1977) and made two visits to the People's Republic of China (1977, 1979). He has taught as Visiting Professor at Stanford, Hawaii, National Taiwan University, and the University of Melbourne.

Professor Birch has published articles on traditional Chinese fiction and drama and on twentieth-century Chinese fiction and poetry. His books include: *Stories from a Ming Collection* (London, 1958); *Chinese Communist Literature* (New York, 1963); *Anthology of Chinese Literature* (2 vols., New York, 1967 and 1972); and *Studies in Chinese Literary Genres* (Berkeley, 1974). In 1976 he completed and published the translation of K'ung Shang-jen's *Peach Blossom Fan* (Berkeley) begun by Chen Shih-hsiang and Sir Harold Acton, and his own complete translation of T'ang Hsien-tsu's *Peony Pavilion* appeared in 1980 (Bloomington). He is currently preparing a volume of critical studies of Ming dramatic romances.

Gary Bjorge received his B.A. in International Relations from the University of Minnesota, Minneapolis. After five years of naval service, part of which was spent completing the eighteen-month course in Mandarin Chinese at the Defense Language Institute in Monterey, California, he began his graduate studies at the University of Wisconsin,

Madison. He has M.A. degrees in Chinese, Political Science, and Library Science. He obtained his Ph.D. in Chinese from Wisconsin with a dissertation on Ting Ling.

Dr. Bjorge has worked as a Library Associate at the Memorial Library, the University of Wisconsin, Madison. He has contributed a number of stories translated from Chinese to the literary journals in Taiwan as well as in this country.

Anita M. Brown received her B.S. from the City College of New York. Upon completing her M.S. in Elementary Education at the University of Oregon, she spent a year of intensive study of Chinese in Taiwan. In 1977 she completed an M.A. degree from the Department of East Asian Languages and Literatures at the University of Wisconsin with a specialization in modern Chinese literature. After an additional year of research and study in Taiwan, two visits to the People's Republic of China, and extensive travel throughout South and Southeast Asia, Ms. Brown is now residing in New York. Employed by a major importing company as an international trade manager, Ms. Brown makes frequent trips to the East Asian region. In addition to her business responsibilities, Ms. Brown continues to remain active in the translation of short stories and maintains a strong interest in the development of modern Chinese literature.

George C. T. Cheng received his B.A. in Chinese literature from National Ch'eng Kung University, Taiwan; M.L.S. from the University of Oregon, and M.A. from San Francisco State University. His writings and translations have appeared frequently in Hong Kong's *Ming Pao Monthly* and *China Monthly*. At present, George Cheng is Librarian at San Francisco State University.

Michael S. Duke received his undergraduate training in anthropology at the University of California, Davis, where he obtained his B.A. in 1962. He took up Chinese language and literature for his graduate studies, and received his Ph.D. from the University of California, Berkeley, in 1975.

Dr. Duke has taught at George Washington University, the University of Vermont, and National Taiwan University. He is the author of *Lu Yu* (Boston, 1977), as well as a number of scholarly articles. He has received a National Endowment for the Humanities Fellowship (1980–1981) to finish a book on Wang An-shih under contract for the Twayne Publishers in Boston. Dr. Duke has served as Resident Director of the Oberlin-in-Taiwan Program in Taipei, and is at present Visiting Assistant Professor of Chinese at the University of Wisconsin, Madison.

Eugene Eoyang studied at Harvard (B.A., 1959), Columbia (M.A., 1960), and Indiana University (Ph.D., 1971), where he is now Professor of Comparative and Chinese Literature. From 1960 he worked as an editor for six years with the Anchor Books division of Doubleday. He spent the 1974–1975 academic year at Princeton as an Alfred Hodder Fellow. He has published in *The Journal of Asian Studies, Yearbook of Comparative and General Literature,* and *Critical Inquiry.*

At present Professor Eoyang is working on an anthology of traditional Chinese stories entitled *Links in the Chain* under contract for Doubleday. He is co-editor of *Chinese Literature: Essays, Articles, Reviews* (CLEAR).

Howard Goldblatt received his Ph.D. in Chinese from Indiana University (1974). One of his first publications in book form is a revised version of his doctoral dissertation entitled *Hsiao Hung* (Boston, 1976). Since then he has published several articles and book reviews, in Chinese and English, on modern and contemporary Chinese literature.

Dr. Goldblatt has been most active recently in the field of translation, having co-translated *The Execution of Mayor Yin* by Chen Jo-hsi (Bloomington, 1978) and *The Field of Life and Death and Tales of Hulan River* by Hsiao Hung (Bloomington, 1979). He has also contributed translations of short stories to several anthologies as well as to translation journals such as *Renditions* and *The Chinese P.E.N.* His latest translation project was an anthology of stories by the Taiwanese writer Hwang Chun-ming, *The Drowning of an Old Cat and Other Stories* (Bloomington, 1980).

Among Dr. Goldblatt's current projects is a literary biography of the Northeastern writer Hsiao Chün. He also plans to translate some of the representative novels by Hsiao Chün, Hsiao Hung, and Chiang Kuei. At present, Howard Goldblatt is Associate Professor of Chinese and Coordinator of the Chinese Program at San Francisco State University, where he offers courses in modern Chinese literature, translation, and research methodology.

Lawrence Herzberg is a graduate student in the Department of East Asian Languages and Cultures, Indiana University, Bloomington, Indiana.

Kai-yu Hsu started his writing career in China in the 1940s. Between his baccalaureate (literature, Tsing Hua University, 1944) and his Ph.D. in modern Chinese literature and thought (Stanford, 1959), he served in the China-Burma-India Theater as a soldier, was on diplomatic assignments in Washington, D. C. and Europe, worked as a journalist in San Francisco's Chinatown, and free-lanced. Since 1959 he has been Professor of Chinese, Comparative Literature, and Humanities, and has chaired the Foreign Language Department and World Literature Department for several terms at San Francisco State University. He started the Chinese Studies Program at San Francisco State, and was the first to organize Chinese language instruction for secondary schools in the western states and Hawaii. He founded the Chinese Language Teachers Association of America.

Among Professor Hsu's major publications are: *Twentieth-Century Chinese Poetry* (New York, 1963; Ithaca, 1970); *Chou En-lai: China's Gray Eminence* (New York, 1968); *Asian-American Authors* (New York, 1972); *The Chinese Literary Scene* (New York, 1975); and *Literature of the People's Republic of China* (Bloomington, 1980), of which he is the editor.

Two of Professor Hsu's most recent works are: *Ch'i Pai-shih's Painting* (Taipei, 1980) and *Wen I-to: Biography of a Modern Chinese Poet* (Boston, 1980).

Dennis T. Hu graduated from Case Institute of Technology with high honors, majoring in mathematics, and continued in computer science at Cornell University to earn his M.S. in 1972. He received his doctorate in Chinese linguistics and literature five years later from the University of Wisconsin, Madison. Subsequently he taught at the Universities of Washington and Oregon, holding visiting appointments. He is at present an assistant professor in the Division of Oriental Languages, University of Virginia. His doctoral research was on Ch'ien Chung-shu's creative prose, the two stories included in this volume being among the works dealt with in his dissertation. A closely related study, entitled "A Linguistic-Literary Approach to Ch'ien Chung-shu's Novel *Wei-ch'eng*," has been published in the *Journal of Asian Studies* 37 (1978). Other anthologies in which his translations have appeared are Joseph S. M. Lau, ed., *Chinese*

Stories from Taiwan: 1960–1970 (New York, 1976), and Y. W. Ma and Joseph S. M. Lau, eds., *Traditional Chinese Stories: Themes and Variations* (New York, 1978).

Frank Kelly began his study of Chinese language and literature at Boston College, receiving his B.A. in 1971. In the same year he started his graduate work in the Department of Far Eastern Languages and Civilizations, the University of Chicago. He got his M.A. degree with a thesis on P'u Sung-ling's *Liao-chai chih-i*. After one year's study at the Inter-University Program for Chinese Language Studies in Taipei (1974–1975), he returned to the University of Chicago. He received his Ph.D. degree in 1979. His dissertation was on the works of Yeh Shao-chün, and he is currently revising that thesis for publication.

Perry Link received his Ph.D. in Chinese from Harvard University. He is at present Assistant Professor of Chinese at the University of California, Los Angeles. He is author of *Mandarin Ducks and Butterflies* (Berkeley, 1980).

Nathan K. Mao was born in Kweiyang, Kweichou Province, China. He was educated at New Asia College (Hong Kong), Yale University, and the University of Wisconsin, Madison. He has taught at the University of Wisconsin, Platteville, the Chinese University of Hong Kong, and York College of Pennsylvania. He was a recipient of the 1978–1979 Commonwealth of Pennsylvania Distinguished Faculty Awards.

Dr. Mao has written *Li Yü* (Boston, 1977) and *Pa Chin* (Boston, 1978). He is an editor of *Classical Chinese Fiction* (Boston, 1978), as well as the translator of *Li Yü's Twelve Towers* (Hong Kong, 1975) and *Cold Nights* (Hong Kong and Seattle, 1978). His most recent publication is *Fortress Besieged* (Bloomington, 1979), of which he is the co-translator. At present, Dr. Mao is Professor of English at Shippensburg State College, Pennsylvania.

Russell McLeod received his Ph.D. in Chinese from Stanford University and is at present Associate Professor of Chinese at the University of Hawaii, Honolulu.

Ronald Miao received his Ph.D. in Chinese from the University of California, Berkeley. He is at present Associate Professor of Chinese at the University of Arizona at Tucson. He is a member of the Advisory Board of *Chinese Literature: Essays, Articles, Reviews* (CLEAR).

William H. Nienhauser, Jr. was educated at the University of Bonn (West Germany) and Indiana University (Ph.D., 1972). He is now Chairman and Associate Professor of Chinese Language and Literature at the University of Wisconsin, Madison. His current fields of interest include traditional fiction, the relation between literature and society, literary history, and theories of reading. He has received fellowships from the Alexander von Humboldt Foundation (University of Hamburg, 1975–1976; University of Munich, summer 1977 and 1979) and the American Council of Learned Societies (1979–1980). Among his publications are a number of articles in learned periodicals: *Liu Tsung-yüan* (co-author; Boston, 1973), *Critical Essays on Chinese Literature* (editor; Hong Kong, 1976), and *P'i Jih-hsiu* (Boston, 1979). He is co-editor of *Chinese Literature: Essays, Articles, Reviews* (CLEAR) and is working on *A Companion to Traditional Chinese Literature* and *A History of Chinese Classical-language Fiction*.

Sidney Shapiro, born in the United States and educated at Cornell University, has been associated with the Peking Foreign Languages Press for over three decades as a veteran translator. Among his major translations are Pa Chin's novel, *Family,* and a number of works of revolutionary literature, including *Tracks in Snowy Forest* and *Annals of a Provincial Town.* He has just completed the translation of the famous sixteenth-century novel, *Outlaws of the Marsh,* which will be jointly published by the Foreign Languages Press and Indiana University Press. Mr. Shapiro is now a Chinese citizen. His latest publication is a book of personal memoirs under the title of *An American in China.*

James Chin-ten Shu received degrees in English literature from National Taiwan Normal University and Oklahoma State University. He is currently a doctoral candidate in Comparative Literature at the University of Wisconsin, Madison. His dissertation is on the problem of allegory in Chinese and Western fiction. His publications have appeared in *Chinese Literature: Essays, Articles, Reviews* (CLEAR), and *Chinese Fiction from Taiwan: Critical Perspectives* (Bloomington, 1980).

Cecile Chu-chin Sun, a doctoral candidate in Comparative Literature at Indiana University, is writing her dissertation on the metaphoric relationship between *ch'ing* (emotion) and *ching* (scene) as a new critical perspective in reading certain kinds of Chinese and English poetry.

Ms. Sun taught Chinese at the New School for Social Research in New York, but most of her professional life has been in English-Chinese and Chinese-English translation. This dates back to 1971, when she began to work as a simultaneous interpreter at the United Nations. After her resignation from the United Nations, she taught graduate courses in Translation and Simultaneous Interpretation at the Monterey Institute of Foreign Studies as an assistant professor until 1976. Currently, Ms. Sun is a freelance interpreter for the U.S. State Department and the Secrétariat d'Etat of Canada as well as private business firms.

Clara S. Y. Sun received her B.A. from Fu-jen University in Peking, and her M.A. from Marquette University, Milwaukee. She is currently a lecturer in Chinese at the University of Wisconsin, Madison.

Jason C. S. Wang received his B.A. in English from Soochow University, Taipei, Taiwan, and his M.A. in Chinese Literature from the University of Wisconsin, Madison. He is currently a Ph.D. candidate at Wisconsin and is working on his dissertation dealing with the date and authorship of the *Lao Tzu.*

Yang Hsien-yi and **Gladys Yang** have always worked as a team in translation. Educated at Oxford University, England, they have since the early fifties translated numerous titles from Chinese literature into English, all of which have been published by the Foreign Languages Press in Peking. Among their outstanding contributions are *Li Sao and Other Poems of Chu Yuan, The Man Who Sold a Ghost, The Dragon King's Daughter, The Courtesan's Jewel Box, The Scholars, Selected Works of Lu Hsün, A Brief History of Chinese Fiction* (by Lu Hsün), *The Sun Shines Over the Sangkan River* (by Ting Ling), and *Changes in Li Village* (by Chao Shu-li). Their latest publication is *A Dream of Red Mansions* (previously known to the Western reader as *Dream of the Red Chamber* or *The Story of the Stone* in different translations). The Yangs serve on the advisory committee of the English journal *Chinese Literature,* to which they have frequently contributed their translations of short stories, drama excerpts, and essays.

Jane Parish Yang received her B.A. at Grinnell College in American Studies and her M.A. in Asian Studies (Chinese) at the University of Iowa in 1977. She previously taught at Lingnan College in Hong Kong (1969–1970) and spent three and one-half years in Taiwan (1972–1976) studying Chinese and teaching English. She is at present a doctoral candidate in Chinese literature at the University of Wisconsin, Madison, writing her dissertation on literature in Taiwan during the Japanese occupation. She has served as Editorial Assistant of *Chinese Literature: Essays, Articles, Reviews* (CLEAR) since September 1977.

Wai-lim Yip received his B.A. in English from National Taiwan University and Ph.D. in Comparative Literature from Princeton University. A prolific author and translator, his major publications include: *Ezra Pound's Cathay* (Princeton, 1969), and *Modern Chinese Poetry: Twenty Poets from the Republic of China, 1955–1965* (Iowa, 1970). At present, Dr. Yip is Professor of Comparative Literature at the Department of Literature, University of California, San Diego.

Checklist of Authors, Dates, and Chinese Titles

Authors and titles of stories are arranged in the order in which they appear in the table of contents. In the case where the author is identified by a pen name, his or her real name is given in parentheses. The dates of the authors are given in the individual biographical sketches. Dates for the stories are those of first publication. In a few cases the date of an initial periodical publication could not be determined, and first appearance in book form is given instead.

1. Lu Hsün 魯迅 (Chou Shu-jen 周樹人)
   K'ung I-chi 孔乙己 (1919)
   Medicine (Yao 藥) (1919)
   My Old Home (Ku-hsiang 故鄉) (1921)
   The New Year's Sacrifice (Chu-fu 祝福) (1924)
   In the Wine Shop (Tsai chiu-lou shang 在酒樓上) (1924)
   Soap (Fei-tsao 肥皂) (1924)
2. Hsü Ti-shan 許地山 (pen name Lo Hua-sheng 落華生)
   The Merchant's Wife (Shang-jen fu 商人婦) (1921)
   Yü-kuan 玉官 (1939)
3. Yeh Shao-chün 葉紹鈞 (Yeh Sheng-t'ao 葉聖陶)
   Rice (Fan 飯) (1921)
   Solitude (Ku-tu 孤獨) (1923)
   Horse-bell Melons (Ma-ling kua 馬鈴瓜) (1923)
   Autumn (Ch'iu 秋) (1932)
4. Yü Ta-fu 郁達夫
   Sinking (Ch'en-lun 沉淪) (1921)
5. Mao Tun 茅盾 (Shen Yen-ping 沈雁冰)
   Spring Silkworms (Ch'un-ts'an 春蠶) (1932)
6. Lao She 老舍 (Shu Ch'ing-ch'un 舒慶春)
   An Old Tragedy in a New Age (Hsin-shih-tai ti chiu-pei-chü 新時代的舊悲劇) (1936)
7. Ling Shu-hua 凌叔華
   Embroidered Pillows (Hsiu-chen 綉枕) (1925)
   The Night of Midautumn Festival (Chung-ch'iu wan) 中秋晚 (1928)
8. Jou Shih 柔石 (Chao P'ing-fu 趙平復)
   A Slave-Mother (Wei nu-li ti mu-ch'in 為奴隸的母親) (1930)
9. Shen Ts'ung-wen 沈從文
   Pai-tzu 柏子 (1928)
   Hsiao-hsiao 蕭蕭 (1929)
   The Lamp (Teng 燈) (1930)
   Quiet (Ching 靜) (1932, rev. 1942)
   Three Men and One Woman (San-ko nan-tzu ho i-ko nü-jen 三個男子和一個女人)
      (1936)

10. Ting Ling 丁玲 (Chiang Ping-chih 蔣冰之)
   When I Was in Hsia Village (Wo tsai Hsia-ts'un ti shih-hou 我在霞村的時候) (1940)
   In the Hospital (Tsai i-yüan chung 在醫院中) (1941)
11. Pa Chin 巴金 (Li Fei-kan 李芾甘)
   Nanny Yang (Yang sao 楊嫂) (1931)
   The General (Chiang-chün 將軍) (1933)
   Sinking Low (Ch'en-lo 沉落) (1934)
   Piglet and Chickens (Chu yü chi 豬與雞) (1942)
12. Chao Shu-li 趙樹理
   Lucky (Fu-kuei 福貴) (1946)
13. Chang T'ien-i 張天翼
   The Bulwark (Ti-chu 砥柱) (1936)
   Midautumn Festival (Chung-ch'iu 中秋) (1936)
14. Hsiao Chün 蕭軍 (Liu Chün 劉均)
   Goats (Yang 羊) (1935)
15. Wu Tsu-hsiang 吳組緗
   Young Master Gets His Tonic (Kuan-kuan ti pu-p'in 官官的補品) (1932)
   Let There Be Peace (T'ien-hsia t'ai-p'ing) 天下太平 (1934)
   Fan Village (Fan-chia p'u 樊家舖) (1934)
16. Ch'ien Chung-shu 錢鍾書
   The Inspiration (Ling-kan 靈感) (1946)
   Souvenir (Chi-nien 紀念) (1946)
17. Hsiao Hung 蕭紅 (Chang Nai-ying 張迺瑩)
   Hands (Shou 手) (1936)
   The Family Outsider (Chia-tsu i-wai ti jen 家族以外的人) (1937)
18. Tuan-mu Hung-liang 端木蕻良 (Ts'ao Ching-p'ing 曹京平)
   The Faraway Wind and Sand (Yao-yüan ti feng-sha 遙遠的風沙) (1936)
   The Rapid Current of the Muddy River (Hun-ho ti chi-liu 渾河的急流) (1937)
19. Lu Ling 路翎 (Hsü Ssu-hsing 徐嗣興)
   The Coffins (Kuan-ts'ai 棺材) (1945)
20. Eileen Chang (Chang Ai-ling 張愛玲)
   The Golden Cangue (Chin-so chi 金鎖記) (1943)

Modern Asian Literature Series

Modern Japanese Drama: An Anthology, ed. and tr. Ted T. Takaya. Also in paperback ed.   1979

Mask and Sword: Two Plays for the Contemporary Japanese Theater, Yamazaki Masa-kazu, tr. J. Thomas Rimer   1980

Yokomitsu Riichi, Modernist, by Dennis Keene   1980

Nepali Visions, Nepali Dreams: The Poetry of Laxmiprasad Devokota, tr. David Rubin   1980

Literature of the Hundred Flowers, Vol. I: *Criticism and Polemics,* ed. Hualing Nieh   1981

Literature of the Hundred Flowers, Vol. II: *Poetry and Fiction,* ed. Hualing Nieh   1981

Modern Chinese Stories and Novellas, 1919–1949, ed. Joseph S. M. Lau, C. T. Hsia, and Leo Ou-fan Lee. Also in paperback ed.   1981

Neo-Confucian Studies

Instructions for Practical Living and Other Neo-Confucian Writings by Wang Yang-ming, tr. Wing-tsit Chan   1963

Reflections on Things at Hand: The Neo-Confucian Anthology, comp. Chu Hsi and Lü Tsu-ch'ien, tr. Wing-tsit Chan   1967

Self and Society in Ming Thought, by Wm. Theodore de Bary and the Conference on Ming Thought. Also in paperback ed.   1970

The Unfolding of Neo-Confucianism, by Wm. Theodore de Bary and the Confer-ence on Seventeenth-Century Chinese Thought. Also in paperback ed.   1975

Principle and Practicality: Essays in Neo-Confucianism and Practical Learning, ed. Wm. Theodore de Bary and Irene Bloom. Also in paperback ed.   1979

The Syncretic Religion of Lin Chao-en, by Judith A. Berling   1980

The Renewal of Buddhism in China: Chu-hung and the Late Ming Synthesis, by Chün-fang Yü   1981

Neo-Confucian Orthodoxy and the Learning of the Mind-and-Heart, by Wm. Theodore de Bary   1981

Translations from the Oriental Classics

Major Plays of Chikamatsu, tr. Donald Keene   1961

Records of the Grand Historian of China, translated from the Shih chi of Ssu-ma Ch'ien, tr. Burton Watson, 2 vols.   1961

Instructions for Practical Living and Other Neo-Confucian Writings by Wang Yang-ming, tr. Wing-tsit Chan   1963

Chuang Tzu: Basic Writings, tr. Burton Watson, paperback ed. only   1964

The Mahābhārata, tr. Chakravarthi V. Narasimhan   1965

The Manyōshū, Nippon Gakujutsu Shinkōkai edition   1965

Su Tung-p'o: Selections from a Sung Dynasty Poet, tr. Burton Watson   1965

Bhartribari: Poems, tr. Barbara Stoler Miller. Also in paperback ed.   1967

Basic Writings of Mo Tzu, Hsün Tzu, and Han Fei Tzu, tr. Burton Watson. Also in separate paperback eds.   1967

The Awakening of Faith, attributed to Aśvaghosha, tr. Yoshito S. Hakeda   1967

Reflections on Things at Hand: The Neo-Confucian Anthology, comp. Chu Hsi and Lü Tsu-ch'ien, tr. Wing-tsit Chan   1967

The Platform Sutra of the Sixth Patriarch, tr. Philip B. Yampolsky   1967
Essays in Idleness: The Tsurezuregusa of Kenkō, tr. Donald Keene   1967
The Pillow Book of Sei Shōnagon, tr. Ivan Morris, 2 vols.   1967
Two Plays of Ancient India: The Little Clay Cart and the Minister's Seal, tr. J. A. B.
    van Buitenen   1968
The Complete Works of Chuang Tzu, tr. Burton Watson   1968
The Romance of the Western Chamber (Hsi Hsiang chi), tr. S. I. Hsiung   1968
The Manyōshū, Nippon Gakujutsu Shinkōkai edition. Paperback text edition.   1969
Records of the Historian: Chapters from the Shih chi of Ssu-ma Ch'ien, Paperback text
    edition, tr. Burton Watson   1969
Cold Mountain: 100 Poems by the T'ang Poet Han-shan, tr. Burton Watson. Also in
    paperback ed.   1970
Twenty Plays of the Nō Theatre, ed. Donald Keene. Also in paperback ed.   1970
Chūshingura: The Treasury of Loyal Retainers, tr. Donald Keene   1971
The Zen Master Hakuin: Selected Writings, tr. Philip B. Yampolsky   1971
Chinese Rhyme-Prose, tr. Burton Watson   1971
Kūkai: Major Works, tr. Yoshito S. Hakeda   1972
The Old Man Who Does as He Pleases: Selections from the Poetry and Prose of Lu Yu,
    tr. Burton Watson   1973
The Lion's Roar of Queen Śrīmālā, tr. Alex & Hideko Wayman   1974
Courtier and Commoner in Ancient China: Selections from the History of The Former
    Han by Pan Ku, tr. Burton Watson   1974
Japanese Literature in Chinese, Vol. I: Poetry and Prose in Chinese by Japanese Writers
    of the Early Period, tr. Burton Watson   1975
Japanese Literature in Chinese. Vol. II: Poetry and Prose in Chinese by Japanese Writers
    of the Later Period, tr. Burton Watson   1976
Scripture of the Lotus Blossom of the Fine Dharma, tr. Leon Hurvitz. Also in paper-
    back ed.   1976
Love Song of the Dark Lord: Jayadeva's Gītagovinda, tr. Barbara Stoler Miller. Also
    in paperback ed. Cloth ed. includes critical text of the Sanskrit.   1977
Ryōkan: Zen Monk-Poet of Japan, tr. Burton Watson   1977
Calming the Mind and Discerning the Real: From the Lam rim chen mo of Tson-kha-pa,
    tr. Alex Wayman   1978
The Hermit and the Love-Thief: Sanskrit Poems of Bhartrihari and Bilhaṇa, tr. Bar-
    bara Stoler Miller. Also in paperback ed.   1978
The Lute: Kao Ming's P'i-p'a chi, tr. Jean Mulligan. Also in paperback ed.   1980
A Chronicle of Gods and Sovereigns: Jinnō Shōtōki of Kitabatake Chikafusa, tr. H. Paul
    Varley   1980

Studies in Oriental Culture

1. The Ōnin War: History of Its Origins and Background, with a Selective Transla-
    tion of the Chronicle of Ōnin, by H. Paul Varley   1967
2. Chinese Government in Ming Times: Seven Studies, ed. Charles O. Hucker   1969
3. The Actors' Analects (Yakusha Rongo), ed. and tr. by Charles J. Dunn and
    Bunzō Torigoe   1969

Companions to Asian Studies

Introduction to Oriental Civilizations

Wm. Theodore de Bary, Editor